THE HANDBOOK OF

REPARATIONS

The International Center for Transitional Justice (ICTJ) assists countries pursuing accountability for past mass atrocity or human rights abuse. The Center works in societies emerging from repressive rule or armed conflict, as well as in established democracies where historical injustices or systemic abuse remain unresolved.

In order to promote justice, peace, and reconciliation, government officials and nongovernmental advocates are likely to consider a variety of transitional justice approaches including both judicial and nonjudicial responses to human rights crimes. The ICTJ assists in the development of integrated, comprehensive, and localized approaches to transitional justice comprising five key elements: prosecuting perpetrators, documenting and acknowledging violations through nonjudicial means such as truth commissions, reforming abusive institutions, providing reparations to victims, and facilitating reconciliation processes.

The field of transitional justice is varied and covers a range of disciplines, including law, public policy, forensics, economics, history, psychology, and the arts. The ICTJ works to develop a rich understanding of the field as a whole, and to identify issues that merit more in-depth research and analysis. Colloborating with colleagues in transitional socieities and often commissioning outside studies, the Center targets its research to address the complex issues confronting policymakers and activists. Identifying and addressing the most important gaps in scholoarship, it provides the benefit of comparative analysis to its staff and to practitioners worldwide.

THE HANDBOOK OF

REPARATIONS

Edited by

PABLO DE GREIFF

The International Center for

Transitional Justice

OXFORD

UNIVERSITY PRESS

This book has been printed digitally and produced in a standard specification in order to ensure its continuing availability

OXFORD
UNIVERSITY PRESS

Great Clarendon Street, Oxford OX2 6DP
Oxford University Press is a department of the University of Oxford.
It furthers the University's objective of excellence in research, scholarship,
and education by publishing worldwide in
Oxford New York
Auckland   Cape Town Dar es Salaam   Hong Kong   Karachi
Kuala Lumpur Madrid Melbourne Mexico City   Nairobi
New Delhi Shanghai Taipei Toronto
With offices in
Argentina Austria Brazil Chile Czech Republic France Greece
Guatemala Hungary Italy Japan South Korea Poland Portugal
Singapore Switzerland Thailand Turkey Ukraine Vietnam

Oxford is a registered trade mark of Oxford University Press
in the UK and in certain other countries

Published in the United States
by Oxford University Press Inc., New York

© International Center for Transitional Justice 2006

'Recommendations and Conclusions' from NUNCÁ MAS: THE REPORT OF
THE ARGENTINE NATIONAL COMMISSION ON THE DISAPPEARED.
Translation copyright © 1986 by Writers and Scholars International Ltd.
Reprinted by permission of Farrar, Straus and Giroux. LLC.
Non-exclusive English Language permission throughout the UK and British
Commonwealth including Canada granted by Faber and Faber Ltd.

'Proposals for Reparation' from REPORT OF THE CHILEAN NATIONAL
COMMISSION ON TRUTH AND RECONCILIATION reprinted by permission
of the Center for Civil and Human Rights, Notre Dame Law School.
Every reasonable attempt was made to contact copyright holders,
and we would be happy to rectify any omissions

The moral rights of the author have been asserted

Database right Oxford University Press (maker)

Reprinted 2010

ISBN 978-0-19-954570-4

CONTENTS

PART II THEMATIC STUDIES

PART III PRIMARY DOCUMENTS
AND LEGISLATION

ACKNOWLEDGMENTS

In the course of developing a project of this magnitude, plenty of debts are acquired. It gives me great pleasure to acknowledge the generous assistance I have received from so many individuals and institutions. First and foremost, I would like to explicitly thank my colleagues at the International Center for Transitional Justice (ICTJ). I cannot think of a more congenial or conducive atmosphere in which to develop work that combines normative theorizing with empirical information.

Like other human rights organizations, the ICTJ carries out intense mission-specific research. Unlike other organizations, especially of a similar size, the ICTJ chose to establish a dedicated Unit to carry out research that goes beyond the specific needs of particular engagements. Among other goals, the projects developed by the Research Unit are supposed to contribute to the ongoing discussion about the nature, content, and boundaries of the conception of transitional justice that the Center promotes. There is an irreducible normative dimension to this discussion. The present project obviously feeds into this ongoing conversation. I find the Center's commitment to this type of research-based reflexive exercise remarkable.

In addition to thanking the institution as a whole, some of its members deserve to be thanked explicitly for their contribution, direct or indirect, to this project. Alex Boraine and Juan Méndez, Presidents of the ICTJ while the project was in course, were sources not just of support but of inspiration. Ian Martin and Paul van Zyl contributed not the least by supporting what became a significant operation. With Lisa Magarrell I had countless discussions on this topic while we grappled with some of the real difficulties stemming from our in-country work on reparations in many places including Peru, Guatemala, and Colombia. Andrea Armstrong and Roger Duthie provided unfailingly reliable assistance, assistance of that type which can only be the expression of commitment and loyalty. Finally, a large group of dedicated interns gave support of various kinds. They include Rachel Cordero, Abby Larson, Miles Norton, Sarah Proescher, and Anthony Triolo. To Anthony this project owes a special debt for absolutely tireless work over a long stretch of time.

The twenty-seven authors whose work is collected here obviously deserve my gratitude as well. A project on a relatively novel field always involves a great deal of back and forth. I am grateful for the patience that the authors exhibited in the face of what others might have begrudged as an endless stream of requests for revisions, updates, and appeals for additional information. The fact that no preexisting friendship was damaged as the project moved forward, and that indeed new ones were formed, gives testimony of the authors' dedication.

This project was supported in part by a grant from the International Development Research Center (IDRC) and by the Rockefeller Foundation, which kindly lent us its conference center in Bellagio, Italy, where we held a meeting of authors, memorable for being as productive as it was pleasant. My deep gratitude to both institutions.

It is difficult for me to imagine a more committed editor than Dominic Byatt at Oxford University Press. To him and his wonderful team, most notably Lyndsey Rice and Anne Hegerty, my gratitude for their contribution to this publication.

Finally, I would like to express my gratitude to my family, both nuclear and extended. I dedicate my share of this project to my two sons, Martín and Simón. May they contribute to the life of a generation that will make the work of their parents truly superfluous by living in such a way that it has nothing to repair.

CONTRIBUTORS

Adila M. Abusharaf is currently a Program Officer with the Center of Arab Women for Training and Research based in Tunisia. Dr. Abusharaf obtained her Doctorate of Juridical Sciences from the university of Toronto in 2000. She has worked on several projects in relation to transitional justice, law and development and gender equality. Her publications include a field-based technical report, 'The Other Side of Oil Wealth: The Case for Compensation of Displaced Southern Sudanese Women' (2003), funded by the Gender Unit of the International Development Research Center (IDRC); 'From Exodus to Resettlement: The Challenges of IDPs in the Sudan' in *The North-South Institute Review* (2003); 'The Legal System of Sudan' in *The Encyclopedia of the Legal Systems of the World* (2002); and 'The Relationship between Multinational Oil Corporations and the Sudan: Problems and Prospects' in *Journal of African Law* (1999).

Andrea Armstrong is a JD candidate at Yale Law School (expected 2007). Prior to returning to school, she worked for the reparations project at the International Center for Transitional Justice (ICTJ) as a Research Associate. Before joining the ICTJ, Armstrong researched regional aspects of conflict in the Great Lakes region of Africa and the area surrounding Afghanistan as a researcher at the Center on International Cooperation at New York University. She has coauthored articles on regional approaches to post-conflict reconstruction and researched a variety of conflict-related issues including refugee protection; Iraq's oil-for-food program; and conflict prevention. Armstrong has a Master's in public affairs from the Woodrow Wilson School of Public and International Affairs at Princeton University and a Bachelor of Arts from New York University.

John Authers is the coauthor of *The Victim's Fortune—Inside the Epic Battle Over the Debts of the Holocaust*, published by HarperCollins in New York, June 2002. A correspondent for the *Financial Times* since 1990, he was based in New York for five years, during which time he researched the campaign for reparations for former concentration camp slave laborers. He is currently the paper's bureau chief in Mexico City. He holds a degree in philosophy, politics, and economics from Oxford University, as well as Master's degrees from Columbia University's School of Journalism and School of Business.

Diana Cammack earned her Ph.D. from the university of California, Irvine, in 1983 and did post-doc work at Oxford University as an SSRC-MacArthur Fellow. As an American living in Malawi, she observed and participated in the democratic transitional process in 1992–2002. In 1995–6 she and other local and international human rights advocates tried without success to start a 'history project' and then a truth commission. She works as a research consultant in the fields of development, human rights, and governance, and her more recent works, such as 'Poorly Performing Countries: Malawi, 1980–2002' (ODI, 2004), have explored the causes of Malawi's poor governance and underdevelopment and the ambiguous role that donors have played in addressing those challenges.

Ignacio Cano is a sociologist and a social psychologist. He received his Ph.D. from the Universidad Complutense de Madrid and spent his post-doc in the universities of Surrey, Michigan, and Arizona, where he specialized in data analysis and evaluation of social programs. He worked in human rights in El Salvador between 1991 and 1993 and was part of the United Nations Truth Commission for El Salvador. He acted as a consultant for human rights projects in Guatemala and other countries of the region. Since 1996, he has worked in Rio de Janeiro in the areas of violence, security, human rights, and education. He is currently a professor of research methodology at the department of social sciences of the Universidade do Estado do Rio de Janeiro.

Arturo J. Carrillo is Associate Professor of Clinical Law and Director of the Human Rights Clinical Program at George Washington University Law School. He taught previously at Columbia Law School, where he was Director of the Human Rights Clinic in 2002–3 and the Henkin Senior Fellow at Columbia's Human Rights Institute from 1999–2003. Professor Carrillo was also associate director of the CLS Transitional Justice Program in 2001–2. Before entering academia full time, he served as a legal adviser to the Human Rights Division of the United Nations Observer Mission to El Salvador (ONUSAL), and worked in Bogotá for the Colombian Commission of Jurists as the Attorney for United Nations Affairs. Professor Carrillo, who holds law degrees from George Washington and Columbia Law Schools, and a BA in Politics and Latin American Studies from Princeton University, has published various works in English and Spanish on topics relating to public international law, the laws of war, and human rights. He is coauthor of the ICTJ-sponsored publication entitled *Design Parameters for a Reparations Program in Peru* (2002). In 2005 Professor Carrillo was named Senior Adviser on Human Rights Policy to the US Agency on International Development (USAID) in Colombia.

Ariel Colonomos holds degrees from Institut d'Etudes Politiques, Université Paris IX (Business and Administration), Université Paris X (Philosophy), and a doctorate in political science from Sciences Po. He has been a CNRS research fellow at the

Center of International Studies (CERI) since 1998. He is lecturer at Sciences Po in Paris and currently an adjunct professor at Columbia (School of International and Public Affairs) where he teaches a course on 'ethical issues in international affairs'. He recently published a book, *La Morale dans les relations internationales—Rendre des compte* (Paris, Odile Jacob, 2005), which explores the various aspects of post-Cold War ethics. He has recently been a guest editor of a special issue on 'Moralising Capitalism' of the *International Social Science Journal* (Unesco, June 2005).

Christopher J. Colvin is currently a postdoctoral fellow at the Center for Comparative Literature and Society at Columbia University, and has a doctorate in cultural anthropology from the university of Virginia. His dissertation re-search was conducted with a victim support and advocacy group in Cape Town, South Africa, and examined the politics of 'traumatic storytelling' among victims of apartheid-era violence. His book chapters include 'Brothers and Sisters, Do Not Be Afraid of Me: Trauma, History and the Therapeutic Imagination in the New South Africa', in *Contested Pasts*, Kate Hodgkins (ed.), and 'Anxious Stories, Natural Histories: Political Violence and Psychological Anthropology' in *Black-well's Companion to Psychological Anthropology*, Conerly Casey (ed.). He has also conducted research on the South African reparations program, on reconciliation and civil society in Southern Africa, on victim's perspectives on the TRC, and on the globalization of both the discourse of 'trauma' and the practice of 'traumatic storytelling'.

Hans Das is a former Director of the Legal Department of the Commission for Real Property Claims of Displaced Persons and Refugees in Bosnia and a former Senior Legal Officer of the Housing and Property Directorate in Kosovo. He has a Ph.D. degree in Law from Leuven University (Belgium) and a Master's degree in inter-national law from the Graduate Institute for International Studies in Geneva. His doctoral thesis examined the administration of evidence and the processing of claims in international mass claims programs. He is currently working at the European Commission in Brussels.

Pablo de Greiff is Director of Research at the International Center for Transitional Justice (ICTJ). Originally from Colombia, he obtained his BA at Yale and his Ph.D. in Philosophy at Northwestern University. Prior to joining ICTJ, he was Associate Professor in the department of philosophy at the State University of New York at Buffalo. He has written extensively on transitions to democracy, democratic theory, and the relationship between morality, politics, and law. He is the editor of five books, most recently *Global Justice and Transnational Politics* (MIT Press, 2002), and Jürgen Habermas' *The Inclusion of the Other* (MIT Press, 1998). From 2000 to 2001, he was the recipient of a fellowship from the National Endowment for the Humanities, and was a Laurance S. Rockefeller Fellow at the Center for Human

Values at Princeton University. He is currently completing a book entitled *Redeeming the Claims of Justice in Transitions to Democracy.*

Bart Delmartino is a researcher at the Katholieke Universiteit Leuven in Belgium. He is preparing a Ph.D. on reparations for property rights violations.

Colleen Duggan is a Senior Program Specialist in the Peace, Conflict, and Development Program Initiative and the Gender Unit at the International Development Research Center (IDRC). She has a Master's in international human rights and humanitarian law from Essex University and holds a postgraduate degree in international development and economic cooperation from Université d'Ottawa. Prior to joining IDRC she worked for ten years with the United Nations, most recently with the Office of the UN High Commissioner for Human Rights in Colombia. She has also worked as a policy analyst with UNDP's Bureau for Crisis Prevention and Recovery in New York and in the field with the UNDP in El Salvador, Guatemala, Honduras and Haiti. She is a trainer for the UN Staff College/UN Department of Political Affairs training program for conflict prevention. Her most recent academic work includes 'UN Strategic and Operational Coordination: Mechanisms for Preventing and Managing Violent Conflict' in *From Rhetoric to Reality: Mainstreaming Conflict Prevention at the Regional Organizations and the UN,* and a contribution to *Entre el Perdón y el Paredón: Preguntas y Dilemas de la Justicia Transicional.*

Liann Ebesugawa received a Juris Doctor degree in 2003 from the William S. Richardson School of Law at the university of Hawaii. She also received a Master of Arts in English from the university of Hawaii with a focus on cultural and literary studies. For 2003–4 she will be the law clerk for Hawaii Supreme Court Justice Simeon Acoba.

Richard Falk is Visiting Distinguished Professor in Global and International Studies at the university of California, Santa Barbara, and Albert G. Milbank Professor Emeritus of International Law at Princeton University. In 2001 he served on a three-person Human Rights Inquiry Commission for the Palestine Territories that was appointed by the United Nations, and previously, on the Independent International Commission on Kosovo. Recent books include *Declining World Order* (2004), and (with Howard Friel) *The Record of the Paper: How the New York Times Misreports American Foreign Policy* (2004). Some of his earlier authored or coauthored books include *Religion and Humane Global Governance; Human Rights Horizons; On Humane Governance: Toward a New Global Politics; Explorations at the Edge of Time; Revolutionaries and Functionaries; The Promise of World Order; Indefensible Weapons; Human Rights and State Sovereignty; A Study of Future Worlds;* and *This Endangered Planet.* He serves as Chair of the Nuclear Age Peace Foundation's Board of Directors and as honorary vice president of the American Society of International Law. Falk also acted as counsel to Ethiopia and Liberia in the Southwest Africa Case before the International Court of Justice. He received his BS from Wharton School, university of Pennsylvania; LLB from Yale Law School; and JSD from Harvard University.

Patrícia Galvão Ferreira is a lawyer. She received her LLM in International Human Rights Law from the university of Notre Dame, Indiana. She has worked for the Center for Justice and International Law (CEJIL) litigating cases on human rights violations in Brazil before the Inter-American System on Human Rights (OAS), has been Executive Secretary of the Association for Prison Reform in Rio de Janeiro, and a consultant for the Ford Foundation in Brazil. She is now the Deputy Representative for the Open Society Initiative for Southern Africa (OSISA) in Angola.

Lucas Sebastián Grosman was born in Buenos Aires in 1971. In 1996 he obtained his law degree from the university of Buenos Aires. Between 1994 and 1998 he practiced law in the areas of civil and commercial litigation, arbitration, and business transactions. In 2000 he obtained his Master of Laws (LLM) degree from Yale University. He has taught several courses, including torts, property, constitutional law, antitrust and law and economics at the universities of Buenos Aires, Palermo, Di Tella and San Andrés, all in Argentina. From 2001 to 2003 he served as Commissioner at the Argentine Antitrust Commission. He is currently pursuing his Doctor of the Science of Law (JSD) degree at Yale University.

María José Guembe currently works as a lawyer at the Human Rights Especial Representation of Argentina's Ministry of Foreign Relations. Born in Argentina, she graduated from the Law School of the university of Buenos Aires, and obtained her Master of Laws (LLM) degree from the university of Notre Dame, Indiana. Previously, she collaborated with the Support Committee to the Special Prosecutor for Social and Political Movements of the Past, in Mexico City. She was director of the 'Memory and Accountability Program' at the Center for Legal and Social Studies [Centro de Estudios Legales y Sociales (CELS)] in Buenos Aires. She has published articles on the Argentine experience in dealing with gross human rights violations including 'The Right to the Truth Before the Courts', 'Recovery of Archives concerning Human Rights Violations during the Argentine Dictatorship', and 'Challenging Amnesty Laws in Argentina'. She has been a junior lecturer at the School of Social Sciences, university of Buenos Aires.

Brandon Hamber was born in South Africa and currently works in Belfast, Northern Ireland. He trained as a clinical psychologist in South Africa and has a Ph.D. from the university of Ulster. He was an Honorary Fellow at the School of Psychology at Queen's University in Belfast in 2001–2. He is currently a Research Associate of the Belfast-based think tank Democratic Dialogue, and a consultant to the Office of Psychosocial Issues based at Free University, Berlin. Prior to moving to Northern Ireland, he coordinated the Transition and Reconciliation Unit at the

Centre for the Study of Violence and Reconciliation in South Africa, of which he remains an Associate. He is a Board member of the South African-based Khulumani Victim Support Group. He was a visiting Tip O'Neill Fellow in Peace Studies at the Initiative on Conflict Resolution and Ethnicity (INCORE) in Northern Ireland in 1997–8. Previously he was the recipient of the Rockefeller Resident Fellowship (1996) and was a visiting fellow at the Centre for the Study of Violence in São Paulo, Brazil. He has written widely on the South African Truth and Reconciliation Commission, the psychological implications of political violence, and the process of transition and reconciliation in South Africa and abroad. He edited the book entitled *Past Imperfect: Dealing with the Past in Northern Ireland and Societies in Transition*, which was published by INCORE/university of Ulster.

Samuel Issacharoff is the Harold R. Medina Professor in Procedural Jurisprudence at Columbia Law School. His wide-ranging research deals with issues in civil procedure (especially complex litigation and class actions), law and economics, constitutional law, particularly with regard to voting rights and electoral systems, and employment law. He is one of the pioneers in the law of the political process. He is also a leading figure in the field of procedure, both in the academy and outside. In addition to ongoing involvement in some of the front-burner cases in this area, he now serves as the Reporter for the newly created Project on Aggregate Litigation of the American Law Institute. He is a 1983 graduate of the Yale Law School. After clerking and practicing, he began his teaching career at the university of Texas in 1989, where he held the Joseph D. Jamail Centennial Chair in Law, before moving to Columbia in 1999. In the summer of 2005, he will join the faculty of New York University School of Law as the Reiss Professor of Constitutional Law. His seventy plus published articles appear in every leading law review, as well as in leading journals in other fields. He is a Fellow of the American Academy of Arts and Sciences.

Elizabeth Lira is a psychotherapist and researcher in the field of mental health and human rights currently working as a researcher and professor in the Centro de Etica, Universidad Alberto Hurtado, Santiago. She worked for ten years at Fundación de Ayuda Social de las Iglesias Cristianas (FASIC), an Ecumenical human rights institution, as a clinical psychologist treating victims of human rights violations. In 1988, she founded with other clinicians the Latin American Institute of Mental Health and Human Rights and was its director for six years. She has published widely on the psychology of abuse and healing, including, among others, *Psicoterapia y represión política/Psychotherapy and Political Repression*, and *Trauma, duelo y reparación/Trauma, Grief and Reparation*, both coauthored with Eugenia Weinstein. She has been working since 1997 as a researcher on political reconciliation in Chile with Brian Loveman, a professor at San Diego State University. She has published several books related to this topic, including *Las suaves cenizas del* *olvido: Vía chilena de reconciliación política 1814–1932* (1999, 2nd edn., 2000) and *Las acusaciones constitucionales en Chile.*

M. Brinton Lykes is Professor of Community/Social Psychology at the Lynch School of Education and Associate Director of the Center for Human Rights and International Justice at Boston College. From 1999 to 2001, she held a chair in Psychology at the university of the Witwatersrand (Johannesburg, South Africa). She is an activist, scholar and teacher and has worked for many years among women and child survivors of war and of state-sponsored economic and political violence in rural Guatemala. She has published extensively about this work in journals and edited volumes, is coeditor of three books including *Myths about the Powerless: Contesting Social Inequalities* (Temple University Press, 1996) and coauthor, with the Association of Maya Ixil Women—New Dawn, of *Voces e imágenes: Mujeres Mayas Ixiles de Chajul/Voices and Images: Maya Ixil Women of Chajul* (2000). She is an associate editor or member of the editorial board of *Action Research, American Journal of Community Psychology*, and *Peace and Conflict: Journal of Peace Psychology*. She is also a community activist and cofounder and participant in many local, national, and international NGOs including Boston Women's Fund, Women's Rights International, and the Ignacio Martín-Baró Fund for Mental Health and Human Rights.

Jaime E. Malamud-Goti, former Solicitor General of Argentina (the equivalent of the Attorney General position in the USA) drew international notice during the administration of President Raul Alfonsin, when he managed the human rights trials of members of the Argentine junta that kidnapped, tortured, and murdered thousands of Argentines (and others) during the military dictatorship's 'dirty war' against 'subversives' in the late 1970s. Since then, Malamud has authored two books, one on state terrorism in Argentina (*Game without End: State Terror and the Politics of Justice*, 1996) and the other on the drug trade in Bolivia (*Smoke and Mirrors*, 1992), and pursued a career as a legal scholar and ethicist. A MacArthur and Guggenheim fellow, he currently teaches morality, ethics, and criminal law at the university of Palermo and is involved with the founding of a new school of law at Universidad de San Andrés.

Anna Morawiec Mansfield received her BA from Mount Holyoke College and her JD from Columbia Law School. She formerly worked for the American Bar Association/Central and East European Law Initiative (ABA/CEELI), a project that promotes the rule of law and strengthens legal institutions in Central and Eastern Europe. Following her work at ABA/CEELI, she was a member of the US delegation to the Organization for Security and Cooperation Mission in Bosnia and Herzegovina, where she served as the Governance Coordinator responsible for the design and direction of governance and political reform programs in that post-conflict nation. She is currently an attorney-adviser in the Office of the Legal Adviser at the Department of State.

Marcie Mersky was born in the USA, and after earning a Master's degree from Harvard University has lived and worked in Latin America for most of the last three decades. She was a senior political officer at the United Nations Verification Mission in Guatemala from 2002 until it closed at the end of 2004. Earlier she worked for the United Nations Office for Project Services on a range of initiatives that included coordinating and editing two books: *The Operations of the Historical Clarification Commission in Guatemala: Systematization of the Experience of the Technical Team* and *Está en sus manos: experiencias de desarrollo local en América Central/It's in Your Hands: Local Development Experiences in Central America*. Prior to that she worked with the Historical Clarification Commission, Guatemala's truth commission, where she headed the team that drafted the volume on the consequences and effects of the violence and served as Coordinator of the Commission's final report. Earlier she was part of the executive team that established and organized 'REHMI', a community-based, nationwide project of the Catholic Church to document human rights violations from the victims' perspective during the armed conflict in that country. She is a member of the ICTJ Managing Truth Commissions Group. She has worked in Guatemala since 1988 and serves on the boards of several NGOs working on justice, development, and peace issues.

Alexander Segovia, a Salvadorean economist, earned a Ph.D. in Economics from London University, a Master's in Latin American Public Policy from Oxford University and a BA in Economics from Central American University José Simeón Cañas (UCA). Currently, he works as an international consultant and is Executive Director of the regional project 'The Societies and Economies of Central America at the Beginning of the XXI Century'. Recently Dr. Segovia has collaborated with the ICTJ on reparations research—both on thematic issues and on country-specific programs (Peru). Between 1997 and 2000, he worked for the United Nations Verification Mission in Guatemala (MINUGUA) as an economic analyst and later as director of the Socioeconomic Division, contributing to the process that culminated in the signing of the Fiscal Pact of Guatemala. From 1996 to 2000, he was a member of an investigation team for a joint project BID-CEPAL-PNUD, which studied poverty and macroeconomic politics in Latin America and the Caribbean; the liberalization of the balance of payments and its effects on distribution; and poverty and growth—the results of which were published in two volumes. Between 1994 and 1996 he was a member of a research team of Ajuste Hacia La Paz of PNUD-El Salvador, which studied the transition and economic dimensions of the Peace Accords and contributed three chapters to the final report. In 2002, Dr Segovia published the book *Structural Transformation and Economic Reform in El Salvador*.

Hans Dieter Seibel is a full Professor of Sociology and Head of the Development Research Center at Cologne University in Germany. He has previously taught at the university of Liberia, Princeton University and the university of Dortmund. He also held visiting professorships at Lagos University and Ohio State University. On leave of absence from Cologne University during 1999–2001, he was Technical Adviser for Rural Finance at the International Fund for Agricultural Development in Rome and prepared IFAD's Rural Finance Policy; during 1988–91, he worked as GTZ teamleader for the central bank of Indonesia and built the first national-scale microfinance project linking banks and self-help groups. In recent years, he has been working on a comprehensive financial systems approach to microfinance, the reform of agricultural development banks, and the establishment of member-owned local financial institutions. He has published some 30 books and 200 articles, among them: 'Finance with the Poor, by the Poor, for the Poor' (*Social Strategies*, 1989); *Self-Help Groups as Financial Intermediaries: A Training Manual* (Breitenbach, 1992); *The Making of a Market Economy: Monetary Reform, Economic Transformation and Rural Finance in Vietnam* (Breitenbach, 1992); *Coping with Scarcity: Microenterprise Strategies in Nigeria* (Breitenbach, 1996); *Financial Systems Development and Microfinance* (TZ-Verlag/GTZ, 1996); *Rural Finance: From Unsustainable Projects to Sustainable Institutions* (IFAD, 2001); *Commercial Aspects of SHG Banking in India* (NABARD, 2002).

Hans van Houtte is Professor in Conflict of Laws, International Business Law and Arbitration at Katholieke Universiteit Leuven in Belgium, where he heads the Institute for International Trade Law and is the Director of the Research Project on Restoration of Property Rights in Post-Conflict Situations. He currently acts as President of the Eritrea-Ethiopia Claims Commission at The Hague. He used to be International Commissioner at the Commission for Real Property Claims in Bosnia, Commissioner at the United Nations Compensation Commission in Geneva, and Senior Judge at the Claims Resolution Tribunal for Dormant Accounts in Switzerland (CRT-1). He has acted as chairman, sole arbitrator or party-appointed arbitrator in more than 120 international arbitration proceedings. He has been appointed as Chairman of Arbitral Tribunals by, *inter alia*, the International Chamber of Commerce (ICC), the London Court of International Arbitration (LCIA), the Geneva Chamber of International Commerce, and the United Nations. He has also acted as counsel in numerous arbitration proceedings. His academic expertise includes his membership in the Commission on International Arbitration (ICC – Paris), more than 100 articles and contributions on arbitration and international trade law, and his serving on the editorial boards of various law journals.

Eric K. Yamamoto is a Professor of Law at the William S. Richardson School of Law at the university of Hawaii. His teaching, scholarship, and public interest litigation work focus on social justice, with an emphasis on reparations for historic injustice. In 1983–4, he served as a member of the legal team representing Fred Korematsu in the successful reopening of his infamous Japanese American internment case from World War II. His book *Interracial Justice: Conflict and Reconciliation in Post-Civil Rights America* won the 2000 Gustavus Meyers Award for Excellence.

ABSTRACTS

PART I CASE STUDIES

'Economic Reparations for Grave Human Rights Violations: The Argentinean Experience'
María José Guembe

Since its return to democracy, Argentina has made great efforts to address the legacy of the last military dictatorship. This chapter presents a complete overview of the Argentinean policy of economic reparations for the victims of human rights violations committed between 1975 and 1983, including the beneficiaries, the crimes for which victims received reparations, the amounts paid, and the forms of payment. The study also analyzes the motivations for redressing the victims, from both national and international perspectives. It identifies the positions adopted by the different actors involved in the measures, especially the State and human rights organizations. The latter gained undeniable legitimacy by representing the victims and has consolidated into a group that has become the main actor on issues related to the legacy of the military dictatorship. The study also focuses on economic, legal, and political questions that have arisen during the process of designing and implementing the reparations policy.

'The Reparations Policy for Human Rights Violations in Chile'
Elizabeth Lira

This chapter describes the reparations programs implemented in Chile from 1990 to 2004. These programs are addressed to victims of violations of human rights committed during the military regime (1973–90): the relatives of disappeared and executed persons; people who were dismissed from their jobs for political motives; peasants who participated in the land reform and were expelled for political reasons from the land; and Chilean exiles returning to the country. Political prisoners and torture victims were considered only in 2003. The creation of the Commission for Political Imprisonment and Torture (2003–5) was followed by a law that provides pensions to political prisoners and torture victims identified by the Commission. Created with different kinds of victims in mind, these programs have been based on pensions, social services, educational benefits, public recognition of the violations of the victims' rights, monuments, sites of memory, and health assistance, mainly in the form of mental health services. The Program for Reparation and Integral Health Assistance for Victims of Human Rights Violations, created in 1991 and reinforced by a law at the end of 2004, has provided health services to all kinds of victims of human rights violations, including third-generation relatives.

'The Reparations Program in Brazil'
Ignacio Cano and Patrícia Galvão Ferreira

This chapter evaluates the federal reparations program for fatal victims of political violence in Brazil. The Brazilian reparations program was born of an amnesty movement for political prisoners, followed by the discovery of mass graves exposing atrocities of the State. In response to pressure from civil society groups and the media, President Cardoso signed the 1995 Law of Victims of Political Assassination and Disappearance. The chapter explores the limitations of the law, among others, its exclusion of many victims of political violence and the charge that the law transferred the burden of proof to victims' families. The chapter examines closely the Commission's structure and operation, as well as the voting patterns of its members. It provides data concerning the cost of the entire reparations process and sheds light on the surprising truth-telling function the Commission acquired in a country in which official truth telling about the years of the dictatorship is still to take place.

'The Reparations Proposals of the Truth Commissions in El Salvador and Haiti: A History of Noncompliance'
Alexander Segovia

As a result of political negotiations in both El Salvador and Haiti, truth commissions were created to investigate human rights violations. The commissions included in their reports recommendations designed to secure reparations for the victims. Despite the gravity of the events and the formal commitment of the governments, neither El Salvador nor Haiti has implemented these recommendations. These two case studies provide an opportunity to examine the economic, social, and political factors that explain noncompliance with truth-commission recommendations on reparations. This report examines the experiences of El Salvador and Haiti, and presents some conclusions and lessons learned. The first and most important conclusion of the study is that in order to ensure that reparations programs will be put into practice, a correlation of political forces that favors such programs is necessary. The report suggests that the construction of such a correlation critically depends on the existence of sufficiently powerful and influential players to promote and defend it.

'Overview of the Reparations Program in South Africa'
Christopher J. Colvin

This chapter explores the reparations debate in post-apartheid South Africa and outlines the recommendations for reparations made by the Truth and Reconciliation Commission (TRC). Although reparations were discussed at the multiparty negotiations at the end of apartheid, the new democratic constitution that came out of those negotiations did not provide for reparations. The legislation that created the TRC, however, established a special committee (the Committee on Reparations and Rehabilitation (CRR)) to formally examine the reparations issue and make policy recommendations to the President. The CRR made its recommendations—widely considered to be one of the world's most ambitious and comprehensive reparations policies—in the TRC's 1998 Report. The South African government, however, did not respond to these recommendations, arguing that since the work of other committees within the TRC was not yet finished, it could not consider the CRR's proposed policy. Victim groups and civil society did not agree, and an acrimonious conflict ensued over the perceived slow pace of government action on reparations. Victims also pursued lawsuits for reparations against multinational corporations that conducted business with the apartheid government. In 2003, the government finally enacted a reduced version of the CRR's original reparations policy.

'Reparations in Malawi'
Diana Cammack

Malawi's five methods of paying reparations (court awards; the government's Disaster Preparedness, Relief and Rehabilitation program; civil service grants; special payments to the political elite; and especially the National Compensation Tribunal (NCT)) have not brought public closure to past rights abuses and the antipathy they engendered. Nor have NCT procedures, which included neither public truth telling nor the identification of perpetrators, fostered democratic consolidation. Growing out of a political compromise during the transition, the NCT has received nearly 20,000 claims and paid interim awards to less than one-third. Eligible are Malawians of any age who, between July 6, 1964 and May 17, 1994, were born in detention or exile or were subjected to wrongful imprisonment, forced exile, personal injury, lost property or business, lost educational opportunities and/ or employment benefits. An autonomous body within the judiciary, the NCT has been underfunded consistently and has limited the bulk of its payments to symbolic 'condolences'. While the public is generally ignorant of the NCT, claimants are frustrated by its procedures, its 'trivializing' their pain and suffering, and its 'favouritism' as well as by its failure to offer them full compensation, information about future payments, or a 'sincere' apology. Yet the existence of the NCT has allowed politicians to counter periodic public demands for a truth commission by asserting that the NCT is addressing the past and nothing more is needed.

'Report on Redress: The Japanese American Internment'
Eric K. Yamamoto and Liann Ebesugawa

How does a country repair its harm to a vulnerable minority targeted during times of national fear because of race? How did the USA redress its then popular yet unconstitutional World War II incarceration of 120,000 innocent Japanese Americans in desolate barbed wire prisons without charges, hearings, or bona fide evidence of military necessity? In response to a congressional inquiry, political lobbying, and lawsuits, the Civil Liberties Act of 1988 directed the President to apologize and authorized over $1 billion in reparations. Congress also created a fund to educate the public about the government's false assertion of 'national security' to restrict civil liberties. Some considered redress a tremendous victory—rewriting history and personal healing. Others questioned reparations for one US group but not others. Japanese American redress served as a catalyst for reparations movements worldwide. This report on redress examines its genesis, legal implementation, and apparent effects. It also explores wide-ranging political mobilization and social meanings of redress and 'unfinished business'. Reparations cannot be measured by laws alone. Diverse communities must engage contested questions of history, justice, and belonging. Reparations claims face often unforeseen benefits and limitations. The report concludes with these 'lessons learned' to date.

'Compensation for the Victims of September 11'
Samuel Issacharoff and Anna Morawiec Mansfield

The September 11th Victims Compensation Fund can only hesitatingly find its place within a comprehensive study of reparations programs. While the origin of the Fund arguably lies in the political exigencies surrounding a perceived threat to the security of the USA, it more accurately reflects the desire by the US Congress to ensure the viability of its nation's air carriers. Unlike traditional reparations, which are closely related to a process of social reintegration of the victim, fostering civic trust and social solidarity, the Fund was not established to bring justice to the victims of the terrorist attacks on September 11, 2001. Also unlike traditional reparations, the Fund did not seek to serve as a mechanism of corrective or distributive justice as a result of an authoritarian domestic regime or internal conflict. Rather, it was initially created out of fear that recourse to the US courts would threaten the precarious financial health of the airline industry. Implicitly, however, such pragmatism reflected a desire by lawmakers that the government be seen as doing all it could to ease the pain of those who suffered so greatly on September 11, 2001. Initial motivations for the program aside, however, there is no question that the compensation scheme has since taken on a life of its own. Ultimately, the Fund's contribution to any reparations case study lies in its cautionary tale about the creation of elaborate administrative schemes that try to individualize recoveries as the mechanisms through which to compensate victims.

'The United Nations Compensation Commission'
Hans van Houtte, Hans Das, and Bart Delmartino

In the aftermath of the 1990–1 Gulf War, the UN Security Council determined that Iraq was liable under international law for any direct damage resulting from its unlawful invasion and occupation of Kuwait. In order to process the claims against Iraq, the United Nations Compensation Commission (UNCC) was established. Since 1991, the UNCC has received approximately 2.6 million claims, which it has subdivided in six categories, depending on the status of the claimant, the type of loss, and the amount claimed. For certain claims, rather than assessing the exact amount of the loss, the UNCC has established fixed compensation standards. Other innovative features include such mass claims resolution techniques and methodologies as data matching, grouping, and sampling. The reparations process was funded through oil exports under the oil-for-food program. A share of originally 30 percent and later 25 percent of the proceeds was reserved for compensation. After the new war in Iraq in 2003, the oil-for-food program was terminated and the share of oil revenues dedicated to reparations was lowered to 5 percent. As of June 2005 the UNCC has decided nearly all claims.

'German Reparations to the Jews after World War II: A Turning Point in the History of Reparations'
Ariel Colonomos and Andrea Armstrong

The post-World War II German–Israeli reparations program is the largest, most comprehensive reparations program ever implemented. Traditionally, reparations were supported by the vanquished and were designed to compensate the victor for the damages caused during the war. The *Wiedergutmachung* (literally 'making good again') program as it is called in Germany, or *Shilumim* (the payments) as Israelis usually prefer to refer to it, innovates in many areas and goes beyond this interstate framework. Jewish leaders participated in the Luxembourg negotiations that led to the signature of the 1952 treaty and community networks played a crucial role in the distribution of the money to the victims. Civil society groups played an instrumental role in the USA as plans for reparations were being discussed during the war. Neither the Federal Republic of Germany (FRG) nor Israel existed during the war. Reparations have been paid to the State of Israel and are paid to Jewish Holocaust survivors regardless of their nationality. The FRG greatly benefited politically and economically from this treaty. As a result, the FRG was able to enter the international arena and establish diplomatic relations with Israel, the economy of which country greatly benefited from the money it received.

'Making Good Again: German Compensation for Forced and Slave Laborers'
John Authers

In 2001, fifty-six years after the cessation of hostilities in World War II, Germany's Federal Government and a group of large German companies entered into a new reparations agreement, aimed at compensating people who had been forced to work for the Third Reich against their will. This chapter examines the confluence of historical circumstances that led to such a belated attempt at righting the injustice, and examines the political factors behind the extremely 'rough' criteria that were used to allocate funds to claimants. It also examines the distribution effort itself, still not quite completed by mid-2005, and finds that the various NGOs and governments involved in the reparations work were surprisingly successful in tracing claimants and making payments to them, given the amount of time that had elapsed.

PART II THEMATIC STUDIES

'Justice and Reparations'
Pablo de Greiff

This chapter represents an effort to articulate a conception of justice in reparations for victims of human rights violations when the aim is to repair a large number of cases, as opposed to individual, isolated cases. It starts with an effort to establish some semantic clarity, at least by trying to distinguish between two different contexts of use of the term 'reparations'. It discusses some of the problems with merely transplanting the ideal of compensation in proportion to harm from its natural home in the resolution of individual judicial cases, and using it as a standard of justice for massive reparations programs. It argues instead in favor of thinking about justice in the context of massive cases in terms of the achievement of three goals, namely, recognition, civic trust, and social solidarity—three goals that, as it turns out, are intimately related to justice. Finally, without pretending that a blueprint for a program of reparations can be designed from a purely theoretical perspective, it tries to shed light on the basic trade-offs that accompany some of the choices that have to be made in the process of constructing a comprehensive and coherent reparations program.

'Reparations, International Law, and Global Justice: A New Frontier'
Richard Falk

This chapter assesses recent trends in international law regarding the availability and character of reparations. Presently, reparations issues have arisen particularly in domestic societies searching for transitional justice in the aftermath of authoritarian rule. These issues are shaped by national legal systems, but are also influenced by international practice. In these transitional settings, the search for justice is affected by political preoccupations, such as the persistent influence of displaced prior authoritarian leadership, as well as by real and alleged limitations on the financial capabilities of transitional states. No general approach can address the interplay between national and international law at this stage. Reliance must be placed on a case-by-case approach, considering matters of context, such as the degree of suffering and disability inflicted on particular categories of claimants, the balance of claims versus the State's demands for resources to fund sustainable and equitable development; remoteness in time bears on the credibility of the claimants as present victims tend to be given priority over victims in the distant past when assessing relative merits; scale and selectivity suggests that if the total of claims overwhelms the administrative capacity of the State, there will be a tendency to substitute apology and symbolic gestures for material ones and award reparations on the basis of individual need associated with the prior deprivation. International law informs background moral and political thinking about reparations, but practical considerations of capability and prudence are decisive in most instances, making the influence of international law indirect, and sometimes marginal.

'Justice in Context: The Relevance of Inter-American Human Rights Law and Practice to Repairing the Past'
Arturo J. Carrillo

This chapter examines how international law contributes to contemporary understandings of transitional justice with respect to reparations for victims of gross and systematic human rights abuses. The author surveys the jurisprudence of the Inter-American Court of Human Rights through 2003 to determine how the Court's practice can be used to guide the formulation of reparatory policies during political transition. Recognizing that the direct application of Inter-American case law to situations of mass atrocity is not always viable in practice, the author analyzes regional human rights jurisprudence, in particular that relating to compensation, to determine what role the Court's rules can—and cannot—play as a reference for policymakers and societies faced with the challenge of designing a reparations program. He concludes that while landmark Court decisions like Velásquez Rodríguez provide general normative guidance, there are significant obstacles to extending to the transitional justice context many of the measures, amounts, and formulae relied upon by the Court in awarding compensation. The fairness of compensation outside the courtroom cannot be determined with reference to predetermined rules, but rather depends on the factual context in which the measures are adopted, including the number of victims involved. A better source of comparative inspiration is found in the Court's growing practice of adopting nonmonetary reparations measures to deal with moral harm.

'Reparations and Civil Litigation: Compensation for Human Rights Violations in Transitional Democracies'
Jaime E. Malamud-Goti and Lucas Sebastián Grosman

Compensation of human rights abuse can be approached from two different perspectives. The first is through principles of tort law, under which the compensation of harm for human rights abuse is no different from the compensation of other, ordinary harm. The second is based on principles of administrative compensation. Under this approach, victims are defined in standardized terms in a statute that provides a relatively fixed, tabulated amount of compensation for all, which is typically smaller than judicial compensation. This chapter analyzes what circumstances justify a shift from the torts to the administrative approach to compensation and how the two approaches should relate to each other. It addresses, in particular, the issue of whether victims should have a right to choose between them in the disposition of their cases and, if so, under what conditions. It finally compares judicial to administrative compensation in relation to the goals a compensation program must pursue, and argues that even in those cases where, for the reasons discussed in the chapter, administrative compensation offers the best option, it is advisable to leave room for the use of judicial compensation as well.

'Narrowing the Micro and Macro: A Psychological Perspective on Reparations in Societies in Transition'
Brandon Hamber

This paper focuses on the relationship between the individual (micro) and the collective (macro) dimensions of reparations. It highlights the gaps and confluences between the two through focusing on symbolic reparations. It argues that massive reparations programs leave a disparity between the individual and the collective dimensions of reparations, i.e. between the needs of victims dealing with extreme trauma and the social and political needs of a transitional society. Through *reparations* the victim seeks some sort of *reparation*, i.e. a psychological state in which they feel adequate amends have been made. However, whether *reparation* at an individual level has taken place is difficult to ascertain, if not impossible. The individual (psychological) and the collective (political) always stand in tension with one another when granting reparations. This dilemma is central to the reparations debate. The chapter argues that the gap between the micro and macro can be narrowed through a better understanding of the impact of extreme political trauma. It shows how steps can be taken at the social and political levels that can potentially increase the impact of reparations on individuals, i.e. through closer consideration of the nature and type of reparations offered, as well as the context, process, and discourses surrounding their delivery.

'Reparations and Mental Health: Psychosocial Interventions Towards Healing, Human Agency, and Rethreading Social Realities'
M. Brinton Lykes and Marcie Mersky

This chapter provides an overview of psychosocial and mental health theory and practice as it has emerged in contexts of war, post-war, and transitional situations. We identify several models that have guided much of this work until now, critically examine their underlying assumptions, and posit a series of limitations inherent in the dominant paradigm of post-traumatic stress disorder, especially as applied in the aftermath of political violence. We then argue that psychosocial work as part of reparations processes must be designed and enacted within specific historical, cultural, sociopolitical contexts, with singular individuals and their particular communities. We suggest that this perspective permits more effective ways of responding to, and working within, the diversity of challenges facing societies seeking to reconstruct in the wake of war and other forms of organized political violence. We propose an alternative framework for this work, rather than a single model, which must be articulated and shaped in practice by individuals, families, and groups in their neighborhoods, communities, and societies. Finally we examine exhumations and reburials, in two distinct contexts, as sites for psychosocial work within reparations processes; and conclude the chapter by describing ongoing questions that challenge psychosocial workers hoping to contribute to reparations work.

'Reparation of Sexual Violence in Democratic Transitions: The Search for Gender Justice'
Colleen Duggan and Adila M. Abusharaf

Although notable advancements have been made in international law, feminists continue to point out that democratic transitions continue to fail to do justice to the victims of gender-based violence. The gendered nature of sexual violence and its ongoing economic, social, and psychological impacts express and reinforce discriminatory public attitudes and gender inequality beyond moments of democratic transition. For this reason, sexual violence against women should figure as a special category under State-sponsored programs for reparations. However, different forms of gender bias can throw up normative and practical barriers that prevent women from accessing the benefits that reparations programs make available. Reparations programs, nevertheless, like many public policies for recovery and redress, continue to be largely gender-blind. This chapter explores the challenge of repairing sexual violence against women and how national reparations programs might provide short-term redress while contributing to the achievement of longer-term goals for gender justice.

'Financing Reparations Programs: Reflections from International Experience'
Alexander Segovia

One of the least studied aspects of programs of reparations, both in theory and in practice, is financing. This is odd if we take into account that mobilizing resources, domestic and foreign, is politically one of the most difficult tasks any society can undertake. This chapter focuses on the subject of financing reparations programs and attempts to answer, even if only in part, the following questions: Which factors play a role in the process of mobilizing domestic and foreign resources to finance reparations? Is financing solely a technical-economic problem, or does it involve political, social, and cultural factors? Why do governments prefer financing social programs instead of programs of reparations? How do the proposals made by truth commissions regarding financing affect the viability of programs of reparations?

Which factors explain the efficacy of financing models of reparations programs? In order to address these questions, this chapter has been divided into three main sections. In the first, programs of reparations are analyzed from the perspective of political economy, which means that both economic and noneconomic factors that influence the mobilization of domestic and foreign resources by a transitional society are taken into consideration. The second section focuses on international experiences in the area of financing programs of reparations, with the purpose of extracting some lessons. Finally, in the third section, the main conclusions are presented.

'Reparations and Microfinance Schemes'
Hans Dieter Seibel with Andrea Armstrong

Allocating reparations benefits to victims of civil rights abuses with a lasting effect on their well-being is a tremendous challenge. By converting benefit payments into shares and beneficiaries into shareholders of microfinance institutions (MFIs), the former victims turn into active partners of aid and owners of local institutions. In many countries, indigenous savings and credit associations are the only civil society institutions that have survived the breakdown of society. They represent the social capital for the reconstruction of local financial institutions. In other countries, such institutions have to be newly built. In either case, experienced international NGOs may be instrumental in building, or reconstructing, MFIs owned by recipients of reparations payments. Part of the funding in a reparations program may thus be allocated directly to the victims-turned-shareholders, and the other part to institution-building. Based on satisfactory performance of the MFI, the share capital may be augmented by donor grants and bank borrowings to increase the volume of loans to the user-owners for income-generating activities. In terms of sustainable impact, there is no alternative to institution-building.

INTRODUCTION

REPAIRING THE PAST: COMPENSATION FOR VICTIMS OF HUMAN RIGHTS VIOLATIONS

PABLO DE GREIFF

This book is intended to provide a broad range of essential information about past experiences with massive reparations programs as well as normative guidance for future practice. That a project such as this one is still necessary is surprising, as a good number of the countries that have emerged from conflict or that have undergone transitions to democracy have at least given some consideration to programs of reparations that seek to make up, in some way, for the harms endured by some members or sectors of society, and more than a few of the countries in transition have actually implemented such programs.[1] A great deal of attention has been paid to what postconflict or transitional countries have attempted to do by way of prosecuting human rights violators, but much less attention has been paid to these countries' efforts by way of reparations for the victims. Clearly, both kinds of efforts, the prosecutorial and the reparative, can be considered elements of justice, but the latter has not received sufficient systematic attention.

It is worth emphasizing that from the standpoint of the victims, reparations programs may occupy a special place in a transition out of conflict or towards democracy. For some victims reparations are the most tangible manifestation of the efforts of the state to remedy the harms they have suffered. Criminal justice—even if it were completely successful both in terms of the number of perpetrators accused (far from being the case in any transition) and in terms of results (which are always affected by the availability of evidence, and by the persistent weaknesses of judicial systems, among other factors)—is, in the end, a struggle *against perpetrators* rather than an effort *on behalf of victims.* Something similar can be said with respect to other transitional justice measures; from truth telling victims will obtain significant benefits that may include a sense of closure derived from knowing the fate of loved ones, and a sense of satisfaction from the official acknowledgment of that fate. But, in the absence of other positive and tangible manifestations truth, by itself, can easily be considered as an empty gesture, as cheap and inconsequential talk. Finally, institutional reform will always be a long-term project that affects the lives of the victims indirectly. Hence, it makes sense to think that at least in terms of potential direct impact on victims, reparations do occupy a special place among transitional measures.

Having said this, the project does not seek to provide an overview of the panoply of initiatives that can be taken in a postconflict or transitional context to improve the lot of victims, and not because these initiatives are either unimportant or not called for by notions of fair governance, sustainable development, moral decency, or even justice itself (understanding the term broadly). In a sense, the project has a much narrower purpose in mind, namely to examine questions around the design and implementation of massive reparations programs, programs that seek to compensate in some way a large universe of victims of human rights violations. Indeed, as the title of this introduction suggests,[2] the project focuses in particular on measures of material compensation. While the research has helped to under-score the importance of designing programs that are 'complex' in the sense that they distribute a variety of benefits (material and 'symbolic') and 'coherent' in the sense that they establish close relations not just between the various benefits that they distribute, but importantly, between the reparations benefits and other transitional initiatives such as prosecutions or truth telling, the main focus of investigation is the material compensation distributed by large-scale, and mostly administrative, programs.[3]

When this project started it was not easy to access even basic information about the sort of program that various transitional or postconflict countries have set in place in order to give some measure of redress to a large universe of victims. There was no systematic work available on the criteria of justice that can be applied to the resolution of large numbers of reparations claims, or on the many questions that frequently arise in the design and implementation of large-scale reparations programs. This project seeks to address this dearth of information and reflection. It is the result of three years of work on the part of an interdisciplinary and international group comprising twenty-seven authors from fourteen different countries.

I

Part I of this book contains a series of highly detailed case studies meant to illustrate international experience with reparations programs and to provide both the empirical grounding and the basis of inquiry for the thematic chapters in Part II. These case studies are both broad in their scope and deep in their scrutiny. They include the history of the discussions leading up to the institutionalization of the reparations initiatives as well as the 'nuts and bolts' of the different programs: their budgets, eligibility criteria, staffing requirements, administrative structure, economic impact, sources of funding, and so on. Whenever possible, the studies were carried out in a way that reflects multiple perspectives, including those of victims, beneficiaries, government officials, participants, and other civil society actors interviewed by the authors. The cases themselves were selected so as to ensure diversity along a variety of axes, including geographical location, the degree of socioeconomic development of the host country or institution, the number of beneficiaries, the complexity and the magnitude of the benefits distributed, and the type of conflict to which the programs responded.

It goes without saying that in a limited sense, there is no such thing as a perfect sample. The set of case studies included here reflects the criteria just mentioned, but also contingent although unavoidable factors such as the availability of resources (material, human, and informational, to name just a few). However, there is nothing arbitrary about the final selection. The reasons for including each case were always various, but they include the following:

- Argentina: This is the earliest reparations program of any in a South American transition. It is also extraordinarily 'munificent' in the sense that its individual awards were very large. It also had interesting features both in terms of delivery (a one-off 'payment') and of financing (government bonds).
- Chile: Despite the geographical proximity, the cultural continuities, the similarities of the predecessor regimes in each country, and the fact that the discussions about reparations in neighboring Argentina could have created path dependence

in Chile, reparations in the latter took a very different form; emphasis was placed from the beginning on providing a wider variety of benefits, and the compensation awards were distributed in the form of a monthly and not particularly large pension.

- Brazil: This was an effort with a very small number of beneficiaries and one that at least in terms of design was disconnected from other transitional justice measures. Although the program was designed as a mere mechanism of distribution, over time it acquired an important truth-telling function. The case therefore raises interesting questions about the relationship between reparations and other justice measures.

- El Salvador and Haiti: Despite the many differences between the two countries, it turns out that some of the reasons why neither ever implemented a reparations program are similar. They have to do with the absence of broad political coalitions in favor of reparations, a factor that is important in its own right, but that acquires especial salience in discussions about the financial challenges that reparations programs always face.

- South Africa: In the field of transitional justice South Africa occupies an important place. Regarding reparations, specifically, in addition to the ambitious program proposed by the Truth and Reconciliation Commission, which in itself makes the case worth studying, the impact that the government's failure to implement these recommendations had on people's perceptions of the work of the commission overall, gives some evidence of the significance of reparations in a transitional process.

- Malawi: This case is interesting both because it comes from a context of severe scarcity and because of the use of an arbitration tribunal that attempted to individualize harms.

- USA: Japanese American Internment: Notwithstanding the fact that it is a reparations case in an affluent country (and that the overall cost was relatively high), the program actually provided to individual beneficiaries what in the US context are not tremendously munificent benefits. Nevertheless, despite inevitable shortcomings, this program is generally considered successful. Part of the explanation may have to do, precisely, with the way in which it established links between material compensation and other measures such as official apologies and education initiatives.

- USA: September 11 Victims' Fund: Although this is not a typical reparations program, the fundamental reason to include a chapter on this case in this book is that it affords the possibility of examining the limitations of procedures that individualize benefits, even in a context in which the availability of resources is guaranteed. Thus, even if the criterion of *restitutio in integrum* can be satisfied, the case suggests that an individualizing procedure generates significant challenges. This is an important cautionary lesson.

- United Nations Compensation Commission (UNCC): This is a case that was designed and operated by the UN, the 'keeper' of the principles of reparations, and that neutralized to a large extent the problem of funding (by relying on the proceeds of Iraqi oil, specifically earmarked for this purpose by the UN). However, it is interesting to consider whether, and regarding which types of claim, the principles were respected by the program. Additionally, the case is important because the UNCC designed and implemented the most sophisticated assessment and mass claims processing system ever devised.
- Germany: Holocaust Reparations: Despite the fact that this case is the historical referent for most reparations programs, it is surprisingly difficult to come by a synthetic presentation of how it actually operated. In addition to offering a detailed overview of this effort, this case study provides an illustration of a truly gargantuan program not just in terms of beneficiaries but also in respect to their geographical dispersion.
- Germany: Forced and Slave Labor Reparations: Despite the nature of the earlier German reparations programs, this case illustrates the difficulties that arise from an insufficiently 'complete' program. Whole categories of victims excluded from the previous program continued the struggle for reparations. The case also provides an illustration of an innovative approach to the problems that are generated when a precise number of beneficiaries that have to be redressed is unavailable, a problem frequently encountered in postconflict situations.

Finally, it is worth pointing out that these case studies include papers on cases that have not been addressed systematically yet outside this project, such as those on Brazil, Malawi, the September 11 Fund, and the unimplemented reparations proposals in El Salvador and Haiti. Even in those cases with respect to which information, albeit from disparate sources, is available, the project includes papers that provide a comprehensive, yet thorough, account of reparations programs (e.g. German Holocaust reparations and the UNCC). The papers present genuinely novel information about some programs, including the paper on Chile, which provides a much more accurate impression of the scale and diversity of that country's reparations efforts than anything available thus far, or the paper on Argentina, which offers one of the few serious attempts to quantify the magnitude of the costs of its different reparations programs.

Rather than summarizing the results of the empirical research, and thus offering help that readers are unlikely to need, I will concentrate on the more useful attempt to provide a taxonomy of reparations efforts, one that in its basic categories presents some of the main challenges faced whenever reparations programs have been undertaken.[4]

Scope

Reparations efforts can have greater or lesser scope according to the total number of beneficiaries they cover.[5] Understood in this manner, there is no inherent merit in a program having greater scope. The fact that one program makes reparation to a larger total number of people than another may simply be indicative of a very large universe of potential beneficiaries. In this respect, it is important to distinguish a program's scope from its 'completeness'.

Completeness

This refers to the ability of a program to cover, at the limit, the whole universe of potential beneficiaries. There is no existing program that satisfies this standard in full, and not only because of the difficulties associated with determining, as a matter of principle, what constitutes the full set of *potential* beneficiaries of a program of reparations. Part of the issue here refers to the selection of the rights whose violation leads to reparations benefits, but this will be addressed below. There are two other types of consideration that have an impact on a program's completeness: the first has to do with evidentiary standards—if the evidentiary bar is set very high, this will of course exclude many people who otherwise deserve to get benefits; the second has to do with structural issues such as the outreach efforts undertaken to publicize the existence of the program, and the hurdles associated with accessing it, including narrow application deadlines, closed lists, requirements to file applications personally, and others. It goes without saying that completeness is a desirable characteristic in a reparations program, and that the mere fact that a program is created will not guarantee it. Rather, serious efforts are called for, particularly considering that a history of both marginalization and abuse might lead large numbers of potential beneficiaries, including entire groups, not to apply to the program at all. The South African reparations effort, despite the outreach initiatives carried out by the Truth and Reconciliation Commission, has become subject to criticism for, among other things, having left many potential beneficiaries out of the commission's closed list.

Comprehensiveness

A not unrelated category is the effort's comprehensiveness, which refers to the distinct types of crimes or harms it tries to redress. Whatever consensus there is in international law about reparations, it is only just emerging, and the boundaries of this obligation remain porous. For instance, there seems to be emerging consensus in international law about the obligation to provide reparations for disappearance and death. But there is much weaker or no consensus on whether the obligation extends to territorial displacement. The situation is still more complicated in practice as, just to mention an example, 'really existing' reparations programs notoriously underrepresent the international law consensus on the obligation to make reparation in cases of torture. Most bodies that have considered the possibility of providing reparations for torture have ended up refraining from doing so, on the basis of evidentiary difficulties (acknowledgedly, not a simple matter to resolve). Programs tend to provide reparations for torture whenever the evidentiary questions can be sidestepped by folding torture into easier-to-prove categories such as illegal detention, and/or when the alleged torture has led to permanent injuries.[6]

In general, and perhaps not surprisingly, most reparations efforts have concentrated on a fairly limited (and traditional) catalog of civil and political rights, leaving the violation of other rights largely unrepaired. Obvious exclusions of various sorts impinge on the reparations efforts' comprehensiveness. In a context in which distinct forms of violence were perpetrated against multiple groups, excluding from benefits either some of the worst or some of the most prevalent forms of violence or some of the targeted groups automatically diminishes the reparations program's comprehensiveness, and as a consequence, its completeness.

All existing reparations programs can be faulted for being insufficiently comprehensive. At the most general level, it can be argued that frequently decisions concerning the catalog of rights whose violation triggers reparations benefits have been made in a way that excludes from the programs those who have been traditionally marginalized, including women and some minority groups. It is not difficult to find the more concrete and specific exclusions for which each reparations program can be arguably faulted. These exclusions have usually fueled continued efforts for increasing each of the programs' comprehensiveness, and in some cases, the struggles have succeeded. Take, for instance, the case of Argentina.[7] There is no such thing as a reparations program in any strict sense of the word 'program' in Argentina. Instead, there are several initiatives, each stemming from a separate piece of legislation and covering a distinct set of victims. The main laws cover the following sets of crimes: disappearance[8] and arbitrary detention and grave injuries and death while in detention.[9] While these laws covered most of the victims of the worst forms of abuse perpetrated under the Juntas, they excluded some important categories of victims: persons who were born while their mothers were illegally detained; minors who remained in detention due to the detention or disappearance of their parents for political reasons or who remained in military areas. Perhaps the most notorious exclusion was that of victims of 'identity substitution', the term used in Argentina to refer to cases of children of disappeared parents and then registered as the legitimate children of other families (in many cases as the children of the military or security personnel who stole them from their biological parents). A recent law redresses these exclusions.[10]

The case of South Africa is particularly challenging in this respect.[11] As is well known, the South African Truth and Reconciliation Commission (TRC), made far-reaching recommendations for the reparation of the victims of apartheid. A 'victim', according to the Act which led to the establishment of the TRC, was someone who had 'suffered harm in the form of physical or mental injury, emotional suffering, pecuniary loss or substantial impairment of human rights (i) as a result of a gross violation of human rights; or (ii) as a result of an act associated with a political objective for which amnesty has been granted'. A gross violation of human rights, in turn, was defined as '(a) the killing, abduction, torture or severe ill-treatment of any person; or (b) any attempt, conspiracy, incitement, instigation, command or procurement to commit [killing, abduction, torture or severe ill-treatment]'.[12] At least in part because of the nature of the apartheid system, a system that involved controlling fundamental aspects of the lives of the majority of South Africans for essentially repressive purposes, the point has been made repeatedly that the conception of 'victims' adopted by the Act was excessively narrow, and that therefore important categories of potential beneficiaries were left out of consideration.[13] Needless to say, a repressive system that affected so many aspects of people's lives—including, of course, their standard of living—can rightly be said to have made victims of virtually all those subject to it. While true, in a sense, this is not particularly helpful from the standpoint of reparations. This general sense of victimhood is best addressed through distributive justice policies leading to the redress of structural imbalances, something that reparations programs are not in a position to do. Having said this, arguably, the recommendations left out of consideration important categories of victims: there were discussions within the TRC about whether to make reparations on behalf of combatants who died during military actions in situations that did not constitute clear violations of international humanitarian law; or victims of the routine violence that accompanied the operation of the social engineering aspects of apartheid, such as people who died not in political demonstrations but, for example, in forced removals; or people who were detained under provisions of the state of emergency. None of them were eligible for reparations as a class, and arguments can be made that they should have been.[14]

In some countries the dynamics tending towards greater comprehensiveness have not borne fruit yet, but it is likely that over time they will. For instance, Brazil's reparations effort was intended to provide reparations only to the victims of disappearance and death for 'non-natural causes in police or similar premises'[15] (notwithstanding how extensively this last criterion was understood by the commission in charge of the program). It therefore left out important categories of victims including the illegally detained, the tortured, and the exiled. However, there continues to be political activism in favor of expanding the reparations program. The last chapter of this story is still to be told.

The pattern of progressively larger comprehensiveness is illustrated by programs in a variety of settings. In Chile, as elsewhere, a good part of the initial reparatory efforts was focused on the crimes covered by the mandate of the Truth and Reconciliation Commission, namely, 'human rights violations under the previous dictatorship that resulted in the death of the victims'. This is to say that the relevant categories of crimes leading to reparations were deadly political violence, political executions, and disappearance while in detention.[16] Other measures intended to benefit additional groups of victims—such as exiles, political prisoners, people who had been dismissed from their jobs for political reasons, and others—were taken over the years. For decades, however, the most significant omission in Chile's reparations efforts was the exclusion of victims of the most prevalent forms of violations during the regime, i.e. illegal detention and torture. Recently, this omission received attention from a commission appointed to examine precisely these crimes, which submitted at the end of 2004 a comprehensive report including recommendations on reparations. The recommendations, accepted by the government, will give victims of these crimes a monthly pension and other symbolic reparatory measures.

The same pattern can be observed in German reparations, notwithstanding a very long delay. Despite the enormity of the reparations afforded by subsequent German laws[17] these programs, until quite recently, excluded important categories of claimants such as those who did not fulfill the law's residency requirements (which meant most people persecuted outside Germany who remained in their native countries) and the Roma, among others.[18] These exclusions led to the reopening of the reparations issue in Germany starting in the late 1980s and running through the mid-1990s, to the conclusion of the now famous slave and forced labor reparations negotiated, at least in part, to avoid litigation against German companies in the USA. This new program not only recognized forced and slave labor but was also open to some of those who had been excluded by the Final Law's residency requirements.[19]

All things considered, comprehensiveness is a desirable characteristic. It is better, both morally and practically, to repair as many categories of crime as feasible. From the standpoint of political morality, the advantages should be obvious; greater comprehensiveness is an expression of what elsewhere I called 'the dynamics of inclusion and ownership behind law making'. Modern societies are no longer content with living under laws stemming from 'our god', or 'our sovereign'; we expect to live under *our* laws. We now recognize a rule as a law not merely because of its capacity to guide our behavior but primarily because of its authority to do so, where this authority is intimately linked to the rule's legitimacy, something it gains precisely in virtue of the fact that we can consider it to be *our* rule, one that we give to ourselves (ownership), where the 'ourselves' keeps growing (inclusion).[20] This dynamic, which applies across all sorts of issues regulated by law, including reparations, explains the familiar pattern whereby over time reparations efforts become increasingly comprehensive.

The pragmatic advantages of such increasing inclusiveness are not unrelated to this account. Leaving important categories of victims unaddressed not only deprives a transitional administration of the gains in legitimacy that it might accrue by establishing a comprehensive reparations program but it also virtually guarantees that the issue of reparations will continue to be on the political agenda, which means it will remain available as the target of legislative or bureaucratic give and take. This may undermine the stability and reliability of reparations agreements, as the Chilean case exemplifies.

Complexity

Whereas comprehensiveness relates to the types of crimes reparations efforts seek to redress, complexity refers to the ways in which the efforts attempt to do so. Thus, rather than focusing on the motivating factors, complexity measures the character of the reactions themselves. A reparations program is more complex if it distributes benefits of more distinct types, and in more distinct ways, than its alternatives. Thus, at one end of the spectrum lie very simple programs that distribute, say, money, exclusively, and in one payment, as in Argentina.[21] Money and an apology (US reparations for Japanese Americans), or money and some measure of truth telling (as the Brazilian program ended up providing), constitute an increase in complexity. Monetary compensation, health care services, educational support, business loans, and pension reform, as in Germany and Chile, increase the complexity of the reparations efforts still more. In general, since there are certain things that money cannot buy, complexity brings with it the possibility of targeting benefits flexibly so as to respond to victims' needs more closely. All other things being equal, then, this is a desirable characteristic. Of course, in most cases not all things remain equal. There are some costs to increased complexity that may make it undesirable beyond a certain threshold.

Integrity or coherence

Reparations programs should, ideally, display what I call integrity or coherence, which can be analyzed in two different dimensions, internal and external. *Internal* coherence refers to the relationship between the different types of benefits a reparations program distributes. Most reparations programs deliver more than one kind of benefit. These may include symbolic as well as material reparations, and each of these categories may include different measures and be distributed individually or collectively. Obviously, in order to reach the desired aims, it is important that benefits internally support one another. Thus, arguably, US reparations for Japanese Americans that included an apology with the reparations check give expression to an internally more coherent plan than Brazil's which distributed money with no official acknowledgment of responsibility, and which acquired an important truth-telling function only incidentally, and not as a matter of design.

External coherence expresses the requirement that the reparations efforts be designed in such a way as to bear a close relationship with other transitional mechanisms, i.e. minimally, with criminal justice, truth telling, and institutional reform. This requirement is both pragmatic and conceptual. The relationship increases the likelihood that each of these mechanisms be perceived as successful (despite the inevitable limitations that accompany each of them), and, more importantly, that the transitional efforts, on the whole, satisfy the expectations of citizens. But beyond this pragmatic advantage, it may be argued that the requirement flows from the relations of complementarity between the different transitional justice mechanisms. Here I can only sketch the basic argument. For example, it is not just that truth telling, in the absence of reparations efforts, can be seen by victims as an empty gesture. The relation holds in the opposite direction as well, since efforts to repair in the absence of truth telling could be seen by beneficiaries as the state's attempt to buy victims' and their families' silence or acquiescence. The same tight and bidirectional relationship may be observed between reparations and institutional reform, since a democratic reform that is not accompanied by any attempt to dignify citizens who were victimized can hardly be understood. By the same token, reparative benefits in the absence of reforms that diminish the probability of the repetition of violence are nothing more than payments whose utility, and furthermore legitimacy, are questionable. Finally, the same bidirectional relationship links criminal justice and reparations. In this sense, from the standpoint of victims, especially once a possible moment of satisfaction derived from the punishment of perpetrators has passed, the condemnation of a few perpetrators, without any effective effort to positively redress victims, could be easily seen by victims as a form of more or less inconsequential revanchism. Reparations without any effort to achieve criminal justice may appear to them as nothing more than blood money. (These complex relations obtain not only between reparations and each of the other components of transitional justice but rather among all of them. That is, parallel arguments may be constructed to describe the relation between criminal justice and truth telling, and between each of these and institutional reform.)

Needless to say, both internal and external coherence are easier to achieve if reparations are designed as a *program*, and if this program is part of a transitional justice policy. Since this is rarely the case, I have for the most part referred to the cases under review here not as reparations 'programs', but 'efforts'.[22] Although the Argentinean and Chilean cases were developed in temporal proximity to other transitional mechanisms, and in the case of Chile, as part of the political platform of the *Concertación*—the alliance of parties that has governed since the end of Pinochet's regime—none of the cases reviewed here were really designed programmatically, either in an internal sense, i.e. in a way that coordinates benefits for distinct crimes in a systematic way, or in an external sense, i.e. so as to coordinate the reparations program with prosecutorial, truth-telling, and institutional reform policies.

Finality

By the 'finality' of a reparations program I refer to whether the program stipulates that receiving its benefits forecloses other avenues of civil redress or not. Not all reparations efforts are final in this sense. In particular, among the cases mentioned, Germany, the USA (the programs to repair both Japanese American internees and the victims of the September 11 attacks), and one of Argentina's laws are final, whereas Brazil and Chile are not. It is difficult to decide, in the abstract, whether it is desirable, in general, for reparations programs to be final. On the one hand, finality means that courts have been made inaccessible to citizens. On the other, once a government has made a good faith effort to create an administrative system that facilitates access to benefits, for reasons mentioned above, allowing beneficiaries to initiate civil litigation poses not just the danger of obtaining double benefits for the same harm but, worse, of destabilizing the whole reparations program also. While the first problem can be easily addressed by stipulating that no one can gain benefits twice for the same violation, the second problem is not so easy to avoid, as the benefits obtained through the courts typically surpass the benefits offered by a massive program. This can lead to a significant shift in expectations and to a generalized sense of disappointment with the program's benefits. Moreover, the shift may be motivated by cases that probably are unrepresentative of the whole universe of victims.[23]

Munificence[24]

This is the characteristic of reparations programs that relates to the magnitude of their benefits (from the individual beneficiary's perspective).[25] Needless to say, there is no absolutely reliable way to measure the absolute *worth* of the benefits, and the difficulties only increase if one aspires to do a cross-country analysis of their comparative worth. Nevertheless, abstracting from other complications, a simple comparison of the dollar value of material benefits directly distributed to victims by some recent reparations programs leads to the following *rough* ascending order of munificence: South Africa, which finally gave a one-off payment of less than $4,000 to victims, would lie on the lower side of the spectrum; the US plan for Japanese Americans, which gave to victims a one-off $20,000 payment, would be followed by Chile, Germany, Brazil, and would end with Argentina's plan, which gave to the families of the victims of the disappeared bonds with face value of $224,000.[26] As this ordering makes clear, it is obvious that munificence, by itself, is not a criterion of success in reparations. It would be difficult to argue that the Argentinean reparations efforts, the most munificent in this list, have been significantly more successful than, say, US reparations for Japanese Americans, which happen to be close to the bottom of the spectrum.

II

Part II of this book examines in detail some of the various challenges that frequently come about in the design and implementation of reparations programs. One of the main goals of this set of chapters is to contribute to the articulation of a conception of justice that can be applied to the massive cases. This involves, to begin with, some normative and conceptual analysis focusing on the boundaries of the concept of reparations—a term whose meaning is not settled either in theory or in practice—examining the relationship between reparations and other transitional justice measures, and attempting to articulate the goals of legitimate reparations programs. Such analysis is particularly important, for while there is solid consensus about the criterion of reparatory justice for the relatively isolated case, namely *restitutio in integrum*—the effort to reestablish the situation prior to the wrongful act (or omission), or to compensate the victim in proportion to the harm suffered—there is no consensus yet around a criterion of justice for the massive cases. That there is a need to work out a conception of justice for these cases is itself a challenging proposition at least in part because it puts to the test our preference for an ordinary conception of compensatory justice ('compensate in proportion to the harm') and for familiar legal procedures (that individualize responsibility, calculations of harm, etc.) Evidence suggests that the criterion of full restitution is rarely, if ever, satisfied by the massive programs.[27] It would be too facile to conclude that those programs that fail this criterion are therefore unfair, among other reasons, for this does not help us much to distinguish earnest reparations efforts from those that are simply a sham. Rather than taking this route, the project takes a fresh look at the legitimate goals of reparations programs and at the very meaning of the term 'reparations' with the aim of articulating a conception of justice that is both normatively thick (so that it can be deployed critically) and empirically informed (so that it does not abstract from the peculiarities of transitional contexts, foremost amongst them, that there is a difference between awarding reparations within a basically operative legal system of which in the relatively isolated case of abuse it can be said that it should have, and could have, fared better and, on the other hand, awarding reparations in a system that in some fundamental ways, precisely because it either condoned or made possible systematic patterns of abuse, needs to be reconstructed, or, as in some countries, built up for the very first time. In the former case it makes sense for the criterion of justice to be exhausted by the aim to make up the *particular* harm suffered by the *particular* victim whose case is in front of the court. In the case of massive abuse, however, an interest in justice calls for more than the attempt to redress the particular harms suffered by particular individuals. Whatever criterion of justice is defended must be one that has an eye also on the preconditions of reconstructing the rule of law, an aim that has a public, collective dimension).[28]

If the case studies in Part I are novel, not the least because some of them constitute the first and only sources of information on these cases, the thematic papers are not any less groundbreaking. Again, without pretending to provide a full summary of their contents, in most cases they tackle questions that have not been addressed elsewhere and that are of deep theoretical and practical interest. Amongst the unexplored issues one can include the relationship between material compensation and symbolic reparations—an issue that has become particularly pressing as reparations proposals become increasingly complex; the seemingly emerging trend of including the provision of mental health care in reparations benefits; the complicated set of questions around the treatment by reparations programs of victims of sexual violence;[29] the possibility of establishing productive links between reparations benefits and microfinancing plans, so as to increase the impact of even modest benefits and to give them some sustainability particularly in economically deprived contexts; and a comparative analysis of the critical issue of how to finance massive reparations programs, a topic that could have been expected to receive close attention before, but has not.

The authors of the chapters in Part II benefited not just from the information in the case studies but also from one additional factor that was intentionally built into the project design: as the research project progressed, the International Center for Transitional Justice (ICTJ), including the Research Director, was involved in advising countries facing the task of implementing reparations programs. This allowed the Center both to feed into these processes the results of the ongoing research, and, more importantly for this project, to fine-tune the research questions in light of some of the real challenges that were being faced on the ground. In this sense, this project is no mere 'academic' exercise. Indeed, the conception of justice in reparations articulated here has been adopted (and adapted) in the chapter on reparations in the report of the Peruvian Truth and Reconciliation Commission,[30] by the recent Commission on Illegal Detention and Torture in Chile,[31] by the Truth and Reconciliation Commission for Sierra Leone,[32] and by various international documents, for example, the 'Independent Study on Best Practices, Including Recommendations, to Assist States in Strengthening Their Domestic Capacity to Combat All Aspects of Impunity', by Diane Orentlicher.[33] The collection includes the most careful articulation of this way of conceptualizing the aims of reparations.

III

Finally, Part III of this book reproduces some basic documents on reparations. Just as Part I did not attempt to become an exhaustive set of case studies examining each and every reparations program ever established, but rather, provides a range of interesting examples, Part III is motivated by a similarly frugal attitude. This part does not aspire to provide an exhaustive list of documents. It does not include, for example, basic international documents on the subject such as the 'Basic Principles and Guidelines on the Right to a Remedy and Reparation for Victims of Gross Violations of International Human Rights Law and Serious Violations of International Humanitarian Law'[34] recently adopted by the UN Human Rights Commission, nor any of the other important international legal instruments on the topic. These documents are not only easily accessible, but reprinted in many other sources, so given the magnitude of this project also, there is no sense in reproducing them here as well. On the same grounds, the collection does not reproduce documents that pertain directly to some of the papers here, such as the case study on the UNCC or the paper on the Inter-American System. Both institutions disseminate their documents widely both in hard and in electronic versions, and the electronic archives have advanced search functions that make moot any editorial process of selection. These archives, furthermore, will certainly be long-lived.

Part III concentrates on making available not only documents that are directly relevant to the chapters in Part I and II and that are illuminating to those who are thinking prospectively about the design and implementation of reparations programs, but also documents that either are difficult to find, or have not been translated into English before. Thus, among other documents, it includes legislation from Argentina, Brazil, Chile, and Germany that is translated here for the first time, as well as documents from Haiti, Malawi, and South Africa that perhaps are not so easy to find. Neither total comprehensiveness nor the desire to achieve great historical depth was the selection criteria used for this part of the collection. Here as elsewhere, this project is interested not only in looking backwards but also in helping us move forward.

NOTES

1. It is not just transitional societies that are considering or have actually implemented programs of reparations. Many non-transitional societies are dealing with the issue. A recent 'best seller' on the topic talks about 'a new international morality' characterized by 'the willingness of the perpetrators to engage and accommodate the victims' demands'. What the author finds especially noteworthy about some of these cases is that they 'involve no coercion but rather evolve from the perpetrators' willingness to acknowledge, and choice to compensate, their victims or their descendants': Elazar Barkan, *The Guilt of Nations: Restitution and Negotiating Historical Injustices* (New York: Norton, 2000), ix.
2. This used to be the title of the project as a whole before it became *The Handbook of Reparations*.
3. Thus, the judicial resolution of individual and sporadic cases of abuse is not the main focus of the project either, although this topic is the subject of detailed examination in several chapters below.
4. The following list of categories tracks closely but also refines and corrects the taxonomy I presented in 'Reparations Efforts in International Perspective; What Compensation Contributes to the Achievement of Imperfect Justice', in *To Repair the Irreparable: Reparation and Reconstruction in South Africa*, Erik Doxtader and Charles Villa-Vicencio, eds. (Claremont, South Africa: David Philip, 2004), and in 'Redressing the Past: Reparations for Gross Human Rights Abuses', in *Rule of Law and Conflict Management: Towards Security, Development and Human Rights?* Agnes Hurwitz, ed. (New York: International Peace Academy, forthcoming).
5. The numbers of beneficiaries, of course, need not correspond to the number of victims of human rights abuses in any given case, not only because a program may fail to provide benefits to all victims (as almost always happens), but also because the program may count as beneficiaries relatives of victims, that is, people who are victims in a 'secondary' or 'indirect' sense, not always counted among victims in the 'primary' or ordinary sense.
6. Argentina provided reparations for 'grave injuries' caused during illegal detention, starting with Decree 70/90 (1990) and continuing with Law 24.043 (1991). Perhaps the most expedient, but not the most accurate, way of dealing with the problem of evidence is that adopted by the Chilean Commission on Torture and Illegal Detention, which, after investigating the *modus operandi* of certain detention centers, asserted that it could safely be assumed that anyone detained in those centers was, indeed, tortured. See *Informe de la Comisión Nacional Sobre Prisión Política y Tortura* (Santiago, 2004).
7. See the paper on Argentina by María José Guembe (Chapter 1, this volume).
8. Law 23.466 (1986) and Law 24.411 (1994). These laws and those referred to below are reproduced in Part III of this collection.

9. Decree 70 (1991), and Law 24.043 (1991).

10. Law 25.914 of August 30, 2004.

11. See the paper on South Africa by Chris Colvin (Chapter 5, this volume).

12. *Promotion of National Unity*, sec. 1(1)(xix)(a), 1(1)(ix).

13. See, for example, Mahmood Mamdani, 'Reconciliation Without Justice', *Southern African Review of Books* Nov. Dec. 3–5 (1996).

14. I am grateful to Paul van Zyl for conversation about these issues.

15. Article 1, Law 9,140/95. See the paper on Brazil by Ignacio Cano and Patrícia Ferreira (Chapter 3, this volume).

16. See Law 19.123 of 8 February 1992, reproduced in Part III.

17. The relevant laws, in addition to the Luxembourg Agreement, were passed in 1953, 1956, and 1965. Part III reproduces the Luxembourg Agreement and extended excerpts of the 1956 and 1965 laws.

18. See the paper on German Holocaust reparations by Ariel Colonomos and Andrea Armstrong (Chapter 10, this volume).

19. See the paper by John Authers on German reparations for concentration camp inmates (Chapter 11, this volume).

20. See my 'Truth-Telling and the Rule of Law', in *Telling the Truths: Truth Telling and Peacebuilding in Post-Conflict Societies*, Tristan Anne Borer, ed. (Notre Dame, IN: University of Notre Dame Press, 2005).

21. This, of course, simplifies reality. It abstracts from the complexities introduced by the fact that the payments were made in bonds, and from other features of the general context like the vagaries of the prosecutorial efforts, the significant amount of information about the past that became available through the CONADEP Report, 'truth trials', and other means, and from institutional reforms that were taking place in Argentina as the reparations laws were being enacted and implemented.

22. As I indicate in my paper in Part II of this collection (Chapter 12), I distinguish between 'reparations efforts' and 'reparations programs'. The latter term should be reserved to designate initiatives that are designed from the outset as a systematically interlinked set of reparations measures. Most countries do not have reparations programs in this sense. Reparations benefits are most often the result of discrete initiatives that come about incrementally rather than from a deliberately designed plan. When no harm is done I use the terms interchangeably.

23. Civil litigation thus raises the risk of entrenching prevalent social biases. Wealthier, more educated, more urban victims usually have a higher chance of successfully pursuing reparations litigation in civil courts than poorer, less educated, more rural individuals, who may also happen to belong to less favored ethnic, racial, or religious groups. For a contrasting perspective on this issue, see Jaime Malamud-Goti and Lucas Grosman, 'Reparations and Civil Litigation' (Chapter 15, this volume). Regardless of one's position on the merits of finality, it is important to acknowledge the very significant catalytic role played by litigation in different instances. In the Latin American context, cases before the Inter-American Human Rights Commission and Court have prodded different governments to establish massive reparations programs.

24. I have chosen this old-fashioned term because I do not want to talk about the 'generosity' of reparations programs. I see reparations as a matter of right, not generosity. Nevertheless, it is clear that even if one considers this an issue of right, there is a large range of options concerning what it takes to satisfy that right.

25. The caveat is important, for in the aggregate, if the number of victims is significant, programs may end up distributing large amounts of money—each victim, of course, receiving a small amount. US reparations for Japanese Americans are a case in point.
26. I emphasize the roughness of the ordering. Part of it is due to the fact that some of the programs gave benefits in a lump sum (US, Brazil, Argentina), and two of them in the form of pensions (Chile and Germany), and establishing the total value of a pension is always a difficult exercise.
27. In the sample of cases included in this collection, only the September 11 Fund has arguably satisfied this criterion of justice. As Issacharoff and Mansfield argue (Chapter 8, this volume), however, it is not clear that the Fund is a reparations program in any ordinary sense. Moreover, interestingly, the fact that this criterion of justice *was* satisfied has not exempted this program from the problems that have usually plagued procedures that individualize the treatment of claims.
28. See my paper in Part II (Chapter 12), as well as the papers by Hamber (Chapter 16), Falk (Chapter 13), Carrillo (Chapter 14), Malamud-Goti and Grosman (Chapter 15).
29. The general topic of gender and reparations has, indeed, become the subject of a new two-year research initiative at the ICTJ.
30. See Comisión de la Verdad y Reconciliación, *Informe Final* (Lima, 2003), vol. 9, ch. 2.
31. See *Informe de la Comisión Nacional Sobre Prisión Política y Tortura* (Santiago, 2004), ch. 9.
32. See *Report of the Truth and Reconciliation Commission for Sierra Leone* [Presented to the President of Sierra Leone on October 5, 2004], vol. 2, ch. 4.
33. UN Document E/CN.4/2004/88, February 27, 2004.
34. UN Document E/CN.4/2005/L.48, April 13, 2005.

PART I

CASE STUDIES

ECONOMIC REPARATIONS FOR GRAVE HUMAN RIGHTS VIOLATIONS: THE ARGENTINEAN EXPERIENCE

MARÍA JOSÉ GUEMBE

Argentina's transition to democracy and its response to serious human rights violations committed between 1975 and 1983 included the creation of the National Commission on the Disappearance of Persons [*Comisión Nacional sobre Desaparición de Personas* (CONADEP)],[1] the prosecution of high-ranking military officials,[2] and a broad policy of economic reparations. The first two measures received both national and international attention and served as examples for transitions to democracy that later took place in many other countries.

Economic reparations for the victims, however, have not received the same attention, despite being quite outstanding in the international arena in terms of their reach. In the significant amount of literature that exists on the Argentinean transition, there is little to be found on economic reparations for the victims of state terrorism. This is probably because the reparations programs were implemented when democracy had already been reestablished for some years in the country, so the attention of analysts and researchers was already focused on other transitional cases. Another reason for this gap in the literature is without a doubt the lack of publicly available and precise information that would enable an in-depth analysis.[3]

The aim of this study is to present a complete overview of the Argentinean policy of economic reparations for the victims of human rights violations committed by the last military dictatorship, including the beneficiaries, the crimes for which victims received reparations, the amounts paid, and the forms of payment. This study also focuses on the motivations for redressing the victims and the positions adopted by the different actors involved in the measures, especially the State and human rights organizations. The latter, created during the period of the military dictatorship, gained undeniable legitimacy by representing the victims and have consolidated into a group that has become the main actor on issues related to the legacy of the military dictatorship.

First, this study analyzes the origins of the policy of reparations. Second, some economic measures adopted shortly after the reestablishment of democracy are considered. Third, reparations for victims of arbitrary detentions, forced disappearances, and assassinations are described. Finally, some general conclusions are presented.

1. ORIGIN OF THE POLICY OF REPARATIONS

As part of the background to Argentina's policy of reparations, it is important to highlight the following recommendation made by CONADEP in its 1984 final report: 'Norms should be enacted in order to provide economic assistance to the children and/or family of the disappeared persons during the repression: scholarships, social assistance, and job positions. Likewise, measures deemed convenient for alleviating the social and family problems created by the forced disappearance of persons should be taken.'[4]

While this recommendation addressed only one crime in particular (disappearance), a series of reparations laws were passed between 1984 and 1985. The benefits established by these laws were not exclusively economic, and they did not comprise an official reparations policy in strict terms; nevertheless, they were very important in repairing the particular situations of the beneficiaries.

Before analyzing these laws, it is necessary to mention the creation of an entity within the executive branch of the government with specific jurisdiction in human rights. When CONADEP was dissolved, the executive branch faced the need to create a body that would systematize the data that had been gathered by the Commission and then present to the courts the conclusions it derived from this information, as well as new denunciations regarding the disappearance of persons. In order to meet this need, as well as to continue with the identification of bodies and the search for disappeared children,[5] the Office of the Undersecretary for Human and Social Rights [*Subsecretaría de Derechos Humanos y Sociales*] was created within the Ministry of the Interior on September 20, 1984—two days after the publication of the '*Informe Nunca Más*' (the 'Never Again Report').[6] The new Office was given the documentation gathered by CONADEP.

When the structure of the Ministry of the Interior was later modified, the Office was given the status of National Directorship for Human Rights [*Dirección Nacional de Derechos Humanos*].[7] Among the duties assigned to this Directorship was promoting compliance with international human rights norms, which involved receiving accusations of discrimination and human rights violations, carrying out proceedings in order to verify their basis, and sending them to the judicial and administrative authorities. The Directorship was also in charge of a document center on human rights issues and coordinating operations with the National Genetic Data Bank [*Banco Nacional de Datos Genéticos*].[8] Later, in 1996, when the structure of the Ministry of the Interior was modified one more time,[9] the National Directorship became, again, the Office of the Undersecretary for Human and Social Rights. In 1999, the Office was transferred to the Ministry of Justice and Human Rights.[10] Finally, in February 2002, it was given the status of Secretariat of Human and Social Rights [*Secretaría de Derechos Humanos y Sociales*].[11] This governmental body, which we will refer to throughout this document using its current name, the Secretariat of Human Rights, was given the authority to apply most of the laws regarding the redress of victims of state terrorism from 1975 to 1983.

Many of these laws that were passed during the first years of the democratic regime aimed to address the situation of public servants who had been dismissed during the dictatorship. Law 23.053 of 1984[12] reincorporated into the Foreign Service those public servants who had been declared redundant and dismissed during the dictatorship. In that same year, Law 23.117[13] called for the reincorporation of employees of State-controlled companies dismissed for political motives or reasons pertaining to their trade union membership.

In 1985, Law 23.238[14] established the reincorporation of teachers who had been dismissed before December 9, 1983, or declared redundant for political or other related reasons (including membership in trade unions), and recognized the time they spent away from work for labor and pension-fund purposes. In the same vein, Law 23.523[15] stated that bank workers who were dismissed for political motives would also be reincorporated. Law 23.278[16] of September 28, 1985 was aimed at those persons who were dismissed, declared redundant, forced to quit their public or private posts, or forced into exile for political motives or reasons pertaining to their trade unions. It established that inactive periods would be calculated for retirement purposes. These laws redressed the unjust situations of specific groups of public servants. They were passed in response, in general terms, to the demands and pressure brought by those groups, independently from the support they received from the rest of society.

At the same time, some persons who had been detained by the Executive under state of siege provisions initiated civil lawsuits in which they demanded indemnification from the State for harms and damages. The state of siege had been declared on November 6, 1974, in a decree in which President María Estela Martínez ordered the 'elimination of subversion', and which led to the application of state terrorism in Argentina. These demands of former political prisoners gave rise to a debate within the judiciary, which later contributed to approving legislative measures of reparations.

Simultaneously, human rights organizations began a slow process of discussion on the possibility of the State economically repairing human rights violations in a broad and far-reaching manner. Together with a number of jurists, these organizations formed the Initiative Group for the Convention against the Forced Disappearance of Persons [*Grupo de Iniciativa para una Convención contra las Desapariciones Forzadas de Personas*],[17] which sought to use national and international legal instruments[18] in its efforts to redress the crime of forced disappearances committed by the former regime.

In October 1988, the Initiative Group organized an international colloquium in Buenos Aires that discussed the topic and formulated the Declaration on the Forced Disappearance of Persons, which was to be presented before the General Assembly of the United Nations, as well as a draft for an international convention for the prevention and sanctioning of this particular crime. This colloquium gathered international experts and nongovernmental organizations (NGOs), as well as the affected persons, and clearly laid out the duties of the State under international law regarding serious human rights violations, including forced disappearances. Debate centered especially on the need to establish the truth about what happened to the victims and to impose sanctions on those responsible.

The colloquium also discussed, for the first time, the State's duty to award economic reparations to victims. Initially, the possibility of receiving economic reparations had provoked resistance among certain human rights organizations formed by those who were directly affected by the crimes: mothers, grandmothers, and other family members. This resistance stemmed from the idea that receiving reparations implied exchanging, for a sum of money, the lives of their disappeared relatives and abandoning their demands for justice. Nevertheless, once it was understood that in the international arena states are required to provide economic compensation for victims of serious human rights violations, among other duties, it was possible to add this demand to those of truth and justice. Hence, human rights organizations understood that economic reparations are a legitimate demand to which the State must respond.

Only one of these human rights groups, Mothers of Plaza de Mayo Association [*Asociación Madres de Plaza de Mayo*], led by Hebe Pastor de Bonafini, maintained its opposition to the idea of reparations. The Association is one of the two groups that make up Mothers of Plaza de Mayo [*Madres de Plaza de Mayo*], along with Mothers of Plaza de Mayo—Founding Group [*Madres de Plaza de Mayo—Línea Fundadora*]. In addition to other important political differences, the issue of reparations divided the organization. The Association is categorically opposed to any policy of reparations, whether it involves either a monetary payment or an act of public recognition, such as an official apology. It contends that economic reparations entail accepting the death of the disappeared. As we shall see later, the rest of the human rights organizations have supported reparations policies and, through active participation, have achieved legislative reforms to this end.[19]

However, despite the specific recommendation made by CONADEP, the support of human rights organizations and those directly affected, as well as willingness on the part of the State, economic reparations took a long time to be awarded. The initial priority in the agenda for the country's democratic transition was the establishment of truth and justice; it was only gradually, however, that these demands were extended to include economic reparations. While some general reparations measures were adopted under the constitutional government of Raúl Alfonsín (1983–9), it was under Carlos Menem's government (1989–99) that the measures comprising an economic reparations policy for serious human rights violations were taken.

2. INITIAL REPARATIONS MEASURES

The first reparations measure adopted by the Argentinean State was granting a pension to the spouses and children of disappeared persons.[20] During the dictatorship and the first years of democracy, human rights organizations undertook the task of providing economic help to the victims. However, after the democratic regime had been in power for some time, due to the country's economic crisis, these organizations could no longer help the families economically. Granting this pension was understood by the victims as the State's duty to provide help to those who were now in a precarious situation because of forced disappearance.

The law defined victims of forced disappearance as those persons who had been deprived of their freedom and had then disappeared, or those who were kept in clandestine detention places or were deprived of their right to due process. Beneficiaries received a pension that was equivalent to the minimum ordinary amount received by a retired public servant. They also benefited from the social coverage of the National Institute of Social Services for Pensioners and Retired Servants [*Instituto Nacional de Servicios Sociales para Jubilados y Pensionados*], which includes health care assistance and medicines.

The persons who could claim both pecuniary and health benefits were the following:

- Children younger than twenty-one years of age whose parents—one or both of them—had disappeared. Benefits expired when the child turned 21, except in cases of disability. Later, the limit was extended to 25 years of age, or when they received their university degrees.
- The surviving husband or wife, legally married, or someone who had lived with the victim for a minimum period of five years, immediately preceding the disappearance. In these cases, benefits do not expire. For this reason, the State still pays them a pension and offers them health care assistance.
- Disabled parents or siblings who do not perform any profitable activity and who do not enjoy pensions, retirement benefits, or tax-free benefits. These benefits also do not expire.
- Orphan siblings under age, who had lived regularly with the victim before the disappearance. This benefit does not expire either.

Forced disappearances had to be proven by filing an accusation before a judicial body, the former CONADEP, or the Secretariat of Human and Social Rights. The law established that in cases without sufficient factual evidence, accusations could be validated by the testimonies of two or more persons. If the petitioner did not have a copy of the accusation, the Secretariat of Human Development and Family [*Secretaría de Desarrollo Humano y Familia*] would issue a report to be sent to the aforementioned bodies.

The pension law did not face opposition from most sectors of society. In the legislative sphere, there were no substantial objections put forth. One of the issues that was discussed in the debates leading to the enactment of this law was the possible incompatibility between receiving the pension awarded and the right of the victims to sue for indemnification under civil law.[21] Nevertheless, there were no disagreements on this point, and the law did not exclude the exercise of any civil law action.

One congressman for the governing party[22] proposed the need to establish a more general law of indemnification that would address the violence committed not just by the military but by other armed groups as well. He argued that in order to achieve national reconciliation, the pain suffered by everyone needed to be considered. This position embodied an idea of Alfonsín's government, commonly referred to as the 'theory of the two demons' [*la teoría de los dos demonios*], an expression that originated in criticism aimed at Alfonsín's attempt to equate the actions of armed groups with State repression. The government contended that terrorist groups had provoked illegal repression, and that both parties were equally criminal. This argument, however, was always unacceptable to human rights organizations and the victims' families. As Emilio Mignone put the point:

[T]he State must remain within the bounds of law and morality, if not, it loses legitimacy. Crimes committed by individual agents cannot serve as justification for moving away from these rules. In the case of crimes, common or political, committed by individual agents, the affected can and must appeal to the protection provided by the State, which holds the monopoly over the legitimate use of force. On the contrary, when it is the State that commits these crimes, the victims are completely defenseless.[23]

This eloquent explanation justified the need to redress victims of State terrorism, which should not in any way be extended to those who, acting as agents of the State, violated the most fundamental human rights.

The draft bill stated that this type of economic reparation did not substitute for the obligation to guarantee the rights of the victims to truth and justice. This would come up again in debates about other norms with economic consequences, as an expression of fear by the victims that the State would neglect its duties after paying a sum of money.

3. The Reparations Laws

At the end of 1989, Carlos S. Menem, of the Justicialist Party [*Partido Justicialista*], was sworn in as President of Argentina. He remained in office for two consecutive terms, his government lasting until the end of 1999. During these terms, the Menem government passed the most important laws concerning economic reparations for victims of human rights violations committed between 1974 and 1983.

During this period the country's judicial system was paralyzed as far as the prosecution of human rights abuses was concerned. At Alfonsín's initiative, two laws had been passed in 1986 and 1987, the 'Final Stop' Law[24] and the Law of 'Due Obedience',[25] which put an end to the prosecution of most members of the military and armed forces for their involvement in state terrorism. Menem then granted Presidential pardons[26] to the members of the military *juntas* who had been convicted in the *Juntas* Trial, and to a few high-ranking military officials whose trials were still underway. At the same time, he also granted pardons to some guerrilla leaders who were being prosecuted.

In response, the victims of state terrorism resorted to the Inter-American Commission on Human Rights (IACHR) to denounce these laws as violations of the American Declaration of the Rights and Duties of Man and the American Convention on Human Rights. On October 2, 1992, the Commission issued Report 28/92 in which it proclaimed the following:

1. Laws Num. 23.492 and 23.521 and Decree Num. 1002/89 are incompatible with article XVIII (right to justice) of the American Declaration of the Rights and Duties of Man, and articles 1, 8, and 25 of the American Convention on Human Rights.
2. [The Commission] [r]ecommends that the Government of Argentina award petitioners with a fair compensation for the violations referred to in the previous paragraph.
3. Recommends that the Government of Argentina adopt the necessary measures to establish the facts and identify those responsible for human rights violations that occurred during the last military dictatorship.
4. Orders the publication of this report.[27]

This recommendation from the IACHR that the Argentinean government economically redress human rights violations gave added support to the incipient demands of the victims.

As mentioned above, a number of persons who had been detained by the Executive under the authority of the state of siege decree initiated legal action against the State after they were released, demanding indemnification for harms and damages. Among them was President Menem himself, who between 1976 and 1981 had been a political prisoner. The number of detained persons under the jurisdiction of the Executive during the dictatorship and the immediately preceding years reached over 10,000. Most had been detained under state of siege, while only a small number were accused of having committed a crime.

Many of the suits brought by these victims were initially rejected on statute of limitation grounds. According to Argentinean legislation,[28] the statute of limitations for these cases is two years. It did not matter, therefore, concluded the judges, whether the courts confirmed that the deprivations of freedom and the conditions in which they took place were against the law. Some of the prisoners who had been released before the military dictatorship came to an end argued that they had been unable to initiate legal action at that time because the State did not provide them with sufficient guarantees. For this reason, they demanded an additional period for filing a suit, according to the provisions of the law.[29] They claimed that the period for calculating the statute of limitations should start on December 10, 1983, when democracy was reestablished. The victims also argued that the responsibility of the State, which would enable them to take legal action against it, was not established until the *Juntas* Trial revealed the systematic plan to physically eliminate political opposition using State apparatus.

Many of these cases were resolved internally by judicial rulings that the statute of limitations should be calculated beginning December 10, 1983, extending the period for filing a lawsuit through December 19, 1985. In these cases, the judges stated that security conditions for presenting accusations only existed after that date, when democracy was reestablished. These cases were not appealed by the State, and the Supreme Court therefore did not review them.

By contrast, those cases in which judges rejected the arguments put forth by the victims reached the Supreme Court and received unfavorable rulings. The Court stated that the passage of time produces legal effects, unless there is a specific law that establishes the contrary. The Supreme Court understood that the statute of limitations—two years—should be calculated from the moment the prisoner was released. Rulings by the Supreme Court only affected the cases it was reviewing, not others, even those where the same questions are at stake, thereby producing conditions of inequality among the victims. Those who won their trials were able to claim indemnification, while those who lost by rulings of the Supreme Court were not able to claim any amount. This situation led the victims whose cases had been rejected to file accusations before the Inter-American Commission on Human Rights.[30]

Petitioners argued before the IACHR that the Supreme Court rulings violated their right to due process established in article XVIII of the American Declaration of the Rights and Duties of Man, and their entitlements established in articles 8 and 25 of the American Convention on Human Rights. They expressed to the Commission their wish to reach a friendly agreement.[31] The government, far from displaying a conciliatory attitude, responded that the case should be declared inadmissible, since the events in question took place before the American Convention was in force.[32]

The State's policy changed, however, when a new government took office. The new President, Carlos Menem, was a member of the *Partido Justicialista* and a former political prisoner, and had in fact won his own case for indemnification against the State.[33] In a hearing with the IACHR, State representatives stated that Menem's government 'was not necessarily in disagreement with petitioners'. They indicated that President Menem himself had been detained for political reasons under the military regime, that he sympathized with petitioners, and that he wanted to award them a fair compensation.[34] The government presented a copy of Decree Num. 798/90[35] to the IACHR, which authorized the creation of an ad hoc commission to formulate a draft bill that would award petitioners the compensation they deserved. Both the IACHR and the petitioners expressed their agreement with this decision by the government. The ad hoc commission elaborated a draft bill that was sent to the National Congress,[36] after which time the commission was dissolved. Due to the delay by the Congress in dealing with this draft bill, and the government's willingness to comply with the IACHR and petitioners, a second decree was issued,[37] which would grant petitioners an adequate compensation. Petitioners accepted this measure and it was adopted by the government.[38] According to the interpretation of his highest-ranked official in human rights,

President Menem's intention was, on the one hand, to earn the respect of the Organization of American States (OAS) by complying with the decisions of its institutions, and on the other, to implement a policy that would redress his own former colleagues involved in political activism who had been victims of the dictatorship just as he had.[39]

Beneficiaries of this decree were persons who under state of siege had been in the custody of the national executive branch, and who complied with the following requirements: they had filed a lawsuit for indemnification for harms and damages before December 10, 1985[40] and a nonappealable judgment had ruled that the statute of limitations had expired; or they had filed a lawsuit whose proceedings were already underway when the decree was enacted. Those with ongoing proceedings could chose to continue with them, and if their cases were eventually dismissed on statute of limitations grounds, they could avail themselves of the benefits offered by this decree. Alternatively, they could withdraw their case and claim the amount for indemnification provided by this decree. This amount equaled one-thirtieth of the monthly salary assigned to the highest category of the Roster of Civil Servants of the National Public Administration [*Escalafón para el Personal Civil de la Administración Pública Nacional*] for each day of detention.

The decision to set the compensation at the level of what is earned by the highest-ranked civil servant had a special meaning for the government. Alicia Pierini, Undersecretary for Human and Social Rights in Menem's government, explains:

The way in which this amount was fixed has to do with the idea of reparation rather than with indemnification. What we wanted was to pay, for each day of the detention, what the State's public servant of the highest rank, who could not work, would have earned. This implied breaking away from labor rights criteria and those of accidents in the workplace. Imprisonment was no accident and Menem agreed, this is why the discussion was won.[41]

The decree explicitly provided for an increase in the amount of compensation for the cases in which the victims died or suffered from severe injuries, in the terms expressed in article 91 of the Penal Code. According to this law, severe injuries are defined as those causing a 'physical or mental illness, certainly or probably incurable, permanent work disabilities, the loss of one sense, an organ, a member, the use of an organ or a member, loss of speech, or the capacity to beget or conceive'. Decree 70/91 proclaimed that if the detainee died during detention, the benefit would be established in the same way as with the other cases of detention for the period calculated until the moment of death, but, owing to the death, would include the amount equivalent to what is provided by this law for five years of detention. In case of severe injuries, there would be an increase in the benefit equivalent to 70 percent of the additional amount awarded in cases of death.

According to this decree, $27 was paid for each day of the detention. Payments were made in cash. According to information provided by the Secretariat of Human and Social Rights, approximately 227 persons received this reparations measure. In cases of death, the benefit was calculated as follows: $27 was paid for each day of the detention plus $49,275, which was the amount for five years of detention. In cases of severe injuries, $27 was paid for each day of the detention plus $34,492, which was the equivalent of 70 percent of the amount for five years. Up to this date, no official data has been published regarding the amounts of the reparations paid. This makes it impossible to estimate the resources that the State has allocated for the implementation of this decree. According to article 12 of the decree, the necessary expenses to comply with this norm were to be charged to the State's assets.

Applications for claiming benefits had to be filed before the Ministry of the Interior, which had to verify 'expeditiously' the duration of detentions, and then the necessary payments. If an application was rejected, an appeal could be filed within ten days before the ordinary courts, which had 20 days to resolve the case. Payments were supposed to be made in cash within 60 days of the approval of the application. In case the payment was not made, it could be judicially claimed through the normal procedure established for the execution of sentences.[42]

Those who received a benefit—in case of the victim's death, his or her successors could claim the benefit[43]—had to renounce any further right to indemnification for damages.[44] In the stated motivation for this decree, the executive branch recognized that this measure was not meant to be a substitute for justice but to correct unfair situations provoked by the strict application of existing law.

4. REPARATIONS FOR VICTIMS OF ARBITRARY DETENTION

Less than a year after Decree Num. 70/91 was sanctioned, the National Congress passed Law 24.043.[45] Like the decree, this law awarded a benefit to those persons who were detained before December 10, 1983 by virtue of state of siege and were in the custody of the Executive. This law was also aimed at those civilians who had been detained as a consequence of decisions made by military tribunals, with or without a sentence, regardless of whether they had brought suit for harms and damages. Those who had already received compensation for the same violations by a judicial ruling could not apply for benefits. Applications for benefits were again presented to the Ministry of the Interior.[46] Authorities had to verify expeditiously the duration of detentions, and then, compliance with the necessary payments. Applicants had to declare under oath that they had been detained under the conditions established by the law between November 6, 1974 and December 10, 1983.[47]

In order to calculate the duration of detentions, the following information was taken into account: on the one hand, the act of the Executive that decreed the detention or the effective arrest without an order from the competent judicial authority, and, on the other, the act that left the previous one without particular effect or as a consequence of the end of state of siege. In case a person died during detention, the end of the period was calculated as the time of his or her death, and an amount equivalent to what is provided by this law for five years of detention was added to the benefit. For those who suffered from severe injuries[48] during detention there was an increase in the benefit equivalent to 70 percent of the amount established in cases of death. This benefit could be received by the beneficiary's successors in case of death or declaration of absence with presumption of death.[49]

Detentions and their duration could be proven with the presentation of copies of habeas corpus appeals or the respective sentence, records from the competent authorities, such as those from the Office of the Undersecretary of Human Rights regarding the accusations in existence in the CONADEP archives, administrative or judicial records, and documentation in existence with the Commission and the Inter-American Court on Human Rights. Documentation in existence with national and international human rights institutions, as well as newspaper articles and bibliographic material, were evaluated together with the accepted proof. In order to prove injuries, the clinical records of the detention place, a copy of the judicial ruling that validated them, and the victim's medical or clinical history from an official health institution were accepted. If necessary, a medical meeting was held at a public hospital. The established guidelines were broad and took into account the conditions in which detentions occurred and the difficulties in proving them. An avenue of legal appeal was established, just as for Decree Num. 70/91, in order to review the partial or total rejection of a benefit claim.

Victims received a sum equivalent, at the time the benefit was claimed, to one-thirtieth of the monthly amount paid to the highest category of the roster of civil servants of the National Public Administration, for each day of the detention. This law established that the considered monthly amount included all aspects of the servant's salary subject to contributions for retirement, excluding certain additions like seniority, degree, etc. According to the provisions of this law and its regulations, $74 was paid for each day of the detention.[50] In the cases in which the victim died during detention, the number of days was counted until the time of death, with an increase in the benefit equivalent to the amount paid for five years of detention, which came to $136,254.50. For those who suffered severe injuries during detention, the compensation awarded for the time of the detention along with an increase in the benefit of 70 percent of the amount established in cases of death came to $94,490.14.

These awards were distributed to victims in the form of bonds of consolidation of public debt—specifically, *Bocon Proveedores Serie II*—documents through which the Argentinean State recognizes the existence of a debt and guarantees its payment. Instead of paying money, the State gives titles of debt that the holders can later exchange for money. Each bond has a nominal value or value in capital, and it pays interest. The bonds can be exchanged at any time at the quoted price in the markets, or they can be exchanged with the State for their total value at the date of their expiration. The *Bocon Proveedores Serie II* bonds expire 16 years after they are issued. It is important to keep in mind that the issuance of bonds has no effect on the national budget before they mature, since there is no immediate distribution of money, but a promise that the titles will be paid in the future.

The benefit had to be claimed within 180 days from the moment the law was in force. The period for filing claims ended on September 17, 1998. According to the Secretariat of Human and Social Rights, approximately 13,600 persons claimed the benefit, of which approximately 7,800 had a favorable resolution.[51] Consulted for the present study, the Secretariat claimed not to have information regarding the amount paid to each person. Those persons who had claimed the benefit established by Decree Num. 70/91 were awarded the difference between the $27 granted for each day of the detention according to that decree and the $74.66 established by this law.[52]

In August 1994, this benefit was extended to cover persons who had initiated legal action and won their cases, but who had received compensation for harms and damages lower than that awarded by Decree Num. 70/90 and Law 24.043.[53]

The implementation of Law 24.043 began in January 1992, only after many political and administrative obstacles had been overcome.[54] A lack of resources in the then Directorship of Human Rights forced it to implement a system for receiving petitions with the help of two nongovernmental human rights organizations.[55] These organizations, which had branches throughout the country, offered their offices for receiving applications. In 1992, the Federal Council for Human Rights [*Consejo Federal de Derechos Humanos*] was created. Its structure enabled the Directorship of Human Rights to appoint an official in each province to administer the reparations payments. In August 1992, the Directorship was upgraded to Office of the Undersecretary for Human and Social Rights.[56]

The application of this law raised a number of new problems. Many persons claiming reparations, for example, had been detained not owing to state of siege, but rather owing to accusations that they had committed crimes. While these were crimes committed during armed resistance, and for this reason the government had the intention of including these people as beneficiaries of reparations, the law did not allow this.[57] In these cases, the benefit was extended despite the existence of legal processes awaiting resolution, and there were no objections by any of the involved parties.

Another question was whether the children of detainees, who were detained with their parents or were born during imprisonment, should be able to claim economic reparations as well. Despite the fact that these cases numbered more than 100, they were not addressed by the law. The Office of the Undersecretary and the Office of the Judge Advocate [*Unidad de Auditoría*], a delegation of the General Trusteeship of the Nation [*Sindicatura General de la Nación*] within the Secretariat of Human Rights, reached conflicting decisions on the issue and the benefit was not awarded. Later, the Secretariat elaborated a draft bill to correct the situation, but it was not approved by Congress. A third difficulty was proving injuries suffered during imprisonment, so many years after they had happened.

Problems like these that arose throughout the implementation of the law were solved in debates between the lawyers of the General Treasury [*Procuración General del Tesoro*] and the Office of the Undersecretary for Human and Social Rights, sometimes with their decisions in writing and other times in verbal discussions. The Office of the Undersecretary decided to work on these problems through critical cases, whose resolutions served as applicable precedents for subsequent cases.

The largest problem was the fact that by 1994 no victim had been paid yet. According to the involved officials, the primary reason for this was an inadequate administrative structure, together with disagreements within the government regarding the employment scale to be used in order to establish the amount of payments.[58] This delay provoked criticism from the affected parties and human rights organizations. In March 1994, a joint resolution issued by the Ministers of the Interior and the Economy[59] established how the payment of benefits would be made and that they would be calculated according to the new roster of civil servants of the National Public Administration. This meant that a larger amount than the one that had been paid according to Decree Num. 70/91 would be awarded this time. As mentioned before, those who had already claimed the amount established by Decree Num. 70/91 were given the difference in order to level their cases with those benefiting from Law 24.043. This resolution enabled the government to start paying the reparations.

5. REPARATIONS FOR FORCED DISAPPEARANCES OF PERSONS AND ASSASSINATIONS

In 1994, Law 24.411[60] was passed, granting economic reparations for victims of forced disappearances and the successors of persons assassinated by the military, members of security forces, or paramilitary groups. This initiative came from the governing party.⁶¹ Without a doubt, this was the law that sparked the most debate about the meaning of economically repairing the crimes of the dictatorship. The issues surrounding the forced disappearances included the denial of information about the victims during the dictatorship, the lack of individualized responses once democracy was reestablished, and the impunity of those responsible.

Economic reparations for political prisoners had provoked neither much debate nor much opposition. By contrast, reparations for disappearances gave rise to many controversies, the majority of which were not discussed publicly. The main concern of the victims was that the State would be exchanging money for silence about what happened and impunity for those responsible. For this reason, they constantly insisted it should be made clear that reparations would not absolve the State of its responsibility to address these matters in other ways. They also demanded that the disappeared would be legally declared as such—disappeared rather than dead—and that any money paid by the State would be given in the victim's name and not in the name of his or her legal successors. If the State declared that the person was still disappeared, this implied an official recognition that the body had not been recovered and that its final whereabouts were not known. Therefore, out of this process of providing reparations a new legal status emerged for persons in the Argentinean legal system: 'absence by forced disappearance'. This was not merely a semantic or political question; it had real consequences for the procedures for claiming the economic reparations granted by the State.

Forced disappearances raised problems for which the legal system could not provide solutions. The Argentinean legal system provides legal solutions applicable in different situations involving the prolonged absence of a person, but none of these solutions could be applied to forced disappearances. The Civil Code distinguishes between living and dead persons, and regards those who are absent, even when presumed dead as in fact dead persons. As explained above, a fundamental demand made by the families, when they had lost all hope that the disappeared would be found alive, was for the authorities not to consider them dead until their bodies were found. The families maintained this demand even when the presumption of death would have removed certain legal obstacles, allowing them, for example, to file a lawsuit to acquire possession of the deceased's property. When Law 24.411 awarded the concession of economic reparations for victims of forced disappearances, the victims themselves could not claim them, but neither could their successors if they refused to declare that their relatives had died.

There existed no specific legal measure to solve this type of problem until 1994, when the government passed the Law of Absence by Forced Disappearance [*Ley de Ausencia por Desaparición Forzada*].⁶² This law does not presume the death of the disappeared person, but forces the State to accept that the person was illegally kidnapped by its agents and that he or she never appeared again, dead or alive. The families, almost unanimously, have applauded this resolution. Alicia Pierini, the Undersecretary for Human Rights at that time, describes the process of approving the law of forced disappearance as a great challenge: '[T]here was no precedent either in national legislation or in comparative law; hence, we had to create the legal formulation from scratch.'[63]

The law created this new legal status for all persons who had involuntarily disappeared before December 10, 1983—the day when democracy was re-established—and for whom there was no news of their whereabouts. As each of these persons was not legally dead, it was necessary to establish who could legitimately request the judge to declare him or her absent by forced disappearance. Those people who were presumed to have a legitimate interest in such a declaration were allowed to make this request: spouses, ancestors, descendants, and relatives to the fourth degree. The request has to be made before a judge and the forced disappearance can be verified with accusations presented before judges, CONA-DEP, or the Secretariat of Human and Social Rights. Once the judge receives the request, he or she has to demand the reports to the authority that received the accusation of disappearance and order the publication of edicts for three consecutive days. After 60 straight days have elapsed, an absence by forced disappearance is declared, fixing as the presumed date of the occurrence the one that appears on the original accusation. Once the victim is declared absent by forced disappearance, proceedings for claiming the economic benefits awarded by Law 24.411 can be initiated by whoever is declared to be his or her successor.

Law 24.411 was the one that provoked the most debate among human rights organizations and within the executive and the legislative branches of the state. Discrepancies were such that the original law only contained some minimal dispositions agreed upon by all parties, but it did not cover all of the aspects that were important for making its application possible. For this reason, years later, this law was complemented with a second one: Law 24.823,[64] known as the 'mending-patch law' [ley parche].

In cases of forced disappearances, the 'mending-patch law' established that as long as the disappearance persists, the benefits provided for by Law 24.411 (de-scribed in detail below) are to be distributed among the victim's assignees in the following order of priority: descendants, spouse, ancestors, and relatives to the fourth degree.[65] The law also applies to common-law marriages as long as the couples had been together for at least two years before the disappearance or death. This had to be proven beyond any doubt. As an exception to the Civil Code, the law established that children who had been given up for adoption as a consequence of the forced disappearance or death of one or both of their parents would have the right to receive economic reparations.

Law 24.823 modified the demand for the declaration of heirs. It established that the person whose forced disappearance had been judicially declared would receive the pecuniary reparations through his or her assignees [causahabientes], who had to validate their status before a court.[66] The judge who had presided over the case of absence by forced disappearance would be competent to dictate the declaration of assignees.[67] This declaration would have similar effects to those of the declaration of heirs.[68]

Law 24.823 proclaimed that '[b]y penalty of nullity, under no circumstance can the intervening judge declare the death, nor fix the presumed date of this death'[69] of a victim of forced disappearance. The 'mending-patch law'[70] declared that the 'constitutional act of the Military *Junta* of April 28, 1983, and the so-called Final Report on the antisubversive fight of the same date' were irrevocably annulled. Both acts had resolved that disappeared persons were declared dead.

Law 24.411 was passed on December 7, 1994, during the early hours of the morning—a strategy frequently employed to avoid the presence of the press whenever controversial measures are discussed—with no relevant parliamentary debate. According to Executive officials at the time, if a debate had been opened, agreement would not have been reached and the law would not have been approved.

Political discussion of the law was contentious not only within the government but also among human rights organizations and within the families of victims. None of these groups openly demanded economic reparations. Even if they knew they had a right to reparations, subjective and political questions prevented them from exercising this right.

While the fight for reparations for former political prisoners had been led by the prisoners themselves, in the case of forced disappearances the families had to speak in the name of the victims and this caused conflicts that are difficult to explain. Some of the subjective questions that were insinuated by the families were never expressed openly by the directly affected persons. The most frequent one is a certain sense of guilt for demanding a payment of money. This sense of guilt is independent from their right to reparations, something the families are quite aware they are entitled to. These questions are a consequence of forced disappearances, or perhaps the way they took place in Argentina, and they affect the possibility of reparations.

In the opinion of Elizabeth Jelín, a sociologist, the debates over economic reparations were haunted by a number of 'ghosts', or unresolved issues. She explains:

The first one is that a reparation would imply the presumption of death. It is important to explain this because it is something that does not come up in all countries suffering from State repression. The second ghost is the idea that a 'transaction' would take place in which the State would buy the silence of the families. The third aspect has to do with abandoning the demand for justice, which is closely related to the second one regarding their silence.[71]

These concerns are clearly present in some of the public statements made by human rights organizations on the subject of economic reparations. The Commission of Families of Disappeared Persons and Detainees for Political Reasons [*Comisión de Familiares de Desaparecidos y Detenidos por Razones Políticas*] released a statement entitled 'We don't sell the blood of our children. We vindicate their cause' ['*No vendemos la sangre de nuestros hijos. Reivindicamos su lucha*']. In this statement, the organization emphasized that each reparations measure entailed the State's recognition of some aspects of its crimes and their consequences. Regarding Law 24.411, it declared the following:

Regarding the project of reparation, our Civil Code points out the duty of repairing economically, and it measures in money, not life, but rather the consequences or the value of the harms suffered.... Compensation is not reduced to mere economic reparation. Most of the families preferred measures of restitution, satisfaction, and above all, guarantees that this would never take place again.[72]

Among human rights organizations there was support for the government's proposals, but nothing more. These organizations did not exert pressure in favor of reparations for forced disappearance but—with the exception of the Association of the Mothers of the Plaza de Mayo—did not oppose them either. Their participation was limited to setting the boundaries of acceptability of the measures the government was considering. They expressed the same reservations as the families of the victims. In relation to the beneficiaries, the role of the NGOs was to counsel victims regarding their rights.[73]

Human rights organizations were also concerned that procedures for claiming benefits should be as easy as possible; they wanted families to avoid repeating the difficult journeys they were subject to during the dictatorship. The original draft bill contemplated some procedures before security agencies, which were clearly unnecessary from every standpoint. However, thanks to the opposition of human rights organizations, these requirements were eliminated from the final bill.

Law 24.411 established the benefit as optional, which meant that it was the victim's family's decision to claim it or not. Which choice those families should make has become a point of contention. As mentioned before, Mothers of Plaza de Mayo Association, led by Hebe P. de Bonafini, contends that families should not claim economic reparations because to do so would amount to prostituting themselves. The other human rights organizations, on the other hand, including Mothers of Plaza de Mayo—Founding Group, for the most part contend that such a decision must be taken individually by each one of the affected. Laura Conte, psychologist and member of the Center for Legal and Social Studies (CELS) and Mothers of Plaza de Mayo—Founding Group, disagrees. According to her:

[T]he law is optional, but in my opinion, it should have been mandatory, for many reasons. Human rights laws are fundamental. Nothing is as important as a law defining matters which are later going to be unquestionable. But reparation laws were never as clear, and moreover, they were even optional. It was important that the State recognized this as its duty: to repair beyond necessities. It was a social necessity and one of each member of society that the State should repair the damage caused by state terrorism.[74]

After much contentious debate, the model for distributing reparations was established as follows. A sum of money would be given to persons who at the time of the law's enactment were disappeared, a sum that would be received by those persons' 'assignees' [*causahabientes*]. This law does not establish a period in which the disappearance had to take place in order to be eligible for reparations, only specifying that it had to extend to the moment when the law was passed. An equal sum of money would be granted to the assignees of persons assassinated by the armed or security forces or paramilitary groups[75] before December 10, 1983. In this case, a deadline was established, but not a starting date for the period in which the assassination had taken place. There was no starting date established in either case because both forced disappearances and assassinations began to happen before the *coup d'état* of 1976. State terrorism began in Argentina under the government of María Estela Martínez (Perón's widow), who was overthrown by the military *coup* of March 24, 1976. During that period, when the actions of the Argentinean Anticommunist Alliance [*Alianza Anticomunista Argentina*], a paramilitary group known as the Triple A, particularly stood out, the first forced disappearances, as well as a significant number of assassinations of members of the political opposition, occurred. Despite opposition from members of the *peronismo,* the law did not exclude these crimes.

The absence of a starting date for the period of the crimes to be repaired created some problems that had to be solved with administrative resolutions. For example, the Secretariat of Human and Social Rights decided to grant reparations in those cases that took place before the *coup d'état* if the methods used were similar to those practiced by the armed, security, or paramilitary forces—as established in the sentence pronounced in the Trial of the Military *Juntas.*[76]

This law excluded from its beneficiaries those who had been victims of forced disappearances, but who had later appeared alive. These cases were included in the reparations for former political prisoners granted by Law 24.043.

Law 24.411 established that a crime of forced disappearance was committed when the victim was detained in nonclandestine detention places, but later disappeared to unknown final whereabouts, or when the victim was imprisoned in clandestine detention places from the beginning.

The range of evidence that can be presented for validating claims of forced disappearances is quite broad. This is of particular importance because repression in Argentina took place under clandestine conditions and no exhaustive investigations had been carried out, which made many of these cases quite difficult to prove. Fortunately, the State accounted for these difficulties, demanding only proof that could actually be provided. In addition, the State determined that the responsibility to prove these cases was held primarily by the State itself and not the families, although it could ask for their help.

A penal accusation of illegitimate deprivation of freedom and a judge's resolution that preliminarily established that the disappearance was due to this reason are accepted as evidence.[77] An accusation filed before CONADEP, of which a certificate is issued by the Secretariat of Human and Social Rights, or an accusation filed before this Secretariat is also accepted. If the disappearance was included in the list of victims published by CONADEP, it is considered to be proven.[78] Finally, other types of accepted evidence include those contemplated in procedural law, such as the testimony of a witness.[79]

Claims of assassination can be validated with a judicial ruling or administrative documents stating that personnel from the armed, security, or paramilitary forces participated in the crime. This participation is presumed when the events took place in the facilities of these forces. The assassination can also be validated with timely accusations presented before CONADEP. In these cases, other types of evidence contemplated in procedural law are also accepted.[80]

Applications for benefits are presented before the Secretariat of Human Rights. Once the beneficiaries have provided all the required documentation, the Ministry of the Interior must decide if the application has a basis within 360 working days. This process involves several stages. Before making any payment, the Secretariat must request from the federal police any possible records of the disappeared person registered after the disappearance occurred. (The State carries this out even though the families were initially expected to do so.)

Once all documents are submitted, and after a ruling by the permanent juridical service of the Ministry of the Interior is made, the Ministry dictates the administrative act by which it is decided whether the claim made by the validated assignees of the victim has a basis or not. These assignees must declare that they have not received indemnification for harms and damages for the same crime, and that they renounce the possibility of filing a lawsuit for the same reasons. Law 24.411 states that when there is doubt about whether to award indemnification, 'whatever is more favorable for the beneficiary, or his or her assignees, should be decided upon, based on the principle of good faith'.[81] It also states that a resolution denying the benefit, partially or totally, is subject to legal review.[82]

For cases both of disappearance and of assassination, the benefit awarded was equivalent to the monthly earnings of employees at Level A of the roster of civil servants of the National Public Administration,[83] multiplied by a coefficient of 100.[84] The awarded benefit was $224,000, which was paid in Bonds of Consolidation of the National Public Debt.[85] In this way, the effective payment of indemnification provided by Law 24.411 was formalized through titles of the Argentinean public debt.

Proposals for payments in bonds were considerably modified after the economic crisis of 2001. For those persons who received the benefit before December 2001, the State's proposal for payment was the following. Back in 1994, when the law was promulgated, the State had offered two types of bonds: one expressed in national currency (pesos), and the other in US dollars. The only difference between the two bonds was the currency in which the amortization of capital and the interests would be paid. In both cases, the public titles were valid for 16 years after they were issued (from 1994 to 2010). During the first 72 months, the State did not have to pay financial services (interests) and amortization (capital) for these bonds. The obligation to pay amortization and interests began in January 2001. From this date on, the State had to make 120 monthly payments including both the interest and capital of these public titles. The State began making these payments in early 2001, but in December 2001 declared the cessation of all payments of public debt titles, including the bonds delivered in payment of Law 24.411. In March 2002, all the bonds that were expressed in dollars were converted to pesos, at a rate of one peso and forty cents per dollar. In May 2002, by Disposition 73 of the Ministry of the Economy, the State decided to exempt from the cessation of payments all bonds that were issued for the payment of indemnification according to Law 24.411, and that were in the possession of the original holders (in other words, the direct family members of the disappeared person).[86] To those whose cases finished their proceedings after December 2001, and those who have not received a benefit yet, payments are and will also be made in bonds, but the foreign currency option no longer exists.

According to the Secretariat of Human Rights, 8,200 claims for reparations for cases of forced disappearance and assassination had been received as of mid-February 2004. Of these cases 200 were rejected and 8,000 were approved. Of the approved claims 7,100 have already received payment, and the rest are still undergoing the necessary administrative proceedings. Law 25.814 of December 1, 2003 extended by 90 days the period for applying for economic reparations for forced disappearances and assassinations. It also accepted the 540 applications that had been filed after the previous deadline, but before the law's approval. According to information provided by the Secretariat of Human Rights, it received a rate of 20 petitions per day after the application period was extended.

The amounts granted by Laws 24.411 and 24.823 were not subject to criticism, but the decision to make the payments in the form of bonds of public debt certainly was. First, coming from a poor and weak state, ownership of public bonds did not guarantee that money would actually be forthcoming.[87] Second, the bonds matured in 16 years, and therefore, the total amount of reparations could only be recovered once that period expired. Those who could not wait that long—for reasons either of need or of age—had to exchange the bonds at their market price, which meant recovering a lesser amount.

We can estimate that $1,170,000,000 was paid for cases of arbitrary detentions[88] and approximately $1,912,960,000 for reparations for forced disappearances and assassinations.[89] According to these figures, the total amount paid as a result of the two laws would be $3,082,960,000.

The development and execution of this policy was, for the most part, carried out by President Menem's government, with outstanding participation at all times by the then Undersecretary for Human Rights, Alicia Pierini, who gave content to this policy.

6. REPARATIONS FOR THE VICTIMS OF OPERATION CONDOR

The coordination of illegal repression carried out by governments throughout South America was called Operation Condor. This coordination started to take shape in 1974 and culminated only with the demise of the military dictatorships in the region. In effect, this was an operation that eliminated national borders for purposes of the exercise of repression. It allowed military regimes to violate the human rights of their citizens living abroad. Thus, murders and kidnappings of foreigners took place in the different southern cone countries. The methods used consisted of the penetration of the repressive apparatus of one country into a neighboring state, or the active collaboration of the host country's security forces in finding those who had sought refuge there.[90]

After the fall of the military regimes in the region, the Argentinean government lobbied governments of the countries where Operation Condor affected Argentinean citizens—including Chile, Uruguay, Paraguay, Bolivia, and Brazil—to enact laws repairing these victims. These efforts were largely unsuccessful.[91] By contrast, foreign victims of human rights violations in Argentina received the same economic compensation available to Argentinean victims, because the legislation did not make distinctions based on the victim's nationality.

7. REPARATIONS FOR MINORS WHO WERE VICTIMS OF STATE TERRORISM

Law 25.914 of August 30, 2004, passed on the initiative of President Néstor Kirchner, completes the policy of economic reparations by the Argentinean State. This law redresses persons who were born while their mothers were illegally detained; minors who remained in detention due to the detention or disappearance of their parents for political reasons by orders of the national executive branch or military tribunals, or those who remained in military areas; and those persons who were the victims of identity substitution.[92]

Those who suffered identity substitution are to receive an indemnification equivalent to the one fixed by Law 24.411, i.e. $224,000 Argentinean pesos.[93] For the victims of the other crimes covered by this law, the benefit consists of a one-time payment equivalent to 20 times the monthly earnings of a government employee Level A, Grade 8, of the National System of the Administrative Profession

[*Sistema Nacional de la Profesión Administrativa*],[94] i.e. $71,288 pesos. The benefit increases by 50 percent for those persons who suffered serious or severe injuries[95] as a consequence of the crimes covered by this law. In the case of the victim's death as a result of these crimes, the amount increases by 100 percent. The payment will be made in money deposits issued in the beneficiary's name, or that of his or her assignee in case of death. The benefit provided by this law cannot be claimed if the person in question has already received indemnification from the courts for the same events. According to estimates by Senator Jorge Capitanich, President of the Budget and Treasury Commission [*Comisión de Presupuesto y Hacienda*], these compensations will cost the Argentinean State up to 200 million pesos.[96]

A person claiming the benefit under this law and who was born during his or her mother's detention and/or imprisonment must certify his or her date of birth, which must be prior to December 10, 1983, and prove, by any possible means, that his or her mother was detained or disappeared. Those boys or girls who were born outside prisons or imprisonment centers must corroborate, by any possible means, their permanence in those places, as well as the detention of at least one of their parents. Those who were the victims of identity substitution must present a judicial sentence rectifying their identity, unless they were adopted in good faith, in which case they must prove, by any possible means, the forced disappearance of their parents.

The application must be filed with the Ministry of Justice, Security, and Human Rights, which then ensures compliance with all requirements. When in doubt about awarding the benefit, the authorities must choose, according to the principle of good faith, what is best for the victim. The law allows appealing the decision if the application is rejected.[97] Expenses for complying with this law are charged to the budgetary allocation for the Ministry of Justice, Security, and Human Rights.

8. REPARATIONS FOR EXILE

The right to economic compensation for those who were forced into exile under the dictatorship has been discussed in Argentinean society for some years. With opinions on the subject divided, exiles were not explicitly included in the laws of reparation. However, on October 14, 2004, the Supreme Court of the Nation ruled that the situation of those who had to abandon the country, due to persecution by the military that endangered their lives, could be compared to the situation of those who were deprived of their freedom, and, for this reason, economic reparation was due to be awarded in such cases.

The resolution was dictated in the case of Susana Yofre de Vaca Narvaja, who, after her husband was murdered and one of her children kidnapped, sought asylum in the Mexican Embassy and then fled to Mexico under the status of political refugee. The Court stated that even if the laws establishing economic reparations did not explicitly include cases of exile, these could be incorporated through interpretation by virtue of the 'reparatory will' behind the laws. The judges established the following:

[T]he conditions in which the plaintiff had to remain and then abandon the country... demonstrate that her decision...far from being considered as 'voluntary' or willfully adopted, was the only and desperate alternative she had in order to save her life in the face of the threat posed by the State or parallel organizations, or at least, of recovering her freedom since...at the moment of her decision to flee the country, she already suffered from the deprivation of th[e] basic right [to freedom].[98]

According to the Court's interpretation, the broad spirit that guided the National Congress to dictate the law that repairs political prisoners 'sought to make the international commitment undertaken by the Republic effective and to repair without restrictions alien to its purpose those serious violations to human dignity committed during those years of our recent history'.[99] The concept of detention, established in Law 24.043, does not exclude—according to the Supreme Court— 'forced confinement of a whole family... in the precinct of a foreign embassy, and its later, inexorable exile as the last resort to avoid the destiny of death that two of its members had already suffered'.[100] By virtue of these considerations, the Court ordered a review of the sentence by the lower court that had denied the right to reparations. The case will now return to the lower court, which will have to establish the due amount to be paid by the State.

Despite the fact that in the Argentinean judicial system Supreme Court verdicts only apply to the cases for which they are issued, through this decision the Court opened up the possibility for those who had to abandon the country during the military dictatorship to be repaired in the same manner as those who were detained in prisons or clandestine centers. Since the ruling, the national government has promoted the passage of a law that specifically contemplates reparations for exiles. As of this date, the bill has been approved by the Chamber of Deputies and is awaiting debate in the Senate.

9. ADMINISTRATIVE STRUCTURE AND COSTS OF THE OVERALL REPARATIONS EFFORT

Decree Num. 70/91 of Necessity and Urgency and Laws 24.043 and 24.411 established that they would all be administered by the Secretariat of Human and Social

Rights, which had already been created when these norms were passed. Law 25.914 established that the Secretariat for Human and Social Rights, a branch of the Ministry of Justice, Security, and Human Rights, would be in charge of its proceedings. None of the reparations laws created specific administrative structures for their application; this task was given to the administrative bodies in charge of all issues related to human rights. For this reason, it is difficult to establish the administrative costs they generated. Furthermore, because the administrative costs of the application of these laws were not contemplated, the funding source for such expenses was not taken into account either.

10. Conclusions

The transitions from authoritarian regimes to democratic systems that have taken place within the past few decades provide quite a valuable background for thinking about measures to address serious human rights violations. The Argentinean experience stands out among these transitions for its efforts regarding truth telling, prosecution of the military *juntas*, and economic reparations for victims. These efforts, however, were eclipsed by other measures that guaranteed the impunity of the majority of those who participated in State terrorism between 1975 and 1983.

The passage of time has not appeased the demands for justice that have gradually found satisfactory institutional responses. Through the 'trials for truth', judges have carried out investigations that attempt to establish what happened to each one of the victims, complementing the information presented by *Nunca Más*. Criminal justice processes have been reopened and laws that previously prevented sanctioning those responsible have been annulled. A proposal has also been made for the creation of a museum for remembering the victims and fostering awareness of the need to respect human rights.

These measures have been taken in the midst of everchanging domestic and international politics. In the international arena, among the most important justice-related developments has been the formation of a strong consensus on Augusto Pinochet's detention in 1998. Argentinean domestic achievements have been less laudable. It is undeniable that, with notable exceptions, the judges, who yesterday were impervious, disinterested, and conservative, today have a more progressive and dynamic interpretation of the law. Such a change in their attitude is linked to the opening created within Argentinean society to debate the past, as well as the aforementioned changes in the international arena. It is also the case, however, that some of the federal judges who have undergone this change did so in response to accusations of complicity with the economic corruption of President

Menem's government, that they began looking into the past as a way of cleaning up their public images. Fortunately, other judges have acted according to their profound convictions.

The development of the policy of economic reparations in Argentina has not been isolated from the ways in which political processes frequently develop in Argentina. Economic reparations were not part of the transition program implemented by Alfonsín's government during the 1980s. In fact, quite the contrary, his government was willing to fight the Inter-American Commission on Human Rights on the subject of reparations for political prisoners, some of whom had been imprisoned without an accusation or sentence for more than a decade. The change of government that instated Menem, a former political prisoner, as President, however, altered the political scene and fostered agreements on thoughtful remedies for all cases of arbitrary detentions. Menem's government combined economic reparations for the victims with pardons for military officials and other measures that were aimed at promoting oblivion and 'reconciliation'. Still, under Menem the first steps toward an effective economic reparations policy for victims of state terrorism were taken.

Despite its eventual scope as well as its political and economic implications, the Argentinean reparations program did not generate a public debate. Within the National Congress, discussion was deliberately avoided because the supporters of reparations feared that any debate opened to the participation of all political groups would not approve any such laws. The political elite's clear inability to seriously debate the past is probably due to its desire to avoid a discussion of each political group's actions during that period and its lack of accountability. Furthermore, the media did not cover economic reparations. Neither arguments for nor against reparations measures were made public. This is particularly surprising since decisions relating to human rights violations during the military dictatorship usually garner a great deal of attention. An even stronger response would have been expected in this case, since it has to do with economic reparations. As a public policy, economic reparations were not subject to an analysis of their feasibility or effectiveness. In fact, one impediment to carrying out this research was the lack of available information for measuring the impact of the reparations policy on the State, the victims, or other parties.

Reparations for crimes of forced disappearances deserve separate mention in this respect. The actions of the human rights movement demonstrate the profound difficulties in addressing this crime. The incapacity of human rights advocates to speak openly about forced disappearances was the most notable feature of these actions. This was due to many factors. First, the families of the victims or the organizations that they created found it very uncomfortable to speak in the name of people who were disappeared. The case of economic reparations for prisoners was different because the victims themselves demanded their rights and claimed the money.

Another factor hampering discussions about reparations for forced disappearances was the amount of money offered by the State. At the time the law was passed, due to the exchange rate (one peso for one US dollar), the reparations represented quite a considerable amount of money. This generated moral and political questioning. There were some who thought that the disappeared had fought for changing the very economic structure of society, and thus it was not appropriate for their relatives to accept so much money. Then there were those who, particularly in the absence of punishment for the perpetrators, saw the payments as a consolation prize, and even as a measure for replacing justice. Rejecting the money was seen by this last group as the politically correct decision. One important human rights organization opposed claiming the reparations, morally and politically condemning those who accepted it, as well as those who awarded it. 'The blood of our disappeared relatives cannot be negotiated. Those who claim economic reparations prostitute themselves', read this organization's banners placed at the Plaza de Mayo. It is easier to understand this position if it is kept in mind that reparations did not emerge after the transition as a right along with truth and justice, but were discussed only once impunity was guaranteed to perpetrators.

While most families of victims accepted reparations, they were influenced by the moral and political questioning. Sadly enough, these objections to the reparations policy did not translate into a dialogue or discussion that could have produced a collective way of addressing the issue. The debate within the human rights movement on this subject was shy, cryptic, and hampered by a strong sense of guilt among the families. In response to these questions, some human rights organizations proposed as a condition that the victims of this crime be declared not dead, but absent by forced disappearance. The State accepted this proposal and made it effective with a national law.

Receiving money as a form of reparations comes as a painful experience for the families of victims; even when they believe that they are exercising a right, doing so actually acts as a reminder of the absence of the disappeared person. In many cases, even if the award constitutes a great help considering the country's economic situation, it is very difficult for the beneficiaries to both receive and spend this money: it is often considered 'tainted' or 'cursed money', as some of the children of the disappeared have called it.

Neither truth nor justice, including economic reparations, has the virtue of repairing the loss of a victim, but measures such as these do provide recognition for the victims, and for the pain and suffering experienced by their families. This quality of economic reparations influences both individual and collective processes of addressing the past, and in this sense, it has a fundamental value.

(Translated from Spanish by Christian Gerzso)

NOTES

1. Decree Num. 157 of December 15, 1983, issued by the executive branch of the government.
2. By decree of the national executive branch, the members of the first three military *juntas* (councils) were prosecuted. The Federal Chamber on the Criminal and Correctional of the Federal Capital [*Cámara Federal en lo Criminal y Correccional de la Capital Federal*] pronounced sentence on December 9, 1985. This historic resolution established that there had been a deliberate and agreed-upon plan to exercise a policy of clandestine repression, and that this policy turned out to be the dictatorship's main vehicle for eliminating subversion. As a result of this process, five commanders of the military *juntas* were sentenced for homicide, illegitimate deprivations of freedom, and torture, among other crimes. Four of these commanders were absolved because the evidence against them was insufficient or inconclusive.
3. Recently, one of the national newspapers launched an investigation of the payments of reparations benefits. The Secretary of Human Rights again claimed that there is no official tally of the amounts paid by the state. See, *La Nación*, October 18, 2004.
4. *Informe Nunca Más; Comisión Nacional sobre Desaparición de Personas*, 2nd edn. (Buenos Aires: Editorial Eudeba, 1984), 477.
5. About 600 of the children of disappeared persons, who were kidnapped together with their parents or were born during their imprisonment, were delivered to other families who illegally registered them as their own biological children. In most of these cases, the adopting families were the families of members of the military or armed forces, although not always. The crime of child kidnapping was one of the few for which amnesties or pardons were not granted.
6. Decree Num. 3090.
7. By Decree Num. 645 of 1991.
8. The National Bank of Genetic Data was created by Law 23.511 in order to facilitate the work of identifying and restituting to their biological families the children of disappeared or assassinated persons who were born during imprisonment or were kidnapped.
9. By Decree Num. 660.
10. Decree Num. 20 of December 13, 1999.
11. By Decree Num. 357/2002.
12. Passed on February 22, 1984.
13. Passed on September 30, 1984.
14. Passed on September 10, 1985.
15. Passed on June 24, 1988.
16. Passed on September 28, 1985, published in the Official Gazette of November 5, 1985.
17. The Group includes: Grandmothers of *Plaza de Mayo* [*Abuelas de Plaza de Mayo*], Permanent Assembly for Human Rights [*Asamblea Permanente por los Derechos Humanos*], Lawyers Association of Buenos Aires [*Asociación de Abogados de Buenos Aires*], American Jurists Association [*Asociación Americana de Juristas*], Latin-American Association of Human Rights [*Asociación Latinoamericana de Derechos Humanos*], Former Disappeared Detainees Association [*Asociación de Ex Detenidos Desaparecidos*], Center for Legal and Social Studies [*Centro de Estudios Legales y Sociales*], Families of Disappeared Persons and Detainees for Political Reasons [*Familiares de Desaparecidos y Detenidos por Razones Políticas*], Latin American Federation of Associations of Relatives

of Disappeared Detainees [*Federación Latinoamericana de Asociaciones de Familiares de Detenidos Desaparecidos (FEDEFAM)*], Institute of International Relations [*Instituto de Relaciones Internacionales*], Argentinean League for the Rights of Man [*Liga Argentina por los Derechos del Hombre*], Mothers of *Plaza de Mayo*—Founding Group [*Madres de Plaza de Mayo—Línea Fundadora*], Ecumenical Movement for Human Rights [*Movimiento Ecuménico por los Derechos Humanos*], Jewish Movement for Human Rights [*Movimiento Judío por los Derechos Humanos*], Office of Solidarity with Argentinean Exiles [*Oficina de Solidaridad con los Exiliados Argentinos*], Peace and Justice Service [*Servicio Paz y Justicia*].

18. *La Desaparición. Crimen contra la humanidad*, Asamblea Permanente por los Derechos Humanos, ed. (Buenos Aires, 1987). This publication compiles the works presented at the convention.

19. The *Asociación Madres de Plaza de Mayo* has publicly stated that 'those who claim an economic reparation prostitute themselves' and that receiving money meant 'selling the blood of our children'. These positions display substantial and explicit political differences from the rest of the human rights movement. Its views can be consulted at http://www.madres.org.ar

20. This was Law 23.466, passed on October 30, 1986. Regulated by Decree Num. 1228/87.

21. This possible incompatibility was argued by Congressman Augusto Conte Mac Donell, the father of a disappeared person.

22. Fernando De La Rúa, who was elected President of the Republic in 1999.

23. Emilio Mignone, *Derechos Humanos y Sociedad, el caso argentino* (Buenos Aires: CELS and Ediciones del Pensamiento Nacional, 1991), 155.

24. Law 23.492, published in the Official Gazette on December 29, 1986.

25. Law 23.521, published in the Official Gazette on June 9, 1987.

26. Decrees Num. 1002, 1003, 1004, and 1005 published in the Official Gazette on October 10, 1989, and Decrees Num. 2.741 through 2.746 of December 29, 1990.

27. IACHR, Report Num. 28/92, cases 10.147, 10.181, 10.240, 10.262, 10.309, and 10.311 Argentina, issued on October 2, 1992. Published in the Annual Report by the IACHR 1992–1993; OEA/Ser.L/V/II.83; Doc. 14, March 12, 1993; Original: Spanish. http://www.oas.org

28. Article 4037 of the Civil Code.

29. The nation's Civil Code establishes the following in article 3980: 'When taking legal action has been impeded due to difficulties or an impossibility, judges are authorized to lift the effects of a prescription that has been reached during the impediment for the holder or proprietor, if after the cessation the holder or proprietor has exercised his or her rights within three months. If the holder did not file a lawsuit that would have interrupted the prescription due to wilful misconduct by the debtor, with the intention of postponing this suit, then judges can apply the provisions of this article.'

30. The first case was filed on February 15, 1989. Then more cases were filed once the Argentinean Supreme Court pronounced a sentence. The petitioners were the following: Miguel Vaca Narvaja, Bernardo Bartoli, Guillermo Alberto Birt, Gerardo Andrés Caletti, Silvia Di Cola, Irma Carolina Ferrero de Fierro, José Enrique Fierro, María Ester Gatica de Giulani, Héctor Lucio Giulani, Rubén Héctor Padula, José Mariano Torregiani, and Guillermo Rolando Puerta.

31. Report Num. 1/93. Report on friendly agreements on cases 10.288, 10.310, 10.436, 10.496, 10.631, and 10.771. Argentina, Annual Report by the IACHR 1992–1993, OEA/Ser.L/V/II.83, March 12, 1993. http://www.oas.org

32. The instrument by which Argentina ratified the Convention was dictated on August 14, 1984. The Argentinean government claimed that at the moment of the ratification it was established that 'the duties owed by virtue of the Convention would only have effect on events occurring after the mentioned instrument'. Response mentioned in Report No. 1/93, quoted above.

33. According to Menem himself, the amount of his indemnification was close to $208,000. *Página/12* Newspaper. http://pagina12.feedback.net.ar/secciones/elpais/index.php?id_nota=8436&seccion=1

34. According to Report Num. 1/93, quoted above.

35. Decree Num. 798/90, issued on April 26, 1990.

36. This draft bill would be later passed as Law 24.043.

37. Decree Num. 70/91, issued on January 10, 1991.

38. Petitioners finally agreed on receiving the following indemnification, established according to the provisions of Decree 70/91: Vaca Narvaja: 56,511 pesos; Bartoli: 36,855 pesos; Birt: 71,739 pesos; Caletti: 24,921 pesos; Di Cola: 58,212 pesos; Ferrero de Fierro: 4,401 pesos; Fierro: 20,655 pesos; Gatica de Giulani: 28,377 pesos; Giulani: 80,514 pesos; Olivares: 46,899 pesos; Padula: 56,403 pesos; Torregiani: 37,773 pesos; Puerta: 67,284 pesos. When this resolution was passed, the exchange rate was one peso per US dollar. These figures were calculated according to the decree, because this was a friendly agreement. Differences between these figures are due to the time each person was detained. In its final resolution, the IACHR expressed 'its acknowledgement of the Argentinean State for its support of the American Convention and for complying with the payment of compensations to petitioners, and of petitioners for accepting the terms of Decree Num. 70/91, complemented with Law 24.043 of December 23, 1991, as part of the process of friendly agreement between the parties. It wishes to express its satisfaction for this friendly agreement and acknowledge that it has been reached to the complete satisfaction of each of the parties and the Commission.'

39. Interview with Alicia Pierini, July 20, 2002. Alicia Pierini was the Undersecretary for Human and Social Rights in Carlos Menem's government. She had a prominent role in the development of the human rights policy of Menem's government.

40. This date is related to the guideline explained above for calculating the statute of limitations. According to this guideline, the period of prescription of two years had to be calculated starting on December 10, 1983, because it was only from this date on that the State guaranteed security for initiating a judicial process.

41. Interview with Alicia Pierini, July 20, 2002.

42. Conf. article 9 of Decree Num. 70/91.

43. Article 7 of Decree Num. 70/91 established: 'The rights awarded by this decree can be exercised by the persons mentioned in article 1, or in case of death, his or her successors.'

44. Article 11 of Decree Num. 70/91 established: 'The payment of the benefit entails renouncing every right to indemnification for harms and damages caused by deprivation of freedom, arrest under the custody of the executive branch, death or injuries, and it will exclude every other benefit or indemnification for the same reasons.'

45. Passed on November 27, 1991, and published in the Official Gazette on January 2, 1992, with the observation expressed in Decree Num. 2722/91. Regulated by Decree Num. 1023/92, modified by Decree Num. 205/97, broadened by Decree Num. 1313/94.

46. To the former Directorship of Human Rights, now Secretariat of Human and Social Rights.

47. This condition was established by regulating Decree Num. 1023/92, and does not appear in the law.
48. According to the classification stipulated by the nation's Penal Code, Art. 91, quoted above.
49. According to Law 14.394. This law allows the declaration of the death of persons whose whereabouts have been unknown for a long period of time.
50. Article 10 of this law established: 'The necessary expenses for complying with this law will be charged to the State's assets.'
51. Information provided by the Secretariat of Human and Social Rights.
52. By Resolution Num. 1768 of the Ministry of Interior, of June 14, 1994, calculations for the benefit provided by Decree Num. 70/91 were made according to the new Roster of Civil Servants of the National Public Administration. Specifically, it establishes that the benefit provided by Decree Num. 70/91 should be calculated according to the provisions of joint-resolutions Num. 15/94 of the Ministry of the Interior and Num. 352/94 of the Ministry of the Economy and Public Works and Services [*Ministerio de Economía y Obras y Servicios Públicos*]. This difference was paid in public-debt bonds.
53. Decree Num. 1313/94 of August 1, 1994.
54. Alicia Pierini, in charge at the time of the Directorship of Human Rights, remembers that implementing this norm 'generated difficulties since the unit in charge of its application did not have the capacity to carry out this process. What was necessary was to create an administrative body within the Ministry of the Interior, but the Minister did not have the will to do it. The first difficulty emerged when the regulating decree needed to be issued through an agreement with the Minister. As Director of Human Rights, I had to negotiate with the Minister, but I did not even have the support of human rights organizations. Furthermore, delays in the payments due to lack of regulations and an adequate administrative structure had generated much criticism, which made it even more difficult to reach the necessary agreement for sanctioning such regulations.'
55. With the exception of the Ecumenical Movement for Human Rights and the Commission of Families of Disappeared Persons and Detainees for Political Reasons, which actively helped with claims for economic reparations, the other organizations for human rights were not opposed, but did not support them decisively either.
56. This decision by President Menem was taken by request of the Association Grandmothers of Plaza de Mayo [*Asociación Abuelas de Plaza de Mayo*]. The 'grandmothers' held a meeting with the President on July 15, 1992, in which they demanded the creation of the National Commission for the Right to Identity [*Comisión Nacional de Derecho a la Identidad*], a body that would help in the task of identifying children born in imprisonment and appropriated illegally. Menem ordered the creation of this commission within the structure of the Secretariat of Human and Social Rights.
57. Even if the government had this intention prior to the passing of the law, this issue was not included in the draft bill because it would have generated much controversy and strong opposition that would have most likely not been overcome in the National Congress. Opposition was based on the fact that the political leaders of the country were not willing to award compensations to those who were accused of committing crimes, but only to those who had been unjustly incarcerated. Moreover, it was certain that if the law included this category it would create strong social discontent. For this reason, this category of prisoners was not included in the law. However, their claims for

economic benefits were later accepted through administrative resolutions of the Secretariat of Human and Social Rights.

58. A few months after the law had begun to be applied, the Roster of the National Public Administration was changed, and the National System of the Public Administration was created [*Sistema Nacional de la Administración Pública (SINAPA)*], which caused problems in determining the 'highest category' of State employees. It also provoked discrepancies in relation to what had been paid to the beneficiaries of Decree Num. 70/91. This gave rise to serious debates about the amount that should be granted to each person.

59. Joint resolution by Ministers Carlos F. Ruckauf, Minister of the Interior and Domingo F. Caballo, Minister of the Economy, of March 10, 1994. The one by the Ministry of the Interior is Resolution Num. 15/94 and the one by the Ministry of the Economy is Resolution Num. 352/94.

60. Passed on December 7, 1994. Regulating Decree Num. 403/95 sanctioned on August 29, 1995.

61. The draft bill was presented by Congressman Marcelo López Arias, of the Justicialista Party.

62. Law 24.321, passed on May 11, 1994.

63. Alicia Pierini. Interview, July 20, 2002.

64. Passed on May 7, 1997. Modified by Laws 24.449 and 24.823, the last one promulgated observing article 5 of Decree Num. 479/97.

65. Article 2b is incorporated by Law 24.823 into Law 24.411. The established order of priority is the same as the one established by the Civil Code for successions without a will, article 3545.

66. Article 4b is incorporated by Law 24.823 into Law 24.411.

67. Before issuing the declaration of successors of the disappeared person, the judge must cite publicly all the interested parties, so that they can claim their rights. Then, the judge declares who the only successors are. Article 4 bis of Law 24.411.

68. Established in article 700 of the Procedural Civil and Commercial Code of the Nation [*Código Procesal Civil y Comercial de la Nación*]. This article proclaims that 'once the period and proceedings referred to in the previous article are completed, and once the successors have been established, the judge will dictate the declaration of heirs. If the ties of one of the heirs presumptive have not been justified, before it is sent to the authority in charge of receiving the vacant inheritance, the declaration will be deferred until the judge deems it appropriate, so that during this period the corresponding proof can be produced. After this period has expired, the judge will either dictate the declaration in favor of those who have proven their ties, or he or she will declare it a vacant inheritance.'

69. Conf. article 4 bis.

70. Article 9 bis incorporated by Law 24.823.

71. Interview with Elizabeth Jelín, sociologist and specialist in human rights issues, social movements, and family and gender. This interview was held in July 2003.

72. The statement was pronounced in December 1994. It is available for reference in the organization's archives.

73. Martín Abregú, who was the Executive Director of the Center for Legal and Social Studies [CELS] when the law was passed, remembered during an interview: 'economic reparations were very difficult for human rights organizations to conceive and discuss.

For instance, when Law 24.411 was passed, CELS decided to provide legal assistance for the victims who decided to claim the reparation. As Director of the Center, I proposed to the board of directors to make this decision known publicly so that the families knew that they could find technical assistance with us. However, the board decided against it for fear of giving the impression that our center profited from this problem. A sense of guilt was felt at all times, so the accusations would have then followed.' Interview held on August 1, 2002. Martín Abregú was Executive Director of CELS between 1994 and 2000.

74. Interview with Laura Conte, August 2002.

75. The regulating decree of this law specified in its article 2 that a paramilitary group would be defined as that which participated in the fight against subversion without identifying its members with either an identification card or a uniform.

76. The Secretariat established a guideline to include 'all the facts proved by the Jurisdictional Power of the State [*Poder Jurisdiccional del Estado*] through the pronouncement of the National Chamber of Appeals on the Federal Criminal and Correctional of the Federal Capital [*Cámara Nacional de Apelaciones en lo Criminal y Correccional Federal de la Capital Federal*], in Cause 13. And for those cases taking place before March 24, 1976, to corroborate whether they were linked to the facts established in Cause 13, and whether they coincide with the methodology employed by the armed or security forces, ordered since March 24, 1976, or if this is not the case, whether they were performed by a paramilitary group.' Resolution of the Secretariat of Human and Social Rights in file 'Ortega Peña, Rodolfo s/solicitud Ley 24.411'.

77. According to Law 24.321.

78. This list was published in an annexed book of the *Nunca Más* Report; in it, all denunciations received by CONADEP are reproduced.

79. Proof produced after the passing of the law is only valid when it serves to corroborate documentation of the time when the disappearance took place.

80. Just as with cases of forced disappearance, proof produced after the passing of the law is only valid when it serves to corroborate documentation of the time when the assassination took place.

81. As previously stated the difficulties in proving these facts are due to the clandestine character of repression, the specific aspects of forced disappearances of persons, and the lack of an investigation carried out by the State.

82. The appeal is presented before the Cámara Nacional en lo Contencioso Administrativo Federal.

83. Approved by Decree Num. 993/91.

84. For the cases in which an indemnification for harms and damages had been granted by a judicial ruling, or the benefit had been awarded according to the provisions of Decree Num. 70/91 or Law 24.043, beneficiaries would only be allowed to receive the difference between what is established by this new law and what they received according to the previous norms. If the received amount was equal to or more than the new one, they would not have a right to this pecuniary reparation.

85. *Bocones Serie II*, according to Decree Num. 726/97.

86. At the present moment, there are many administrative petitions being presented by elderly persons with health problems before the Ministry of Economy. These persons decided to transfer their bonds to their children or other family members so that they could claim the amounts; at the moment, they cannot do so because the children, or

other family members who actually have custody of the bonds, do not appear as the original holders in the State's records. This is one of the problems caused by the way in which the payment of the benefit is made according to Law 24.411.

87. On different occasions, such as the economic crisis of 2001, the Argentinean state failed to meet the obligations it had acquired with internal creditors.

88. This figure was arrived at by assuming that each one of the 7,800 persons who claimed the reparation was paid an average of 150,000 pesos.

89. Each one of the 8,540 persons would have received $224,000.

90. An example of this operation is the murder in 1974 in Argentina by members of Chile's National Intelligence Directorate [*Dirección de Inteligencia Nacional (DINA)*] of General Carlos Prats, former chief of the army during the government of Salvador Allende. DINA agents, with Argentinean collaboration, traveled to Buenos Aires to carry out this assassination.

91. The exception is Brazil, where Law 9,140 enacted, in December 1995, included in its annex the names of the victims to be repaired, among whom there were three Argentineans. For an account of the reparations effort in Brazil, see Ignacio Cano and Patrícia Ferreira (Chapter 3, this volume).

92. Identity substitution refers to cases of children of disappeared parents who were then registered as the legitimate children of other families (in many cases as the children of the military or security personnel who stole them from their biological parents).

93. Of course, the exchange rate had changed dramatically since the days of parity between the dollar and the peso. As of this writing (November 2004) the exchange rate is 2.80 pesos for one dollar.

94. According to Decree Num. 993/91, text ordered in 1995.

95. According to the classification of the Argentinean Penal Code.

96. Slightly less than US$71.5 million at the current exchange rate. *La Nación* Newspaper, August 5, 2004. Available at: http://www.lanacion.com.ar/04/08/04/dp_624571.asp?origen=rss

97. The appeal must be presented before the Cámara Nacional de Apelaciones en lo Contencioso Administrativo Federal de la Capital Federal.

98. 'Yofre de Vaca Narvaja, Susana v. Ministry of the Interior—resolution. M.J.D.H. 221/00' (file 443.459/98).

99. Ibid.

100. Ibid.

CHAPTER 2

THE REPARATIONS POLICY FOR HUMAN RIGHTS VIOLATIONS IN CHILE

ELIZABETH LIRA

INTRODUCTION

For almost seventeen years, from 1973 to 1990, Chile was governed by a military dictatorship that first ruled under states of constitutional exception (internal war, martial law, and others) and then under a new constitution promulgated in 1980. Throughout this period, the regime was characterized by systematic human rights violations. Its repressive actions were beyond public scrutiny and control, and petitions before the courts had no effects. Political repression subjected hundreds of thousands of people to extreme pain and fear. Persecution forced thousands to abandon their homes and go into exile, both inside and outside the country, in order to protect their lives. It also, however, provoked an institutional response from the nation's churches, which interceded in various ways on behalf of the persecuted, with various strategies for protection, assistance, and legal defense. These initiatives foreshadowed many aspects of the reparations policies and programs established after the end of the dictatorship.

In 1988, a plebiscite was held to determine whether General Augusto Pinochet should remain President of the country. The majority of the people voted against the continuation of his regime. Subsequently, democratic elections for President and Congress took place, which brought Patricio Aylwin into office as the new President. Aylwin inaugurated his government by emphasizing the importance of human rights. The aims of the new administration centered on (*a*) the establishment of the truth regarding the human rights violations that took place under the dictatorship; (*b*) the provision of reparations for those affected; and (*c*) the development of social, legal, and political conditions that would prevent these violations from happening again.

This chapter examines the reparations programs implemented in Chile from 1990 to 2003. These programs were directed toward the families of disappeared detainees and victims of political executions, returning exiles, those who had been dismissed from their jobs for political reasons, and peasants who had been excluded from agrarian reform and expelled from their land. In the case of political prisoners, the government's immediate goal in 1990 was to release them from prison; at the time it did not consider any measure of reparations, and did not do so, in earnest, until 2003. All of the groups listed above have been beneficiaries of the Program of Reparations and Comprehensive Health Care [*Programa de Reparación y Atención Integral de Salud* (PRAIS)], which has offered medical assistance, including psychological care, free of charge in the public health care system. Another type of reparations has resulted from civil lawsuits brought against the State; however, the discussion about the relationship between the legal avenue to reparations and the massive reparations programs has not concluded yet. In recent rulings, the Supreme Court has pronounced itself against compensation through such lawsuits, arguing that victims receive proper reparations through the established programs.

In mid-2003, public debate on the existing reparations policy was reopened, primarily around the following issues: (*a*) the unsatisfactory results in the search for disappeared detainees; (*b*) the need for reviewing the reparations programs for the families of disappeared detainees; and (*c*) the demand for recognition of, and reparation for, former political prisoners. In terms of reparations for the families of disappeared detainees, some proposals from right-wing groups have suggested a one-time payment as compensation in exchange for waiving the right to judicial processes. In addition to this, the families would have to recognize explicitly the presumed death of their disappeared relatives. The hope of these right-wing groups is that such recognition would eliminate the legal category of qualified kidnapping, which has prevented those responsible from benefiting from the amnesty decree law passed in 1978. That amnesty covers homicides in cases of disappearance and political execution that occurred between 1973 and 1978, but not kidnappings.

In the course of this debate President Ricardo Lagos received more than fifty proposals from different groups covering the entire political spectrum in the country, including right-wing groups that had been part of Pinochet's government. In response, the President formulated a comprehensive proposal on human rights, which resulted in three draft bills being sent to Congress. These bills are aimed at reforming the reparations laws, institutionalizing PRAIS, generating incentives for delivering information on disappeared detainees, and expunging the records of former political prisoners. In addition, President Lagos created the Commission of Political Imprisonment and Torture [*Comisión de Prisión Política y Tortura*] in order to examine the cases of former political prisoners and victims of torture during the dictatorship and propose measures for reparation.[1]

1. Program of Reparations for the Families of Victims of Political Violence, Political Executions, and Disappeared Detainees[2]

Origins of the Program of Reparations

In March 1990, Patricio Aylwin was sworn in as President of the Republic of Chile. One month later, he created the National Truth and Reconciliation Commission [*Comisión Nacional de Verdad y Reconciliación*] with the purpose of disclosing the truth about human rights violations under the previous dictatorship that resulted in the death of the victims. In February 1991, the Commission delivered a report to the President, who then presented it to the country, asking the victims for forgiveness in the name of the Chilean State.[3]

The Commission established that 2,298 persons had died for political reasons between September 11, 1973 and March 11, 1990. It determined that 2,130 of these were victims of human rights violations and 168 were victims of political violence. The latter cases did not fall strictly under human rights violations definitions because of the various circumstances surrounding the victims' deaths, from confrontations on September 11, 1973 to accidental deaths from a tear-gas bomb at a protest rally.[4] A total of 979 persons were classified as disappeared detainees and 1,319 as deceased. The Commission could not reach a satisfactory conclusion regarding 634 cases.

The Chilean armed forces and the Supreme Court officially rejected the report, arguing that it did not take into account the historical and political context in which these acts occurred. The Army repudiated 'the campaign surrounding the report, which targeted innocent people, making them suffer inhuman pressures and punishment'.[5] The Navy made a similar statement, justifying its repressive actions and pointing out the inconvenience of establishing commemorative acts to teach future generations, arguing that such acts 'would contradict the precepts of reconciliation, pardon and oblivion which should characterize this period in the historic Chilean process'.[6] The Navy insisted that the amnesty law was a valuable instrument for reconciliation, 'a first step towards the pacification of the country'.[7] The Air Force and *Carabineros* rejected the report on similar grounds, arguing that the past should be left behind in order to reach reconciliation in the country. The Supreme Court strongly denied that the judicial branch of government had any responsibility for the victims' defenselessness. Despite such criticism, however, the actual content of the report was not denied and it was published in a special edition of the newspaper *La Nación*.[8]

Almost a month later, Jaime Guzmán, Senator and ideologue of the former military regime, was assassinated. This incident weakened the political impact of the report, and gave new impetus to the arguments of different groups in favor of a 'final stop' [*punto final*] in the name of social peace and reconciliation.

The Commission recommended various measures of reparations for the victims identified by the Commission's report. The President then sent Congress a draft bill for the implementation of these measures.[9] The draft bill understood reparations as

a set of acts that express the recognition and responsibility that may be owed by the State for the circumstances described in the report. ...Reparations should be a process aiming towards the recognition of the facts in accordance with the truth, the moral dignifying of the victims, and the achievement of a better quality of life for the families most directly affected.[10]

The Group of Families of Disappeared Detainees [*La Agrupación de Familiares de Detenidos Desaparecidos* (AFDD)] criticized the reparations measures proposed by the government, objecting to the proposal to declare the presumed death of the victims, expressing mistrust in the creation of a public interest corporation with no juridical faculties to investigate the whereabouts of disappeared detainees, and condemning as unfair the 'single pension' [*pensión única*] for not taking into account the number of members in each family.[11] In a public statement, the AFDD declared:

[T]he public should remember that the priority for the families of disappeared detainees is to know the truth and to obtain justice. We can only agree with the reparation policies on the understanding that the State assumes its responsibility for the harm done by the actions of its agents during the dictatorship. This would be the only way of restoring the rights of the victims.[12]

In the end, the law that was approved incorporated the proposal by the AFDD regarding the declaration of presumed death, modified the life pensions, and included benefits for the mothers of the victims.

The Reparations Pension

Law 19.123 of February 8, 1992 established a monthly reparations pension for the families of the victims of human rights violations or political violence identified in the report by the National Truth and Reconciliation Commission. It stated that the pension should be expressly requested.[13] Additional cases validated by the newly created National Corporation for Reparations and Reconciliation [*Corporación Nacional de Reparación y Reconciliación*] were incorporated into the Commission's list. Article 24 of the law established that the reparations pension was compatible with any other benefits that the beneficiary was receiving at that moment, or would receive in the future, as well as any other social security benefits. Furthermore, the reparations pension could not be seized under any circumstances. According to the currency value in 1996, the monthly pension amounted to $226,667 Chilean pesos (US$537). This figure was used as a reference for estimating the different amounts provided to each type of beneficiary. The surviving spouse received 40 percent of the total or $90,667 pesos (US$215);[14] the mother of the petitioner or, in her absence, the father, received 30 percent of the total or $68,000 pesos (US$161); the surviving mother or father of a victim's out-of-wedlock offspring would receive 15 percent or $34,000 pesos (US$80); and each of the children of a disappeared person would receive 15 percent or $34,000 pesos (US$80) until the age of twenty-five, or with no age limit in the case of handicapped children.[15] A one-time compensatory bonus equivalent to twelve months of pension payments was also awarded. The law defined all the percentages assigned to each of the categories of beneficiaries for all effects. Consequently, a beneficiary would receive the pension in the proportion determined by the law, even if there were no other beneficiaries in the family. By the same token, if the amount required by the number of beneficiaries exceeded the reference amount, each one of them still received the percentage established by the law.

The Institute of Pension Normalization [*Instituto de Normalización Previsional* (INP)] has been in charge of paying the pensions throughout the country since 1992 (Table 2.1). The initial number of beneficiaries was 5,794, which had diminished to 4,570 when the Corporation for Reparations and Reconciliation closed down in 1996. By late 2001, there were 3,210 beneficiaries left. The cost of the initial compensatory bonus was $2,473,455 pesos (US$708,280). The cost of the pensions from 1992 to 2001 totaled $52,329,750,000 pesos (US$8,240,905). The State also spent $7,296,200,000 pesos (US$1,149,008) on higher education for the beneficiaries during the same period.[16]

Table 2.1 Pensions: Annual expenditures by the State[17]

Year	1992	1993	1994	1995
Pesos	6,926,398,000	5,116,674,000	5,769,755,000	5,774,229,000
Dollars	2,582,370	1,711,327	1,719,415	1,458,263

National Corporation for Reparations and Reconciliation

According to Law Num. 19.123,[18] the National Corporation for Reparations and Reconciliation was to implement the recommendations of the Truth and Reconciliation Commission and promote reparations for the moral harm done to the victims. The Corporation was directed by a council formed by six members, who were appointed by the President and ratified by the Senate. They were appointed by Supreme Decree Num. 540. The law also stated that the Corporation should promote and support the search to determine the late and final whereabouts of disappeared detainees, even those who had been confirmed deceased but whose bodies had not been found. The Corporation was intended to function for two years, starting in 1992. However, it lasted two additional years, finally closing down in December 1996.[19] Annual contributions from the National Budget and other national and international sources financed its operation.[20]

The Corporation organized its work around six different fields of action, each one of them functioning as a separate program.

1. *The Qualifying Program [Programa de Calificación]* gathered records, analyzed pending cases, and assessed the accusations that were received within the legal time frame.[21] In all 2,188 cases were examined, 988 of which came from the Truth and Reconciliation Commission with no decision, which therefore had to be reviewed by the Corporation. Among the latter cases, the Corporation accepted (i.e. qualified the persons involved as victims) 347 and rejected 641. The Corporation received 1,200 accusations directly, of which 522 were accepted and 678 rejected, either because they did not correspond to the definitions under the law or because the records were insufficient. At the end, 869 cases were accepted by the Corporation. The Truth and Reconciliation Commission and the Corporation received 4,750 accusations altogether, of which 3,197 qualified as victims. Among them, there were 1,102 disappeared detainees and 2,095 deceased, which included cases of political violence.[22]

2. *The Investigation Program Regarding the Final Whereabouts of the Victims [Programa de Investigación sobre el Destino Final de las Víctimas]* had as its main goal determining the whereabouts of disappeared detainees and of those whose mortal remains had not been found, even if there existed legal

documents certifying their death. In total 1,251 cases were investigated, and the bodies of 144 persons were found.[23]

3. *The Social and Legal Assistance Program* [*Programa de Asistencia Social y Legal*] expedited proceedings so that the families could enjoy the benefits established by the law. The benefits were: (*a*) the reparations pension; (*b*) educational benefits for the disappeared person's children up to thirty-five years of age, who were allowed to attend the institution of their choice at any level. The educational benefits included tuition and other fees, as well as a monthly stipend of 1.24 Monthly Fiscal Units (UTM) for other expenses during the school year in the case of primary education.[24] Beneficiaries who attended technical or higher education institutions were exempt from tuition and other fees, and each student received a stipend of 1.24 UTM for the duration of his or her degrees. Payments were made through a savings account at the State Bank [*Banco del Estado*], once the status of the student was confirmed every semester; (*c*) exemption from mandatory military service through an agreement with the Ministry of Defense; (*d*) health care through the PRAIS program starting in 1991 (including the parents and siblings of the victim, even if they were not direct beneficiaries of the reparations pension). The nation's most important newspapers published the list of victims who qualified for benefits in 1992, so that their families could submit their requests. In 1994, the list of victims who did not have any beneficiaries registered yet was published.

4. *The Education and Cultural Promotion Program* [*Programa de Educación y Promoción Cultural*] introduced human rights education programs in schools with the purpose of strengthening a culture of human rights in the country.[25] When the Corporation closed down, the work team of this program became part of the Ministry of Education.

5. *The Legal Studies and Research Program* [*Programa de Estudios e Investigaciones Jurídicas*] was formed according to the recommendations made by the Truth and Reconciliation Commission. After a short period of exploratory work, it decided to focus on the following areas of study: military justice, penal processes, and penal justice.[26] There were also other projects on constitutional studies and the right to a defense. Some of these were published by the Corporation.[27]

6. *The Archive and Documentation Center Program of the Corporation* [*Programa Centro de Documentación y Archivos de la Corporación*] had the purpose of building the foundations for an archive that would host historical, documentary, and bibliographic material from all the information gathered, analyzed, and processed by the Corporation.[28]

Finally, in 1991, the government accepted the proposals by the AFDD and the Group of Families of Victims of Political Executions [*Agrupación de Familiares de*

Ejecutados Políticos] and decided to build a memorial plaza and a mausoleum at the General Cemetery in Santiago, so that the mortal remains of the victims could be given proper burial when found.[29] The support for such constructions was conceived as part of the moral reparations for, and vindication of, the victims.

The Corporation's final report stated that the work of the institution had contributed effectively to political reconciliation, but that the pending cases of more than 1,000 disappeared detainees undermined these efforts. It pointed out that political reconciliation depended on finding a fair solution to pending cases, especially those related to disappeared detainees. The Corporation concluded that eluding this responsibility and 'turning the page', as many would have wished for, had become increasingly impossible.

Evaluation

The Corporation met most of the objectives established by Law 19.123, with the exception of the search for disappeared detainees, which continues to be one of the most difficult and complex problems of the transition. The government believed that having complied with the other obligations this phase of the transition had been completed.

The beneficiaries appreciated the economic reparations they received. However, they demanded further recognition for the harms they had suffered, as well as vindication of the dignity and good names of their families. They emphasized that no benefits would appease the need for 'justice and truth'. In other words, in order to 'feel compensated', they demanded that the other forms of reparations contemplated in the recommendations by the Truth and Reconciliation Commission be implemented. Moreover, economic reparations generated tensions and difficulties and, in some cases, had negative consequences for the beneficiaries, such as the following:

1. *Moral and Psychological Conflicts Caused by Economic Reparations.* Some of the families of disappeared detainees expressed reluctance and doubts on moral grounds about accepting economic reparations, even if for many of them these helped put an end to years of economic scarcity. Some groups also feared that such benefits could compromise everyone's commitment to pursuing 'truth and justice'. Family groups and human rights organizations insisted that accepting reparations pensions did not entail renouncing their search for truth and justice regarding the fate of the victims. In turn, the authorities stated clearly, and it was thus established by the law, that these reparations pensions were not incompatible with any other type of pension. The authorities also stated that requesting the reparations pensions did not impose restrictions or conditions of any kind on a family's right to bring civil lawsuits against the State

or any person related to these cases. During the debates on the draft bill for Law 19.123, the government had stated as well that reparations were an *obligation* of the Chilean State and that the victims had the *right* to such reparations. Many beneficiaries conceded that they were relieved to learn that they could exercise their rights without moral or political pressure or restrictions of any kind from the government or other groups.

2. *Insufficiencies of Law 19.123 Left Uncorrected.* Unmarried partners of disappeared detainees or victims of political executions without children, as well as the mothers of illegitimate children, were excluded from receiving pensions under the guidelines established by the law.[30] These cases were still pending in 2003. The delay in resolving these cases shows how the political framework that had given meaning to the policy of reparations has been diluted, and without it, the reparative sense of pensions and any form of assistance for the victims has also been disappearing. There have been attempts by right-wing groups to reject the policy of reparations or reinterpret it as a 'privilege', disassociating it completely from cases of human rights violations. A news story in *El Mercurio* newspaper in March 2003 on policies of reparation—the only one in that paper since 1990—was entitled 'Vivir del Fisco' ('Living on Our Tax Money'), referring to the pensions awarded to the victims.[31]

3. *Impact of Economic Reparations in the Mapuche Communities.* A research team that studied the impact of reparations measures on the families of Mapuche victims in the Araucanía region[32] observed that in very poor communities the economic reparations distorted family relations of solidarity and negatively affected family and community networks. Researchers pointed out that this culture's conceptions of reparations, as well as its ways of mourning, had been disregarded. For these reasons, many of the interviewed people concluded that it would have been better to use non-monetary forms of compensation, such as payments in kind with land or animals.

The Corporation closed down on December 31, 1996, stating explicitly that some of the obligations assigned to it by the law had not been fulfilled. Prior to this, members of the AFDD met with representatives of the Ministry of Interior and the Corporation to remind them that Law Num. 19.123 recognized the right of the families to know the final whereabouts of their missing relatives. Article 6 of the law recognized

the inalienable rights of the families of the victims and of Chilean society to know the final whereabouts of their relatives and their mortal remains. These rights have persistent effects and can be exercised at any time. The State has the duty to contribute with all its power, within the bounds of its authority, in the search for disappeared persons, and reveal the circumstances surrounding their disappearance or death.[33]

Henceforth, the State had the obligation to carry on with its efforts to search for the disappeared victims, even after closing down the institution created for this purpose. Taking this into account, the government decided to continue with some of the tasks that had been undertaken by the Corporation. Supreme Decree Num. 1.005, issued on April 25, 1997, established that a new program would be created under the responsibility of the Undersecretary of the Interior.

Follow-up Program for Law Num. 19.123

The Follow-up Program for the Corporation had the following aims: (*a*) the implementation of the recommendations by the Truth and Reconciliation Commission on all pending points; (*b*) the provision of legal and social assistance for the families of the victims upon request; and (*c*) the preservation and safekeeping of documents and archival records collected by the National Truth and Reconciliation Commission and the former National Corporation of Reparations (it was expressly indicated that these records were to be kept confidential, except when the Courts needed to have access to them).

Alejandro González, former President of the Corporation, was put in charge of this program. A team of fifteen people formed the program's staff and its budget for 1997 was $128,867,000 pesos (US$303,330). The same amount was allocated in 1998; in 1999 the budget was $152,063,000 pesos (US$300,000), and an equivalent amount was assigned until 2000. The investigation into the final whereabouts and the circumstances surrounding the disappearances of victims became the main task of the program.

Evaluation

The Program did not publish a report on its work during the 1997–2000 period. Nevertheless, it continued with the activities specified by Law 19.123, in a limited fashion and with little visibility, assigning resources to assisting the families of the victims and performing judicial and extrajudicial investigations to determine the whereabouts of the victims.

Human Rights Program of the Ministry of the Interior

President Eduardo Frei's government initiated a roundtable discussion [*Mesa de diálogo*] on human rights between 1999 and 2000. The participants included human rights attorneys, academics, and representatives of the churches, human rights organizations, and the armed forces. After ten months of work, the participants reached a final agreement committing the armed forces to deliver information regarding the whereabouts of the disappeared detainees. Six months later, as agreed, the armed forces delivered a report regarding 200 cases, in which they indicated that most of the victims had been killed and thrown into the ocean. In his capacity as President of the Republic, Ricardo Lagos announced the findings of the report and delivered it to the President of the Supreme Court, who in turn assigned special judges to investigate the information. As a result of the armed forces report, the Follow-up Program for Law 19.123 was reorganized, thus creating the Human Rights Program of the Ministry of the Interior. Lawyer Luciano Fouillioux was appointed Executive Secretary in April 2001. In 2002, the work team grew to thirty-two members.

The framework of the Human Rights Program was still based on Law 19.123 and Decree 1.005. The social program continued to work with the families, addressing more than 1,300 cases in 2002. The judicial program was reorganized in order to provide logistical support to the special judges conducting investigations in regiments, clandestine cemeteries, and other places indicated in the report by the armed forces. These special judges were dedicated exclusively to the program from 2001 until 2003. The projects and studies program was in charge of symbolic reparations, conducting new projects, and working with some of the families' groups throughout the country. The budget for the Program was part of the Interior Ministry's budget, and its annual expenditures are shown in Table 2.2.

In 2002, a registry was compiled of the 134 symbolic reparations projects that had been constructed up until then, including memorials, monoliths, parks, sculptures, and other public monuments and places.[34] According to the Undersecretary of the Interior, Jorge Correa:

[T]he majority of these constructions have been the initiative of the families with some support from civil and governmental organizations....At the moment, we have signed agreements for seven memorial projects that will honor the deaths of 215 men and women who were executed or detained without due process in Tocopilla (30), La Serena (55), Paine (70), Coronel (12), Chihuío (18), Osorno (30) and Villa Grimaldi. This is a commitment to memorialize, signed by the families of the victims with the Chilean Government.[35]

Table 2.2 Annual expenditures by the Ministry of the Interior

Year	2000	2001	2002	2003
Pesos	252,000,000	516,000,000	516,642,000	523.000.000
Dollars	400,000	748,000	735,000	756,875

Source: www.dipres.cl

Evaluation

The results of the Human Rights Program were publicly evaluated during the twelfth anniversary celebration of the Truth and Reconciliation Commission report in 2003. There was evidence of greater awareness in the country that social reparations and the necessity to dignify the memory of the victims 'is a challenge of our democracy, a commitment for all of us, but above all, the State, to fulfill the duties specified by Law Num. 19.123'.[36] Hence, the objectives of the Human Rights Program continued to be the following: (a) strengthening collaboration with the judicial branch of government in order to search for the disappeared and determine the circumstances of their disappearances or deaths; (b) broadening the reach of, and improving social and material reparations for, the families of the victims; (c) promoting cultural and symbolic actions that foster respect for human rights in all of society and preserve historic truth.

The families of the disappeared detainees and victims of political executions have not changed their position, insisting 'that social or symbolic reparations are relevant and important contributions to the families; however, they can never replace the value, not only for the victims, but also for the country, of applying sanctions to those who committed these atrocious human rights violations'.[37]

In June 2003, during new debates on human rights issues, the AFDD put forth a proposal called 'Truth, Justice, and Reparation Measures' ['Verdad, Justicia y Medidas Reparatorias'], on behalf of all the families of victims' organizations throughout the country.[38] Among other things, it proposed applying the legal status of 'absence due to forced disappearance' in place of 'presumed death' for the remaining unsolved cases. The proposal included demands related to historical memory, education, and recognition of pending cases in the Human Rights Program of the Ministry of the Interior. It requested raising the minimum amount of reparation pensions to $600,000 pesos (approx. US$900) as well as the inclusion of parents and siblings as eventual beneficiaries.

Government Proposal 'No hay mañana sin ayer' ('There is No Tomorrow without a Yesterday') and Draft Bills

In August 2003, the President of the Republic made a proposal to the country regarding pending issues related to the consequences of human rights violations that occurred between September 11, 1973 and March 10, 1990. The President declared that it was his duty, as well as the duty of all Chileans, to confront these issues and to take the necessary steps towards achieving 'truth, justice, and reparation'.[39] His ideas were further developed in the presidential message sent to Congress for three draft bills on these issues. Noting that '[m]any have believed that in order to overcome the traumas of the past, we need to bury memory and have a "fresh start", the President argued that the human rights violations of the dictatorship represented a social, political, and moral scar that required meaningful reparation measures and a responsible recognition of the magnitude of the problem.[40] One of the draft bills proposed incentives for delivering information on the whereabouts of disappeared detainees, and another proposed, among other things, the following modifications to Law Num. 19.123 of 1992: (*a*) an increase in the monthly reparations pension by 50 percent; (*b*) the redefinition of beneficiaries;[41] (*c*) the redefinition of educational benefits for victims' children; and (*d*) a reparations bonus of $10,000,000 pesos (approx. US$15,700) for children who had never received a reparations pension, and for those who had received it for only a limited time, the difference between the amount received and the bonus (this was a one-time bonus awarded to each of the victim's children who were alive at the time of the publication of the law and who were not enjoying a monthly pension; the bonus had to be requested within a year of the publication of the law). At the end of October 2004, the draft bill was approved in the third phase of constitutional proceedings.

2. Program of Reparations and Comprehensive Health Care for Victims of Human Rights Violations (PRAIS)[42]

Background

Human rights violations committed under Pinochet severely affected the mental and physical health of the victims. Many experienced severe emotional and psychosomatic problems, including anxiety, depression, and sleep disorders. Faced with this situation, during the dictatorship, human rights organizations offered medical care, first through a network of volunteers, and later on, through specialized teams.

Origins of the Program of Reparations

These mental health teams not only offered direct assistance to the victims and their families but also drew public attention to the psychosocial and psychological consequences of human rights violations, specifically torture and the disappearance of family members, as well as of suffering constant threats and fear. The clinical approach of these teams took into account the patient's suffering, his or her resources, and pointed out the therapeutic value of social recognition and reparation.

Many professionals from these teams participated in developing the proposals for human rights violations reparations led by the Government of the Concertación.[43] They cooperated with the Truth and Reconciliation Commission and later with the government agencies responsible for the creation of reparations programs, especially PRAIS, the comprehensive health care program established for the victims of human rights violations that took place between 1973 and 1990.[44]

These teams' analysis of the consequences of political repression on the mental and physical health of victims became the basis for the following recommendation made by the Truth and Reconciliation Commission:

From a medical point of view, we have received important opinions which point to serious concern for the health of the families of the victims and, hence, recommend that they should be provided with special care due to the consequences these abuses have caused in their health.[45]

According to expert opinions, these were extreme traumas

which presented severe symptoms in their mental health. These traumatic experiences are of such magnitude and quality that they cannot be processed or assimilated by the psychological structure of a person. Consequently, all of his or her subsequent attempts to reorganize his or her life will be marred by the inflicted damage, unless specialized treatment is provided.[46]

The Commission determined that it was the State's responsibility to provide reparations for the victims in the form of facilitating access to health services and developing mental health programs through the Ministry of Health. The Commission added:

[A]ccording to our previous experience and the suggestions we have received, we propose that all persons who were subject to extreme mental and physical traumas as a consequence of severe violations of their human rights by agents of the State or individuals acting for clear political ends should be the beneficiaries of these programs. We suggest that access be provided to the resources and programs of the private health sector to be able to offer a wider range of alternatives to the beneficiaries.[47]

The Program

The idea for PRAIS was conceived in proposals made in the platform of the Concertación in 1989. The Truth and Reconciliation Commission recommended that the program be created within the Ministry of Health. PRAIS began its work in 1991 thanks to funding from the United States Agency for International Development (USAID) in the amount of $205,823,739 pesos (US$600,000). After the first phase was completed, it became a program of the Ministry of Health and was financed with funds allocated to the Ministry's budget.[48]

The aim of the program was to provide comprehensive physical and psychological health care for those who were most severely affected by human rights violations. This aim received concrete expression in the proceedings that regulated and still regulate the way in which this sector of the population was integrated into the public health care system.[49] An internal Ministry of Health document from 1993, 'Norms for Qualifying as PRAIS Beneficiaries' ['*Normas para la Calificación de Beneficiarios PRAIS*'] established the guidelines for awarding PRAIS identification cards, which provided access to the services of the public health care system, free of charge. These 'Norms' stated that the following categories of people qualified as beneficiaries: former political prisoners, family members of disappeared detainees, family members of victims of political executions, those fired from their jobs for political reasons, those who had been exiled and returned to the country as well as their families, victims of torture and their families, and every person who had suffered human rights violations of any kind during the military regime (other examples include the *relegados*, or people who were forced to live in a confined region and subject to periodic controls by the police instead of being imprisoned, and peasants expelled from their land). In 2000, the technical requirements for qualifying for medical care were established, defining more clearly the types of beneficiaries and adding the following to the list: 'persons who had been working on human rights, providing assistance to those who were directly affected by the political repression between 1973 and 1990'. This referred to people who worked in human rights organizations, including health care professionals who provided their services.[50]

The procedures for qualifying a person as a victim of repression have been varied. The majority of the beneficiaries come from other programs that have established their status as victims already, or they possess the appropriate documentation. Others have qualified by demonstrating, in a number of ways, that they received assistance from human rights programs under the dictatorship. Since a main goal of the program has been to protect victims from humiliating and discriminatory proceedings, they are not forced to demonstrate that their present ailments were caused by political repression.

Population Covered and Beneficiaries of PRAIS[51]

By the end of 2002, there were 93,272 registered beneficiaries of PRAIS throughout the country. By June 2003, this number had risen to 132,000.[52] As explained above, these beneficiaries had the right to receive primary and emergency medical care from public health establishments, free of charge; they also received priority where there were delays, depending on the requested treatment.

While the infrastructure of Chile's public health care system enables its qualified professionals to provide care to the majority of the country's population, there are some limitations that affect the quality of the services. One of these limitations has to do with the rate between the demand and the availability of professional resources. Since 80 percent of the Chilean population receives care from the public system, there are, for example, frequent delays in providing access to specialized assistance, surgeries, and even some laboratory examinations. Nevertheless, despite these limitations, PRAIS beneficiaries have positively evaluated the services they receive, particularly mental health care assistance.

From the moment PRAIS was included in the ordinary budget for regional health services, it became impossible to determine the cost of the program, since its expenses are absorbed throughout the public health care system. A differentiated record of the assistance provided is not kept, with the exception of mental health care services offered by PRAIS teams.

Evaluation of the Program until 2003

PRAIS represents the reparations program with the widest coverage throughout Chile. In one sense, therefore, the State's responsibility to provide reparations for the victims of human rights violations has largely materialized in the form of the provision of specialized health and mental health programs. At the same time, however, the development of PRAIS embodies an expression of the contradictions regarding topics related to the past in Chilean society.

The first evaluation of the program, carried out in 1994, demonstrated that team members possessed high professional standards and technical qualifications, and that they were providing an increasing amount of services to beneficiaries across the country. However, from that year on there was no follow-up training of personnel, and the teams ceased to provide exclusive care to victims of human rights violations, incorporating domestic violence assistance into their services, and therefore diluting the sense of reparations that gave birth to the program.

The mobilization of the program's beneficiaries and their decision to form a national organization in 1998, along with the political situation created by Pinochet's detention in the UK, contributed to the recovery, by the following year, of PRAIS's original role as a health program within the framework of reparations. This generated, in turn, proposals for a reformulation of the program's working methods, contractual relations, and its publicity in mass media. Beneficiaries, who were nationally and regionally organized, played a prominent role in this evolution.[53] Since 2000, victims' organizations, and in particular groups of former political prisoners, have demanded that PRAIS should become national law in order to secure its permanence and national coverage, as well as more substantial financing.[54]

Despite the praise PRAIS received and the satisfaction its beneficiaries expressed, the program depended greatly on the individual motivation of the professionals who formed its teams, rather than on institutional compliance with its objectives. After ten years of operation, changes in the demand for mental health care services had not been examined, there was no clear profile of a PRAIS 'beneficiary', and the efficacy of psychological treatments for patients and their families had not been evaluated.

In the context of the general discussion of all reparations policies begun in 2003 previously described, the government proposed the institutionalization of PRAIS as a reparations program as part of the modifications to Law Num. 19.123. The message from the executive branch accompanying the draft bill modifying Law 19.123 stated that PRAIS would become a specific program of the Ministry of Health and defined its aim as providing reparative and comprehensive health care, i.e. physical and mental care, for the following people: (a) the beneficiaries defined in Article 28, Law Num. 19.123; (b) the beneficiaries registered before August 30, 2003; and (c) professionals who worked in human rights, providing direct assistance to the persons mentioned above for a period of ten years—these services had to be validated by PRAIS, according to regulations. The bill stated that these beneficiaries had the right to health services, free of charge. The necessary resources for creating specialized teams for providing mental health care would be considered in the course of formulating the health care budget and available resources would be allocated throughout the public health care network. The bill provided an annual budget of $1,000,000,000 pesos (approx. US$1,562,500) from 2004 to 2007.[55] At the end of October 2004, the draft bill was in the third phase of constitutional proceedings.

3. Program of Reparations for Returning Exiles to Chile[56]

Origins of the Program of Reparations

After the military coup in 1973, thousands of people requested asylum in foreign embassies. Thousands of others fled across the borders and applied for asylum in other countries. Many were expelled from Chile. Others left temporarily, but were not allowed back into the country; their passports were stamped with the letter 'L' indicating that they had been put on the 'National List' and would need authorization to return. Thousands of political prisoners who had been found guilty by military tribunals had their long prison sentences commuted to banishment from the country (Law Decree Num. 504). Later, more than 6,000 people left the country under a program of family reunification. It was not until the end of the state of constitutional exception, on August 30, 1988, that exile was abandoned as an administrative measure. The Program of the Concertación prepared for Aylwin's government stated that the government would lead an active effort to promote the return to the country of all Chileans who had fled or been exiled. On April 23, 1990, President Aylwin sent a draft bill to the Chamber of Deputies [*Cámara de Diputados*], which proposed the creation of the National Office for Returning Exiles [*Oficina Nacional del Retorno* (ONR)]. The message he sent to the House explained the concept of reparations behind the initiative, estimating that 160,000 people would potentially benefit from the program.

National Office for Returning Exiles

The National Office for Returning Exiles was created by Law Num. 18.994, published in the Official Gazette, on August 20, 1990. The law stated that exiles were those who had left the country during the dictatorship, who had or used to have Chilean nationality, as well as children born abroad to exiled Chilean parents who were or had been Chilean, and who intended to return to Chile or had already done so. The following cases were also considered exiles: persons whose prison sentences had been commuted to banishment; persons expelled or forced to abandon the national territory by administrative resolutions; those who had left Chile legally, but were not allowed back; those who sought refuge in consulates or embassies and who became subject of United Nations Convention on the Status of Refugees; those who were given refuge for humanitarian reasons in other countries; and those who had to leave the country because they had lost their jobs for political reasons, and were subsequently denied permission to return. The families of all of the above cases were also considered exiles, provided that they had had residence in a foreign country for three or more years. All of these circumstances had to be verified.

The responsibilities of the ONR were established by Law Num. 18.994. In addition, two complementary laws were passed: in 1991, Law Num. 19.074, which allowed exiled Chileans to work in Chile with the foreign degrees obtained during exile;[57] and in 1992, Law Num. 19.128, which awarded concessions to returning exiles and modified customs taxes for luggage, merchandise, and art owned by Chileans.[58]

Institutional Features and Organization of the National Office for Returning Exiles

Once the ONR had verified a returning exile's situation, it awarded him or her an identity card. It published the benefits exiles were to receive in newspapers and in an ONR brochure distributed throughout the country and abroad. Specialized nongovernmental organizations (NGOs) and some human rights organization programs provided most of the assistance for returning exiles, which consisted of the following: (a) economic and job market reincorporation; (b) health and mental health care through incorporation into the PRAIS program of the Ministry of Health in 1991; (c) access to basic and middle education for returning students; and (d) legal and other types of assistance.

The ONR had seven regional agencies. It ended its operations on September 20, 1994. According to official figures, it had served 18,042 beneficiaries and their families, totaling 52,557 persons. The registered returning exiles came from seventy different countries.[59]

Financing for the National Office for Returning Exiles

Financing for the ONR came from the Chilean government and international assistance. According to available information, the Office's budget expressed in Chilean pesos of 1994 is given in Table 2.3.[60]

The total five-year budget amounted to US$12,711,072. A 1994 Ministry of Justice report stated that 'the majority of the funds were designated to programs that help foster the development of the country'. The same report indicated that during a three-year period the international community contributed US$19,000,000 for these programs. The funds that were not spent were made available to the Ministry of Justice. The report stated that ONR reported annually its work and expenses to the Chamber of Deputies.[61]

Table 2.3 Budget for the ONR

Year	1990	1991	1992	1993	1994
Pesos	57,623,000	876,977,000	1,823,032,000	1,212,921,000	832,479,000
Dollars	189,000	2,511,245	5,027,944	3,001,017	1,981,866

Evaluation

The policy of reparations for returning exiles was implemented over the course of five years (1990–4), with the collaboration and coordination between the ONR, other State institutions, NGOs, and international organizations. Years have elapsed since the program came to an end, and during this time returning exiles have expressed conflicting opinions about it, valuing its efforts, but pointing out that it failed to take fully into account the great emotional impact of the experience of exile. There is no reference in any official reports or in those of NGO programs of the emotional cost, that intangible dimension of exile, which was part of the collective and personal backgrounds of those returning to the country after banishment, and which sheds light on why some returnees were able to reencounter their lost personal histories, but decided they had to leave their children behind, while others who could have returned decided to stay definitively in their countries of exile.

The policy focused on the reincorporation of returning exiles into the economy and workforce, providing services that helped achieve this aim. The cultural, social, and psychological aspects of returning were not considered important. As a result, the experience of loss and the frustrations of returning exiles remained, in the end, the private problems of the families and the individuals. Mental health programs provided help to deal with these issues, but these did not translate into political or social projects at a public level.

In spite of its flaws, however, the policy's most evident success was that it helped to change the social perception of exile, canceling, in this way, a social debt of the country to a sector of Chilean society. In other words, the political aim of this policy was fulfilled even though more than half of the Chileans in exile did not return to the country, many beneficiaries were quite critical of these programs, and many important aspects about the experience of exile and return were left out of the public debate and of the sense of political responsibility for the past.

4. Program of Reparations and Reincorporation for Political Prisoners[62]

Background

The forms of repression that political prisoners experienced under the military dictatorship deeply affected their lives and their family environment in particular ways. They suffered from the ways in which they were incarcerated, the trauma of torture, the social stigmas attached to their imprisonment, the difficulties experienced upon being released from jail, and the subsequent difficulties of becoming employed or self-employed afterwards, which considerably hampered their economic subsistence and that of their families. Under the military regime, human rights groups, particularly the Social Aid Foundation of Christian Churches [*Fundación de Ayuda Social de las Iglesias Cristianas* (FASIC)] and, during the 1980s, the Committee for the Defense of Peoples Rights [*Comité de Defensa de los Derechos del Pueblo* (CODEPU)], provided legal defense, as well as health, social, and economic assistance for political prisoners and their families. The electoral platform of the Concertación had expressly formulated its commitment to free all political prisoners incarcerated during the military regime, in the belief that neither due process nor their right to justice had been respected.

Initiatives by President Aylwin's Government Regarding Political Prisoners

At the beginning of President Aylwin's term in office, 397 political prisoners remained in detention. According to available information: '89% had been processed by military justice for violations under the State Security Laws (NE 12.927), the Arms and Explosives Control Laws (NE 17.798), and the Terrorist Conduct Laws (Num. 18.314). Some were also tried for violations under the Military Justice Code.'[63] Owing to procedural constraints, only forty-five of these detainees could be freed when the new government took office. The government developed the following three initiatives regarding the remaining prisoners:

1. The '*Cumplido* Laws':[64] Despite modifications during their approval, these laws (*a*) eliminated the jurisdiction of military tribunals to try civilians for some violations under the Military Justice Code (threats and offenses against the armed forces and *Carabineros*); (*b*) revised the Arms Control Laws (bearing and ownership of arms, ammunition, and explosives); and (*c*) revised the Terrorist Conduct Laws, whoever the victims might have been. Crimes established by legislation under the military regime were suppressed, such as infractions to the political bannings and unlawful entry into the country. It was determined to transfer most of the military tribunals' functions to the ordinary justice system in order to expedite proceedings and finalize cases against political prisoners.[65]
2. The '*Acuerdo-Marco*' (frame-agreement): This agreement was intended to reduce sentences through transitory norms both for prisoners accused of

terrorist actions and for state agents accused of human rights violations, with the exception of the so-called 'blood cases' violent actions [*casos de sangre*].[66] However, this agreement was never concluded, despite various efforts running until April 1991.

3. Reform to Article 9 of the Political Constitution: This reform allowed the President to grant pardons at his discretion to individuals condemned under the Terrorist Conduct Laws and to authorize judges to order provisional freedom on bail.[67] As many as 169 political prisoners received presidential pardons. Prisoners were freed gradually every year, as proceedings for their pardons got underway.

Freedom for Political Prisoners

Between 1990 and 1992, a social and economic reincorporation program for former political prisoners was implemented. It was aimed at those who had been liberated after 1990, although some exceptional cases of prisoners freed before this date were accepted. Former political prisoners who benefited from the program claimed that it was very limited and that it could not be considered an effective form of reparation. One of the beneficiaries, 'PR', a sixty-three-year-old former political prisoner, said that the program consisted of a one-time payment of $400,000 pesos (US$1,312 in 1990), which was intended to help him get established in an economic activity that would provide for his subsistence.[68] The Group of Families of Political Prisoners declared that this payment only helped beneficiaries pay 'their most urgent debts'.[69]

In 1994, a CODEPU report described the cases and problems still pending in relation to political prisoners of the military regime, including some cases in which a pardon had been granted. The report identified the following problems: (*a*) prisoners who had been accused, but had no sentence, and were under provisional freedom; (*b*) prisoners who had been sentenced while under provisional freedom, and were serving their terms because proceedings for their pardons were still underway; (*c*) the existence of arrest warrants pronounced under military justice that could take effect at any time; (*d*) former prisoners whose criminal records had not been expunged, thus hampering their reincorporation into society (the civil and political rights of these former political prisoners were not fully reestablished during the years these proceedings took to be resolved); and (*e*) the lack of economic reparations for time served in prison.[70] To make matters worse, many prisoners had multiple cases against them, which meant that proceedings were quite slow.

Evaluation

Debate on the *Cumplido* Laws provoked strong disagreement among different sectors of Chilean society regarding the sentences for political prisoners. These disagreements extended to the relevance of the distinction between conscientious objectors and prisoners accused of 'blood' crimes [*delitos de sangre*], and the political justification and efficacy of violence, which came under question. While within the government the will to honor the President's commitment to political prisoners predominated, there was also awareness of the armed forces' sensibility to measures having to do with political prisoners. Once all political prisoners were pardoned [*indultados*], the governments of the Concertación considered the case closed and they did not advance any new initiatives specifically aimed at the reparation of former political prisoners. They did not recognize left-wing militants detained after 1990 as political prisoners either, even though these prisoners argued that their actions had been politically motivated. Finally, the governments of the Concertación did not consider economic compensation for time spent in prison during the dictatorship.

Some lawyers estimated that there were almost 1,500 political prisoners under the military dictatorship, including the 397 who were still incarcerated when Aylwin was sworn in as President.[71] With the exception of a few cases that were granted nonmandatory or grace pensions by the President between 1990 and 1992, there was no reparations policy for these political prisoners for physical or mental harm, loss of opportunities, including education, damage to property, or loss of income. There was no compensation for time spent in prison, or for the harm done to the dignity and reputation of prisoners' families. Former political prisoners and victims of torture were, however, beneficiaries of PRAIS and the programs for the politically dismissed when they qualified.

V. PROGRAM OF RECOGNITION FOR THE POLITICALLY DISMISSED[72]

Background

Massive dismissals of public servants and employees working in companies controlled by the Government of Popular Unity [*Gobierno de la Unidad Popular*] (1970–3) represented one form of political repression practiced by the military regime once it came to power. Layoffs also took place in universities and other educational institutions. After the dictatorship ended, concern for the situation of those who had been politically dismissed from their jobs was manifested in various initiatives. The first was a memo written by President Aylwin that instructed public sector institutions to rehire all employees who had been laid off for political reasons. Meanwhile the National *Commando* for the Politically Dismissed [Commando Nacional de Exonerados de Chile] had been formed in 1986. This organization submitted several petitions to the government demanding reparations for the dismissed and providing it with background documents and information about the consequences of dismissals. In response, the government offered a minimal, single pension, which was deemed not satisfactory by the affected. Long negotiations followed between the government and the Commando, finally reaching agreement in 1992 on a draft bill that would provide reparations to this sector.

Origins of the Program of Reparations

On August 4, 1992, the President sent to the Chamber of Deputies a draft bill along with the customary message to Congress, in which he explained that the bill established social security benefits for public servants and employees of State-controlled companies who had been dismissed under the military regime. According to the President, this bill would repair, in part, the negative effects that political dismissals had had on thousands of people. The draft bill was intended to promote the recognition of their rights and to guarantee them a fixed pension.

The draft bill defined dismissals for political motives as 'those which were associated with the imputation by civil or military authorities of political activism or participation in political parties during the period between September 11, 1973 and March 10, 1990. There should be proof of these imputations beyond any doubt.'[73] The text established the requirements for the validation of these cases and stated that it was 'the exclusive attribution of the President of the Republic to qualify the political character of dismissals'. The President would grant pensions at his discretion [*gracia*] according to this law. The initial qualification of the beneficiary was the responsibility of the Ministry of the Interior. This draft bill excluded members of the armed forces, *Carabineros*, and Chilean Civil Police [Policía de Investigaciones de Chile]. During congressional debate, arguments in favor of this bill pointed out that layoffs based on political and ideological discrimination constituted a 'violation of norms and principles contained in the Universal Declaration of Human Rights and constitutional guarantees in the Magna Carta of our country'. Furthermore, it was contended that

compensation for the harm inflicted on the victims is based on international and domestic laws in force, and that the reparation for these harms is the responsibility owed by the State, since the State or its agents, through action or negligence, were the ones legally responsible for these serious transgressions of the labor rights of its citizens.[74]

In August 1993, after a long controversy, Law Num. 19.234 was promulgated by a qualified quorum.[75]

Once the period for requesting benefits was opened starting with the enactment of the law in September 1993 and running until August 1994, 43,302 applications were filed. By the end of 1996, 30,077 cases had been classified as political dismissals, 7,000 were discarded for not meeting the requirements, and 6,000 were still pending. A total of 24,187 cases were granted a time bonus for purposes of calculating retirement pensions (a bonus that could be as high as thirty-six months). Only 4,650 cases received the monetary pension established by this law, at their minimum level, i.e. $80,000 pesos (US$120).

Second Draft Bill

After evaluating the results of Law 19.234, the *Commando* for the Politically Dismissed insisted on modifying the program. In response, President Frei sent a new draft bill to the Chamber of Deputies. In his message, he pointed out the deficiencies of Law 19.234 that more than three years of its implementation had revealed. The main weakness was its exclusion of certain groups of public servants such as personnel from the Chilean Army, and the Chilean Civil Police, as well as members of the National Congress, which had been dissolved during the military coup. The time bonus limit for awarding benefits was also increased from thirty-six months to fifty-four months. Despite controversy, the draft bill was approved in the name of national reconciliation by the senators of both the Concertación and the opposition. It was published as Law Num. 19.582 on August 31, 1998. The period for requesting benefits began on September 1, 1998 and ended on September 1, 1999. On June 27, 2003, Law Num. 19.881 was published in the Official Gazette, establishing a new period of twelve months, starting on July 11, for requesting the pension benefits for the politically dismissed provided by Law 19.234. The period ended on June 30, 2004. The results of applications were to be given individually to those qualified by a commission of lawyers named by the Ministry of the Interior in May 2004.

Program of Recognition for the Politically Dismissed

The Program of Recognition for the Politically Dismissed [*Programa de Reconocimiento al Exonerado Político* (PREP)] was established by Law Num. 19.234 in 1993. It is part of the Ministry of the Interior, but has a specific administrative body

Table 2.4 Budget for the PREP

Year	1999	2000	2001	2002	2003
Pesos	278,120,000	287,000,000	294,960,000	291,032,000	291,032
Dollars	546,641	531,984	464,547	422,434	421,175

Source: www.dipres.cl

assigned to it in order to receive and review the cases. The PREP has a National Coordinator and four staff members.

The duties of the PREP are the following: to qualify candidates as having been dismissed for political reasons; to produce decrees that grant grace time bonuses, decrees that grant tax-free pensions, and decrees that derogate other benefits. The final qualification of the cases is the exclusive attribution of the President of the Republic; once he qualifies them they cannot be objected to under any circumstance. The program is financed with funds from the National Budget.

The State spent $11,631,736,000 pesos (US$1,688,355.41) in PREP pension payments up until 2001. The PREP's budget for the years following 2001 is given in Table 2.4.

Access to Benefits and Validation of Dismissals for Political Reasons

Dismissals for political reasons were determined according to the information and documents presented in each case, which had to be properly validated. People dismissed between September 11 and December 31, 1973 had their status as 'politically dismissed' validated automatically, as did those who were exiled for national security reasons or through expulsion decrees. Families (spouses or children younger than twenty-four years of age) of disappeared persons or persons killed by agents of the State could also access the benefits distributed by this program.

Those dismissed between September 11, 1973 and February 9, 1979 had to validate fifteen years of pension contributions [*imposiciones previsionales*] at the time of the dismissal. Those dismissed between February 10, 1979 and March 10, 1990 had to validate twenty years of contributions at the time of the dismissal. These requirements were completed with the time bonuses mentioned before. As stated, Law Num. 19.582 increased the bonus limit to fifty-four months for all of the cases, according to the date of dismissal. Those dismissed in 1973 would receive a six-month bonus per year of contributions. Those laid off between January 1, 1974 and December 31, 1976 would receive a four-month bonus per year. Finally, those dismissed between January 1, 1977 and March 10, 1990 would receive a three-month bonus per year. For the resolution of those cases without proper documentation, alternative proceedings existed that allowed substitutions for missing documents. Once the cases were validated, the files and documents were submitted to the Institute of Pension Normalization, which calculated and determined the benefits.

The law established the following benefits for those who qualified: (*a*) a special time bonus; (*b*) a grace tax-free pension (similar to pensions for seniority, old age, handicap, widowhood); (*c*) a retirement pension for forced dismissals; (*d*) compensation for dismissal; (*e*) recalculation of pensions taking into account the time bonuses granted and the consequences this would have given the choice of pension system now open to beneficiaries (applicable only to beneficiaries who had pension savings with the pre-1981 pension system, or in the new, private, pension funds); and (*f*) health care in the public system through PRAIS. The aim of time bonuses is to fill in gaps when the politically dismissed could not make contributions to their pensions. The time bonuses allow them to reach the time requirements necessary to obtain a tax-free pension.

The program's benefits expire with the death of the beneficiary, as long as there is no surviving spouse or offspring younger than twenty-four who can claim the pension. As stated by the law, benefits can also be claimed by exiled beneficiaries, even when they continue to live abroad. There exist no incompatibilities with other pensions awarded by other reparation laws, or with civil lawsuits brought against the State. Only when a beneficiary is already receiving an assistance pension granted by the State does the law require him to choose one or the other.

Administration of Benefits

The INP handles the administration of PREP benefits. Its functions are to (*a*) receive applications; (*b*) compile the pension history of each applicant in order to determine the benefits; (*c*) calculate time bonuses and tax-free pensions; (*d*) pay the entitled benefits; (*e*) assign time bonuses to the individual account of each beneficiary; and (*f*) reliquidate pensions from the old system and the 'recognition bonus' (the amount accumulated in the previous pension system that is transferred to the new pension fund).

Evaluation

In the debates over the reparations laws for the politically dismissed, a broad consensus emerged between different political groups behind granting pensions as compensation. The number of applications for these pensions reached 103,000, and by February 28, 2003, a total of 71,404 persons had directly received some kind of benefit. Of these, 40,696 persons had received a tax-free pension. During 2002, 7,694 persons were able to reliquidate their pension package, thus being able to increase the amount received each month. As many as 7,416 persons have benefited from time bonuses, which are registered in their individual accounts.

Due to various circumstances, a large number of those who should have qualified for PREP benefits were not able to do so before the application period expired. A third draft bill was therefore approved by Congress in June 2003. This law extended the period for receiving applications for one more year. Since then, the PREP has received more than 100,000 new applications, with an estimated 25,000 of these pending. Given this 'boom' in new claims, there have been reforms made to the qualifying commission, seeking a strict application of the qualifying criteria established by the law. The qualifying of these cases had just begun at the time of this writing.

It is important to note that, despite the large numbers of beneficiaries under this program, the majority of them receive only the minimum amount of $80,000 pesos (US$112) per month; interviewed beneficiaries who expressed satisfaction with the program tended to be those for whom the PREP pension is merely a complement to other sources of income, such as other pensions or salaries. Those who count this pension as their only source of income, on the other hand, hope that a new law will increase the minimum amounts. They believe that it is unfair that the minimum amount from a reparations program equals the payments from a regular pension program.

The purpose of these laws has been to offer reparations to those who were dismissed from their jobs as part of the repressive measures taken by the military regime. The dismissals were massive in 1973, and it has been calculated that more than half of the total number took place within the first two years of the regime's rule. The politically dismissed as a category of reparations beneficiaries also includes released political prisoners, victims of torture, exiles, and the families of victims of executions and disappeared detainees. In most cases, beneficiaries can legally obtain more than one reparations pension, since the various programs are not incompatible. However, the sense of reparations embodied by the PREP program has been questioned because there have been cases in which members of the military regime have requested and obtained pensions. The 1998 law technically allowed some former members of parliament, among others, to be granted a pension even though they had been immediately rehired by the military government after the coup.[76] The *Commando* for the Politically Dismissed has denounced these cases on several occasions, naming the beneficiaries publicly, including Sergio Onofre Jarpa, former Minister of the Interior under Pinochet, who stated that if the law awarded him a benefit, he was going to claim it. Preferring to follow a policy of 'no conflict', neither the government nor members of Congress have responded to these denunciations.

6. PROGRAM OF REPARATIONS FOR PEASANTS EXCLUDED FROM AGRARIAN REFORM OR EXPELLED FROM THEIR LAND

Background[77]

When the military regime came to power in 1973, it put an end to the agrarian reform that had been ongoing since the previous decade. In doing so, it gave back some of the land to its previous owners, and assigned plots from reformed pieces of land to other peasants. The government also reformulated the criteria for assigning the land. Law Decree (DL) 208 of December 1973 excluded most of the peasant leaders from land assignments, while DL 1600 of 1976 broadened the categories of exclusion in the assignment of land. The leaders of peasant organizations (unions, cooperatives, agrarian reform centers, and others) were not only excluded from the new agrarian reform process but in most cases they were also persecuted and expelled from their lands and homes, without any compensation for their years of service.

From the very day of the military coup, thousands of peasants were detained and more than 600 were executed or made to 'disappear',[78] being considered up to now disappeared detainees. According to the report of the Truth and Reconciliation Commission, 686 (more than 30 percent) of the 2,279 identified victims of the military regime were peasants, and, in most cases, these peasants had lived in agricultural lands under reform. The surviving families of these victims were also affected by exclusion from the assignment of land.[79]

Origins of the Program of Reparations

The idea of reparations for peasants excluded from agrarian reform or expelled from their land under the military regime was initially proposed by the bishops of the Catholic Church in 1979, after witnessing the economic and social damage caused by the exclusion from land assignment of those who had worked to make land reform possible. This damage was exacerbated by the ideological discrimination and political persecution the victims had to suffer. Peasant organizations themselves proposed some solutions, which were then incorporated into the platform of the Concertación in 1989. The purpose of this program was to estimate damages, both personal and patrimonial, in order to determine an eventual compensation amount for victims. It was also supposed to lead to the creation of a 'land fund' to be distributed among beneficiaries.

Since 1990, a number of different approaches to addressing this issue have been discussed. Frei's government offered the organizations grace pensions to be awarded at the discretion of the President. With the agreement of the peasant organizations, the government formulated a reparations policy for the loss of land rights and the damage caused by exclusion from land assignments. This policy consisted of a grace pension for the affected peasants. The amounts to be received were determined according to three different age groups: (*a*) sixty-five years of age or older; (*b*) fifty to sixty-four years of age; and (*c*) forty-nine years of age or younger. The program began in 1995, organizing administrative procedures to advertise its existence and identify the beneficiaries.[80]

Several State institutions coordinated their efforts to work with peasant organizations in order to identify beneficiaries and publicize and award the benefits. Beneficiaries have to validate their qualifications, for which a certificate from the Agriculture and Husbandry Service [*Servicio Agrícola y Ganadero* (SAG)] is needed. Requests for these certificates can be presented throughout the country at the offices of the Institute for Agrarian and Livestock Development [*Instituto de Desarrollo Agropecuario*], or in the town councils. Once a claimant's qualifications are established, a monthly pension is paid by the National General Treasury [*Tesorería General de la República*] throughout the country. The funds come from the National Budget. The State allotted the funds shown in Table 2.5 for the payment of these pensions in 2002 (expressed in 2002 values).

Table 2.5 Funds allotted by the State

	Monthly Payment (Pesos)	Monthly Payment (US Dollars)	2002 Cost (Pesos)	2002 Cost (US Dollars)
65 years or more 1089 awarded	77,411	112	1,011,606,948	1,468,352
50–64 years 1684 awarded	61,929	90	1,251,461,232	1,816,502
49 years or less 226 awarded	30,965	45	83,977,080	121,895

The 2002 total cost was $2,347,045,260 pesos (US$3,406,748). There are no updated data regarding the number of beneficiaries after 2000; nor is there any more detailed information regarding the costs of this program since the start of pension payments in 1996.

This pension is compatible with other pension benefits and with other reparations pensions and it expires with the death of the beneficiary. It is an individual, nontransferable, life pension. Being a beneficiary of this program does not preclude taking any type of legal action, including civil lawsuits, against the State. To date, however, there have not been any lawsuits filed by peasants for their expulsion from their land or exclusion from agrarian reform during the dictatorship. Beneficiaries of this program also have access to PRAIS. Information about this program has been provided by peasant organizations and public rural services. The official estimate, from the SAG,[81] of the number of beneficiaries is 4,579. Under President Frei's government, 2,999 peasants received benefits. When he left office, 374 requests were still pending (93 persons sixty-five years of age or older, 190 persons fifty to sixty-four years of age, and 91 persons forty-nine years of age or younger).

Evaluation

The program that was implemented in 1995 ended up being something completely different from what peasant organizations had demanded as reparation. The idea of a 'land fund' was left behind and the authorities did not incorporate the benefits requested by these organizations into this or any other programs. The organizations had demanded, in addition to a 'productive plot', family housing, educational assistance, and other measures.

Although in theory the grace pensions were not offered in exchange for the rights to the lost land, in practice, at least in part due to the advanced age of many of the petitioners, and to the fact that a good number of them had left the region where they had their land, as was mentioned before, no legal action to recover the land has been initiated.

Interviews conducted for this research, including many of beneficiaries of these grace pensions, suggested that these payments were far from constituting reparations for damage and losses to peasants caused by expulsion from their lands. Interviewees were frustrated that their efforts to obtain reparations corresponding to their losses did not succeed. In spite of this, they tended to value and express gratitude for the aid they had received. For many of the beneficiaries, this gratitude was for the certainty of receiving a secure monthly amount after the precarious times they had suffered through. This program has had little publicity beyond the beneficiaries, a common trait among most reparations programs implemented in Chile since 1990.

There has been no new assignment of pensions (as of this writing, October 2004), but the program has not been closed down either. The interruption of this process reflects, on the one hand, the weakness of peasant organizations nowadays, and on the other, the difficulties of relating these measures of reparations to a wider political framework of human rights violations under the dictatorship.

7. CIVIL LAWSUITS[82]

Chilean legislation establishes that civil lawsuit can only be brought against a properly identified person, so that his or her responsibility in the facts can be established beyond any doubt and thereby the corresponding indemnification payments can be determined. Due to the application of the Amnesty Law Decree Num. 2.191 of 1978, the identification of those responsible for human rights violations was obstructed for several years, particularly in cases involving disappeared detainees. For more than fifteen years, amnesties were granted for most crimes without any investigation or identification of the persons responsible. This was the case even though the Amnesty Decree differentiated between perpetrators, accomplices, and those who obstruct investigations, and instructed the judge, according to the provisions of the Penal Code, to establish the type of participation of each individual in the crime in order to be able to award an amnesty. According to the decree, a judge needs to conduct a previous investigation before awarding an amnesty. However, during the 1980s, the Supreme Court rejected this interpretation of the Penal Code, going as far as sanctioning Judge Carlos Cerda for continuing to perform investigations without applying DL 2.191. Judge Cerda had investigated cases of disappeared detainees and did not consider it proper to apply the Amnesty Decree prematurely as the Supreme Court had ruled in one case. This discussion was revived in the 1990s as other cases of disappeared detainees came before the courts. Finally, Judge Cerda's thesis prevailed: the amnesty could be applied only if the requirements established by DL 2.191 were met, that is, if an investigation was carried out and the investigation confirmed that a homicide was involved and the type of participation of those responsible for the crime could be identified. To award an amnesty without an investigation does not allow the identification of the responsible individuals, and therefore hinders an individual's right to use the civil courts to obtain reparations.

Many accusations against the Chilean State had been filed in the Human Rights Commission of the Organization of American States (OAS). One accusation, dated March 27, 1991, was for the State's 'violation of the right to justice and the impunity in the detention and disappearance of 70 persons' who were identified individually. This document pointed out that the Supreme Court had stated that the 'auto-amnesty' in DL 2.191

did not preclude the right of the affected to be properly compensated by the civil courts for the harm these crimes might have caused to their assets. But if this DL of 'auto-amnesty,' as the Supreme Court interprets it, constitutes a norm that even impedes a judge from ordering an investigation, and in cases where one has already been initiated, requires the judge to close it immediately, then the right to an indemnification for harm is not only illusory, but legally impossible. The unanimous jurisprudence of Chilean tribunals indicates that civil lawsuits can proceed once the *corpus delicti* has been proven and hence, the responsible parties against whom these lawsuits are taken have been identified. Article 40 of the Penal Code explicitly prescribes this by pointing out that a civil lawsuit can be placed against the one personally responsible and against his or her heirs, and article 254, Num. 3 of the Civil Code prescribes imperatively that it is mandatory for the civil lawsuit to contain the name, address, and profession or trade of the individual against whom it is placed.[83]

The use of civil lawsuits based on existing legislation in order to seek indemnification for harms and damages caused by political repression under the military regime has been limited. No more than 170 civil lawsuits had been filed by March 2003, although the exact number of these lawsuits varies according to the source.[84] Occasionally, civil lawsuits have attracted some media attention, especially when large amounts have been sought as compensation. None of the laws establishing reparations programs has expressly stated any incompatibility between receiving benefits and filing a civil lawsuit against the State; nor was there any incompatibility with the provisions of the Office for Returning Exiles or with pensions for peasants expelled from their land.

Lawsuits have been filed for different damages, including harm caused by torture, attempted homicide, and the disappearance or execution of a family member. There was also a class action suit filed that sought reparations for exile. The results of these lawsuits have been varied. In many cases, the ruling has not been favorable to the plaintiffs, and has subsequently been appealed. In other cases, the ruling has been favorable to the plaintiffs, but the compensation has been lower than requested, also resulting in appeal. Until 2002, civil lawsuits for cases of human rights violations had always been brought against the State, and have required demonstrating evidence of repressive actions causing harm to mental and physical health, social damage, or negative economic and material consequences.

In the case opened after the homicide of Orlando Letelier and Ronnie Moffit, in Washington, DC in 1976, US courts ruled that the masterminds of the crime were agents of Chile's National Intelligence [*Dirección de Inteligencia Nacional* (DINA)]. The Bryan Commission therefore determined that the Chilean State had to pay US$2,500,000 to the victims' families as compensation, which represents the largest amount it has paid so far.[85] In 2002, in the case of the Spanish diplomat

Carmelo Soria, the Chilean government came to an agreement through the Inter-American Human Rights System with the victim's family to reopen the judicial investigation and pay a compensation, later fixed at US$1,000,000, in exchange for waving the US$3,200,000 civil lawsuit the family had filed against the Chilean State.

Other cases filed for human rights violations committed by the military regime include the following:

1. In August 1997, the Courts, in response to a 1990 lawsuit filed by Carmen Gloria Quintana against the State for damages, ruled that she had the right to compensation in the amount of $240,000,000 pesos (US$741,600). Gloria had been seriously injured by burns and her companion, Rodrigo Rojas Denegri, had been killed during a public demonstration on July 2, 1986. Denegri, whose mother was an exile, had been a US resident on a short trip to Chile. The perpetrator of the crime was Pedro Fernández Dittus, an officer in the Army, who was sentenced to 600 days in prison. The requested compensation rose to $251,000,000 pesos (US$820,261). The State Defense Council [*Consejo de Defensa del Estado* (CDE)] appealed this resolution, even though many political and human rights sectors had expressly asked the government to abstain from appealing. Finally, the lawyers for the plaintiff requested an extrajudicial settlement, which amounted to $200,000,000 pesos (US $485,119).

2. A lawsuit[86] was filed in 1997 seeking $1,600,000,000 pesos (US$2,322,408 in 2002), filed by the families of four young men who were killed by agents of the National Center of Information [*Central Nacional de Informaciones* (CNI)] during an operation called 'Operación Albania' that took place between June 15 and 16, 1987.[87]

3. On November 20, 2000, a class action suit was filed, combining sixteen individual lawsuits brought by four different categories of exiles: the expelled, those who were granted asylum, political refugees, and former prisoners who had exchanged their sentences for banishment. The suit was presented by Leopoldo Letelier Linque and twelve other Chileans, who argued that 'violent actions forced them to request diplomatic protection in various embassies throughout the country, between 1973 and 1974'. They based their suit on the harm caused by these actions. On May 29, 2001, the State Defense Council, in its response, restated the legality of the act of exile. The lawyer for the plaintiffs, Adil Brkovic, commented:

It is completely incongruous that the State Defense Council, directed by someone who was exiled himself, states that exile is legal because it is founded on a law decree. It was a decree established by the dictatorship! If this is the case, then the executions and everything the dictatorship did was legal, simply because a legal document exists. But does just having a document make it legal? Then what would be the difference between a democratic State and a dictatorial State?[88]

4. In January 2001, legal action was initiated against the National Treasury in order to declare the nullity of the public right to summon, constitute, and operate military courts [*Consejos de Guerra*] that were formed under the dictatorship. This broadened the scope of matters addressed by these lawsuits.[89] Attorney Fabiola Letelier stated that she was specifically requesting compensation from the State for the thirteen victims of one of these tribunals, which ruled against them in Punta Arenas, in November 1973.[90]

5. On May 14, 2002, Judge Rubén Palma Mejías of the Thirteenth Civil Court in Santiago pronounced a sentence of the first instance that ordered the Treasury to pay $50,000,000 pesos (US$ 72,674) to the family of former Director of the State Railways [*Ferrocarriles del Estado*], civil engineer and Socialist Party militant Alfredo Rojas Castañeda. He had disappeared in March 1975 when agents of DINA detained him. In his resolution, Judge Mejías stated that the families of victims of human rights violations have the legitimate right to an indemnification, but that there could be no sum of money that could repair the harm suffered by these families. He added that it was unacceptable for the State Defense Council to invoke the statute of limitations or argue that the plaintiffs had already benefited from reparation pensions. Nor was it acceptable that the Council had disregarded the evidence presented by the Retting Report. Because this evidence had established systematic human rights violations under the military regime as well-known facts, their occurrence did not have to be proven formally, 'more so when the State itself, by many means, has recognized their existence and proposed reparations'. However, the CDE disregarded this argument and appealed the sentence.[91]

Search for Justice and Reparations through Civil Lawsuits

Civil lawsuits increased during the last months of 2002. This was due to the dismissal of the case against Pinochet for 'relative dementia'. In the opinion of a human rights attorney:

[W]ith the certainty that other penal processes against the General will not prosper, representatives of the victims will file civil lawsuits against the State with the purpose of putting on the record that it was he who gave the order to kill....Lawsuits brought by human rights attorneys aspire to a higher aim: to leave a legal record, and therefore a historical one, that Pinochet was guilty of the crimes he was prosecuted for.[92]

The final outcome of a number of the civil lawsuits (although no more than five), and the generally favorable sentences dictated by the lower courts, produced a difficult precedent for the Chilean State and its reparations policy, since the amounts of compensation awarded were hundreds of times higher than the amounts of the reparation pensions.[93] As the number of lawsuits increased, the CDE hardened its defense of the State's assets, even though, in doing so, it contradicted in the civil cases some of the positions it had adopted as a party in the penal processes. It appears that not all judges use the same criteria for determining compensation amounts. Furthermore, neither the defense lawyers of the CDE nor the government seem to share the same legal principles in these matters. Until now, the arguments made by the CDE against indemnification have been based on two principles: (a) the lawsuit has been filed after the statute of limitations, which establishes a four-year period for taking legal action, has expired; (b) the State has already repaired the harms done to these persons, in the cases of disappeared detainees and victims of political executions, referring to Law Num. 19.123; it cannot repair the damage twice. As yet, these arguments have not presented an obstacle to the families of victims of human rights violations in their pursuit of reparations. However, this could change if the decision taken by the Fourth Chamber of the Supreme Court on April 25, 2003 is upheld. In this case, the Chamber annulled a court ruling that had ordered the payment of compensation to the family of a disappeared detainee, accepting the two main arguments of the CDE.

8. Reparations for the Tortured

The military regime's methods of repression included the regular use of torture and rough treatment in police stations and detention places. Complaints about these practices were filed starting in the first months of military rule and continued throughout. Examples of this include the 1981 excommunication by Chilean dioceses of everyone who had participated in torture; the formation, in 1983, of a National Commission Against Torture within the Human Rights Commission; and simultaneously, the peaceful rallies held by a group of priests and nuns in front of the places where torture was practiced, displaying a banner that read: 'Torture Happens Here'.[94] Under the dictatorship, human rights organizations offered legal defense, social support, and health and psychological care for the victims of torture. Professionals involved in these groups publicly denounced the effects of torture to academia and to their unions. Since the rule of the military regime ended, PRAIS has continued to provide health and psychotherapeutic assistance to the tortured. However, because of the large numbers of victims, torture was not addressed by the Truth and Reconciliation Commission, nor was it considered for any other type of reparations program.

The Ethical Commission against Torture

The Ethical Commission against Torture was created in March 2001, on the tenth anniversary of the presentation of the report by the Truth and Reconciliation Commission. The Ethical Commission comprises diverse organizations and personalities that have fought for the defense of human rights in Chile. One of its first tasks was to publish the magnitude, reach, seriousness, and systematic character of torture practices under the military regime. According to the Commission, the number of victims of torture could reach 500,000.[95] The Commission has emphasized the effects of torture on the victims, their families, and society. It has proposed

to put an end to impunity and oblivion for the crime of torture in Chile, since this situation leads inevitably to the repetition of these acts in the future as they have been practiced until today. The Chilean State must recognize that torture is a crime, and that it has been massively practiced in our country; with it, the State has caused enormous damage to a large number of people. The sense of moral reparation and public recognition will generate, in our judgment, the basis to prevent the repetition of this practice in our country, and therefore, the beginning of its eradication.[96]

The Commission proposed the enactment of a Comprehensive Reparation Law [*Ley de Reparación Integral*] for those who had experienced torture. It pointed out the necessity of restoring to all former political prisoners the civil and political rights that had been restricted by legal processes which were based on the results of the practice of torture. 'Said processes were based on confessions extracted through torture, explained the Commission, which resulted in police records that impede the social and labor reincorporation of these former prisoners.'[97] With respect to health reparations, the Commission declared that, according to the International Convention against Torture, which Chile has signed, the State should guarantee appropriate medical and psychological treatment for victims for life.

The Commission requested that the government create a Truth, Justice, and Reparation Investigating Commission [*Comisión Investigadora de Verdad, Justicia y Reparación*] for the survivors of torture in Chile, a proposal it had insisted upon since its inception, and which it had bolstered through a campaign of denunciations about the consequences of torture and the obligations of the Chilean state to repair its victims. On December 10, 2002, the Commission made public a new report, which reminded the government again of the 'commitment of the government' towards the victims of torture, to create a new truth commission and design reparations policies for the survivors.[98]

On the other hand, starting in the year 2000, there was a proliferation of demands for reparations presented by the different groups of former political prisoners. These demands were generally supported by a variety of political parties and institutional sectors. In response to all of this, a number of congressmen in the Concertación presented a draft bill to the Chamber of Deputies [*Cámara de*

Diputados], seeking to create a commission that would investigate the situation of persons who had suffered from torture and deprivation of freedom for political motives. This was a debt, argued the congressmen, still owed to Chilean society. The aims of this commission would be to define 'the criteria for validating, as a former political prisoner, a case in order to be able to petition reparation in the moral sphere, as well as the juridical, social, labor, and pecuniary spheres'.[99] However, the claim that hundreds of thousands had been tortured and imprisoned for political reasons by the military regime also offered an excuse to postpone the matter; it was argued by the opposition that it would be impossible to carry out a task of such magnitude.

In the midst of this debate, and despite difficulties and the ambivalence of many political sectors, the President of the Republic created the Commission on Political Imprisonment and Torture, which began its work in November 2003. The Commission received more than 35,000 testimonies over a six-month period, out of a total of more than 42,000 denounced detentions. More than 60 percent of those who testified before the Commission were detained in 1973. Because more than half of them did not have the proper documentation, the qualification of cases forced the Commission to extend its period of operations. It was estimated that its work would end with a report to the President in November 2004. The President, after making the report available to the general public, would send a draft bill to Congress in order to implement the recommendations made by the Commission and the measures of reparations for the victims.

CONCLUDING REMARKS

The Chilean reparations policy has been an important part of a set of initiatives designed to address some of the consequences of human rights violations committed by the military regime that ruled the country from 1973 to 1990. During the first two years of his administration, President Aylwin was particularly concerned with explaining the meaning of these initiatives, usually relating them to the achievement of political reconciliation. He emphasized the importance of promoting truth and justice, but only 'as far as it was possible'. While the victims demanded complete truth and justice, the armed forces, with Pinochet still as Commander in Chief, maintained an important political role and demanded oblivion and impunity. Despite this conflict, most reparations programs were initiated under Aylwin's government; and while these programs have received little publicity, beneficiary organizations and word of mouth have extended their reach widely.

Most reparations programs have granted life pensions to those who have qualified as beneficiaries. The amounts have generally been equivalent to the minimum amounts disbursed by the pension system in the country, with the exception of the families of disappeared detainees, victims of political executions, and victims of political violence resulting in death, who have received larger amounts.

The reparations program for the politically dismissed has been based on a long tradition of indemnification, pensions, and time bonuses, developed since the nineteenth century, for those dismissed from their posts as part of an overthrown government. The large number of politically dismissed claims is the result of the lengthy duration of the military regime and its continually implemented policy of massive layoffs. It includes the initial dismissals of those who were detained, dismissals of trusted and well-established employees, and dismissals due to the regime's progressive reduction of the State apparatus. The main criteria for targeting the dismissed were always their ideological adherences. However, it has also been a program that has favored the political clientele of different political sectors, given the 'flexibility' with which eventual beneficiaries have been qualified. Beneficiaries have received tax-free pensions of a minimal amount, i.e. $82,000 pesos, which does not exceed the amount of US$125 a month.

Victims' organizations have emphasized the insufficiency of a reparations policy based for the most part on subsidies. They have argued that 'true reparation' is based on the achievement of truth and justice. Justice, they insist, is the only way to amend the profound harm caused by the impunity of perpetrators and the only way for the victims and their families to reach some degree of peace.

Without a doubt, systematic human rights violations affected the entire Chilean nation; therefore, the demand for truth and justice involves more than what can be attained in each individual case. Many had hoped true reparation would immediately become an issue of social relevance throughout the country once the dictatorship came to an end. However, it has been a long process, and its focus has varied with time. In the beginning, granting pensions as a form of reparation generated tensions between the economic needs of the families of victims and the concept of reparations as an institutional, political, and cultural process in society. This tension has resurfaced in the past few years, though in a different manner, with lawsuits being filed by the tortured seeking compensation or pensions as forms of economic reparations.

There is generally a more positive perception of pensions as such, because there is a clear awareness that true reparation is not exhausted by these pensions, and that reparation is a right. Following this notion, some victims have sought to obtain, through civil lawsuits, compensation amounts far superior to the life pensions established by the reparations policy of the governments of the Concertación. However, as of 2004, these lawsuits have not achieved any results. Furthermore, between 2002 and 2003, the Supreme Court signaled that it would not accept civil lawsuits brought against the State for cases of human rights violations. Going against previous rulings of the lower courts, the Supreme Court has ruled, in three definitive verdicts, against indemnification. This has had the effect of strengthening the existing reparations programs. Civil lawsuits have involved long, cumbersome, and costly processes, which in some cases have been absorbed by human rights NGOs, but have inevitably created unequal access to justice and reparations (even if up until now this has had little significance, given the meager results of such lawsuits). Very few people, in fact, would be able to afford taking cases before international legal bodies.

Since 1990, debates over how to address human rights violations, and the different proposals made both within and outside the government, have revealed an issue that changes over time, always generates new dilemmas, and continually reopens active discussion of the past in very dynamic ways. The pursuit of truth and justice has become an aim not only of victims and human rights organizations but also more and more of Chilean society as a whole. The media attention that judicial processes have received, the public acknowledgment by some agents of the State of the crimes they committed, and the progressive deterioration of Pinochet's image among his supporters have together allowed Chileans to see more clearly how their society is addressing the human rights violations committed under the military regime. This, in turn, has led to legislation in support of the victims.

At the time of this writing, two of three of the new laws sent to Congress in 2003 had been approved, and were awaiting their promulgation, meaning that only one of the three laws was still pending. The report by the Commission of Political Imprisonment and Torture, including its proposals for reparations, has yet to be made public. Perhaps, by the end of Lagos's term in office, a long phase lasting fifteen years will finally come to an end. A new President, in 2006, will have to face the outcome of trials for human rights violations. There will be more justice and truth, and new measures in the matter of reparations will be undertaken. However, the human rights violations of the Pinochet regime have left their mark not only on the victims, but also on the political and cultural life of the country. The task for making reparations is only beginning to become visible.

(Translated from Spanish by Christian Gerzso)

Notes

1. President Ricardo Lagos's proposal, '*No hay mañana sin ayer*' ('There is No Tomorrow without a Yesterday') of August 12, 2003, summarized reparation policies implemented since 1990 and made proposals on pending issues. See: http://www.lanacion.cl/p4_lanacion/antialone.html?page=http://www.lanacion.cl/p4_lanacion/site/artic/20030812/pags/20030812212921.html and http://www.ddhh.gov.cl/DDHH_propuesta.html

2. This section is based on documents compiled by Professor Yuri Gahona, as well as interviews conducted by Gahona and the author. Gahona interviewed Sara Carrasco, social assistant, and Victoria Baeza, social assistant and current chief of the social section of the Human Rights Program of the Ministry of the Interior. Within this program, Gahona interviewed Raquel Mejías, lawyer, who at the time was chief of the legal section of the program, Loreto Meza, lawyer, Cristina Cárcamo, social assistant, Jenny León, chief of personnel, Olga Bascuñán, Director's secretary since 1997, María Isabel Rojas, in charge of the Center of Documentation, and María Luisa Ortiz, documentation employee. He also interviewed the president of the Group of Families of Disappeared Detainees [Agrupación de Familiares de Detenidos Desaparecidos], Viviana Díaz, and from CINTRAS [*Centro de Salud Mental y Derectos Humanos*], José Miguel Guzmán, social assistant, who filled out applications for grace pensions for victims of human rights violations not included in Law 19.123. The author interviewed Alejandro González (deceased), President of the National Corporation for Reparations and Reconciliation [*Corporación Nacional de Reparación y Reconciliación*] and later Executive Secretary of the Follow-up Program for Law 19.123 until 2001; she also interviewed Lorena Escalona, who was in charge of the Education Program of the Corporation, Andrés Domínguez, Executive Secretary, María Paz Vergara, Director of the Archive and Documentation Foundation of the Solidarity Vicariate [*Fundación Documentación y Archivo de la Vicaría de la Solidaridad*], and Nelson Caucoto, lawyer for the Human Rights Department of the Corporation of Judicial Assistance [*Corporación de Asistencia Judicial*].

3. The families of victims each received a copy of the report.

4. For information on the criteria for the classification of political violence see *Informe de la Comisión de Verdad y Reconciliación*, Volume I (Santiago: Edición de la Corporación de Reparación y Reconciliación, Santiago, [1991] 1996). For final figures on the cases analyzed by the Commission, see Vol. II, 945. See also in: http://www.ddhh.gov.cl/DDHH_informes_rettig.html

5. 'Informe presentado ante el Consejo de Seguridad Nacional por el Comandante en Jefe del Ejército de Chile, General Augusto Pinochet Ugarte, el día 27 de marzo de 1991', *Estudios Públicos* 41 (Santiago, 1991), 459.

6. See 'Informe presentado ante el Consejo de Seguridad Nacional por el Comandante en Jefe de la Armada de Chile, Almirante Jorge Martínez Busch', March 27, 1991. *Estudios Públicos* 41 (Santiago, 1991), 449–504.

7. Ibid., 488–9.

8. See *La Nación* (March 5 and 6, 1991) (287 pages in total).

9. *Diputados* (session 41, April 3, 1991), 4865.

10. Ibid.

11. 'Declaración Pública' (March 27, 1991). AFDD – *Resumen de Actividades Año 1991* (Santiago, 1991), 38–40.

12. Ibid.

13. The complete text of the law can be found in Spanish at http://www.ddhh.gov.cl/DDHH_ley19123.html, and in English in Part III of this volume.

14. The currency exchange rate in December 1996 was 422 Chilean pesos per US dollar. See http://s:2bcentral.cl/Basededatoseconomicos/951_417.asp?Llamada Portada-SI

15. See Corporación Nacional de Reparación y Reconciliación, *Informe final de la Corporación Nacional de Reparación y Reconciliación* (Santiago, 1996), 119–20. See also the

web page of the Human Rights Program of the Ministry of the Interior: http://www.
ddhh.gov.cl/DDHH_informes_cnrr.html

16. Ana María Sanhueza and Vanessa Bravo: 'Indemnizaciones por violaciones de DD.HH:
el otro costo de la dictadura', *Siete + 7*, December 27, 2002, 40–3.

17. See Corporación Nacional de Reparación y Reconciliación, *Informe final* ... (1996),
120.

18. Published in the *Diario Oficial* (February 8, 1992).

19. Law Num. 19.274 (Extension from March–December, 1994); Law Num. 19.738 (1995);
Law Num. 19.441 (1996).

20. See Corporación Nacional de Reparación y Reconciliación, *Informe final*... (1996),
121–2. See also http://www.ddhh.gov.cl/

21. Law 19.209 published on April 19, 1993 extended the deadline for the presentation of
cases to the *Corporación* until June 18, 1993.

22. See *Informe sobre calificación de víctimas de violaciones de derechos humanos y de la
violencia política* (Santiago: Corporación Nacional de Reparación y Reconciliación,
1996), 580–1.

23. Ibid., 51.

24. *Unidad Tributaria Mensual* (UTM) (Monthly Fiscal Unit) was equivalent to $29,860
Chilean pesos on April 30, 2003. This corresponds to between US$42 and US$45.

25. See details on each one of the activities by the Education Program in Corporación
Nacional de Reparación y Reconciliación, *Informe a su Excelencia el Presidente de la
República sobre las actividades desarrolladas al 15 de mayo de 1996* (Santiago, 1996), 58–74.

26. For details on the authors and subjects see *Informe a su Excelencia* ... (1996), 78–9.

27. Ibid., 131–2.

28. Ibid., 85–8.

29. Supreme Decree No. 294 (March 13, 1991).

30. Before the Filiation Law Num. 19.585 of October 27, 1999, illegitimate children lacked
the rights and benefits granted to legitimate children.

31. 'Vivir del Fisco'. Reportaje. Economía y Negocios. *El Mercurio* (Santiago, March 8,
2003).

32. Basic, Roberta, Teresa Durán, Roberto Arroyo, and Pau Pérez. *Memorias recientes de mi
pueblo. 1973–1990: muerte y desaparición forzada en la Araucanía: una aproximación
étnica* (Temuco: Centro de Estudios Socioculturales, Universidad Católica de Temuco,
1997). See the complete text at http://www.derechos.org/koaga/x/mapuches

33. Decree 1.005 of the Ministry of the Interior 'dictates the rules to be followed by the
Ministry in relation to the tasks which used to be under the responsibility of the former
National Corporation for Reparation and Reconciliation created by Law N. 19.123.'

34. See http://www.ddhh.gov.cl/

35. Speech given by the Undersecretary of the Interior, Jorge Correa, on the twelfth
anniversary of the Report by the Truth and Reconciliation Commission (March 3,
2003). Programa de Derechos Humanos. Ministerio del Interior. Documento Interno.

36. Ibid.

37. May 20, 2002. Mercedes Castro 'Comando Conjunto, Aldoney y Cuesta Barriga:
Finalizados interrogatorios y alistan autos de procesamiento'. In this article, the letter
from the regional groups of the AFDD of the 9th, 10th and 11th regions addressed to the
Human Rights Program is reproduced. See http://www.lanacion.cl

38. 'Proyecto de la Agrupación de Familiares de Detenidos Desaparecidos: Verdad, Justicia y Medidas Reparatorias', June 25, 2003. It included: 1. Nuestra Propuesta para la Paz y la Reconciliación en Chile (Our Proposal for Peace and Reconciliation in Chile); 2. Anteproyecto Ley PRAIS (Draft Bill PRAIS); 3. Ley 24.321 sobre Declaración de Ausencia vigente en Argentina (Law 24.321 on Declaration of Absence in Force in Argentina); 4. Proyecto de Ley interpretativa del DL 2.191 (Interpretative Draft Bill for DL 2.191). http://www.lanacion.cl/p4_lanacion/antialone.html?page=http://www.lanacion.cl/p4_lanacion/site/artic/20030624/pags/20030624153213.html

39. http://www.ddhh.gov.cl/DDHH_propuesta_mensaje.html

40. 'Mensaje de S.E. el Vicepresidente de la República con el que se inicia un proyecto de ley que establece incentivos para la entrega de información en los delitos vinculados a los detenidos desaparecidos y ejecutados políticos.' *Cámara de Diputados* (Bulletin No. 3391–17).

41. The main change allowed fathers of victims to inherit the pensions received by the mothers when the latter died, and in that sense, fathers became potential beneficiaries. (Law 19.123 allowed fathers to receive the pension only in the absence of the mother. The recent modification allows fathers to inherit the pension previously received by the mother.) A change of a different type was to bring the portion of pensions received by the unmarried partner of a victim into line with what his wife receives. Law 19.123 assigned 40 percent of the pension to the wife, 15 percent to the unmarried partner. After the modification, unmarried partners also receive 40 percent of the pension.

42. This section was written using information from research on PRAIS by the author and Brian Loveman, political scientist at the Center for Latin American Studies, San Diego State University, conducted between 1999 and 2002 at the Centro de Ética de la Universidad Alberto Hurtado (Ethical Studies Center, Alberto Hurtado University). The research focused on PRAIS and reparation policies since 1990.

43. The *Concertación de Partidos por la Democracia* is the coalition formed in 1988 in the face of the plebiscite that took place on October 5 of that year. The coalition has governed the country since 1990. It is an alliance between the Socialist Party (PS), the Christian Democrat Party (PDC), the Party for Democracy (PPD) and the Radical Social Democrat Party.

44. A study conducted between 1989 and 1992 documented the work done by human rights organizations regarding mental health in Chile. See Inger, Agger and Sören Buus Jensen, *Trauma and Healing under State Terrorism* (London and New Jersey: ZED Books, 1996; *Trauma y cura en situaciones de terrorismo de estado*, Santiago: Editorial CESOC, 1996).

45. *Informe de la Comisión de Verdad y Reconciliación*, vol. 2 (Santiago: Edición Oficial, 1991), 830–2.

46. Ibid.

47. Ibid.

48. See 'Decreto de creación de PRAIS' in Brian Loveman and Elizabeth Lira, *Leyes de Reconciliación en Chile: Amnistías, Indultos y Reparaciones 1819–1999* (Santiago: Fuentes para la historia de la República Volume XVII, Centro de Investigaciones Diego Barros Arana, Dirección de Bibliotecas, Archivos y Museos y Universidad Alberto Hurtado, 2001), 258.

49. If there were modifications to the institutional features of PRAIS, there could be changes in proceedings, which could be reflected in 2005.

50. *Norma técnica para la atención de personas afectadas por la represión política ejercida por el Estado en el período 1973–1990* (Santiago: Ministerio de Salud, Unidad de Salud Mental, 2002), 55–6.

51. These figures were given by the Servicio de Salud Metropolitano Sur. Unidad de Salud Mental Programa PRAIS (South-Metropolitan Health Services. Mental Health Services Unit PRAIS Program), 'Informe de la primera jornada nacional de beneficiarios y funcionarios del programa de reparación y atención integral de salud PRAIS' (Santiago, 1999).

52. Gobierno de Chile, Ministerio de Salud, Unidad de Salud Mental, *Boletín Informativo*, N. 14, Year III, September, 2003, Edición Especial.

53. See Corporación Metropolitana de Beneficiarios PRAIS, '¿Qué es el programa de salud PRAIS?' (brochure, 2001).

54. 'No en nuestro nombre' ('Not in Our Name'). Declaration made by the Coordinadora de Organizaciones de Ex Presos Políticos de Chile (Coordinator of Former Political Prisoners' Organizations in Chile), Santiago, July 17, 2003.

55. The exchange rate in August 2004 was 640 pesos per US dollar. The average exchange rate during 2003 was 691 pesos.

56. This section was written using information compiled by Mario Rodríguez, journalist. The following people were interviewed: Jaime Esponda Fernández, lawyer and former director of the National Office for Returning Exiles [*Oficina Nacional del Retorno*, ONR]; Carlos Espinoza, Vice Director of the ONR; Patricio Reyes and Juan Carlos Vega of the Committee for the Defence of Peoples Rights [*Comité de Defensa de los Derechos del Pueblo* (CODEPU)]; Humberto Lagos F., lawyer for the ONR; Maura Brescia, journalist; Augusto Ugarte, President of the Corporation of Returning Exiles; and three returning exiles who had been political prisoners, who requested anonymity. The author interviewed Soledad Falabella, professor of literature who returned from Holland, Norma Muñoz, social assistant who worked at the Solidarity Vicariate [*Vicaría de la Solidaridad*], Verónica Reyna, lawyer for FASIC, and Teresa Gómez, social assistant for FASIC. Notes from a previous study on problems of psychosocial reincorporation were also used. In this study, the following experts participated: María Isabel Castillo, psychologist, Germán Morales, psychologist, and Niels Biedermann, psychiatrist; all of them from the Latin American Institute of Mental Health and Human Rights [*Instituto Latinoamericano de Salud Mental y Derechos Humanos*].

57. There were more than 1,000 professionals who had obtained their degrees abroad, who returned during the dictatorship. According to the ONR, 1,300 professionals had returned, of which 550 were covered by this law. See Ministerio de Justicia, *Memoria del Ministerio de Justicia—1990–1994.* (Santiago, 1995), 142.

58. The quoted laws can be found in Brian Loveman and Elizabeth Lira, *Leyes de Reconciliación en Chile...* (2001): 228–39; 251–6; and 277–9.

59. See 'El polémico balance final de los retornados del exilio', *La Segunda* (September 9, 1994), 42–5.

60. Ibid., p. 138. The sources are unspecified.

61. Ministerio de Justicia *Memoria...* *1990–1994* (1995), 142.

62. This section was written using research information compiled by Mario Rodríguez, as well as information provided by the following interviewed specialists: Verónica Reyna,

lawyer for FASIC, Martita Wörner Tapia, Undersecretary of the Ministry of Justice during Patricio Aylwin's government, Francisco Cumplido, Minister of Justice during the same period, Carlos Fresno, lawyer, María Isabel Bobadilla, Secretary, María Paz Vergara, Director of the Archive and Documentation Foundation of the Vicaría de Solidaridad, and Norma Muñoz, social assistant of the Vicaría.

63. See Comité de Derechos del Pueblo (CODEPU) *Informe 1994*, www.codepu.cl

64. These laws were named after the Minister of Justice at the time (Mr Francisco Cumplido).

65. The '*Cumplido* Laws' were an important step in adapting Chilean procedural penal law to international norms of human rights. They established norms of protection for detainees that prevented torture and exceptions in detentions, and promoted equality under the law.

66. See Ascanio Cavallo, *La historia oculta de la transición, Memoria de una Época, 1990–1998* (Santiago: Grijalbo, 1998), 41–5.

67. Law Num. 19.005 (April 1, 1991).

68. This program has not been documented. The information comes from interviews with beneficiaries and professionals who worked in it. The program was financed with funding from international organizations and an unidentified NGO from Holland, and is subject to the scrutiny of the Ministry of Justice.

69. *La Nación* (March 16, 1992).

70. Comité de Derechos del Pueblo (CODEPU) *Informe 1994*. Available at www.codepu.cl

71. These figures were estimated taking into account that in 1989 there were 1,902 freed prisoners, including 862 who were on parole. On the number of prisoners on parole, see Verónica Reyna, 'Situación jurídica y social de los presos políticos en Chile', in *Jornada de abogados defensores de presos políticos en Chile* (Santiago: FASIC, 1989), 15–18.

72. This section was written using documented information researched by Yuri Gahona, as well as information from his interviews with members of the Recognition Program for the Politically Dismissed [*Programa de Reconocimiento del Exonerado Político*] of the Ministry of the Interior, such as the following: Humberto Lagos, National Coordinator for the Program, Lenia Pizarro, member of the Evaluation Commission, Héctor Cereceda, member of the Evaluation Commission, and Guillermo Grovarí, social assistant. Zaida Araya, Secretary of the National *Commando* for the Politically Dismissed [*Comando Nacional de Exonerados Políticos*], was also interviewed. Several beneficiaries of the program who had been dismissed from public service in 1973 were interviewed as well, but requested anonymity.

73. *Diputados* (Session 23, August 4, 1992), 1923.

74. *Diputados* (Session 37, September 8, 1992), 2840–41.

75. See Brian Loveman and Elizabeth Lira, *Leyes de Reconciliación en Chile...* (2001): 270–6.

76. 'Denunciarion diputados socialistas: Colaboradores de Pinochet se acogieron a la ley de exonerados políticos', www.latercera.cl. (June 10, 2000).

77. A summary of this program can be found in Brian Loveman and Elizabeth Lira, *Leyes de Reconciliación en Chile...* (2001): 285–9. This section was written using press archives, institutional documents, books and magazines, and information extracted from interviews with key participants. Oscar Torres from the Group of Agro-regional Studies [*Grupo de Estudios Agro-regionales*] conducted the interviews and compiled the

information. The interviewees were: Humberto Vergara Muñoz, leader of the Confederación Unidad Obrero Campesina, Pedro Minay, leader of the MUCECH [*Movimento Unitario Campesino de Chile*] and of the National Peasants Confederation [*Confederación Nacional Campesina*], Orlando Avendaño, leader of MUCECH and of the Peasant Victory Confederation [*Confederación El Triunfo Campesino*], Carlos Ulloa, leader of the Confederación Unidad Obrero Campesina, Orlando Céspedes, leader of the Peasant Victory Confederation, Liliana Barría, member of the Central Team at INDAP [*Instituto de Desarrollo Agropecuario*], and Sara Mangiamarchi, in charge of the INDAP archives. Sergio Gómez, sociologist, Luis Enrique Salinas, agricultural engineer, and Fernando Arancibia, Doctor in Agricultural Science, cooperated with the study.

78. See chapters II and III in *Labradores de la Esperanza. La región del Maule, CODEPU-DIT* for an illustration of the situation of repression experienced in some rural sectors of the country. See the entire book at www.derechos.org/nizkor/chile/libros/maule; see Máximo Pacheco, '*Lonquén*' (Santiago: Editorial Aconcagua, 1980).

79. News Story: 'Las listas del despojo'. *Análisis* (Year XIV Num. 367, Janaury 28–February 3, 1991).

80. This modality was established in Law Num. 18.056 of Grace Pensions (November 9, 1981).

81. The original information regarding those who were assigned benefits and those excluded was registered by the Agrarian Reform Corporation [*Corporación de la Reforma Agraria* (CORA)] until 1976, and is kept today by the SAG.

82. This section was written using documents and press articles. Mario Rodríguez assisted with compiling the information. The following persons were interviewed: María Eliana Rique, lawyer for the State Defence Council, Héctor Salazar Ardiles, Adil Brkovic, and Nelson Caucoto, lawyers, and the Ministers of the Court of Appeals, Carlos Cerda Fernández and Juan Guzmán Tapia.

83. See www.cidh.oas.org/annualrep/96span/Chile10843.htm *Garay Hermosilla et al. v. Chile*, Case 10.843; Report Num. 36/96, CIDH OEA/Ser.L/V/II.95 Doc. 7 rev. in 156 (1997). Report No 36/96 CASE 10.843 CHILE (October 15, 1996).

84. According to information from the State Defence Council, by August 28, 2002, 126 civil lawsuits had been filed.

85. The Bryan-Suárez Mujica Commission is a dispute resolution mechanism agreed upon by Chile and the USA since 1914 to deal with matters that are not resolved through normal diplomatic channels.

86. ROL N° 2686–97.

87. In this case, the Defense Council had contradictory arguments. From the penal standpoint the CDE identified the crime as qualified homicide. In the civil lawsuit, and with the aim of denying compensation, however, it stated that the harms were the result of 'confrontations' [enfrentamientos].

88. See www.memoriayjusticia.cl/

89. See 'Presentan demanda civil para anular consejos de guerra', January 23, 2001; www.elmostrador.cl

90. Ibid.

91. Fundación Documentación y Archivo de la Vicaría de la Solidaridad Santiago, 'Informe de derechos humanos del Primer Semestre de 2002'; www.vicariadelasolidaridad.cl

92. Malú Urzúa R. 'Más que indemnización, querellantes buscan verificación histórica. Por la vía civil se buscará establecer que Pinochet es culpable de crímenes', (July 5, 2002); www.elmostrador.cl

93. Apart from the Letelier and Soria cases, which sought amounts that were negotiated in international institutions, the only other case of a single person that appeared in the Rettig Report, and whose family had been compensated in 1998, was the one of Julio Cabezas, who had been a member of the State Defense Council and who was executed in Pisagua in 1973. Legal action in this case prevented the application of the statute of limitations, an argument wielded by the Supreme Court in order to accept the appeals made by the CDE in other cases. There are two other cases in which the State has paid indemnification: the case of Carmen Gloria Quintana (who suffered from burns) and that of María Paz Santibáñez, pianist (shot in the head). All of the other cases have been appealed or have been definitely closed after rulings by the Supreme Court (2002 and 2003).

94. See Hernán Vidal, *El Movimiento contra la Tortura Sebastián Acevedo. Derechos humanos y la producción de símbolos nacionales bajo el fascismo chileno*, 2nd edn. (Santiago: Biblioteca 7&3, Mosquito Editores, 2002).

95. This number is more than double the estimate of the Fundación Documentación y Archivo de la Vicaría de la Solidaridad, namely 214,000 victims.

96. Comisión Ética contra la Tortura (handwritten original of the presentation), no date, 3.

97. Ibid.

98. Mercedes Castro, 'Informe contra la tortura. Compilación de 587 flagelaciones y sus responsables' (December 10, 2002); www.primeralinea.cl

99. *Diputados*, Session 7a, June 17, 2003, 36–7.

CHAPTER 3

THE REPARATIONS PROGRAM IN BRAZIL[1]

IGNACIO CANO

PATRÍCIA GALVÃO FERREIRA

INTRODUCTION

Unlike other countries, Brazil did not establish a comprehensive national program to redress all human rights violations perpetrated by the military regime. A series of unrelated laws and decrees dealing separately with banishment, illegal imprisonment, and other issues were enacted at different moments in time starting in 1973, even during the dictatorship, and there are complementary measures regarding the reinstatement and compensation of dismissed public servants and workers still being studied by Congress and by the government to this day. Several states created local programs directed towards the compensation of victims of torture. Nevertheless, Brazil has only one federal program of reparations for fatal victims of political violence and that will be the object of this study.[2]

1. HISTORICAL BACKGROUND

The Brazilian dictatorship started with a coup d'état against President João Goulart on March 31, 1964, and lasted twenty-one years. Backed by civilian allies, members of the armed forces took control of the country's political institutions, suspended civil and political rights and initiated a violent repression of dissidents, a formula that would be followed by many other Latin American countries in the coming years. However, the Brazilian military regime had many unique features, which would later influence the way Brazilian authorities would deal with the violations of basic human rights during that period.

In Brazil, the intensity of political repression increased over time during the first years of the dictatorship and, likewise, later on democratization was also an incremental process that lasted several years. The regime's first Institutional Act deposed João Goulart, the country's elected vice president who had just been appointed president after Janio Quadros' early resignation. The Act established indirect elections to Congress (i.e. only parliamentary authorities would be allowed to vote) and cancelled the political rights of six state governors, two senators, sixty-three federal representatives and hundreds of state- and county-level politicians. It took more than one year for the regime to enact Institutional Act No. 2, in October 1965. This second Act banned all political parties, gave the president the power to close Congress, and established indirect elections also for president and vice president. In 1967, the military regime imposed a new constitution and enacted the National Security Law, which gave broad powers to the armed forces and the police to fight all political opposition to the regime.

As political opposition to the dictatorship mounted, repression against dissidents became increasingly common. The year 1968 marked the beginning of the most violent phase of the military regime, which lasted until 1973. In 1968 a student was killed by the police at a university cafeteria during a demonstration. As a result, student organizations, progressive sectors of the Catholic Church and members of civil society organized a massive demonstration in downtown Rio de Janeiro, the so-called 'One Hundred Thousand Rally', which was brutally dispersed by the police. The first armed operations against the regime also started in 1968, with a spectacular assault on a train and an unsuccessful attempt to bomb the American consulate.

In response to the various demonstrations against the regime, the military government issued Institutional Act No. 5, which suspended many constitutional rights, including habeas corpus, and established censorship for cultural and social manifestations. Congress was closed and state-level legislatures were declared 'in recess'. The capital cities of all states and almost 100 municipalities were declared 'national security areas', their mayors being appointed by the president. From 1968, some units of the military regime started using torture, executions, banishment, summary dismissals, suspension of political rights and censorship in a systematic way. Armed groups opposed to the regime responded by kidnapping foreign ambassadors, who were later exchanged for political prisoners. To finance their operations, they robbed banks.

By 1973, the violent military repression had completely neutralized urban armed groups.[3] A group from the clandestine Communist Party of Brazil [*Partido Comunista do Brasil: PC do B*] then attempted to establish Brazil's only armed rural movement, based in the lower Amazon region of Araguaia. In 1972, there were approximately sixty-nine militants in Araguaia, who were joined by seventeen peasants. From 1972 to 1974, the armed forces made three operations to eliminate the guerrillas. These operations were never officially recognized. Accounts from the survivors estimate that seventy guerrilla members and rural workers died in Araguaia. There is no known estimate of the number of members of the armed forces who perished in the operations.

Also in 1973, President Ernesto Geisel took office, starting a period called 'slow, safe and gradual opening'. He adopted a series of measures aimed at dismantling the 'emergency legislation' imposed after 1968. One year later, Congress restored most political rights. The Brazilian military remained in power until October 1985, when General Figueiredo handed over power to José Sarney, the vice president indirectly elected by Congress, since the president-elect had fallen ill and died before taking office. He was the first civilian president in twenty years.

There is no accurate information on how many people were arrested for political crimes and tortured during the military regime, since many of the detentions were not notified to the judiciary. The same could be said of other kinds of violations of human rights, but unofficial estimates are around the thousands: thousands left Brazil in voluntary exile or were banished after forcibly losing Brazilian citizenship and thousands were fired from public jobs owing to political persecution. In the Project Brasil Nunca Mais (Brazil Never Again), lawyers working for the Catholic Church obtained statements from 1,843 prisoners who reported having suffered torture while being tried by military tribunals.

Yet the perpetration of gross human rights violations by military and police officers during Brazil's dictatorship was not as widespread a phenomenon as in other Latin American countries. There were scattered episodes in many different parts of the country, but systematic torture, assassination and disappearances were restricted to specific sectors of the armed forces and the police, like the DOI-CODI Division of the Federal Police. Most analysts would agree that the Brazilian dictatorship caused fewer fatal victims than most of its Latin American counterparts.

2. ORIGINS OF THE FEDERAL BRAZILIAN REPARATIONS PROGRAM: THE MOVEMENT FOR AMNESTY

It was still during the process of political opening-up, in the 1970s, that various organizations were established to fight for amnesty for the thousands of Brazilians who were imprisoned, in exile, or in hiding. Entities like the Women's Movement for Amnesty and Political Liberties [*Movimento Feminino pela Anistia e Liberdades Políticas*], organized by mothers, wives, and sisters of political prisoners and several Brazilian Committees for Amnesty [*Comitês Brasileiros de Anistia*] were created throughout the country by relatives of the victims. Backed by sectors of the Catholic Church and of other civil society organizations, these entities fought for a broad, general, and unrestricted amnesty. The families of the dead victims and of those who had disappeared joined these entities.

Indeed, the Law of Amnesty was finally issued by the military regime on August 28, 1979. This Law, though not as unrestricted and comprehensive as the movements had demanded, still allowed for the return of thousands of persons who had been exiled, banished, or driven into hiding, and freed thousands of political prisoners. Yet many of them were freed by judicial orders not based on the Law of Amnesty itself. Political prisoners accused of so-called 'blood crimes' [*crimes de sangue*][4] did not benefit from amnesty and remained in prison. They would be freed only after amendments were made to the National Security Law [*Lei de Segurança Nacional*] in the following years, reducing their sentences.

The Law of Amnesty did not benefit all the banished people either and failed to restore the rights of all public servants who had been fired or otherwise professionally affected on political grounds. Hence, celebrated as an important achievement on the one hand, the act was much criticized, on the other. The Law of Amnesty would later be broadened by other legislative measures. With the new democratic constitution of 1988, a commission was created at the Ministry of Justice to analyze allegations from public servants who had lost their jobs or suffered illegal administrative sanctions due to political persecution.

According to Nilmário Miranda, a House Representative from the Workers' Party [*Partido dos Trabalhadores*] who has been a key figure in promoting reparations, the approval of the Law of Amnesty was possible thanks to a political agreement between the military and the opposition. The military accepted the granting of the amnesty to the opposition in exchange for a promise not to investigate, let alone punish, human rights violations committed during the dictatorship. Despite all the limitations, the interviewees, without exception, stressed that the 1979 Law of Amnesty was a turning point and had a huge impact on Brazilian society.

In the years that followed, as those who had been banished, exiled, imprisoned, or forced to live in hiding started to return to normal life, Brazilian civil society turned its energy to fight for the full reestablishment of democracy. Other liberalizing measures would be gradually adopted, abolishing the two-party system and legalizing all political parties. Direct elections were also restored at the municipality and state levels. A proposal for an amendment to the Constitution, allowing for direct presidential elections, was presented in 1983 with the support of broad sectors of society. This movement was called *Diretas Já* (Direct Elections Now). In November 1984, the amendment was defeated in Congress. In January 1985, the Electoral College elected a civilian from the opposition alliance, Tancredo Neves, President of Brazil. Neves died right after the election and Vice President José Sarney took office. For the next three years, a newly elected Congress, backed by civil society, drafted the democratic 1988 Constitution, which finally restored the direct election of the president.

Although the Law of Amnesty did not contemplate the plight of the families of the dead and disappeared who wanted to clarify the facts and recover the bodies, most of the political energies from the opposition forces were channeled toward the process of redemocratization. Thus, despite the demobilization of the Brazilian Committees for Amnesty [*Comitês Brasileiros de Anistia*], families of the victims of political assassination and disappearance decided to renew their personal battle for truth and reparation. In 1979, the relatives delivered a file relating cases of deaths and disappearances to Senator Teotônio Vilela, then president of the Amnesty Commission of the National Congress. This file was subsequently organized and expanded by the Commission of Relatives of the Dead and Disappeared [*Comissão de Familiares de Mortos e Desaparecidos*] and the Brazilian Committee for Amnesty, section Rio Grande do Sul [*Comitê Brasileiro pela Anistia/RS*]. It was published by the Legislative Assembly of Rio Grande do Sul in 1984 under the name of *Dossiê dos Mortos e Desaparecidos* (Dossier on the Missing and Assassinated). The *Dossiê* was updated in 1996. It refers to 217 victims of assassination and 152 victims of forced disappearance committed by State agents.

One year later, in 1985, the first *Grupo Tortura Nunca Mais* (Torture Never Again) was established in Rio de Janeiro by family members and activists, in order to fight for the truth about the political assassinations and forced disappearances. Other similar groups were later established in other parts of the country. These organizations, in partnership with the *Comissão de Familiares de Mortos e Desaparecidos*, played a crucial role in maintaining this issue on the political agenda and in the establishment of a reparations program.

3. THE CLANDESTINE MASS GRAVES

Several actors in this process consider the discovery of clandestine graves in various states in the 1990s as a turning point in the struggle for truth. On September 4, 1990, a mass clandestine grave was discovered in the Dom Bosco Cemetery, in São Paulo. This grave, known as *Vala de Perus* (Perus Ditch), was used mainly to bury indigents but, according to official cemetery records, six political prisoners were also buried in it as if they were indigents. Excavations found the remains of a total of 1,049 people in the grave.

In 1990, a reporter named Caco Barcellos, while investigating police violence by means of forensic reports at the Legal Medical Institute (IML) of São Paulo, discovered the history of the clandestine grave. In fact, the practice of burying political victims as indigents had been discovered by relatives as early as 1973. The family of two missing brothers, Iuri and Alex de Paula Xavier Pereira, tried to find their remains in municipal cemeteries throughout São Paulo and finally discovered that Iuri had been buried in the Perus Grave in December 1973, under the alias he used at the time.[5] This discovery alerted the families of victims to the practice of using false names for the burial of assassinated political militants. In 1979, Suzana Lisbôa discovered the remains of her husband, who had been missing, also buried in Perus.[6] Many years would pass until the mass grave was revealed to the whole country.

When the mass grave became known, family members of the dead and missing obtained critical support from the mayor of the City of São Paulo, Luiza Erundina, who created a Special Commission for the Investigation of the Remains of the Grave of Perus. The Municipal Chamber of São Paulo also created a Parliamentary Commission of Inquiry (CPI) in order to investigate the history of that grave.

In Rio de Janeiro, relatives were also carrying out various investigations to locate the remains in the archives of the IML, the State Institute of Criminology (Carlos Éboli), and public hospital (Santa Casa de Misericórdia). They discovered that at least sixteen political activists had been buried in three different cemeteries in Rio de Janeiro. On September 16, 1991, the *Grupo Tortura Nunca Mais*, section Rio de Janeiro, obtained support from the mayor to exhume 2,100 remains from a mass grave in the Ricardo de Albuquerque Cemetery, where they believed that fourteen activists had been buried.[7] As in São Paulo, the Municipal Chamber of Rio de Janeiro also created a Parliamentary Commission of Inquiry (CPI) in order to investigate the cases of missing activists and identify the responsibilities for the clandestine graves in Ricardo de Albuquerque Cemetery. Finally in Recife, state of Pernambuco, at least six political activists were buried as indigents at the Cemetery of Santo Amaro. Unfortunately, the possibility of identifying the bodies of political victims among a high number of indigents proved to be very slim.

The exhumation of the clandestine graves marked a pivotal moment in the struggle to preserve the memory of the victims. Family members and entities demanded public access to police and military archives of the dictatorship. The governors of the states of Paraná and Pernambuco transferred their respective archives from the confidential Department of Public and Social Order [*Departa-mento de Ordem Política e Social* (DOPS)] to public archives, thereby permitting access to the documents. The archives of the states of São Paulo and Rio had been transferred to the Federal Police in Brasilia, but family members insisted that President Fernando Collor de Mello release the archives, and he transferred them back to the states in January 22, 1992. As a result, governors of both states were able to send them to public archives.

4. THE EXTERNAL COMMISSION OF THE HOUSE OF REPRESENTATIVES

All these developments encouraged House Representative Nilmário Miranda to create the External Commission for the Search for the Victims of Political Disap-pearance [*Comissão de Representação Externa de Busca dos Desaparecidos Políticos*] in the Chamber in December 1991. He tried to create a Parliamentary Commission of Inquiry, which would have more powers, but he could only create a Special Commission, which lacked the binding power to request documents or subpoena witnesses. Despite its limitations, the Commission lasted three years—the only Special Commission in the history of the Brazilian Congress to last that long—from December 10, 1991 to December 31, 1994.

This commission organized hearings with relatives of dead victims and victims of torture. Some military officials also gave testimony, bringing forward new information on the missing and assassinated. This commission paid a visit to seven different states, listening to the accounts of relatives. It also requested information about a list of missing activists (the list presented in the *Dossiê*) and received as a result a series of 'confidential' documents from the armed forces. The documents released by the Army and the Air Force did not bring any new information. Nevertheless, the report released by the Navy recognized, for the first time, the death of forty-three activists in Araguaia. Although many of the documents were contradictory and incomplete, the State had finally recognized officially the existence of the *Guerrilha do Araguaia*. The Navy Report also recognized the death of five missing activists in the area, and the detention of at least ten.

5. The Search for the Missing in Araguaia

Of the 152 reported victims of forced disappearance in Brazil, 59 were probably killed during the Guerrilha do Araguaia, according to a report from the PC do B. During a hearing at the Special Commission, journalist Ronaldo Brasiliense related he had had access to confidential documents from the Army, where he saw reference to 92 casualties. This figure did not include Army casualties. However, the exact number of victims is not known since the armed forces have kept total silence.

Families of those missing in Araguaia had undertaken various attempts to clarify the circumstances of the deaths and the location of the remains. In October 1980, they made a first visit to the region in an attempt to find information. In order to finance the visit, relatives reportedly received support from famous Brazilian artists and personalities. They spent three weeks in Araguaia, talking to peasants and inhabitants of the region. Soon they learned that State agents had recently threatened the peasants so they would not talk. Yet some were moved by the families' plight and decided to tell what they knew. Their testimony revealed the systematic use of torture against peasants during the military operations. They also indicated the existence of clandestine graves in several different regions in Araguaia.

As was to be expected, relatives did not receive official support to investigate the clandestine graves. In 1982, families filed a judicial action asking for the State to clarify the circumstances surrounding the deaths and to indicate the location of the remains. The judiciary has not analyzed the merits as yet.

In April 1991, relatives undertook a second mission to Araguaia, initiating excavations in the Xambioá Cemetery, where the remains of two individuals were found. One of them was that of a young woman who would several years later be identified as Maria Lucia Petit. In January 1993, relatives returned to the region, trying in vain to find the remains of Helenira Rezende in Fazenda Oito Barracas.

As a result of this lack of official cooperation in the case of those missing in Araguaia, families of twenty-five missing militants in Araguaia presented a petition before the Inter-American Commission of Human Rights of the Organization of American States in June 1995. It requested the Commission to declare the State responsible for the violation of the right to know the truth and the right to legal protection, included in the Inter-American Convention of Human Rights. The Commission is still analyzing the case.

6. OTHER LEGAL ACTIONS AGAINST THE STATE

Even during the dictatorship some relatives defied the oppressive climate and started to file judicial actions against the State, to force acknowledgment of responsibility, to issue death certificates, and to demand access to information and reparations. The first judicial action against the State was presented by the family of Wladimir Herzog, a journalist who, the State alleged, had committed suicide in custody in 1975. On October 25, 1978, federal judge Márcio José de Morais declared the responsibility of the State for the detention, torture, and death of Herzog, ordering reparations for his widow, Clarice Herzog. It was the first time that the State was found responsible for these violations. The decision was confirmed by the Federal Court of Appeal on June 21, 1983. However, Clarice did not accept the economic reparations. In 1979, the widow of Manoel Fiel Filho, who was officially declared to have committed suicide while in custody in 1976, also presented a judicial action. In 1980, the State was condemned to pay a monthly pension of six minimum wages to the widow. The sentence was confirmed in April 1987.

In 1981, the family of Mario Alves presented a legal action asking the judiciary to declare the responsibility of the State in his illegal detention, torture, and disappearance. The family did not want pecuniary reparations. They just wanted the State to be declared responsible for his death, which they obtained in a sentence issued in October 1981. The Regional Tribunal upheld the decision on December 1, 1987.[8] In 1991, the courts issued a sentence declaring State responsibility for the detention of another missing activist, Rui Frazão Soares, granting the family a compensation of 6,558,272.16 réis (around US$2,732,613 at the May 2002 exchange rate) for material and moral damages. In 1999, the Federal Regional Tribunal confirmed the sentence.[9] The State appealed the amount to be paid.

7. THE IMMEDIATE ANTECEDENTS OF LAW 9,140/95

In 1993, the Commission of Relatives, the *Tortura Nunca Mais* groups, human rights organizations and the House of Representatives' External Commission for the Search for the Victims of Political Disappearance held a national conference to discuss legal projects that would allow the recognition of responsibility by the State for such cases.

The resulting proposal, presented to the then Minister of Justice, Maurício Correia, advocated the establishment of a Commission that was to be organized by the Executive and coordinated by the Ministry of Justice, but would also include members of the legislative, judiciary, and representatives of civil society. This Commission would study every case of assassination and disappearance between 1964 and 1985. It would be entrusted with investigating, as far as possible, how, where, and under what circumstances the deaths and disappearances occurred and who was responsible for them.[10] The Minister promised to present a bill creating this Commission. However, the government was divided on the issue and the bill never reached Parliament.

In August 1994, in order to mark the fifteenth anniversary of the Law of Amnesty, the *Comissão de Familiares de Mortos e Desaparecidos Políticos* and the *Tortura Nunca Mais* groups formally delivered a 'Letter of Intent'[11] to the representatives of the leading presidential candidates. This letter had a list of ten commitments to which candidates were asked to subscribe. Among them were 'public and official recognition by the Brazilian State of its total responsibility for the imprisonment, torture, assassination and disappearance of political dissidents between 1964 and 1985'; immediate establishment of a Special Commission of Investigation and Reparation; opening of the 'archives of repression'. The letter received the signatures of several candidates and parties, such as Miguel Reale Junior, who signed on behalf of PSDB, the party of candidate Fernando Henrique Cardoso. Cardoso was elected in 1994, and started his mandate in January 1995.

Several interviewees mentioned the visit to Brazil of Pierre Sané, Secretary General of Amnesty International, in March and April 1995, as an important milestone in the process. Sané paid a visit in order to acquaint himself with the human rights situation in the country. In his assessment of the visit, he made the following statement to the press:

The President maybe does not understand that the crime of forced disappearance, being a crime against humanity, has no statute of limitation. A President cannot say 'Let's forget the past.' This must be investigated. The families must receive compensation, the identities of the victims must be restored and their bodies must receive a dignified burial. ... The President was not interested in discussing this issue. He said it was too complicated.[12]

This declaration and the prompt response of the government denying Sané's interpretation had a huge impact on the Brazilian media.[13] The political assassinations and disappearances were suddenly back on the national agenda.

The subsequent report of Amnesty International attracted international attention to this issue. In May of the same year, during a press conference in Washington, a journalist, who happened to be the sister of an activist who disappeared in Araguaia, asked President Cardoso why he had not undertaken any measure to redress the violations of the military dictatorship. Many consider the government's fear of international condemnation as an important factor that contributed to the law on reparations.[14] Also in May 1995, Nelson Jobim, then Minister of Justice, attended a hearing at the newly created Human Rights Commission of the House of Representatives, where relatives presented a proposal for the establishment of a Special Commission to discuss each case cited in the *Dossiê*.[15]

The Chief of Staff of the Ministry of Justice, José Gregori, was then charged with the task of negotiating and elaborating a bill to be sent to Congress, creating a Commission to grant reparations to the families of those missing. The relatives themselves and human rights organizations were not consulted. In July 1995, the television station Rede Globo finally broadcast a documentary produced by reporter Caco Barcellos in 1990 about the mass graves in Perus and concomitantly announced that the government would present a bill to Congress, in August, recognizing responsibility and giving compensation to the families.

Relatives, sensing that the bill would be too limited, pressed for a meeting with José Gregori, which they held under the auspices of the Secretary of Justice of São Paulo, Belisário dos Santos Jr. In a meeting described by several people as 'emotional', Gregori listened to the requests of relatives and human rights activists. According to participants, one of the achievements of this meeting was that the government accepted the inclusion of an article permitting the submission of new cases after the creation of the Special Commission. A second concession was the inclusion of a representative of the families in the Commission. Finally, relatives obtained the official recognition of the list of missing persons documented by the *Dossiê*.

Army General Murillo Neves Silva, commander of the 7th Military Region, publicly opposed such a commission. He was due to retire, but resigned instead in protest. The Minister of the Navy, Admiral Mauro César Pereira, also criticized the payment of reparations, claiming that 'there are many people missing who are still alive',[16] but he later backed down from this position. However, most of the high-rank officers in command remained silent. The Minister of the Army, General Zenildo de Lucena, organized a meeting with the President at the Vila Militar in Rio so officers could be reassured that compensations would not affect the Law of Amnesty.

On August 28, 1995, relatives attended a ceremonial session in the House of Representatives to pay homage to the victims of assassination and forced disappearance and to publicly emphasize that an amnesty did not forbid the right to know the truth. Leaders from all political parties demanded a congressional debate to discuss the bill. Representative Gilney Viana made an official pronouncement proposing amendments.[17] However, the government put the bill to the vote in Congress before a thorough debate could take place by using the procedure of urgency. Representatives loyal to the government in Congress defeated each and every proposal for amendments and the bill was approved in exactly the same terms as it was presented. On December 4, 1995, during the celebrations of the anniversary of the Universal Declaration of Human Rights, President Cardoso signed Bill 9,140, which came to be known as the Law of Victims of Political Assassination and Disappearance [*Lei dos Mortos e Desaparecidos Políticos*].

Relatives held meetings to decide whether they would participate in the process that originated from Law 9,140. Not everybody was in favor, since the Law did not contemplate several of their historic demands and seemed to be centered around the question of economic reparations, which had certainly not been a traditional demand on their agenda. A majority vote decided for active participation in the process unleashed by the Law.

8. Contents of Law 9,140/95

The Law officially recognizes the death of 136 persons who disappeared between 1961 and 1979 owing to their participation in political activities:

People related in Annex I of this Law are recognized as dead, for all legal purposes, for having participated or having been accused of participating in political activities in the period starting on September 2, 1961 and ending on August 15, 1979, and for having been arrested by public agents because of this, given that they became missing since then and that there has been no more information about them.[18]

The Law also stipulated an economic compensation for the families of the victims and determined that efforts be undertaken to locate their remains. Thus, official recognition of death, economic compensation, and location of remains are the three practical initiatives contemplated by the Law with respect to the victims and their families.

From the list presented in the *Dossiê* elaborated by the relatives, Annex I of the Law included all names except those who disappeared abroad and those whose names were incomplete. Apart from the victims enumerated in Annex I, the Law created a Special Commission, which would, among other tasks, consider the inclusion of other dead victims who fulfilled the following conditions:

A Special Commission shall be created which, regarding the political situation mentioned in Article 1 and in conformity with the present article, will have the following attributions:
I – Proceed to the recognition of people:
  a) missing but not related in Annex I of the present Law;
  b) who, because of having participated or having been accused of participating in political activities during the period from September 2, 1961 until August 15, 1979, have died of non-natural causes in police or similar premises.

II – Try as far as possible to locate the corpses of people missing in cases where there are indications of their possible location.

III – Issue an opinion as to the petitions of reparation which come to be filed by people mentioned in Article 10 of this Law.[19]

Hence, the Law was not restricted to victims of disappearance but encompassed people who had died in a violent way too, provided they met the criteria set out in paragraph I (b). A period of 120 days was established for relatives to present their cases to the Commission. Relatives entitled to compensation included spouse, common-law spouse, descendants, ancestors, and collateral relatives up to fourth kin, in this order.

The Special Commission, located within the Ministry of Justice, was composed of seven members to be appointed by the President of the Republic, who would also designate the President of the Commission (Article 5). The Law determined that four out of the seven members had to be chosen from among each of the following categories of people:

1. Members of the Human Rights Commission of the House of Representatives;
2. Relatives of the victims;
3. Federal public prosecutors; and
4. Members of the armed forces.

The Commission was to be assisted by federal public servants and had the power to request documents from any public institution and demand forensic reports and testimonies from witnesses. However, there was no provision to ensure that collaboration with the Commission would be legally binding for either institutions or witnesses.

The time span contemplated by the Law started in 1961, three years before the beginning of the dictatorship, allegedly to include cases related to unsuccessful coups d'états before 1964 and also considering that other amnesties already in effect reached the period until 1961. The period covered by the Law ended on August 15, 1979. It was exactly the same period established by the Law of Amnesty. Hence, the legislator apparently wanted to make sure all the cases addressed would be covered by the amnesty.

The economic compensation accorded to the victims consisted of 3,000 réis[20] for every year of life lost, considering the difference between the age at death and the life expectancy for an average person of that same age and sex (Article 11). Even though several interviewees mentioned that they thought this figure was established according to other civil compensations, nobody knew exactly how it had originated. Annex 2 of the Law provides the corresponding values for the life expectancy table. However, the Law dictated that no payment could be lower than 100,000 réis.[21] Payments were made in a lump sum and were nontaxable.

The Commission did not have a prespecified deadline to complete its work. The Law specified that the Commission was entrusted with issuing a trimonthly report of its work and a final report once its task had been accomplished. The Commission was to be dissolved after the publication of this final report (Article 13). The Law does not establish any restrictions as to families who had presented a legal action in the courts, who could also petition the Commission. Likewise, petitioning the Commission did not preclude future legal actions against the State.

Law 9,140 also prescribes that, in cases of court sentences condemning the State for political assassinations or disappearances during the dictatorship, any appeal by the State should not prevent it from paying the stipulated amount while the appeal is decided (Article 14).

9. LIMITATIONS OF LAW 9,140

In this section, we will relate the relatives' assessment of the terms of the Law as they were published. However, the final evaluation that all relevant actors accorded to the Law and to the reparations process depended substantially on the way it was implemented. Therefore, a more thorough evaluation will be presented in a subsequent section, after a full account of the whole process has been offered.

From the relatives' point of view, some of the main limitations of the text of the Law are:

- The Law excludes many victims of political violence. Since it restricts new cases to victims who died of nonnatural causes in 'police or similar premises', some of the victims of political repression, such as those that died during public demonstrations, for example, might not be considered. Nevertheless, the precise nature of the limitation was not totally clear beforehand as it depended crucially on the interpretation of this notion of 'police or similar premises'.
- The period contemplated by the Law definitely excludes victims who disappeared or died in custody after 1979. Several disappearances were documented during 1980, for example, so these victims would be left out even if the crimes they suffered were exactly the same as those in 1979.
- The length of the period opened to present petitions consisted of only 120 days. To many, this seemed too short an interval. As one relative put it: 'The violations went back thirty years, so why give the families such a tiny period of submission?'
- The burden of proof was placed with the relatives. In fact, this is not a simple issue. In the case of those victims enumerated in the annex of the Law, the burden of proof does not lie with the families since the State has already accepted its responsibility. Furthermore, in other cases of disappearance not mentioned in

the Annex, Article 1 of the Law only requires that victims who were arrested by state agents remain missing since then. Hence, it could be thought that the principle of 'presumed death' would be applied here and so relatives would not have to prove that the victim was killed by the State. Had it been so, it would have been up to the State to prove that it did not kill these persons. Yet, in reality, families had to present the proof of arrest by the State in the cases not contained in the Annex, and had to file their petitions 'with information and documents that can prove their claim' (Article 7). In addition to that, in cases of death where there was an official version that needed to be contradicted, for instance as to whether the person had or had not been taken into custody prior to the death, families envisaged they would bear the full burden of proof. Relatives also complained that the burden of proof remained entirely in their hands regarding the clarification of the circumstances of the deaths and disappearances, which was not mentioned by the Law, and regarding the location of the bodies. Indeed, Article 8 of Law 9,140 determined that the Commission act to locate the remains after an 'express request' of the relatives and only if there are *indications* as to the probable location. There is no provision for an initiative of the state to find evidence that might lead to the location of the bodies. In any case, a final balance of the question of the burden of proof depended on how the work of the Commission would actually unfold, so this question will be dealt with again in the last section.

10. THE WORK OF THE COMMISSION

The seven members of the Special Commission appointed by the President of the Republic were the following: President Miguel Reale; Eunice Paiva; Suzana Lisbôa; General Oswaldo Gomes; João Grandino; Paulo Gonet; and Nilmário Miranda. After a few months, Paiva resigned and was replaced by Luiz Francisco Carvalho. A profile of each member is presented in Appendix 3.1.

The Commission met for the first time on January 9, 1996. President Reale explained that the list of victims contained in the Annex of the Law had been compiled out of nongovernmental reports, press articles, and also government investigations, such as the one carried out under the Minister of Justice of the previous administration, Mauricio Corrêa. Suzana Lisbôa, representative of the relatives, requested access to the original files of the Army from which the 1993 reports had been elaborated. She also asked, in the name of the families, that the meetings of the Commission be public, but the other members agreed that this might disrupt the meetings and it was decided that they would be closed. Upon reflection, she also accepted retrospectively that open meetings might have jeopardized normal functioning.

The proceedings of the Commission were established as follows. Each case was distributed to a rapporteur who would analyze and prepare all the relevant information, present it in written form to the Commission, and propose a verdict. Each member of the Commission served as rapporteur for a different group of cases. If the other members were convinced by the presentation, the case could be voted on straightaway, either granting or rejecting the application by a majority vote. Since the number of members is uneven (seven), the vote of the President of the Commission does not carry any special weight. If any other member had doubts, he or she could ask to review the documentation and the case would then be postponed for a later date. In some cases, the petition was voted on but then withdrawn for reconsideration by one of the members, who presented it again to be voted on at a later meeting. After the resolution, petitioners could still ask for their cases to be reopened if they found any further evidence to back up their claim. No formal code of procedures was elaborated; members just reached and followed informal agreements.

The second meeting took place on January 18, 1996, and it discussed the proceedings to request a death certificate for the victims, as the Law contemplated. Suzana Lisbôa stated that many relatives refused to request the death certificate before the cause of death and the date could be determined. However, Nilmário Miranda and Miguel Reale argued that the Civil Registry could issue the certificates even when some pieces of information were missing and could alter them later, should the evidence be found. In practice, this would mean that the Offices of the Civil Registry would start giving out certificates with an explicit reference to Law 9,140 as a way to justify the missing information. In this second meeting, Suzana Lisbôa presented eight cases that had been selected by her adviser and all of them were approved unanimously. Indeed, the strategy of the relatives was to present cases that were relatively uncontroversial first so as to establish a pattern.

From the third meeting, which took place on February 8, 1996, different rapporteurs started to present their cases. Cases were all granted by unanimous decision or were delayed so that more information could be gathered. It was only at the fourth meeting, on February 29, 1996, that a petition had dissenting votes. The case of Ângelo Arroyo was approved by four votes to three, the minority votes being expressed by President Reale, General Gomes, and Eunice Paiva. From then on, different cases were either approved or refused in majority decisions: four to three, five to two and six to one.

Even though Law 9,140 specified that some members of the Commission should belong to certain institutions (Federal Prosecutor's Office, the Army, the Foreign Office), none of them seemed to function as a formal representative of his or her institution. There was no evidence that any of them followed the decisions or criteria from their institutions when voting, with the exception of Suzana Lisbôa, who, as representative of the families of the victims, attended regular meetings with the relatives where the strategy was discussed. In fact, it was decided that she should vote together with House Representative Nilmário Miranda, a victim of political repression himself and also a participant in many of these meetings with the families. As for General Gomes, he declared that, in the beginning, he sought the advice of each of the military ministers (Army, Navy, and Air Force) before each meeting but they offered no orientation, so he started to act according to his own criteria.

Relatives' organizations were working actively to gather and organize evidence in a meaningful way for each of the cases, so they could be presented before the Commission. Iara Xavier Pereira, adviser to Suzana Lisbôa and as such a participant in the meetings, performed a crucial task in organizing and setting up the cases for presentation. The relationships between the relatives seem to have been marked by a degree of political involvement. Some relatives were political militants who valued the political impact of the process above all, whereas others did not have a clear political aim and basically desired to somehow address the emotional loss suffered many years ago or to obtain compensation. Even though this difference appears to have caused some strain at times, it was the more militant and organized relatives who helped the others present their cases before the Commission, and they seemed to enjoy the legitimacy derived from the fact that it had been their militant strategy and persistence that finally made it possible to obtain such reparations.

Soon relatives were alarmed by the rejection of cases of victims who had apparently been executed, and feared that many other cases could be excluded.

A clear pattern started to emerge. If the person had disappeared, evidence of political participation and of arrest by State agents, together with the statement of the family concerning the disappearance, were deemed sufficient to apply the principle of presumed death. If the person had ostensibly died of nonnatural causes while in custody, the petition was also approved. In this respect, the Law did not distinguish between homicides or suicides as long as they happened to political prisoners for whose life the State was considered responsible. If, however, the official version for the death referred to an armed combat, a car accident, or some other fatal outcome for people who were not arrested, it was up to the relatives to prove that the government version was untruthful. So the burden of proof seemed to fall primarily on the heads of the relatives for cases of deaths (in alleged accidents, suicides, or armed combats) but on the State in the case of disappearances where there was no official acknowledgment of the death. This notwithstanding the fact that the situation of victims was often the same in both categories except for the fact that in the cases of disappearances the corpses had not been found or identified. This paradox implied that victims who had been taken out of the list of disappeared, after the remains had been found, now became much harder to seek compensation for.

Cases were based on testimonies from survivors and on documents uncovered by the investigations that relatives themselves carried out in the official archives that were available. When the official version had to be proven false, photographs and original forensic reports were crucial as they allowed the elaboration of new forensic analyses that often contradicted the original ones. Thus, pictures portraying marks of torture and bullet trajectories incompatible with combat situations played an important role in uncovering the truth. Also, exhumations were carried out to allow for new forensic evidence. However, cases in which no documents supported the alternative version received no compensation, even if the story and the context were very similar to those that did. Indeed, there were episodes with several victims where some, which had more accurate pictures or forensic reports, obtained compensation while others, whose pictures or reports were not clear enough, did not.

Even though it lacked subpoena powers, the Commission summoned several military officers to request information that could shed light on the fate and the remains of several victims. Not one of them turned up to testify. Also, the Commission formally demanded from the armed forces the present address of several officers so they could be contacted. The armed forces never answered.

It soon became clear that the crux of the decisions to be taken by the Commission lay in the interpretation of the concept of 'police or similar premises' contained in Article 4 of Law 9,140. In the more restrictive interpretation, this meant that compensations would be granted only to people who had been killed or disappeared after having been detained in police stations, military headquarters, or even in buildings or facilities owned by secret or irregular forces, such as intelligence units. In this view, 'police or similar premises' should be interpreted in a geographical sense.

In a wider interpretation, this notion would apply also to victims who had been killed while technically under custody, even if not previously arrested, which would include people who had been killed when they could offer no resistance. This would be the case of those militants who were executed after having been wounded in combat. In this case, 'similar premises' would not refer to a location but to a situation of violation of the right to life of those who were under custody and for whose integrity the State was fully responsible.

Yet an even wider interpretation, held by the representatives of the families, maintained that the concept should cover also the deaths resulting from any illegal use of force from agents of the State, wherever it occurred. This understanding would include not only combatants who were executed but also people who were killed in the repression of demonstrations and victims of torture who ended up committing suicide after being released.

Tensions related to these different interpretations peaked around the emblematic cases of Marighella and Lamarca between May and September 1996.

Carlos Marighella was an old communist leader with a long history of opposition to several regimes. This set him apart from most of his younger colleagues in militant leftist organizations. Also, the fact that he had allegedly killed a policeman in an armed confrontation implied that he was perceived as a great threat by the regime. He was ambushed in São Paulo where he was shot dead in gunfire so intense and indiscriminate that two other people were also killed accidentally. He carried a gun but did not have time to use it.

Carlos Lamarca's was an even more controversial case that aroused intense feelings. A captain in the Army, he decided to desert because of his political ideas, taking with him guns and ammunition to supply the guerrilla forces. Hence, he was considered a deserter and, moreover, a traitor. Some officers said publicly that he should at least have resigned from the Army before he joined the guerrillas. Lamarca engaged in several armed combats with State agents and went to the region of Araguaia to promote a rural guerilla force. In an incident, his group reportedly executed, through blows to the head, an officer who had been taken prisoner, since gunshots might have been heard by their pursuers. This increased the hatred against Lamarca, and he became probably the figure most detested by the military regime. He and another militant were surprised after a long chase in the wilderness by a military party that shot them dead before they could react. Lamarca's gun was in his bag and was not used in the incident.

The Commission first considered Lamarca's case in its ninth meeting, on May 30, 1996. Paulo Gonet was the rapporteur. Marighella's case was presented in the eleventh meeting, on August 1, 1996, by its rapporteur, Luiz Francisco Carvalho. However, several members asked to review the files and both cases were only settled on September 11, 1996, during the thirteenth meeting. Both cases were of paramount importance from the point of view of the standard they would set and also in terms of the political significance they had in, and of, themselves.

Paulo Gonet voted to deny the compensation for the widow of captain Lamarca,[22] based on the argument that the Law would apply only to victims who died in police buildings or other buildings where prisoners were held, and arguing against the, in his view, free exegesis that his widow's lawyers made of Law 9,140. He reasoned that House Representative Nilmário Miranda had placed an amendment to the original bill proposing that Article 4b have the following text added to it: 'or in any other circumstances as a result of the actions of agents at the service of the State'. This amendment was rejected by Congress. In his view, the very decision to present the amendment could be interpreted to mean that representatives were conscious that the Law, as it stood, would not include cases that happened outside detention centers. Likewise, he mentioned that several members of Parliament made personal statements commenting on the 'fact' that the Law had excluded cases 'such as Lamarca and Marighella'. General Gomes, for his part, agreed with this restrictive interpretation of the notion of 'similar premises' and added that Lamarca was a dangerous opponent, was armed, and hence the shooting was fully justified under war conditions.

Luiz Francisco Carvalho, on the other hand, adhered to the wider interpretation that covered all deaths of victims who were under custody of the State,[23] including those of victims who could have been arrested and were killed instead—a situation that would apply to both Lamarca and Marighella. Indeed, he argued that the overwhelming superiority of State agents in the incident, the number of shots fired, the lack of armed reaction on the part of the victim, and the military documents that prescribed the objective of 'destroying' Lamarca's group, all agreed with the conclusion of a summary execution. Suzana Lisbôa, the representative of the relatives, agreed with this position as expected, and her report described the forensic evidence that proved that the lethal wound had a downward trajectory and corresponded to somebody who was shot while lying, probably after having been wounded by previous shots.[24]

A number of senior legal experts also expressed their opinion on the interpretation of 'police and similar premises'. Belisário dos Santos, Secretary of Justice of the State of São Paulo, published an article stating that it was the State's obligation to respect life and integrity that was at stake rather than the location of the event.[25] In the same vein, the Brazilian Institute of Criminal Sciences [*Instituto Brasileiro de Ciências Criminais*] and the association of Judges for Democracy [*Juízes para a Democracia*] created a study group on the issue that concluded that it was the situation rather than the location that mattered, and that people submitted to the same situations deserved equal legal treatment regardless of the place of occurrence. The Association of American Jurists [*Associação Americana de Juristas*] sent a legal opinion to the Commission, elaborated by Lenio Luiz Streck, which underlined that the people who fought against the dictatorship were exercising their legitimate right to resistance and that the *ratio essendi* of Law 9,140 was the recognition of the State having acted against the rule of law. As a result, the place where incidents happened was, in their perception, an irrelevant matter. Otherwise, they claimed, one would have to believe that the State only broke the law within the prison walls. Further, they argued that Law 9,140 did not require the victims who disappeared to have died within police premises in order to grant them reparations. Hence, they favored a teleological rather than a grammatical interpretation.

On September 11, 1996, the final vote was five to two in favor of the families of Lamarca and Marighella, with only General Gomes and Paulo Gonet voting against. The repercussions were significant,[26] with relatives celebrating and the military expressing outrage. General Gomes expressed his intention to resign from the Commission and was only dissuaded after a meeting with the President of the Republic in which he blamed the verdict on a political decision originating in the government. When interviewed, he declared that in his memoirs he would reveal who, in his opinion, gave the order to approve these cases. Another retired general gave up his medals in protest, and the Army stated through its internal official channels that Lamarca died in combat against legal forces and that he would always represent 'treason, desertion, terrorism and betrayal of the sacred oath of an officer'.[27] The commander of the Military School in Porto Alegre had Lamarca's files destroyed and his name covered on the corresponding plaque.[28]

The Military Club [*Clube Militar*], whose members are retired army officers, together with its Navy and Air Force counterparts [*Clube Naval, Clube de Aeronáutica*], gave a more thoughtful response and presented an administrative action to the President arguing that the whole Commission was unconstitutional and should be dismantled.[29] According to them, the Commission violated the following constitutional principles: the principle of equality, since it ignored other similar victims; the principle of legality; the principle of access to the judiciary and the principle of a natural judge, since judges were left out of this process; the principle of due process, for the State could not defend itself and had to pay the compensations without appealing; the principle of administrative legality, since there were no proceedings or rules officially approved for the work of the Commission; the principle of 'impersonality', since the Law cited many beneficiaries by name; and the principle of publicity, since meetings were closed.

The President did not formally answer this action. Military clubs are supposed to reflect the deep underlying views of the Army, transmitted by veteran officers who, being retired, can express their views without the constraints of officers who are still active. This is why disagreements of the Army are usually channeled through these clubs rather than through officers in command who could be disciplined for dissenting publicly.

Interestingly enough, military protests for the Lamarca case seemed to be based often on the resentment and contempt they felt for the person rather than on objective principles. Indeed, it was particularly Lamarca's case that caused such rejection while other cases in similar circumstances did not.

The President, in a statement apparently directed at soothing the military's reaction, asked his spokesperson to say publicly that he agreed with the view of the military that Lamarca had been a traitor, but that this was not what was being judged in the Commission.[30] Military ministers repeated their attacks against Lamarca but respected the autonomy of the Commission to decide.

In fact, the military's outrage seemed to stem, at least partially, from the surprise at seeing those two cases approved, as if that contradicted an implicit pact to the contrary. Nilmário Miranda wrote in his book that he had always suspected that the wording of 'police and similar premises' was meant to exclude those two cases.[31] The relatives' perception that the Commission was expanded beyond its original limits and the blame that some officers attributed to the government for this verdict both fit within this interpretation that the decision contradicted previous pacts or orientations. José Gregori, Chief of Cabinet of the Ministry of

Justice in 1995 and one of the main negotiators of the Law, is reported to have said that the Commission was too hasty in its decisions on these cases, again hinting that the verdict was unexpected. Nevertheless, there are grounds to believe that at least some sectors of the government had had a different view all along. Thus, Minister of Justice Jobim convinced some relatives to participate in the process by telling them that all victims who had been executed rather than killed in combat would be covered by the Law. This opened up relatives' hopes that victims would not be limited to those who died in prison.

In any case, these resolutions set the standards that would be accepted for the remaining cases. Victims who had been executed when technically 'under custody', whether previously arrested or not, would be covered, but deaths in demonstrations or suicides of victims of torture once they had left the prisons would not.

The official deadline to present cases was basically observed by the Commission. Cases that arrived after the deadline were not analyzed, with one single exception. A woman now living in Sweden was allowed a longer period to present her documents, given the obvious communication difficulties.

After 1998, the Commission met only twice, once on June 27, 2001 and once on May 9, 2002. Both sessions were devoted to locating the bodies. Thus, the Commission has met officially a total of twenty-eight times as of this writing.

In general, relationships within the Commission were reportedly pleasant, with a few exceptions. Representatives of relatives and relatives themselves declared that their relationship with General Gomes was difficult, both because of his position and what he represented and also because he allegedly referred to victims as 'terrorists', and was perceived to have a 'sneering' attitude toward the whole issue at times. In an isolated and embarrassing incident, the son of a victim called the general an 'assassin' in the hall. On another occasion, the general had a bitter interchange with the widow of Marighella as she tried in vain to obtain a copy of his report on the case.

In seven cases, two persons or groups presented different petitions, knowingly or unknowingly, for the same victim. The Commission tried to ask the plaintiffs to reach an agreement as to how the reparations would be divided, if granted, and followed these informal agreements. However, a few cases could not be settled by agreements and the petitioners went to court. In one case, for example, the court established that the common-law wife rather than the legal wife would receive the compensation, thus confirming the decision of the Commission. In another case, the courts also backed the Commission resolution to grant the compensation to the wife rather than to the children.

There is one exceptional case where two families entered the petition, one of them after the deadline. The courts decided that the family that acted within the deadline would obtain the compensation.

When the work of the Commission started, there was no certainty as to whether, in the case of a civil suit presented directly before the courts, the judge would deduct the money already paid through the Commission from the total amount due. A legal opinion elaborated by an adviser to the Commission in 1996 stated that the civil court reparations and that of the Special Commission would be of different nature and therefore independent and fully compatible without deduction. Yet the opinion asserted that some judges might still ask for the amount given by the Commission to be deducted from the total civil lawsuit awarded. As we shall see in a later section, this was indeed the case in a few petitions but not in others.

In only one case did the victim 'reappear' after the family had received compensation. When they applied for a pension for the supposed widow, once they were in possession of the death certificate, they were informed that the person was still alive. An official enquiry was opened but, since it had all happened in good faith, the family was not forced to return the money. Indeed, Article 12 of Law 9,140 only stipulated the obligation to return the lump sum in cases where relatives had intentionally acted to mislead the Commission.

11. THE COMPENSATIONS PAID

Commission meetings occurred regularly until the twenty-sixth session, held on May 5, 1998, when the last pending cases were decided. By 1999, all compensations had been effectively paid, except for very few that were awaiting court resolutions. The lowest lump sum was 100,000 réis, as the Law indicated, and the highest actually paid was 138,300 réis.

In short, the Commission received 373 petitions for reparations referring to 366 victims. A further two applications demanded a death certificate and the remains of the victims but explicitly refused economic compensation because of moral and political considerations.

From the 366 victims, a total of 132 appeared in the Annex of Law 9,140 and therefore were recognized automatically. The Annex contained 136 victims but in four cases the Commission did not receive any petition from the relatives. Among these four cases that were not presented to the Commission, one of them was that of a person found out to have died of natural causes long after he had allegedly disappeared. This case was included in the Annex even though he was not part of the *Dossiê*, because the *Tortura Nunca Mais* group from Rio de Janeiro had a statement indicating that the person had been arrested and killed, even though there was no confirmation from the family. This decision, which caused some controversy within the relatives' organizations, proved wrong, but since the family did not claim compensation the government decided not to alter the Law.[32] Another of these four was that of the husband of one of the members of the Commission, Eunice Paiva. She preferred to wait for the sentence on the lawsuit rather than resort to the Commission where she herself was a member. In the other two cases—one of which is that of a victim whose full name is still uncertain—the relatives could not be found.

As a result, leaving aside the victims contained in the Annex, the Commission had to decide on a total of 234 petitions for reparations. Out of these, 148 (63 percent) were granted and 86 (37 percent) refused. Considering also the cases in the Annex, the Commission granted a total of 280 reparations. Table 3.1 summarizes the results.

The refusals were based on several grounds. A total of fifteen applications were not considered since they arrived after the deadline. A few cases were also disregarded because the disappearance had occurred in another country or after the period established in the Law. There were also cases where the petitioner was deemed not to be entitled to the benefit, i.e. he or she was not a relative in the terms defined by Article 3 of the Law. On some occasions, the victim had no apparent political activity. The rest were rejected on the merits of the case.

Out of the 358 victims contained in the *Dossiê* elaborated by the relatives, 298 produced a petition for reparations before the Commission. This was considered a success by their organizations, given the time constraints and the difficulties. In the end, 262 victims from the *Dossiê* obtained reparations: 132 who were already in the Annex and a further 130 who were judged by the Commission. Hence, only 36 cases from the *Dossiê* were turned down by the Commission.

Despite the tension that surrounded some of the most famous cases, most of the decisions in the Commission were taken unanimously. In fact, 168 out of the 234 decisions (72%) were unanimous: 103 were approvals and 65 refusals. Tables 3.2 and 3.3 show how the approving votes were distributed.

Table 3.1 Summary of applications and victims

Petitions that requested death certificates or location of remains but no economic reparations: 2

Total number of petitions for reparations received: 373

Total number of victims in petitions for reparations: 366

From these: 132 were contained in Annex of Law 9,140 automatically approved

234 to be judged by the Commission

From these: 148 granted

86 refused

Total number of victims for which reparations was granted: 280

Table 3.2 Number of approving votes*

Number of votes	Number of cases	%
0	65	27.8
2	13	5.6
3	8	3.4
4	13	5.6
5	20	8.5
6	34	14.5
7	81	34.6
Total	234	100.0

*Data for this table were obtained from the Acts of every Commission meeting. When one case was voted several times, we considered only the last and final vote.

Table 3.3 Configuration of approving and dissenting votes*

Approving to dissenting votes	Number of cases	Verdict
7 to 0	81	
6 to 0	10	
5 to 0	12	
6 to 1	24	APPROVED
5 to 2	8	
4 to 2	4	
4 to 3	9	
TOTAL	148	
3 to 4	8	
2 to 4	2	
2 to 5	11	REJECTED
0 to 6	17	
0 to 7	48	
TOTAL	86	

*Votes do not always add to seven, the total number of members, since occasionally one or two members were absent from the session.

A total of nine petitions were granted by just one vote while eight were rejected by the same margin.

Several members of the Commission expressed difficulties sometimes with trying to simultaneously uphold two principles in their votes: the first was following the Law, and the second, granting fair reparations to the relatives. Thus, they sometimes felt they had to deny a petition that they considered just because it was not covered by the Law. Those members with a legal background were more inclined to follow the Law, whereas those who represented groups—such as the relatives or the Army—were more prone to defend certain criteria regardless of the content of the Law or, in other words, more likely to try to stretch the Law as far as possible. In any case, all members expressed at least a certain inclination to follow the Law, even when that occasionally clashed with the expectations of the groups they represented.

12. THE SEARCH FOR THE BODIES

Article 3, II, of Law 9,140 established that the Special Commission should 'try as far as possible to locate the corpses of people missing in cases where there are indications of their possible location'.

In April 1996, the newspaper *O Globo* published a series of articles on the guerilla campaign of Araguaia, with unpublished photographs of deceased militants in the region and the location of seven clandestine burial sites. The articles confirmed the information of the families of the missing militants, who shortly thereafter petitioned the Commission to investigate. In the document, they insisted on the clarification of the circumstances of the disappearances and assassinations, asking for a search for the bodies.

The Commission made the first official mission to search for the remains between May 7 and 11, 1996. Among the members of the mission were Cristiano Morini, senior assistant, Criméia de Almeida, widow of a missing militant, and Luis Fondebrider, member of the Argentine Forensic Archeology Team (EAAF). As a result, three areas possibly used as clandestine graves were identified and marked.

A second visit to excavate these sites and identify others was carried out between June 29 and July 24, 1996. They found three skeletons in a site named Xambioá, two of which presented traits compatible with the burial of a guerrilla combatant. In a site at an indigenous area, they found two other skeletons, which were in such a bad state that it was not possible to apply DNA testing.

13. FURTHER LEGAL ACTIONS AGAINST THE STATE

Many families decided to take their cases to court even after the enactment of Law 9,140. The decisions of the judiciary have varied with respect to the compatibility between the administrative reparations granted by the Commission and the reparations awarded by the courts.

The son of Fernando Santa Cruz Oliveira presented a legal action in 1995. He stated that the compensation contemplated in Law 9,140 was insufficient and arbitrary, and did not involve an unequivocal declaration of State responsibility for the disappearance of his father. He demanded a formal declaration in this sense, information on the circumstances of his death, the location of the remains, and compensation for material and moral damages. In 1997, the judge declared that Law 9,140 had not established clearly the responsibility of the State for the disappearance and death of his father, stating instead that he would be presumed dead.[33] The verdict also established that the compensation of Law 9,140 referred only to material damage, and awarded Santa Cruz moral damages of 225,000 réis.[34] The case of Sonia Maria Angel Jones received a similar decision. In the cases of Lincoln Bicalho Roque and Honestino Monteiro Guimarães, however, the decisions were that the amount paid by Law 9,140 should be deducted from the total amount of material damages awarded, and also granted moral damages.

In the case of Rubens Paiva, as already explained, his family decided not to request the reparations under Law 9,140. The legal sentence established an amount of material damage according to the criteria of Law 9,140, and also gave moral damages to the widow and each of his sons and daughters. As a rule, compensations awarded by the courts have exceeded by far those granted by Law 9,140.

14. STAFF, STRUCTURE, AND COST OF THE COMMISSION

The staff of the Commission was composed as follows:

- one Executive Secretary;
- two senior assistants;

- one civil servant of the Ministry of Justice;
- one secretary;
- two interns, one undergraduate and one high-school intern, who joined the team in 2002.

Apart from these permanent members of staff, the Commission counted on the technical advice of other civil servants. Thus, one adviser elaborated legal opinions and another one contributed as a technical consultant for the calculation of the exact amount to be paid to each victim according to his or her age and gender.

Since the applications were all judged in 1999, the Commission has been in a state of 'stand-by', with only Helder Pereira, the Executive Secretary, actively involved in it. The new efforts to locate the bodies that started in 2001 and the foreseeable extension of the period considered by the Law allowed for an expansion of the team. At present, the team is composed of Pereira, a senior assistant, a secretary, and two interns.[35]

Members of staff who were interviewed expressed their commitment and their satisfaction at having been part of the Commission, despite its limitations. They related some difficulties in dealing with some relatives of the victims but reported having achieved a good working relationship in most cases. The adviser to the Chief of Cabinet of the Ministry of Justice in 1995, Ana Samico, was allegedly careful in appointing staff for the Commission, so as not to incorporate civil servants with a bureaucratic mentality but rather people with a certain commitment to this kind of enterprise.

The seven appointed members of the Commission had no personal support staff while at home, though they could obviously make use of the administrative staff while in Brasilia.

Members, and occasionally staff, had their travel expenses paid by the Commission. This was mainly meant for attending the meetings in Brasilia, since several members lived elsewhere, but also included trips to collect relevant information such as the investigations in the Araguaia area. When the travel required an overnight stay, accommodation and per diem were also granted. However, several members reported having traveled for purposes related to the Commission with expenses paid by their own institutions (e.g. State Assemblies or the House of Representatives), and some costs pertaining to the investigations were covered by other institutions. For instance, one of the visits of the EAAF was paid, at least in part, by the state assembly of Rio Grande do Sul.

15. The Cost of the Commission

It is widely accepted that the Commission had a limited budget for expenses but the president, Luiz Francisco Carvalho, insisted that all expenses considered crucial would be covered.

The money for the compensations was obtained through amendments to the federal budget presented in Congress by Representative Nilmário Miranda, a member of the Commission, and by Representative Hélio Bicudo. The amounts budgeted for every year tended to be very close to the money that was in fact paid.

As for other expenses, they were treated as normal expenses within the Ministry of Justice and were not budgeted or processed separately. Hence, it is difficult to establish the exact cost of the Commission, with the exception of the money paid in compensations. Nevertheless, we attempted, with the help of the Commission staff, to estimate the total cost, which will be divided into three categories: (*a*) compensations paid; (*b*) travel expenses; (*c*) salaries.

Unlike the money for compensations that can be determined to the penny, travel expenses have been estimated by the Budget and Financial Execution Service of the Ministry of Justice [*Serviço de Execução Orçamentária Financeira*].

As for salaries, we have estimated the numbers ourselves based on the approximate salaries reported by the members of staff interviewed. Since salaries increased over time, we considered an average of the initial and the last values reported. Therefore, this should be considered as a rougher estimation than the previous one.

Current expenses (stationery, furniture, etc.) as well as the cost of office reform to accommodate the Commission were deemed impossible to estimate, though they should have a very minor impact on the overall cost.

Money budgeted and spent on *compensations* every year (until July 2002) can be broken down as shown in Table 3.4.

As can be seen, most of the lump sums were paid during the first two years: 1996 and 1997. In 1999, nearly all cases were settled, except for a few that were pending court decisions and were finally paid in 2000 and 2002.

Travel expenses for every year (until July 2002) can be estimated as shown in Table 3.5.

Costs related to *salaries* per year (until July 2002) can be estimated as shown in Table 3.6.

These are salaries effectively paid. In order to calculate the salary costs one would also have to add social and labor costs paid by the State to its servants.

The overall costs of the Commission, including the three types of expenses, would add up as shown in Table 3.7.

Even though the actual figures may be slightly higher than estimated here, it is clear that the administrative cost of the Commission is reasonably small. As it

Table 3.4 Amount budgeted and paid in compensations per year (in réis)

Year	Amount budgeted	Amount effectively paid
1996	15,000,000.00	14,939,639.94
1997	17,360,400.00	17,247,974.93
1998	0.00	0.00
1999	1,068,670.00	1,068,670.00
2000	700,000.00	100,000.00
2001	744,000.00	0.00
2002	397,208.00	100,000.00
Total	35,270,278.00	33,456,284.87

Table 3.5 Travel expenses estimated per year (in réis)

Year	Tickets	Accommodation	Per diem	Total
1996	23,310.58	9,658.65	1,136.97	34,106.20
1997	24,639.95	0.00	38,591.11	63,231.06
1998	10,998.78	0.00	0.00	10,998.78
1999	280.79	0.00	0.00	280.79
2000	0.00	0.00	0.00	0.00
2001	27,606.45	540.48	4,383.48	32,530.41
2002	9,173.95	0.00	240.53	9,414.48
Total	96,010.50	10,199.13	44,352.09	150,561.72

stands, less than 2 percent of the cost of the Commission was spent on administration and running costs while the other 98 percent was directly paid in compensations. In other words, 53 réis were paid out to victims' relatives for every real spent in internal costs.

Table 3.6 Salaries estimated per year (in réis)

Year	Number of persons	Estimated average monthly salary	Estimated period	Estimated number of persons/months	Total
Executive Secretary	1	5,000.00	Jan 96–Feb 99	38	190,000.00
Senior assistant	2	1,300.00	Jan 96–Feb 99 (2) Jan 02–July 02 (1)	83	107,900.00
Civil servant	1	1,500.00	Jan 96–July 02 Jan 96–Feb 99	79	118,500.00
Secretary	1	1,300.00	Jan 02–July 02	45	58,500.00
Intern	2	300.00	Jan 02–July 02	14	4,200.00
Total					479,100.00

Table 3.7 Estimated total cost of the Commission per year (in réis)

Year	Compensations	Travel expenses	Salaries	Total
1996	14,939,639.94	34,106.20	124,800.00	15,098,546.14
1997	17,247,974.93	63,231.06	124,800.00	17,436,005.99
1998	0.00	10,998.78	124,800.00	135,798.78
1999	1,068,670.00	280.79	35,800.00	1,104,750.79
2000	100,000.00	0.00	18,000.00	118,000.00
2001	0.00	32,530.41	18,000.00	50,530.41
2002	100,000.00	9,414.48	32,900.00	142,314.48
Total	33,456,284.87	150,561.72	479,100.00	34,085,946.59

16. THE IMPACT OF THE FEDERAL REPARATIONS PROGRAM

It should be pointed out that we will be attempting to evaluate a Law and a Commission whose task has not yet been thoroughly completed, even less now that both the deadline for filing applications and the period contemplated under the mandate of the Law have been extended.[36] Nevertheless, we are confident that the process and its impact can be evaluated now since all relevant actors have a clear idea of the achievements and limitations and they envision its future work as a mere continuation. No major change in the pattern of functioning of the Commission or in its results is expected.

From the relatives' point of view, the Law and the Commission were a very important accomplishment, despite all the limitations. One of the reasons behind this positive evaluation is that they obtained from the Commission process more than they envisaged at first. In the words of a relative: 'We had no idea of the dimension of the Commission in the beginning.' This exceeding of initial expectations is based mainly on the amplified interpretation of the concept of 'police and similar premises', which allowed for the inclusion of victims who had been executed without having been arrested first, like Lamarca and Marighella. The relatives unanimously define the granting of reparations for these two famous cases as a great victory, due to their political significance. Even the relatives who had misgivings about being involved in the process at first have not regretted their decision to take part, and see the final balance definitely as a positive one. One of the reasons behind this optimistic summary is the fact that the truth-telling outcome of the whole process ended up being wider than the limited recognition of responsibility by the State reflected in Law 9,140. Indeed, the Law accepts State responsibility for the disappearances and deaths only indirectly, through the application of the principle of 'presumed death'. However, since many of the cases had to be argued before the Commission to contradict official accounts of deaths as a result of supposed accidents, suicides, or armed combats, the fact that reparations were granted for such cases implied that the alternative version presented by the relatives was considered true by the Commission, i.e. by the State. In a way, the pains that the relatives had to go through in order to gather evidence and build up a case against the State served at least to foster the interpretation, in those cases that were approved, that it was *their* truth that had been acknowledged.

As a matter of fact, rescuing historical truth and collective memory was deemed by many as the most relevant contribution of the process. As such, moral reparation, limited though it may be, was considered far more important than economic compensation or the regularization of the juridical status of the disappeared. Even though the State did not issue a formal apology or an official recognition of the memory of the victims, relatives could at least, after so many years, have the truth about the deaths officially recognized. The work of the Commission was able to prove that most of the official versions given at the time of the deaths were false and most victims either were summarily executed or died as a result of brutal tortures. This recognition enabled the relatives to vindicate the memory of their loved ones and to deny the claim that they had been criminals or that they had simply run away from home. In only one case was it true that the alleged victim had in fact deserted the family rather than been killed, but the relatives acted in good faith.

Until very recently, mentions of tortures or executions were private, either by victims or by a few perpetrators, and there were no official documents that attested to these facts. This was the first time that the Brazilian State recognized them. Even the existence of guerrilla warfare in the region of Araguaia in the 1970s and the subsequent repression were systematically denied by the military.

Therefore, the work of the Commission allowed setting the record straight, even though many cases may not have been considered due to lack of evidence or information. Furthermore, the proof that the dictatorship lied in most of these cases enables the relatives to cast all similar cases in the same light and vindicate their memory even when the evidence was not enough to obtain compensation. As an activist put it: 'History was hazy and different versions coexisted in society. Now, we went on to have one single true version.'

One can also judge the importance of this official acknowledgment by the angry reaction of its opponents, that is, some members of the military who were suddenly portrayed as executioners and torturers rather than as brave combatants.

On the other hand, several interviewees said that they believed public opinion was not in favor of the economic compensation, which was considered excessive by many of the letters of readers published by newspapers over the past few years. Somebody working for the Commission specified that 'enlightened people' understand, though, that the Commission was an important step. Yet, the prevailing feeling among relatives is that the whole process, including not only the performance of the Commission itself but also all the actions carried out by other actors alongside, succeeded in attracting more attention for their cause and awakening the sensibility of several social sectors. A good example is the role of the federal prosecutors, several of whom participated actively and are still participating in attempts to find the truth of the facts. A relative said that the prosecutors in Araguaia performed the role that the Commission itself should have undertaken and they were a decisive factor in the new impetus of the Commission toward locating the bodies.

All members of the Commission who were interviewed expressed satisfaction with the final result and a certain pride in having been part of it, even though several expressed that it was also a painful and stressful process to have to deal repeatedly with evidence of torture and execution and with the grief of the relatives. General Gomes himself asserted in the interview that the Law and the Commission were positive events since they 'fitted within the country's tradition of amnesty' and were meant to solve the question of 'politically motivated crime,' even though he resented that the occasion had been grasped by some in order to 'tarnish the image of the armed forces as a whole'. He added that the Commission 'eased tensions' and showed, once and for all, that the military did not command the country since many of the decisions were taken against the will of the Army. He insisted that torture and executions were perpetrated by uncontrolled individuals and could not be blamed on the institution itself, despite the fact that some very high military officers, like former president General Ernesto Geisel, had publicly defended the use of torture in some circumstances.[37] General Gomes declared himself to be against torture because of the harm that it did to the Army and also based on the need to uphold the Law.

Several crucial actors in this process see Law 9,140 as a step in a long process of increased focus on human rights that started back with amnesty in 1979 and continued, through the Special Commission, into the National Plan for Human Rights and the Law that defined the crime of torture in 1997. Indeed, the first compensation paid under Law 9,140 was granted the same day that the National Plan of Human Rights was launched in 1995.

As for the role of the Commission in the transition toward democracy, one should bear in mind that by the time the Law was issued, Brazil had been a normally operating democracy for a number of years. Even if some interviewees stated that the transition to democracy was not complete and there remained a few structural and cultural components inherited from the dictatorship, none denied that Brazil fulfilled the basic requisites of a democracy well before 1995. In this respect, the role of the Commission in this process was limited, unlike other countries where such reparations commissions were formed shortly after the fall of the dictatorship. In any case, many people agreed that rescuing the truth can be seen as something that fosters democracy.

As for the shortcomings of the Commission, there is unanimous frustration with its inability to uncover the circumstances of many deaths and, mainly, the remains of the victims. It has to be remembered that discovering the remains of the victims was an important part of its mandate while unveiling the circumstances of the deaths was an important step in this direction. Indeed, it would be difficult to locate the bodies without researching the historical facts first. Members of the Commission are very conscious of this shortcoming, given that, despite several attempts, very few bodies have been located or identified during the work of the Commission.

Apart from this main consensual criticism, different sectors have other complaints as well, directed not only at the way the Commission has conducted its work but also at the limitations of the reparations process as a whole. The relatives' organizations, for instance, continue to demand punishment of those responsible for the crimes, though no other social group seems to support this claim.

Another criticism of relatives' organizations that has a wider backing in society is the inability of the Commission and, in turn, of the government to find and open the 'archives of political repression'. Linked to this, some members of the Commission underlined the fact that some decisions concerning individual petitions for reparations had not been fair due to lack of sufficient evidence or poor presentation of cases. This meant that some victims of the same event achieved official recognition and reparations while others did not. Access to official archives might help redress this unfairness by providing all relevant information.

There is no evidence that there is a single archive containing all the relevant information on what happened during those years, and the military has sometimes denied that such archives exist at all. However, those partial archives that have been made public so far (DOPS in Rio de Janeiro and São Paulo) did contain information of great significance and the investigations of the relatives in the Forensic Institutes have also unveiled crucial documents. In fact, when Minister Corrêa asked the Army, the Navy, and the Air Force for information on the disappeared in 1993, the reports that were sent as an answer contained information that had obviously been extracted from a wider source. A member of the Commission believes that some of the evidence that General Gomes brought to bear on some cases could only have been taken from archives that are not public. General Gomes himself holds the view that archives could not be made public, according to the Law of National Security still valid today, 'if they exist at all, since they could have been burned'.

Furthermore, Uruguaian intelligence monitoring a Uruguaian political dissident in Porto Alegre, Brazil, sent a report back to Montevideo in 1983 that included a copy of the complete file of a Brazilian citizen elaborated by Brazilian intelligence sources. These files had supposedly been burned publicly by the governor some time before. In short, there is a widespread conviction that relevant information that could be used to clarify the truth and to locate the remains still lies within the archives of different organizations of the Brazilian State. Miguel Reale, first president of the Commission who then became Minister of Justice, promised he would open all relevant archives of the Federal Police, under his jurisdiction, but resigned in July 2002 without having accomplished it.

The visit of the Federal Prosecutors to the area of Araguaia in 2001 underlined both the existence of information that remains unavailable and the lack of cooperation of the Army. During this visit, prosecutors gathered evidence that indicated that the Army still had an intelligence unit in the area after so many years, that food and weapons were still being distributed to civilians who collaborated with the Army during the military campaign in the 1970s, and that witnesses were being threatened if they told what they knew. Prosecutors themselves had their investigations obstructed by members of the military and decided to confiscate the materials in the would-be 'intelligence center' of the Army in the area. A lieutenant in the Army threatened the prosecutors who carried out this search. This episode raised serious concerns about the will or the ability of the government to obtain information and cooperation from the military on this issue. This in turn underscores the possibility that some areas of military power are still immune to civilian authority. In the words of the president of the Commission, Carvalho: '[T]he Brazilian state shows a double personality. It is a surreal situation: there is the state that investigates the facts and there is the state that hides the evidence.'

The four limitations of the Law pointed out at the time it was enacted can be reiterated at the time of a final evaluation of the Commission: (*a*) that many victims of political violence were excluded from the Law; (*b*) that the period was covered only until 1979 and excluded victims in similar episodes between 1980 and 1985; (*c*) the short application period and the lack of an official campaign to call for relatives of those deceased and disappeared; and (*d*) that the burden of proof lay with the relatives.

1. Some of the deceased victims of political violence who were finally excluded were those killed in combat and those killed in demonstrations or in contexts where they could not be considered under the custody of the State, such as militants who committed suicide after being released from long periods of torture. The relatives have been campaigning to include these cases, since they do not want to draw distinctions among the victims of political violence depending on the circumstances of their deaths. Several members of the Commission understand the principles behind the idea of including such cases, but maintain that they are not covered by the present Law.[38] In any case, victims of genuine combats do certainly deserve a different treatment from a humanitarian law or from a human rights perspective. Furthermore, some members of the Commission, like General Gomes and Representative Nilmário Miranda, believe that deceased victims of the leftist insurgents, such as the peasants killed by the Araguaia guerrillas for having helped the Army, and victims accidentally killed in the armed encounters should also receive compensation. Indeed, this is the only group of deceased victims that has never received any kind of compensation. Agents of the State who were killed had a pension for their families and the relatives of the disappeared and executed obtained their reparations through Law 9,140, but the former categories have never been contemplated. The relatives' organizations accept that these groups, including those civil victims of the guerrillas, could be somehow benefited, but they insist that they be covered through some other mechanism. Their position is that Law 9,140 was devised according to the principle of the responsibility of the State, which would not apply to victims of the insurgents. There is reportedly another bill in Congress, proposed by retired army officer and right-wing Representative Jair Bolsonaro, to pay compensations to the victims of the armed groups that opposed the government, but there is no sign of this bill having a chance of being approved in the immediate future.

2. As for the period contemplated by the Law, the main criticism relates to the fact that the Law excluded those who disappeared after 1979, as already explained. Bill number 4.908 of 2001 [*projeto de lei 4.908 de 2001*] reformulates Articles 1 and 4 of Law 9,140 to include all cases between September 2, 1961 and October 5, 1988, the day the new Constitution was adopted. This will satisfy everybody's demands. Several interviewees related that the pressure of the Argentinean relatives and the Argentinean government has been very important for the Brazilian government to introduce this change. Since one Argentinean who disappeared in 1980 had been included in the Annex of Law 9,140 despite being outside the period of the Law, reportedly because he was a priest and the Brazilian government did not want to leave him out, the relatives of the three other Argentineans who disappeared the same year had been persuading the Brazilian government to include them too. In any case, all interviewees accept that it is a fair principle to extend the Law until the end of the dictatorship in order to cover the remaining cases, and there is no real opposition to this new piece of legislation.[39]

3. Bill number 4.908 will also alter Articles 2 and 3 of Law 9,140 so as to open a new period of application of 120 days, starting from the publication of the Law. The new application period will make it possible not only to incorporate cases that occurred after 1979 but also all previous cases whose relatives had not known about the Law or had not had time to prepare the documents. Likewise, this will open a new chance for the government to publicize the Law more widely. In fact, the lack of an official campaign to publicize the Law has been a consistent criticism of the relatives' organizations. The last information we received is that Bill 4.908 would be awaiting presidential sanction to become law.[40] Notwithstanding the fact that these alterations to Law 9,140 are well received, there are people who would like the period of petitions to be left open indefinitely, particularly since the state has not been able to produce all relevant documents related to political repression, and it is therefore very difficult for the families to obtain the necessary evidence.

4. As for the question of the burden of proof, the initial impression of the relatives was confirmed. In the case of those victims enumerated in the Annex of the Law, families did not have to prove anything since the State had already accepted its responsibility, indirectly though it may be. Furthermore, in other cases of disappearance not mentioned in the Annex but where there was evidence of political participation of the victim and of an arrest, the principle of 'presumed death' was applied and the relatives did not have to prove that the victim was killed by the State. Indeed, in these cases it was up to the State to prove that it did not kill the victim. In this sense, there was a 'limited inversion' of the burden of proof, for the families still had to prove both political participation and the arrest by State agents. Nevertheless, the burden of proof concerning the cases of executions where there was an official version that had to be challenged

remained entirely in the relatives' hands. Not to mention the clarification of the circumstances of the deaths and disappearances and particularly the location of the remains, both depending completely on the relatives' own sources of information. In fact, it is the members of the State forces who could provide exact information on both the circumstances of the deaths and the location of the remains provided they decided to cooperate.

Overall, the Law and the Commission came to legitimize and provide an official character to investigations and actions carried out by relatives for many years. Even during these last few years, it has been the work of the relatives that has made it possible to document many cases and to mobilize other organs of the State, such as the prosecutors, to act accordingly.

Many of the relatives declared that the Commission was an attempt by the government to put an end to their demands and protests by recognizing the deaths and offering a compensation, which was interpreted by some as an attempt to 'shut up our mouths'. The relatives who are politically committed, in particular, deeply resent the fact that the whole approach of the Law and the Commission is to treat the problem as one between the families and the State, i.e. as somewhat of a private issue that can be settled through compensation. This can be interpreted from the fact that reparations have to be solicited by the families and that investigations of the remains, as already mentioned, have to be started by the relatives. Instead, they firmly argue that it is a problem for society at large, crucial for democratic citizenship. As such, it should be the State that takes the initiative to clarify the facts, grant reparations, and locate the remains.

Hence, the offer of the money, which had not been a traditional demand of the relatives, was perceived by some as a way to try to 'buy them out'. This is why two families demanded the official recognition of the death but rejected the money. One of these mothers wrote to the Commission:

It will not be through coins stained with their [the victims'] own blood, profaned by violence, tortures and indignities that the dignity of their lives will be restored and returned to them. We just fight for the truth, which was what they believed in. The reparation does not belong to us or any of the relatives, since in this way we will be able to close our eyes one day in peace with our conscience, for the coins offered will remain in the hands of those who profane them. Only in this way will our sons rest in peace.

The accusations of members of the organization Madres de la Plaza de Mayo in Buenos Aires, declaring that the families in Brazil had 'sold' their sons, did not help. Yet there is not a unanimous view among the relatives about the extent to which this alleged attempt by the State to muffle its critics and their political struggle has succeeded. Some say that as time goes by the number of people actively participating in the relatives' movements is diminishing, particularly after the reparations. They also note that some relatives who were not politically active participated only as a way to prepare their applications to the Commission but discontinued their participation afterwards. Others, however, underline that their cause has obtained a lot of attention as a result of the Law and the ensuing process, has attracted other social sectors that did not show the same sensitivity before, and has been strengthened economically by the reparations. Indeed, some of the recipients used the lump sums for initiatives like setting up and maintaining a website on this topic (www.desaparecidospoliticos.org.br), creating a park in the memory of the victim, or simply paying up travel expenses to continue fighting for their objectives. On the other hand, others, particularly those who were in a worse financial situation, used the money to buy an apartment or to otherwise improve their living condition. Some of them expressed feelings of guilt over this 'private' use of the money, even when they had devoted their lives and considerable resources to this cause in the past.

In short, despite all ambiguities and limitations, most of the actors involved in this process, including the victims' families, consider the reparations process a positive milestone for society and for the cause of addressing the violations of the past.

17. Afterword (October 2004)

Since the main part of this paper was completed, two new laws have been issued, altering Law 9,140. Also, the composition of the Special Commission has changed almost completely. Another important development has been a new official attempt to search for the remains of the missing victims in Araguaia.

On August 15, 2002, Law 10,536/02 was issued, reformulating Articles 1 and 4 of Law 9,140 to include all cases that took place between September 2, 1961 and October 5, 1988, the day the new democratic Constitution was adopted.

Law 10,536/02 also altered Articles 7 and 10 of Law 9,140 so as to open a new period of application of 120 days, starting from the publication of the Law. The new application period made it possible not only to incorporate cases that occurred between 1979 and October 5, 1988 but also all previous cases whose relatives had not known about the Law or had not had time to prepare the necessary documents.

The approval of this new Law was expected, as indicated above in the text. The new piece of legislation resulted from the pressure of family members and civil society, and addressed two of the limitations of Law 9,140, pointed out by many actors involved in the process: the time period covered and the insufficient time of application, as described earlier.

Furthermore, Law 10,875 was issued on June 1, 2004, reformulating Articles 4, 5, 6, and 10 of Law 9,140 to include victims who had died due to police repression during public demonstrations or during armed conflicts with public agents. Additionally, it also contemplated those who had died due to suicide committed in the imminence of an arrest or due to psychological damages resulting from acts of torture by public agents. The Law opened a new period of application of 120 days, starting from the date of its publication, to cover only the cases under these new situations.

Indeed, the exclusion of victims falling under these two categories by original Law 9,140 had been one of the main criticisms of many actors involved, as explained above.

On August 14, 2003, the Special Commission was reinstalled, with an almost completely new composition. The new Commission members were Maria do Rosário Nunes, House Representative, João Batista da Silva Fagundes, from the Army, Maria Eliane Menezes de Farias, from the Federal Prosecutor's Office, André Sabóia Martins, from the Foreign Office, and Belisário dos Santos Júnior, lawyer. The new president of the Commission was João Luiz Duboc Pinaud.

Nilmário Miranda, who had been representing the House of Representatives in the Special Commission in the past, assumed the post of Special Secretary for Human Rights, with status of minister, when President Luis Ignácio Lula da Silva took office in January 2003. Belisário dos Santos Júnior, one of the current members, was one of the persons interviewed for this work, owing to his participation in the preparation of Law 9140. Maria Eliane Menezes de Farias used to head a division called Federal Prosecution for Citizens' Rights [*Procuradoria Federal dos Direitos do Cidadão*] in the Federal Prosecutor's Office.

After the publication of Laws 10,536 and 10,875, the Special Commission received 139 petitions. The final deadline for new petitions, according to Law 10,875, was September 29, 2004. A total of four meetings have been held and thirty-five petitions were analyzed. In nineteen cases the Special Commission recognized State responsibility, granting reparations for the family members, and thirteen petitions were denied. The meetings were held on December 19, 2003, April 22, 2004, August 10, 2004, and August 26, 2004.

These new pieces of legislation addressed three of the main limitations of Law 9,140: the short application period, restriction in the types of victims covered, and violations in periods not contemplated by the Law. Still remaining are the limitations regarding the burden of proof and the inability to extract all relevant information from the State and to locate the remains of the victims.

On March 1, 2004, a weekly magazine, *Época*, published an article quoting former soldiers who claimed to know the spots where the remains of the disappeared in Araguaia had been buried. That month the Special Commission organized another mission to Xambioá, Araguaia, to try to locate the remains of the victims of political disappearance. The group formed by the Commission included two geologists from the Federal University of Minas Gerais, three forensic anthropologists from Argentina, a geneticist, and members of the Special Commission, as well as relatives of the disappeared. The mission did not find any skeletons in the burial site, but delimited the area, and the Special Secretary on Human Rights promised that a long-term search would be made.

APPENDIX 3.1

Profile of Members of the Commission

- Miguel Reale, a reputable lawyer from São Paulo and a personal friend of President Cardoso, was appointed president of the Commission. He left the Commission in March 2001 to become Minister of Justice.[41]
- Eunice Paiva is also a lawyer from São Paulo and a friend of President Cardoso. She is the widow of Rubens Beirodt Paiva, who had been arrested and disappeared during the dictatorship. She had been invited by the government to the ceremony in which Law 9,140 was published on December 4, 1995. Ironically, she did not present her case to the Commission since she had started a legal process long before, which was near conclusion. In the meantime, the courts have granted her petition and awarded compensation far above what she would have received through the Commission. She participated in the Commission until the fifth meeting, in March 1996, after which she resigned. Interviewed by the press, she gave two main reasons for her decision.[42] First, she was receiving angry letters from some of the relatives of the victims after she had voted against granting the petition in a number of cases. She clarified that she understood their position and she believed they deserved compensation but, as a lawyer, she had to follow what the Law said rather than her feelings, which led to an internal conflict on her part. Second, she confessed the hardships of confronting all these documents, photographs, and other evidence of the tortures and executions, which forced her to relive those painful years when she was herself arrested and witnessed tortures.
- Suzana Lisbôa was a representative of the relatives of the victims. Her husband was the first case of a disappeared person whose body was located and identified in 1979. However, he was not removed from the list of the disappeared of the organizations so as to maximize the social impact of the case. She refused to participate in the Commission at first, but was convinced after the Minister of Justice made it clear that all victims who had been executed rather than killed in a genuine confrontation might be included in the Law. Concerned that the government might appoint Eunice Paiva as their representative in the Commission, even though she was not an active member of the relatives' organizations, the

organizations postulated Lisbôa's name and the President accepted it. After several years of very intense and demanding work in the Commission, she wanted to step aside and the relatives' organizations already had the name of the person to replace her. However, the then president of the Commission, Miguel Reale, asked her to stay in case some of the decisions were appealed by the victims' families so that the same members who gave the first resolutions would consider the appeals.

- General Oswaldo Pereira Gomes from the Army was the representative of the armed forces. He is a lawyer too and had been an elected member of the House of Representatives in past legislatures. He had also worked as a lobbyist for the Army during the constitutional period and had been a legal and political adviser for the Army, participating, for instance, in the negotiations on the Law of Amnesty. He had himself given a negative legal opinion concerning a previous project of reparations during the government of Itamar Franco. The then Minister of the Army, Zenildo Lucena, apparently suggested his name and he had had personal contact with President Cardoso at the time when the constitution was being negotiated. Before he was appointed, his past was investigated to guarantee that he had not been involved in tortures, executions, or other types of criminal behavior. He declared that there was some opposition among his peers to his participating in the Commission and that he received enormous pressure and criticisms both from the relatives of the victims and from some members of the military during the whole process. When the Commission approved the reparations for the family of former Captain Lamarca, Gomes expressed his intention to resign in protest, but later changed his mind after a meeting with the president. In his own words, he decided to continue 'so as not to be accused of being afraid or of having something to hide in his own past'.

- João Grandino Rodas was a legal adviser to the Brazilian Ministry of Foreign Affairs, vice president of the Juridical Commission of the Organization of American States (OAS), and president of the Administrative Council of Economic Defense (CADE), an organ that enforces free competition rules.

- Paulo Gustavo Gonet was a federal prosecutor from the Regional Prosecutor's Office in Brasilia.

- Nilmário Miranda was a House Representative for the Workers' Party [*Partido dos Trabalhadores*: PT] and the President of the Human Rights Commission in the Chamber, which he had been involved in creating. He was a victim of political repression himself and had been involved in several attempts to draft a Law of reparations in the past. Likewise, he had been personally involved in the negotiations that resulted in Law 9,140.

- After Eunice Paiva resigned, she was replaced by Luiz Francisco Carvalho, a criminal lawyer from São Paulo, apparently recommended by the President of the Commission, Miguel Reale. When Reale left the Commission to take over the Ministry of Justice in March 2001, Luiz Francisco Carvalho was appointed new president.

APPENDIX 3.2

State laws of reparations

Since the Federal Program of Reparations represented by Law 9,140 was restricted to dead victims, several states issued laws to offer compensation to surviving victims of gross human rights violations, mainly to victims of torture. Hence, these laws were passed after Law 9,140 as a complement to it. Some of them mention the Federal Program explicitly in their wordings.

We cannot claim to have compiled all state laws since there is not a central institution where all of them can be found. We requested such laws through networks of victims' relatives and through state assemblies and obtained the laws of nine states, but we cannot guarantee that no other cases exist. In the case of Rio de Janeiro, the Law is still awaiting the publication of the Regulations so it can be applied.

Indeed, some of the details of how each program will be implemented do not appear in the Law itself but in the Regulations that are issued by the Executive after the publication of the Law. For some states we received the text of the Law and of the Regulations, but in other cases we only obtained the former.

As a result, the present Annex should not be understood as a comprehensive review of all state reparations programs in Brazil, but as an overview of the type of programs being applied in the country. The analysis presented in this Annex is based mainly on documents (laws and regulations). In a few states, interviewees also discussed these programs. In the case of Rio Grande do Sul, we had access to a report that summarized the results of the program.

The nine laws that will be analyzed correspond to the following states: Ceará, Paraná, Rio Grande do Sul, Espírito Santo, Minas Gerais, Santa Catarina, Goiás, São Paulo, and Rio de Janeiro.

The first conclusion is that most state laws are remarkably similar to one another. In fact, some interviewees confirmed that laws from other states were analyzed in the process of elaboration of the Law in their state. In short, we can assume that many of them are modeled from similar laws elsewhere. Tables A3.1 and A3.2 summarize the main elements that can be extracted out of the Laws and Regulations of each state. Among these are dates, beneficiaries, period covered, deadline for petitions, type of Commission, compensation, and restrictions.

All of these laws create Special Commissions, under the model of Federal Law 9,140, to judge the applications but, unlike the Federal Law, do not include an Annex with victims already approved. The members and the President of the Commission are usually appointed by the governor, although in some cases

Table A3.1

State	Date of the law	Beneficiaries	Period covered	Perpetrators	Time for petitions	Evidence requested	Restrictions
Ceará	10 Jan. 02	Victims of torture with physical or psychological impairment because of political activities	2 Sept. 61– 15 Aug. 79	State agents	180 days	Medical report (whenever necessary)	Not having received compensation through the courts and not having sued the state for that reason, unless the action is withdrawn
Paraná	21 Dec. 95	Victims of torture with physical or psychological impairment because of political activities	2 Sept. 61– 15 Aug. 79	State agents	60 days		Compensation by the Federal Government is not incompatible
Rio Grande do Sul	18 Nov. 97	Victims of torture with physical or psychological impairment because of political activities	2 Sept. 61– 15 Aug. 79	State agents	180 days		Not having received compensation through the courts and not having sued the state for that reason, unless the action is withdrawn
Espírito Santo	11 May 98	Victims of professional restrictions and torture resulting in physical or psychological impairment because of political activities	2 Sept. 61– 15 Aug. 79	State agents	90 days		Not having received compensation through the courts and not having sued the state for that reason, unless the action is withdrawn

Table A3.1 (Cont.)

State	Date of the law	Beneficiaries	Period covered	Perpetrators	Time for petitions	Evidence requested	Restrictions
Minas Gerais	20 Jan. 99	Victims of torture with physical or psychological impairment because of political activities	2 Sept. 61–15 Aug. 79	State agents	60 days	Forensic report (whenever necessary)	Compensation by the Federal Government is not incompatible
Santa Catarina	13 Jan. 98	Victims of arrest and torture with physical or psychological impairment because of political activities	2 Sept. 61–15 Aug. 79	State agents	60 days		Not having received compensation through the courts and not having asked for it
Goiás	17 Dec. 01	Victims of arrest, banishment, removal from their job, and torture because of political activities	18 Sept. 46–5 Oct. 88				Not having received compensation by the Federal Government for the same reason
São Paulo	8 Jan. 01	Victims of torture with the result of death or physical or psychological impairment because of political activities	31 Mar. 64–15 Aug. 79	State agents	180 days	Psychological forensic report for cases of psychological impairment	Not having received compensation for the same reason
Rio de Janeiro	21 Dec. 01	Victims of physical or psychological torture because of political activities	1 Apr. 64–15 Aug. 79	State agents	180 days	Testimonies, documents or similar proofs of arrest	

Table A3.2

State	Judicial sentences	Investigation of facts	Members of the Commission	President of the Commission	Minimum compensation (réis)	Maximum compensation (réis)	Other benefits
Ceará			11 members from 8 categories.	Appointed by the governor	5,000	30,000	
Paraná			9 members from 7 categories: 3 appointed by the governor and 4 by other organs	Appointed by the governor	5,000	30,000	
Rio Grande do Sul			7 members from 7 categories: all appointed by the governor	Appointed by the governor	5,000	30,000	
Espírito Santo	Executive is authorized not to appeal against judicial sentences granting reparations	Judicial enquiry on penal actions	7 members from 6 categories	Elected by members	5,000	30,000	Pension for work impairment can be requested instead of lump sum
Minas Gerais			7 members from 2 categories		5,000 for injuries; 10,000 for partial disability; 20,000 for total disability	10,000 for injuries; 20,000 for partial disability; 30,000 for total disability	

Table A3.2 (cont.)

Santa Catarina	9 members: 4 appointed by the governor and 5 appointed by different institutions	Appointed by the governor	5,000	30,000	Medical expenses
Goiás	8 full members and 8 reserve members from 6 categories: all appointed by the governor	Appointed by the governor	5,000; pensions cannot be lower than 15% of the salary of a state secretary	30,000; pensions cannot be higher than the salary of a state secretary	Pension for work impairment can be requested instead of lump sum. The value of the pension increases by 3% for every month in prison
São Paulo	13 members from 9 categories	Appointed by the governor	39,000 for death; 26,300 for permanent disability; 14,600 for psychological impairment; 7,800 for partial disability; 3,900 for injuries		
Rio de Janeiro	9 members: 4 appointed by the governor and 5 appointed by different institutions	Appointed by the governor	5,000	50,000	

(Paraná and Rio de Janeiro) the institutions represented can nominate their representatives, or the President of the Commission can be chosen by the members (Espírito Santo). The period considered is, as a rule, the same as in Law 9,140: September 2, 1961 to August 15, 1979. São Paulo and Rio de Janeiro postpone the beginning of the period to 1964, the beginning of the dictatorship, rather than 1961. And Goiás is the only State with a far longer period: 1946 to 1988.

The period open to present petitions can be as short as two months or as long as six months. No state has opted for a Law that can be applied indefinitely. As in the federal case, this appears to be an attempt to end the problem in a short term.

Beneficiaries of these programs are, above all, victims of torture, particularly if they suffer from any disabilities as a result. A few states, such as Goiás and Santa Catarina, contemplate compensation also for victims who were just arrested for political reasons or for those who were sacked or prevented from working in their professions as a result of their political ideas.

In general, state laws limit their application to episodes where victims were held or tortured by agents of that state, i.e. not by federal agents or agents of other states. This presents further problems since people who were tortured in that state but by federal forces might be left out of any existing law, given that there is no federal program for victims of torture. Considering that state and federal agents acted in a coordinated manner at the time, some Commissions apparently decided to accept also victims of federal agents whose rights were violated in that state, but the decision on this point seems to have varied from state to state.

The amounts to be paid in compensation are, to say the least, very modest, far short of what the judges would grant in similar cases. The minimum amount is usually 5,000 réis[43] and the maximum is normally set at 30,000 réis.[44] The state of São Paulo has slightly wider limits: the minimum is 3,900 réis and the maximum 39,000 réis, but only in cases of death. The state of Rio de Janeiro establishes the highest maximum amount at 50,000 réis. As such, it is obvious that the compensations have a moral rather than an economic character. Compensations are paid in lump sums but in two states it is possible to request a life pension instead. The state of Santa Catarina also covers medical expenses for injuries or impairment resulting from torture.

Most of the state laws restrict their applications to victims who have neither obtained nor asked for compensations in the courts, unless they withdraw their demands. The laws from Paraná and Minas Gerais explicitly acknowledge that a federal compensation for the same reasons is compatible with the one granted through this law. In some cases, the state is authorized not to appeal against judicial sentences awarding compensations for the same motives, as an alternative way to obtain reparations. The execution of these sentences, customarily appealed to the highest level, takes many years, so this lack of appeal is important to expedite the process.

The Law of the state of Espírito Santo is the only one to mention the investigation of the facts and the opening of a legal enquiry to ascertain the circumstances and the responsibility of State agents. However, we have no information of cases that have been duly investigated or whose responsibilities were sought as a result of this Law.

The main point of controversy involved in this kind of legislation is the fact that compensations are awarded to victims who suffer physical or psychological impairment [*dano físico ou psicológico*]. This means that victims are asked to relate the tortures they suffered and in some cases also to *prove* the impairment. Organizations of victims always resented the attempt to distinguish the cases according to their specific characteristics and, particularly, the proposal to grant different compensations according to the severity of the torture. Different pieces of legislation seemed to have dealt with this question in slightly different ways and, even within the same State Commission, not all members seem to share the same criterion in this area. The laws of the states of Minas Gerais and Ceará request medical and forensic reports to prove the harm, 'whenever necessary'. The law of Rio Grande do Sul mentions the need of forensic reports in cases of psychological damage. In this state, some members of the Commission hold the view and apply the criterion that any torture necessarily leads to some kind of harm or impairment, so this would not have to be proven in each case.

The state of São Paulo is reportedly among those that insist most in proving harm and in offering compensation proportional to that harm.

A further complication is that when the victims are dead, the possibility of a forensic report for these cases is severely limited. In Rio Grande do Sul, the Commission accepted the so-called 'indirect forensic reports' on dead victims based on the evidence presented by others. The impressions we have collected so far indicate that this is a painful and difficult process, where evidence is scarce. The pain and even potential psychological damage for victims who have to relate again and prove the tortures they suffered cannot be overestimated, especially in the cases that are settled without reparations for lack of enough evidence. On the other hand, the possibility that some people may try to abuse the law simply to obtain some money, undeservedly, keeps all actors alert in order not to delegitimize the whole process.

As for the final impact of these laws, we can describe the case of Rio Grande do Sul[45] where nearly all applications have been judged, even though a new period to present petitions may be opened in the near future. This is arguably the state with the highest number of compensations awarded so far. In Rio Grande do Sul, a total of 1,378 petitions were filed until 2002. A total of 1,000 (72 percent) were approved and 343 (25 percent) rejected. The total amount to be paid comes to 18,160,000 réis,[46] but many victims have not received the money yet.

NOTES

1. The following persons were interviewed to complete this report:
   (a) Members of the Commission: Luiz Francisco Carvalho, president of the Commission; General Oswaldo Gomes, member representing the armed forces; Suzana Lisbôa, member representing the relatives of victims; Nilmário Miranda, House Representative, and member of the Commission representing the Human Rights Commission of the House, who also participated in the negotiations leading to Law 9,140; Helder Pereira, Executive Secretary of the Commission; Rodrigo Ribeiro, senior assistant to the Commission.
   (b) Others: Criméia de Almeida, member of the 'Commission of Relatives of the Dead and Disappeared' in São Paulo; Cecília Coimbra, former president of the relatives' organization 'Tortura Nunca Mais' in Rio de Janeiro; Belisário dos Santos, former Secretary of Justice of the state of São Paulo, who actively participated in the negotiations which led to Law 9,140; Vitória Grabois, member of the relatives' organization 'Tortura Nunca Mais' in Rio de Janeiro; Eloísa Greco, member of the relatives' organization 'Tortura Nunca Mais' in the state of Minas Gerais; Jair Krischke, president of the human rights organization 'Movimento de Justiça e Direitos Humanos' in Porto Alegre, state of Rio Grande do Sul; Ana Miller, lawyer who conducted several legal actions in court on behalf of the relatives of the victims; Elizabeth Silveira, president of the relatives' organization 'Tortura Nunca Mais' in Rio de Janeiro; Gilney Viana, former House Representative who participated in the negotiations on Law 9,140.
   Most people who were contacted agreed readily to be interviewed. We found special difficulties in contacting members of the military opposed to the Commission and families of victims who were not actively engaged in relatives' organizations. General Hélio Ibiapina, president of the Military Club, was contacted on the phone and sent relevant documents but refused to be interviewed in person. We want to thank all interviewees and, in particular, the group 'Tortura Nunca Mais' for their fundamental cooperation with this work, which is nevertheless the exclusive responsibility of its authors.
2. This is the program created by Law 9,140 enacted in 1995, which is the main focus of this paper. Two laws were passed subsequently, Law 10,536 on August 15, 2002, and Law 10,875, on June 1, 2004. These two laws addressed some of the problems with Law 9,140 but do not modify it in any fundamental way. The two latter laws are the subject of the Afterword. The state programs to redress the victims of torture are briefly analyzed in Appendix 3.2.
3. Nilmário Miranda and Carlos Tibúrcio, eds., *Dos Filhos deste Solo: Mortos e desaparecidos politicos durante a ditadur* (São Paulo: Boitempo Editorial, 1999).
4. This includes all crimes that involved physical violence against other people, such as murder or bodily harm.
5. 'A luta pela reparação', in *Mortos e Desaparecidos Políticos: Reparação ou Impunidade?* Janaina Teles, ed. (São Paulo: Editora Humanitas, 2001), 164.
6. 'A luta pela reparação', op. cit., 161.
7. Gazette of Grupo Tortura Nunca Mais, Year 3, No. 12 (December 1991).
8. Decision of Federal Court of Appeals on Case *Relatives of Mario Alves versus Federal Union* (December 1, 1997).

9. Sentence on Case *Relatives of Rui Frazâo Soares versus Federal Union*, December 19, 1997.

10. 'A luta pela reparação', op. cit., 180.

11. Gazette of Grupo Tortura Nunca Mais, Year 8, No. 17 (August 1994).

12. Suzana Keniger Lisbôa, 'Recontando a Nossa História', *Relatório Azul* (1998), 182.

13. 'Diretor Mundial da Anistia Critica FHC', *Journal Folha de São Paulo* (April 12, 1995).

14. Coimbra, Cecília, 'Cidadania ainda Recusada', presented in October 1997 during Seminar coordinated by the Commission on Human Rights of the Federal Council of Psychology.

15. 'União poderá ter de indenizar as famílias dos desaparecidos', *Jornal do Brasil* (March 10, 1995).

16. Nilson, Borges Filho, *Democracia de Incertezas*, available at www.tre-sc.gov.br/sj/cjd/doutrinas/borges.htm

17. Official Pronouncement in the House by Representative Gilney Viana on September 4, 1995.

18. Article 1 of Law 9,140/95.

19. Article 3 of Law 9,140/95.

20. This was equivalent to approximately US$3,000 or 37.5 times the minimum monthly wage at the time the legislation was passed in 1995, and to approximately US$1,250 or 16 times the minimum monthly wage in May 2002.

21. This was tantamount to approximately US$100,000 and 1,250 times the minimum wage at the time and around US$43,500 or 555 times the minimum wage in May 2002.

22. Report on the Case of Carlos Lamarca by Paulo Gonet.

23. Report on the Case of Carlos Lamarca by Luiz Francisco Carvalho.

24. Report on the Case of Carlos Lamarca by Suzana Lisbôa.

25. Belisário dos Santos, Jr., in *A Revolução Possivel: Homenagem às Vitimes do Regime Militar*, J. C. K. Q. em Moraes, ed. (São Paulo: Fundação de Amparo à Pesguisa do Estado de São Paulo (FAPESP), 1996).

26. 'União indenizará famílias de Lamarca e Marighella: Militares reagem e FH diz que decisão foi técnica e que ex-capitão é desertor', *O Globo* (September 12, 1996).

27. Informex (Informativo do Ministério do Exército) from September 11, 1996.

28. 'Colégio Militar queima fichas de Lamarca', *Zero Hora* (October 2, 1996).

29. 'Recurso Administrativo Interposto Ao Exmo. Sr. Presidente da República pelos presidentes dos Clubes Naval, Militar e de Aeronáutica'.

30. 'União indenizará famílias de Lamarca e Marighella: Militares reagem e FH diz que decisão foi técnica e que ex-capitão é desertor', *O Globo* (September 12, 1996).

31. Miranda and Tibúrcio, op. cit., 16.

32. See Nilmário Miranda's book on the issue. Miranda and Tibúrcio, op. cit.

33. See the sentence *Relatives of Fernando de Santa Cruz Oliveira versus Federal Union* (May 7, 1997).

34. This was equivalent to around US$93,750 in May 2002.

35. As mentioned in n. 2, above, Laws 10,536/02, and 10,875/04 led to an expansion of the terms of the Commission and therefore to its reactivation with new membership. See Afterword.

36. For details about recent changes, see Afterword.

37. The former president admitted the use of torture in some circumstances in an interview that was later published in D'Araujo, Maria Celina, and Celso Castro, eds., *Biography of Ernesto Geisel* (Rio de Janeiro: Fundação Getúlio Vargas (FGV): 1998).

38. This was subsequently resolved by Law 10,875 of June 1, 2004, to which we turn in the Afterword.
39. This was accomplished through Law 10,536 of August 15, 2002. See Afterword.
40. Both Laws 10,536/02 and 10,875/04 extend the relevant period of application. See Afterword.
41. He later resigned from the Ministry in July 2002, when the president refused to back his proposal of a federal intervention in a state where organized crime had appeared to infiltrate the state government and the judiciary and where human rights activists were being threatened.
42. See *Jornal do Brasil* (March 31, 1996), 16, and *Zero Hora* (April 1, 1996).
43. This was equivalent to around US$2,000 in May 2002.
44. This was equivalent to around US$12,500 in May 2002.
45. See *Relatório Azul 2000/2001*, Comissão de Cidadania e Direitos Humanos, Assembléia Legislativa do Rio Grande do Sul.
46. This was equivalent to approximately US$7.5 million in May 2002.

CHAPTER 4

THE REPARATIONS PROPOSALS OF THE TRUTH COMMISSIONS IN EL SALVADOR AND HAITI:

A HISTORY OF NONCOMPLIANCE

ALEXANDER SEGOVIA[1]

BACKGROUND

As a result of political negotiations in both El Salvador and Haiti, truth commissions were created to investigate human rights violations. The commissions included in their reports recommendations designed to secure reparations for the victims. Despite the gravity of the events and the formal commitment of the governments, neither government has implemented these recommendations.

Hence, El Salvador and Haiti are interesting case studies of the economic, social, and political factors that explain the noncompliance with the recommendations on reparations. This analysis can contribute not only to the theoretical debate regarding reparations programs but also to their successful design and implementation in other countries facing the challenge of providing reparations to victims of political violence.

This chapter is organized into three main sections. Section 1 examines the experience of El Salvador; Section 2 analyzes the experience of Haiti; and Section 3 presents the main conclusions and lessons learned.

1. The Experience in El Salvador

Introduction

On March 15, 1993, the Truth Commission of El Salvador (CVES) publicly presented its final report.[2] The report included recommendations designed to provide reparations to the victims of political violence, which occurred in the country from 1980 until July 1991. Although the publication of the report had a strong political impact at the national and international levels, the majority of its recommendations, including those related to reparations, were never implemented, despite their binding character for the signatory parties of the peace agreements.[3] This situation stands in stark contrast to the high degree of compliance with the rest of the commitments negotiated as part of the Peace Accords between the government of El Salvador (GOES) and the 'Frente Farabundo Martí para la Liberación Nacional' (FMLN). These commitments enabled the realization of profound political reform in the country through the dismantling of the repressive State apparatus and the establishment of a basic foundation for the creation of an open, inclusive, and participatory democratic system.[4]

Several questions immediately arise: Why were the recommendations by the Truth Commission in general, and in particular those related to reparations, not adhered to as were the rest of the commitments of peace? From the State's perspective, was the reason for noncompliance a result of the design, technical, and financial dimensions of the CVES's program or just simply a problem of the political will within the government? Why did the FMLN not insist on the implementation of the recommendations in the report by the CVES in reference to reparations? What were the position and the role of social organizations and the international community in relation to the issue of reparations? The following pages will attempt to at least partially answer these questions.

The Reparations Program Proposed by the Truth Commission

In El Salvador, the topic of reparations was introduced in the national agenda by the Truth Commission as part of the peace agreements negotiated between the Salvadoran government and the FMLN in Mexico in April 1991. According to the text creating the CVES, the Commission was to consist of three persons appointed by the Secretary General of the United Nations after hearing the opinions of the two concerned parties. The resulting Commission consisted solely of foreign personalities.[5] According to its mandate, the CVES was assigned 'the investigation of grave cases of violence that occurred from 1980 whose impact on society demands with the utmost urgency a public acknowledgement of the truth'.[6] Furthermore, the Commission was charged with 'recommending legal, political or administrative measures that could be devised from the outcome of the investigation', which could include 'measures aimed at preventing the recurrence of such acts, as well as measures tending to national reconciliation'.[7]

Based on its mandate, the CVES recommended in its final report measures to facilitate national reconciliation, including recommendations of material and moral reparations. The most important of the reparations recommendations was the creation of a special fund, as an autonomous entity, with the appropriate legal and administrative faculties, meant to secure appropriate material compensation for the victims of violence. In the Commission's opinion, the fund should have been financed primarily by the international community because of the domestic financial constraints. The Commission recommended that 1 percent of the total international aid to El Salvador be devoted to this fund.[8]

Regarding moral reparations, the CVES recommended the creation of a national monument in San Salvador displaying the names of all of the identified victims of the conflict, honorably acknowledging these victims and the grave acts they were subjected to. In addition, the CVES recommended the establishment of a national holiday in remembrance of the victims of the conflict and as an expression of national reconciliation.[9] Finally, in order to allow Salvadoran society to analyze in detail the Commission's report, the creation of a Truth and Reconciliation Forum was recommended, in which representative sectors of the country could participate.[10]

More than ten years have passed since the Truth Commission made its recommendations. To date, almost none has been observed.[11] This failure is noteworthy considering the enormous number of victims of political violence and of the political repression by the Salvadoran State during the 12 years of conflict,[12] and the existence of a powerful political and military force (the FMLN and its base organizations), for whom the issue of human rights violations historically had been an important point in its political agenda. The remainder of this part of the chapter will attempt to provide a general explanation of this failure.

Toward a General Interpretation of the Causes Leading to the Failure to Implement the Reparations Program Proposed by the Truth Commission

The reasons that explain the failure to adopt the reparations measures recommended by the CVES are directly related to at least three factors. The first and most important is that the recommendations included in the Commission's report did not arise from the negotiation process between the signatory parties to the Peace Accord. Therefore, they did not benefit from the balance of political and military forces that favored compliance with the remainder of the peace agreements. The second factor is the lack of political will of the Salvadoran government to comply with the Commission's recommendations and the absence of a political force willing to defend the reparations program proposed by the CVES. The third factor relates to flaws in the design of the reparations program proposed by the CVES, to the composition of the Commission, and to the position assumed by the international community in respect to the reparations program and its financing. The following sections will analyze each of these factors in turn.

The CVES Recommendations and the Remainder of the Peace Agreements: Their Different Natures

The reparations recommended by the El Salvador Truth Commission were not part of the direct negotiations between the GOES and the FMLN. Therefore, they did not obtain the same level of political backing as the remainder of the agreements included in the Peace Accord, nor did they benefit from the relative balance of political and military forces among the negotiating parties. This balance resulted in good measure from the enormous military capacity of the FMLN, which in the end was the principal factor explaining the compliance with the remainder of the fundamental agreements within the El Salvador Peace Accord.[13]

Indeed, as one of the principal leaders of the ex-guerillas pointed out, reparations were never an issue negotiated between the GOES and the FMLN, but rather one addressed always in the broader context of human rights.[14] During the negotiation phase, the main topics for the human rights organizations and the FMLN (which was serving as an intermediary between the organizations and the government) were the finding of the truth, and to a lesser extent, the achievement of justice.[15] The subject of negotiation between the parties was the creation of the Truth Commission itself and not the content of the report this commission would produce. As was pointed out by one of the FMLN negotiators:

[T]he Truth Commission is one of the few products of the negotiation of the Peace Accords that was totally left out of the political control of the government and FMLN negotiators. The negotiators agreed to create a commission, and they entrusted it with an aim ... but the end product of the commission was never the subject of negotiation.[16]

In fact, when the CVES presented its report in March 1993, the peace negotiations had already concluded and the process was in the implementation phase of the signed agreements. For the signatories, especially for the FMLN, the peace agreements were critically important as the movement's political livelihood and its future access to State power depended on their implementation. But when the CVES published its report, the balance of political and military forces that enabled the peace negotiations had substantially changed in favor of the government and the right-wing sector. The GOES, unencumbered by military pressure from the FMLN, chose to abide by only those agreements previously negotiated.

On the other hand, the FMLN was totally absorbed by the process of political and military reform and by its own process of converting from a military organization to a political party. The following quote from the present coordinator of the FMLN serves to illustrate this point:

All negotiations have their correlations: the military negotiation had the military correlation, and this led to certain results, which caused the implementation (of the items already negotiated). Later on, the process was not totally favorable since the government that assumed the commitment questioned the Truth Commission. That is, one of the parties that stood under the obligation to comply undermined the credibility of the Commission's resolutions, and the correlation between civil society and political forces was insufficient to make the implementation of the recommendations made by the CVES possible.[17]

The Lack of Political Will of the Government to Comply with the Commission's Recommendations and the Absence of Social Forces to Defend Them

The second factor explaining the notable lack of compliance with the CVES's reparations recommendations was the lack of political will of the government of Alfredo Cristiani. His administration faced pressure from right-wing groups and the armed forces, who forcefully criticized the contents of the Truth Commission report because of its conclusion stating that the largest share of the human rights violations were carried out by the State apparatus (armed forces, Security Corps, and death squads),[18] and because it recommended the vetting of the principals responsible for such violations.

Indeed, and as has been pointed out by the United Nations:

[T]he publication of the report gave rise to a chain of protest reactions by the higher ranks of the Armed Forces, the Supreme Court President and high-ranking government officials. . . . Tensions in El Salvador were exacerbated by the fact that the people mentioned in the report, as well as the political and media leaders, vehemently and publicly rejected the conclusions and recommendations of the Commission. It was said that the Commission exceeded its mandate and that it had tried to assign itself judicial functions. The United Nations was violently criticized and there were anonymous threats against ONUSAL [United Nations Observer Mission in El Salvador]. There was concern that the report would generate violence, for example, vengeful acts that might destabilize in some way the country at a critical stage in the peace process. Further complicating the situation was the fact that the vetting of the Armed Forces had not concluded.[19]

In this context, President Cristiani expressed to the United Nations some reservations regarding the report. He declared that

he was willing to comply strictly with those recommendations of the Commission that fell under his power, that accorded with the Constitution of the Republic, that were also in harmony with the Accords derived from direct negotiations, that would contribute to the reconciliation of the Salvadorian society, and that would not involve the assumption of competencies which would threaten the system and the institutional order established in the country.[20]

In spite of the previous agreements, the government did not comply with most of the recommendations in the Commission's report. On the contrary, five days after it was published, on the initiative of President Cristiani, the Legislative Assembly approved the general amnesty law that protected the persons involved in the violations and abuses committed during the war.[21]

The Cristiani government never formally opposed those recommendations regarding reparations. Its lack of political will was reflected in its unwillingness to assign any resources to finance the reparations fund, claiming a lack of public resources and the need to assign the available resources to the task of reconstruction.

This failure of Cristiani's government to abide by the recommendations concerning reparations was also encouraged by the absence of social and political forces to promote and defend reparations. In particular, the low profile of victims' organizations, except for those representing wounded war veterans, is notable. Other nongovernmental organizations (NGOs) were relatively passive actors and had little influence on the post-Truth Commission process.[22]

The Truth Commission's report also aggravated the internal divisions within the FMLN because it recommended a political ban of all the heads of the guerilla groups for a period of ten years on account of their policy of systematically eliminating city mayors.[23] This not only eroded the FMLN's support of the

Commission's report but it also generated strong infighting within the organization.

In addition, some in the leadership within the FMLN perceived the reparations recommendations as counterproductive and nonviable from a financial point of view. The following quote by Salvador Samayoa, one of the negotiators of the FMLN, clearly illustrates the point:

[T]he subject of material reparation ... made no sense, not only was it un-payable but it couldn't be operationalized practically (due to the huge amount of casualties and the lack of a trustworthy registry of the victims). Furthermore ... it would have been a bit offensive that the State would give you some funds for the victims. ... The thing about the monument and that type of thing are symbolic and as such they have more value to certain types of people than others. ... In my judgment (the construction of the monument) would have brought back the subject of the lists (of the dead); which ones did you kill, who did I kill? ... In my judgment, putting us back into that mud pit with the only purpose of having a plaque, sincerely does not repair anything of what happened. ... On the topic of reparations I have a pretty political criterion, which is the most ethical—and at the same time the most practical—of all, and that is, that the only reparation which could truly be carried out in this society was to stop the killing ... stop the tortures, stop the persecutions, stop the repression. ... But above everything, to change the structures in such a way that we could be sure these things would not happen again.[24]

As can be deduced from the quote, within the FMLN there was not only little support for the reparations recommendations made by the Truth Commission but there was also frank opposition to the measures. This was due in part to a short-term and biased view of the Salvadoran reality as well as to the lack of knowledge about the subject of reparations at a conceptual and operative level. Given these circumstances it should not be surprising that the issue of reparations was never seriously debated by those charged with the follow-up of the Peace Accords, that is, the National Commission for the Consolidation of the Peace (COPAZ). According to Salvador Samayoa, reparations measures

never had a major debate (within COPAZ) because the subject was simply unthinkable. ... In reality it never was debated seriously; there were people within the FMLN that carried those flags, I believe without considering the total implications ... but never, never was it seriously discussed.[25]

The Flaws in the Design of the Reparations Program, the Composition of the CVES, and the Posture of the International Community

The third factor that contributed to the failure to implement the reparations program recommended by the CVES comprises flaws in the design of the finance proposal, the composition of the CVES, and the posture of the international community (including the United Nations) regarding reparations.

The proposed financing of the reparations fund (international and domestic contributions, plus 1 percent of all international aid to El Salvador) instead of favoring the movement of internal and external resources to fund the program actually had the opposite impact and discouraged contributions. This was so for two reasons. The first was that the proposal to finance the fund with external resources was formulated under the premise that this was a poor country, which did not have enough internal resources.[26] The CVES inadvertently provided legitimacy to the claims by the Salvadoran government that resources were scarce and otherwise already earmarked.[27]

The second reason was that the Commission's proposal did not anticipate the international community's unwillingness to finance the reparations program because it considered reparations a fundamental responsibility of the State and took a State's contribution to a reparations program to have a reparative value in and of itself. In their view, assigning internal resources to finance reparations was firm proof of the government's and the people's resolve to break away from the past.[28]

Furthermore, the CVES concentrated exclusively on producing the report, without attention to the task of creating the necessary political conditions to ensure effective execution of the recommendations. In part, this oversight was due to commissioners optimistically assuming that just by having a formal agreement between the signatory parties in the Peace Accords and under the vigilance of the United Nations, the parties would comply with the recommendations. The other factor that explains this oversight was the lack of international experience with the political tasks of truth commissions, including reparations.[29] The Commission did not consider it necessary to implement a strategy of political dialogue with the rest of the national players, in particular with civil society organizations and with the political parties represented in the Legislative Assembly. This explains partly why the political forces shifted in favor of the right wing during the implementation phase of the Accords. The reparations program was left without any social or political base strong enough to defend it.

Finally, the composition of the CVES did not help in this respect, either. As stated previously, the commissioners as well as the technical personnel were foreigners. In fact, the primary concern for supposed neutrality in the human rights investigations created a barrier for members of Salvadoran society for being part of the commissioners' teams. Even though this favored the perceived neutrality of the Commission, it detracted from its operations and political performance since there was never an adequate dialogue between the Commission and the rest of Salvadoran society. In fact, once the final report had been delivered, the commissioners left the country without achieving a true collaboration with the victims' organizations and the other NGOs, which were ultimately the ones that needed to defend and promote the reparations program.

The Lessons Learned from the Salvadoran Experience

The analysis of the Salvadoran experience allows us to extract important lessons regarding the design of reparations programs and of strategies to assure their political viability. The following are the main findings:

1. Effective implementation requires an interdependence of political forces and the formation of political alliances and coalitions among different sectors (domestic and international) with sufficient political strength and capacity to defend and move forward the program.

2. The Salvadoran experience warns of the necessity to distinguish between formal and real agreements by the political forces, as well as the necessity of establishing a permanent monitoring system to oversee the changes in the political balance over time. In other words, it is important to evaluate constantly the positions of the various actors, for these can change during the different phases of the process that leads from negotiation to the implementation of the accords.

3. In relationship to the previous point, truth commissions and other social players must provide an arena to acquire broad knowledge and information about the reach and content of the reparations program. Even the natural allies of the program had very little understanding of the topic and therefore there was neither the knowledge nor the interest to defend it.

4. A financial strategy based on the assumption that the resources would be mainly foreign is unreal and counterproductive. In the long run, it not only contributes to the justification of the position of those who oppose the program but it also sends the wrong message to the international community for whom the use of internal resources shows the political will of the State and the society, and represents in itself an act of reparations.

2. THE HAITIAN EXPERIENCE

Introduction

In December 1994,[30] a few weeks after his return to Haiti, President Jean-Bertrand Aristide created, through presidential decree, the National Truth and Justice Commission (CNVJ). In March 1995, another presidential decree defined the mandate and appointed seven commissioners (four nationals and three foreigners).[31] The CNVJ was mandated to document the most serious human rights violations committed during the de facto military regime that governed Haiti in the period between September 29, 1991 and October 15, 1994, placing special emphasis on crimes against humanity and sexual crimes against women. Furthermore, it had to investigate the nature of the paramilitary groups, identify and find the authors of the abuses, and prepare a public report of the findings with recommendations to the Haitian government on reparations for, and rehabilitation of, the victims, as well as legal and administrative measures to prevent the recurrence of such violations.[32]

A six-month term was originally given to the Commission to complete its work. It was later extended to nine months. Due to internal disorganization, poor performance, and lack of financial resources, the period was extended to close to a year.[33] Therefore, on February 5, 1996, just a few hours before President Aristide concluded his first term, the CNVJ delivered its final report, titled 'Si M Pa Rele' ('If I Don't Cry Out'), which, among its many points, recommended reparations measures.

As in El Salvador, the vast majority of the recommendations embodied in the CNVJ report were not implemented. As stated by Commissioner Freud Jean: '[W]hat has been done with the report is practically nil. The report was filed just after it was delivered.'[34]

The Reparations Measures Suggested by the CNVJ

Even though most of the suggestions by the CNVJ in the final report focused on institutional and judicial systems reform,[35] there were some recommendations in relation to reparations for victims. The most important recommendation was the creation of a 'Special Commission for reparations of the harm caused to the victims of the de facto regime' whose main task would be to assure the reparations of harms to victims identified by the CNVJ and to 'other victims who would be identified in accordance with criteria proposed by the CNVJ'.[36]

It was also recommended that the special commission should have a temporary character and the status of a mixed entity (led by a diverse administrative council and including representatives of the victims), whose resources would come from the State, private national and foreign donors, or from international or United Nations assistance, in particular from the United Nations Fund for the Victims of Torture.

According to the CNVJ recommendations, the special commission would assign victims an indemnity based on a previously established scale and offer other forms of assistance and services that would answer the legitimate needs of the victims. It was further indicated that the Reparations Commission should function without prejudice for the victims' right to obtain integral reparations through judicial means and that the commission could eventually work with the victims to establish a system of legal aid for victims who lacked the resources to try to get a judgment against the authors of the violations. Finally, the CNVJ recommended that for children 15 years or younger, orphaned as a result of the violence, the government should insure a decent education and quality of life.

The Haitian government has not implemented the recommendations contained in the report, including those pertaining to reparations.[37] According to a report from the United Nations Secretary General,[38] the Preval government created an office called *Bureau Poursuite et Suivi*, which was charged with examining the issue of reparations for victims of the military coup, with a budget of 60 million gourdes (approx. US$3.5 million).[39] Nevertheless, the office ceased activities later on. As ascertained by Commissioner Freud Jean: 'After the CNVJ, there was an attempt to establish a Reparations Commission within the Ministry of Justice. Some people received reparations through social programs. However, this Commission disappeared suddenly, the same way it had originated.'[40]

Toward a General Interpretation of the Causes of Noncompliance with the Reparations Recommendations of the CNVJ

In the Haitian case, the reasons for noncompliance with the reparations measures suggested by the CNVJ are both structural and contingent, that is, some have to do with the nature of the government, and others merely with happenstance. In the first place, the Aristide and Preval governments were enormously weak and limited. They were occupied with trying to survive in the midst of a profound political crisis and severe economic limitations, and thus had less flexibility in the definition and implementation of public policies, reinforcing the traditional dependence of the country on international aid.

Second, the failure to realize the CNVJ's recommendations stems from the lack of importance given to the reparations by the government, by the different players in the national arena, and by the international community, who prioritized institutional reform (especially the reform of the judicial system) and the achievement of minimal political stability over reparations. The third reason relates to the serious problems faced by the CNVJ in fulfilling its mandate, mistakes in the handling of the report, and the CNVJ's relations with the other social actors. The following sections will present a detailed analysis of these factors.

The Weakness of the Aristide and Preval Governments and the Structural Nature of the Haitian Political Crisis

One of the main factors that explain the failure to implement the CNVJ's recommendations is the notable weakness of the Aristide government (October 1994–February 1996) and its successor, Rene Preval's government (February 1996–February 2001). The weakness of the Aristide government stemmed from the nature of his return to power, made possible by a foreign military intervention and by the very complex negotiations among the US government and the military coup leaders that preceded the intervention.[41] Another factor in the weakness of the Aristide government was the economic conditions inherited from the military regime[42] characterized by a profound crisis that had provoked the collapse of public finances.[43]

This situation, in addition to the pressure exerted by the USA and international financial institutions in favor of orthodox measures of adjustment, forced the government to forgo its reform agenda and apply a program of economic adjustment that implied heavy social costs.[44] Although the adoption of said program provided access to international resources to deal with the economic crisis, it contributed to the erosion of the already weak social and political base of the government.[45] The application of adjustment policies suggested by international financial institutions provoked an important rupture between the government and the social movement that had brought it into power, which found itself divided.

Preval's government officially inherited the responsibility to comply with the recommendations of the CNVJ. However, through most of his term he was involved in a political crisis arising from accusations of electoral fraud during the senatorial elections in April 1997, and the subsequent resignation of his prime minister.[46] The crisis had grave repercussions including the suspension of international aid,[47] placing the State in jeopardy,[48] and negatively impacting the institutional reform program that the government had pledged to realize.

With such reduced margins of action, the Aristide government and the Preval government had to define intervention priorities, which had the support of the international community and the political underwriting of the USA. As we will see, in neither case was the reparations policy a priority.

The Political Priority of the National and International Actors: Institutional Reforms versus the Reparations Policies

Due to the structural nature of the recurring political and institutional crisis in Haiti, during the period after Aristide's return there was ample consensus between the national and international actors that the only viable way to establish democracy in the country was through the strengthening of the democratic institutions.

To that effect, both the Aristide and the Preval governments defined, at least formally, institutional reform as a political priority.⁴⁹

The priority of institutional reform affected other policies, including reparations, which were relegated to the backseat of, or even excluded from, the government's agenda. This helps to explain the Aristide government's lack of support for the CNVJ and its attention to the victims,⁵⁰ as well as the notable lack of political will of the Preval government to comply with the recommendations of the Commission's report, despite its expressed commitment to do so.⁵¹

It is important to underline that the CNVJ itself placed a higher priority on institutional reforms than reparations. According to Commissioner Freud Jean: 'Even for the CNVJ, the reform of the judicial system was of clear importance (more important than reparations to the victims) because it corresponds to justice. The CNVJ presented a true reform plan. It cohered with the interest of the international community as it pertained to reforms to the judicial system.'⁵²

Finally, it is worth mentioning that there was an additional element that influenced the fact that the reparations recommendations had no political support. This was the notion, apparently widespread in Haiti, that reparations could not be separated from judicial procedures and therefore that priority should be given to justice. The following quote from Commissioner Freud Jean brings into evidence this point: 'The idea of reparations should not leave the context of a trial. To create a reparation process independent of the judicial system would legitimize the fact that justice is not important or that there will always be reparations even if justice does not work.'⁵³

The Reach of the CNVJ's Mandate and other Internal Problems

The mandate of the Commission, as well as its internal operational problems, is a third factor contributing to the failure to implement the CNVJ's reparations recommendations. In the first place, the mandate of the CNVJ was extremely limited since it was restricted to investigating the human rights violations of the de facto government of Cedras, which interrupted Aristide's first term from September 27, 1991 to October 14, 1994. The mandate did not address the systematic and grave human rights violations of previous years, including the decades of the dictatorial government of the Duvaliers.⁵⁴ For that reason the mandate placed upon the Commission by President Aristide did not correspond to the public's expectations and those of the human rights NGOs, which were for a greater reach.

This was compounded by accusations that the CNVJ paid more attention to the victims in Aristide's political movement (Fanmi Lavalas), which eroded the Commission's credibility since it reinforced the belief that the CNVJ was just a political instrument to exact revenge from those responsible for the coup. According to Jean-Claude Bejeux of the *Centre Oecumenique de Droits de l'Homme*: '[F]rom the first moment it was decided to focus only on the victims that belonged to the Fanmi Lavalas. There was nothing said about the victims that did not belong to

Aristide's party. Obviously, this generated conflict and lack of interest towards the commission.'[55]

Having said this, it is also fair to recognize that the CNVJ's task was performed in an adverse environment. In the first place, the Commission lacked financial resources to achieve its mandate. According to some studies[56] the CNVJ worked with little more than US$1 million. The main share came from international aid. In fact the CNVJ final report complained that the lack of sufficient funds considerably reduced its capacity to complete the assigned task.[57]

Second, the CNVJ faced serious difficulties gathering and systematizing the information pertaining to the political violence and the perpetrators of the human rights violations.[58] The lack of cooperation by the USA also hampered the investigation. The USA refused to deliver about 60,000 miscellaneous pages it had recovered, which were from the Revolutionary Front for Haitian Advancement and Progress [*Front révolutionaries pour l'avancement et le progrès haïtiens*, FRAPH], an organization that was one of those principally responsible for the human rights violations during the military government.[59]

All of the above, including the presence of important divisions within the Commission,[60] kept the CNVJ from meeting the preestablished deadlines for the delivery of the report, which, in turn, affected the political viability of its recommendations. In effect, the report was delivered to President Aristide just a few hours before he left power. Obviously, this foreclosed any possibility for him to take any action that could lead to the implementation of the recommendations. Instead, the responsibility for implementing the recommendations landed on the new government, which delayed the report's publication by several months—a situation that seriously affected any possibility of support by the population.

Finally, the CNVJ committed a grave error in not defining and putting into place a communications policy that would allow it to share its work with Haitian society and in not establishing permanent consultation relationships with different national and international social sectors. This failure hindered the formation of the minimal political conditions that the recommendations required for an effective implementation. This mistake by the Commission resulted in the final report being rapidly forgotten by some and filed away indefinitely by others.

The Lessons Learned from the Haitian Experience

The Haitian experience regarding reparations allows us to extract the following lessons:

1. Effectively implementing a reparations policy is intimately connected with structural factors, such as the functioning of State institutions and the presence of financial and economic restrictions.

2. A fundamental prerequisite for the application of a reparations policy is that this policy needs to be part of the national agenda. This entails designing and implementing political strategies to sensitize the general public, particularly the political elite, to the pertinence and convenience of reparations for the sake of the consolidation of democracy and governance.

3. Utilizing the Truth Commission for short-term political objectives can undermine the political viability of the recommendations included in the final report.

4. The Haitian case shows the inconvenience of mechanically binding the issue of reparations with judicial proceedings. It is important to remember that the judicial system finds itself overwhelmed when human rights violations are not the exception but are massive and systematic:[61] it is here that adopting a political perspective regarding reparations can contribute to the general purpose of doing justice.[62]

3. Conclusions

The study of the Salvadoran and Haitian experiences with reparations and the respective lessons learned allows us to draw some general conclusions about the factors that determine the fate of reparations programs, factors that have an impact on their effective implementation. The first and most evident of these is that in order to ensure that reparations programs will be put into practice, a balance of political forces that favor such programs is necessary.

This raises two questions: What does the balance of these political forces depend on? Who is in charge of promoting their formation? First, the construction of a political force favorable to reparations critically depends on the existence of sufficiently powerful and influential players to promote and defend it. In both cases, the only defenders of the recommendations were basically the NGOs, which are generally weak. In the Salvadoran case, only handicapped war victims from the FMLN and armed forces got any type of reparations, precisely because they were organized and had the capacity to mobilize and protest.[63]

Second, national and international players that are in favor of reparations must assume responsibility for constructing and/or strengthening a social and political force able to promote and defend reparations. In this sense, all of the interested sectors in the reparations for victims of political violence (the truth commissions, the victims' organizations, human rights NGOs, the government or public servants who sympathize with reparations, and the international community) should include within their own agendas the definition and implementation of political

strategies conducive to creating a strong *political coalition* that allows the introduction of the issue of reparations to the national agenda and that will exert
pressure over those responsible for the design and implementation of public policy.

Third, in both cases, victims' organizations, with few exceptions, had a low
profile in the post-Commission processes and were not capable of mobilizing, or
forming alliances with, other social or political sectors. As a result, the possibilities
of constructing a coalition in favor of reparations were very limited, and, as a
consequence, the possibility of victims and their families actually receiving reparations diminished considerably. In this sense, the experiences of El Salvador and
Haiti suggest the necessity of having victims' organizations play a central role in the
construction of coalitions in favor of reparations. Hence, it is necessary that both
internal and external agents who sympathize with them avoid the temptation of
substituting for victims' organizations and instead assist them to become effective
actors in the political process.

In this task, truth commissions can and should play a central role throughout
their operations, from the starting date of their mandate until the date their report
is delivered, since they are perceived as the leaders in the process by national and
international players. The cases of El Salvador and Haiti both show that the truth
commissions committed the grave mistake of becoming isolated from the social
and political, national and international actors. They concentrated on elaborating
the final report and overlooked the importance of systematically revealing their
findings and establishing the sort of communication that forms the basis of future
implementation. Such a strategy would sensitize key political actors about the
benefits for the country as a whole of implementing public policies of reparations.
As a result of this behavior, and given the weakness of the few players in favor of
reparations, when the reports came to light, they did not find enough political
support to make the implementation of their recommendations plausible.

These two cases suggest that it is necessary that beyond the mandate entrusted to
truth commissions, they ought to implement strategies of political impact that
allow for the creation of the minimal necessary conditions for the political viability
of their recommendations regarding reparations. Otherwise, they will continue to
act with the best intentions but without achieving any of the objectives they are
supposed to achieve.

(Translated from Spanish by Christian Gerzso)

Notes

1. The author wishes to express his gratitude to Patricia Moral and Julie Guillerot for their
contribution to the elaboration of this study, particularly for their job collecting and
systematizing information about El Salvador and Haiti, respectively, as well as for
interviewing different actors.

2. United Nations Security Council, *From Madness to Hope: the 12-year war in El Salvador: Report of the Commission on the Truth for El Salvador*, S/25500 (1993). ['CVES Report' hereafter.]

3. See letter dated March 29, 1993 addressed to the President of the Security Council by the United Nations Secretary General reprinted in United Nations, *The United Nations and El Salvador 1990–1995*, vol. IV (United Nations Blue Book Series, 1995), 307.

4. The political reforms included: (i) the elimination of the repressive apparatus of the State (paramilitary groups, Civil Defense, National Guard, National Police, Treasury Police); (ii) the reform and purging of the armed forces; (iii) the creation of a new Civil National Police; (iv) the creation of the Public Security Academy; (v) the dissolution of the National Directory of Intelligence and the creation of a State intelligence entity independent from the army and with direct responsibility to the President of the Republic; (vi) the approval of reforms to the Constitution and the judicial system; and (vii) the reform of the electoral system (including the creation of the Supreme Electoral Tribunal, the establishment of the right of political parties to supervise the elaboration, organization, publication, and updating of the electoral registry, the legalization of the FMLN as a political party, and the guarantee of its civil, political and institutional rights).

5. The members of the Commission were: Belisario Betancur (President), ex-president of Colombia; Reinaldo Figueredo Planchart, former foreign minister of Venezuela; and Thomas Buergenthal, ex-president of the Inter-American Court of Human Rights.

6. See El Salvador Peace Accords. Mexico Accord, April 27, 1991.

7. Ibid.

8. 'The fund should receive an appropriate contribution from the State but, in view of prevailing economic conditions, should receive a substantial contribution from the international community. Therefore, without prejudice to the obligations of the State and of FMLN, the Commission urgently appeals to the international community, especially the wealthier countries and those that showed most interest in the conflict and its settlement, to establish a fund for that purpose. It also suggests that the United Nations Secretariat promote and coordinate this initiative. It further recommends that not less than 1 per cent of all international assistance that reaches El Salvador be set aside for this purpose' (CVES Report, 186).

9. Ibid.

10. The CVES recommended that the National Commission for the Consolidation of Peace (COPAZ), the entity charged with the follow-up of the peace agreements—made up of representatives of the government, the FMLN, and the political parties represented in the National Assembly—be made responsible for the Reconciliation Forum. To that end, it suggested increasing the membership of COPAZ so that 'sectors of civilian society that are not directly represented in COPAZ can participate in this analysis' (CVES Report, 187).

11. The monument to honor the victims never got beyond ground breaking in the Cuscatlan park. Today the 'Committee in favor of the Monument Construction' is trying to create it by private sponsorship of each of the victim's names. The national holiday in remembrance of victims is celebrated mostly by FMLN ex-combatants who observe it every January 16th, the anniversary of the Peace Accords, for Congress has not approved the proposed law declaring a specific day for such a holiday. The only reparations measures that have been awarded are for handicapped ex-combatants of

the army and the FMLN, who, in the face of the failure to implement reinsertion programs have become organized and have staged several demonstrations, marches, and the occupation of public buildings. The main organization of handicapped ex-combatants is the *Asociación de Lisiados de Guerra de El Salvador* (ALGES), established in 1997, and currently with approximately 4,500 members from the FMLN and the army. One of its main achievements is the reform of the law of the special fund for the handicapped of the armed conflict (Decree 416) so that it covers a larger number of people and includes medical and psychological services for those wounded and handicapped as a result of the armed conflict.

12. Although there are no official figures of the total number of victims of the armed conflict and State repression, it is estimated that 30,000 persons lost their lives and hundreds of thousands were injured. As far as the disappeared go, more than 2,000 claims were presented to international human rights organizations, of which only a few have been resolved.

13. The political and military force of the FMLN was demonstrated throughout the 12-year war by its ability to defeat all counterinsurgency strategies applied by the US-supported Salvadoran army; by the military capacity displayed in the November 1989 offensive during which it was able to control for several days ample sectors of the San Salvador metropolitan area; and in the last phases of the war, by the use of land-to-air missiles, which gave a strategic turn to the conflict.

14. Interview with Salvador Sanchez Ceren, present General Coordinator of the FMLN (late 2002).

15. The following quote by Sanchez Ceren eloquently illustrates the point: '... during the first moments of the debate (between the FMLN and the human rights organizations) the need to clarify, that was the word, that there had to be total clarity, to recover the trust of society, and not only that, there should be events where justice could operate....' (Interview at the end of 2002).

16. Interview with Salvador Samoya, President of the Public Security Council (late 2002).

17. Interview with Salvador Sanchez Ceren, Coordinator of FMLN (late 2002).

18. The commission received more than 22,000 complaints of 'grave acts of violence' that took place between January 1980 and July 1991, but it elected to focus on 32 cases chosen to illustrate different types of acts of violence, which were classified as violent acts committed by agents of the State; peasant massacres by the armed forces; murder committed by death squads; violent acts committed by the FMLN and magistrate killings. Ninety-five percent of such violent acts, according to the Commission, were committed by the military establishment, the State security forces and the death squads, primarily against civilians. The FMLN for its part was responsible for the remaining 5 per cent of violent cases that included a killing campaign against 30 city mayors. See CVES Report, 41–2.

19. United Nations (1995), op. cit., 40–1.

20. After several exchanges of ideas between ONUSAL and the Salvadoran government, President Cristiani, in a letter dated July 13, 1993, stated to the Secretary General that after an analysis done by the government of the recommendations suggested by the Commission, the government was in a position to apply all of them, except the following: (*a*) the dismissal of public officials and their barring from holding office again; (*b*) the constitutional reforms; and (*c*) the recommendations whose initiative and execution depended on the judicial system through the Supreme Court. United

Nations, 'Report by the Secretary General in relation to the application of the suggested recommendations by the Truth Commission' (UN:S/26581, October 14, 1993).

21. The report of the CVES named 40 individuals responsible for human right violations, including high-ranking military officers, members of the Supreme Court and the Secretary of Defense, among others.

22. The scant visibility of victims' organizations can also be noted in the existing analyses of the compliance with the Truth Commission's recommendations. See for example, *Instituto de Derechos Humanos de la UCA* (IDHUCA), 'Cumplimiento de las Recomendaciones de la Comisión de la Verdad en El Salvador', *Revista ECA*, 655(58), Mayo (2003).

23. The ban affected the leaders of the *Ejército Revolucionario del Pueblo* (ERP), led by Joaquín Villalobos, considered to be the military strategist of the FMLN. Owing to the strong political opposition from diverse sectors that considered this recommendation from the CVES to be contrary to the incorporation of the former guerrilla movements to the democratic process, it was never implemented. Villalobos later resigned from the FMLN and formed a new political party.

24. Interview with Salvador Samayoa (late 2002).

25. Ibid.

26. Obviously, the CVES's proposal of financing the reparations program with external funds was also a political message for the international community, particularly the USA, which had been deeply involved in the Salvadoran conflict. The message was: 'You financed the war, now you should finance its consequences.' But this message was never taken up.

27. For a detailed analysis of the financing of the Salvadoran peace process, and the position of the government and international institutions on the subject, see Alexander Segovia, 'Domestic Resources Mobilization', in *Economic Policy for Building Peace*, James Boyce, ed. (London: Lynne Rienner Publishers, 1996).

28. This same position has been assumed by the international community in the case of Guatemala, where it has refused to replace the State as the principal provider of resources to finance the peace agreements. For a detailed analysis on the subject see Alexander Segovia (2001), 'The Role of the International Community in the Guatemalan Peace Process: Lessons from the Fiscal Point of View.' To be published.

29. In general, the Truth Commission dedicated its main efforts and resources to the elaboration of the final report rather than worrying about the political viability of the proposed recommendations.

30. On September 19, 1994 a multinational force authorized by the United Nations Security Council under the direction of the United States intervened in Haiti to restore to power President Jean-Bertrand Aristide, who was elected in December of 1990 and had assumed power on February 7, 1991. His government lasted only seven months before it was deposed by a military coup on September 29, 1991 led by General Raoul Cedras. Once reinstated, Aristide's first term lasted until February 1996.

31. Later on, the Commission was reduced to six members: Françoise Boucard (President); Ertha Elysée and Freud Jean of Haitian nationality; Oliver Jackman from Barbados; Patric Robinson from Jamaica; and Bacre Waly Ndiaye from Senegal.

32. See 'Haiti: Human Rights after President Aristide's Return', *Human Rights Watch*, 7(11) (1995).

33. Audrey R. Chapman and Patrick Ball, 'The Truth of Truth Commissions: Comparative Lessons from Haiti, South Africa and Guatemala', *Human Rights Quarterly*, 23(1)

(2001); Amnesty International, 'Haiti: A Question of Justice', *AI Index: AMR 36/01/96*. Patrick Costello and José Antonio Sanahuja, 'Haití: The Challenges of Reconstruction' (1996) available at: www.cip.fuhem.es/observatorio/informes/hait.htm

34. Interview with Commissioner Freud James in late 2003.

35. Chapter 8 of the CNVJ final report contains the recommendations, grouped in five sections: reparations measures (1.5 pages), violations and sexual violence against women (1 page), institutional and judicial systems reforms (34 pages), procedures and sanctions (4 pages), and other recommendations (1 page).

36. According to the CNVJ the commission for reparations could give benefits to other victims if they satisfied the following criteria: (*a*) having suffered a grave violation of human rights as defined by the CNVJ, (*b*) applying to the Special Commission within six months of its establishment.

37. Some measures of reparations have been implemented by nongovernmental organizations. For example, the NGO Map Viv procures medical and psychological assistance for the victims of human rights violations. See Amnesty International, 'Haiti: Steps Forward, Steps Back', *AI Index: AMR 36/010/2001*. September 2001.

38. United Nations, 'The Situation of Democracy and Human Rights in Haiti', report by the United Nations Secretary General, A/52/986. July 20, 1998.

39. According to the United Nations the office had three lines of work: social aid, economic aid, and legal/medical aid. The UN document also states that the office was, at that time, in the final part of the design of a home reconstruction project for those dwellings destroyed by the army in the central region (United Nations, 1998, op.cit.).

40. Interview, February 2003.

41. For example, Aristide had to accept an amnesty for the military involved in the coup, which permitted them to leave the country. (In reference to this point see documents by Amnesty International from 1996 and 2001 already cited.) On the economic front, in August 1994 representatives of the Aristide government in exile met in Paris with the principal donors and international institutions, where the rules of the economic game to be followed by the Aristide government once he returned to the country were settled. For more details see Costello and Sanahuja (1996, op.cit.).

42. The economic situation during the military regime had deteriorated in good measure due to the suspension of international aid and the imposition of a commercial embargo decreed by the United Nations Security Council in June 1993. On this subject, see Costello and Sanahuja (1996, op. cit.).

43. The Gross National Product (GNP) in real terms decreased by 30 percent between 1990–94 and the GNP per capita decreased to the levels of around US$260 in 1994, confirming Haiti to be the poorest country in the Western Hemisphere. The fiscal revenues of the central government decreased from 7.3 percent of the GNP in 1990 to 3.3 percent of the GNP in 1994 and inflation reached a rate of 18 percent per year in the period 1990–1993. Minimum wages in 1994 represented just 21.8 percent of their 1981 level. See International Monetary Fund (IMF), 'IMF approves Stand-by Credit for Haiti', Press release No. 95/14, March 8, 1995, and IMF, 'Haiti: Recent Economic Developments', IMF Staff Country Report No. 98/101, 1998.

44. Aristide's social program, with which he had won the elections, included agrarian reform, support for the rural sector, and increased spending in education, health, and public sector reform (see Costello and Sanahula, 1996, op. cit.). All of that was abandoned and instead an IMF-promoted stabilization program was put in place.

It consisted of the reduction and simplification of the tariff system, a new policy regarding petroleum prices with automatic adjustments in accordance with changes in the import costs, a first phase of privatization of public entities, and the reform to the power company (IMF, 1995, op. cit.).

45. Aristide won the elections thanks to the Lavalas coalition (Avalanche), formed by diverse social groups and the National Front for Change and Democracy (FNCD). Cedras' de facto government heavily repressed the coalition. As per Costello and Sanahuja (1996, op. cit.), when Aristide returned to power in October of 1994, the social base that had facilitated the election was already destroyed.

46. The crisis arose due to the accusations of fraud during the elections and was aggravated by the resignation of the Prime Minister and the impossibility of reaching a political accord to replace him, which forced Preval to make unilateral decisions that worsened the situation. A detailed analysis of this point can be found in Amnesty International, 'Haiti: Still Crying Out', *AI Index: AMR 36/02/98.* 1998.

47. According to Amnesty International (1998, op. cit.), in 1998 around US$500 million of international aid was frozen.

48. The following quote by the United Nations (1998, op. cit.) reflects with clarity the severity of the situation: 'The prolonged crisis has taken a toll on the stability of the political institutions that underpin the democratic process and has exacerbated the fragility of State structures. As the center of these political confrontations, the Parliament has been distracted from its legislative and executive oversight responsibilities and has become increasingly dysfunctional.... The impartiality and good faith of the Presidency ... have been called into question by some sectors, as it assumed the responsibilities of the vacant Prime Minister's office is a manner reminiscent of the traditional presidential-type regime.'

49. Aristide, in an important institutional reform program, instituted reforms in the security forces, the prison system, and in a lesser way in the judicial system. For his part, Preval pledged to continue with Aristide's reforms and tried to advance the judicial reform. This choice earned strong national and international support, which was emphasized by all the persons interviewed for this chapter.

50. President Aristide opened complaint offices for the victims, but the offices were not well run or well financed, and closed shortly after being established. Furthermore, there were no efforts to preserve the files of local victims (Human Rights Watch, 1996, op. cit.). See Costello and Sanahuja (1996, op. cit.). On another matter, the Aristide government abandoned the CNVJ in its quest for funds, which substantially delayed the start of its work. (Interview with Freud Jean, at the end of February 2003.)

51. The Preval government through the Minister of Justice refused to implement the reparations recommendations, alleging lack of funds. Nor did it support the distribution of the CNVJ final report, alleging that the photocopies were excessively expensive, and offering instead an electronic copy of the report to those who would procure a diskette (Human Rights Watch, 1996, op. cit.).

52. Interview, February 2003.

53. Ibid.

54. Even after the Duvaliers there were several coups and systematic violence. For example, during the 1988 and 1990 elections there was a substantial increase in violence (see Costello and Sanahuja, 1996, op. cit.).

55. Interview carried out in late February 2003. In the same vein Micha Gaillard of *Haiti Solidarité Internationalé* (HIS) stated that since the creation of the CNVJ certain sides had been chosen, 'first in relation to the victims, since the only ones considered were the ones openly involved with the Lavalas Family. The persons who fought for Aristide's return but were not identified as Lavalas Group were not considered. Second, Aristide only spoke about the coup against him as if previous coups had not taken place.' (Interview at the end of February 2003.)

56. Audrey R. Chapman and Patrick Ball, 2001, op. cit.

57. For its political value, it is worth mentioning the behavior of the USA on this issue. According to Human Rights Watch (1995 and 1996) in May of 1995 the US government offered US$250,000 to support the Commission, an offer that it subsequently withdrew. In the end, it gave the Commission only US$50,000 and just a month before the end of its mandate. The funds were used to pay for supplies that were previously given by other donors.

58. The international composition of the technical personnel of the CNVJ—who did not know the terrain and were not fluent in Creole, which is the language used by 95 percent of the Haitian population—had an impact on this. Another fact was the constant threats to the members of the Commission in the field. (Interview with Maxine Rony, from the Alternative Justice Program, end of February 2003.)

59. See Amnesty International (1996, 1998 and 2001).

60. According to Commissioner Freud Jean, within the CNVJ there were existing conflicts in the definition of basic strategy and methodologies, and general lack of understanding among those responsible for the working groups.

61. The CNVJ report was based on interviews with 8,500 persons that reported 19,308 human rights violations.

62. See Pablo de Greiff, 'Justice and Reparations' (Chapter 12, this volume).

63. The Guatemalan case is paradoxical in this respect, for it is in virtue of the social and political force of ex-patrollers belonging to the former Civil Self-Defense Patrol—who were in part responsible for the human rights violations in Guatemala—that the government has been forced to revisit the topic of reparations for both victims and victimizers.

CHAPTER 5

OVERVIEW OF THE REPARATIONS PROGRAM IN SOUTH AFRICA

CHRISTOPHER J. COLVIN

The South African Truth and Reconciliation Commission (TRC) ushered in what was probably the most publicized and celebrated postconflict transition process undertaken in the last fifty years. During the course of the Commission's work, the spotlight was thrown in particular on the applications submitted to the Amnesty Committee (AC) by those who had perpetrated gross violations of human rights and on the stories of victims as they testified at the hearings of the Committee on Human Rights Violations (CHRV). Less visible, but equally important to those involved in the process was the work of the Committee on Reparations and Rehabilitation (CRR). Although most of the focus during the transition out of apartheid centered on the problem of amnesties for those involved in the conflict, the importance of reparations has featured at every stage of the process as an integral and necessary part of South Africa's transition and reconciliation project.

Although the *principle* of reparations has always, in one form or another, accompanied the development of the amnesty framework, victims have still not benefited from a full and binding elaboration of what reparations would mean for them. Despite various legal obligations to provide reparations, and despite the growing anger of victims and those in civil society who support them, the South African government, almost four years after the CRR made its final recommendations, has only now begun the process of implementing a reparations program. At the time of writing, however, the only concrete aspect of its reparations policy that the government has committed to is a one-time payment of R30,000 (US$3,750) to those identified by the TRC as victims of gross human rights violations.

This chapter traces the development in South Africa of the debates around reparations and the recommendations made by the TRC. It begins with the negotiations that brought about the end of apartheid rule, continues through the drafting of the TRC legislation, and examines the TRC process itself along with the recommendations for reparations made by the CRR. Up until this point in the process, the debate over reparations was largely overshadowed by the discussions around amnesty and reconciliation. When the TRC submitted its 1998 Report, however, the call for reparations grew louder and the government's apparent reluctance to deliver reparations in the form recommended by the TRC became more evident. In its final section, this chapter briefly addresses a number of unanswered questions that have evolved out of the reparations debate in South Africa.[1]

1. Reparations During the Transition from Apartheid

Reparations and the Negotiations to End Apartheid

The negotiations that eventually brought an end to both National Party (NP) rule in South Africa and the legislative framework of apartheid were a slow and painful affair. Secret negotiations between the NP and the African National Congress (ANC) began under President Botha and were concluded under President de Klerk when he announced, on February 2, 1990, the release of all political prisoners and the unbanning of antiapartheid organizations. This announcement in turn led to the beginning of formal (nonsecret) negotiations between the liberation movement and the apartheid government. These discussions took place during the first few years of the 1990s in the midst of a severe, largely state-sponsored escalation of political violence in the country.

The question of amnesties proved to be one of the most difficult hurdles in the negotiating process. A 'blanket amnesty' was considered at the South African negotiations, but was rejected by representatives of the democratic movements. The full prosecution of those who committed gross violations for human rights during apartheid, however, was not something the apartheid government was willing to accept either. In the end, a compromise of individual amnesty was concluded at the last minute.[2]

The negotiations that brought about the end of apartheid rule in South Africa are notable, though not unique, for their singular lack of attention to the question of reparations. Except for the Interim Constitution, none of the documents produced during the negotiations even mentions reparations; they are instead concerned almost exclusively with amnesty and indemnity for those on either side of the conflict.

Although some have argued that the liberation movement was in a weaker bargaining position than the apartheid government, it is not self-evident that reparations would have necessarily been left off the agenda. Throughout the 1980s and 1990s, reparations, along with amnesties, came to be seen as a key element of democratic transitions. A number of Latin American countries have, through their own truth commissions, implemented reparations programs. Many of these countries pointed to the 1948 Universal Declaration of Human Rights, which asserted that an 'effective remedy' should be provided for violations of fundamental rights. This principle has found widespread, if not unequivocal, support since then in a number of international legal conventions, covenants, and declarations, as well as in regional agreements.[3]

Despite the historical and legal precedents for including reparations as part of the bargaining process, the issue of amnesty seems to have captured the attention of those negotiating the end of apartheid rule. Reparations were discussed, but a policy on reparations was never codified. When they did consider reparations, the negotiators focused on offering the opportunity for storytelling to victims and truth telling by perpetrators. Both kinds of information were deemed vital to the rehabilitation of victims: victim narratives because they offered the chance for recognition and psychological healing, and perpetrator narratives because they offered the equally restorative chance to hear the truth of what happened.[4] Beyond the production of these narratives, however, the negotiations failed to further engage with the question of reparations after apartheid.

Reparations do appear as a concern in the Interim Constitution, but, as with the negotiations more broadly, it seems to have been more of an afterthought. The Interim Constitution's provision for amnesty reads 'amnesty *shall* be granted in respect of acts, omissions and offences associated with political objectives and committed in the course of the conflicts of the past'. The Postamble continues that Parliament *must* design the 'mechanism, criteria and procedures' for granting amnesty to individuals.[5] There are no such imperatives attached to reparations, however. Instead, the idea of reparations seems to serve more of a rhetorical function in the text. In the paragraph before the amnesty provision, it declares that the violent effects of apartheid 'can now be addressed on the basis that there is a need for understanding but not for vengeance, a need for reparations but not for retaliation, a need for ubuntu but not for victimization'.[6] This is the only mention of reparations in the Interim Constitution. Reparations are left as abstract as the notions of 'ubuntu' and 'understanding', neither of which have any legal character in the Interim Constitution.

By the time the final Constitution of the Republic of South Africa was enacted on December 10, 1996, however, direct mention of reparations had been removed altogether. Schedule 6 of the Constitution states that 'all the provisions *relating to amnesty* contained in the previous Constitution . . . are deemed to be part of the new Constitution . . . *for the purposes of* the Promotion of National Unity and Reconciliation Act, 1995 (Act 34 of 1995), as amended, *including for the purposes of its validity*'.[7]

Reparations and Civil Society in the Creation of the TRC

Reparations do, however, feature prominently (if still indeterminately) in the Promotion of National Unity and Reconciliation Act (hereafter, 'the Act' or 'the TRC Act'), the act that created the Truth and Reconciliation Commission. This act was the product of not only the negotiations mentioned above but also of a number of government and civil society initiatives and debates in 1994 and 1995 that led to the drafting of the Act.

The two most prominent forums where recommendations for an institution like the TRC were considered were two conferences held in 1994 organized by the Institute for Democracy in South Africa (IDASA) and Justice in Transition. These conferences brought local stakeholders in the transition process together with people who had experienced, and participated in, similar transitions throughout the world. Experts from Latin America and eastern and western Europe met together with representatives from South African political parties, civil society, and academic institutions to debate how best to deal with the many challenges of the transition.[8]

The discussion around reparations, however, was minimal. Several speakers briefly outlined the reparations measures undertaken by their governments. Other speakers either downplayed the question of reparations as 'not an enormously important part of the process' or argued that the 'moral reconstruction' of society was the most important kind of reparations.[9] There were a number of other venues, however, where the debate around reparations was developed in greater detail. Much of this local consultative work was coordinated by Justice in Transition.[10] The Justice Ministry relied on Justice in Transition and the other individuals and organizations it liaised with to do much of the initial consultation and drafting of the TRC legislation. Justice in Transition ran a series of workshops and conferences on the draft TRC policies as well as an informal technical committee to work on the actual legislation.[11]

Representatives from peace and conflict resolution NGOs, from various church groups and from victims' organizations all made inputs regarding the need for reparations in the final policy.[12] There has been criticism, though, about the level of civil society participation in these various fora. Some have argued:

> The establishment of the TRC was...largely a process driven by a limited number of concerned political parties, non-governmental organisations and individuals. It was not a process which was instituted through grass-roots and collective civil society ground swell and pressure.[13]

Others concur that 'very few NGOs were involved in the initial conceptualizations of the broad policy concerns around the TRC...most organizations were called upon for the individual expertise of some of their staff'.[14]

The NGO sector (if not all of civil society) did manage to make its voice heard more clearly when the draft legislation was made public and sent from Justice in Transition to the Parliamentary Portfolio Committee on Justice. This committee had to draft the final bill and it held a series of public hearings to consider comments.[15] It began its work in March 1995, entertaining 20 hours of public comment on the submissions and putting more than 100 additional hours into drafting the final legislation.[16]

The Portfolio Committee did discuss submissions on reparations, but it is unclear how widespread, sustained, and public the conversation around reparations actually was during this period. Simpson and van Zyl report in 1995 that '[t]he whole area of compensation/reparation in relation to the Truth Commission has become fairly controversial', but their perspective is largely informed by debates within the victim community itself.[17] Elsewhere, Lowell Fernandez, in 1996, argues that '[v]ery little, if anything, has been discussed in public on what form reparations will take'.[18] Several of those close to the process recount that reparations were often raised, but never dealt with intensively as a topic of discussion.[19] Reparations seem to have been promoted in principle by most actors as a just and necessary part of transition, but discussion of the details of reparations was always delayed until later in the process.

2. THE TRC ACT ITSELF

Principles and Definitions

Despite the lack of a developed public debate around reparations during the drafting of the TRC Bill, the TRC Act identified the problem of reparations and the rehabilitation of victims as one of its three major concerns. The Promotion of National Unity and Reconciliation Act of 1995 (No. 34 of 1995), which formed the TRC, created three committees within the Commission. The AC was empowered to receive and consider applications for amnesty from those who had perpetrated gross violations of human rights associated with a 'political objective'. The Act further required that applicants for amnesty make a 'full disclosure of all the relevant facts relating to [these] acts'. The CHRV was required to compile as comprehensive a picture as possible of the nature and extent of gross human rights violations during the time period under review (between March 1, 1960 and May 10, 1994). This included holding public hearings where victims would be afforded 'an opportunity to relate the violations they suffered'.[20] Finally, the CRR was to determine whether or not individual victims qualified as victims for the purposes of reparations and to make recommendations to the President for both an urgent and a final reparations policy.

The Preamble to the Act says that the TRC is to 'provide for... the taking of measures aimed at the granting of reparations to, and the rehabilitation and restoration of the human and civil dignity of, victims of violations of human rights' and also restates the Interim Constitution's text about the 'need for understanding, but not for vengeance, a need for reparations but not for retaliation'.[21] Section 3 of the Act requires the Commission to

promote national unity and reconciliation... by... establishing and making known the fate or whereabouts of victims and by restoring the human and civil dignity of such victims by granting them an opportunity to relate their own accounts of the violations of which they are the victims, and by recommending reparation measures in respect of them.[22]

The concept of the 'rehabilitation and restoration of the human and civil dignity of victims' features prominently throughout the TRC Act. Most frequently, it seems to involve the production and circulation of information about human rights violations, whether through 'making known the fate or whereabouts of victims' or by allowing victims to 'relate their own accounts of the violations'. This is the extent to which the TRC is empowered to engage with the 'restoration' of the dignity of victims. It is beyond the power of the Commission to do anything but make recommendations about what other forms of reparations might look like.

The Act defines 'reparations' as including 'any form of compensation, *ex gratia* payment, restitution, rehabilitation or recognition'.[23] The Act's definition of 'reparations' is intentionally open-ended and it was up to the CRR to make specific recommendations and definitions. The Act also makes a distinction between recommendations for a broad, longer-term reparations policy and those for an urgent interim reparations policy:

The . . . Commission shall . . . make recommendations to the President with regard to (i) the policy which should be followed or measures which should be taken with regard to the granting of reparations to victims or the taking of other measures aimed at rehabilitating and restoring the human and civil dignity of victims; (ii) measures which should be taken to grant urgent interim reparation to victims.[24]

The urgent interim reparations were intended for those victims who needed the assistance of reparations immediately. Those eligible included victims not expected to outlive the Commission as well as those who had 'urgent medical, emotional, educational, material and/or symbolic needs'.[25]

A 'victim' according to the Act was someone who had 'suffered harm in the form of physical or mental injury, emotional suffering, pecuniary loss or substantial impairment of human rights, (i) as a result of a gross violation of human rights; or (ii) as a result of an act associated with a political objective for which amnesty has been granted'. A gross violation of human rights is defined as '(a) the killing, abduction, torture or severe ill-treatment of any person; or (b) any attempt, conspiracy, incitement, instigation, command or procurement to commit [killing, abduction, torture or severe ill-treatment].'[26]

The Committee on Reparations and Rehabilitation: Form and Function

The CRR was to consist of a chairperson, a vice chairperson, and up to five other members. Committee members had to be 'suitably qualified, South African citizens and broadly representative of the South African community'.[27] The committee members were to be selected by the Commission at large.

The CRR was asked to deal with referrals from the other two committees or from the Commission itself and 'facilitate, and initiate or coordinate, the gathering of information and the receiving of evidence . . . which establish the identity of victims of such [human rights] violations'. All of the relevant information relating to these individuals was to be conveyed to the CRR which would then make a determination as to whether the individual qualified as an 'official' victim. After consulting the evidence, and in terms of the criteria set out in the Act for being found to be a victim, the CRR had to 'make recommendations . . . in an endeavor to restore the human and civil dignity of such victim'. It also had to refer these applicants to the CHRV so that the CHRV could deal with the victim's case in terms of its own powers and mandate.[28]

The main work of the CRR, besides determining who qualified as a victim for the purposes of the TRC, was to make recommendations on an urgent interim and final reparations policy. The urgent interim recommendations were to be made as soon as possible during the life of the CRR and the final reparations policy was to be included in the TRC's Final Report to the President. The CRR could consider the possibility of financial, symbolic, and community forms of reparations. It was also empowered to make recommendations regarding the 'creation of institutions conducive to a stable and fair society and the institutional, administrative and legislative measures which should be taken or introduced in order to prevent the commission of violations of human rights.'[29]

After the Submission of the TRC Recommendations

The Act requires the CRR to make its final recommendations (the CRR recommendations from 1998) to the President. The President must then consider these recommendations and make his or her own recommendations to Parliament. The joint committee of the Houses of Parliament that deals with TRC matters must consider these Presidential recommendations and formulate its own recommendations. Their recommendations are to be put before Parliament to be debated and approved in the form of a Parliamentary Resolution. The President is then required to publish the appropriate regulations to enact this resolution.

These regulations 'shall determine the basis and conditions upon which reparations shall be granted; [and] determine the authority responsible for the application of regulations'. Furthermore, these regulations 'may provide for the revision and, in appropriate cases, the discontinuance or reduction of any reparation and ... provide for any other matter which the President may deem fit to prescribe in order to ensure an efficient application of the regulations'. It was also up to the government to decide what kind of institutional framework, if any, would be put in place to implement reparations.[30]

The President's Fund

Finally, Section 42 of the Act provides for the creation of a Fund that would hold and later disburse any funds that might be made available to victims as reparations. It was not a requirement that such a Fund be created. Money not required for immediate use (i.e. through urgent interim reparations) could be invested. The Fund would contain all money appropriated to it by Parliament, donated to it by nongovernmental sources, and accruing to it from any investments. 'Officers in the Public Service designated by the Minister [of Justice]' would administer the Fund. The Fund would be subject to audit by the Auditor-General.[31]

Amnesty Clauses in the TRC Act

There are several amnesty clauses in the Act relevant to this discussion. In particular, the ones involving the immunity from criminal and civil prosecution need mention. One controversy that raged from the beginning of discussions about a truth commission involved the fact that the victims of those granted amnesty would lose the right to pursue civil claims against perpetrators. Since the South African Constitution guarantees the rights of citizens to pursue such legal remedies, many argued that any amnesty provision that made civil claims impossible was unconstitutional (see discussion of the AZAPO case below).

In the end, the TRC Act did provide for immunity from civil claims, both for perpetrators individually and for the State itself. Section 20(7)(a) declares:

No person who has been granted amnesty in respect of an act, omission or offence shall be criminally or civilly liable in respect of such an act, omission or offence and no body or organisation or the State shall be liable, and no person shall be vicariously liable, for any such act, omission or offence.

Section 20(7)(c) continues that neither the State nor any individual person or organisation can be held liable for the acts, omissions, or offences of any deceased person who *could have qualified* for amnesty.[32]

The only concession made was for those victims who had already secured a civil judgment against a perpetrator of human rights violations. However, those previously prosecuted criminally for human rights violations would, if granted amnesty, be released and have their records expunged of the conviction.

3. REPARATIONS DURING THE TRC

The AZAPO Case

Six months into the life of the TRC, the Amnesty Committee (and the whole TRC process) faced a serious legal challenge from the widows of three victims of the apartheid security forces. N. M. Biko, C. M. Mxenge, and C. Ribeiro, along with the

Azanian People's Organization (AZAPO), challenged the constitutionality of the key amnesty provision in the TRC Act. As mentioned above, Section 20(7) of the Act releases both individuals and the State from civil or criminal liability in respect of those offenses for which amnesty is granted. The claimants alleged that this provision violated Section 22 of the Constitution, which holds that '[e]very person shall have the right to have justiciable disputes settled by a court of law or, where appropriate, another independent or impartial forum'.[33] This attack on the constitutionality of the TRC Act cut to the heart of the TRC's work and, though explicitly about the amnesty provision, also had consequences for the issue of reparations.

Judge Mahomed of the Constitutional Court argued in a unanimous opinion that though the TRC Act did seem to abrogate the right to judicial recourse, other clauses in the Constitution ensured the constitutionality of the TRC Act.[34] Judge Mahomed further argued that the amnesty clause was constitutional since amnesties made it possible for the truth of human rights violations to be known and the cause of reconciliation and reconstruction to be furthered.[35] The Constitution includes reconstruction and reconciliation as protected goals of the new State and authorizes Parliament to balance the rights of victims against the broad reconstructive goals of the Constitution. The abrogation of victims' rights to civil and criminal redress was, therefore, constitutionally certified.[36]

Another issue engaged by the Court concerned the distinction between individual and State liability for civil claims. The claimants argued that even if individuals could be granted freedom from criminal and civil liability, the State was in no position to immunize itself against civil claims with respect to violations that occurred under its authority. Judge Mahomed dismissed this argument on three grounds. First, he held that the cost of subjecting the State to civil claims was prohibitive and ran against the Constitutionally protected aims of developing the social welfare of the country as a whole. He further argued that there were many more people who had suffered under apartheid than just those who could have filed a provable claim of violation against the government. Finally, he held that the pursuit of truth was a constitutionally protected mission of the State and that the withdrawal of the amnesty provision would have removed the incentive for truth telling.[37]

Judge Didcott, writing in a separate but concurring opinion, offered a different reason for immunizing the State. He argued that cost was not a relevant or appropriate concern in terms of the question of the statute's constitutionality. He continued that the presence of many people who could not file a provable claim against the government should not remove the right of those who could. And he argued that maintaining the State's civil liability would not be a barrier to truth telling by individuals, but would rather enhance the aim of truth. Nonetheless, he argued that opening the State up to a long process of civil actions that could run for many years and with great (and probably negative) publicity would not further the broad aims of reconciliation as the Constitution required.[38]

I have detailed these arguments behind the Constitutional Court decision because the case impacts in several ways on the question of reparations. Since the decision was handed down, many have argued that it provides the legal foundation for reparations for victims. Their basic argument is that by immunizing itself and those individuals responsible for human rights violations, the State has assumed the burden of responsibility to compensate those victims whose right to criminal and civil redress was denied.[39] The Legal Resources Centre has argued that 'it was only on the basis of the duty to provide reparations that the Constitutional Court upheld the validity of the amnesty provision in section 20(7) of the Act'.[40] Judge Mahomed seems to confirm this when he writes:

[T]he reparations authorised in the Act are not alien to the [amnesty] legislation contemplated by the [Postamble]. Indeed, they are perfectly consistent with, and give expression to, the extraordinarily generous and imaginative commitment of the Constitution to a philosophy which has brought unprecedented international acclaim for the people of our country.[41]

Other language in the Court's decision, however, as well as the surrounding legislation, is less clear. In fact, the questions of amnesty and reparations are not directly or explicitly linked in Mahomed's decision. His decision states:

The election of the makers of the Constitution was to permit Parliament to favor the 'reconstruction of society' involving in the process a wider concept of 'reparation', which would allow the state to take into account the competing claims on its resources but, at the same time, to have regard for the 'untold suffering' of individuals and families whose fundamental human rights had been invaded during the conflict of the past.[42]

He continued that the Postamble to the Constitution allowed 'Parliament to decide upon the ambit of the amnesty, the permissible form and extent of reparations and the procedures to be followed'. He also argued that Parliament was not required to make an 'irrational differentiation' between those who had enforceable claims against the State and those who did not.[43] That is, reparations were not necessarily the province of only those whose rights were limited by amnesties. Although his argument around reparations is decidedly noncommittal, he does imply that (a) competing needs and lack of resources are legitimate concerns in developing a reparations program; (b) Parliament is allowed wide latitude in designing a reparations package; and (c) reparations need not be limited to those specific individuals whose rights were denied by the amnesty provision but instead could be part of a broader government plan aimed at the 'reconstruction of society'. In other words, reparations to particular individuals were not part of the fundamental condition for amnesties.

Judge Didcott is more forthcoming in his opinion about the positive duty of the government to provide reparations. He writes:

Reparations are usually payable by States and there is no reason to doubt the [Postamble] envisages our own state shouldering the national responsibility for those. . . . I believe an actual commitment on the point is implicit in its terms, a commitment in principle to the assumption by the state of the burden.[44]

Didcott's opinion, though, does not carry the same weight as Mahomed's (since Didcott was its only signatory). The Center for Applied Legal Studies, along with the claimants, argued that this was not a sufficient guarantee that the government would adequately compensate the rights lost by victims. It 'merely [gave victims] an opportunity to apply for reparations'.[45] Didcott agreed that there were no 'legally enforceable rights in lieu of those lost by claimants who amnesties hit'.[46] He did assert, though, that 'machinery for determining such alternative redress' was nonetheless put in place by the TRC Act. He added that provisions for reparations could not have reasonably been part of the drafting of the Act (or the Constitution) given the circumstances of the times.

In the end, neither Didcott nor Mahomed asserts that any *particular* form of reparations must be forthcoming to those denied the rights to civil and criminal redress through amnesties. The question of reparations was not the central issue at hand in the case and reparations only appear as a kind of undefined requirement in exchange for amnesty. Didcott comes closest to assigning the responsibility for reparations to the State, but Mahomed's (majority) opinion makes clear that a reparations program could take any number of forms and need not necessarily be tied down to the specific question of the loss of rights of redress of particular individuals.

4. THE URGENT INTERIM REPARATIONS PROGRAM

Once the AZAPO case had been resolved, the CRR got down to work. Its two principal mandates were to make determinations on applications for reparations (compiling the official list of victims) and formulate recommendations on urgent and final reparations. The CRR also took on the responsibility of implementing the Urgent Interim Reparations (UIR) program, a function not originally envisioned (or provided for materially) by the TRC Act.

After the AZAPO case, one of the CRR's first tasks was to complete its recommendations for UIR. As with the final reparations package, the CRR was only empowered to recommend policy to the government. The policies for UIR were discussed from the start of the CRR's work and recommendations were sent to the government in September 1996. Regulations were only promulgated, however, in April 1998 and the first payments began in July 1998, as the TRC was winding down its work.

Final Policy and Regulations

The TRC's policy for UIR stated that beneficiaries should receive 'information about and/or referral to appropriate services' as well as 'financial assistance in order to access and/or pay for services deemed necessary to meet specifically identified urgent needs'. Those in urgent need included 'victims or their relatives and dependants who have urgent medical, emotional, educational, material and/or symbolic needs'.[47] The urgency of an applicant's needs (and thus their eligibility for UIR) was determined by the CRR according to a detailed set of criteria. Those applicants considered especially urgent included terminally ill victims, both young and old, who would not survive beyond the life of the TRC, those who had no fixed home or shelter, those who were orphaned as a result of the violation, those whose physical impairments markedly affected their social functioning, and victims requiring special education because of mental or physical disability.

The UIR payments were calculated according to need and according to the number of dependants the victim supported. An applicant with no dependants was eligible for up to R2000 (US$250). One dependant raised the maximum possible payment to R2900 (US$363). The ceiling for a victim with two dependants was R3750 (US$469), for three dependants was R4530 (US$566), for four dependants was R5205 (US$651), and for five or more dependants was R5705 (US$713).[48]

The government regulations protected the funds dispersed for UIR in several ways. The award could not be transferred or ceded by victims, could not be attached as part of a judgment of a court of law, and could not form part of the estate of the victim.[49] In these ways, it was hoped that the funds would go directly toward meeting the identified urgent needs of victims and not other financial obligations the victims might possess.

The process of delivering UIR took longer than expected and UIR payments only began in July 1998. The process the CRR had to go through included:

- identifying a list of victims who qualified under the Act;
- sorting through their applications to identify, categorize, and rank urgent needs;
- consulting with victims, civil society, and others to design a UIR policy;
- making recommendations to the government about how to meet those urgent needs;
- waiting for the government to respond with regulations;
- organizing a body to implement the final policy;

- setting up the President's Fund;
- disbursing the funds to those who qualified for urgent reparations; and
- communicating the reasons for any UIR applications that were turned down.

This process was mostly completed in April 2001, almost three years after the first payments were made. In the end, the Fund paid out approximately R44,000,000 (US$5.5 million) to approximately 14,000 victims in the form of cash payments ranging from R2000 (US$250) to R5600 (US$700).

The TRC's 1998 Report states that one problem with implementation of the program was the government's delay in promulgating the necessary regulations. This delay resulted in a second complication. Although a 'multidisciplinary implementing body' was the originally intended means for coordinating and disbursing UIR, the CRR felt there was no time to set this body up given that regulations for UIR came so late. The CRR decided that it would take responsibility for processing reparations application forms and forwarding cash payment recommendations to the President's Fund as well as referrals for appropriate services to victims.[50] This administrative function of the CRR was not envisioned by the TRC Act and placed a strain on the Committee.[51]

Outcomes

Anna Crawford-Pinnerup has completed the most in-depth analysis of the impact of UIR on victims of gross human rights violations.[52] The main complaint lodged by victims is that the process of UIR took too long to be implemented. Her research indicated that most of those who received UIR payments were 'pleased' to have received them but all agreed that the amounts involved made little material difference in their lives. Some victims interpreted the funds more as symbolic gestures of acknowledgment to victims and thus held fewer expectations about the lasting material effects of UIR payments. Others saw the UIR funds as inadequate, even on a symbolic level, and felt even more alienated from the TRC's mission of reconciliation and forgiveness. None of the victims, however, felt that reparations were 'blood money' used to buy their silence in the face of amnesties that dishonoured the dead. This has been a problem with other reparations programs.[53]

Almost all of the victims reported that many of those who did not receive UIR—because they were not considered urgent cases—'"became jealous or mad", and sometimes threatened violence'.[54] Similarly, almost all those who did receive UIR reported increases in family and community conflicts. Often those receiving UIR informed neither their neighbors nor even their immediate family members for fear of creating conflict or having the money simply taken away. Women, the elderly, and the disabled in South Africa face similar problems of conflict and abuse with monthly pension and grant money from the government.

Those who did finally receive payments tended to use the funds for 'essentials' (food, clothing, school fees), tombstones, and/or memorial celebrations for those who had died in the struggle. It is not clear how many victims who received UIR payments used the money to access or pay for the specific services recommended by the CRR. The TRC's detailed policy on UIR measures recommended providing a range of specific services to victims, but Hlengiwe Mkhize, the chairperson of the CRR, has admitted that the 'service component... didn't work'.[55]

Victims receiving UIR seemed to be divided on the issues of the adequacy of UIR, the fairness of the selection process, and the relationships between UIR payments and 'healing', 'forgiveness', and 'reconciliation'. One group of victims demonstrated a more positive feeling about the UIR process, emphasizing the symbolic nature of the program and downplaying the fact that the payments had little lasting material value. The other group focused on the inability of UIR funds to meet the tangible challenges of daily suffering. Crawford-Pinnerup's research suggests that those in greater material need or greater psychological distress tended to have higher expectations of the UIR and hoped for a more substantial material change to flow from reparations. Those who were coping financially and/or psychologically seemed, instead, to highlight the symbolic importance of UIR.

Crawford-Pinnerup argues that, in general, none of the recipients were empowered psychologically or politically by the UIR process. They did not understand the legal foundations of their access to reparations (either before or after the payments). They lacked basic knowledge about how the Commission was organized or how it functioned vis-à-vis reparations and were thus not empowered to engage fully with the TRC. And they were often completely unclear as to the next steps in the reparations process (i.e. the Act's designated process of recommendation, Cabinet and Parliamentary debate, and final implementation). They also complained about receiving little information on the perpetrators that the Amnesty Committee was dealing with. She concludes that UIR has not 'made a meaningful and substantial impact on the lives of recipients and cannot, therefore, be considered a significant or even an adequate attempt at reparations'.[56]

5. REPARATIONS AND REHABILITATION HEARINGS AND PREPARATIONS FOR FINAL RECOMMENDATIONS

The CRR had the responsibility of crafting the final reparations policy to be presented to the government. Since the government refused to discuss what it understood as 'reparations' with the CRR in terms beyond those outlined in the Act, the CRR turned to the international literature on reparations and to South Africans in general for guidance. Its original working definition of reparations was derived from common international definitions of reparations, organized in terms of the '5 R's: redress, restitution, rehabilitation, restoration of dignity and reassurance of non-recurrence'.[57] It then began a national consultative process with individual victims, victim advocacy groups, NGOs, churches, civil society, and human rights organizations to refine and develop a policy around final reparations.

Wendy Orr, one of the CRR Commissioners, writes that the consultations with victims were the most important and the most difficult. The danger of raising expectations among victims was very real, but often unavoidable. Additionally, many victims did not understand the restricted policy role of the CRR and thought that the Committee itself would be disbursing final reparations according to the answers they gave to the CRR about their needs.[58] Although some have noted (and celebrated) the fact that victims made 'exceedingly modest requests for reparations' at TRC hearings,[59] when asked in private, most victims listed money or compensation as their first priority and need. Their second most common request was for investigations into the violations they suffered. Orr recounts that in debates over the question of financial versus symbolic reparations, victims never seemed to have difficulty asking for money (in private, at least) but nonvictims seemed much more reluctant to equate reparations with cash.[60]

The CRR also held a series of public meetings throughout the country to open up debate on the final reparations policy. These hearings were held in 1997 and 1998 as the CRR was polishing its final reparations policy and enabled a wide range of inputs from victims, NGOs, community-based organizations, academic institutions, churches, and other organs of civil society.

In the course of the consultative process, several key issues emerged. The question of the relationship between financial and symbolic reparations was a frequent point of conflict (and has since become the most enduring debate in the reparations issue). Hamber reports that the CRR was initially 'reluctant to suggest any form of financial reparation and spoke more of the need for collective and symbolic reparation'.[61] He recounts, however, how the CRR shifted its emphasis during the course of the Commission and came to integrate financial reparations as a central part of their policy recommendations.

The issue of the final list of victims identified by the CRR raised further problems. Many argued that the list should be kept 'open' so that those victims who did not go to the TRC for whatever reason would have a chance to add their names to the list of victims eligible for reparations. Others argued that the terms of the Act for defining victims were too restrictive and should be broadened. The CRR decided in the end that government was unlikely to accept an open-ended list (and thus an open-ended bill) for reparations and that it was not allowed to expand the definition of 'victim' under the Act.

Another debate centered on whether straight monetary payments or 'service packages' would be the most appropriate. Some argued that simple monetary payments were crass forms of reparations, would cost the government too much, and sustained the impossibility of translating suffering into numbers. They added that grants would not be spent 'wisely'. Others replied, though, that a package of social services geared toward each victim's needs would be too costly and difficult to administer. They added that the differences between rural and urban levels of service might make service packages unfair.[62]

The issue of the 'sustainability' of final reparations payments has animated several of the discussions around reparations. Orr describes the debate within the CRR as falling loosely along racial lines, with white members patronizingly implying that black victims could not be trusted to make good use of their money. In other forums, however, this situation was reversed. Members of the victim support group, Khumbula, argued strongly that reparations should be accompanied by training workshops in financial planning and legal protection from those who might defraud victims. This was dismissed by representatives of the Cape Town NGOs as irrelevant and patronizing. They explained that financial reparations were actually 'symbolic' and not meant to be a victim's means of support. Khumbula representatives felt this argument was dismissive of the precarious financial and legal situation of most victims.

In the end, the CRR did decide to recommend straight financial payments (in addition to the other reparations measures outlined below) called 'individual reparation grants'. The formula for calculating these grants was also debated, sometimes heatedly. Some argued that there should be a distinction between the 'severity' of violations as well as the 'present financial status' of victims. The CRR recommended making no distinctions based on severity or financial status. Severity was too difficult to quantify, they argued, and financial status required the kind of complicated and costly 'means testing' that would be too difficult to apply to the 22,000 applicants on the final list of victims.[63]

Orr argues that despite the many debates about what recommendations to make, the delays by the government, in implementing both the UIR and final reparations programs, have run the risk of undermining the goals of reparations by raising and then frustrating victims' expectations. The optimism the CRR often displayed in public meetings and to the media about the prospects for reparations did not help either. Commissioner Piet Meiring told an audience in 1997:

The R&R Committee's work is ... to start drafting proposals on reparation and rehabilitation. ... Those proposals then have to go to Government who have to adopt them and then, hopefully, at the beginning of next year [1998] ... all the proposals on reparation should have gone through the process so that the first people in line, the first victim standing in the queue, should be already receiving their reparations.[64]

The delays experienced in the UIR program and since then in the final reparations program have been, Orr argues, the most damaging aspects of the Truth Commission's work and threaten to undermine the nascent healing process the TRC may have facilitated in some of the victims. They stand in marked contrast to the 'immediate delivery' of amnesty to perpetrators.[65] In a similar vein, Yazir Henry has argued that the delays experienced in UIR payments served to disconnect the testimonial experience of the TRC from the reparations measures, reducing 'the symbolic sense of the reparation', and in the process often doing more harm than good.[66]

6. THE TRC'S 1998 AND 2003 FINAL REPORT(S)

In October 1998, the TRC handed over its 'interim' Final Report to the President. The report is an interim report because the work of the AC was still continuing when the other two committees finished their work. The recommendations of the CRR appear in Volume 5, Chapter 5 of this report. The final two volumes of the TRC Final Report appeared in March 2003. At the time of writing, neither volume was available for examination.

The Reparations and Rehabilitation Policy: Development, Rationale, and Principles

The CRR's final reparations and rehabilitation (R&R) policy stated two reasons for reparations. First, it argued that 'without adequate reparation and rehabilitation measures, there can be no healing or reconciliation'. It added that reparations were necessary to 'counterbalance amnesty'.[67] Expanding on these themes, the Commission states elsewhere that 'the granting of reparation awards to victims of gross violations of human rights adds value to the "truth-seeking" phase by

- Enabling the survivors to experience in a concrete way the state's acknowledgement of wrongs done to victims and survivors, family members, communities and the nation at large,
- Restoring the survivors' dignity,
- Affirming the values, interests, aspirations and rights advanced by those who suffered, and;
- Raising consciousness about the public's moral responsibility to participate in healing the wounded and facilitating nation-building.'[68]

The report reminds the government that these 'international instruments [laws, declarations, etc.] . . . place it under an obligation to provide victims of human rights abuse with fair and adequate compensation . . . it is not sufficient to award 'token' or nominal compensation to victims'. It continues that 'the term "compensation" implies that the award to victims should be substantial'. The report also makes the case that reparations are a moral requirement of the transition out of apartheid. The report links reparations to the moral integrity of the TRC process and reminds the government that it is 'morally obliged to carry the debts of its predecessors and is thus equally responsible for reparations'.[69]

The report also reviews the principles that guided the development of the R&R policy. It argues that the implementation of reparations should be a *development-centred* 'participatory process . . . [that] strengthens collective community development and local reconstruction and development initiatives'.[70] It continues that the broad reparations program should be *simple* and *effective, culturally appropriate,* and *community-based*. Finally, it maintains that the reparations should serve to *develop capacity* in communities and *promote healing and reconciliation*. The broad principles that guided the development of the specific R&R policy recommendations are outlined below.

The Five Components of Reparations and Rehabilitation

UIR

UIR have been discussed above and the final reparations policy simply describes the recommendations and measures put in place for this program.

Individual Reparations Grants

The Final Report reiterates the major arguments in favor of 'individual reparations grants in the form of money'. The grant is based on a 'benchmark amount of R21,700' (US$2713), the median annual household income in 1997 for a family of five in South Africa, and comprises three components. The acknowledgment of suffering component would constitute 50 percent of the grant total. The access to services and the daily living costs components would each constitute 25 percent of the remaining grant total. Those in rural areas or with large numbers of dependants would receive more. The highest possible grant per year would thus be R23,023 (US$2878) and the smallest would be R17,029 (US$2129). These grants would be paid out in six-month installments and would continue for six years. The Final Report calculates the overall expense involved to be R477,400,000 (US$59,675,000) per year or R2,864,400,000 (US$358,050,000) over six years (based on an estimate of

22,000 eligible victims). The CRR further recommended that the President's Fund, which has the responsibility of disbursing reparations payments, would work with a 'multi-disciplinary Reparation Panel to assess application forms and to advise appropriately'.[71]

Symbolic Reparations/Legal and Administrative Measures

Symbolic reparations were designed to facilitate the restoration of the dignity of victims of gross human rights violations. These reparations come in three kinds in the final reparations policy.

1. Individual interventions include:
   - issuing of death certificates;
   - exhumations, reburials, and ceremonies;
   - headstones and tombstones;
   - declarations of death;
   - expunging of criminal records; and
   - expediting outstanding legal matters related to the violations.

2. Community interventions include:
   - renaming of streets and facilities;
   - memorials and monuments; and
   - culturally appropriate ceremonies.

3. National interventions include:
   - renaming of public facilities;
   - monuments and memorials; and
   - a Day of Remembrance.[72]

Community Rehabilitation

Since UIR, individual reparations grants, and most of the symbolic reparations measures are aimed at individuals, the CRR recommended that communities also be the focus of a special type of reparations. The CRR added that these community rehabilitation measures should be integrated into the broader attempt to transform services in South Africa. Community rehabilitation includes:

- national demilitarization;
- resettlement of displaced persons and communities;
- construction of appropriate local treatment centers;
- rehabilitation of perpetrators and their families;
- support for mental health services and community-based victim support groups;
- skills training;
- specialized trauma counseling services;

- family-based therapy;
- educational reform at the national level;
- study bursaries;
- building and improvement of schools; and
- provision of housing.[73]

Institutional Reform

The CRR was also mandated to make recommendations on institutional, legislative, and administrative matters that would help to prevent the recurrence of human rights violations. The CRR recommended 'that the measures and programs outlined in the chapter on *Recommendations* [Volume 5, Chapter 8 of the 1998 Report] become part of the operational plans and ethos of a wide range of sectors in society including the judiciary, media, security forces, business, education and correctional services'.[74] This chapter of recommendations is a wide-ranging discussion of many possible avenues of reform that could be undertaken by South African government, business, and civil society in order to promote a human rights culture and prevent the kinds of violations that characterized apartheid.

Implementation Process and Responsibility

The CRR recommendations include plans for the implementation process itself. They suggest that 'a structure be developed in the President's office, with a limited secretariat and a fixed life-span, whose function will be to oversee the implementation of reparation and rehabilitation policy proposals and recommendations'.[75] The CRR outlines several broad issues it says must be taken into consideration as the government designs the implementation structure:

- Implementation must take place at national, provincial, and local levels.
- The national implementing body should be located in the office of the State President or Deputy President. The body should not be allocated to one particular ministry, as its functions will require access to the resources, infrastructure, and services of a number of ministries.
- The national body should be headed by a National Director of Reparation and Rehabilitation, who will be advised by a panel or board of trustees, composed of appropriately qualified members from relevant ministries and human rights organizations.[76]

The national body would perform the following functions:

- implementing and administering any financial reparations policy;

- maintaining regular contact with relevant ministries, to ensure appropriate service provision;
- establishing provincial reparations desks;
- facilitating the formation of partnerships with NGOs, the private sector, faith communities, and other appropriate groupings, in order to meet victims' needs;
- promoting fund raising and communication strategies;
- monitoring, evaluating, and documenting the national implementation of reparations and rehabilitation; and
- reporting to the Inter-Ministerial Committee.[77]

The provincial reparations desk would

- ensure that reparations recipients are linked to appropriate service providers;
- monitor dispersal of financial reparations and provide suitable financial counseling to recipients;
- take particular responsibility for community reparations and symbolic reparations at a local level;
- monitor, evaluate, and document implementation of reparations at a provincial level; and
- report to the National Director of Reparation and Rehabilitation.[78]

Economic and Budgetary Analysis of the Recommendations on Reparations

Since the government has, so far, not released any specific details of its final reparations policy recommendations beyond the one-time payment of R30,000 to each victim, there are not many concrete ways to analyze the fiscal and budgetary ramifications of a full reparations program. With the exception of the urgent interim reparations (mostly already paid out) and final individual reparations grants, the TRC's recommendations on reparations do not give much guidance either about how it understood the potential economic burden of its recommendations. Most of its recommendations comprise simple lists of possible reparative measures. No indication is given about priority. Few suggestions are provided about how long such programs might run and who might be eligible for them. There are no recommendations, outside of the financial grants, about how much money should be put into, for example, skills training, trauma counseling, or housing.

Assuming the government does not embark on a massive symbolic, community, and institutional reparations program and generously fund each of the many kinds of possible reparations listed by the TRC in these areas, it would seem that even at the reduced level of R30,000 per victim, the individual reparations grants would comprise the majority of probable expenditure on the reparations program, followed most likely by the administrative costs. At R30,000 per victim, total expenditure directly to victims would amount to approximately R660,000,000 (US$82,500,000).

Administration costs for the grants and for the rest of the reparations program would be significant but are harder to estimate. Speculating about the possible costs of the symbolic, community, and institutional reparations programs becomes futile without specific details from the government on concrete reparations plans in these areas. Many of the community reparations could conceivably involve little more than the prioritization of victim needs within already existing social services. Symbolic reparations, unless they involved separate and significant expenditures in the form of large memorials or museums, would also presumably fold into the ongoing work of local community councils and government departments like the South African Heritage Resources Agency. The recommendations for institutional reparations are so vague that their costs are likely to be difficult to estimate even if a detailed plan were in hand.

Since individual reparations grants would be the costliest component of any reparations program, it might be useful to contextualize the recommended expenditure on these grants in terms of the broader budgetary and economic profile in South Africa. At R30,000 per grant, the total expenditure for all victims would be R660,000,000. In Table 5.1, adapted from Hamber and Rasmussen,[79] but updated with current figures, this total expenditure is compared to various economic indicators and budgetary items.[80]

Table 5.1 Total expenditure compared to various economic indicators and budgetary items

Indicator or budget item	Amount (R)	R660,000,000 as a percentage of item
Gross domestic product	990,000,000,000	0.067
Total government expenditure	262,289,759,000	0.25
Defense	16,052,950,000	4.1
Education	8,117,060,000	8.1
Health	6,706,368,000	9.8
Arms Procurement Bill	5,400,000,000	12.2
Housing	3,711,275,000	17.8
Social development	2,334,847,000	28.2
National Parliament	423,669,000	155.8

At present, the individual financial grants would comprise 0.067 percent of the gross domestic product (GDP) or 0.25 percent of total government expenditure. Grants would cost the equivalent of 4.1 percent of the annual defense budget, 8.1 percent of the education budget, 9.8 percent of the health budget, 17.8 percent of the housing budget or 28.2 percent of the yearly welfare budget. Reparations would cost roughly 50 percent more than the annual cost of running Parliament.

The money for the proposed R30,000 grants has already been set aside in the President's Fund. However, the TRC included in its report several alternative schemes for financing reparations as well, including:

- a wealth tax;
- a one-off levy on corporate and private income;
- each company listed on the Johannesburg Stock Exchange to make a one-off donation of 1 percent of its market capitalization;
- a retrospective surcharge on corporate profits extending back to a date to be suggested;
- responsibility for the payment of the previous government's debt to be critically considered;
- a surcharge on 'golden handshakes' given to senior public servants since 1990; and
- the suspension of all taxes on land and other material donations to formerly disadvantaged communities.[81]

These ideas were offered not only as ways to finance reparations but also as part of broader macroeconomic policies that would support reconstruction and development.[82] Extra ideas have emerged for funding reparations and reconstruction more generally, including:

- reallocation of resources from the budget of the defense force;
- donations of individuals, international aid organizations, and the business sector;
- asking the European Union to divert unspent funds earmarked for development projects into the President's Fund;
- pressuring Swiss (or other) governments and banks for contributions;
- restructuring GEAR social spending limits,[83] the tax system, and the Government Employees Pension Fund in order to release more money for social spending; and
- cancellation of foreign debt.[84]

Jubilee South Africa has also pointed out that the multinational corporations that helped to finance the apartheid government in its final, most repressive years removed roughly R3 billion (US$375,000,000) a year between 1985 and 1993 from the country. Jubilee argues that if 1.5 percent of these profits was returned each year for six years, financial reparations at the level of the original TRC recommendations could be paid.[85]

The government has already ruled out a wealth tax. Given that it already has the money for the individual grants, it is unlikely to require much more money for the rest of the reparations program. These financial grants, however, seem unlikely to impact substantially on the lives of victims. Roughly half of the South African population lives in 'abject poverty',[86] and it has been suggested that for reparations to have any 'appreciable impact', they must match the average household income in South Africa and be continually adjusted for inflation.[87] The proposed one-time R30,000 grants do not come close to providing this level of support.

7. REPARATIONS AFTER THE TRC—THE 'FIGHT FOR REPARATIONS'

Victims' reactions to the 1998 CRR recommendations were documented in several places. The Centre for the Study of Violence and Reconciliation found support for the proposed amounts of financial reparations among victims it interviewed. Early meetings of the Ex-Political Prisoners Group in Cape Town revealed a slightly more ambivalent attitude. From the beginning, it has insisted that a one-off payment of a token amount of money would not be acceptable and the recent announcement has confirmed its fears that the TRC recommendations would be trimmed back.[88]

With the conclusion of most of the TRC's work in 1998, it fell on civil society to pursue and monitor the implementation of the TRC's recommendations.[89] A number of organizations and individuals responded to this call to take up the fight for reparations in the subsequent years. The lack of meaningful integration of the NGO and victim advocacy sectors into the work of the TRC, however, meant that much of this lobbying was uncoordinated and fitful in the beginning. As the years passed, though, and as the government was increasingly perceived to be ignoring the plight of 'victims of the TRC',[90] a core group of victim advocacy organizations and the NGOs that they (sometimes) worked with emerged.

One commentator, who participated in the TRC as both victim and perpetrator, captured the feelings of most victims, NGOs, and observers when he wrote that the government's response to the reparations issue 'has been confusing, inadequate and disconcerting'.[91] This is perhaps a mild indication of the growing discontent with, and alienation from, government over the lack of forward movement in the reparations process. Some have argued that the dismissive attitude toward some victims (labeling them 'opportunists' and 'unrepresentative') was part of the government's perspective even during the hearings.[92]

Indeed, the government's input on reparations has generally been offhanded and inconsistent. No sustained or meaningful conversation has taken place between government and representatives of victims or civil society. Although the difficulties around funding and administering reparations have been prominent in government communications, probably the most frequently repeated reason for the delay in taking the reparations process further was that the TRC had not finished its work until its final two volumes were handed over in 2003. The Department of Justice and the Presidency argued that the TRC was not officially and legally 'over' until this Final Report was submitted. They contended that they were not in the position to do anything on the question of reparations until the report was received.

Despite the government's reliance on this line of reasoning, the debate between the government and civil society has been less over whether any *final decisions* should or could be made before the TRC finished and more over the question of the *process* involved. More specifically, advocates for victims claimed that (*a*) it was possible to begin debating the content of a final policy without reaching a final policy recommendation; and (*b*) civil society in general, and victims in particular, must be part of these debates and negotiations.

Early communications from the government seemed to imply that there might be room for this kind of consultation at some point in the process (either before or after the TRC completely finished). Justice Minister Maduna and others, however, emphasized several times that they were under no obligation to consult with victims at any point in the process.[93] A columnist in the *Sunday Independent* recently summarized what many victims have often expressed about these various arguments concerning procedure, legal obligation, and government privilege: 'By stealth, a new technical language of procedures and prerogatives emerges to explain why policies cannot be implemented. Procedural fundamentalism takes precedence over moral reflection.'[94]

Part of the difficulty in understanding the deeper reasons and motivations behind the government's (frequently haphazard) position on reparations is that it has failed to engage victims, NGOs, and other groups in the kind of ongoing dialogue that might better illuminate their perspective. Government and civil society interactions have generally taken the form of an offhanded 'call and response' where government officials make a brief comment on one aspect of reparations, civil society responds with its counterarguments and pleas for consultation, and the government remains silent. The next round only begins when some other government official makes another, usually unrelated, comment and the cycle begins anew.

In general, the range of the government's objections to reparations, especially to individual reparations, seems to be congruent with a broader, emerging neoliberal model of government. Under this model, the government is expected to reduce social spending and provide incentives for individual initiative, economic or otherwise. The government may have an ideological objection to what some could consider a 'handout'. They may want to fold reparations into the government's broader, and more community- and structure-oriented, poverty alleviation programs, a basket of programs that it is already under market pressure to reduce.

The embrace of neoliberal modes of governance has also entailed a heightened proceduralism in the State. Officials often explain, in exasperation, that they are only trying to be transparent and accountable in their adherence to the forms of procedure that they contend are delaying the reparations process. They argue that there is only one possible legal and bureaucratic route that reparations policy development can take, and they are powerless (and indeed completely averse) to speeding it up.

Many victims and organs of civil society believe that the privatizing and bureaucratizing tendencies of the state reflects a 'betrayal' of victims. Arguments that government officials 'don't care about victims' almost certainly overstate (and oversimplify) their case, but they do point to a growing feeling that the ruling elite in the government is increasingly out of touch with the concerns of 'ordinary' South Africans, especially the poor. The leadership of the ANC has always been fairly distant from its constituency in terms of class position and levels of education. Its time in government seems to have revealed this gap more openly and more painfully.

Whether the government's apparent reluctance to commit to reparations reflects (*a*) reasonable concerns about the perils of social welfare and the importance of bureaucratic rationality and transparency *and/or* (*b*) a marginalization of social and economic justice in favor of elite interests ultimately depends on one's particular political and economic perspective. The many questions in the reparations fight over the affordability and individual focus of reparations, the representativeness and comprehensiveness of the victim list, and the question of consultation are answered differently by different sides. Few elements of the arguments for and against reparations seem wildly unreasonable. Reparations *are* affordable but the cost is certainly not inconsequential. The victim list is incomplete but perhaps not absurdly so. Individual reparations grants do privilege individuals over communities, but this is just a continuation of the logic of the TRC. However, whatever the government's motivations (if indeed there is a coherent set of motivations), one thing seems clear: the lack of dialogue between the government and advocates for reparations has meant that the nature and reasonableness of the government's motivations have remained unexamined and beyond the scope of meaningful debate.

Since dialogue seemed unlikely to produce the desired results, victims turned to legal activism in their case against the government. The question of a legal challenge to the government had been discussed for several years. The victim community was sanguine about the potential (and the appeal) of legal action, but in general lacked knowledge about what form legal options might take and certainly lacked resources to pursue these options. With the help of local legal aid organizations, however, one victim support group, Khulumani Western Cape, filed suit under the terms of the Access to Information Act for access to the government's draft policy on reparations. Khulumani has recently been considering another possible avenue of legal action on reparations of a different sort through its connection with Jubilee South Africa, a network of organizations devoted to debt relief and reparations for developing and postcolonial countries.

8. Discussion

The marginal role played by reparations in the negotiated end of apartheid and the subsequent controversy over the implementation of final reparations raise a number of broader issues about reparations in South Africa. These issues include the insufficient legal guarantees for reparations in South Africa, the difficulty in defining the full scope of what reparations mean and who should be involved, and the political and social causes and consequences of the fight for reparations. These subjects are addressed in the following sections.

Legal Ambiguity Around Reparations

The place of reparations in South African statutory and constitutional law is ambiguous at best. The Interim Constitution only suggested that there was a 'need for reparations' as part of South Africa's transition, but it mandated the implementation of an amnesty process. The provisions concerning the required amnesty and the need for reparations were included in the Final Constitution, but only insofar as these provisions related to, and legitimated, the TRC Act. As the Legal Resources Centre (LRC) has pointed out, there is therefore 'no free-floating constitutional right to reparation outside of the terms of the [TRC] Act'.[95]

The TRC Act itself allows the TRC to develop a wide-ranging conceptualization of reparations but limits the Truth Commission to making recommendations to the government. It allows that reparations can mean any number of things, but once the TRC makes its recommendations, it is up to the government to decide on a final definition and program. It seems that the government would not be allowed to dismiss the question of reparations altogether, but the final form and content is up to the government.[96]

The AZAPO case has been cited by many who argue that it provides a constitutional requirement for reparations. While this seems true in its broadest sense, the Court left it up to the government as to who would qualify for reparations and in what form. Judge Mahomed in his majority opinion made it clear that those specific individuals who lost the right to pursue civil damages because of amnesties are not necessarily the same individuals who could or should qualify for reparations. His opinion also contains no suggestion that by granting amnesty, the State takes on the responsibility of granting reparations in the equivalent amount that civil damage claims might have secured. Therefore, the burden assumed by the State is neither an equivalent burden (in terms of monetary compensation) nor does it necessarily apply to the specific individuals whose rights were abrogated.

International law has been another avenue victim advocates have pursued in mounting their demands for reparations. It is true that there are many legal instruments of international law that require states that commit, sponsor, or allow gross violations of human rights to provide significant and 'effective remedies'. For the victims of human rights abuses in South Africa, however, two interrelated difficulties emerge. First, while the South African Constitution recognizes and affirms the commitments the South African State engages in by signing treaties, declarations, conventions, and other instruments of international law, it makes clear that the South African State is empowered to override any of these obligations either through the Constitution or through individual Acts of Parliament.[97]

This raises the second issue of how to hold states accountable for their obligations under international law. In particular, how can *individual citizens* hold their states accountable to international law? Most international laws only recognize states, and not individuals, as possible claimants and there are few international agreements that provide individuals with access to tribunals, courts, or other mechanisms of accountability. Outside of the terms of the United States Alien Claims Tort Act or the conditions of the recently created International Criminal Court, there are few if any ways for individuals in South Africa to force their government to honor its international obligations.

None of this is offered as a way of undermining the potential legal avenues and arguments that victims of apartheid have pursued. There are several lines of argument victims could follow in their attempts to force a speedier conclusion to the reparations process, but success in these applications is not likely, at this point at least. What I seek to highlight here is the ambiguous and inadequate attention paid to the legal character of reparations in South Africa. The right to amnesty was firmly defined and secured in both Constitutions, the TRC Act and the AZAPO case opinion (as well as a series of indemnity acts before the transition). Reparations, however, have never enjoyed the same legal security or clarity of definition as amnesty.

Opening Up the Debate: Defining Reparations in the Broader Context

The debate around reparations has taken on a narrow and inflexible character in recent years. In spite of the TRC's thoughtful and comprehensive recommendations on reparations and despite the protests of victims, civil society, academics, and others that reparations have always been about more than money, the fight for reparations has consistently been reduced to the problem of individual grants. The question of reparations, however, radiates into many domains of social, political, and economic life.

The most commonly rehearsed debates around reparations involve the meanings of and relationships amongst individual, symbolic, community, and institutional forms of reparations. Less discussed, or perhaps more difficult, are the relationships between the kinds of reparations outlined in the TRC's report and other postconflict reconstruction and development programs that have a reparative component or potential. These include land restitution, special pensions, poverty alleviation, affirmative action, and heritage resources management.

The fight for reparations has also had the unfortunate consequence of sidelining the responsibility of other role players besides the government. The complicity of foreign corporations and governments in supporting the apartheid regime has only recently entered the discussion. Jubilee South Africa has consistently looked abroad for debt relief and reparations, but its campaign and the local campaign for reparations from the South African government have never been meaningfully integrated. Despite the TRC's fairly strongly worded condemnation of business's role in apartheid, the culpability of domestic business has also not been seriously considered. Business either ignores the question or makes absurd offers to 'manage' the disbursement of reparations funds.

The problem of incorporating 'beneficiaries' into the transition process has plagued the TRC at all stages of its work and continues to be another of the unanswered questions in the debate over reparations. There have been various calls for a 'wealth tax' or a 'reparations tax' but they have gone unelaborated. The recent Declaration of Commitment by white South Africans (the so-called 'white apology') has highlighted the roles and responsibilities of the beneficiaries of apartheid. Some have argued, however, that this declaration has been more about making sure white South Africans feel included in the transition process and less about their positive duties to contribute to reparations and reconstruction.[98]

The *Realpolitik* of Reparations: Victim/State Politics Since the Report

As the fight for reparations has grown more rancorous, the terms of the debate have narrowed and made it increasingly difficult to discuss at any length the broader dimensions of reparations. A key irony of the whole quarrel has been that most of the concerns raised by the government around reparations are fully endorsed by victims. The TRC was too limited both in its mandate and in its life span, and many victims were left out. Reparations should contribute to the broader program of social and economic development. Those individuals and organizations that benefited from apartheid should be part of the reparations process. No victim joined the struggle against apartheid for monetary gain.

So why has the conversation been reduced to the question of individual financial grants? In fact, it does not seem that the provisions of financial reparations are as much the real issue as is the reluctance of the government to provide them. That is, by implying that it was not prepared to offer financial reparations (and by insulting those victims who later demanded them), the government ended up making the disbursement of financial reparations the key moral indicator of its commitment to victims.

Some observers have argued that this was an important political mistake on the part of the government. They argue that if the government had simply included victims in the process from the beginning or implemented a limited but speedy and efficient reparations program right after the TRC's 1998 report, it could have avoided the stand-off it currently finds itself in. Instead, it has chosen to retreat from consultation with victims and civil society and has treated critics of its approach with contempt.

Victims complain that this reflects a broader transformation in state political practice that dismisses dissent as 'antitransformation' and highlights the 'procedures and prerogatives' of an increasingly unapproachable and unaccountable bureaucratic State. Whether or not this is true, the degeneration of the reparations debate does indicate a failure of the political process to address the need for reparations among victims of apartheid. The recourse to legal activism highlights the inability of the government to craft a political solution to the problem (though it does reveal the potential strength of legal and judicial guarantees of rights).

Reparations and the Sustainability of Victim Activism

Just as the government has failed to engage with the difficulties of reparations in a creative (or at least politically clever) way, victims' organizations and civil society have had difficulty developing a rich and sustainable political program in their fight for reparations. None of the groups involved has developed detailed proposals on how it envisions a just and adequate reparations program. Even the recent legal actions against the government center on narrow legal and procedural issues of access to information.

One could blame the government for not releasing the documents earlier and therefore making alternative policy development impossible. This may be part of the problem, but the focus on individual reparations grants has nonetheless made it difficult for victim groups to think more broadly, both in terms of the reparations issue and in terms of the more general concerns and needs of victims. The fight for reparations has consumed too much of the attention and resources of victims' organizations. Members of one victim support group in the Western Cape have said that they fear the day reparations are paid out because (*a*) they are not sure where the group would find its broader purpose and motivation after reparations; and (*b*) most of the members would not qualify for reparations and would be left dissatisfied with, and unaided by, the whole process.

This perspective may overstate this particular group's reliance on the reparations fight for its purpose and energy, but it is not without merit. Victims and the organizations they create exist in a precarious social, economic, and political position. The reparations fight has given great energy to these groups, bringing them together around a common cause and identifying a common enemy against whom they can unite. It has also garnered a great (if still inadequate) amount of attention from media, civil society, and even those outside of South Africa who have come to support their cause. The bigger and more long-term challenges of these organizations, however, lie in much less dramatic and newsworthy work—in economic empowerment projects, in ensuring access to social services like health and education, and in providing the kinds of local, daily support to victims they will need over the next few decades. Reparations may be part of the solution to these problems, but they are only one part.

Reparations, Reconciliation, and Theodicies of Suffering and Responsibility

The problems faced by government and by victims and civil society in finding a solution to reparations do not simply involve questions of adequate financing, effective social services, or political maturity. Reparations also play a key role in the process of reconciliation. The ways particular reparations programs are designed and implemented reflect particular theodicies, or theories of suffering, justice, and responsibility. They can play a very specific and important role in the moral and political negotiations and transactions that take place after conflict. Likewise, disagreements over the form and meaning of reparations can reflect divisions over the meaning of reconciliation and can even disrupt the process of reconciling for those involved.

Not only does the conflict over financial reparations threaten to upset emerging processes and meanings of reconciliation but it also threatens to reduce the problem of reparations to one of exchange, and thereby also limit the notion of reconciliation. Just as reconciliation is usually a long and difficult process, many have argued that reparations should also be regarded as a multidimensional process, unfolding and changing over time, rather than a narrow set of exchanges concluded at the supposed end of a transition process.[99]

Victims have frequently raised the objection that both the TRC and the government have been much more interested in placating perpetrators than in meeting the needs of victims. In this context, reparations have come to mean much more than a means of support or a kind of recognition of suffering. They have become the unfulfilled answer to the question of whether or not justice has been done in the transition process. This may be too much pressure to put on the limited question of reparations when there are so many other pressing concerns that the postapartheid government must engage with. Nonetheless, in the minds of most victims and the NGOs that support them, reparations have come to occupy a central, if not the central, role in their theories of suffering, justice, and responsibility. Accordingly, what kind of answer the government provides in the form of reparations will, for victims at least, affect the bigger process of reconciliation as much as it serves to meet the material needs of victims.

9. AFTERWORD

In late 2002, while waiting for a final government reparations policy, a number of individual victims and victim support groups—in collaboration with other civil society organizations and lawyers from South Africa, Germany, and the USA—filed lawsuits in a US federal court against a range of multinational corporations that had done business with the South African government during apartheid. These 'apartheid lawsuits' were all filed under the Alien Tort Claims Act (ATCA). ATCA is a federal law from 1789 that allows foreign citizens to bring lawsuits for damages in US courts against individuals and institutions with a 'presence' in the USA, regardless of where the violations occurred. The two major apartheid suits filed under ATCA were *Ntzebeza et al. v. Citigroup et al.* and *Khulumani et al. v. Barclays et al.* Although the two suits share a number of defendants (including Citigroup,

Credit Suisse, Ford, and GM) as well as legal arguments, there are also significant differences between them. The Ntzebeza suit is a class action suit filed on behalf of a wide range of black South Africans born between 1948 and 1994 who were killed, tortured, or imprisoned and seeks damages from a number of US-based corporations for doing business with the apartheid government. It argues that their business involvement helped to perpetuate apartheid and asks for restitution, compensatory and punitive damages, and the establishment of a 'humanitarian trust' fund. In contrast, the Khulumani suit focuses on individual plaintiffs and defendants, and on specific acts by corporations that Khulumani alleges contributed to specific violations of human rights, and asks for compensatory and punitive damages from these corporations.

Because of their similarities, the federal court decided to coordinate (though not consolidate) the suits. In November 2003, the corporations presented a defense in a pretrial hearing on a motion for dismissal and argued that (*a*) the issues at stake were political, not legal; (*b*) the alleged actions did not fall under the purview of ATCA; and (*c*) the time limits for considering violations had lapsed. The South African government also took the unusual step of sending a letter to the US court protesting the lawsuits. It argued that the suits undermined South African sovereignty, that they interfered with the existing processes of reconciliation, and that they made foreign investors nervous. A year later, the judge hearing the cases, Judge John Sprizzo, dismissed the lawsuits, ruling that there was insufficient evidence of wrongdoing and that profiting from apartheid, while perhaps a moral problem, did not constitute a legal problem. In April 2005, Khulumani filed an appeal with the Second Circuit Court of Appeals in New York.

In April 2003, while the lawsuits were in an early stage of development, the South African government announced that it had decided to provide victims a one-off payment of R30,000 (approx. US$4,000 at the time) as reparations for the gross violations of human rights they had suffered during apartheid. While rejecting calls (from Desmond Tutu and others) for a 'wealth tax' to supplement reparations funding from the government, President Mbeki said that 'community reparations and assistance through opportunities and services' would be made available with the remaining funds in the President's Fund. He also agreed to the TRC's suggestion for renewed attention to memorials and the changing of place names, and said that a National Day of Prayer and Traditional Sacrifice would be instituted. Few details, however, for any of these programs beyond individual reparations payouts were (or have since been) made available. The government has also said it would work further with the business sector to encourage corporations to voluntarily contribute to the reparations effort, though the Business Trust insisted on calling this work 'nation-building'.

Reparations payouts began in November 2003. After some initial delays, the majority of payments were made over the next four months. A year later, however, about 10 percent of victims had still not been paid due to problems finding them or obtaining correct bank account information. The overall cost to the government of this final reparations plan was R571.5 million, roughly one-fifth of the TRC's original recommended reparations payment of R2.9 billion. Information on how victims spent their reparations and on the impact of these payouts is still being developed.

Notes

1. Information for this chapter came from academic articles and reports, newspaper clippings, primary documents (legislation, budgets, the TRC Report, government speeches, etc.), correspondence and minutes from relevant meetings, and interviews done with various role players.
2. Alex Boraine, Janet Levy, and Ronel Scheffer, eds., *Dealing with the Past: Truth and Reconciliation in South Africa* (Cape Town: Institute for Democracy in South Africa, 1994), 140; Graeme Simpson and Paul van Zyl, 'South Africa's Truth and Reconciliation Commission', *Temps Moderne* 585(1995): 394, 398.
3. Lowell Fernandez, 'Possibilities and Limitations of Reparations for the Victims of Human Rights Violations in South Africa', in *Confronting Past Injustices: Approaches to Amnesty, Punishment, Reparations and Restitution in South Africa and Germany,* Medard Rwelamira and Gerhard Werle, eds. (Durban: Butterworths, 1996), 65–78.
4. Simpson and van Zyl, op. cit.
5. South African Interim Constitution, Postamble, emphasis added.
6. Ibid.
7. South African Constitution, sch. 6, para. 22, emphasis added. This clause was inserted to ensure the constitutionality of the amnesty provisions in the 1995 TRC Act. Judge Mahomed of the Constitutional Court later ruled that the entire Postamble (not just those sentences strictly dealing with amnesty) should be considered to be part of the new Constitution. *Judgment in Case CCT 17/96*, Constitutional Court of South Africa (1996), para. 48. The Legal Resources Centre (LRC) has pointed out, however, that since the Postamble was included only for the purposes of the TRC Act, 'there can, accordingly, be no free floating constitutional right to reparations outside of the terms of the [TRC] Act'. Gilbert Marcus and Matthew Chaskalson, 'Amnesty, Pardons and Reparations Memorandum' (Johannesburg: LRC, 2002), para. 16.
8. Boraine et al., op. cit.; Alex Boraine and Janet Levy, *The Healing of a Nation?*, eds. (Cape Town: Justice in Transition, 1995).
9. Boraine et al., op. cit., 6, 10, 55, 85; Boraine and Levy, op. cit., 39–41.
10. Hugo van der Merwe, Polly Dewhirst, and Brandon Hamber, 'Non-Governmental Organisations and the Truth and Reconciliation Commission: An Impact Assessment', *Politikon* 26(1)(1999): 55–79.
11. Ibid., 57.
12. Ibid., Thloki Mofokeng, interview by author, Johannesburg, July 19, 2002.
13. Brandon Hamber, Thloki Mofokeng, and Graeme Simpson, 'Evaluating the Role and Function of Civil Society in a Changing South Africa' (paper presented at The Role of Southern Civil Organisations in the Promotion of Peace Seminar, London, 1997), 3.

14. Merwe et al., op. cit., 58.
15. Ibid.
16. Antjie Krog, *Country of My Skull* (Johannesburg: Random House, 1998), 4, 9.
17. Simpson and van Zyl, op. cit., 8.
18. Fernandez, op. cit., 70.
19. Mofokeng, interview; Piers Pigou, interview by author, Johannesburg, July 19, 2002.
20. Promotion of National Unity and Reconciliation Act of 1995, Preamble.
21. Ibid.
22. Ibid., sec. 3(c).
23. Ibid., sec. 1(1)(xiv).
24. Ibid., sec. 4(f).
25. Truth and Reconciliation Commission, *Report of the Truth and Reconciliation Commission of South Africa* (Cape Town: TRC, 1998), vol. 5, ch. 5, para. 56.
26. Promotion of National Unity, sec. 1(1)(xix)(a), 1(1)(ix).
27. Ibid., sec. 24(3).
28. Ibid., sec. 4(b), 26(3).
29. Ibid., sec. 4(h).
30. Ibid., sec. 27(3)(a)(i–ii), 27(3)(b)(i–iv).
31. Ibid., sec. 42(3), 42(5).
32. Ibid., sec. 20(7)(a), 20(7)(c); emphasis added.
33. South African Constitution, sec. 22.
34. Ismail Mahomed, *Judgment in Case CCT 17/96*, Constitutional Court of South Africa (1996). The Postamble from the Interim Constitution (which was indirectly included in the Final Constitution) stated that 'amnesty *shall* be granted in respect of acts, omissions and offenses associated with political objectives and committed in the course of the conflicts of the past'. Interim Constitution, Postamble (emphasis added). The Postamble would thus seem to be in contradiction with the requirements of Section 22. However, elsewhere (Section 33(2)) the Constitution provides that 'save as provided for in subsection (1) *or any other provision of this Constitution*, no law, whether a rule of common law, customary law or legislation, shall limit any rights entrenched in this Chapter'. Constitution, sec. 33(2) (emphasis added). Judge Mahomed argued that the Postamble conferring amnesty is fully part of the Constitution and therefore the amnesty provisions were protected under Section 33(2). The rights under Section 22 were, therefore, legitimately limited. *Judgment*, para. 14.
35. Mahomed, op. cit., paras. 19, 21, 42–3.
36. The claimants in this case also argued that amnesty was prohibited under international law. Judge Mahomed argued that amnesty, in fact, did have a precedent in international law, but that the question of international law was irrelevant to the constitutionality of a particular South African statute. The state does have limited obligations to international law, but this was not part of the Court's jurisdiction (para. 26).
37. Ibid., paras. 42–5.
38. Ibid., paras. 55, 57, 59.
39. Mpho Leseka, 'The TRC's Recommendations on Rehabilitation and Reparation', in *From Rhetoric to Responsibility: Making Reparations to the Survivors of Past Political Violence in South Africa*, Brandon Hamber and Thloki Mofokeng, eds. (Johannesburg: Centre for the Study of Violence and Reconciliation, 2000), 2.

40. Marcus and Chaskalson, op. cit., para. 3.
41. Mahomed, op. cit., para. 48.
42. Ibid., para. 45.
43. Ibid., para. 47.
44. Ibid., para. 63.
45. D. Davis, *Written Argument of the Amicus Curiae* (Johannesburg: Centre for Applied Legal Studies, 1996), para. 8.1.
46. Mahomed, op. cit., para. 65.
47. TRC, *Report*, vol. 5, ch. 5, para. 56.
48. Ibid., para. 55.
49. Department of Justice, 'Measures to Provide Urgent Interim Reparation to Victims', in *Government Gazette, Regulation Gazette* 6154, no. 18822 (1998).
50. Wendy Orr, 'Reparations Delayed is Healing Retarded', in *Looking Back, Reaching Forward: Reflections on the Truth and Reconciliation Commission of South Africa*, Charles Villa-Vicencio and Willem Verwoerd, eds. (Cape Town: University of Cape Town Press, 2000); Yasmin Sooka, 'The Unfinished Business of the TRC', in Hamber and Mofokeng, op. cit.
51. Claire Keeton, 'Parliament Must Act on Reparations', *The Sowetan* (February 16, 1999).
52. Anna Crawford-Pinnerup, 'An Assessment of the Impact of Urgent Interim Reparations', in Hamber and Mofokeng, op. cit.
53. Brandon Hamber and Richard Wilson, 'Symbolic Closure Through Memory, Reparation and Revenge in Post-Conflict Societies' (paper presented at the Traumatic Stress in South Africa Conference, Johannesburg, 1999); Martha Minow, *Between Vengeance and Forgiveness: Facing History After Genocide and Mass Violence* (Boston: Beacon Press, 1998); Sooka, op. cit.
54. Crawford-Pinnerup, op. cit., 2.
55. Keeton, op. cit. According to Mkhize, the failure of government ministries in providing the requested targeted reparative services for victims was partly explained by the fact that 'at each occasion, the Commission had to push the [Joint Ministerial Committee in charge of implementing UIR measures], there was no impetus from them and they had to be led by us'. NGO Working Group on Reparations, 'Minutes of the TRC Workshop', March 24, 2000.
56. Crawford-Pinnerup, op. cit., 9.
57. Orr, op. cit., 240–1.
58. Ibid., 242.
59. Minow, op. cit., 105.
60. Orr, op. cit., 241–2.
61. Brandon Hamber, 'Repairing the Irreparable: Dealing with the Double-Binds of Making Reparations for Crimes of the Past', *Ethnicity and Health* 5 (2000): 221.
62. Orr, op. cit., 244–5.
63. Ibid., 245.
64. Committee on Reparations and Rehabilitation, 'Minutes of the CRR Hearings', 1998.
65. Orr, op. cit., 242–3, 247.
66. Yazir Henry, 'Where Healing Begins', in Villa-Vicencio and Verwoerd, op. cit.
67. TRC, *Report*, vol. 5, ch. 5, paras. 2, 3.

68. Ibid., vol. 5, ch. 8.
69. Ibid., vol. 5, ch. 5, paras. 11, 16, 20.
70. Ibid., vol. 5, ch. 5, para. 47.
71. Ibid., vol. 5, ch. 5, paras. 49, 65, 76.
72. Ibid., vol. 5, ch. 5, para. 78.
73. Ibid., vol. 5, ch. 5, para. 95.
74. Ibid., vol. 5, ch. 5, para. 115.
75. Ibid., vol. 5, ch. 8, para. 23.
76. Ibid., vol, 5, ch. 5, para. 116.
77. Ibid., vol, 5, ch. 5, para. 117.
78. Ibid., vol, 5, ch. 5, para. 119.
79. Brandon Hamber and Kamilla Rasmussen, 'Financing a Reparations Scheme for Victims of Political Violence', in Hamber and Mofokeng, op. cit.
80. Republic of South Africa, 'Overview: National Medium Term Expenditure Estimates' (Pretoria: Department of Treasury, 2002).
81. TRC, *Report*, vol. 5, ch. 8, para. 38.
82. Kamilla Rasmussen, 'Ten Strategies to Finance Individual Reparations', Research Report (Johannesburg: Centre for the Study of Violence and Reconciliation, 1999), 7.
83. GEAR (Growth, Employment and Redistribution) is the government's macroeconomic policy that sets limits on social spending.
84. Rasmussen, op. cit., 7–8; Shirley Gunn, 'Report on the Khulumani Reparations Indaba' (Cape Town: Khulumani Support Group, 2001), 7–9.
85. N. Gabriel, 'Time for Business to Pay Up', *The Sowetan* (June 20, 2002).
86. Ibid.
87. Fernandez, op. cit., 74.
88. Khulumani Support Group (Western Cape), 'Iphephandaba No. 1' (Cape Town: Khulumani, 1999).
89. Brandon Hamber and Steve Kibble, *From Truth to Transformation: The Truth and Reconciliation Commission in South Africa* (London: Catholic Institute for International Relations, 1999), 19.
90. Lars Buur, ' "In the Name of the Victims": The Politics of Compensation in the Work of the South African Truth and Reconciliation Commission' (unpublished paper, 2001).
91. Henry, op. cit., 172.
92. Thloki Mofokeng and Brandon Hamber, 'Contextualising Reconciliation and Reparation', in Hamber and Mofokeng, op. cit.
93. Johnny de Lange, 'Final Reparations Emanating From The Truth And Reconciliation Commission Process: Access To An Alleged Policy Document', letter to Khulumani Support Group (2002); Christelle Terreblanche, 'Apartheid Victims Go to War With Maduna', *Daily News* (March 22, 2002).
94. Xolile Mangcu, 'Alleged Minister of Health has Become Menace to Society', *Sunday Independent* (July 21, 2002).
95. Marcus and Chaskalson, op. cit., para. 16.
96. Ibid., para. 5.4.
97. Constitution, sec. 231–3.

98. A. Johnstone, 'The Politics of Apology and Acknowledgement: White Engagement with South Africa's Reconciliation Process: A Discussion Paper' (unpublished report, Johannesburg: Centre for the Study of Violence and Reconciliation, 2001).

99. Minow, op. cit.; Boraine and Levy, op. cit.

CHAPTER 6

REPARATIONS IN MALAWI

DIANA CAMMACK

INTRODUCTION

A well-designed and implemented transitional justice program can accomplish two
goals: it can bring closure to past rights abuses and the divisions and antipathy they
engendered; and it can set the stage for a new democratic dispensation where rights
are emphasized and protected. Bringing closure requires truth seeking, fair payment to victims, naming of perpetrators and their sincere contrition, while establishing a new democratic order requires justice and reestablishing the rule of law.
While several methods have been used in Malawi to come to terms with the
atrocities and abuses committed by the government of Dr H. Kamuzu Banda and
members of the Malawi Congress Party (MCP), most of these initiatives have
sought neither justice, truth, nor disclosure, but have mainly concentrated instead
on the making of small payments to victims. As such these programs have
contributed little to national reconciliation or democratic consolidation and so
both remain elusive.

Malawi was ruled for thirty years, from independence from Britain until 1994, by
Life President Banda. He retained power by using the law, especially the Public
Security Act,[1] and the so-called traditional courts to imprison political opponents

and any others thought to be disloyal. The primary instruments of State repression were the police and paramilitary forces, an extensive spy network, the Young Pioneers (MYP), and the MCP Youth League. These were used to detain, beat, humiliate, and otherwise harass anyone who was deemed disloyal. This included whole villages known to associate with opposition political figures. Dr Banda's most powerful opponents were detained, killed, or 'disappeared'—some reportedly by 'feeding them to the crocodiles' in the Shire River. Many fled with their families and set up homes in Zambia, Zimbabwe, and especially Tanzania, though some professionals ended up in South Africa, Europe, and the USA. Jehovah's Witnesses were special targets because Dr Banda labeled their refusal to participate in politics and buy MCP membership cards as sedition. After being overheard saying something critical of the government, ordinary people such as shopkeepers, factory workers, and civil servants would be picked up by the police, while anyone who (even accidentally) wrote or broadcast something deemed unfavorable was arrested. Once in prison people might be held for long periods of time in solitary confinement, tortured, kept naked and hungry, and subjected to humiliating treatment and unsanitary conditions. Some victims still suffer psychologically and physically (depression, nightmares, eye problems, headaches, injuries to joints and bones, etc). Many of those who fled or were arrested lost their personal property, houses, land, businesses, and vehicles through the Forfeiture Act.[2] In a fit of nationalism, Dr Banda ordered Asians to move into towns in the 1970s, and took their rural properties and businesses away from them. In the early 1990s political activists were detained for promoting multipartyism.

At the same time many loyalists profited from the Banda regime. Civil servants and party leaders were given estates (carved from communal land) and licenses to grow and export tobacco, bank loans and technical assistance, school fees for their children, trips and training abroad, as well as the properties 'forfeited' by those who fled or were imprisoned. Party stalwarts ran the Press companies in the interest of Dr Banda, John Tembo[3] and his niece (and Dr Banda's 'official hostess') Mama Kadzamira, and the MCP. Britain and the USA, 'pariah states' such as Israel and Taiwan, and apartheid South Africa supported his regime because Dr Banda was anticommunist and provided rear bases to reactionary elements fighting in Mozambique and because he opened full diplomatic relations with Pretoria.

During the transition to multiparty democracy in 1993–4 opponents of the regime and the MCP negotiated a settlement that allowed exiles to return home; freed political prisoners; permitted the formation of new movements and eventually political parties; initiated the production of a new Constitution; and oversaw a referendum on multipartyism, multiparty elections, and, importantly, a peaceful transfer of power. Amongst other issues, their discussions focused on ways to address the past, and how to return property to those who had forcibly 'forfeited' it and to compensate those who had been forced to flee, or were imprisoned, tortured, or otherwise abused. These debates were molded, first, by the civil and political leaders' desire to ensure the transition remained peaceful and the opposition united; and, second, by the interests of specific participants, especially the MCP representatives and those leaders of the multiparty movement, most of them in the United Democratic Front (UDF), who had been senior officials in Dr Banda's government and allegedly involved, either directly or indirectly, in past rights abuses and atrocities.[4]

To keep the transition on track, proposals that were put forth by radicals were unlikely to gain widespread support. For instance, repatriation of exiles and compensation for the imprisonment or murder of family and friends were generally acceptable, but 'excavating the past', naming names, or punishing perpetrators were less so. The UDF, instead of calling for a truth-seeking process covering the whole Banda period, focused on the 1983 Mwanza murders,[5] while the smaller party, the United Front for Multiparty Democracy (UFMD), concerned itself with repatriation and compensation. On the other hand, the more radical Alliance for Democracy (AFORD), a northern party comprising exiles and professionals, initiated 'accountability discussions' amongst the party leaders and in the constitutional drafting subcommittee. AFORD's leaders were well aware that 'the issue of accountability is hotly contested because a lot of abusers have returned to politics under the banner of [multiparty] democracy. There have been attempts [by the abusers] to downplay the role they played and to blame it all on President Banda.' The Malawi Democratic Party (whose leaders were influenced by their exile in South Africa) agreed and insisted that the truth must be told and names should be named.

Although aware that the 'presence of old-style politicians in the leadership of opposition political parties has compromised public debate about the past', AFORD was unable to hold a firm line in favor of truth seeking because it had to prove to the MCP and UDF that it did not intend to 'use the accountability issue to blackmail and marginalize them [the MCP and UDF] in a democratic Malawi'. AFORD was also afraid that it would split the opposition movement and the country along regional lines if it called for 'individual sanction' against ex-MCP politicians (most from the southern and central regions) in the opposition. In the end all it did was to ask that a record of 'what happened' be made for posterity. In other words, because 'a lot of compromises' were needed to keep the negotiations on track, the search for truth was cut short before it had begun.[6]

1. Addressing the Past

Five methods of helping victims of past abuse were utilized between 1992 and 2002: in 1992–5 awards were granted by the high court to victims of unlawful acts; the Department for Disaster Preparedness, Relief and Rehabilitation (DDPRR) provided assistance to returning exiles and others from 1993 to 1996; back wages and pensions were granted from 1995 to civil servants who had been unfairly dismissed; unspecified payments were made by the new government to prominent people soon after the transition; and the National Compensation Tribunal (NCT) was established to operate from 1995 through 2004.

A number of factors have affected the success of these various methods of addressing past abuses and atrocities. These factors include the already mentioned need for compromise during the negotiations leading to multiparty elections as well as the new ruling party's (the UDF's) need since then to establish and maintain parliamentary party alliances, the poverty of the nation and its people, the aforementioned lack of political will amongst members of government to 'excavate the past', and the weakness of civil society institutions. Only in the courts in 1992–5 was truth seeking, fair compensation, and the naming of perpetrators high on the agenda, and even then abuses committed by politicians and government officials were generally assumed to be infringements by agents of the State and so damages were paid by government, rarely by the MCP or individual abusers. Perpetrators of abuse have not been barred reentry to political office. Nor have they been named publicly, even by the NCT, which could rely on the ample testimony it has collected from victims. The weakness of civil society and its institutions (including the media) and of parliament and opposition parties—all of which is a legacy of the Banda regime but has been encouraged by the UDF leadership as well—means that since 1994 the issue of transitional justice could generally be ignored by the new government. This has been made easier by the neopatrimonial nature of Malawian society, which results in the relative powerlessness of villagers. The poverty and cynicism of ordinary people mean that they are willing to accept money rather than hold out for truth or justice from the nation's leaders.[7]

The public's ignorance of, and indifference to, claims for reparations, combined with the persistent impotence of victims, insufficient government (and donor) funding, and powerful politicians' antipathy to truth telling, have resulted in reparations programs that have attained neither fair compensation for victims nor social justice. The NCT's inefficiency and lack of funds mean that many of the claimants who have come into contact with it have left frustrated and bitter, demanding more personal consideration and respect, a more transparent and speedy process, and an honest apology and more faithful compensation. At the same time, the existence of the NCT, regardless of its shortcomings, has allowed UDF politicians to counter periodic public demands for a truth commission by asserting that the NCT is addressing the past and nothing more is needed.

2. CIVIL COURT AWARDS

Malawi's multiparty movement was part of democracy's 'third wave', which emerged in eastern Europe and sub-Saharan Africa at the end of the cold war. It was linked to the transition in South Africa, when Dr Banda lost the support of the apartheid regime and of western governments that focused increasingly on regional economic growth and stability and were willing to impose conditionality to foster democracy. In 1992–4 local churchmen led what was essentially a reformist movement promoting liberal political and economic reforms and civil rights. Radical students, trade unionists, and exiles were soon sidelined by those who took over the leadership of the movement: businessmen and civil servants, sometimes referred to as MCP Team B, who had been marginalized (including exiled, arrested, and imprisoned) in the previous three decades by MCP Team A, i.e. by Dr Banda and John Tembo. Part and parcel of Malawi's transition to multiparty democracy was a handful of high court cases filed by intrepid individuals and lawyers starting in 1992. These people sued government and sometimes the MCP or MYP for damages arising from false imprisonment and other abuses.

One of the first cases was taken by Catherine Nyondo, who had been detained for three months because her husband had made disrespectful comments about Dr Banda. She was awarded K40,000 (approx. US$10,000)[8] in general and exemplary damages. Early in 1993 a much higher award—K4.5 million (approx. US$1.1 million)—was given to Machipisa Munthali for having unjustly spent nineteen years in prison. Not surprisingly, following his case there was a 300 percent increase in the number of similar cases registered with the court.[9] In the following three years several dozen awards—most ranging from K40,000 to K120,000 (approx. US$2,700–8,000) though a few reached into the millions of kwacha—were made by the court to individuals who had been beaten by the police, MYP, or Youth Leaguers, detained and tortured in prison, shot during multiparty demonstrations, or had lost property through forfeiture. A number of these cases were not contested by the government, as it was harder for its lawyers to defend repression while the national democratic movement was strengthening and winning concessions from the regime.[10] Other cases were settled out of court probably for sums lower than might have been paid had the litigants gone to trial.[11]

These rulings influenced the longer-term reparations process and later the NCT's work in a number of ways. The judges faced difficult legal questions, but they had few local precedents upon which to base their judgments. They had no choice but to set precedents (some of which were conflicting) that were used thereafter.[12] They also established local guidelines for awarding compensation.[13] Most of the judgments delivered in these cases placed the justices at the forefront of the transition, articulating liberal principles and rights protection at a time when it was not wholly safe to do so. Their exemplary awards, which reached into millions of kwacha, were explicitly meant to halt future state-sponsored repression and violence.

During their judgments they sometimes castigated government, giving the Ministry of Justice and others little reason to believe that the courts would turn away further rights-related cases or that future awards would be lower. At the same time pressure was building from impoverished victims who found themselves unable to take their cases to court because of the high cost, and also from people whose cases were time-barred and who demanded changes in the law that would allow them to take their abuse cases to court.[14] As such, members of the civil service could see more cases and high awards coming, and wondered how government was going to pay for them.[15] In light of their concerns it is not surprising that the regulatory act governing the NCT explicitly closed off to victims the relatively expensive avenue of the high court and channeled all claims arising from abuses during the Banda years to the NCT.

3. Government Assistance to Returnees and Victims

After the Amnesty Act was passed in 1993 people began returning to Malawi from neighboring states and abroad.[16] The General Amnesty (Amendment) Act of November 1993 outlined government's obligation to help resettle and rehabilitate returnees. That and government's advertisements, which claimed that it had changed and that it wanted Malawians to come home, encouraged people to repatriate. With raised expectations exiles left schools and jobs and came back to Malawi hoping to find work, funds, and a program that would help them resettle.

The first exiles returned in the last week of June 1993 (just after the referendum on multipartyism) and they continued coming at a rate of about 100 per quarter until after the general elections in May 1994, when the rate increased to more than 300 in July–September 1994. The rate stabilized at about 200 per month (i.e. 40 adults per month plus children) by mid-1995. Then the number of registered returnees requiring assistance numbered about 5,000 (of whom 1,300 were adults).[17]

At the end of 1993, after the army forcibly disarmed the MYP in Operation Bwezani, Dr Banda established a fund to 'assist people who suffered injuries' during that campaign.[18] The office of the Commissioner for Disaster Preparedness (now known as the DDPRR) was appointed as secretariat to the fund as well as the manager of the returnee program. The fund's committee comprised representatives of the National Insurance Company, the Ministry of Labor, medical practitioners, and the Workman's Compensation fund. In the three years it existed it assisted 222 people, 191 of whom were injured, and the beneficiaries of a further 31 people, who had died during Operation Bwezani. Nearly K1 million (approx. US$66,000) was paid to this group, while a further 53 minors were assisted with long-term education grants and other awards, totaling just over K1.5 million (approx. US$33,000).[19]

Assessing the exiles' claims was a separate committee comprising returnees. Its task was to investigate whether a claimant had been a political exile rather than an economic migrant by collecting documentation (from the United Nations High Commissioner for Refugees (UNHCR) and other agencies) and interviewing returnees. Starting in January 1994[20] families were given K500 per month (approx. US$125) by the Commission and after February 1995, K1,000 per month (approx. US$66). This 'upkeep' allowance continued until the end of 1996[21] when the returnee program was closed. One special issue of concern to most adult returnees was land: 86 percent of registered returnees did not have access to farms and expected the NCT to help them gain access to plots when it began operations.[22]

In March 1995 the returnees' resentment that 'no meaningful mechanism' had been put into place to relieve their suffering and improve their condition permanently culminated in a peaceful march to the Ministry of Social Welfare and eventually the President's Sanjika Palace in Blantyre. Other efforts initiated by nongovernmental organizations (NGOs) to assist the returnees using UN support[23] came to nothing, as (the NGOs felt) there was 'no commitment in government' to assist these people because politicians and bureaucrats, few of whom had been in exile, had little understanding of the plight of returnees. On the other hand, questions were being asked by civil servants about the suitability of assisting returnees in particular, when poverty amongst all Malawians was so widespread. Ever since then some people have questioned whether claimants for reparations are any poorer, more in need, or were more victimized by the Banda regime than the mass of Malawians.

4. CIVIL SERVICE AWARDS AND GOVERNMENT GRANTS

During the Banda years many people were dismissed from the civil service with little or no reason given. After the transition these people began making demands for back wages and pensions. To regularize payments in mid-1995 the Office of the President and Cabinet (OPC) instructed ministries to reinstate from the date they were dismissed 'civil servants who suffered detention and dismissal from the service on political grounds'. Anyone over fifty-five was deemed to have retired on his fifty-fifth birthday and anyone under fifty-five was deemed to have retired on May 21, 1994 (a few days after the transitional election). Back wages and terminal benefits were calculated on that basis. Several months later employees of statutory corporations were included. Also added to the list of those receiving benefits were civil servants who had been neither detained nor dismissed, but who had been 'victimized by being retired prematurely on political grounds following Presidential directives'.[24] In recent years the Ombudsman's office has heard 'a lot of cases' brought by civil servants who have not been able for one reason or another to obtain benefits from their former ministries in accordance with these directives.[25]

Some observers are quite skeptical about these OPC instructions, arguing that they were promulgated to justify huge payments made by government directly to senior political figures. Indeed, reports of payments by government to prominent UDF members circulated in this period. In mid-1995 a senior MCP politician published a list of thirty-nine people who had, he said, been given money by government before the rules for the NCT had been laid down. He labeled these payments 'an abuse of public funds' and called on government to explain them.[26] The NCT's first chairman denies that these 'huge' payments were paid through his agency.[27] Nor, according to the then high court registrar, did the money come from or through the courts.[28] While evidence that some 'big shots' received money 'without transparency' or public explanation is lacking, many people, even those close to power, believe that soon after the UDF came to power, inordinately high awards were made without public oversight to well-connected people, directly by the Treasury or the Office of the President. This belief contributes to the frustration now expressed by NCT claimants about their delayed and much smaller awards.

5. National Compensation Tribunal

The most wide-ranging method of paying reparations to victims has been through the National Compensation Tribunal. The NCT pays compensation for wrongful imprisonment, forced exile, personal injury, and loss of property/business/employment benefits and educational opportunities during the Banda years. It was established by the 1995 Constitution (Chapter XIII) and is governed by the NCT Act and provisions.[29] The NCT began operating in 1995, has been functioning for ten years, and is chaired by a high court judge working with the aid of lawyers and accountants. Claimants may appeal their assessments and final awards to the high court. By mid-2003 some 23,600 people had registered claims with the tribunal, and over 7,000 interim awards and less than 500 final awards had been paid.

Origins

In 1993–4, while ordinary Malawians were largely unaware of the details of the political negotiations underway in Lilongwe, a subcommittee representing all political parties was charged by party bosses with drafting the new Constitution. One of its concerns was whether to create a commission of inquiry to look at past atrocities or to form a bureau to pay reparations.[30] In keeping with the decision made by party leaders explained above, members of the subcommittee opted for a compensation tribunal rather than a truth commission. Foreign technical advisers working with the subcommittee provided the subcommittee with details about international precedents for paying compensation.[31] Aiming to finalize the Constitution before the multiparty elections scheduled for May 1994,[32] the subcommittee presented its draft to the public in March. For four days politicians and representatives of civil society (traditional chiefs and leaders of NGOs) met in Blantyre to discuss the proposed Constitution, including its section on 'reconciliation of past breaches of rights, for example confiscated land'.[33] This was as close as Malawians got to holding public consultations on how to deal with its past.

A legal adviser to the subcommittee, Mordecai Msisha, told the audience that the constitutional subcommittee recommended the creation of a National Compensation Fund (NCF) supported by public monies, and a National Compensation Tribunal (NCT) chaired by a judge with a lawyer, representing the claimants' interests, and an accountant as members. The subcommittee proposed that the NCT would function for ten years, and would consider 'abuse of civil liberties and matters related to land'. He described the claims process proposed by the subcommittee: a victim would approach the tribunal and make his case, after which the

NCT would deliberate and make a determination. If matters concerned the interest of a third party, he or she would be invited to attend and would be provided with the services of a government lawyer if necessary. To address the issue of confiscated (i.e. forfeited) land, the subcommittee suggested that all titles of land up to 1964 should be recognized as valid, but that the titles of all property acquired by government after that, which were still vesting in a public authority, should not be recognized as valid. Any land that was publicly acquired since 1964 should be vested in the NCF. Thus citizens would be able to come to the NCT and present claims regarding property, and the tribunal would adjudicate those claims and determine the rightful owner. The issue of forfeiture needed to be looked into further, he said, as there had been no judicial review of decisions made by the executive at the time forfeitures were ordered.

The subcommittee also proposed that the tribunal would deal with detentions, the direct injury to victims, and the indirect injury to the families of victims. The question of compensating civil servants who lost their jobs and pensions and other rights also needed to be looked into. Another matter needing resolution was the Asians, who were expelled wholesale from parts of the country and had lost their properties. Some Malawians were also subject to forfeiture 'for no clear or clearly defensible reasons'. Other people had been subjected to 'internal deportation'. That is, people were uprooted by the MCP and told to go elsewhere (e.g. from the lower Shire valley where Dr Banda carved out a cattle ranch and from the Sucoma sugar estates).

In an effort to get beyond the proposed NCT and to open up the discussion, Msisha tried to get these leaders of civil society to consider the issue of truth and reconciliation, asking them if reconciliation is possible without full disclosure.

[At] the end of the day this topic raise[s] moral as well as legal questions. You can bury the past and call it forgiveness, you can expose the past and forgive after exposing it, or you can pretend the past never was and simply move on. Some decision will have to be taken as to the course which the delegates wish to adopt.

He was supported in this view by Vera Chirwa, Malawi's first woman lawyer and a political prisoner during the Banda years, who eloquently pleaded that a truth commission be formed, 'not a means of revenge but rather...a way of discovering the truth about what happened in the past and also of looking critically at ourselves and at our institutions, of laying those spirits, that is victims of atrocities that still haunt us, to rest'.

He went on to raise a related issue: whether immunity from prosecution should be considered to promote truth telling. And who might be considered for immunity—civil servants or political leaders? He then asked the audience to consider the difficult question of whether people should be barred access to the courts once the tribunal was established since the 'right of access to the courts is a fundamental right'. Finally, he wanted their view about the statute of limitations, explaining that the law says that claims must be presented within six years of when all the facts relating to a claim arise. He asked whether they should set a similar limitation on claims related to abuses of civil liberties and the expropriation of assets, such as land, for illegal purposes.

Unfortunately, the delegates were not up to the task and they did not answer the questions he posed. Instead the audience focused on the death penalty, and on how to get back the land that had been taken from the rural people, as much for private estates as by forfeiture, during the Banda years.

Land is a major problem, Msisha acknowledged, but other issues need further discussion before the Constitution is completed. He pleaded with the audience to reconsider the issue of 'compensation as a protocol for reconciliation'. While the country 'needs to move on' beyond the Banda era with its rights abuses and antagonisms, it is important, he said, that 'those who have questions which require answers [about what happened in the past] should have those answers as part of process of reconciliation. Otherwise we will always have a sector of our community believing that there was a cover-up, not a process of reconciliation.' The nation needs 'full exposure [of] what went wrong as a method of guaranteeing what went wrong won't happen again'. His arguments were largely ignored.

There were several members of the audience who spoke against the formation of the NCT: not only would it be too costly but its existence would also undermine the reconciliation process, as it would not be able to rectify long-standing complaints. Others countered that justice was needed to ensure reconciliation and the NCT could provide that. As such, the NCT should be written into the Constitution 'as a symbol of the new basis for life in Malawi and as a warning to others in the future who might turn to abuse power and if they do they will come under the scrutiny of the Constitution's instruments that are put in place'. Others were afraid that the NCT's activities might undermine land titles, though some people noted that there was wisdom in enumerating the NCT's rights over confiscated property in the Constitution. Others suggested that the decision to create the NCT should be postponed until the new government came to power in May 1994, though others were suspicious, stating that if the NCT was not written into the Constitution before the election, it would not be done afterwards. But its very existence was unfair to the MCP, another asserted, because that was based on a prejudgment of the old party's actions. The party would be protected though, another countered, as judgment of guilt will be a matter for the tribunal and a tribunal under a judge would ensure that justice prevailed.

There was then a vote by hands and the motion that the NCT should be included in the new Constitution 'was overwhelmingly carried by the conference'. Still dissatisfied by the limited nature of the body, the leader of the Malawi Democratic Party (MDP) urged that a Commission of Inquiry to investigate and report on atrocities be formed. His motion was seconded by a spokesman for AFORD, who added that 'reconciliation would be meaningful if we establish the truth'.[34]

Thus, in the two years before the NCT was created important decisions were made about the way Malawi would address the past and about the NCT's mandate—decisions that had long-term implications for justice and reconciliation, and ultimately for democracy. The more radical and prescient politicians could see that Malawi's future hung in the balance. At the same time other policymakers had a more narrow focus: they were more concerned with the structure and function of the NCT, how it should be funded, the amount to be paid to victims, the type of claims it should handle, how to sort out competing claims to property, and whether dissatisfied claimants might take their cases to court.

Early Concerns about the NCT

In the years immediately after the NCT was formed, debates about its structure and function continued because of its mention in the Constitution, which was not ratified until 1995, and because its early operation did not meet expectations. One local human rights lawyer summarized concerns held then, some of which were the same as before (e.g. whether the NCT should be written into the Constitution) and some of which were new. Of the latter, he said he found it a

big surprise...that the decisions of this court [the NCT] would be subject to judicial review. In other words a high court shall be reviewing the decision of a fellow high court judge sitting as a chairman of the tribunal.... It would be otherwise if the tribunal was manned by a Resident Magistrate or a Legal Practitioner [or if] cases [came] from the Tribunal to the Supreme Court of Appeal.[35]

He focused attention on issues that had only been mentioned briefly earlier, such as the question of why the tribunal did away with the question of 'individual responsibility [and] replaces it with the concept of "past government"—i.e. collective responsibility'. When he wrote this the UDF had been in power for a year, and so this observation was quite pointed. More so, when he argued that in order to deal with the problem of culpability and with abuses by the new government (which had already become apparent) he recommended 'that the tribunal should form part of the Human Rights Commission and it should be of perpetual duration'.[36]

As a trial lawyer who represented victims of abuse, he and others like him were keenly aware of what many saw as the problematic relationship between the tribunal and courts. He restated earlier worries that the

tribunal is in all practical terms inconsistent with the bill of rights in so far as it attempts to deny the people their right [of access] to the ordinary courts. This is exacerbated by the fact that up to now (a period of nine months) people who intended to sue the Government for acts committed [during the Banda years] and had not done so by the [multiparty election] cannot pursue their claims in the ordinary courts. As a result some of the claims are now [in

1995] statute-barred, which means that they are now at the mercy of the courts as to whether the statutory [time] limits will be waived or not.[37]

As it turned out, the Constitution was very clear about the NCT's jurisdiction, and since then the courts have upheld the view that the tribunal has initial jurisdiction over cases where claims against government arise from atrocities committed in the Banda years.[38] The decision to give the NCT initial[39] jurisdiction was taken because that would reduce the cost to government of settling claims in court, where high awards for exemplary damages were being paid. Some also expected that the NCT would have few claims and few awards.[40] Clearly, too, some sort of standardization of awards for various types of cases was needed and victims, many of whom were illiterate and/or had lost documentary evidence, needed access to a hearing where the standard of proof was less stringent and the procedures less rigorous than in a court of law. The tribunal was also preferred because it would be less expensive for claimants, many of whom were unable to afford lawyers and full-blown court proceedings. Moreover, the tribunal could waive the statute of limitations for everyone and it could pay compensation to claimants quickly. Some policymakers also believed that it could overlook some issues of law—e.g. whether the government ought to be paying compensation for actions committed by individual members of the MCP, the Youth League, and the MYP. For perpetrators especially, it was relevant that abusers were less likely to be publicly named in the NCT than in court.

Ruling party (UDF) politicians had other concerns as well. These emerged in mid-1995 during the parliamentary debate on the NCT Act. Their discussion initially focused on how to pay claimants, but quickly turned to individual culpability.[41] In an eloquent speech about truth and transparency the UDF Minister of Information (who had been imprisoned by Dr Banda) argued that perpetrators of past abuse ought to be held accountable. The way to do that, he said, is to hold the MCP and its individual members responsible and for them 'to pay... compensation [rather than it being paid] just [by] the [new] Government'. Other MPs concurred: '[T]he party is guilty. That party, the Malawi Congress Party, has got assets. . . . The contribution must not be left to the [new] Government. . . . They have assets. Their leaders are still alive, they must be brought before the book.'

In its defense the MCP's parliamentary members argued that when the nation moved from a single to a multiparty system, all of Malawi's new political parties inherited MCP leaders as well as the MCP's obligations. Indeed, one stated that some old MCP members 'have changed their colours' and now belonged to other parties.[42] Because President Muluzi was one of these, as was his vice president and a number of cabinet ministers, the UDF MPs dropped the question of individual politicians bearing responsibility and thereafter in the debate highlighted the guilt and financial responsibility of the MCP as a party. One AFORD MP, also searching for a way to make MCP members responsible for compensation payments, pointed to the Press companies Press Bakeries and Press Transport, suggesting that those who benefited from confiscated riches should pay the old regime's victims. A UDF MP agreed: some MCP members were living in confiscated houses, which ought to be given back. Another added that the MCP supposedly had K2 billion (approx. US$130 million) stashed away somewhere, which should 'come back' to pay compensation. In the end, the NCT Bill passed and the government remained responsible for compensation payments. Within months the UDF government divested the MCP of Press Corporation,[43] a move that impoverished the old party and that made any further discussion about the MCP paying reparations to victims a moot point. In 1997 the second NCT chairman approached President Muluzi and asked that Press Trust funds be given to the NCT to do its work and pay compensation. Although the President told him he favored the idea and encouraged him to write to the trustees directly, no support was forthcoming from the Trust.[44]

Operations

The NCT is an autonomous body within the judiciary. It is chaired on a part-time basis by a high court judge, who continues to work within the court system, assisted by professional and administrative staff. There are frequently a number of staff vacancies, largely due to funding problems. There are no investigators on staff and the tribunal relies upon the victims, who approached the police, prison authorities, refugee agencies, and other officials for documentation, to prove their claims.

The NCT began operations on August 1, 1995 and paid its first claimant in June 1996.[45] In 2001 it made a public request for all victims to file their claims before December 31, 2001, but after that date there were a large number of new claims filed and so it has continued to open case files. It announced in June 2003 that it has stopped receiving new claims and will close operations in May 2004.[46] As the NCT office is located in Limbe in the southern region, it is harder and more expensive for people from the north especially to visit the tribunal. Therefore, when claimants come for their assessments, the NCT tries to ensure that they receive their interim payments right away—the following day generally—to avoid further costs to the beneficiaries.

Funding

The NCT is reliant upon government money. Donor funding has been used for equipment, training, outreach, and a few special events such as workshops to sort out payment guidelines. Agencies have also supplied technical advisers.[47] The NCT has requested funds from donors to help pay compensation to victims, but this the donors have refused to do because they reportedly feel that such payments are the responsibility of a successor government: if donors went around paying compensation it would not encourage governments to maintain clean human rights records. Moreover, the current government ought to recognize that something wrong was done in the past.[48]

The establishment of the tribunal was delayed by the slow passage of the NCT Miscellaneous Provisions bill, which finally passed during the March–April 1996 session of parliament. Financing of the NCT's payments also depended on Constitutional Amendment Bill 2 and when it was delayed, the NCT had to find another way to pay awards. Instead of quantifying the claims and making final settlements, which the tribunal had no legal power to do, it decided to make 'interim payments' starting in June 1996. Within four months it had paid nearly 500 claimants interim payments totaling over K8 million (approx. US$500,000)[49] and in the next couple of years, significant funds went into interim reparations payments. This was not to last, though, and funding problems have plagued the tribunal since the late 1990s. As a result the agency has been understaffed and inefficient, unable to take special trips or to hold workshops without donor grants, and most importantly, unable to make final awards to those claimants who have already been assessed and given interim payments.

Virtually all informants feel that government 'is not serious' about compensating victims or it would find the funds to run the tribunal and make payments. If government can buy three dozen Mercedes Benz, run forty ministries, and pay for foreign trips for the President and for dozens of advisers, government can afford to support the NCT and pay compensation to claimants. If it can borrow money to support the work of line ministries, it can do the same to pay compensation.[50] Another potential source of funds, as yet untapped, is the property to which NCT has rights—property that was wrongfully seized by government during the Banda years and still in government hands.[51] Why it is not being exploited baffles some observers. Others have suggested that government sell bonds to raise money for the NCT.

That these fund-raising efforts are not pursued is proof to many beneficiaries that the current administration lacks the political will to make amends. The stories (true or not) that prominent people received large awards soon after the transition, paid either by the OPC or the Treasury, and later by the NCT, support such an interpretation of events: once the politicians were given their money, government no longer cared about compensating victims, and so the NCT and ordinary claimants have been starved of funds. Recently the funding situation has gone from bad to worse; in the midst of a government budget crisis in mid-2002, the NCT chairman said he had received no funds at all from the Treasury.[52]

Eligibility

Those eligible to claim for compensation are Malawians of any age who, between July 6, 1964 and May 17, 1994 (the period of Banda's rule), were subjected to wrongful imprisonment,[53] forced exile, personal injury, lost property or business, lost educational opportunities, and/or employment benefits. Also eligible are persons who were born in exile or detention. Victims of Operation Bwezani may also claim compensation from the NCT. There is no age limit and estates can benefit from claims made on behalf of deceased persons. Anyone who has made claims before the high court or whose claims were settled or dismissed there, is ineligible to claim compensation from the NCT. On the other hand, with the NCT's permission, people have been known to divide their claims between the court and the NCT, with for instance, claims for compensation for imprisonment being dealt with by the tribunal while claims for personal injury are filed in the high court.

There was some question early on about whether those who were tried by the traditional courts or otherwise imprisoned legally under valid laws such as the Public Security Act were eligible for assistance. In 1996 the Law Commissioner argued that such people were not eligible[54] but this view did not prevail. The chairman of the NCT wrote instead:

[T]hose laws or trials that did not conform to the minimum standards of the bill of rights in the 1964 Constitution, did not pass to be lawful. For example, some people that were jailed for belonging to [the] Jehovah's Witnesses, [which was declared] ... [an] unlawful society, do receive compensation ... [from the] NCT.

They are paid, he said, because 'both the law and the trial upon which the victims were tried offended the bill of rights, which was completely ignored during one party dictatorship'.[55]

The NCT decided that two groups of former prisoners were ineligible for compensation. First, there were those who were falsely imprisoned for crimes. Specifically, being arrested and held for a crime such as theft or murder and later released for lack of evidence was not the same as being imprisoned for, say, expressing political views or championing reform. Second, 'criminals' were denied compensation by the NCT, which ruled that senior party and government officials, police, and others in the Banda government, who had ill-treated people and abused their positions, but were later arrested themselves, were ineligible for payments. These people, the NCT said, who make claims for the ill-treatment they subsequently suffered at the hands of Banda's officials, 'have forgotten that their suffering was due as wages for their sin of causing untold suffering to many innocent Malawians'. In other words, a person 'who seeks equity [i.e. justice] must come with clean hands', i.e. they must not be a perpetrator of any human rights abuse.

Outreach

On several occasions the NCT has made an effort to reach potential claimants to explain their rights and the tribunal's procedures. For instance, NCT staff visited Nkhotakota and Malindi on the lakeshore (December 2001), Mchinji on the border with Zambia (January 2002), as well as Zimbabwe (December 2001) where a number of people (especially Jehovah's Witnesses) still live in exile. In mid-2002 staff of the NCT hoped to visit London, where a number of exiled Asians and Malawians still live.[56] To inform the wider public about the NCT and its functions, the second chairman of the tribunal produced weekly columns for *The Nation*, in which he explained how people could make claims, what the NCT's mandate and goals are, etc. These articles have since been reproduced as single-page pamphlets, each covering a different topic, and distributed.[57]

The NCT is required by law to produce monthly reports for the government *Gazette* that include the total number of claims received, the number of claims and the awards made in each category, the total amount awarded, other forms of compensation awarded, the number of claims dismissed, and other 'appropriate' information.[58] A search of the *Gazette* and its supplementary volumes for 1995–2001 failed to turn up any NCT reports of this nature. Nor was the parliamentary librarian able to put his hands on any NCT reports. According to the Constitution (S.144(7)), the Auditor-General should make an annual report to parliament on the conduct and status of the NCF.

Discussions are underway between donors and the NCT about hiring a historian to write about the NCT's work and its claimants' cases. This project would provide the tribunal with the opportunity to draw lessons about the structure, system, and methods of State-sponsored repression in Malawi, and to name names where appropriate. But there remains some ambivalence about the openness now and in the future of the tribunal's files, the claimants' hearings, and its compensation guidelines, and it is not certain that this initiative will go ahead.[59]

To date, the NCT has not publicized its findings, or the events outlined, or the perpetrators named during the claimants' hearings. It asserts that some people who approach the tribunal do not want their cases discussed publicly because some things that happened to them and their spouses are deeply personal and humiliating.[60] Others, though, would like their stories known and their abusers named publicly. Malawians are largely ignorant of the work of the tribunal, its funding problems, and its frustrations. Their ignorance deprives the NCT of potential allies in its quest for money and staff. More importantly, the end result of the NCT's silence is that the tales told by claimants at their hearings have had no instructional value for the public, and the structures and methods of State repression used in the Banda era are being replicated by the new government, sometimes by the same perpetrators, with impunity.

Procedures

According to the administrator, both the tribunal and claimants are following the principles elaborated in the 1995 Constitution and the 1997 procedures, as intended in the founding legislation.

- The NCT will establish and publish assessment guidelines and tariffs for the processing of claims.[61] Tribunal procedures should conform to the standards of proof in normal civil courts, unless the tribunal determines otherwise in the interest of justice in any particular case or class of cases. Procedures should also conform with the standards of justice set out in the Constitution and the principles of natural justice.
- After the claimant submits information about the claim, NCT provides forms to the person to facilitate their claim.
- Once the forms are received, a number is assigned to the claim and within two weeks the NCT is to notify the claimant that the case has been registered.[62] Claimants and claims may be grouped together by the NCT if they are associated (e.g. Moto villagers filed their claims together). Claims can be registered up to one year before the NCT is to cease operations.
- Cases for claimants older than sixty or in ill health may receive priority.
- The NCT is to determine claims in 'ascending order of size', dealing with the smallest claims on hand before the larger ones.
- After the claim is filed, the NCT will review it and the evidence and notify the claimant to appear after at least fourteen days' written notice. Save where the tribunal may otherwise order, an oral hearing will be heard in public.[63]
- Agents, such as lawyers, working for the claimant(s) must inform the NCT, and provide evidence, of their authority to act. The claimant has the right to terminate the arrangement with the agent at any time and must notify the tribunal by letter of the termination.
- Claims can be abandoned and reinstated (with permission of the NCT).

Evidence

- The claimant will provide evidence regarding the claim to the NCT. A list of acceptable evidence includes medical reports, detention orders, letters from the police or prison, prison discharge certificate, dismissal letters from a school or employer, refugee identity card, a letter from UNHCR or the Ministry of Relief and Rehabilitation, blue books for vehicles, documents proving property ownership, letters from witnesses (e.g. religious ministers, other refugees, ambassadors), letters from churches such as the Watch Tower Society, photos, newspaper articles, etc.[64] At the same time, the NCT has all powers of investigation necessary to establish the facts of any case before it.[65] Witnesses and experts may also be summoned to provide evidence.

Property restitution

- In restitution of property cases, the new property holder will be notified and informed of his or her rights. The new property holder should submit information about the property and his or her claims to it to the NCT.
- Where a third party disputes a claim and has an interest in money or property that is the subject of a claim, he or she will be given adequate notification and will be entitled to legal representation and legal assistance.
- Once all of the evidence has been reviewed and all other outstanding matters are resolved, the claim will be determined and within a week, the NCT will notify the claimant of its determination.

Awards

- The NCT can make interim awards that do not exceed the total value of the claim. Lump sum payments should be made as expeditiously as possible. The NCT can also order a nonmonetary award, such as restitution of property.
- Payments to minors may be made through the District Commissioners' offices.
- If a claimant dies, the award is payable to his or her estate.

Appeal

- The claimant can file, within twenty-one days of receiving notification of an award, a request for a review of the amount or type of award by the tribunal. The tribunal can amend its previous decisions.

Administration

- NCT records are to be kept so that periodic reporting is possible and transparency of the fund is assured.
- The NCT is to publish in the *Gazette* a monthly progress report covering the total number of claims received and awarded by category, the total amount awarded, other forms of compensation awarded, the number of claims dismissed, and other information that the NCT considers appropriate.[66]

Payments

Before these procedures were adopted in 1997, the method of collecting, assessing, and paying claims was less well defined, and prominent people could more easily obtain compensation regardless of their file registration numbers, which were supposed to be followed in order to pay the earliest claimants first. Also in those years some prominent claimants were paid large sums of money, much more than the interim payments now made.[67] Also, at times, politicians encouraged the NCT to advance their friends' claims or to pay their friends' full awards immediately. This type of interference was unwelcome and was reported by the chairman to the President. (Now only in emergencies or in 'exceptional circumstances'—where people are aged or infirm—are cases advanced and dealt with out of numerical order.)[68] Criminal behavior amongst staff at the NCT has been reported periodically (e.g. kickbacks demanded from, and payments made to, staff to ensure that 'lost' files are found or that claims are paid, or false claims paid knowingly by staff to impostors). There is no reason to doubt the current chairman when he states that whenever such misdeeds have been discovered, they have been halted. Members of the tribunal complain that a number of people have approached the NCT and told lies, for example, about how they received their injuries (in prison, not 'during a beer party'). There has also been evidence of collusion between individuals making false claims separately. Such cases add to the staff's level of frustration and cynicism about claimants.[69]

NCT Claims and Interim Payments[70]

Supposedly it can take six months for a person to move from the stage of filing a claim to receiving an interim payment. But it can take two or more years, depending on the amount of time needed to collect evidence and complete a file, the amount of money the tribunal has been given to function and pay claims, and whether the claimant's file is 'lost' or not.[71] In the past a panel sat for an assessment, but nowadays, to get through the cases quickly (reportedly, in as little as a couple of minutes), one assessor and a clerk hear a case. The papers arising from the case are countersigned by a second assessor after reading them. A number of assessments (e.g. 100) are gathered together and then heard during a single day and if a person's claim is upheld, an interim payment in the form of a check is ready for him or her the following day (see Table 6.1). If the total award is small, a final payment (e.g., K5,000–10,000) will be made instead of an interim one.

Table 6.1 NCT claims and interim payments

Date	Claims made to NCT	Interim payments made
October 1996	4000+	496
April 1997	5096	'about one-sixth of claimants'
September 2000	13,104	4208
March 2002	19,500	6000
June 2003	23,600	7000

Generally, when interim awards are quantified and paid, final payments are not calculated. Nor are suggested amounts announced by the assessor because to tell the beneficiaries the final amount to be paid might cause arguments. Besides there is almost no money available to pay what will in theory be much larger final awards.[72] Members of the tribunal do not expect its final awards to reach the high level set by the high court in the early 1990s, for that would 'run government out of money'.[73] To date, few (less than 500) final payments have been made and many close observers, including people working with the NCT, fear that because of the NCT's funding problems, most final payments will never be made.[74]

In the early years a few significant payments were made to claimants: K1.5 million was paid to a claimant in installments between 1996 and 1998; another claimant received K200,000 in the same period; and another received K345,000 between 1997 and 2002. Other large claims have been paid in recent years (e.g. claimant no. 2624 received K685,000 in 1999–2000) but these are more rare.[75] Recently final payments have mostly been small amounts (e.g. K5,000 or US$55 in late 2002), which the NCT could pay immediately. Most final payments went to victims who are elderly or ill and cannot wait for years to receive compensation. In 2001, the Chairman quantified 150–200 final awards (starting with the lowest claim numbers first) and made submissions to Treasury for final payments, but government had not given the tribunal money to pay these claims. Quantifying final awards was thus seen to be a 'wasted exercise' and was stopped.[76]

Guidelines, which are not widely available to the public or claimants, have been established by the NCT to govern the amount to be paid. The guidelines provide the assessors with a means of determining interim and final awards, based on the suffering that claimants have endured. In this case suffering is equated with the amount of time a person spent in exile or detention rather than the treatment meted out.

Interim Payments for Imprisonment and Exile[77]

False imprisonment:

- Below 1 month   Discretionary
- Below 6 months   K10,000
- Below 12 months   K15,000
- Above 12 months   K20,000

Forced exile:

- Below 10 years   K10,000
- Below 25 years   K15,000
- Above 25 years   K20,000

The NCT pays awards to people forced into exile, but initially it refused to deal with claims from children born in exile. Now it recognizes that children born to exiled parents would have been harassed or detained had they tried to return to Malawi before 1993. Thus the tribunal has agreed to pay them compensation and some 1,500 young people had claimed compensation by mid-2002.[78]

Property Restitution and Compensation

In mid-2000 the NCT held a workshop attended by various experts to devise a set of principles governing the award of interim and final payments to people who claim compensation for loss of property,[79] private employment benefits and business, and for personal injuries.[80] Up until then most claims made on these bases had been deferred.

A set of principles for property claims was created:

- Maximum compensation for loss of property, including detention and loss of property, should be K10 million (approx. US$140,000).
- Title would not be determined by the NCT until a claim is made.
- *Nemo dat* rule should apply with modifications, i.e. purchaser with notice should not obtain title.
- Anyone making a claim must come with 'clean hands', i.e. cannot be a perpetrator of a human rights abuse.
- All claims should be registered by December 31, 2001.
- Where the NCT can trace title to property, the NCT should pass that title (restitution) 'unconditionally if there are no added improvements to the property'; if improvements by a third party are added, the value of the improvements should be assessed and the claimant should pay the third party for these improvements (in installments if necessary) before title is passed; or if the claimant is unable to pay for the improvements, the NCT will sell the property and give the claimant 20 percent of the current market value as full compensation. The balance will go to the NCF to pay compensation to the third party for the improvements. If government has an interest in the property, it should be given the second offer to buy (if the claimant cannot pay for improvements).

A set of guidelines for property claims were also laid out:

- Interim payments for houses should be

Urban	K50,000
Urban traditional	K20,000
Rural	K15,000

- Final payments for vehicles should be (depending on age, depreciation, etc.)

Saloon	K100,000
Light truck	K150,000–200,000
Truck	K350,000
Buses	K500,000

- Full compensation for livestock should be

Cattle	K10,000
Goats, sheep, pigs	K2,000
Chickens, ducks, etc.	K500

Household property values will be obtained from court assessments.

At that point the NCT adopted other recommendations as well:

- Civic education ought to focus on the fact that the tribunal cannot pay full damages, as did the high court earlier, because the country and government are poor. It can only pay symbolic awards.
- The government should acquire land that the NCT can use for restitution.
- A final date for claims should be established and legislation drafted to implement that order.
- The Ministry of Lands ought to inform the NCT about any government lands acquired through forfeiture.
- The Ministry of Education ought to consider allocating funds to returnees' children for secondary school fees.

When victims fled their homes their property was sometimes destroyed and, at other times, it was disposed of in unknown ways. Some properties were burnt by the MYP while other goods were stolen or confiscated. Oftentimes people's proof of ownership was lost when their homes were destroyed. Making matters worse, most claimants have no receipts to prove what personal property they purchased, held, or lost. 'What happened to [people's] property is the million dollar question which the tribunal has to answer,' says one source. In any event, the NCT agreed that people must demonstrate that their property was unlawfully taken away or destroyed in circumstances known to be an abuse of power.

The Banda government used the Forfeiture Act to take property from people it said had sabotaged the economy and State. In reality the Act was often used to settle political vendettas or to 'fuel political lust'.[81] Even if the forfeiture decree was lifted, people did not have an automatic right to get their property back. While the NCT has the power to deal with cases where property was placed under forfeiture, it has yet to compensate victims. First, it does not have adequate funds: claims would run into billions of kwacha now. Second, though it does not condone or encourage property grabbing, the NCT feels it must protect the interests of people who have innocently acquired forfeited property. So, thus far, interim payments have been made for property claims—to a maximum of K20,000 (approx. US$270 in mid-2002)—and a final solution has not been found.

In spite of the fact that agricultural land is in short supply in Malawi and that much of the property taken from rural victims was communally owned, the issue of the return of, or compensation for the withdrawal of rights to, communal land has not been brought to the NCT. Thus far the question of how to compensate people who lost the right to use customary land (which is allocated to families by chiefs generally) has not been raised by any claimant.[82]

Personal Injury Claims

The NCT admits that it is not 'very articulate in the area of personal injury claims'.[83] Over the years many people were beaten while in prison. Particularly in 1992, some people were shot by the police during public protests against the one-party state. Some of these victims were permanently disabled. What the NCT feels it must do is to establish a link between a political atrocity and a resultant injury. For the moment the tribunal is giving K20,000 (approx. US$270 in mid-2002) interim awards for loss of life and it hopes to get experts (such as insurance brokers) to establish clear guidelines for the assessment of injuries.[84]

'Symbolic' Awards

By mid-2002 some 19,500 people had made claims for compensation. Of the 19,500 claims filed for compensation with the NCT, 3,969 applicants filed petitions claiming false imprisonment, 4,826 filed petitions claiming forced exile, 884 filed petitions claiming they were born in exile, and 546 filed petitions claiming loss of property. New claimants have continued to arrive at the NCT office on a daily basis. According to law the NCT will function for a full ten years, after which it will stand down, and any remaining funds will be available for future reparations payments. One reason the tribunal wanted to cease registering new claims at the end of 2001 was because it hoped to finalize its list of claimants and calculate how much money it will need in order to pay final compensation. In mid-2002 estimates ran to K24 billion (approx. US$324 million).[85]

That it will be able to make full final payments appears highly unlikely given the fact that, first, less than 5 percent of final claims had been paid and only a third of claimants had received interim payments by the end of 2002; second, the government as a whole and the NCT especially is chronically short of funds; and third, there seems to be little political will to prioritize reparations payments. People in touch with the NCT, including some members of the tribunal, are skeptical about final awards ever being paid.[86]

The fact that the tribunal makes small interim awards and generally postpones final payments has given rise to debates about what the tribunal's awards are really meant to be—damages and real restitution or just a 'symbol', a token to say 'sorry'.[87] According to its own literature the original aim of the NCT was to put people into a 'state of *restitutio in integrum*, back to way it was before' they were victimized.[88] It hoped to pay exemplary damages similar to those paid by the high court. Soon, though—probably as the number of claimants grew beyond expectations—it realized this would mean a 'huge cost to government' and that idea was abandoned. Now in giving compensation 'fellow Malawians are extending their condolences. [The NCT] is not as a matter of policy a mechanism for awarding damages.... the Tribunal will not give full restoration arising from the past sufferings'. Acknowledging that some claimants are insulted by the small interim grants, the NCT explains that payments are 'mere compensation and not an award'.[89]

Nonetheless, public expectations have remained high:

[C]laimants [expect]...that the Tribunal will compensate them up to the levels of High Court award of damages for similar claims. For example, claimants peg their claim[s] to that of Machipisa Munthali who was awarded over K4 million by the High Court. There are times when you hear names of leading politicians... [whose] claims [were] settled out of court by the Attorney General... [and actually] relate to defamation or wrongful dismissal but not unlawful detention.... [The NCT has] no mathematical formula for [setting amounts]. However, general principles are there and these are guided by precedents, economic factors and general policy at any given time. At the moment...the policy is that the awards of compensation by the Tribunal shall be lower than the High Court and shall follow the tradition of condolences.[90]

In its defense the NCT notes that it is more flexible and accommodating than the courts. If the strictness of courts were to apply to the tribunal, 'most of the claims would have been dismissed for lack of evidence or lapse of time'. Moreover

it is clear in the minds of everyone that the Tribunal was established through the people's wish for extending an olive branch to those afflicted souls, political and economic development of Mother Malawi[sic]. It would be wrong to think that Malawians thought of restituting the afflicted claimant to the position they would have been but for the wrong. The Tribunal would therefore wish to appear to all claimants who were wrongfully imprisoned to bear in mind that the spirit behind the establishment of the Tribunal was to say sorry to our brothers and sisters who suffered for no fault of their own.[91]

People talking about the interim payments as 'tokens' or symbols, through which government (in the form of the NCT) says *pepani kwambiri* (very sorry), have noted that the idea of symbols resonates culturally with locals. Malawians recognize the difference between *kulipira*, which means to pay the full value of something (like reparations or compensation) as opposed to *kupupesa*, which has more of a sense of 'we identify with the trouble you have gone through [such as a death of a family member].... Sorry, this [token] is not enough, but it is as much as we can do.'

But for Malawians the *spirit* in which this token is given, more than the *amount* of the payment, determines the extent to which it contributes to the healing process. If payment of tokens or symbols (rather than full compensation or reparations) is to repair a relationship and bring about reconciliation, people need to receive their adversary's *pepani* and token payment in person and in a spirit of 'let's come together'. Culturally, because the token is now paid without this face-to-face interaction between victim and perpetrator, but rather by the NCT to the victim in a relatively impersonal manner, without any real evidence that the perpetrator is 'sorry', it just does not convey an apology or a desire to reconcile on the part of government or the perpetrator. It will not, therefore, repair the social fabric.[92]

Claimants anticipate being fully compensated for their losses and suffering, they expect their full awards to be given to them quickly, and they anticipate that in giving them their money, government (in the form of the NCT) will be open, humble, and repentant. Many are disappointed. If the government is ever going to convince the victims that their awards cannot be full compensation, but must remain symbols of the government's genuine effort to say it is sorry, transparency and sincerity on the part of the NCT are necessary. In other words, reconciliation may come without full compensation only if the government's *pepani* is felt by beneficiaries to be sincere. But that is only half of the battle won. Also undermining the NCT's hope that symbolic payments will be sufficient is the fact that the public believes that a number of prominent individuals received huge awards, not symbols, soon after the transition, some through the NCT and some directly from Treasury and/or the OPC. Some beneficiaries therefore believe that the reparations system has been perverted and that justice cannot be achieved.

One lawyer who has taken cases to the NCT said that 'most people feel good' after having gone to the NCT because someone in government has 'recognized that they were wronged' and that reparations should be paid. The tribunal's administrator would agree with this, for he said that the NCT 'restores the dignity of the human being, brings back confidence in themselves, and reconciles people with the property they have lost'. Reconciliation is achieved, he added, because people are 'reconciled with themselves' and because people at the NCT understand the pain they went through, listen to their stories, and see their scars and tears. This, and their returning to the village to tell their neighbors that government has given them a little money and that it has said *pepani* and has acknowledged its fault, helps restore their pride and reconcile them to their communities.[93]

It seems, though, that this view is not widely held by beneficiaries and other observers. Almost without exception beneficiaries are dissatisfied with the NCT.[94]

They complain that people do not know how much money they will eventually receive or when it will arrive, and they, in their ignorance, must just wait.[95] Promises of final payment or restitution of property are only a 'mirage', said one lawyer.[96] Not surprisingly the Ombudsman's office is now getting complaints about the delay in final NCT payments.[97] People also object to the fact that the NCT has not paid as much to victims as the courts did earlier. 'The basis of the compensation is biased'; some prominent people received huge awards yet ordinary people suffered the same as they did. As a result, 'people are disappointed and frustrated.'[98] And because the NCT does not pay 'aggravated damages' or exemplary awards, it does not differentiate between the treatment meted out to, and the suffering experienced by, different people.[99] Also, it is asserted that the NCT still prioritizes some claimants over others, displaying 'favoritism'. But because the assessments are done in secret it is hard to know how 'objective' the procedures are.[100] The fact that it loses claimants' files and/or it delays assessments and payments without providing good reasons to the victims has caused considerable anger. Some claimants go so far as to state that their files have been deliberately lost to 'punish' them because they openly oppose the UDF government, while others state that files are lost in order to force them to pay bribes to NCT staff.[101] Neither assertion can be substantiated.

Next, the NCT is accused of 'trivializing' claimants' pain and suffering. Claimants who approach the NCT complain that its procedures have 'bureaucratized' what are essentially very deep and personal experiences. Some blame this on the fact that the NCT has not hired people who were exiled or victimized by the Banda regime and its staff therefore lacks 'sensitivity'. Dr Kanyongolo, a claimant and lawyer, explained in detail: he had been part of a small leftist group at Chancellor College that was picked up on February 3, 1983 and was detained until mid-May 1984. He did not approach the NCT for a long time because, though 'it is a convenient way of closure' for others, he 'did not want closure on this matter'. In mid-2000, urged on by his family, he wrote to the NCT and 'there began my frustration'. He was told to collect evidence. He wrote to the police, who did not answer. He wrote again to the NCT and it reiterated his need for evidence. He complained to the Ombudsman about the police's lack of response. The Ombudsman's office set up a board of enquiry but neither the Ombudsman nor the police appeared at the hearing. Eventually he approached the prison, from which he received a letter noting the dates of his incarceration, a letter that he sent to the tribunal. He then received a date for his assessment and went to the NCT office in Limbe. This, he said, 'is exactly what I did not want to get involved in': four people met (the chairman, a clerk, Dr Kanyongolo, and his lawyer) for two minutes 'at most' and he was awarded K10,000 (approx. US$130) interim compensation. 'Fifteen months in jail was resolved in two minutes: this did not bring closure.' Money is not the issue, he explained. He would have preferred to have had a chance to explain the facts of the case. Nor did the NCT explain to him how much his final award will be, or when it will be paid. He also noted that the current Minister of Home Affairs is the man who signed his detention papers years before. It is 'not only the biggest fraud, but the final humiliation, to be lied to by the state'. Another claimant put it similarly: 'the NCT is a subtle continuation of the same treatment by the same people with different faces'.[102]

Finally, some claimants report that the NCT process and staff make them feel like supplicants rather than people claiming their due. The lectures the NCT gives to claimants ('the government is giving you this ...') are humiliating: they treat a person like a 'nuisance' not a person with a right to be compensated. Many claimants are frustrated by the process and few feel reconciled to their government as a result of going through it. 'To assume that people have forgiven is wrong, people have not been given a chance to forgive,' said one politician.[103] Nor is there evidence of healing: 'What proof is there that people are accepting the government's apology or that there is reconciliation?'[104]

6. CONCLUSION: REPARATIONS AND DEMOCRATIC CONSOLIDATION

Key to understanding Malawi's reparation process has been the nation's poverty and the political context in which the courts and ministries have functioned and in which the NCT was established and has worked. Politics and poverty have molded the tribunal's mandate and goals, operations, budget, reporting policy, structure, and personnel choices, and therefore its impact. Since 1993 the political will to open up and 'excavate' the past has been largely lacking amongst key decision-makers in the UDF, and so the NCT's mandate has been limited to paying compensation. Even when performing that limited task it has been underfunded and understaffed, which has generated frustration amongst the NCT's own workforce and certainly amongst the claimants.

Much about the payment of compensation for past atrocities remains shrouded in secrecy, but reconciliation without truth or justice is difficult to achieve. The administrator admits that 'the truth [about the past] has not quite surfaced'. Making matters worse for some beneficiaries is the fact that the perpetrators of their abuse are still in government, unnamed and unpunished. ' "Look at my [worn out] shoes," they say, "but he is chauffeur driven".'[105]

Not only are beneficiaries and the general public kept in the dark but information about reparations procedures and payments has also been concealed from policymakers, legal professionals, politicians, and donors. Who has been paid what amount and by which agency and for what abuses is not widely known. Nor do people understand the various policies and rules governing the methods of making reparations payments in the last decade, whether used by the NCT, Treasury, OPC, or DDPRR. Only the Ombudsman's office regularly publicizes its findings and awards.

As a result, rights activists are unhappy: 'What is the point of giving all these people money if we do not know what happened? What is the truth? Who caused what?'[106] The truth has still not been told or widely heard, yet 'we want to excavate the truth'.[107] 'Nobody is really looking for truth. [Instead] truth is only used to get money.'[108] The NCT has not named perpetrators publicly. 'Who are they holding responsible?' It has 'run away' from the 'details' and the past is being 'packaged as a whole' for which the government pays.[109] The end result is that the NCT has paid awards to people and in doing this it has 'given the complainant something [and] it closes them up. [It] keeps everybody quiet' that way.[110] For some victims the NCT has created more dissatisfaction, frustration, and bitterness than they felt before approaching it. It is 'more a cause of mistrust and suspicion' than of reconciliation and has not contributed to healing.[111] Secrecy continues to serve the perpetrators and those who raised no objection to Banda's method of government, including for some time, churchmen and donors.

On a national scale the reparations process has played another role. Early in the transition, awards—whether paid by the courts or by the DDPRR—released tensions around the atrocities of the past, allowed exiles to come home, negotiations to start, and the 1994 elections to proceed relatively peacefully. In a similar way the existence since the mid-1990s of the NCT has reduced public demand for truth telling and the naming of names, for it permits the argument to be made that stories about the past are being collected and compensation is paid by the tribunal—even when these payments are delayed and the testimonies remain secret—so further truth seeking is not needed. Information Minister Clement Stambuli explained not long ago that a truth commission is not necessary because Malawians need to 'forget the past without humiliating each other.... The present leadership is undertaking most measures to foster genuine reconciliation. Everyone was affected [by] the past, [and] the best would be to forget and forge ahead with a unified Malawi.'[112]

Thus by remaining silent about the past the NCT has helped push the democratic transition off course. By not publicizing its findings or the stories of claimants, by not identifying perpetrators or explaining how the state apparatus functioned to eliminate Dr Banda's opponents, the NCT has allowed perpetrators to reenter government, has permitted the retention of repressive laws and the recreation of oppressive systems. Its very existence, however flawed, makes it harder to start a truth commission, where truth and justice can be prioritized rather than token payments.

First, because the 'NCT has brought no healing...[and] it just brings anger [and]...no reconciliation', other options for addressing national divisions should be explored.[113] One lawyer suggested that since the NCT is not accessible to the most vulnerable people and its emphasis is on compensation rather than healing, reparations funds should instead be used to raise community consciousness at the local level about the structures and methods of oppression used in the past. He added that perpetrators also need healing and some method should be devised to address their problems and promote their reintegration into society.[114] In other words, a community-based program could address injuries done not just to individuals but also to the society as a whole.

Second, because the NCT 'is a closed thing and [it has] never been an open kind of process where the public knows what is happening', its findings, procedures, and payments should now be widely publicized.[115] Parliament might start by 'probing' the NCT to find out what it has done—what its findings are, what money has been paid out, and for what reason.[116] Parliament's findings should be made public. Then it might undertake to rewrite the NCT's mandate and procedures, amend the Constitution, and pass new laws to extend its life and make it fully functional. It could be funded through loans and the other, normal methods of raising government revenue, including international support, once donors understand the importance of truth telling for democratic consolidation. Its findings—about past events, perpetrators, and State structures of repression—could easily be made public through open hearings broadcast on public radio and reported in the press. At the same time, as one historian put it, truth should be told in a structured way, for memories about the past are still fresh, people have not forgotten. There can be 'no peace and reconciliation if people are taken for a ride. You need truth—and an accounting: when, where and how'. Creating a 'history project' to collect and disseminate the truth is possible.[117]

Alternatively, Malawi's Human Rights Commission might form its own truth commission. 'It is never too late, you just need a different [membership of the] Human Rights Commission. If there is a vision within the Commission it could still take up the truth commission.' Civil society should push for this, said one of its leaders,[118] but so should parliament.

Finally, since 2002, rights activists have expressed an interest in seeing abuses by officials within President Muluzi's administration held accountable too. 'The winds are blowing towards us from Zambia. It won't come as [a] surprise if our parliament will face the same test which our neighbors have been battling with,' wrote *The Weekly Chronicle* in August 2002. Since then Malawians have been directly confronted with the question of whether to lift President Muluzi's immunity from prosecution.[119] Events in nearby Zimbabwe, Zambia, and Kenya have brought home the importance of holding the posttransitional government accountable. Extending the life of a restructured NCT or creating a different agency to investigate and report on abuses from 1964 until the present could promote justice and reconciliation and help put Malawi's democratic transition back on course.

7. POSTSCRIPT[120]

Truth and reconciliation still elude the people of Malawi, for little has changed in the last two years except that the date for the closure of the NCT has passed—on May 18, 2004, two days before the national elections. Most trends identified in the above report were still evident at that time, especially the politicization of disclosure, funding problems at the NCT, complaints about its operations, rumors of large payments to the political elite, unsubstantiated accusations about past abuses committed by sitting politicians, and calls for the establishment of a truth commission that would cover the period 1964–2004.

For some time it had been expected that the new (from October 2003) NCT chairperson, Justice Jane Ansah, would try to extend the life of the tribunal beyond its mandated ten years. Her aim in doing so was not to accept new cases, but to wrap up the existing caseload. (New claims were not to be filed after July 13, 2003.)[121] When the Attorney General introduced the Constitutional amendment proposal in March 2004, he admitted that the NCT's term had to be extended because the 'number of people compensated was negligible. "Of the 25,000 registered claimants, only 600 have received full compensation while only 7,000 have been paid interim compensation. A total of 23,900 claimants are on the waiting list for payment of full compensation, while 17,500 are waiting for interim compensation."'

As it turned out, there were insufficient MPs in the Assembly to vote on the amendment and parliament rose without extending the NCT's life. When asked what this meant for the claimants, the Attorney General said: '[C]laims not yet attended to will not receive their reparations. There will be no legal mandate for the NCT to exist and administer the NCF, and the Minister of Finance will have no legal basis for allocating money to the fund.'[122] In the event that the NCT actually wraps up operations, its files and staff are likely to go to the high court, and the remaining claims will be processed at an even slower pace.[123] It is also probable that cases not addressed or only partially dealt with by the NCT will start appearing in court, though the government is no better able to pay settlements now than it was in the early 1990s.

As in the previous decade, politicians used any discussion about the NCT amendment and about the larger issue of truth telling to score political points. For instance, the Attorney General warned claimants: '[T]he only remedy [for the failure of the amendment to pass] I can see is for them to vote for the UDF/AFORD alliance. Because if we win they can rest assured the [NCT] bill would be brought back. I do not see that happening if the opposition wins, especially the MCP who opposed the bill.' On the contrary, the MCP said that while it

subscribes to the principle of the Tribunal, it had reservations with the 'selective' targeting of the period between 1964 and 1994. 'What shall we say of the period between 1994 and 2004? This [Muluzi] period has also seen atrocities. The vehicle of Gwanda Chakuamba was burnt to ashes in Chiradzulu, Chief Wimbe was beaten in Kasungu, Reverend Kalebe was beaten in Mzuzu. [Lieutenant James] Njoloma, General [Manken] Chigawa, [musician Evison] Matafale and [Kalonga] Stambuli all died mysteriously. What shall we do about them?'

Furthermore, the MCP demanded an accounting of all reparations given so far, as 'most of them have been given to supporters of the ruling party', an unsubstantiated view shared by other opposition politicians and members of the public.[124]

Funding at the NCT remained a problem throughout 2002–4 as the government continued to spend its money elsewhere. The withholding of budgetary support by major donors may have played a role in government not giving the NCT enough funds to operate, let alone to pay off claimants, but misappropriation of State funds[125] and waste were surely to blame as well. At the same time the fact that major political figures managed to get significant reparations from the State did not escape notice.[126] Before it closed, the NCT was unable to give K15,000 to all victims, as a previous chairman claimed it wanted to do, let alone pay full reparations, because it was financially impossible.[127]

Also heard after 2002 were complaints that abusers from the Banda era were still unpunished, including President Muluzi. In defense, UDF politicians again argued that 'none of the parties . . . should apportion blame on the other and claim to have suffered more than others. "All of us [including UDF members] suffered because there was one party." '

Such words were unlikely to pacify all Malawians. For instance, one wrote:

When considering the question of voting [for] Hon. John Tembo [MCP] as our next president [what] should we remember? It is very important to firstly ask, has any victim forgotten? Could they ever forget? Secondly we should ask, who wants to forget? Who benefits when all the atrocities stay silent in the past? The question, 'should we remember[?]' is usually asked by people who have a choice. For many of the people in Malawi . . . there is no choice about remembering. Many of those who have been traumatically affected by armed conflict and political oppression wake up in the night with nightmares. Every time they pass a particular street or place, they remember the dreadful event that took place there. When the calendar moves towards certain dates, anniversaries of deaths or losses, the memories come flooding back uninvited. Remembering is not an option—it is a daily torture, a voice inside the head that has no 'on/off' switch and no volume control.[128]

There is little chance that recriminations will stop or that politicization of past abuses will subside as long as no mechanism is developed to name names or publicly open up the past. Periodically a prominent Malawian will still stand up and ask that a truth commission be created. For instance, AFORD MP Frank Mwenifumbo said in March 2004, when discussing the NCT, that he would have loved to see the tribunal run 'in chorus with the truth and reconciliation commission', saying, 'money alone cannot atone for the suffering that the previous regime inflicted on the people'.[129] The closest Malawi has thus far come to exploring the past is a 'history project' funded by the European Union, which should result in a book in the near future.[130]

NOTES

The author would like to thank Cuthbert Mwale for his assistance in the preparation of this chapter.

1. Preservation of Public Security Act, No. 1 of 1960 as amended in 1965 (Laws of Malawi Cap. 14:02). This act allowed for arrests without warrants and the imprisonment of persons deemed a threat to order for up to 28 days without detention orders. The arrest of persons publishing material that was deemed prejudicial to public security or that promoted a feeling of ill will, hostility or industrial unrest was permitted as was the 'control' (house arrest) of individuals.

2. Forfeiture Act, No 1 of 1969 (Laws of Malawi, Cap. 14:06). People who were declared subversive or prejudicial to the safety or economy of the State, who were accused or convicted of stealing public funds, could have their personal and real property transferred to the State. The person had no right to appeal, and the property could be transferred to new owners.

3. A ruthless and cunning politician, John Tembo was Dr Banda's right-hand man. He held a variety of senior positions in finance, including Minister of Finance and head of the central bank.

4. For instance, Mr Bakili Muluzi, who heads the UDF and was President (1994–2004), had been a General Secretary of the MCP. Vice President Justin Malewezi was a senior civil servant in Dr Banda's government, while Aleke Banda, a UDF Vice President and a senior member of Mr Muluzi's cabinet, was head of Dr Banda's notorious Young Pioneers. At the beginning the UDF was mostly comprised of businessmen and senior civil servants.

5. Four senior MCP politicians were murdered at Mwanza and their deaths disguised as a car accident. A commission of enquiry was appointed by Mr Muluzi soon after the 1994 election, which named Dr Banda, John Tembo and others culpable, though the trial that followed could not prove their guilt on the higher standards of evidence. The death of several key witnesses in the intervening years did not help the judicial cause either.

6. The Robert F. Kennedy Memorial Center for Human Rights, *Confronting the Past: Accountability for Human Rights Violations in Malawi*, May 1994, citing Mapopa Chipeta of AFORD. Also interviews with Max Mbendera (July 4); Wiseman Chirwa (July 5); Unandi Banda and Kamlepo Kalua (July 10); and Kapote Mwakasungura (July 22, 2002). Ralph Mhone (July 1, 2002) explained that the transition in Malawi was unlike that in South Africa, where there was a complete change of government, and where new leaders replaced old ones. There the search for truth and reconciliation was part and parcel of the transition, where in Malawi that was not possible.

7. Malawi's per capita GDP is about US$160, over 80 percent of the population are subsistence farmers, one-half of Malawi's children are malnourished, and the country has high rates of unemployment, illiteracy and HIV/AIDS. For a discussion of neopatrimonialism, see Diana Cammack, *Malawi at the Threshold: Ingenuity, Resources and Conflict in a Newly Democratic State* (American Academy of Arts and Sciences, USA and University of Toronto, Project on Environment, Population and Security, 2001).

8. The value of the Malawi kwacha fell considerably between 1992 and 2002. US dollar values are given throughout the paper, based on approximate exchange rates at the time noted. Until February 1994 there were about four kwacha to the dollar, at which time the government let the exchange rate slide, and by December 1994 it had reached 15 to the dollar and by the end of 1996, 16 to the dollar. By August 1998 it was 27 to the dollar, and by July 2002, 74. It has remained fairly stable at K90 to the dollar since late 2002. For comparison sake, a driver would earn K10,000–12,000 per month in late 2002.

9. Interview with then high court registrar, Justice Dustain Mwaungulu (July 9, 2002).

10. Dr Banda was forced by donors and activists to hold a referendum in June 1993 that determined whether the country would retain the single-party state. Three-quarters of the electorate voted for multipartyism. Immediately after that, meetings began between government/MCP representatives, opposition politicians and churchmen. Their task was to guide the transitional process: to oversee the legislation of reforms by abolishing laws and amending the old Constitution, the preparation of a new Constitution, and the administration of multiparty elections (held in May 1994). A General Amnesty Act was passed in 1993, which granted reprieves to residents and exiles who had supported the formation of alternative political parties, advocated change in the form of government, and/or held banned political, religious or personal convictions. Alternative political parties were allowed, the Forfeiture Act and the Life Presidency were repealed, the ban on Jehovah's Witnesses was lifted, and the dress code was relaxed. Concerned that elements in the MYP would undermine the transition, they were forcibly disarmed by the army in December 1993 in what was known as *Operation Bwezani*.

11. Interviews with Ralph Mhone (July 1, 2002) and Justice Chimasula Phiri (July 9).

12. For instance a number of cases were denied a hearing because of the statute of limitations, though other judges ruled that cases could be heard because it would be unrealistic to think cases could be filed against the government or MCP before the 1990s.

13. Justice Mwaungulu tried to set a standard for awards: 1–6 mo false imprisonment would bring K60,000 (approximately US$15,000) while 6–12 mo would earn the plaintiff K100,000 (approximately US$25,000). Cause 1455 of 1993. Interview with Justice Mwaungulu (July 9, 2002). These are much higher than the interim awards given to people in 2002, added to the fact that the kwacha was worth in 2002 about a sixth of what it was in 1993.

14. Interview with Viva Nyimba (July 4, 2002). People were coming to the Legal Aid office, asking for assistance with cases.

15. Interviews with Anthony Kamanga (July 15); Max Mbendera (July 4); Jewel Amoah and Martin Nkuna (June 19, 2002).

16. Interviews with James Chiusiwa (July 16 and 17); Olin Mwalunbunju and Kapote Mwakasungura (July 22); and Lyson Milazi (July 17, 2002).

17. Centre for Human Rights and Rehabilitation, 'A Report on the Needs and Opportunities for Malawi Returnees' (November 1995) and interview with Olin Mwalunbunju (July 22, 2002). This survey shows that the largest number of exiles (more than 240) left in 1964–5 after the 'cabinet crisis', in 1972 when the Jehovah's Witnesses were specially targeted by government (more than 250), and in 1983 (almost 50) after the Mwanza murders. Overall, from 1964–92 the number of people leaving the country, who later requested government assistance, ranged from 8 to 20 per year. It is likely that many more exiles returned in the 1990s without registering with government, especially farm families, who just walked back across the border. As such, they were not included in this survey or on the DDPRR register.

18. OPC General Notice 114, 1993.

19. Telephone interview with James Chiusiwa of DDPRR (July 17, 2002).

20. Interview with James Chiusiwa (July 16, 2002). Centre for Human Rights and Rehabilitation, op. cit., notes 'it was not until August 1994 that they started receiving relief support from government'.

21. Interview with James Chiusiwa (July 16, 2002).

22. Interviews with Olin Mwalunbunju of CHRR (July 22) and James Chiusiwa (July 16, 2002).

23. Proposed were skills training, temporary employment for professionals, income-generating activities for vulnerable people, legal reform to allow lawyers trained outside Malawi to practice in Malawi etc. Counselling and medical treatment were provided by the Danes' International Rehabilitation Centre for Torture Victims to more than 500 people and UNICEF provided clothes to the poorest returnees. A legal aid project was also started by CHRR to assist people who approached the NCT for compensation. Centre for Human Rights and Rehabilitation, op. cit.

24. OPC Circulars 5/06/4 dated July 28, 1995 and April 2, 1996, both entitled 'Processing of Terminal Benefits for Civil Servants Dismissed on Political Grounds'.

25. Interview with the Ombudsman, Enoch Chibwana (July 11, 2002). Typically, in mid-2002 the Ombudsman directed the government to pay wages and a pension to Gomo Michongwe, who was dismissed in 1965 by Dr Banda for shaking hands in Zambia with Malawians who had fled the country after the 1964 cabinet crisis. (In the following years Michongwe escaped two assassination attempts.) After returning home he filed a claim with the NCT and received K20,000, but the tribunal was unable to help him with his terminal benefits. When the Ministry of Foreign Affairs refused to pay him, he took his case to the Ombudsman. *The Nation* (July 10, 2002).

26. *The Daily Times* (August 1, 1995) reporting Dr Ntaba's complaints. Payments allegedly ranged from those to Vice President Malewezi (K612,000) to G. Mbaluka (K40,000), and included Malawi's first woman lawyer, Vera Chirwa (K64,000), the then Minister of Information Brown Mpinganjira (K449,311), and Alfred Upindi, now Secretary to the President and Cabinet (K450,000). (The US dollar was worth approximately K15 in August 1995.) Vera Chirwa (interview, July 10, 2002) says she did not receive these funds though she received compensation later through a different channel.

27. Interview with Justice M. P. Mkandawire (July 9, 2002).

28. Interview with Justice Mwaungulu (July 9, 2002).

29. National Compensation Tribunal (Miscellaneous Provision) Act No 8 of 1995 and National Compensation Tribunal (Procedures Rules) of 1997, Notice No 59, appearing in the Government of Malawi *Gazette* (October 17, 1997).

30. Email from John Barker (July 11, 2002) and interviews with Viva Nyimba (July 4) and Unandi Banda and Kamlepo Kalua (July 10, 2002).

31. Interviews with Justice Chimasula Phiri (July 9); Garton Kamchedzera (July 5); and Edge Kanyongolo (July 16, 2002). For instance, experience of the UK Foreign Compensation Commission was made available to the subcommittee.

32. Many politicians and donors wanted the Constitution written and its provisions (e.g. its Bill of Rights) entrenched before the multiparty election, for it was assumed that after that, party politics would more easily influence its content. This has proven to be the case, for since 1994 several amendments have been initiated by the UDF government aimed at increasing party control and at undermining civil liberties.

33. National Consultative Council Verbatim Report for the Kwacha Constitutional Conference, Blantyre (March 21–24, 1994), 216ff.

34. National Consultative Council Verbatim Report for the Kwacha Constitutional Conference, Blantyre (March 21–24, 1994), 293–302.

35. In the same volume Justice Tambala also wrote about the composition of the tribunal, arguing that the legal assessor on the tribunal should not 'represent a claimant and be an assessor at the same time. That would contravene a principle of natural justice.' He also raised the issue of the standard of evidence required by the NCT and whether it ought to be the same as in a court of law. Justice Duncan G. Tambala, 'Views on the Provisional Constitution', in *Building Blocks for the Republic of Malawi Constitution 1995*, Emmillias Dokali, ed.

36. Raphael Z. M. Kasambara 'Promoting, Protecting and Enforcing Human Rights under the Constitution', in Dokali, op. cit.

37. In the end the Constitution stated that 'any statutory time limitation may be waived by the tribunal or by a court if it seems...equitable to do so'.

38. Section 138(1): 'No person shall institute proceedings against any Government in power after the commencement of this Constitution in respect of any alleged criminal or civil liability of the Government of Malawi in power before the commencement of this Constitution arising from abuse of power or office, save by application to the National Compensation Tribunal, which shall hear cases initiated by persons with sufficient interest.' Also see Cause No 1325 of 1994, *Walter Chona vs. Attorney General*, and Cause 1980 of 1994, *Estate of Flora Kapito vs. Attorney General*. Interview with Desmond Kaunda (June 17, 2002).

39. Two clauses of the Constitution—S. 138(3) and S. 142(1)—open up the possibility that first, the NCT can remit a case to the courts 'in the interest of justice' and secondly, after a determination is made by the NCT, its decision can be taken to the high court for review. One lawyer reported that such cases have begun to appear. Interview with Bazuka Mhango (July 11, 2002).

40. According to ex-chairman of the NCT Justice Chimasula Phiri, policymakers believed that some politicians would take their claims to the NCT but they did not 'expect so many commoners to come to the NCT' for compensation. Interview (July 9, 2002).

41. Malawi National Assembly, *Hansard* (May 10, 1995).

42. This point would not have been lost on observers. A year earlier, for instance, the leader of the Malawi Democratic Party noted that it 'was sad...[that some people are saying] that they [MCP] have to face the tune. If you say the Malawi Congress Party, it's just a name of a political party but there were people who were in the Malawi Congress Party, some of them are in the opposition now. They have also to come up and face what we want to build for the future. Because now they are pointing the wrong finger at the people in the Malawi Congress Party because they are now hiding in the multiparty.' National Consultative Council Verbatim Report for the Kwacha Constitutional Conference (March 21–24, 1994), 183ff.

43. Press Corporation consisted of several companies, including bahevier, fisheries, newspapers and printing presses. It was extremely powerful, dominating the economy. Nominally held in trust for the nation, it was in fact owned by Dr Banda and the MCP, and generated money for the MCP and its leadership.

44. There appears to be a sense of 'why should Press Trust pay for things done by the government?' Interview with the current NCT chairman, Justice Isaac Mtambo (July 22, 2002).

45. NCT Project Proposal to Government of Malawi/European Union Rule of Law Programme. n.d. re. proposed trip to Zimbabwe; Government of Malawi/European Development Fund, Promotion of the Rule of Law and Improvement of Justice Programme. *Annual Report 2001; Minutes of the 5th Roundtable Meeting of the Case-*

handling Institutions in Malawi (March 1, 2002) and *Minutes of the 6th Roundtable Meeting of the Case-handling Institutions in Malawi* (April 12, 2002).

46. See the Postscript for recent developments.

47. For instance, 'Report on Study Tour to South Africa's Truth and Reconciliation Commission'; Government of Malawi/European Union Development Fund, Promotion of the Rule of Law and Improvement of Justice Programme, *Annual Report 2001*, 'National Compensation Tribunal'; UNCHR, 'Report of the Barker Mission' (May 1, 1997).

48. Donors 'say they will not fund atrocities'. Interviews with lawyer to the NCT, Viva Nyimba (July 4, 2002) and with former chairman, Chimasula Phiri (July 9, 2002). Making compensation payments, they said, is meant to keep the present government from abusing rights.

49. *Understanding the Past to Safeguard the Future, Proceedings of a Conference Convened by the University of Malawi and the Robert F Kennedy Memorial Center for Human Rights* (October 18–29, 1996), 36. Interview with Justice Mkandawire (July 9, 2002), who noted that 'funding was a problem from the word go'.

50. For instance, government expenditure was K3.85 billion for the month of January 2002, while annual NCT expenditure runs around K33 million (two-thirds of which was paid to claimants). See Malawi Government, National Economic Council of Malawi, *Monthly Economic Report* (January 2002), www.malawi.gov.mw/finance/nec/erjan2002.htm.

51. Government of Malawi, *The Constitution of the Republic of Malawi*, 1995, section 209. Also see UNCHR, op. cit.

52. Interview with Justice Isaac Mtambo (July 22, 2002).

53. According to the first chairman people who were held in private detention, not prisons, would not be compensated. *Understanding the Past to Safeguard the Future, Proceedings of a Conference Convened by the University of Malawi and the Robert F Kennedy Memorial Center for Human Rights* (October 18–29, 1996), 42.

54. '...the Constitution did not envision that those cases would go before the Tribunal. ...If you open that up, you will open a completely different affair. Compensation does not come into it. What has happened is that only the cases of abuse outside the law are to be compensated by the Tribunal. Abuses committed within the law are excluded. The only exception is if people were made to leave the country under threats or circumstances of duress. Otherwise, compensation will be given purely for acts that were done unlawfully....If [a] person was detained under the Security Act, then it was a lawful detention. Compensation is only for detentions outside the law.' If people were detained under the Public Security Act but subsequent procedures were not followed, they may claim, he concluded. *Understanding the Past to Safeguard the Future, Proceedings of a Conference Convened by the University of Malawi and the Robert F Kennedy Memorial Center for Human Rights* (October 18–29, 1996), 44.

55. Viva Nyimba, NCT lawyer (email, August 3, 2002).

56. Government of Malawi/European Union Development Fund, Promotion of the Rule of Law and Improvement of Justice Programme, *Annual Report 2001*, 'Track Records: National Compensation Tribunal'; NCT Project Proposal to Government of Malawi/European Union/European Union Rule of Law Programme, n.d. re proposed trip to London; NCT Project Proposal to Government of Malawi/European Union Programme, n.d. re. proposed trip to Zimbabwe. Also interview with Jewel Amoah and Martin Nkuna (June 19, 2002).

57. *National Compensation Tribunal,* set of articles provided by ex-chairman of the NCT Justice Chimasula Phiri (July 9, 2002), and pamphlets provided by NCT administrator (July 4, 2002).

58. The National Compensation Tribunal (Procedures Rules) 1997, sec. 34 (2).

59. On July 4, 2002 the NCT administrator said that neither the guidelines, the claimants' files nor their hearings were open to the public. The guidelines, he said, were withheld to ensure that the claimants did not see them, though the NCT 'knows they are fair for them'. Other researchers reported being told that the guidelines were not publicized because the tribunal did not want the claimants to argue about their awards. Interview with Jewel Amoah and Martin Nkuna (June 19, 2002). Viva Nyimba (July 10, 2002), one of the NCT's lawyer-assessors, as well as the current and past chairmen said the files, guidelines and proceedings are open. Justice Chimasula Phiri did note though that some foreign 'experts' recommended closing the files for 25 years. Interviews with Justices Mkandawire and Chimasula Phiri (July 9, 2002), Justice Mtambo (July 22, 2002) and Hendrik Wittenberg (April 14, 2003).

60. When suggested to the current chairman of the tribunal that it might be instructive to publicize some of the basic information provided by the claimants, he said he had not thought of it before, but that he would consider it. Interview (July 22, 2002). Lawyer Ralph Mhone (July 1, 2002) suggested that the reason why stories have not been published by the media is because they 'are not newsworthy'. Interview (July 1, 2002). The NCT administrator (July 4, 2002) said that the NCT 'can't allow media coverage'.

61. As noted above and proposed here, the guidelines are not widely circulated by the NCT

62. One person explained that the letter to the NCT for his grandfather went to the NCT in late 2001 and seven months later they were still waiting for their claim number. Interview with Lyson Milazi (July 17, 2002). Others complained that they had to file their claims two or three times before receiving a number.

63. As noted earlier, the NCT administrator was not comfortable with the notion of open, public hearings, though the NCT's lawyer and current chairmen were.

64. Complicating matters, it is sometimes difficult for claimants to get letters from police or prison wardens without a payment, therefore making it difficult for them to complete their NCT files. Interview with Lyson Milazi (July 17, 2002).

65. In fact the NCT has rarely had the resources to do independent investigations.

66. As noted previously, a search of the *Gazette* failed to turn up progress reports.

67. One lawyer put it a different way: early on there were few rules set in the NCT, and most cases taken to the tribunal were by people who had been in public office. They received large awards because there were no guidelines or rules to follow. Interview with Bazuka Mhango (July 11, 2002). Interview with the current chairman, Justice Mtambo (July 22, 2002). It is estimated that perhaps ten people were awarded large sums by the NCT in that period. The first chairman provided an example of one such case at a meeting in 1996. At the same meeting the Law Commissioner Singini outlined the problem: 'My suggestion would be to consider altogether suspending payment of these interim funds until such time as the entire legal framework for the administration of the Fund is in place. . . . My fear . . . is that you might find that when the legal framework is in force, and it is as intended, then what you are doing now is not the norm then, and that you will have compensated people today with money that you may not do for future claimants. You might be accused of double standards . . .' *Understanding the Past to*

Safeguard the Future, Proceedings of a Conference Convened by the University of Malawi and the Robert F Kennedy Memorial Center for Human Rights (October 18–29, 1996), 39.

68. Interviews with Harold S. Khombe (July 4, 2002) and Justice Chimasula Phiri (July 9, 2002). Others who may be assisted prematurely are people in need of funeral fees or people with children without school fees. In order to address such problems, perhaps 10–20% of scheduled assessments might be reserved for people in special circumstances.

69. For reports of lost files, interviews with Lyson Milazi (July 17, 2002), Vera Chirwa (July 10, 2002), Unandi Banda and Kamlepo Kalua (July 10, 2002), and for a frank and open discussion of these problems and the criminal behaviour of staff, interview with the current chairman, Justice Isaac Mtambo (July 22, 2002).

70. These statistics were drawn from *Understanding the Past to Safeguard the Future, Proceedings of a Conference Convened by the University of Malawi and the Robert F Kennedy Memorial Center for Human Rights* (October 18–29, 1996), 35–6; *Minutes of the 5th Roundtable Meeting of the Case-handling Institutions in Malawi* (March 1, 2002); National Compensation Tribunal, 'Workshop No. 4: Paper Guidelines and Recommendations' (September 29, 2000); UNCHR, op. cit.; Government of Malawi/European Development Fund, Promotion of the Rule of Law and Improvement of Justice Programme. *Annual Report 2001, 'Track Records: National Compersation Tribunal'*, and *The Nation* (June 13, 2003).

71. Interview with NCT administrator, Mr Khombe (July 4, 2002); NCT pamphlet n.d. Those beneficiaries interviewed noted that the time between filing their claim and getting them interim awards was closer to two to five years.

72. Interviews with Mr Khombe (July 4), Justice Mkandawire (July 9), Vera Chirwa (July 10), and Justice Chimasula Phiri (July 9, 2002).

73. Two letters to the Treasury were shown to us, dated mid-2001, with approximately three dozen claimants, with final payments totalling about K16.5m (approximately US$240,000). Interviews with Viva Nyimba (July 4, 2002), Mr Khombe (July 4, 2002), and Justice Mtambo (July 22, 2002).

74. In mid-2003 Mr Khombe told the press that a total of K100 million had been paid out, but he did not indicate if this covered interim or final payments or both. *The Nation* (June 13, 2003).

75. National Compensation Tribunal database (June 2002). It does not differentiate between final and interim payments.

76. Interview with Justice Mtambo (July 22, 2002).

77. National Compensation Tribunal, 'Guidelines for Interim Compensation', n.d. The US dollar was worth K74 in July 2002, when the undated guidelines were provided to the authors. At that time a skilled urban worker might earn K10,000 per month.

78. National Compensation Tribunal, 'Forced Exile', pamphlet, n.d. Also, National Compensation Tribunal database (June 2002).

79. Ralph Mhone (July 1, 2002) said that a few properties that had been forfeited by individuals and retained by government had been returned but that such cases were rare.

80. National Compensation Tribunal, 'Workshop No. 4: Paper Guidelines and Recommendations' (September 29, 2000). In September 2000 the kwacha was valued at K72 = US$1. At the end of 2002 it was closer to K90=US$1, meaning the real value of the awards had been reduced by 25 percent.

81. National Compensation Tribunal, 'Loss of Property Claims', pamphlet, n.d.

82. Interview with Viva Nyimba (July 4, 2002). It is an interesting problem, for customary rights to land are not the same in all regions and they are different for different pieces of land and different classes of persons (e.g. men and women, outsiders, returnees, etc.). Interview with Wiseman Chirwa (July 5, 2002). Note that in the mid-1990s over 80 percent of registered returnees had no access to land and wanted the NCT to obtain that for them.

83. National Compensation Tribunal, 'Claims for Personal Injury', pamphlet, n.d.

84. As of mid-2002, the NCT database held approximately 120 cases related to loss of life. National Compensation Tribunal database (June 2002).

85. Interview with Mr Khombe (July 4, 2002). This figure is high compared to earlier estimates, but must include confiscated property cases. See UNCHR, op. cit. 6, which notes that 'it is estimated that there will be in excess of 10,000 claims involving awards expected to exceed K650 million, or US$45 million, approximately six times what the Government is able to contribute from Treasury' (US$45m is closer to K4 billion in 2003).

86. Interviews with Justice Mtambo (July 22), Mr Khombe (July 4), Max Mbendera (July 4), and Viva Nyimba (July 4, 2002). Mr Khombe noted that if (relatively wealthy) South Africa is having trouble paying final awards, surely Malawi will too.

87. Interview with NCT lawyer Viva Nyimba (July 4, 2002).

88. National Compensation Tribunal, 'Protection of Third Party Rights', pamphlet, n.d.

89. National Compensation Tribunal, 'National Compensation Tribunal', pamphlet, n.d.

90. National Compensation Tribunal, 'Problems Associated with Assessments in Respect of Wrongful Imprisonment', pamphlet, n.d.

91. Ibid.

92. Interview with Garton Kamchedzera (July 5, 2002) and with Wiseman Chirwa (July 5, 2002). Others discussed the difference between reparation/compensation and the symbols being given by the NCT in similar terms, e.g. Max Mbendera, Mr Khombe, Chimasula Phiri, and Viva Nyimba.

93. Interviews with Ralph Mhone (July 1, 2002) and Mr Khombe (July 4, 2002).

94. Olin Mwalunbunju, who has run a legal aid project supporting NCT claimants, estimated that 90 percent of the people CHRR has worked with are dissatisfied with the NCT's operations. Interview (July 22, 2002). All beneficiaries and many lawyers interviewed for this study expressed frustration.

95. Interview with Edge Kanyongolo (July 16) and Olin Mwalunbunju (July 22, 2002).

96. Interview with Max Mbendera (July 4, 2002).

97. Interview with Enoch Chibwana (July 11, 2002).

98. Interview with Olin Mwalunbunju (July 22, 2002).

99. Interview with Max Mbendera (July 4, 2002).

100. Interviews with Dan Msowoya and Manifesto Kayira (July 1, 2002) and with Olin Mwalunbunju (July 16, 2002).

101. One opposition politician noted he filed a claim in 1996, was not given a number and his file was lost. He refiled in 1997 and the file was lost again, and so he filed in 1998 and was then given a number. He is now waiting for his hearing. He thought the NCT chairman was probably unaware of what had happened, but felt that his file had been lost deliberately because of his political stance. Another thought a lost file could be found by paying a small sum of money.

102. Edge Kanyongolo (July 16, 2002), and interview with John Soo Phiri (July 16, 2002). Kapote Mwakasungura (July 22, 2002) agreed: the NCT process 'trivializes' the ordeal. It is a 'travesty'.

103. Dan Msowoya, in interview with Dan Msowoya and Manifesto Kayira (July 1, 2002). The UN should have been involved in the return of the exiles and refugees, said Kapote Mwakasungura (July 22, 2002), but the government refused. Since then the government has treated returnees as if 'you are a nuisance after all. You were rude to Kamuzu [Banda] and do not deserve help.' Also interview with Vera Chirwa (July 10, 2002).

104. Interview with Wiseman Chirwa (July 5, 2002). 'I doubt very much' that reconciliation emerges from this process, agreed the NCT's lawyer, Viva Nyimba (July 4, 2002).

105. Interview with Mr Khombe (July 4, 2002), who cited an unnamed claimant.

106. Emmie Chanika in *Understanding the Past to Safeguard the Future, Proceedings of a Conference Convened by the University of Malawi and the Robert F Kennedy Memorial Center for Human Rights* (October 18–29, 1996), 42.

107. Interviews with Desmond Kaunda (June 17), and with Dan Msowoya and Manifesto Kayira (July 1, 2002).

108. Interview with Garton Kamchedzera (July 5, 2002).

109. Interview with Dan Msowoya and Manifesto Kayira (July 1, 2002).

110. Interview with Desmond Kaunda (June 17, 2002).

111. Interview with former NCT chairman Justice Chimasula Phiri (July 9, 2002).

112. *The Nation* (June 29, 2001). At a public meeting celebrating the UN Day against Torture, UDF spokesman Ken Lipenga said that Malawi had improved on South Africa's Truth and Reconciliation Commission because the NTC was 'helping to resettle people'. Neither Mr Stambuli's nor Mr Lipenga's statements were questioned.

113. Interviews with John Soo Phiri (July 16), and Edge Kanyongolo (July 16, 2002).

114. Interview with Garton Kamchedzera (July 5, 2002).

115. Interviews with Desmond Kaunda (June 17), and Justice Msosa (July 9, 2002).

116. Interviews with Dan Msowoya and Manifesto Kayira (July 1, 2002), and with Olin Mwalunbunju (July 16, 2002). Interview with Chimasula Phiri (July 9, 2002). There is always the possibility, though, that a parliamentary debate on the NCT might result in its closure.

117. Interview with Wiseman Chirwa (July 5, 2002). He, three other lecturers and two international human rights activists tried unsuccessfully in 1995–6 to start a 'history project', where victims' oral testimonies were to be collected by university students, archived and used to write newspaper articles, a monograph, curricula and textbooks on rights and governance, and civic education materials. This group held a meeting in Lilongwe where international experts met with victims to discuss truth commissions: *Understanding the Past to Safeguard the Future, Proceedings of a Conference Convened by the University of Malawi and the Robert F Kennedy Memorial Center for Human Rights* (October 18–29, 1996).

118. Interview with Olin Mwalunbunju of CHRR (July 22, 2002).

119. *The Weekly Chronicle* (August 5–11, 2002). In early 2003 Mr Muluzi's designated successor said that he would protect the President after 2004, promising him that his immunity from prosecution would not be removed as has been the case for former President Chiluba in Zambia. This statement was condemned by civil society, the media, and even President Muluzi, who said he had done nothing while in office for which he needed immunity.

120. Postscript added on July 30, 2004.

121. *The Weekend Nation* (May 3, 2003), cited in Malawi Discussion Forum (May 6, 2003), www.mailtalk.ac.uk/archives/malawitalk.html

122. *The Nation* (March 14 and 21, 2004).

123. Anonymous email to Cammack (March 4, 2004).

124. *The Nation* (March 4 and 21, 2004).

125. *The Nation* (March 4, 2004), and Business *Report* (SA) (July 23, 2004). ' "I am sad to report to the entire nation and donor community that 10 billion kwacha . . . [$92 m] were lost through fraud and corruption involving some former cabinet ministers," said Ishmael Wadi, newly appointed director of public prosecutions.' This claim the UDF calls 'outrageous'. *The Nation* (July 30, 2004).

126. Old accusations continued to surface, e.g. that Vice President Justin Malewezi and (Minister) Brown Mpinganjira received money quickly after the UDF came into power, while others 'were toiling' to get funds from the NCT. See Nyasanet (April 14, 2004) (http:maelstrom.stjohns.edu/archives/nyasanet.html). For a new case, see Malawi Discussion Forum (January 31, 2004), www.mailtalk.ac.uk/archives/malawitalk.html. Presidential candidate Gwanda Chakuamba asked for K38m for a house confiscated by Banda's government in 1980. Soon after the 2004 election, which he lost, and when he joined the UDF 'unity' government, he moved into a new farm.

127. *The Weekend Nation* (May 3, 2003), cited in Malawi Discussion Forum (May 6, 2003), www.mailtalk.ac.uk/archives/malawitalk.html

128. Malawi Discussion Forum (March 4, 2004), www.mailtalk.ac.uk/archives/malawitalk.html

129. *The Nation* (March 21, 2004).

130. Anonymous email to Cammack (March 4, 2004).

CHAPTER 7

REPORT ON REDRESS: THE JAPANESE AMERICAN INTERNMENT

ERIC K. YAMAMOTO

LIANN EBESUGAWA

INTRODUCTION

The Japanese American reparations movement culminated in the Civil Liberties Act of 1988. Through the Act Congress authorized a presidential apology and the payment of $1.2 billion in reparations to Japanese Americans incarcerated by the USA without charges or trial on account of their race during World War II. Indeed, the Act is the culmination of the reparations movement. This chapter therefore emphasizes the Japanese American internment and the Civil Liberties Act—its genesis, implementation, and apparent effects. In addition, it looks beyond the legislation itself and explores the mobilization of various political groups, the Japanese American community, and the psychological healing for many Japanese Americans.

Finally, this chapter looks at the broader social meanings of reparations emerging from the Japanese American redress effort and some of redress' 'unfinished business', even after 15 years. It does this because a reparations movement cannot be measured solely by legal enactments. In a successful reparations movement an entire community reengages with the issues of justice and belonging. The community reassesses its history and attempts to reestablish group goals. The community benefits from the group work and from the links it forges across racial lines. And other groups look to the movement for 'lessons learned'. For this reason the chapter concludes with an assessment of the Japanese American reparations movement's unfinished business.

1. ORIGINS OF THE JAPANESE AMERICAN INTERNMENT AND REPARATIONS

The reparations movement's roots lie in the incarceration of 120,000 innocent Americans of Japanese ancestry (mostly US citizens) by the US government in 1942. The internment's social and political setting, the government's decisions, the legal challenges in the 1940s and again in the 1980s, and Congressional legislation in 1988 are key components of Japanese American redress. A brief overview is in order.

The World War II internment process developed in three stages.[1] First, military orders imposed a nighttime curfew on Japanese Americans. In 1942, Gordon Hirabayashi and Minoru Yasui tested the constitutionality of the curfew. Second, the orders implemented the exclusion of people of Japanese ancestry from protected areas. Hirabayashi and Fred Korematsu violated the initial order to report to an assembly center to prepare for exclusion. Third, without explicitly stating it, the orders created the conditions of continued *detention*. It was not until Mitsuye Endo filed her habeas corpus petition in 1944 that the Court addressed the indefinite incarceration. Together, these phases—the curfew, exclusion, and continued detention, all without charges or trial—constituted 'the internment'. Well before the internment process officially began, however, Americans of Japanese ancestry were targeted both formally and informally.

Before Pearl Harbor

Before the bombing of Pearl Harbor, the federal government prepared for possible conflict with Japan. In the late 1930s, the Justice Department compiled a list of

2,000 Japanese resident aliens who were potentially 'subversive' and 'dangerous'.[2] Among them were leaders of Japanese civic groups, businessmen, language teachers, Buddhist priests, and martial arts instructors.

The government also engaged in careful intelligence gathering and analysis. In March 1941, Lieutenant Commander Kenneth D. Ringle of Naval Intelligence was chosen by President Roosevelt to investigate the West Coast 'Japanese Problem'. Ringle broke into the Japanese Consulate in Los Angeles and helped uncover an espionage operation, which led to the arrest of a Japanese naval officer posing as a language student.[3]

After the arrest, military intelligence maintained that a credible threat of espionage persisted (although it concluded that any Japanese espionage would likely have minimal impact). FBI Director J. Edgar Hoover, however, believed that the military overstated the risks.[4]

The federal government also conducted broader studies of Japanese American loyalty. One early inquiry was conducted by Chicago businessman Curtis B. Munson. Munson's report to the White House was contradictory. He warned that 'there are still Japanese in the United States who will tie dynamite around their waist and make a human bomb out of themselves' and he was 'horrified to note that dams, bridges, harbors, power stations, etc. are wholly unguarded everywhere'.[5] Yet he did not recommend detention of Japanese Americans as a group. In an extensive memo to Roosevelt, he wrote: 'We do not believe that they would be any more disloyal than any other group in the United States with whom we went to war. Those being here are on a spot and they know it.'

Finally, the Justice Department and the War Department developed specific contingency plans. In March 1941, they reached a secret agreement for 'transferring [only] enemy aliens to the custody of military authorities for permanent detention'. The departments, however, did not contemplate mass detention, and their agreement explicitly provided for arrest under warrant issued by a federal prosecutor, a preliminary hearing, and a Justice Department determination of each individual's loyalty. In this initial agreement, citizens were distinguished from aliens.[6]

After Pearl Harbor

On the day of the Pearl Harbor attack, the Justice Department immediately arrested enemy aliens. The initial arrests took into custody more than 2,000 individuals. In accordance with the Justice and War Departments' plan, enemy alien review boards quickly processed these people through individual loyalty hearings. Two-thirds of the Japanese aliens but less than half of the German and Italian aliens were then detained in Immigration and Naturalization Service internment camps in Montana, New Mexico, and North Dakota.[7]

By December 10, just three days after Pearl Harbor, FBI Director Hoover reported that most of the persons whom the FBI had intended to arrest had been taken into custody. However, on that same day, the head of the Western Defense Command (covering the western portion of the USA), Lieutenant General John L. DeWitt, began to raise 'certain questions relative to the problem of apprehension, segregation and detention of Japanese in the San Francisco Bay Area'.[8]

Heightening military anxieties, between December 17 and December 23, Japanese submarines sank two tankers and damaged one freighter along the West Coast. General DeWitt feared (inaccurately) that Japanese Americans were aiding the submarines by signaling them from shore. By December 19, DeWitt advocated 'collect[ing] all alien subjects fourteen years of age and over, of enemy nations and remov[ing] them to the Zone of the Interior'.[9] Still, throughout the month of December, there was no government-wide consensus. Even as General DeWitt was starting to envision mass internment, US Attorney General Francis Biddle was assuring the public that arrested aliens were given individualized assessments and that '[n]o alien was apprehended, and none will be, on the score of nationality alone'.[10] There was no serious talk of interning American citizens.

But with the New Year and the declaration of war, public opinion began to turn against all persons of Japanese ancestry including American citizens. The Commission on Wartime Relocation and Internment of Civilians[11] (CWRIC) in *Personal Justice Denied: Report of the Commission on Wartime Relocation and Internment* (*Personal Justice Denied*, 1983) documented the changing tide of opinion against the Japanese Americans.

On January 2, the Joint Immigration Committee [of the California legislature] sent a manifesto to California newspapers that summed up the historical catalog of charges against the ethnic Japanese. It put them in the new context of reported fifth column activity in Hawaii and the Philippines and a war that turned the Japanese into a problem for the nation, not California alone. Repeating the fundamental claim that the ethnic Japanese are 'totally unassimilable', the manifesto declared that 'those born in this country are American citizens by right of birth, but they are also Japanese citizens, liable . . . to be called to bear arms for their Emperor, either in front of, or behind, enemy lines'. Japanese language schools were attacked as 'a blind to cover instruction similar to that received by a young student in Japan— that his is a superior race, the divinity of the Japanese Emperor, the loyalty that every Japanese, wherever born, or residing, owes his Emperor and Japan'. In these attacks the Joint Immigration Committee had the support of the Native Sons and Daughters of the Golden West and the California Department of the American Legion, which in January began to demand that 'all Japanese who are known to hold dual citizenship . . . be placed in concentration camps'. By early February, Earl Warren, then attorney general of California, and U.S. Webb, a former attorney general and coauthor of the Alien Land Law, were actively advising the Joint

Immigration Committee how to persuade the federal government that all ethnic Japanese should be removed from the West Coast.[12]

Deep-rooted prejudices and economic self-interests emerged. For example, a white American manager of the Salinas Vegetable Grower-Shipper Association stated:

We're charged with wanting to get rid of the Japs for selfish reasons. We might as well be honest. We do. It's a question of whether the white man lives on the Pacific Coast or the brown man. They came into this valley to work, and they stayed to take over. . . . If all the Japs were removed tomorrow, we'd never miss them in two weeks, because the white farmers can take over and produce everything the Jap grows. And we don't want them back when the war ends, either.[13]

Such views supported earlier anti-Japanese immigrant laws like the Alien Land Law (which prohibited Japanese immigrants from owning land) and gained pseudo-legitimacy with the January release of a report commissioned by President Roosevelt. Authored quickly by Supreme Court Justice Owen Roberts, the Roberts Commission report wrongly concluded that Japanese living in America had committed espionage, contributing to the Pearl Harbor disaster.[14]

General DeWitt also claimed forthrightly the racial justification for his 'final recommendation'. DeWitt is well known for stating publicly that 'a Jap's a Jap'.[15] Although German and Italian immigrants could be treated as individuals in determining their guilt or innocence, he made clear that the Japanese—immigrants and citizens alike—were inherently disloyal:

I have little confidence that the enemy aliens are law abiding or loyal in any sense of the word. Some of them, yes; many, no. Particularly the Japanese, I have no confidence in their loyalty whatsoever. I am speaking now of the native born Japanese—117,000—and 42,000 in California alone. In the war in which we are now engaged racial affinities are not severed by migration. The Japanese race is an enemy race and while many second and third generation Japanese born on United States soil, possessed of United States citizenship have become 'Americanized' the racial strains are undiluted.

I have the mission of defending this coast and securing vital installations. The danger of the Japanese was, and is now—if they are permitted to come back—espionage and sabotage. It makes no difference whether he is an American citizen, he is still a Japanese. American citizenship does not necessarily determine loyalty.

You needn't worry about the Italians at all except in certain cases. Also, the same for the Germans except in individual cases. But we must worry about the Japanese all the time until he is wiped off the map. Sabotage and espionage will make problems as long as he is allowed in this area—problems which I don't want to have to worry about.[16]

General DeWitt's views were communicated by prominent newspaper journalists. By February, the popular syndicated columnist Walter Lippman also recommended internment. To civilian government officials, the widely circulated Lippman essay confirmed popular sentiments favoring internment.[17] On February 13,

DeWitt made his 'final recommendation' on the 'Evacuation of Japanese and Other Subversive Persons from the Pacific Coast'.

Although the bombing of Pearl Harbor rekindled anti-Asian sentiment, it was the media and government that propagated and reinforced the growing animus. Significantly, despite all the military and media pronouncements of Japanese American disloyalty in the court of public opinion, as the government's intelligence services found, Japanese Americans did not commit a single action of espionage or sabotage.

The Internment: Military, Congressional, and Executive Actions

Several high-ranking government officials, including Attorney General Francis Biddle, opposed the exclusion of Japanese Americans. On February 19, President Roosevelt nevertheless signed Executive Order 9066 granting the military the power to exclude persons from specified areas.[18] On its face, the order made no mention of persons of Japanese ancestry. Race was implied.

EXECUTIVE ORDER NO. 9066
Authorizing the Secretary of War to Prescribe Military Areas
Whereas the successful prosecution of the war requires every possible protection against espionage and against sabotage to national defense material, national defense premises, and national defense utilities:

Now, therefore, by virtue of the authority vested in me as President of the United States, and Commander in Chief of the Army and Navy, I hereby authorize and direct the Secretary of War, and the Military Commanders who he may from time to time designate, whenever he or any designated Commander deems such action necessary or desirable, to prescribe military areas in such places and of such extent as he or the appropriate Military Commander may determine, from which any or all persons may be excluded, and with respect to which, the right of any person to enter, remain in, or leave shall be subject to whatever restrictions the Secretary of War or the appropriate Military Commander may impose in his discretion.

I hereby further authorize and direct the Secretary of War and the said Military Commanders to take such other steps as he or the appropriate Military Commander may deem advisable to enforce compliance with the restrictions applicable to each Military area hereinabove authorized to be designated, including the use of Federal troops and other Federal Agencies, with authority to accept assistance of state and local agencies.

I hereby further authorize and direct all Executive Departments, independent establishments and other Federal Agencies to assist the Secretary of War or the said Military Commanders in carrying out this Executive Order, including the furnishing of medical aid, hospitalization, food, clothing, transportation, use of land, shelter, and other supplies, equipment utilities, facilities, and services.

The White House
February 19, 1942

General DeWitt then issued a series of military orders that eventually led to the mass detention of approximately 120,000 people of Japanese descent, over 70,000 of whom were US citizens.[19]

On March 21, 1942, Congress passed Public Law 503, which criminalized violations of the military orders.[20] Congress had been conducting hearings throughout February and March in San Francisco, Portland, Seattle, and Los Angeles. The Tolan Committee 'National Defense Migration' hearings generated many witnesses sympathetic to European aliens but almost none favorable to Japanese Americans and Japanese immigrants. With the passage of Public Law 503, both the executive and legislative branches stood together behind the exclusion of Japanese Americans.

Three days after the law's enactment, General DeWitt began issuing a series of 108 Civilian Exclusion Orders. Japanese Americans were given seven days to leave their homes, jobs, and businesses, carrying only whatever belongings they could evacuate. They were shipped first to 16 different assembly centers operated by the army, such as the Puyallup racetrack in Washington and the Santa Anita racetrack in Southern California. They were later moved to 13 permanent internment prisons (or 'camps') run by a civilian agency called the War Relocation Authority (WRA), created by executive order on March 18. There, most of them remained for several years, in desolate surroundings, behind barbed wire and watched by armed guards.[21] Many were separated from family members. They lost their homes, jobs, businesses, and personal belongings. With the military in the lead, the executive branch following, and, finally, Congress attaching federal criminal penalties to disobedience, all but one branch of government—the judiciary—had approved the internment process. The lower federal courts, and ultimately the Supreme Court, began to consider the cases that challenged the constitutionality of the internment.

Legal Challenges

In 1942, shortly after DeWitt's evening curfew order, Minoru Yasui demanded that Portland, Oregon, police arrest him for a curfew violation. Yasui was eventually convicted of curfew violation, and his conviction was upheld by the US Supreme Court.[22]

On May 16, 1942, Gordon Hirabayashi turned himself into FBI headquarters in Seattle, Washington, to challenge the exclusion. Hirabayashi was convicted for violating the exclusion and the curfew orders. His conviction on the curfew charge was upheld by the US Supreme Court (the Court found it unnecessary to rule on his exclusion conviction).[23]

On May 30, 1942, Fred Korematsu was arrested in San Leandro, California, three weeks after the exclusion order had been issued. His conviction was affirmed by the US Supreme Court.[24]

From an internment camp Mitsuye Endo applied administratively for leave clearance on February 19, 1943 (which was granted on August 16, 1943). She also filed with a federal court a petition for habeas corpus stating that she was a loyal and law-abiding citizen of the USA, that no charge had been made against her, and that she was being unlawfully detained. The Supreme Court affirmed the granting of her release because Endo, as found by the District Court, was a loyal citizen.[25] She was being detained by a civilian agency, not the military, and she could not be held indefinitely without good cause.

The four test cases against the government's internment orders originated independently. Each raised different procedural and substantive claims. Each was tried by a different court.[26] Yet they eventually became essential pieces of a single internment whole. The government charged Yasui, Korematsu, and Hirabayashi with related crimes—violating General DeWitt's military orders. They responded by asserting that the military orders were illegal because they singled out a racial group and were unsupported by genuine military necessity. The defense strategies in these individual cases were loosely coordinated and were subject to contradictory interventions by both the national and local chapters of the American Civil Liberties Union (ACLU) as well as the Japanese American Citizens' League (JACL).[27] The government's lawyers were also split by disagreements about ethical, political, and legal strategy choices (discussed later).

The Supreme Court's opinions in the internment cases each built on the opinions issued earlier. Briefly stated, the Court affirmed the curfew convictions of Hirabayashi and Yasui, and on the basis of those decisions affirmed Korematsu's exclusion conviction, deferring to the government's assertion that military necessity justified the internment. In these three cases the Court rejected the petitioners' equal protection of laws challenge (grounded in the Fifth Amendment's Due Process clause) to the varying aspects of the internment. In Endo's case, the Court affirmed the order of her release from detention not on constitutional grounds but because the WRA statute did not authorize continued detention of innocent individuals.[28]

The Supreme Court's reasoning and holdings in these internment cases are further discussed in connection with the *coram nobis* litigation that reopened those same cases 40 years later.[29]

2. HISTORY OF 1988 CIVIL LIBERTIES ACT

The Japanese American redress movement provided more than reparations for former internees.[30] It also provided political and legal insights into the earlier breakdown of a democratic system of checks and balances during a time of national stress.[31] Tracing the history of the Civil Liberties Act of 1988 offers a more complex understanding of a democratic government's efforts to address historic injustice.

The foundational question is this: *How does a government repair serious harm it inflicts upon its own citizens, particularly when those citizens are members of a minority racial group targeted because of their race?*[32] On the road to redress Asian Americans challenged, used, and changed American law through political struggle and litigation.

The modern redress movement's roots date back to the late 1960s when a second-generation Japanese American started a reparations campaign of public education and legislative lobbying. That informal campaign gradually gained momentum, expanding its base through newly formed university ethnic studies programs and engendering organizational support, media curiosity, and legislative interest. Various groups provided general support for a nationwide coalition for redress.[33]

Progress stalled in the late 1970s, however. The legal basis for reparations was ill-defined. Although many came to realize the historical injustice of the internment, public support for legislative reparations, and even support within the Japanese American communities, diminished.

Two events in the early 1980s galvanized the reparations movement. First, Japanese American congresspersons from California and Hawaii pushed through legislation creating a congressional study commission.[34] The commission's thorough and aggressive investigation, discussed below, unearthed new information and provided the solid factual record for reparations.[35]

The second event involved lawsuits: the *coram nobis* litigation in 1983 that reopened the World War II court cases challenging the constitutionality of the internment and the *Hohri* class action suit that sought damages for the internees' loss of freedom and property.[36]

In order to better understand the coalescence of these two events and their impact, it is helpful to assess the ways that the Japanese American redress and reparations movement targeted each branch of the federal government.

As discussed in greater detail below, on the judicial front, Japanese Americans initiated two different kinds of lawsuits. The first was the *coram nobis* litigation brought by the three individuals who had been convicted of violating the wartime curfew and exclusion orders. This litigation sought a judicial declaration of injustice and did not seek monetary relief. The second was a class action damages lawsuit, filed by former internees in an attempt to obtain monetary compensation for the material and psychological harms of the internment. This case, *Hohri v. United States,* was ultimately dismissed by the federal courts as untimely filed.

On the executive level, intense lobbying culminated in President Ford's 1976 repeal of Executive Order 9066 during the nation's bicentennial. In the legislative arena, congresspersons from California and Hawaii successfully pushed through federal legislation creating a study commission, the CWRIC. The CWRIC's 1983 report *Personal Justice Denied* is a revealing historical investigation of government racism and an in-depth report on the continuing harms of the internment.

In response to the various redress efforts—the lawsuits, the CWRIC hearings and report, and extensive lobbying by diverse civil rights and community groups—Congress passed the Civil Liberties Act of 1988. The Act committed the President to apologize to the former internees and established a $1.25 billion, later increased to $1.6 billion, trust fund for reparations payments of $20,000 to each surviving internee.

The individual, executive, and legislative actions, collectively leading to, and comprising, Japanese American redress, are summarized below.

Judicial Action

Coram Nobis *Litigation*

Toward the end of World War II the US Supreme Court ruled in the infamous *Korematsu* case that internment did not transgress the Fifth Amendment's Due Process clause because 'military necessity' justified it.[37] Fred Korematsu's legal challenge failed at that time, and the government imprisoned him for refusing to abide by the military's exclusion orders leading to the internment. That same case was reopened by Korematsu in 1983 through a highly unusual petition for a writ of *coram nobis*. Korematsu renewed his legal challenge on the basis of newly discovered, now declassified, government documents from World War II that revealed three extraordinary facts: first, before the internment, all government intelligence services involved unequivocally informed the highest officials of the military and the War and Justice Departments that the West Coast Americans of Japanese ancestry as a group posed no serious danger, and that there existed no justification for mass internment; second, the key West Coast military commander based his internment decisions on invidious racial stereotypes about the inscrutable, inherently disloyal Japanese American; and third, the military and the War and Justice Departments concealed and destroyed evidence and deliberately misled the Supreme Court in 1944 when it was considering the *Korematsu* case and the asserted military necessity justification for the internment.[38]

The Supreme Court in 1944 had accepted as true the government's false statements about military necessity without close scrutiny—and with tragic consequences. The Court's unquestioning acceptance of racial stereotypes and false statements of necessity 'not only legitimized the dislocation and imprisonment of loyal citizens without trial solely on account of race, but it also weakened a fundamental tenet of American democracy—government accountability for military control over civilians'.[39] Justice Jackson, in his scathing dissent, pinpointed the dangerous latent legal principle of the 1944 *Korematsu* decision: 'What the Court appears to be doing, whether consciously or not ... [is] to distort the Constitution to approve all the military may deem expedient.'[40]

The 1983 reopening of the *Korematsu* case,[41] with its revelations of egregious government misconduct in destroying key evidence and lying to the Court, highlighted the danger to citizens, and to minorities particularly, of unscrutinized military and government national security power. That danger led the federal court hearing the case in 1984 to observe:

As historical precedent [*Korematsu*] stands ... as a caution that in times of distress the shield of military necessity and national security must not be used to protect governmental actions from close scrutiny and accountability. It stands as a caution that in times of international hostility and antagonisms our institutions, legislative, executive and judicial, must be prepared to exercise their authority [to enforce constitutional guarantees] to protect all citizens from the petty fears and prejudices that are so easily aroused.[42]

Thereafter, similar results were achieved in the *Hirabayashi*[43] and *Yasui*[44] *coram nobis* cases.

Hohri *Class Action*

Additionally, William Hohri of Chicago, supported by the National Council for Japanese American Redress (NCJAR), filed a class action civil damages suit in Washington, DC in March 1983, after the *coram nobis* petitions were filed, on behalf of all internment camp survivors as a class. The suit listed 21 separate legal injuries the government had caused the internees and asked that each class member be awarded damages of $10,000 for each violation, a total potential award of some $24 billion. The injuries claimed by the camp survivors included 'summary removal from their homes, imprisonment in racially segregated prison camps, and mass deprivations of their constitutional rights' by the government.[45]

Although the *coram nobis* petitions and the class action suit were pursued as distinct legal cases, both were facets of the overall redress movement, and lawyers in the two efforts maintained contact. Several of the documents from the *coram nobis* petition were included in the class action suit as 'direct evidence that the government knew of the falsity of its claim of military necessity' in defending the internment before the Supreme Court.[46]

On May 17, 1984, Federal District Judge Louis Oberdorfer dismissed the class action suit as untimely, holding that the government records refuting the army's 'military necessity' claim had been available in the 1940s.[47] The DC Court of Appeals reversed in part. It held that the internees as a class stated a claim for property deprivation—a claim not barred by the statute of limitations because of the government's concealment of critical evidence.

In 1987, the Supreme Court vacated that decision, and remanded the case to the Court of Appeals for the Federal District. The Supreme Court held that the DC Court of Appeals (where the case was initially appealed)[48] lacked jurisdiction. On remand, in 1988, the Court of Appeals for the Federal Circuit[49] dismissed the entire case on statute of limitations grounds.[50]

The NCJAR first chose to pursue monetary redress in the courts rather than the legislature for several reasons. Unlike the passage of legislation, judicial success did not require huge constituency support.[51] Second, the NCJAR believed that the injuries suffered by Japanese Americans were of a constitutional nature and were best addressed by the courts. Third, the judicial route allowed the NCJAR to operate independently. The NCJAR and William Hohri in particular were motivated by disagreements with the National JACL. Hohri disliked the JACL for its willing compliance with the exclusion orders during World War II and for its decision not to pursue direct redress legislation.[52]

The NCJAR lawsuit helped galvanize the overall redress effort. The NCJAR research helped educate public officials and society at large that constitutional violations were the central issue in the Japanese Americans' internment.[53] Most important, the high potential damage claim made the legislative reparations demand appear moderate in comparison.

Executive Action

For Japanese American internees, presidential action entailed both the repeal of Executive Order 9066 and a formal governmental apology.

Repeal of Executive Order 9066

President Roosevelt's executive action in 1942, Executive Order 9066, initiated the internment. President Ford's repeal of that order in 1976, the year of America's bicentennial, marked the beginning of the lengthy redress process. In his proclamation, President Ford acknowledged: 'We now know what we should have known then—not only was the evacuation wrong, but Japanese Americans were and are loyal Americans.'[54]

President's Apology to Japanese Americans

A presidential apology accompanied reparations payments authorized by Congress in 1988 to former internees. President George Bush sent a letter to each of the surviving internees, apologizing on behalf of the USA in the following words:

A monetary sum and words alone cannot restore lost years or erase painful memories; neither can they fully convey our Nation's resolve to rectify injustice and to uphold the rights of individuals. We can never fully right the wrongs of the past. But we can take a clear stand for justice and recognize that serious injustices were done to Japanese Americans during World War II.

In enacting a law calling for restitution and offering a sincere apology, your fellow Americans have, in a very real sense, renewed their traditional commitment to the ideals of freedom, equality, and justice. You and your family have our best wishes for the future.

Congressional Action

Congressional action lay at the heart of Japanese American redress.

The Commission on Wartime Relocation and Internment of Civilians

Through HR 5499 Congress established the CWRIC. The bill was introduced on September 28, 1979 by nine Democrats and an additional 105 cosponsors. Only Representative Robert E. Bauman (Republican from Maryland) spoke in opposition to the bill. He argued that the Evacuation Claims Act of 1948,[55] regarded largely as ineffectual in returning less than ten cents on the dollar for property losses, had been the proper vehicle to address the incarceration. HR 5499, with bipartisan support, passed by a vote of 279 to 109.[56]

Congress directed the CWRIC to

1. review the facts and circumstances surrounding Executive Order 9066, issued February 19, 1942, and the impact of such Executive Order on American citizens and permanent resident aliens;
2. review directives of the USA military forces requiring relocation and, in some cases, detention in internment camps of American citizens, and permanent resident aliens of the Aleutian and Pribilof Islands; and
3. recommend appropriate remedies.[57]

The CWRIC played a pivotal role in the Japanese American redress process. It held public hearings in ten cities throughout the USA[58] over 20 days, during which more than 750 witnesses and internees told their stories of suffering then and their continuing pain. Its findings of no military necessity for, and governmental misconduct in, justifying the internment laid the foundation for the court rulings in the *Korematsu* and *Hirabayashi coram nobis* cases.

Equally important, the Commission's unexpected recommendations that the government apologize and provide monetary reparations for surviving internees spurred on the Japanese American reparations movement.

1988 Civil Liberties Act

Through the 1988 Civil Liberties Act,[59] Congress built upon the foundation laid by the CWRIC and the *coram nobis* and *Hohri* cases. The legislation was several years in the making.

The Civil Liberties Act's increasing number of cosponsors reflected growing congressional support.[60] Many former internees, for the first time, also actively pushed for redress, joined by civil liberties groups. Public education programs[61] and community fund-raising efforts flourished. Other minority group organizations lent support.[62]

Additionally, support from the general American public grew as 'efforts of community activists across the nation produced some monetary redress policies and scores of supportive proclamations and resolutions from a broad array of groups'.[63] These groups included national church organizations,[64] veteran affiliations,[65] civil rights groups,[66] labor unions,[67] and professional associations.[68] State governments also passed resolutions in favor of redress.[69]

The Civil Liberties Act became law on August 10, 1988, when Ronald Reagan signed Public Law 100–383.

Before signing the bill President Reagan remarked that 'we gather here today to right a grave wrong.... More than forty years ago ... 120,000 persons of Japanese ancestry living in the United States were forcibly removed from their homes and placed in makeshift internment camps. This action was taken without trial, without jury. It was based solely on race.'[70]

The President captured the essence of the bill by stating:

[N]o payment can make up for those lost years. So, what is most important in this bill has less to do with property than with honor. For here we admit a wrong; here we affirm our commitment as a nation to equal justice under the law.... the ideal of liberty and justice for all—that is still the American way.[71]

The Civil Liberties Act created the Office of Redress Administration to administer the reparations program. It also committed the President to a formal apology and authorized reparations in the amount of $20,000 for each surviving internee who was a US citizen or legal resident alien at the time of internment.[72] Securing congressional funding over subsequent years required additional rounds of intense political maneuvering. Reparations payments, along with the presidential letter of apology, commenced in 1991 and continued (as new eligibility was determined) through the Act's sunset in 1998.[73]

In addition to the payment of individual claims, the Act established a Civil Liberties Public Education Fund Board to 'sponsor research and public educational activities, and to publish and distribute the hearings, findings, and recommendations of the Commission [CWRIC]'.[74] The significant impact of this fund for public education is discussed below.

3. IMPLEMENTATION OF THE 1988 CIVIL LIBERTIES ACT

Office of Redress Administration

The 1988 Civil Liberties Act created the Office of Redress Administration (ORA). Although the Act establishes a blueprint for reparations, it delegates responsibility for implementation to the Attorney General. The Attorney General established the ORA within the Justice Department under the Civil Rights Division in September 1988. The Act authorized a ten-year period in which the ORA was to identify, register, verify, and administer reparations payments to eligible individuals. The ORA's influence rested in its interpretation of the Civil Liberties Act's eligibility provisions. Many Japanese American activists agreed that the ORA and its leadership brought a sympathetic openness to the interpretation of the legislation.[75] The ORA worked with the National Coalition for Redress/Reparations (NCRR) and the Japanese American Citizens League (JACL) to disseminate redress information through Japanese American newspapers, community meetings, and organizational newsletters. The tightly knit Japanese American community also passed redress information through word of mouth.[76] The ORA also implemented a toll-free telephone line, literature and informational publications, direct mailings, advertisements, and press releases to aid in locating eligible individuals.[77] In addition, the ORA minimized the paperwork in applying for redress. Within six months of the signing of the Civil Liberties Act of 1988 the ORA had identified over 48,000 potential recipients.[78]

On January 1989, President Reagan's budget for fiscal year 1990 only allocated $300,000 to Aleuts and $20 million to Japanese Americans for redress payments. This appropriation represented only 1.6 percent of the amount authorized for Japanese American redress and would compensate only 1,000 of the then estimated

60,000 eligible Japanese Americans.[79] At this rate the completion of redress payments would take 60 years.[80]

To assure prompt payment of reparations, in 1989 Congress passed a bill that made redress an entitlement.[81] Senator Daniel Inouye (Hawaii) was instrumental in passing the entitlement bill. He stated: 'By making it [redress] into an entitlement program, we will be assured to pay off everyone in three years.... Otherwise, it might take 50 years—$20 million one year, $10 million the next.... Each year, we would have to fight the same battle over and over again.'[82]

Eligibility Requirements and Payments

On August 10, 1989 the ORA finalized its implementing regulations, which would aid in the processing of cases.[83] The Act specifies that the attorney general must identify and locate persons who may be eligible for redress. According to Robert Bratt,[84] Administrator of the ORA from its inception in 1988 until 1992: 'It is the government that must prove each individual's eligibility for redress, rather than the opposite.... This makes the redress program truly unprecedented.'[85] The Civil Liberties Act of 1988 provided that former internees who were alive at the time of the Civil Liberties Act's enactment would be eligible for payments. Eligible individuals were identified by the ORA, or an individual could notify the ORA of potential eligibility and submit affidavits or other documentary evidence to support his or her assertion of eligibility.[86] To identify potential eligible individuals, the ORA researched historical records over an 18-month period.[87] Further verification of eligibility was obtained by declarations, citing the name and address of the person along with proof of date of birth and internment camp.[88] Additionally, the legislation provided for payments to the heirs of those alive at the time of enactment but who passed away before receiving their reparations payment.[89] The reparations payments were to be made first to the surviving spouse; if no spouse, then in equal shares to all children living at the time of the payment; if no children, then in equal shares to parents living on the date of the payment. If a deceased individual had no one in any of these categories the money would be returned. The Congressional conference report on the legislation instructed the Justice Department to attempt to make payments to the oldest survivors first.[90]

The Civil Liberties Act of 1988 also included $12,000 each for Aleuts.[91] Aleuts and Pribilof Islanders were evacuated from their homes and relocated to camps in southeastern Alaska to protect them from Japanese invasion.[92] Although many Aleuts were allowed to return to their homes in 1944, they found that their houses had been looted and destroyed.[93] The CRWIC ruled that there was 'no persuasive showing that evacuation of the Aleuts was motivated by racism or that it was undertaken for any reason but their safety. The evacuation of the Aleuts was a rational wartime measure taken to safeguard them.'[94] The Aleuts were included in the Civil Liberties Act of 1988 because the compensation for evacuation was a shared experience of both groups.[95] Furthermore, inclusion of the Aleuts extended the benefit of the legislation beyond Japanese Americans, making the legislation more attractive to some legislators.[96] Congress was given ten years to make all monetary payments. In addition, the bill capped the amount Congress could appropriate per fiscal year at $500 million. Finally, the payments were subject to availability of appropriated funds and the Act immediately extinguished all other claims against the government.[97]

The Act, although carefully drawn, contained gaps. In the ORA implementation process, several ambiguous eligibility categories emerged. These categories included:

- children of parents who were excluded but not incarcerated;[98]
- children born outside the camp whose mothers left camp under the 'indefinite leave' program or 'voluntarily' reentered before or just after giving birth;[99]
- individuals and their children relocated from the concentration camps to teach in the naval language schools;
- children whose fathers were in the famous 442nd infantry company and whose mothers voluntarily returned to camp;
- children who accompanied parents who were sent to Japan in exchange for American civilians (most of whom were white Americans);
- individuals in Phoenix and Glendale, which were split down the middle by the exclusion zone;[100]
- individuals born outside of the military and exclusion zones after January 1945;[101]
- Japanese Latin Americans;[102]
- railroad mining employees;[103] and
- individuals displaced from their homes in Hawaii.[104]

The ORA responded to reparations demands from people from these categories sometimes by finding eligibility and sometimes by denying eligibility. In some cases of denial, further challenges were successfully lodged in the courts.[105]

In addition to questions of eligibility, many key implementation issues, procedural and substantive, needed clarification or further legislative support.[106] The 1992 amendment to the Civil Liberties Act of 1988 attempted to address these needs:

1. The amount authorized for the Civil Liberties Act of 1988 was increased from $1.25 to $1.65 billion. This amount provided for an additional 20,000 redress payments, while maintaining the original reserve of $50 million to be made available for educational purposes.

2. Individuals not of Japanese ancestry became eligible for redress if they had been incarcerated with their spouse or children. These payments would come from discretionary appropriations.

3. The US Claims Court acquired exclusive judicial review over decisions concerning eligibility of individuals.

4. The benefit of the doubt in determining eligibility was given to claimants by the Justice Department; redress payments were not viewed as income when making eligibility determinations for veterans' benefits.

5. The Justice Department's ORA was given 180 days to complete its administrative activities following termination of the Civil Liberties Public Education Fund.[107]

One case proved highly compelling and deeply problematic for the ORA. During World War II, the USA helped kidnap 2,260 Japanese Latin Americans from 12 Latin American countries and incarcerated them in US internment camps.[108] Those largely Peruvian citizens were uninvolved in the war. They were initially held in the American internment camps for possible hostage exchanges with Japan. Most simply languished there, having lost homes, businesses, jobs, and families. After World War II, they were released from the internment camps and, astonishingly, branded 'illegal aliens' in the USA. Because they were not 'legal residents' in the USA at the time of the internment, the Civil Liberties Act barred them from receiving reparations. The ORA had also worked with the Immigration and Naturalization Service to identify those internees whose permanent residency status had been misclassified, barring them from receiving reparations.[109]

Carmen Mochizuki and other former Japanese Latin American internees filed a federal class action suit, *Mochizuki et al. v. United States*.[110] They sought full reparations for Japanese Latin Americans. The suit settled in June 1998. The partial settlement resulted in the US government issuing an apology and redress payments of $5,000 to each eligible Japanese Latin American.[111] Other Japanese Latin Americans objected to the settlement as discriminatory and thereafter continued to pursue litigation to achieve the full $20,000 reparations payment.[112]

At the end of the ORA's 11-year tenure, over $1.6 billion dollars had been paid out to more than 82,250 persons of Japanese ancestry who had been interned during World War II.[113]

Form of Delivery

The apology mandated by the Civil Liberties Act of 1988 was ultimately made through a letter from President George Bush to each person eligible for reparations.[114] The reparations check accompanied the letter, both of which were sent by registered mail.

Civil Liberties Public Education Fund

In addition to authorizing the apology and payments, the Civil Liberties Act established the Civil Liberties Public Education Fund (CLPEF) to educate the public and facilitate general public understanding about the redress legislation and in order to curb future racism and governmental abuses of power.[115] The Act also established the CLPEF Board of Directors for making disbursements from the fund to 'sponsor research and public educational activities, and to publish and distribute the hearings, findings, and recommendations of the Commission... [and] for reasonable administrative expenses of the Board'.[116]

The Civil Liberties Act of 1988 authorized $50 million for CLPEF. By 1994, however, only $5 million had been appropriated and nothing had been disbursed.[117] In 1996, President Bill Clinton appointed eight individuals to sit on the board of CLPEF, and the Senate approved those appointments.[118]

In March 1997, 100 recipients received grants totaling $2.7 million from the CLPEF. This number was subsequently raised to 132, which included 19 national fellowships and brought the total award to $3.3 million. The grants ranged from $2,000 to $100,000.[119] Seven different categories of projects were funded: curriculum, landmarks and institutions, community development, arts and media, research, national fellowships, and research resources.[120]

The projects included development of internment curriculum for elementary and high school students; development of materials and a book for teaching law and the internment; new research on reparations for historic injustice; oral histories of internment artists; books on the internee draft registers; documentaries on internment camp life; psychological studies on the effects of the internment; and numerous others. Because Congress appropriated only $5 million of the authorized $50 million, and because so many additional projects were proposed, the California legislature created its own version of CLPEF in 2000 to support many of those internment public education initiatives.

For some reparations supporters, the public education projects have become the most important aspect of Japanese American redress. In addition to giving voice to those who experienced the internment, the projects also targeted mainstream USA and policymakers to bring home the political and legal lessons of the internment.

Relationship to Civil Suits

Acceptance of reparations payments barred the recipients from filing any other reparations claims against the government. Under section 105 of the Civil Liberties Act of 1988: 'The acceptance of payment by an eligible individual under this section shall be in full satisfaction of all claims against the United States.'[121] Thus, the *Hohri* class action, which had already been dismissed, and other possible reparations lawsuits were foreclosed. In addition, the Act also stated expressly that it did not serve as legal precedent for

recognition of any claim of Mexico or any other country or any Indian tribe (except as expressly provided in this Act with respect to the Aleut tribe of Alaska) to any territory or other property of the United States, nor shall this Act be construed as providing any basis for compensation in connection with any such claim.[122]

Economic Impact

The economic impact of Japanese American reparations is difficult to assess. The payment of $20,000 per surviving internee was very helpful financially to some, particularly to the elderly. The payments, however, were intended to be largely symbolic. They were not intended to have a direct impact on the US economy.

Those individual payments, however, along with the CLPEF projects, had an economic impact on Japanese American institutions, especially those with a social justice component. Donations from individuals, sometimes a direct donation of reparations checks, helped fund the Korematsu Civil Liberties Foundation fellowship with the Asian Law Caucus in San Francisco. They aided in the creation of the Japanese American National Museum in Los Angeles, which has featured several major internment exhibitions. They helped endow chairs and establish historical archives at the University of California Los Angeles Asian American Studies Program.

The long-delayed ORA report on its administrative operations may shed additional light on the specific economic and institutional effects. As of the date of this chapter, the Justice Department authors of the ORA report were not willing to share their research or preliminary findings.

4. CONCLUSION

The Japanese American redress process was arduous. Many Japanese Americans contributed, and their communities overwhelmingly considered reparations a great victory. The trauma of racial incarceration, without charges or trial, and the lingering self-doubt over two generations left scars on the soul. The government's apology and bestowal of symbolic reparations fostered long overdue healing for many. Redress was cathartic for internees. A measure of dignity was restored. Former internees could finally talk about the internment. Feelings, long repressed, surfaced. Yet some of the support from within Japanese American communities and from other groups seemed grudging. One thoughtful African American put it succinctly: 'Why them and not us?' Reparations for Japanese Americans thus lead us to ask the larger question about justice: What political role will Japanese American redress and Japanese Americans themselves play in ongoing and future struggles for racial justice in the USA and indeed throughout the world?

The view that redress demonstrates that the USA does the right thing, that the Constitution works (if belatedly), and that the USA is far along on its march to racial justice for all is unrealistically bright. The danger lies in the possibility of enabling people to feel good about each other for the moment, while leaving undisturbed the attendant social realities creating the underlying conflict.[123] Another view is that reparations legislation has the potential for becoming a civil rights law that at best delivers far less than it promises and that at worst creates illusions of progress, functioning as a hegemonic device to preserve the status quo. There is, however, another perspective: true, reparations legislation and court rulings such as the *Korematsu coram nobis* case do not inevitably lead to a restructuring of governmental institutions, a changing of societal attitudes, or a transformation of social relationships, and thus, the dangers of illusory progress and co-optation are real. At the same time, reparations claims, and the rights discourse they engender in attempts to harness the power of the State, can and should be appreciated as intensely powerful and calculated political acts that challenge racial assumptions underlying past and present social arrangements. They bear potential for contributing to institutional and attitudinal restructuring.

From these colliding perspectives emerge pertinent questions that will continue to shape the legacy and impact of Japanese American reparations. What are the long-term societal effects of reparations—the social legacy of Japanese American redress beyond personal benefits? Will societal attitudes toward Asian Americans and other racial minorities change? Will institutions, especially those that curtailed civil liberties in the name of national security, be restructured? Will Japanese American reparations serve as a catalyst for redress for others?

At bottom, the social meaning of Japanese American redress has yet to be determined. The key to the legacy of redress is likely to be how Japanese Americans act when faced with continuing racial subordination of African Americans, Native Americans, Native Hawaiians, Latinas/os and Asian Americans, and with reparations claims of deserving groups throughout the world.

NOTES

1. The accounts in Section I are drawn principally from Professor Yamamoto's coauthored book, Eric Yamamoto, Magaret Chon, Carol Izumi, Jerry Kang, and Frank Wu, *Race, Rights and Reparation: Law and the Japanese American Internment* (New York: Aspen Publishers, 2001). Other later accounts, particularly those of the reparations political process, are drawn principally from the excellent book by Mitchell T. Maki, Harry H. L. Kitano, and S. Megan Berthold, *Achieving the Impossible Dream: How Japanese Americans Obtained Redress* (Chicago: University of Illinois Press, 1999). We express our appreciation to the authors of these works.

2. Yamamoto et al., op. cit., 96.

3. Ibid., 96.

4. Ibid., 96–7.

5. Ibid., 97.

6. Ibid., 97.

7. Ibid., 97.

8. Ibid., 97.

9. Ibid., 98.

10. Ibid., 98.

11. The Commission on Wartime Relocation and Internment of Civilians (CWRIC) was a congressional commission set up in 1980 and authorized to investigate the internment of Japanese Americans during World War II. For another excellent account of the internment, see Michi Weglyn, *Years of Infamy: The Untold Story of America's Concentration Camps* (Seattle: University of Washington Press, 1996).

12. Report of Congressional Commission on Wartime Relocation and Internment of Civilians, *Personal Justice Denied* (1983) (hereinafter *Personal Justice Denied*), 67–8.

13. Frank J. Taylor, 'The People Nobody Wants', *Saturday Evening Post* 24 (66) (May 9, 1942), quoted in *Korematsu v. United States*, 323 U.S. 214 (1944) (Justice Murphy, dissenting).

14. Yamamoto et al., op. cit., 99.

15. Ibid., 99.

16. *Personal Justice Denied*, 65–6 (quoting transcript of meeting in DeWitt's office (January 4, 1942); testimony before House Naval Affairs Subcommittee (April 13, 1943).

17. Yamamoto et al., op. cit., 99–100.

18. Ibid., 100.

19. Ibid., 101.

20. Ibid., 101.

21. Ibid., 101.

22. *Yasui v. United States*, 310 U.S. 115 (1942).

23. *Hirabayashi v. United States*, 320 U.S. 81 (1943).

24. *Korematsu v. United States*, 323 U.S. 214 (1944). Yamamoto et al., op. cit., 137–8.

25. Ex Parte Endo, 323 U.S. 283 (1944).

26. Yamamoto et al., op. cit., 101.

27. Ibid., 101.

28. Ibid., 102.

29. A detailed historical account of these legal cases may be found in Peter Irons, *Justice at War: The Story of the Japanese American Interment Cases* (Berkeley, CA: University of California Press, 1993); Yamamoto et al., op. cit.

30. Eric K. Yamamoto, 'Friend or Foe or Something Else: Social Meanings of Redress and Reparations', *Denver Journal of International Law and Policy* 20 (2) (1992): 225 (hereinafter 'Social Meanings of Redress').

31. Yamamoto, 'Social Meanings of Redress', 225.

32. Yamamoto et al., *Race, Rights and Reparation*, 278.

33. Yamamoto, 'Social Meanings of Redress', 225. The history of the Japanese American redress and reparations movement is well documented. See, for example, William Minoru Hohri, *Repairing America: An Account of the Movement for Japanese American Redress* (Pullman, WA: Washington State University Press, 1988); Leslie T. Hatamiya,

Righting a Wrong: Japanese Americans and the Passage of the Civil Liberties Act of 1988 (Palo Alto, CA: Stanford University Press, 1993); Roger Daniels, Harry H. L. Kitano and Sandra C. Taylor, *Japanese Americans: From Relocation to Redress* (Salt Lake City: University of Utah Press, 1986); Peter Irons, ed., *Justice Delayed: The Record of the Japanese American Internment*, (Middletown, CT: Wesleyan University Press, 1989).

34. There was disagreement between the JACL and other groups as to the appropriateness of a congressional commission. Some groups pushed for judicial remedies rather than establishing a legislative investigative commission. Maki et al., *Achieving the Impossible Dream*, 122.

35. Yamamoto, 'Social Meanings of Redress', 225. CWRIC, *Personal Justice Denied*.

36. Yamamoto, 'Social Meanings of Redress', 225. Professor Yamamoto's views on reparations are informed by his participation in 1983 and 1984 on the *coram nobis* legal team that litigated the reopening of *Korematsu v. United States*, 323 U.S. 214 (1944). The *Hohri* class action was ultimately dismissed on statute of limitations grounds. *Hohri v. United States*, 586 F.Supp. 769 (D.D.C. 1984), affirmed in part and reversed in part 782 F.2d 227 (1986), vacated 482 U.S. 64 (1987), on remand 847 F.3D 779 (1988), certiorary denied 488 U.S. 925 (1988). While the suit was pending on appeal, its threat of a possible multibillion dollar recovery exerted pressure on Congress concerning reparations.

37. Yamamoto, 'Social Meanings of Redress', 225. *Korematsu v. United States*, 323 U.S. 214 (1944).

38. Eric K. Yamamoto, 'Korematsu Revisited—Correcting the Injustice of Extraordinary Government Excess and Lax Judicial Review: Time for a Better Accommodation of National Security Concerns and Civil Liberties', *Santa Clara Law Review* 26, (1986): 2, 24–6. See also Peter Irons, *Justice at War*, op. cit.

39. Yamamoto et al., *Race, Rights and Reparation*, 3.

40. Ibid., 3.

41. *Korematsu v. United States*, 584 F.Supp. 1406 (N.D. Cal. 1984).

42. *Korematsu v. United States*, 584 F.Supp. 1406, 1418 (N.D. Cal. 1984). See also 'Note, Developments in the Law: The National Security Interest and Civil Liberties', *Harvard Law Review* 85 (6) (1972): 1134 (observing characteristic political branches' overestimated 'threats to national security to the detriment of civil liberties').

43. *Hirabayashi v. United States*, 828 F.2d 591 (9th Cir. 1987). Hirabayashi's 1942 conviction was also vacated. The U.S. Court of Appeals for the Ninth Circuit affirmed the district court on the evacuation charge and reversed on the curfew charge. In doing so, it issued a strongly worded opinion that both condemned the government's litigation strategies during the original internment cases and criticized the government's approach to the *coram nobis* litigation itself. Yamamoto et al., *Race, Rights and Reparation*, 319.

44. In Min Yasui's *coram nobis* action, filed with the federal district court in Portland, Oregon, the federal judge issued a brief order vacating Yasui's conviction, but did not provide a revised factual record about the validity of the curfew or internment. Yamamoto et al., *Race, Rights and Reparation*, 318.

45. Yamamoto et al., *Race Rights and Reparations*, 392 (quoting Irons (ed.), *Justice Delayed*, 27–32).

46. Irons (ed.), *Justice Delayed*, 27–32.

47. Yamamoto et al., *Race, Rights and Reparations*, 393. *Hohri v. United States*, 586 F. Supp. 769 (D.C. 1984).
48. *Hohri v. United States*, 782 F.2d 227 (D.C. Cir. 1986).
49. *Hohri v. United States*, 847 F.2d 779 (Fed. Cir. 1988).
50. For a more detailed explanation of the *Hohri* decisions, see Yamamoto et al., *Race, Rights and Reparation*, 392–9.
51. Maki et al., *Achieving the Impossible Dream*, 122. Several of the descriptions in this section and following sections are drawn principally and directly from this excellent book.
52. Ibid., 122.
53. Ibid., 128.
54. Yamamoto et al., *Race, Rights and Reparations*, 399.
55. The Evacuation Claims Act of 1948 did not address the illegality of the internment, but provided compensation to voluntary evacuees for documented property loss. Although the Act did not specify any appropriations, any award above $2,500 had to be approved by Congress. Maki et al., *Achieving the Impossible Dream*, 249, n. 9.
56. Maki et al., *Achieving the Impossible Dream*, 91–5.
57. *Personal Justice Denied*, 1.
58. Washington, DC, Los Angeles, San Francisco, Seattle, Anchorage, Unalaska, St. Paul, Chicago, New York and Boston. Maki et al., *Achieving the Impossible Dream*, 99.
59. Excerpts of the Civil Liberties Act of 1988 are reproduced in Part III of this volume.
60. Maki et al., *Achieving the Impossible Dream*, 145.
61. The Smithsonian Institution Exhibit was one of the most significant public education programs which lent support to the Japanese American reparations movement. The exhibit was entitled 'A More Perfect Union', and opened on October 1, 1987. The exhibit highlighted the wartime treatment of Japanese Americans, as well as the heroism of the Japanese American military units the 442nd R.C.T. and the 100th Battalion. The exhibit helped to reframe the reparations movement in the eyes of the American public as a '"story about fifty years worth of citizen involvement with the Constitution".... [and] as an American issue and its potential as a positive political issue.' Maki et al., *Achieving the Impossible Dream*, 160 (quoting Tom Crouch; interview by Mitchell Maki, Harry Kitano, and S. Megan Berthoed, Washington, DC, July 11, 1995.) The exhibit was attended by congressional members and members of the Japanese American community.
62. Yamamoto, 'Social Meanings of Redress', 227.
63. Maki et al., *Achieving the Impossible Dream*, 145.
64. The American Baptist Churches, USA; the United Methodist Church; the Presbyterian Church, USA; the United Church of Christ; the Buddhist Churches of America; and the American Jewish Committee passed proclamations endorsing redress. Maki et al., *Achieving the Impossible Dream*, 265, n. 33.
65. American Legion; the Veterans of Foreign Wars, Department of California; and the Jewish War Veterans. Maki et al., *Achieving the Impossible Dream*, 145.
66. The International Longshoremen's and Warehousemen's Union (ILWU) and the American Federation of Labor and Congress of Industrial Organizations (AFL-CIO). Maki et al., *Achieving the Impossible Dream*, 145.
67. The Anti-Defamation League of B'nai B'rith (ADL); the American Civil Liberties Union (ACLU); the National Association for the Advancement of Colored People

(NAACP); the National Council of La Raza; and the Leadership Conference of Civil Rights (LCCR). Maki et al., *Achieving the Impossible Dream*, 145.

68. The American Bar Association (ABA); the National Association of Social Workers (NASW); the National Education Association (NEA); and the American Psychiatric Association (APA). Ibid., 146.

69. Hawaii, Minnesota, Wisconsin, Oregon, and New Jersey. Ibid., 146.

70. Ibid., 195. Ronald Reagan, *Public Papers of the Presidents of the United States: Ronald Reagan, 1988–1989, Book II, July 2, 1988 to Jan. 19, 1989* (Washington, DC: US Government Printing Office, 1991), 1054.

71. Reagan, *Public Papers*, op. cit., 105–55.

72. Yamamoto et al., *Race, Rights and Reparation*, 406.

73. Ibid., 406.

74. Yamamoto et al., *Race, Rights and Reparation*, 409. Civil Liberties Act of 1988, section 106.

75. Maki et al., *Achieving the Impossible Dream*, 199. Kay, Ochi interview by authors Maki, Kitano, and Berthold, Los Angeles, CA (May 31, 1995).

76. Ibid., 199.

77. US Newswire, *Redress Payments to Japanese-Americans to Begin Oct. 9* (October 2, 1990).

78. Maki et al., *Achieving the Impossible Dream*, 199. Rita Takahashi, JACL LEC press release, January 20, 1989, citing Bob Bratt in January 26, 1989, public forum meeting.

79. 'With every passing month approximately two hundred elderly Japanese Americans died without having the promise of redress fulfilled.' Maki et al., *Achieving the Impossible Dream*, 200.

80. Ibid., 200.

81. Ibid., 208.

82. Ibid., 208 (quoting Arnold T. Hiura, 'Entitlement Plan Passes Congress: Hawaii Sen. Dan Inouye Engineers a Way to Guarantee Full Redress Funding', *Hawaii Herald* (November 3, 1989), 11.

83. US Newswire, *Redress Payments to Japanese-Americans*.

84. The ORA had three executive directors during its existence: Robert Bratt (1988–1992), Paul Suddes (1992–1994), and Irva 'DeDe' Greene (1994–1998). Deserene Worsley served as acting administrator for ORA from June to October 1994.

85. US Newswire, *Redress Payments to Japanese-Americans*.

86. 50 App. U.S.C.A. § 1989b–4 Restitution explains the procedures for locating eligible individuals. 28 C.F.R. § 74.5 lists the sources from which the ORA shall establish eligibility. The sources include the National Archives, the Department of Justice, the Social Security Administration, and the Internal Revenue Service.

87. U.S. Newswire, *Redress Payments to Japanese-Americans*.

88. 28 C.F.R. § 74.7 Notification of Eligibility.

89. Maki et al., *Achieving the Impossible Dream*, 185.

90. For a more detailed explanation of the compromise between the House and Senate version of the H.R. 442 that eventually became the Civil Liberties Act of 1988 see Maki et al., *Achieving the Impossible Dream*, 185–6.

91. See 50 App. U.S.C.A. § 1989 Purposes, which explains why restitution was made to the Aleuts.

92. *Personal Justice Denied*, 317–59.

93. Ibid., 317–59.

94. Ibid., 317–59, 463.

95. Maki et al., *Achieving the Impossible Dream*, 91.

96. Ibid.

97. Civil Liberties Act of 1988, section 105(a)(3)(A).

98. This group included children of parents who were excluded from the West Coast by Executive Order 9066, but moved to the interior regions of the United States before they were forcibly removed by the military. Maki et al., *Achieving the Impossible Dream*, 217.

99. Children who were born outside of the camp but were voluntarily brought back into the camp because of the lack of community support and/or lack of job opportunities. Maki et al., *Achieving the Impossible Dream*, 219.

100. Although individuals were not incarcerated in these cities, because of the exclusion zone, excluded individuals were barred from going to work, school or church, and from participating in other daily activities. At least 76 individuals were compensated for these losses. Maki et al., *Achieving the Impossible Dream*, 221.

101. As of January 20, 1945, Proclamation 21 repealed the exclusion orders and allowed individuals to travel freely. Therefore, individuals who voluntarily returned to the camps and were born after January 20, 1945 were not eligible for reparations. The controversy erupted over the January 2, 1945 cut-off date that was later extended to January 20, 1945, a date that more accurately reflected when all Japanese Americans would probably have been notified of Proclamation 21. Maki et al., *Achieving the Impossible Dream*, 221.

102. Individuals living in Latin America who were incarcerated by the US government, deported, or sent back to Japan in exchange for white Americans in Japan. Maki et al., *Achieving the Impossible Dream*, 222.

103. Railroad and mine workers were people who lived far from the exclusion zones, but felt the effects of the racial exclusion when they were fired from their jobs because of government interference. Maki et al., *Achieving the Impossible Dream*, 221–3.

104. Maki et al., *Achieving the Impossible Dream*, 217.

105. A listing of those cases and overall ORA eligibility rulings awaits completion of the long-overdue ORA Final Report. Most recently, that report was promised by November 2002. For a more detailed explanation of how each category was resolved see Maki et al., *Achieving the Impossible Dream*, 217–25.

106. Maki et al., *Achieving the Impossible Dream*, 215–16.

107. Ibid., 216.

108. Ibid., 222.

109. Northwest Nikkei, *ORA Updates Community On Redress: Almost 80,000 payments made*, November 20, 1995.

110. *Mochizuki et al. v. United States*, U.S. (19—). The citation is not complete because the case was settled, therefore the case was never recorded.

111. Maki et al., *Achieving the Impossible Dream*, 222.

112. Ibid., 222.

113. Department of Justice, 'Ten-Year Program to Compensate Japanese Americans Interned During World War II Closes Its Doors', *News Release* (February 19, 1999).

114. See above under 'Executive Action'.

115. Maki et al., *Achieving the Impossible Dream*, 225.
116. Yamamoto et al., *Race, Rights and Reparation*, 409. Civil Liberties Act of 1988, section 106.
117. Maki et al., *Achieving the Impossible Dream*, 225–6.
118. Ibid., 226.
119. Ibid., 227.
120. Ibid., 227.
121. Yamamoto et al., *Race, Rights and Reparation*, 408.
122. Civil Liberties Act of 1988, section 301.
123. Yamamoto, *Social Meanings of Redress*, 232.

COMPENSATION FOR THE VICTIMS OF SEPTEMBER 11

SAMUEL ISSACHAROFF

ANNA MORAWIEC

MANSFIELD[1]

INTRODUCTION

On September 22, 2001, Congress enacted Public Law 107–42, the Air Transportation Safety and System Stabilization Act. The Act was an immediate response to the perceived need to save air carriers from the possibility of devastating tort liability or the inability to secure insurance coverage for losses resulting from the terrorist attacks on the USA on September 11, 2001. The prospect of a disruption to domestic air service and the attendant economic consequences prompted a congressional response of stunning breadth and magnitude. Alongside the desire to protect a vital national industry came the additional decision to provide a compensatory regime for the victims of the terrorist attacks. Thus, in addition to compensating the air carriers, Title IV of the Act established the 'September 11th Victim Compensation Fund of 2001' (the 'Fund'). The stated purpose of the Fund was to provide compensation, and a no-fault alternative to tort litigation, to any individual or personal representative of an individual who was killed or physically injured as a result of the aircraft crashes on that day. The Act provided that the Fund be administered by a Special Master appointed by the Attorney General. On November 26, 2001, Attorney General John Ashcroft appointed Kenneth R. Feinberg as Special Master. The roughly $4 billion Fund, as part of the Act's $15 billion bailout of the airline industry, was intended to provide for an average payout of $1.85 million to each victim's family—an unprecedented level of federal financial assistance, and a level of payment that was faithfully achieved by the time the Fund terminated.[2]

The inclusion of the Fund in a study of reparations programs requires some introductory exposition. Although the origin of the Fund may well lie in the political exigencies surrounding a perceived threat to the viability of the nation's air carriers, there is no question that the compensation program has taken on a life of its own. In loosely categorizing this Fund within the broad outlines of a reparations program, we can identify certain critical aspects that distinguish the Fund from a damages pool or even an administrative version of civil tort recovery. It is because of the unique characteristics of the Fund that its inclusion within a comparative evaluation of international reparations efforts is justified. But we should be clear at the outset that there are as many differences as there are similarities. Perhaps most central to this premise, those who were injured or killed on September 11 were not singled out for harm or targeted on the basis of a salient group characteristic. Nor was it the intent of Congress to create a reparations program; as we will develop below, Congress entered the arena in a desire to provide financial security for the airline industry and backed into the victim compensation scheme as a result of the perceived unseemliness of providing compensation to companies, but not individuals. Due to the imperfect fit, the Fund's contribution to any reparations case study lies in its cautionary tale about the creation of elaborate administrative schemes that try to individualize recoveries as the mechanisms through which to compensate victims—initial motivations for the program aside. Nonetheless, this chapter will attempt to situate the Fund, albeit imperfectly, within a conception of reparations based upon the following five critical factors:

1. Reparations seek to compensate for harms beyond the ordinary risks associated within any specific society, that is, that category of harms that are not considered part of what happens to citizens in the normal course of life in that society, no matter how unpleasant or unwarranted. In this way, reparations are distinct from programs of social insurance compensating for disease or death or economic harm, or even for the misfortune of being a victim of crime.

2. Reparations hold as their ultimate objective the creation of an after-the-fact form of social insurance for harms whose existence and scope were not anticipated as within those encountered in the normal course of life in any

given society. Unlike typical social insurance schemes, they tend to be one-time affairs attempting redress for a specific occurrence.

3. Reparations seek to compensate for harms that are suffered as tears in the social fabric rather than a matter of individual fate or fault. Reparations generally correspond to a perceived sense of societal failure to provide for the security of the individual citizen or a defined community within the broader society.

4. Reparations do not conform to any easy conception of corrective or distributive justice. The aim is to provide compensation for those who suffered the identified harm, and in many cases to allow the social reintegration of those who were victimized.

5. The source of the funds in a reparations program need not be the wrongdoer. Although many reparations programs, particularly those imposed by a militarily victorious force over the vanquished, do obligate the wrongdoers to undertake the financial burden of reparations, the object is independent of the source of the funds.

Put in the affirmative, the general outlines of a reparations program are defined by compensation outside the normal operations of the civil or criminal justice systems; compensation to victims outside general measures of social insurance; and the use of no-fault/no-trial administrative structures to award compensation for the victims. With these governing criteria, we turn to the origins, scope, and structure of the Fund.

1. SCOPE OF COVERAGE

The events of September 11 have spawned a program of reparations unparalleled by any other public compensation program in US history. What is it that differentiates September 11 victims from people who suffer severe harm unrelated to such acts of terror? Reparations are not a generalized form of social insurance, made available by a government to its citizens as a safety net in the event of death, unemployment, or lack of individual resources, but a form of relief offered for calamities outside the realm of a civilized world. An act of international terrorism on the scale of that which the USA experienced on September 11 goes beyond the normal risks associated with living in this democratic society. The US government, even without any acceptance of charges that it might not have done enough to identify and prevent such devastating security breaches, felt itself compelled to act on behalf of the significant loss of life, injury, property damage, and potentially crippling economic fallout that resulted from the terror of that day.[3] The tragedy of September 11 is therefore distinguishable from street crimes, most natural calamities, and even from instances of domestic terror, in that it was carried out by foreign nationals and presumably funded and coordinated overseas. The perpetrators methodically penetrated American institutions and security for an orchestrated attack on several strategic targets. The harm was imposed from outside the borders of the country by an entity whose sole purpose was to destroy American life and property.

It is because the attack on Americans symbolized an attack on America itself that lawmakers expedited passage of the Act to compensate families for wrongs committed against their deceased and injured family members.[4] Although proposals were also put forward to expand the Fund to include other victims of international terror independent of September 11, namely, those involved in the 1998 bombings of US Embassies in East Africa,[5] the focus remained firmly on the events of September 11.

The Fund seeks to compensate victims financially for the wrongs they have suffered in a campaign of terror. A notable difference between the Fund and other programs is that the source of the harm was not an authoritarian domestic regime or internal conflict. Consistent with other models, however, the Fund seeks to provide a guaranteed financial settlement intended to allow families immediate economic benefits and a sense of closure to their ordeal by inducing them to seek compensation outside the civil tort system. Implicit in public discussions of the Fund, there is also a desire by lawmakers that the government is seen as doing all it can to ease the pain of those who have suffered as a result of September 11.

Nonetheless, we would misstate the origins of the Fund if we did not acknowledge that the original and immediate concern was the fate of the airline industry, not the victims of the terrorist attacks. It is possible to distinguish the September 11 attacks from earlier acts of terror, such as the Oklahoma City bombing, based on the foreign origin of the perpetrators of September 11. This might serve as a salient distinction in addressing the limitation of the Fund to the recent attacks, but it would obscure the fact that the program orignated in a congressional desire to forestall potential tort claims against the airlines for arguable negligence in the safety precautions they undertook. The Fund thus stems from complicated and often inconsistent motivations. It is for this reason that the Fund neither fits neatly within the parameters of a traditional reparations program nor wholly dismisses the underlying compensatory goals of such a program.

2. THE CONGRESSIONAL RESPONSE

Public Law 107–42, the Air Transportation Safety and System Stabilization Act (the 'Act'), was introduced, debated and passed by Congress in a matter of hours the evening of September 21, 2001. Owing to the imminent economic disaster to befall the airline industry, and in turn the US economy, as a result of the terrorist attacks, Congress expedited passage of the law and enacted swift remedies for the airlines and victims alike. The legislative process leading up to enactment of the Act demonstrates the speed and urgency with which members of Congress acted. At 6:08 PM on Friday, September 21, 2001, the House Committee on Rules presented to the House of Representatives House Resolution 244 (H.R. 244) for consideration of a bill to preserve the continued viability of the United States air transportation system (H.R. 2926 Air Transportation Safety and System Stabilization Act). At 8:49 PM, H.R. 244 passed with a vote of 285 in favor and 130 against. Immediately thereafter, consideration of H.R. 2926 commenced, introduced by Representative Don Young (R-AK). At 11:06 PM, upon conclusion of the floor debate, H.R. 2926 passed with 356 votes in favor and 54 votes against. The companion bill in the Senate (S. 1450) was introduced by Senator Thomas Daschle (D-SD) and passed the same day with 96 votes in favor and one against. A unanimous consent agreement provided for passage of the House bill in the Senate if it remained identical to the Senate bill. Shortly before midnight on September 21, a mere three hours after substantive discussion of the bill began, it was presented to President Bush, and signed into law as Public Law 107–42 the morning of September 22, 2001.

Although the Act received overwhelming support in congressional debates on September 21, 2001, its drafting history prior to passage suggests a more troubled route to the floor of Congress. While no public officials disagreed that the tragic events of September 11 required immediate government response and financial support for those directly affected, the extent and scope of that support was nonetheless the subject of considerable congressional wrangling and compromise. At its inception, the purpose of the Act's precursor bill, H.R. 2891, A Bill to Preserve the Continued Viability of the United States Air Transportation System, was, simply, to meet the significant needs of the airline industry mounting in the wake of the terrorist attacks. It was intended purely as an economic bailout scheme, with provisions to provide loans, loan guarantees, and other compensation to carriers that suffered direct losses on September 11. Compensation for victims killed and injured on September 11 was not an original consideration by H.R. 2891's sponsors when initially introduced in the House.

A week before passage of the Act, on Friday, September 14, 2001, Chairman of the House Committee on Transportation and Infrastructure Don Young (R-AK) and Representative and Ranking Member of the Committee Jim Oberstar (D-MN) introduced in the House H.R. 2891. In urging the House to pass the bill, Rep. Young declared:

[O]n September 11, 2001, the FAA grounded every air carrier in this country within a 2-hour period. This is absolutely necessary for the safety and protection of our country and our people.... As private industries, they put the welfare of the American people above their own profit and their own welfare. Unfortunately, we are now facing a serious crisis that may result in a severe reduction in our air transportation system. We will be, in the very near future, facing layoffs of the airline industry, reductions in flights.... The ripple effect on our economy will be enormous.... The purpose of H.R. 2891 is to keep our U.S. air transportation system alive and able to serve its important functions for our country, because we shut down the industry. The bill will provide an immediate ability to the President to provide loans and other assistance to U.S. air carriers, and also to compensate those carriers who can document direct losses because of the actions of our government to protect our national security. The current crisis requires this action be taken as quickly as possible to preserve not only the financial viability of the airlines, but also to protect the general public welfare.[6]

Rep. Oberstar echoed the sentiments of Rep. Young in underscoring the bill's necessity to safeguard the economy. In doing so, he also hoped to preempt concern that they were seeking passage of the bill too rapidly for thoughtful discussion and review. Rep. Oberstar declared:

What we are proposing to do tonight is to get an authorization in place so that when financial markets open on Monday, airline stocks do not tank and airlines do not go under and they shut down forever. That is what this is about. Yes, it is on short notice; no, we did not go through the hearing process. We did not have time. We consulted with all that we could in the very short period of time. We are facing an airline crisis and the airlines need some recognition that Congress will act to prevent a financial liquidation of the airline industry.[7]

Rep. Oberstar's preemptive warning did not succeed in garnering support for the bill from his fellow members. Despite Rep. Oberstar's and Rep. Young's requests for unanimous consent to discharge the bill from committee and consider the measure on the floor, an objection to do so was heard and upheld.[8] H.R. 2891 thus failed to pass in the House, and was consequently sent to the House Committee on Transportation and Infrastructure for hearings to review and revise the bill. On Wednesday, September 19, 2001, Chairman Young opened his Committee's hearings with repeated calls for support of the bill.[9] Such calls warned that without assistance from the federal government, major airlines would begin layoffs and other downsizing schemes that could lead to full-scale economic crisis. Warnings that September 11 victims and their families would suffer severe financial hardship without government support remained conspicuously absent.

Representatives of all major airlines, including aerospace labor organizations and the Teamsters Union, attended the hearing. Concerns voiced by representatives of the airline industry about their economic losses dominated the Committee hearing. Beyond their federally grounded planes, the silence in airport terminals, and potential airline industry layoffs and stock tumbles, airline executives were especially anxious about exposure to liability through civil suits and obtaining insurance at affordable premiums, if at all. Leo Mullin, Chairman and CEO of Delta Airlines, addressed such concerns to the Committee, stating:

I must discuss...the liability issues arising out of the tragic role cast on aviation in this attack on America. The events of September 11 are unique, with terrorists for the first time in history using a commercial aircraft as an instrument of destruction. We believe, however, that the resolution of claims arising from the act of war should be resolved by Congress enacting appropriate federal laws rather than by resorting to the widely divergent principles of state common law. If that is not the case, then while...airlines named as defendants will necessarily defend themselves in litigation, the massive response time and uncertainty as to the outcome of litigation will almost certainly frustrate an airline's ability to raise needed capital in the short term. In addition, it may well prevent airlines from purchasing necessary insurance until such time as the litigation is concluded. And what's more, some carriers are reporting drastic increases in premiums, and other carriers fear that insurance may not be available at any price...Mr. Chairman, it is absolutely critical that this issue be addressed in your legislation as it is a critical element of the overall financial impact of the tragedy on our industry.[10]

What little was said on behalf of the victims and their families during the Committee hearing was initiated by Rep. Max A. Sandlin, Jr. (D-TX) in response to the concern over airline liability. Discussions between Rep. Sandlin, Hollis Harris, Chairman and CEO of World Airways, and Kerry Skeen, Chairman and CEO of Atlantic Coast Airlines, illustrate the secondary role that a fund to support the victims and their families played in comparison to the desire to provide financial support to the airlines.

Sandlin: Is there any advice you could have to us on how we could work together as an industry and as a Congress to provide relief to the families and the victims without further victimizing the victims?
Harris: Well, are you talking about now the victims on the ground?
Sandlin: Yes, sir.
Harris: I think the...basic insurance that we carriers have had would take care of the passengers and the victims...on the airplane, but I don't know the answer to the third party body and...property. It is so vast. I don't know exactly where you have to draw the line there.
Sandlin: Do you think some of the money that we've set aside to help the airlines, and certainly we want to help the airlines, should some of that be set aside for a claim fund by the victims? Would that be something to consider or not?
Harris: Technically, I'm sure you could put it in the bill and it could be set aside. I don't know—I really don't know if it's workable...because of the large number of people involved...

Skeen: My comment on that, if you don't mind, would be that . . . those type of funds are not in the . . . request, as I understand it. [It] is my understanding, that those numbers were not built into Mr. Mullin [Leo Mullin, Chairman and CEO of Delta Airlines] and ATA's model. Sandlin: I think that's correct, but I was just asking generally, without getting into dollars, if you had any ideas, and you might want to think on that and talk with us later . . . You said the government should absorb the liability of [the airlines]. One, do you think we have enough information right now to move on those issues or should we pause and do a little more research? [S]econdly, do you have any suggestions—maybe some sort of creative suggestions on what we might do . . . to address the immediate and current needs of our families as a whole? Maybe part of the money should be set aside in a relief fund and delivered immediately. . . . I'm asking for some input or something that you think might be helpful to families.[11]

Following the Committee hearing, and the increasingly divergent opinions over the scope of compensation for the airline industry, congressional members initiated talks on a new compromise bill. Dubious of the perceived overly generous support the federal government was intending to bestow upon the airlines, some Democrats, echoing the concerns of Rep. Sandlin, sought complementary measures that would ensure victim and airline employee relief.[12] Some Republicans, however, maintained concern that a victim relief fund could cost the government untold sums, arguing that the liability issue should be dealt with at a later date.[13]

In the week following H.R. 2891's failure to pass in the house, a bipartisan emergency package emerged that would accommodate the needs of the airline industry and those of the victims and their families. Finally, late in the evening on Thursday, September 20, 2001, following President Bush's address to a joint meeting of Congress, Senate lawmakers and White House officials met behind closed doors to hammer out a final deal on a consensus bill to be introduced to Congress the next day.[14] In exchange for capping the liability of the airlines at their insurance levels should victims or their families pursue civil actions against them, a provision for compensating victims and their families on a no-fault basis was swiftly added. Uncertainty over how the tort system would facilitate the provision of damage awards for economic and noneconomic losses of victims and their families contributed to the addition of this provision that would guarantee such compensation without further burdening the airlines.

The provision, now Title IV of the Air Transportation Safety and System Stabilization Act, otherwise known as the September 11th Victim Compensation Fund, was added to H.R. 2926 under the guidance of House Democratic Leader Richard Gephardt (D-MO), House Speaker Dennis Hastert (R-IL), Rep. Oberstar and Ranking Member of the House Judiciary Committee Rep. John Conyers, Jr. (D-MI). H.R. 2926, the product of the House Committee on Transportation and Infrastructure hearings and other extensive bi-partisan negotiations, subsequently went on to win congressional approval and passage into law the next day.[15]

The Fund, due in large part to the haste with which it was drafted and enacted into law, is thus a precarious prescription for the losses suffered by victims and their families as a result of the terrorist acts of September 11. Included as Title IV of the Act, it nonetheless bears little connection to other provisions of the Act, reaffirming its conception as a sudden afterthought to remedies sought for the beleaguered airlines. Indeed, the Fund's very inclusion within legislation entitled 'Air Transportation Safety and Stabilization Act' bespeaks its secondary import-ance. Absent any preamble discussing the context and general intent of the provision, the Fund is instead encapsulated by a simple purpose briefly stated in section 403: 'It is the purpose of this title to provide compensation to any individual (or relatives of a deceased individual) who was physically injured or killed as a result of the terrorist-related aircraft crashes of September 11, 2001.'[16]

Details on the administrative procedures necessary for the Fund's efficient and effective disbursement were scant. Although the Fund provides for a claims process to be completed by those eligible, it left all details of the claims forms, eligibility criteria, and methodology for determination of award amounts to the Special Master alone. The Special Master was accorded significant discretion in his power to issue all regulations to administer the Fund according to section 407. Specifically, he was authorized to promulgate all regulations with respect to:

1. Forms to be used in submitting claims under this title [Title IV];
2. Information to be included in such forms;
3. Procedures for hearing and the presentation of evidence;
4. Procedures to assist an individual in filing and pursuing claims under this title; and
5. Other matters determined appropriate by the Attorney General.[17]

By contrast, the administrative procedures specified by the Fund itself included only that claims be made before December 31, 2003; that the Special Master complete a review and make a determination of compensation no later than 120 days after the submission of a claim; that payment to the claimant be authorized no later than 20 days after a determination is made; and that claimants waive their right to file a civil action. Strikingly, under section 405 subsection (b)(4)(c), the Fund also vested in the Special Master authority to determine the due process rights of the claimants. This power, together with the rule in section 405 subsection (b)(3) that the decision of the Special Master is final and not subject to judicial review, granted overwhelming and almost unprecedented authority to a single individual charged with administering a victim compensation program. Such powers exceed even those vested in the judges who would hear civil actions brought by victims and their families who opt out of the Fund.

In its haste to provide compensation to the victims and their families, Congress appeared to have sacrificed clear and explicit directives on how that compensation would be provided. The resultant Fund was therefore highly susceptible to criticism and inertia given the extensive provisions that were to be drafted and executed by one man. Fortunately, at the end of the day, the extraordinary diligence and ability of the Special Master deflected much of the criticism.

3. SOURCE OF FUNDS

The Fund, subsidized entirely by the federal government through a congressional appropriation, differs substantially from most of its international counterparts in that there is no connection between the source of reparations and the wrongdoers. In almost all other cases, reparations have been established by governments seeking to compensate people they have victimized through past state action (or those victimized by predecessor regimes). The well-known German, Argentinean, and Chilean schemes, as well as the scheme involving Japanese Americans interned in World War II, all share this characteristic.[18] By contrast, the US government played no role in perpetrating the September 11 attacks. It did, however, possess the means—political and logistic—to potentially have minimized its vulnerability to such devastating attacks, at least in theory. It is only under this hypothetical account, in which the US government is seen as not having done enough to prevent the terror of September 11, that the Fund's benefits can be considered genuine reparations for wrongs committed. Absent this point, the Fund is merely a compensatory and restorative scheme for lives and livelihoods lost. The lack of direct connection between the source of compensation and the perpetrators of the attacks has several important ramifications that make the September 11 compensation scheme fundamentally different from other initiatives that fall more comfortably within the reparations rubric. In particular, the notions of justice, reconciliation and restitution, typically central goals of reparation programs, are entirely absent from the September 11 scheme.

Justice is an abstract notion, but invariably it comprises both an effort to render whole a victim of wrongdoing and the punishment of the wrongdoer. For example, a burglary case is not considered resolved when the victim receives an insurance payment covering his loss. Through payments to victims by wrongdoing states or their successors, most reparation programs inherently seek to provide their beneficiaries with a sense that justice is being carried out. Such payments typically are accompanied and justified by expressions of remorse by the State for the past wrongdoing, with the explicit or implicit goal of providing victims with closure and a secondary goal, again often tacit, to attempt to preclude any recurrence. However, conspicuously absent from the congressional debates regarding the Fund is the suggestion that it was intended to give a sense of justice to the victims of the attacks. Indeed, none of the September 11 victims' groups or individual victims have made any public statement that the reparations will give them such a sense. To the extent that providing solace to victims is an objective of reparations programs, this calls into question the likely incorporation of the American effort into the general framework of reparations.

Closely related to the notion of justice is that of reconciliation. Most reparations programs are intended to mitigate or eliminate the resentment and desire for vengeance instilled in victims of massive human rights abuses, so as to reduce the potential of an ongoing cycle of violence and allow a country to put the wrongdoing in the past. For example, implicit in the Argentine and Chilean reparations schemes was a desire by the respective governments to ease the bitter political divisions that had ravaged those countries.[19] By contrast, President Bush and Congress in no way sought to reconcile the beneficiaries of the Fund to their attackers. To the contrary, through its repeated public pledges to capture or kill those deemed responsible for the attacks, its military campaign in Afghanistan and other related actions, the US government has demonstrated its commitment to vigilantly pursue the September 11 perpetrators.

Restitution is another common component of reparation programs. For example, a December 1999 agreement provided, in principle, that German companies that profited from slave labor during World War II would pay $5.1 billion in compensation to the victims of such practices.[20] The government of New Zealand established a process through which land confiscated by the British in the 19th century may be returned to the Maori.[21] Such examples are informed by the notion that those who benefit from systematic human rights abuses (or their successors) should disgorge their ill-gotten gains to the victims of the abuses. Whether or not anyone can be said to have profited unjustly from the September 11 attacks, there is no question that restitutionary principles are not found within the Act or the Fund.

The minimal legislative history related to the creation of the Fund suggests that its purpose was quite limited in comparison to the rationales behind most reparations programs for human rights abuses. The purpose of the Fund was simply to provide monetary compensation to victims and their survivors for their losses, so as to reduce consequent economic hardship. In this sense the September 11 scheme more closely resembles emergency relief funds for victims of natural disasters than it does reparations programs addressing human rights abuses. It is worth noting that unlike in the cases of prior reparation schemes, the wrongdoers in the September 11 attacks are not viable sources of reparations funds. Al-Qaeda is an international terrorist network, whose suspected financial backers have had assets frozen and rendered inaccessible. The Taliban government that most directly harbored and supported it no longer exists, and its successor lacks the resources to fund reparations.

4. MODE OF COMPENSATION

Typically, reparations are handled on an administrative basis that assumes the fungibility of the human experience under the conditions being repaired. In coming to terms with his country's 'Dirty War', Argentinean President Menem signed a decree providing that persons who had suffered detention by virtue of acts of military tribunals during the years 1976–83 would be eligible for reparations. Compensation would be based on the number of days in detention, and a fraction of the length of detention commensurate to injury sustained as a result.[22] Such calculations do not try to make a fine-grained analysis of the nature of the individual experience. In other words, they do not try to replicate the award of individualized legal damages under a tort system. The Fund is curious in that it seeks to induce individuals away from the tort system. As stated in the Act's 'final rule', promulgated on March 13, 2002, the Fund 'provides an alternative to the significant risk, expense, and delay inherent in civil litigation by offering victims and their families an opportunity to receive swift, inexpensive, and predictable resolution of claims'.[23] As a consequence, its most difficult and most controversial aspects are the determinations of individual desert that Special Master Feinberg had to make.

The Act provides that the Special Master issue the rules no later than 90 days after its enactment. On December 21, 2001, the Department of Justice and the Special Master's Office released the 'interim final rule' governing the Fund.[24] The interim final rule, effective immediately as law, allowed for the submission of claims to begin and, more importantly, granted a 30-day public comment period. Upon publication of the interim final rule, the Special Master's Office was inundated with thousands of emails, letters and calls commenting on the relative justice of the Fund's distribution. The public comment period presented a unique addition to a reparations program because it specifically asked people to come forward with thoughts on how their individual experiences could best be compensated and accommodated. It deliberately sought contributions to the development of a final rule that would be attractive enough to lure individuals away from the tort system. This comment process resulted in some changes to the interim final rule as evidenced in the release of the final rule on March 13, 2002.

The comments that flooded the Department of Justice website represented opinions from a cross-section of society, including those directly and indirectly affected by the tragedy.[25] The comments also reflected a deep divide in perspectives as to the purpose of the Fund itself. Those who supported the Fund and its distributional scheme supported it as a symbol of national healing, providing families of innocent victims with the means for their continued existence without having to revisit the tragedy year after year in protracted civil lawsuits. Others criticized its unsuccessful attempt to replicate the tort system and mirror past jury awards in airline litigation, citing the areas of compensation that are not equivalent to damages eligible in court. Still others criticized its overall approach to reparation, declaring that if any money was to be distributed, it should be distributed equally to all. These critics viewed the loss suffered by each family as indistinguishable and argued that quantifying awards based on income levels effectively declared a dishwasher's life less valuable than that of a stockbroker. One commentator on the website stated 'rich people do not deserve more because they are rich'. Special Master Feinberg has defended the Fund's hybrid of quasi-reparation program and quasi-tort scheme as the most effective means of delivering a fair and equitable sum to each eligible claimant.

Of concern to most who commented was the level of compensation, given the required forbearance of civil litigation that feasibly could have awarded higher damages than those provided for by the interim final rule. Others perceived the cold calculus of the award as forcing them to view the deceased instrumentally, much the same way courts handle wrongful death suits. Following common legal practice, the equation the Fund uses to calculate loss is based primarily on economic loss derived from an individual's earning potential in life. It is in this manner that the Fund strays from other reparations programs, where the intent is to make victims psychologically whole irrespective of financial circumstances. The Fund values different lives differently, and refuses to weigh, individually, other noneconomic harms, such as lost household services or pain and suffering (even in court, the latter harms would be compensated in a manner designed for 'make whole' reparation).

The award calculation prior to the final rule was a product of explicit economic variables, with specific value allocations for each, including collateral offsets. First, tables of income projections, based upon 'expected remaining years of workforce participation', multiplied by average yearly salary for the years 1998–2000, qualified by wage growth rates, estimated presumptive awards. For example, according to one projection, the spouse of a victim who earned $225,000 per year, caring for two young children, would be eligible for $3.8 million in compensation prior to offsets.[26] Next, in addition to the economic calculation, the family would be eligible for a one-time, flat award of $250,000 for noneconomic damages plus $50,000 for each dependent (including the spouse). Subsequently, the award would be offset by compensation received from other sources, such as life insurance, pension benefits, social security and workers' compensation. Additional offsets included the victim's share of household expenditures or consumption as a percentage of income as well as a factor to account for risk of unemployment, all presented with assigned numerical values. Critics have referred to this as Special Master Feinberg's 'Robin Hood Strategy' given its resemblance to the adage of taking from the rich to benefit the poor.[27] The collateral offsets remove from the calculus any supplemental financial sources that could have conceivably added up to a windfall for some families if they were awarded a sizable compensation package in addition to other insurance benefits. The offsets thus diminished the marked differences in the awards that would have resulted from a simple compensatory model.

Beyond opinions on the merits of the Fund as a reparations program, comments on the interim rule included concerns about the specific methods of award calculation. They raised issues regarding the fact that the Special Master's schedules, tables and charts identified presumed economic determinations that were discriminatory against women and minorities. The projections, commentators argued, were based upon outdated statistics of predominantly male workers and underestimated the advances made by women towards greater participation in the workforce, in addition to their longer life expectancy. Some comments suggested that income growth rates were too low, or that consumption rates were too high. Other comments raised concerns that domestic partners, heterosexual and homosexual, were being discriminated against because the rules relied upon applicable state law to determine one's eligibility as a personal representative. To the extent that a state did not recognize gay partners or fiancés as comprising domestic partnership, those individuals would not be eligible to claim compensation. The Fund sought to defuse these issues by erring on the side of inclusion and negotiation, even where state law might prove an obstacle.

However, a significant share of comments seemed to be devoted to the calculations of the collateral offsets. The Act mandated that the total amount of compensation be reduced by the amount of money received through collateral sources, defined as 'life insurance, pension funds, death benefit programs, and payments by Federal, State, or local governments related to the terrorist-related aircraft crashes of September 11, 2001', that the victim or family has received or is entitled to receive. Many commentators claimed that deducting collateral compensation from the final award penalized those individuals who bought life insurance or invested wisely to provide for their families. Moreover, the personal representative, from whose award the collateral proceeds would be deducted, may not necessarily be the beneficiary of the deceased's life insurance or pension but would be penalized nonetheless. The potential for offsetting contributions made to victims and their families by charitable organizations was also raised as an inappropriate interference in private financial arrangements. Similar criticism met the suggestion that pension funds, retirement savings plans (401(k) plans), and Individual Retirement Accounts (IRAs) be offset; those benefits, critics argued, are essentially personal savings plans and should not be introduced into the calculus of economic loss. Partly as a result of the vague language of the Act, and the resulting confusion over what would and would not fall within its definition of a collateral source, an overwhelming number of comments consistently raised the unfairness of any such collateral offsets.

Families of public safety officers killed in the line of duty on September 11 suggested that offsets affecting their compensation would be especially unjust, given the sacrifice made by the officers in risking their lives to protect those of their fellow citizens. Consequently, attempts to distinguish between civilian victims and public safety officers for purposes of calculating compensation amounts and collateral offsets engendered debate and disagreement among families of victims. Speaking on behalf of public safety officers killed as a result of the attacks, some commentators emphasized that these men and women earn generous collateral benefits precisely because they place themselves in dangerous conditions such as those that cost them their lives on September 11.[28] Such commentators felt that the benefits should therefore not be denied. By contrast, families of civilian victims urged Special Master Feinberg to treat all victims equally when making decisions regarding economic loss calculations. Administrative decisions, they argued, should not be applied according to the victim's line of work.

Congress, however, initiated the practice of granting public safety officers and their families priority and particular attention with respect to compensation, when it passed Public Law 107–37, entitled 'Public Safety Officer Benefits Act', on September 18, 2001—four days before establishing the Fund to compensate all other victims of the terrorist attacks. The stated purpose of the bill was '[t]o provide for the expedited payment of certain benefits for a public safety officer who was killed or suffered a catastrophic injury as a direct and proximate result of a personal injury sustained in the line of duty in connection with the terrorist attacks of September 11, 2001.'[29] Impassioned discussions of the bill reiterated the acts of heroism and bravery on the part of the firefighters, police officers, and other rescue workers who rushed to the scene of the attacks on September 11.[30] Families of fallen officers had looked upon this bill as the strongest support of their position that collateral resources would not offset any compensation they would receive through the Fund. The offsets, they claimed, would be contrary to the congressional goal of swift payment of death benefits to which they are uniquely entitled and the Fund again read the possible offset against recovery by uniformed officers narrowly, permitting a more generous award than a more technical reading might have prompted.

Finally, an area that has also raised a significant amount of questions had been the fixed noneconomic loss awards of $250,000 and $50,000 per dependent. Those who disagreed with the income-basis of award calculation argued that the fixed noneconomic awards should have been higher to compensate for the differences in income levels. Others claimed that the figures were simply too low to adequately compensate for the emotional hardship they had endured since September 11. Discontent regarding the amount of compensation soon grew into disagreement among the families over how to calculate increases in the figures commensurate with the grief suffered. Some recommended basing noneconomic loss awards on whether or not the victim was able to communicate with the outside world prior to his or her death (and thus able to say goodbye), or, in the case of World Trade Center victims, whether the victim was trapped above the impact area as opposed to those located physically below it. Ultimately, most public complainants were only able to agree upon the fact that they disapproved of the approach proposed by the Special Master to compensate for noneconomic losses.

5. IMPLEMENTATION DIFFICULTIES

The comments submitted to the Department of Justice and Special Master's Office illustrated the sharp divide in approaches to reparations for the attacks on September 11. In a statement accompanying his release of the final rule on March 13, 2002, Special Master Feinberg recognized the differences:

I have listened carefully to both supporters and critics of the interim final rule. I have benefited tremendously from their input. I believe that, as a direct result of that varying input, this final rule constitutes a product worthy of support by all those interested in a just, fair and efficient compensation program. No amount of money can right the horrific wrongs done on September 11, 2001. Nor can any of us who has not shared such immediate and irrevocable loss fully understand the depths of suffering that families and victims are enduring.... [M]y goal has always been to provide the most fair and appropriate compensation within the parameters established by Congress.[31]

The final rule indeed took into consideration most of the concerns voiced and incorporated changes based on the public's comments. Figures used to calculate economic losses were amended to increase, in most cases, the amount of compensation in the Special Master's presumed award charts.[32] In response to complaints of outdated and discriminatory data, the final rule declared that 'in order to increase awards for all claimants by maximizing the duration of foregone earnings and accommodating potential increases by women in the labor force, the Special Master's revised presumed economic loss methodology uses the most generous data available.'[33] Income growth assumptions were expanded to ensure higher calculations and consumption levels were adjusted to reflect after-tax discount rates.

Further, the final rule interpreted the definition of collateral benefits from sources other than the Fund such that certain government benefits need not be treated as collateral sources of compensation. Specifically, benefits such as social security and workers' compensation would be offset only to the extent they had already been paid, given the impossibility to calculate such benefits with reasonable certainty. Other offsets, based upon private investments, would be subject to a case-by-case analysis as deemed appropriate by the Special Master. As stated in the final rule, 'While Congress left...little choice on whether or not to make certain collateral source deductions [the Special Master] has slightly more discretion in how to calculate the appropriate deduction.'[34] Most importantly for families of public safety officers killed on September 11, an 'Explanation of Economic Loss Calculations for FDNY or NYPD Victims', as revised on May 15, 2002, explicitly stated, 'The Fund will not offset the...Public Safety Officers Benefit'.[35] The 'Explanation' also made clear that the methodology of economic loss calculation for public safety officers, unlike for civilian victims, 'is set up so that the Fund will not include in the offset the amount of the pension that was vested as of September

11'.[36] Hence, in line with Congress' recent legislative actions and the wishes of families of fallen officers, Special Master Feinberg made the distinction between civilian and public safety victims of September 11 a prominent one as it relates to the determination of economic loss calculations.

Finally, the amount of noneconomic loss awards was increased to $100,000 per dependent, rather than the previous $50,000 figure. The one-time award of $250,000 remained unchanged; the final rule described it as an appropriate starting point because it was the same level of compensation that Congress has historically made available to public safety officers and soldiers killed in the line of duty. Payments for economic loss, which compensated for what the victim would have earned in his or her lifetime had the attacks never happened, were thus liberalized as a result of public comments and concerns. Noneconomic loss also played a key role in determining awards for personal injury claims.

6. PERSONAL INJURY CLAIMS

Personal injury claims proved to be one of the most difficult and vexing aspects of the Compensation Fund. Since most of the attention had been paid to the deceased victims, injury claims largely slipped below the radar screen. Special Master Feinberg noted, 'We received five times more personal injury claims than we thought we would,' and described his reaction as 'stunned'.[37] According to some statements, Feinberg did not expect the number to exceed 300, much less than the 4,400 that were actually filed.[38] The vast majority of those cases dealt with respiratory problems 'from breathing in gunk at the site'. Feinberg stated that he simply did not 'anticipate the number of respiratory claims'.[39] Despite the large number of filings, some attorneys believed it was only the tip of the iceberg, with many response workers suffering from serious health problems but unable to attain any compensation from the Fund because they missed the December 22, 2003 deadline. Michael Barasch of Barasch, McGarry, Salzman, Penson & Lim represented 120 individuals, including many firefighters rejected from the Fund because they only showed respiratory problems after December 22. 'They missed it because their lungs didn't get the message that the deadline was Dec. 22, 2003,' Barasch noted.[40]

The interim and final rules set down strict limitations on eligibility for compensation. Only people who suffered 'physical harm' were eligible for compensation, and the interim rule's definition of 'physical harm' required treatment by a medical professional within a 24-hour period either after the injury was sustained or after rescue. Additionally, it required hospitalization for at least 24 hours, and the injury must have caused temporary or permanent, partial or total physical disability, incapacity, or disfigurement. The final rule would later expand the period before seeing a medical professional from 24 to 72 hours. This accounted for situations where either someone did not realize the extent of his or her injury until later or no appropriate health care was available. The Special Master also had the option of granting a time extension in the case of rescue workers.[41] The Fund's restrictions also applied to location. Only victims present at the sites (World Trade Center, Pentagon, or Shanksville, Pennsylvania) were included in the Fund. For nonrescue workers, they had to have been either in a building or the area contiguous to the building during the period 12 hours after the crash. For rescue workers, this time frame was extended to 96 hours.[42]

Personal injury claims also posed some problems that were not encountered in the claims for deceased victims. According to John C. Jeannopoulos, a lawyer from Trial Lawyers Care, evaluating someone who was still alive posed the unique problem of putting a number on his or her experience.[43] This 'subjectivity' caused great difficulties for Fund officials and was something that Special Master Feinberg specifically tried to avoid: 'We do not make distinctions between claimants on the basis of pain and suffering and emotional distress...I will not play Solomon. I cannot make those distinctions and I won't make those distinctions.'[44] Policy—at least regarding compensation for death—reflected this sentiment in two ways: a standard amount was used to compensate for the pain caused by death; and the 'pain and suffering' of the victim's death was not included in calculating the final award. Feinberg tried to avoid these subjective judgments so that there would not be an arbitrary weighing of different people's experiences and pains, which could lead to more divisiveness, insult, and injury. Unfortunately, in the case of personal injury awards, this type of subjectivity had to be a factor in the final calculations. While a strict formula could not be applied, two guiding principles would be used to try and provide a criterion for determining the size of the award. First, for people totally or permanently disabled, the economic award would be calculated in a manner similar to victims who were deceased. It would be based upon loss of earnings, other benefits related to employment, medical expense loss, replacement services loss, and loss of business or employment. There would be no deduction for projected consumptions, and finally, compensation for lost earnings would be reduced by any collateral source offset.[45] The collateral source offset was in turn based upon whether (1) the offset fitted the definition of a collateral source (charity was excluded for instance), (2) victims were 'entitled' to compensation from collateral sources, (3) the collateral compensation was guaranteed, and (4) the appropriate amount of deduction would include considerations of the time-value of money and contributions made by the victim (for instance to taxes or charities).[46] Second, the noneconomic component of the award would be based on the nature, severity, and duration of the injury. Burn-related injuries were expected to require the largest noneconomic award due to the pain being more permanent and the high probability of disfigurement. Because of the severity of some injuries, the personal injury award could exceed the awards to deceased victims.[47]

Personal injury claims reflected a tension inherent in both trying to compensate individuals based upon their particularized circumstances, and trying to craft an administrative compensation system that, to a great degree, must abstract from any particular claimant. In the context of reparations, they further raise the question whether the attempt to provide individual-specific compensation, as opposed to a societally determined fixed amount, is truly viable. Injury claims may also cast a negative light on the legislation's attempt to rapidly provide aid. Many victims had been and may continue to be unaware of their injuries until far past the deadline; hence, the ability to compensate all victims may be seriously undermined. It still remains to be seen how many victims will remain uncompensated because of the expedited nature of the compensation process.

7. Born Difficult

While the methodology of compensation may have been amended to provide for 'fair, predictable and consistent' compensation in an expedited and efficient manner, the claims process suggests otherwise. It is not accidental that administrative difficulties initially plagued the Fund, given its inception amidst confused purpose and intentions—a rushed amalgam of congressional desire to induce families out of the tort system while attempting to reflect a more altruistic national purpose. As a result, the process remained cumbersome and complicated. Indeed, given the administrative burden, the claim forms themselves encouraged families to enlist the assistance of an attorney to complete the process.[48]

The instructions and form for compensation for deceased victims and the instructions and form for personal injury compensation were 33 and 31 pages long, respectively. The supporting documentation necessary to file for compensation for a deceased victim included over 20 different types of certificates, affidavits, and other forms requesting detailed information that may be dauntingly difficult to amass.[49] To help facilitate the processing of claims and queries, the Department of Justice and the Special Master's Office established toll-free hotlines, several claims assistance sites, and a website for claimants. The Fund's attempt to provide an alternative to the tort system, while maintaining an equitable balance in award distributions, thus resulted in a complex administrative scheme.

Over seven months after the publication of the interim final rule and the official start of claim submissions, only 605 of approximately 3200 eligible families filed even partial applications for compensation from the Fund. The slow pace of applications was not only disappointing to supporters of the Fund and surprising to its detractors, it raised concerns that families were opting out of the Fund and into civil litigation.

Many of the families who delayed their application seemed to be participating in a waiting game for the results of the applications first filed. Some of the test cases involved young victims who worked for multinational firms and had significant earning potential. The cases were expected to illustrate how the families of young, financially promising victims were going to be compensated. Given some of these victims' potential future earnings, the economic loss calculation for the awards were expected to exceed the average $1.85 million payout per family. In admitting that the formula used to calculate loss could result in a much higher than average award, Special Master Feinberg explained, 'After all is said and done, a formula is just that—a formula—and in individual cases, I do have the discretion to divert, or to part from the formula in an effort to do justice in an individual case.'[50]

To settle the concerns over the Fund's distributional scheme, Special Master Feinberg also needed to address the vague, or at worst absent, legal guidelines that governed the awards. The ambiguities in the regulations led to wary families waiting for the results before they decided whether to opt in. Among US citizens entitled to benefits, the potential awards from the Fund had sparked discord between family members vying for official recognition as 'personal representative' of the deceased's estate, or the one to whom compensation would be paid. Although the final rule specified that the personal representative shall be a spouse, child or parent, and preferably in that order, it did little to ease the confusion that many of the non-nuclear family members felt in determining who fit this description. Biological parents challenged the legitimacy of those who raised the victim. Children from a previous marriage challenged the status of the unwed partner of the victim. Siblings challenged other siblings. The permutations seemed endless and Special Master Feinberg had offered no clear instructions other than the requirement that one who intends to be named personal representative notify all other family members of that fact.

Among the most baffling tests of fairness presented to Special Master Feinberg were those that concerned foreign beneficiaries, including the illegal aliens whose eligibility for compensation from the Fund Congress had approved. Because the Fund relied upon state law, based upon the domicile of the personal representative, to answer the questions of legal entitlement posed by nontraditional marital, family, or dependency status, it followed that the Fund had to look to foreign national laws to determine the beneficiary status of those families of victims not resident in the USA. Such a proposition posed a significant problem if one accepts the myriad of relevant religious laws and ethnic customs that often determine the basis of inheritance. In some Muslim countries, for example, the Koran allows a husband to marry multiple wives; should the husband die, they each inherit a prescribed share of the estate, as do the children. In some Latin-American countries, where common-law marriages are recognized, unlike in New York, the number of beneficiaries based upon extensive family ties could easily multiply; this affected the families of the many Mexican and Dominican victims of September 11. Sharing his own uncertainty over how such laws will apply, Feinberg stated:

It's one thing to look at the law of New York or New Jersey; it's quite another when I have to look to the law of Norway, or Yemen, or the People's Republic of China. ... It's very unclear to me at this stage of the process exactly how we will mesh with those laws in determining who gets what.[51]

In attempting to gain insight as to how such matters should be resolved, Special Master Feinberg consulted with over 50 consulates and embassies. In sum, by attempting to replicate a tort system, the Fund introduced substantial legal uncertainty that could have been avoided by adopting a simpler administrative scheme.

The victims and their families had until December 21, 2003 to file claims for compensation from the Fund. The slow start caused Special Master Feinberg to redouble his efforts to promote the Fund, conducting outreach initiatives across the country in person and on television broadcasts. At one point, Feinberg stated pithily, 'It's all part of an effort to ease the access of the claimant to a very unique program, which is unprecedented in history... We'll try to make it efficient and reasonable.'[52] Unfortunately, his commendable promises did not seem to be encouraging those victims and their families who still preferred to wait and see how the current cases developed before submitting their own claims. One commentator aptly noted, 'What's going on is kind of a sad game of chicken. Do the families and their lawyers push Mr. Feinberg—and Congress—for more money? Or do they risk trying to persuade a jury that the airlines should have foreseen what nobody else foresaw?'[53] Whether one agrees with the tactics employed by the families, it is indisputable that the nation's largest and most generous financial compensation scheme was, at that time, largely untouched by the thousands whose welfare depended on its generosity.

Due to the low number of applicants, some legislators including Senator Frank R. Lautenberg tried but failed to extend the deadline for a year. Lautenberg expressed disbelief that anyone could vote against the measure, but several Republican leaders explained their reasons for maintaining the deadline. They thought the last-second change would cause confusion among families, anger families who already filed claims, and create incentives for procrastination. Special Master Feinberg, despite concerns over the low number of claims, did not express support for the extension, and several officials remained optimistic that the number of claims would increase as the deadline approached.[54] Indeed, Feinberg later described the role deadlines played as one of forcing parties to come to terms with the decisions that had to be made, under any circumstances.[55]

In the end, the concerns over lack of participation proved to be unfounded. During the last six weeks before the deadline, hundreds of families rushed to file a claim, and fully a third of the total claims were filed during that period. The final results exceeded Feinberg's hopes of 90 percent participation with over 98 percent of eligible participants filing claims.[56] The reasons for filing claims at the last second varied from family to family. Some families reported only hearing about the Fund very late in the process. Others noted a change in Feinberg's approach after conceding that he 'underestimated the depth and extent of the families' grief'.[57] Some families simply needed as much time as possible to deal with the grief. Feinberg reported that victims' relatives would come up to him in tears and say, simply, 'I'm not ready' when told that the deadline was approaching.[58] The stories from families who had already filed claims with the Fund also were very important. There had been fairly widespread criticism of the Fund as 'complicated, cold-hearted, and ungenerous',[59] and Feinberg had been criticized as insensitive and inconsistent as well. These negative accounts made people cautious about submitting claims and forgoing the option of civil suits. But as people began to share their experiences with the Fund, these concerns dissipated. Claimants uniformly described Feinberg as fair and generous. As a result, more people were willing to file claims rather than take the risky path of litigation. Some of Feinberg's harshest critics would even end up switching sides to support the Fund, including Charles Wolf, who lost his wife on September 11 and started a website, www.fixthefund.org, because of his opposition to Feinberg.[60]

By the official closing of the Fund on June 15, 2004, 7,397 families had participated in the program. Around 98 percent of the 2,973 eligible families of deceased victims filed claims, with only 70 choosing litigation and 30 doing nothing.[61] Of the 4,400 physical injuries claims filed, 2,678 awards were issued, ranging from a low of $500 to a high of $8.6 million.[62] The total amount of awards paid was $6.9 billion, which included injury claims amounting to $888.2 million. The awards for the deceased averaged at $2.1 million, with a median of $1.7 million. The award ranges after collateral offsets are shown in Table 8.1.[63]

Table 8.1 The award ranges after collateral offsets

Income level	Age	Range
$50,000 or less	35 or under	$250,000 to $3.2 million
$50,000 or less	Over 35	$250,000 to $4.1 million
$50,000 to $100,000	35 or under	$250,000 to $4.2 million
$50,000 to $100,000	Over 35	$250,000 to $4.3 million
$100,000 to $200,000	All ages	$250,000 to $5.5 million
Over $200,000	All ages	$250,000 to $7.1 million

The man responsible for bestowing that munificence[64] upon those who sought it, Special Master Kenneth Feinberg, undoubtedly deserves mention in this study for the role he has undertaken to play since November 2001. Although he inherited a program contentious from the start, and thus a position equally controversial, Special Master Feinberg conducted a heroic effort to compensate victims and their families, uncompensated and unshaken in his resolve to impart fair decisions and awards. Acting as permanent grief-catcher for the thousands profoundly affected by the tragedy of September 11 is by no means an easy task; engendering their trust and confidence is a significantly more difficult one. Feinberg came to this task uniquely qualified as perhaps the most experienced mediator and administrator of mass tort remedies in the USA. He had previously dealt with tremendously complicated and socially charged claims for compensation in cases as disparate as Agent Orange and the Dalkon Shield claims. Although a life-long Democrat, Feinberg's expertise was sufficient to immediately make him the Special Master of choice to Republican Attorney General John Ashcroft. Special Master Feinberg has undertaken the difficult task at the head of the Fund with both professionalism and humility.

8. Relation to Other Restorative Mechanisms

The Fund, unlike most traditional reparations programs, is unrelated to any other mechanism traditionally employed for dealing with massive abuse or human rights violations. In other words, the typical sequencing of programs undertaken by countries in response to past atrocities is not found within the context of the Fund. The Fund is not supported by the work of any truth commission or commission of inquiry, nor will it be followed by institutional reform of, or amnesties granted to, the regime responsible for the attack. There has been no public apology issued by the perpetrator, and the US government envisages no formal reconciliation procedures. The reason for the lack of interrelationships between measures is the absence of an internal complicit entity.

Interestingly, however, despite bearing no responsibility for the terrorist attacks on September 11, the US government has nonetheless initiated some measures analogous to those implemented by other countries in response to a history of atrocities. In addition to financial reparations through the Fund, the US government (in conjunction with the state and local governments of New York,

Pennsylvania, and Virginia) has supported the establishment of symbolic reparations through the erection of monuments and memorials, and the dedication of days of remembrance to the victims of September 11. Further, the US government has also launched a full-scale investigation into the actions and omissions of government agencies responsible for gathering intelligence that could have detected and perhaps thwarted some of the airliner hijackings that led to the tragedy of September 11. Finally, the US government seeks the punishment of the perpetrators of the terrorist attacks, despite in no way linking the distribution of financial compensation to the victims to the successful prosecution of those responsible for the wrongs committed.

The weeks following September 11 saw the organization of hundreds of events and services, both secular and religious, devoted to the commemoration of those who were killed and injured in the attacks. In honor of the memory of the thousands of lives lost, President George W. Bush proclaimed Friday, September 14, 2001 as a 'National Day of Prayer and Remembrance for the Victims of the Terrorist Attacks on September 11, 2001'. He called upon all Americans to mark the National Day of Prayer and Remembrance with noontime memorial services, the ringing of bells at that hour, and evening candlelight vigils. In addition to such commemorations, government officials, family members and civic leaders commenced discussions of the physical structures that would forever preserve the memory of the victims of September 11.

Most notable among the discussions is the ongoing debate in New York City over the composition of the permanent memorial to be erected on the site of the World Trade Center. Business developers of the 16-acre lot would like to see the land used primarily for commercial real estate, citing the lack of adequate office space as both a logistic and an economic problem for the city.[65] An estimated 10 million square feet of rentable space (or an acre of rentable space on each floor of each tower) was lost when the towers collapsed, driving many businesses to neighboring New Jersey. Families of the victims, on the other hand, urge the committees responsible for developing the site to dedicate significant space to a memorial honoring the lives lost and injured in the attacks.[66] As the remains of many of those killed were not found in the recovery effort, families claim the site is hallowed ground, equivalent to a burial place where they should be free to come and pay their respects. New York City Mayor Michael Bloomberg has called for compromise between the two sides. Although he agrees with family members of the victims that a memorial be the centerpiece of the site, it must host a variety of uses, including commercial and residential property. Mayor Bloomberg advises that a balance be struck, to accommodate not only the wishes of the business community and the victims' families, but also the residents of the adjacent Battery Park City who, he observes, do not want to live in a 'graveyard'.[67] As we go to press, the disputes over the development of the site and the claims of families of victims to a special role in designing the future remain largely unresolved.

Further, reparations programs often occur subsequent to truth commissions or other commissions of inquiry; on occasion the two mechanisms of reconciliation are employed in tandem. The reason is clear: truth seeking efforts aim to discover and identify legacies of abuse so as to create an official, unbiased record of past events for victims, their families and perpetrators. The record serves as public acknowledgment of the abuses suffered by victims and their families and provides a sense of closure to a painful past. The results of those efforts can then serve to shape the extent and scope of subsequent reparations programs. The Fund follows neither prescription.

However, one could look upon the US government's efforts to identify potential intelligence community oversights as attempts to fulfill similar goals to those of official truth commissions. Congressional investigations into the actions, or inactions, of the Central Intelligence Agency (CIA), the Federal Bureau of Investigation (FBI) and the National Security Agency (NSA) seek to uncover truths about the operations of those agencies in the months and weeks prior to September 11. The complicated and overlapping responsibility of offices engaged in intelligence and security matters within the US government often clouds their ability to easily detect, and correct, official errors. Moreover, sensitive information suggesting careless errors, the avoidance of which could have altered the outcome of September 11, may even be suppressed by the intelligence agencies themselves. Therefore, the launching of a congressional inquiry into the work and knowledge of those offices signals official government recognition of the compelling need to prevent future intelligence lapses, and, more importantly, future atrocities.

On February 14, 2002, the Senate Select Committee on Intelligence (SSCI) and the House Permanent Select Committee on Intelligence (HPSCI) announced a joint inquiry into the September 11 terrorist attacks. A press release accompanying the announcement declared:

Among the purposes of this joint effort is ascertaining why the Intelligence Community did not learn of the September 11th attacks in advance, and to identify what, if anything, might be done to better the position of the Intelligence Community to warn of and prevent future terrorist attacks and other threats of the 21st century. The Committees may seek to legislate changes to remedy any systemic deficiencies revealed by the joint inquiry.[68]

Further, on June 4, 2002, the SSCI and HPSCI adopted an Initial Scope of Joint Inquiry officially authorizing an investigation into the intelligence community's activities before and after the September 11, 2001 terrorist attacks on the USA. The stated purpose of the joint inquiry was telling in its desire to uncover information that may have easily been concealed, whether intentionally or not, by the intelligence community. The inquiry sought to conduct a thorough investigation of, among other things,

all matters that may have any tendency to reveal the full facts about ... what the Intelligence Community had, has, or should have learned from all the sources of information, including any terrorist attacks or attempted ones, about the international terrorist threat to the United States; what the Intelligence Community knew prior to September 11 about the scope and nature of any possible attacks against the United States . . . and what was done with that information; what the Intelligence Community has learned since the events of September 11 about the persons associated with those events, and whether any of that information suggests actions that could or should have been taken to learn of, or prevent, those events; whether any information developed before or after September 11 indicates systemic problems that may have impeded the Intelligence Community from learning of or preventing the attacks in advance, or that, if remedied, could help the Community identify and prevent such attacks in the future.[69]

The answers to such inquiries are intended to produce an accurate picture of the security measures adopted and implemented both before and after September 11, and seek the development of recommendations to improve intelligence gathering to avoid future attacks. Similar to the work of truth commissions, the congressional investigations also hope to provide some measure of relief to the victims and their families in publicly accepting responsibility for any errors that may have contributed to the tragedy of September 11.

Nonetheless, the most significant effort by the US government is undoubtedly the ongoing effort to find and punish the perpetrators of the attack. Prosecution of wrongdoers in cases of human rights violations sends a clear message both to the perpetrators and victims that acts of violence are not tolerated nor will they be relegated to the annals of history. Punishment not only serves future, deterrent, purposes, but it offers victims retributive justice for past abuses. In his statement to the nation on the evening of the terrorist attacks, President Bush declared:

The search is underway for those who are behind these evil acts. I've directed the full resources of our intelligence and law enforcement communities to find those responsible and to bring them to justice. We will make no distinction between the terrorists who committed these acts and those who harbor them.[70]

The search for the perpetrators, as well as those who aid in their terror, remains the chief goal of American law enforcement agencies within the USA and abroad.

Since the President's declaration, the US military has led a full-scale offensive, Operation Enduring Freedom, against the Taliban regime in Afghanistan—considered by many to have been harboring and encouraging the development of future terrorist attacks by Osama Bin Laden's al-Qaeda network. As a result of the Afghanistan campaign, the military has detained hundreds of men on the US Naval base in Guantanamo Bay, Cuba. The detainees recently had their challenge to continued detention heard by the Supreme Court and now, in light of the Court's ruling, are being processed by military tribunals. In addition, the Department of Justice and the Immigration and Naturalization Service has detained approximately 460 individuals, some of whom face criminal charges, while others have been deported for technical immigration violations. The US government has also named 22 'most wanted' terrorists, including Osama Bin Laden, and is offering up to $25 million for information leading to their arrest.[71]

Finally, the misfit between the Fund and classic reparations programs may be further reflected in the strong ongoing private efforts to assist the victims of September 11. Prominent among the organizations who established such programs were the American Red Cross, a joint initiative of the United Way of New York City and the New York Community Trust,[72] and The Salvation Army. In the months following September 11, individuals who met eligibility requirements set by the organizations could apply for assistance in areas as diverse as cash assistance for short- and long-term financial needs, job training, placement and counseling, and mental health and health care. Although eligibility requirements varied somewhat between organizations, the plans offered commonly applied not only to those individuals who were injured or families of those who died as a result of the events of September 11, but also to those who worked south of Canal Street in Manhattan as of September 11 and who lost their jobs.[73]

The American Red Cross established perhaps the largest charitable program, the 'Red Cross Liberty Fund', for families who suffered losses and those who were seriously injured in the September 11 attacks. According to a press release from the organization on June 21, 2002, the American Red Cross anticipated the total expenditures for the Liberty Fund to come to approximately $765 million by September 2002.[74] The Liberty Fund established programs tailored to meeting the needs of discrete groups of individuals, such as the Red Cross Family Gift Program, which provided financial assistance for one year to those families in need of basic living expenses, averaging $51,000 per family.

9. THE FUND AS REPARATIONS

The Compensation Fund can only hesitatingly be described as a reparations program. Reparations are closely related to a process of social reintegration of the victims. They involve both recognizing the victims as victims and citizens (i.e. as rights holders), and fostering civic trust and social solidarity.[75] This makes reparations conceptually out of place for September 11. Rather than being looked down upon, outcast from society or suffering from negative stigmatization, the victims were widely seen as heroes and embraced by the nation. As a result, the Fund's status as a reparations program would be limited to its ability to provide compensation. But the central factor is that the Fund was not initially aimed at the victims. The Fund was not established to bring justice or even, strictly speaking, provide compensation to the victims; rather, it was initially created out of fear that recourse to the courts would threaten the precarious financial health of the airline industry. The discussion and deliberation on 'just' compensation for victims must be considered within the context of the overarching theme of protecting the airline industry. Even the public comment period must be viewed in the light of an incentive-based system, attracting people away from litigation. This inevitably influenced the shape that the Fund would eventually take.

While the Fund would begin to take on its own life in pursuing compensation, its conceptual integrity would remain significantly compromised by the purpose behind its establishment. At its most simple, there was no discernible rationale for separating the September 11 victims from those of the bombings in Oklahoma City, on the U.S.S. Cole and at the embassies in Africa. As cogently asked by Kathleen Treanor, whose 14-year-old daughter was among the victims in Oklahoma, and who filed a lawsuit after the Victim Compensation Fund was established for September 11, 'Why is it right for a New York stockbroker's widow to be given millions of dollars and not a poor farmer's family in Oklahoma? It's been nearly eight years since the Oklahoma City bombing. It took them days to pass this legislation.... They told me that my daughter was not worth as much as a New York victim, and that's an ugly, ugly thing to say.'[76] A similar story was told by relatives of victims of the embassy bombings in Africa, including Howard Kavaler, who lost his wife in Nairobi on August 7, 1998. He noted simply, 'We've been forgotten.'[77] As families pushed for inclusion, they inevitably debated over which similarities to September 11 were relevant to the scope of the Fund.[78]

The individualized method of payment also raised tensions among victims because it invited comparative judgments. Families of firefighters and rescue workers with large amounts of life insurance and pensions worried that they would not get anything from the Fund due to collateral offsets.[79] Issues were also raised with Feinberg's method of calculating the awards. Cantor Fitzgerald, a firm that lost 658 employees, noted that Feinberg used national averages to calculate the projected earnings, but that a typical Fitzgerald employee substantially exceeded the national average. It suggested that a lump sum or cap on the payments would have been better (even if it resulted in a smaller award), simply because it was fairer and would create less division among victims.[80]

Strictly speaking, the program was successful in its goals. A tiny minority of people filed suits, the solid majority accepted payments, and the airlines were insulated from expensive tort litigation. But if we evaluate the Fund in the context of a reparations program or restorative justice, its success may be far more constrained. The Fund was crafted to serve a set of goals distinctly removed from the goals of reparation. Rather than being tailored specifically to the needs of the victims, it was a more complicated undertaking that responded not just to the sense of national horror following September 11, but also to some less exalted expedient concerns over potential liabilities of powerful economic actors.

10. CONCLUDING NOTES

The Fund stands as a curious hybrid between the make-whole aspirations of the civil tort system and a reparations-style public compensation system. There are a few historic examples of such public compensation schemes in the USA, such as funds created to compensate victims of the war of 1812 and civil war widow pensions. But the Fund is unique in trying to marry the idea of a societal cost to the individual-specific calculations that underlie the civil liability system.

Part of the unique feature is no doubt attributable to the rushed origins of the Fund in trying to shore up the insurance ratings of the suddenly vulnerable airline industry. But a large part has to do with the unfamiliarity of American social insurance with collective harms and the relation between the customary operation of our legal system and foreign insults that test its ability to respond. The more familiar form of this debate is presented in the question of whether the ordinary operation of the criminal justice system can address the problem posed by terrorism. The Fund, however, was an attempt to induce families away from the civil justice system by trying to replicate the results of the tort system through administrative means, and at public expense. The mix of a private compensation system run through an ad hoc administrative agency, together with the uneasy blend of individual benefit and societal cost, introduces necessarily difficult questions about the nature of societal risk.

The result was largely successful, assuming success is defined as the use of unlimited public funds to secure acquiescence of the victims' families to nonlitigated outcomes. To that extent, the force of Special Master Feinberg's personality and the sheer energy brought to the task are stunning. Unfortunately, that measure of success leaves unresolved what the society owes to those who are befallen by either misfortune or a broadly delivered attack on the society writ large. By and large, we leave individuals to the markets for first-party insurance and do not try to assign either a life value to all individuals or a safety net of social insurance against death generally. At best, we pay limited amounts of survivors' benefits from social security or for the heirs of military personnel. But these systems are defined by their cold, administrative calculus, paying out according to a strict formula of either age and number of dependents, or contributions through lifetime wages.

It is only when we assign blame to a culpable wrongdoer that we attempt to make fine-grained distinctions between the value of two distinct lives, finding the life circumstances and prospects of one to be more deserving than that of another. These fine-grained distinctions are confined to the compensatory role of the tort system and are intended to compel the wrongdoer to return the victim and his or her descendants to a state equivalent to the status quo ante, in order to assume the cost of the harms rendered. To this elaborate assessment of the value of a life, the tort system adds the additional costs occasioned by the loss, measured by such soft variables as pain and suffering, emotional distress, and lack of consortium. While this is the core of the civil tort system, its strained attempts to fine-tune the value of a particular life have never been translated to any administrative compensation system.

Thus, our account of the Fund raises, but cannot answer, two fundamental issues. The first has to do with the role of social insurance for extraordinary harms directed at the society as a whole, but falling upon discrete individuals. It is by no means a given that the victims at the World Trade Center are more deserving of social compensation than are the individuals killed by a runaway van a few weeks earlier at Herald Square. If they are, it must be because the random road accident is internalized as a customary cost in a society dependent upon motor vehicles. But even if we draw the distinction between the unique and the quotidian, it does not follow at all that the exceptional response must take the form of recreating the ordinary workings of the civil justice system. Indeed, Feinberg's own account of his experience indicates that in many instances the need to document the value of a life through contested proceedings may very well have compromised the best of humanitarian impulses. Thus Feinberg summarizes:

I've become convinced that the 9/11 fund formula was defective. Instead, if Congress decides to provide compensation in the event of a new terrorist attack, all eligible claimants should receive the same amount. . . .

[I]t is essential to understand the nature of public compensation. It should be viewed as an expression of the collective cohesive spirit of the nation and its citizens toward the victims of a foreign terrorist attack here at home. It is a recognition of the emotional suffering of surviving families, regardless of economic wherewithal and financial circumstances. In this sense, the economic impact of the award is almost irrelevant; the fact that the award is authorized by Congress at all is what matters. The rest is window dressing, expensive window dressing to be sure, but window dressing nonetheless.[81]

NOTES

1. Darren Geist, an intern at the ICTJ, contributed to updating this paper in late 2004. The paper was updated again, by the authors, in May 2005.
2. The actual average for loss of life was $2.1 million, as we see in this chapter.
3. It is noteworthy that the September 11 Fund was created and administered independently of the 9/11 Commission, whose mandate was an overview of government functioning both in anticipation of the September 11 attacks and in the aftermath.
4. During discussion of the Act on the Senate floor, Senator Arlen Specter (R-PA) declared that 'The terrorist attack is really an attack against the United States as a whole, and when we have losses directly attributable to that attack, it seems fair to me that the entire Nation should sustain those damages.' Senator John McCain (R-AZ) added that 'The intent of the fund is to ensure that the victims of this unprecedented, unforeseeable, and horrific event, and their families do not suffer financial hardship in addition to the

terrible hardships they already have been forced to endure.' 147 Cong. Rec. S9593 (daily ed., September 21, 2001) (statements of Sen. Specter and Sen. McCain).

5. Representative Roy Blunt introduced the 'Embassy Employee Compensation Act' on November 29, 2001. The Act has since passed the House (H.R. 33775) and was referred to Senate committee on May 22, 2002. Its stated goal was to provide compensation for the US citizens who were victims of the bombings of the US Embassy in Nairobi, Kenya and of the US Embassy in Dar es Salaam, Tanzania on August 7, 1998 on the same basis as compensation is provided to victims of the terrorist-related aircraft crashes on September 11, 2001. The bill died in Senate committee and never became law.

6. 147 Cong. Rec. H5685 (daily ed., September 14, 2001) (statement of Rep. Young).

7. Ibid.

8. In objecting to continued debate over H.R. 2891, Rep. Lloyd Doggett (D-TX) requested that the bill be sent to committee. He stated, 'I feel that the taxpayers of this country are owed a better explanation than to hear about a bill at 4, with promises and and's, if's, or's and but's, that is going to take perhaps not just $2.5 billion, but perhaps $15 billion out of that Social Security money, that they are entitled to know a little more about it. If it is so desperate and if it is so essential that this be accomplished before Monday, then I suggest we stay and work on it. I am prepared to do that. I suggest that we stay and have a hearing. If the gentleman has so much wisdom and insight on this, I suggest he convey it to us in the course of an ordinary hearing.... So, for all of those reasons, I object to doing this tonight.' 147 Cong. Rec. H5690-1 (daily ed., September 14, 2001) (statement of Rep. Doggett).

9. Chairman Young reminded Committee members that 'We are here today to address the threat to the continued stability and viability of our U.S. air transportation system. The terrorists who attacked our country last week, were trying to destroy our way of life and our economy—but we must not let them do that. They have murdered thousands of innocent people, destroyed billions of dollars in property and have dealt a terrible blow to an air transportation system that is vital to the economic health of our country.... Unfortunately, we are now facing a serious crisis in our air transportation system. The reductions in schedules and flights have started and layoffs are being announced. The capital markets are not coming to the aid of most of the airlines. We are seeing the ripple effect in our economy as layoffs occur in other related industries. Our economy is at risk.... This assistance is intended as a short term, emergency response to keep the air transportation system operating for the benefit of the American people.' Press release, US House Committee on Transportation and Infrastructure, Hearing on Needs of Airline Industry Following Terrorist Attacks (September 19, 2001), http://www.house.gov/transportation/press/press2001/release112.html (last visited August 11, 2002) (on file with authors).

10. Needs of the Airline Industry Following the September 11 Terrorist Attacks: Hearing on H.R. 2891 Before the House Comm. on Transp. and Infrastructure, 107 Cong. (2001) (statement of Leo Mullin, Chairman and CEO, Delta Airlines).

11. Needs of the Airline Industry Following the September 11 Terrorist Attacks: Hearing on H.R. 2891 Before the House Comm. on Transp. and Infrastructure, 107 Cong. (2001) (statements of Rep. Sandlin, Hollis Harris, Chairman and CEO of World Airways, and Kerry Skeen, Chairman and CEO of Atlantic Coast Airlines).

12. In debates on H.R. 2891's ultimately successful successor bill, H.R. 2926, Representative Jim McDermott (D-WA) reiterated his continuing concerns regarding the bill's

munificent support of the airline industry: 'Congress blew an ideal opportunity to continue the bipartisan unity it has so nobly demonstrated during the past ten days .... Instead, Congress is handing airline executives golden parachutes while over 90,000 American workers—to date—are left without so much as a safety net! Congress may have blown an opportunity but the Republicans have demonstrated their opportunistic aims. They neatly wrapped this one-sided bill in a patriotic package, enveloped not by the American flag mind you, but with the American Airlines logo. There is no question that the airlines desperately need this bailout, but why should the government shoulder the brunt of the responsibility—to resuscitate an industry that has shown its true colors.... Does anyone here seriously believe that the American public will seriously consider returning to the airways when they can't really be sure that these planes are safe or even properly maintained? There isn't any money in this bill that ensures the future safety of our citizens. After all, isn't this an industry that resists government regulation and abhors collective bargaining agreements. And now they are asking us to bail them out ... It's time our leadership got their priorities straight. They should have brought a more responsible bill to the floor for our consideration and not wasted this body's precious time.' 147 Cong. Rec. H5899 (daily ed., September 21, 2001) (statement of Rep. McDermott).

13. Lizette Alvarez with Stephen Labaton, 'A Nation Challenged: The Bailout; An Airline Bailout,' *New York Times*, September 22, 2001: A1.

14. At his appearance on *CNN Live at Daybreak* at 7:00 AM on Friday, September 21, 2001, Sen. Daschle (D-SD) was asked by John King: '[S]ir, as the country listened to the president last night, the Congress also acting on his request and the concerns in the Congress that more be done quickly to help the airline industry, which obviously is struggling right now. We understand a deal was reached on this late last night. Will that be passed today in the House and the Senate and give us the highlights, sir.' Sen. Daschle responded, 'Well, all four leaders are going to be presenting what we will recommend as a way to respond to our caucuses this morning. Depending on what kind of response we get from our caucuses, we'll be in a better position to make some decision about whether we can pass it and send it off to the president quickly. It involves direct assistance, about $5 billion. It involves loan guarantees, about $10 billion. And it provides for liability protection for the airlines and direct assistance to all of the victims of the tragedy of September 11th.' Television interview with Sen. Tom Daschle, Majority Leader, US Senate (September 21, 2001).

15. In supporting H.R. 2926 during discussions on September 21, 2001, Rep. Gephardt spoke to the considerable debate and disagreement that drafting the bill engendered: '[T]his has been a very difficult process of putting this bill together.... We are here to disagree. That is what we do. We do that because we each represent a half a million people who all disagree most of the time. If we were not here expressing their heartfelt views, democracy would not work and we would not be doing our job.... Tonight, in my humble opinion, agreeing and acting to save this industry and keep it going forward is in the highest and best interest of all the people of our country. There are good things in this bill, and I want the Members to know that it is not an airline bill. It is a bill to keep these airlines going.... It is also not the bill that I wanted. It has some glaring omissions from my viewpoint.... So we are learning tonight, in many ways, that bipartisanship is hard. You cannot get everything you want. You never do.... Bipartisanship means you get

some things you really want and you give up some things that you really want.' 147 Cong. Rec. H5898 (daily ed., September 21, 2001) (statement of Rep. Gephardt).

In voicing his support of the newly added provision for victims and their families of September 11, Representative Jim Turner (D-TX) stated, 'I want to address these remarks to the families of the victims, those who were injured on September 11. One of the best provisions of this bill is that this Congress has provided a method whereby all those injured, the victims of those who have died, will have full recovery for their economic and noneconomic damages by the establishment of a special master. The Treasury of the USA has been opened by the Members of this Congress to ensure that every family will receive just recovery. It is one of the best provisions of the bill, and I urge my colleagues to support it.' 147 Cong. Rec. H5906 (daily ed., September 21, 2001) (statement of Rep. Turner).

16. Air Transportation Safety and System Stabilization Act of 2001, Pub. L. No. 107–42, § 403, 115 Stat. 230, 237 (2001).

17. Air Transportation Safety and System Stabilization Act of 2001, Pub. L. No. 107–42, § 403, 115 Stat. 230, 240 (2001).

18. One possible exception is the 1994 Florida law providing $2.1 million in state-funded reparations to descendants of the victims of the Rosewood massacre, in which white lynch mobs killed six blacks and drove many black families from their homes. The perpetrators were not officials of the state of Florida. Nevertheless, given the tacit official support that often surrounded such attacks and the state-mandated discrimination against blacks, one can argue that a nexus between Florida and the perpetrators of the crime did exist. See the studies on the German, Argentinean, and Chilean reparations efforts in this volume.

19. The State organ created by Chile to provide compensation to victims of the Pinochet dictatorship was called the 'National Corporation for Reparations *and Reconciliation*' (emphasis added). See the study on Chile by Elizabeth Lira (Chapter 2, this volume).

20. The fund was announced after months of negotiations between German companies that used slave and forced labor during World War II, attorneys representing the laborers, and Jewish organizations.

21. Public Act 1993 No 4, entitled 'Te Ture Whenua Maori' (Maori Land Act) provided for the establishment of a court and other mechanisms to assist the Maori people in achieving the implementation of the principles set out in the Treaty of Waitangi, which established the relationship between the Maori people and the Crown. The Treaty embodied principles of protection of land of special significance to the Maori people; it sought to facilitate the occupation, development and utilization of that land for the benefit of the Maori.

22. Although some compensation was premised on tortlike calculations pursuant to recommendations of the Inter-American Human Rights Commission, the most common method for calculation of reparations was based on factors such as detention rates. See the study by María José Guembe (Chapter 1, this volume).

23. September 11th Victim Compensation Fund of 2001 Final Rule, 67 Fed. Reg. 11,233 (March 13, 2002) (to be codified at 28 C.F.R. pt. 104); available at http://www.usdoj.gov/ victimcompensation/finalrule.pdf (last visited August 11, 2002) [hereinafter 'final rule'].

24. September 11th Victim Compensation Fund of 2001 Interim Final Rule With Request for Comments, 66 Fed. Reg. 66,274 (December 21, 2001) (to be codified at 28 C.F.R. pt.

104); available at http://www.usdoj.gov/victimcompensation/victimcompfedreg.pdf (last visited August 11, 2002) (on file with the ICTJ) [hereinafter 'interim final rule'].

25. All comments can be viewed on the website created by the Department of Justice for the Victim Compensation Fund, at http://www.usdoj.gov/victimcompensation/ civil_03.html (last visited August 11, 2002).

26. The victim's expected remaining years of workforce participation were not based on his or her individual health or other personal characteristics, but precalculated according to 'A Markov Process Model of Work-Life Expectancies Based on Labor Market Activity in 1997–98', by James Ciecka, Thomas Donley, and Jerry Goldman in the *Journal of Legal Economics*, 9(3) (Winter 1999–2000): 33–68. Likewise, a prepared table of presumed age-specific wage growth rates was calculated based on life-cycle, inflation, and overall productivity increases of the average male worker from the 2001 Current Population Survey.

27. Amanda Ripley, 'What Is a Life Worth?', *Time*, February 11, 2002: 22.

28. One commentator noted, 'The City of New York lures young men to very dangerous jobs as firefighters paying them relatively low wages for years with the promise of a healthy pension . . . it is deferred compensation. Why should this deferred compensation be considered any different than savings in a bank account?' http://www.usdoj.org /victimcompensation/interim/nfeb11/N002586.htm (last visited August 11, 2002) (on file with authors).

29. Public Safety Officer Benefits Act of 2001, Pub. L. No. 107–37, 115 Stat. 219, 219.

30. Senator Hillary Clinton (D-NY), in introducing the bill to the Senate floor, stated, '[W]hen we look at who is on the front lines, it is not me carrying the ax. It is not me as one of the ironworkers who rushed down to volunteer their services to help remove some of the debris. It is not me as a police officer who is on the front lines. It is these men and women who have made the sacrifice to protect us, and to respond as they would have at a time of battle. And, in effect, when this act of war took place, they were our front-line soldiers. The Federal Government provides a one-time benefit payment to the families of public safety officers lost in the line of duty through the public safety officer benefit program. Unfortunately, these benefits are often delayed for long periods of time because of very burdensome regulatory applications . . . . It is imperative that we take action now to ensure that the family members of those brave men and women who lost their lives in this terrorist attack are not confronted with the same onerous process.' 147 Cong. Rec. S9360 (daily ed., September 13, 2001) (statement of Sen. Clinton).

Representative F. James Sensenbrenner (R-WI), on the floor of the House of Representatives, declared, 'The purpose of this resolution is simple and clearly warranted: that is, to provide swift aid and comfort to the survivors of the public safety officers who perished in the wake of the terrorist attacks on the World Trade Center in New York City. Their loss and the loss incurred by the New York City fire and police departments is unfathomable. The bravery exhibited by these men and women was of the greatest magnitude, and was the embodiment of noble service to our Nation and to the citizens of this country . . . . In the towers and on the ground, New York City public safety officers were unflinching in carrying out their mission of saving and protecting thousands of people who now owe their lives to these devoted officers. Because of their dedication to duty, many officers made the ultimate sacrifice for their fellow citizens. May God bless their souls and their families. They will never be forgotten, and their heroism will always be cherished by a grateful Nation, State and city.' 147 Cong. Rec. H5599 (daily ed., September 13, 2001) (statement of Rep. Sensen-brenner).

31. Final rule, *supra* n. 20, at 11,233.

32. The hypothetical spouse discussed above could now receive $4.5 million before offsets.

33. Final rule, *supra* n. 20, at 11,238.

34. Final rule, *supra* n. 20, at 11,234.

35. Explanation for Economic Loss Calculations for FDNY or NYPD Victims (May 15, 2002), http://www.usdoj.gov/victimcompensation/fdny_nypd.pdf (last visited August 11, 2002).

36. Ibid.

37. Quoted in Ted Sherman, 'Head of 9/11 Fund "stunned" by volume of injury claims', *Star-Ledger*, Monday, June 21, 2004.

38. Leslie Eaton, 'Threats and Responses: The Wounded', *The New York Times*, September 10, 2002.

39. Quoted in Sherman, op. cit.

40. Quoted in Thomas Adcock, 'NY Firm Spurs 9/11 Controversy', *New York Lawyer*, July 9, 2004.

41. *Victim Compensation Fund Frequently Asked Questions.* Section 2.6 at http://www.usdoj.gov/victimcompensation/faq2.pdf

42. *Victim Compensation Fund, Frequently Asked Questions.* Section 2.3 at http://www.usdoj.gov/victimcompensation/faq2.pdf

43. Quoted in Rudy Larini, 'Victims Fund Concludes Last Ground Zero Cases: Federal Compensation Totals Nearly $6B', *Star-Ledger*, Wednesday, June 16, 2004.

44. Special Master Kenneth R. Feinberg Transcript, *News Conference Announcing Regulations Concerning 9/11 Victim Compensation Fund*, December 20, 2001 at http://www.usdoj.gov/ag/1220kenfeinbergnewsconference.htm

45. September 11th Victim Compensation Fund of 2001, 'Compensation for Personal Injury Victims: Award Payment Statistics' at http://www.usdoj.gov/victimcompensation/payments_injury.html

46. *Victim Compensation Fund Frequently Asked Questions.* Section 6—Compensation for Personal Injury at http: //www.usdoj.gov/victimcompensation/faq6.pdf

47. September 11th Victim Compensation Fund of 2001, 'Compensation for Personal Injury Victims: Award Payment Statistics' at http://www.usdoj.gov/victimcompensation/payments_injury.html

48. The Association of Trial Lawyers agreed to provide pro bono counseling on processing the claims.

49. The required documentation includes: a certified death certificate; written proof that the victim was at the World Trade Center (for World Trade Center victims only and does not apply to those who died in Virginia or in Pennsylvania); a court order proving personal representative status or, in the absence of such an order, the victim's will and proof that the claimant is the first in line of succession under the laws of intestacy in the victim's domicile; written consent of dependants for advance benefits and a cancelled check for direct deposit; tax returns for the victim for tax years 1998–2000; information proving the victim's base salary/wages for the years 1998–2001, including pay stubs, year-end pay statements or a salary letter; additional information regarding compensation the victim received in the years 1998–2001 including bonuses, commissions, or overtime; employer-provided benefit information including health benefits, pension

plans, 401(k) funds, and other fringe benefits; proof of burial/memorial costs and medical costs; proof of collateral sources of compensation including life insurance, social security payments, and workers' compensation payments; a proposed distribution plan for compensation award; certification of dismissal of legal action; a signed list of individuals notified of claim filing; and any other information relevant to the claim.

50. *CBS Morning News* (CBS Television Broadcast, July 22, 2002).

51. David Chen, 'Struggling to Sort Out 9/11 Aid to Foreigners', *New York Times*, June 27, 2002: A1.

52. Ibid.

53. 'Victim's Compensation', *St. Louis Post-Dispatch*, July 21, 2002: B2.

54. David Chen, 'Senate Rejects Bid for Extra Year for Sept. 11 Compensation', *New York Times*, November 26, 2003.

55. Kenneth R. Feinberg, *What is Life Worth?: The Unprecedented Effort to Compensate the Victims of 9/11* (New York: Public Affairs, 2005), 161.

56. *Closing Statement from the Special Master, Mr. Kenneth R. Feinberg, on the Shutdown of the September 11th Victim Compensation Fund*, at http://www.usdoj.gov/victimcompensation/closingstatement.pdf

57. David Chen, 'Applicants Rush to Meet Deadline for Sept. 11 Fund', *New York Times*, December 23, 2003.

58. Diana B. Henriques, 'Concern growing as families bypass 9/11 Victims' Fund', *New York Times*, August 31, 2003.

59. David Chen, 'Applicants Rush to Meet Deadline for Sept. 11 Fund', *New York Times*, December 23, 2003.

60. Ibid.

61. Editorial Desk, '9/11 Fund Closes Its Doors', *New York Times*, June 18, 2004.

62. Ibid.

63. September 11 Victim Compensation Fund of 2001, 'Compensation for Deceased Victims', at http://www.usdoj.gov/victimcompensation/payments_deceased.html

64. Pablo de Greiff, 'Justice and Reparations' (Chapter 12, this volume), uses the term 'munificence' to refer to the magnitude of individual awards distributed by reparations programs.

65. Larry A. Silverstein, who holds the lease on the site, has commissioned a team of architects from the firms of Skidmore Owings & Merrill and Cooper Robertson & Partners to draw up plans for four 50-story buildings and a park that would include a memorial.

66. Architects, artists and members of the business and political communities are serving on a special Memorial Process Team, which will weigh competing plans for a memorial on the site of the collapsed World Trade Center towers. In addition, an advisory committee to the Lower Manhattan Development Corporation consisting of family members of the victims has also begun discussions about the memorial.

67. Edward Wyatt, 'Less is More, Mayor Suggests on World Trade Center Site', *New York Times*, June 16, 2003: B1.

68. During the announcement of the inquiry, Senate and House Intelligence Committee Chairman Senator Bob Graham (D-FL) added that 'When the Intelligence Community fails to provide timely and accurate threat information, it is a grave matter. We are launching this inquiry without preconceived notions of what may have gone wrong in the Intelligence Community leading up to September 11th of last year. I have no interest

in simply looking in the rearview mirror and playing the 'blame game' about what went wrong from an intelligence perspective. Rather, I wish to identify any systemic short-comings in our intelligence community and fix those problems as soon as possible. We have a solemn obligation to the 3,000 people who died, their families and the rest of the American people to insure that any deficiencies in the organization and operation of the intelligence community are remedied to prevent a recurrence of September 11th.' Press Release, US Senate Select Comm. on Intelligence, Senate and House Intelligence Committees Announce Joint Inquiry Into the September 11th Terrorist Attacks (February 14, 2002), http://intelligence.senate.gov/020214.htm (last visited August 11, 2002) (on file with authors).

69. Initial Scope of Joint Inquiry Preamble, Senate Select Comm. on Intelligence & H.R. Permanent Select Comm. on Intelligence, http://intelligence.senate.gov/preamble.pdf (last visited August 11, 2002) (on file with authors).
70. President's Address to the Nation, 37 Pub. Papers (September 11, 2001) available at http://www.whitehouse.gov/news/releases/2001/09/20010911-16.html (last visited August 11, 2002) (on file with authors).
71. See Rewards for Justice, *Most Wanted Terrorists*, http://www.rewardsforjustice.net/mostwanted.html (last visited July 31, 2002) (on file with authors).
72. The United Way and the New York Community Trust established the Fund hours after the terrorist attacks. The Fund has since raised over $500 million to help those directly affected by the terrorist attacks. http://www.uwnyc.org/sep11/faq.htm (last visited August 6, 2002) (on file with authors).
73. See Press Release, American Red Cross, *Deadline Nears for Workers Impacted by 9/11* (March 3, 2002) available at http://www.redcross.org/press/disaster/ds_pr/020304wtcdeadline.htm (last visited August 6, 2002) (on file with authors).
74. See Press Release, American Red Cross, *Red Cross Begins Final Phase of September 11 Family Gifts* (June 21, 2002) available at http://www.redcross.org/press/disaster/ds_pr/02062fam.htm (last visited August 6, 2002) (on file with authors).
75. See de Greiff, op.cit.
76. Ibid.
77. Richard Leiby, 'Working Wounded', *Washington Post*, February 12, 2002.
78. Belkin, 'Just Money', *New York Times*, December 8, 2002.
79. David Chen, 'Victims' Fund Announces First Awards', *New York Times*, August 23, 2002.
80. Belkin, op. cit.
81. Feinberg, *supra* n. 55, at 183, 186.

CHAPTER 9

THE UNITED NATIONS COMPENSATION COMMISSION

HANS VAN HOUTTE

HANS DAS

BART DELMARTINO

INTRODUCTION

This chapter is meant to provide systematic and detailed answers to a number of questions pertaining to the origins and the institutional structure of the United Nations Compensation Commission (UNCC), its mandate and eligibility requirements, the procedures and forms of delivery as well as the relationship with domestic courts.

Throughout the text, the authors have aimed to identify the main obstacles encountered by the UNCC as well as the lessons learned in each of these domains. It is believed that by showing the obstacles and challenges encountered in implementing the largest postconflict compensation program in history, valuable lessons for future operations begin to emerge. The main focus of this chapter is therefore on the practical and legal elements that may be relevant to other postconflict or transitional situations.[1]

The chapter is structured into six separate sections, as follows:

In Section 1, the origins of the UNCC are examined. The factual background of the Iraq-Kuwait conflict is summarized and the different steps leading to the determination of Iraq's liability and the establishment of the reparations program are outlined.

Section 2 relates to the UNCC's institutional design. The Commission has a tripartite structure, which is characterized by a functional distinction between policy questions, legal determinations, and operational aspects. The three main organs are the Governing Council, the Panels of Commissioners and the Secretariat.

Section 3 deals with the UNCC's mandate. It describes the various categories and subcategories of claims which the UNCC is mandated to receive and decide, examines the eligibility requirements and the way the Commission dealt with the required causal link.

In Section 4, the authors examine the general procedures that apply to the presentation, verification and determination of claims in the UNCC. Particular attention is devoted to relatively sophisticated mass claims processing techniques, such as data matching and the grouping and sampling of claims. It concludes by examining the procedural fairness requirements in the UNCC's mass claims context and the procedural rights of Iraq in the process.

Section 5 relates to the delivery of compensation, and focuses first on the mechanism of fixed amounts of compensation for certain claims categories and the priority accorded to urgent claims. Subsequent sections are devoted to the mechanism established for the payment of compensation sums and the financing of the Compensation Fund.

Section 6 deals with the relationship between the UNCC and domestic courts. Since the UNCC does not have exclusive competence to consider claims arising from Iraq's invasion and occupation of Kuwait, specific measures have been taken to avoid multiple recovery of losses.[2]

1. ORIGINS OF THE REPARATIONS PROGRAM

The Conflict and Its Origins

Iraq's claim that Kuwait is historically and legally an integral part of Iraq's Basrah province has a long history. The territorial dispute has its origins in the history of both entities during the Ottoman Empire and already came before the Security

Council in 1961, when Kuwait gained independence and Iraq massed troops on the border. Failing agreement between the permanent members of the Security Council, the UN was not in a position to take action at the time and a solution was devised in the Arab League. The threat of military confrontation was eased and, except for one Iraqi incursion into Kuwaiti territory in 1973, the border between the two countries remained relatively calm.[3]

From February through July 1990, the Iraqi leadership commenced a political campaign against Kuwait, advancing several political, territorial, and financial claims, including:

- Allegations that Kuwait had extracted Iraqi crude oil worth US$2.4 billion by 'slant-drilling' into the Rumaila oilfield;
- A claim that Kuwait's illegal possession of the Warba, Bubiyan, and Failaka islands in the Persian Gulf obstructed Iraq's access to Gulf waters; and
- Accusations that Kuwait and other members of the Organization of Petroleum Exporting Countries (OPEC) were not respecting the OPEC oil-export quotas, causing a worldwide depression of oil prices and depriving Iraq of the resources it needed to pay its debts and to recover from the devastating eight-year war with the Islamic Republic of Iran.

Kuwait denied all of these allegations.[4]

In July 1990, Iraq started to deploy military forces along the border with Kuwait. Negotiations organized by Egyptian President Mubarak on July 31, 1990 failed and on August 2, 1990, at 1 a.m. local time, Iraqi troops crossed the international frontier and started their invasion and occupation of Kuwait.[5]

Within hours of the Iraqi attack, the Security Council met and unanimously adopted Resolution 660 (1990), in which it condemned the invasion, demanded that Iraq withdraw immediately and unconditionally all its forces and called upon both parties to begin intensive negotiations for the resolution of their differences. Individual UN member states, the European Community, the League of Arab States, the Gulf Co-operation Council, the Organisation of the Islamic Conference and others voiced equally strong protest against the occupation of Kuwait.[6]

The Iraqi occupation of Kuwait lasted several months. Thousands lost their lives and millions of others their homes, employment, savings, real property, and personal possessions. More than a million people, mostly workers from Bangladesh, Egypt, Jordan, India, Pakistan, the Philippines, and Sri Lanka, had to leave Iraq or Kuwait. Businesses and individuals suffered losses valued in billions of dollars.

After intense political pressure and a forceful military campaign a ceasefire was reached in April 1991. The Security Council's actions and positions in the immediate aftermath of the Gulf conflict reveal a clear willingness and determination to restore legal order and remedy the injustices inflicted upon individuals and businesses. The Council adopted several resolutions, leading to the creation of the

UNCC. Two of its decisions were crucial in this context: first, the Council ascertained Iraq's liability for the invasion and occupation of Kuwait; and, second, it decided that appropriate compensation should be provided to injured parties.[7] The genesis and evolution of both decisions will be briefly outlined in the following sections.

The Determination of Iraq's Liability

Successive Security Council Resolutions show an evolution in the nature and the extent of Iraq's liability.[8]

- In paragraph 13 of Resolution 670 (1990) the Security Council simply '[r]eaffirm[s] that the Fourth Geneva Convention applies to Kuwait and that as a High Contracting Party to the Convention Iraq is bound to comply fully with all its terms and, in particular, is liable under the Convention in respect of the grave breaches committed by it, as are individuals who commit or order the commission of grave breaches.'[9]
- In paragraph 8 of Resolution 674 (1991) the Security Council reminds Iraq that 'under international law it is liable for any loss, damage or injury arising in regard to Kuwait and third States, and their nationals and corporations, as a result of the invasion and illegal occupation of Kuwait by Iraq'.
- The Security Council took a slightly different approach in Resolution 686 (1991). In paragraph 2(b), the Council 'demands that...Iraq accept in principle its liability' for any loss, damage or injury arising as a result of the invasion and illegal occupation of Kuwait by Iraq.
- Subsequently, Resolution 687 (1991) limits Iraq's liability to losses which are a *direct* result of its invasion and occupation of Kuwait. Moreover, the Resolution no longer requires an acceptance by Iraq. Paragraph 16 unequivocally states that the Council '[r]eaffirms that Iraq, without prejudice to the debts and obligations of Iraq arising prior to 2 August 1990, which will be addressed through the normal mechanisms, is liable *under international law* for any *direct* loss, damage, including *environmental damage* and the depletion of natural resources, or injury to foreign Governments, nationals and corporations, as a result of Iraq's unlawful invasion and occupation of Kuwait' (emphasis added). The explicit reference to compensation for environmental damage and the depletion of natural resources is a first in the history of postwar claims settlement. Although Iraq was by no means the first State to have deliberately harmed the environment as an act of war, the UNCC is the first international body dealing with reparations for deliberate environmental damage.[10]

The Establishment of the United Nations Compensation Fund and Commission

To give effect to its findings on liability, the Security Council also took responsibility for establishing the mechanism that would be used to award compensation. Indeed, for the first time in its history, the United Nations 'has organized an operation to provide compensation for war damage, and in the process created a new system for its implementation, while establishing sources for its funding'.[11]

In paragraph 18 of Resolution 687 (1991), the Security Council resolved 'to create a fund to pay compensation for claims that fall within [Iraq's liability] and to establish a Commission that will administer the fund'. In the following paragraph, the Security Council requested the Secretary-General to formulate concrete recommendations concerning the 'administration of the fund; the mechanisms for determining the appropriate level of Iraq's contributions to the fund...; the process by which funds will be allocated and claims paid; appropriate procedures...; and the composition of the Commission'.

The Secretary-General submitted a report on May 2, 1991 (S/22559), in which he stressed 'the need for maximum transparency, efficiency, flexibility and economy in the institutional framework' and formulated a number of recommendations concerning the institutional and procedural framework of the institution to be created.[12]

Taking note of the Secretary-General's report, the Security Council, in paragraph 3 of Resolution 692 (1991), decided 'to establish the Fund and Commission...in accordance with Part I of the Secretary-General's report' and requested 'the Secretary-General to take the actions necessary to implement [this decision]'. The United Nations Compensation Fund was created as a special account of the United Nations, and the UNCC was established as a subsidiary organ functioning under the authority of the Security Council.

Conclusion

The early establishment of the UNCC and the Compensation Fund was made possible by a number of factors. For our purposes, the following elements are relevant:

• First, it was nearly universally accepted in 1991 that Iraq had breached fundamental norms of international law and that it was liable for the direct losses resulting from these wrongful acts. In addition, the Government of Iraq itself accepted—be it reluctantly—its liability in a letter to the UN Security Council dated April 6, 1991.[13]

- Second, individual victims of the conflict represented over 90 different nationalities, therefore making the majority of the international community of States directly concerned.
- A third—and perhaps most important—factor is the availability of natural resources in Iraq. Obviously, the accessibility of financial resources is a key factor in the design and establishment of any compensation process. In order to be effective, the compensating party must have a form of wealth that has a high degree of liquidity, that is easily accessible, that is not privately owned, and that was not destroyed during the conflict.[14] All these conditions are met in the case of Iraq and its oil supplies.
- Fourth, several key players in the Security Council, including the USA, UK, and France, had been actively involved in the military operations, creating a certain opening towards reparations.

The combination of these factors enabled the UN to move swiftly and take concrete steps towards establishing a compensation mechanism. Nevertheless, some aspects of the Security Council's actions, and in particular the adoption of Resolution 687, have caused much debate in the international legal community. A detailed analysis of these legal concerns would be beyond the scope of the present paper, but it is worthwhile summarizing briefly the main controversies.

First, different views exist on whether it was within the Security Council's powers to unilaterally determine Iraq's liability and whether a formal acceptance by Iraq was required. Some scholars have argued that from a legal point of view a formal Iraqi acceptance of its liability was not necessary since the Security Council was acting under Chapter VII of the United Nations Charter. Decisions taken under Chapter VII are binding on all UN member states.[15] Iraq's acceptance of Resolution 687 (1991) then merely established an additional 'specific consensual basis for the basic claims provisions'.[16] Others have questioned the UN's authority to impose automatic liability on the basis of nothing more than the illegality of Iraq's original invasion and occupation of Kuwait, regardless of the question whether compensation claims have been based on individual showings of violations of precise rules of armed combat.[17] This discussion, however, was largely moved to a theoretical level when Iraq formally accepted its liability.

A second controversy relates specifically to the establishment of the UNCC and the question whether the Security Council was competent to create the Compensation Commission. Bernhard Graefrath, for instance, argued that:

[t]here is no reason why the Security Council should not have the right to find that there exists a duty to make reparation, if it has the power to determine that a breach of the peace occurred.... Only when the Security Council established the Resolution 692(1991) procedure, and took decisions on individual reparation-claims (on the assessment of the damage, which amounts should be paid etc), did the Security Council clearly misuse its competences under Chapter VII. The establishment of the United Nations Compensation Commission, a

subsidiary organ of the Security Council, which exercises legislative and quasi-judicial powers, was clearly outside the competence of the Security Council, and its creation was simply an *ultra vires* act.[18]

Nevertheless, the competence of the Security Council to establish the UNCC as its subsidiary organ has been accepted by the majority of scholars.[19]

This discussion is closely related to a third dispute, which concerns the fact that the UNCC was established as a subsidiary organ, and functions under the authority of the Security Council. The political supervision by the Security Council is surprising and has caused concerns about the legitimacy of the institution.[20]

A few observations need to be made in this respect. First, as discussed above, Iraq's liability had already been determined, which made it possible for the compensation program to be designed as an administrative or fact-finding exercise rather than a judicial scheme. Second, it was clear from the outset that the overwhelming volume of claims would prevent the UNCC from functioning as a traditional judicial body. The institution was immediately conceived as a mass claims facility rather than a court or tribunal. Third, given the extent of the losses and the uncertainty about the amount of compensation funds available, it was correctly assumed that setting up an effective and fair compensation process would require balancing the needs of claimants against other competing interests, including the humanitarian situation of the Iraqi people and the viability of the Iraqi economy. This balancing exercise involves difficult political—as opposed to legal—determinations and is best achieved through a political process. It was therefore preferred to create an institutional structure which could accommodate both the legal and political process, with a Governing Council responsible for policy guidelines and functioning as a reflection of the Security Council, and Panels of Commissioners, responsible for the resolution of compensation claims and acting in full independence from any national or international authority.[21]

2. INSTITUTIONAL STRUCTURE

From an institutional perspective, the UNCC is a creation of a *sui generis* character: as one author has noted, it assumes the form of a hybrid between an administrative mass claims program and an international tribunal.[22] Or, as the Secretary-General has stated in his report of May 2, 1991:

The Commission is not a court or an arbitral tribunal before which the parties appear; it is a political organ that performs an essentially fact-finding function of examining claims, verifying their validity, evaluating losses, assessing payments and resolving disputed claims. It is only in this last respect that a quasi-judicial function may be involved.[23]

In his report, the Secretary-General further highlighted the distinction between policy questions, legal determinations, and operational aspects. This functional distinction is reflected in the institutional design of the UNCC and has led to a tripartite structure with a Governing Council, Panels of Commissioners, and a Secretariat.

Governing Council

The principal policymaking organ of the UNCC is a 15-member Governing Council composed of the representatives of the members of the Security Council.[24] The Council sets the Commission's policy within the framework of relevant Security Council resolutions. As such, it has the responsibility 'for establishing guidelines on all policy matters, in particular, those relating to the administration and financing of the Fund, the organisation of the work of the Commission and the procedures to be applied to the processing of claims and to the settlement of disputed claims, as well as to the payments to be made from the Fund'.[25]

In addition to this policymaking role, the Governing Council has the crucial task of approving the reports and recommendations made by the Panels of Commissioners.[26] The Council may adjust the sums recommended by the panels, but it cannot alter their legal and factual conclusions. The Council's decisions on compensation awards are final and not subject to appeal or review.

Although the composition of the Governing Council is a reflection of the Security Council, the right of veto, which is held in the latter by the five permanent members, has been expressly excluded in the UNCC.[27] Decisions can be taken by a majority of at least nine members. Only for decisions concerning the financing of the Compensation Fund must a consensus be reached.

The Governing Council usually holds four formal sessions per year, with occasional special sessions to deal with particular issues as they arise. In addition, a number of informal meetings take place between the formal sessions.

Commissioners

The Commissioners' task is to evaluate the claims: they verify claims, determine whether the claimed losses are directly attributable to Iraq's invasion and occupation of Kuwait, assess the amount of loss or damage, and recommend compensation awards for the Governing Council to approve.[28] As such, they serve as the backbone of the entire decision-making structure.[29]

Panels of usually three Commissioners each are established to review specific categories or subcategories of claims (Articles 28 and 32 of the Provisional Rules for Claims Procedure).[30] Any recommendation or other decision of the panel has to be made by a majority of Commissioners (Article 33). They meet at the Commission's headquarters in Geneva. Expert consultants can be contracted to assist the panels in the valuation and quantification of claims (Article 36, b).

The Commissioners act in their personal capacity. They do not have financial interests in any of the claims submitted to their panel, nor are they associated with nor have financial interests in any corporations whose claims have been submitted to them. They are not allowed to represent or advise any party or claimant concerning the claims process during or for two years after their service as Commissioners (Article 21).

The Governing Council appoints the Commissioners upon recommendation by the Executive Secretary and nomination by the UN Secretary-General (Article 18). They are appointed paying due regard to the need for geographical representation and based on professional qualifications, experience, integrity and expertise in fields such as finance, law, accounting, insurance, environmental damage assessment, oil, trade, and engineering. The selection process takes account of the nature of the claims that will be assigned to the Commissioners in question (Articles 19 and 20).

All Commissioners are under an obligation to disclose to the Executive Secretary any prior, actual, or newly arisen relationship with governments, corporations or individuals, or any other circumstances, that are likely to give rise to justifiable doubts as to their impartiality or independence with respect to their tasks. If any claimant or Commissioner becomes aware of such circumstances, they must be communicated in due time to the Executive Secretary. He then informs the Governing Council, which determines whether the Commissioner concerned should cease to act, either generally or with respect to a particular claim (Article 22). Before taking up his or her duties, every Commissioner must solemnly declare to perform his or her duties 'honourably, faithfully, independently, impartially, and conscientiously' (Article 27).

Resignations have to be communicated through the Executive Secretary to the Governing Council. A resigning Commissioner has to continue to perform his/her functions until the Governing Council accepts the resignation. If he/she resigns during the consideration of claims, the Commissioner will continue to serve for the limited purpose of completing work on a particular claim or group of claims unless excused by the Governing Council (Articles 23 and 24).

If a Commissioner fails to act, or in the event of a de jure or de facto impossibility of performing his/her functions, the Executive Secretary informs the Governing Council, which may replace the Commissioner concerned (Article 25).

When performing tasks for the UNCC, Commissioners have the status of experts on mission within the meaning of Article VI of the Convention on the Privileges and Immunities of the United Nations of February 13, 1946 (Article 26).

To date, the Governing Council has appointed 56 Commissioners, representing 40 nationalities. Of this number, 33 are still active, while the remaining 23 have completed their work.

Secretariat

The UNCC Secretariat services the Governing Council and the Commissioners.[31] It also administers the Compensation Fund. Being an active and central organ in the preparation and processing of claims, the Secretariat has been called 'the seat of real power' of the UNCC.[32]

The Secretariat provides administrative, technical, and legal support to the Commissioners, which includes the development and maintenance of a compu-terized database for claims, and assistance in obtaining additional information (Article 34, 1, of the Provisional Rules for Claims Procedure). To this end, members of the Secretariat may attend sessions of the panels (Article 34, 3).

To ensure uniformity in handling similar claims, and to facilitate the Commis-sioners' work, the Secretariat categorizes claims according to, *inter alia,* the type or size of the claims and the similarity of legal and factual issues (Article 17). The Executive Secretary, who heads the Secretariat, submits the claims to the panels, together with related documentation, containing the result of the Secretariat's preliminary assessment and any other information deemed useful for the work of the Commissioners (Article 32). In handling the claims, the Commissioners have to take into account the information provided by the Secretariat (Article 34, 2).

The Secretariat is headed by an Executive Secretary, who is appointed by the UN Secretary-General. In addition to the Office of the Executive Secretary, the Secre-tariat comprises the Governing Council Secretariat, the Claims Processing Division and the Support Services Division.

The Secretariat staff comprised initially no more than a handful of lawyers[33] and support staff. The number of staff increased gradually over the years. In the early years of its work and until 1996, the UNCC faced chronic financial problems that also placed constraints on the recruitment of Secretariat staff. At the peak of its activity (i.e. from 1998 to the present), the Secretariat has employed approximately 250 staff members. Approximately half of these are professional staff, including a majority of lawyers but also 21 accountants, five loss adjusters, ten IT specialists, two statisticians and a few others. The support staff includes secretaries, recep-tionists, registry clerks, but also a large number of paralegals or claims analysts who assist the lawyers and accountants in their work.[34]

Conclusion

The institutional set-up of the UNCC, based on three key organs, reflects the various functions of the institution and demonstrates a clear division of tasks among the three pillars. As outlined in the Secretary-General's report of May 2, 1991, the Governing Council has the responsibility for establishing guidelines on all policy matters, the Commissioners are in charge of the verification and valuation of claims in accordance with the guidelines established by the Council and subject to approval by the Governing Council, and the Secretariat provides services to, and carries out such tasks assigned to it by, the Council and Commissioners.

This institutional structure provides an interesting model for mass claims resolution in a postconflict context. It combines within one institution three key functions—political, legal and technical—and is based on a clear division of responsibilities. For instance, the task of making a determination as to the merits of the claims has been kept separate from the question of the extent to which awards based on such determinations would be paid. At the outset, it was not known how much money would eventually be available for compensation purposes and in fact, it was never assumed that the available funds would be sufficient to satisfy all claims. By keeping the legal determination of claims—which in itself already constitutes a form of redress—separate from the actual payment of moneys, the Commissioners were in a position to proceed at full speed with the verification and evaluation of claims despite the uncertainty as to the availability of funds for compensation.

Secretariat

The extensive role of the Secretariat is another interesting feature of the UNCC's institutional design. In practice, the role of the Secretariat as an intermediary between the Governing Council and the Panels of Commissioners has been extremely important. As the Commissioners were not employed full-time by the Commission, the Secretariat has been the driving force behind the design and development of efficient and fair mass claims processing techniques. As one author states, 'the Secretariat is not only the "glue" holding the UNCC together on a number of levels; it is necessarily, at least with respect to C claims (see 'Claims Categories' below), the workhorse for generating the substantive ideas, methodologies, and criteria for evaluating, processing and compensating the claims'.[35]

In view of this role, it is important to note that the Secretariat staff, and especially the lawyers in the Secretariat, come from extremely varied backgrounds and represent some 20 different nationalities. Cultural differences, including different legal and conceptual approaches to fairness and efficiency in the context of mass claims resolution, have led to a balanced and flexible approach to problems.

More important perhaps, the relatively young and dynamic Secretariat has been driven 'more by "doability" than by *stare decisis,* but it is a doability consistent with the demands of fundamental fairness'.[36]

Commissioners

The selection of Commissioners has equally been inspired by the need for geographical distribution. The Commissioners represent a wide variety of nationalities and backgrounds and the selection process has guaranteed the appointment of independent and neutral personalities. Given the nature of their work, it is critical that they act in their personal capacity and are independent from their national authorities. Moreover, by working with Panels of Commissioners, the composition has been kept flexible and recruitments could take place as the caseload increased. It has also proven wise to recruit Commissioners on a less than full-time basis: in all likelihood, it would have been far more difficult to attract senior-level experts for these posts if a full-time engagement had been expected.

Governing Council

The composition of the Governing Council as a reflection of the Security Council has raised concerns.

First, on a practical level, it has been noted that problems or conflicts in the Security Council could easily affect decision-making in the Governing Council. However, the absence of the right of veto in the Governing Council mitigates this problem.

Second, as a matter of legal principle, the supervision by the Governing Council of the Commissioners is questionable. Although the Commissioners act in their personal capacity and are independent in their functioning, the Governing Council may adjust the compensation amounts recommended by the Commissioners. Although this intervention is limited to an adjustment of the actual amount of compensation and does not extend to the reasoning underlying the award, the mere possibility of such political interference in an essentially legal process is surprising. Two observations need to be borne in mind.

- The Compensation Fund is an open-ended fund and the total amount of funds was not known from the outset. It was therefore necessary to provide a mechanism for the possible adjustment of compensation sums recommended by the Panels of Commissioners: otherwise, one would run the risk of fully compensating the first successful claimants and running out of resources when the last claims are processed.
- An analysis of the practice of the Governing Council reveals that it has been extremely cautious and reluctant to adjust the recommendations of the Com-

missioners. Only on one occasion has the Governing Council found it impossible to agree on a recommended US$15.9 billion award to the Kuwait Petroleum Corporation. Instead of risking a negative vote, and the diplomatic problems that would inevitably ensue, the discussion was postponed. In the end, a compromise was reached, which consisted of approving the award, but at the same time lowering the level of Iraq's contribution to the Compensation Fund.[37]

3. Mandate

The UNCC was established to process claims and pay compensation for loss, damage or injury suffered by individuals, corporations, Governments and international organizations as a direct result of Iraq's unlawful invasion and occupation of Kuwait.[38]

Eligibility

Who Can Claim?

States can submit claims on behalf of individuals and corporations. As one author notes, the submission of individual and corporate claims through their governments does not alter the fact that the claims are those of the individuals and corporations concerned.[39] The submission through Governments was merely a practicality dictated by the massive number of claimants and the impossibility of managing direct contact with a claimant population spread over several countries.

Claims have to be submitted in a consolidated form by Governments on behalf of their nationals, and, if they so choose, of other persons resident in their territory.[40] In the latter category, claims have been filed on behalf of permanent residents, refugees and asylum seekers.[41] In the case of Governments existing in the territory of a former federal State, such as the former Yugoslavia and the Soviet Union, one such Government could submit claims on behalf of nationals, corporations or other entities of another such Government, if both Governments agree.[42]

In addition, the Governing Council may 'request an appropriate person, authority or body to submit claims on behalf of persons who are not in a position to have their claims submitted by a Government',[43] i.e. claims from stateless persons. The United Nations Development Programme (UNDP), the United Nations High

Commissioner for Refugees (UNHCR), and the United Nations Relief and Works Agency for Palestine Refugees (UNRWA) have been appointed according to this provision and have each submitted large numbers of claims, mostly on behalf of Palestinians.

Claims by Iraq will not be considered, nor will those on behalf of Iraqi nationals who do not have the bona fide nationality of another State.[44]

Concerning claims by corporations, a distinction has been made between partnerships and shareholdings.[45] Losses suffered by a partnership without legal personality have to be claimed jointly by all partners, except when one of the partners has Iraqi nationality, in which case each of the other partners may claim pro rata for his proportionate interest. A partnership with legal personality may claim for its own losses, unless it has Iraqi nationality. In the latter case, each of the eligible partners may claim pro rata for his proportionate interest. A shareholding may claim for its own losses. If, however, it is not able or, because of its Iraqi nationality, not eligible to claim, the shareholders may jointly claim for the losses of the shareholding. The important question of the nationality of a corporation is dealt with by Governing Council Decision 10, which states that a government 'may submit claims on behalf of corporations or other entities that, on the date on which the claim arose, were incorporated or organized under the law of that state'.[46] Only corporations incorporated under Iraqi law are therefore excluded from the UNCC compensation scheme.[47] If the State of incorporation fails to submit the claim of a corporation, that corporation may itself make a claim to the UNCC.

Governments and international organizations, finally, may claim on their own behalf.[48] International organizations are defined in Article 1 of the Provisional Rules for Claims Procedure as 'international organizations of States', thereby excluding NGOs.

Directness of Loss

In order for losses, damages or injuries to be compensable, they need to be a direct result of Iraq's invasion and occupation of Kuwait. In an effort to simplify and facilitate the evaluation of the directness of losses by the Panels of Commissioners, the Governing Council has defined five types of actions and situations, which, if present in a particular claim, establish the required causal link:[49]

1. *Military operations or threat of military action by either side during the period from 2 August 1990* (the date of the invasion) *to 2 March 1991* (the date of Resolution 686, which marked the end of hostilities). Iraq's responsibility embraces the full range of its military operations, including missile attacks on other States. Losses resulting from the coalition's military operations are also considered a direct consequence of Iraq's invasion and occupation of Kuwait.[50]

2. *Departure from or inability to leave Iraq or Kuwait (or a decision not to return) during that period.* The Governing Council expected that many potential claimants in this group would lack documentary or other evidence and therefore created a presumption that the mass departures from Iraq and Kuwait were caused by Iraq's illegal attack and occupation.[51]

3. *Actions by officials, employees or agents of the Government of Iraq or its controlled entities during that period in connection with the invasion or occupation.* This results from Resolution 687, which establishes Iraq's responsibility for all direct losses stemming from its unlawful invasion and occupation. This liability even covers actions which, but for the invasion, are not violations of international law attributable to the State.[52] Additionally, under Article 3 of the Fourth Hague Convention of 1907, Iraq is responsible for all acts committed by members of its armed forces.[53]

4. *The breakdown of civil order in Kuwait or Iraq during that period.* Anticipating that certain claimants who suffered damage to property might not be able to prove the specific circumstances of their losses, the Governing Council created this general area of responsibility, which again is considered in accordance with Iraq's liability under the law of war (Article 43 of the 1907 Hague Regulations).[54]

5. *Hostage-taking or other illegal detention.* No relevant period is indicated, which means that incarcerations continuing after 2 March 1991 are also included.[55] This conduct is also forbidden by the Geneva Conventions and other instruments of international law.[56]

Claims Categories

Since 1991, the Commission has received approximately 2.7 million claims, which it has subdivided into six categories, according to the nature of the injured party (individual, corporation, government or international organization), the type of loss (physical, moral, commercial...) and the nature of the procedure (expedited or normal).[57]

Category A claims are those submitted by individuals who had to leave Iraq or Kuwait between the date of the invasion of Kuwait, i.e. August 2, 1990, and the date on which the Iraqi occupation came to an end, i.e. March 2, 1991. These claims are handled through an expedited procedure with relaxed standards of proof: no proof has to be shown of the circumstances or amount of loss, and proof of eligibility requires only simple documentation of the fact and date of departure.[58] The UNCC received 923,158 category A claims, seeking a total of US$3,455,088,000.[59]

Category B claims are those of individuals for serious personal injury and death. Just as for category A claims, the Governing Council decided that these claims should be handled with priority, and that no proof of the actual amount of damage is necessary: compensation is paid on the basis of simple documentation of the fact and date of the injury, or of the death and family relationship.[60] 'Serious personal injury' is defined in Governing Council Decision 3, and includes both physical and mental damage.[61] It includes dismemberment; significant disfigurement; loss or limitation of use of a body organ, member, function or system; and any injury requiring a course of medical treatment to result in full recovery. It further includes physical or mental injury arising from sexual or aggravated physical assault, torture, hostage-taking or illegal detention for more than three days, or being forced to hide for more than three days on account of a 'manifestly well-founded fear for one's life or of being taken hostage or illegally detained'. As was stated in the panel report on the first instalment of category B claims, such a mental injury is a psychological trauma, which is 'more serious than mere psychological pain or anguish'.[62] Therefore, claims for mental pain and anguish have to be put forward under categories C or D, dependent on the amount of the damage, where more elaborate evidence is required. The distinction is not always clear, however, which resulted in many claims being filed in the wrong category.[63] The UNCC received 5,734 category B claims, seeking a total of US$20,100,000.

Category C claims cover all types of individual loss up to US$100,000. Compensation is provided for 21 different types of loss, including damages not fully covered under categories A and B, as well as loss of personal property; loss of bank accounts, stocks, and other securities; loss of income; loss of real property; and individual business losses.[64] As stated in the previous paragraph, claims for mental pain and anguish can also be filed under this category. As to the scope of allowable claims, the Governing Council found little helpful international precedent.[65] It was agreed to provide compensation for pecuniary losses resulting from mental pain and anguish, as well as for the following mentally burdensome nonpecuniary losses: death of the claimant's spouse, child, or parent; his or her suffering serious personal injury; his or her suffering sexual or aggravated assault or torture; his or her witnessing the intentional infliction of these events on his spouse, child, or parent; his or her being taken hostage, or being illegally detained or forced to hide, under certain circumstances; or his or her being deprived of all economic resources, threatening his or her survival.[66] Category C claims are handled with priority and on an expedited basis, and 'must be documented by appropriate evidence of the circumstances and the amount of the claimed loss. The evidence required will be the reasonable minimum that is appropriate under the circumstances involved, and a lesser degree of documentary evidence would ordinarily be required for smaller claims, such as those below $20,000.'[67] The UNCC received 1,736,265 category C claims, seeking a total of US$11,504,564,653.

Category D claims are individual claims for damages above US$100,000. The types of compensable loss are similar to those under category C, with the most frequent being the loss of personal property, the loss of real property, the loss of income and individual business-related losses.[68] In addition, compensation is available for payments made or relief provided by individuals to others for losses covered by any of the criteria adopted by the Governing Council.[69] Since these claims may be for substantial amounts, they must be supported 'by documentary and other appropriate evidence, sufficient to demonstrate the circumstances and the amount of the claimed loss'.[70] The UNCC received 13,876 category D claims, seeking a total of US$16,555,170,488.

Category E claims are those of corporations, other private legal entities and public sector enterprises. These claims are mainly dealt with by Governing Council Decision 9, drawing its rules from public and private international law and commercial practice.[71] They include claims for: construction or other contract losses; losses from non-payment for goods or services; losses relating to the destruction or seizure of business assets; loss of profits; and oil sector losses.[72] For processing purposes, the claims have been divided into four subcategories: oil sector claims (E1), claims by non-Kuwaiti corporations not falling into any other subcategory (E2), claims by non-Kuwaiti corporations related to construction and engineering (E3), and claims by Kuwaiti corporations, except for oil sector claims (E4). Like category D claims, these claims must be 'supported by documentary and other appropriate evidence, sufficient to demonstrate the circumstances and the amount of the claimed loss'.[73] The UNCC received 6,569 category E claims, seeking a total of US$78,730,169,724.

Category F claims are claims filed by Governments and international organizations for losses incurred in evacuating citizens; providing relief to citizens; damage to diplomatic premises and loss of, and damage to, other government property; and damage to the environment.[74] These claims are organized into four subcategories: claims for losses incurred in connection with the departure and evacuation of individuals and for damage to property (F1), claims filed by the Governments of Jordan and Saudi Arabia (F2), claims filed by the Government of Kuwait (F3), and claims for damage to the environment (F4). Since these claims, like those of categories D and E, are for substantial amounts, they must be 'supported by documentary and other appropriate evidence, sufficient to demonstrate the circumstances and the amount of the claimed loss'.[75] The UNCC received 393 category F claims, seeking a total of US$237,430,840,289.

E/F claims are export guarantee and insurance claims submitted under both categories E and F.[76] Each export guarantee or insurance claim normally covers a number of corporate claims, the compensability of which must first be established in order to verify the guarantee claim. The UNCC received 123 category E/F claims, seeking a total of US$6,147,780,045.

Table 9.1 gives an overview of the number of claims received and the total amount of compensation sought.

Table 9.1 Claims received and compensation sought

Category	No. of claims received	Compensation sought (US$)
A	923,158	3,455,088,000
B	5,734	20,100,000
C	1,736,265	11,504,564,653
D	13,876	16,555,170,488
E	6,569	78,730,169,724
E/F	123	6,147,780,045
F	393	237,430,840,289
Total	2,686,118	353,843,713,199

Note: Figures as of July 1, 2005.

Individual claimants may file claims in more than one category. Consequently, claimants under categories A or B can also file a claim under the other category, or under categories C or D, if their loss amounts to more than the amount of fixed compensation provided by the UNCC.[77] If they choose to do so, claimants under category A have to file their category A claim for the lowest amount of fixed compensation.[78] An individual can also claim under category D for losses in excess of the US$100,000 compensable under category C. A claimant may choose to file a claim only under the category that could provide him with the highest amount of compensation. It might be more appropriate, however, to file multiple claims, since the evidentiary standard for D claims is higher than the standard for C claims, which in turn is higher than for A and B claims. In other words, higher amounts of compensation are harder to obtain. For claimants with larger claims pending, the compensation they receive from their 'priority claims' (categories A, B, and C) is considered to be interim relief.[79]

Priority for Small Individual Claims

In Decision 1, the Governing Council decided that small individual claims (categories A, B, and C) would be processed with priority and on an expedited basis.[80] This decision marked a clear break with previous claims resolution processes, where the emphasis had traditionally been on claims by governments and corporations.[81]

Specific Cases

Concerning the special situation of the Allied Coalition Armed Forces, the Governing Council has decided that their costs are not eligible for compensation (Decision 19), nor are their members eligible for compensation for loss or injury, except if three cumulative conditions are met. Those conditions are that (*a*) the compensation is awarded in accordance with the general criteria already adopted; (*b*) they were prisoners of war as a consequence of their involvement in coalition military operations against Iraq in response to its unlawful invasion and occupation of Kuwait; and (*c*) the loss or injury resulted from mistreatment in violation of international humanitarian law (including the Geneva Conventions of 1949).[82]

Another issue is that of losses resulting from the embargo against Iraq, established by Security Council Resolution 661. Governing Council Decisions 1 and 7 stated that compensation was not to be provided for losses suffered as a result of the trade embargo, reflecting a legal judgment that the causal link, required by Resolution 687, between the invasion and occupation and the loss was not sufficiently direct.[83] In Decision 9, the Governing Council changed its position, establishing that 'compensation will be provided to the extent that Iraq's unlawful invasion and occupation of Kuwait constituted a cause of direct loss . . . which is separate and distinct from the trade embargo and related measures.'[84] This evolution was confirmed and further elaborated upon by Decision 15.[85]

Deadlines

Deadlines were established for the filing of the various categories of claims. The deadline of January 1, 1995 was set for the filing of category A, B, C, and D claims and January 1, 1996 for the filing of category E and F claims, with the exception of environmental claims in category F which had to be filed before February 1, 1997.[86]

All of the filing deadlines have now expired with the exception of claims put forward on behalf of missing persons and claims for damage and losses resulting from land mine or ordnance explosions.[87]

As in all mass claims programs, a mechanism had to be established to deal with the inevitable occurrence of claims filed only after the expiration of the time limits. Article 12 of the Provisional Rules for Claims Procedure provides that such late-filed claims are reported by the Secretariat to the Governing Council, which decides whether to accept the claims or not.

Conclusion

The UNCC's mandate has been defined in very broad terms and covers all losses which are a direct result of Iraq's invasion and occupation of Kuwait. The compensable losses include a wide range of different loss types, including departure-related losses, personal injury and death, real property and personal property losses, environmental harm, business losses and many others.

The UNCC has different processes for different types of claims. It is important to note that in principle the claimants themselves select the type of claim they wish to submit. A claimant who does not desire to go through an extensive proof process can select 'a payment option that will result in a lower monetary benefit based upon a less extensive investigation'.[88] Furthermore, the possibility of filing multicategory claims further improves the flexibility of the system.

In accordance with Security Council Resolution 687 (1991), losses are only compensable to the extent that they constitute a direct result of the invasion and occupation of Kuwait. Rather than examining the causality requirement in each individual claim, the Governing Council as the policymaking organ of the UNCC has established general criteria and guidelines on the compensability of losses in the various claims categories. In particular, it has defined five types of actions and situations, which, if present in a particular claim, establish the required causal link.

The technique of issuing clear and comprehensive instructions to be applied to groups or categories of claims has greatly facilitated decision-making by the Commissioners. In particular, it has enabled the Commissioners to proceed quickly and to ensure consistency and uniformity in the determination of claims. As the former Chief of the Legal Services Branch of the UNCC Norbert Wühler notes, in a system that handles large volumes of claims, 'clear criteria and guidelines that are to be followed by all decision-makers are essential for the fairness and efficiency of the process'.[89]

Moreover, decision-making on individual claims has greatly benefited from the presumption that certain losses are the result of Iraq's invasion and occupation of Kuwait. For category A claims, for instance, claimants do not need to demonstrate that their departure constituted a direct result of the invasion and occupation; instead, it is sufficient that the fact and time of the departure is established. Any other approach, it is submitted, would have been highly impractical and fundamentally unfair, as many claimants would not be in a position to demonstrate the precise reasons leading to their departure.

The implementation of the UNCC's mandate has been characterized by a clear humanitarian approach, prioritizing small individual claims over the larger claims submitted by corporations and Governments.

As Wühler notes, 'given the traditional emphasis in previous claims resolution processes on the losses suffered by Governments and corporations, this humanitarian decision to focus first on urgent individual claims marked a significant step in the evolution of international claims practice'.[90]

The privileged treatment accorded to individuals is indeed based on humanitarian considerations: claimants in these categories—often nationals of developing countries—had to leave their livelihood behind, suffered an injury which reduced their quality of life, or saw their already limited possessions destroyed.[91] For these claimants, receiving compensation through the UNCC is an important precondition for rebuilding their lives.

The focus on the individual claimants is further illustrated by the mechanism that was set up to collect claims from stateless persons: UNRWA, UNDP and UNHCR have collected individual claims of approximately 3,000 stateless persons. Without any doubt, this effort is unprecedented in the history of international mass claims settlement and represents an important contribution to the practice of claims resolution.

4. MASS CLAIMS PROCEDURES

General Introduction

The UNCC received approximately 2.7 million claims, the vast majority of which were considered 'urgent' and had to be resolved within a reasonably short period of time. With such a large caseload and given these time constraints, the methods used to process claims had to depart from traditional approaches to arbitration or claims determination.

From the outset the UNCC has focused on the development of a mass claims resolution system geared for processing the massive claims population in categories A, B, and C within an acceptable time period. Indeed, already in its first decision, the Governing Council instructed the Panels of Commissioners responsible for urgent claims to use simple and expedited procedures, 'such as checking individual claims on a sample basis, with further verification only if circumstances warranted'.[92] The UNCC's goal has been to 'create a system that will lead to the fair, expeditious and efficient processing of claims' and to adopt an approach 'that renders practical and simple justice, while weighing the interests of the claimants and Iraq'.[93]

The claims resolution procedures developed by the UNCC include a wide range of different techniques and methodologies. For the large claims in categories E and F, as well as for the individual claims in category B, which were fewer in number, a claim-by-claim (or 'individualized') review and decision-making process was feasible. For the host of small individual claims in categories A and C, however, the UNCC relied extensively on computer support and relatively new and sophisticated techniques of data matching, grouping and sampling and other forms of statistical modeling.

The use of these techniques has enabled the UNCC to resolve the vast majority of its caseload, as is shown in Table 9.2.

In the following sections, the general decision-making procedures of the UNCC will be explained. The part first concentrates on the procedures governing the presentation and registration of claims, the initial screening by the Secretariat and the procedures governing the work of the panel. Subsequent sections focus on the administration of evidence and the use of sophisticated mass claims processing techniques. The part concludes by examining the procedural fairness requirements in a mass claims context.

Presentation and Registration of Claims

The procedure for the submission and registration of claims is governed by section II of the Provisional Rules for Claims Procedure. The basic rules were already explained above in part three, and will not be repeated here. It is worth looking at some of the practicalities of the claims registration procedure, however, because these were largely dictated by the technical requirements of the UNCC's computerized software and database system and by the demands of efficient and fair mass claims processing methodologies.

Table 9.2 Claims received, resolved, and to be resolved

Category	Number of claims received	Claims resolved	Claims to be resolved
A	923,158	922,997	161
B	5,734	5,734	0
C	1,736,265	1,704,200	32,065
D	13,876	13,449	427
E	6,569	6,569	0
E/F	123	123	0
F	393	374	19
Total	2,686,118	2,653,446	32,672

Note: Figures as of July 1, 2005.

Standard claim forms were designed and distributed by the Secretariat to capture data in a consistent and uniform manner.[94] Consistency and uniformity in data capture are critical in any mass claims process, since they determine to a large extent the feasibility, efficiency and accuracy of automated processing techniques, such as data matching and sampling.

Claim forms in category A had to be submitted in the computer format distributed by the Secretariat. The governments kept custody of the original paper copies of the form and of the supporting documents and had to make them available to the Commission upon request. For all other categories, claim forms had to be submitted on paper.[95]

Claim forms could be submitted in any of the official languages of the United Nations. However, since the UNCC's software and database system was designed in English, a translation into English had to be provided in all cases where claim forms were submitted in a language other than English.[96] This additional burden placed upon governments was needed to reduce the ambiguities associated with expressing concepts in many different languages and to overcome technical hurdles in the automated processing of hundreds of thousands of claims.

Despite the efforts made to ensure consistency and accuracy in claims registration, significant differences were noted in the quality of presentation of the claims and in the relevance and materiality of the evidence submitted by claimants. Some claims were carefully prepared, presenting extensive explanations of the bases for compensation and reliable documentation of the claimed losses. Others, however, were rather poorly prepared, confused or inaccurate.[97] These patterns reflect certain differences among claimant countries and within countries, in level of income, literacy and education:[98]

- Some Governments have established well-organized national claims programs and provided extensive assistance to individual claimants. Other governments served only as a forwarding service, without providing any guidance or assistance to claimants.
- For well-educated or relatively sophisticated claimants, the proper completion of the claim forms did not present too many problems. For others, however, the proper filing of the claim form may have been a very difficult exercise, especially when they received no guidance or assistance from their government.

Bearing in mind these inequalities, the UNCC has sought to create a mass claims program that treats all claimants as fairly as possible. The Secretariat has prepared 'country reports' detailing the socioeconomic backgrounds of claimant populations from particular countries and explaining the national claims programs and other forms of assistance available to claimants. The purpose of these reports is to facilitate the commissioners' understanding of the factual and legal issues raised by the claims from a particular country and to draw their attention to existing inequalities between different claimant groups. The Secretariat has also engaged in its own evidence collection and verification efforts for claims that presented little explanation and evidence, trying to fill the gaps in certain groups of claims.[99]

Initial Screening by the Secretariat

Upon receipt of the claims, the Registry Unit in the Secretariat issues a filing receipt and carries out a preliminary assessment of the claims. This preliminary assessment is designed to determine whether the claims meet the formal requirements established by the Governing Council. If it is found that a claim does not meet these formal requirements, the Secretariat notifies the Government that submitted the claim and gives it 60 days to remedy the defect.[100]

In accordance with Article 16 of the Provisional Rules, the Executive Secretary prepares periodic reports (so-called 'Article 16 Reports') listing the total number of claims covered, the relevant category and the total amount of compensation sought. The reports also indicate all significant factual and legal issues raised by the claims under review. The reports are made available to the Governing Council, the Government of Iraq and to all governments and international organizations that have filed claims with an invitation to submit within 30 or 90 days any additional information and views they may have on the issues raised.

The Executive Secretary then submits the claims in 'instalments' to the Panels of Commissioners appointed to review the group of claims in question. Responses received to Article 16 Reports and any additional information provided by claimants is included in the submission.

Procedures Governing the Work of the Panels

Section IV of the Provisional Rules for Claims Procedure governs the work of the Panels of Commissioners.

Composition of the Panels

The requirement in Article 28(1) that the three members of a panel shall be of different nationality stems from the need for geographical representation that the Council is bound to respect in the selection of Commissioners. Priority is given to the establishment of panels to deal with the urgent claims in categories A, B, and C.

In our view, it would have been preferable to include in this provision a further requirement that the three members of a panel should be from different regions or parts of the world. Although this was the general practice in the UNCC, it is not strictly required by Article 28(1).

The Role of the Chairmen

Article 29 defines the role of the chairmen of the panels in terms of ensuring the expeditious processing of the claims and the consistent application of the relevant criteria and the Rules.

Meetings of the chairmen and the Secretariat take place on a regular basis to discuss matters of general interest. In practice, however, it is mainly the Secretariat that ensures consistency between the various panels and continuously informs them how other panels decided similar or related issues.

Confidentiality

Article 30 protects the confidentiality of the records received or developed by the Commission (except for the normal status updates prepared by the Secretariat) and the private nature of the work of the panels. Commissioners are obliged not to disclose, even after the termination of their functions, any information that is not in the public domain and which they have learned of by reason of their working for the Commission.

Applicable Law

The applicable law is laid down in Article 31, which provides that the Commissioners apply Security Council Resolution 687 (1991) and other resolutions as well as the criteria and other decisions issued by the Governing Council. Where necessary, the Commissioners shall apply other relevant rules of international law.[101]

Review of Claims and Preparation of Recommendations

As mentioned above, the Executive Secretary assigns the claims to a Panel of Commissioners and may, after consultation with the chairmen, reallocate claims from one panel to another in the interest of the efficient processing of claims. This provision is actually a safety net permitting the realignment of claims to alternative categories to which they may be deemed to be more properly suited.[102] Failure to submit a claim in the proper category should not be detrimental to a claimant's efforts to obtain compensation.

Upon receipt of the claims from the Executive Secretary, the Commissioners examine the claims, deliberate and prepare their recommendations. In considering the claims, the Commissioners will take into account the information and views provided by the Executive Secretary. Members of the Secretariat attend the sessions of the panel and may, if required, provide information to the Commissioners, i.e. on what other panels are deciding on similar or related issues. Any recommendation or other decision of a panel shall be made by a majority of the Commissioners.

With respect to the processing of urgent claims, Article 37 authorizes the panels to use expedited processing techniques such as data matching and sampling. For other claims, Article 38 provides that 'in so far as possible, claims with significant common legal and factual issues will be processed together' and that 'Panels may adopt special procedures appropriate to the character, amount and subject-matter of the particular types of claims under consideration.'

A time limit (normally 120 days for urgent claims, 180 days for other claims, 12 months for unusually large or complex claims) is set for the Panels of Commissioners to deal with each instalment of claims.[103] Upon completion of its review of a particular instalment of claims, the panel submits a written report to the Governing Council on the claims received and, for each claim, the amount of compensation recommended. The reports provide detailed explanations as to the reasons for the recommendations.

Approval by the Governing Council

The Governing Council then considers the report and recommended awards. Article 40 provides that the recommended amounts are subject to approval by the Governing Council, which may increase or reduce them.[104] The Governing Council may, in its discretion, return a particular claim or group of claims to the panel for further review. The decisions taken by the Council are final and 'are not subject to appeal or review on procedural, substantive or other grounds'.[105] Once the Council has decided, the panel reports are made public, with the exception of the identities of individual claimants and other confidential or privileged information.

The Administration of Evidence

In accordance with the general principles on burden of proof, Article 35 of the Provisional Rules for Claims Procedure provides that each claimant is responsible for submitting evidence to prove that his/her claim is eligible for compensation. Although it is up to the claimants to prove their cases, it should be underlined that Iraq's liability has already been established by the Security Council: individual claimants are therefore 'relieved from the otherwise heavy burden of proving the liability of a sovereign state'.[106]

The same article also emphasizes that it is up to the panels to assess and consider the available evidence. It states that '[e]ach Panel will determine the admissibility, relevance, materiality and weight of any documents and other evidence submitted'. This approach is based on the—correct—assumption that it is only through working with the actual claims and identifying the main problems that a pragmatic and fair administration of evidence can be ensured.[107] Nevertheless, Article 35 of the Provisional Rules gives broad guidelines and general directions to the Commissioners to ensure consistency among the different panels.

The general standard of evidence for individual claimants is a lenient or 'relaxed' standard, which makes the submission of claims and the gathering of evidence as simple as possible for individuals. Article 35 of the Provisional Rules makes the following distinctions between the various categories of claims:

- For departure claims (category A), claimants are required to provide simple documentation of the fact and date of departure from Iraq or Kuwait. Documentation of the actual amount of loss is not required, since the UNCC awards fixed amounts of compensation to successful claimants in this category. As explained in part three, the causal link between the departure and invasion or occupation of Iraq is presumed. Consequently, only the fact and date of departure need to be established.
- For the payment of fixed amounts in the case of serious personal injury or death (category B), claimants are required to provide simple documentation of the fact and date of the injury or death (and in the latter case of the family relationship with the deceased). Documentation of the actual amount of loss is not required.
- Claims for individual losses up to US$100,000 (category C) must be documented by appropriate evidence of the circumstances and the amount of the claimed loss. The required evidence is 'the reasonable minimum that is appropriate under the particular circumstances of the case'.[108] The article adds that a lesser degree of documentary evidence ordinarily will be sufficient for smaller claims such as those below US$20,000.
- Large claims (especially those in categories E and F), however, must be 'supported by documentary and other appropriate evidence sufficient to demonstrate the circumstances and amount of the claimed loss'.[109]

The evidentiary standards therefore vary according to the category of claims. Lenient standards have been set for smaller individual claims; more demanding standards apply in the case of larger claims. The rationale for applying lenient standards of evidence to individual claims is clearly a humanitarian one and relates to the difficulties for individual claimants of documenting their claims. The first report of the category D panel illustrates this point:

Considering the difficult circumstances of the invasion and occupation of Kuwait by Iraq…many claimants cannot, and cannot be expected to, document all aspects of a claim. In many cases, relevant documents do not exist, have been destroyed, or were left behind by claimants who fled Kuwait or Iraq. Accordingly, the level of proof the Panel has considered appropriate is close to what has been called the 'balance of probability' as distinguished from the concept of 'beyond reasonable doubt' required in some jurisdictions to prove guilt in a criminal trial. Moreover, the test of 'balance of probability' has to be applied having regard to the circumstances existing at the time of the invasion and the loss.[110]

Based on the same reasoning, the D panel has found it possible to give 'significant weight' to clear explanatory statements. To be acceptable, however, a statement must 'clearly state the nature and extent of the loss, it must make clear that the loss was a direct result of the Iraqi invasion and occupation, and it must clearly explain the reasons, regarded as credible and sufficient by the panel, for the absence of any additional documentary evidence'.[111] However, the Governing Council has emphasized that in large claims 'no loss shall be compensated by the Commission solely on the basis of an explanatory statement provided by the claimant'.[112]

For certain loss types, the Panels of Commissioners had to acknowledge that it was simply not possible to arrive at fair and objective compensation awards on the basis of the evidence presented by claimants. This occurred for instance with claims for personal property losses, for which the Commissioners acknowledged that the evidence presented by the claimants alone was insufficient for providing a fair and objective standard for valuing the loss and determining the corresponding amount to be compensated for each claim. For example, some claimants have listed losses on a replacement cost basis while others have presented estimates based on the depreciated value of the lost objects. To supplement the evidence, a statistical computer model was developed to estimate an upper limit to the amount each claimant might reasonably be expected to claim. The model was based on the amounts claimed by similarly situated claimants in the claimant population and certain individual characteristics.[113]

Mass Claims Resolution Techniques and Methodologies

The UNCC employed a variety of different techniques and methodologies to verify claims and to determine the appropriate level of compensation. The selection of the proper methodology for a particular group of claims is made by the relevant Panel of Commissioners, in accordance with the guidelines established by the Security Council resolutions, the decisions of the Governing Council and the Provisional Rules for Claims Procedure.

In some cases, claims could be resolved by a straightforward application of the criteria established by the Governing Council. For mental pain and anguish claims based on hostage-taking or illegal detention for more than three days, for instance, Decision 8 of the Governing Council provided a simple scheme for calculating compensation: the claimant receives US$1,500 for the first three days of detention and US$100 for each additional day.

In other cases, however, the verification of claims and the precise determination of compensation required the application of complex and sophisticated methodologies. In view of the large number of claims received in certain categories, the use of modern information technology and statistical techniques was inevitable. In the following subsections, two particular techniques will be examined: the automated matching of claims data against independent evidentiary sources and the use of grouping and sampling techniques.

Data Matching

'Data matching' is an automated process of cross-checking claims against independent and objectively verified data. Whenever a perfect match is found, claims can be decided without further investigation.

The approximately one million departure claims were verified to a large extent through computerized data matching. The Secretariat had managed to reduce the category A claims to a relatively simple computer program which was distributed to claimant governments. The requested information included numeric elements such as passport and ID numbers, year of birth, etc. as well as non-numeric details such as name, sex and nationality. In addition, the Secretariat gathered a vast volume of information and documentation on departures from Iraq and Kuwait in the relevant time period, including lists of residents in Kuwait and Iraq as of August 2, 1990, flight manifests, border control records, lists of evacuees kept by international organizations, etc.[114] The data in the claims forms were checked through specially designed matching software against the information in these records.[115] Where a perfect match was found, the claims were considered verified and no further investigation was required. The claims for which no perfect match was found were reviewed using sampling and other techniques.

Data matching techniques, it is submitted, do not represent a radical departure from conventional methods of decision-making. In many ways, data matching is merely an automated form of individualized decision-making, whereby each claim is examined on its own merits. As such, it needs to be distinguished from sampling, which constitutes a more radical departure from conventional approaches.

Grouping and Sampling

The A panel summarized the rationale for the use of sampling and related methods as follows:

Faced with situations of mass claims and other situations where a large number of cases involving common issues of law and fact arise, courts, tribunals and commissions have adopted methodologies, including that of sampling, recognizing that the traditional method of individualized adjudication if applied to such cases would not be appropriate as it would result in unacceptable delays and substantially increase the burden of costs for such claimants and more so for the respondents. The legal principle involved may be stated as follows: in situations involving mass claims or analogous situations raising common factual and legal issues, it is permissible in the interest of effective justice to apply methodologies and procedures which provide for an examination and determination of a representative sample of these claims.[116]

Grouping and sampling techniques were for instance applied in category C. In general terms, the methodology relied 'on computerized support, the categorization and grouping of claims presenting similar factual and legal issues, the individualized review of sample claims from the relevant groupings, the analysis of statistical data regarding the claims, the extrapolation of findings with respect to sample claims to the nonsampled claims, and additional verification of individual claims only when necessary'.[117]

Although there are significant differences as to the scope and methodology of sampling among the various groups and subgroups of claims, the general process can be summarized as follows. As a first step, evaluation and compensation criteria are established for each loss element. On the basis of these criteria, the Secretariat proceeds to the grouping and categorizing of claims.[118] From each grouping or subgrouping of claims, a sample is selected for individual review by the Commissioners. The size of the sample depends on the total number of claims in a particular group and the complexity of the factual and legal issues presented by the claims in the group. The results of the Commissioners' review of the sample claims and the issues contained therein are then applied by the Secretariat to the remainder of the claims in the subgrouping. The Secretariat presents the results of the extrapolation to the panel, which will verify and determine:

1. whether the extrapolation leads to a fair and equitable result;
2. whether the groupings from which the claims were taken are representative of the issues presented by the claims in each instalment; and
3. whether a particular grouping of claims is sufficiently homogeneous, so that the decisions made with respect to the sample claims from a particular group may be applied to the non-sampled claims.[119]

Obviously, this type of claims processing cannot be used for all loss types and has to be applied in a careful and balanced manner. An extensive or unconditional use of sampling techniques can easily lead to absurd or unfair results. If applied carefully and properly, however, sampling may be a great help and lead to expedient and fair results. It is therefore not possible to give a general assessment of sampling techniques *in abstracto*. Whether a specific extrapolation leads to a fair and equitable result must be assessed in each particular case, and the role of the panels is crucial in this regard.

For category C, the claims which exclusively contained loss elements that could be processed through database-assisted techniques and that did not otherwise present special problems were grouped together in the second instalment of category C claims. The claims resolved on this basis represent the losses most frequently suffered by category C claimants, including: losses of food, transportation, lodging, relocation and related losses; clothing, personal effects, household furnishings and other personal property-related losses; loss or theft of motor vehicles; losses related to bank accounts located in Kuwait; and wage and salary losses.[120]

Iraq's Participation in the Proceedings

Not surprisingly, the Government of Iraq has criticized the limited procedural opportunities that were offered in the UNCC proceedings. In its 'Presentation' of February 26–27, 2001, the Government of Iraq alleged that the UNCC's work 'is purely political, lacks any element of fairness and ignores the principle of due process of law required by natural justice'.[121] In the same document, Iraq asserts that the Governing Council in effect decided 'in favour of speed rather than justice'. Certain scholars have voiced similar criticisms, arguing for instance that 'Iraq's right to be heard is not just violated, it has simply not been foreseen. The basic concept on which the system is built assumes that there is no need for Iraq to be heard.'[122]

According to UNCC officials, the participation of Iraq in the proceedings is only required to the extent that it is necessary for the Panels of Commissioners to make their just determinations on the claims.[123]

In this respect, a distinction needs to be made between the categories of claims for which the UNCC operates as a mass claims facility, and those categories for which more conventional individualized approaches are taken.

Mass Claims Processing and Iraq's Participation

The Article 16 reporting mechanism is the primary mechanism through which Iraq's participation in the proceedings is structured. Article 16 applies to all categories of claims. For the categories A, B, and C it is the only mechanism available to Iraq.

The so-called Article 16 reports list the total number of claims covered, the relevant category and the total amount of compensation sought, and indicate all significant factual and legal issues raised by the claims under review. The reports are circulated to the Government of Iraq, which is invited to present within 30 (for categories A, B, and C) or 90 days (for other categories) any additional information and views it may have on the issues raised. These views are transmitted to the Panels of Commissioners, who are required to take them into account when formulating recommendations to the Governing Council.

Needless to say, the deadline of 30 or 90 days is extremely short to prepare a fully informed and documented response. In the interest of the overall fairness of the process, a longer time period would have been desirable.

Individualized Review of Large or Complex Claims

More extensive procedural opportunities are granted to Iraq when it comes to the conventional procedures used to process larger claims. As mentioned above, such claims are resolved through an individualized review of the claims by the panels.

(a) *Transmission of files.* In unusually large or complex claims, the relevant panel may decide to make claim files available to the Government of Iraq and to request additional written submissions from Iraq. Especially where it may be thought that Iraq has information relevant to the claim or where the claimed amount is particularly high, the panel will issue a procedural order that directs the Commission to send the claim files to Iraq and invite the Government to offer its comments and views on the claims. According to the Executive Secretary, the practice of transmitting claim files to Iraq is applied in the following situations:

- when the Government of Iraq is a party to a contract forming part of the subject-matter of the claim;
- when the *situs* of the alleged loss is in Iraq;
- when Iraq's view is otherwise helpful in order to verify or evaluate the claim; and
- when the amount claimed is more than US$100 million.[124]

In these cases, the full claim file, consisting of the claim form, statement of claim and all of the supporting documents, is sent to Iraq. According to Carron and Morris, this procedure is frequently used: 'a typical instalment in the E2 category of claims may include approximately 60–80 claims being sent to Iraq out of 200 total claims in the instalment'.[125]

In September 2000, the Security Council decided to review the UNCC procedures. A number of proposals were considered and in December 2000 the Governing Council issued Decision 114. Concerning the transmission of claim files to Iraq, the Governing Council decided that the discretion to send claim files to Iraq should remain with the Panels of Commissioners. However, the Council encourages the panels to continue to apply the above-mentioned criteria and to make claim files available to Iraq prior to the formal commencement of the review of an instalment of claims. This should allow some flexibility in the application of the six-month response rule for Iraq. Moreover, the Council recommends that an additional six months should be given to Iraq to respond to claims with an asserted value of US$1 billion or more.

(b) *Oral proceedings.* The panel may also invite Iraq (as well as others) to present its views in oral proceedings. Although such occurrences were rare in the initial phases of the UNCC's work, recent practice reflects a policy change and an increase in the use of oral proceedings, especially in sensitive cases.

In the first few oral proceedings, Iraq unfortunately used these occasions to express its general objections against the UNCC mechanism rather than addressing in a technical way the specific legal and factual issues that arose from the claims concerned.

According to Decision 114 of the Governing Council, discretion in convening oral proceedings remains with the Panels of Commissioners.[126] The Council recommends, however, that oral proceedings always be convened when the panels determine that it would be useful to hear the views of Iraq and when:

- the claim has an asserted value of US$1 billion or more;
- the claim contains significant technical, legal and factual issues;
- the claims are substantive 'F4' environmental claims.

In Decision 114, the Governing Council also requested concrete recommendations concerning the issue of making funds available to Iraq for purposes of hiring experts to assist in preparing Iraq's responses to claims, in particular to environmental claims.

Conclusion

With Iraq's liability established by the Security Council and accepted by Iraq, the UNCC was from the outset conceived as a mass claims resolution facility rather than a court or tribunal with an elaborate adversarial process. Its main purpose was to provide redress to all injured parties and to make determinations on a large number of claims within a reasonable period of time.

Mass claims processing techniques are well known in some domestic law systems. Proceedings in the context of mass torts, primarily in the USA, have led to the development of sophisticated methods for resolving masses of claims. Procedural and technical innovations have been introduced and tested, such as making use of computer support, standardized forms and questionnaires, sampling and aggregation techniques, statistical analysis and rule-based systems for processing many thousands of cases.

These developments have begun to show that there may be significant advantages in using statistical and computer-supported techniques in the face of mass claims, including judicial economy and the expediting of proceedings. Moreover, it is felt that these techniques, when applied properly, may increase the general level of accuracy while reducing the bias that may be present in any individualized case.[127]

Until recently, however, there was little experience in this area in international law. The UNCC was the first institution to employ these techniques in the context of an international claims resolution process.[128] Not surprisingly, the use of statistical and computer-supported methodologies, the close interaction between the law and information technology and the different approach to conventional procedural principles have led to objections from Iraq and have caused discomfort among certain legal scholars.

Creating a procedural framework that would enable the institution to process a caseload of 2.7 million claims within a reasonable timeframe, while ensuring fair and just outcomes to both the claimants and Iraq, was without any doubt the most important challenge facing the UNCC. In the following sections, we will first consider why the UNCC was established as a mass claims resolution facility rather than a traditional court. Subsequently, we address the difficulty of balancing procedural fairness requirements and the need for speedy and effective remedies in a mass claims context. Finally, we outline some of the procedural innovations that were introduced by the UNCC and which may be of relevance to future mass compensation programs.

Mass Claims Resolution versus Traditional Adjudication

International human rights standards allow a considerable variety of legal proceedings, depending on the circumstances. The circumstances in which the UNCC has operated are by any account extreme:

- The volume of claims received by the UNCC is the largest caseload ever dealt with by an international claims program: the UNCC received almost 2.7 million claims, including some 2.5 million individual claims, many of which were deemed urgent because of humanitarian reasons. The traditional method of individualized adjudication, if applied to this caseload, would result in unacceptable delays and substantially increased costs for claimants and the Respondent Government.
- The UNCC's claimant population was spread over ninety different countries. Organizing traditional judicial proceedings—with adversarial proceedings, public hearings, oral submissions, appeals, etc.—would be impossible in such a context.
- Providing compensation to those who have suffered losses as a result of the invasion and occupation of Kuwait was recognized by the UN Security Council and the international community at large as an important part of the post-conflict settlement.
- To be effective, compensation needs to be awarded within a reasonable period of time. A claim-by-claim review would require either very significant staff resources or very long waiting periods for claimants or—most likely—both. Hence the need for innovative and speedy remedies.

In such extreme circumstances, the need to provide a speedy and effective remedy to claimants must balance in the human rights equation together with the procedural rights of parties. The UNCC must have procedures which enable it to process claims expeditiously. If not, the UNCC could take many years to complete its work, leaving its hundreds of thousands of claimants without an effective remedy in the meantime. Such delays would effectively amount to a denial of justice.

In this regard, the specificity of the UNCC's mandate needs to be borne in mind. Iraq's liability for losses resulting directly from its invasion and occupation of Kuwait had already been established by the Security Council and formally—although reluctantly—accepted by the Government of Iraq. The UNCC's role was therefore confined to verifying and evaluating claimed losses.

Balancing Procedural Fairness and Efficiency

The main challenge in designing a mass claims procedure is to seek a balance between speed and efficiency, on the one hand, and justice and fairness on the other. Norbert Wühler, former Chief of the Legal Services Branch of the UNCC, explains that:

In every mass claims program, a tension exists between the search for individual justice and fairness and the requirement of an expedient process that resolves the whole claims population within a reasonable time period. For the UNCC, as one Commissioner stated it, 'the vast number of claims before the Commission, and the time limits adopted by the Rules, necessitated the employment of legal standards and valuation methods that were administrable and which carefully balanced the twin objectives of speed and accuracy'. The larger the number of claims, the more difficult this balance is to achieve.[129]

The following two subsections aim to assess the use of data matching and sampling techniques as well as Iraq's participation in the proceedings.

(a) *Data matching and sampling.* Iraq has repeatedly objected to the use of so-called mass claims processing techniques. In its 'Presentation' of February 26–27, 2001, for instance, the Government of Iraq repeated its objections against sampling, which 'is not the approved procedure under international law which requires proof and causation in respect to every claim'.[130]

It is submitted, however, that this criticism fails to take into account the specific circumstances surrounding the establishment and continued operation of the UNCC, as set out above. In our view, the use of these techniques can be assessed as follows:

- The use of data matching techniques is legitimate and acceptable. As shown above, it allows efficient and fair decision-making on large numbers of claims without departing radically from conventional decision-making standards and principles.

• The use of sampling and extrapolation techniques is more intrusive. Given the specific context, these techniques may constitute a legitimate and acceptable means of deciding masses of individual claims. In order to be acceptable, however, their application must meet a number of conditions, including the proper selection of a representative sample and the homogeneous composition of the group. Most importantly, the commissioners must thoroughly review the results of the extrapolation and determine whether it leads to a fair and equitable result in the specific claims at hand.

(b) *Iraq's participation in the proceedings.* Given the specific nature of the UNCC and the overwhelming volume of claims it received, there are no clear precedents or rules against which Iraq's procedural rights can be assessed. Most critics of the UNCC procedures appear to approach the notion of due process in terms of case-by-case adjudication, an approach, it is submitted, that would have been highly impractical given the volume of claims and time constraints. In our view, any assessment of the UNCC rules should start from the basic premise that the volume of claims does not permit a conventional individualized approach to claims resolution. The traditional understanding of the legal notions of fair trial and due process is not particularly helpful in the context of mass claims processing.[131] Clearly, the UNCC has had to develop innovative rules and seek a delicate balance between the requirements of procedural fairness and the need to establish a process which can operate expediently and efficiently.

In this respect, a distinction needs to be made between the individual claims, which are resolved through mass claims resolution procedures, and the large claims that were resolved through a more conventional individualized process. For the many small individual claims, the Article 16 reports are the only vehicle for Iraqi participation. These reports provide the Government of Iraq with an opportunity to learn of the facts underlying the claims and the legal issues presented by the claims. Iraq is given the opportunity to make its views and positions on these issues known to the Panels of Commissioners. As explained above, it is in our view regrettable that Iraq was given only a very brief period of time for the preparation of its responses. As a matter of principle, however, it is submitted that the use of such reports is acceptable and sufficient in the context of the small individual claims.

First, with Iraq's liability established and with clear and transparent criteria for compensability set by the Governing Council, the processing of these claims is a relatively straightforward process. Once the facts of the claims are determined, they rarely present complex legal problems.

Second, it is hard to see how Iraq's participation could have been organized differently, without jeopardizing the efficiency of the process. Indeed, if Iraq were granted a right to review each and every individual claim, long delays would have been an inevitable consequence. How much time should Iraq be given to review all individual claims? Should any opportunity for Iraq to comment on individual claims be matched with a corresponding opportunity for individual claimants to respond to Iraq's comments? Inevitably, this would lead to a very lengthy and individualized claims resolution process, which, as we have seen, is not a viable option in the case of the UNCC.

Third, for the small claims in categories A and B, it is not immediately clear how Iraq could usefully make comments on individual claims. The departure claims, for instance, were checked against a body of independent and objective data on departures. The accuracy and comprehensiveness of these records had been objectively verified and established. The checking of claims against these records, as explained above, is a simple and largely automated process, which leaves little or no scope for disputes or arguments.

It is therefore concluded that the Article 16 reports constitute a proper mechanism to reconcile procedural fairness and the requirements of efficiency, at least to the extent that the Article 16 reports are drawn up in an impartial and objective manner and provide a full and unbiased account of all the factual and legal issues arising from the claims. For the larger claims, which are resolved through a more individualized review process, Iraq's procedural rights are protected through the Article 16 reports, the transmission of actual claim files and the convening of oral proceedings where necessary. As shown above, these last two techniques are used mainly in cases where Iraq has direct knowledge that may be helpful to resolve the merits of the claim, in complex and large claims and in claims with a high value. Moreover, through the use of precedent-setting techniques and the guarantees for consistency and uniformity among the various panels, the Iraqi interventions in such claims will also affect the determination of other claims.

In contrast to the relatively straightforward nature of most individual claims, the verification of large claims often presents complex issues. In many of the large cases Iraq may have information and documentation that sheds light on some of the more contentious issues. Even where Iraq has no direct knowledge of the facts underlying the case, its views and positions may be particularly relevant to the resolution of complex legal and valuation issues.

It is submitted, therefore, that the accuracy and fairness of the UNCC process will benefit from an extensive use of these two mechanisms. The views and observations of Iraq—which has a great financial interest in these claims—will certainly inform the resolution process and enhance its legitimacy. The Governing Council appears to be aware and supportive of such extensive use, as is shown by recent practice and the review of the UNCC procedures.

Finally, it is noteworthy that in the UNCC institutional structure, it is the responsibility of the Commissioners to establish the facts and evaluate the claims. The process is inquisitorial rather than adversarial and it is up to the Commissioners to seek the information and documentation required to arrive at a fair determination of the claims. The recommendations of the various panels, especially those dealing with larger claims, clearly demonstrate an awareness of the responsibility that is entrusted to them. The following observation of the D panel may serve to illustrate this attitude:

The Panel is mindful that the Government of Iraq has, under the Rules, limited procedural opportunities to put its case and make submissions. The Panel views its role as balancing the interests of claimants fleeing a war zone often under difficult circumstances and who are therefore in many cases unable to submit extensive evidence to document legitimate claims, with the interests of the Government of Iraq, which is only liable for damage and loss caused as a direct result of the invasion and occupation of Kuwait. Keeping these considerations in view...the Panel directed that the [largest claim file in the instalment] be provided to the Government of Iraq for comments and submissions. In all other cases, the factors set out above were carefully taken into account, along with the factual background, the applicable law, and the Article 16 responses of Governments (in particular the Government of Iraq) in setting the criteria for all methodologies and evidentiary standards and when claims...were individually reviewed.[132]

Procedural Innovations

The UNCC procedures reflect a number of novel and important procedural features, some of which may be relevant to similar undertakings in the future. The most important procedural features can be summarized as follows:

- The UNCC has developed unique mass claims procedures, relying largely on computer support, the use of standard claim forms designed to capture data in a uniform and consistent manner, the grouping and categorization of claims which present identical or similar legal and factual issues, the use of precedent-setting techniques, data matching and sampling. Common issues have been decided on the basis of sample claims and the results were extrapolated to the remaining claims in the group. These mass claims procedures probably represent the most important contribution of the UNCC to international claims resolution.
- The UNCC rules on the administration of evidence recognize the difficult conditions under which many claimants had to leave Kuwait or Iraq. Many individual claimants were unable to take their documents or even passports. In recognition of these problems, the UNCC has established lenient or relaxed evidentiary standards for small individual claims. For the urgent individual claims in categories A, B, and C, simple documentation of the loss is sufficient and the applicable standard is 'the reasonable minimum appropriate under the circumstances'. More demanding standards have been set for larger claims.
- In an international compensation process, with a claimant population spread over several countries, inequalities among different groups of claimants are inevitable. These inequalities may affect the presentation of claims and must be taken into account when making determinations on these claims. In the UNCC, this was largely done through the presentation of so-called country reports to the

Commissioners. These reports explained the various forms of assistance that claimants had received from their national authority when submitting the claims and described the socioeconomic composition of the claimant population of a particular country.

5. DELIVERY

Fixed Compensation

For small individual claims, fixed compensation standards were established by the Governing Council:[133]

- In category A, compensation for successful claimants was set at the fixed amount of US$2,500 for individuals, and up to US$5,000 for families. However, if a claim was filed only in category A, the claimant was eligible to receive a maximum sum of US$4,000 for individuals, and US$8,000 for families.[134]
- In category B, compensation for successful claimants was set at US$2,500 for individuals, and up to US$10,000 for families.

These figures were established after extensive discussion between the members of the Governing Council. Initially, it was planned to calculate the average salary earned by foreign workers in Kuwait and to set the standard compensation for category A claimants at the level of an average one-year salary. During the discussions, other elements were taken into account and eventually the sum of US$2,500 was agreed upon as a lump sum.

The sums were deliberately set at a relatively low level. Claims in these categories were classified as urgent claims for humanitarian reasons and were processed under the so-called expedited procedures.[135] The figures were intended as a minimum amount of compensation that could be paid to successful claimants.

If claimants wished to claim for greater amounts in respect of these losses, they remained free to do so under categories C and D. In other words, using fixed compensation sums is a matter of balancing speed with fairness: small urgent claims are subject to a lower burden of proof and are reviewed and paid quickly, while larger claims are subjected to a more demanding review process.

The use of fixed compensation sums has enabled the UNCC to achieve impressive results in these claims categories. A total of US$3,212,600,000 has been awarded in compensation to 859,258 successful claimants under category A. As for category B claims, a total amount of US$13,450,000 has been paid out to 3,941 successful claimants.[136]

Timing of Payments

From the outset, it was anticipated that the value of claims approved by the Commission would at any given time far exceed the resources of the Fund.[137] In March 1994, the Governing Council therefore established two basic principles for the allocation of available funds to successful claimants.[138] First, 'similarly situated claimants within each category of claims are treated equally... regardless of the chronological order in which their claims are decided'. Second, '[c]laimants with claims in the three categories of urgent claims (categories "A", "B", and "C") shall receive priority of treatment, including at both the processing and the payment stages, in accordance with the prior decisions and statements of the Governing Council.'

Actual payments have been made in three successive phases. In 1994, the Governing Council adopted the mechanism for the first phase of payments, providing that only after each successful claimant in categories A, B and C had received an initial amount of US$2,500 would payments to claimants in other categories commence.[139] However, for humanitarian reasons, all category B claims were paid in full by the end of 1996.[140] Under this first phase of payments, a total of US$3,252,337,997.09 was made available to 1,498,119 successful claimants in categories A, B, and C.[141] The first phase ended in September 1999.

The mechanism for the second phase of payments was adopted in June 1999.[142] It determined that priority of payments would continue to be given to urgent claims, while also providing 'meaningful compensation' to claimants in categories D, E, and F 'at the earliest possible date'. Payments of up to US$100,000 were made available to approved claims in all these categories, comprising subsequent amounts of up to US$25,000 and up to US$75,000 respectively. The priority payment of claims under categories A and C was completed during this second phase of payments, which ended in September 2000.

In June 2000, the Governing Council adopted the mechanism for the third phase of payments, which commenced in October 2000.[143] It was decided that successful claimants in categories D, E, and F would receive an initial amount of up to US$5 million, later followed by a payment of up to US$10 million. In contradiction with one of the basic principles put forward in Decision 17, payments will be made 'in the order in which [the claims] have been approved provided that all initial payments of newly approved claims will have priority over subsequent payments'. In line with past statements, priority of payment was accorded to successful environmental monitoring and assessment claims.

Table 9.3 indicates the status of the claims processing and payment mechanism.[144]

Table 9.3 Claims processing and payment mechanism*

Category	No. of claims to be resolved	Compensation sought by claims to be resolved (US$ approx.)	No. of claims resolved	Compensation sought by claims resolved (US$)	No. of resolved claims awarded compensation	Compensation awarded (US$)	US$ paid
A	161	454,000	922,997	3,454,634,000	859,258	3,212,600,000	3,202,591,638
B	0	0	5,734	20,100,000	3,941	13,450,000	13,450,000
C	32,065	103,910,000	1,704,200	11,400,654,653	640,918	5,121,222,180	5,114,302,767
D	427	886,000,000	13,449	15,669,170,488	10,041	3,317,362,266	2,651,810,816
E1	0	0	105	44,740,422,417	67	21,520,820,521	676,041,475
E2	0	0	2,445	13,661,076,541	954	916,054,517	827,494,413
E3	0	0	398	8,538,543,367	159	402,562,327	349,032,589
E4	0	0	3,621	11,790,127,399	2,867	3,457,004,569	3,165,344,646
E/F	0	0	123	6,147,780,045	57	311,282,668	180,071,703
F1	0	0	100	18,902,591,737	70	291,171,423	253,987,026
F2	0	0	63	18,417,163,597	46	264,422,123	256,121,518
F3	0	0	62	113,905,394,877	60	8,261,985,226	2,148,055,723
F4	19	50,000,000,000	149	36,205,690,078	101	5,009,717,982	328,434,672
Total	32,672	50,990,364,000	2,653,446	302,853,349,199	1,518,539	52,099,655,802	19,166,738,987

* Figures as of July 1, 2005.

Payment Procedure

The compensation awarded by the UNCC is made available to the Governments that submitted the relevant claims and those Governments are responsible for the distribution of the compensation to successful claimants.[145]

A specific problem arose with regard to individuals who owned and/or operated Kuwaiti companies and who filed claims in categories C and D for direct losses sustained by these companies. Some of these claims concerned losses for which claims were also filed by the company in category E ('overlapping claims'); others concerned losses for which no such duplicate claims had been filed ('stand alone claims'). The Governing Council considered that it was not within the UNCC's mandate to determine whether these individuals were entitled to all or part of the compensation awarded to the company. Instead, bilateral committees were established to make these determinations. Kuwait delegated to the UNCC the responsibility for disbursing to the Governments and other submitting entities the amounts to which these individual claimants are entitled.[146]

Governments are required to distribute funds received from the UNCC within six months to successful claimants.[147] Prior to or immediately following the receipt of the first payment from the UNCC, each Government has to provide information to the Governing Council on the arrangements that it has made for the distribution of funds to claimants.[148] Within three months after the expiration of the time limit for the distribution of each UNCC payment, Governments have to report to the Commission on the amounts of payments distributed.[149] These reports enable the UNCC to monitor the distribution of compensation.

The Governing Council decided that Governments have to return any funds that have not been distributed within 12 months of their receipt, a problem which mainly occurs when a claimant cannot be located.[150] The UNCC secretariat holds the returned compensation in reserve for a further 12 months: if the Government notifies the Secretariat that it has located the claimant, payment is made. After 12 months, undistributed funds will no longer be held in reserve. However, payments will be made to claimants, as soon as they have been located, from any balances in the Compensation Fund that are not needed for the Commission's administrative budget or operating reserve, or for scheduled payments of approved awards.

If a government fails to return funds in time or if the above-mentioned reports are not submitted in time, the Governing Council may ask for an explanation or further information, and may decide, in the absence of a satisfactory response, not to distribute further funds to that government.[151]

A government may offset its costs of processing claims by deducting a small fee from payments made to claimants. The processing fee should be commensurate with the actual expenditure incurred, and explanations for any deductions have to be reported to the UNCC. The fee should not exceed 1.5 percent in the case of awards payable to claimants in categories A, B, and C, or 3 percent in categories D, E, and F.[152]

Interest will be awarded on successful claims from the date the loss occurred until the date of payment, at a rate sufficient to compensate successful claimants for the loss of use of the principal amount of the award.[153] These interest payments will only be made after the principal amounts of all awards have been paid.

These provisions also apply to the distribution of payments by any person, authority or body which has been requested to collect and submit claims on behalf of persons who are not in a position to have their claims submitted by a government.[154]

Financing Mechanism

On August 6, 1990, the Security Council adopted Resolution 661 (1990), imposing comprehensive sanctions on Iraq, including a prohibition on the import of Iraqi oil by UN member States.[155] Eight months later, in April 1991, the Security Council decided in Resolution 687 to establish the Compensation Fund and requested the Secretary-General to make recommendations on the appropriate level of Iraq's contribution to the Fund, taking into account Iraq's payment capacity, the requirements of its people, and the needs of its economy.[156] A balance had to be struck between compensating the victims of Iraq's aggression and ensuring the current and future well-being of the Iraqi population. Having formulated recommendations for the creation of the Fund in his Report of May 2, 1991, the Secretary-General determined, in a note thereto, the appropriate level of Iraq's contribution.[157]

Having first observed that Iraq derives almost its entire export earnings from the export of oil, the Secretary-General then looked in more detail at the Iraqi economy, drawing upon data taken from the Government of Iraq, the International Monetary Fund (IMF), the UN Economic and Social Commission for Western Asia (ESCWA), OPEC and the UN Statistical Office. Consequently, he could estimate Iraq's total oil export earnings, its foreign exchange expenditure for strictly civilian purposes, and its debt servicing requirements. Since the latter two constituted respectively 48 percent and 22 percent of the former, the Secretary-General concluded that Iraq's contribution to the compensation fund should not exceed 30 percent of Iraq's annual oil export earnings. This figure was officially adopted by the Security Council in Resolution 705 (1991).[158]

The step that necessarily had to follow was to partially lift the ban on imports of Iraqi oil, in order to ameliorate the humanitarian situation in Iraq and to start compensating the victims of Iraq's aggression. To that end, Resolutions 706 (1991) and 712 (1991) were adopted, respectively in August and September 1991. Iraq refused to accept them.[159] In October 1992, the Security Council adopted Resolution 778 (1992), which urged the member states to transfer funds into the escrow account established by Resolution 706 to meet its purposes. These funds included frozen Iraqi assets and voluntary contributions.[160] On April 14, 1995, the Security Council adopted Resolution 986 (1995), which marked a new effort to establish an 'oil-for-food' program, allowing US$2 billion in Iraqi oil sales every period of 180 days (the so-called 'phases'). Iraq initially refused to accept its terms, but on May 20, 1996, following extensive negotiations, the Government of Iraq and the UN Secretariat signed a Memorandum of Understanding regarding the implementation of Resolution 986 (1995).[161]

The first oil under the program was exported on December 10, 1996. For phases I to III, the Security Council set a ceiling of US$2 billion on oil exports in each six-month phase. For phases IV and V, the ceiling was raised to US$5.2 billion. Iraq was permitted to export an additional US$3 billion worth of oil in phase VI. Finally, Security Council Resolution 1284 (1999) removed the ceiling on future Iraqi oil exports.[162]

Between the first exports of Iraqi oil in December 1996 and the end of the oil-for-food program in November 2003, some 3.4 billion barrels of Iraqi oil were exported for a total revenue of approximately US$65 billion.[163]

As the Secretary-General pointed out in his note of 30 May 1991, and the Security Council confirmed in Resolution 705, a constant review is necessary of the premises on which the level of Iraq's contribution to the Fund is determined. In March 1999, a Humanitarian Panel report pointed out 'the insufficiency of present levels of revenue to deal with pressing humanitarian needs', and therefore recommended that 'the Security Council could authorize ... reducing by an agreed percentage the revenue allocated to the United Nations Compensation Commission'.[164] Such a revision was also envisaged in an Anglo-Dutch draft resolution, which preceded Resolution 1284 and proposed that out of the 30 percent which is channelled from the escrow account to the Compensation Fund, 10 percent would be loaned back to the escrow account for humanitarian purposes, therefore practically reducing to 20 percent the percentage of Iraq's oil income allocated to the Compensation Fund.[165] Eventually, in Resolution 1330 (2000), the Security Council decided to reduce the level of Iraq's contribution from 30 to 25 percent, which was the result of a compromise to solve the controversy regarding the US$15.9 billion award for the Kuwait Petroleum Corporation.[166] A subsequent French draft resolution even proposed a further reduction to 20 percent, but has not been adopted.[167]

Conclusion

Fixed Compensation

The mechanism of fixed compensation sums in categories A and B combined with the lenient evidentiary standards for these claims categories is 'perhaps the [UNCC's] most significant procedural innovation'.[168] The use of fixed compensation sums indeed presents clear advantages:

- Fixing the compensation sums at a relatively low amount makes it feasible to establish lenient or relaxed evidentiary requirements, which helps to ensure that claimants who suffered losses but who are not in a position to fully document these losses, can participate in the claims process and will be compensated;
- Fixed compensation sums ensure full equality among all successful claimants within the same category. All claimants who meet the criteria will eventually receive the same amount;
- Fixed compensation sums increase the efficiency of the process, by reducing the scope for lengthy arguments about the exact extent of damages, which could otherwise seriously delay the processing and payment of claims;
- If applied properly, the use of fixed compensation sums does not exclude differentiation between fundamentally different types of losses and respects the freedom of choice of claimants. Where claimants wish to claim greater amounts, they remain free to do so under categories C or D. In this case, however, they will be subject to a more demanding burden of proof and review process.[169]

It might have been possible, especially for category B, to define more narrow subgroupings of claims on the basis of the various loss types (various degrees of serious personal injury, death of spouse or other relative, etc.) and to set different amounts for the various subgroupings. Such an approach would present the advantage of allowing further differentiation between various degrees of losses or injuries. However, it would complicate decision-making and require a rather cumbersome exercise of establishing a hierarchy of different losses or victims, which almost certainly would cause frustration among certain claimant groups.

Priority of Payment

As stated above, priority has been given to urgent individual claims for humanitarian reasons.[170] The priority treatment in the payment stage is a logical extension of the priority accorded in the processing stage.

Payment Procedure

The Governments that submitted the claims are also responsible for the distribution of any compensation awarded for those claims. However, the governments have no discretionary power to determine their own priorities: they are bound by UNCC rules and have to report meticulously to the Commission on their arrangements and progress.

It has been argued that a more important role should be given to the governments, since they would normally be in a better position to assess the needs of their nationals.[171] This view is not convincing, however, since it would inevitably entail inequalities among claimant groups in different countries and increase the risk that not all compensation would arrive in the hands of those entitled to it.

Financing Mechanism

After the war, a comprehensive sanctions regime was imposed on Iraq. As a result, the local humanitarian situation grew ever more precarious. At the same time, millions of victims eagerly awaited compensation for their losses. In an attempt to address both challenges simultaneously, the oil-for-food program was established, allowing Iraq to export oil and using the revenues mainly for humanitarian and compensatory purposes.

Although Iraqi oil production increased from 550,000 barrels per day in November 1996 to around 2.5 million barrels per day during 2001, the program still faced a persistent revenue shortfall as a result of a price collapse caused by the renewed presence of Iraqi oil on the world market.[172] Consequently, the resources generated through the program were insufficient to address both the humanitarian crisis and the compensation question. Two options were open to improve the situation: either to increase the amount of Iraqi oil exports, or, depending on what was deemed most urgent, to adjust the percentages of Iraqi revenues destined for humanitarian purposes and compensation. Since the extent of the Iraqi oil production is the sole responsibility of the Government of Iraq, the international community could only alter the allocation of funds. After several studies had exposed the deteriorating humanitarian situation in Iraq and once the most urgent compensation claims had been handled, the Security Council decided—as part of a compromise to accept the huge compensation recommended for the Kuwaiti Oil Company—to lower the level of Iraq's contribution to the Compensation Fund from 30 to 25 percent of its oil export revenues.

Although the generation of revenue for the Fund is in principle clearly regulated and its level is set, the actual flow of income is in practice rather volatile. As the amounts of Iraqi oil exports have dropped again during 2002, prospects for the future are not particularly promising. (See Postscript.)

6. RELATION TO DOMESTIC COURTS

General Observations

In his report of May 2, 1991, the Secretary-General stated that 'Resolution 687 (1991) could not, and does not, establish the [UNCC] as an organ with exclusive competence to consider claims arising from Iraq's unlawful invasion and occupation of Kuwait.'[173] Therefore, not only can claims against Iraq for losses that are not compensable by the UNCC[174] be pursued in other fora, particularly domestic courts, but also claims that are compensable. Parallel procedures have been developed, particularly in countries where Iraqi assets were frozen after the invasion, as part of national measures or in implementation of the trade embargo against Iraq.[175]

To avoid multiple recoveries in these situations, the Secretary-General 'recommended that the Governing Council establish guidelines regarding the non-exclusivity of claims and the appropriate mechanisms for coordination of actions at the international and domestic levels'.[176] The Council has repeatedly stated that any compensation already received from any source has to be declared by the claimant and will be deducted from the total amount of losses suffered.[177] This concerns compensation awarded by national courts, as well as payments made or relief provided by individuals, corporations, international organizations or States.[178] The Governments of Iraq and other States have also been asked to provide the UNCC with this information.[179]

Additionally, claimants are obliged to inform the Commission about any parallel proceedings they have initiated seeking compensation from Iraq.[180] Again, the governments of Iraq and other countries have also been requested to provide the UNCC with information about claims against Iraq in the courts of their jurisdiction.[181] If the Commission finds out, through means other than the claimant, about such parallel proceedings, the claim before the UNCC will be suspended, either until it is no longer pending elsewhere, or until all other claims in the same category have been processed.[182]

Conclusion

There is no statistical record of the number of UNCC claimants who have sought or received compensation from sources outside the Commission. However, it is clear that these instances have occurred mainly in the corporate claims of category E.

There have been a number of instances where deductions have been made for compensation payments already received from other sources, *inter alia*, from insurers, employers, governments or organizations, or through settlement agreements between the parties to a contract.[183]

The measures introduced by the UNCC do not exclude the risk of claimants filing for compensation in a domestic court after they have already received compensation from the UNCC. However, a safeguard lies in the fact that Iraq would be a party to the proceedings both before the Commission and before the national court. Consequently, it would be in a position to inform the national court that the claimant had received or is about to receive compensation from the UNCC. Iraq is in a position to do so, since it receives information regarding corporate and Government claims, including the identity of the claimants, either during the UNCC review process or in the approved reports and recommendations made by the Panels of Commissioners.

Information regarding proceedings in other fora has been and continues to be provided by the Government of Iraq and other Governments pursuant to Decision 13, and this has been useful for the claims review process.

A related problem is the issue of withdrawals of large corporate claims. In the past four years, some 185 companies have quietly dropped a total of US$2.9 billion in claims.[184] Apparently, Iraq exerted strong pressure on these companies and made the withdrawal of their claims a precondition for winning aid contracts and other business opportunities.

7. EVALUATION

General Observations

In 1991, the international community acting through the UN showed a clear willingness and determination to provide effective remedies for the many individuals, corporations, international organizations and governments who suffered losses as a direct result of the Iraqi invasion and occupation of Kuwait. To this end, the UNCC was created with a mandate to provide a measure of practical justice to those who suffered damage.

The UNCC's overall success in implementing this mandate cannot be disputed. The UNCC registered a total of approximately 2.7 million claims, including approximately 2.5 million claims by individuals in categories A, B, and C. The merits of these individual claims were determined and compensation was paid within less than ten years. Work continues on the larger claims and is scheduled for completion by the end of 2003. (See Postscript.)

Setting up a mass compensation program on such a scale has required innovative and sometimes creative approaches to the problems and challenges that inevitably arise when providing reparations after armed conflict. The humanitarian approach prioritizing 'urgent' individual claims, the use of computer-supported mass claims techniques such as data matching and sampling, the application of fixed compensation sums for certain claims categories, the elaboration of a unique evidentiary framework: these are just a few examples of the procedural innovations that have greatly contributed to the expedient delivery of compensation to millions of individuals.

In the following two sections, we will examine the applicability of the UNCC model to other situations and the main challenges encountered and lessons learned.

Applicability to Other Situations

By establishing the UNCC, the Security Council has aimed to ensure that the party responsible for the invasion and occupation of Kuwait was held responsible for its violations of international law and was held liable for the damages and losses it caused. Whether the UNCC concept as such is applicable to other situations is questionable. Schoolbook examples of the Iraqi type are rare. Most armed conflicts present more complicated interactions between various parties and a less clear pattern of responsibility. The nearly universal support for reparations in the aftermath of the Iraqi aggression was clearly exceptional and can largely be explained by the fact that many countries had victims among their nationals, the clear-cut responsibility of Iraq and the availability of compensation funds from that country. The combination of these factors is rare in international or internal armed conflicts. To date, there have been no indications that the Security Council will establish similar reparations programs in the near future.

This does not mean, however, that the UNCC is an isolated process, the relevance of which is limited to the specific conflict it has been established for. Although many of the practical and procedural innovations introduced by the UNCC were designed to deal with specific problems and related to the unique circumstances surrounding its establishment and activities, it is submitted that the experience of the UNCC in determining mass compensation claims provides valuable lessons for similar undertakings in the future.

In recent years, the international community has witnessed a proliferation of mass claims programs, designed to provide compensation or restitution to victims of armed conflicts.[185] Although the particularities may differ, the broad concepts and approaches will often be quite similar and some of the recently established institutions have already benefited from the experience and expertise of the UNCC.[186]

Main Challenges and Lessons Learned

This final section aims to identify the main challenges encountered in the implementation of the UNCC's mandate and to formulate a few lessons arising from the UNCC experience that may be relevant to future mass compensation claims programs. Rather than repeating the conclusions formulated in previous parts, the focus will be on issues that are likely to arise in other mass compensation programs.

Funding of UNCC Operations

Funding has been a significant challenge, especially in the early years of the UNCC's existence. The UNCC's operational budget, covered by the Compensation Fund, is prepared by the Secretariat and approved by the Governing Council. Although the generation of revenue for the Fund is in principle clearly regulated and its level is set, the actual flow of income has been and to some extent continues to be rather volatile.

Detailed financial data on the UNCC operations are not publicly available. For the years 1998–9, the UNCC's (biennium) budget amounted to US$82.3 million. According to one source, it was to reach US$100 million in 2000–1.[187]

Establishing an international compensation process on a mass scale evidently requires a significant investment in terms of human resources, legal and other expertise, information technology, and technical support. It is submitted, however, that a more conventional approach to claims resolution—based on a claim-by-claim review and some sort of adversarial proceedings—would have been substantially more expensive.[188]

Balancing Compensation Needs and Competing Interests

The UNCC compensation process was made possible by the fact that Iraq disposes of significant oil resources and that compensation money could be generated through Iraqi oil exports. Based on an analysis of Iraq's payment capacity and its civilian needs, Iraq's contribution to the Compensation Fund was initially set at a level of 30 percent of its oil export earnings. The remaining 70 percent was deemed sufficient to cover Iraq's humanitarian and other civilian needs.

However, when the humanitarian condition of the Iraqi population continued to deteriorate during the 1990s, some observers, especially those active in the field, and a few countries have strongly argued in favour of prioritizing humanitarian aid over compensation. In 2000, the Security Council determined to reduce the level of Iraq's contribution to 25 percent.

A comprehensive analysis of the proper balance between reparations for past injustices and urgent humanitarian needs would be beyond the scope of the present chapter. However, on the basis of our research, three general recommendations for future compensation programs can be formulated.

1. The decision to establish a compensation program depends on the availability of money and requires a reliable estimate of the resources needed.
2. The proper balance between reparations and humanitarian needs should be established at the earliest possible stage, to allow clear information to claimants about the extent and timing of compensation payments and to avoid frustration.
3. Once actual compensation sums have been awarded or paid, the level and standards of compensation should not be altered or adjusted. Any compensation program must ensure equal treatment of all claimants and must be nondiscriminatory. Any reduction in the amount of resources available for compensation purposes during the process may lead to inequalities between claimants whose claims were processed first and claimants whose claims were processed only after the reduction occurred.

Practical Measures to Organize a Large and Diverse Caseload

The UNCC's mandate was defined in very broad terms, covering all losses resulting directly from the invasion and occupation of Kuwait. Claims could be submitted on behalf of individuals, corporations, international organizations, and governments. Many different types of losses were considered compensable under the scheme. The claimed losses ranged from very small amounts to billions of dollars.

The large number of claims, their different nature, and the variety and size of the losses has required the introduction of a number of practical measures.

- **Establishing claims categories:** The UNCC has chosen to divide its claims into six neatly defined and relatively simple claims categories, according to the status of the injured party, the type of loss and the nature of the procedure. Within each category, further subdivisions were made. Depending on which claims category is concerned, different rules and criteria apply. This grouping of claims has allowed the UNCC to develop tailor-made solutions and methodologies for each group of claims.
- **Prioritizing 'urgent' individual claims:** Facing a caseload of 2.7 million claims, the UNCC was forced to give priority to certain categories of claims. Specifically, the Commission decided to expedite and treat on an urgent basis the resolution of claims of individuals in categories A, B, and C. This priority treatment extended from the processing phase to the payment phase. As mentioned above, the privileged position of individual claimants in the system marks a significant departure from the traditional emphasis on corporate and Government claims in previous mass claims processes.

- **The need for clear criteria and guidelines:** In accordance with its general policy-making role, the Governing Council has set the general guidelines and criteria for the determination of the claims by the Commissioners. These criteria and guidelines have enabled the Commissioners to proceed quickly and have ensured consistency and uniformity in the determination of claims. Clear criteria and uniform guidelines that are to be followed by all decision-makers are essential elements of any compensation program that handles large volumes of claims.[189]
- **Precedent-setting techniques and the management of the docket:** To the extent that claims in a particular category or subcategory present similar legal and factual characteristics, the panels have attempted to resolve such common issues and develop standard valuation methods during the review of the first instalment of such claims. Once relevant legal and factual precedents had been established, the panels were in a position to apply them to the subsequent instalments of claims and in effect limit their work. Without such grouping and precedent-setting techniques, the UNCC could not have resolved its large number of claims within the set time frames. The use of these techniques, however, implies that claims cannot be processed on a 'first in, first out' basis. Instead, claims are submitted to the panels for determination on the basis of efficiency-related considerations, including the similarity of loss types and of legal and factual issues as well as the homogeneity of the instalment.[190]

Setting Fair and Appropriate Evidentiary Standards

The UNCC quickly recognized that many individual claimants faced serious difficulties in providing documentary evidence of the losses they suffered. Many individual claimants left Iraq or Kuwait in extremely chaotic circumstances and were not in a position to produce extensive documentation.

The UNCC therefore adopted specific rules on the administration of evidence. These rules explicitly take into account these difficulties and provide for a differentiation among various categories of claims: while lenient evidentiary standards were established for smaller individual claims, requiring only a 'reasonable minimum appropriate under the circumstances', more demanding standards were adopted for larger claims.

This evidentiary framework is well balanced and provides an important procedural innovation that may be relevant in other postconflict situations.

Using Fixed Compensation Sums for Small Individual Claims

Evaluating losses is often a difficult and time-consuming exercise. This is especially so in the absence of reliable documentation on the basis of which the extent of the loss can be established.

For categories A and B, the UNCC established fixed compensation sums. The sums were deliberately set at a relatively low level and were intended as a minimum amount of compensation that could be paid to successful claimants on the basis of a lenient evidentiary basis. If claimants wished to claim greater amounts for the losses they suffered, they remained free to do so under categories C and D, subject to a more demanding burden of proof and review process.

The use of fixed compensation sums linked to lenient evidentiary standards has made it possible to ensure that claimants who suffered relatively small losses and who are not in a position to fully document these losses can still participate in the process. At the same time, the rights and entitlements of claimants who suffered significant losses and who are in a position to present full documentation of their losses, are safeguarded. This system has also enabled expedient decision-making on large numbers of claims and has greatly contributed to the UNCC's success in terms of resolving its caseload.

Using Computer-Supported Mass Claims Resolution Techniques

Without any doubt, one of the most important contributions of the UNCC to modern claims resolution is the development of expedited claims processing systems making maximum use of computer technology. The guiding principle in resolving A, B, and C claims has been one of 'practical justice: that is, a justice that would be swift and efficient, yet not rough'.[191] The use of mass claims processing techniques has enabled the UNCC to decide the vast majority of individual claims within a short period of time. In addition to judicial economy and the expediting of procedures, it is submitted that these techniques, when applied properly, increase the general level of accuracy and efficiency while reducing the bias that may be present in any individualized claims review. Working with these techniques, however, also entails several practical implications.

- **Initial investment:** First, the development of database and software systems to process large numbers of relatively complex claims requires a significant initial investment in terms of time and resources. This initial investment and the time needed to set up the systems should not be underestimated. This implies that no decisions can be made in the first few months or even years of the compensation process.
- **Consistency and uniformity in claims data:** For the use of such techniques to be efficient and fair, consistent and uniform capturing of all claims data is essential. Standard claim forms, containing all data that may be relevant to the processing of claims, need to be developed and entered into a database. This requires a relatively good idea of how the claims processing procedures will be organized and which substantive rules or considerations will affect the outcome of the claims. Moreover, clear instructions governing the presentation and registration

of claims are needed as well as screening mechanisms to avoid inconsistent data entry.

- **Language:** In addition, computer-supported techniques greatly benefit from the use of one standard language in claim forms. Although relatively sophisticated translation programs exist nowadays, the use of one standard language helps to reduce the ambiguities associated with expressing complex legal concepts in different languages. The problem of different languages also appears in the review of evidence by the Commissioners, who often had to decide issues on the basis of documentation written in a language that they had not mastered themselves. Although translation services are provided by the Secretariat, this aspect further complicates decision-making by the Commissioners and forces them to rely on the processing of documents undertaken by the Secretariat.

Moreover, on a more general level, mass claims processing techniques present specific conceptual problems, including:

- **Balancing procedural fairness and efficiency:** As seen above, one of the main challenges in designing procedures for mass compensation claims is to define a proper balance between the procedural rights of all parties concerned and the need to provide justice expeditiously.
- **Transparency and claimants' involvement:** When using mass claims processing techniques, the involvement of the claimants in the process is by definition very limited. Claimants only get the opportunity to 'tell their story' through the statement of claim and the subsequent notification (request for additional information). Apart from these two instances, they are not directly involved in the proceedings. In addition, the motivation given in final decisions is often very short and relatively general. This can easily lead to alienation, frustration and distrust. Although this problem is to some extent inevitable in a process that handles millions of claims, it should be taken seriously when designing compensation processes. In particular, it is important to ensure maximum transparency and clear information and communication about the methodologies and the substantive rules that determine the outcomes of claims. Appropriate motivation of decisions and awards is also of great importance in this respect.

Avoiding Multiple Recovery

The UNCC was not granted exclusive jurisdiction to decide compensation claims against Iraq, therefore creating the risk of claimants approaching domestic courts or other compensation sources in addition to the UNCC. The UNCC introduced a number of measures designed to avoid multiple recovery. The overall effectiveness of these measures can only be assessed in the years to come.

As one author wisely notes, 'the risk of flooding national courts with lawsuits or other proceedings against Iraq is inversely proportional to the degree of "customer satisfaction" provided by the UNCC'.[192] The temptation by some to circumvent the UNCC, by asking a national judge or an arbitrator to reexamine their case, can only be countered to the extent that the UNCC imposes its authority and lives up to the highest standards of fairness and efficiency. Customer satisfaction, as mentioned above, depends to a large extent upon the transparency of the process, the proper motivation of awards, and clear information and communication to claimants.

8. POSTSCRIPT: THE IMPACT OF THE 2003 WAR AND STATISTICS

The Impact of the 2003 War

UN Security Council Resolutions 1483 and 1546

The situation in Iraq changed drastically as a result of the new war of early 2003. With regard to the UNCC, the major changes related to the source of funds and the payment procedure. These measures were part of a larger framework established by UN Security Council Resolutions 1483 (2003) and 1546 (2004).

Security Council Resolution 1483 called upon the Secretary-General to terminate the oil-for-food program.[193] This decision did not, however, put a stop to Iraqi oil exports. Paragraph 20 of the Resolution allowed internationally monitored exports of 'petroleum, petroleum products, and natural gas from Iraq', the proceeds of which, except for the contribution to the UNCC Compensation Fund, were to be transferred to the Iraqi Development Fund. This Fund was 'to be held by the Central Bank of Iraq and to be audited by independent public accountants' (paragraph 12). The Development Fund was to be monitored by an International Advisory and Monitoring Board (IAMB) and its funds disbursed 'at the direction of the [Coalition Provisional] Authority [i.e. the Coalition body which exercised the powers of government over Iraq between May 2003 and June 2004],[194] in consultation with the Iraqi interim administration' (paragraph 13).

With regard to the funding of the UNCC Compensation Fund, paragraph 21 of Resolution 1483 established a mechanism similar to the one under the oil-for-food program, based upon the Iraqi contribution of a certain percentage of oil sales revenues:

[The Security Council] [d]ecides further that 5 percent of the proceeds referred to in paragraph 20 above [i.e. the proceeds of 'all export sales of petroleum, petroleum products, and natural gas from Iraq'] shall be deposited into the Compensation Fund established in accordance with resolution 687 (1991) and subsequent relevant resolutions and that, unless an internationally recognized, representative government of Iraq and the Governing Council of the United Nations Compensation Commission, in the exercise of its authority over methods of ensuring that payments are made into the Compensation Fund, decide otherwise, this requirement shall be binding on a properly constituted, internationally recognized, representative government of Iraq and any successor thereto.

Anticipating the end of the occupation and Iraq's reassertion of full sovereignty by the end of June 2004, the Security Council adopted Resolution 1546.[195] This Resolution, although it '[r]eaffirm[ed] the right of the Iraqi people... to exercise full authority and control over their financial and natural resources' (paragraph 3), essentially confirmed the above mechanism. Paragraph 24 provided as follows:

[The Security Council] [n]otes that, upon dissolution of the Coalition Provisional Authority, the funds in the Development Fund for Iraq shall be disbursed solely at the direction of the Government of Iraq, and decides that the Development Fund for Iraq shall be utilized in a transparent and equitable manner and through the Iraqi budget including to satisfy outstanding obligations against the Development Fund for Iraq, that the arrangements for the depositing of proceeds from export sales of petroleum, petroleum products, and natural gas established in paragraph 20 of resolution 1483 (2003) shall continue to apply, that the International Advisory and Monitoring Board shall continue its activities in monitoring the Development Fund for Iraq... and that appropriate arrangements shall be made for the continuation of deposits of the proceeds referred to in paragraph 21 of resolution 1483 (2003).

Paragraph 25 of Resolution 1546 addressed the future of the Development Fund:

[The Security Council] [d]ecides further that the provisions in the above paragraph for the deposit of proceeds into the Development Fund for Iraq and for the role of the IAMB shall be reviewed at the request of the Transitional Government of Iraq or twelve months from the date of this resolution, and shall expire upon the completion of the political process set out in paragraph four above.[196]

It follows from these provisions that the deposit of oil sales proceeds into the Development Fund will cease on December 31, 2005, whereas the contribution to the UNCC Compensation Fund will continue until it is cancelled pursuant to an agreement between the Governing Council and the Government of Iraq or by a new Security Council Resolution.

UNCC Governing Council Decisions 197 and 227

As a result of Security Council Resolutions 1483 and 1546, the UNCC Compensation Fund would only receive 5 percent instead of 25 percent of Iraq's oil export revenues. Accordingly, the envisaged timing of payments was disturbed. Therefore, the UNCC Governing Council decided to suspend the applicability of Decision 100 regarding the third phase of payments and to establish a temporary payment mechanism:

The Governing Council, Considering that, the income into the Compensation Fund is expected to be inadequate to allow for payments under decision 100 (S/AC.26/Dec.100 (2000)/Rev.1) on all claims expected to be approved during the next year,

1. Decides that, due to the circumstances described above ... the provisions of decision 100 shall be temporarily suspended and that the funds available to the Commission for the payment of claims will be allocated as follows:

   (*a*) The amount of USD200 million will be made available for payments every three months for distribution among successful claimants;

   (*b*) Successful claimants in all categories will receive an initial amount of USD100,000 or the unpaid principal amount of the award, if less;

   (*c*) Subsequent rounds of payments of USD100,000 (or the unpaid principal amount of the award, if less) will be made to successful claimants in all categories of newly approved claims and of claims approved at any previous session of the sessions described above in the order in which they have been approved, until the available funds for distribution have been exhausted.[197]

Statistics

The UNCC status of claims processing and payment was updated most recently at the end of June 2005. The table reproduced below shows that a total of nearly 2.69 million claims have been filed. Over 98 percent of these claims have been processed, about 57 percent of them successfully. A total of just over US$52 billion has been awarded to successful claimants, of which approximately 37 percent has been paid.

The outstanding claims include 19 category F4 claims for a total of US$50 billion, about 32,000 category C claims, 427 category D claims and 161 category A claims.

The bulk of the caseload of individual claims consists of so-called 'late claims'. These claims are accepted after the general claims deadlines laid down for the different categories of claims.[198] The Governing Council has allowed such claims on behalf of certain categories of victims whose claims could not be filed in time.[199]

Decision 219 of the Governing Council provided that no more late claims would be accepted after March 11, 2004.[200] Nevertheless, Decision 225 of July 2, 2004 created 'an accelerated, special claims programme' for Kuwaiti claims on behalf of the bedoun, who are stateless or undocumented Arabs.[201] Table 9.4 illustrates claims and compensation as of July 1, 2005.

Table 9.4 Claims and compensation*

Category	Number of claims to be resolved	Compensation sought by claims to be resolved (US$ approx.)	Number of claims resolved	Compensation sought by claims resolved (US$)	Number of resolved claims awarded compensation	Compensation awarded (US$)	US$ paid
A	161	454,000	922,997	3,454,634,000	859,258	3,212,600,000	3,202,591,638
B	–	–	5,734	20,100,000	3,941	13,450,000	13,450,000
C	32,065	103,910,000	1,704,200	11,400,654,653	640,918	5,121,222,180	5,114,302,767
D	427	886,000,000	13,449	15,669,170,488	10,041	3,317,362,266	2,651,810,816
E1	–	–	105	44,740,422,417	67	21,520,820,521	676,041,475
E2	–	–	2,445	13,661,076,541	954	916,054,517	827,494,413
E3	–	–	398	8,538,543,367	159	402,562,327	349,032,589
E4	–	–	3,621	11,790,127,399	2,867	3,457,004,569	3,165,344,646
E/F	–	–	123	6,147,780,045	57	311,282,668	180,071,703
F1	–	–	100	18,902,591,737	70	291,171,423	253,987,026
F2	–	–	63	18,417,163,597	46	264,422,123	256,121,518
F3	–	–	62	113,905,394,877	60	8,261,985,226	2,148,055,723
F4	19	50,000,000,000	149	36,205,690,078	101	5,009,717,982	328,434,672
Total	32,672	50,990,364,000	2,653,446	302,853,349,199	1,518,539	52,099,655,802	19,166,738,987

* Figures as of July 1, 2005.

Notes

1. In preparing this chapter, we have relied upon a number of sources, including:
   - Relevant United Nations documents: the resolutions of the Security Council together with the reports of the Secretary-General and the decisions of the Governing Council of the UNCC provide an elaborate normative framework governing the entire compensation program. In addition, certain reports prepared by Panels of Commissioners and reports of the Executive Secretary have been studied.
   - Certain Iraqi documents and positions, which are publicly available and have been included in the research.
   - International legal literature concerning the UNCC.
   Professor van Houtte, who is the Director of the Research Project, and has served as a Commissioner in the UNCC for several years, Mr Mojtaba Kazazi, the Executive Secretary of the UNCC, and Mr Michael Raboin, Deputy Executive Secretary of the UNCC, have provided additional information on certain topics. The authors wish to express their gratitude for this help. (As a former Commissioner, Professor van Houtte continues to be bound by the UNCC rules on confidentiality. Moreover, the views expressed in this chapter represent his personal opinions and cannot be interpreted as the official views of the UNCC.) All positions, views, and opinions expressed in this report are attributable solely to the authors.
2. After the main body of this chapter was completed, a postscript was added (in the second half of 2004). Recent events in Iraq raise important (and yet to be decided) questions about the future of the UNCC.
3. Boutros Boutros-Ghali, introduction to *The United Nations and the Iraq-Kuwait Conflict, 1990–1996*, The United Nations Blue Books Series, vol. IX (New york: UN Department of Public Information, 1996), 18, 19, 33.
4. Ibid., 35.
5. Ibid., 36.
6. Ibid., 38.
7. Carlos Alzamora, 'The UN Compensation Commission: An Overview', in *The United Nations Compensation Commission*, Richard Lillich, ed. [Thirteenth Sokol Colloquium] (Irvington, NY: Transnational Publishers, 1995), 3.
8. John R. Crook, 'The United Nations Compensation Commission: A New Structure to Enforce State Responsibility', *American Journal of International Law* 87 (1993): 144, 147–8; Pierre d'Argent, 'Le Fonds et la Commission de Compensation des Nations Unies', *Revue belge de droit international* 25 (1992): 485, 490.
9. Article 147 of the Fourth Geneva Convention defines 'grave breaches' as 'those involving any of the following acts, if committed against persons or property protected by the present Convention: wilful killing, torture or inhuman treatment, including biological experiments, wilfully causing great suffering or serious injury to body or health, unlawful deportation or transfer or unlawful confinement of a protected person, compelling a protected person to serve in the forces of a hostile Power, or wilfully depriving a protected person of the rights of fair and regular trial prescribed in the present Convention, taking of hostages and extensive destruction and appropriation of property, not justified by military necessity and carried out unlawfully and wantonly'.

10. Mariano J. Aznar-Gómez, 'Environmental Damages and the 1991 Gulf War: Some Yardsticks Before the UNCC', *Leiden Journal of International Law* 14 (2001): 301, 331.

11. Alzamora, op. cit., 3.

12. UN, *Report of the Secretary-General of 2 May 1991* in pursuance of Paragraph 19 of *Security Council Resolution 687*, S/RES/687, 1991. The institutional recommendations formulated by the Secretary-General appear to reflect to a large extent the suggestions made by the USA. See Ronald J. Bettauer, 'Establishment of the United Nations Compensation Commission: The U.S. Government Perspective', in Lillich, op. cit. 29, 33.

13. Identical letters dated 6 April 1991 from the Permanent Representative of Iraq to the United Nations addressed respectively to the Secretary-General and the President of the Security Council, S/22456. The Security Council promptly notified Iraq that its acceptance of liability was 'irrevocable and ... legally binding on the Republic of Iraq'.

14. Rosemary E. Libera, 'Divide, Conquer, and Pay: Civil Compensation for Wartime Damages', *Boston College International & Comparative Law Review* 24 (2001): 291, 301, http://www.bc.edu/schools/law/lawreviews/meta-elements/journals/bciclr/24_2/03_FMS.htm.

15. Peter van der Auweraert, 'How the UN Decides on Damages for the Victims of the Gulf War (pt. 1)', *The Daily Star* (Beirut) (February 27, 1997), 7, http://www.soas.ac.uk/Centres/IslamicLaw/DS27-2-97UNCC.html; Bettauer, op. cit., 30; Pierre d'Argent, op. cit., 493.

16. Bettauer, op. cit., 30; *contra* Michael E. Schneider, 'How Fair and Efficient is the UNCC System? A Model to Emulate?', *Journal of International Arbitration* (March 1998): 15, 25.

17. Rex J. Zedalis, 'Gulf War Compensation Standard: Concerns Under the Charter', *Revue belge de droit international* 26 (1993): 333, 334.

18. Bernhard Graefrath, 'International Crimes and Collective Security', in *International Law: Theory and Practice. Essays in Honour of Eric Suy*, Karel Wellens, ed. (New York: Aspen Publishers, 1998), 237, 244–5.

19. Nicolas C. Ulmer, 'Claimants' Expectations From the United Nations Compensation Commission', *Journal of International Arbitration* (March 1998): 7, 10; Frederic L. Kirgis Jr., 'Claims Settlement and the United Nations Legal Structure', in Lillich, op. cit., 103, 110; *contra* Bernhard Graefrath, 'Iraqi Reparations and the Security Council', *Heidelberg Journal of International Law* 55 (1995): 1, 47; Graefrath, 'International Crimes', op. cit.

20. Kirgis, op. cit.

21. *Report of the Secretary-General of 2 May 1991*, 8.

22. Hans Wassgren, 'The UN Compensation Commission: Lessons of Legitimacy, State Responsibility, and War Reparations', *Leiden Journal of International Law* 11 (1998): 473, 490.

23. *Report of the Secretary-General of 2 May 1991*, 20.

24. States generally are represented on the Governing Council by their ambassadorial permanent representatives in Geneva, often assisted by experts.

25. *Report of the Secretary-General of 2 May 1991*, 10.

26. United Nations Compensation Commission, *Provisional Rules for Claims Procedure*, S/AC.26/1992/10, Article 40, 1991.

27. *Report of the Secretary-General of 2 May 1991*, 10.

28. Ibid., 25–6.

29. Wassgren, op. cit., 476.

30. *Provisional Rules for Claims Procedure*, 26.

31. *Report of the Secretary-General of 2 May 1991*, 12.

32. 'Oil for Food: The True Story. How the UNCC Works', *Le Monde Diplomatique* (Paris), October 2000, http://mondediplo.com/2000/10/03iraquncc; Nicolas C. Ulmer, 'The Gulf War Claims Institution', *Journal of International Arbitration* (March 1993): 85, 91.

33. Several staff members served previously at the Iran–US Claims Tribunal and the UNCC has benefited greatly from this experience in a vaguely similar context; see Crook, op. cit., 145.

34. Data provided by Mr Mojtaba Kazazi, July 22, 2002.

35. Christopher S. Gibson, 'Mass Claims Processing: Techniques for Processing over 400,000 Claims for Individual Loss at the UNCC', in. op. cit., Lillich, 155, 162.

36. Francis E. McGovern, 'The Intellectual Heritage of Claims Processing at the UNCC', in Lillich, op. cit., 187, 200.

37. *Campaign Against Sanctions on Iraq Newsletter* (February 2001): 8; 'Kuwait Oil Deal on Hold as Powers Seek Deal on Iraq', *Turkish Daily News* (28 September 2000), http://www.turkishdailynews.com/old_editions/09_28_00/for3.htm#f31.

38. United Nations Security Council, *Security Council Resolution 687*, S/RES/687, 1991, 16, 18; United Nations Security Council, *Security Council Resolution 692*, S/RES/692, 1991, 3; *Report of the Secretary-General of 2 May 1991*, Part 1.

39. Norbert Wühler, 'The United Nations Compensation Commission: A New Contribution to the Process of International Claims Resolution', *Journal of International Economic Law* 2 (1999): 249, 253.

40. United Nations Compensation Commission, *Criteria for Expedited Processing of Urgent Claims*, S/AC.26/1991/1, 1991, 19.

41. Wühler, op. cit., 253.

42. *Provisional Rules for Claims Procedure*, Article 5, 1, b.

43. Ibid.; United Nations Compensation Commission, *Guidelines Relating to Paragraph 19 of the Criteria for Expedited Processing of Urgent Claims*, S/AC.26/1991/5, 1991; Crook, op. cit., 150.

44. *Criteria for Expedited Processing of Urgent Claims*, 17; d'Argent, op. cit., 499.

45. United Nations Compensation Commission, *Business Losses of Individuals Eligible for Consideration Under the Expedited Procedures*, S/AC.26/1991/4, 1991; d'Argent, op. cit., 500.

46. *Provisional Rules for Claims Procedure*, Article 5, 1, b.

47. d'Argent, op. cit., 501.

48. United Nations Compensation Commission, *Criteria for Additional Categories of Claims*, S/AC.26/1991/Rev.1, 1991, 30.

49. Ibid., 6, 21, 34; *Criteria for Expedited Processing of Urgent Claims*, 18. These guidelines are not intended to be exhaustive, according to the UNCC, *Compensation for Business Losses Resulting from Iraq's Unlawful Invasion and Occupation of Kuwait Where the Trade Embargo and Related Measures Were Also a Cause*, S/AC.26/1992/15, 1992, 6.

50. Crook, op. cit., 147–8.

51. Ibid., 148.

52. Ibid., 147–8; Zedalis, op. cit., 333–4.

53. Crook, op. cit., 148.

54. Ibid., 149.

55. d'Argent, op. cit., 503.

56. Crook, op. cit., 149.

57. d'Argent, op. cit., 503.

58. *Criteria for Expedited Processing of Urgent Claims*, 11.

59. Figures as of July 1, 2005. United Nations Compensation Commission, *Status of Claims Processing*, http://www.unog.ch/uncc/status.htm.

60. *Criteria for Expedited Processing of Urgent Claims*, 12.

61. United Nations Compensation Commission, *Personal Injury and Mental Pain and Anguish*, S/AC.26/1991/3, 1991.

62. United Nations Compensation Commission, *Recommendations Made by the Panel of Commissioners Concerning Individual Claims for Serious Personal Injury or Death (Category 'B' Claims)*, S/AC.26/1994/1, 1994, 22.

63. Ibid.

64. *Criteria for Expedited Processing of Urgent Claims*, 11, 12, 14; Wühler, op. cit., 255; see United Nations Compensation Commission, *Category 'C' Claims*, http://www.unog.ch/uncc/claims/c_claims.htm.

65. Crook, op. cit., 153.

66. *Personal Injury and Mental Pain and Anguish*, op. cit.

67. *Criteria for Expedited Processing of Urgent Claims*, 15.

68. Wühler, op. cit., 255; see United Nations Compensation Commission, *Category 'D' Claims*, http://www.unog.ch/uncc/claims/d_claims.htm.

69. *Criteria for Additional Categories of Claims*, 7. This kind of compensation is also granted to corporations, international organizations and States: *Criteria for Additional Categories of Claims*, 22, 36.

70. Ibid., 8.

71. Crook, op. cit., 154.

72. Wühler, op. cit., 255–6; see United Nations Compensation Commission, *Category 'E' Claims*, http://www.unog.ch/uncc/claims/e_claims.htm.

73. *Criteria for Additional Categories of Claims*, 23.

74. Wühler, op. cit., 256; see United Nations Compensation Commission, *Category 'F' Claims*, http://www.unog.ch/uncc/claims/f_claims.htm.

75. *Criteria for Additional Categories of Claims*, 37.

76. Wühler, op. cit., 256; see *Category 'F' Claims*.

77. *Criteria for Expedited Processing of Urgent Claims*, 11–13; United Nations Compensation Commission, *Report and Recommendations Made by the Panel of Commissioners Concerning the First Instalment of Individual Claims for Damages up to US$100,000 (Category 'C' Claims)*, S/AC.26/1994/3, 1994, 54–8; Graefrath, 'Iraqi Reparations', op. cit., 57. On fixed compensation, see Section 5.

78. United Nations Compensation Commission, *Multi-category Claims*, S/AC.26/Dec. 21, 1994; United Nations Compensation Commission, *Report and Recommendations Made by the Panel of Commissioners Concerning the Second Instalment of Claims for Departure From Iraq or Kuwait (Category 'A' Claims)*, S/AC.26/1995/2, 1995, 8–11.

79. *Criteria for Expedited Processing of Urgent Claims*, 1; United Nations Compensation Commission, *Report and Recommendations Made by the Panel of Commissioners*

Concerning Part One of the First Instalment of Individual Claims for Damages Above US$100,000 (Category 'D' Claims), S/AC.26/1998/1, 1998, 6.

80. Ibid., 1, 8.

81. Wühler, op. cit., 261.

82. United Nations Compensation Commission, *Eligibility for Compensation of Members of the Allied Coalition Forces*, S/AC.26/1992/11, 1992.

83. Crook, op. cit., 154.

84. United Nations Compensation Commission, *Propositions and Conclusions on Compensation for Business Losses: Types of Damages and Their Valuation*, S/AC.26/1992/9, 1992, paragraph 6.

85. United Nations Compensation Commission, *Compensation for Business Losses Resulting from Iraq's Unlawful Invasion and Occupation of Kuwait Where the Trade Embargo and Related Measures Were Also a Cause*, S/AC.26/1992/15, 1992.

86. Maren Zeriffi, *Refugee Compensation: Selected Cases and Source Materials*, http://www.arts.mcgill.ca/MEPP/PRRN/biblo1.html.

87. United Nations Compensation Commission, *The Claims*, http://www.unog.ch/uncc/theclaims.htm.

88. McGovern, op. cit., 196.

89. Wühler, op. cit., 257.

90. Ibid., 261.

91. The Briefing Book on International Organizations in Geneva 2000–2001, *United Nations Compensation Commission*, http://www.genevabriefingbook.com/chapters/uncc.html.

92. *Criteria for Expedited Processing of Urgent Claims*, 8.

93. *Category C Claims, First Instalment*, 43.

94. On the importance of comprehensive and detailed forms and loading these into computer format, see Christopher Gibson, 'Using Computers to Evaluate Claims at the United Nations Compensation Commission', *Arbitration International* 13 (1997): 167, 179.

95. *Provisional Rules for Claims Procedure*, Article 7. In addition to the paper form, governments could also submit them in a computer format.

96. Ibid., Article 6, 3. The translation serves as the basis for the evaluation of the claim.

97. Some claims have been forwarded to the UNCC in tattered condition or poor quality photocopies. Such claims have obviously complicated the work of the Secretariat.

98. On the problem of differences between claimant groups, see especially Gibson, 'Mass Claims Processing', op. cit., 169–71.

99. Ibid.

100. *Provisional Rules for Claims Procedure*, Articles 13–14. If the deficiencies are not remedied within 60 days, the claim shall not be considered as filed.

101. Although this limited, almost subsidiary role given to international law may surprise, it is submitted that Article 31 accurately reflects the relevance of the various sources of law. Given that the Security Council already established Iraq's liability under international law, the Commissioners' role is confined to establishing whether the claimants suffered direct losses and the value of the claimed losses. The relevant Security Council resolutions and the decisions of the Governing Council are likely to be more important in this regard than the traditional rules of international law. See also

Michael F. Raboin, 'The Provisional Rules for Claims Procedure of the UNCC: A Practical Approach to Mass Claims Processing', in Lillich, op. cit., 119, 138.

102. Ibid., 139.

103. If a panel considering a claim or group of claims cannot complete its work within the allotted time, the Panel will notify the Governing Council through the Executive Secretary. The Council may grant additional time or allocate the claims to another panel. See *Provisional Rules for Claims Procedure*, Article 39.

104. In practice, the Governing Council has been extremely reluctant to adjust recommended amounts. See *Provisional Rules for Claims Procedure*, Section 2.5.3.

105. *Provisional Rules for Claims Procedure*, Article 40, 4.

106. Mojtaba Kazazi, 'An Overview of Evidence before the UNCC', *International Law Forum* 1 (1999): 219, 221.

107. See for instance Gibson, 'Using Computers', op. cit., 174.

108. In determining what was to be considered the 'reasonable minimum appropriate under the particular circumstances of the case' the panel was free to consider many factors including: (1) the instructions on the claim form itself, some of which were ambiguous, (2) the types of evidence routinely submitted, (3) the circumstances in Iraq and Kuwait during the invasion and occupation, (4) transactional practices in Iraq and Kuwait prior to the invasion (e.g. both were cash-only economies), (5) the socioeconomic characteristics of claimants from different countries, and (6) the national claims programs of the various governments. All of these factors were taken into account as establishing a significant evidentiary 'platform' or context for the C claims.

109. *Provisional Rules for Claims Procedure*, Article 35, 3.

110. *Category D Claims, First Instalment*, Part One, 72.

111. Ibid., 75.

112. United Nations Compensation Commission, *Explanatory Statements by Claimants in Categories 'D', 'E' and 'F'*, S/AC.26/Dec.46, 1991, 3.

113. *Category C Claims, First Instalment*, 143.

114. The A Panel verified and assessed the evidentiary value of these records. While most of the records supplied by governments and international organizations were considered reliable and sufficient for this purpose, several others were excluded from the process.

115. See United Nations Compensation Commission, *Report and Recommendations Made by the Panel of Commissioners Concerning the First Instalment of Claims for Departure From Iraq or Kuwait (Category 'A' Claims)*, S/AC.26/1994/2, 1994, 24: 'the computerized methodology used for the verification of the A claims involves the comparison of the information in the claims with information obtained from outside sources relating to the departure of individuals from Kuwait and Iraq during the Gulf crisis'.

116. United Nations Compensation Commission, *Report and Recommendations Made by the Panel of Commissioners Concerning the Fourth Instalment of Claims for Departure From Iraq or Kuwait (Category 'A' Claims)*, S/AC.26/1995/4, 1995, 9.

117. *Category C Claims, First Instalment*, 44.

118. See also *Provisional Rules for Claims Procedure*, Article 26: claims are to be categorized 'according to, inter alia, the type or size of the claims and the similarity of legal and factual issues'.

119. Gibson, 'Mass Claims Processing', op. cit., 183–4.

120. United Nations Compensation Commission, *Report and Recommendations Made by the Panel of Commissioners Concerning the Second Instalment of Individual Claims for Damages up to US$100,000 (Category 'C' Claims)*, S/AC.26/1996/1, 1996, 13.

121. Presentation of the Delegation of the Republic of Iraq in the Dialogue with the Secretary-General of the United Nations, February 26–27, 2001, 26, http://www. iraqi-mission.org/untalks1.htm.

122. Schneider, op. cit., 18; Mr Schneider represented Iraq before the UNCC.

123. Wühler, op. cit., 261.

124. United Nations Compensation Commission, *Review of Current UNCC Procedures*, S/ AC.26/Dec.114, 2000, 14; see also Andrea Gattini, 'The UN Compensation Commission: Old Rules, New Procedures on War Reparations', *European Journal of International Law* 13 (2002): 161, 169.

125. David B. Carron and Brian Morris, 'The UN Compensation Commission: Practical Justice, Not Retribution', *European Journal of International Law* 13 (2002): 183, 192.

126. *Review of Current UNCC Procedures*, 14.

127. On the advantages of mass claims processing techniques, see McGovern, op. cit., 187.

128. It was only during the 1990s that the creation and experience of institutions such as the United Nations Compensation Commission, the Swiss Claims Resolution Tribunal for Dormant Accounts, and the Commission for Real Property Claims in Bosnia and Herzegovina brought mass claims processing to the forefront of the international domain. These initial experiments have been followed by the creation of other bodies such as the Housing and Property Claims Commission in Kosovo and the Eritrea-Ethiopia Claims Commission. Simultaneously, a number of mass claims programs have been established to provide compensation for losses incurred during World War II. Mass claims processing, with all its advantages and disadvantages, is slowly becoming a feature of international procedure.

129. Wühler, op. cit., 265–6.

130. Presentation of the Delegation of the Republic of Iraq in the Dialogue with the Secretary-General of the United Nations, February 26–27, 2001, 26, http://www. iraqi-mission.org/untalks1.htm.

131. This is illustrated by the practice of other mass claims programs. The Commission for Real Property Claims in Bosnia, for instance, issues final and binding decisions on property title through single-party proceedings. The Housing and Property Claims Commission in Kosovo applies specific adversarial procedures to complex cases involving ethnic discrimination and operates through single-party proceedings for other claims.

132. *Category D Claims, First Instalment*, Part One, 76.

133. *Criteria for Expedited Processing of Urgent Claims*, 11–13.

134. United Nations Compensation Commission, *Category 'A' Claims*, http://www.unog.ch/ uncc/claims/a_claims.htm.

135. See *Criteria for Expedited Processing of Urgent Claims*, 19.

136. *Status of Claims Processing*, http://www.unog.ch/uncc/status.htm.

137. *Report of the Secretary-General of 2 May 1991*, 28.

138. United Nations Compensation Commission, *Priority of Payment and Payment Mechanism. Guiding Principles*, S/AC.26/Dec. 17, 1994, 1, A.

139. Ibid., 2, 5.

140. United Nations Compensation Commission, *Payment Procedure*, http://www.unog. ch/uncc/paymproc.htm.

141. Ibid.

142. United Nations Compensation Commission, *Decision Concerning the Priority of Payment and Payment Mechanism for the Second Phase of Payment*, S/AC.26/Dec. 73, 1999.

143. United Nations Compensation Commission, *Decision Concerning the Priority of Payment and Payment Mechanism for the Third Phase of Payment*, S/AC.26/Dec. 100/Rev. 1, 2000.

144. *Status of Claims Processing*, http://www.unog.ch/uncc/status.htm.

145. United Nations Compensation Commission, *Distribution of Payments and Transparency*, S/AC.26/Dec. 18, 1994.

146. United Nations Compensation Commission, *Claims Filed by Individuals Seeking Compensation for Direct Losses Sustained by Kuwaiti Companies*, S/AC.26/Dec. 123, 2001.

147. *Distribution of Payments and Transparency*, I, 3.

148. Ibid., 2.

149. Ibid., 4.

150. United Nations Compensation Commission, *Decision Concerning the Return of Undistributed Funds*, S/AC.26/Dec. 48, 1998.

151. *Distribution of Payments and Transparency*, 5.

152. Ibid., I, 1.

153. United Nations Compensation Commission, *Awards of Interest*, S/AC.26/1992/16, 1992.

154. *Distribution of Payments and Transparency*, II; see *Awards of Interest*, Section 3.1.

155. United Nations Security Council, *Security Council Resolution 661*, S/RES/661, 1990, 3.

156. United Nations Security Council, *Security Council Resolution 687*, S/RES/687, 1991, 19; see Section 1.

157. Note of the Secretary-General Pursuant to Paragraph 13 of his Report of May 2, 1991 (S/22559), S/22661 of 30 May 1991.

158. United Nations Security Council, *Security Council Resolution 705*, S/RES/705, 1991, 2.

159. Office of the Iraq Programme Oil-for-Food, *Oil-for-food—the basic facts 1996 to 2002*, http://www.un.org/Depts/oip/background/basicfacts.html.

160. United Nations Security Council, *Security Council Resolution 778*, S/RES/778, 1992.

161. *Oil-for-food—the basic facts*.

162. Office of the Iraq Programme Oil-for-Food, *Basic Figures*, http://www.un.org/Depts/ oip/background/basicfigures.html.

163. Office of the Iraq Programme Oil-for-Food, Press Release of November 19, 2003. On the termination of the oil-for-food program pursuant to *United Nations Security Council Resolution 1483 (2003)*, see Postscript.

164. Report of the second panel established pursuant to the note by the president of the Security Council of 30 January 1999 (S/1999/100), concerning the current humanitarian situation in Iraq, S/1999/356, Annex II, 54, http://www.cam.ac.uk/societies/casi/ info/panelrep.html; *cf.* The Human Rights Impact of Economic Sanctions on Iraq, Background Paper prepared by the Office of the High Commissioner for Human Rights for the Meeting of the Executive Committee on Humanitarian Affairs, December 5, 2000, 4, http://www.cam.ac.uk/societies/casi/info/undocs/sanct31.pdf.

165. UK/Netherlands draft resolution, http://www.cam.ac.uk/societies/casi/info/ uk-dutch.html.

166. United Nations Security Council, *Security Council Resolution 1330*, S/RES/1330, 2000, 12; the maximum level of Iraq's contribution is still set at 30 percent, but the actual level has been lowered to 25 percent.

167. France's Second Draft Resolution for the UN Security Council, June 19, 2001, http://www.cam.ac.uk/societies/casi/info/france010619a.html.

168. Crook, op. cit., 152.

169. On multi-category claims, see *supra* Section 3.

170. See *supra* Section 3.

171. Graefrath, 'Iraqi Reparations', op. cit., 46, 51.

172. *Weekly Update* (July 6–12, 2002); Energy Information Administration, *OPEC Revenues: Country Details* (June 2002), http://www.eia.doe.gov/emeu/cabs/orevcoun.html.

173. *Report of the Secretary-General* of 2 May 1991, 22.

174. Noncompensable claims are those concerning Iraq's debt and obligations arising prior to August 2, 1990; for indirect loss or damage; for losses attributable to the trade embargo, which are not separate and distinct from that embargo; for claims preparation; for costs of the Allied Coalition Forces; and for loss or injury of members of the Allied Coalition Armed Forces, except if three cumulative conditions are met.

175. Wühler, op. cit., 260.

176. *Report of the Secretary-General* of 2 May 1991, 22.

177. *Criteria for Expedited Processing of Urgent Claims*, 16, 20(a) (iii); *Criteria for Additional Categories of Claims*, 7, 13(a) (iii), 25, 27(a) (iv), 39, 40(a) (iii); United Nations Compensation Commission, *Further Measures to Avoid Multiple Recovery of Compensation by Claimants*, S/AC.26/1992/13, 1992, 3(b).

178. d'Argent, op. cit., 507.

179. *Further Measures to Avoid Multiple Recovery of Compensation by Claimants*, 1–2.

180. Wühler, op. cit., 260.

181. *Further Measures to Avoid Multiple Recovery of Compensation by Claimants*, 1–2.

182. Wühler, op. cit., 260.

183. See for category D claims *First Instalment*, Part One, 341 (compensation provided by employer); *Second Instalment*, Part One, 32–3 (end of term indemnities), 39–40 (hostage-taking), 113–14; *Third Instalment*, 26–8 (end of service indemnities); for category E claims Category E1, *Second Instalment*, 338 (reimbursement of insurance premium), 482–3 (payments by insurers); Category E1, *Fifth Instalment*, 78–82 (re-negotiation of contract after liberation of Kuwait), 135 (Government of Saudi Arabia and Allied Coalition Forces); Category E2, *Fourth Instalment*, 138 (partial payment in settlement of dispute), 205–6 (judgment or other award), 207 (payment received from insurers); Category E2, *Fifth Instalment*, 67–72 (partial payment in settlement of dispute); Category E3, *Fourth Instalment*, 98 (retention monies), 99–108 (guarantees, bonds and like securities), 109–17 (export credit guarantees), 119 (business losses, construction), 237–40 (advance payments); Category E3, *Eighth Instalment*, 70 (arbitration award); Category E4, *First Instalment*, 152–4 (salary payments, loss of income); Category E4, *Third Instalment*, 107–9 (loss of cash); Category E4, *Fifth Instalment*, 71 (salaries, loss of profits), 87–9; Category E4, *Sixth Instalment*, 73 (claim for reward paid by claimant company to its owner for efforts to restore contracts after liberation); Category E4, *Fifteenth Instalment*, 159–64 (payments received from insurers); for category F claims Category F1, *Second Instalment*, 112; Category F1, *Fourth Instalment*,

(136–7 European Commission's financial contributions), 145–6 (European Commission's financial contributions), 158 (contributions received from other governments or international organizations); Category F1, *Fifth Instalment*, 84–151 (grant received from another government); Category F3, *First Instalment*, 31–48 (relief provided by Kuwaiti Government to employees).

184. Steve Stecklow and Alix M. Freedman, 'Iraq Presses Firms to Forgo Billions in War Reparations', *Wall Street Journal* (June 19, 2002): 1.

185. Examples are: the Commission for Real Property Claims (CRPC) in Bosnia, the Housing and Property Claims Commission (HPCC) in Kosovo, the Claims Resolution Tribunal (CRT) for Dormant Accounts in Switzerland and other mass claims programs recently established to provide reparations to victims of Nazi aggression during World War II.

186. See Wühler, op. cit., 265.

187. 'Oil for Food: The True Story. How the UNCC Works,' http://mondediplo.com/2000/10/03iraqunc; see also the UNCC's website: http://www.unog.ch/uncc at the Governing Council's page.

188. It can be roughly estimated that in order to process 2.7 million claims within 15 years through conventional methods, a minimum of 250 adjudicators would be required, working seven days a week and deciding an average of two claims per day. Staffing levels in the Secretariat would equally have to be increased to provide the necessary support to these adjudicators.

189. Wühler, op. cit., 257.

190. Ibid., 266–7. The criteria that determine the order in which claims are submitted to the panels include: the date of filing of the claims, the homogeneity of the instalment with respect to the type of losses claimed, the size, volume and complexity of the claims, as well as the legal, factual and valuation issues raised by the claims.

191. Carron and Morris, op. cit., 188.

192. Gattini, op. cit., 181.

193. United Nations Security Council, *Security Council Resolution 1483*, S/RES/1483, 2003 at para. 16. In line with this provision, the program officially ended on November 21, 2003.

194. See Coalition Provisional Authority Regulation No. 1, CPA/REG/16 May 2003/1.

195. United Nations Security Council, *Security Council Resolution 1546*, S/RES/1546, 2004.

196. Para. 4 endorsed 'the proposed timetable for Iraq's political transition to democratic government', which would eventually lead to 'a constitutionally elected government by December 31, 2005'.

197. UNCC Governing Council Decision 197 concerning a Temporary Payment Mechanism, S/AC.26/Dec. 197, 2003. See also Decision 227 'concerning the extension of the temporary payment mechanism' established by Decision 197, S/AC.26/Dec. 227, 2004, which confirmed and continued the application of Decision 197.

198. These deadlines were set at January 1, 1995 for categories A, B, C, and D, at January 1, 1996 for categories E and F, and at February 1, 1997 for environmental category F claims.

199. So far, all late category C claims decided have been claims on behalf of Palestinians. See United Nations Compensation Commission, *Decisions concerning the first and*

second instalments of Palestinian late claims for damages up to US$ 100,000 (category 'C' *claims)*, S/AC.26/Dec. 207, 2003 and S/AC.26/Dec. 216, 2004.

200. United Nations Compensation Commission, *Decision concerning requests for the late filing of claims*, S/AC.26/Dec. 219, 2004.

201. United Nations Compensation Commission, *Decision concerning the filing of 'late' claims on behalf of the 'bedoun'*, S/AC.26/Dec. 225, 2004.

GERMAN REPARATIONS TO THE JEWS AFTER WORLD WAR II: A TURNING POINT IN THE HISTORY OF REPARATIONS

A R I E L   C O L O N O M O S
A N D R E A   A R M S T R O N G[1]

INTRODUCTION: POST-WORLD WAR II GERMAN REPARATIONS TO THE JEWS AND TRADITIONAL INTERSTATE REPARATIONS: SIMILARITIES AND DIFFERENCES

West German payments to the State of Israel and Jewish victims of the Holocaust since 1950 are an unprecedented landmark in the history of reparations. Traditionally, reparations were part of the framework of relations between nations following a conflict and obligated the losing State to compensate damages incurred by its opponents during the course of the war. German postwar reparations were not limited to this sort of interstate compensation. Certain aspects of the reparations policy proposed by Konrad Adenauer, the first Chancellor of the Federal Republic of Germany (West Germany or FRG), are rather unique and hence, German reparations to Jews after World War II are a model of an entirely new kind of reparations.

Briefly, the West German reparations program contained several new innovations: First, the reparations addressed both the Holocaust (also known as the Shoah), beginning with the rise of Nazism in the 1930s, and the war against other countries; all preceding reparations had addressed the damages caused by war, exclusively. Second, they were negotiated by representatives of two countries, West Germany and Israel, which did not exist at the time the atrocities or the war took place. Third, these reparations compensated two categories of people: individual victims of the Holocaust, including citizens of the State paying reparations; and citizens of a new country, Israel. Fourth, also unprecedented, the negotiations included both representatives of states and nongovernmental organizations, such as international Jewish associations. Last, in contrast to the reparations following World War I, West Germany established this policy because Adenauer was convinced of its political necessity and of its just and moral character, and not necessarily because the FRG was held legally responsible.

The specifics of the West German reparations program were the result of almost six months of negotiations that started in Wassenaar, the Netherlands, and culminated in the signing of the agreement in Luxemburg on September 10, 1952. The agreement consisted of two broad categories of measures. The first category compensated the State of Israel for the pain suffered by survivors of the Shoah who emigrated to the new state. The German government allocated funds to Jewish organizations to support their development of an outreach program for these victims of Nazi persecution. The second category of measures in the agreement obligated Germany to enact a series of laws that allowed individuals to request reparations because of physical and moral sufferings during the time of the Nazi persecution. The Bundestag, the West German Parliament, also enacted a restitution law in 1957 that allowed individuals to reclaim confiscated property.[2]

This chapter concentrates on the following five points. First, it examines the genesis and development of the idea of German reparations. Before describing the various measures in detail, it will be useful to understand the different objectives of the negotiating parties. This section will also consider the role of civil society, especially in the USA, in promoting the idea of reparations, and German and Israeli reactions to the proposals made by the negotiating parties. Second, it examines the agreements signed between West Germany, Israel, and the Claims Conference in Luxemburg 1952, as well as the laws promulgated in Germany starting in 1952. Third, it assesses the current state of the German reparations policy. Fourth, it considers to what degree the recent demands in the 1990s, for reparations and restitution are linked to the limits of the previous arrangements of the 1950s and concludes with some general observations on reparations.

1. The Emergence of the Idea of Reparations and the Negotiations Between the Federal Republic of Germany, Israel, and the Claims Conference

German reparations were not established by Adenauer and his government *de novo*. Reparation discussions began before the creation of the Federal Republic of Germany. The first measures were introduced in the framework of laws imposed by the Allies. The Allied Restitution Law of 1947 foresaw the restitution of goods that had been 'aryanized'—but was silent on the issue of compensation of victims.[3] As a result, the Jewish Restitution Successor Organization (JRSO), which began its work in 1948,[4] received about 50 million deutschmarks.[5] In April 1949, the Council of States in the American-occupied zone established a law of compensation.[6] By defining important concepts such as the right of 'displaced people' from Eastern Europe to compensation and the categories of harm considered persecution, this law established the foundations of the first nationwide law on reparations enacted in 1953.[7] This law, written primarily by Otto Küster, the Württemburg state commissioner for reparations, also became the model of reparations legislation in other provinces including Bayern, Bremen, and Hessen (known as *Ländergesetze*), which became federal laws once the Federal Republic of Germany was founded in 1949.[8]

Indeed, in the fourth part of the treaty that established the sovereignty of the Federal Republic of Germany and ended its occupied status on February 26, 1952, the Allies requested the German authorities to prepare a federal law of reparations, which included the following points:

(1) effective and accelerated negotiation, decision, and fulfillment of restitution claims with no discrimination against groups or classes of persecutees;
(2) a procedural and evidentiary arrangement for restitution that takes account of the difficulties of proof resulting from persecution—loss of documents, disappearance of witnesses;
(3) creation of opportunities for reopening claims made under older legal arrangements when newer, more favorable restitution laws were adopted; and
(4) appropriation of funds to satisfy restitution claims.[9]

The laws of 1947, 1949 and the provision of the 1952 treaty were just the starting point for the larger reparations program set up by West Germany a few years later. Morally, reparations were necessary, in Adenauer's eyes, for the new Germany to underscore the extent of atrocities committed by the Nazis. Reparations would also demonstrate to the world Germany's repentance, thereby achieving the political objective of assuring Germany's entrance into the concert of nations. From an economic standpoint, although reparations involved considerable costs, Adenauer wagered that over the long term, Germany could eventually benefit from its good will. And so, on September 27, 1951, Adenauer declared '...unspeakable crimes were committed in the name of the German people, which create a duty of moral and material reparations.... Initial steps have been taken in this area. But much remains to be done. The Federal Government will ensure rapid adoption of reparation legislation and its just implementation.'[10]

For West Germany, this policy was referred to as *Wiedergutmachung* ('making good again'). Germany was not forced into such a program, and major powers did not insist that international law obliged Germany to adopt it. The name, however, was unacceptable to many victims and to several Israeli leaders who participated in the negotiations. For them, it was impossible to 'make good' the atrocities of the Holocaust. They deemed the reparations and restitutions as necessary, and referred to them as *shilumim*, meaning 'payments', instead.

The Emergence of Compensation Claims within the Jewish World

The idea of making Germany pay for the wrongs that it committed against the Jews was discussed from the very beginning of the war within the Jewish community and then took hold in the USA. It was evoked as early as 1939 by Shalom Adler-Rudel, the leader of the German Jewish community, exiled in London.[11] At that time, the proposition fell on deaf ears, but beginning in 1941, advocacy groups regularly raised the issue, including Jewish organizations in Palestine since 1943. The topic was also at the center of the 'War Emergency Conference' held in Atlantic City in 1944, organized by the World Jewish Congress.

American civil society was predisposed to assist Jewish reparation efforts through disseminating Jewish claims against Germany in the public realm, given the important role played by religious associations in American social movements and their legal approach to issues of equality and justice. In the postwar years, Jewish organizations, whose main goal was to assist refugees, increased their influence and were naturally interested in obtaining compensation to further provide for the refugees. The World Jewish Congress and the American Jewish Committee were two of the most important of such organizations. A new organization was rapidly created in order to coordinate the efforts of the different movements and associations representing Jewish needs. The Claims Conference on Jewish Claims Against Germany—an umbrella organization of 23 groups—was founded in 1951 after a meeting in New York among representatives of the Jewish associations and individuals who had survived the Holocaust. Leaders from the Claims Conference would later take part in the negotiations with the Federal Republic of Germany.

Secret Meetings between Israel and Germany

Nahum Goldmann—the head of the World Jewish Congress—emerged as the most important Jewish leader in the negotiations between the Germans and the Israelis. Goldman was inspired by the perspective developed by Nehemiah Robinson—a Lithuanian jurist with a German law degree who had an influential role in crafting the legal framework for the final agreement—and by the debates concerning reparations that took place in the USA. In 1949 Adenauer publicly declared his wish to rectify the wrongs caused by the Germans, only two months after his election as the first Chancellor of the Federal Republic of Germany.[12] Adenauer's public statements were unambiguous and convinced Jews and their representatives that meeting with the Germans could be worthwhile.

However, because of the chronological proximity of the Shoah, a harsh debate had broken out in Jewish communities within the diaspora as well as in Israeli society concerning the legitimacy of engaging with one's former executioners. Faced with the reticence of certain members of Israeli society, Israeli leaders authorized Goldman to have clandestine discussions with Adenauer at least until they could produce a possible agreement acceptable for both parties.[13] Goldman met Adenauer secretly on December 6, 1951 in London and later served as mediator between the German and Israeli authorities.

Accepting the Idea of Reparations

Adenauer's reparations initiative engendered less than full support from German citizens. Polls showed that many Germans considered themselves victims of the war and therefore entitled to whatever assistance could be given, especially if it was to come from the German government. The idea of paying attention to the victims of the Holocaust was not commonly accepted.[14] Just after the war Germans were asked which groups should receive economic support for having been victims of the Third Reich. A majority of them thought that it was the German widows and orphans that should be the first recipients of support. Next came the people who had suffered material losses, the refugees and people who had been expelled from the country, relatives of people executed because of participation in the attempt on Hitler's life, and finally, Jewish victims.[15]

This resistance towards paying reparations to Jewish victims could be found in government circles as well. Within the German government, the idea of German reparations to Jewish people was opposed not just because it conflicted with an idea of who should be the first recipients of assistance, but also because of the feasibility of such a large expenditure given Germany's delicate financial position at the time.[16]

When Adenauer attempted to implement the *Wiedergutmachung* agreement, several political figures of Bavaria singled themselves out by their opposition to a program of reparations.[17] Such was the case of Fritz Schäffer, Minister of Finance of the Federal Republic of Germany until 1957 and in 1961, Minister of Justice. He proudly defended German economic interests, particularly its currency, and his skepticism vis-à-vis the *Wiedergutmachung* policy led to heated political battles with some of its advocates, such as Otto Küster.

In the end, however, the German government rallied around the necessity of engaging in a reparations policy, convinced that reparations best promoted German interests. Perhaps cynically, the decision to pay Israel and the Jewish organizations a significant amount of money was dictated by considerations of interest and reconciliation/integration with the West and the North Atlantic Treaty Organization. Indeed, it is arguable that the economic rehabilitation of the new Germany with the aid of the Marshall plan and its subsequent economic integration with the West occurred because of the provision of benefits for Germany's former victims.

Within German society, especially in circles of intellectuals, judges, journalists, and theologians, some defended the *Wiedergutmachung* on moral grounds, convinced that Germany should fulfill this obligation.[18] Some, like Küster, were deeply influenced by Protestant culture, which emphasizes repentance and asking for forgiveness after an individual accounts for their behavior. These Christian initiatives of accountability and transparency provided considerable support to Jews trying to marshal their efforts in Germany.

Justifying Claims in Israel

Within Israeli society, the years before the signature of the reparations treaty between Israel and Germany in 1952 were marked by acrimonious debates between advocates and opponents of German reparations. If the idea was born within the diaspora and within the principal Jewish-American organizations, its reception in Israel was much more complicated.

Once again, the economic rationale was a decisive variable for the different Israeli protagonists in charge of negotiations with the Germans. However, the economic explanation is not sufficient to fully understand the reasons that encouraged the Knesset, the Israeli Parliament, to choose to accept reparations.

David Ben Gurion, Israel's Prime Minister, in agreement with the leaders of the Jewish World Congress like Nahum Goldmann, declared himself in favor of demanding compensation from Germany. They emphasized the needs of the young State of Israel, which faced serious economic hardships soon after its creation. The money collected from diaspora donations did not suffice and more was needed in order to absorb the costs of the influx of people. The diaspora remitted US$118 million in 1949 and US$90 million in 1950, while the country's commercial deficit was US$220 million for 1949 and US$282 million for 1950.[19]

However, this logic of economic necessity met with sharp opposition. Opponents mobilized political and moral arguments against accepting compensation. They insisted on the peculiarity of the State of Israel, which should not sacrifice the principles of its uniqueness by accepting compromises in the name of material interest. The political sense of Zionism, the willingness of its leaders to define an autonomous path for the Jews, and the determination to be independent of a foreign country whose leaders had previously sought to exterminate the Jews were threatened by accepting compensation. Morally, the Zionist project itself was thought to be at stake in so far as it was based on a criticism of materialism. In addition, many Israelis adopted an even more radical position that advocated abstaining from all contact, including commerce, with Germany in order not to suffer the effects of its impurity. Putting the monstrous German State in quarantine seemed to them the most appropriate action. Opponents of negotiating with Germany put forward two principal arguments: (*a*) Jewish national dignity must be preserved as the legacy of the Holocaust, as a form of respect for the murdered victims, (*b*) collective sentiments should override cold logic—the legacy of Jewish history and the Zionist rebirth must prevail.[20]

These political and moral arguments were at the center of bitter debates that took place in the Knesset in 1951 when the young deputy Menahem Begin accused Ben Gurion of being an assassin. Begin denounced the procedure through which Germany would pay reparations to Israel, which involved accepting German goods that Israel would resell afterward. According to Begin, this scheme meant that Israel participated in an economic chain that directly linked it to the work of their torturers.[21] Consequently, in the long run, Israelis would support the work of their torturers, essentially profiting from their own suffering. Hence, he argued that Israelis would, after the fact, become partners in their own genocide.[22]

The debates were passionate. In defense, those favoring compensation relied on religious arguments. The Talmud teaches that a criminal should not profit from his crime.[23] Consequently, the demand for compensation from Germany seemed justified and made sense in the context of a country that was founded on religion. This argument, which became the mantra of those who defended negotiations with the Germans, was not without controversy. The Talmud also teaches that one must not rob the robber.

Thus at the founding meeting of the Claims Conference, Rabbi Isaac Lewin disagreed in the name of the Agudat Israel organization. This organization claimed that for a period of one thousand years no generation could acquit itself of such a debt as the Germans had acquired; Germany's debt was one that could not be paid off.[24] Rabbi Lewin referred to the following passage: 'Ye shall not take ransom for the life of a murderer that is guilty of death' (Numbers 35:31).

In this context, proponents of negotiations with Adenauer's Germany encountered a wave of particularly fierce opposition. At first, Golda Meir also criticized Ben Gurion's proposal. However, she later changed her mind and came to the conclusion that Israeli policy had to be pragmatic and that reparations could be used to sustain the development of the Israeli State. 'Why was it placed upon us, a small people, to bear such a large part of the terrible cruelties that have befallen the world? There is only one answer. We were weak, we had no independence, we had no state... we must make ourselves stronger in every way in order to save quickly... Jews from all over the world.'[25]

From a religious and moral point of view, this question was difficult to resolve. From a political point of view, there was a clear response and pragmatic argument in favor of reparations. From a legal perspective, experts such as Nehemiah Robinson clearly distinguished between the legal issue of addressing demands for compensation and restitution to the Germans on the one hand, and the moral debt contracted by the Germans on the other. The legal admissibility of demanding compensation for victims of war and genocide was not to be confused with the moral debt to victims. The latter could not be quantified and hence would remain eternal.[26]

2. THE LUXEMBURG AGREEMENT AND THE PROMULGATION OF GERMAN REPARATIONS LAWS

Eventually, the Israeli delegation and the Claims Conference were ready to negotiate with Germany and a neutral country was chosen to stage the negotiations, the

Netherlands. Jewish negotiators defined a detailed scheme of the claims to be presented to Germany:

(1) existing laws on restitution and compensation should be more effectively implemented;

(2) existing general claims legislation should be extended to the whole Federal Republic;

(3) the existing general claims legislation should be amended to correct omissions and defective provisions arising from the limitations on place of residence and the upper limit set to claims;

(4) additional legislation should be enacted to ensure that compensation for economic loss inflicted by the Reich, whether it directly accrued to the Reich or to the Nazi party, should be identical; and

(5) the successor organizations should be recognized, wherever necessary, as the proper recipients of heirless property and unclaimed portions of assets which accrued to the Nazi state and party.[27]

As far as individual claims were concerned, the following demands were presented:

(1) indemnification for deprivation of liberty;

(2) compensation for various kinds of economic loss;

(3) simplification of the procedure for verifying compensation claims when the relevant documents had been lost or destroyed;

(4) according relatives the right to present claims on the deceased's behalf;

(5) linking the level of compensation to the cost of living in Germany;

(6) acceptance of responsibility for payment of pensions to officials and employees of Jewish communities and institutions;

(7) amendment of legislation in the French zone and West Berlin;

(8) amendment of claim laws in the British zone;

(9) legislation on compensation and indemnification should be extended to cover additional categories of claimants: compensation for forced levies imposed on the Jews in Germany such as the Flight tax, compensation for property seized by institutions of the Reich and Nazi party inside the frontiers of greater Germany, compensation for property seized by institutions of the Reich and Nazi party outside the frontiers of greater Germany;

(10) implementation of the above obligations within 5 years;

(11) exemption from the equalization of burden tax for survivors of Nazi persecution;

(12) assumption of responsibility by the federal government for acts of the Third Reich in matters related to property restitution.[28]

The Luxemburg Agreement

As noted earlier, the agreement compensated two groups of beneficiaries: (*a*) the newly formed State of Israel populated mainly by the victims of the Holocaust who had decided to leave Europe; and (*b*) the Jewish victims in the diaspora. The terms for the former were easier to determine than those in the latter group because the victims in the diaspora were spread out over several countries. It was also easier to determine the needs of a state, because this question was part of the traditional kind of reparations between states, compared to estimating the needs of individual victims who belonged to a vastly dispersed collective.

To find a solution to this last problem, the agreement was divided into different parts. The first part dealt with the sum that Germany agreed to pay to Israel: DM3 billion (US$882 million) between 1953 and 1965. The agreement also foresaw two protocols. Protocol number one addressed the legislative acts concerning individual compensation that had to be ratified, within the framework of a series of federal laws examined in more detail below. Protocol number two detailed the payment of a total amount of DM450 million (US$107 million) to the Claims Conference. This amount was actually paid to Israel, which then gave it to the Claims Conference.[29]

In the first meeting of negotiations among the Israelis, the representatives of the Claims Conference, and the German delegation, in March 1952, Israel and the Jewish groups demanded compensation of DM4.2 billion to help construct the State of Israel and DM500 million for the Claims Conference to be used in relief, rehabilitation (social and cultural) and resettlement of Jewish victims of Nazi persecution living outside of Israel.

The Israeli government's demand arose out of calculations of integrating the 500,000 victims of the Holocaust who fled Europe since 1933 into the new Israeli State. German experts from the Ministry for Refugees agreed with an Israeli government estimate, which calculated that US$3,000 per person would be necessary.[30] Although Adenauer agreed to the sum in principle, after the negotiations, Israel only received DM3 billion out of an initial demand for DM4.2 billion.

The Claims Conference's demand for DM500 million was based on the following principle: 'The West German government should pay the Conference a commensurate share for heirless and unclaimed Jewish assets which accrued to Germany other than those which will be reclaimed by individuals and successor organizations.'[31] The sum requested by the Claims Conference was also for past expenditures and anticipated costs of the different Jewish relief organizations assisting refugees.[32] The needs of these organizations were enormous; there were an estimated 22,000 very serious cases of mental disease in the diaspora and 150,000 less serious ones.[33] The Claims Conference needed to cover their expenses for as long as the survivors needed, which in a number of cases meant until their death. As for individual reparations, the Jewish parties to the negotiations expected these to be paid directly to victims by Germany under a federal law to be debated in 1952.

The German delegation was incapable of clearly responding to these requests and the Israeli delegation accused the Germans of haggling and withdrew from negotiations in April 1952. Back in Germany, the delegation met with Adenauer who opposed the reticence of his own government, which in his view harmed the negotiations. The negotiations started again when Germany offered to pay DM3 billion to Israel, not including the US$450 million earmarked to help finance the program of the Claims Conference, which was subsequently accepted.[34]

The Signing of the Treaty and the Allocation of the Reparation Money to Israel

The treaty, which enabled the payments to be delivered to Israel, was ratified by the Bundestag on March 18, 1952. Two hundred and fifty-five members voted in favor, thirty-five voted against it, and eighty-nine members abstained.[35] Israelis and Germans now had to agree on the financial modalities. The ideal terms of the financial settlement would be ones that met both the needs of the Israelis and the capacity of the Germans. The payments were to be made over the course of thirteen years, starting from 1953 until 1965. Germany transferred funds into the Israeli Mission bank account at the German Bundesbank, which was solely to be used to buy goods produced in Germany. In addition to the transfer of goods, Israel received foreign exchange to purchase oil from the UK.[36] The treaty listed five categories of goods, each with a corresponding spending limit, totaling DM200 million, including DM75 million for the purchase of oil:

> Group I: steel, iron and non-ferrous metals, DM26.5 million;
> Group II: steel and metal-processing industries, DM45 million;
> Group III: chemical and other industries, DM35 million;
> Group IV: agricultural and food products, DM3.5 million;
> Group V: services (including shipping, insurance, and administration), DM15 million.[37]

A large percentage of these payments, up to 80 percent, was invested in Groups I and II, i.e., capital goods.[38] This was crucial for the industrial development of Israel and consisted of 12 percent of the total value of its imports. The output of electric generating stations in Israel increased almost fourfold, from 175,000 kW to 635,000 kW, with the delivery of five power stations.[39] The following shipping goods were also delivered: forty-one cargo vessels, four oil tankers, two passenger ships, two combined passenger-cargo vessels, trawlers, customs launches, and a floating dock. In the field of production, a copper and an iron works were built with the payments. Building equipment was also delivered. Public infrastructure was largely enhanced through the delivery of telephone and telegraph systems, diesel locomotives, railway coaches, hospital and medicine facilities. Most important-ly, German disbursements for oil deliveries from the UK paid for approximately

28 percent of Israel's consumption needs. These deliveries lasted for thirteen years and amounted to DM1,050 million.[40]

These goods were not to be sold to other countries, unless it was otherwise specified in the agreements between the Israelis and the Germans. Israel was notably able to re-export oil. Israel was also able to take advantage of the selling of certain commodities. For example, when iron was cheap on the German market, it was purchased in large quantities, only to be sold for a profit when the prices changed.

Every year, the Claims Conference received a percentage of the sum of German payments to Israel.[41] In October 1953, the Israeli government notified the Conference that the agency would receive a payment every three months of 15 percent of the income from the sale of German goods reaching Israel during the previous nine months.[42]

The main Jewish organizations that preexisted the formation of the Claims Conference were in charge of the distribution of the reparations money, since they could more easily reach the victims through their own existing networks. The American Joint Distribution Committee (JDC) and the Jewish Relief Survivor Organization (JRSO) benefited the most from the money delivered by the Claims.[43] The Conference budget for 1954 was US$9,500,000, of which the JDC received US$6,724,250,[44] greatly increasing the revenue of the JDC in comparison to other Jewish organizations. The relief programs organized by the JDC fell into different categories: cash relief, medical aid, childcare, and care for the elderly. By the end of 1954, the Conference, through the JDC, had assisted 27,500 Jewish victims including 11,500 people in 'Displaced Persons' countries (Germany, Austria, Italy) and 16,150 in France, Belgium, and other Continental countries.[45]

A large portion of the sum received by the Claims Conference (18.5 percent) was also used to finance the activities of the Jewish Agency (JA).[46] The JA used 90–95 percent of this money to finance its own resettlement and rehabilitation programs. The JA also financed Israeli organizations with the money received from the Claims. These funds were used to finance educational and cultural activities at Hebrew University, Haifa Technion University and some 150 yeshivot.[47]

The money the Claims Conference spent directly, primarily financing its own logistics, was a minor portion of the total sum delivered to it by Germany through Israel. As the Claims Conference is an umbrella organization, it used most of the money from Germany to finance other organizations. After the allocations by the Jewish Agency and the Jewish Distribution Committee, the amount to be allocated in the form of grants by the Claims Conference among Jewish assistance organizations was approximately US$2,500,000 per year.[48]

Since two-thirds of West European Jews lived in France, the Claims Conference decided to give priority to this country through its country-specific programs. The *Fonds Social Juif Unifié* (FSJU) was the main network through which these funds were channeled. The FSJU distributed a total of US$22,129,000 through the end of the Conference-administered reparations in 1965.[49]

Jewish populations in other countries, such as Belgium, were also in great need. There were vast disparities between the established Belgian Jewish community and the much larger refugee community that arrived in 1945. The JDC financed a community center in Belgium and invested in the improvement of welfare services.[50] In Holland, the provision of communal services focused on cultural work, restoration of synagogues, and assistance to children and the elderly. The Conference allocated US$1,146,263 to this country.[51]

3. THE FEDERAL REPARATIONS LAWS

The 1953 Federal Supplementary Law for the compensation of Victims of National Socialist Persecution— (Bundesergänzungs gesetz zur Entschädigung für Opfer der national sozialistischen Verfolgung)

Under the first nationwide compensation law, the Federal Supplementary Law, direct compensation was limited to former German citizens, refugees, and stateless persons.[52] Holocaust survivors living in the Soviet Bloc countries received no indemnification. During the period of détente between the USA and the Soviet Union, many survivors emigrated to the West, thus qualifying as refugees. But most of them were still excluded from German compensation programs, because the filing period had ended in 1966.[53]

The first indemnification law was passed on July 29, 1953 by the Bundestag and went into force on October 1, 1953.[54] Although this law offered more compensation to the victims than the former state laws did, the reparations and restitutions it offered were still lower than those offered within the legal framework of the US-occupied zone immediately after the war.[55] Victims had to file individual claims that would be sent to provincial (*Land*) reparations agencies. They had to follow very precise bureaucratic procedures and notably be interviewed by doctors if they wanted to be compensated for physical or psychological damages.[56] If the claimant disagreed with the agency's decision, he or she could contest the settlement first in provincial courts (*Landgerichte*), then courts of appeal (*Oberlandsgerichte*), and finally the Federal Supreme Court (*Bundesgerichthof*). Claimants over 60 years old, the needy, and those sick and infirm whose earning capacity had been reduced by at least 50 percent received priority within the decision process.[57]

The 1953 law outlined categories of damage eligible for compensation, including 'harm to life, body, health and freedom; harm to possessions and assets; harm to career and economic advancement'. Claimants could simultaneously pursue damages in each of the various categories for persecution from January 30, 1933 until May 8, 1945. The main benefits are as follows:

- *Compensation for life*: Widows, children, dependent relatives could apply for an annuity for wrongful death, based on the amount paid to families of civil servants who suffered accidental death on duty, depending on the civil servant's seniority.[58] The average income from the last three years before the death was the basis for determining to which category of civil servants the deceased belonged, and thus the relevant annuity. Claimants were also eligible to receive a one-time capital payment for the time between the death of the victim of persecution and the beginning of the annuity payments. As of December 2001, the German government has paid approximately US$3.5 billion (€3.9 billion) in claims for compensation for life.[59] In 2001, the average pension awarded under this category was approximately US$697 per month (€792).
- *Compensation for health*: For 'not insignificant' damage to health or spirit, claimants were entitled to medical care. For damages beyond the provision of medical care, claimants could apply for an annuity and needed to prove that persecution caused certain health damages that led to at least a 30 percent reduction in their earning capacity. Doctors often relied on tables for quantifying the damage, such that loss of an eye constituted a 30 percent reduction, while loss of arm constituted a 50 percent reduction in earning capacity.[60] The reduction in earning capacity is based on the average income of the persecuted for the three years before persecution against him or her began.[61] The percentage reduction in earning capacity is then equaled to a percentage of civil servants' salary, such that for a 30–39 percent reduction in earning capacity a claimant was entitled to 15–40 percent of the relevant civil servants' disability pay. For the time between the injury (or reduction in earning capacity) and the annuity, claimants were entitled to a one-time capital payment. As of December 2001, the German government has paid approximately US$21.8 billion (€24.7 billion) in health-related claims.[62] In 2001, the average pension awarded under this category was approximately US$450 per month (€510).
- *Compensation for damages to freedom*: This category includes claimants subjected to political or military jail, interrogation custody, correctional custody, concentration camp, ghetto, or *Wehrmacht* punishment entity. It also includes forced labor insofar as the persecuted lived under jail-like conditions. Claimants were entitled to DM150 per month of custody (approximately US$35).[63] As of December 2001, the German government has paid approximately US$1.27 billion (€1.4 billion) in claims for damages to freedom.[64]

- *Compensation for property, assets,*[65] *discriminatory taxes*: Claimants were entitled to compensation (note: not restitution) for damage to property, assets lost due to boycotts or payment of discriminatory taxes such as the Reich Flight tax.[66] The loss of property must have occurred because the claimant fled the country or emigrated, or was 'robbed of his freedom'(§18). The maximum amount (including all three categories) was DM75,000, approximately US$18,750 at the then exchange rate of US$1 to DM4.[67] Of that DM75,000, claims for personal belongings could only constitute DM5,000 or one and a half times the claimant's annual salary in 1932. As of December 2001, the German government had paid approximately US$568 million (€645 million) in property, assets and tax claims.[68]
- *Compensation for damages to career or economic advancement*: Self-employed and privately employed claimants (or dependent relatives) were entitled to a maximum payment of DM25,000 (approximately US$6,250 at the exchange rate of US$1 to DM4 at the time) for the time that persecution (firing or restriction of duties) began, until January 1, 1947, the assumed date that victims could attain an adequate standard of living. The exact amount was calculated as at least two-thirds of the relevant civil servant's pay for that time period. If a victim was unable to resume their career, they could choose to receive their retirement pension early, calculated as two-thirds of the pension for the relevant category of civil servants. Additional provisions for these victims included a loan of a maximum of DM30,000 to restart their businesses and reaccreditation with the relevant authorities. Compensation for public officials was covered under separate laws on public officials more generally.[69] Victims can also claim assistance to make up their missed education, up to DM5,000. As of December 2001, the German government has paid approximately US$8.8 billion (€9.9 billion) in claims for damages to career or economic advancement.[70]
- *Compensation for loss of life or pension insurance*: Maximum of DM10,000 awarded.

The 1956 Federal Compensation Law

The 1953 Federal Supplementary law excluded several categories of victims. Additionally, the processing of the claims was extremely slow and some of the victims complained that the administrative procedure was extremely complex, including, notably, the reparations claims form they had to fill in.[71] Victims also complained that the evaluation procedure and the interviews with the doctors were a rather unpleasant and inhumane experience. Not surprisingly, many Holocaust survivors abstained from filing a claim. Filing a claim and being examined by a doctor, who would coldly judge the impact of the injuries on the victims' earning capability, was emotionally too difficult to bear for many victims, some of whom felt guilt for surviving, or shame, not to mention the pain of reliving these traumatic experiences.

Many German bureaucrats and deputies of the Bundestag, dissatisfied with the provisions of the 1953 law, initiated a process of reform. This movement led to the drafting and the ratification of a new Federal Compensation Law (*Bundesentschädigungsgesetz*—BEG) in 1956. This law implied several improvements over the former, most notably in terms of the residence and deadline requirements. Victims could benefit from reparations if they had arrived in Germany prior to 1952 (instead of 1947 as stipulated by the former law). Individuals who had lived in the borders of the German Reich of 1937 (i.e. Eastern part of the former Reich, East Germany, and former German territories in Poland) and who would meet all other requirements also became eligible for reparations.[72]

The main changes in the law are as follows:

- *Compensation for health*: The minimum 30 percent reduction in earning capacity necessary to claim monetary damages was lowered to 25 percent. Funds were available to assist claimants with retraining exercises necessary to recover or improve their capacity. The law also recognized that if a claimant died as a result of harm to his health of body, the surviving kin were eligible for compensation under the provisions for 'loss of life'[73] (§31, 40, 41).
- *Compensation for damages to freedom*: This category was expanded to include claimants forced to wear the Star of David or to live illegally in inhuman conditions (§47).
- *Compensation for property, assets, discriminatory taxes*: This category was divided into three separate categories, each with separate ceilings on compensation (except for discriminatory taxes, which were no longer subject to a ceiling). For property, claimants could file for the replacement value, not to exceed a maximum award of DM75,000 (§55). The law also recognizes other instances in which claims for property are eligible, including being expelled or deported and forced to flee and live in inhuman conditions (§51). Claims for assets were also subject to a ceiling of DM75,000 (§58).
- *Compensation for damages to career or economic advancement*: Regulations were eased for privately and self-employed claimants to choose an annuity instead of the one-time capital payment.[74] The monthly maximum was raised from DM500 to DM600. Eligibility for career compensation was quantified as a reduction in earning capacity of at least 25 percent for privately and self-employed claimants (§76, 82, 83, 87).
- *Compensation for loss of life or pension insurance*: Maximum of DM25,000 awarded (§133).

For example, if the victim was assigned a middle-level category for civil servants, based on his average earning capacity for the three years before his injury, a person in his or her mid-fifties with a 50 percent reduction in earning capacity would have received DM243 a month (about US$60) in 1961.[75]

The status of the eligible victims was also different from what was stipulated in the 1953 law. In the 1956 law, if victims had been persecuted for either their political opposition to the Nazi regime or on the grounds of race, religion, or ideology, then they were eligible for reparations. In contrast, the 1953 law required victims to be persecuted for their political convictions as well as on the grounds of race, religion, or ideology.[76] The new law designated more specific but overall more inclusive categories, thus making benefits accessible to more victims.

Despite the expansion of beneficiaries, the 1956 law still excluded several groups of victims:

(1) all those who had been persecuted outside Germany by German killing squads, who, because they had remained in their native countries, did not fulfill the law's residency requirements;

(2) forced laborers;

(3) victims of forced sterilization;

(4) the 'antisocial';[77]

(5) Communists;

(6) gypsies; and

(7) homosexuals.[78]

Individuals in the first category, who lived in Western European countries, were entitled to claim monetary damages through a series of interstate treaties. Between 1959 and 1964, Germany agreed to pay damages (a total of DM977 million) to the governments of Austria, Belgium, Denmark, France, Great Britain, Greece, Italy, Luxembourg, the Netherlands, Norway, Sweden, and Switzerland, who would then distribute the money among their citizens who had been harmed by the Nazi regime.[79] As far as victims from Eastern Europe were concerned, they would be eligible for compensation only if they had immigrated to Western countries before the deadline for application, October 1957.[80] The October 1957 deadline, which was an extension of the previous deadline in the 1953 law, caused great difficulties for many survivors who were dispersed all over the world and who were cut off from reliable sources of information. It was eventually extended until April 1958.[81]

There was another limitation to eligibility for compensation. The BEG ($6 (1) 4) specified that victims who had committed criminal acts after May 8, 1945 and who had been imprisoned for more than three years were not entitled to compensation.[82] This limitation was harshly criticized for its lack of humanity. Indeed, marginality and social problems had, in some cases, been the consequences of the trauma survivors had suffered during the war. The victims' lack of integration and their attitude vis-à-vis the law could also be correlated with their traumatic experiences during the Holocaust.

The 1965 BEG Schlussgesetz—the Federal Compensation Final Law, and later developments

The 1956 BEG law was criticized by several Jewish organizations, most notably by the Claims Conference. Many politicians and German bureaucrats had also expressed divergent opinions about this legislation. Therefore, at the beginning of the 1960s a second process of reform was initiated. It would lead to the promulgation of the BEG Final Law in 1965, which was published in the German legal bulletin on September 18, 1965.[83]

First, it created a hardship fund of DM1.2 billion (US$300 million) to support refugees from Eastern Europe who were previously ineligible for compensation under the BEG, primarily emigrants from 1953 to 1965. The fund distributed lump-sum payments beginning at DM1,000–3,000, depending on the damage incurred.[84] Second, the 1965 law contained the presumption that if a claimant had been incarcerated for a year in a concentration camp, subsequent health problems could be causally linked to their persecution under the Nazi regime. This significantly eased the burden on claimants to prove that damages to their health were linked to their earlier persecution. Third, eligibility for compensation for loss of life was expanded to recognize deaths that had occurred either during persecution or within eight months (§15). Similarly, if the victim died more than eight months after the end of persecution from harm to his body or health, then surviving relatives could claim compensation under the category 'loss of life' (§41). Fourth, the BEG Final Law raised the ceiling on claims for education to DM10,000 (then approximately US$1,250).[85] Last, already adjudicated claims were to be revised based on the new provisions.[86]

The Final Law did little to compensate those excluded by previous laws, as mentioned:

(1) all those who had been persecuted outside Germany by German killing squads, who, because they had remained in their native countries, did not fulfill the law's residency requirements;
(2) forced laborers;
(3) victims of forced sterilization;
(4) the 'antisocial';
(5) Communists;
(6) gypsies; and
(7) homosexuals.

In addition, the Final Law recognized slave or forced labor but only in terms of the 'jail-like' conditions that victims lived under. Compensation for their work, whether in concentration camps or for private German companies, was not legally recognized.

During the 1970s, the Claims Conference negotiated with the German author-ities to provide some compensation for survivors who were refugees from Soviet Bloc countries. Many of them fled those countries during the détente period and therefore were excluded on the basis of the 1965 deadline. In 1980, the FRG agreed to create a new 'Hardship Fund' for this later group of emigrants of DM400 million. Five percent of this was for institutional grants; the rest was to be paid to survivors in the form of one-time grants of DM5,000 each (approximately US$2,500 at 2001 rate), based on demonstrated financial need and failure to receive compensation under the German Federal Compensation Final Law.[87] The Claims Conference repeatedly, and successfully, negotiated with the German government additional contributions to the Hardship Fund including DM135 million till 1992, DM200 million from 1993–9 and a commitment for funding from 2000–3.[88]

4. ASSESSING GERMAN REPARATIONS

German reparations are the biggest reparations program that has ever been imple-mented.[89] The German government received over 4.3 million applications for individual reparations, of which approximately 2 million were approved.[90] Overall, its economic magnitude is impressive. On September 30, 1965, according to differ-ent estimations, Germany had paid more than DM18 billion (US$4.5 billion), on January 1, 1986, that figure rose to more than DM59 billion (US$27.5 billion) and in 2000 it was estimated to have reached more than DM82 billion (US$38.6 billion).[91] Added together, the different kinds of payments issuing from the BEG, of certain laws outside of the BEG, the Federal Restitution Law, the agreements reached in Luxemburg, the treaties Germany made with twelve Western countries, payments made to individuals who underwent medical experiments and other various payments, the German government has paid approximately US$61.5 billion (€70 billion) in reparations, including US$37.5 billion (€42.5 billion) under federal individual indemnification laws as of December 2001.[92]

This program of reparations had important economic and political conse-quences. First, it has directly impacted Israel and Germany. Not only have both countries benefited from this agreement, had this program of reparations not been implemented, German–Israeli relations would have been dramatically different. For the victims themselves, it is extremely difficult to make a general assessment other than to calculate the sums given so far by Germany to claimants. However, indi-vidual victims have testified to a variety of experiences with the claims procedure, illustrating the complexity of the process and obstacles victims had to overcome.[93]

Economic and Political Relations between Israel and Germany

Israel did not use the reparations money to directly support the resettlement of the half million Holocaust survivors, instead using the funds to foster economic development more generally. This incoming capital boosted the Israeli economy, ultimately benefiting Holocaust survivors.[94]

The treaty between Israel and the FRG enabled these two countries to engage in a substantial trade relationship. In 1964, Germany's imports from Israel amounted to DM157 million (US$39.6 million) and Germany's exports to Israel to DM243.3 million (US$61.2 million).[95] German imports consisted of fruits, precious stones, and motor fuels. Israel purchased from Germany machinery, ships, chemicals, and vehicles. Germany became Israel's third trading partner.[96] The German economy developed and benefited from the reparations program. Economic investment was stimulated from the reparations plan and the FRG benefited from the Marshall plan. In part because of the reparations, the FRG benefited from US aid and also engaged in profitable trade relations with Western countries, particularly with the USA.

Reparations also facilitated the sale of arms and military equipment when Israel needed it most. At the end of the 1950s, Israel had some difficulty procuring equipment for its military. The USA refused to sell arms to Israel, and France could only supply a portion of its needs. Contacts established during the reparations negotiations facilitated new negotiations with the FRG and created a favorable context. Germany agreed to the sale and deliveries began in 1959. It sold motor vehicles, training aircraft, and helicopters to Israel.[97]

From a strictly political and diplomatic perspective, Germany and Israel had no official relations other than the necessary institutional arrangements that had been settled by the treaty in order to enforce the agreement. During the thirteen years when Germany delivered these goods to Israel, the two countries abstained from any other political relationship. To a certain extent, reparations served as an excuse and as a shield for the nonrelations between these two countries.[98] This phase was considered as a period of transition.

When the reparations payments to Israel ceased in 1965, political relations were gradually initiated. The process started with the establishment of diplomatic relations and the opening of embassies in 1965. These political relations were accompanied by German aid and continued good trade relations between Israel and the FRG. However, deep political tensions emerged when the Israelis criticized Germany's double-edge diplomacy in the Middle East. Indeed, Germany was selling military equipment to Israel, but it was also helping Egypt and had through the years developed a pro-Arab foreign policy. German ties with Arab countries had already begun during the Suez crisis. At the beginning of the 1960s, Israel discovered that the FRG had provided Egypt with military experts. This caused some tension between Israel and Germany and diplomatic relations largely declined with the advent of the Six Days war.[99]

Nevertheless, it is arguable that the relationship that was established around the reparations allowed the two countries to weather the ups and downs, contributing to the stabilization of a relationship between two states that would have been hard to conceive of under different circumstances.

Individual Reparations and Their Impact

The procedure leading to compensation was strenuous for the victims. This was particularly so in the case of body and health damages. Unlike restitution, where the claimant could bring objective evidence of the looting, the compensation for body and health damages is more complex and obliges the victim to expose his or her most intimate wounds in order to access reparations benefits. After the victim had filed a claim for body and health damages,[100] the file was sent to the reparations office in Germany, where it was processed and was either accepted or denied. If it was denied, the victim could bring his or her case to court. The victim had to hire a lawyer and the court nominated experts. The victim would be interviewed by regular physicians, specialists, and in the case of psychological problems, by psychiatrists. Such an experience by definition brings back memories of the war. This process also obliged victims to face the judgment of evaluators, bureaucrats, doctors, and sometimes court judges.

Numerous victims complained about the complexity of the procedure. They stated that they had to suffer the cold, impersonal, and inhumane tone of the evaluators. The assessment of any harm is, of course, a very difficult process. It is even more so when the claims are so numerous. Indeed, by December 31, 1966, the ultimate deadline for the submission of claims for individual reparations under the BEG Final Law, 550,000 petitions had been submitted.[101] Germany needed a standardized procedure to efficiently process and monitor those claims. But the need for standardized efficiency often increased the risk of further traumatizing former victims.

The most difficult task facing the examiners was analyzing the connection between persecution and the harms the victims claimed. In a great many cases, it was difficult to assess the impact certain persecution-related illnesses had on victims' earning capacity. It was also difficult to determine the extent to which persecution had caused certain illnesses such as neurological disorders. Establishing the relationship itself needed very close examination. Indeed, every victim deserved close attention, because many cases were complex and because the victims themselves felt they needed attention.

However, in practice, victims were confronted with a cold bureaucracy, because of the necessity of processing a large number of cases and because of the nature of bureaucracy itself. Examiners were said to apply the procedure earnestly, but were criticized for being insensitive. Their insensitivity, the sense of routine examiners experienced, came from the great number of cases they had to evaluate. Those examiners—doctors and judges—were getting used to human suffering.

The German bureaucracy had difficulty evaluating the subjective dimension of pain and suffering. Especially in the case of psychological harm—a large number of victims suffered from post-traumatic disorders and anxiety neuroses—German bureaucracy had to assess a subjective and personal harm that had been done to the victim and that was potentially related to the genocide. Medicine is not a precise science. But it is all the more difficult when attempting to establish connections between a patient's personal history, physiology, and psychological state.[102]

Despite the tremendous challenges, it is arguable here, again, that the reparations program, however glaring its shortcomings, provided services and funds without which the victims' lives would have been harder than they actually were under this program. Given the overall magnitude of the effort this is no empty praise on the lines of 'something is better than nothing'. In fact, the German reparations program, as has been seen, dwarfs other reparations efforts all over the world.

CONCLUSION: *WIEDERGUTMACHUNG-SHILUMIM* AND THE 1990S REPARATIONS CLAIMS

Reparations are part of the history of twentieth-century world politics. Indeed, reparations claims have gained considerable strength over the years, as is made obvious by the new wave of reparations starting in the 1990s. This development of new claims owes a great deal to German reparations after World War II, which set a precedent for, and constitutes a turning point in, victims' rights.

Strictly speaking, mass reparations stem from a moral interpretation of the law. As such, reparations have been criticized since their first implementation. Reparations can be seen as a manifestation of a phenomenon criticized by the jurist and German philosopher Carl Schmitt: the criminalization of politics. Schmitt made this critique in his analysis of the Versailles treaty that followed World War I.[103] This treaty—particularly its indictment of Emperor William II as a war criminal and the reparations program it imposed on Germany—radically put into question both the maximalist interpretation of state sovereignty and the Hobbesean conception of the relationship between states that Schmitt defended. For him, this meant the betrayal of politics in the name of a dangerous and inappropriate morality.

Reparations are a threat to the traditional vision of the state, notably because they strengthen accusations of collective responsibility against the state. After the war, Israelis wanted Germany to acknowledge its collective responsibility, but Adenauer never complied with this demand. However, when a state pays reparations and when its taxpayers bear the burden of an extensive program of payments, it is not far fetched to interpret this as an acceptance of its collective responsibility. Despite those refusals to accept collective responsibility, the issue is still haunting many of the debates for new claims of reparations and restitution in the 1990s. Historians still argue about the responsibility of states in the genocide and this accusation is regularly brought against governments. In its final report, the Bergier Commission considered the role of anti-Semitism in the definition of a discriminatory migration policy that resulted in the death of many Jews who had wanted to cross the Swiss borders and who had been rejected by Swiss customs officers.[104] The Commission also took a moral stance in its conclusion when it wrote that, 'the reliance on "raison d'état" in the name of which many measures were justified, was not appropriate even at the time'.[105]

At the substate level, the attribution, in practice, of corporate responsibility has strengthened over the years. The development of human rights in business circles has made it easier for corporate responsibility, and therefore collective responsibility at the company level, to be accepted. Such a vision was implicit in the moral critiques made against German businesses and European companies in the late 1990s. This public bashing transformed itself into a juridical battle. Diplomacy then entered this arena and a program of compensation for slavery and forced labor, partly financed by German industries, was accepted by the German government.[106]

The *Wiedergutmachung-shilumim* process testifies to the power of victims and nonstate actors in their claims against perpetrators of genocide. Such a step is essential in the development of human rights politics and is a major turning point in world politics. This historical experience also paved the way for the definition of new claims.[107] The postwar period had seen the accusation of perpetrators. During the 1990s, victims and their representatives targeted new actors: the beneficiaries of the Holocaust and the accomplices of its perpetrators. Swiss banks and European companies that had benefited from the politics of the Holocaust were criticized and brought to court in the USA. From the perspective of the victims, there is a shift from direct responsibility that characterized post-World War II claims to indirect responsibility.

This extension of responsibility goes beyond the borders of the Western world. In the early 1990s, when Stuart Eizenstat was the US ambassador at the European Union, he clearly foresaw that Europe would be confronted with another unsolved question: the double spoliation that victims of Nazism and Communism had to suffer in Eastern European countries.[108] Jewish organizations had indeed tried to help Jewish victims from Eastern Europe, but they could be compensated only if they had migrated to the West. They were also unable to access restitution of their property.

In the 1990s, there were talks with Eastern European countries regarding the matter of double spoliation. Within those countries, their citizens—mostly non-Jews—had only benefited from the slave and forced labor compensation initiatives. However, those countries continue to face severe economic problems, which makes it all the more difficult to compensate their own forgotten victims of World War II and the cold war. As for now, the problem of the double spoliation has not been solved and the solutions that have been offered to the victims are far from satisfactory. For example, in the 1990s, Poland issued a law according to which victims could get some restitution, notably land property confiscated by the Communist regime. Yet, former victims must be Polish and reside in Poland.

The complexity of the *Wiedergutmachung-shilumim* process illustrates a difficult and unsolvable problem. Identifying a morally satisfactory financial settlement that compensates genocide victims for their suffering is impossible. Morality and the politics of shaming[109] have certainly enabled the emergence of reparations claims and their development in the 1990s. New laws have given victims access to reparations and have laid the basis for individuals to be compensated by their own state. However, the price of compensation is not settled by criteria of morality; it is the result of a bargaining process that lies at the intersection of law and post-cold war politics. Reparations have certainly facilitated our departure from a strictly amoral realist stance of 'great power politics', to the extent that reparation obliges states to take into account moral claims and, to a certain extent, individuals' suffering. Yet, more concretely, the standard of fairness that reparations benefits satisfy remains to be defined.

Notes

1. This paper benefited from suggestions, comments, and revisions from Anthony Triolo and Pablo de Greiff.
2. Building on restitution laws in three of the Allied Occupation zones, the Federal Restitution Law of 1957 (*Bundesrückerstattungsgesetz*—BRüG) sought to restore, or replace, identifiable items wrongfully seized by the Third Reich. If the item could not be returned, an individual would receive compensation based on the item's value as of April 1, 1956 and, before the law's revision in 1964, a percentage of the item's worth. As of January 2000, the German government had paid approximately DM4 billion in claims. The FRG also negotiated payments with the Jewish representative organizations, 'global settlements', to oversee recovered heirless items or payment for said items within a lump

sum payment of DM75 million (US$18.75 million). See United States Court for the Eastern District of New York, Special Master's Proposal, *in re Holocaust Victim Assets Litigation (Swiss Banks)* (September 11, 2000), http://www.nyed.uscourts.gov/pub/rulings/cv/1996/665994.pdf and German government, 'Press Release: State Payments Made by the Federal Republic of Germany in the Area of Indemnification', January 2000. Available at http://www.germanemb.org.il/messages/318.html

3. Christian Pross, *Paying for the Past: The Struggle Over Reparations for the Surviving Victims of the Nazi Terror* (Baltimore, MD: Johns Hopkins University Press, 1998), 20.

4. Ronald Zweig, *German Reparations and the Jewish World: A History of the Claims Conference*, 2nd ed. (London: Frank Cass, 2001), 57.

5. The exchange rate in the early 1950s was approximately DM4.2 to US$1. The equivalent would be approximately US$11,900,000. See Constantin Goschler, *Wiedergutmachung: Westdeutschland und die Verfolgeten des Nazionalsozialismus (1945–54)* (Munchen: R. Oldenbourg, 1992), 11.

6. Similar laws were put in place in equal measure in the British and French zones.

7. Pross, op. cit., 20.

8. Bundesministerium der Finanzen, 'Fachblich: Entschädigung NS-Unrecht', December 2001, http://www.lbv.bwl.de/lbv_internet/pdfs/Entschaedigung-von-NS-Unrecht.pdf (website of the Landesamt für Besoldung und Versorgung of the Baden-Württemburg administration of the German government). See Axel Frohn, *Holocaust and Shilumim: The Policy of Wiedergutmachung in the Early 1950s* (Washington, DC: German Historical Institute, 1991), 3.

9. Pross, op. cit., 20.

10. Ibid., 22.

11. Nana Sagi, *German Reparations: A History of the Negotiations* (New York: St Martin's Press, 1986), 10.

12. Zweig, op. cit., 18.

13. Sagi, op. cit.

14. Kurt Grossman, *Germany's Moral Debt: The German-Israeli Agreement* (Washington, DC: Public Affairs Press, 1954), 18–19.

15. Ibid.

16. Pross, op. cit.

17. Ibid., 8–9.

18. Ibid., 7.

19. Michael Brecher, 'Images, Process, and Feedback in Foreign Policy: Israel's Decisions on German Reparations', *American Political Science Review* 67 (March 1973): 73–102.

20. Neima Barzel, 'Dignity, Hatred, and Memory-reparations from Germany: The Debates in the 1950s', *Yad Vashem Studies* 24 (1994): 258.

21. Ibid., 258.

22. Brecher, op. cit., 93.

23. Talmud, Gittin, 55b.

24. Zweig, op. cit., 29–30.

25. Brecher, op. cit., 82.

26. See Barzel, op. cit., 255.

27. Sagi, op. cit., 84.

28. Ibid., 92.

29. Ibid., 3.

30. Pross, op. cit., 24.
31. Zweig, op. cit., 34.
32. Ibid., 35.
33. Ibid.
34. Pross, op. cit., 28.
35. *Brücke in die Zukunft das Deutsch Israelische Abkommen von 10 September 1952.*
36. This amount was included in the 1952 Luxemburg agreement under Letters Nos. 4a and b. See Nicholas Balabkins, *West German Reparations to Israel* (New Brunswick, NJ Rutgers University Press, 1971), 171, 186.
37. These figures were changed over the course of the payments through additional Protocols signed by Germany and Israel after discussion in the Mixed Commission, the main agency created to oversee implementation and settle disputes. See Table 8.6 in Balabkins for amounts spent in each category by 1965, the end of the Luxemburg payments (Balabkins, op. cit., 144, 169–170, 184, Table 8.6).
38. Ibid., 204.
39. Ibid., 185.
40. Ibid., 186–87.
41. See Table 6.3 in Zweig, op. cit., 150.
42. See Ibid., 112.
43. See Ibid., 148, Table 6.1.
44. Ibid., 113.
45. Ibid., 121.
46. Ibid., 115.
47. Ibid., 116.
48. Ibid., 117.
49. Ibid., 135.
50. Ibid., 138.
51. Ibid.
52. The 1953 Agreement in §68 defines these groups as those of German citizenship or who are culturally German as defined in the *Bundesvertriebenengesetz* (Federal Expellee Law) of May 19, 1953. It also later references the 1951 Geneva Convention on refugees to disqualify certain individuals under Article 1 (F): 'The provisions of this Convention shall not apply to any person with respect to whom there are serious reasons for considering that:
    (b) he has committed a serious non-political crime outside the country of refuge prior to his admission to that country as a refugee;
    (c) he has been guilty of acts contrary to the purposes and principles of the United Nations.'
53. The final filing deadline, after several extensions, was March 31, 1967 if a preliminary application had been filed by September 1, 1966. Otherwise, the September 1, 1966 date was regarded as final.
54. Pross, op. cit., 39.
55. For example, Pross notes that the 1949 Council of States' law on reparations does not exclude victims of persecution from compensation based on their political views. The Federal Supplementary Law of 1953 excludes those 'who combat the free, democratic, order', which at the beginning of the Cold War meant Communists. Pross, op. cit., 39, 51.

56. Pross, in the Annex to *Paying for the Past*, reproduces the application form for accessing reparations benefits.

57. *Bundesergänzungs gesetz zur Entschädigung, 1953, Vierter Abschnitt, Zweiter Titel §85.*

58. Civil servants were divided into four earning categories (junior, middle-level, upper-level, senior).

59. See German Consulate, New York, 'Leistungen der öffentlichen Hand auf dem Gebiet der Wiedergutmachung: Stand 31.Dezember 2001', received via fax.

60. Pross, op. cit., 72.

61. Neither compensation for life or health take into account the reduction of income due to persecution, when basing their benefit calculations on the previous income of the victim.

62. See German Consulate, New York, op. cit., 2001.

63. United States Court for the Eastern District of New York, Special Master's Proposal, *in re Holocaust Victim Assets Litigation (Swiss Banks)* (New York, 2000), http://www.nyed.uscourts.gov/pub/rulings/cv/1996/665994.pdf

64. See German Consulate, New York, op. cit., 2001.

65. 'Assets', or 'possessions', were not defined within the compensation laws of 1953, 1956 or 1965. German case law has interpreted 'assets' (as distinct from property) as including 'inventions, patents, goodwill, business connections, and reversionary interests'. See United States Court for the Eastern District of New York, E-26.

66. The Reich Flight tax or *Reichsfluchtsteuer* was a tax for those seeking to emigrate from Germany.

67. United States Court for the Eastern District of New York, E-26.

68. See German Consulate, New York, op. cit., 2001.

69. This law, the Law to Settle Reparations for Members of the Public Service (*Gesetz zur Regelung der Wiedergutmachung für Angehörige des Öffentlichen Dienstes vom 11.Mai 1951*), is described by Pross as 'far more generous' than for non-civil servants (i.e. no deadlines to fulfill). Pross, op. cit., 21, 228. Kurt Schwerin notes that former civil servants, including former officers, judges, teachers, and professors, were reinstated to their 'position, salary, or pension group which the claimant would have reached had the persecution not taken place'. Kurt Schwerin, 'German Compensation for Victims of Nazi Persecution', in *Transitional Justice*, vol. 2, Neil Kritz, ed. (Washington, DC: United States Institute of Peace, 1995), 60. Also known as the '131' Law, after Article 131 of the Basic Law of Germany (the constitution), this law was passed before any nationwide law on reparations to Jewish victims of the Nazi regime (Pross, op. cit., 21–2).

70. See German Consulate, New York, op. cit., 2001.

71. Pross, op. cit., 198.

72. Ibid., 50.

73. Schwerin points out that refugees and stateless persons were only able to claim compensation for loss of life if it fulfilled the critieria in the 1953 law, while other eligible claimants were allowed to claim compensation for loss of life under §15 in the 1953 law (wrongful death as a result of persecution) but not §41 (death as a result of injury to body or health). Schwerin, op. cit., 51.

74. In the 1953 law, claimants had to prove that they were no longer capable of practicing their earlier occupation. In the 1956 law, they only had to show that at the time of application, they were not earning enough for an adequate standard of living

and that attaining such a standard of living was not to be expected (§33, 1953 and §82, 1956).

75. Zweig, op. cit., 73. US dollar equivalent calculated using average of 1961 US$-DM exchange rate (DM4.017 per US$). Exchange rate information from the Long-Term Financial Database of the *Global Financial Database*.

76. Eligibility is addressed in Article 1 in both the 1953 and the 1956 laws.

77. The 'antisocial' referred to the 'so-called "work-shy", prostitutes, vagabonds, and beggars'. These individuals, some of whom were forced into concentration camps or otherwise harmed by the Third Reich, were not eligible for compensation because their treatment was not based on the grounds of 'race, religion, or political convictions' as stated in §1 of the BEG. Zweig, op. cit., 53.

78. Pross, op. cit., 52.

79. See *Bundesministerium der Finanzen*, 'Fachblich: Entschädigung NS-Unrecht' (December 2001), 6. The rules for distribution and eligibility varied by country. Some states compensated for property and persecution, such as the Netherlands, and some only for disabilities and detection as in UK and Norway. See United States Court for the Eastern District of New York.

80. Pross, op. cit., 52.

81. Ibid., 56.

82. Ibid., 55.

83. Ibid., 65

84. Article V, BEG *Schlussgesetz*. For individual suffering beyond six months of detainment or an 80 percent reduction in earning capacity, the 1965 law includes provisions for doubling, tripling, etc. the minimum award based on years of incarceration, etc. This initiative had been of great concern for the Claims Conference. Many Jews who had been persecuted by the Nazis emigrated to Western countries after the deadline stipulated in the 1953 BEG law.

85. United States Court for the Eastern District of New York, E-27. Article 1, 69, 70, 71.

86. Pross, op. cit., 65.

87. Claims Conference, 'Hardship Fund: Eligibility'. Jewish victims of Nazi persecution are eligible for the Hardship Fund if: (1) The applicant did not receive any previous compensation under the German Federal Indemnification Law (BEG); and (2) The annual income of an applicant does not exceed $16,000 and $21,000 for single and married persons, respectively; and (3) The applicant suffered considerable damage to health which the applicant may prove by demonstrating that either: (a) The applicant's earning capacity was reduced by 80 percent or (b) The applicant suffered deprivation of liberty for at least one year on Nazi-occupied territory or in the following Nazi allied countries: Hungary, Slovakia, Bulgaria, Romania and Yugoslavia. See Claims Conference website: http://www.claimscon.org/index.asp?url=hardship/eligibility

88. United States Court for the Eastern District of New York, E-42.

89. Although the UNCC will be larger still if carried out to completion. See the study on the UNCC by van Houtte, Das, and Delmartino (Chapter 9, this volume).

90. Of the 4,384,138 applications, 2,014,142 were approved; 1,246,571 were denied; and 1,123,425 were otherwise resolved (applications rescinded etc.). The German government has not published figures on the total number of beneficiaries, since each individual may have submitted multiple applications (i.e. one under each category of

harm). See German Consulate, New York, op. cit., 2001. Figures were calculated using December 2001 exchange rate of €1 = US$0.8813.

91. For details concerning the number of individual claims, the number of claims approved and denied by the German administration, the different types of damages, see Tables 1 to 8, Appendix B (Pross, op. cit., 170). Dollar equivalents: Average of US$-DM exchange rate in 1965 (DM3.9959 per US$); in 1986 (DM2.15 per US$) from the Long-Term Financial Database of the *Global Financial Database*. Average US$-DM exchange rate in 2000 (DM2.122 per US$) from OANDA FXHistory, available online: www.oanda.com.

92. German Consulate, New York, op. cit., 2001. Figures were calculated using December 2001 exchange rate of €1=US$0.8813.

93. Pross, op. cit., 106–64.

94. Yeshayahu Jelinek, 'Implementing the Luxembourg Agreement: The Purchasing Mission and the Israeli Economy', *Journal of Israeli History* (Summer/Autumn 1997): 191.

95. *Brücke in die Zukunft das Deutsch Israelische Abkommen von 10 September 1952.* Figures were calculated using average 1964 US$-DM exchange rate (DM3.975 per US$). Figures from the Long-Term Financial Database of the *Global Financial Database*.

96. Jelinek, op. cit., 204.

97. George Lavy, *Germany and Israel: Moral Debt and National Interest* (London: Frank Cass, 1996), 53.

98. Jelinek, op. cit., 204.

99. Lavy, op. cit.

100. See Pross, op. cit., Appendix A.

101. Ibid., Appendix B: Table 1.

102. Here is an example of such complexity. 'While hiding from the Germans in a French convent, Frau E. suffered from depression. Incidentally, while she was staying in that convent, she fell from a ladder in 1944. After the war, she discovered that her entire family had been exterminated. She continued to suffer from depression and filed a claim. When traveling to Spain, she had a car accident that caused her injury. She had to be examined by a doctor after the German commission received her claim. The doctor who examined her found stiffening in the right hip joint as well as a chronic infectious process with joint disorders. Several years passed until the commission rejected her claim on grounds that the illnesses were "due to fate". Several months later, Frau E. suffered from a stroke that caused paralysis to the right side of her body. The next doctor who examined her stated that there could be some connection between the skull trauma caused by her fall from the ladder and the stroke. Several doctors express divergent opinions on her case, especially when they had to determine the correlation between the physiological harms caused by the fall, their neurological consequences, and the psychological depression. Finally, Frau E. went to court arguing that her psychological and physiological sufferings were deeply correlated to the persecution and the genocide. However, the court did not acknowledge the validity of such connection. Twenty-four years after the end of the war and thirteen years after she had made her claim, Frau E. was granted only a 25% reduction in earning capacity' (Pross, op. cit., 116). Although this case is extreme, it illustrates the complexity and the difficulty of evaluation and the frustration this process and its results can cause to claimants.

103. Carl Schmitt, *Le nomos de la terre* (Paris: Presse Universitaire Francaise, 2001).

104. Commission Bergier, *Final Report of the Independent Commission of Experts Switzerland: Second World War* (Zurich: Pendo, 2002), 477 onward, accessed French version online, http://www.uek.ch/fr/schlussbericht/synthese/uekf.pdf

105. Ibid., 521.

106. See the paper by John Authers (Chapter 11, this volume).

107. Ariel Colonomos, 'Unilateral Jurisdiction: Universal Jurisdiction 'à l'Américaine' in the Age of Post-Realist Power', *Human Rights Review* (2005).

108. Ariel Colonomos, 'L'exigence croissante de justice sans frontières: le cas des demandes de restitutions de biens juifs spoliés', *Études du Ceri* (July 2001): 8.

109. Robert F. Drinan, *The Mobilization of Shame: A World View of Human Rights* (New Haven, CT: Yale University Press, 2001).

MAKING GOOD AGAIN: GERMAN COMPENSATION FOR FORCED AND SLAVE LABORERS

JOHN AUTHERS

INTRODUCTION

In June 2001, fifty-six years after the end of World War II, the *Bundestag*, Germany's parliament, voted to approve a law that would create a new foundation charged with giving DM10 billion (approx. US$5 billion at the exchange rates prevailing at the time) to former laborers forced to work for the Third Reich.[1] In addition, the money would also be used to restitute beneficiaries of unpaid life insurance policies written on the lives of Holocaust victims, and owners of businesses that had been confiscated, or 'Aryanized', by the Nazis. The German lawmakers believed that more than 2 million people still living might qualify for payments, which would be distributed via five national governments and two large international nongovernmental organizations (NGOs).

Half of the funds for the foundation came from the German government, with the rest coming from German companies that had profited from using slave labor during World War II. The law came into being only after lawsuits in the USA against many of Germany's largest and most powerful companies were initiated, and involved international negotiations among eight different governments.

The first former laborers received their payments in June 2001. Payments continue at the time of this writing. By June 2005, after four years of the process, a total of €4.18 billion (approx. US$1.93 billion) had been paid to 1.62 million claimants.[2] This accounted for 96 percent of the funds that had been earmarked for laborers, leaving the German organizers content that the process had moved swiftly by comparison with similar mass-claims exercises. 'Slave laborers'—those, mostly Jewish, who had worked in concentration camps in conditions of extreme cruelty—received DM15,000 (about US$7,500) each. 'Forced laborers'—those, mostly Slavic, who had been forced to work for the Nazi effort, but in more humane conditions—received about DM5,000 each.

Why did the world wait so long before trying to compensate the laborers? And why did the issue suddenly reemerge? How could any value be put on such suffering? Were the reparations in any way proportional to the suffering caused? And was it practical to attempt to pay reparations to a population so large, aged, and dispersed?

This chapter will try to answer these questions.[3] After a brief summary of the crime and of earlier reparations efforts by Germany for its human rights violations during World War II—which are covered elsewhere in this volume[4]—it will examine the philosophical justifications used by both sides for reopening the issue in the late 1990s. Then it will examine the forces leading to the new law of 2001, and the negotiations that determined the amounts. Finally it will examine the mechanics that were adopted for distributing the money, and try to assess whether a degree of justice was achieved.

1. THE CRIME

Little need be said about the Nazi scheme to work slaves to death in concentration camps, since it formed part of the most notorious—and most examined—crime of the twentieth century. As part of the Nazi war effort, people from the occupied territories of Eastern Europe were forced to work in German factories. The demand for such workers became more acute as the war continued and more young German men went to serve at the front. By the fall of 1944, 7.7 million foreign workers were in Germany, including 2.8 million Russians and 1.7 million Poles.[5] Most were young women.

Separately, as part of the 'Final Solution' that envisaged the liquidation of the Jewish population in the occupied territories, as well as other smaller ethnic or religious groups including the Sinti and Roma gypsies, and Jehovah's Witnesses, the Nazis embarked on *Vernichtung durch Arbeit* ('death through work'). This entailed working slaves to death, doing unnecessarily hard labor with little or no nourishment. Once too weak to work, they would either die naturally or be killed.[6]

Although the program was intended to kill them, their work was gainful for the regime, and particularly for the companies who used them—finding laborers to work twenty hours a day for no pay would be little short of a godsend for any company. Slaves performed such vital tasks as building weapons in caves underneath the Austrian Alps, or making chemicals in the labor camp adjoining Auschwitz.

However, 'slave labor' was not a uniform phenomenon. The picture grows more complicated when those (mostly Slavic) who worked against their will but were not subject to such extreme conditions are included.

The treatment they received even at the hands of one company could vary widely. Manfred Gentz, the current chief financial officer of DaimlerChrysler, stressed the range of conditions under which his company's laborers had worked. Some lived in basic concentration camp conditions, without food, and had been grossly abused. But others had a different experience.

In our company we had people coming from the western part of Europe living in small hotels, or even living within families. They were treated quite well and they also got some money for the work they had to do. In our plants further south on the Bodensee, we even had a form of forced laborers returning every year for their vacation. They tell us it was the nicest time of their life.[7]

While this assertion startled survivors of Auschwitz and Mauthausen, it is plain that not all those forced to work in the service of the Reich suffered equally. This point has serious implications for the design of a compensation program. The majority of slave laborers who had suffered the most were Jewish, while the majority of the more leniently treated forced laborers were gentile. Jewish groups and East European governments were separately represented in their talks with the Germans, but both were paid out of the same foundation. They wanted to adopt different criteria for allocating reparations among claimants, with the Jewish groups proposing proportionality for the harm suffered, and East Europeans preferring relatively uniform payments.

2. PHILOSOPHICAL AND PRACTICAL JUSTIFICATIONS

As has been seen elsewhere, Germany paid significant reparations soon after World War II. By 1999, when the attempt to fashion reparations for slave laborers began in earnest, more than forty years had passed since the last substantive talks on reparations, and the issue could only be reopened due to gaps in the compensation. These were largely due to cold war preoccupations. US foreign policy could not countenance large flows of reparations money to the many former concentration camp inmates and forced laborers trapped on the Communist side of the Iron Curtain. Thus little money flowed to them.[8]

Further, all this money was paid by the German government. Companies did not have to pay compensation directly to the victims who had worked for them, under a legal fiction agreed with the Allies in 1953 that all such claims must await the 'final resolution' of World War II. This did not happen while Germany was divided. Even in the '4 plus 2' talks that reunified Germany in 1990, the then Chancellor Helmut Kohl insisted on excluding the words 'final settlement' or 'peace treaty'.[9]

Reparations for former slave laborers did not involve the companies that had benefited from their labor, and were not officially connected with their hardship.

Over a period from 1958 to 1966, five companies that had been particularly heavily involved in concentration camp labor made voluntary contributions to their former slaves, following negotiations with the Conference on Jewish Material Claims Against Germany, the NGO established to negotiate with the Germans on behalf of the Jewish Diaspora. But the amounts were tiny compared to the sums that had been paid directly by the German State and could fairly be described as tokens. By the end of 1973, according to a study by Benjamin Ferencz, a total of DM51.9 million had been paid to 14,878 former slaves. While the amounts paid, at about US$3,000 per person, compared reasonably favorably with the settlement reached in 2000, only a tiny proportion of the number of slaves who were at that time alive were paid, including nobody living in the Soviet Bloc. More than half of this had been paid by IG Farben, the Nazi-era conglomerate that operated the labor camp at Auschwitz, and was subsequently split into Agfa, BASF, Bayer, and Hoechst.[10]

Although in total the German government had paid vast sums to Israel, beneficiaries in the following categories were excluded:

- survivors living in Communist countries;
- survivors who had worked in Austria;
- many non-Germans—specifically those from Bulgaria, Czechoslovakia, Hungary, and Romania;
- slave laborers; and
- those who had been tortured or tattooed.[11]

Both sides faced problems when framing the justification for making the payments. For the Germans—from Adenauer to Schröder—the problem was to avoid accepting that they were under a legal obligation to make payments, because to do so would open them to wider claims for reparations.[12] They also had internal political problems. Amid continued attempts at de-Nazification, successive governments wanted to avoid anything that could be portrayed as German weakness or vacillation in the face of the Jewish lobby. This might have played into the hands of anti-Semites looking for propaganda. In 2000 and 2001, the pronouncements of Jorg Haider, the leader of the far-right Freedom Party in Austria, showed that this risk was not imaginary.[13]

For the Jewish side, the problem was to avoid any appearance that they had allowed Germans to buy absolution, or that the paying of material reparations meant that they had gained moral atonement.

Within the Jewish world, moral debate hinged on the same biblical injunctions that had infused the debate over the first reparations treaty almost fifty years earlier. It was necessary to ensure that nobody profited from murder, without allowing a murderer to buy absolution with money.[14]

The organization put together in 1951 to negotiate on behalf of the Jewish Diaspora—the Conference on Jewish Material Claims Against Germany—deliberately emphasized in its name that it aimed only to correct material debt. Payments were not intended to have a moral purpose. 'Moral' and 'material' claims were kept separate. But, as with Adenauer half a century earlier, the latter could help lead to the former.

Problems over vocabulary demonstrate the sensitivities. The German word most commonly translated into English as 'reparations'—*Wiedergutmachung*—was coined by Adenauer in the 1950s, and means 'making good again'. It was chosen for internal political reasons, as the German public believed that 'reparations'— which first entered the international political vocabulary after the 1919 Treaty of Versailles—were unfair, and connoted a unilateral payment by the losers of a war to the victors. *Wiedergutmachung* after World War II was meant to involve paying money to right specific problems that other people had suffered as a result of Germany's actions. According to a historical report into the reparations paid by Switzerland, written by an international panel of historians led by Jean-Francois Bergier, one lawyer regarded the concept as 'fateful' because it 'tended to substitute material debt for moral guilt'.[15] Some Nazi officials regarded themselves as 'victims' of the war and claimed *Wiedergutmachung* of their own.

By the 1990s, with memories less raw, and both Germany and Israel firmly established, Jewish leaders could be more explicit about their attempt to win justice. With World War I relegated to history, and the generation who could remember the Nazis retiring from public life, leading German figures could also approach the past more directly.

'We all agree that there's no such thing in law as *Wiedergutmachung*,' said Hans Heinrich von Stackelberg, the New York German consul and an expert in German–Jewish relations, addressing German and Jewish legal students in 2000. 'I hate the word. If your mother tongue is German you feel there's something wrong with the word. There's a living lie incorporated in it.'[16]

At the time the word was invented, he said, 'nobody knew how to deal' with the consequences of Nazi actions. 'The inability to form an appropriate word shows the inability to deal with it intellectually,' he said.

Objections rose on the Jewish side as well. 'You don't hear me using the word reparations,' said Israel Singer, the secretary-general of the World Jewish Congress (WJC) and arguably the single most important figure in the campaign to achieve compensation for laborers. 'We take good care to avoid it. Reparations denote the concept of repairing. And you can't repair the dead. And just as there's no way to make the dead good again, there's no way to take 58 months of slave labor where the objective was to kill the person through work. The only way is to say sorry.'[17]

The foundation the German government established emphasized a different approach. It was named 'Remembrance, Responsibility, and the Future', stressing that the new compensation effort was about coming to terms with history and acknowledging responsibility, rather than 'making good again' after one of history's worst crimes.[18]

The body set up to negotiate on behalf of survivors caught on the eastern side of the Iron Curtain in 1991 was named the World Jewish Restitution Organization. Unlike with the Claims Conference, it was no longer felt necessary to emphasize the lack of a moral component.[19] The campaigners leading Jewish civil society asked for 'moral and material restitution'—continuing to separate the moral from the material, but suggesting that they were linked. In layman's terms, this meant that they wanted the Germans to say sorry, and to pay at least some money to show that they meant it. They did not expect Germany to pay enough to make good all of the consequences of its actions.

Singer clarified the approach in early 1998, before the start of negotiations with Germany:

We need moral and material restitution for one reason and one reason alone. The Nazis dehumanized the Jews. It became legal to steal their property because they no longer were human. What we are doing today is rehumanizing these individuals posthumously and saying that the grand theft that took place in fifteen countries was not permissible. That rehumanization and rebreathing of life into these people, into these dry bones, is what our activity is all about. It's not about money.[20]

Note that the first round of reparations had explicitly concerned payment for the material problems caused by the influx of refugees to Israel.[21] Both sides then made clear that the reparations were 'about money'. In the late 1990s, according to Singer, the payment of money was a symbolic acceptance of responsibility and acknowledgment of a wrong done. He was not trying to achieve full justice for the suffering, or come up with some sum of money that could compensate for the wrong caused.

The Claims Conference's executive vice president, Gideon Taylor, said he wanted a 'measure of justice' for Holocaust survivors. 'Justice' as such, he recognized, was impossible to achieve in the circumstances.[22]

Another aim was simple punishment. Alan Hevesi, the New York City comptroller, who took a leading role in the campaign to win reparations, drew a comparison with the Israeli government's decision to chase down all the perpetrators of the massacre at the Munich Olympics of 1972. For him the point was to show that no matter how much time had elapsed, criminals could not escape with impunity. If the companies had profited, they should be forced to disgorge their profits.[23]

Elan Steinberg, executive director of the WJC and one of the coordinators of the campaign for restitution, put this point more pungently: 'We beat their brains out. It's like Pharaoh. This is punishment.'[24]

The basis for class action lawsuits was different again. The laborers' rights had been violated, and therefore they should receive compensation. As putting a value on such suffering was impossible, they sued for 'all their unjust enrichment' that companies had gained as a result of the use of slave labor.[25] This sum itself was impossible to calculate, as the accounts from the era no longer existed but the lawyers initially estimated that the figure could be as high as US$60 billion.

But even the lawyers, forced by the requirements of US law to provide precise measurements of the harm done, conceded that reparations should be a symbolic acknowledgment of responsibility, rather than provide a 'just' outcome. Professor Burt Neuborne of New York University's school of law, the attorney who led the lawsuit in its later stages, conceded: 'They [the reparations] weren't about justice. They were about symbolism and some form of material relief and most importantly about getting into the future by closing the past.'[26]

From a broader legal point of view, he hoped that the case—in combination with other restitution cases—would establish a form of international civil law to accompany the international criminal law that was already emerging.

It's one thing to put the people in jail who built the concentration camps, but it's another thing to find the people who sold them the barbed wire, who claim they have no duty to disgorge their profits to the victims. That's what I hope these cases will stand for—that customary international law can be used in a forum to force the disgorgement of illegally made profits.[27]

Another imperative that had not existed half a century earlier was to acknowledge what had happened. Jewish leaders did not want the Holocaust to be forgotten, and wanted to make clear that companies had profited from it. Thus it was written into the reparations agreement that both the Federal Republic of Germany and German companies accepted 'moral and historical responsibility arising from the use of slave and forced laborers, from property damage suffered as a consequence of racial persecution and from other injustices of the National Socialist era and World War II'.[28]

To make the symbolic intent of the reparations clear, every check to a slave laborer was accompanied by a note of apology from Johannes Rau, the President of Germany and Hitler's legal successor. Israel Singer believed this note was more important than the money that accompanied it.[29]

The statement went further than Adenauer had done. Made in December 1999, it included the words:

This compensation comes too late for all of those who lost their lives back then, just as it is for all those who have died in the intervening years. It is now therefore even more important that all survivors receive, as soon as possible, the humanitarian agreement agreed today. I know that for many it is not really money that matters. What they want is for their suffering to be recognized as suffering and for the injustice done to them to be named injustice.

I pay tribute to all those who were subjected to slave and forced labor under German rule and, in the name of the German people, beg forgiveness. We will not forget their suffering.[30]

3. RESTITUTION

A second concept that bulked large in the issue of reparations was restitution. Restitution means the return to somebody of something that is theirs. Unlike 'reparations', which covers other means of trying to redress past wrongs, restitution should be susceptible of a precise value. If an object was stolen, the victim is entitled to the value of that object in return. If the person who committed the theft can be identified, they should be responsible for making the payment.

The Holocaust involved one of the biggest robberies in human history. This largely predated the wholesale murder at the end of World War II, but the two crimes were often dealt with simultaneously.

Separate restitution laws were passed by the *Bundestag* in 1953, 1956, 1957, and 1964. These increased the net of compensation schemes, and provided one-off compensation, or even in some cases pensions, for those who had been robbed. These payments did not entail any compensation for the suffering these same people had often undergone as slave laborers.[31]

Had the attempt to make amends taken place immediately after the war, the two processes would have been conducted separately with little difficulty. But after an interval of half a century, claims for stolen property could not be assessed with precision. While ethical precepts insisted that an attempt be made to restitute to individuals anything that was theirs, in practical terms it was simpler to treat the issue of stolen property as one of 'rough justice'. If people had circumstantial evidence of a claim without clear proof, some token payment seemed acceptable. Similarly, if businesses or houses had been confiscated and subsequently destroyed during the war, it made sense to make a large token payment, but it was impractical to devote great energy to an assessment of exactly how much the property had been worth.

Even greater complexities attended insurance claims. While an insurance policy should have a determinate value, a number of imponderables made values difficult to ascertain. Often policies had been paid by companies, but to Nazis rather than to claimants. Usually for good reasons, eventual victims stopped paying premiums well before they met their fate, thus arguably releasing the company from the moral or legal obligation to pay in full. Currencies collapsed in Eastern Europe after the war, rendering such policies virtually worthless.

Despite these problems, Allianz, Germany's largest insurer, was involved in an effort at restitution, through a specially established international commission, at the time the issue of slave labor reparations was first broached. Established under the auspices of US insurance commissioners, and chaired by the former Secretary of State Lawrence Eagleburger, it attempted to place a value on unpaid insurance policies, with groups of experts drawing up rules for the various accounting issues.

Eagleburger's commission (the International Commission on Holocaust-Era Insurance Claims) has received more criticism than any other body involved in the contemporary attempt to pay restitution to Holocaust survivors. While it has successfully reached compromise positions on all the technical issues that had been disputed, insurance companies, which bear the cost, complain that it has done so at unnecessary expense, while survivors and their advocates complain that payouts have so far been negligible.[32] Having been founded in September 1998, and having started inviting claims in February 2000, the Commission had by the beginning of 2003 incurred total expenses of slightly more than US$40 million. Offers, at the same stage, came to US$23.9 million. Many claimants regarded their offers as insultingly low, with the result that only 36 percent had been accepted. Of 88,665 claims received by the Commission by the end of November 2002, only 14,712 had been decided, and only 1,674 had resulted in offers. This payout rate improved over time, and by May 27, 2005, the Commission had made 5,805 offers totaling US$90.21 million. But many claimants, already aged at the beginning of the process, were disappointed and frustrated by the slow progress.

However, the problems with the insurance claims process were not fully apparent during the negotiations leading to the establishment of the German foundation. Thus, it was decided that the foundation should be required to pay holders of unpaid insurance policies issued by German insurers, even if the holders had never been slave laborers. To do this, it would supply money to Eagleburger's Commission, and would also be responsible for ensuring that it had enough information from German insurance companies' records to enable the claims process to proceed. In particular, it was envisaged that German insurers would publish lists of names of potential claimants.

A remaining problem concerned looted property, and specifically 'Aryanization'—the practice of seizing Jewish-owned businesses. The foundation would also be required to compensate victims of such theft, even if they were not slave laborers.

4. THE FORCES LEADING TO SLAVE LABOR REPARATIONS

Several factors converged to put Holocaust compensation back on the agenda.

German Internal Political Pressures

Ahead of the federal elections in 1998, when the opposition Social Democratic Party (SPD) under Gerhard Schröder unseated Helmut Kohl's Christian Democrats, the SPD wanted to show it was more able to face up to Germany's past. Kohl, who had been in power for sixteen years, belonged to the generation that fought World War II, and so the issue gave Schröder a symbol of the generational shift that would take place under his leadership.

The Greens, with which the SPD allied in power, were to the left of the SPD on most issues, and took a much stronger line on the issue of reparations, saying it was outrageous to leave the slave laborers unpaid. With expectations raised among the electorate, and strong persistent pressure from his coalition partners, Chancellor Schröder had to push on with the issue once in power.

International Civil Society

The WJC and the Conference on Jewish Material Claims Against Germany, both based in New York and both involved in negotiating the first reparations treaty, started to put pressure on German companies, pointing out that they had never been held accountable for their direct role in exploiting slave labor.

These organizations benefited from momentum from separate but related issues concerning the Holocaust. Starting in 1995, the WJC had led a campaign against the largest Swiss banks over allegations that they had deliberately held on to money deposited with them before the war by Jews who subsequently perished in the Holocaust.[33] Numerous witnesses were brought forward to testify that they had gone looking for their accounts, but had been rebuffed by Swiss banking officialdom.

One survivor, Estelle Sapir, famously recounted how an official at the Swiss bank Credit Suisse had asked for her father's death certificate. She said: 'I answer[ed] him, "How can I have a death certificate? I have to go find Himmler, Hitler, Eichmann and Mengele." '[34]

International press attention on the Swiss issue had been intense, spawning a number of quickly written books and a documentary that won an Emmy award in the USA.[35] The Swiss banks eventually agreed to a settlement in 1998, paying US$1.25 billion in restitution to the relatives of account holders. This sum also included money for those who had done slave labor in concentration camps for Swiss companies, such as Nestlé, and those whose concentration camp 'employers' had banked in Switzerland.[36] Thus precedents already existed for corporations to pay damages to former slave laborers.

The Swiss banks issue also galvanized the Jewish community, particularly in the USA, to look at other financial aspects of the Holocaust. By the time Schröder came to power in late 1998, Allianz had already agreed to join the international commission on Holocaust victims' life insurance policies.[37] The participation of Allianz, a pillar of the German economy both during the war and at the end of the twentieth century, heightened the impression that Germany's corporate establishment had unpaid debts from the Holocaust.

In another case, the WJC succeeded in persuading the former allied governments to pay over the last remaining looted Nazi gold to a special humanitarian fund for needy Holocaust survivors. The victorious powers of the USA, UK, and France had set up the so-called Tripartite Gold Commission in 1946, which took possession of 337 tons of looted gold and aimed to receive looted gold and distribute it to its owners after the war. A few gold bars had remained in the vaults of the Federal Reserve and the Bank of England. The image of modern-day central banks still holding gold, which in some cases had been pulled from Holocaust victims' teeth, was similarly powerful, and also helped to galvanize opinion.[38] This discovery led to the creation of the 'Nazi Persecutee Relief Fund', to which seventeen countries donated their remaining entitlements of gold. This money is being spent on welfare programs for survivors, mostly in Eastern Europe and the former Soviet Union, where the need is believed to be greatest.

The momentum created in US public opinion, and the precedents set in the other cases, virtually required that Germany offer some compensation to laborers.

External Political Pressure

There was also external political pressure from foreign governments, although not from international organizations such as the United Nations (UN).

President Bill Clinton had close links with Edgar Bronfman, the billionaire president of the WJC and one of his most faithful donors. Acting largely at Bronfman's instigation, he had appointed a senior political appointee at the State Department, Ambassador Stuart Eizenstat, to head a special team looking into the financial aspects of the Holocaust. Eizenstat wrote a highly critical report of the Swiss banks, and attempted to mediate a resolution to the Swiss banks dispute. The US government was thus actively promoting settlements with Holocaust survivors.

The Israeli government also wanted reparations for its nationals, although it kept a lower profile than the Americans, guarding its strong relations with Germany.

Five Central and Eastern European nations which provided a home to former forced laborers—Belarus, the Czech Republic, Poland, Russia, and the Ukraine—also pressured the German government to pay reparations. Newly subject to democratic pressures, Eastern European governments realized that their populace resented its exclusion from previous reparations, and wanted to deliver something. It was thus in Germany's foreign policy interests to settle the issue of reparations.

US Civil Lawsuits

Arguably most importantly, civil lawsuits in the USA added to the pressure. Class action lawyers, who had already helped extract a US$1.25 billion settlement from the Swiss banks, sued large German companies with subsidiaries in the USA for all their ill-gotten profits. This amount was in practice almost impossible to quantify, but lawyers initially requested US$37 billion[39]—enough to make a huge dent in German corporate profits. The lawyers were experienced and well financed.[40]

While the Germans contended (successfully in the judgment of some US judges) that the matter was a subject for international treaties and not for civil law,[41] the threat scared them. Any German company with a subsidiary operating in the USA was liable to US law, and US juries could award high amounts. With suits filed in New Jersey, home to many Holocaust survivors, it would be difficult to find a sympathetic jury.

The German government could not countenance any settlement with victims that left open the possibility of continued legal action against German companies.

But it would also not countenance framing reparations as the settlement of a civil lawsuit, as this would effectively make the German government subject to a US judge. This added a crucial extra dimension of pressure on it to negotiate reparations with the surviving laborers and their representatives.

5. THE NEGOTIATIONS

The foundation that came into being in 2001 was the result of direct negotiations between the German government and international civil society organizations, with no overseeing body such as the UN or a court. Thus the amounts paid were contingent far more on the balance of negotiating strength than on any objective factors for assessing a fair amount to pay for the damage caused.

Instead, the foundation was endowed with a fixed amount after much argument. This was divided among the claiming parties, again as the result of a negotiating process.

These negotiations started in early 1999, at the behest of the governments of the USA and Germany. They lasted—amid great rancor—until the formal signing of the agreement in July 2000. At this stage, Germany still required 'legal peace'—the dismissal of the lawsuits against German companies. This took a year to achieve. The German *Bundestag* ratified the agreement, allowing payments to start in June 2001.

The number of parties involved ensured that finding a consensus would be difficult. Eight sovereign governments (Germany, the USA, Israel, Poland, the Czech Republic, Russia, Belarus, and the Ukraine) had seats at the table. So did the Conference on Jewish Material Claims Against Germany (representing the interests of Jewish survivors), the German 'Industry Initiative' (the organization set up by German industrial groups to represent them on the issue), and fifty-one different law firms, mostly from the USA. The talks were further complicated by the decision to include property restitution, as well as compensation for slave labor. This meant that once a size for the overall pie had been fixed, there were disputes between the claimants over distribution.

First, the negotiators agreed on a structure, choosing an executive international agreement (short of a treaty). The class action lawyers agreed to recommend dismissal of their lawsuits in return for receiving the money, thereby denying US judges power over its implementation. Instead, they agreed to create a foundation with a majority of German members, and representatives from the lawyers, victims' groups, and all the foreign governments involved.[42] Once all outstanding lawsuits had been dismissed in the USA, this foundation would raise the money, and distribute it to 'partner organizations'—governments or NGOs—who would then pay survivors.

Over the course of a year, the lead negotiators for the US and German governments—Stuart Eizenstat and Otto Graf Lambsdorff respectively—cajoled the two sides into agreeing to an amount of DM10 billion. This required German industry to provide a substantially larger amount than it had wanted to, and also required the German government to match it deutsche mark for deutsche mark, something that the politicians had not originally contemplated. The class action lawyers and Eastern European governments, meanwhile, were forced to moderate their demands.

Once the DM10 billion figure had been settled in December 1999, the issue of how to distribute the money remained. This led to a falling out between the Jewish organizations and the representatives of the Eastern Europeans over the distinctions that should be made between 'slave laborers' and 'forced laborers'. Jewish campaigners, arguing that reparations should be to some extent proportional to the degree of suffering inflicted, accused Jewish lawyers who wanted to equate or minimize the difference in payments to the different kinds of laborers as 'a disgrace to the memory of the Holocaust'.[43] There were also issues over dividing the money between those who had property claims against the German government and laborers. The main casualty in this process was the 'Future Fund' backed by the governments of Germany and Israel, which was intended to pay for Holocaust education and commemoration programs in Germany, rather than to make payments directly to survivors. Originally accounting for as much as half of the fund in some projections, it eventually received only DM700 million, or 7 percent of the total.

At this stage, it was necessary to decide on terms of 'legal peace'. The Germans would not pay any money until such peace had been achieved. However, the US government could not make promises on behalf of the judicial branch, and was not prepared to attempt to write such legal guarantees into law.[44] Defeat in Congress seemed assured for any law that limited the rights of Holocaust survivors. After many months, a compromise was reached in which the US State Department agreed to write a letter or 'statement of interest' to judges adjudicating the different cases, recommending dismissal. This told judges that it was in the foreign policy interests of the USA for such cases to be dismissed. However, its constitutional validity was limited. While the federal government's opinion could be expected to have weight with judges, the separation of powers meant that the executive had no power to compel the judiciary into a specific action. To do so would have required a formal intergovernmental treaty, which would in turn have required the consent of the Senate—which would have been very difficult to obtain. On the more limited basis of the federal government's 'statement of interest', the agreement was signed by all parties in July 2000.

However, one US district judge refused to dismiss the case, citing conflict of interest among the lawyers, expressing her doubts over the soundness of the German foundation, and raising doubts over the constitutionality of the 'statement of interest'.[45] After five more months of legal argument, in which the possibility of changing the terms of the foundation was raised, an appeals court overruled the district judge. This allowed the foundation to come into existence and payments to start in June 2001.

6. THE MECHANICS

Slave and forced laborers each received a fixed 'rough justice' amount. Former slaves received DM15,000 each (approx. US$7,500), while former forced laborers received DM5,000 (approx. US$2,500). These were maximum figures. If there proved to be more eligible claimants than expected, they might receive less, and for this reason claimants would only receive a first installment when first making a successful claim. This could vary between 50 and 70 percent. The final balance was payable once all claims had been received and assessed.

Two 'rough justice' levels of payment were deemed the fairest way to treat the problem in the circumstances, as this allowed for swift and easily made payments. These numbers were determined on the basis of what was available. Other claimants from the foundation—the 'Future Fund' for memorials, claims for unpaid insurance policies, and for other property losses—took DM1.9 billion between them. This left DM8.1 billion to compensate laborers. This amount was divided by an estimated number of survivors, which had been determined by a historical commission, to arrive at the figures of DM15,000 and 5,000. The author is unaware of anybody on either side of the negotiations at any stage claiming that these amounts were intended to be proportional reparations for the suffering the victims endured—although the Jewish negotiators could at least say that there had been some crude attempt at proportionality.

In another move to enable swift payments, the burden of proof was set very low. The Jewish survivors had mostly been covered by previous reparations efforts, and therefore could be traced swiftly.[46] Definitions with arbitrary cut-off points made the justice rougher, but also allowed for ease of administration. No attempt was made to assess applicants' current needs. Prior compensation that the victims had received was also excluded from calculations—those already compensated separately by other German restitution schemes received no less than those who had received nothing. There was also no differentiation in terms of how long they had served as a laborer, a possibility that had been mooted at one point by the Jewish side in the negotiations.

Definitions were as follows. 'Slave labor' was:

Work performed by force in a concentration camp (as defined in the German Indemnification Law) or a ghetto or another place of confinement under comparable conditions of hardship, as determined by the German Foundation.

'Forced labor' was:

Work performed by force (other than 'slave labor') in the territory of the German Reich or in a German-occupied area, and outside the territory of Austria, under conditions resembling imprisonment or extremely harsh living conditions; or work performed by force under a program of implementing the National Socialist policy of 'extermination through work' (*Vernichtung durch Arbeit*) outside the territory of Austria.[47]

Applicants had to fill out a form to prove that they had been through these experiences. To speed the process, a 'cut-off date' of December 31, 2001 was agreed. All claims had to be made by this point, although in practice this was treated leniently. If people had made themselves known as potential claimants without actually filling in the necessary forms, they were generally given more time.[48]

Payments were for the laborers only and not for their descendants. However, there was one important exception to this, again involving an essentially arbitrary cut-off point. When the negotiations over compensation began, in February 1999, the Jewish side and others had been anxious to avoid the risk that the German side could simply reduce its liability by continuing to talk while potential claimants died. Thus the heirs of anyone who had died on or after February 16, 1999 could apply to the fund.[49]

'Heirs' was defined narrowly so that people were eligible only if they were the spouse, child, grandchild, sibling, or testamentary heir of the original claimant. They needed to provide proof of relationship (usually in the form of a birth certificate), or a notarized will.

The German foundation designed the process so as to keep very tight control of payments. This was necessary. With many survivors distrusting the Claims Conference,[50] to say nothing of the various East European governments involved, the process had to minimize the opportunity for corruption. Money in proportion to the expected number of the claimants was given to each government (and to the Conference on Jewish Material Claims Against Germany for the Jewish claimants, and the International Organization for Migration (IOM) for all non-Jewish claimants outside the Central and Eastern European countries). If any government, or the NGOs, failed to find as many survivors as expected, the remainder was to be returned to the German foundation, where it could be redirected to other countries where there were more claimants than expected. Partner organizations had to submit claims for money to the central German foundation, and would be reimbursed with money intended for immediate distribution to claimants. Thus the only element of discretion over the funds for slave laborers rested with the German foundation. None of the distributing organizations was allowed to hold on to any of the money.[51]

This proved a necessary precaution, as the pattern of claims proved very different from the projections on which the original allocations had been based. The greatest anomaly was in the claims received by the International Organization for Migration—306,000 against an estimate of 61,000. The Claims Conference received 243,000, compared to an estimate of 156,000, while the Russian government received about 500,000 against an estimate of 382,000. Overestimates occurred in the cases of Poland, Belarus, and the Czech Republic, and most startlingly the Ukraine, which was projected to receive 846,000 claims, and in fact only received 558,000.[52] The disparities showed the difficulty of attempting to catch up with such a large population after the passage of more than half a century, and underlined the wisdom of designing a flexible process.

The forms that claimants needed to fill proved time-consuming, even with the attempt to achieve 'rough justice'. The Claims Conference offered its claimants a choice of eight languages for correspondence—German, Hebrew, English, Yiddish, Russian, Hungarian, Spanish, and French. They had to include a photocopy of their ID and provide details of their previous claims from other German compensation programs. They were also required to declare if they had ever received slave labor compensation directly from a German company. The question on 'internment' was probably the hardest to answer:

Please list all the places where you were interned, imprisoned or confined, to the best of your ability. If you have a Liberation Certificate, Repatriation Document or Displaced Persons ID card, please attach a photocopy. If you wish to provide a more detailed description, you may attach an additional sheet. Please include the name of the company(ies) for which you were forced to work, if known.[53]

There were separate codes to indicate concentration camps, ghettos, labor camps, and prisons.

Those who had not applied for previous compensation programs had to list all their countries of residence since liberation from labor, and their last residence, including the city, town, or village, before they had been interned, imprisoned, or confined.

Most importantly, they had to sign a declaration that they had been forced to perform slave or forced labor, and to name at least one place where they had been forced to perform it. They also had to waive their legal rights in connection with forced and slave labor or property damage against the German government and in connection with all claims in connection with Nazi-era injustices against all German companies.

Many survivors found the process of filling out the forms both distressing and demeaning, and so great sensitivity was needed in helping them with the paperwork. The Claims Conference trained volunteers to help survivors fill out forms, and made them available through Jewish day care centers. Many law students volunteered to help in the process.

Reaching all the survivors in itself cost money. The Claims Conference's first 10,000 payments, made only days after the Bundestag had signed the law that created the foundation, went to claimants in twenty-five different countries.[54] Claims were received from such unlikely places as Zimbabwe and Costa Rica. 'Outreach' campaigns to reach such a far-flung population were necessarily expensive. For example, the Claims Conference spent an estimated US$1 million on an advertising campaign to cover forty countries. It involved placing advertisements in 149 different newspapers.

The Geneva-based International Organization for Migration, charged with compensating all non-Jewish survivors living outside the five Eastern European countries that had their own systems, had an even harder job. Unlike Jewish survivors, many gentiles had never received any compensation before, and they tended not to have the strong community organizations developed by Jewish survivors.

By the deadline for claims, which fell on December 31, 2001, the IOM had received 306,000 claims for slave and forced labor—four times the original estimate. Within a month they had paid first installments to 6,070 former laborers, roughly 10 percent of the total they expected to make eligible claims.

Confusion over eligibility standards worsened the problems for the IOM. Among those claiming were more than 100,000 former Italian military internees. The ultimate decision on their case sat with the German foundation, which ruled that they were not eligible for reparations, along with 40,000 Western European victims who had made claims. In both cases they were held ineligible unless they had actually spent time in a concentration camp. About 4,000 Algerian residents also claimed, and again were almost all found to be ineligible. People who were subjected to *Service du Travail Obligatoire en Allemagne* (STO) and who were subsequently granted the status of *Personne Contrainte au Travail en Pays Ennemi* (PCT) were held not generally to be eligible for compensation, unless they had been held under guard and been subjected to 'constant searches and controls by guards or police and were not allowed to leave the camp except for transfer to and from the work site'.[55]

The majority of the IOM's claimants could not provide documents or any other evidence to back their claims. As they came from ethnic groups such as the Romani and Sinti gypsies, without the strong history of community organization enjoyed by the Jews, the process of tracing them was also harder than for other categories.

The IOM had the most difficult task, and thus paid its compensation more slowly than the other groups, leading to complaints by affected claimants that the decision to divide the work among partner organizations had discriminated against them. Some non-Jews living outside Eastern Europe argued they would have been served better by a process run entirely by the German government.

By the end of 2002, fewer payments had been made by the IOM—€68 million, to 32,350 claimants—than by any of the other organizations involved, despite its high number of original claims. By comparison the Claims Conference, with a similarly dispersed population but with far better information to help them track claimants, had paid €578 million to 114,000 claimants.[56]

Eventually, the IOM reached its target of completing its reparations project by the end of 2004,[57] partly because it received extra help with administrative expenses from the German foundation.[58] Under the law, such expenses are to be met from the interest made on the funds held by the foundation, and there should be room to do this. It completed the processing of slave labor claims in the fall of 2004, and began sending out second checks to successful claimants in May 2005. By June 2005, it had made payments to about 75 percent of its successful claimants.[59]

The mechanism for restitution for people who had suffered property losses—particularly Jews whose businesses had been 'Aryanized'—was more complicated. DM200 million is administered by the IOM. Payments are determined by a three-person commission including delegates from the German finance ministry and the US State Department, with a neutral chairman decided by these two members.[60]

A further DM500 million was offered to the International Commission on Holocaust-Era Insurance Claims (a body that had already been set up independently of the German slave labor process) to compensate relatives of Holocaust victims who had never received payouts on life insurance policies. Negotiations over the way in which the Commission should interact with the foundation (covering such details as the publication of policyholders' names, and the payment of administrative expenses) were only resolved in October 2002, more than two years after the signing of the agreement that would bring the foundation into being, due to a disagreement over how much of the Commission's administrative expenses should be paid by German insurers. The plans for restituting insurance should—both the Jewish and the German negotiators hope—add greatly to the historical record, as the process will involve compiling a list of all the Jews resident in Germany between 1933 and 1945, drawing on eighty-six archives to do so.[61]

Finally, DM300 million was paid to the Claims Conference for the humanitarian and welfare needs of Jewish Holocaust survivors. Although this was technically a restitution payment, intended to compensate for individual property losses, it was made as a general humanitarian payout, to be directed at the discretion of the Conference's officers. The Claims Conference already had a series of established programs for making grants to established Jewish welfare organizations around the globe, and this money was destined for such work.

7. CONCLUSIONS

Virtually no party to the reparations process was satisfied by the outcome. The lengthy legal delays clearing the foundation meant that by some estimates as many as 10 percent of the eligible population alive at the time the reparations agreement was signed in principle in July 2000 died in the year which then elapsed before money started to be disbursed.[62] The process also raised hopes and increased frustrations for the remaining survivors. Many Jewish Holocaust survivors objected to the designation of the Conference on Jewish Material Claims Against Germany to receive their money, claiming that it was insufficiently accountable.

On the German side, many complain—although generally not in public—that they are victims of moral blackmail, and that their Jewish interlocutors understated the importance of money already paid out to them in the reparations programs of the 1950s.

However, by comparison with other attempts at restitution at about the same time (regarding stolen property in Austria and France, unpaid insurance policies across Europe, laundered stolen gold, and dormant Swiss bank accounts), the process was a relative success.[63] Many Jewish organizations put great weight on the German president's decision to accompany the payouts with a formal apology. This gave the gesture much more moral and symbolic value. There was a general acceptance on all sides that the crimes being compensated were so terrible that full justice was impossible. Thus even a token gesture commanded a wide degree of assent.

Israel Singer, a chief negotiator on the Jewish side, reconfirmed this at the ceremony when the first payments were made. 'You can't make the dead good again', he said. 'We can only take a modicum of justice—a modicum of attempting to somehow right wrongs in a small way for those who are still alive.'[64] However, on the subject of the adequacy of the payments themselves, he was as aggressive as anyone. 'At most, the justice we are doing is going to be very rough,' he said. 'If we are paying someone who worked for 58 months in conditions which should have killed them DM15,000, I would like to say it's a pittance and an insult, rather than being a good gesture.'[65]

While always stressing that the payments were tokens, other Jewish compensation campaigners placed more value on the payments themselves. Gideon Taylor, executive vice president of the Claims Conference, said that one of his happiest moments from the campaign came when a Latvian woman due to receive a payment told him she would use it to buy herself the new washing machine she had been needing for years.[66] Particularly for the more needy survivors in Eastern European countries, a check for a few thousand dollars could make a real difference to their standard of living, he said.

Singer suggested instead that the attempt to pinpoint the financial reckoning of the Holocaust had had one positive side effect. By trying to pinpoint financial liability, and by attempting to find a way to make it good, it had forced people on all sides to come to terms with the truth, and to reconcile with their own history. Money, despite the elaborate mechanisms for paying survivors, was a secondary consideration.

'Truth telling is what the fifteen commissions[67] that were established throughout Europe, North America, and South America accomplished,' he said. 'Money was an important material expression of remorse and restitution. The struggle for justice, however, was not about money, and those who chose to make it so, whether they were Jews or non-Jews, tried one more time to revise history and failed.'

The attempt to compensate laborers also seemed to leave more satisfaction in its wake than the various restitution campaigns that took place at the same time. At least two reasons account for this. First, with no possibility of calculating a precise figure, everyone agreed that a final payment to laborers could only be a token. In the restitution cases, arguments persisted over valuations. Second, it was accompanied by an emphatic admission of guilt, responsibility, and contrition. A check for US$7,500 accompanied by a letter from the President of Germany apologizing and admitting that any amount of money could never be enough had a much more positive effect on its recipients than checks for much larger amounts of money paid by banks or insurance companies. With no contrition, and with lingering suspicions that the financial services companies had escaped lightly, claimants from banks and insurers tended to be much less happy with their money.[68]

It also helped that the German slave labor talks, while acrimonious behind closed doors, were conducted relatively swiftly, and with public dignity. This was in large part due to the presence of two of the world's most powerful governments—the USA and Germany—leading the talks. A lesson from this might be that international organizations have a legitimate role in brokering negotiations of this type in future.

The lessons for the efficacy of lawsuits are harder to discern. Two of the many lawsuits were thrown out by US judges. This drastically weakened the lawyers' negotiating power, but there was agreement on all sides that the sum would have been far lower without the lawsuits. Once there was a risk of ongoing litigation in the USA, German negotiators were adamant that any settlement must include legal peace. Their anger was understandable and Otto Graf Lambsdorff, who headed the German side at the negotiations, told lawyers: 'I wish to stress that none of these lawsuits, neither in Germany nor anywhere else in the world, were ever won by any claimant.'[69] With cases resting on the recollections of elderly victims, and legal concerns over whether the USA was an appropriate forum for trying such cases, it is doubtful whether the cases would have been successful if pursued to trial. However, the reaction of the German and other companies sued demonstrates that lawsuits were perceived as a clear and serious risk.

Another problem with US litigation is that it is expensive. Attorneys normally expect to be paid about a third of the money they recover. This compensates them for the risk of paying all administrative costs in advance with no guarantee of receiving payment. The attorneys in the German case agreed to take very low fees— 1.25 percent of the total recovery. Without any lawsuits, it is almost inconceivable that Germany would have paid as much as DM10 billion, and so the lawyers argued that their fee represented good value for money.[70]

However, although low in percentage terms, this represented DM125 million. The single best-paid lawyer in the case, Melvyn Weiss, received a fee of US$7.5 million (a figure three orders of magnitude higher than the highest compensation paid to one of his victim-clients). Further apparent injustice was created by the mechanism the Germans adopted to ensure legal peace. Numerous US lawyers had brought cases, and all of them had to be persuaded to withdraw the cases in order for 'legal peace' to be achieved. This involved paying off fifty-two law firms in total, some of which had done little or no work, and had certainly not contributed to the huge settlement on behalf of survivors.[71]

Roman Kent, president of the American Gathering of Holocaust Survivors and a negotiator on the Jewish side, seemed particularly hurt by the notion that anyone could profit from the campaign—after all, a central aim of the campaigners was to prevent people from profiting from the Holocaust, and this was exactly what the lawyers had done.

My attitude towards the lawyers is that I would have greatly appreciated help because they certainly had a place to do so, but what I did resent was the greed. This was not an issue for which the lawyers should be making millions of dollars. To take money from a case like this was, I considered, obscene. In addition many of the lawyers tried to drum business from the survivors by making ads and calling meetings and trying to sign the survivors. They gave misleading information that they could not collect the money without a lawyer.[72]

The episode in which a judge refused to dismiss the case, thereby holding up payments to survivors for many months, demonstrated another shortcoming of US litigation—once started, it is difficult to stop. Although all lawyers on both sides wanted the case dismissed, they needed the consent of a US judge. This meant that the Germans eventually fell under the jurisdiction of a US judge, despite having gone to great lengths to avoid such an outcome.

This episode also demonstrated the practical limitations of a legalistic approach to solving the problem. Holocaust survivors reacted with great anger to the delay. Both the German government and the various representatives of survivors had agreed in principle to make payments, and they had given wide and detailed publicity to the amounts they proposed to pay. Caviling over legal points drastically diminished the moral content of the gesture. In Poland, a group of eight survivors, reacting to the German companies' pleas that they could not afford to pay money until they had legal peace, held an ironic collection for German industry, each donating a fraction of their pensions into a hat.[73] Roman Kent felt that the long legal delays robbed the settlement of its moral value. 'This moral gesture amounts to words, and words only,' he said. 'This is the best proof of what morality means for them. For them it's strictly business, cold-blooded business.'[74]

In the final analysis the most potent judgment on the reparations program must be left to the survivors. And very few, if any, appear to have derived any sense of closure when they received their payments. The views of two survivors interviewed by the author in June 2001, at the New York ceremony where they finally received their checks, are representative and serve as an appropriate epitaph on the entire attempt at slave labor reparations. To judge by their comments, an earlier and more generous response would have made them feel better, but both seemed to think that any attempt at reparations using money to compensate for their hardship was doomed to failure.

One survivor, Mendel Rosenfeld, said: 'This is very far from justice. It's very far from that. There's no such thing as money that can pay for what I went through in my life.'

And his colleague Jaime Rothman said: 'Truly it's not a big thing. It's not justice. Whenever you touch the subject and you put the money and the suffering together, it's not the way to do it. This is not justice. It is too little and too late, but even if it had been much earlier and much more, it would have been no more moral.'

NOTES

1. Details are included in 'The Law on the Creation of a Foundation "Remembrance, Responsibility and the Future"', a bill which entered the *Bundestag* on August 2, 2000, and entered into force on August 11, 2001.
2. These figures were provided to the author by Kai Hennig, chief of public affairs for the foundation. The statistics on payments are continuously updated on the foundation's website, http://www.stiftung-evz.de/, and were accurate as of June 22, 2005.
3. The author has already covered several of these questions in a book written jointly with Richard Wolffe: *The Victim's Fortune—Inside the Epic Battle over the Debts of the Holocaust* (New York: HarperCollins, 2002). Much of the information in this paper is drawn from the research for that book. It has been supplemented by further interviews in a period from May 2002 to February 2003, to discuss the more technical issues of the reparations payments, and to respond to the experience of the reparations process in action. The author's earlier book gives a detailed narrative of how the various decisions on German reparations were made.
4. See Ariel Colonomos and Andrea Armstrong (Chapter 10, this volume).
5. These figures are taken from Michael Pinto-Duschinsky, *Nazi Slave Labour: The Unfinished Campaign for Compensation* (London: Holocaust Educational Trust, 1998), 13. Precise figures are contestable, but these figures are in line with other published estimates.

6. Many books have covered the phenomenon. For a first-person account emphasizing the extent and depth of the human rights violations committed, see *If This Is A Man* by Primo Levi, English edition (New York: Orion Press, 1960).

7. Mr Gentz said this in an interview in Stuttgart in April 2001 with Richard Wolffe, the author's coauthor on *The Victim's Fortune*, op. cit., 208.

8. See Stuart Eizenstat, *Imperfect Justice* (New York: Public Affairs Press, 2003), 207–8. Eizenstat was the chief negotiator for the US government in the contemporary talks on slave labor, and discusses why reparations were not paid to Soviet bloc countries.

9. See Pinto-Duschinsky, op. cit., 20.

10. See Benjamin Forencz, *Less Than Slaves: Jewish Forced Labor and the Quest for Compensation* (Cambridge, MA: Harvard University Press, 1979), cited in Pinto-Duschinsky, op. cit., 19.

11. See Pinto-Duschinsky, op. cit., 26–7.

12. 'Legal peace' was a basic condition laid out by the German government's negotiators at all points during the talks to design the reparations program.

13. Numerous articles traced the 'Haider phenomenon', and his success in joining the Austrian government coalition in January 2000. An excellent journalistic treatment of Germany's ongoing political debate over responses to the Holocaust is Judith Miller, *One by One by One* (New York: Simon & Schuster, 1990).

14. See Colonomos and Armstrong, op. cit.

15. See *Final Report of the Independent Commission of Experts Switzerland* [the Bergier report] (Zurich: Perdo, 2002), 428.

16. His comments were made at a symposium on the slave labor reparations agreement held at Columbia University's Law School, in New York, in April 2001.

17. Singer's comments are taken from a speech made at the same symposium.

18. The original plan for the foundation envisaged that half of its money should be devoted to a so-called 'future fund', funding museums, monuments, and educational efforts (see Eizenstat, op. cit., 212). This proportion was reduced after negotiation, but the attempt to make a symbolic moral gesture, and not to attempt specific financial redress for harms done, remained in place.

19. Elan Steinberg, executive director of the World Jewish Congress (a constituent member of both the World Jewish Restitution Organization and the Claims Conference), made this point to the author in an interview in January 2000.

20. Singer's comments were made in a symposium on Holocaust restitution at the Cardozo Law School in New York, in March 1998.

21. See Colonomos and Armstrong, op. cit.

22. The phrase became a slogan, with the words 'A Measure of Justice for Holocaust Survivors' emblazoned on the cover of the Claims Conference's annual reports.

23. These comments are taken from a speech Hevesi made to a group of Holocaust survivors in New York in January 2000, in a meeting attended by the author.

24. Elan Steinberg made this comment in an interview with the author in January 2001.

25. Nathan Associates, an economic analysis firm, made an attempt to quantify the damage, after being commissioned by one of the law firms involved. It estimated that the average economic loss suffered by the laborers was US$460 per year labored, in wartime dollars. Applying a discount rate of 7.0 percent, this implied an economic value of US$17,760 in 1999. The figure was highly dependent on the discount rate—an assumption of 7.5 percent would raise the amount to US$22,850 per year worked. It

further estimated that the laborers still alive in 1999 had worked 5,025,806 years between them. This implied a total payout—without making any attempt to compensate the more harshly treated prisoners for the abuses of their human rights—of between US$90 billion and US$110 billion. See Dr John C. Beyer and Dr Stephen A. Schneider, 'Forced Labor Under the Third Reich', study paper produced for the Washington law firm of Cohen, Milstein, Hausfeld & Toll in 1999.

26. Professor Neuborne was speaking at the symposium on German reparations at Columbia University's Law School mentioned before.

27. This comment is also drawn from the Columbia Law School symposium.

28. See German foundation law, op. cit.

29. Mr Singer made this statement addressing a meeting of Holocaust survivors in New York City in January 2000.

30. President Rau's speech was widely reported at the time. It is quoted at length in *The Victim's Fortune*, op. cit., 229.

31. The chapter by Colonomos and Armstrong (Chapter 10, this volume) summarizes the basic components of these laws.

32. See *The Victim's Fortune*, op. cit., 253–79, and Michael Bazyler, *Holocaust Justice—The Battle for Restitution in America's Courts* (New York and London: New York University Press, 2003), 110–71, for detailed and strongly critical accounts of the Holocaust insurance claims process. While claimants are supposed to have the advantage of 'relaxed' standards of proof, an independent study commissioned by the commission itself found that insurers were instead using very high standards of proof, in some cases not even accepting an insurance certificate as evidence that a claimant or his and her ancestor held a policy, if this did not cohere with their own records.

33. See *The Victim's Fortune*, op. cit., 5–106 and 350–64, for a detailed narrative of the Swiss banks affair.

34. See the transcript for the field hearing by the Senate Banking Committee in New York, October 1996.

35. Gaylen Ross, 'Blood Money', 1998.

36. The special master appointed by the judge in the Swiss banks litigation to decide on an allocation of funds to claimants made clear that he regarded the claims against the banks on these grounds to be dubious. Each surviving laborer was entitled to a token payment of US$1,000 under the original allocation agreed in November 2000, and they started to receive this money in the summer of 2001. Subsequently the interest on the money the Swiss banks had paid into court accumulated to such an extent that all claimants were given an extra US$400. A total of about 115,000 people were covered.

37. Known as the International Commission on Holocaust-Era Insurance Claims (ICHEIC), and chaired by the former US Secretary of State Lawrence Eagleburger, the commission included representatives of the government of Israel and of Jewish NGOs, as well as state insurance commissioners from the US, and representatives of the insurance companies themselves. All decisions were to be reached by consensus.

38. Studies of this issue include Moshe Sanbar and Raul Teitelbaum, *Holocaust Gold* (Tel Aviv: Moreshet Publishers, 2001), and Tom Bower, *Nazi Gold* (New York: Harper-Collins, 1997).

39. See Eizenstat, op. cit., 240–1.

40. The two largest class action legal firms in the US, Milberg Weiss Hynes & Lerach and Lieff Cabraser Hyman & Bernstein, both took leading roles in the litigation.

41. See the decisions by US District Judges Dickinson Debevoise and Joseph Greenaway, September 13, 1999. They dismissed a lawsuit against Ford because the claims exceed time limits imposed under German and US law and because Germany has not allowed individual claims. 'Although courts are not bound by a foreign government's pronouncement of which claims are cognizable, "international customs" dictate that a court not interfere with a foreign sovereign's pronouncement of its law,' Greenaway wrote. In a separate ruling on cases against Siemens and Degussa-Huls, Judge Debevoise said that 'to structure a reparations scheme would be to express the ultimate lack of respect' for the US government leaders who ratified those pacts.
42. The full composition of the 27-member board of trustees, as laid out in the German law, op. cit., was as follows:
    1 chairman (named by the German chancellor);
    4 members named by German companies contributing to the foundation;
    5 members named by the Bundestag;
    2 members named by the Bundesrat;
    1 representative of the German finance ministry;
    1 representative of the German foreign affairs ministry;
    1 representative of the Claims Conference;
    1 representative of the three main bodies representing Roma and Sinti gypsies in Germany;
    1 representative each from the governments of Israel, the USA, Poland, Russia, Ukraine, Belarus, and the Czech Republic;
    1 US lawyer (nominated by the US government);
    1 representative of the UN High Commissioner for Refugees;
    1 representative of the International Organization for Migration; and
    1 member of Germany's Federal Information and Counseling Association for Victims of National Socialism.
43. This comment was made by Roman Kent, one of the leading negotiators for the Holocaust survivors, against the attorney Michael Hausfeld (who was himself the son of survivors).
44. See Eizenstat, op. cit., 269–74, for an account of the Justice Department's strenuous objections to the proposed structure for legal peace.
45. See the Memorandum Opinion and Order, in re Austrian and German Bank Litigation, issued by Judge Shirley Wohl Kram (March 7, 2001).
46. See the Processing Report of March 13, 2001, produced by the Claims Conference, which gives details. The Federal German Indemnification Laws (known as the BEG for their initials in German) had a database of 96,000 survivors who were in receipt of pensions. All of these people had already provided details of their history, and all of them were sent mailings asking them to declare if they were eligible (through having performed slave labor). Of the first 37,000 to apply, 95 percent proved to be eligible. Thus it was possible to reach the large population of potential claimants with relative speed.
47. These definitions are included in 'Eligible Persons', Section 11 of the German reparations law, op. cit.
48. Author's interview with Claims Conference official. Other 'partner organizations' involved in apportioning funds also interpreted the deadline leniently.
49. See the German foundation law, op. cit.

50. The Claims Conference is unpopular with many survivors because of its perceived inefficiency and bureaucracy. Also, many object that there is little involvement by survivors' organizations in the board which controls it. For a vitriolic attack on the organization, which well summarizes the criticisms of the Claims Conference, see Normal Finkelstein, *The Holocaust Industry—Reflections on the Exploitation of Jewish Suffering* (New York and London: Verso, 2000).

51. Details are in the reparations law. Both Kai Hennig, head of communications for the German foundation, and Greg Schneider, the official charged with organizing payments for the Claims Conference, helped the author by explaining the process in detail.

52. These figures were collated for the author by Claims Conference officials, comparing the final returns reported by each partner organization against the official projections made by the historical commissioner.

53. Compensation forms were made widely available in 2001, at the start of the payment process, and copies are in the possession of the author.

54. These figures are drawn from a statement released by the Claims Conference on June 19, 2001, the day of the first payments.

55. These terms were laid down by the IOM, which made an interpretation of the German law. The criteria for those deserving compensation included that they must have been deported from their home country to Germany or to a German-occupied territory, that they must have been subjected to forced labor, and that they must have been subjected to 'extremely harsh conditions'. People working under the somewhat more lenient programs presided over by the Vichy regime did not necessarily satisfy any of these criteria, although some were kept in prison-like conditions. See 'Compensation for Forced Labour During the Nazi Era—All Former Forced Labourers Resident in France Are Invited to Contact the IOM in Geneva', Press Release issued by the IOM, February 2001.

56. These figures, correct as of December 31, 2002, were provided by the German foundation.

57. See the comments by Dirk de Winter, head of the IOM's compensation program, in the second edition of the organization's newsletter on compensation.

58. Kai Hennig, of the foundation, indicated this to the author in an interview in January 2003.

59. These figures are taken from the foundation's seventh press release of 2005, issued in June 2005.

60. It is still too early to make any confident judgments on the success of this restitution effort. The IOM had received 14,000 completed claims forms and 'several thousand' claims without forms by the deadline for claims, which fell on December 31, 2001. The first decisions were announced on January 28, 2003, although no payments will be made until all claims have been examined, an event that had still not happened by mid-2005. The total sum available for restitution is capped, and so claimants' awards may have to be reduced *pro rata*. The IOM received 'about 35,000 claims', of which 'over 25 percent' were fully or partially approved. Subsequently, there were 8,081 appeals, which slowed the process down further. According to the IOM, the most common reason for a rejection was a failure to demonstrate 'essential, direct and harm-causing participation of a German enterprise'. General war damage caused as a result of military attacks, for example, was excluded. So was any property loss which would not have been eligible for compensation under earlier restitution schemes run by the German government

during the 1950s. Perhaps ironically, given the opprobrium heaped on Switzerland during the contemporary efforts to achieve Holocaust restitution, the US and German representatives chose the president of the Swiss Arbitration Association to act as the property claims commission's chairman. See the IOM's press release 'IOM Issues First Decisions on Property Claims', Geneva, January 2003, and the 2005 edition of its 'Compensation News'.

61. The full legal document establishing the process for German insurance restitution is available on the International Commission on Holocaust-Era Insurance Claims' website: www.icheic.org. At the time of writing, it is hoped that the publication of names will greatly aid the commission's work, which has been much criticized. The potential amount to be paid out to claimants from German insurers has been capped at DM500 million as part of the negotiation. At present it appears likely that this will more than cover all claims, although heated controversy persists over whether this is due to a small number of claims existing, or to inadequate publicity meaning that many with valid claims have not come forward. Most claims generated by this process are likely to come from holders of policies issued by insurers operating in Eastern Europe before the war, which have since been bought by German insurers.

62. The 10 percent figure was cited by numerous campaigners on the survivors' behalf during the negotiations. While the figure is plausible, the author is unaware of any precise documentation to substantiate it.

63. For comparative purposes, the insurance commission, which had started work in late 1998, two and a half years before the German foundation, had paid out on only 1.9 percent of the claims it had received by the end of 2002.

64. Singer made these comments in his speech at Cardozo Law School, op. cit.

65. See his comments made at Columbia Law School, op. cit.

66. He made the comments in an interview with the author in New York, in May 2000.

67. He was referring to the number of countries which had set up special commissions of enquiry (often referred to as 'truth commissions') to examine outstanding financial issues arising from the Holocaust. The number has since increased. According to the United States Holocaust Museum, which keeps a register, the following 23 countries have established historical commissions to examine property and financial issues arising from the Holocaust: Argentina, Austria, Belgium, Brazil, Croatia, the Czech Republic, Estonia, France, the Holy See, Hungary, Israel, Italy, Latvia, Lithuania, Luxembourg, the Netherlands, Norway, Poland, Portugal, Spain, Sweden, Switzerland, and the US.

68. In this regard, responses by potential beneficiaries to the planned payouts by the Swiss banks, held in the docket for the case *Weisshaus vs UBS* in the courthouse for the East District of New York in Brooklyn, are particularly constructive. Canvassed for their views by the court, many said they would not accept money from the Swiss without an admission of responsibility. One survivor wrote to the court to say that to do so would be to surrender his right 'to call a spade a spade, a thief a thief, and a bastard a bastard'. The letter is available in the official case docket at the courthouse in Brooklyn.

69. Graf Lambsdorff said this at the annual conference of the American Corporate Counsel Association in Berlin, on June 25, 2001.

70. In response to complaints by survivors, Burt Neuborne, who represented the US lawyers on the board of the German foundation and was rewarded with US$5 million

for his efforts, commented to the author: 'If they complain about this, let them see a world without lawyers, and see how just they think it is.'

71. Plaintiff counsel awards, published on June 11, 2001, were made by arbitrators led by Kenneth Feinberg, later to be appointed Special Master in the September 11 compensation scheme.

72. He was speaking in an interview with the author in February 2001.

73. See *The Financial Times* (February 28, 2001).

74. Mr Kent was speaking to the author in New York in June 2001.

PART II

THEMATIC STUDIES

CHAPTER 12

JUSTICE AND REPARATIONS

PABLO DE GREIFF

The aim of this chapter is to articulate a conception of justice that can be applied to massive reparations efforts. The task is particularly urgent because if there is such a thing as a 'common' or ordinary understanding of reparations, it is heavily influenced by a 'juridical' understanding of the term. While I have absolutely no interest in launching a critique of legal approaches to transitional problems, the juridical approach to reparations is problematic; it is so not because of its juridical nature per se, but because it is an understanding that has been developed, for good reasons, with an eye to the resolution of relatively isolated cases.[1] By contrast, the aim of this chapter—and of this research project as a whole—is to think about what is fair, proper, and efficient in the resolution of massive and systematic cases of abuse.

Hence, I will start with a modest effort to establish some semantic clarity, at least by trying to distinguish between two different contexts of use of the term 'reparations' (Section 1). I then proceed to a brief discussion of what justice in reparations may mean when the idea is to repair a large number of cases, as opposed to individual, isolated cases. I discuss some of the problems with merely transplanting the ideal of compensation in proportion to harm from its natural home in the resolution of individual judicial cases, and using it as a standard of justice for massive reparations programs. I argue instead in favor of thinking about justice in the context of massive cases in terms of the achievement of three goals, namely, recognition, civic trust and social solidarity—three goals that, as it turns out, are intimately related to justice (Section 2). Finally, without ever pretending that a blue print for a program of reparations can be designed from a purely theoretical perspective, I try to shed light on the basic trade-offs that accompany some of the choices that have to be made in the process of constructing a comprehensive and coherent reparations program (Section 3).

1. CONCEPTUAL CLARIFICATION: THE MEANING OF THE TERM

I start by concentrating on a fact that, surprisingly, has not received sufficient attention in discussions of reparations thus far, namely, that there are two different contexts of use of the term 'reparations' (and that within each of them the term is used in different ways). The first context is the juridical one, particularly, the context of international law, in which the term is used in a wide sense to refer to all those measures that may be employed to redress the various types of harms that victims may have suffered as a consequence of certain crimes.[2] The breadth of the meaning of the term 'reparations' in this context can be seen by considering the diversity of forms reparations can take under international law. These include:

- *Restitution*, which refers to those measures that seek to reestablish the victim's *status quo ante*. These measures can range from the restorations of rights such as citizenship and liberty, to the reinstatement of job and benefits, to the restitution of property.
- *Compensation*, which refers to those measures that seek to make up for the harms suffered through the quantification of harms, where harm is understood to go far beyond mere economic loss, encompassing physical and mental injury, and in some cases moral injury as well.
- *Rehabilitation*, which refers to measures that provide social, medical, and psychological care, as well as legal services.
- *Satisfaction and guarantees of nonrecurrence*, which are especially broad categories that include such dissimilar measures as the cessation of violations, verification of facts, official apologies and judicial rulings that establish the dignity and reputation of the victim, full public disclosure of the truth, searching for, identifying, and turning over the remains of dead and disappeared persons, along with the application of judicial or administrative sanctions for perpetrators, and institutional reform.[3]

The other context in which the term 'reparations' is frequently used is in the design of programs (i.e. more or less coordinated sets of reparative measures) with massive coverage. For example, Germany, Chile, and Argentina can be said to have established 'reparations programs'.[4] In this context, and despite the relations that each one of those programs may have with other efforts to achieve justice, the term is used in a narrower sense. Here 'reparations' refers to the attempts to provide benefits directly to the victims of certain types of crimes. In this sense, programs of reparations do not take truth-telling, criminal justice, or institutional reform, for example, as parts of reparations.

The categories used in the context of the design of programs in order to analyze reparations are different from those proposed by international law. In this context the two fundamental distinctions are between material and symbolic reparations, and between the individual and the collective distribution of either kind. Material and symbolic reparations can take different forms. Material reparations may assume the form of compensation, that is, of payments in either cash or negotiable instruments, or of service packages, which may in turn include provisions for education, health, and housing. Symbolic reparations may include, for instance, official apologies, rehabilitation, the change of names of public spaces, the establishment of days of commemoration, the creation of museums and parks dedicated to the memory of victims, etc.

There are, then, two different contexts of use of the term 'reparations', and they differ significantly from one another. In the sphere of definitions, the fundamental question is not so much about the correctness of a particular definition, but rather, about the relative advantages of understanding a term in a particular way. In the case at hand, the advantage of the breadth of the legal understanding of the term consists in the fact that it provides an incentive to design programs of reparations that cohere with other measures of justice, a topic to which I will return shortly. Nevertheless, the breadth of this understanding also carries a price: a program of reparations can hardly be designed from the beginning so as to include, as parts of a single whole, all the measures which international law takes to be forms of reparations.

The more restricted use of the term characteristic of discussions about the design of programs also has advantages and disadvantages. One of the advantages is that it suggests certain limits to the responsibilities of those in charge of designing such programs, which in principle makes their task satisfiable. However, this narrower use also poses the risk that the program of reparations will be completely unrelated to other justice measures. Although I insist on the importance of preserving the links between the program of reparations and other measures of justice in times of transition, I defend the use of the term 'reparations' in the narrower sense described above, that is, to refer to measures that provide benefits to victims directly. This use contrasts with measures which may have reparative effects, and which may be very important (such as the punishment of perpetrators, or institutional reforms), but which do not distribute a direct benefit to victims themselves.

2. NORMATIVE CONSIDERATIONS: THE AIMS OF REPARATIONS PROGRAMS

Reparations as a Political Project

Now, these differences in use are of course motivated and not simply arbitrary. Part of the underlying motivation is functional in nature; in the juridical context, the meaning of the term is tied to the specific aim pursued in judicial settings, that is, the achievement of justice for individuals, where the means of achieving justice, namely, the trial of isolated cases, has an impact on the concrete content of justice. This approach to the concept of justice differs significantly from that which those who are responsible for the design of reparations programs may and should adopt. Courts do not have an option but to consider each case in its own terms.[5] By contrast, whoever is in charge of designing a massive program of reparations has to respond to a much wider and complex universe of victims, and has to employ, per force, methods and forms of reparation suitable to these circumstances.

Although reparations are well-established legal measures in different systems all over the world, in transitional periods reparations seek, in the last analysis, as most transitional measures do, to contribute (modestly) to the reconstitution or the constitution of a new political community. In this sense also, they are best thought of as part of a political project.[6]

There are two fundamental reasons that justify thinking about reparations in relation to a broader political agenda rather than in terms of a narrowly conceived juridical approach.[7] In the first place, and from a negative perspective, a massive program of reparations cannot reproduce the results which could be obtained in the legal system, because all legal systems work on the assumption that norm-breaking behavior is more or less exceptional. But this is not the case when programs of reparations are being designed, for such programs attempt to respond to violations that, far from being infrequent and exceptional, are massive and systematic. The norms of the typical legal system are not devised for this sort of situation. It is worth pointing out that this problem is not limited to national jurisdictions. Most human rights treatises are conceived and configured to respond to violations in an individualized fashion, and not through massive programs.[8] General international law has not formulated clear norms or principles on this matter either. In any case, the capacity of the state to redress victims on a case-by-case basis is overtaken when the violations cease to be the exception and become very frequent. I will return to this point shortly.

In the second place, and from a positive perspective, to assume a political perspective on reparations opens up the possibility of pursuing ends through the reparations program that would be more difficult to pursue if the sole aim of the program could be victims' redress in accordance with a legal formula. Some of these ends, as it will be argued below, have to do with a broad conception of justice that goes beyond the satisfaction of individual claims, and that involves recognition, civic trust, and social solidarity.[9]

JUSTICE

The most general aim of a program of reparations is to do justice to victims. The question, of course is, what should victims in fairness receive?

Perhaps, rather than approaching the question in a vacuum, it would be easier to start by examining what international law and jurisprudence have to say about the issue. Needless to say, here I can only do so in the most cursory manner.[10] There seems to be growing consensus among international lawyers that victims of human rights abuses are entitled to reparations. This emerging consensus is grounded, in part, on the general principle that all violations of international law entail some responsibilities. But responsibilities to do what? Here is what some international human rights instruments say: Article 8 of the Universal Declaration of Human Rights talks about 'effective remedies'.[11] Article 10 of the American Convention, about 'adequate compensation', Article 63 about 'fair compensation', and Article 68 talks about 'compensatory damages'.[12] Article 9 of the International Covenant on Civil and Political Rights includes vocabulary about 'an enforceable right to compensation',[13] Article 14 of the Convention against Torture speaks about 'fair and adequate compensation including the means for as full rehabilitation as possible',[14] and Article 50 of the European Convention about 'just satisfaction to the victim'.[15]

This, of course, does not settle the issue. What do the expressions 'effective remedies', 'fair and adequate compensation', and 'just satisfaction' mean, precisely? Once again, perhaps it is easier to approach the subject by examining what different bodies responsible for interpreting these norms have said about the subject. Both the Inter-American and the European human rights systems have dealt extensively with the issue, the courts in both systems having decided well over one hundred cases involving reparations. Although there are important differences between the decisions in the two systems, I will not deal with these here.[16] In general, it can be said that they agree on the following interpretation of 'fair and adequate compensation' and other cognate terms: the ideal behind reparations is 'full restitution' (*restitutio in integrum*), that is, the restoration of the *status quo ante*. In cases where this is impossible, for example, when a death has occurred, compensation is required, and this means, for the Inter-American Court, for instance, that material and moral damages are called for. To pay material and moral damages means to cover 'any damages of economic value such as physical or mental damages, psychological pain or suffering, opportunity cost, loss of wages and the capacity to earn a living, reasonable medical and other expenses in rehabilitation, damages to goods and trade; including loss earnings; damages to reputation or dignity and reasonable expert fees'.[17] Procedurally, the Court has calculated these damages by projecting the victim's actual income, multiplying it by whatever was left of his or her professional life (based on national professional and life expectancy averages), and subtracting 25 percent of this amount (assuming that this was the portion of income that the victim would have consumed for personal use, and therefore not available to relatives). In cases where it is difficult to estimate the victim's income, the Court has used national minimum wages, and in at least one case, where it determined that the national minimum wage was too low, it went as far as using the average of regional minimum wages.[18] To this amount, the Inter-American Court has then added its calculation of subjective, or 'moral', damages, which try to compensate for pain and suffering. In sum, decisions by the Court have typically required payments of between $150,000 and $200,000 per victim.[19]

Now, in an isolated case of a human rights violation, this ideal of complete reparation (*restitutio in integrum*) understood in terms of the restoration of the *status quo ante* or of compensation in proportion to the harm suffered, is unimpeachable. Its justification should be obvious: from the perspective of victims and survivors, it attempts to neutralize the consequences of the violation they have suffered. From another perspective the ideal hopes to prevent perpetrators from enjoying any benefit they may have derived from their criminal actions, or to obligate the state to take responsibility for having allowed, by act or omission, certain violations to occur.

But there are circumstances in which this ideal is unrealizable, either due to insurmountable constraints such as the impossibility of bringing someone back to life, or due to constraints that although not absolute, are still severe, such as real scarcity of resources of the sort that makes it unfeasible to satisfy, simultaneously, the claims of all victims and of other sectors of society that in fairness, also require the attention of the state.[20]

Let me illustrate with a concrete example some of the problems generated by the prevalent interpretation of 'adequate compensation'. I want to say that it not only fails to provide guidance, but may actually have some pernicious effects.

As the Peruvian Truth and Reconciliation Commission discussed its reparations recommendations, the Inter-American Commission and the Court kept deciding cases of torture and disappearances in the country, making the familiar sorts of awards, involving sums between $100,000 and $200,000 per victim. These decisions formed the backdrop against which the TRC was articulating its position on reparations, which naturally awakened expectations that it would recommend a reparations plan featuring similar measures. But, of course, it could not possibly do that. If the plan aspired to follow the Inter-American Court's criteria, assuming that it would give each of the families of the more than 69,000 victims of death $150,000, not counting any of the additional services that the Court usually requires, this would have consumed more than $10 billion. Now, Peru's total national budget for 2003 was around $9 billion. This is to say that this part of the reparations plan alone would have consumed more than the entire national yearly budget. Clearly, this was completely unfeasible for the country, even if the costs could have been spread over a number of years, and even if the reparations plan had enjoyed unconditional political support (which it did not, for different reasons, including the generalized perception that the plan would give benefits to a large number of people who are deemed not to deserve them, namely former insurgents, people who do not have 'clean hands'). For a long while there was a very strong probability that given these expectations, whatever the TRC proposed it would have been a huge disappointment. And, given the impact that perceptions concerning reparations have on people's assessment of the success or failure of the *general* work of a truth commission, this is no insignificant matter. In South Africa, for example, the failure to implement the TRC's recommendations on reparations has affected the overall perception of its success, despite the fact that the South African TRC was not at all responsible for the implementation of the plan![21]

But the fact that there is no transitional or postconflict reparations program that has managed to compensate victims in proportion to the harm they suffered, that the very quantification of these harms is problematic, and that even the idea that this should be attempted might generate unfulfillable expectations, are not the only problems that accompany the effort to import this criterion of justice to the domain of massive programs. Ultimately, I think that there is a difference between, on the one hand, awarding reparations within a basically operative legal system of which, in the relatively isolated case of abuse, it can be said that it should have and could have fared better, and, on the other hand, awarding reparations in a system that in some fundamental ways, precisely because it either condoned or made possible systematic patterns of abuse, needs to be reconstructed (or, as in some countries, built up for the very first time). In the former case it makes sense for the criterion of justice to be exhausted by the aim to make up the *particular* harm suffered by the *particular* victim whose case is in front of the court. In the case of massive abuse, however, an interest in justice calls for more than the attempt to redress the particular harms suffered by particular individuals. Whatever criterion of justice is defended must be one that has an eye also on the preconditions of reconstructing the rule of law, an aim that has a public, collective dimension.

In such contexts, some additional difficulties with the attempt to import the received criterion of reparative justice to the massive cases are worth highlighting. These difficulties stem from the *procedure* that would have to be implemented if the criterion of *restitutio in integrum* were to be satisfied. This criterion calls for procedures that individualize the treatment of cases, for the criterion defines justice in terms of rendering *each* victim whole. Again, there is nothing objectionable about this in the sporadic, isolated case of abuse. For massive cases of abuse, and of abuse that comes about as the result of a deliberate policy, however, a case-by-case procedure generates the following two complex problems: first, such procedure would disaggregate victims (in at least two ways), and second, it would disaggregate the reparations efforts (again, in at least two ways).

A case-by-case procedure for settling reparations claims disaggregates *victims* because of unequal access to courts, and of the unequal awards courts make. Even legal systems that do not have to deal with massive and systematic crime find it difficult to ensure that all victims have an equal chance of accessing the courts, and even if they do, that they have a fair chance of getting similar results. The more frequent case is that wealthier, better-educated, urban victims have not only a first, but also a better chance of obtaining justice through these case-by-case procedures.[22]

Furthermore, since doing justice to victims on a case-by-case basis inevitably involves trying to assess individual harms and compensating accordingly, and this, in turn naturally leads to awards of different magnitude for different victims, the difference in the awards may send a message that the violation of the rights of some people is worse than the violation of the same rights of others, thereby undermining an important egalitarian concern and resulting in a hierarchy of victims. Notice that while in general equity does not require equal treatment, in cases of systematic abuse in which people feel that they are victims of the same system and in which they are being redressed through the same procedure and more or less simultaneously—which makes them particularly likely to compare the outcomes—this becomes a serious issue.[23] Even in the rare case in which respect for the equality of rights is not the real concern, disparities in the magnitude of the awards has a deeply divisive effect on the victims, as witnessed, for example, in the operation of the September 11 Victim Compensation Fund in the US. The divisive effect obtained regardless of the high baseline of the awards. ($2.1 million was the average award for families of the deceased. The median was $1.7 million. The awards were made on the basis of sophisticated calculations of the victims' expected income.)[24]

The second problem entailed by the effort to apply the case-by-case procedure that the satisfaction of the criterion of *restitutio in integrum* requires is that it ends up disaggregating not only the victims, but also the reparations efforts. Part of the difficulty here has to do with issues of publicity: due to reasons of privacy, case-by-case approaches might find obstacles to full disclosure of facts needed to treat like cases alike. Moreover, the piecemeal nature of the process makes it comparatively more difficult to provide a comprehensive view of the nature and magnitude of the reparations efforts. Compounded by the disparity in the magnitude of the awards mentioned before, headlines are usually grabbed by the largest awards, to the detriment of the overall efforts.

Finally, because it is easy, in employing a case-by-case approach, to conclude that justice is exhausted by the satisfaction of the criterion of full restitution (what is it, after all, that victims could want in addition to this?), benefits distributed in this manner tend not to be coordinated with other justice measures that are also important. In purely procedural terms, case-by-case approaches tend to produce a certain amount of frustration among beneficiaries, who complain that the proceedings concentrated on financial considerations alone, that whereas they wanted to talk about the experiences of victimization, program officials concentrated on evidence regarding income and assets.[25]

Despite these complications, the state cannot simply ignore the claims of victims with the argument that there are no resources to cover the corresponding costs, or alleging that there is simply no way to overcome the problems described. This would be tantamount to acknowledging that it is in no position to sustain a fair regime. Part of the aim of this project, in fact, is to block the inference from premises regarding how difficult it is to establish fair and effective reparations programs to a conclusion claiming the impossibility of doing so. The state's responsibility consists in designing a program of reparations of which it might be said that it satisfies conditions of justice, even though its benefits are not the same as those that would be determined by a court resolving infrequent or at least isolated suits. But what is involved in 'satisfying conditions of justice' if one cannot rely upon the standard of compensation in proportion to harm?[26]

Before addressing the question directly, it is worth making a preliminary remark. Mere disparities in the awards distributed by courts relative to those distributed by mass programs do not necessarily manifest a flaw, let alone a lack of fairness, in mass programs. For this reason, reparation programs need not to be considered simply as second best alternatives to judicial procedures. Reparation programs at their best are administrative procedures that, among other things, obviate some of the difficulties and costs associated with litigation. These include long delays, high costs, the need to gather evidence that might withstand close scrutiny (which in some cases may be simply unavailable), the pain associated with cross-examination and with reliving sorrowful events, and finally, the very real risk of a contrary decision, which may prove to be devastating, adding insult to injury. A well-designed reparations program may distribute awards which are lower in absolute terms, but comparatively higher than those granted by courts, especially if the comparison factors in the faster results, lower costs, relaxed standards of evidence, nonadversarial procedures, and virtual certainty that accompanies the administrative nature of a reparations program.

In the second place, it is important to keep in mind that most programs of reparations are designed in the context of a transition to democracy.[27] This in my mind has an impact on how justice—and the different measures applied to achieve it—should be understood. There are three specific aims, closely related to the notion of justice, but particularly salient during times of transition, that I think can help structure an answer to the question of what is fair in terms of reparations. These aims are simultaneously necessary conditions and consequences of justice.

Recognition

One of the main aims of transitional justice is to return (or, in some cases to establish anew) the status of citizens to individuals. To the extent that a reparations program aims to contribute to the achievement of justice, and that recognition is both a condition and a consequence of justice, this links reparations and recognition. In order to recognize individuals as citizens it is necessary to recognize them as *individuals* first. That is to say, it is necessary to recognize them not only as members of groups (as important as this might be), but also as irreplaceable and unsubstitutable human beings. Citizenship in a constitutional democracy is a condition that individuals grant to one another, each one of whom is conceived as having value on his or her own.

One of the ways of recognizing another person as an individual, in addition to recognizing the peculiarities of his or her chosen form of life[28] (which is to recognize the person's *agency*), is to recognize the ways in which the person is affected by the environment, that is, to recognize that the person is not only the *subject* of his or her own actions, but the *object* of the actions of others. In other words, there is a form of injustice that consists, not in illegitimately preventing her from exercising her agency through, say, the deprivation of liberty, but in depriving her of the sort of consideration which is owed to whoever is negatively and severely affected by the actions of others. A minimum condition for the attribution of moral standing, without which individuals cannot be recognized as such, is the acknowledgment that my actions impinge on them. The denial of this sort of standing, of this sort of consideration, reveals clearly that I have failed to recognize that I am dealing with individuals.[29]

As if this were not enough, in a constitutional democracy it matters that members recognize one another not only as individuals, but also as *citizens*. To withhold from victims the type of consideration we are talking about makes the mutual attribution of this status impossible. In a democracy, citizenship is a condition that rests upon the equality of rights of those who enjoy such status. And this equality of rights determines that those whose rights have been violated deserve special treatment, treatment that tends towards the reestablishment of the conditions of equality.

From my standpoint, the various transitional mechanisms can be usefully seen through the lens of recognition. That is, all of them can be interpreted as efforts to institutionalize the recognition of individuals as citizens with equal rights. Thus, criminal justice can be interpreted as an attempt to reestablish equality between the criminal and his or her victim, after the criminal severed that relationship with an act that suggested his superiority over the victim.[30] Truth-telling provides recognition in ways that are perfectly familiar, and which are still probably best articulated by the old difference proposed by Thomas Nagel between knowledge and acknowledgment, when he argued that although truth commissions rarely disclose facts that were previously unknown, they still make an indispensable contribution in acknowledging these facts.[31] The acknowledgment is important, precisely because it constitutes a form of recognizing the significance and value of persons—again, as individuals, as citizens, and as victims. Finally, institutional reform is guided by the ideal of guaranteeing the conditions under which citizens can relate to one another and to the authorities as equals.

The exact way in which reparations contribute to justice is complex. On the one hand, it is one aspect of the close relationship that binds the different elements of transitional justice together, and specifically, of the ways in which reparations complement other transitional justice processes. Let me illustrate. Truth-telling in the absence of reparations can be seen by victims as an empty gesture, as cheap talk. The relation holds in the opposite direction as well: reparations in the absence of truth-telling can be seen by beneficiaries as the attempt, on the part of the state, to buy the silence or acquiescence of victims and their families, turning the benefits into 'blood money'. The same tight and bidirectional relationship may be observed between reparations and institutional reform, since a democratic reform that is not accompanied by any attempt to dignify citizens that were victimized can hardly be understood. By the same token, reparative benefits in the absence of reforms that diminish the probability of the repetition of violence are nothing more than payments whose utility, and furthermore legitimacy, are questionable. Finally, the same bidirectional relationship links criminal justice and reparations: from the standpoint of victims, especially once a possible moment of satisfaction derived from the punishment of perpetrators has passed, the punishment of a few perpetrators without any effective effort to positively redress victims could be easily seen by victims as a form of more or less inconsequential revanchism. In summary, reparations contribute to justice not only because they complement transitional justice measures generally, but because they do so in a particular way, namely by helping to keep those other measures from fading into irrelevance for most victims.

On the other hand, reparations can play this 'supportive role' precisely because they constitute, in themselves, a form of recognition. They are, in a sense, the material form of the recognition *owed* to fellow citizens whose fundamental rights have been violated.[32]

Civic Trust

Another legitimate aim of a program of reparations as an instrument of justice is the formation or the restoration of trust among citizens.

Needless to say, whether the hypothesis is reasonable and testable depends on what 'civic trust' means. Thus, some explanation is in order. First, let us start with a broad understanding of trust: trust in general, as a disposition that mediates social interactions, 'is an alternative to vigilance and reliance on the threat of sanctions, [and] trustworthiness... an alternative to constant watching to see what one can and cannot get away with, to recurrent recalculations of costs and benefits'.[33]

Still by way of indirection, it can be said that while trusting someone involves relying on that person to do or refrain from doing certain things, trust is not the same thing as mere predictability or empirical regularity. If that were so, the paradigm of trust would obtain in our relationship with particularly reliable machines. That reliability is not the same as trustworthiness can be seen in our reluctance to say that we *trust* someone about whose behavior we feel a great deal of certainty but only because we both monitor and control it (e.g. through enforcing the terms of a contract), or because we take defensive or preemptive action.[34] Trust involves an expectation of a shared normative commitment. I trust someone when I have reasons to expect a certain pattern of behavior from her, and those reasons include not just her consistent past behavior, but also, crucially, the expectation that among her reasons for action is the commitment to the norms and values we share. In this sense, although trust does not involve normative symmetry—trust is possible within largely asymmetrical relationships including those within deeply hierarchical institutions—it does involve normative reciprocity: trust develops out of a mutual sense of commitment to shared norms and values. This explains both the advantages of trust and the risks it always involves: in dispensing with the need to monitor and control, it facilitates cooperation immensely, and not only by lowering transaction costs; but as a wager (no matter how 'safe'), that at least in part for *normative reasons* those we trust will not take advantage of our vulnerabilities, we risk having our expectations defeated.

Now, the term 'civic' in 'civic trust', I understand basically as a limiting qualifier. Trust can be thought of as a scalar relationship, as one that allows for degrees. The sense of trust at issue here is not the thick form of trust characteristic of relations between intimates, but rather, 'civic' trust, which I take to be the sort of disposition that can develop among citizens who are strangers to one another, and who are members of the same community only in the sense in which they are fellow members of the same *political* community. True, the dimension of a wager is more salient in this case than in that of trust towards intimates, since we have much less information about others' reasons for actions. However, the principles that we assume we share with others and the domain of application of these principles are much more general. To illustrate, the loyalty that binds me to intimates is significantly thicker than the loyalty (e.g. to a common political project) that binds me to fellow citizens.

Just like recognition, civic trust is at one and the same time a condition and a consequence of justice. There are myriad ways in which a legal system relies on the trust of citizens.[35] At the broadest level, a legal system works only on the basis of the citizens' generalized norm-compliance. In other words, the legal system can cope with norm-breaking behavior only when it is exceptional. This means that most social interactions are not directly mediated by law, but rather, at some level, by trust between citizens. Closer to home, however, all legal systems rely not just on the trust that citizens have towards one another but on the trust that they have in the systems themselves. In the absence of total(itarian) surveillance, criminal legal systems must rely upon the citizens' willingness to report both crimes that they witness and crimes that they suffer.[36] And this willingness to report, of course, rests upon their trust that the system will reliably produce the expected outcomes. This is actually a complex sort of trust: in police investigations, in the efficiency of the court systems, in the honesty of judges, in the independence of the judiciary (and therefore on the executive's willingness to protect and promote that independence), in the at least minimal wisdom of the legislature, and in the strictness (but perhaps also the simultaneous humaneness) of the prison system, etc. Needless to say, each of these objects of trust can be further analyzed.

On the other hand, it is not just that legal systems rely upon the trust of citizens both among one another and in the system itself. Legal systems, when they operate well, also catalyze trust, once again, both among citizens themselves, and in the system itself. Indeed, Rawls takes the rule of law's ability to generate social trust—which he understands in terms of the reliability of expectations—as a definitional aspect of the rule of law:

A legal system is a coercive order of public rules addressed to rational persons for the purpose of regulating their conduct and providing the framework for social cooperation. When these rules are just they establish a basis for legitimate expectations. They constitute grounds upon which persons can *rely on one another* and rightly object when their expectations are not fulfilled.[37]

To the extent that law helps to stabilize expectations, and that it helps to diminish the risks involved in trusting others, especially strangers, it contributes to the generation of trust among citizens.

As for the catalytic role of law in generating trust in legal institutions, the underlying argument should be clear: legal institutions, insofar as they are reliable, provide further reasons for citizens to rely upon them for the resolution of their conflicts. This simply follows from the fact that trust is something that is earned, rather than arbitrarily bestowed, and this is true just as much for institutions as it is for individuals. The easier way of seeing this is by noticing attitudes towards law in societies where the legal system is perceived as inaccessible or otherwise unreliable.

The fundamental point, of course, is to clarify the relationship between reparations and civic trust. Again, for victims, reparations constitute a manifestation of the seriousness of the state and of their fellow citizens in their efforts to reestablish relations of equality and respect. In the absence of reparations, victims will always have reasons to suspect that even if the other transitional mechanisms are applied with some degree of sincerity, the 'new' democratic society is one that is being constructed on their shoulders, ignoring their justified claims. By contrast, if, even under conditions of scarcity, funds are allocated for former victims, a strong message is sent to them and others about their (perhaps new) inclusion in the political community. Former victims of abuse are given a material manifest-ation of the fact that they are now living among a group of fellow citizens and under institutions that aspire to be trustworthy. Reparations, in summary, can be seen as a method to achieve one of the aims of a just state, namely, inclusiveness, in the sense that all citizens are equal participants in a common political pro-ject.

Solidarity

Finally, another legitimate aim of a program of reparations, considered once again as one of the forms of promoting justice, may be the strengthening or the generation of another attitude which—like recognition and civic trust—is also a condition and a consequence of justice. This is the attitude of social solidarity.[38]

Just like civic trust, solidarity also comes in different types and degrees. Social solidarity is the type of empathy characteristic of those who have the disposition and the willingness to put themselves in the place of others. That this attitude is a condition of justice may be seen in the following way: an impartial perspective, an indispensable requisite of justice, is not achievable unless the person that judges is prepared to assume the place of the contesting parties. Moreover, in a democratic system which distinguishes legitimacy from mere balances of power, the only way to assure that the legitimacy of a law has been attained is by making sure that the law incorporates the interests of all that are affected by it. And this implies having an interest in the interests of others.[39] This is precisely what social solidarity is.

Reparations can be seen as an expression of this type of interest, and, at the same time, as generators of this form of solidarity. In societies divided and stratified by the differences between the urban and the rural, by ethnic, cultural, class, and gender factors, reparations manifest the interest of the traditionally most advan-taged in the interests of the least favored. Although it cannot be assumed that the former will immediately support a reparations program, this is a point at which the relations between reparations and other transitional mechanisms, especially truth-telling, may play an important role, for historical clarification can awaken empathy with victims. On the other hand, to the extent that victims feel that a new 'social contract' in which their dignity and their interests are amply recognized is being offered, they will have reasons to take an interest in common interests, contributing in this way to the strengthening of the basis of a just society.

Here it is particularly important not to overstate the case; it is unlikely that a reparations program, on its own, can generate a sense of social solidarity where there is none. In this sense, it becomes obvious that reparations manifest, that is, rest upon, preexisting commitments. Nevertheless, a well-crafted reparations program can play a (modest) role catalyzing solidarity. It is true that transitional moments are periods of heightened normative sensitivity, where both institutions and individuals have strong incentives to articulate the principles, norms, and values to which they commit themselves. However, they are also moments still marked by the signs of social bonds strained and broken by conflict or authoritarian rule, and of bankrupt and largely unreliable institutions. Complexity beyond a certain threshold can undermine social virtues not so much by undermining the virtues of individuals, at least initially, as by leaving clear no avenue of action that expresses those virtues. Over time, commitments may weaken. Under such circumstances, normative talk, including talk about solidarity with victims, may turn into nothing more than talk, unless it receives adequate and effective institutional expression. A carefully designed and well-implemented reparations program *may* catalyze social solidarity precisely by giving concrete expression to commitments that, if they remain free floating, are always at risk of dissipating.

Notice, to conclude this section, three additional advantages of thinking about the aims of reparations in these explicitly political terms rather than in the more judicial terms of compensation in proportion to harm. First, this way of thinking about reparations, although based on principled normative considerations, permits crafting reparations in a way that attends to contextual features in two important senses: as I have pointed out before, it suits the peculiarities and the needs of transitional situations, taking advantage of the aspects of such contexts that call for a 'constitutional moment'. However, it is not just that in thinking about the aims of reparations in terms of recognition and the reconstitution of civic trust and social solidarity important transitional goals are explicitly assumed as guides for the design of an important transitional tool, thereby helping to guarantee the success of both the reparations program and the transitional policy, but that taking these as the main goals of the reparations program gives it a beneficial forward-looking character. One of the main sources of dissatisfaction with most reparations awards is the fact that beneficiaries frequently consider them insufficient compensation. In this, they are usually correct, independently of the magnitude of the award, for reasons that have to do with the difficulty—and ultimately, the impossibility—of quantifying great harm; there is no amount of money that can make up for the loss of a parent, a child, a spouse. There is no amount of money that can adequately compensate for the nightmare and the trauma of torture. In my view, reparations programs, not least because of the financial difficulties that arise in cases with massive numbers of claimants, should not even attempt, and should always avoid using the vocabulary of, proportional compensation. There should not be anything in a reparations program that invites either their designers or their beneficiaries to interpret them as an effort to put a price on the life of victims or on the experiences of horror. Rather, they should be interpreted as making a contribution to the quality of life of survivors. Thinking about reparations in terms of recognition and of the promotion of civic trust and social solidarity invites the assumption of this forward-looking perspective.

Second, there is another sense in which taking the more political aims of granting recognition, and promoting civic trust and social solidarity, allows for a healthy form of contextualism: for instance, what in a given society is sufficient to provide adequate recognition to victims is largely a matter of context. What US citizens expect by way of recognition may differ widely from what the potential beneficiaries in different contexts may expect. And satisfying those different expectations, despite their differences, is obviously not a bad thing.

Another advantage of thinking about reparations in explicitly political terms, rather than in terms of judicial considerations, is that it places another thorny issue in the design of reparations programs in its proper context. I am talking about the question of finances. A political perspective on reparations introduces some clarity in discussions about financing strategies. Basically, this happens because it takes the question of finances out of the exclusive domain of technicians and lawyers and returns it where it should properly lie, namely, in the domain of competing social priorities. Most governments respond to recommendations concerning reparations with one of two responses. Either 'reparations are too expensive and we cannot afford them', or, 'if we repair, let's do it collectively'. To the first response, the adequate reaction is to point out that questions about what can and cannot be afforded at public expense are always questions about priorities. Perhaps, unless there is a budget surplus, nothing can be afforded by leaving everything else untouched. The question is about what is deemed urgent, and this is always a matter of politics.[40] To the second response, which usually accompanies the preference of governments for folding reparations into development programs, the proper reaction is to point out that the bias in favor of the collective is nothing more than that; the collective can be quite expensive, more expensive than the individual (in fact, given the generally dismal record of development programs, these, in particular can be very expensive).[41]

3. STRUCTURAL CONSIDERATIONS

Integrity or Coherence

Up to this point I have said virtually nothing about the characteristics of reparations programs. Part of the reason is that, needless to say, I do not think that their design follows deductively from matters of principle. Nevertheless, I am prepared to make two general points.

The first is a remark about a desirable characteristic that I think all programs should have. Reparations programs should display what I call integrity or coherence, which I analyze into two different dimensions, internal and external. *External* coherence expresses the requirement that the reparations program be designed in such a way as to bear a close relationship with the other transitional mechanisms, that is, with criminal justice, truth-telling, and institutional reform. This requirement is both pragmatic and conceptual. The relationship increases the likelihood that each of these mechanisms be perceived as successful (despite the inevitable limitations that accompany each of them), and, more importantly, that the transitional efforts, on the whole, satisfy the expectations of citizens. But beyond this pragmatic advantage, it may be argued that the requirement flows from the relations of complementarity between the different transitional justice procedures that I sketched before.

Reparations programs ought to display integrity or coherence in another dimension: a program of reparations, if it is to attain its proper goals, must always be a complex program that distributes different benefits, and the different components of the plan ought to be mutually coherent. That is, the program ought to be *internally* coherent. Most reparations programs distribute more than one kind of benefit. These may include symbolic as well as material reparations, and each of these categories may include different measures and be distributed individually or collectively. Obviously, in order to reach the desired aims, it is important that benefits be part of a plan whose elements internally support one another.

Forms of Reparations and Their Trade-offs

The second set of points about the structure of reparations programs that can be safely made from a relatively abstract perspective is the following. Although the final details of a program for a particular country will depend on heeding many contextual features, the trade-offs between different measures can be clarified in very general terms. So although I do not think that theorists can properly get into the business of writing up blueprints of such programs—at least not in their capacity as mere theorists—there is a great deal of work that can be done in the clarification of the advantages and disadvantages that may accompany different design choices. The following scheme illustrates the basic orientation:

1. *Symbolic Measures*
   Individual (personal letters of apology, copies of truth commission reports, proper burial for the victims, etc.)
   (*a*) Advantages

   - Constitute a way to show respect for individuals.
   - Express recognition for the harm suffered.
   - Low cost.

   (*b*) Disadvantages

   - May create the impression that by themselves they constitute sufficient reparations for the victims.

   Collective (public acts of atonement, commemorative days, establishment of museums, changing of street names and other public places, etc.)
   (*a*) Advantages

   - Promote the development of:
     – Collective memory;
     – Social solidarity; and
     – A critical stance toward, and oversight of, state institutions.

   (*b*) Disadvantages

   - May be socially divisive.
   - In societies or social sectors with a proclivity toward feeling victimized, this feeling may be heightened.
   - May create the impression that they alone constitute sufficient reparations for the victims.

2. *Service Packages*
   Service packages may include medical, educational, and housing assistance, etc.
   (*a*) Advantages

   - Satisfy real needs.
   - May have a positive effect in terms of equal treatment.
   - May be cost-effective if already existing institutions are used.
   - May stimulate the development of social institutions.

(*b*) Disadvantages

- Do not maximize personal autonomy.
- May reflect paternalistic attitudes.
- Quality of benefits will depend on the services provided by current institutions.
- The more the program concentrates on a basic service package, the less force the reparations will have, as citizens will naturally think that the benefits being distributed are ones they have a right to as citizens, not as victims.

3. *Individual Grants*
   (*a*) Advantages

- Respect personal autonomy.
- Satisfy perceived needs and preferences.
- Promote the recognition of individuals.
- May improve the quality of life of the beneficiaries.
- May be easier to administer than alternative distribution methods.

(*b*) Disadvantages

- If they are perceived solely as a way of quantifying the harm, they will always be viewed as unsatisfactory and inadequate.
- If the payments fall under a certain level, they will not significantly affect the quality of life of the victims.
- This method of distributing benefits presupposes a certain institutional structure. (The payments can satisfy needs only if institutions exist to 'sell' the services that citizens wish to purchase.)
- If they are not made within a comprehensive framework of reparations, these measures may be viewed as a way to 'buy' the silence and acquiescence of the victims.
- Politically difficult to bring about, as the payments would compete with other urgently needed programs, may be costly, and may be controversial as they would probably include ex-combatants from both sides as beneficiaries.

There are those who think that reparations can also take the shape of development programs. I do not agree with that option, but to complete the analysis, the following may be said.

4. *Development and Social Investment*
   (*a*) Apparent Advantages

- Gives the appearance of being directed toward the underlying causes of the violence.

- Would appear to allow due recognition to be given to entire communities.
- Gives the impression of making it possible to reach goals of justice as well as development.
- Politically attractive.

(b) Disadvantages

- Has very low reparative capacity, as the development measures are too inclusive (are not directed toward the victims) and they are normally focused on basic and urgent needs, which make the beneficiaries perceive them as a matter of right and not as a response to their situation as a victim.
- In places characterized by a fragmented citizenry, these measures do nothing to promote respect for people as individuals rather than as members of marginal groups.
- Uncertain success: development programs are complex and long-term programs. This threatens the success of the institutions responsible for making recommendations regarding reparations, which may lead to questions regarding the seriousness of the transitional measures in general.
- Development plans easily become the victims of partisan politics.

In principle, there is no conflict at all between the distribution of symbolic and material reparations. In fact, ideally, these benefits can lend mutual support to each other, something that will be especially important in contexts characterized by scarce resources, where symbolic reparations will surely play a particularly visible role. Nor is there any conflict at all, in principle, between individual and collective measures. As long as there is a substantial individual component, the exact balance between the two kinds of measures should be established taking into consideration, among other factors, the kind of violence sought to be redressed. In those places where the violence was predominantly collective, it makes sense to design a program that also places special emphasis on these kinds of methods.

Having said this, it should be obvious from considerations under point 4, above, that I am skeptical of the effort to turn a program of reparations into the means of solving structural problems of poverty and inequality.

Strictly speaking, a development program is not a program of reparations. In fact, development programs have a very low reparative capacity, for they do not target victims specifically, and what they normally try to achieve is to satisfy basic and urgent needs, which makes their beneficiaries perceive such programs, correctly, as ones that distribute goods to which they have rights as citizens, and not necessarily as victims. In the second place, development programs are affected by a very high degree of uncertainty, for development aims are both complex and long-term. This threatens the success of the institutions responsible for making recommendations concerning reparations, and may raise questions about the seriousness of the transitional process in general. Given the importance of reparations in a transitional process, to propose a program with a very uncertain or very extended horizon of success could generate questions about the commitment to democratic renewal.

Here it is worth distinguishing between reparations in their strict sense, and the reparative effects of other programs. Development, just like criminal justice, for example, may have reparative effects. Nevertheless, this does not make either of them part of the domain of responsibility of those who design programs of reparation. Naturally, we may reiterate here that the latter must cohere with other aspects of the transitional policy. That is to say, the program must be internally and externally coherent, and it must avoid reproducing and perpetuating unjust social structures. In the last analysis, a transitional government in a poor country will most likely propose a development plan, and ideally, the program of reparations must also cohere with that plan. But the point I have emphasized is that it is important to set boundaries of responsibilities between different policies, for strictly speaking, the responsibilities of a program of reparation are not the same as that of a development or social investment plan.

4. CONCLUSION

The conception of justice in reparations presented here takes as its starting point the difference between the requirements of fairness in isolated cases and those requirements in the design of massive programs. It tries to spell out some legitimate aims of these programs, heeding the constraints under which they usually operate. It has insisted on the importance of individual reparations, allowing all the while that there are situations in which a collective dimension is perfectly proper. It has defended both the differentiation of benefits and the need for both external and internal coherence.

None of this offers a formula that embodies what justice in reparations requires—one of the reasons why the principle of *restitutio in integrum* continues to be appealing in the domain of massive programs despite its patent inapplicability. The three goals around which I have defined the requirements of justice for these cases require the exercise of political judgment, understood in the broad sense of a judgment about what is both in the common good and feasibly achievable. This type of judgment is never in plentiful supply. However, there is no substitute for it—not even legalistic abstractions, for in the domain of massive reparations, experience shows that even these are unavailable. We do well, then, in asking ourselves seriously what justice in reparations requires.

Notes

I gave a first expression to some of the ideas presented here in a document prepared for the ICTJ in association with the *Asociación Pro Derechos Humanos* (APRODEH) for discussion in Peru, *Parámetros para el diseño de un programa de reparacions en el Perú*, September, 2002. Since then, this conceptualization of reparations has been adopted—and adapted—in the chapter on reparations of the Peruvian Truth and Reconciliation Commission (see Comisión de la Verdad y Reconciliación, *Informe Final* (Lima, 2003), vol. 9, ch. 2), by the recent Commission on Illegal Detention and Torture in Chile (see Comisión Nacional Sobre Prisión Política y Tortura (Santiago, 2004), ch. 9), by the Truth and Reconciliation Commission for Sierra Leone (see *Report of the Truth and Reconciliation Commission for Sierra Leone* [presented to the President of Sierra Leone on 5 October 2005], vol. 2, ch. 4), and by various international documents, for example, the 'Independent Study On Best Practices, Including Recommendations, To Assist States In Strengthening Their Domestic Capacity To Combat All Aspects Of Impunity', by Diane Orentlicher, UN Doc. E/CN.4/2004/88, February 27, 2004.

I am grateful to my partners in the ICTJ-APRODEH project, Arturo Carrillo, Alex Segovia, Julie Guillerot, Humberto Ortiz, and Lisa Magarrell. Some actual as well as a few imagined conversations with Lisa forced me to clarify my position, so I owe a special debt to her. I presented earlier versions of this paper at the ICTJ; University of California, Riverside; Queens University, Kingston, Ontario; The Carnegie Council on Ethics and International Affairs in New York; at the meeting of authors who participated in this project at the Rockefeller Foundation's Conference Center in Bellagio, Italy; at a meeting, organized by the International Development Research Center (IDRC) in Ottawa, at Brown University; at a meeting organized by the International Peace Academy in Pocantico; and at the International Criminal Court in The Hague. My gratitude to commentators and discussants, and to the institutions mentioned above. The views expressed here do not necessarily represent the position of the ICTJ.

1. Despite the difficulties associated with the effort to transplant the juridical approach to the resolution of massive cases, reparations litigation before both national and regional jurisdictions such as the Inter-American Court or the European Court can play a tremendously important role in massive reparations. First, such litigation can act as a catalyst for the adoption of reparations programs. Arguably, this happened in Argentina, Peru, and might happen in Guatemala as well. Second, notwithstanding the near impossibility of fulfilling the juridical criterion of justice in reparations in massive cases, this criterion may be used by victims and their representatives to exercise pressure for large benefits. Given the usual reluctance of governments to establish reparations programs in the first place, this leverage becomes particularly important.
2. In this collection, see Falk (Chapter 13) and Carrillo (Chapter 14). See also the papers in *State Responsibility and the Individual: Reparation in Instances of Grave Violations of Human Rights*, Albrecht Randelzhofer and Christian Tomuschat, eds. (The Hague: Martinus Nijhott Publishers, 1999).

3. See, for example, Theo van Boven, 'Study Concerning the Right to Restitution, Compensation and Rehabilitation for Victims of Gross Violations of Human Rights and Fundamental Freedoms', UN Commission on Human Rights, Sub-Commission on Prevention of Discrimination and Protection of Minorities, UN Doc. E/CN.4.Sub.2/1993/8. More recent updates have not changed the categories. For an interesting discussion of the development of these principles, see Dinah Shelton, 'The United Nations Draft Principles on Reparations for Human Rights Violations: Context and Contents', in *Out of the Ashes: Reparation for Victims of Gross and Systematic Human Rights Violations*, Marc Bossuyt, Paul Lemmens, Koen de Feyter and Stephan Parmentier, eds. (Antwerp: Intersentia, 2005).

4. In my 'Reparations Efforts in International Perspective; What Compensation Contributes to the Achievement of Imperfect Justice', in *To Repair the Irreparable: Reparation and Reconstruction in South Africa*, Erik Doxtader and Charles Villa-Vicencio, eds. (Claremont, South Africa: David Philip, 2004), I distinguish between 'reparations efforts' and 'reparations programs' more precisely; the latter term should be reserved to designate initiatives that are designed from the outset as a systematically interlinked set of reparations measures. Most countries do not have reparations programs in this sense. Reparations benefits are most often the result of discrete initiatives that come about incrementally rather than from a deliberately designed plan. When no harm is done I will use the terms interchangeably.

5. Except, of course, when dealing with mass claims. There are interesting parallels between mass claims and reparations programs, including a similar shift in the understanding of what is fair to particular claimants. I cannot pursue the parallels here.

6. When it is claimed that reparations are part of a political project it is assumed that the 'political' refers to, among other things, the (ideally deliberative) exercise of power in the distribution of public goods and benefits for the good of all, rather than to the partisan exercise of power for the good of a few. A strong defender of the constitutive role of truth commissions and their recommendations—including those on the issue of reparations—is Andre du Toit. See his 'The Moral Foundation of the South African TRC', in *Truth v. Justice*, Robert Rothberg and Dennis Thompson, eds. (Princeton, NJ: Princeton University Press, 2001), 122–40.

7. It goes without saying that in arguing in favor of a 'political' approach to reparations I am not denying that there is a *legal* right to reparations. The target of my criticism is the attempt to transplant the juridical criterion of full restitution—and the procedures that accompany the application of this criterion—from the domain of the resolution of individual cases to that of programs that deal with a massive number of cases. It should also be obvious that nothing in my argument raises questions about the need to give legal expression to reparations measures.

8. Christian Tomuschat, 'Individual Reparation Claims in Instances of Grave Human Rights Violations: The Position under General International Law', in Randelzhofer and Tomuschat, op. cit.

9. The move involved in attributing these goals to reparations programs is not so much descriptive as 'reconstructive'. So, my claim is not that these are the goals that reparations programs have in fact pursued, but rather, that it makes sense to think that these are goals that they may be said to pursue, or, in any case, that given the close relationship between these goals and the goal of achieving justice, these are aims that reparations programs *should* pursue.

Incidentally, the possibility that reparations programs may make a modest contribution to the attainment of broader political goals explains some of my initial reservations concerning the tendency to juridify discussions about reparations. The discussion about reparations for African-Americans in the US is part of a long series that demonstrates the increasing tendency to juridify political issues (not just) in the US. Of course, the motivation to do so is unobjectionable, especially considering the obstacles that would have to be overcome in order to gain a political solution to this issue. Nevertheless, the case both illustrates and entrenches what in the end is a suspicious attitude about politics, an attitude that is not a positive symptom in a democracy. For a very useful analysis of this issue, see Thomas McCarthy, 'Vergangen-heitsbewältigung in the US: On the Politics of Memory of Slavery', Political Theory 30 (2002): 623–48, and 'Coming to Terms with Our Past, Part II: On the Morality and Politics of Reparations for Slavery', Political Theory 32 (2004): 750–72.

10. The papers by Falk and Carrillo in this collection address this issue, specifically.

11. Universal Declaration of Human Rights, UN Doc. A/RES/217A (III) of December 10, 1948.

12. American Convention on Human Rights, O.A.S. Treaty Series No. 36, 1144 U.N.T.S 123 entered into force July 18, 1978, reprinted in Basic Documents Pertaining to Human Rights in the Inter-American System, OEA/Ser.L.V/II.82 doc.6 rev.1 at 25 (1992).

13. International Covenant on Civil and Political Rights, UN Doc. A/RES/2200A (XXI) of December 16, 1966.

14. Convention against Torture and Other Cruel, Inhuman or Degrading Treatment or Punishment, UN Doc. A/RES/39/46 of December 10, 1984.

15. The European Convention on Human Rights, Council of Europe, Rome, November 4, 1950.

16. For a useful but undertheorized survey see Dinah Shelton, Remedies in International Human Rights Law (Oxford: Oxford University Press, 1999).

17. Victor Rodríguez Rescia, 'Reparations in the Inter-American System for the Protection of Human Rights', ILSA Journal of International and Comparative Law 5(3) (1999): 583–601, here at 594.

18. See the following cases: El Amparo, Panel Blanca, Castillo Paéz, Niños de la Calle, Ricardo Baena, Bámaca Velásquez, Barrios Altos. In Neira Alegría the Court decided to use the average of Latin American wages, considering the Peruvian minimum wage too low.

19. Arturo Carrillo, in his paper in this volume, examines thoroughly the criteria and procedures employed by the court.

20. The idea of compensation in proportion to harm ignores three very real problems. First, the quantification of harm. The ideal of making victims whole assumes harms can be measured in some reliable way. It should be obvious that this is not so easy. To illustrate, one of the relevant questions here is how to assign values to different sorts of harms. What is more 'costly': the loss of a limb, or of an eye, for example, or the psychological trauma of torture? How can the relative costs of physical and psycho-logical harms be compared? And those stemming from the loss of a relative? How can these 'costs' be sensibly assessed? The second challenge arises from difficulties stem-ming from interpersonal comparisons. This challenge comes about, ultimately, because there is a fundamental difference between losses and harms; two persons who suffer the same loss are not necessarily equally harmed, for harms depend to some degree on the

individual's reactions to circumstances. For example, not everyone who loses a hand reacts in the same way. Even if having both hands is equally important for two persons—say, because both are manual laborers—it is possible that the experience will sink one of them into depression, while the other may live the experience as a challenge, a painful one of course, but one that she is determined to overcome. Finally, in order to show that even seemingly precise reparations based on calculations of past income and earning potential have some degree of arbitrariness to them, consider that they must rely both on generalizations and on questionable assumptions; the most questionable assumption is that the world remains in a steady state; when a lifetime income is calculated, it is taken for granted that there will be no sharp economic cycles, that the demand for professionals in a given career will remain steady (the use of an 'unemployment risk factor' in calculations of potential lifetime earnings does not neutralize the need to make assumptions about general economic stability or demand), that the person in question would not have died before the expected average age, that he or she would not have become an alcoholic, a failure, etc. The generalizations refers to among other things, calculations about average projected incomes for different professions, which are notoriously sensitive to, for example, geographical location. I cannot deal with these difficulties here. But they are certainly worth flagging. Debra Satz at the conference at the University of California, Riverside, where I presented an initial draft of this chapter, discussed the last set of complications.

21. See Colvin on the South African case (Chapter 5, this volume).

22. This is true both of court procedures (in national *or* international courts) and of administrative procedures that adopt a case-by-case approach. To illustrate these claims: the report of the Guatemalan Commission of Historical Clarification contains a detailed analysis of how courts in that country were traditionally inaccessible to rural, and particularly to indigenous, populations. See Comisión de Esclarecimiento Histórico (CEH), *Guatemala Memoria del Silencio*, 'Denegación de Justicia', vol. 3, ch. 16 (UN Office for Project Services: June 1999). Ten years after the signing of the peace accords, and five years after the CEH produced its report, no one in Guatemala considers courts a viable mechanism for the distribution of reparations benefits. Similarly, the cases that end up reaching the Inter-American Court tend to be those that largely urban human rights NGOs decide to pursue during the years-long winding process leading to the regional system. Finally, the Arbitration Commission established in Morocco in 1999 to redress mostly victims of 'disappearance' (illegal detention) during the reign of Hassan II was subject to criticism for, among other reasons, the order in which it took cases.

23. This set of considerations, i.e. that equity does not require equal treatment, but that in the context of massive abuse people are bound to make comparisons and are likely to view differential treatment with (justified) suspicion, is what explains why I speak about the 'disaggregation' of victims, rather than claiming that the procedure is actually unfair (although it frequently is, as when equal access to courts is not guaranteed). The tendency to make comparisons under these circumstances seems to me to be well grounded, and not merely a psychological curiosity; when the violations result from the implementation of a policy, people who have suffered similar violations are not unreasonable in expecting similar benefits. For a contrasting view of this issue, see Malamud-Goti and Grosman (Chapter 15, this volume).

24. On this case, see Issacharoff and Mansfield (Chapter 8, this volume).

25. See, for instance, Cammack (Chapter 6, this volume).

26. Some people defend the idea that for massive cases, at least, international law should not try to set criteria for determining the magnitude of awards, but rather criteria that would have to be satisfied by the processes used to determine the magnitude of awards. More concretely, the idea is that international law should give some impetus to deliberative, consultative processes at the national level, processes that would lead to the choice of award levels. This, presumably, would consist mainly in ensuring that victims and victims groups have a say in the determination of award levels. See, for instance, Heidy Rombouts, 'Reparation for Victims of Human Rights Violations: A Socio-Political Approach', Paper presented at the Expert Seminar on Reparation for Victims of Gross and Systematic Human Rights Violations in the Context of Political Transitions, Katholieke Universteit, Leuven, Belgium, March 10, 2002. In general, I am supportive of this idea, but with the following cautionary note. In the end, and for reasons that are very easy to understand, victims will always want more benefits. Although I do not mean this derogatorily at all, victim groups will in the end behave like other interest groups—this one with a cause that is particularly compelling to me. In order for this proposal to make sense, one would have to include victim groups in discussions not just about the reparations plan, but about the national budget, so that they have an adequate perception of the other legitimate projects (such as health, education, justice, and development, to mention only a few) reparations always competes with.

27. There are of course important exceptions. Some so-called 'well-established democracies' have instituted reparations programs. These include the US (for Japanese-American internees during World War II), Canada (for mistreatment of indigenous groups), and others. See Yamamoto and Ebesugawa on US reparations for Japanese-American internees (Chapter 7, this volume).

28. For a philosophical elaboration of the notion of recognition, and one that takes seriously choices about forms of life, see Axel Honneth, *The Struggle for Recognition: The Moral Grammar of Social Conflicts*, Joel Anderson, trans. (Cambridge, MA: MIT Press, 1995). See the interesting debate between Honneth and Nancy Fraser in their joint work, *Redistribution or Recognition? A Political–Philosophical Debate* (London: Verso, 2003).

29. See Onora O'Neill's attractive account of moral standing in *Towards Justice and Virtue* (Cambridge: Cambridge University Press, 1996), ch. 4.

30. See Jean Hampton, 'The Moral Education Theory of Punishment', *Philosophy and Public Affairs* (1981): 209–38; 'A New Theory of Retribution', in *Liability and Responsibility*, R. G. Frey and Christopher W. Morris, eds. (Cambridge: Cambridge University Press, 1991); and her essays in *Forgiveness and Mercy*, Jeffrie Murphy and Jean Hampton, eds. (Cambridge: Cambridge University Press, 1988).

31. Nagel argues that there is 'a difference between knowledge and acknowledgment. It is what happens and can only happen to knowledge when it becomes officially sanctioned, when it is made part of the public cognitive scene.' Quoted in Lawrence Weschler, 'Afterword', in *State Crimes: Punishment or Pardon* (Washington, DC: Aspen Institute, 1989).

32. The fact that recognition is one of the aims of reparations programs invites the participation of victims in the process of designing and implementing such programs, for recognition is not something that can merely be given, as if the views of those to be

recognized did not matter! Participatory processes may themselves provide useful forms of recognizing not just the status of victims as victims, but also, importantly, as *agents*. Stating this, however, does not detract from the force of the caveats stated in n. 26 above.

33. Annette Baier, 'Trust and its Vulnerabilities', in her *Moral Prejudices* (Cambridge, MA: Harvard University Press, 1994), 133.

34. Laurence Mordekhai Thomas illustrates the point with a telling example: 'Trust does not amount to prediction: if I put everything under lock and key and invite you into my home, I can quite confidently predict that you will not steal anything, yet nothing is clearer than that I do not trust you.' See his 'Power, Trust, and Evil', in *Overcoming Racism and Sexism*, Linda Bell and David Blumenfeld, eds. (Lanham, MD: Rowman and Littlefield, 1995), 160.

35. For a closer analysis of this issue and of how truth-telling efforts, in particular, can contribute to the rule of law in transitional situations precisely by fostering civic trust, see my 'Truth-Telling and the Rule of Law', in *Telling the Truths: Truth Telling and Peacebuilding*, Tristan Anne Borer, ed. (Notre Dame, IN: University of Notre Dame Press, 2005).

36. From the perspective of well-ordered societies it is hard to conceive of circumstances in which people would not bother reporting even serious crimes like murder. But this indeed happens. In Colombia, for example, during the late 1980s more than 35 percent of murders were never even reported. See Mauricio Rubio, *Crimen e Impunidad* (Bogotá: TM Editores, 1999).

37. John Rawls, *A Theory of Justice* (Cambridge, MA: Harvard University Press, 1972), 235 (emphasis added).

38. Hauke Brunkhorst offers a sophisticated analysis of the concept of solidarity in *Solidarity: From Civic Friendship to a Global Legal Community*, Jeffrey Flynn, trans. (Cambridge, MA: MIT Press, forthcoming).

39. See Jürgen Habermas, 'Justice and Solidarity', in *The Moral Domain*, Thomas Wren, ed. (Cambridge, MA: MIT Press, 1990), and William Rehg, *Insight and Solidarity: The Discourse Ethics of Jürgen Habermas* (Berkeley, CA: University of California Press, 1994).

40. Perhaps the best illustration of this point comes from South Africa where efforts to restart the stalled discussions of reparations at one point were taking place with the government arguing that there was no money for the program while at the same time it was proposing the purchase of two new submarines. See Brandon Hamber and Kamilla Rasmussen, 'Financing a Reparations Scheme for Victims of Political Violence', in *From Rhetoric to Responsibility: Making Reparations to the Survivors of Past Political Violence in South Africa*, Brandon Hamber and Thloki Mofokeng, eds. (Johannesburg: Centre for the Study of Violence and Reconciliation, 2000), 52–9.

41. Of course, placing reparations in the political arena rather than in the judicial sphere puts a premium on an effective strategy of effective coalition building in favor of reparations.

CHAPTER 13

REPARATIONS, INTERNATIONAL LAW, AND GLOBAL JUSTICE: A NEW FRONTIER

RICHARD FALK

1. POINTS OF DEPARTURE

It is only in the last decade or so that international law has moved significantly in the direction of providing the means to pursue global justice, that is, in global arenas or by reference to global standards and procedures, on behalf of the individual and collective victims of severe injustices of the sort associated with oppressive governing regimes.[1] Prior to that time this class of issues pertaining to global justice was treated as marginal, at best, to the endeavors of international law, although overseas economic interests of individuals from the North received periodic protection if encroached upon by governments in the South. But in the 1990s the combination of the end of the cold war, the rise to prominence of international human rights, trends away from authoritarianism and toward constitutional democracy, and the partial eclipse of sovereignty in a globalizing world gave unexpected attention to the many facets of global justice, hitherto mainly neglected, including steps designed to rectify the harm endured by individuals at the hands of dictatorial and abusive governments.

At the forefront of these moves was the reinvigoration of efforts to impose accountability on individuals associated with the perpetration of crimes of state, highlighted by such high-profile cases as those associated with the transnational pursuit of Augusto Pinochet and of Slodoban Milosevic.[2] This emphasis on accountability by leaders was reinforced by institutional and procedural innovations enabling indictment and prosecution.

Of almost equal prominence was the temporarily increased acceptance of an international responsibility on the part of the organized international community to protect vulnerable populations facing catastrophic challenges, whether from an abusive government or from an inability to provide governing authority, giving rise to a series of humanitarian interventions as responses to chaos and oppression. This historical climate of concern reached its climax with the Kosovo War under NATO auspices in 1999, and has subsequently declined markedly. Here, the duty to protect an oppressed and endangered Kosovar Albanian majority in the province of Kosovo was assumed by a regional security alliance to validate military action against a sovereign state, in this instance Serbia, even without the benefit of a prior mandate from the United Nations Security Council. Such a use of force even if credibly undertaken for protective purposes was always controversial from the perspective of international law, and depends upon the presence of political factors that were selectively present in the 1990s to a greater degree than at any other historical moment, and have subsequently almost disappeared.[3] The inability to mobilize support for humanitarian intervention in the setting of ongoing, massive ethnic cleansing and genocidal tactics in western Sudan during mid-2004 is indicative of how restricted to context was the surge of humanitarian diplomacy in the 1990s. And even then, without the presence of more strategic objectives of the sort present in Kosovo, but absent in Rwanda during the genocide of 1994, the prospects for humanitarian intervention by either the UN or a coalition of the willing are minimal.

As part of this climate of global opinion that seemed in the 1990s more sensitive to injustice than ever before, a new disposition to consider historic injustices endured by individuals and groups was evident in international relations. As Elazar Barkan, one of the more perceptive analysts of this welcome mutation in international attitudes, notes, there was 'the sudden appearance of restitution cases all over the world', leading him to postulate the possible beginnings of 'a potentially new international morality'.[4] It is in this setting of a redress of historic grievances that the issue of reparations makes its appearance, especially in the setting of transitional justice arrangements, but not only. Part of this incipient normative revolution of the 1990s was a concern with rectifying harm previously done to individuals and groups, as well as punishing perpetrators and repudiating their documented wrongdoing in an authoritative forum. What accounted for this focus on this redress agenda at such a historical moment is uncertain, but it undoubtedly reflected a loss of a guiding geopolitical purpose after the end of the cold war combined with the growing prominence of human rights and an impulse in leadership circles to overcome the chorus of criticisms directed at the amorality of neoliberal globalization.

Barkan and others, for entirely persuasive reasons, approach these issues of restitution and reparations as primarily matters of morality and politics rather than law, that is, treating these humanitarian initiatives as reflecting the impact of moral and political pressures, rather than exhibiting adherence to previously established or newly emerging legal standards and procedures.[5] The sea changes in the 1990s reflected almost exclusively a combination of special circumstances generating political pressures and a mysteriously supportive moral 'window of opportunity' in a global setting. But to the extent that morality and politics created new widely shared expectations about appropriate behavior by governments, international law was being generated, even if it did not assume in most instances the positivist formality of treaty arrangements or the specificity of a meaningful legal obligation that included measures designed to ensure consistent implementation. Throughout the history of international society, the evolution of international law has been closely related to prevailing political currents, evolving moral standards, and dominant trends in religious thought. Such a linkage has been particularly evident in the war/peace context, international law essentially embodying the just war tradition as evolved by theologians, but it is also true with respect to the recent prominence of a global justice agenda in which redress and restitution play such a large part. In one sense the role of international law has been generally one of codifying behavioral trends in state practice and shifting political attitudes on the part of governments with the intention of stabilizing and clarifying expectations about the future.

It seems essential to distinguish three sets of circumstances: the first, the main preoccupation of international law and lawyers, involves disputes between states, and increasingly other actors, in which the complaining party seeks relief from alleged wrongs attributed to the defending party; the second involves war/peace settings in which the victorious side imposes obligations on the losing side, 'victors' justice, which may or may not correspond with justice as perceived from a more detached outlook; the third, achieving attention recently, involves transitions to democracy settings in which the prior governing authority is held accountable for alleged wrongs, and again reflect political outcomes of sustained struggle, but not international war. These three contexts should be kept distinct for both analytical and prescriptive purposes. In the first and second, there exists a more obvious role for international norms, procedures, and institutions than in the third, which is treated for most purposes as a matter of domestic discretion, although influenced by wider trends of *national* practice in comparable instances, and by wider global trends toward individual accountability for crimes against humanity.

To what extent these mainly encouraging developments involving the rendering of global justice have been stymied, the window closed, by the September 11 attacks and the American-led response are matters of uncertainty and conjecture at the present.[6] The refocusing of attention on global security issues seems to have remarginalized in general the pursuit of the global justice agenda, including the drive for reparations associated with various forms of historic redress other than those associated with transitional issues in a given country relating to the recent past.[7] As developments in 2003 within Argentina suggest, a change of governmental leadership at the national level can affect the approach taken to justice claims in a transition process, including those involving a renewed resolve related to individual criminal accountability and compensation for past abuse. Against this double background of an inchoate normative revolution in the 1990s and the altered historical setting of the early twenty-first century, this chapter analyzes the relevance of international law to reparations, and especially whether and to what extent reparations have acquired an international obligatory character of any practical significance.[8] Such significance is difficult to assess, especially as its most tangible impact may be to encourage the provision by national legal systems of remedies for various categories of losses sustained due to prior abuses of human rights. To the extent that international law is relevant at all, it is to provide *legal* arguments or *jurisprudential* background useful for representatives and advocates of victims' rights in *domestic* political arenas to the effect that victims are legally entitled to reparations, and that the domestic system is obliged to make this right tangible by providing meaningful procedures.

2. INTERNATIONAL LAW: AUTHORITY AND INSTRUMENTS

The fundamental norms of international law are contained in customary international law, and reflect widely accepted basic ideas about the nature of law, its relation to legal wrongs, and the duty to provide recompense. The Permanent Court of Justice, set up after World War I, gave the most authoritative renderings of this foundation for the legal obligation to provide reparations. This most general international law imperative was set forth most authoritatively, although without any equally general prospect of implementation, in the *Chorzow Factory (Jurisdiction) Case*: 'It is a principle of international law that the breach of an engagement involves an obligation to make reparation in an adequate form.'[9] The Advisory

Opinion by the International Court of Justice involving the Israeli Security Wall reaffirmed this cardinal principle in ruling that Israel was under an obligation to provide reparations to the Palestinians for damages sustained due to the illegal wall built on their territory.[10]

A second equally important idea embodied in customary international law had to do with the nationality of claims associated with wrongs done to individuals. In essence, this norm expressed the prevailing understanding that only states were *subjects* within the international legal order, and that wrongs done to foreign individuals were in actuality inflicted upon their state of nationality. Accordingly, if the individual was stateless, a national of the wrongdoing state, or a national of a state unwilling to support the claim for reparations, there was no basis on which to proceed. This limiting notion was expressed succinctly by the Permanent Court of International Justice in the *Mavrommatis Palestine Case*: '[b]y taking up the case of one of its subjects and by resorting to diplomatic action or international judicial proceedings on his behalf, a state is in reality asserting its own rights—its right to ensure, in the person of its subjects, respect for the rules of international law.'[11] It is important to appreciate that these formulations were made before there existed any pretense of *internationally* protected human rights.

A third important idea in customary international law, that has persisted, forbids a state to invoke national law as a legal defense in an international dispute involving allegations of wrongdoing by the injured state. Such a principle pertains to the setting of international disputes, which is where the main precedents and doctrines of international law relative to reparations are fashioned. Somewhat surprisingly, the International Law Commission (ILC) Articles on State Responsibility, despite years of work, clarified to some extent this earlier teaching, refining and codifying it conceptually more than changing it substantively.[12] The ILC approach to remedial or corrective justice was based on distinguishing between restitution, compensation, and satisfaction. *Restitution* is defined in Article 35 as the effort 'to re-establish the situation which existed before the wrongful act was committed'. Such a remedy is rather exceptional. It is usually illustrated by reference to the *Temple* case before the International Court of Justice (ICJ) in which Thailand was ordered to return religious relics taken from a Buddhist temple located in Cambodia.[13] This primary reliance on restitution where practicable has been recently reaffirmed by the ICJ in its ruling on Israel's security wall, an important restatement of international law although contained in an advisory opinion, because it was endorsed by fourteen of the fifteen judges. The language of the Advisory Opinion expresses this viewpoint with clarity in paragraph 153: 'Israel is accordingly under an obligation to return the land, orchards, olive groves and other immovable property seized from any natural or legal person for purposes of construction of the wall in the Occupied Palestinian Territory. In the event that such restitution should prove to be materially impossible, Israel has an obligation to compensate the persons in question for the damage suffered. The Court considers that Israel also has an obligation to compensate, in accordance with the applicable rules of international law, all natural or legal persons having suffered any form of material damage as a result of the wall's construction.'[14]

Article 35(a) and (b) of the ILC Draft Articles indicates that restitution is not the appropriate form of reparations in circumstances where it is 'materially impossible' or would 'involve a burden out of all proportion to the benefit deriving from restitution instead of compensation'.

Compensation, resting on the fungibility of money, is more widely used to overcome the adverse consequences caused by illegal acts. In the *Chorzow* case it was declared that where restitution cannot be provided to the wronged state, then the wrongdoer should be required to compensate up to the level of the value attributed to whatever was lost, including loss of profits. Articles 36 and 37 go along with this approach of full reimbursement, without qualifications based on capacity to pay.

Satisfaction is the third, and lesser known, manner of providing reparations. The ILC Articles make it a residual category in relation to restitution and compensation. As explained by du Plessis, '[s]atisfaction provides reparation in particular for moral damage such as emotional injury, mental suffering, injury to reputation and similar damage suffered by nationals of the injured state'.[15]

Customary international law, as well as the ILC Draft Articles of State Responsibility, impose an undifferentiated burden, as stated in Article 37, on the wrongdoing state 'to make full reparation for the injury caused by the internationally wrongful act'. As such, it gives very little guidance in specific situations where a variety of considerations may make the grant of full reparation undesirable for various reasons, although commentary by the ILC on each article does go well beyond the statement of the abstract rule.

International treaty law does no more than to restate these very general legal ideas in a variety of instruments, and without the benefit of commentary attached to the ILC articles. Because property rights are of paramount concern, the language of reparation is not used, and the more common formulations emphasize compensation for the wrongs suffered. The basic direction of these treaty norms also derives from international customary law, especially legal doctrine associated with the confiscation of foreign-owned property. The legal formula for overcoming the legal wrong accepted in international law involved 'prompt, adequate, and effective compensation'. Discussion of 'restitution' and 'satisfaction' is abandoned as the wrongdoing states are acknowledged by the United Nations to possess 'permanent sovereignty' over natural resources.[16]

The Universal Declaration of Human Rights shifts the locus of relief to national arenas and away from international disputes between sovereign states. Individuals are endowed with competence, and the notion of wrongdoing is generalized to encompass the entirety of human rights. Article 8 reads: 'Everyone has the right to an effective remedy by the competent national tribunals for acts violating the fundamental human rights granted him by the constitution or by the law.' Of course, such a right tends to be unavailable where it is needed most, although the existence of the right does provide a legal foundation for reparation in future circumstances when political conditions have changed.

Article 10 of the American Convention on Human Rights (1978) particularizes a 'Right of Compensation' in a limited and overly specific manner: 'Every person has the right to be compensated in accordance with the law in the event that he has been sentenced by a final judgment through a miscarriage of justice.' It seems to refer exclusively to improper behavior of the state associated with criminal prosecution and punishment within the judicial system. It is available only on the basis of an individual initiative.

Article 14 of the Convention Against Torture and Other Cruel Inhuman and Other Degrading Treatment or Punishment (1984) imposes on parties the obligation to 'ensure in its legal system that the victim of an act of torture obtains redress and has an enforceable right to fair and adequate compensation, including the means for as full rehabilitation as possible'. Again, the emphasis is on the legal duty of the state to provide individuals who are victims with a remedy within the domestic system of laws. That is, victims are not dependent on governments of their nationality pursuing claims on their behalf, nor are nationals barred from relief by the obstacle of sovereign immunity. Article 9 of the Inter-American Convention to Prevent and Punish Torture (1985) similarly obligates parties to 'undertake to incorporate into their national laws regulations guaranteeing suitable compensation for victims of torture'.[17] In the absence of case law it is difficult to know what this standard might mean in practice, and whether it is purely aspirational or represents a genuine effort to acknowledge the full spectrum of injury that often results from torture and severe abuse. Beyond this duty of the state, Article 8 allows persons alleging torture to internationalize their claims for relief '[a]fter all the domestic legal procedures of the respective State...have been exhausted' by submitting their case 'to the international fora whose competence has been recognized by that State'.

Within the European regional system there is a right of an individual in Article 50 of the European Convention for the Protection of Human Rights and Fundamental Freedoms (1950) to seek 'just satisfaction' in the event that national law provides 'partial reparation' due to injury sustained as a result of a violation of the Convention. A proceeding of this nature would fall within the authority of the European Court of Human Rights. Here, too, the idea is to provide individuals with a remedy at the regional level beyond what is available within the national legal system.

These international law developments over the last half century have several different important consequences for the wider interest in reparations as provided to a victimized group, especially in the context of transition from authoritarian regimes:

- first, there is the shift in the emphasis of international law from the protection of aliens abroad, and especially their property, to the protection of individuals who experience abuses of human rights;
- second, there is a legal recognition that the state responsible for the abuse should legally empower those who claim to have been victimized to pursue relief by way of compensation through recourse to the national judicial system;
- third, the national identity of the victim and the sovereign immunity of the state should not affect the availability of legal relief in the event of abuse;
- fourth, in the event of frustration at the national level, then some further mechanism for providing relief is becoming available at either the regional or global level, or both.

In summary, the importance of these international law developments is probably indirect, but the shift from a concern with dispute settlement to human rights does involve a major reorientation. The obligations embodied in legal instruments are vague and abstract, and are difficult and cumbersome to implement, but they do contribute to what might be called the formation of 'a reparations ethos' to the effect that individuals who have been wronged by applicable international human rights standards, especially in the setting of torture and kindred maltreatment, should be compensated as fully as possible. This ethos is a challenge to notions of sovereignty associated with earlier ideas that a state can do no wrong that is legally actionable, and that the wrong done to an individual is *legally* relevant only if understood as a wrong done to the state of which he or she is a national.

At the same time, the most important circumstances of reparations, leaving aside postwar arrangements, are not really addressed directly by contemporary international law. In authoritarian political settings, by definition, there is an absence of judicial independence, and there is no prospect of relief even in extreme situations. In postauthoritarian political settings, where there is an impulse to achieve redress, the magnitude of the challenge requires some categorization of the victims as well as a recognition of severe limits on the capacity of the new government to provide anything approaching 'adequate compensation'. In this sense, the contributions of international law at this stage must be mainly viewed as indirect, and the actual dynamics of reparations arrangements reflect a variety of specific circumstances that exist in particular states. These arrangements have an ad hoc character that makes it impossible to draw any firm conclusions about *legal* expectations, much less frame this practice in the form of *legal doctrine*. For this reason, among others, it is appropriate to view reparations as primarily an expression of *moral* and *political* forces at work in particular contexts.[18]

3. SHADOWS OF MISUNDERSTANDING

Any broad consideration of the relevance of international law to the subject matter of reparations needs to be sensitive to several background factors that could invite misunderstanding if not addressed. Such factors illuminate the tensions that have historically existed between considerations of global justice and political relationships shaped by hierarchical relations between the strong and the weak.

For most people (other than specialists in international law concerned with international disputes about wrongdoing), the idea of 'international reparations' recalls the burdens imposed on Germany at the end of World War I that were embodied in the Versailles Treaty.[19] These burdens were widely interpreted as accentuating the hardships faced by German society in the 1920s, and were viewed in retrospect as a damaging example of a 'punitive peace' that contributed to a surge of German ultranationalism, producing a political climate conducive to extremism of the sort represented by the Nazi movement. From an international law perspective, the reparations imposed were perfectly legal, indeed specified in a peace treaty formally accepted by Germany, but from a political perspective such reparations were viewed as imprudent, if not disastrous, and from a moral perspective, they were widely viewed as ill-deserved, mainly exhibiting the vengeful appetite of the victors in the preceding war in which neither side could convincingly claim the moral high ground. This 'lesson of Versailles' was heeded after World War II, Germany being assisted in economic recovery and political normalization despite the existence of a far stronger case for collective punishment of German society than existed in 1918, given the multiple legacy of crime and tragedy generated by Hitler's regime.[20] And the results are generally viewed as vindicating the soft approach, reinforcing the repudiation of Versailles.

And yet, somewhat surprisingly, the 'peace' imposed on Iraq after the Gulf War seems to have adopted the previously discredited Versailles model of punitive peace, although the terminology of reparations was largely displaced in this instance by the language of sanctions and claims, perhaps to avoid evoking bad memories. At the same time, extensive assets and oil revenues were made available, along with a procedure within the UN, to provide compensation to victims of Iraqi harm arising out of its invasion of Kuwait in 1990, and so there was a justice dimension so far as individual victims of Iraqi wrongdoing were concerned.[21] Thus, overall, an important ambiguity emerges: the Iraqi people were punished collectively and severely despite being entrapped in a brutal dictatorship, while the various categories of victims arising from the *international* crimes of Iraq as committed in Kuwait were the recipient of substantial reparative efforts to compensate for losses sustained. In this respect, the positive side of reparations was present. This whole framework of 'sanctions', combining the punitive with the compensatory, was given legal stature in the form of unanimous UN Security

Resolution 687, the harsh terms of which were accepted by a defeated and devastated Iraq in the 1991 ceasefire that ratified the results of the Gulf War.[22]

There are two observations to be made. First, in the sphere of interstate reparations, there is a confusing association of 'reparations' in language and policy both with a largely discredited process of imposing collective punishment upon a defeated state and its civilian population, and as seeking to give the victims of illegal and criminal conduct on behalf of a state a meaningful remedy for harm sustained in the form of substantial monetary compensation. Second, there is a flexible capacity for international law to provide a legal imprimatur, either by treaty or Security Council decision that ratifies a mechanism for the award of 'reparations', and gives legal expression to the geopolitical relationship that exists at the end of a war, without regard to whether the motivations for reparations are punitive or compensatory, or a mixture of the two. If the outcome of the war is 'just', and the victors are 'prudent', then the reparations imposed may contribute to global justice, but if not, not. International law provides at this point no substantive guidelines as to these assessments, and its main role is to provide victorious powers with a flexible *instrument* by which to give a peace process in accord with their goals and values an authoritative status.

The analogous dynamics of establishing reparations in the context of transitional societies also reflects power variables, although there is often not a clear dividing line between victory and defeat, but rather a political process that produces a negotiated compromise that inhibits to varying degrees the redress of past injustices by the newly emerging constitutional leadership. The arrangement is formalized exclusively through a reliance on mechanisms provided by the governing authorities enlisting the national legal system and establishing special administrative procedures. There is no direct role for international law, except to the extent of taking account of past wrongdoing as instances of 'crimes against humanity', or indirectly, as responsive to international pressures associated with imposing national means to determine accountability and rectifying past wrongs to the extent possible, given the political and economic realities. In the context of the Holocaust, and to some extent in relation to authoritarian antecedents to constitutional government, the goal of reparations is also a deterrent message to future leaders and a pledge of sorts by present leaders to repudiate the past and build a just constitutional order.

Certainly, in the background of the sort of moral and political pressures effectively brought to bear on Swiss banks by Holocaust survivors and their representatives during the 1990s was the strong sense that these individuals, or in this case sometimes their descendants, had truly been victims of internationally criminal conduct and deserved some sort of redress even if belatedly.[23] Decades had passed since the occasions of wrongdoing, and it was only a change in global setting that abruptly lent *political* credibility to claims that always had been actionable from *legal* or *moral perspectives*. It was this credibility that overcame the impulse to disregard old claims as stale, and allegedly avoid opening old wounds. Such belated redress went against the traditional disposition of law to reach finality with respect to claims, both for the sake of stability and because evidence becomes less reliable and often unavailable with the passage of time.

An additional source of misunderstanding pertaining to international law relates to its state-centric orientation and traditions, which have been increasingly challenged in a variety of ways in the last few decades. The modern structure of international law was based on the idea that states were the only formal members of international society, and that the legal interests of individuals if associated with the actions of foreign governments were protected, if at all, by one's country of nationality on a discretionary basis.[24] International wrongs of aliens were thus treated as generating potential legal claims by a government on behalf of their aggrieved nationals, but purely as a matter of political and moral discretion, and under international law the wrong was done to the state, not to the individual who was harmed. The practice by states of reacting to such wrongs was described as 'the diplomatic protection' of nationals or aliens abroad, and was usually associated with the protection of foreign property rights. The individual beneficiary of such claims had no *legal* entitlement, and a government could ignore or waive the claims of its nationals. This statist pattern was further reinforced by ideas of nonaccountability with respect to wrongs inflicted on nations, both internationally and domestically. The doctrine of sovereign immunity meant that an individual suffering injury could not initiate any legal action in the courts of either the country where the harm took place or the country of his or her nationality. Claims of allegedly injured aliens in Third World settings were sometimes addressed by claims commissions assessing the merits of particular claims or by a lump sum settlement the funds of which were then allocated on some basis to the claimants. This background of international law is highly relevant to the circumstance of societies in the midst of transitions to democracy. There are three further observations that are relevant to this inquiry. First, the political reality of such dynamics reflected the geopolitical and hierarchical structures of the colonial era. These claims made by governments in the North involved only losses sustained by Western individuals in Third World settings. There was no reciprocity or equality given the manner with which investment and property rights were dealt with in international law. A bit later these claims for compensation involved opposition to socialist approaches to both private investment and economic development, and resisted the legal effects, as far as possible, of the rise of economic nationalism in the decades following World War II. The protection of nationals abroad was not at all in the spirit of 'reparations' (conceived as corrective justice) and reflected an opposite policy generally associated with protecting foreign investors who had characteristically been beneficiaries of 'unjust enrichment' in a variety of exploitative center–periphery relations. Ideas of state responsibility were also formulated with an eye toward fashioning an international law instrument designed for the protection of transnational private property interests, especially in the face of allegedly confiscatory forms of nationalization. Even the most recent formulation of the law of state responsibility by the International Law Commission treats the state as the sole subject of wrongs whose victims are its nationals, and fails to address the existence of rights under international law of the victims if they are conceived of as individuals or groups. With moves toward neoliberal globalization since 1990, there has emerged a widespread intergovernmental consensus supportive of private sector autonomy, which has ended the widespread emphasis on balancing territorial rights against those of foreign investors in Third World countries. In this regard, the capitalist ethos has prevailed, at least for the foreseeable future.

Second, the kind of concerns that have been associated with transitions to democracy were completely absent from these earlier concerns of international law with harm sustained by individuals. For one thing, victims *within* society were left completely vulnerable to abuse by their own governments due to ideas of territorial supremacy of sovereign states, and thus the abuses of oppressive government toward their own citizenries remained outside the legal loop of potential responsibility. International law was completely silent as to state–society abuses so long as the victims were nationals.[25] The emergence of international human rights, by way of the Universal Declaration of Human Rights in 1948 and the 1966 Covenants were at first only *politically* feasible because there were no expectations of *legal* implementation, much less remedies for victims seeking reparations. The majority of governments were authoritarian, fully dedicated to traditional notions of sovereign rights, and would have opposed a legal structure that had explicit ambitions associated with implementation of individual rights. It is here where the emergence of transnational civil society actors changed the political equation, creating pressures to promote degrees of implementation for human rights that went far beyond what had been anticipated at intergovernmental levels.[26]

Third, since international law failed to protect the human rights of individuals as a matter of law until after World War II, there was little pressure on national legal procedures to do so. But in more than a half century since the adoption of the Universal Declaration of Human Rights there has been an extraordinary set of regional and global developments enhancing the position of the individual as the formal holder or subject of rights.[27] What is important here is less the exceptional *international* initiative on behalf of the victims of human rights abuse, than the influence on the erosion of sovereign exemptions from accountability in *domestic* legal arenas.[28] Here the indirect impact of the human rights movement has been strongly felt. It includes the empowerment of civil society actors, creating intense perceptions of injustices endured by individuals, expectations of some sort of remedial process, and the importance of taking official steps toward corrective justice by a government in the struggle to renew an atmosphere of political legitimacy. This is the case with respect to its own citizens by means of a signal of the repudiation in the past and also to aid efforts to acquire or reacquire legitimacy within international society.[29] In effect, some of the traditional veils of sovereignty are lifted to facilitate transition, but this is overwhelmingly disguised directly by the adoption of a self-interested national political and moral discourse. But what seems national, even nationalistic, is undoubtedly influenced by varying degrees by what has been going on internationally, transnationally, and in other kindred states. What is most evident, particularly in Latin America, which provided the main experimental frontier, was the degree to which justice for victims was complementary to what often from the outside appeared to be a more strident insistence, effectively promoted by civil society actors, on combating what came to be described as 'the culture of impunity' toward past wrongdoing by leaders. More properly considered, this effort to impose accountability on leaders was integral to restoring the dignity of victims, constituting a direct repudiation of the past, and was thus an aspect of rendering justice to the victims, however retrospectively.[30] There is also evidence of a mimetic element in which national dialogues listen to one another, while adapting to their own particularities, building a trend that establishes a new pattern of expectations about justice in transitional circumstances. Such a drive for corrective justice was tempered by resource constraints and by the search for normalcy or social peace, tending to produce compromise approaches, especially encouraging an approach to feasible levels of 'satisfaction' for victims by reliance on truth and reconciliation processes adapted to the particularities of a given country. The end result is an acknowledgment of the past, but without great efforts either to punish perpetrators or to compensate victims. Symbolic forms of redress prevail, with both corrective and deterrent goals.

Such a historical process of innovative practice is somewhat puzzling from an interpretative perspective. Whether we call such patterns 'law' or 'international law' is a matter of the jurisprudential outlook, either positivist or constructivist. It is also a question of what might be called the politics and epistemology of law. A positivist approach would not regard the existing rules of international law as sufficiently clarifying as to permissible behavior to qualify fully as law. A constructivist jurisprudence attributes to the interpreters of law, both judges and scholars, a dynamic role in imparting authoritative meaning, and proceeds from the belief that legal standards cannot be objectified by language and strict canons of interpretation. I favor such an acknowledgment of the uncertainty of law on the books as a means to encourage those with discretion to interpret, apply, and enforce the law to act responsibly, which I regard as meaning that ambiguities be resolved by opting for morally guided outcomes to decision-making. Of course, discretion is not unlimited, but confined by rules of reason that identify the boundaries of interpretative reasonableness and thus accord with the idea that those interpreting the law are not free to give expression to private ideas of morality and political prudence. Legality as a clarifying condition is left in abeyance until patterns of expectations are shaped by interpretative trends and practice.[31] Such a prism of evaluation would seek to relate law to widely endorsed expectations about behavior that exist in society, but would not 'legalize' moral sentiments that lacked such backing, however appealing, by pretending that these sentiments qualified as 'law'. From such a perspective, then, there is a greater relevance for international legal obligations in relation to reparations practice, and wider issues of corrective or remedial justice, than would seem to derive from a strictly positivist jurisprudence. The normative revolution that seemed to get underway in the 1990s had a law-making potential if expectations of legality are created by influential institutional and societal actors. Such expectations would acknowledge as valid specific claims and demands for justice, and thereby set precedents that shape perceptions as to the evolving character of 'the law'. If victims' rights become established legally, expectations of participants alter in circumstances of future victimization.

4. SOME LIMITING CONDITIONS

Reparations, if conceived as central to corrective justice, pose difficulties from the perspective of international law, but these are encountered in analogous form in transitional justice settings. Even more than efforts to impose individual account-ability, a reliance on reparations, especially as a means to address the various dimensions of harm endured by victims, is inevitably to be context-driven.[32] And because context is so decisive, the guidance functions of international law tend to be minimal beyond affirming the existence of an underlying obligation as a generality. As the 2004 Advisory Opinion on the legal status of the Israeli security wall clearly reaffirmed, there does exist in international law a well-established entitlement for the victim of legal wrongs to appropriate reparations. But between the affirmation of the legal right/duty and its satisfaction there exists a huge contextual gap. In this instance, Israel, backed by the US government, immediately repudiated the World Court decision, and the prospects of compliance are nil. The international legal standard is authoritative and context-free, but its implementa-tion is context-dependent.

Several dimensions of this unavoidable contextuality can be identified, but such a reality also pertains at least as much to reparations within national settings, where a wide measure of prosecutorial discretion has been an attribute of efforts to bring justice to perpetrators and victims in transitional situations. So what is set forth as applicable in international contexts is also relevant with some adjustments to national contexts.

Unevenness of Material circumstances

To the extent that reparations attempt to compensate victims for losses endured, some assessment of an ability to pay needs to be made. This assessment should take account, as well, of the extent of victimization, and whether certain forms of vicitimization need to be excluded from the reparations program. But in the end, the question of fiscal capabilities at the disposal of the perpetrators, or their successors, is crucial. Of course, this is true, as well, for prosecutorial efforts to impose accountability on perpetrators, which also reflects the unevenness of national capacities to sustain the 'shock' of prosecutions. Iraq after the Gulf War, with extensive oil revenues, and South Africa, with an impoverished population, are at opposite ends of the spectrum in two respects: Iraq was an instance of reparations doubling as sanctions, whereas in South Africa any attempt to provide monetary reparations would involve a massive diversion from the priorities of the new leadership to promote economic growth and address the challenge of massive poverty.

The case of South Africa is significant for this inquiry.[33] The new political order had repudiated its criminal past mainly by way of a truth and reconciliation process. It was deeply committed to the improvement of the material circumstances of an extremely poor majority black population. Of course, the new leadership could have taken greater account of the high degree of victimization, as well as the unjust enrichment of the white minority, by combining constitutionalism with a program for the redistribution of wealth based on past injustice. To have done so, however, would likely have doomed the political miracle of a bloodless transition from apartheid, and might have led to prolonged civil strife. The role of reparations in transitions to democracy is especially complicated, taking into consideration the entrenched interests of those associated to varying degrees with the old order, seeking to avoid overtaxing available capabilities to ensure the success of the newly emerging order, and yet providing some needs-based relief to those who suffered incapacitating harms due to prior wrongdoing. As well, in the setting of many African countries that are extremely poor, it seems unrealistic because of resource constraints to impose corrective burdens of a monetary character.[34] This is especially so for national settings where prolonged civil strife has victimized many, if not all, living in the society; many severely, if massive atrocities were committed on a large scale. Normally more appropriate would be symbolic measures of acknowledgment (via truth and reconciliation) along with a needs-based conception of reparations that tries, at least, to enable those who have been disabled, or find themselves in acutely vulnerable circumstances, to be given the means by which to restore a modicum of dignity to their lives.[35]

Remoteness in Time

Because some claims for redress of grievances arise from events that seem in the remote past, and their redress is of a magnitude that would be disruptive to present social and economic arrangements, there is a vigorous resistance to material forms of compensation.[36] It is partly a matter of responsibility, the unwillingness of most members of a present generation to believe that they owe obligations to the ancestors of claimants. It is partly a matter of changed mores, a sense that 'injustice' needs to be measured within the historical setting of the contested behavior. It is partly a matter of scale and impact, the realization that restoring the rights of victims would be enormously expensive and subversive of currently vested property interests. And it is partly a refusal to treat those in the present as truly vicitimized by occurrences that took place long ago. The reality is complicated, as old wounds often have not healed despite the passage of many generations.

At the same time, remoteness has not altogether stymied efforts to obtain redress in the form of reparations under certain conditions. The exemplary case is the pursuit of Swiss bank deposits by Holocaust survivors and their heirs, as well as claims on behalf of those who had been compelled to do forced labor in Nazi times. Swiss banks agreed to pay survivors $1.25 billion, and the German government agreed to pay compensation for slave labor.[37] Related efforts produced agreements with France to compensate for stolen assets during the Vichy period, 'truth' commissions have been set up in as many as twenty-three countries that are continuing to assess claims relating to looted works of art and unpaid insurance proceeds owed to relatives of Holocaust victims. At the same time, beneficiaries are disappointed by the level of compensation received, and more than this, distressed by the monetization of their suffering that can never be compensated. When one survivor of Auschwitz, Roman Kent, was asked whether he was happy about the results, his reply was typical: 'Why did it take the German nation 60 years to engage the morals of the most brutal form of death, death through work?'[38] The pursuit of these claims on behalf of Holocaust victims has produced mixed assessments from observers, but the main relevant point is that the process has been primarily driven by moral and political pressures, with law playing a facilitative role, although lawyers have played a rather controversial role by siphoning off a considerable proportion of negotiated settlements as legal fees.[39] In a technical sense, the recovery of wrongfully taken property is an instance of reparations, but in its more unusual mode of restitution rather than as a means of providing compensation for injuries sustained.

In some respects, the relative success of Holocaust claimants has stimulated other categories of remote victims to be more assertive about seeking redress, although not necessarily in the form of reparations. To begin with, Asian victims of imperial Japan mounted pressures on behalf of survivors who had been engaged in forced labor, as did representatives of 'comfort women'. Asian claimants were able to take advantage of national laws in the USA that had been drafted in response to pressures associated with the Holocaust, although in the end were unable to proceed as potential claims had been waived in the peace treaty concluded with Japan, an exemption from responsibility that the US State Department continues to support in litigation brought before American courts. Note here that the obligations to compensate written into American law do not pretend to be 'international legal obligations', but are instances of discretionary national legislation that results from moral appeals and political leverage.

Yet remoteness has not inhibited certain categories of claims for reparative justice, especially those associated with indigenous peoples and the institutions of slavery and slave trading. These claims, building credibility in the wake of efforts on behalf of Holocaust survivors, gained unprecedented visibility in the atmosphere of the 1990s.[40] To the extent that symbolic reparations were pursued there were positive results in the form of acknowledgments, apologies, and media attentions to past injustices.

Remoteness definitely limited the capacity of such claimants to implement the very broad legal imperative to give victims remedies for harms endured, but it did not formally preclude relief. There was no statute of limitations applicable to bar claims. Those with limited claims and a small constituency, most notably Japanese-Americans who had suffered enforced detention in World War II, were recipients of nominal compensation payments.[41] These payments were important to the victims as much, if not more so, as acknowledgments of past injustice, that is, as symbolic reparations in the sense of acknowledgment and apology even though a nominal payment was involved. In contrast, descendants of slaves, although receiving some satisfaction, including a legal affirmation in authoritative global settings that slavery constituted a crime against humanity, have not been able to gain satisfaction in the form of compensation.[42] Unlike the case of Japanese-Americans where compensation was not a huge financial tax on the present and unlike Holocaust survivors who had formal American pressures behind them (which appeared to push the Swiss banks and others into accommodating gestures), indigenous peoples and descendants of slaves found themselves without political leverage, despite generating significant moral pressures arising from the documentation of horrendous past atrocities. Beyond this, redress in these latter instances would have been economically and politically disruptive, imposing a major and politically unacceptable burden on present public revenue flows.

Absence of Individuation

The magnitude of the harm done, especially when directed at a large class of victims, makes it impractical to evaluate individual claims on a case-by-case basis in most instances, and therefore is not consistent with the international law approach based on the individual that is embedded in human rights.[43] It has been historically possible under certain circumstances to create claims commissions to deal with efforts to achieve restitution of property and compensation arrangements, as was done in relation to the Iranian Revolution and the first Gulf War. In both instances, there were large pools of resources available that belonged to the accused governments, as well as antagonistic international attitudes toward the government that was being charged with improper taking of private property rights. And redress for claimants did not impose any burdens on the states that established the reparations mechanism, which distinguishes the situation from those where payment of reparations would be imposed from within. That is, the geopolitical climate was supportive of efforts to implement reparations on an individuated basis in Iran and Iraq. But these instances are the exception rather than the rule. No such redress occurs when the accused government is victorious or beyond the reach of the international community, as has been the case in relation to the USA, considering the wrongs associated with its conduct of wars in Vietnam, Panama, Afghanistan, and Iraq in the course of the last forty years, as well as in relation to both world wars of the twentieth century.

More common are those many circumstances in a wide range of countries where an oppressive past has been finally repudiated by a new political leadership, but not necessarily in a conclusive fashion. Beyond this, there are neither the administrative nor financial capabilities to process claims on an individual basis, particularly if the abuses do not involve property rights that can be established by the claimants. In such circumstances, the dynamic of redress has tended to emphasize accountability for the main perpetrators of atrocities and a collective truth-telling procedure for the community of victims, especially reliance on truth and reconciliation commissions.[44] Reparations are certainly not excluded, but they have not been consistently part of the process, and rarely reach the majority of victims except in pitifully small amounts. In Latin America several countries have implemented significant reparations programs, including Argentina, Chile, and Brazil, others have made efforts that are more than token. Reparations have received less attention than efforts at criminalizing the perpetrators of gross wrongs, but have been at least as significant an aspect of attempts at overall rectification.

Generality of Obligation

Any attempt to evolve a law-centered approach to reparations must accept the frequent inability to specify the level of responsibility with the kind of precision that makes it more likely that equal circumstances will be treated equally. Of course, this difficulty with reparations should not be exaggerated, and it should be appreciated that the more demanding rules of evidence and standards of persuasion that apply to criminal prosecution make problems of ascertaining responsibility and entitlement with respect to reparations somewhat manageable. The provision of reparations, however constructed, usually must depend in the end on a rule of reason, which accords those who administer the program, whether judicially or administratively, wide discretionary authority. Only where the idea of full compensation for losses is sustained, as in Kuwait after the Gulf War, is there operational guidance for those making decisions. Or where uniform payments are decreed, which overlook the unevenness of harm sustained, as with compensation accorded to Japanese-Americans detained during World War II, is specificity attained. In other settings, the legal mandate to award reparations operates in a manner similar to other areas of the law where the specific and the general are only loosely connected, as when such standards as 'due process' or 'the reasonable person' are used to judge legal responsibility in particular circumstances. Where the number of claimants is very large, there is a greater disposition to rely on administrative procedures that compensate victims by category of harm, and usually with no pretension that the level of reparations corresponds to the level of harm. Again, the human rights approach based on individual rights challenges this flexibility.

Extreme Selectivity

To the extent that reparation claims are given support in national legal systems, there are present critical geopolitical factors that inhibit any kind of standardization of treatment. It is one thing to initiate litigation to give some remedial relief to Holocaust victims, but it would be inconceivable that comparable relief, even of a symbolic character, were to be accorded to Indochinese victims of the Vietnam War or to Palestinian victims of Israeli abuses of international human rights and international humanitarian law during the period of extended occupation of the West Bank and Gaza. The victims require political leverage, and the target of remedial abuse must be discredited or defeated for such remedies to exist. Whenever geopolitical factors become relevant to the application of legal standards, the issue of legitimacy casts a shadow over discussions of legality, especially because selective implementation means that equals cannot be and are not treated as equals. Should such a realization be allowed to taint those applications of law that can be explained by reference to geopolitical patterns of influence?[45]

5. WHAT INTERNATIONAL LAW CAN DO

So far the emphasis has been placed on the limitations of international law in relation to the imposition of obligations to provide reparations to victims of past injustices and deprivations of rights, especially in the setting of transitions to democracy. But international law also has contributed to a generalized atmosphere of support, a reparations ethos, for compensating victims as part of its overall dedication to global justice and the enforcement of claims, and thus lends support to the domestic willingness to provide reparations when contextual factors are favorable. Beyond this, international law is part of the normative context, giving a higher level of credence to victims and their supporters who insist on reparations as part of a new political regime of 'fairness'. Such a change in the climate of credibility with respect to claims of reparations for past wrongs is perhaps most evident in the greater seriousness accorded to the grievances associated with the descendants of slaves and the representatives of indigenous peoples. These claims had previously been hardly ever mentioned in influential settings, being treated as too frivolous to warrant attention, much less action.

International law also helps by clarifying those forms of governmental abuse that constitute international crimes, and therefore cannot be shielded from legal accountability.[46] Certainly, the establishment of the International Criminal Court (ICC) is a step in the direction of accountability for perpetrators, and by its provisions of funds for reparations of victims, there is an agreed-upon framework that should exert an indirect influence upon those transitions to democracy that occur against an established background of gross abuse and international criminality. That is, by linking accountability for perpetrators to compensation for victims there is encoded in international law a conception of fairness and rectification of past harm that includes victims.[47] This is a major conceptual step forward, with policy consequences, although disappointments also arise to the extent that compensatory steps are either trivial in relation to the quantum of harm endured or are never implemented beyond nominal awards.[48] Perhaps the most important impact of this level of generalized obligation is to influence the approach of national legal systems, which in any event have the most opportunity to actualize international standards, including those associated with human rights, in relation to the persons who endured the wrongs or their representatives. To the extent that national programs of reparations are enacted, there are expectations generated that a transition to democracy is incomplete if it does not include efforts to address as well as possible, given contextual constraints, the harms endured by victims of a prior oppressive regime. At the same time, there exists a margin of appreciation that allows a given national government a wide range of discretion in determining what it is reasonable to appropriate for the satisfaction of past claimants.

To the extent corrective justice is taken into account, then the pressure to overcome the culture of impunity relating to transitions to democracy is of at least symbolic benefit to the victims, as well as to their families and friends. The difficulties of providing material compensation are offset to some extent by publicly and officially acknowledging past abuses, documenting the record of wrongdoing associated with a prior regime, discrediting perpetrators while expressing solidarity with a community of victims, issuing apologies, and challenging self-serving grants of amnesty. In this process, not only is the harm to those most victimized repudiated as wrong, but the general public is educated about the limits on permissible behavior by governments.

Given the degree to which transitions to democracy are carried on within national legal frameworks, where the contours of arrangements are determined exclusively by reference to domestic law, the role of international law is inherently limited. Of course, to the extent that international human rights and criminal law are internalized, they push the national approach, in circumstances of transitional justice, in the direction of providing 'just compensation' for victims as determined contextually. Beyond this, international law could impose obligations on states and other actors to provide financial capabilities via the ICC, and elsewhere, to enable those countries with limited resources and very widespread claims of victimization to receive special credits and loans for the purpose of satisfying certain categories of victimization. Whether such an undertaking could fit within the mandate of existing international financial institutions such as the World Bank or IMF is doubtful, but a special commission could be created within the UN system to receive voluntary contributions earmarked for such purposes. The record to date is not encouraging if the UN Voluntary Fund for Victims of Torture established by GA Res. 36/151 on December 16, 1981, is taken as indicative. The Fund receives contributions from governments, nongovernmental organizations, and individuals, but has managed to raise only $54 million during its entire course since coming into existence in 1983. Another possibility, undoubtedly remote, would be to affix a 'Tobin Tax' on international currency transactions or on activities that pollute the commons, such as commercial jet international travel, thereby providing a pool of funds to be used to bolster the capabilities to realize the goals of corrective justice in transitional societies and other circumstances where international victimization has occurred. This kind of mechanism could also be used to address categories of claimants on a group basis, thereby circumventing the extraordinary bureaucratic burdens associated with judicial and administrative approaches that are based on assessing the merits of individualized claims.

NOTES

1. For review of this dynamic see Falk, 'Reviving the 1990s Trend toward Transnational Justice: Innovations and Institutions', *Journal of Human Development* 3 (2) (2002): 169–97.

2. See Falk, 'Assessing the Pinochet Legislation: Whither Universal Jurisdiction?' and the reply by Pablo de Greiff, 'Universal Jurisdiction and Transitions to Democracy', in *Universal Jurisdiction: National Courts and the Prosecution of Serious Crimes Under International Law*, Stephen Macedo, ed. (Philadelphia, PA: University of Pennsylvania Press, 2004).

3. The conclusion of the Independent International Commission on Kosovo was that the action was 'legitimate' (as it prevented an imminent instance of ethnic cleansing), but 'illegal' (as it lacked a required UNSC mandate). See the report of the commission, *The Kosovo Report: Conflict, International Response, Lessons Learned* (Oxford: Oxford University Press, 2000); along similar lines, but with a more comprehensive approach, see the report of the International Commission on Intervention and State Sovereignty, *The Responsibility to Protect* (Ottawa, Canada: International Development Research Centre, 2001).

4. Elazar Barkan, *The Guilt of Nations: Restitution and Negotiating Historical Injustices* (New York: Norton, 2000), ix.

5. In this collection, de Greiff defends a nuanced position with respect to the issue of the relationship between reparations and international law: the main point is that what international law has to say about this issue is still mostly geared to the case-by-case resolution of claims, and that both this and the (related) adoption of *restitutio in integrum* as the criterion of justice in reparations, make the guidance provided by international law less than clear when the task is to create a massive program. See de Greiff, 'Justice and Reparations' (Chapter 12, this volume).

6. For a consideration of this dynamic of distraction see Falk, *The Great Terror War* (Northampton, MA: Olive Branch Press, 2003); also, Falk, 'Reviving Global Civil Society after September 11', in *Traditions, Values, and Humanitarian Action*, Kevin M. Cahill, ed. (Fordham, NY: Fordham University Press, 2003), 344–67.

7. Even in the aftermath of the Afghanistan War and the Iraq War there does not seem to be a disposition to set up a procedure to provide reparations for the numerous victims of these brutal regimes. Unlike after World War II or the Gulf War, the main goals of the occupying powers, aside from selective criminal prosecution of the leaders of the former regime, seem to involve the establishment of stability and a sense of normalcy.

8. Of course, there are a series of affirmations of a legal obligation to compensate victims of abuses that can be found in such influential documents as Article 8 of the Universal Declaration of Human Rights, Articles 2(3), 9(5), 14 of the International Covenant on Civil and Political Rights, Article 14 of the UN Convention against Torture, and Article 6 of the International Convention on the Elimination of All Forms of Racial Discrimination, as well as the elaborate consideration of victims' rights in the Statute of the International Criminal Court. See also Theo van Boven, 'Basic Principles and Guidelines', E/CN.4/2000/62, January 18, 2000. It is to be noted that most of the assertions of this right to compensation situate the remedy within national legal systems. With the

exception of the ICC approach there is no attempt at an *international* remedial option made available to a victim even in the event that there is no meaningful national remedy. The Basic Principles document, in Principle 12, affirms the victim's right to pursue a remedy in all legal arenas 'under existing domestic laws as well as under international law', but without any clarification as to how such rights can be upheld in concrete circumstances. States are obliged to '[m]ake available all appropriate diplomatic and legal means to ensure that victims exercise their rights to a remedy and reparation for violations of international human rights or humanitarian law'.

9. Case concerning the Factory at Chorzow, 1927 P.C.I.J. (Ser. A) No. 9, at 29; in explaining the bearing of international law I have adapted the framework clearly set forth by Max du Plessis, 'Historical Injustice and International Law: An Exploratory Discussion of Reparation for Slavery', *Human Rights Quarterly* 25 (2003): 624–59.

10. 'On the Legal Consequences of the Construction of a Wall in the Occupied Palestinian Territories', ICJ Reports, July 9, 2004, para. 152.

11. Mavrommatis Palestine Concessions Case (*Greece v. UK*), 1924 P.C.I.J. Reports (Ser. A) No. 2, at 12; for fuller account see Ian Brownlie, *Principles of Public International Law*, 3rd edn. (New York: Oxford University Press, 1982).

12. For the definitive account of the ILC treatment of reparations see James Crawford, *The International Law Commission's Articles on State Responsibility: Introduction, Text and Commentaries* (Cambridge: Cambridge University Press, 2002); for useful assessment see Dinah Shelton, 'Righting Wrongs: Reparations in the Articles on State Responsibilities', *American Journal of International Law* 96 (4) (2002): 833–56. Professor Shelton asserts that these draft articles, that is, not yet in the form of an international convention, combine persuasively the descriptive function of 'codification' with the prescriptive function of 'progressive development' in accord with the mission of the International Law Commission. She also confirms the influence of this statement of the law despite its lack of a formally obligatory character, including extensive reliance by the International Court of Justice in its decisions, and by parties in their submissions.

13. The Temple Case, 1962, ICJ, 6.

14. See 'On the Legal Consequences', para. 152.

15. du Plessis, op. cit., at 631.

16. See especially GA Res. 1803, December 14, 1962, Res. 3171, December 17, 1973; also Declaration on the Right to Development, December 4, 1986.

17. For a careful study of reparations in the Inter-American Human Rights System see Carrillo (Chapter 14, this volume).

18. Which is one of the conclusions at which de Greiff, Segovia, and others in this volume arrive.

19. For a sense of the professional viewpoint on reparations associated with international law practice see Shelton, op. cit. A typical view of the Versailles approach, primarily because the reparations features were regarded as symbolically humiliating and substantively burdensome for Germany and Germans, and thereby leading to a backlash, is the following: 'The Treaty of Versailles...represented a peace without justice. The desire of the First World War victors to seek revenge against the vanquished is widely believed to have contributed to conditions which led to the Second World War.' Stuart Rees, *Passion for Peace* (Sydney: New South Wales University Press, 2003), 21. Of course, it would be simplistic to explain the rise of Hitler by reference only to an extremist reaction to Versailles. See Hannah Arendt, *The Origins of Totalitarianism*

(London: Allen and Unwin, 1951). For a recent inquiry into the origins of 'radical evil' as a political reality see Ira Katznelson, *Desolation and Enlightenment: Political Knowledge After Total War, Totalitarianism, and The Holocaust* (New York: Columbia University Press, 2003).

20. The issue of punishment and responsibility was individualized after World War II, as exemplified by the Nuremberg trials. See the instructive account in Gary Jonathan Bass, *Stay the Hand of Vengeance: The Politics of War Crimes Tribunals* (Princeton, NJ: Princeton University Press, 2000), esp. 14–205. For the international law foundations of the Nuremberg approach see Richard Falk, Gabriel Kolko, and Robert Jay Lifton, eds., *Crimes of War* (New York: Random House, 1971), 73–176. The lesson of Versailles was reinforced by geopolitical considerations that regarded the reconstruction of Germany (and Japan) as an essential element in the containment of the Soviet Union as the cold war unfolded and came to dominate the political imagination of those shaping the policies of leading Western states in the 1940s and 1950s.

21. See the study of the UNCC by van Houtte et al. (Chapter 9, this volume); and David Bederman, 'The UN Compensation Commission and the Tradition of International Claims Assessment', *NYU Journal of International Law and Politics* 27 (1) (1998).

22. For a range of critical assessments of sanctions imposed on Iraq see Anthony Arnove, ed., *Iraq Under Siege: The Deadly Impact of Sanctions and War* (Cambridge, MA: South End Press, 2000); a broader perspective is to be found in David Cortright and George A. Lopez, eds., *The Sanctions Decade: Assessing UN Strategies in the 1990s* (Boulder, CO: Lynne Rienner, 2000), esp. 37–61. Also, Falk, 'Iraq, the United States, and International Law: Beyond the Sanctions', in *Iraq: The Human Cost of History*, Tareq Ismail and William W. Haddad, eds. (London: Pluto Press, 2004).

23. See Michael J. Bazyler, 'Nuremberg in America: Litigating the Holocaust in United States Courts', *University of Richmond Law Review* 34 (1) (2000). For a general study see Gregg J. Richman, *Swiss Banks and Jewish Souls* (New Brunswick, NJ: Transaction, 1999).

24. See Richard B. Lillich, *International Claims: Their Adjudication by National Commissions* (Syracuse, NY: Syracuse University Press, 1962) on the nationality of claims, and their discretionary prosecution, as well as international practice; discussed earlier in this chapter.

25. The role of sovereignty in creating sanctuaries for state wrongs is impressively depicted in Ken Booth, 'Human Wrongs and International Relations', *International Affairs* 71 (1) (1993): 103–26.

26. This argument is set forth in greater detail in Falk, 'The Challenges of Humane Governance', in *Concepts and Strategies in International Human Rights*, George J. Andreopoulos, ed. (New York: Peter Lang, 2002), 21–50; for scholarly treatment that fails to address this hypothesis of nonimplementation see Johannes Morsink, *The Universal Declaration of Human Rights: Origins, Drafting, Intent* (Philadelphia, PA: University of Pennsylvania Press, 1999).

27. For various aspects of this evolution see Andreopoulos, op. cit.; also Falk, *Human Rights Horizons: The Prospect of Justice in a Globalizing World* (New York: Routledge, 2000); for theoretical inquiry into the expanding status of individual rights see Jack Donnelly, *Universal Human Rights: In Theory & Practice* (Ithaca, NY: Cornell University Press, 2003); the most comprehensive assessment of this trend can be found in Henry J. Steiner and Philip Alston, eds., *International Human Rights in Context*, 2nd edn. (New York: Oxford University Press, 2000).

28. Donnelly makes this point strongly.

29. For a pioneering study of legitimacy see Thomas M. Franck, *The Power of Legitimacy among Nations* (New York: Oxford University Press, 1990); further elaborated and explored in impressive detail in Thomas M. Franck, *Fairness in International Law and Institutions* (New York: Oxford University Press, 1995). Despite the sweep of coverage in this latter study, Franck gives no attention whatsoever to issues of corrective justice, and limits his relevant coverage to issues of 'fairness' associated with alien property claims (453–73).

30. Of course, from another perspective, Germany after 1945 could be described in a similar manner, but Germany was taking steps in the aftermath of a devastating military and political defeat, and in the midst of a foreign occupation, to restore its standing as a legitimate state. It seems like an antecedent case to that of victim-oriented reparations as conferred by Latin American legal initiatives. See the studies on German reparations by Ariel Colonomos and Andrea Armstrong (Chapter 10, this volume) and John Authers (Chapter 11, this volume).

31. Although not so formulated, this jurisprudence derives from the work of the New Haven School, especially Myres McDougal, Harold Lasswell, and Michael Reisman. For the most comprehensive overview see McDougal and Lasswell, *Jurisprudence for a Free Society: Studies in Law, Science and Policy* (New Haven, CT: Yale University Press, 1992). A constructivist account of political and conceptual reality is most explicitly set forth by Alexander Wendt in *Social Theory of International Politics* (Cambridge: Cambridge University Press, 1999).

32. Reparations can also be conceived, in part, as punitive, or at least directed toward burdening perpetrators with obligations. For insightful discussion of some of these issues see Martha Minow, *Between Vengeance and Forgiveness: Facing History After Genocide and Mass Violence* (Boston, MA: Beacon, 1998).

33. See the study of South African reparations by Colvin (Chapter 5, this volume).

34. For one such example, see the study of reparations in Malawi by Cammack (Chapter 6, this volume).

35. A harm-based conception is more in accord with ideas of corrective justice, treating the victim as an autonomous subject entitled to compensation, at least to the extent otherwise feasible.

36. The issue of intertemporality is carefully considered by du Plessis, op. cit., in relation to efforts to obtain reparations on behalf of descendants of slaves. Interesting issues are posed as to the nature of victimization, and whether the grant of reparations, even in symbolic amounts, would not heal the inherited wounds of slavery and past forms of racial persecution and discrimination.

37. See study by Authers (Chapter 11, this volume).

38. Quoted in 'Satisfaction not Guaranteed', a review of books on the Holocaust dynamic by John Authers, *Financial Times*, August 23, 2003.

39. Among the treatments of this process see Stuart Eizenstat, *Imperfect Justice* (New York: Public Affairs Press, 2003); Michael Bazyler, *Holocaust Justice* (New York: New York University Press, 2003); and for a skeptical account see Norman Finkelstein, *The Holocaust Industry* (London: Verso, 2000).

40. These claims categories are included in Barkan, op. cit., and du Plessis, op. cit.; see also Falk, 'Reviving the 1990s Trend toward Transnational Justice', op. cit.

41. See study on reparations for Japanese-Americans by Yamamoto and Ebesugawa (Chapter 7, this volume).

42. For instance, in the declaration adopted at the 2001 Durban UN Conference on Racism and Development. It is notable that the US government withdrew its delegation from the conference, partly to protest criticism of Israel and partly because of reparation claims advanced in relation to the condemnation of slavery. On this issue generally see du Plessis, op. cit., for extensive treatment.

43. de Greiff spells out the possible consequences of a case-by-case approach (Chapter 12, this volume).

44. For an admirable overview see Priscilla B. Hayner, *Unspeakable Truths: Confronting State Terror and Atrocity* (New York: Routledge, 2001).

45. It should be noted that this same selectivity applies in many crucial areas of international law, including that of humanitarian intervention, regulation of nonproliferation of weaponry of mass destruction, and enforcement of UN Security Council resolutions. It is an aspect of the balancing act that conjoins law and power within *any* social order, but its influence is more salient and pronounced in relation to global policy concerns.

46. See a useful overview in Geoffrey Robertson, *Crimes Against Humanity: The Struggle for Global Justice* (New York: Norton, 1999).

47. For an analysis of reparations and the ICC see Pablo de Greiff and Marieke Wierda, 'The Trust Fund for Victims of the International Criminal Court: Between Possibilities and Constraints', in *Out of the Ashes: Reparation for Victims of Gross and Systematic Human Rights Violations*, Marc Bossuyt, Paul Lemmens, Koen de Feyter, and Stephan Parmentier, eds. (Antwerp: Intersentia, 2005).

48. Such nominal forms of satisfaction can be worse than nothing to the extent that the claimant continues to feel the anguish associated with harm while the impression is spread that reparative justice has been rendered, setting the stage for reconciliation.

CHAPTER 14

JUSTICE IN CONTEXT:
THE RELEVANCE OF
INTER-AMERICAN
HUMAN RIGHTS LAW
AND PRACTICE TO
REPAIRING THE PAST[1]

ARTURO J. CARRILLO

1. INTRODUCTION

This chapter examines the question of how international law contributes to contemporary understandings of transitional justice with respect to reparations for victims of gross and systematic human rights abuses. Transitional justice can be defined as 'the conception of justice associated with periods of political change, characterized by legal responses to confront the wrongdoing of repressive predecessor regimes'.[2] As conditions have changed globally and locally over time, so too have the objectives and methods that characterize the conception of justice during periods of political transition. Historically, what today is commonly referred to as transitional justice dates back to the post-World War II era, starting with the Nuremberg Trials. At Nuremberg and in the other postwar trials, human rights abuses were criminalized by the victorious Allies through the invocation of universal norms and the international rule of law to secure individual accountability for wartime atrocities. This postwar justice, though not limited to criminal proceedings, had a distinctly retributive flavor.[3]

In the final quarter of the twentieth century, transitional justice became a central theme of the political transformations taking place *within* states. This new context produced new challenges. In Latin America and elsewhere the leaders of countries transitioning from dictatorship to democracy found it necessary to forgo criminal prosecutions as a rule 'in favor of alternative methods of truth-seeking and accountability', most notably truth commissions.[4] After the end of the cold war similar situations of political change arose in response to the waves of democratization that followed the demise of the Soviet Union. By the beginning of the twenty-first century, the concept of transitional justice was evolving from one largely defined by Nuremberg-style international justice and punishment to one contingent on local conditions associated with democratization and nation-building. In this context, the pursuit of criminal accountability, though still very much a part of the transitional calculus, had been found in practice to be highly problematic. For new and reforming democratic regimes, prosecutions for past atrocities generated complex legal problems and deep political tensions within society that tended to conflict with the overriding objectives of consolidating democratic institutions, securing peace, and promoting national reconciliation.

The rise to prominence of the truth commission during this period was emblematic of the growing debate juxtaposing truth and reconciliation with accountability, sometimes referred to as the 'truth versus justice' dichotomy.[5] To a great extent, truth commissions came to reflect the shift in emphasis away from retribution and towards more restorative and reparatory aims in the fashioning of transitional justice policy. Transitional justice issues 'were framed in terms more comprehensive than simply confronting or holding accountable the predecessor regime, and included questions about how to heal an entire society and incorporate diverse rule of law values, such as peace and reconciliation, that had previously been treated as largely external to the transitional justice project'.[6] Local political forces and the goals associated with achieving a stable democratic regime became the primary factors defining the course of political transitions and shaping their conception of postconflict justice.

Towards the end of the last century, the difficulties involved in securing criminal accountability domestically and the emergence of the 'truth versus justice' debate had called into question the role of law during periods of radical political change. Even so, international law had continued to exert a normative influence on the policies of transitional states searching for justice in context. Indeed, during this period international law itself underwent a radical transformation through the development of a new and far-reaching human rights jurisprudence. At the forefront of the legal revolution was the Inter-American Court of Human Rights, which in a landmark case decided in 1988 dramatically expanded and defined the duties of states in redressing past wrongdoing. The Court's decision in the *Velásquez-Rodríguez* case was the first to articulate the duty to prevent, investigate and punish human rights violations alongside the state's separate duty to make moral and material reparations to individual victims. The judgment introduced a new legal paradigm of justice for human rights violations by illuminating the interaction between criminal and civil remedies and establishing that even where punishment was unavailable, other legal responsibilities were owed to victims in the form of reparations, especially compensation.

No subject better encapsulates the legal and political dilemmas of transitional justice than reparations. The *Velásquez-Rodríguez* case, which dealt with forced disappearances in Honduras, established new ground rules with respect to reparations that were 'manifestly transitional', i.e. directly relevant to situations of political transformation involving past wrongdoing by prior regimes.[7] The decision had an enormous impact on the processes of political transformation ongoing in various Latin American countries at the time. In Chile, President Patricio Aylwin, based on the national Truth and Reconciliation Commission's 1991 report, accepted responsibility for the prior regime's wrongdoing on behalf of the state and assumed the corresponding obligation to pay reparations.[8] President Aylwin's promises to carry out an official investigation into military abuses and the implementation by his government of a range of reparatory measures conformed de facto to the *Velásquez-Rodríguez* framework. In fact, Chile not only adopted an innovative compensation program but also took novel steps to provide moral reparations for victims who were killed or disappeared and their families.[9] The Chilean experience can be said to reflect the new international human rights law principles on individual reparations in repairing a legacy of widespread human rights abuses in the context of a nation's political transition and its struggle to come to terms with the past.

The government of Carlos Menem in Argentina after 1989 was similarly susceptible to legal pressure by the Inter-American human rights system. It eventually adopted a compensation scheme that was broader and more generous than Chile's. In 1992, after three years of litigation, the Inter-American Commission on Human Rights, relying on the Court's decision in *Velásquez-Rodríguez*, found that several laws adopted by Argentina to foreclose the possibility of criminal investigations of official abuses were incompatible with the American Convention on Human Rights and international law. In that case, the Commission affirmed 'the right [of victims] to be compensated by the State for its failure to ensure the right to life, human treatment and freedom [as well as for] the denial of justice that was the legal consequence of the laws...at issue'.[10] The litigation, which involved a number of related cases consolidated into one by the Commission, provided impetus to the intense debate around reparations ongoing in Argentina at the time, with positive results. The government of Carlos Menem eventually implemented a series of legal measures establishing one of the most generous and comprehensive compensation regimes ever.[11]

It is important to stress that the influence of Inter-American jurisprudence during this period was not limited to policymakers and government officials. Victims and other civil society actors seeking justice for serious human rights violations were also impacted. In late 1988 the human rights movement in Argentina began to debate the question of reparations for forced disappearances, which generated a resistance among certain victims' groups uncomfortable with the notion of receiving monetary payments as compensation for the disappearance of their loved ones. The idea was rejected by many victims as being tantamount to accepting 'blood money' from the government to buy off their claims to justice; many viewed it as an unacceptable trade on the disappeared family member's life. Most (though not all) of the victims' groups in opposition to the idea of economic reparations changed their position when it was made clear to them that, under international law, any state responsible for violating human rights had a *duty* to pay compensation to the victims and their families. This, of course, was the rule that had recently been articulated by the Inter-American Court in *Velásquez-Rodríguez*. The result was much needed public support for the ambitious plans of the Menem government to compensate the families of the disappeared.[12]

The ruling in *Velásquez-Rodríguez* and its subsequent development by the Inter-American Court and Inter-American Commission have continued to contribute to our understanding of reparatory justice. These are the two principal organs of the regional human rights system erected by the Organization of American States (OAS). The law and practice of the Inter-American system on the subject of reparations for individual human rights violations are the most advanced of any international legal regime.[13] Though scholars have studied rule-of-law values and their complex interaction with the search for justice during political transitions, none has engaged in a comprehensive study of the Inter-American system for this purpose. This chapter is intended to fill this lacuna. It considers what guidance contemporary international human rights law can contribute to the eminently political challenge of providing adequate reparations to the victims of past repression and mass atrocity.

In this chapter I survey the jurisprudence and current practice of the Inter-American human rights system to shed new light on the process through which transitional societies address certain fundamental questions relating to reparatory justice. How can fair compensation for gross and systematic human rights violations be made to the victims of such atrocities? What elements and values in international law are relevant to the process of shaping reparatory policies during political transitions? Which are not? As a practical matter, how can the appropriate elements and values be applied to meet the legitimate expectations of victims and achieve acceptable levels of justice? How do these elements and values contribute to securing the broader restorative goals of transitional reparations policy? Because the Inter-American system focuses on individual case litigation it cannot answer or even address all of the difficult questions arising from the design of a mass reparations program. It nevertheless offers an underexplored source of insight and inspiration in the analysis of the difficult issues raised by the aforementioned questions.

To most observers, the exacting standards for legal reparations in specific cases decided under international law cannot and should not be reproduced *in toto* when designing programs seeking to redress widespread human rights abuses. Pablo de Greiff in particular has argued that such 'reparations programs' are predominantly, and rightly, products of the political process. He views the international law of reparations for human rights violations in individual cases as representing an ideal that, if followed rigorously, would tend to complicate rather than clarify the duty of successor regimes and policymakers when confronting the complex realities of designing a mass reparations program. For example, de Greiff points to the pragmatic difficulties that would arise with the importation into the domestic political realm of international legal ideals like the principle of *restitutio in integrum*, which would require in most cases the payment of 'full' monetary compensation to the countless victims produced by gross and systematic human rights abuses.[14] He is not alone in believing that such a measure in most circumstances would be neither economically nor politically viable; it could to the contrary prove to be disastrous given the enormous drain it would place on the state's financial and political resources.[15] In short, based on strong arguments of practical necessity, most commentators argue against the excessive convergence of the two spheres (juridical/international and political/domestic) in the design of reparations programs for the aggregated victims of past wrongdoing.

It is true that a direct extrapolation of reparations jurisprudence under international human rights law to the primarily political plane on which most reparations programs are designed may be unworkable and counterproductive in many respects. But that is the starting point, not the end, of our inquiry. Few would dispute the predominance of politics in shaping modern conceptions of transitional justice. Yet international law has continued to play an important role in defining these conceptions as well, not least through the consolidation of the Nuremberg legacy in the establishment of the International Criminal Court. International norms have also contributed to shaping the national constitutions and legislation of numerous transitional societies since World War II. Similarly, international human rights law, despite its particular contextual framework, remains a pertinent source of inspiration for national actors engaged in the process of defining policies of reparatory justice during political transitions. By analyzing Inter-American jurisprudence in detail and observing its influence on modern conceptions of transitional justice in Latin America, I intend to illustrate the role international human rights law can—and cannot—play in guiding governments and societies confronted by the challenge of designing a mass reparations program.

In this chapter I survey the case law of the Inter-American Court through 2003. The paper emphasizes when and how monetary compensation is awarded by the Inter-American human rights system, since that is traditionally the preferred method of making reparations under international law. It also highlights certain basic principles recognized as guarantees of fairness in the adjudication of individual cases with respect to reparations.

2. Reparations and the Inter-American Human Rights System

This section provides a technical analysis of the Inter-American system's practice and jurisprudence around reparations in the context of individual human rights cases. The Inter-American experience demonstrates how this system has developed and applied international law principles to redress human rights violations in practice. Under the aegis of the Inter-American Court, the American Convention's duty to provide compensation to persons injured in breach of its protections has evolved dramatically since *Velásquez-Rodríguez* was decided in 1988, with potentially far-reaching implications for the field of transitional justice. In the concluding observations to this second section, I analyze the legal principles and practices of the Inter-American system to determine which, if any, are relevant to the broader analysis of achieving justice through the design and implementation of mass reparations programs. Building upon this foundation, I return in the final section to the basic questions raised in the introduction regarding how reparatory justice may best be defined in the context of widespread or systematic human rights violations.

Prior to surveying the Court's jurisprudence and the Commission's practice, it is necessary to introduce some of the relevant rules and procedures involved.[16] The American Convention recognizes two main tribunals: the Inter-American Commission and the Inter-American Court of Human Rights. The Commission receives 'petitions containing denunciations or complaints of violation of [the] Convention by a state party'.[17] Its functions in relevant part are to receive communications from individual victims, process and investigate their claims, and propose diplomatic solutions which, if unsuccessful, open the door to invoking the Court's judicial authority. Petitions may be lodged by any person (individually or collectively) or by any nongovernmental entity of a member state of the American Convention. For the Commission to process a complaint, the petitioner must meet a number of threshold requirements, including the exhaustion of domestic remedies prescribed in Convention Article 46. Once the complaint is lodged, the Commission is authorized by the Convention to request information concerning the petition from the respondent state and, if possible, to mediate between the parties and broker a friendly settlement. If unsuccessful in bringing the parties together voluntarily, the Commission will draft a preliminary nonpublic report setting forth its findings and recommendations, to which the state must respond.

In situations where the state concerned does not accept or implement the confidential report's findings and recommendations, the Commission may submit the matter to the Inter-American Court for formal adjudication if the state has agreed to be subject to the Court's jurisdiction. Or it may decide instead to publish the final report pursuant to Convention Article 51, which authorizes such action. Only states party to the American Convention, or the Commission, may present a case directly to the Court, whose rulings are final and binding. Unlike the judgments of the Inter-American Court, or those of other tribunals set up under international law, the Commission's findings and recommendations are neither binding nor, in cases taken to the Court, final.[18] This, of course, does not mean that the Commission's recommendations are without legal weight. As both the primary human rights authority of the Organization of American States under the OAS Charter, and a treaty body granted jurisdictional functions by the American Convention, the Commission is unquestionably a source of authoritative legal interpretation within the system.

Reparations and the Jurisprudence of the Inter-American Court of Human Rights

The Inter-American Court has recognized that its judgments on reparations are governed by international law in all respects: scope, nature, modality, and determination of beneficiaries. When a state violates an international obligation it is legally bound to respect, it is held responsible for the wrongful act and all its harmful effects, which the state is consequently under a duty to repair. As regards the violations of human rights in individual cases, the offending state is bound under international law to grant victims 'adequate, effective and prompt reparations'.[19] Where such a violation takes place and the state is held responsible, the victim is entitled to reparations regardless of whether the perpetrator has been identified, apprehended, prosecuted or convicted. Nor is a person's status as a 'victim' under these circumstances affected by any relationship that might exist or may have existed between the victim and the perpetrator of the violation.[20] It should be noted that the Court has reiterated in its judgments that none of the international rules governing the subject of reparations may be altered or disregarded by invoking provisions of the state's domestic law.[21]

States have a duty not only to respect the internationally protected human rights of their subjects, but also to guarantee them the full and free exercise and enjoyment of those rights. A state, in other words, must exercise 'due diligence' under international human rights law, which means that it 'has a legal duty to take reasonable steps to prevent human rights violations and to use the means at its disposal to carry out a serious investigation of violations committed within its jurisdiction, to identify those responsible, to impose the appropriate punishment and to ensure the victim adequate compensation'.[22] Consequently, the state may still be held responsible even where the violation alleged was committed by a private or unidentified person and is therefore not directly imputable to the state. Such is the case where the state either failed to exercise 'due diligence' to prevent the violation or did not respond adequately to investigate and punish those responsible.[23] This obligation, which was first articulated judicially by the Inter-American Court in the *Velásquez-Rodríguez* case, is significant because it establishes the principle that human rights abuses committed by private, nonstate or unidentified actors may under certain circumstances give rise to state responsibility and thus the duty to provide reparations to the victims of those abuses.

Though regulated by international law principles, Article 63(1) of the American Convention furnishes the immediate authority for the Inter-American system's reparations regime. This article declares that

[i]f the [Inter-American] Court finds that there has been a violation of a right or freedom protected by this Convention, the Court shall rule that the injured party be ensured the enjoyment of his right or freedom that was violated. It shall also rule, if appropriate, that the consequences of the measure or situation that constituted the breach of such right or freedom be remedied and that fair compensation be paid to the injured party.

There are three types of remedy contemplated in Article 63. The first is a kind of injunctive relief, which is an order from the Court to act, or desist from acting, in order to prevent harm from occurring to persons involved in a case.[24] The other two remedies relate to reparations for injuries sustained as a result of a state's illegal conduct. They refer essentially to adjustments in the social and legal structures that gave rise to the violations, and to fair compensation for the persons aggrieved.[25] The remainder of this section focuses on the second and third types of remedies mandated by Article 63(1), with special consideration for the Court's extensive practice of awarding monetary compensation.

Reparations

The Inter-American Court views reparations as the generic term encompassing the various ways in which a state found responsible can make amends for its wrongful acts in compliance with its obligations under the American Convention. It has interpreted Convention Article 63(1) in light of international law to authorize a broad array of reparatory measures intended, among other things, to guarantee victims 'fair compensation' for pecuniary and nonpecuniary (moral) damages, as well as a degree of reimbursement for costs and expenses. Reparations under international law fall into a number of categories which are useful in analyzing the Court's jurisprudence in this regard, namely, restitution, rehabilitation, compensation (*indemnización*), satisfaction, and guarantees of nonrepetition.[26] Each of these is examined in turn, but it is important to stress that monetary compensation for both material and moral harm is still the predominant means of redress adopted by the Court. In every one of its judgments on reparations through 2003, the Court has ordered that an indemnification be paid to victims or their beneficiaries.

(*a*) *Restitution.* Restitution means restoring the victim to his or her original situation as it existed before the violations were committed. Where possible, it normally entails the restoration of the victim's liberty, legal rights or social status, but can also apply to the recuperation of his or her lost residence, employment or property. Although full restitution for most serious human rights violations is impossible, the Inter-American Court has on several occasions ordered measures seeking to reestablish the victim's *status quo ante*. These include liberating arbitrarily detained persons,[27] vacating criminal judgments due to procedural irregularities,[28] and expunging criminal convictions that resulted from proceedings held in violation of basic judicial guarantees.[29] The Court has also ordered on two occasions the full reinstatement of public employees wrongfully dismissed from their jobs or, in the alternative, the opportunity to access employment alternatives matching the conditions, salaries and compensation they enjoyed at the time of their unfair termination.[30]

(*b*) *Rehabilitation.* Rehabilitation is a modality characteristic of reparations under international human rights law. It is intended to assist the victim in his or her recovery from serious physical or psychological harm in the wake of a violation. This kind of reparation encompasses all *future* medical and clinical treatment aimed at caring for the victim's short- or long-term injuries, thus distinguishing it from simple compensation for past medical or professional expenses. Rehabilitation may include not only medical and psychological care but also legal and social services. The Court began only recently to adopt measures recognizing the distinct importance of rehabilitation as a form of reparation. In the *Loayza Tamayo Case* decided in 1998, the victim was a university professor in Peru suspected of belonging to the hard-core Shining Path guerrillas and of being involved in 'terrorist' activities. In 1993 she was detained by the Peruvian police and severely tortured to make her confess to the crimes alleged. As a result of the torture she was subjected to, the victim suffered from acute post-traumatic stress syndrome, in addition to other disabilities. The Court ordered a lump sum payment which, for the first time, specifically included an item for the *future* medical treatment of the victim and her two children, both of whom were gravely affected by the ordeal and obliged to receive medical and psychological treatment.[31]

Subsequently, the Court has reaffirmed the importance of medical and psycho-logical care for victims as reparations to assist them in overcoming the various traumas resulting from the violation.[32] In the *El Caracazo Case,* discussed in more detail below, the Court awarded compensation for 'expenses incurred *or to be incurred* for medical treatment...' required by the survivors of a massacre *and* the numerous next of kin of the deceased victims.[33] It has also expanded the rehabilitation rubric to cover situations of general medical treatment under certain circumstances.[34] In the *Barrios Altos Case,* as part of an anti-insurgency campaign, a covert hit squad belonging to Peruvian military intelligence carried out the massacre of over a dozen persons attending a party at a private residence in Lima. Four victims survived the attack but were severely injured. Here the Court ratified a comprehensive agreement reached between the parties stipulating that the Peruvian government would grant the survivors as well as the next of kin of the deceased victims free access for life to a range of social and health services concentrated in (although not limited to) those areas associated with the injuries suffered: traumatological rehabilitation, mental health, outpatient consultation, diagnostic support procedures, specialized care, and hospitalization.[35]

(c) Compensation. Compensation is the most common mode of reparation under international law. In the human rights context, it usually refers to monetary payments that must be made to victims and other beneficiaries for material losses incurred as a result of the violation, on the one hand, and for certain kinds of moral harm, such as pain and suffering, on the other. All of the Court's decisions on reparations through 2003 award such payments for material or moral injury. A large majority include indemnification for both. This section provides a detailed ac-count of the Inter-American Court's practice with respect to compensation. It begins with a brief explanation of how the Court identifies the beneficiaries in a given case, i.e. the persons with a right to make a claim to compensation. The rest of the discussion largely mirrors the Court's own approach to the subject, begin-ning with a study of compensation for 'pecuniary damages', which comprise mainly lost earnings and consequential damages, followed by an analysis of the compensation paid for those 'nonpecuniary' or moral damages susceptible to assessment in economic terms. The Court in its recent judgments tends to award legal costs and expenses related to bringing the case before domestic and inter-

national tribunals under a separate rubric. However, these can properly and more conveniently be considered as part of the section on consequential damages since they are incurred directly by victims and their next of kin as part of their efforts to address the harmful consequences of the violation.

(*i*) *Beneficiaries of Compensation.* The victims of human rights violations adjudicated by the Inter-American Court are, of course, the primary beneficiaries of the reparations awarded. For purposes of its reparations mandate, the Court has distinguished between two types of victims: those immediately injured by the violation, the direct victim, and his or her next of kin, who later suffer the consequences of their loved one's ordeal.[36] Under certain circumstances, the next of kin may themselves become direct victims of violations under the Convention in their own right, as when the state fails to duly investigate or punish the perpetrators of the crime suffered by their family member.[37] In any event, the term 'injured party' in Article 63(1) of the American Convention refers both to the direct victim of a human rights violation as well as any other persons, usually close family members or dependants, who as a result experience material loss, personal suffering or prejudice to other basic values.[38]

(*ii*) *Compensation for Pecuniary Damages.* Material or 'pecuniary damages' are those that can be objectively quantified in monetary terms, and are divided by the Inter-American Court into *loss of earnings* and *consequential damages*. The Court has developed a practice for determining and distributing lost earnings, which is described below. Consequential damages are those expenses incurred by victims and their next of kin in dealing with the effects of the state's violation.

The Court has established certain judicial presumptions in connection with some material damages, which means these do not have to be proven to be compensated. In cases where the victim is deceased, the Court will presume with respect to lost earnings that he or she would have spent most of their lost income on caring for their immediate family members; as concerns consequential damages, the Court will presume that the next of kin covered the costs of the victim's funeral.[39] As a general rule all other material losses and expenses should be 'pleaded [and] proven opportunely' to be compensated.[40] For instance, if a third party claims to have been dependent on a deceased victim and thus entitled to compensation, he or she must meet three conditions established by the Court in the landmark *Aloeboetoe Case* to qualify as a beneficiary.

In the *Aloeboetoe Case*, a group of men from an ethnic tribe in Suriname known as Bushnegroes or Maroons were beaten, tortured and then murdered by a jungle unit of the Surinamese army. One of the victims escaped from his captors and survived long enough to testify to the massacre before dying from his injuries. The case presented a series of novel legal issues regarding reparations, many arising from the unique social structure and customs of the tribe to which the victims belonged. For one thing, polygamy was common and family dynamics were communal in stark contrast to the nuclear family unit prevalent in Western culture. As a result, the Inter-American Court adopted to a certain extent a culturally sensitive approach that took into account the tribe's particular customs and practices. It fashioned a series of presumptions (discussed in more detail below) to aid in the identification of beneficiaries, and devised a flexible formula to allow third party, non-successor dependants not covered by the presumptions to prove their status as beneficiaries of the deceased victim. Under this formula, a third party claimant must first prove that he or she was receiving regular and periodic payments of money, services or goods from the victim during his or her life. The second condition is to demonstrate that these payments to the third party would have continued if the victim had not been killed, due to the relationship that existed between the two. And finally, the third party claimant must show that said payments met a financial need and would have continued to do so had the victim survived.[41]

Lost Earnings. Direct pecuniary damages take the form of lost earnings, which refers exclusively to the loss of economic income, past or future. Where the victim has been killed or disappeared, which is the case in the majority of Inter-American cases, the object is to provide compensation for income that, had the violation not occurred, would have entered the victim's patrimony 'based upon the income the victim would have received...up to the time of his [or her] possible natural death'.[42] If the deceased or disappeared victim is a minor, lost earnings are calculated starting from the age of legal maturity.[43] In those situations where the victim survives the violation, the Court compensates for lost wages as well as for any prejudicial effects of the wrongful act on future employment. For example, if the events in question result in disabilities that limit the victim's ability to work normally, the Court will compensate lost earnings based on a calculation of the reduction in salary and the loss of those benefits to which the victim would have been entitled under the relevant national legislation if fully employed.[44] As a general rule, the Court will adjust its projected figures to determine their present value and factor in any interest accruing between the time of the violation and the judgment.

To quantify this type of future loss to patrimony as fairly as possible, the Court has developed certain objective indicators and a functional perspective. The first indicator relied upon by the Court is the salary earned by the victim when the violation occurred, or the minimum salary then in effect if no evidence of higher earnings is submitted.[45] At the same time that the Court relies on indicators in determining lost earnings, it maintains a flexible approach adopted in its first case, *Velásquez-Rodríguez*. There the Court affirmed that 'it is not correct...to adhere to rigid criteria...but rather to arrive at a prudent estimate of the damages, given the circumstances of each case'.[46] Thus, it will apply the minimum wage baseline even where there is evidence that the victim performed only informal or sporadic work, or was unemployed at the time of the violation.[47] Similarly, in the *Neira Alegría Case*, the first decided against Peru, the Court departed from its usual practice. The judgment addressed the violations that occurred when the victims, who were political prisoners in a Peruvian jail, 'disappeared' after the violent suppression by the army of a prison uprising. In that case the Court adopted as its base indicator an average or representative minimum salary based on 'the actual economic and social situation in Latin America', because it considered the minimum salary prevailing in Peru to be too low.[48]

The Court has made clear that lost earnings projections should be based on real expectations that, although uncertain, must be substantiated to be recognized and compensated.[49] In determining lost earnings, consideration is also given to the period of time during which the victim is unable to work due to the violation or to obtain the benefits thereof, such as a pension. In those cases involving death or disappearance, this indicator consists of the difference between the victim's age upon death and the probable years of life remaining to him or her, calculated according to the average life expectancy in the state concerned.[50] In principle and practice, the Court presumes that the victim, if married or accompanied, would have allocated 75 percent of his or her income to immediate family, and spent the remaining 25 percent in personal expenses. Accordingly, unless specific proof is presented to the effect that the victim spent more or less on him or herself, the final compensation payment awarded for loss of earnings will be reduced by 25 per-cent.[51] This general approach developed by the Court for calculating lost earnings has evolved slightly over time, but has been applied more or less consistently in the majority of its decisions on reparations.[52]

By and large the Court has developed a consistent practice in granting compen-sation for a victim's lost earnings as reflected in *El Caracazo*, a judgment against Venezuela from 2002. In that case, widespread demonstrations to protest a rise in transportation costs resulted in a national state of emergency and the heavy-handed repression of the protests by the Venezuelan authorities. Hundreds of people were killed, disappeared or injured over the course of several days. Thirty-seven victims executed or disappeared by the police received compensation for lost earnings ranging between $33,000 and $38,000, which was calculated according to the formula just described. For instance, the Court adopted for its calculations Venezuela's legal minimum wage in effect for 1989 when the events in question occurred. Other awards for lost earnings in prior cases presenting similar circumstances have ranged between $28,000 and $50,000. This range is shaped by the precise characteristics of a victim's situation, that is, age at time of death, salary level recognized, life expectancy in the country where the violation occurred.[53] In a few cases, significantly higher awards of over $100,000 have been made on the grounds of a victim's elevated professional status or increased income.[54]

One area that has evolved is that relating to beneficiaries. If the victim survived the violation, he or she obviously will receive the corresponding compensation directly; if not, the Court tends to award the bulk of the victim's lost earnings to his or her immediate family or heirs.[55] The exact pattern of distribution will vary with each victim's family situation. In its earlier jurisprudence, the Court routinely awarded one-third of its damages for lost earnings to the victim's spouse, and the remaining two-thirds to his or her children. Only when the victim did not have a spouse or children did the parents become beneficiaries.[56] In a recent decision, however, the Court seemed to acknowledge that a deceased or disappeared victim in certain circumstances may have spent some personal income on his or her parents (or close relatives acting as parents). Thus, in the 2002 reparations decision in *El Caracazo*, the Court allotted half of the compensation awarded for lost earnings in equal part to the victim's children; a quarter to his or her spouse or permanent companion; and a quarter to the parents.[57] If the victim did not have a spouse or children, then one half was awarded to the parents and the other to his or her siblings in equal part. This, too, represents a change over prior cases where lost earnings were typically not shared with siblings, but rather awarded entirely to the spouse, children or parents.[58]

The Court's supposedly 'flexible' approach to calculating future income is, nonetheless, rather formulaic and two dimensional. It does not, for example, adequately take into account a number of other realistic factors affecting future income, including potential earning increases (or decreases) over time. 'Concerning the suggestion to the Court that a lump-sum compensation be awarded on the premise that an improvement in the victim's future income was a "probable certainty", the Court considers that compensation must be calculated on the basis of a definite injury that is sufficiently substantiated to find that the injury likely occurred.'[59] Because estimating increases in long-term potential income due to unrealized employment opportunities or promotions is speculative and therefore extremely difficult to prove, the Court has consistently refused to take any such factor into consideration in its determination of compensation. As a practical matter, the Court will take into account a victim's education and professional trajectory only to the extent that these factors—or any other that cannot be definitively established by evidence—are reflected in the salary earned by the victim at the time of the violation.[60]

The Court on one occasion formally acknowledged a more comprehensive alternative, the so-called 'life plan' of the victim.[61] This category of damages centers on the victim's self-realization and personal fulfillment. The notion goes well beyond even a flexible approach to the lost future earnings and consequential damages rubrics to address the truncated personal development of a victim deprived of the opportunity to live her life to its fullest reasonable potential. It explicitly takes into account 'her calling in life, her particular circumstances, her potentialities and her ambitions, [which would have permitted] her to set for herself, in a reasonable manner, specific goals and to attain those goals'.[62] It thus advances a multifaceted concept of expected future benefits qualitatively distinct from the limited formulae generally relied upon by the Court to calculate pecuniary injury. In the *Loayza Tamayo* case, the Court accepted this far-reaching concept of damages and held that the state had impeded the victim's realization of her particular 'life plan' by violating her human rights and disrupting her personal and professional development.[63] It refrained, however, from awarding compensation under this heading because 'neither case law nor doctrine has evolved to the point where acknowledgment of damage to a life plan can be translated into economic terms'.[64] Nor has the Court revisited the concept of 'life plan' injury in any subsequent cases, raising serious questions as to its status as viable legal precedent.

Consequential Damages. The concept of indirect or consequential damages centers on the material losses or expenses that victims and their families incur as a result of the violations. In compensating them, the Court has addressed different types of economic harm emanating from Convention violations. Consequential damages normally refer to conventional costs associated with serious human rights violations, such as medical bills or funeral expenses, but may, in certain circumstances, include extraordinary expenditures or losses related to counteracting the prejudicial effects of the underlying violation. These damages are usually compensated based on actual expenses incurred and proven before the Court in a specific case, although certain presumptions may apply, as noted already.

The Inter-American Court routinely covers the costs related to searching for victims who have disappeared and/or the funeral expenses of those who have died. Another common form of reimbursement awarded is for medical costs assumed by the victims and/or their next of kin in dealing with the aftermath of the violation.[65] In one case, for instance, the Court ordered the reimbursement of all expenses assumed by the disappeared victim's family in their search for him, which includes 'outlays for travel, communications, administrative inquiries, visits to jails, hospitals and public institutions', as well as costs corresponding to medical treatment for his parents and siblings.[66] As a general rule, compensation relating to these basic expenditures tends to consist of a few to several thousand US dollars, depending on the precise nature of the activities covered and the gravity of the injuries treated. However, on one occasion that represents the exception rather than the rule, the Court awarded a considerably higher amount ($25,000) to compensate for material harm 'to the family group' caused by the victim's disappearance, which 'caused economic and other types of problems for the family that must be redressed based on principles of equity'.[67]

But the Court may also compensate victims who can prove they have incurred greater or different expenses than the ones normally associated with a violation as a consequence of their efforts to deal with it. In one action, where the disappeared victim was a US national, the Court ordered reimbursement for nearly two dozen trips to Guatemala by the victim's relatives who were searching for their loved one, amounting to $20,000.[68] In another, when the victim's next of kin fled to Holland to avoid persecution and then applied for political asylum there, compensation was ordered to defray the corresponding costs; the total awarded for all consequential damages, including the family's relocation, was $25,000.[69]

The Court on one occasion even recognized and compensated the lost earnings of a victim's next of kin. In *Bámaca Velásquez* the victim was a guerrilla captured in combat by the Guatemalan army. He was clandestinely tortured and executed by his military captors, who then 'disappeared' the cadaver leaving no trace of his final whereabouts. His American wife launched a crusade to uncover what had happened to her husband and to locate his remains. The Court subsequently ordered that she be compensated $80,000 for her lost income suffered as result of her intensive dedication to the case during the five years that the litigation lasted. The total amount awarded as consequential damages to the victim's wife was $125,000, which included an additional $25,000 for her medical treatment and another $20,000 for other expenses related to pursuing the case.[70] These extraordinary reparation measures have not been repeated in subsequent judgments, presumably because the unique circumstances presented in the cases have not been repeated.

In its current practice, the Court will also compensate victims for the costs of appearing before national and international tribunals.[71] Attorneys' fees and legal costs are 'understood to fall under the concept of reparations set forth in Article 63(1)'.[72] The Court began by ordering legal fees and costs as part of its consequential damages award, but in recent decisions has assigned them a separate rubric.[73] In any event, the Court has clearly established that 'the activities carried out by the victim or victims, their next of kin or their representatives to obtain justice under domestic and international jurisdiction [*sic*] involve ... expenses and financial commitments for which there must be compensation. ...'[74] Such costs include hiring legal counsel or other authorized representatives. This represents a welcome advance over prior practice, in which the Court was resistant to recognizing and reimbursing the victim's direct representation in the proceedings before it.[75]

(iii) Compensation for Nonpecuniary Damages. The Inter-American Court also recognizes and compensates 'nonpecuniary damages', commonly referred to as moral damages. 'This nonpecuniary damage may include both the suffering and distress caused to the direct victims and their next of kin, and the impairment of values that are highly significant to them, as well as other sufferings that cannot be assessed in financial terms.'[76] The Court thereby recognizes two categories of moral harm: that which can be compensated in monetary terms, emphasized here, and that which must be redressed through other, noneconomic means, which is the subject of the final reparations subsection dealing with satisfaction and guarantees of nonrepetition.

The present section concentrates on reviewing the practice relating to the kind of moral harm that is routinely assessed by the Court in financial terms: the victim's mental anguish, emotional distress, and pain and suffering. Because the subjective nature of these injuries makes them difficult to measure, they are treated quite differently from other types of harm redressed through monetary compensation. Unlike material damages, which are calculated based on supposedly objective criteria such as receipts, expense records and mathematical projections of future income, moral damages must be 'determined on the basis of equity and by a prudent assessment..., which cannot be measured by any absolute rule'.[77] A determination based 'upon the principles of equity', which is the standard followed by the Court,[78] means that it will take into account the special circumstances of each case and give weight to certain factors to determine the amounts to be awarded 'in fairness'.[79] These factors and a number of related considerations are discussed below.

Although perhaps alien to nonlawyers, the notion of equity is a widely recognized concept characteristic of nearly all domestic and international legal systems.[80] At the local level, it is central to the judicial processes involved in redressing the moral and other intangible harms commonly recognized by national courts. For similar reasons it is also a concept of significant relevance to the work of tribunals operating under international law, which, as we saw, provides the normative framework for the Inter-American Court's reparations jurisprudence. Equity in international law refers to 'considerations of fairness, reasonableness, and policy often necessary for the sensible application of the more settled rules of law'.[81] The Inter-American Court's longstanding practice of invoking equity to award compensation for pain, suffering and other kinds of moral injury to victims and their next of kin is thus firmly rooted in general principles of law.

The Court's authority to compensate moral harm is express in the text of Convention Article 63(1), but it may also be understood as derived from the inherent remedial powers enjoyed by all courts in equity.[82] The Court over time has given a good indication of how it will apply this standard. 'Bearing in mind the economic and social position of the beneficiaries, such reparations [for moral damages] should take the form of a lump-sum payment in the same amount for all the victims [in the case].'[83] Variations in the amount of compensation awarded by the Court within a given case tend to reflect 'differences in the injuries and ill-treatment suffered by the... victims',[84] or factors such as the egregiousness of the state's wrongdoing and the persuasiveness of the evidence on the extent of emotional and psychological suffering.[85] Another example of the factors that influence the Court's deliberations on moral damages are attempts by the authorities to cover up the truth or deny information about the whereabouts of loved ones to family members.[86]

To aid it in its task, the Court has developed a series of judicial presumptions that originated with the *Aloeboetoe Case* allowing it to indemnify victims automatically for the subjective moral injury that is presumed to have occurred with respect to certain violations. In these situations no proof is required other than an admission or finding that the violation—an execution, a disappearance or torture or other serious abuse attributable to state agents—occurred. As a rule, then, moral harm will be presumed by the Court with respect to the primary or immediate victim, who may be dead or disappeared, because 'it is characteristic of human nature that anybody subjected to the aggression and abuse [of a serious violation] will experience moral suffering', regardless of whether evidence of this suffering is available.[87] A similar presumption operates in relation to the victim's close relatives, given that 'violations of human rights and a situation of impunity regarding those violations cause grief, anguish and sadness, both to the victims *and to their next of kin*'.[88] This means that the parents, spouse, children, and siblings are, like the victim, entitled to a degree of compensation in grave cases due to the subjective distress the wrongful act is assumed to have caused them.[89] The Court affirmed, for example, how 'it can be presumed that the parents have suffered morally as a result of the cruel death of their offspring, for it is essentially human for all persons to feel pain at the torment of their child'.[90] A similar reasoning, *mutatis mutandis*, operates with respect to the primary victim's other close family members: husbands and wives (or companions), sons and daughters, brothers and sisters. How much is actually awarded based on the application of these presumptions depends, of course, on the circumstances of the case.[91]

Any condition that can be viewed as contributing to the victim's or the next of kin's suffering may be taken into account when fashioning compensation amounts. In *El Caracazo*, the Court distinguished between similarly situated victims and ordered additional compensation to a number of them based on aggravating factors. Where the victim was a minor at the time of his death, $5,000 was added to a baseline amount of $15,000 awarded to compensate for the deceased adult victims' presumed pain and suffering, raising the total paid for each minor to $20,000. The Court reasoned that as 'especially vulnerable persons..., [the minors] should have received special protection by the state [and it] can be presumed that the suffering caused [by the violation] was especially intense'.[92] Similarly, if the remains of the victim had not been handed over to the next of kin for proper burial, the state was required to pay an additional 30 percent on top of the baseline compensation for moral harm paid to each family member of the deceased person. This baseline was fixed at $20,000 respectively for the mother, the father, the spouse or companion, as well as each son or daughter; and $5,000 for each brother or sister.[93] The Court in *El Caracazo* lamented that:

[t]he remains of several of the homicide victims and missing persons have not been delivered to their next of kin. This omission is linked to a set of highly reprehensible patterns of State action in connection with the handling of the victims, such as the irregular use of common graves and denial of existence of the latter.[94]

To the Court this 'reprehensible' conduct exacerbated the anguish of the family members and, in all fairness, justified increasing the baseline compensation award for moral injury by a full 30 percent. In sum, the Court determines what constitutes 'fair compensation' for moral injury under Convention Article 63(1) through the equitable assessment of the factors it deems relevant. In doing so, the Court follows what is commonly accepted as the 'guiding principle in most courts for calculating damages for non-monetary injury as an intangible loss'.[95]

Moral injury was recognized and compensated in virtually every reparations decision adopted by the Court through 2003. Indemnification was awarded without exception where violations of the rights to life, liberty, and personal integrity occurred; as noted already, these comprise the bulk of the Court's jurisprudence.[96] But such compensation has not always been made consistently or in accordance with easily identifiable criteria, objective or otherwise. Perhaps the only rule in this regard is the Court's insistence 'that jurisprudence can serve as a guide to establish principles in this matter [of compensating nonmonetary harm], although it cannot be invoked as an absolute criterion, since the particularities of each case must be examined individually'.[97] This approach has led to unevenness in the Court's jurisprudence in certain key areas.

For instance, in *Aloeboetoe*, the Court calculated subjective moral damages to be US$29,000 for each of the victims abducted and executed, with an extra one-third added on for one who survived longer than the rest and thus 'was subjected to greater suffering as a result of his agony'.[98] Of this award, one quarter went to the victim's parents, one quarter to the spouse or companion, and one half to the children, to be divided equally among the members of each group.[99] This was a separate arrangement from that adopted with respect to the distribution of the primary victim's lost earnings, which were divided between the spouse or companion (one-third) and the children (two-thirds). In the more recent *El Caracazo Case*, however, the Court ordered that the moral damages awarded to the next of kin for the victim's pain and suffering ($15,000 to $20,000) be distributed according to the same formula applied to pecuniary damages (lost earnings), that is, half for the children, and a quarter each to the spouse or companion and the parents, to be divided in equal part among those in each category.[100] Whether this represents a new standard to be applied prospectively to subsequent cases remains to be seen; it is more likely that the Court continues to weigh the circumstances of each case in deciding how to distribute such compensation.[101]

The amounts awarded by the Court in the *Aloeboetoe* and *El Caracazo* cases reflect the high end of a range applied in some, but not all, similar cases.[102] In the *Street Children Case,* five indigent Guatemalan youths, including three minors, were clandestinely abducted, tortured and executed by state agents. The Court provided for the intense pain and suffering experienced by the victims with compensation ranging from $23,000 to $30,000 to be paid to their mothers or, in one case, to the grandmother; the same mothers and grandmother were also awarded $26,000 for their own personal emotional distress and suffering. The victims' siblings received $3,000 for the presumed moral injury their brothers' deaths caused them, largely as recognition for their blood ties to the victims.[103] In another action against Guatemala involving forced abductions, torture and executions, the *White Van Case*, the Court ordered that sums ranging between $22,000 and $54,000 be paid to the beneficiaries of the six victims who were assassinated by state agents.[104] But here, despite the suggested similarities, the disaggregated sums were significantly lower than those in the decisions already mentioned, possibly because the moral injury of the next of kin was not backed by supporting evidence. Each of the lump sum payments for moral damages in the *White Van Case* encompasses a standard $20,000 award for the victim's pain and suffering, with the remainder, sometimes no more than $2,000 or $3,000, covering all of the next of kin's moral injury. In a few instances, this meant only a nominal amount of $1,000 paid to each family member for moral injury.[105]

Cases of forced disappearance, not surprisingly, tend to produce the largest individual awards, with respect to both the direct victims and the next of kin. In *Bámaca Velásquez*, a judgment from 2002, Guatemala was ordered to pay $100,000 in equal part to the disappeared victim's heirs (wife, father, and two sisters) by virtue of his presumed pain and suffering. This was augmented by direct payments to the same family members for their own moral injury of $80,000 for the victim's wife, $25,000 for his father, and $20,000 for his sisters.[106] It is worth noting that the Court in the same case had already ordered a large compensatory payment for pecuniary damages: it awarded $100,000 to the same beneficiaries as heirs to the victim's lost earnings, as well as a total of nearly $150,000 for consequential damages, including $80,000 for his wife's lost income during the litigation. In another action for reparations relating to a forced disappearance in Bolivia, the *Trujillo Oroza Case* decided in 2002, the young victim's mother alone was awarded compensation totaling nearly $350,000. The Court held that as the primary beneficiary, she was entitled to $100,000 for the victim's presumed moral injury and $80,000 for her own emotional distress and suffering; in addition, she was entitled to $130,000 for her son's lost earnings, $20,000 for her medical expenses, and $8,400 other consequential damages.[107] Perhaps a better indication of the prevailing payment for moral injury to next of kin for the forced disappearance of a loved one can be found in the *Blake Case*, where the members of the victim's nuclear family—the mother, father and two siblings—each received payments of $30,000.[108]

Though they are few, the Court's decisions involving the survivors of arbitrary detention and torture are illustrative. Recall that in *Loayza Tamayo*, the victim, a university professor, was captured by the Peruvian anti-terrorist police, held incommunicado and brutally tortured as a suspected insurgent. The Court not only found that the victim's pain and suffering was extensive but also accepted that her 'life plan' had been gravely impaired by the state's action (the 'life plan' theory of damages was discussed above under lost earnings). For the reasons already discussed, however, it chose not to compensate the latter harm, but did award $50,000 to the primary victim in recognition of her conventional moral injury.[109] Each of her children and both her parents were awarded $10,000 for their mental, emotional and, in some cases, physical distress. Her six siblings each received $3,000 because 'as members of a close family [they] could not have been indifferent to [the victim's] terrible suffering, a presumption not disproved by the State'.[110] In a similar but more recent case involving two brothers, also against Peru, one of the main victims was tortured after being arbitrarily detained and was given $60,000 in moral damages; his mother received $40,000.[111]

With respect to moral damages, it does not seem possible to draw useful parallels between groups of judgments (or even among cases in the same category) since each action presents its own unique blend of circumstances and factors influencing compensation. As discussed, the variables are many. The nature and number of the violations, their interrelation and duration, the intensity of the victim's subjective suffering, the egregiousness of the government's wrongdoing or conduct, all of these are elements that will go into the Court's deliberations around how best to indemnify the injured parties before it. Some of the difficulty in finding a pattern or specific criteria emanates from the fact that many of the cases examined involve overlapping violations, which the Court usually lumps together for purposes of considering the moral harm suffered.[112] Nor does the Court provide much insight into the process of how it fixes compensation amounts based on the conjugation of the circumstances and factors in a given case. In any event, the Court's prior awards and practice around moral damages, while not dispositive, will continue to represent a valuable reference point and to serve as a source of guidance in its deliberations.

Although in most cases damages are made to individual victims, the Court has also recognized circumstances in which collective compensation may be required. In a case concerning the group rights of an indigenous tribe, the Court recognized that an illicit state act may impact upon an indigenous community and its traditional values such that the corresponding reparation, including compensation for moral damages, should be directed at the injured community as a whole.[113] In the *Mayagna (Sumo) Awas Tingni Community Case,* the only one to date addressing the issue, the Court held that compensation should be awarded for the moral harm caused by Nicaragua to the traditional values held by the indigenous tribe with respect to its communal property. Nicaragua had awarded licenses to a private contractor to exploit natural resources on indigenous lands in the absence of formal title or ownership rights in favor of the Awas Tingni Indians living there. The Court held, among other things, that the granting of such contracts without taking into account the tribe's legitimate claims to the land violated the community's right to property. It determined that since the injury was, in fact, communal in nature, equity (fairness) dictated a form of collective compensation. It thus ordered the state to invest 'as reparation for the immaterial damages...the total amount of $50,000...in works or services of collective interest for the benefit of the Awas Tingni Community, by common agreement with the Community.'[114]

Finally, the Inter-American Court has set out certain guidelines and developed rules pertaining to the payment of compensation and modes of compliance.[115] The Court regularly includes in the operative paragraphs of its judgments that compensation must be paid directly to the beneficiaries and that it should be free from any tax or lien—present or future—imposed by the state. Where said payment is in arrears, the state will be obliged to pay interest on the amounts due as determined by the applicable banking rates in the state's jurisdiction. Likewise the Court has reiterated that the right to indemnification for damages suffered by the victims up to their death is transmitted to their heirs by succession, even where those heirs remain unidentified at the time the judgment is handed down.[116] And, in those cases where the beneficiaries are minors, the Court tends to decree the establishment of a trust. This measure is taken so that the item allocated to compensate the minors is carefully administered and delivered to the trustees upon reaching maturity.

(d) *Satisfaction and Guarantees of Nonrepetition.* Although the Court's growing practice of awarding nonmonetary reparations is a very important dimension of its jurisprudence requiring deeper study, it will not be analyzed extensively here.[117] Instead, an overview of the most salient measures relating to satisfaction and guarantees of nonrepetition is provided to round out our discussion of the Inter-American Court's reparations jurisprudence. As noted in the prior section, the concept of nonpecuniary damages extends beyond emotional distress to encompass other prejudicial effects on the dignity and well-being of the victims that, unlike personal suffering, cannot be compensated financially even in nominal terms. The Court tends to deal with these consequences of a violation under a rubric created for 'other forms of reparation', to distinguish them from those material and immaterial injuries compensated in monetary terms. This type of injury is of a symbolic character, and typically involves an affront to the dignity or humanity of the victim and his or her family. It may revolve around the failure by a state to accept responsibility for its illegal actions, or to disclose the truth about what happened to the victims or the whereabouts of their mortal remains. It frequently arises from a failure to investigate, prosecute and punish the perpetrators, or to adopt measures to ensure that the violations never happen again.

(i) *Satisfaction.* When injury cannot be fully redressed solely through restitution or compensation, the state responsible is obliged to provide 'satisfaction' for the harm caused to a victim's dignity and reputation.[118] The Court has recognized that some moral harm can only be compensated through symbolic or nonmonetary means that provide satisfaction in addition to, or in lieu of, restitution or compensation. It has reiterated, for instance, that judicial decisions favorable to the victims including its own constitute per se a form of reparation that addresses this type of moral injury.[119] At the same time the Court has recognized a wide range of other nonpecuniary measures aimed at remedying grave human rights violations and providing satisfaction. The most common are to order the cessation of repeated violations;[120] a full and public disclosure of the 'truth';[121] the identification of a deceased or disappeared person's remains, and delivery of their remains to the next of kin;[122] as well as the issuance of official statements accepting responsibility and apologizing.[123] I will briefly touch upon each of these.

Most importantly, the state itself may take steps to provide satisfaction 'by the execution of acts or works of a public nature or repercussion, which have effects such as recovering the memory of the victims, reestablishing their reputation, consoling their next of kin or transmitting a message of official condemnation of the human rights violations in question and commitment to the efforts to ensure that they do not happen again'.[124] These acts or works are usually aimed at recognizing the wrong done to the victims and reestablishing their dignity. They may entail, for example, an official acceptance of responsibility by the state or an expression of regret, together with an official apology or the publication of the Court's judgment by the government in the local media.[125] On a few occasions, the Court has determined that the state should also provide the victims or their beneficiaries with academic scholarships, or should construct monuments or community education centers in honor of the victims' memory and to benefit the community affected by the violations.[126]

Of special relevance to providing satisfaction are those measures consistently ordered by the Court to ensure that violations are duly investigated and their perpetrators identified, brought to justice, and punished. The Court has reiterated that this obligation is not a mere formality and 'must be complied with seriously'.[127] It mandates, among other things, that states may 'not ... resort to measures such as amnesty, extinguishment and [others] designed to eliminate responsibility'.[128] Such actions are themselves incompatible with the American Convention because 'they are intended to prevent the investigation and punishment of those responsible for serious human rights violations such as torture, extrajudicial, summary or arbitrary execution and forced disappearance, all of them prohibited because they violate non-derogable rights recognized by international human rights law'.[129] It is worth underscoring here that fulfillment of the responsible state's duty to investigate violations and bring the perpetrators to justice—to ensure accountability—is part and parcel of the reparations formula in the context of individual cases decided under international law. In contrast, punishment plays no formal role in the design or implementation of 'reparations programs' per se, because the latter are expressly intended as measures adopted *for* the benefit of victims and not *against* the perpetrators of the violations. Criminal accountability is thus largely separated out from the prevailing conception of reparatory justice in political transitions, and is pursued separately through other 'external' measures.[130]

(ii) Guarantees of Nonrepetition. Under international law, the first duty of an infringing state is to put an end to the illicit act, if it persists, and then to guarantee that it will not reoccur. To suspend or cease the action in violation is not necessarily a complicated endeavor. For instance, the Inter-American Court may determine that a person arbitrarily detained during the ongoing judicial proceedings should be released.[131] When the illegal act entails a more complex violation of the Inter-American Convention, the Court will order appropriate measures. In the *Mayagna*

Awas Tingni Case, where the communal property of an indigenous tribe was exploited economically by the state in detriment of the group and its members' property rights, the Court, to put an end to the ongoing exploitation, ordered the state to 'abstain from carrying out . . . actions that might lead the agents of the state itself, or third parties acting with its acquiescence or its tolerance, to affect the existence, value, use or enjoyment of the property located in the geographical area where the members of the Community live and carry out their activities'.[132]

The Inter-American Court, when it adopts measures aimed at ensuring the nonrepetition of a violatory act or practice, may order legislative or other reforms affecting the state's social, legal or political institutions and policies. As a general rule, the Court will require that the state's laws conform to its international obligations, particularly under the American Convention.[133] In a recent case, the Court ordered the responsible state to ratify and enforce a particular treaty, the Inter-American Convention on Forced Disappearance of Persons.[134] When the rules of a state's domestic legal system are deemed incompatible with the American Convention, the Court may order that they be modified[135] or, in extreme cases, annulled. Thus, in the landmark *Barrios Altos* case, the Court held in no uncertain terms that amnesty laws passed in relation to gross human rights violations do not comply with the dictates of the American Convention or international human rights law generally.[136] Sometimes the problem is that there are no local rules against the human rights violations prohibited by the Convention; in those cases the Court may order that certain abuses such as forced disappearance[137] and extrajudicial execution[138] be made crimes under the laws of the responsible state. It may also require the implementation of other human rights obligations ratified but not yet implemented by the state.[139]

3. Concluding Observations

The starting point of our study is the recognition that there are substantial differences between reparations in the adjudication of individual cases and reparations in the transitional justice context, and that these differences militate against presuming the direct extrapolation or transference of international law rules from the former context to the latter. It is evident to most observers, for instance, that international human rights regimes like the one set up under the American Convention are intended to address primarily violations occurring at the individual level; they simply are not configured to deal with gross and systematic violations in the same way.[140] Nevertheless, the normative guidance of the

Velásquez-Rodríguez decision on the fashioning of reparatory policies in Chile and especially Argentina at the end of the last century confirms that there is indeed a constructive role for international human rights law to play in the transitional context. The foregoing survey of Inter-American Court case law opens the door to examining which elements of the Court's jurisprudence are relevant to the design of a reparations policy and which are not. It permits a deeper analysis of those elements that would be inappropriate or counterproductive as standards for public and private actors in transitional societies responsible for developing such policies. At the same time, the survey points to other aspects of the Court's jurisprudence that may contribute positively to the design of a reparations program in practice.

A degree of caution is in order when consulting the Court's reparations juris-prudence for guidance in the design of a domestic policy. The emphasis on compensation as a primary modality for reparations in both the individual adju-dication and the transitional contexts can be especially misleading.[141] It implies that the Inter-American Court's extensive practice of adopting pecuniary measures may or should provide a suitable map for policymakers and other national actors seeking reparatory justice in the wake of mass atrocity. In reality, it does not, nor could it. More than any other modality, the determination of fair compensation is constrained, first, by the factual context in which it takes place and, second, by the quantitative challenges raised by the number of victims involved. Whether mon-etary payments are made to individual victims in a case before the Court or to large groups of victims through the implementation of a reparations program is itself a decisive factor in establishing whether the adopted measures are adequate and fair. Contrast this to the adoption of nonpecuniary measures, such as those seeking satisfaction or the guarantee of nonrepetition of the underlying violations, whose impact is not measured as a function of circumstances or the numbers of benefi-ciaries affected. Many of the measures ordered by the Court of this nature—full disclosure of the 'truth', public apologies, memorials, legal reform—are also hall-marks of most reparations programs; they are comparable to similar measures adopted by the Inter-American Court in a way that compensation awards are not. This is because, qualitatively speaking, neither the content nor the effectiveness or fairness of these nonpecuniary measures is substantially affected by the context or the numbers of victims involved.[142]

A shared emphasis aside, there are a number of other elements characteristic of compensation as ordered by the Court that are inappropriate or uncertain sources for normative guidance in the transitional context. As recognized already in the Introduction, a general consensus exists to the effect that the substantial amounts awarded as damages in individual human rights cases usually cannot and should not be emulated by most countries facing legacies of widespread human rights abuses. The reason is obvious. Providing full compensation in the same way as the Court does to tens of thousands of victims of mass atrocity is a practical impos-sibility for most transitional states; some commentators even suggest that when dealing with poor or developing nations it may be wrong to subject the entire populace to the effects of such a budgetary strain.[143] And there is the added complication that the Court's sizable awards can lead to inflated expectations on the part of the countless victims who cannot access the Inter-American human rights system, or who otherwise must rely on a state's domestic reparations policies to obtain compensation of any sort. For these reasons, unqualified comparisons between the amounts of compensation ordered by the Inter-American Court and those contemplated for a national reparations program will likely do more harm than good.

Working backwards from these principles it is possible to identify certain aspects of the Court's practice that are probably unworkable in transitional settings. With respect to compensation for material loss, for example, economic reality indicates that even a conservative formula for calculating lost earnings like the one utilized by the Court would be inappropriate for situations involving very large numbers of victims, as the resulting economic burden would be too great for most countries to bear.[144] Similarly, the tribunal's generosity in paying most if not all out-of-pocket expenses of its successful claimants as consequential damages is probably not suited to a mass reparations program where resources are severely limited. It is likely that, all else being equal, scarce economic resources will be directed at redressing to some degree lost earnings or moral harm suffered by victims and their next of kin rather than most types of out-of-pocket expenses. Which brings us to the next question: What normative guidance does the Court's experience offer in the way of recognizing and compensating moral harm?

Aside from reaffirming the rule that moral harm where it exists should be compensated, even with respect to victims that are deceased or disappeared, the Court's jurisprudence regulating monetary awards for moral harm is muddled in several important respects. A central difficulty is that Inter-American Court judgments in cases involving similar violations and circumstances are not always decided in a consistent manner. The amounts awarded vary considerably from case to case, even where the facts are similar; the manner in which compensation is distributed to next of kin defies uniformity. The Court claims to reference prior precedent in this area as a guide for its deliberations, but offers little insight into how, as a practical matter, it does so. In reality differing approaches are adopted and variable outcomes achieved in cases with similar facts and related issues. There is often little indication or comparative analysis with respect to the reasoning behind the disparate treatment of similar cases. In short, the Court could be clearer in its analysis of how the circumstances in a particular case give rise to specific award amounts and lines of succession, and how these stand in relation to prior determinations in similar actions. The failure to do so is problematic, to say the least, especially from the point of view of external observers seeking guidance from the Court on how to deal with substantially similar questions arising in the transitional justice context. As noted by one long-time observer:

There are serious problems caused by variability of awards in human rights tribunals. First, fundamental fairness requires that similarly situated parties be treated in a similar fashion by the legal system. The inability to achieve consistency in awards tends to erode general confidence in justice and the integrity of the human rights systems. In addition, highly variable, unpredictable valuations undercut the deterrence function of ... law.[145]

Finally, it is apparent for the same reasons explored above with respect to compensation for material loss that the frequently high amounts fixed by the Court for monetary awards redressing moral harm are, on the whole, unsuitable as benchmarks in any context other than that of individual adjudications. It simply is not possible, for example, to reproduce the figures for moral damages awarded by the Court to victims in a case of disappearance in situations where the violations were systematic or widespread and the victims number in the thousands. This is especially true where the moral harm suffered by the next of kin would have to be redressed as well. In any event, it is evident that the Court's jurisprudence in this respect will be of limited use to those charged at a national level with the design of a viable reparations program seeking to provide fair reparations, especially where compensation for both material and moral harm *together* is contemplated.

Even so, not all of the Inter-American Court's jurisprudence on compensation is unhelpful outside the courtroom. It cannot be denied that the Court's judgments as a whole continue to 'provide the most wide-reaching remedies afforded in international human rights law'.[146] For example, the tribunal's growing recourse to broad nonpecuniary measures to redress moral harm (satisfaction) and to guarantee that violations are not repeated is a prime example of constructive legal innovation that holds great potential for the transitional justice field; this is an area ripe for greater academic study. And despite its inherent limitations, the Court's recent jurisprudence canvassed in the preceding section is undoubtedly significant in its own right, not least because it sets strong precedent to the effect that states have a duty to repair, and compensate, human rights violations under international law.[147] It has also contributed to the progressive development of international human rights law in other ways that may be of great practical utility for the architects of a national reparations policy.

NOTES

1. I am indebted to several other authors in this volume who provided comments on earlier versions of the manuscript, especially Richard Falk, Pablo de Greiff, and Colleen Duggan. Dinah Shelton, Lisa Magarrell and Thomas Antkowiak also provided invaluable feedback. Finally, I would like to thank my research assistants, Angela Suárez Álvarez, María Paula Barrantes, Anne Janet De Ases and Zachary Redman for their efforts.

2. Ruti Teitel, 'Transitional Justice Genealogy', *Harvard Human Rights Law Journal* 16 (2003): 69.
3. Postwar reparations were another important component. The practice of defeated states paying reparations to victor states to compensate for losses suffered during war was, of course, not new. War reparations in the traditional sense, however, did not evolve to reach individual victims of gross and systematic human rights abuses until after World War II, beginning with the German reparations to victims of Nazi persecution in the 1950s. See the paper by Ariel Colonomos and Andrea Armstrong (Chapter 10, this volume), and Dinah Shelton, *Remedies in International Human Rights Law* (New York: Oxford University Press, 1999), 332–44.
4. Teitel, op. cit., 77.
5. Whether or not the perception of a dichotomy is justified is itself part of the debate. See Priscilla Hayner, *Unspeakable Truths: Confronting State Terror and Atrocity* (New York: Routledge, 2001), ch. 7. For another articulation of this dichotomy, see Miriam J. Aukerman, 'Extraordinary Evil, Ordinary Crime: A Framework for Understanding Transitional Justice', *Harvard Human Rights Journal* 15 (2002): 39.
6. Teitel, op. cit., 77.
7. Ruti Teitel, *Transitional Justice* (New York: Oxford University Press, 2000), 125.
8. See the paper on reparations in Chile by Elizabeth Lira (Chapter 2, this volume).
9. Ibid.
10. *Decision on Full Stop and Due Obedience Laws*, Inter-Am. C.H.R., Report No. 28/92 (Argentina, 1992), 51.
11. See the paper by María José Guembe (Chapter 1, this volume). The Argentine experience is contrasted with that of other countries in Pablo de Greiff, 'Reparations Efforts in International Perspective: What Compensation Contributes to the Achievement of Imperfect Justice', in *To Repair the Irreparable: Reparation and Reconstruction in South Africa*, Erik Doxtader and Charles Villa-Vicencio, eds. (Claremont, South Africa: David Philip, 2004).
12. See Guembe, op. cit.
13. While the Inter-American human rights system is not the only one that adjudicates individual claims, it is the international regime where the state's duty to provide compensation for human rights violations is most developed. This is also true with respect to other modes of reparations. Shelton, op. cit., 173–4, 195, 279.
14. Pablo de Greiff, 'Justice and Reparations' (Chapter 12, this volume).
15. See Christian Tomuschat, 'Individual Reparation Claims in Instances of Grave Human Rights Violations: The Position under General International Law', in *State Responsibility and the Individual: Reparation in Instances of Grave Violations of Human Rights*, Albrecht Randelzhofer and Christian Tomuschat, eds. (The Hague: Martinus Nijhoff Publishers, 1999), 20–1.
16. For more on Inter-American procedure in relation to compensation, see W. Michael Reisman, 'Compensation for Human Rights Violations: The Practice of the Past Decade in the Americas', in Randelzhofer and Tomuschat, op. cit.
17. American Convention on Human Rights, opened for signature, November 22, 1969, Art. 44, 1144 U.N.T.S. 144 (entered into force, July 18, 1978).
18. See *Caballero Delgado and Santana Case Judgment*, Inter-Am. C.H.R., Ser. C, No. 22 (1995), 67.

19. 'Basic Principles and Guidelines on the Right to a Remedy and Reparations for Victims of Violations of International Human Rights and Humanitarian Law', Annex to *Final Report of the Special Rapporteur: Mr. M. Cherif Bassouini: The Right to Restitution, Compensation and Rehabilitation for Victims of Gross Violations of Human Rights and Fundamental Freedoms*, E/CN.4/2000/62 (January 18, 2000), 15.

20. Ibid., 9.

21. *Loayza Tamayo Case Judgment on Reparations*, Inter-Am. C.H.R., Ser. C, No. 42 (1998), 129(d); *El Caracazo Case*, Inter-Am. C.H.R., Ser. C, No. 95 (2002), 77; *Castillo Páez Case Judgment on Reparations*, Inter-Am. C.H.R., Ser. C, No. 43 (1998), 49; *Garrido and Baigorria Case Judgment on Reparations*, Inter-Am. C.H.R., Ser. C, No. 39 (1998), 42.

22. *Velásquez-Rodríguez Judgment*, Inter-Am. C.H.R., Ser. C, No. 4 (1988), 174.

23. Ibid., 172.

24. Jo M. Pasqualucci, *The Practice and Procedure of the Inter-American Court of Human Rights* (Cambridge: Cambridge University Press, 2003), 240–3.

25. Reisman, op. cit., 73.

26. See 'Basic Principles and Guidelines', 21; see also the International Law Commission's Draft Articles on Responsibility of States for Internationally Wrongful Acts, Part II, Chapter II, Articles 34–9, in James Crawford, *The International Law Commission's Articles on State Responsibility: Introduction, Text and Commentaries* (Cambridge: Cambridge University Press, 2002), 67–8.

27. *Loayza Tamayo Case (Reparations)*, 155–8.

28. *Castillo Petruzzi et al. Case*, Inter-Am. C.H.R., Ser. C, No. 52 (1999); *Cantoral Benavides Case Judgment on Reparations*, Inter-Am. C.H.R., Ser. C, No. 88 (2001), 42. See also *Hilaire et al. Case*, Inter-Am. C.H.R., Ser. C, No. 94 (2002), 214, 223, where the Court ordered that the petitioners who were sentenced to death be retried under a reformed criminal system incorporating the legal guarantees and other protections of the American Convention.

29. *Loayza Tamayo Case (Reparations)*, 121–2; *Suárez Rosero Case Judgment on Reparations*, Inter-Am. C.H.R., Ser. C, No. 44 (1999), 113; *Cantoral Benavides Case (Reparations)*.

30. *Loayza Tamayo Case (Reparations)*, 113; *Ricardo Baena Case*, Inter-Am. C.H.R., Ser. C, No. 72 (2001), 214.

31. *Loayza Tamayo Case (Reparations)*.

32. *Blake Case Judgment on Reparations*, Inter-Am. C.H.R., Ser. C, No. 48 (1999).

33. *El Caracazo Case*, 86–7 (emphasis added).

34. See *Villagrán Morales et al. Case Judgment on Reparations*, Inter-Am. C.H.R., Ser. C, No. 77 (2001), 86–7; *Durand and Ugarte Case*, Inter-Am. C.H.R., Ser. C, No. 89 (2001); *Cantoral Benavides Case (Reparations)*, 51–2; *Trujillo Oroza Case Judgement on Reparations*, Inter-Am. C.H.R., Ser. C, No. 92 (2002); and *Barrios Altos Case Judgment on Reparations*, Inter-Am. C.H.R., Ser. C, No. 87 (2001).

35. *Barrios Altos Case (Reparations)*, 42.

36. The Court's Rules of Procedure define next of kin as the 'direct ascendants and descendants, siblings, spouses or permanent companions, or those determined by the Court, if applicable', 2001 Rules of Procedure of the Inter-American Court of Human Rights, Art. 2(15).

37. *Las Palmeras Case*, Inter-Am. C.H.R., Ser. C, No. 90 (2001); *El Caracazo Case* (violations of American Convention Articles 8 and 25).

38. See *El Caracazo Case*, 67. While all victims are in theory beneficiaries, not all beneficiaries have to be victims or even injured parties. In some instances, relatives may become beneficiaries through succession, even though they have suffered no loss or harm. This is because, as the Court has held, 'the right to compensation for damages suffered by the victims up to the time of their death is transmitted to their heirs by succession'. *Garrido and Baigorria Case*, 42; *Loayza Tamayo Case (Reparations)*, 92.

39. *El Caracazo Case*, 50.

40. *Velásquez-Rodríguez Case Judgment on Compensation*, Inter-Am. C.H.R., Ser. C, No. 7 (1989), 42; see also *Garrido and Baigorria Case (Reparations)*.

41. *Aloeboetoe Case Judgment on Reparations*, Inter-Am. C.H.R., Ser. C, No. 15 (1993), 68. For a deeper analysis of this seminal case, see Reisman, op. cit., 85–91.

42. *Velásquez-Rodríguez Case (Compensation)*, 146.

43. *El Caracazo Case*, 88; *Villagrán Morales et al. Case (Reparations)*, 74(a), n.68.

44. See *Constitutional Court Case*, Inter-Am. C.H.R., Ser. C, No. 71 (2001); *Blake Case (Reparations)*.

45. See, for example, *El Amparo Case Judgment on Reparations*, Inter-Am. C.H.R., Ser. C, No. 28 (1996); *Paniagua Morales et al. Case Judgment on Reparations*, Inter-Am. C.H.R., Ser. C, No. 76 (2001); *Bámaca Velásquez Case Judgment on Reparations*, Inter-Am. C.H.R., Ser. C., No. 91 (2002); *Castillo Páez Case (Reparations)*; *Villagrán Morales et al. Case (Reparations)*; *Ricardo Baena Case*; *Barrios Altos Case (Reparations)*.

46. *Velásquez-Rodríguez Case (Compensation)*, 48.

47. *El Caracazo Case*, 50.

48. *Neira Alegría Case Judgment on Reparations*, Inter-Am. C.H.R., Ser. C, No. 29 (1996), 50.

49. See *Velásquez-Rodríguez Case (Compensation)*; *Aloeboetoe Case (Reparations)*; *Neira Alegría Case (Reparations)*; *El Amparo Case (Reparations)*; *Paniagua Morales et al. Case (Reparations)*.

50. See, for example, *Aloeboetoe Case (Reparations)*; *Castillo Páez Case (Reparations)*.

51. The first time when this presumption was applied was in *El Amparo*. *El Amparo Case (Reparations)*, 28. See also *Castillo Páez Case (Reparations)*, 71(a); *Villagrán Morales et al. Case (Reparations)*, 81.

52. The Court in its very first case calculated lost earnings but did not subtract the amount that the victim presumably would have spent on himself. This practice was first applied in *El Amparo*, another of the Court's early decisions on reparations, and is now commonly followed. *El Amparo Case (Reparations)*, 28.

53. *Villagrán Morales et al. Case (Reparations)*, 70; *Castillo Páez (Reparations)*; *El Amparo Case (Reparations)*; *Aloeboetoe Case (Reparations)*.

54. *Paniagua Morales et al. Case (Reparations)*; *Bámaca Velásquez (Reparations)*. In *Paniagua Morales*, the beneficiary of a victim who was a bookkeeper received an award over $100,000 for the amount the victim was expected to earn in a lifetime, as determined by the life expectancy tables provided by each party. Similarly, in *Bámaca Velásquez*, the victim's elevated professional status, as an indigenous leader and participant in negotiating the Guatemalan peace accords, resulted in an award over $100,000.

55. See *Myrna Mack Case*, Inter-Am. C.H.R., Ser. C., No. 101 (2003), 13 (operative paragraphs)(awarding all $235,000 in lost earnings to victim's daughter); *Bámaca Velásquez (Reparations)*.

56. *El Amparo Case (Reparations)*, 41; *Neira Alegria Case (Reparations)*, 19; *Aloeboetoe Case (Reparations)*. See also Reisman, op. cit., 97.

57. *El Caracazo Case*, 91. It is interesting to note that the aunts of two of the victims who lived 'under the same roof as their aforementioned nephews and had close ties of affection with them [were] assimilated, for purposes of their participation in compensation for pecuniary damage, to the condition of mothers of those victims'. Ibid.

58. *Villagrán Morales et al. Case (Reparations)*; *Paniagua Morales et al. Case (Reparations)*. But see *Bámaca Velásquez (Reparations)*, in which the Court assigned compensation for pecuniary harm to the surviving wife, father and two sisters. The manner in which the Court has distributed the lost earnings of deceased victims lacks consistency and has given rise to debate on what is the most appropriate approach. For one critique, see Jo M. Pasqualucci, op. cit., 260–1.

59. *Castillo Páez Case (Reparations)*, 74.

60. See *Loayza Tamayo (Reparations)*; *Trujillo Oroza Case*.

61. *Loayza Tamayo Case (Reparations)*, 144–54.

62. Ibid., 147.

63. Ibid., 144–53. See also Shelton, op. cit., 229–31.

64. *Loayza Tamayo Case (Reparations)*, 153.

65. *Loayza Tamayo Case (Reparations)*; *El Caracazo Case*, 86–7 (medical). See, for example, *Blake Case (Reparations)*; *Villagrán Morales et al. Case (Reparations)*; *Bámaca Velásquez Case (Reparations)*; *Trujillo Oroza Case Judgment on Reparations*, 141(8) (funerals).

66. *Castillo Páez Case (Reparations)*, 77.

67. Ibid., 76. This appears to be an isolated decision and may be due to the fact that the respondent government in the case (Peru) did not contest the victim's claim that such a collective injury had occurred. This very rubric, that the victim's personal services to the family be calculated in terms of the group's lost economic benefit, has been pleaded in subsequent cases but ignored by the Court. See, for example, *El Caracazo Case*, 80, 88.

68. *Blake Case (Reparations)*, 49, 66.

69. *Castillo Páez Case (Reparations)*, 77 (total compensation for consequential damages was $25,000).

70. *Bámaca Velásquez Case (Reparations)*, 54.

71. See, for example, *Aloeboetoe Case (Reparations)*; *Neira Alegría Case (Reparations)*, 5; *Paniagua Morales et al. Case (Reparations)* (providing national litigation costs); *Blake Case (Reparations)*; *Villagrán Morales et al. Case (Reparations)*, 107–9; *Baruch Ivcher Bronstein Case*, Inter-Am. C.H.R., Ser. C, No. 74 (2001), 189 (providing international litigation costs); *Garrido and Baigorria Case (Reparations)*; *Suárez Rosero Case (Reparations)*, 88, 93, 100; *Trujillo Oroza Case Judgement on Reparations*, 129 (providing costs and expenses for counsel).

72. *El Caracazo Case*, 130.

73. See *Myrna Mack Case*, 290; *Bámaca Velásquez (Reparations)*, 91; see *Garrido and Baigorria Case (Reparations)*, 75–85 for the earlier approach.

74. *El Caracazo Case*, 130.

75. See Shelton, op. cit., 315–18.

76. *Villagrán Morales et al. Case (Reparations)*, 84.

77. *Castillo Páez Case (Reparations)*, 78–90.

78. *Velásquez-Rodríguez Case (Compensation)*, 27.

79. *El Caracazo Case*, 99 (citing previous decisions).

80. Shelton, op. cit., 71–2, 78.

81. Ian Brownlie, *Principles of Public International Law*, 5th edn. (Oxford: Oxford University Press, 1998), 25–6.

82. 'The authority of human rights tribunals to afford remedies is uncontested. Judicial bodies have inherent power to remedy breaches of law in cases within their jurisdiction.' Shelton, op. cit., 181. See also *Cantoral Benavides Case (Reparations)*, 53. The Court awards compensation for nonpecuniary damages 'through payment of a sum of money or delivery of goods and services of appreciable cash value, which the Court determines in reasonable exercise of its judicial authority and on the basis of equity'. See also Shelton, op. cit., 226–9.

83. *Aloeboetoe Case (Reparations)*, 91.

84. Ibid.

85. See, for example, *El Caracazo Case; Aloeboetoe Case (Reparations)*; see also Reisman, op. cit., 78, 81, 87–9; Shelton, op. cit., 228–32, 239.

86. *Aloeboetoe Case (Reparations); El Caracazo Case*.

87. *Aloeboetoe Case (Reparations)*, 52. See also *Castillo Páez Case (Reparations)*, 86.

88. *El Caracazo Case*, 50(e) (emphasis added).

89. For parents, see *Aloeboetoe Case (Reparations); Neira Alegría Case (Reparations); Genie Lacayo Case*, Inter-Am. C.H.R., Ser. C, No. 30 (1997); *Loayza Tamayo Case (Reparations)*. For spouses, see *El Amparo Case (Reparations); Suárez Rosero Case (Reparations); Bámaca Velásquez Case (Reparations)*. Spouse is defined as the wife, husband or partner, even if there is more than one. For children, see *Velásquez-Rodríguez Case (Compensation); Aloeboetoe Case (Reparations); Myrna Mack Case*. The Court has also recognized the right to compensation of the victims' children born out of wedlock. *Garrido and Baigorria Case (Reparations)*, 65. For siblings, see *Paniagua Morales et al. Case (Reparations)*, 109; *Castillo Páez Case (Reparations); Garrido and Baigorria Case (Reparations); Blake Case (Reparations)*, 51–8.

90. *Aloeboetoe Case (Reparations)*, 76. See also *Castillo Páez Case (Reparations)*, 88.

91. For instance, the Court has indicated that, at least with respect to siblings, 'it is necessary to take into account the degree of relationship and affection' that existed between them and the victim. *Paniagua Morales et al. Case (Reparations)*, 109.

92. *El Caracazo Case*, 102.

93. Ibid., 104. It is important to note that the Court gave no rationale for how it arrived at these baseline figures, i.e. the $15,000 set for the deceased *victims'* pain and suffering, as well as the $20,000 set for the next of kins' *own* moral harm arising from their loved one's death.

94. Ibid.

95. Shelton, op. cit., 262.

96. Through 2003 the two cases where no compensation for moral damages was ordered are *Petruzzi et al. Case*, Inter-Am. C.H.R., Ser. C, No. 52 (1999); *'The Last Temptation of Christ' Case*, Inter-Am. C.H.R., Ser. C, No. 73 (2001).

97. *Paniagua Morales et al. Case (Reparations)*, 104; *Blake Case (Reparations)*, 54; *Castillo Páez Case (Reparations)*, 83; *Neira Alegría Case (Reparations)*, 55; *El Amparo Case (Reparations)*, 34.

98. *Aloeboetoe Case (Reparations)*, 91.

99. Ibid., 97.

100. *El Caracazo Case*, 101, 111.

101. Thus in the 2003 *Myrna Mack Case*, the Court awarded the full $40,000 in damages arising from the victim's moral harm to her daughter, to the exclusion of her parents and several siblings. *Myrna Mack Case*, 263, 267.

102. *Barrios Altos Case (Reparations)*, 33–4; *Benavides Ceballos Case*, Inter-Am. C.H.R., Ser. C, No. 38 (1998) (granting $1,000,000). *Barrios Altos* and *Benavides Ceballos* were negotiated as friendly settlements, and thus somewhat exceptional.

103. *Villagrán Morales et al. Case (Reparations)*, 93.

104. *Paniagua Morales et al. Case (Reparations)*, 111, 160, 229.

105. Ibid., 111, 127, 145, 160, 217, 229. The siblings of several of the victims received only $1,000 in recognition of the presumption of moral injury.

106. *Bámaca Velásquez Case (Reparations)*, 106.

107. *Trujillo Oroza Case (Reparations)*, 141(7). Compensation was awarded to the victim's half brothers and sisters too.

108. *Blake Case (Reparations)*, 58. No compensation for pain and suffering to the primary victim was made in this case because the forced disappearance took place before Guatemala's ratification of the American Convention. Instead, the Court held that the disappearance was a continuing violation and compensated only that harm to the next of kin accruing after said ratification took place.

109. *Loayza Tamayo Case (Reparations)*, 139.

110. Ibid., 143.

111. *Cantoral Benavides Case (Reparations)*, 62. The Court is not entirely clear why the victim's mother received such an elevated sum, but suggests that it is justified by the fact that two of her sons were direct victims, and that as a result her family 'broke apart'.

112. See, for example, *Loayza Tamayo Case (Reparations)*.

113. *Mayagna Awas Tingni Community Case*, Inter-Am. C.H.R., Ser. C, No. 79 (2001) (compensation for moral damages).

114. *Mayagna Awas Tingni Community Case*, 167.

115. See generally *El Caracazo Case*, 134–42 (discussing modes of compliance).

116. See, for example, *El Caracazo Case*; *Aloeboetoe Case (Reparations)*; *Villagrán Morales et al. Case (Reparations)*, 67; *Paniagua Morales et al. Case (Reparations)*, 84; *Neira Alegría Case (Reparations)*.

117. For a good introduction to the nature of these nonpecuniary measures and their significance in the reparations field generally, see Jo M. Pasqualucci, op. cit., 242–54. 'The Inter-American Court until the 1998 *Loayza Tamayo* decision manifested a reluctance to utilize its power to order nonpecuniary reparations, although these can be extremely important in remedying human rights violations', Shelton, op. cit., 359.

118. See 'Basic Principles and Guidelines', 21, 25. See also Crawford, op. cit., 231.

119. *Mayagna Awas Tingni Community Case*, 166; *Suárez Rosero Case (Reparations)*, 72. See also *Castillo Páez Case (Reparations)*, 84, stating that this principle prevails likewise in the European Court of Human Rights' jurisprudence.

120. See, for example, *Loayza Tamayo Case (Reparations)*.

121. See *Villagrán Morales et al. Case (Reparations)*; *Durand and Ugarte Case*; *Cantoral Benavides Case (Reparations)*; *Bámaca Velásquez Case (Reparations)*; *Trujillo Oroza Case (Reparations)*; *Barrios Altos Case (Reparations)*, 41. In several of these cases the Court ordered the publication of the operative part of its judgments in the official

gazette or another daily with national circulation. The Court has recognized that every person has the right to truth, which includes the right of the victim's relatives, where possible, to know what happened to him/her and, as the case may be, where his/her remains are. In this regard, to disclose the truth 'is a means of reparation, and therefore an expectation regarding which the State must satisfy the next of kin of the victims and society as a whole', *Bámaca Velásquez Case (Reparations)*, 76. See also *Cantoral Benavides Case (Reparations)*, 79; *Villagrán Morales et al. Case (Reparations)*, 100; *Paniagua Morales et al. Case (Reparations)*, 200.

122. The Court has always acknowledged that establishing the whereabouts of a victim's mortal remains and returning them to the next of kin constitute 'an act of reparation as it leads to restore the dignity of the victims, to honor the value of their memory to those who were their beloved ones, and to allow them to adequately bury them'. *El Caracazo Case*, 123; *Velásquez-Rodríguez Case Judgment*, 181. This frequently leads the Court to order the exhumation and identification of victims' remains, as well as their delivery for proper burial to the next of kin. See *Neira Alegría (Reparations)*; *Castillo Páez Case (Reparations)*; *Trujillo Oroza Case (Reparations)*; *Caballero Delgado and Santana Case*.

123. See, for example, *Durand and Ugarte Case*; *Bámaca Velásquez Case (Reparations)*; *Barrios Altos Case (Reparations)*.

124. *Villagrán Morales et al. Case (Reparations)*, 84.

125. *Barrios Altos Case (Reparations)*, 44. In *Barrios Altos*, the Court ordered the state to include 'a public expression of apology to the victims for the grave damages caused' as well as to publish the judgment of the Court in the official gazette *Diario Oficial El Peruano*. Peru was also obliged to disseminate its content through other media 'deemed appropriate for that purpose, within 30 days from the date the agreement is signed'. Ibid. See also 'Basic Principles and Guidelines', 25.

126. See *Aloeboetoe Case (Reparations)*; *Villagrán Morales et al. Case (Reparations)*; *Trujillo Oroza Case (Reparations)*, 122; *Cantoral Benavides Case (Reparations)*; *Barrios Altos Case (Reparations)*, 43.

127. *Villagrán Morales et al. Case (Reparations)*, 100. See also *Suárez Rosero Case (Reparations)*, 79, 80.

128. *El Caracazo Case*, 119.

129. *Barrios Altos Case Judgment*, Inter-Am. C.H.R., Ser. C, No. 75 (2001), 41.

130. *Parámetros para el diseño de un programa de reparaciones en el Perú* (Lima: International Center for Transitional Justice (ICTJ)-Asociación Pro Derechos Humanos (APRODEH), 2002), 8.

131. See *Loayza Tamayo Case (Reparations)*.

132. *Mayagna Awas Tingni Community Case*, 153. See also *Hilaire et al. Case*, 113, 212, 215.

133. See, for example, *Loayza Tamayo Case (Reparations)*; *Suarez Rosero Case (Reparations)*; *Trujillo Oroza Case (Reparations)*.

134. *Benavides Ceballos Case*, 51–2.

135. See, for example, *Castillo Petruzzi et al.*, 222; *Suárez Rosero Case (Reparations)*, 80; '*The Last Temptation of Christ*' Case.

136. See *Barrios Altos Case (Judgment)*, 41–4.

137. See *Trujillo Oroza Case (Reparations)*.

138. See *Barrios Altos Case (Judgment)*, 41; *Bámaca Velásquez Case (Reparations)*.

139. See *Villagrán Morales et al. Case (Reparations)*, 123.

140. See Tomuschat, op. cit., 18–20.

141. Regarding the practice in the transitional justice context, see the country case studies in Part I of this volume.

142. A simple example illustrates this point. A case before the Inter-American Court of forced disappearance may result in a compensation award of several hundred thousands of dollars for the next of kin. A reparations program for surviving family members of tens of thousands of disappearance victims will most likely approve awards in the thousands or perhaps tens of thousands of dollars per victim. Generally speaking, it is not possible to invert the two sums and still consider the award fair *and* viable in the respective contexts. On the other hand, disclosure of the truth and a public apology by the authorities, whether ordered by the Court in an individual case or by a legislature as part of its national reparations policy, are substantially identical and equally effective measures irrespective of whether they are granted to one victim by a court or to 30,000 beneficiaries of a reparations program.

143. See Christian Tomuschat, 'Reparations for Victims of Grave Human Rights Violations', *Tulane Journal of International and Comparative Law*, 10 (2002): 175–6.

144. There may be exceptions, of course, for rich countries like the USA, as the post-9/11 reparations experience will attest. This is not the case for most other countries obliged to develop a mass reparations program, since on the whole they tend to be developing nations with severe economic restraints. The case study of Argentina provides an important illustration of the challenges involved in adopting such an approach. See Guembe, op. cit.

145. Shelton, op. cit., 279.

146. Ibid., 222.

147. This precedent is frequently contrasted with that set by the European Court of Human Rights, which has to date been exceedingly restrained in exercising its discretion to order compensation. See Tomuschat, 'Reparations for Victims of Grave Human Rights Violations', 161–3.

....

CHAPTER 15

REPARATIONS AND CIVIL LITIGATION: COMPENSATION FOR HUMAN RIGHTS VIOLATIONS IN TRANSITIONAL DEMOCRACIES

....

JAIME E. MALAMUD-GOTI

LUCAS SEBASTIÁN GROSMAN

1. INTRODUCTION

....

Although the precise scope of the right of victims of human rights abuse to reparation is controversial, it is generally accepted that it must include some form of monetary compensation for the harm suffered. This compensation—its justification, the substantive and procedural standards for its distribution, the institutions most qualified to distribute it—can be approached from two different perspectives. The first is through principles of tort. Under tort law, the compensation of harm for human rights abuse is no different from the compensation of other, ordinary harm. The same substantive criteria and procedural requirements apply to both in connection with matters such as burden of proof, statute of limitations, identification of the individual defendant, assessment of damages, and so forth. Under this approach, it is a judge, in the context of a specific case, who awards compensation based on the specific harm experienced by each particular victim. The second is based on principles of administrative compensation. Under this approach, victims are defined in standardized terms in a statute that provides a relatively fixed, tabulated amount of compensation for all. The procedure to access that compensation, typically, is not judicial but administrative (hence the label we use to describe it), and usually requires the victims to provide perfunctory evidence on only some very basic facts, under standards more lenient than in an ordinary lawsuit, to receive a monetary award.

In this chapter, we compare these approaches and analyze the way they should complement each other in the furtherance of a policy of just reparation. Our analysis will be informed by both moral and practical considerations. In our view, justice ought to be assessed within the constraints imposed by particular contexts. To be able to perceive the nature and strictness of these constraints within concrete situations, we will refer throughout to the experience of the transitional democracies in Argentina and Chile.

The chapter unfolds as follows. First, we will analyze what circumstances justify, or even require, a shift from the torts to the administrative approach to compensation. Second, we turn to how the two approaches should relate to each other. We will address, in particular, the issue of whether victims should have a right to choose between them in the disposition of their cases and, if so, under what conditions. Finally, we compare judicial to administrative compensation in relation to the goals a compensation program must pursue. We hope this comparison will show that even in those cases where, for the reasons we discuss, administrative compensation offers the best option, it is advisable to leave room for the use of judicial compensation as well.

2. THE TORTS APPROACH AND ITS LIMITS

It is a general principle of law that the breach of a duty not to cause harm gives rise to a right to restitution and, where restitution is materially impossible, to compensation. This principle is also present at the international level: its applicability in the context of state liability under international law can be traced back, at least, to a dictum by the Permanent Court of International Justice in *Chorzow Factory*.[1] Moreover, the international documents that set forth the obligation of reparation include restitution and compensation at the top of the list.[2]

The issue, however, is whether in the context of mass human rights abuse we should construe the obligation to compensate victims along the lines of the traditional torts approach. Such an approach would require that a court of justice award damages to each individual victim on the basis of the evidence supplied by the victim as to the magnitude of the harm, assessed under standard procedural and substantive rules. Moreover, because damages are intended to fully compensate a victim for the harm suffered, under a torts approach nothing short of full compensation will meet the requirements of justice.

One way of approaching this issue is to make reference to the general goals a reparations program must pursue and that, as one among many purposes, compensation to the victims is supposed to serve. Conceived in this way, however, one could easily undermine the victims' interests in the name of social well-being or social goals that only remotely relate to those interests. This is not the route we wish to take. We believe that, in the context of a transitional democracy, the specific goal of compensation to victims of human rights abuse is to restore their dignity and to reintegrate them into society as equal citizens. It is in reference to this more specific goal that the justice of a compensation scheme should be assessed.

The key question, therefore, is whether there are justifications for preferring the administrative to the judicial approach that can be invoked for the victims' sake, and not only in the name of broader societal goals. The former approach suggests that victims will receive a smaller amount of money than a judge would award to them in an ordinary torts action and it thus may not seem obvious, at first glance, how that approach can be reconciled to the overarching goal of doing justice to the victims—but such, we believe, is the case. Specifically, there are four reasons that cast doubt on the applicability of the torts approach to human rights abuse: (*a*) the nature of the harm; (*b*) the number of victims; (*c*) the institutional inadequacy of the judiciary; and (*d*) legal obstacles. While we do not find (*a*) to be compelling, and our position on (*b*) is ambivalent, we believe that (*c*) and (*d*) offer decisive reasons to resort to the administrative approach.[3]

The Nature of the Harm

It may be tempting to distinguish human rights violations from ordinary torts based on the nature of the harms involved; however, we do not find this line of argument convincing. Torture, murder, and deprivation of freedom are not actions alien to, or that do not fit, the law of torts of most countries. No amount of money, of course, may fully compensate the death of a beloved, torture, or the deprivation of freedom. But this is hardly specific to human rights violations. If the murder of a spouse at the hands of a death squad is not compensable, neither is that person's death in a car accident or their intentional killing by a bank robber. Yet in such cases courts provide compensation everyday by applying nothing more than ordinary tort law. Indeed, the whole system of civil liability is based upon the assumption that what victims or their heirs receive in a like case is an adequate compensation for their pain and suffering. One could claim that this is merely a legal fiction, but that, again, is no less true in an auto accident than in a human rights case. Consequently, it is not the nature of the harm that makes the traditional torts approach inadequate.

We do not mean by this that auto accidents and illegal executions perpetrated by death squads deserve equal compensation. Most certainly, the fact that the killing was intentional and perpetrated by state agents, as well as all the other elements present in the latter case, may substantially increase the damages. The point we wish to stress is that the evaluation and award of such damages are neither conceptually nor practically alien to tort law and to ordinary courts of justice. The fact that human rights violations are in more than one sense more serious than auto accidents and other typical torts, one might further argue, suggests the value of compensating human rights violations through a torts rather than an adminis-trative approach. After all, resorting to the administrative approach could imply that terrible crimes would elicit less compensation than auto accidents. Emphasiz-ing the nature of the harm at stake thus cannot justify rejecting the torts approach; rather, it has the opposite effect.

The Number of Victims

The number of victims is a natural place to look to distinguish ordinary tort cases from human rights abuse. But it is more difficult to distinguish human rights violations from ordinary torts on these grounds than it may seem at first glance. Car accidents, for instance, usually cause more deaths than dictatorships' hench-men over equal periods of time.[4] This fact reveals that we cannot merely assume that violations of human rights are too large to be dealt with by the judiciary.

Having said this, the truth is that in certain contexts the number of victims may be far beyond an ordinary torts case. Guatemala in the 1980s, where the victims of state sponsored violence numbered in the hundreds of thousands, is a paradig-matic example. Furthermore, the burden put on the judiciary by the compensation of human rights abuse may become overwhelming when actions are filed in a short period of time following a triggering event, such as the fall of the abusive regime or the repeal of a statute. In the face of such a situation, ordinary civil procedures may prove impractical or unfeasible. But the number of victims may also be relevant in connection with a different concern, namely, the financial burden that the compensation of human rights abuse places upon the transitional government. We will deal with this issue in the next section.

The Inadequacy of the Judiciary

Governments in transitional situations usually wish to move forward to leave behind a difficult past and start anew. Victims and their sympathizers do not want to move forward at any cost, but they have a strong interest in the compensation process being expedient. This is the case not only for the obvious reason—present in an ordinary torts case as well—that the sooner the damages are collected the better, but also because of the more specific circumstances of human rights abuse that make it especially traumatic for the victims and their heirs to go through an extended process.

Traditional legal procedures may be inadequate to respond to this concern. Expediency is a characteristic more frequently found in administrative procedures, and this makes them attractive as a way to cope with the particular timeframe imposed on transitional democracies. Moreover, in certain cases, the transitional state may lack a judiciary capable of dealing with compensation in an adequate and timely fashion. The judges in office may have been appointed largely by the perpetrators and may be ideologically disinclined to favor victims. In other cases, the structure of the state may be so dismantled, for instance due to a civil war, as to prevent conducting procedures in a proper way. Although these deficiencies must be addressed, and eventually solved, by the transitional government, the truth is that the process of doing so may be quite slow—probably too slow for the victims and the transitional government alike. Administrative compensation may prove to be a more feasible alternative under those circumstances.

In addition, in some contexts access to justice may be particularly difficult for the victims or their heirs, especially if they are poor or members of a socially subordinate class. This situation also must be addressed, and hopefully solved, by the transitional government, but the time demanded for that most certainly will not meet the requirements typical of transitional situations, again, not only from the government's but also from the victims' point of view.

Finally, as a consequence of the adversarial nature of the procedure, judicial actions typically are characterized by antagonism. This means that the new government will have to endeavor to rebut victims' allegations of both fact and law. Public lawyers have a general yet stringent duty to discharge, and they must be expected to perform their role zealously, in accordance with the norms of professional responsibility. They cannot be expected to be negligent or lenient; they must try to win the case. This may put the transitional government in a difficult position, since it must aim to reinsert victims into society as equal citizens, not to confront them in the harsh terms a judicial procedure imposes. The procedure by which victims would obtain administrative compensation has no such antagonizing dynamics. The bureaucratic obstacles that may appear in that procedure may affect the victims' perception of the government's efficiency, but not of its good will more generally.

Legal Obstacles

As we noted above, the torts approach is premised on the notion that claims related to harms derived from human rights abuse should follow the same procedure, and meet the same standards, as ordinary torts claims. But this, in fact, would leave most victims of human rights abuse without compensation. To see this point more clearly, we turn to the experience of Argentina and Chile.

In Argentina, most of the lawsuits seeking compensation for harms derived from human rights abuse that were filed after the end of the military dictatorship were rejected due to the statute of limitations, whose term is of two years for torts (Article 4037 of the Argentine Civil Code).[5] Only a few plaintiffs managed to succeed, and they did so only after facing numerous legal obstacles. The difficulties faced by plaintiff Daniel Tarnopolsky to dodge the statute of limitations offer a fine illustration.[6] Daniel Tarnopolsky filed an action in 1987 against the Argentine state, Armando Lambruschini, and Emilio E. Massera (former heads of the Navy), seeking damages resulting from the arbitrary detention and subsequent killing of his parents, his brother, and his sister in July of 1976. The position of the Argentine government was that the starting point of the two-year term established in the statute of limitations was the moment when the wrongful detentions took place, or when the plaintiff learned of it. In the alternative, the government argued that the two-year term started with the publication of Presidential Decree 158/83, which launched the trial against nine members of the Juntas.

The Court of Appeals decided in this case that the two-year term started when the authors of the criminal action that caused the harm could be reasonably identified.[7] That, according to the Court of Appeals, occurred when the decision in case 13/84 (the trial against the Juntas) was handed down—October 9, 1985. However, the Court of Appeals emphasized that the harms to compensate in these cases were of a continuous nature. As it had been established in the *Hagelin* case,[8] in cases in which the harm was continuous, if the two-year term started the moment the tort became known, as the government alleged, the right to sue would have expired before the harms had even occurred—a clear absurdity.

The Supreme Court agreed with the argument that, although the general rule was that the starting point for the term in the statute of limitation is the commission of the tort, a different criterion may apply when the harm cannot be fully appreciated until the end of a continuous act.[9] Moreover, it claimed, although the plaintiff could reasonably link the illegal actions committed in July of 1976 to the government, the initial deprivation of freedom was followed by the disappearance of the plaintiff's family members, and the plaintiff did not know about their imprisonment or death, which meant that he could not fully appreciate the harm.[10]

A similar conclusion was reached by the Supreme Court in the *Guastavino* case, in which the District Court and the Court of Appeals considered that the plaintiff's action had to be rejected, since the starting point of the two-year term established in the statute of limitations was April 1979, when the plaintiff had become a detainee 'under the terms of the state of siege'. The Supreme Court reversed the decision resorting to the same argument used in *Tarnopolsky* that the harm was continuous. The detention of the plaintiff had lasted until March 1983, so only then could the two-year term start.

In Chile, in turn, a decisive obstacle for the victims of the military dictatorship and their heirs was the impossibility of identifying the specific perpetrators of the tort. Under Chilean law, a torts claim must be addressed against a specific person: Article 40 of the Chilean Code of Criminal Procedure establishes that the civil action can be filed against the person who is criminally liable and his or her heirs, while Article 254 of the Code of Civil Procedure establishes that the civil lawsuit must include, as a sine qua non requirement, the name of the defendant. For the tortfeasor to be identified, however, judicial investigation was necessary. The problem was that the Self-Amnesty Decree of 1978 was construed for more than 15 years as barring not only the punishment of the perpetrators but also the investigation of the cases (it was not until the mid-1990s that the contrary interpretation, which established the duty to investigate, prevailed). As a result of this (initial) interpretation of the Amnesty Decree, the victims and their heirs were unable to seek compensation because they could not identify the specific individuals who had committed the tort.[11]

We believe that the experiences of Argentina and Chile speak to a more general point, namely, that the harms derived from human rights violations frequently will not fit the ordinary legal requirements in matters such as evidence, statutes of limitations, and identification of the tortfeasors. This is so because those standards were not developed for the kind of situation that human rights abuse typically involves. Take statutes of limitations in Argentina. The purpose of a statute of limitations is to prevent claims from being pending forever, creating a state of perpetual uncertainty. Statutes of limitations are premised on the assumption that diligent and interested plaintiffs do not wait long before filing an action. In that sense, failure to file an action in due time is presumed to be an indication of a lack of interest on the part of the plaintiff. This assumption, of course, does not hold in most cases of human rights abuse. Failure to file an action in due time may more likely derive from fear of the perpetrators or from the belief, often justified, that the action will be unsuccessful while the perpetrators remain in power. After all, the judiciary is not outside the political system that promoted or conducted the human rights violations in the first place. These considerations may be taken into account by the democratic judiciary at the time of enforcing the statutes of limitations, as the Argentine cases cited above illustrate. But, as the Argentine experience also illustrates, ingenuous, pro-victim interpretations need not be the rule, and most plaintiffs are likely to leave the courts with empty hands. This injustice is not necessarily due to the bad faith of the courts, but is rather the natural consequence of applying the law to situations that do not fit its factual premises.

The case of Chile described above provides a further illustration of this point, in particular with regards to the precise identification of the defendant. The requirement that the tortfeasor be accurately identified becomes a decisive impediment in cases in which the identification of the perpetrator has become impossible as a result of laws passed by the very government under scrutiny—the Self-Amnesty in Chile being a paradigmatic case.

The extent to which these legal obstacles turn out to be fatal for the victims as plaintiffs depends to a large extent on how the courts react to them, a point we consider further below. But when they *are* fatal, they constitute a strong argument for the government to resort to administrative compensation as a way of bringing justice to the victims.[12]

3. THE COEXISTENCE OF THE TWO APPROACHES TO COMPENSATION

Human rights violations frequently occur in poor countries that cannot afford to compensate all victims in full. As Christian Tomuschat points out, the more extensive the violations, the less likely that the victims will be adequately compensated.[13] A variety of case studies show that awards following ordinary torts actions are far above the administrative compensation provided by general reparation programs.[14] It may be argued that this, on its own, is a reason for resorting to administrative compensation instead of the torts approach, at least from the point of view of affordability.

It is worth noting that this argument cannot be sustained in cases where the government offers administrative compensation but does not prevent victims from choosing to resort to the courts instead, since the natural consequence of that is adverse selection: most victims who will choose administrative compensation will be those who have reason to believe that they would not prevail in a judicial lawsuit, or that, even if they were to prevail, they would not obtain an award large enough to justify the risk. This would imply that, so long as the victims' assessment of the probabilities of judicial success is roughly correct, the government will end up paying more than if it did not offer administrative compensation.[15]

If, in turn, victims of human rights abuse are barred from suing in court and are offered administrative compensation as their sole option (we will refer to this as 'judicial closure'),[16] the government may or may not spend less money on compensation than in the case where only judicial compensation is available. This depends on how many victims would eventually win their lawsuit and what amount of damages they would be awarded if they do. But the important question here is, would judicial closure be compatible with the goal of treating the victims with justice? We do not think so. Given the fact that judicial compensation tends to be much higher, for each victim, than administrative compensation, judicial closure implies, quite plainly, that victims of human rights abuse would be treated worse than victims of ordinary torts.

Consider the following hypothesis. Person A is hit by a fire engine and suffers various injuries. Person B is abducted, tortured, and kept in a clandestine detention camp for three years. The harms, both psychological and physical, suffered by B dwarf those suffered by A. A, however, sues the state in court and obtains full compensation (say, $300,000). B, in turn, does not have an option to sue; he receives administrative compensation (say, $50,000) whose level does not come close to adequate compensation. The unfairness of the situation is obvious. And it could not be argued, in response, that horrendous crimes never can be fully compensated. The difficulty, or impossibility, of assessing and compensating certain harms does not mean that any damages constitute fair compensation, or that a 'reduced' compensation is as fair as a larger one. Otherwise, one would fallaciously conclude, as was common in early torts analysis, that since pain and suffering are difficult to assess, no compensation should be provided for them. What renders this argument a fallacy is that providing no compensation for pain and suffering in fact implicitly assesses them as 'zero'.[17]

The above argument may seem to suggest that it is not only judicial closure but also administrative compensation more generally that is at odds with the purpose of treating the victims of human rights abuse with justice. This is not the case. So long as the judicial option is open, the fact that administrative compensation is lower than what a judge would award in a torts action is unproblematic. Victims of human rights abuse will not find it easy to overcome the hurdles typically involved in the legal process in this type of case. As we saw in the previous section, these hurdles very well may be decisive. That may give many victims—in fact, most— objectively good reasons to choose the administrative option. It is when victims are *forced* to receive a 'reduced' compensation, and not when they so choose, that they are treated unjustly.

The existence of legal obstacles determines that leaving the judicial option open may not turn out to make a large difference as to what the government will eventually have to pay. But what would happen if legal obstacles were not decisive and a very large number of victims in fact obtained judicial compensation? Even in this case, the argument based on financial restrictions lacks normative significance. That argument assumes that the scarcity of resources faced by the transitional government is a problem that affects victims of human rights abuse alone. It is not. Why should B's compensation be reduced due to financial constraints, while A's remains untouched? There is no reason for the consequences of economic scarcity to be borne disproportionately by victims of human rights abuse. Rather, those consequences should be more evenly distributed among all persons with a claim against the state. We do not mean by this that restrictions to compensation must be identical or mathematically proportionate for all state creditors. The concept of justice is more complex than that, and different considerations, for instance, a preferential treatment of those persons in a more urgent need, may be justified, or even required.[18]

Needless to say, the approach we are defending does not guarantee that victims of human rights abuse will effectively collect the compensation awarded by the courts. Nothing can guarantee that. But for the compensation of human rights abuse to be just, it is important that it be implemented in such a way that it respects the victims' equality, and this needs to be judged with reference to the way the government treats them vis-à-vis other creditors.

In sum, even though most victims are likely to find the judicial option un-attractive for the reasons discussed above, there is no justification for denying that option to those victims who, right or wrong, believe that they can prevail in a judicial action. Closing that option is incompatible with treating victims with justice. Judicial closure would imply that victims of human rights abuse were denied the alternative, available to ordinary torts victims, of seeking full compen-sation. But it is one thing to close the judicial option from the start and quite another to do it only after administrative compensation is chosen. In other words, our argument is not intended to suggest that the government may not demand that each victim waive the right to sue before the courts as a condition for his or her receiving administrative compensation. In Argentina, for example, Article 11 of Presidential Decree 70 of 1991 established that the payment of the administrative benefits provided thereto implied that the victim had waived the right to receive any other damages in connection to human rights violations addressed in the Decree (among others, deprivation of freedom, torture, lesions, and death).[19]

There are other reasons, described by Pablo de Greiff, why the government may be tempted to close the judicial option.[20] First, in a scenario in which some victims end up receiving larger judicial compensation, the smaller administrative benefits may appear insignificant. This may undermine the government's effort to restore the victims and leave many feeling frustrated, thereby jeopardizing the success of the reparations program. Second, in certain contexts it may be the case that the decision whether to sue or to accept the administrative benefits will be determined by the victim's social status, since urban, middle-class victims may objectively have a much better chance of succeeding in court than poor, rural victims.

Regarding the first concern, we believe the frustration the victims may feel, and the consequent impact of such frustration on their evaluation of the government's efforts, is likely to be worse in case of judicial closure. To see this, recall the hypothesis presented above in which B, a victim of human rights abuse, received a much smaller compensation than A, who had been hit by a fire engine. The frustration felt by victim B, illustrating the consequences of judicial closure, must certainly be more severe than in the alternative, in which the victim *chooses* to seek administrative benefits.

The second concern actually challenges the notion that the victim can actually be said to choose the administrative option in the first place. In those instances in which access to justice is much more difficult for certain people of lower social status, the normative value of choosing the administrative program diminishes. The challenge posed by this concern is significant, but not decisive. First, the problem of unequal access to justice is a general one and must be addressed by the transitional government in a more structural way. This problem would affect the entire system of justice, and not just cases related to compensation of human rights abuse. Among the more general ways to deal with this problem, it is worth emphasizing the importance of the legal aid institutions sponsored by the government itself or by law schools; and, in certain cases, a pro bono system, whereby private law firms represent poor litigants, could be fostered.

Furthermore, to respond to this problem by appealing to judicial closure would imply leveling down: since some victims of human rights abuse find it difficult to access the courts, so the argument goes, nobody should be allowed to do so. Leveling down is premised on the notion that harming some while benefiting no one can be morally good. It might be argued that this could be justified when the fact that some people obtained a given benefit would imply that they will relate to others who cannot access that benefit in a way that is incompatible with an egalitarian society. Without discussing the merits of such argument in general, which would exceed the purpose of this paper, it must be noted that its relevance to the cases at stake is far from obvious. The argument assumes that for the representative victim of human rights abuse, it is more important to compare oneself with other victims of such abuse than with victims in general (including victims of other types of torts). The intuitive discomfort provoked by our hypothesis involving A and B tends to challenge the plausibility of this assumption. Moreover, the argument we are entertaining presupposes that only by giving all victims of human rights abuse the same amount of money regardless of the particularities of their harm can they be treated 'as equals'. This is a strong assumption. We return to it when dealing with the problem of 'disaggregation' of victims.

There is a final scenario we wish to examine at this point. What happens if the government does not require that each victim waive the right to sue before the courts as a condition for joining the administrative compensation program? As we noted above, we do not believe that the ideal of doing justice to the victims *requires* this more 'flexible' scenario. All that is required is that the victims have the possibility of choosing at some point whether to resort to the courts, but the option need not be open forever. The government has a legitimate interest in being able to assess the total cost of the compensation sooner rather than later, and that implies that it may need to know, early enough in the process, how many victims are likely to resort to the courts.

Yet there is an interesting variation of this scenario that deserves discussion. The government may allow the victims to try to obtain the judicial compensation first, and only if this action is rejected *for certain reasons*—namely, legal obstacles—allow them to access the administrative program. This is the system that the Argentine reparations scheme established for certain cases.[21] The problem with this system is that, as we noted above, it may render the government unable to assess in advance how much it will have to pay to victims overall. Nonetheless, there is an argument to make in favor of this option. As we will argue in the next section, we believe that judicial compensation has certain special virtues that are absent, at least to some extent, in administrative compensation. The pursuit of these virtues may induce the government to resort to administrative compensation only after being certain that judicial compensation is not a valid alternative—that is, only after being certain that the 'legal obstacles' and the 'inadequacy of the judiciary' will have a decisive weight. However, the existence and the importance of such obstacles may not be clear to the government at the moment of designing the reparations program, and therefore it may prefer to remain flexible until the panorama is more certain. After all, it is sometimes difficult to predict what courts will do.

Let us return to the experiences of Chile and Argentina to illustrate this point. As we described above, the Chilean courts rejected numerous claims because victims could not precisely identify the tortfeasor as required by the applicable law. This situation, however, is not unknown to courts, and some of them have devised doctrines to circumvent the difficulties faced by plaintiffs in cases where the strict application of certain legal requirements would lead to unjust results. In common law, for instance, one such doctrine is *res ipsa loquitur*, which has been invoked by courts to relieve the plaintiff of the burden of proving the identity of the actual tortfeasor.[22] The doctrine known in some civil law countries as 'dynamic burden of proof' tends to perform a similar function. It seems that the application of this type of doctrine by the Chilean courts in the cases discussed above would have made a difference. Arguably, they could have found ways to relieve the plaintiffs of certain formalistic requirements that seemed unwarranted in the cases at stake. In fact, this is what eventually happened, at least to some extent, in the Argentine experience: after initially tending to construe the statute of limitations rigidly, Argentine courts started to resort to more ingenious arguments that allowed victims to recover.

The problem is that it may be difficult for the transitional government to predict *ex ante* whether, and to what extent, courts will be willing to engage in this kind of reasoning. Inasmuch as those conditions of uncertainty apply and the government finds the alternative of judicial compensation to be more attractive in principle, it may be justified to wait and see what happens in the courts before designing an administrative compensation program. Alternatively, the government may choose to design such a program in a way that allows for certain flexibility to adapt it to the courts' evolving jurisprudence.

Needless to say, this would make no sense in cases where the judiciary is dismantled or where, for whatever reason, it is clear that it will not provide just compensation. In other words, the alternative we are discussing can only be attractive in those cases where the judicial system is generally trustworthy. Otherwise, it would simply be a waste of time, an exercise in demagogy, or both.

4. THE TORTS APPROACH AND ITS VIRTUES

The analysis presented so far reveals that resorting to administrative compensation is a likely outcome in the particular context of transitional democracies, and one that may turn out to be the right way to deal with the conditions such a context imposes. But the approach imposes a cost as well. As we hope to show, administrative compensation is not a perfect substitute for judicial compensation. This implies that the need to supplement compensation with other forms of remedy is particularly strong if compensation is administrative instead of judicial. There also is a further reason why the comparison is important. As we noted above, we believe that the central goal of compensation to the victims of human rights abuse is to restore their dignity and reintegrate them into society as equal citizens. The special connection that judicial compensation may have with this goal suggests that there are reasons, other than the ones exposed in the prior section, to avoid judicial closure. As we will argue, even if only a small fraction of cases reach the courts, that may be enough for these purposes. Therefore, by emphasizing these positive features of judicial compensation, we are not necessarily arguing in favor of resorting to it exclusively and rejecting administrative compensation. In many transitional contexts, there may be good reasons for this not to be the case. But the following considerations further argue against judicial closure.

Truth

The discovery and disclosure of the truth is a crucial issue in any attempt to repair the victims of human rights abuse. The best-known way to achieve this goal has consisted in devising bodies, such as truth commissions, whose precise aim is to discover and disclose the truth about the human rights abuse perpetrated by state agents.

A similar function can be performed through individual cases brought by each victim before the courts seeking compensation. In fact, judicial determination of the truth even has certain advantages over truth commissions. Usually, judicial fact-finding is more rigorous—and, therefore, more reliable—than the findings of a truth commission. The fact that witnesses render their testimony under oath and can be cross-examined, together with the vast array of procedural institutions devised to guarantee the fairness of the fact-finding process, foster such reliability. Having said this, it is nonetheless clear that the question of whether a truth commission or judicial civil proceedings are a better way of finding truth is highly contextual. It depends on issues such as what the authority of the commission is, how its members are appointed, and the general opinion of its work. The question, therefore, can be answered only on a case-by-case basis. However, it is beyond doubt that whatever the advantages of truth commissions, judicial civil proceedings can at least complement them. And, of course, the truth-seeking role of the courts becomes far more important where there are no truth commissions.

It can also be argued that a judicial decision tends to be more authoritative than the findings of a truth commission as a result of the particular role the judge plays in society. This point is not true of all countries and all situations. Judges may lack prestige, especially if they are perceived as having been actively or passively complicit with the perpetrators. Conversely, as 'newcomers' whose only credentials are their political contacts with the new authorities, members of truth commissions may prove to be unreliable to the populace at large.[23] Having said that, it is worth emphasizing that the decision by a judge is especially meaningful as an act of authority, and can hardly be matched in those terms by the findings of a truth commission.[24]

In contrast with judicial compensation, administrative compensation lacks these truth-finding virtues. In fact, administrative compensation is easily associated with silence-seeking plans, as was the case in Argentina, where President Carlos Menem's reparation program was perceived by many as 'pardon to the perpetrators, money to the victims'. We will return to this point below when dealing with the problem of political manipulation.

We wish to emphasize that, as we suggested above, even if only a small fraction of cases reaches the courts, this may be enough to perform this essential truth-finding function. Once the courts establish the facts in one case, those facts become the basis for understanding the truth. And establishing the truth in this way will benefit not only the plaintiffs in the instant case, but also victims more generally. After all, however narrow a judicial case may seem, general issues must necessarily be discussed; those issues, inevitably, will go far beyond the plaintiffs' situation. For this purpose, individual plaintiffs may act as representatives of victims more generally.

Punishment

Punishing the perpetrator is an important way—probably the most important—of restoring victims' dignity. Although no one can deny that the paradigmatic mechanism of punishment by the state is the criminal system, civil compensation performs a similar role. Of course, this is true insofar as it is actually the perpetrator, and not the state, who ends up paying. A serious analysis of that issue would exceed the scope of this paper.[25] However, it may be noted that under the administrative compensation programs it is *never* the perpetrator who pays for the compensation, not even as the result of a subsequent action by the state, and therefore there is no punishment involved.

In the cases where criminal prosecution is not available, the punishment that can derive from a civil action becomes more relevant. That scenario, of course, is not unlikely in transitional democracies. The new democratic state may lack the power to conduct criminal trials against the perpetrators. Civil proceedings, however, are a different story. They usually do not give rise to the kind of uneasiness among the group of perpetrators that the threat of criminal trials involves, and therefore the transitional government may be able to cope with them.

The Chilean experience illustrates that dynamic. After former dictator Augusto Pinochet was acquitted by local courts in late 2002, the number of civil lawsuits increased. This trend is explained as follows. After the acquittal, and knowing for certain that criminal procedures would not succeed, representatives of victims filed civil actions to try to obtain a judicial decision that stated that Pinochet ordered the killings and was guilty of the crimes for which he was prosecuted.[26] In other words, civil actions were the second best alternative to achieve punishment of the perpetrator. This example also speaks to the truth-finding virtues of judicial proceedings, discussed above, for the victims sought not only punishment, but the truth.

As we stated, punishment of the perpetrators plays a central role in restoring victims' dignity. This dignifying effect, too, will obtain even if only a small fraction of the civil actions succeeds. The fact that a perpetrator is made to pay in one case will have symbolic importance for the other victims as well. In this respect, compensation to a few victims, it could be said, has positive externalities for all of them. Again, one could see individual plaintiffs as representatives of victims more generally, as far as the pursuit of punishment to the perpetrators is concerned.

Personal Dignity and 'Homogenization' of Victims

A torts claim aims, *inter alia*, at understanding how the harmful event impacted the plaintiff. The damages awarded thereby are a recognition that *that* victim underwent certain pain and suffering as a result of the actions of the defendant. Administrative compensation, conversely, treats all the victims in the same way. It does not allow victims to prove the ordeal *they* went through and how *their* lives were affected. For example, in the *Tarnopolsky* case, the damages award of about $1 million was based upon due consideration of the fact that the plaintiff had suffered the loss of four members of his family and had gone through a long-lasting exile.[27]

All these specific features of the victims' personal ordeal are emphasized by the torts approach and overlooked by administrative compensation. Pablo de Greiff, in 'Justice and Reparations' (Chapter 12, this volume), finds in this fact a reason to favor the administrative approach. In his view, the torts approach, in emphasizing the victims' differences, tends to disaggregate them; this, he argues, is problematic from the point of view of equality.

To address this concern, it is useful to distinguish between treating victims equally and treating them as equals.[28] De Greiff is, of course, aware of this distinction, but we tend to disagree with him on what the relevant dimension of equality is in this type of case. To assert that people should receive equal compensation regardless of their actual harm is not plausible as a general claim. There is no principled way of arguing that a person who suffered a $1 million loss and another one who suffered a $10 loss should receive the same compensation in the name of equality. This would clearly not be the relevant dimension to equalize in such a case; rather, it seems that only by compensating people in accordance with the harm suffered can they be treated as equals. To compensate people equally regardless of their actual harm is as egalitarian as it is to collect the same amount of tax from everyone regardless of their actual income or wealth.[29]

The argument about 'disaggregation' of victims presupposes that, in the case of victims of human rights abuse, this general conclusion does not hold. But only very strong reasons could justify such a dramatic departure from what equality requires in cases of reparative justice generally. We fail to see such reasons present in the case of human rights abuse. Quite to the contrary, we find the *aggregation* of victims problematic in terms of restoring the victim's dignity. By treating the harms of all the victims alike, the sense of uniqueness of each victim is diluted. The victim is viewed as forming part of a large, uniform mass or, in any case, a mass whose heterogeneity is deemed irrelevant by the policy maker. The fact that the human rights abuse was massive does not imply that the redress should be massive as well. Human dignity implies being respected for what one is as an individual. Judicial actions, by emphasizing the individuality of each victim, contribute to the restoration of lost dignity. Administrative compensation, conversely, by overlooking relevant differences, reproduces the sense of a diluted individuality attached to mass human rights violations.

It is true, nevertheless, that our argument loses strength when it is precisely the fact of belonging to a discrete group that motivated the human rights abuse in the first place. When it is a discrete group that was the target of abuse, the link between mass compensation and restoration of dignity can be clearer. But we cannot take these cases to be the rule. Moreover, the argument about 'disaggregation' of victims does not presuppose the existence of a discrete group that was the target of human rights abuse, but rather that the mere fact of being a victim of such abuse binds people together in morally relevant ways, and that it is therefore essential to preserve such bonds. We fail to see why this would be so.

In sum, we believe that the torts approach can serve the goal of restoring victims' dignity by emphasizing their individuality. But, also here, it is not necessary that all lawsuits be successful, or even that a large number of cases reach the courts, for this effect to obtain. What is important is that the option should exist, even if the reasons discussed throughout make it improbable that most victims will actually choose it. Choosing is an important—probably the most important—way of emphasizing one's individuality. The positive consequences of leaving some room for choice should therefore not be undervalued.

Personal Dignity and Political Manipulation

Any reparation program may be rightly considered a failure if it is deemed by the majority of the population, or at least by the majority of the victims, as an instance of political manipulation. But we do not wish to be misunderstood on this point. It is to be expected in a transitional democracy that a reparation program be politically negotiated, and that the democratic government be responsive to the political reactions such a program generates. However, the problem arises when as a result of either the form or the content of the reparation program, the public considers that the program has been a kind of bargain or concession by the government to mollify a political group.

The Argentine experience with reparations could, on some readings, be one of those cases. The administrative compensations promoted by then President Carlos Menem gave the impression, at least to some, that their purpose was to 'buy' the silence of a politically active group, and that they worked as a kind of counterbalance to the recent presidential pardon to the perpetrators of human rights violations. As de Greiff remarks: 'In the Argentinean case, it must be remembered, most of the programs came in the wake of the cessation of attempts to achieve criminal justice and of presidential pardons for the very few perpetrators who had been convicted. The overall combination suggested that the policy was something like "pardon for perpetrators, money for victims", where each of the measures was itself quite controversial; the pardons were the result of politically divisive decisions, and the money for reparations distributed in ways that either encouraged or allowed the wrong associations.'[30]

Of course, this does not mean that any program of administrative compensation will be regarded as a case of political manipulation. And, conversely, the judiciary could also deal with compensation in a manipulative manner. However, there are many reasons related to the institutional design of the courts that make such a scenario less probable. One might mention their relative political independence, the length of the proceedings (which precludes short-run political speculation) and the atomization of decision-making (which makes a unified scheme leading to manipulative maneuvers less likely).

As we have seen throughout this section, here, too, the mere existence of the possibility of resorting to the courts may in itself be helpful. So long as the victims know that the judicial option is available, it is less likely that they will see themselves as objects being traded as part of a political bargain. After all, they can rightly think, if the government cannot fully control their decision on how to seek compensation, this may limit its ability to negotiate.

In Argentina, the judicial option was not closed.[31] Although we cannot assess the precise impact that this fact had on victims' opinion on the issue we are discussing, it seems safe to assume that judicial closure could only have worsened that opinion. The government may have good reasons to endeavor to leave behind a 'sad chapter' of the country's history as promptly as possible. If, however, this approach is pushed too far or is done in ways that give rise to perceptions of political manipulation, the success of the compensation scheme may be in danger. It is imperative to strike a delicate balance.

5. CONCLUSION

In Section 4, we pinpointed some advantages of the torts approach over the administrative one. By this, we do not mean to argue that the former should necessarily be preferred over the latter. Quite the contrary, as we noted, there may be reasons to prefer administrative compensation in certain cases. But this does not mean that, in those cases, we should forget the torts approach altogether. The goal of bringing justice to victims of human rights abuse may often be attained by establishing the appropriate relation between administrative and judicial compensation.

Moreover, we believe that our analysis helps to illuminate what is lost through administrative compensation, and what risks should be adequately considered. This, in turn, speaks to the importance of devising a comprehensive reparation program in which the different remedies are viewed as complementary. In that vein, we note that civil remedies are indispensable, and yet they do not suffice to provide full redress to the victims. Some authors have claimed that restorative justice may be preferable to retributive justice.[32] Our analysis, however, does not support that position. Although it may be difficult at times to prosecute and convict powerful perpetrators, not only punishment but criminal proceedings themselves are the strongest statement of condemnation available.

In this chapter we have dealt with matters that are highly context-specific, depend on myriad variables of an elusive nature. No clear-cut answers, therefore, should be expected, and we have not sought to provide them. Our purpose, rather, has been to illuminate some of the relevant factors that are at play and to seek principled arguments for addressing them.

NOTES

1. PCIJ Ser. A No. 17, 67, 80, 86, 99, 121.
2. See Draft Articles on Responsibility of States for internationally wrongful acts of the International Law Commission, Articles 35 and 36; United Nations Convention against Torture and Other Cruel, Inhuman or Degrading Treatment or Punishment, Article 14.1; United Nations Declaration of Basic Principles of Justice for Victims of Crime and Abuse of Power; Basic Principles and Guidelines on the Right to a Remedy and Reparation for Victims of Violations of International Human Rights and Humanitarian Law, Section IX; Set of Principles for the Protection and Promotion of Human Rights through Action to Combat Impunity, Principle 36; General Recommendation XXVI of the Committee on the Elimination of Racial Discrimination; Statute of the International Criminal Court, Article 75; American Convention on Human Rights, Article 63.

3. In Sections 3 and 4 we analyze, and reject, two other arguments in favor of the administrative approach. The first claims that administrative compensation should be preferred because it is cheaper; the second, that it must be preferred because it does not 'disaggregate' the victims. These arguments raise problems that relate to topics specifically dealt with in those sections, and for that reason we chose to address them there.

4. The Argentine newspaper *La Nación* reported on January 23, 2004 that some 9,000 persons were killed in auto accidents in Argentina in the year 2003 alone.

5. For a detailed account of Argentina's reparations efforts, see María José Guembe (Chapter 1, this volume).

6. But they are also an illustration of how case law can evolve on these matters in favor of victims, a point we address in other sections.

7. *T.D. c. Estado Nacional y otros*, Cámara Nacional en lo Contencioso administrativo Federal, sala III, February 9, 1996. The decision was confirmed by the Argentine Supreme Court *in re Tarnopolsky, Daniel c. Estado Nacional*, August 31, 1999.

8. *Cámara Nacional de Apelaciones en lo Contencioso Administrativo Federal, sala III*, March 31, 1992, Case No 27294, *Hagelin, Ragnar c. Estado Nacional (PEN)*.

9. Argentine Supreme Court *in re Tarnopolsky, Daniel c. Estado Nacional*, August 31, 1999.

10. Ibid.

11. For an overview of Chile's reparations efforts, see Elizabeth Lira (Chapter 2, this volume). For specific cases, see *Garay Hermosilla et al. v. Chile*, Case 10.843, Report No. 36/96, Inter-Am. C.H.R., OEA/Ser.L/V/II.95 Doc. 7 rev. in 156 (1997). Report No 36/96 Case 10.843 Chile, October 15, 1996.

12. While it is true that these legal obstacles could be removed by passing a law to that effect, the torts approach is based upon the notion that compensation of human rights abuse should be judged by the same substantive and procedural standards as ordinary torts. Therefore, passing ad hoc laws that single out cases of human rights abuse in order to treat them differently runs counter to the torts approach. And, in any case, no ad hoc law could remove the obstacles related to the structure of the judiciary analyzed above.

13. Christian Tomuschat, 'Individual Reparation Claims in Instances of Grave Human Rights Violations', in *State Responsibility and the Individual: Reparation in Instances of Grave Violations of Human Rights*, Albrecht Randelzhofer and Christian Tomuschat, eds. (The Hague/London/Boston: Martinus Nijhoff Publishers, 1999), 20. On the issue of the economic constraints to compensation, see also, in the same volume, Michael Reisman, 'Compensation for Human Rights Violations: The Practice of the Past Decade in the Americas'.

14. Systematized information on the amounts of the awards can be found in Pablo de Greiff, 'Reparations Efforts in International Perspective: What Compensation Contributes to the Achievement of Imperfect Justice', in *To Repair the Irreparable: Reparation and Reconstruction in South Africa*, Erik Doxtader and Charles Villa-Vicencio, eds. (Claremont, South Africa: David Philip, 2004).

15. For the purposes of this argument, we are assuming that the awards obtained through the torts approach will be eventually paid by the government, not the perpetrators. To the extent that this assumption does not hold, the administrative approach may actually imply more expenditures for the government than the torts approach.

16. This is what de Greiff calls 'finality' in 'Reparations Efforts in International Perspective', op. cit.

17. In line with that fallacy, civil systems that followed the Napoleon Code were very restrictive in granting compensation for moral damage; in general, they limited compensation for moral damages to torts involving a criminal offense. Most civil codes have been amended in that respect but others still hold that restriction, e.g. the Bolivian Civil Code.

18. The idea here is not to modify the substantive rules that determine how ordinary torts should be compensated, but rather to pass general laws establishing limitations on the extent to which credits against the government can be collected. Such laws do not affect the way compensations are awarded by the courts; they affect the ability to collect the awards in full.

19. See Guembe, op. cit.

20. See de Greiff, 'Justice and Reparations' (Chapter 12, this volume).

21. See Guembe, op. cit.

22. A leading case on the matter is *Ybarra v. Spangard*, 25 Cal. 2d at 486, 154 P.2d at 687. Joseph Ybarra suffered paralysis and atrophy in his shoulder while going through surgery. He could not identify who, of all the doctors and nurses who attended him, had actually caused the injury, since he was under the effects of anesthesia when it occurred. Invoking the doctrine of *res ipsa loquitur,* the court decided to shift the burden of proof to the defendants, who in this case had better access to the relevant information as to who was the actual tortfeasor.

23. The Argentine experience in the trial of the Juntas was probably successful in this respect, since the judges were generally perceived as reasonably impartial.

24. It may be claimed that many of the arguments in favor of the courts as truth-finders apply better to criminal procedures than to civil procedures. Even if such was the case, there is still room for a strong argument in favor of civil procedures in those cases where criminal actions are not available—not a rare scenario in transitional democracies (more on this issue in Section 4, in connection with criminal punishment).

25. As Michael Reisman (op. cit., 68) claims: 'Because the "State" is identified as the responsible party, it is often innocent people who, in effect, pay the compensation for the human rights violations that have been effected by others. . . .'

26. See Lira, op. cit.

27. See n. 6.

28. See Ronald Dworkin, *Taking Rights Seriously* (London: Duckworth, 1977).

29. This argument is focused on the monetary compensation of material loss. This is not the only relevant aspect of a reparation scheme, but, since it is a crucial component of it, it cannot be overlooked.

30. de Greiff, 'Reparations Efforts in International Perspective', op. cit.

31. See Guembe, op. cit.

32. This was suggested by Elazar Barkan, *The Guilt of Nations* (New York: Norton, 2000).

CHAPTER 16

NARROWING THE MICRO AND MACRO: A PSYCHOLOGICAL PERSPECTIVE ON REPARATIONS IN SOCIETIES IN TRANSITION

BRANDON HAMBER

1. INTRODUCTION

Tantalus was the son of Zeus and was the king of Sipylos. He was uniquely favored among mortals since he was invited to share the food of the gods. However, he abused the guest–host relationship and was punished by being 'tantalized' with hunger and thirst in Tartarus: he was immersed up to his neck in water, but when he bent to drink, it all drained away; luscious fruit hung on trees above him, but when he reached for it the winds blew the branches beyond his reach.[1]

This chapter is concerned with the relationship between the individual (micro) and the collective (macro) dimensions of reparations. Specifically, it seeks to highlight the gaps and confluences between the two, especially when thinking about symbolic reparations. To expand: a reparations program might be judged to represent a judicious and legitimate effort to repair in terms of macro considerations, but individual recipients, given their personal loss, may consider it insufficient and it may fail to meet their psychological needs. The gap between the micro and the macro dimensions of reparations, it will be argued, can leave massive reparations programs, in the metaphorical sense of the story of Tantalus, stuck between two worlds, that of the individual victims as they struggle over a long period of time to come to terms with the extreme trauma inflicted upon them, and the world of the social and the political, which is cut through by a range of pragmatic concerns especially during times of transition.

This chapter demonstrates that this gap can be narrowed through a better understanding of what happens to individuals when subject to extreme political trauma. It will also outline the benefits and limits of symbolic reparations in this regard. It further highlights how steps can be taken at the social and political level that can potentially increase the impact of reparations on individuals, namely, through considering more carefully the nature and type of reparations offered, and the context, process, and discourses surrounding their delivery.

2. The Individual and Collective Dimensions of the Impact of Political Violence

Understanding the relationship between what reparations can or cannot do at an individual or collective level is partially dependent on how one understands the impact of political violence. Lykes and Mersky (Chapter 17, this volume) identify at least two competing philosophical traditions in terms of trauma theory and practice. Lykes and Mersky highlight an etic perspective that suggests that individuals subject to politically organized or state-sponsored violence and/ or war trauma generally display a set of identifiable and universal symptoms that can be ameliorated through individual and small group interventions such as counseling. They also identify a more emic approach that seeks to understand the uniqueness of those affected within a social and historical context. This approach, as they note, is not one single model, but rather an orientation that aspires to reestablish community, cultural, and social life and bonds as constituent parts of healing.

The approach adopted in this paper is in line with the more emic approach to political trauma. From this perspective, coming to terms with the past for the victims and survivors of political violence has both a psychological and socio-political dimension. Strategies for addressing the interpersonal consequences of trauma may be necessary (e.g. counseling, community support, dealing with bereavement through culturally relevant mourning processes), but addressing the socio-political context itself will require attention to fully address the impact of the trauma.

Attempts to rebuild society (e.g. guaranteeing nonrepetition, ensuring socioeconomic equality, doing justice, and developing a fair and accountable political system) are important for an individual who is struggling to come to terms with extreme political trauma. Reparations can also be very significant in this regard. As de Greiff notes (Chapter 12, this volume), reparations programs, from the standpoint of the victims, generally occupy a special place as they are the most tangible manifestation of the efforts of the state to remedy the harms they have suffered.

In societies coming out of political violence, strategies to address the past such as massive reparations programs can bolster national attempts to 'reestablish' society. Using the emic approach outlined above, reparations are in themselves potentially one of the constituent components of healing, although they are not free from their risks and challenges. This is discussed later in this chapter.

3. DEFINING REPARATIONS: A PSYCHOLOGICAL APPROACH

Reparations can imply a range of responses and actions. Generally reparations entail, amongst others, acts of restoring what has been lost, giving something to a victim equivalent to a loss, or making amends for what has been done whether symbolic or material, and may even entail specific gestures such as an apology. Most often, drawing on largely legal notions, reparations are understood as the effort to restore someone (or something) to the state it was before harm was done. From this perspective, *reparations* generally implies a structured and procedurally just way of trying to redress or compensate harm.

However, the term *reparations* also has a specific meaning in psychology, and particularly in psychoanalytic thinking. Historically it is mostly closely associated with the work of Melanie Klein.[2] Space does not permit a thorough examination of this, but suffice to say that in psychoanalytic thinking, reparation generally deals with internal psychic processes. It is closely associated with intrapsychic guilt, i.e. the profound (psychological) urge to 'make good' for injuries done to others. As Klein writes:

[s]ide by side with the destructive impulses in the unconscious mind both of the child and the adult, there exists a profound urge to make sacrifices, in order to help and put right people who in phantasy have been harmed or destroyed. In the depths of the mind, the urge to make people happy is linked up with a strong feeling of responsibility and concern for them, which manifests itself in genuine sympathy with other people and in the ability to understand them, as they are and as they feel.[3]

Thus, for Klein, the human need to make amends for perceived and actual harm[4] is closely tied to developing the capacity (i.e. in the infant as it develops psychologically) for taking responsibility. In the same way, the capacity to understand others and have sympathy for them is developed each time the infant engages in the psychological process of making reparation.[5] In this sense, the psychological ability to make reparation is considered an essential component in the psychological development of the child, and ultimately necessary in the formation of all relationships.

Klein's analysis tells us that not only do most people have an urge to try to set things right that have been damaged in some way, we also internalize this and expect it from others. If this theory is correct then reparation (and the urge to make amends for perceived or actual wrongs to others) holds a fairly central place in human psychology. This goes some way to explaining the 'special place' afforded to reparations by victims that de Greiff mentions. The theory also highlights the complexity of thinking about reparations from an individual perspective (this is discussed throughout this chapter). That said, and in line with the so-called emic approach outlined earlier, we also need to begin to think about the social dimension of reparations.[6]

Reparation and Reparations

To understand the relationship between the individual (micro) and collective (macro) processes at play during the implementation of a massive reparations program I believe a distinction between the term *reparation* (singular) and *reparations* (plural) can be useful.

I define *reparations* (plural) as the acts or objects associated with attempts to make amends, e.g. compensation payments, building a memorial. *Reparations* can also be representational in form or intent, such as the act of stating an apology.

Simply put, reparations are the things done or given as an attempt to deal with the consequences of political violence. In line with the approach taken in this book, I understand reparations in the narrow sense, that is, to refer to 'the attempts to provide benefits directly to the victims of certain types of crimes' (quoted from de Greiff, Chapter 12, this volume). Such a definition of reparations does not include broader strategies such as institutional reform or truth-telling as de Greiff notes. This fits neatly with my understanding of *reparations* as acts and objects, or things done or given. In addition, and again in line with the focus of this book, this chapter is mainly concerned with what are termed symbolic *reparations* (e.g. memorials, apologies) insofar as they are granted under the auspices of a massive reparations program.

At the same time, a massive reparations program, and the reparations it dispenses, are generally going to be associated with a much more expansive set of aims. In this book, for example, de Greiff argues that the general aim of a program of reparations is to do justice and this can include the goals of recognition, civic trust, and social solidarity. This is a useful conceptualization and assists in focusing the reparations debate. However, if we are to understand the psychological processes at play for victims, I would like to suggest that the goals of reparations may need to be understood in a wider sense. From an *individual* psychological perspective it is helpful to think about the aim of *reparations*, as obvious as it may sound on first reading, as being about making *reparation*, or from the Kleinian perspective to 'make good' psychologically for what has been damaged, lost, or destroyed.

The advantage of using the terms in this way is that it can assist in understanding how an individual victim may think about reparations and what they may ultimately desire from them (whether this is practically possible or achievable is another matter). At the individual level the victim is generally seeking through the granting of *reparations* some sort of *reparation*, that is, a psychological state in which they will feel that adequate amends have been made for a wrong committed. A government may also aspire (or at least hope) that its reparations program will broadly satisfy victims in this way. That said, whether reparation has taken place for an individual is difficult to measure, if not impossible to satisfy—a point to which I will return later.

At the macro level, a massive reparations program may also seek to make social or collective *reparation* in the society at large (i.e. achieving a socio-political context in which past wrongs can be said to have been adequately addressed). Some psychologists take this broad approach, calling this 'social reparation'. For them 'social reparation' embodies the revelation and condemnation of past human rights violations, the formal 'doing of justice', and setting up structures to prevent future violations.[7] Still for others, 'social reparation' is understood to be a socio-political and psychological process, which aims to establish the truth of political repression and demands justice for human rights violations, while taking account of individual mental health needs.[8]

In the interests of conceptual clarity, however, I will not address *reparation* in this collective sense. Thinking about the broader aims of reparations is, as de Greiff argues in this book, generally much more of a political project. As he notes, this may require, especially in a society in transition, to take a broader conception of justice that goes beyond the satisfaction of individual claims and seeks more modest goals such as recognition, social solidarity and increased levels of civic trust.

But why do I make a distinction between reparations and reparation *at the individual level*? First, conceptualizing the reparations debate using the reparations and reparation distinction assists in sensitizing us to the micro and macro processes implicit in granting reparations in a more nuanced and detailed way. At the individual level, it draws our attention to the fact that individual victims have an extremely deep set of relationships to what is granted to them and what it is they desire for reparations to achieve. A disjuncture will exist between the reparations and what can be achieved through them at a personal psychological level.

Second, the conceptualization proposed highlights how what is needed (or possible) at the macro level may be at odds with what can be achieved (or is desired) in terms of individual reparation. The gap can no doubt be narrowed through developing reparations programs that are complex and internally and externally coherent (de Greiff in this volume). These types of factors are important because from a psychosocial perspective how the process of *reparations* is structured, publicly spoken about and dealt with is one of the factors that psychologically communicates to victims how their plight is understood in the wider social context.[9] The actual type of reparations is also important. Before turning to these points, however, it is necessary to make some additional points on the benefits and challenges of granting reparations from the individual perspective (micro level).

4. THE INDIVIDUAL LEVEL

Benefits of Symbolic Reparations

All objects or acts of reparations have a symbolic meaning *to individuals*—they are never merely acts or objects. This symbolism to individuals operates at two levels:

1. Reparations generally *symbolize something to individuals*, that is, in form, quality, shape, or image they represent or indirectly express something abstract or invisible such as the memory of a loved one. Such acts and objects can be profoundly meaningful to victims or survivors at a psychological level.

2. Reparations also represent or indirectly express something abstract or invisible to victims *about those giving or granting* the reparations, for example, an admission of guilt, benevolence, care for citizens by society, and/or a willingness to pay back what has been lost.

In terms of the first point, acts of reparations (e.g. reburials) and material acts of reparations (e.g. payments) serve the same symbolic end, that is, they stand as 'symbolic' markers of redress, recognition, or acknowledgment in their own right. This is not to say, however, that political conflict cannot have very real material impacts (e.g. goods being stolen or destroyed, and/or a breadwinner's income being lost) that may need to be redressed in a financial or compensatory way, but this focuses on reparations of the more symbolic kind.

At an individual level, financial reparations and other acts of reparations (e.g. building a monument) have the potential to play an important role in any process of healing, coping with bereavement, and addressing the impact of violence for victims. They can symbolically acknowledge and recognize the individual's suffering. Symbolic representations (e.g. a memorial) of what happened, particularly if the symbol is personalized (e.g., contains the name of a loved one) and culturally relevant, can help concretize a traumatic event, aid an individual to come to terms with it, and help label responsibility. The final point is important because labeling responsibility can appropriately redirect blame toward those responsible and relieve the guilt that survivors often feel.

In addition, reparations can serve as focal points in the grieving process, i.e. as a place or object (e.g. memorial garden or memorial) that can serve as a physical or visual representation of what was lost, allowing individuals space to channel their emotions and address them in a focused or specific way. This can aid recovery by allowing individuals to focus exclusively on their grief through the symbol. Reparations (such as the building of a memorial), and even compensation payments in some instances, can also symbolically mark the point of moving on to a new phase and symbolize an individual's mastery over the past.

In terms of the second level of symbolism, that is, what the granting of reparations represents to victims *about those giving or granting* them, a few points are also worth making. First, the establishment of a massive reparations program can represent to victims societal or community willingness to deal with and part from the past. This can assist victims to feel a greater level of integration, recognition and acceptance into society. At the same time, this can combat feelings of isolation and silence, both common consequences of political violence. It is also possible, as de Greiff argues in this book, that reparations can lead, at the individual level, to greater feelings of recognition by the state and increase levels of civic trust. If victims feel their hurt is recognized and adequately acknowledged it is completely plausible that this will contribute to a sense of citizenship and social belonging for the recipients. This, from an emic understanding of the impact of trauma, can be vital in terms of healing insofar as reconnecting an individual with their society is a crucial dimension of dealing with trauma.

Monuments and museums, plaques and other markers are some of the ways that governments, as well as social actors, can try to embody memories—these can serve as vehicles for the intergenerational transmission of historical memory.[10] Spatial markers of memory (e.g., memorials and monuments) are also attempts to make affirmations and statements, and are both objects and gestures which embody individual, political, collective and public meaning. A public monument, writes Kirk Savage, 'represents a collective recognition—in short, legitimacy—for the memory deposited there'.[11] The establishment of monuments and museums, plaques, and other markers demonstrates a societal or community willingness to deal with and acknowledge the hurts of the past. They may result in lessons from the past being carried into the future and convince victims of the possibility of nonrepetition. They are as de Greiff suggests in this volume, a materialization of society's willingness to do things differently.

At a more micro level, in restorative justice, restitution paid by the perpetrator to the victim can also help symbolize the perpetrator's commitment to apologizing, making amends, and taking responsibility. There is research to show that many victims (of criminal violence) want reparations in the form of a sincere apology from their offender, as well as compensation from them for damages, promises not to reoffend and the taking of responsibility by the offender for their actions.[12] Similar needs have been expressed in relation to truth commission processes. For example, a victim who testified at the South African Truth and Reconciliation Commission commented:

> In my opinion, I think the best way to demonstrate a truthful commitment to peace and a truthful commitment to repentance is that perpetrators of acts of violence would make a contribution, a financial contribution to the families of victims and, in that way, they would then cleanse themselves of their own guilt, and they will then demonstrate with extreme confidence that in fact they are sorry about what they did.[13]

Hugo van der Merwe, in his study of a community in South Africa over the life of the South African Truth and Reconciliation Commission, found that it was common for victims to want to confront the perpetrator and tell their story—they wanted perpetrators to be made aware of their suffering and in some cases wanted them to explain their actions and apologize.[14]

Challenges Facing the Granting of Reparations

From an individual perspective, reparations for human rights violations are trying to repair the irreparable.[15] From the perspective of direct victims of political violence, and even at times from the collective perspective, acknowledgment, apology, recognition, and even substantial material assistance do not 'bring back the dead', nor are they guaranteed to converge with, and ameliorate, all the levels of psychological pain suffered. No matter what the motive, all reparations strategies face this intractable problem. Reparations can never wholly meet all the psychological needs of survivors of political violence. All reparations, in the context of trying to redress the impact of political violence, whether financial or in the form of an object (e.g. a memorial) are nominal in nature. It is impossible to wholly close the gap between an individual's personal psychological needs and what the society can offer at a social and political level.

Furthermore, the difficulties of trying to repair the irreparable can be compounded in transitional contexts. For example, one of the needs often highlighted by victims following human rights violations is the need for justice.[16] Bringing perpetrators to justice is also considered an important and sometimes essential component of a victim's recovery and psychological healing.[17] However, in societies in transition, justice through the courts is a need seldom met, for example, in cases where concessions to former combatants and amnesties to state officials are part of a peace agreement, or where there are insufficient resources or evidence to prosecute human rights violators. In the South African context, for example, there is little doubt that the granting of amnesty to perpetrators of human rights violations compounded the sense and feelings of the 'irreparability' of the situation for some survivors, whether retributive justice through the courts was a pragmatic possibility or not.[18]

Reparations, however, can also add tensions to the process of dealing with human rights violations. For example, passively accepting reparations can be experienced by some survivors as a disrespectful act that betrays the loss they have endured, or the memory of those killed. In the case of families of the disappeared, for example, accepting reparations can (often unconsciously) make the survivor feel complicit in betraying the final memory of their missing relatives. Some of the mothers of the disappeared in Argentina do not accept reparations because it compels them to 'psychologically kill and bury their children and to finally become their own children's "executioners"'.[19] Accepting reparations can be guilt-inducing, and can imply, say in the case of 'disappearances', giving up hope, or psychologically rendering the lives of the missing meaningless.[20]

From these brief examples it is evident that trying to psychologically come to terms with human rights violations is a difficult, complex and lengthy process, not to mention highly individualized, as was noted in the introduction to this chapter. For the most part, when reparations are granted, the survivors will not be ready to put the past behind them at that specific point. It is likely that their personal process of coming to terms with what has happened to them will not fully overlap with the protracted process or political timing of granting reparations. The granting of reparations is a political act with its own time frame, and potent social dynamic.

In addition, it is critical that reparations are not conditional or make demands on the recipient. For example, victims should not be expected, either implicitly or explicitly, to forgive the perpetrators or forget about the past because some form of reparations has been made. Any form of reparation can be expected to leave the survivor feeling dissatisfied. Reparations designed or granted with the naïve aim of 'closure' are starting on the wrong trajectory. This is not to say, however, that reparations cannot be psychologically beneficial, or open personal and social space to assist with dealing with a violent past, but the gap between what they can achieve at an individual and internal level, and what can be offered at a collective and political level will remain.

Thus, when thinking about consequences of extreme political violence and trauma, *reparation* can never be fully achieved at an individual level. The psychological impact can never be totally ameliorated and actual harm done cannot, psychologically speaking, be *completely* 'made good' in the Kleinian sense.

This is not to say that all victims of political violence remain completely damaged. Degrees of dealing with the consequences of extreme political violence and trauma are possible, many victims are indeed survivors and highly resilient. It is possible to reach a situation where a substantial degree of mental resolution takes place, that is, where the trauma is no longer seen as unfinished business, requiring, for instance, a compulsion to take revenge. Grief and loss no longer plague the individual consciously or unconsciously, and the victim moves to a place where the loss is to a large degree accepted and incorporated into the functioning of everyday life.[21]

Having said this, given that what has been lost can never be fully replaced, the type of reparation that reparations can contribute to *individual victims* can at best be psychologically 'good enough';[22] that is, the victim feels subjectively satisfied that sufficient actions have been taken to make amends for their suffering and a psychological state is achieved in which some sort of mental resolution concerning past trauma is reached.

Admittedly, this is a less than conclusive way of thinking about the issue, especially for policymakers. It reminds us of the debate introduced by de Greiff in this volume regarding Article 50 of the European Convention that states reparations should be about the 'just satisfaction to the victim'. Correctly de Greiff asks, 'what does "just satisfaction" mean, precisely?' In a sense, I am asking the same question. One way would be to try and quantify a fair level of compensation based on calculating material and moral loss as the Inter-American Court does, but as de Greiff notes, this in itself can be impractical in the transitional justice context.

From the psychological perspective, however, we cannot take the question of 'satisfaction' out of the equation. It is ever present from the victim perspective at the same time as being illusive, differing from individual to individual, and never fully attainable. That said some level of satisfaction is attainable. Macro strategies, if developed and operationalized in certain ways, which I discuss in the next section, can move the reparation process somewhat up the continuum of satisfaction for victims.

5. Narrowing the Gap between the Micro and Macro

This section highlights some steps that can be taken at a social and political level to potentially increase the impact of reparations on individuals. It considers (*a*) the nature and type of reparations offered and (*b*) the context, process and discourses surrounding their delivery.

Nature and Types of Reparations

It is difficult to categorize or discuss the potential impact of all the different types of reparations (e.g. apologies, memorials, service packages). In line with the focus of this chapter, however, I restrict my perspective to those types of reparations considered more symbolic in nature.

One psychological theory that I find useful for framing an analysis of what symbolic reparations can mean and achieve is the theory about human development proposed by Winnicott concerning what he calls 'transitional objects'. In child development, Winnicott argues, a child begins its life focused inwardly—he or she lives in a subjective inner world. To make the transition to experiencing the objective reality of the outer world, the child uses objects (typically a blanket or teddy bear, specifically objects to which the child seems very attached) as vehicles for fantasized thought and action. This object becomes the first external object that gets woven into their personal or individual pattern. The object becomes the child's symbolic bridge between the outer and inner world.[23] The object becomes 'sacred'. Often the parents collude with this because they know not to risk altering, washing, or throwing the object away for fear of seriously upsetting the child. They understand the object's 'magical' significance to the child.

In a similar sense, one could understand reparations objects (memorials and the like) as objects that assist in bridging the gaps between the interpersonal world and the social world for victims and individuals in the society. Reparations objects of this kind bridge inner-directed grief and suffering, and mirror (to the world and individual) how that suffering is understood and accepted (or not) within the real socio-political world. Through the object the reactions of the real world are tested and messages are sent back (at a deep psychological level) to the victim about their personal value and psychological sense of belonging in society.

How the object (e.g. the memorial) comes into being, and how it is treated by others and society is of great significance to victims. The context in which reparations are granted needs to be one that demonstrates adequate levels of recognition, responsibility, social change and acknowledgment of the individual (and the collective to a degree) within an environment where its meaning is felt to be genuine by those it directly affects. If not, the object itself can become (metaphorically speaking) the vehicle for re-evoking inner pain and suffering. Instead of helping bridge and externalize suffering and convince victims that the outer world or the society is a safe and caring place in which the victim has a place, the object and those who supported its establishment become 'persecutory' in a very profound psychological sense, driving suffering inward once again.

Reparations are a deep interpersonal and social barometer for victims. They tell the victim much about their place in society and signal whether there is social space for their grief, anger and feelings of injustice. This is important because generally in political violence it is 'the society' (the social world) that is the cause of their suffering, and without social recognition of this their suffering runs the risk of continuing to exist only in their 'internal world' where it can be acute and isolating. Reparations, like the 'transitional object', must have something 'sacred' or even 'magical' about them to have an interpersonal (individual) and social (collective) meaning simultaneously.

But what does this mean practically? Can reparations acquire these characteristics? How does an object become 'sacred' or 'magical'? This is a difficult question to answer as it can depend on many factors. Some of these concern the process of how the object came into being and contextual factors (this is dealt with later). Other factors can relate directly to the object itself.[24] On the whole, if victims are part of the process of creating the meaning and symbolism of an object such as a memorial, and the symbol relates personally to them and their suffering, it is more likely to have increased 'inner' significance to them.[25] This is something seen in many community-based memorial projects.

One initiative that demonstrates this, although not directly related to political violence, is the development of the Aids Quilt, which is the largest ongoing community arts project in the world.[26] To date, 44,000 colorful panels have been sewn by family members and loved ones of those who have died of AIDS. The individual squares were then sewn into a massive memorial that is now large enough to cover the entire Mall in Washington, DC. I have seen this process replicated in various political contexts, including a quilt being developed by victims of state violence in Northern Ireland,[27] as well as the production of small stained glass windows which were amalgamated into one large window by another group of victims.

The reason for the popularity of this approach is that it allows for individual symbolism to be created and controlled by the family and loved ones, whilst being part of a bigger memorialization process. Most symbols on the squares, say of the Remembering Quilt in Northern Ireland, are highly individualized. They include highly personalized symbols, photos, and images that have deep meaning to the families. For example, one family placed a photo of their dead relative in the center of the square. In the photo the relative 'is wearing a shirt and tie. The tie he is wearing has been used to border the square... many more squares have used similar sacrifices from families dearest treasures.'[28]

Names, as part of the process of individualizing those lost, are also important in these projects. It is also common practice to put the name of individuals onto such squares. For example, in the Aids Quilt Project (now under the banner of a foundation known, interestingly, as the Names Project Foundation), the reading of names is now a tradition followed at nearly every Quilt display. On a much larger scale, and directly related to political violence, the worldwide Holocaust memorial project, 'Unto Every Person There Is A Name', now in its eleventh consecutive year, attempts to perpetuate the memory of the Jewish victims of the Shoah as individuals by the public recitation of their names on Yom Hashoah, or Holocaust Martyrs and Heroes Remembrance Day.[29]

Another example is the Vietnam War Memorial in Washington.[30] One of the strengths of the memorial is the way it personalizes individuals through the names on it, whilst recognizing the suffering of others and drawing (reflective) relevance to the present. As Sutherland writes:

Looking at the Wall, we see the world reflected: sun, moon, clouds, the trees in the distance, the people standing next to us. Finally, we see ourselves on its surface. These reflections remind us that the Wall is as much about the present as the past. We see our world mirrored in the names we find there and realise that the slightest movement changes the view. No image is permanent on the Wall. Only the names are eternal.[31]

Clearly, therefore, the individual content of memorials is important to many victims, as well as their active participation in the process. Another way of putting this is that reparations of this kind need to contain personal symbolic capital to contribute to greater levels of reparation at an individual level. That said, for massive reparations programs it would be difficult to recommend the type of community development processes (such as the quilting projects) outlined above. Such initiatives generally work better when they come from communities or groups themselves than when 'recommended' say by an outside body such as a truth commission. This is not to say, however, that such initiatives could not be supported financially through reparations processes. It also highlights the importance of how memorials come into being, and whether they do in fact represent community aspirations and the local ways of memorialization. For example, some of the memorials set up to commemorate victims and remember the atrocities committed under apartheid have been criticized for failing to reflect local African cultural traditions and practices.[32] They have taken on, in some cases, a Holocaust identity as the processes of establishing such memorials have often been run by external (western) consultants.[33]

The lessons therefore for massive reparations program considering various symbolic forms of reparations (e.g. memorials, monuments, plaques) is that although they may often have to balance a range of macro factors (e.g. reaching as many people as possible with limited resources), from a psychological perspective the personalized and individual content of such processes requires attention.[34] If symbolic reparations are delivered (e.g. memorials, apologies), the individual generally (but not always) needs to feel that *their* suffering, or their relative's suffering, is adequately reflected in these measures. This can be difficult to achieve and in short cannot be assumed without adequate participation and public involvement of key stakeholders in their development and conceptualization.

The debate in South Africa concerning what has been termed 'community reparations' can also be illustrative in this regard. 'Community reparations' can be defined as strategies aimed at providing broad access to some form of collective service for a large but select group of individuals said to have jointly suffered in some way. One example cited in the international literature is the provision of better and more accessible health services to previously oppressed minorities in remote areas.[35]

In South Africa, however, community reparations generally seem to have a wider meaning. For example, when President Mbeki made his announcement about final Truth and Reconciliation Commission (TRC) reparations, he noted these should be 'combined with *community reparations*, and assistance through opportunities and services'.[36] He did not fully define what he meant by community reparations. Based on the context of his statement one can surmise he meant actions that would benefit whole communities in some way rather than just individuals. He adds services to his list of reparations as distinct from community reparations, so presumably he means general social upliftment (e.g. building schools, and providing access to water) when he talks of community reparations. In South Africa, community reparations, therefore, seem to have a wider meaning than simply a section of a population targeted for additional services. No reparations have been granted in this way to date, or more to the point no development program has officially been called 'reparations'.

Such an approach could, at least in theory, be considered to contribute to reparation for individuals, that is, the government's commitment to assisting with development could symbolically represent recognition of individual hurts and demonstrate a willingness to build a better future through tangible redress that directly benefits individuals. This makes pragmatic sense and may even make egalitarian sense; if whole swathes of individuals were disadvantaged by apartheid, surely whole swathes of individuals should benefit from reparations?

However, the principle of repairing whole communities in South Africa, and thinking of this as reparations, although a noble endeavor, is also not free from its own problems when applying a psychosocial analysis.

First, perhaps like most reparations, if it is the only mechanism available it is unlikely to achieve its aims outside of other types of reparations and acknowledgment. One of the central problems in the debate about 'social development' in South Africa and its relationship to any concept of reparation is that it is presently almost exclusively forward-looking in its approach. Although social upliftment implicitly recognizes that communities suffered under apartheid, the direct links to who was responsible for this are seldom made publicly. This point is extensively discussed by de Greiff, as well as Segovia, in this volume.

The business community in South Africa sees its contribution as one focused on the future (which is of course important), but this is not matched by their unequivocal acknowledgment of their role in the past. This was startlingly evident in a recent meeting between the Business Trust[37] and government. At the meeting the Business Trust continued to pledge a further five-year term of support for development in a range of areas. However, the condition to the support from business was that the program had to be referred to as 'nation-building' and not 'community reparations'.[38]

Without a more contrite acknowledgment of the TRC's findings concerning the business community's complicity with the apartheid state,[39] it is unlikely that 'community reparations' will be accepted or have a significant impact. The government would argue that a range of urgent initiatives is underway (and many are), but seemingly something is missing regarding acknowledgment for the past. This is impeding how acts of social development (community reparations if you will in the South African case) are or might be interpreted. Thus, although the Business Trust may be able to offer a range of supports and development, as the government itself also does, it is likely that these measures will be interpreted as being insufficient reparation by individuals as they are not implicitly linked to recognition and acknowledgment at a social level. The current refusal by the business community in South Africa to label some of the development work they are funding as being about 'community reparations' undermines the reparative social and psychological value of such actions.

Second, at an individual level, social reconstruction as reparations will have a limited psychological impact, especially for those seeking individual reparations. Individuals who suffered the brunt of the *direct* brutality of apartheid violence will probably need more. At an individual level, the substitution of social reconstruction for individual reparations will probably not work because for reparations to be psychologically restorative at the individual level they need some level of personal symbolic capital, as was explained earlier in this section. But it is not only this personal significance community reparations may fall short on; due to their generic nature they may also provide insufficient recognition of the suffering of victims in the way de Greiff outlines it in this volume.

Although the broader system may have been responsible for creating a context conducive to human rights violations, and the system itself may have caused additional structural violations, individuals primarily experience violence through their own personal universe. As has been noted, the consequences of political violence are interpersonal, social, political and cultural, and all of these dimensions need to be taken into account when conceptualizing reparations. This is where the notion of recognition (de Greiff) intersects with the much more profound and personalized psychological processes unfolding for the victim.

Although socioeconomic development (social reconstruction) is necessary, the physical and psychological impact of violence has to be addressed directly and simultaneously at the individual level. There may be some hope if collective approaches to reparations are personalized (e.g. by naming new schools after individual people who died); however, it is unlikely that broad social reconstruction would carry sufficient recognition at an individual level, or contain sufficient symbolic capital for those who directly suffered the brunt of extreme political violence.

Thirdly, and perhaps most importantly, for most people in South Africa, the upgrading of their communities is considered a right, and is expected anyway, regardless of reparations debate. The majority cast their vote for the new government in April 1994 with the expectation of social reconstruction in mind. To define this as reparations, or think it will make adequate reparation, misses this point, as de Greiff and Segovia also argue in this volume.

Thus, specific violations and individuals need to somehow feel personally recognized (and recognize themselves) in the process. On the whole, and based on the psychological analysis presented here, I share the views expressed by de Greiff and Segovia in this volume, that development programs (community reparations) are not really programs of reparations.

This is not to say that such development programs are not needed or should not be set up, but their ability to contribute to reparation at the individual level is limited. If such strategies are undertaken they need to take place in addition to, and not instead of, individualized reparations or collective reparations strategies (e.g. monuments, memorials, commemoration services). In the *Guatemala: Memory of Silence* report, collective reparations are recommended, particularly for the wholesale destruction of indigenous villages. It is noted:

Collective reparatory measures for survivors of collective human rights violations and acts of violence, and their relatives, should be carried out within a framework of territorially based projects to promote reconciliation, so that in addition to addressing reparation, their other actions and benefits also favor the entire population, without distinction between victims and perpetrators.[40]

This is important and an interesting development, especially in the Guatemalan context where indigenous understandings of suffering can be collective. However, the report also notes that depending on the type of violation, the reparatory measures should be individual and/or collective. It also states that communities should have a say in the process of how community reparations are conceptualized and delivered. In so doing it recognizes the individual and collective impact of the extreme trauma of political repression and violence, as well as the importance of process, and in that regard points to some ways forward.

Context, Process and Discourses

The issue of recognition of suffering must not be underestimated when trying to understand how victims interpret reparations, or react when reparations are offered or granted. Reparations are laden with value judgments for victims. According to Sharon Lean, reparations demonstrate a government's interest in, and the state's acceptance of responsibility for, the well-being of its citizens.[41] For many victims of direct political violence it is the denial of their victim status, the social and political silence about their victimization, and/or the untruths told through official sources about the reason for their victimization that is the most difficult to bear. From the perspective of many victims these are often the fundamental injustices they wish to see set right, at least to some degree, through reparations.

The Bloody Sunday killings in 1972 in Northern Ireland are a good example of this.[42] One of the driving forces behind the families' push to secure an inquiry decades after the event is that many still feel that the general perception, perpetuated by the first inquiry held in 1972, is that those killed were committing 'terrorist' activity and not on a peaceful demonstration.[43] One of the demands of the Charter adopted by the families of the victims when campaigning for the inquiry was 'the formal, explicit acknowledgement of the innocence of all those killed and wounded'.[44]

It is how individuals perceive their suffering is understood, accepted and acknowledged in the social and political context that is one of the most important factors in determining how reparations will be sought and accepted. This is where the distinction between reparations and reparation can be helpful. That is, although in some objective sense adequate acts of reparations may have taken place in a society (e.g. a program may be developed that is well resourced relative to other social priorities, and is externally and internally coherent, to use the terms de Greiff suggests in this volume), the context and process in which they were granted may have been unsatisfactory to many of those they concern. Reparations may be interpreted as being insufficient as reparation at the individual level. The context and discourse around the granting of reparations is one of the mediating variables that can change this situation.

Some of the most important factors in this regard are the issues of truth and justice. It is worth mentioning the 'mothers of the disappeared' group in Argentina, *Madres de la Plaza de Mayo* (the Mothers of the Plaza de Mayo), who still refuse compensation.[45] Similarly, in Brazil some of the families of the murdered and disappeared during the Brazilian dictatorship see the most recent attempts to compensate them as the government's final attempt to buy their silence and close the book on the past without revealing the true facts of what happened.[46]

Another example, from a slightly different perspective, as examined at length by Yamamoto and Ebesugawa in this study,[47] is the 1996 class action suit against the US government for the seizure of Japanese Latin Americans from their homes in Latin America and subsequent internment in the USA during World War II.[48] Despite heated debate between different survivors about whether the group should accept a compromise that all qualified class members were to receive a presidential apology letter and $5,000 in compensation, the settlement was finally agreed.[49] However, the settlement meant that the US government did not need to give an explanation for the internment of this particular group of people of Japanese ancestry, an issue which remains unclarified to this day.[50]

The responses from the Japanese Latin Americans involved, typical of a case like this, ranged on the negative side from 'a bittersweet victory', 'incomplete justice', 'empty gestures', 'compromised injustice' to, on the more positive side, 'healing of wounds', 'closing a chapter' and 'bringing to an end the uncertainties of litigation'.[51] The variety of responses is no doubt a reflection of the complexity of making reparation for such a violation, but also highlights the diversity of expectations and needs that were supposed to be met through the reparation. Yamamoto and Ebesugawa (Chapter 7, this volume) also note that the redress offered was cathartic for internees and a measure of dignity was restored.

That said, when some survivors or families of victims talk of reparations as a form of 'blood money' (as some do in Chile, Brazil, Argentina and Northern Ireland), this is because the national process of 'moving forward and making amends' is not coinciding with the individual process of reparation, or the type and context of reparations may be militating against it. This is particularly the case when survivors feel that reparations are being used to buy their silence in the absence of the truth and justice.

Reparations, justice, and truth recovery need to be linked for reparation to be 'good enough' at the individual level. Without this, pain can remain internal, denied and silenced. Without being integrally linked with the processes of uncovering the truth, seeking justice, and offering support to victims, reparations run the danger of being seen by the survivors as a governmental strategy to close the chapter on the past prematurely and leave the secrets of the past hidden, victims still in pain, and justice unresolved. This will only serve to exacerbate the gap between the individual (micro) and political (macro) process. To this end, my view fits well with de Greiff's notion of reparations programs needing to be externally coherent; for de Greiff they must bear a close relationship with the other transitional mechanisms, with criminal justice, truth-telling, and institutional reform.

One further factor, which is more difficult to address, is that the socioeconomic status of the society more broadly could undermine the reparative value of reparations. Where society remains unjust on different levels, or power is unequally distributed, claims for reparations are likely to be more evident, especially where the injustice of the present can be explained through the continuities of historical oppression. The seemingly increasing number of claims for reparations (especially for historical crimes and oppression against individuals who are no longer living) is a direct reflection of ongoing injustice and inequality within society—they cannot be understood outside of this. Structural inequality and ongoing oppression are two of the most destructive factors that undermine a conducive context for granting reparations.

South Africa provides an interesting example of all these factors at play. In South Africa, for example, one cannot remove the impact of the current government's initial negative rhetoric about claims for reparation following the South African TRC from subsequent claims, most notably a larger suit for reparations from companies that did business with the apartheid government.[52] The case focuses on corporations who did business with South Africa during apartheid. However, through public discourse, and politicking, the entire process has become intertwined with the current South African government and the work of the TRC.

The South African President Thabo Mbeki undermined initial claims for reparations by victims from the TRC by saying: 'Did our people engage in a gigantic struggle, with some deciding to lay down their lives, with the prospect of financial reward in their minds? I have said, and I will say again, that any such suggestion is an insult to them and to all of us who now enjoy the freedom that they fought for.'[53] Such comments served to fuel the resentment many victims bore towards the government's seeming reticence in responding to the TRC's recommendations on reparations promptly when it received them in October 1998. This is one reason why victim groups have sought alternative redress through the apartheid lawsuits, which incidentally the government also opposes.[54]

Arguably, in the South African context, a process which began with a very wide range of reparations options being presented, including both acts and objects of reparations (such as building memorials, paying for tombstones for the dead) and financial compensation as recommended by the South African TRC,[55] has been reduced to legal battles and financial claims. The official announcement made by the South African government about long-term TRC-related reparations, which finally came in April 2003,[56] was largely understood by the public and the media as being only about financial compensation. The President did mention the issue of community reparations, and the need for ongoing social transformation, as well as the importance of other forms of support and memorialization. However, the vagueness of his comments in some cases, and the lack of definition of terms such as community reparations, led to an increased focus on the monetary component of the reparations as they were the most concrete of his suggestions.

The response from victims to the government's eventual offer of reparations for those found to be victims by the TRC (some 20,000 individuals) was predictable. Victims were quoted as saying that Mr Mbeki's words stung like salt in a wound and Ntombi Mosikare, co-ordinator of the Khulumani Support Group, added, 'we only want the country to acknowledge us. What they are giving us is too little.'[57] On one level this comment could be simply read as an objective statement about the relatively small amount of money offered. However, on another level, the degree of animosity developed over the course of the process between the victim groups and the government has left a bitter legacy. If more sizable grants were made it is possible that this might not have resulted in the immediate retort that the amount of money was insufficient. But given the residue anger left over from the clash with government and that many in the group feel the government has consistently failed to recognize their reparations claims as legitimate, it is possible that the group would have judged any compensation no matter the size as insufficient.

The reduction of the debate largely to the financial in South Africa serves as a good reminder of how the context and the broad political environment affect how reparations are defined, fought for and received. In South Africa, if symbolic gestures (say a monument to apartheid victims) were now made, one might predict that these would be more contested (especially by victims who went to the TRC) given the way the debate has been handled so far.

One cannot simply separate out the call for reparations for victims from the politics of how people feel and perceive they are treated. Many survivors are acutely attuned to having being mistreated in the past. It is for this reason that in the South African context, and in the absence of substantial reparations, money has taken on a negative symbolic significance, that is, it symbolically represents the new governments' lack of willingness to listen to the voices of those who were victimized in the past. In essence, it has been the *process* of making reparations, marked by the government's failure to act promptly, as well as negative public *discourse* about those seeking reparations, which has turned the debate into a struggle over amounts of money and soured relationships.[58]

One of the missed opportunities in South Africa was the failure to deliver substantial reparations to victims (e.g. the offering of tombstones and the renaming of streets after activists) early on in the transition process, and shortly after the

TRC report was tabled, when the context was conducive for their constructive delivery and reception. Instead, as it currently stands, the struggle for reparations has been converted into a bureaucratic and political one through delays, inefficiency and seeming governmental reticence (and obstinacy). This is very interesting considering that in the first year of the South African Commission, Commissioners often said that in the TRC Act the word 'reparation' and not 'compensation' had been used because the latter implied financial payouts which were going to be unlikely as reparations would probably be more collective and symbolic.[59]

We cannot expect those who have suffered to want to remove their grief and anger from the reparations process, and we cannot ignore the challenges that thinking about the issue from an individual level poses. In fact these, along with anger and grief, are integral to the reparations process and need to be managed accordingly. Genuine reparation, and the process of healing, does *not occur only or mainly through the delivery* of an object (e.g. a pension, a monument), or acts of reparations (e.g. an apology), but also *through the process* that takes place around the object or act. The task is to create a conducive environment that allows the process to unfold in such a way that the dilemmas that arise when making reparations are verbalized, dealt with, and appreciated as important components of any massive reparations program. The process, context and discourses surrounding delivery need to be given as much attention as debates about what will ultimately be delivered.

6. Conclusion

The aspiration of satisfying the psychological needs of victims is part of the equation in the reparations debate regardless of whether doing so is possible or measurable. At the same time, the constraints imposed on a society at a macro level during times of transition cannot be wished away. *Reparations* such as symbolic processes (e.g. memorials), reburials or even material acts (e.g. payments) all have symbolic meaning in and of themselves. If they are part of a stated *reparations program* they are doubly significant insofar as they relate to the broader goals of the program.

That said, from a psychological perspective, I do not believe that *reparations* can be defined outside of the concept of *reparation*, certainly at an individual level. Sensitivity to the question of the degree to which we can satisfy victims psychologically through reparations is needed. This may not be completely possible, but

I have argued throughout this paper that the reparative nature of reparations at the individual level can be maximized in several ways.

Greater attention can be paid in the design of massive reparations programs to the nature and type of reparations offered and their psychological meaning. The value of personal symbolic capital must not be underestimated in this regard. Reparations acts and objects have a greater likelihood of being considered meaningful and of being of value to recipients if they have a direct and personalized reference to the issue or form of suffering they are trying to deal with.

Reparations objects too need to embody a good mix of individual, political and social symbolism. For example, as was argued with regard to the Vietnam Memorial in Washington, symbolic imagery that connects the past, present and future, as well as being deeply personal for survivor and visitor alike, is needed. Sharing de Greiff's view in this volume, concepts such as recognition will also need to be grappled with by those designing reparations programs. The context, relationships, processes of delivery, and how reparations are spoken about at the macro level, are also important.

In order for reparations to have a powerful impact, an adequate reparations context needs to be fostered. Such an environment would be one where the attempts to address the needs of those harmed are acted upon in a timely fashion, and reparations are in some objective sense considered to be substantial relative to other social priorities (not to mention the program being internally and externally coherent as de Greiff in this volume suggests). Although difficult to measure, there is no doubt that reparations programs that are considered to be built on sincerity will be better received by victims. This is often dependent on the way those that represent the program present themselves publicly. Those making the reparations, whether a government or truth commissioners for example, need to be seen to be trying by all means to set the past wrongs right, acknowledge past injustices in their entirety, and ensure responsibility and blame are appropriately apportioned and recognized. There is no blueprint on how to do this, but an awareness of the value of the issues raised above may influence the design and process of massive reparations programs.

But reparation, and acts and objects of reparations, are fraught with complexity. Psychologically, the victims and survivors have to deal with the inner reality of what they have lost and the impossibility of it being externally replaced. They have to confront attempts to 'symbolically' represent their loss in social reality (the outer world), which is inevitably fraught with conflict over identity, nation, politics and power. The inner world inescapably gets drawn into the political and public realm when a massive public reparation program is conceptualized and operationalized (e.g. the perceived personal motivations of those demanding reparations being publicly discussed by the society and politicians). A political sensitivity to this is required.

The individual (psychological) and the collective (political) always stand in a relationship, and often in tension to one another when granting reparations. For this reason, an acceptance of the inherent conflict in a reparations program and the delivery of reparations is crucial. Reparations are not a quick fix to deal with individual psychological distress. For reparation to take place, ongoing space has to be provided for survivors to express their feelings of sadness and rage as they struggle to come to terms with the psychological and emotional impact of their loss—a loss that reparations can only nominally acknowledge.

The gap between what the delivery of a massive reparations program aspires to do in a society in transition and what it can actually do in terms of delivering adequate reparation to individuals is a core dilemma in any reparations program. Like the story of Tantalus introduced at the beginning of this paper, reparations programs have to try in many senses to reach for the impossible, i.e. simultaneously satisfy individual and socio-political needs. Although the gap between the micro and macro may never be completely narrowed, unlike Tantalus, reparations programs can, under the right circumstances, provide a level of satisfaction that will be a 'good enough' form of reparation for a substantial number of victims.

NOTES

1. James Hunter (1999), 'Tantalus', *Encyclopedia Mythica* Online, http://www.partheon. org/articles/t/tan₁alus.html. Accessed November 14, 2005.
2. Melanie Klein and Joan Riviere, *Love, Hate and Reparation* (New York: Norton, 1964).
3. Ibid., 65–66.
4. It is important to note that the concept of 'reparation' (used by Klein in the singular) in psychoanalytic thinking concerns internal processes. I speak here of 'actual harm' to make the theories more accessible to thinking about reparations in the context of this chapter. Klein does not refer to 'actual harm' but is concerned with infant 'phantasies'. She purposefully uses the word 'phantasy' rather than 'fantasy', i.e. for Klein fantasies are *conscious* such as daydreaming, but 'phantasy' largely concerns *unconscious* thoughts linked to instincts. Thus, the infant when not provided by its parents with everything it needs can have 'phantasies' of hate or aggression. Subsequent to having them the infant can be filled with guilt and an urge to make some form of 'reparation' or to try and 'make good' what they have 'done' in 'phantasy'.
5. Space does not permit a more detailed discussion of this point, but it is central to much psychoanalytic thinking. It is probably best expressed by D. W. Winnicott's notion (drawn from Klein's work) of the beginning of the socialization process being described by him as the development of the 'capacity for concern'. Maturity is seen by Winnicott as the ability of individuals to compromise, to feel and act responsibly; see Madeleine Davis and David Wallbridge, eds. *Boundary and Space: An Introduction to the Work of D. W. Winnicott,* (New York: Brunner, Mazel, Karnac Books, 1981). The notion of reparation is woven into

reaching this milestone insofar as feelings of personal guilt in respect of aggression lead to the urge for reparation and the beginnings of social responsibility.

6. Inger Agger and Soren Buus Jensen, *Trauma and Healing under State Terrorism* (London: Zed Books, 1996); and David Becker, Elizabeth Lira, Maria Isabel Castillo, Elana Gomez, and Juana Kovalskys, 'Therapy with Victims of Political Repressions in Chile: The Challenge of Social Reparations', in *Transitional Justice: How Emerging Democracies Reckon with Former Regimes*, Neil J. Kritz, ed. (Washington, DC: United States Institute of Peace, 1995).

7. Agger and Jensen, op. cit.

8. Becker et al., op. cit.

9. This is not to say that I think that the outcomes of a reparations process are not important. However, in this chapter I have chosen to focus more on the process of delivery, because it is an area which has received little attention in the field.

10. Elizabeth Jelin, 'The Minefields of Memory', *NACLA Report on the Americas* XXXII (1998): 23–9.

11. Sanford Levinson, *Written in Stone: Public Monuments in Changing Societies* (Durham and London: Duke University Press, 1998).

12. Carrie J. Petrucci, 'Research Evidence: What We Know about Apology', *Behavioral Science and the Law* 20 (2002): 337–62.

13. Quote from Cynthia Ngewu, mother of one of the so-called Guguletu Seven, at the forum on Reconciliation, Reconstruction and Economic Justice in Cape Town, March 19, 1997, cited in the *Report of the South African Truth and Reconciliation Commission*, vol. 5 (Cape Town: Juta, 1998), ch. 9, 99.

14. Hugo van der Merwe, *The South African Truth and Reconciliation Commission and Community Resolution* (Johannesburg: Centre for the Study of Violence and Reconciliation, 1998).

15. Martha Minow, 'Breaking Cycles of Hatred', in *Breaking the Cycles of Hatred: Memory, Law and Repair*, Martha Minow and Nancy L. Rosenblum, eds. (Princeton, NJ: Princeton University Press, 2002); Brandon Hamber, 'Repairing the Irreparable: Dealing with the Double-Binds of Making Reparations for Crimes of the Past', *Ethnicity and Health* 5 (2000): 215–26.

16. See Becker et al., op. cit. and Brandon Hamber, Dineo Nageng, and Gabriel O'Malley, 'Telling It Like It Is: Survivors' Perceptions of the Truth and Reconciliation Commission', *Psychology in Society* 26 (2000): 18–42.

17. Debra Kaminer, Dan J. Stein, Irene Mbanga, and Nompumelelo Zungu-Dirwayi, 'The Truth and Reconciliation Commission in South Africa: Relation to Psychiatric Status and Forgiveness Among Survivors of Human Rights Abuses', *British Journal of Psychiatry* 178 (2001): 373–7; Daniel W. Shuman and Alexander McCall Smith, *Justice and the Prosecution of Old Crimes: Balancing Legal, Psychological and Moral Concerns* (Washington, DC: American Psychological Association, 2000).

18. See Hamber, Nageng, and O'Malley, op. cit . Which is not to say that even if justice was forthcoming (say in the retributive sense through the courts), a past wrong of the extreme kind (murder) can ever be totally set right from a psychological perspective. That said, justice through the courts certainly can assist some survivors a great deal and is found to be favored by many.

19. Marcelo Suarez-Orozco, 'The Heritage of Enduring a Dirty War: Psychosocial Aspects of Terror in Argentina', *The Journal of Psychohistory* 18(1991): 469–505.

20. Brandon Hamber and Richard Wilson, 'Symbolic Closure Through Memory, Reparation and Revenge in Post-Conflict Societies', in *The Role of Memory in Ethnic Conflict*, Ed Cairns and Michael Roe, eds. (New York: Palgrave/Macmillan, 2003), 144–68.

21. Ibid.

22. The concept of 'good enough' is borrowed from psychoanalyst D. W. Winnicott, some of whose theories are discussed later in the chapter. He uses the concept in relation to parenting, arguing that parents need not be perfect but simply 'good enough' and that the mother needs to treat the child with a 'primary maternal preoccupation' and create a 'holding environment'. I think these concepts are a fitting way to think of reparations, which can never be perfect from an individual perspective, but can be 'good enough'. The environment in which they are delivered is also essential.

23. I have simplified this theory a great deal here—the bridging for the child comes from the fantasy and thinking the child starts to link with the object that is neither 'me' nor 'not me' object. Winnicott himself also acknowledged that the line between the object being used positively and negatively (in a regressive way) was also a thin one. For an introduction to this work, see Davis and Wallbridge, op. cit.

24. My focus here is reparations other than money or compensation directly. Although there is no doubt these have a significance and meaning in society. I restricted my view here to the types of reparations considered more symbolic in nature.

25. This is not always the case as sometimes memorials can in themselves take on significance after they have been created despite opposition during the process of their development. The Vietnam War Memorial in Washington, DC, is a case in point. Many veterans and members of the public were opposed to Maya Lin's proposed design, but once the memorial was built 'the debate about aesthetics and remembrance surrounding its design simply disappeared.... The experience of viewing Lin's work was so powerful for the general public that criticism of its design vanished.' Jenny Edkins, *Trauma and the Memory of Politics* (New York: Cambridge University Press, 2003), 79.

26. See http://www.aidsquilt.org/about.htm

27. For information on the Relatives for Justice Remembering Quilt, visit http://www.relativesforjustice.com/projects/quilt.htm

28. Speech by Andree Murphy on the launch of the Quilt, August 6, 2001, at http://www.relativesforjustice.com/projects/quiltspeech.htm

29. See http://www.yad-vashem.org.il/remembrance/index_remembrance.html

30. This is not to say that we can simply define the Vietnam War Memorial in Washington as reparation as such. Of course, whether memorials are a form of reparations, or about reparation, is a difficult and complex question in itself. If they flow directly from documents such as a truth commission report we would probably say they are—if they come later it is much more difficult to judge. Perhaps the defining line should be whether they are in some way aimed at making 'amends' for the past, acknowledging suffering, or seeking to make some repair in a broad way (reparation). Using the proposed framework, perhaps the dividing line is if some judgment can be made regarding whether the act being undertaken (setting up a truth commission, building a memorial) is broadly spoken about as some form of reparation, or, if not referred to directly as such, is at a broad level about trying to symbolically represent something else, e.g. addressing the past, making peace, etc.

31. Cara Sutherland, 'Preface', in *Hunger of the Heart: Communion at the Wall*, Larry Powell, ed. (Dubuque, IA: Islewest, 1995), ix–xi, x, cited in Edkins, op. cit., 89.

32. Ereshnee Naidu, 'Memorialisation and Symbolic Reparations in South Africa', in *Trauma and Transitional Justice in Divided Societies* (Warrington, VA: Airlie House, 2004).

33. Ibid.

34. Although not the direct focus of this chapter, it is interesting to consider this point with regard to financial compensation. If we accept the premise of my argument, i.e. from a psychological perspective the personalized and individual content of reparations processes is important, then it is likely that compensation schemes that assess and compensate relative to personal loss/damage (a common law approach) rather than a standardized grant (tariff system) may have the potential to contain a greater degree of personal symbolic capital and thus contribute to greater levels of reparation at an individual level. Equally, however, if compensation schemes are personalized relative to individual loss/damage, but are judged to be inadequate by victims anyway, then their personal symbolic capital could have the opposite effect, i.e. the money granted is seen as an 'insult' to the loss endured. This is one reason why most truth commissions probably favour a more standardized approach to compensation. From this perspective the personal symbolic capital can be 'given' to the money by the victims or survivors in how they choose to use it (say, purchasing a tombstone), rather than through the process of assessing how much an individual should get based on their individual circumstances or loss. This can then be complemented by alternative symbolic measures (e.g. memorials, plaques) recommended by a truth commission. That said, the debate about the 'symbolic' value of financial compensation is one that still needs to be developed in the literature, and there are certainly many victims who would favor a more personalized compensation process. More work remains to be done in this area.

35. Stef Vandeginste, 'Reparation', in *Reconciliation after Violent Conflict: A Handbook*, David Bloomfield, Teresa Barnes, and Luc Huyse, eds. (Stockholm: International Institute for Democracy and Electoral Assistance, 2003).

36. Extract from Statement to the National Houses of Parliament and the Nation, at the tabling of the *Report of the South African Truth and Reconciliation Commission*, April 15, 2003 by Thabo Mbeki.

37. The Business Trust is an initiative of 145 companies in South Africa that work in partnership with the South African government to undertake job creation and capacity building: see http://www.btrust.org.za/

38. Christelle Terreblanche, 'Business Says "No" to Apartheid Payouts', *Cape Argus* (November 14, 2003): 2.

39. The TRC found that 'Business was central to the economy that sustained the South African state during the apartheid years. Certain businesses, especially the mining industry, were involved in helping to design and implement apartheid policies. Other businesses benefited from co-operating with the security structures of the former state. Most businesses benefited from operating in a racially structured context.' *Report of the South African Truth and Reconciliation Commission*, vol. 4, ch. 2, 106.

40. Summary of the *Guatemala: Memory of Silence* report, published at http://shr.aaas.org/guatemala/ceh/report/english/recs3.html, Point 10.

41. Sharon E. Lean, 'Is Truth Enough? Reparations and Reconciliation in Latin America', in *Politics and the Past: On Repairing Historical Injustices*, John Torpey, ed. (Lanham, MD: Rowman & Littlefield, 2003), 169–79.

42. On January 30, 1972, soldiers from the British Army's 1st Parachute Regiment opened fire on demonstrators in Derry, Northern Ireland. Thirteen people were killed and a number of others wounded. One wounded man later died in the hospital.

43. The Bloody Sunday Inquiry was announced by Prime Minister Tony Blair in a statement to the House of Commons on January 29, 1998. The Commission of Inquiry's terms of reference were to inquire into 'the events of Sunday, 30th January 1972 which led to loss of life in connection with the procession in Londonderry on that day, taking account of any new information relevant to events on that day'. The Inquiry interviewed and received statements from over 1,700 civilians, clergymen, journalists, photographers, and soldiers. As of the end of June 2003, the total cost of the Inquiry to Government was £113.2 million. The current estimated out-turn cost of the Inquiry to Government is £155 million. The Inquiry ended its hearings in February 2004. At the time of going to print the most recent press statement from the Inquiry (August 12, 2005) noted that the report was currently in preparation, and, given the large quantity of material it was not possible at that stage to give any firm estimate of when the report was likely to be finished. However, in all likelihood the report should be released in 2006. For more information see http://www.bloody-sunday-inquiry.org.uk

44. http://www.bloodysundaytrust.org/updates/charter.htm

45. The group is split. The *Madres de la Plaza de Mayo-Linea Fundadora* accepts government reparations.

46. See Cano and Ferreira, 'The Reparations Programs in Brazil' (Chapter 3, this volume); and Hamber, 'Living with the Legacy of Impunity: Lessons for South Africa about Truth, Justice and Crime in Brazil', *Latin American Report* 13 (1998): 4–16. Cano and Ferreira also note, however, that there is not a unanimous view among the relatives as to whether the state has in fact managed to stifle demands for truth. Some say, Cano and Ferreira add, that as time passes the number of people participating in the relatives' movements is diminishing, particularly since reparations measures have been put in place.

47. Yamamoto and Ebesugawa, 'Report on Redress: The Japanese American Internment' (Chapter 7, this volume).

48. The case was brought by four such individuals led by Carmen Mochizuki. For more details on the entire Japanese American reparations movement in the USA see Yamamoto and Ebesugawa, op. cit.

49. See Yamamoto and Ebesugawa, op. cit.; and Eric K. Yamamoto, 'Reluctant Redress: The U.S. Kidnapping and Internment of Japanese Latin Americans', in *Breaking the Cycles of Hatred: Memory, Law and Repair*, Martha Minow and Nancy L. Rosenblum, eds. (Princeton, NJ: Princeton University Press, 2002). One of the difficulties with accepting the settlement was that previous claims for the unjust internment of Japanese (US) citizens had resulted in higher payments, leaving some victims dissatisfied with the compromise. The Mochizuki case was separate to the compensation paid out by the USA for detaining US citizens of Japanese descent living on the West Coast of the USA and sending them to internment camps located further inland. Under a 1988 law, the surviving internees were given $20,000 in compensation and an apology. According to a US Department of Justice Press Release on February 19, 1999, some 82,219 eligible claimants were compensated, totalling more than $1.6 billion, and amongst this group were 189 Japanese Latin American claimants eligible for the full $20,000 in redress

compensation under the Act because they had the required permanent residency status or US citizenship during the defined war period. Again see Yamamoto and Ebesugawa, op. cit.

50. The most often cited reason is that internees were held as potential hostages to be exchanged for US prisoners, with more than 800 Japanese Latin Americans actually being used in this way.

51. See Yamamoto, 'Reluctant Redress', op. cit., 137.

52. On November 11, 2002, the Khulumani Victim Support Group (a group of victims of past political violence in South Africa) filed a lawsuit in its name, as well as that of 85 of its 33,000 members, in the New York Eastern District Court against 21 multinational corporations and leading international banks for helping prop up the apartheid state. The companies and banks named in the lawsuit are: Citigroup, JP Morgan Chase, Exxon Mobil, Caltex Petroleum, Fluor Corporation, Ford, General Motors and IBM in the USA; German-based Commerzbank, Deutsche Bank, Dresdner Bank, Daimler-Chrysler, and Rheinmetall; Credit Suisse and UBS in Switzerland; Barclays Bank, British Petroleum, Rio Tinto and Fujitsu ICL in the UK; Total-Fina-Elf from France; and Royal Dutch Shell from the Netherlands. The list is expected to grow. Khulumani is supported by Jubilee 2000 South Africa through a group known as the Apartheid Debt and Reparations Campaign (ADRC), an umbrella body campaigning for the scrapping of developing-world debt. Additional class action lawsuits modelled on compensation claims by Holocaust survivors are being made through US lawyer Ed Fagan. Figures of anywhere between US$50 billion (A$93.5 billion) and US$100 billion (A$187 billion) have been bandied about for the apartheid claims. The Apartheid Debt and Reparations Campaign, which initially supported the claim, has distanced itself from Fagan's lawsuits. The lawsuits continue.

53. Source: President Thabo Mbeki, May 2000, Parliament. A short time after this statement Archbishop Tutu criticized this position and others who made similar comments, when he wrote: 'It has been deeply distressing over the past year to see the insensitive comments being made by some government spokespersons implying that victims who approached the truth commission were "in the struggle for money". No one would dare suggest that those who underwent the agony of exile, imprisonment, banning and other harassment, and who now earn relatively good salaries in the government, were in the struggle for the money that is coming their way. Why then should it be implied, and by people who have jobs moreover, that those who underwent the same sacrifices, but who are now destitute, entered the struggle with the prospect of financial rewards?' Cited in *Sunday Independent*, May 21, 2000.

54. The South African government does not support the litigation. In fact, the government has dismissed the lawsuits out of hand. It is worth quoting President Mbeki on the issue as it highlights the government's unequivocal position: 'In the recent past, the issue of litigation and civil suits against corporations that benefited from the apartheid system has sharply arisen. In this regard, we wish to reiterate that the South African government is not and will not be party to such litigation. In addition, we consider it completely unacceptable that matters that are central to the future of our country should be adjudicated in foreign courts which bear no responsibility for the well-being of our country and the observance of the perspective contained in our constitution of the promotion of national reconciliation.' (Extract from Statement to the National Houses of Parliament and the Nation, at the tabling of the Report of the Truth and

Reconciliation Commission, April 15, 2003 by Thabo Mbeki.) In June 2003, the South African Minister of Justice, Penuell Maduna, took the process one step forward by writing to the US District Judge John Sprizzo, who was presiding over the cases, asking him to dismiss them. See *Business Day*, http://www.bday.co.za/bday/content/direct/ 1,3523,1478932-6078-0,00.html. In the nine-page affidavit the minister reiterates that the government is opposed to the lawsuits; sees the issues they concern as being about sovereign domain of South Africa; notes the various achievements made by the government in terms of development; and dismisses the victims' actions as akin to wanting to set up 'a surrogate government'.

55. See Colvin (Chapter 5, this volume).

56. Statement to the National Houses of Parliament and the Nation, at the tabling of the *Report of the South African Truth and Reconciliation Commission*, April 15, 2003 by Thabo Mbeki. On April 15, 2003, South African President Thabo Mbeki announced that victims of apartheid who testified before the TRC would receive a once-off final reparations grant of R30,000 (US$3,842). A total of US$85 million would be paid to 19,000 victims, considerably less than the US$360 million recommended by the TRC. The South African government received the TRC's recommendations in October 1998.

57. Ginger Thompson, 'South Africa to Pay $3,900 to Each Family of Apartheid Victims', *New York Times International* (New York, 2003), A5.

58. See Hamber, 'Repairing the Irreparable', op. cit.

59. These statements were made despite the fact that the TRC Act explicitly says that reparations can include compensation and/or *ex gratia* payments.

CHAPTER 17

REPARATIONS AND MENTAL HEALTH: PSYCHOSOCIAL INTERVENTIONS TOWARDS HEALING, HUMAN AGENCY, AND RETHREADING SOCIAL REALITIES

M. BRINTON LYKES AND
MARCIE MERSKY

1. INTRODUCTION

Since World War II there have been important advances in codifying the rights of victims of human rights violations and/or violations of international humanitarian law to remedy and reparation.[1] Until the 1980s, the right to reparation was generally exercised as part of the outcome to some form of legal proceedings. More recently, however, in the aftermath of repressive regimes or internal armed conflicts, access to reparations is often divorced from court proceedings. Instead, reparatory measures or reparations programs are integrated into wider social, political, and judicial reform processes, which together are intended to contribute to what is commonly termed 'social reconstruction' or 'reconciliation'. In this context, reparations schemes represent a certain political acknowledgment of wrongdoing and a commitment to provide redress through specifically defined measures for the victims and their families.

In the centuries-old legal tradition, reparations are considered to be an integral part of justice;[2] in their newer, more political incarnation, especially in transitional contexts, in addition to their relationship to justice, reparations programs—explicitly or implicitly—seek to heal individual and social wounds. It is in this latter framework that psychosocial interventions have received increasing attention as part of multifaceted reparations schemes.

The 'Principles and Guidelines on the Right to Reparation', prepared in 2000 and still under consideration by the United Nations Commission on Human Rights, built on a fundamentally juridical model. They establish four broad forms of reparations: (a) restitution, (b) compensation, (c) rehabilitation, and (d) satisfaction and guarantees of nonrepetition. Direct attention to mental health is contemplated within compensation, which should address 'physical or mental harm, including pain, suffering and emotional distress', and rehabilitation, which 'should include medical and psychological care, as well as legal and social services'.[3] A number of the measures considered as part of restitution or satisfaction and guarantees of nonrepetition also may have clear psychosocial implications for victims and their societies. Specifically, diverse actions aimed at restoring or establishing victims' equality and dignity as human beings and as citizens respond to their right to know and permit mourning, psychological processes identified by many as important in social reconstruction and reconciliation.

Recently, in the design of specific reparations programs to address situations where violations were committed on a massive scale, a somewhat different terminology has been introduced, to refer to material and symbolic forms of reparation, which may be provided individually or collectively. In this volume, de Greiff suggests that the latter conceptualization may be more useful in transitional situations, and Hamber argues further that all reparations measures are fundamentally symbolic. In any case, even within the more juridical framework, the specific measures suggested by the United Nations often have both material and symbolic value and implications.

There is a general sense among mental health and psychosocial researchers and practitioners that all of these forms, including those that focus on material well-being, restoration of legal rights or property, judicial actions, truth-seeking processes, apologies, or institutional reform, can have important effects on psychosocial conditions at the individual and national or collective levels.[4] And while there are few empirically based studies of these issues, there is growing awareness that the potential healing effects of any one measure may often depend on its congruence with other measures—on what de Greiff calls the external coherence or integrity of reparations programs—or more generally, with other actions being taken in the society to address the structural problems that gave rise to the conflicts, and especially to end impunity, impart justice, and strengthen the rule of law.

With the notable exception of Chile, however, there is almost no experience with mental health services being provided to large numbers of victims or their families, as part of an intentionally designed, national reparations program. The programs being established in Guatemala and Peru, as part of truth commission recommendations, both contemplate attention to mental health needs, but neither program, for differing reasons, has actually been implemented at this time.[5]

Nonetheless, there is an increasingly rich experience in a number of countries with psychosocial interventions or mental health accompaniment of victims and survivors, often associated with exhumations or larger truth-seeking initiatives, and mostly developed by nongovernmental organizations (NGOs). For example, in both Peru and South Africa, psychological support was provided for many victims who gave their testimonies before truth commissions, especially in public hearings, and there has been some limited, follow-up support, as well. In Guatemala several organizations have emerged, using differing methodologies of psychosocial interventions, to work with family members during exhumation and reburial processes, or more generally to work with victim groups or with communities where army massacres or local paramilitary actions have left deep ruptures. There is also a growing body of literature that examines autochthonous healing processes at the community level. These experiences, and others like them, have played an important role in raising awareness about the need to address the psychosocial dimensions of postconflict/postwar situations and the importance of developing effective intervention strategies as part of a comprehensive reparations program.

Unfortunately, serious evaluations and comparative studies of these and other initiatives are still pending, making it difficult to establish clear patterns or emergent practical guidelines. Moreover, despite the moral and political arguments to support psychological attention to victims/survivors, there is limited, and sometimes contradictory, empirical research about the effects of mental health services provided for direct victims.[6] While this chapter cannot possibly make amends for the absence of comprehensive and in-depth research on these issues, we have attempted to provide an overview of psychosocial and mental health theory and practice as it has emerged in contexts of war, postwar, and transitional situations. Specifically, we:

1. identify theoretical and applied models that dominate work within war and postwar contexts and critically examine the epistemological assumptions underlying these models;
2. elaborate complementary and contrasting principles that inform this work;
3. present a 'proposed framework' that integrates three principles and three cross-cutting factors that we recommend for consideration in the design of psychosocial work within reparations programs;
4. examine exhumations and reburials, in two distinct contexts, as sites for psychosocial work within reparation processes; and
5. conclude the chapter by briefly describing a set of ongoing questions that continue to challenge psychosocial workers within reparations processes.

This chapter is posited on, and grounded in, some core understandings based on many years of work in war-torn societies and a growing literature describing the experiences of others. First, while we will often use the language of 'recovery', 'reparation', or 'healing' when referring to psychosocial interventions with survivors of torture, massacres, rape, and other politically motivated atrocities, or for relatives of victims of forced disappearance, we share a view held by many other practitioners that these are, at best, relative terms. As understood and analyzed here, they may provide important solace and some sense of closure to individuals through recognition, support services, and resources, and can contribute to social reconstruction processes by helping to rebuild civic trust and solidarity (as de Greiff argues in this volume). In this sense, they are just and necessary measures for peace building in postwar or transitional situations. But experience has also shown that reparation measures and the processes they generate are insufficient, fundamentally partial in their impact, and/or symbolic (see also Hamber, Chapter 16, this volume).

There is increasing awareness that wounds to the person and the collectivity run deep and across generations when they are the result of actions that erased fundamental moral boundaries in a society, yet were broadly permitted and often continue to be justified by the perpetrators and others in that society. On both individual and social levels, 'where gross human rights violations take place, predictability, trust, belonging, sense of self-agency and control—and hence meaning and meaning construction—are destroyed or severely affected'.[7]

This brings us to a second core understanding, namely that repair from political violence (or systematic human rights violations, organized or state-sponsored violence, or trauma of human origin, as others have referred to it) must be distinguished from repair from the psychological distresses caused by severe natural disaster or even as the result of individual criminal action.[8] The former has a singular moral dimension; this moral dimension characterizes not only the violence/violation, but also must characterize the efforts to 'heal'. If reparation processes are developed in ways that are devoid of values or ignore moral dimensions in the wider social context, then it will be difficult to move forward in meaningful ways towards recovery. This has at least two important implications for practitioners and for the design of reparations programs. In our work with victims and survivors, it means that we must 'share the moral condemnation of the moral transgression' committed against that person; and that 'this sharing of a common moral standard is not only a private agreement', but also implies broader social and political obligations.[9] Moreover, reparations programs for victims and survivors need to be complemented by efforts directed towards 'nonvictims' (or those not directly affected), which opens discussion on fundamental values and the need to establish and defend moral boundaries in the society. And then there is the virtually unexplored terrain of work with perpetrators, many of whom may still retain much power.

Thus, this chapter begins by situating the challenges facing those seeking to design psychosocial reparations programs for survivors of politically generated violence within a broader theoretical and applied discussion of psychosocial work in war-torn societies. Moreover, it explores potential contributions of this work among individuals and in societies seeking to rethread social relations and rebuild in the wake of mass violations of human rights, proposes an alternative framework for developing a psychosocial reparations program and offers several examples. Finally, it discusses ongoing challenges to those seeking to implement psychosocial programs within reparations processes in the absence of full disclosure and justice.

2. Psychosocial Work in War and 'Postwar' Contexts: Some Theoretical and Applied Issues

As the number of civilian casualties of war has increased, there has been a parallel upsurge in the recognition of psychological or mental health consequences of armed conflict.[10] Health workers (including psychiatrists, psychologists, psychiatric nurses, and social workers) increasingly can be found in zones of armed conflict and, more specifically, as protagonists in the multiple arenas of recovery, reparations, and reconciliation that emerge in their wake. One indicator, among many, of the growth of psychosocial resources directed towards survivors of political violence is the *Global Directory of Centres and Programmes for the Rehabilitation of Torture Victims*.[11] This directory describes the work of 177 centers or programs in seventy-five countries worldwide engaged in medical and psychosocial work with survivors of human rights abuses and in preventative work that typically includes education and advocacy. In addition to suggesting the proliferation of these resources, a quick review also confirms that most are situated within the general health context and assume that a medical approach works most effectively in treating psychological problems. In effect, much mental health work carried out in contexts of war and postconflict is grounded in a medical model that informs both the definition of the problem and the strategies for responding.

The Dominant Paradigm: Post-traumatic Stress Disorder

The general consensus among psychiatrists, psychologists, and other mental health professionals working with survivors of war and organized violence has been that a major impact of organized political violence (including torture) on individuals is reflected in a confluence of symptoms first identified in 1980 as post-traumatic stress disorder (PTSD).[12] Diagnosis for this disorder is made based on one's exposure to a traumatic event that includes 'actual or threatened death or serious injury, or a threat to physical integrity to the self or others' and to which one responds with 'intense fear, helplessness, and horror'.[13] Much work has focused on veterans and survivors of rape. In general, the term is associated with major stressors, including concentration-camp experiences, torture, bombings, combat experiences, and natural disasters, and subsumes previous diagnostic categories including post-torture syndrome and rape-trauma syndrome. Rarely does this theory, and the practice it informs, distinguish between trauma caused by natural disasters and that caused by humans.

This apparently contemporary illness discourse for survivors of political violence is neither altogether new, nor recent. Indeed, this set of responses was first identified in a study of soldiers' reactions to warfare and has a long tradition within psychiatry and psychology. Some, including Starcevic and Durdic,[14] trace its origins to the soldier's 'irritable heart' in the wake of the US Civil War. According to Scott,[15] among others, characterizations of the psychological effects of World War I for soldiers included 'shell shock' and 'war neurosis', and of fighters in World War II, 'survivor syndrome', 'combat exhaustion', and 'battle fatigue'—all clinical antecedents of the symptoms and syndromes reflected by the diagnosis PTSD.

What is perhaps new is the extent to which discussion of PTSD has been popularized within Western societies, and the extent to which this disorder is increasingly identified as a major effect of war and state-sponsored violence, wherever these occur.[16] Moreover, in the late twentieth century, psychologists, psychiatrists, and other mental health workers made great progress in convincing international institutions, including the United Nations, of the importance of incorporating mental-health work within the rapid and long-term responses to war, natural disasters and other 'exceptionally difficult circumstances'. In this context, mental health workers increasingly focus on the *effects* of war on civilian populations, describing psychological symptoms and behaviors observed, and one of the dominant narratives in postwar discourse is that of the 'victim/survivor' who suffers from 'post-traumatic stress disorder'.[17]

Initially, therapeutic interventions for those diagnosed with PTSD included some combination of 'talking therapies' with medication. In the USA this treatment combination dominated individual and small group work with Vietnam veterans, among others, for years.[18] Moreover, clinical practice in this area has contributed to an intense interest in the physiology underlying trauma, with a growing focus on the brain, as well as on mental processes, for example, cognitive appraisals and schemas.[19] In the process, talking therapies have ceded dominance to shorter-term behaviorally or physiologically based intervention strategies or therapies that stress reduction of symptoms through cognitively reframing the traumatic experience and its effects[20] or through eye movement desensitization and reprocessing (EMDR).[21] Critical incident stress debriefing[22] is another short-term intervention strategy that draws on insights from cognitive and behavioral psychology and is widely used with individuals, communities, and crisis-intervention workers.

What these seemingly divergent approaches have in common is a traditional biomedical conception of the problem, in which selected symptoms and behavioral indices provide evidence of a 'disease or disorder', in this case PTSD, which can then be treated with specific therapeutic protocols. In addition, and perhaps most importantly, they share an underlying assumption that PTSD represents a universal human phenomenon present in most (some say, all) children and adults who have lived through war and organized violence.[23] Treatment modalities in these contexts have focused primarily on short-term individual and small group psychotherapy. When available, this work has been supplemented by drugs, some of which have been found to be helpful in reducing symptoms.

Breaking Epistemological Set

Despite important contributions made through the recognition of and responses to the psychological needs of survivors of war and state-sponsored violence, many researchers and field workers[24] argue that the tendency to describe and analyze the effects of war, state-sponsored violence, and structural oppression within the biomedical framework of PTSD deeply reduces and constrains the understandings available to those who seek to accompany survivors. The developing critique covers several issues:

1. an assumption of the universal nature of trauma and its effects, when much field experience demonstrates otherwise;

2. an assumption that trauma is a single event and that its effects are linearly and causally related in time, when much recent theory and research suggests that it is chronic and/or intergenerational;

3. a tendency to medicalize, pathologize, or psychologize what are fundamentally political, economic, cultural, and psychosocial phenomena; and

4. an emphasis on individual, 'innocent' victims of organized political violence, despite growing recognition that these individuals are also survivors, many of whom were historical actors in a struggle, and all of whom are members of families, communities and societies that have also been deeply affected.

These concerns are particularly important for psychosocial workers seeking to contribute to processes of reparation where specific legal and political instruments, agreed upon by the international community and multiple parties within conflicts, are recommended as resources for rethreading and rebuilding war-torn or postconflict societies.

In many ways, this critique is rooted in a questioning of the epistemological underpinnings of dominant notions of trauma, in general, and of PTSD, in particular. Raija-Leena Punamaki's[25] introduction to a three-volume special issue of the *International Journal of Mental Health* identified several severe limitations of traditional psychological and psychiatric theories of trauma. She suggested that these theories 'portray the *essence* of being a *victim* of politically induced violence and repression'.[26] The theories' 'implicit concept of the human being, the assumption of the universality of psychological responses, and the inability to describe accurately the interaction between social-political and psychological developments and to catch both the collective and the individualistic dimensions of the human psyche'[27] limit their usefulness in understanding war and its effects. Bracken, Giller, and Summerfield[28] argue further that the ontology underlying the psychiatric and biomedical model of PTSD reveals an individual at the center of morality and cosmology as well as a presumed universalism of forms and content of mental disorder. And Bracken[29] took the critique further by demonstrating how the PTSD paradigm incorrectly posits that trauma and its effects are universal, linearly and causally related, and that this relationship is trans-historical and cross-cultural.

Despite these challenges, therapeutic models developed to respond to PTSD, drawing primarily on 'talking cures' or 'biomedical interventions' are presumed by many psychosocial workers to be relevant and effective across cultures. However, as Arthur Kleinman[30] observed, simply because we can identify a similar phenomenon in different situations does not mean that it is universal. An increasing body of literature, including Bracken,[31] Das et. al.,[32] Kleinman,[33] and Marsella and White,[34] among many others, have challenged the biomedical model of trauma. For example, through field work with Salvadoran refugees in the USA who suffered *nervios*,[35] with Cambodian orphans grieving murdered parents,[36] and with survivors of chronic depression and trauma,[37] researchers and practitioners have identified particular psychosocial responses to traumatic events that can only be fully understood within the cultural discourse of the society/culture in which they are situated and its historical, political and social realities (i.e. the Salvadoran civil war, the Pol Pot regime in Cambodia, China's single child policy, respectively).

Moreover, Young challenges the ahistoricity of most accounts of PTSD, arguing that it is neither timeless, nor universal, but rather an historical product, 'glued together by the practices, technologies, and narratives with which it is diagnosed, studied, treated, and represented and by the various interests, institutions, and moral arguments that mobilized these efforts and resources'.[38]

Ignacio Martín-Baró's work, based on the Central American experience in the 1970s and 1980s, also took on these epistemological issues and in doing so contributed importantly to shifting psychologists' and mental health workers' thinking about survivors of war and organized violence. He spoke about the need to understand mental health:

in broader, more positive terms ... The problem is rooted in a limited conception of human beings that reduces them to individual organisms whose functioning can be understood in terms of their individual characteristics and features. Such a conception denies their existence as historical beings whose life is developed and fulfilled in a complex web of social relations. If the uniqueness of human beings consists less in their being endowed with life (that is, in their organic existence), and more in the kind of life they construct historically, then mental health ceases to be a secondary problem during times of war and becomes a fundamental one. It is not a matter of the individual's satisfactory functioning; rather, it is a matter of the basic character of human relations, for this is what defines the possibilities for humanization that open up for the members of each society and group. *To put it more plainly, mental health is a dimension of the relations between persons and groups more than an individual state, even though this dimension may take root differently in the body of each of the individuals in these relations, thereby producing a diversity of manifestations ('symptoms') and states ('syndromes'). .... we want to emphasize how enlightening it is to change the lens and see mental health or illness not ... as the result of an individual's internal functioning but as the manifestation, in a person or group, of the humanizing or alienating character of a framework of historical relationships.*[39] (emphasis added)

During war, communities are ruptured and relationships are stressed, sometimes irrevocably fractured. Martín-Baró[40] described the trauma of war as the concrete crystallization of dehumanizing social relations of exploitation and structural oppression. Friends and family members choose opposite sides of a conflict and many civilians are slaughtered in local attacks. Neighbors turn against each other, sometimes using the national/nation-wide political conflict to legitimize long-standing local conflicts over land or religious differences. While he emphasizes the importance of personal suffering, he situates it within the family, the community, and the wider society, thereby characterizing the trauma as 'psychosocial'.

The inability of traditional trauma theory to deal with what Punamaki[41] calls the 'collective dimension of the human psyche' is not only reminiscent of Martín-Baró but is also echoed in recent work by Summerfield.[42] He draws on his experiences in Nicaragua, as well as his reading of Vietnam survival tales, of the British Falklands/ Malvinas experience, of Palestinian youth in Gaza, and of grieving mothers in the streets of Soweto. In each context he argues that it is not only the individual that is traumatized, but the social setting wherein social and cultural institutions are ruptured. Thus, the trauma of war—whether an individual's or a community's— must be read and responded to within its social, cultural, political meanings over time, rather than located and addressed exclusively or even primarily within affected individuals.

Psychologists and psychiatrists in the Southern Cone of Latin America were some of the first to systematize a response to the psychological effects of torture, disappearances, and political imprisonment in the 1970s. Trained as physicians and in psychoanalytic psychiatry and psychology, they were challenged to articulate a set of resources that responded to the extreme situations of the authoritarian regime in which they and their patients/clients were living. Although much of their therapeutic work was conducted with individuals and families and many were trained in the biomedical model described above, they departed from several of its assumptions and made critical contributions to the development of an emergent model that could contribute importantly to work within a reparations context.

The work in Chile reflects an effort to conceptualize the ongoing or sequential aspects of trauma, the collective nature of the experience, the intricate interrelationship between the individual and the society in contexts of extreme political violence, and the role of the psychologist in this context. Based on these experiences, David Becker characterized traumatization as 'extreme', that is, as an individual and collective process of 'extremely long duration' that exceeds 'the capacity of the individual and of social structures to respond adequately.... Its aim is the destruction of the individual, of his sense of belonging to society and of his social activities.'[43] This reconceptualization of trauma situates it within socio-political, economic, and historical contexts of power and its abuse, and focuses on the singular experience of a person, within particular social circumstances, across time, in sharp contrast to the universalizing biomedical model described above.

During the worst years of the dictatorship, Ana Julia Cienfuegos and Christina Monelli,[44] among others, recognized that under conditions of ongoing violence and state terror the relationships they were establishing with their clients/patients differed significantly from a traditional client/patient-therapist alliance. One response to the realities confronting them was to encourage the patient/client to tell her or his story. Using tape recordings and working in various sessions, the therapist carefully documented the story in all its details and then this 'testimony' was presented to human rights activists, becoming part of the public denunciation of and discourse about the Chilean dictatorship and gross violations of human rights.

This process implicated the therapists in a new way in relationships with survivors of political violence, a relationship they described as a 'bond of commitment'.

This bond arose in a 'historical context where, amidst the harsh political repression of the dictatorship, it was necessary to make explicit the political, social, and psychological alliance established between patients and the therapists who chose to work with victims of the regime'.[45] The therapist positioned him or herself on the side of the victim/survivor, shedding the notions of distance and moral neutrality that characterize classic psychotherapeutic patient-therapist alliances. As significantly, Becker writes that through this work he and his colleagues learned that the experiences of the people with whom they worked 'could only be integrated into a perspective of life if we, ourselves, were willing to recognize that death. We had to look at its causes and make it a part of a lively relationship . . . to cure means not so much to repair destruction, rather it emphasizes a willingness to share it'.[46] The advocacy role of the 'therapeutic relationship' and the potential of testimony were thus core contributions made by Chilean mental health workers and have been incorporated into similar work in other contexts.[47]

Comparing and Contrasting Theory and Practice

Within trauma theorizing and practice, then, we can speak of at least two underlying philosophical traditions that are at odds. This seemingly academic debate about cause and effect actually informs radically different responses to work with individuals and communities living in conflict and postconflict situations and has, therefore, important implications for the design of psychosocial reparations programs.

On the one hand, the dominant model for thinking about the psychological sequelae of war and state-sponsored or politically organized violence is a biomedical, positivist perspective. Within this framework the most salient points posit the individual traumatized man, woman, or child, who is diagnosed as suffering from PTSD. Although there are variations on the details, a disease entity is identified, and the emphasis is clearly placed on the individual's pathology. Preferred treatment today includes drugs and cognitive-behavioral interventions, among others discussed above, and, less and less frequently, the talking cures of psychotherapy. The model suggests that identifiable symptoms are universal in character; research seeks to test the causal models towards refining individual and small group intervention strategies, and many believe these will heal the illness.

In contrast, many anthropologists, cultural psychologists, social and community psychologists, and indigenous healers stress a more descriptive, contextualized approach based on narrative and testimony as resources for understanding the psychosocial experiences of victims/survivors (see examples from Eisenbruch, Jenkins, Kleinman). Within this orientation, rather than focus on a general pathology within a single individual, researchers and practitioners press to understand the uniqueness of each participant, that is, the victim/survivor's story, within a social, historical, and cultural context.

These critical perspectives suggest that in order to better understand and more effectively respond to the sequelae of political violence, we must understand trauma and its wake, not in terms of a universal syndrome of symptoms that may be manifest among individuals, but rather within the specific contexts that are defining of, and defined by, the experiences of violence that gave rise to the trauma. As the observational lens widens, the family and community come into focus, as well as the cultural, social, and political particularities constitutive of the psychosocial trauma. Culture and communities are core dimensions within this perspective. Understanding the particular experiences deepens descriptive as well as explanatory possibilities, enriching our understanding of the phenomena and suggesting a range of creative responses for accompaniment and/or reparations.

3. TOWARDS AN ALTERNATIVE FRAMEWORK: PSYCHOSOCIAL WORK WITHIN REPARATIONS

Based on the above, we argue that psychosocial work within reparations processes be integrated and enacted within specific historical, cultural, and socio-political contexts, with singular individuals and their particular communities. We suggest that this perspective permits more effective ways of responding to and working within the diversity of challenges facing societies seeking to reconstruct themselves in the wake of war and the multiple forms of organized political violence described in this volume. In contrast to the PTSD framework, this perspective does not propose one single model, but rather an orientation which must be articulated within and shaped by individuals, families, and groups in their neighborhoods, their communities, their towns and cities, and their societies.

Developing an 'alternative framework' for situating work with survivors of politically organized violence as part of a reparations process requires us to address psychosocial effects of gross human rights violations as doing justice with and for victims. This challenge requires an understanding of each person as fundamentally active in the world and acting on/with others in producing and reproducing themselves and their communities, in nexuses of social relations.[48] This person lives in a particular social context and is culturally rooted in processes that constrain, facilitate, and give meaning to her or his social subjectivity.[49] In addition, working within an alternative framework implies not only seeking means to address individual suffering, but also understanding that individual and social healing both depend in a fundamental way on regenerating, under new terms, the social relations and the moral boundaries that were destroyed.

We describe three principles that are central to this alternative framework: the individual-community dialectic, the importance of 'thinking culturally' about social experience, and the victim/survivor as historical agent. We then identify three cross-cutting factors that must be clarified in all psychosocial work. Taken together, these six issues constitute, not a model, but rather a set of lenses through which to view postwar contexts and a framework for designing psychosocial reparations processes and programs (see Table 17.1).

Individuality and Community

An exploration of the ways in which the relationship between the individual and society varies across cultures is one important step in reorienting psychosocial work in war-torn societies. In the USA and in most of Western Europe an individual is thought of as autonomous and independent, interacting with other individuals to form families, groups, neighborhoods, and communities.[50] In contrast, in other societies (including many Asian countries, much of Latin America, etc.) social relations are core and social structures are sociocentric where social individuality is embedded in and emergent from wider concentric circles of

Table 17.1 Alternative framework for psychosocial reparations work

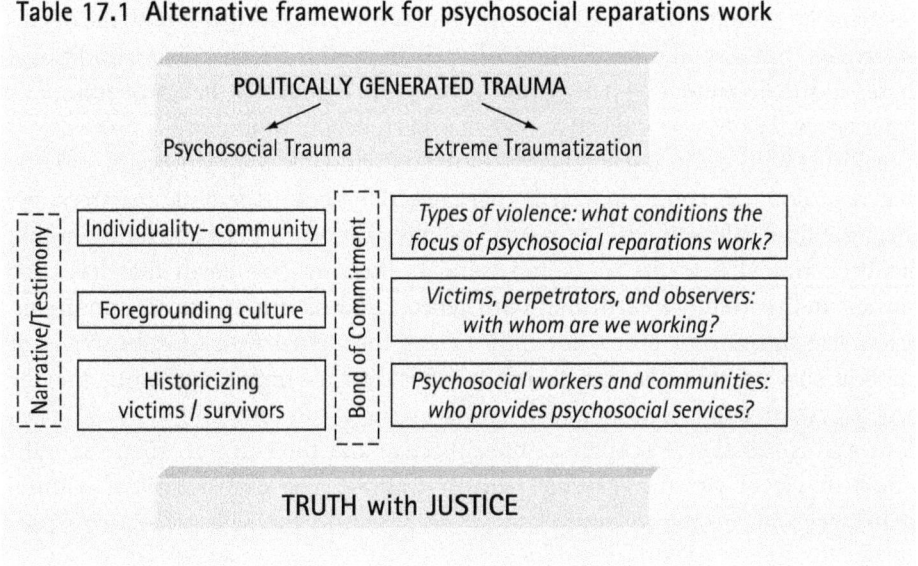

relationality. Notions of autonomy are less emphasized and have lesser social value than interdependence or sociality.[51]

Within both worldviews social relations are most frequently expressed in and lived through community of one kind or another. Community, traditionally, is understood as a locality or place, for example neighborhood, that is, a context in which interactions and social ties draw people together, wherein they develop shared interests, purpose and goals, and frequently develop collective political power. Communities may also be less location-specific and reflect a sense of 'groupness' or collectivity based on shared ideas, beliefs or experiences, among other factors, that generate identifications.[52] In general, communities foster 'the perception of similarity to others, an acknowledged interdependence with others, a willingness to maintain this interdependence by giving to or doing for others what one expects from them, and the feeling that one is part of a larger dependable and stable structure'.[53] Communities are thus sites where individuality and collectivity are co-constructed or, put another way, develop at the interstices of multiple subjectivities, cultural diversities, and social systems and structures. Thus psychosocial assistance with survivors of extreme traumatization needs to be developed through their communities.

Foregrounding Culture

As argued above, listing symptoms or diagnosing syndromes barely scratches the surface of the experience of politically generated trauma. Mayan children, for example, who came from communities targeted for scorched-earth tactics by the Guatemalan military, described the horrors of war highlighting not only the deaths of parents, but also the destruction of their homes, their crops and traditional dress, and their animals.[54] This is not simply the cumulative effect of traumatic experiences. The Mayan collective body has been deeply wounded—a body that is constituted in its deepest particularity in the individual lives of survivors—a body that is profoundly communal. It is that collective body—the ants, the trees, the corn, the domestic animals, the human beings gathered across generations—that has been ripped from its roots and wanders the earth, an earth that has been burned and scarred, an earth that both reflects and constructs the communities' scars. The burning of crops not only means the destruction of subsistence or physical survival, but also represents an attack on a symbol that embodies the people of corn, and is thus an attack on Mayan social subjectivity.[55] What has been destroyed is broader in scope (i.e. the collective and the cultural) than the individual or his or her intrapsychic pain or trauma. The destruction of cultural archetypes and metaphors annihilates or deeply limits the next generation's possibility of affirming aspects of their cultural life, so that psychosocial trauma is, once again, extended in time. Only a deeper reading of indigenous life and traditions can yield more adequate theories for work with these child survivors.

There is relatively little psychological or psychiatric work on trauma that directly informs accompaniment of survivors of war and political violence in contexts such as these Mayan communities. However, a large and growing body of anthropological and cross-cultural research on mental health and illness is informative. While a comprehensive review of this work is beyond the scope of this chapter, we present some selected examples to argue for the importance of a cultural perspective in any psychosocial work within the context of reparations processes.

Perhaps best known within the anthropological literature is the work of Arthur Kleinman and his colleagues. His extensive work in China as well as the more recent three-volume study of 'social suffering'[56] is filled with rich ethnographic observation and interpretations of participants' narratives. In case after case authors' efforts to stand within the cultural specificity offer dramatic alternatives to the biomedical model described above. Moreover, Kleinman's re-representation of PTSD as 'social suffering' destigmatizes the survivor, removes the terror of war and its effects from the domain of illness, and focuses on the survivor's interpretations of his or her experiences.

For example, Jenkins[57] sought to reveal the multiple meanings of *nervios* among Salvadoran refugees. This construct has been used by Latinos/as to describe a wide range of physical and psychological ailments and is frequently described by US-based mental health professionals as evidence of the poor Latino's tendency to somaticize psychic trauma. Moreover, PTSD diagnostic criteria ignore somatic and psychosomatic symptoms.[58] In contrast, Jenkins suggests that a deeper analysis of survivor narratives clarifies the socio-political dimensions of their complaints and how neither medical nor narrowly defined psychological interventions will address the depth of this pain.

The implications of a cultural perspective for resituating trauma are multiple. Minimally it requires an exploration and revalorization of traditional understandings and practices. Indigenous healing processes are fundamentally cultural processes. Trauma and healing are configured within local practices and historic beliefs. These include, among others, conceptions of time as a cyclical process where ancestors and spirits are as intimately engaged in everyday life as are living sisters and brothers, sons and daughters. Within such an understanding, the acknowledgment of the past and/or recognition and acknowledgment within the family and/or community is often several generations later, perhaps long after reparations have been paid to immediate survivors.

In one revealing case, United Nations workers described the importance of *conselho* or the advice and consolation offered by family members, neighbors, and church groups to Angolan children who had been displaced and/or lost one or both parents in the war there.[59] They highlight ways in which traditional forms of support that focus on the 'naturalness' and 'inevitability' of suffering and death as well as its cyclical, rather than linear, nature, contribute to the survival of families and communities. Further, the suffering that accompanies those who survived the war was seen as characteristic of all people, not a particular stigma attached to some. Based on similar experiences, Wessells and Monteiro,[60] working within the Angolan context, argued that these rich cultural resources and historical traditions, among others that they identified, must be incorporated into war and postwar interventions.

In one of the few efforts to evaluate reparations work within indigenous or traditional communities affected by war and organized violence, Durán Pérez and her colleagues[61] concluded that economic reparations for families of detained and disappeared of Mapuche origin negatively affected local traditions and distorted relations of solidarity within the community. The authors argued that material reparations should have reflected the needs and traditional norms within the community. Moreover, they suggested that much of the psychosocial support offered by mental health workers ignored Mapuche practices and beliefs, including but not limited to traditional understanding of causality and mourning processes.

Many psychologists working in South Africa, both in the context of the Truth and Reconciliation Commission and more widely with survivors of community violence there, also argue that it is critical to understand and incorporate indigenous healing resources in work with trauma survivors. Gill Eagle[62] shows, for example, that despite the difficulties in characterizing the diversity within African societies and the risk of reductionism, African worldviews contrast with Euro-American along multiple dimensions. The African worldview is, generally, more holistic, wherein 'physical, emotional, cognitive, and spiritual functioning are viewed as integrally related'.[63] The relationship between the individual and the spiritual is more permeable and immediate than in Euro-American cultures. For example, Noel Muchenga Chicuecue[64] describes reconcilation processes in Mozambique as about 'building a relationship between parties in conflict' and having as much to do with the dead and their presence among the living as with the living. Traditional healers frequently have a role in these contexts, in which the basis of the conflict or 'wrong-doing' is core to the healing process. He argues that these traditions have contributed to work among child-soldiers, refugees, and others affected by the civil war there.

Yet it is also the case that local traditions and cultural practices are not static, nor should they be accepted uncritically. Within an increasingly global community, they intersect with Euro-American theories and practices. Euro-American social scientists and mental health workers laboring in ongoing and postconflict societies (e.g. Eagle, Lykes, Wessells) maintain that it is challenging but necessary to work at the interstices of these cultural diversities and facilitate active participation among a diversity of practitioners. Thus we argue for an 'alternative framework' that foregrounds culture to better accompany individuals and societies in transition from war and seeking reparations.

Historicizing the Victim/Survivor

The need to historicize the victim/survivor responds to several challenges of working effectively with the psychosocial consequences of war, including transgenerational issues and what might be called social healing. A range of efforts in this respect suggests the importance for survivors and for their children and grandchildren of reconstructing identities, recognizing the agency of victims/survivors in historical, social and political processes, and providing some explanation for what happened to them. In addition, doing this and taking it to the public sphere represents a potential tool for 'rehumanizing' the victims/survivors in their societies, where they may often have been stigmatized and criminalized, and for opening wider discussions on the underlying social and moral dilemmas in postwar situations.

Research with Holocaust survivors[65] provides critical insight into how political trauma in the past is experienced directly and indirectly several generations beyond the events. Those working with grandchildren of survivors have found, for example, that the past enters the present through the intergenerational dynamics of families. In both instances silence has been found, perhaps paradoxically, to be a source of transmission of the unspeakable. The silence of secrets reappears as the 'ghosts' of the next generations.[66] Thus, while it protects the survivors, their silence 'gives voice' in the imaginations of the children of survivors, and even their offspring, so that fantasies and speculations sometimes approximate or surpass historical horrors and lived experiences. Extensive therapeutic and narrative work, mostly at the level of the individual or the family, with the children and grandchildren of victims/survivors, and more recently perpetrators, of the Holocaust has been documented through case studies and qualitative research. This work confirms that 'breaking silence' has contributed importantly to individual and familial well-being[67] as well as important historical protagonism in current political conflict involving this generation.

Historicizing the victims/survivors of massive human rights violations will depend, to a greater or lesser degree, on the use of methodologies that permit people to speak about what happened, about their own experiences, and about those who were lost. Testimony, narration, and storytelling can be key in the effort to locate victims/survivors in a specific historical context and reconstruct their identities and roles in that context.[68] In the work developed by Cienfuegos and Monelli,[69] described above, they reported that the use of testimony gathered through multiple sessions was key to their therapeutic approach, a way to aid the victims/survivors in reconstructing a sense of themselves as actors and agents, by focusing not only on the traumatic experience of torture or disappearance, that is, not only on the victimhood, but also on their lives in their families and organizations, as activists and professionals, as the case might be, in a concrete political context.

It is important to note, however, that in some contexts silence has been a resource for survival, and perhaps contributed to some victims sustaining their dignity through horrifically dehumanizing experiences. Frequently read as denial, silence can conversely be an extremely important coping mechanism within contexts of ongoing violence and destruction. For example, silence and secrecy have been identified by some within local Mayan communities as strategies for survival and as resources for developing a collective sense of identity within a repressive social order. Others there argue that while silence was an adaptive form of coping during the worst years of violence there, it may no longer be so.[70] As a minimum, caution should be exercised by those who seek to facilitate testimony or storytelling among survivors/victims, and an attempt made to understand the role and kinds of silences that are present in their communities.

Truth commissions, while not intentionally designed in most cases to historicize the victims/survivors, have often made important contributions, in practice, in this regard. Established by countries emerging from armed conflict as part of the measures to acknowledge and address atrocities committed during the years of political violence, these commissions generally depend greatly on testimony from local survivors to carry out their work. In effect they create spaces for survivors to recount what happened, identify victims and/or perpetrators, provide background to events, and in some cases, retrieve the 'missing links' in the death of a child or parent. Such individual testimonies are then situated within the broader 'truth-seeking' processes, by others, to document human rights violations and, increasingly, to construct an historical and political explanation of periods of extreme repression and political strife. In few cases are victims/survivors brought to life, historicized, on an individual basis (although public hearings may provide some venue for this); rather truth commission findings can provide a more general historical context for groups of victims/survivors.

Although there is relatively little empirical research evaluating the impacts of these processes, a recent comparative study[71] offers some initial evidence of how victims/survivors and human rights workers experienced them in five countries. Similar to earlier evidence based on single sites or smaller samples, they found that many survivors affirmed the historical and societal importance of the commission and its work (although there was not total consensus on this). However, individual survivors had very mixed evaluations of the impact of the truth-telling and associated reparations processes for themselves and their families.

Testimony, storytelling, and historical reconstruction function differently in time and space, and within and across generations. For example, in Argentina the grandchildren of the Grandmothers of the Plaza de Mayo have created a process of 'historicizing the subject' through their Family Biography Archive. They are collecting and preserving family testimonies of the disappeared, as well as the stories of those close to them, in order to dispel the notion that the disappeared were nothing more than 'innocent victims'. Project participants argue that this characterization of 'victimhood' was perpetuated, perhaps by historical necessity, by the widely published *Nunca Más* and by the Grandmothers themselves. Today these fuller, historicized accounts make possible a more complete and human characterization of the disappeared, so that their children and others can know and identify with them as more than victims, as people 'who were capable of desire—and of acting with consequence'.[72] The private and political lives of individuals are firmly situated in significant periods of political conflict and social trauma by this research project that reunites a decontextualized individual with the historical, collective experience of identity-giving groups.

Intergenerational trauma doubtless marks the present and the future, but shifts in socio-political realities in Argentina have created new opportunities for renarrating and revaluing the past. This work has been found to be an important personal resource by many children of the disappeared. Moreover, through this remembering project, their parents, the disappeared, are yielding their historical place as 'victims' and claiming, through their children, a collective protagonism as seekers of social change. By linking intimate stories with public accounts, the project helps restitute a socio-cultural and political identity to the disappeared and facilitate the recovery of a fuller historical memory, creating a much richer opportunity for dialogue between the past and the present.

The three principles we outlined above, wherein the victim/survivor is repositioned within history, culture, and community, offer critical resources for psychosocial work within reparations processes. We are careful not to suggest that they form a model that can be applied directly; rather they provide orientation and a set of lenses through which to enter a process with a group of victims/survivors and/or a local community. Psychosocial workers bring important resources to this process, but the complexities and conflicts are cautionary tales suggesting how difficult it is for psychosocial resources to 'heal' in the absence of wider legal and political processes.

Below we discuss three cross-cutting factors in psychosocial work within reparations processes, which should be addressed by mental health workers in postwar contexts. Again, these are not solutions, but rather factors that help frame and situate the work and challenge those who seek to engage it. Although these factors are specific to psychosocial reparations work, they are not isolated concerns, but are rather inserted into and emergent from broader cultural and socio-political processes within a given society. We suggest that they should inform how we think and act psychosocially within reparations processes and programs.

Types of Violence: What Conditions the Focus of Psychosocial Reparations Work?

Prior to or concurrent with designing a reparations process, it is critical to situate and characterize the violence that has occurred, including who was or is responsible for it, in order to assess its effects, as well as to begin to visualize the categories of victims and perpetrators, and the often very complex relationships between them. This is importantly linked to our initial discussion above, that is, that politically motivated violence has distinctive social and moral dimensions. Its effects are, therefore, distinct from those caused by individual, criminal acts, natural disasters or other exceptionally difficult circumstances. Thus, the first cross-cutting factor involves developing an analysis of the types of violence. Those who hope to develop psychosocial reparations programs for victims/survivors must distinguish, for example, between vertical violence, that is, violence exercised directly by a powerful state against its opponents or perceived opponents, and horizontal violence, that is, violence exercised by one social group against another. The typology must also capture complex, local variations, in which both types of violence are engaged in simultaneously, or when the state overtly or covertly supports one or another faction, or when individuals may be both victims and perpetrators of violations. The Civil Defense Patrols (PAC) in Guatemala, wherein all men between the ages of 16 and 65 were forced to collaborate with army operations, including participation in torture and massacres, is one example of that complexity. Northern Ireland offers another example wherein paramilitary organizations engaged in horizontal violence while the British military exerted control. The conflicts in South Africa between the African National Congress (ANC) and the Inkatha Freedom Party (IFP) towards the end of the apartheid regime reflect another complex intersection of types of organized violence. Other examples include family members or neighbors who took advantage of the wider social conflicts to enact longstanding disputes, frequently resulting in death, destruction or usurpation of property. Thus the analysis of the types of violence should be comprehensive, taking these complex forms into account, while avoiding frequent pitfalls characteristic of some truth-seeking and reparations processes, that is, that of equating all forms of violence.

Victims/Survivors, Perpetrators and Observers: With Whom Are We Working?

Organized political violence and war involves perpetrators, victims, and observers. Sometimes these categories are clear-cut and permanent, but often people and communities move between these experiences and actions. While reparations programs generally focus directly on victims and their needs, attending to these needs does not necessarily imply only working with them. Those working with individuals, communities, and the wider society in psychosocial accompaniment efforts are likely also to be working with those indirectly affected by war, that is, the observers, and/or family members absent during the worst of the violence but who have returned to find a devastated community, and in some cases, even with perpetrators. In fact, as we have suggested throughout this chapter, the effectiveness of psychosocial interventions or other reparation efforts may actually depend in a significant fashion on the restoration or re-creation of victim/survivor relationships in their communities and in society as a whole. Providing health services or mental health accompaniment to victims/survivors may be useful to those who receive the services, but the reparatory effect may well be limited, if the stigma of victimhood is attached to those services, or if the state— or neighbors—continues to deny pertinent responsibilities or justify repressive actions. Thus, identifying those with whom we work is a second cross-cutting factor for psychosocial work in reparations programs.

Although most psychosocial reparations work has been directed, appropriately, towards victims/survivors, there are a small number of lawyers and psychologists who have argued for the importance of including perpetrators in such work. For example, some psychosocial workers are accompanying perpetrators in their testimonies before truth and reconciliation processes and beyond.[73] Moreover, community workers in war-torn societies frequently find perpetrators and victims in the same small group programs, where material conditions often drive neighbors who fought on opposite sides of a conflict to see their own and their families' survival as dependent upon these former enemies.[74] There is strong disagreement among psychosocial workers about whether or not victims/survivors and perpetrators can achieve some form of healing within the same psychosocial programs, and there has been even less attention to those who were both victims and victimizers and to those who were observers. Although there are no clear resolutions of these contested issues, our alternative framework offers a set of parameters that enable those designing reparations programs to be cognizant of these complex dynamics within local, regional, and national reparations processes.

Psychosocial Workers and Communities: Who Provides Psychosocial Services?

As discussed above, many of those currently engaged in psychosocial work are trained as psychiatrists, psychologists, social workers, or, more broadly, as mental health professionals. Although it is difficult to argue that such training is not necessary for those who operate within the dominant paradigm wherein PTSD is most frequently identified as the 'problem' for victims/survivors of war and politically organized violence, it is less clear what training is required for those who would work within the alternative framework identified here. Specifically, the mandate to foreground culture, historicize victims/survivors, and attend to individual and community-level dynamics and processes suggests the importance of involving interdisciplinary and intercultural teams in the design of psychosocial reparations processes. The central importance of justice and truth in the healing process argues for legal and/or human rights involvement. Moreover, the growing pressure to shift psychosocial reparations processes from an 'emergency aid orientation' towards development work argues for some representatives skilled in economic development.[75] Across all domains, it is critical to involve local or indigenous expertise. Thus, a third and final cross-cutting factor in the design of any reparations program requires careful attention to those who carry out, that is, design and implement, psychosocial programs.[76]

In addition to the suggestion above that teams should be interdisciplinary and rely importantly on local and/or indigenous workers in the design and implementation of programs,[77] our framework recognizes the potential of local communities and their leaders. The War-Torn Societies Project, piloted over six years in Eritrea, Guatemala, Mozambique, and Somalia, represents one kind of model.[78] The program focuses on the recovery and strengthening of societies emerging from conflicts through bringing together local actors and internationalists who work together to build consensus and formulate responses. Although not intended directly as a psychosocial program or as reparations per se, these initiatives included the reintegration of demobilized soldiers in Mozambique, the establishment of women's development centers in Somalia and the development of cross-ethnic organizing models among Maya in Guatemala. In each case local leaders developed their capacities for naming the problem, situating it within its socio-historical and cultural context and working collaboratively to design solutions.

On a more modest level, but with an explicit psychosocial focus, the first author of this chapter collaborated with Ixil and Quiché Maya women over an eight-year process during which the women developed several economic development projects, a bilingual educational program for children of their town and psychosocial creative workshops for women of the town and six of its surrounding villages.

Women from differing religious groups, political affiliations, widows of soldiers and guerrillas, as well as members of the latter group and internationalists, joined together through a participatory action research process to create a photoessay that recounts the community's story of war and survival, as well as current efforts to rethread social relations and rebuild institutions.[79]

Those planning psychosocial reparations programs must also situate their work within some institutional base—and there is much debate about the pros and cons of governmental and nongovernmental sites for such work. To address this issue, one must clarify the possibilities and limitations facing a repressor/oppressor government that seeks to provide psychosocial resources for survivors/victims when it is the alleged perpetrator of the violence. Yet, to hand these responsibilities over to NGOs sends a potentially contradictory message about the state's 'responsibility' for the violations, as well as for transition and transformation. The extent to which medical services, the conventional site of psychosocial treatment, are identified with the repressor may differ from country to country and even from community to community. Moreover, the medical professions' direct involvement in repressive activities may also differ according to the context.

Within insight or psychoanalytically based therapeutic interventions, this issue is additionally complex. The signification of the 'healer' and the transference and counter transference processes suggest that in some contexts the government or its representatives may not be in the best position to provide psychosocial assistance. We know that for many years in contexts of long-term political and military conflict, for example, in Northern Ireland, those on one side of the political conflict rejected outright 'treatment' provided by those on the other.

Alternatively, reparations processes are also about the reconstruction of the state and of local governing institutions, including the reconstruction of social services. If all resources for psychosocial assistance are invested in NGOs rather than the government, the latter's institutions may be weakened, depending, in part, on the level of infusion of international resources. This is ever more acute in countries where mental health resources were sparse or nonexistent prior to the conflict. Moreover, in the domain of international law, it is an obligation of the state to provide such resources. Further, if indigenous populations or specific ethnic or racial groups or communities were the primary victims in the conflict and continue to be marginalized from state resources and processes in postconflict, are there obligations of international organizations to support them in the provision of psychosocial resources to meet their needs? Thus, there are two intertwined questions here that must be addressed: who should provide the services and who should pay for them?

4. EXHUMATIONS AS A SITE OF HEALING

Exhumations of clandestine graves, frequently at the sites of massacres or where the bodies of the disappeared have been found, are increasingly considered to be an important piece of a reparations process. They offer one concrete example of a way in which complex psychosocial, cultural, ethical, legal, and political challenges converge. They may serve to facilitate closure of grieving processes, permit fulfillment of long-delayed, cultural and religious obligations around death, honor the victims, square the historical record, acquire critical evidence for bringing legal actions, and confront grievances between opposing factions.

Space does not permit an exhaustive examination of this issue and, as with other experiences discussed in this chapter, there is relatively little empirical data to support all aspects of this argument. However, in both Guatemala and Zimbabwe there have been efforts to document and evaluate the different procedures and accompaniment strategies used in exhumations and in reburials. Each of these contexts offers an example of how the three principles described above as well as the three cross-cutting factors come into play in the psychosocial processes that imbue and embed an exhumation of victims of gross human rights violations and their reburial. Critical reflections on the processes suggest ways in which the framework can be used creatively to design and evaluate psychosocial programs within a reparations framework.

In Guatemala, close to 450 grave sites have been exhumed in more than 150 communities over the past ten years.[80] During the first years, victim/survivor groups were the major advocates for exhumations and they continue to be strong protagonists in the process. More recently, the Catholic Church, a number of human rights organizations, and an important array of international donor agencies have also become important actors. Virtually all of the exhumations have been carried out by teams of forensic anthropologists. Once the remains are exhumed, they are taken to Guatemala City for detailed forensic analysis, to determine and confirm the identification of the victims, as well as the cause and circumstances of death, actions that can be important for implicating perpetrators. It generally takes several months for the forensic analysis to be completed, before the remains can be returned to the communities for burial.

After decades of unresolved grief and having lived through the deeply painful process of recovering the remains of family members, people have differing responses: some may want to press charges and open legal proceedings, while others hope only to rebury their loved ones immediately in local cemeteries. In the words of one Mayan widow who had identified her mother's bones by the coins that were on her earrings, what she longed for most was to take the dead to the cemetery where the dead should be.[81]

Analyzing this situation through the 'alternative framework' suggested above reveals multiple complexities. Experts using painstaking forensic methods to develop evidence for legal and judicial processes must also engage and respond to the intense emotions and needs of families and communities. Human rights activists working with exhumations often provide protection to participants threatened by former paramilitary members still in the community, yet they are also sometimes implicated in local conflicts, as residents remain divided on whether or not to bring charges against alleged perpetrators for their crimes. Moreover, local communities are generally fractured, with fissures sometimes following the lines that gave rise to the war and frequently complicated by new factors that have developed within contexts of unresolved grief and continuing extreme poverty.

The psychosocial issues raised for those hoping to contribute to a reparatory process go well beyond the symptomatology and responses offered by the PTSD model. Rather they emerge within and reflect the kinds of individual, familial, cultural and historical processes presented in the alternative framework, which offers a lens for analyzing and suggesting changes for ongoing work as the context shifts in the postwar context.

As forensic workers, community activists and others in Guatemala became more conscious of the kinds of problems that frequently arise before, during, and after an exhumation, psychosocial assistance teams coordinated by NGOs were incorporated into the exhumation processes. While using a range of methodologies, in general the tendency has been towards giving greater attention to culture, community and history in attempts to improve accompaniment in highly complex emotional and political processes. The importance of this work cannot be overestimated, nor can the challenges that the communities and mental health workers face.

A second site of exhumations and reburials from East Africa offers a different example of how local communities and those accompanying them responded in the wake of massive violations of human rights. Thousands were massacred, others tortured, and entire homesteads destroyed in a matter of weeks in Matabeleland in Western Zimbabwe during five years of intense violence in the early 1980s. Fractious internal conflicts followed on the heels of the 1960s and 1970s liberation struggle and were violently repressed by Prime Minister Mugabe.

Political instability has prohibited the more active involvement of forensic teams and legal action against perpetrators to date, but the AMANI Trust, a small NGO concerned with the rehabilitation of survivors of torture and organized violence, has taken important leadership in Matabeleland.[82] Exhumations were initiated there with a primary purpose of 'facilitating community healing processes.'

The community-rebuilding work undertaken by the Trust draws heavily on traditional cultural practices, including, for example, *umbuyiso*, 'during which the spirit of the dead is officially brought home and inaugurated as an ancestor'.[83]

These rituals are community-wide events, responses to the absence of culturally appropriate funerals that had left hundreds of people in states of suspended mourning. Community-rebuilding exercises and activities facilitated by AMANI contributed to previously warring groups and individuals being able to witness collectively to the murders. Testimonies about the past also served to call the dead back into life. Moreover, the rituals provided opportunities for victims and by-standers to narrate a future, rethreading social relations while recognizing publicly the injustices wrought on their communities. Psychosocial social accompaniment has, thus, enabled individuals to mourn their murdered relatives and enabled local communities to reestablish relations among the living and the dead. Although ongoing political instability contributes to an uncertain future, AMANI and the communities they serve see this work as important to an ongoing struggle that seeks truth with justice.

In both countries, then, exhumations and reburials are sites where individuals and collectivities converge in history and culture. In lieu of providing individual therapy for victims/survivors, teams of psychosocial workers and community leaders have accompanied families and communities in complex processes and programs at the intersection of psychology, forensic science, and human rights. Bonds of commitment between the workers and local community members create possibilities, bounded by particular political contexts, for seeking truth, approximating healing and striving for justice.

5. Some Persistent Concerns

We have outlined the dominant paradigm in which most psychosocial work with victims/survivors of politically organized violence and war has developed. We have argued strongly that an 'alternative framework' that is socially, historically, and culturally embedded offers important lenses through which to engage in psycho-social work, particularly in and with local communities. As argued above, this is not a model but a set of orienting principles and issues that enable psychosocial workers to foreground the moral and ethical dimensions of their possible contributions to reparations processes.

Significantly, our reflections here and our field work in contexts of war and truth-seeking, have generated several continuing concerns. The first is an unexamined assumption underlying much psychosocial work, that is, the expected outcomes from this work are 'recovery and healing'. As mental health workers and human rights activists, we interrogate the multiple meanings of words like recovery, healing, and reparation, and strongly resist claims of reconciliation as the logical outcome of reparations program. We argue here that work with victims/survivors of extreme violence of human origin directly implicates questions of justice and truth. Thus psychological language of 'recovery' is insufficient to characterize the processes described herein. Moreover, we interrogate the assumption that there are identifiable and specific outcomes to be achieved 'once and for all' through reparations processes or psychosocial interventions. The intergenerational, historical, and cultural factors that imbue all psychosocial work with victims/survivors discussed in this chapter and elsewhere suggest otherwise. Perhaps we are paraphrasing the words of Lawrence Langer[84] when he faced the impenetrability of the Holocaust, reading meaning where there may be none. He suggested that those of us who work among victims/survivors create meaning in order to heal our own pain, to quiet our own rage. Moreover, if all reparations are symbolic and justice is 'pending', what are the possible consequences of psychosocial interventions in the absence of justice?

A second persistent concern centers on testimony and truth-seeking/truth-telling processes in psychosocial programs and reparations. The involvement of former combatants, lawyers, religious leaders, ethicists, political activists, and social scientists within truth and reconciliation processes has contributed to growing debates about the 'nature of truth' and the possibilities or impossibilities of achieving justice.[85] For example, truth is sometimes contrasted to facticity, that is, what 'really happened'. Others argue that while getting 'the facts' is clearly very important, truth-telling at times may reflect a stronger emphasis on the meaning that the victim/survivor makes of the experience, that is, his or her interpretations. Others have engaged truth-telling as a negotiated process at the community level, wherein survivors from a variety of political perspectives, religious convictions, ethnicities, etc. engage in developing an understanding of what happened within which they can live together and build a future.[86]

Yet, in each of these understandings, and among most of the informants in Espinoza Cuevas et al.'s comparative study,[87] truth-seeking/truth-telling was described as a critical basis for justice and, in some cases, as a foundation for political action. These efforts, then, should be understood as part of ongoing social processes that develop an historical record and interpretation, which can serve as a tool for critical reflection in the present and for the future. Moreover, each of these understandings of 'truth' and 'truth-seeking/truth-telling' has psychological and social consequences for those who hold them. As importantly, Espinoza Cuevas et al.[88] found consensus, perhaps not surprisingly, about the damaging impact of impunity in the context of a search for truth. The absence of justice, more so than many other factors, diminishes the potential positive impact of psychosocial healing efforts.

Third, psychosocial programs carry possible risks for victims/survivors. Victims may be restigmatized by being 'selected out' for special services or resources. Diagnostic categories per se sometimes marginalize or restigmatize survivors, objectifying them rather than engaging them as active collaborators in a healing process. Alternatively, victims may become 'stuck in victimhood', that is, they may repeat their story of traumatization so frequently that they become the story; they 'may no longer exist' outside of the testimony of survival.

A final persistent concern has to do with time limits in reparations processes. Beyond the question of whether it is possible to heal politically generated traumas, victims/survivors may only recognize their pain or loss years after the violation, therefore not seeking help at the time reparations are offered. As argued above, psychosocial processes are long term and often intergenerational. In addition, the cyclical nature of time in some indigenous communities challenges those negotiating current truth commissions and reparations processes to envision and plan for the possibilities of inter- or multiple generational processes. Minimally these diversities and constraints must be recognized and acknowledged by and to all parties in reparations processes.

In raising each of these complexities we are reminded of the centrality of the moral positioning of psychosocial workers. We write from a position as human rights activists and psychosocial workers and argue that continued impunity and the absence of justice greatly limit, or may even annul, the potential for healing in reparatory measures, including material compensation or even well-intentioned psychological attention. We share with many colleagues the conviction that 'reparations without justice' is not reparatory and that the wider social-political struggles for justice and against impunity and specific psychosocial interventions need to be increasingly consonant and integrated in a unified strategy.[89] Unfortunately, psychological interventions, frequently appropriated as technical instruments divorced from socio-political processes and from a struggle against impunity, may have little reparatory potential and could well even undermine the impact of other forms of reparations.

In this chapter we have presented and critically analyzed a range of psychosocial processes developed for work with survivors/victims of war and organized political violence. We have identified an 'alternative framework' which we offer as a resource to those seeking to design psychosocial assistance within reparations processes. Moreover, we have identified three principles and three cross-cutting factors that must be addressed if these programs are to successfully complement the wider reparations and transitions processes facing many states today. We recognize that each component of reparations has psychosocial dimensions and implications, yet we have argued here for a role for specific psychosocial processes and components that would both resonate with and complement broader reparations projects. Rather than negating the psychosocial dimension of all reparations processes, this work would enhance them, offering a deeply contextualized process of psychosocial accompaniment.

NOTES

1. Paul Dalton, 'Some Perspectives on Torture Victims, Reparation and Mental Recovery', *Article 21*(6) (2002), http://www.article2.org/mainfile.php/0106/63/; accessed January 17, 2003.

2. Naomi Roht-Arriaza, 'Punishment, Redress, and Pardon: Theoretical and Psychological Approaches', in *Impunity and Human Rights in International Law and Practice*, Naomi Roht-Arriaza, ed. (Oxford: Oxford University Press, 1995), 13–23.

3. M. Cherif Bassiouni, 'Civil and Political Rights, Including the Questions of Independence of the Judiciary, Administration of Justice, Impunity: The Right to Restitution, Compensation and Rehabilitation for Victims of Gross Violations of Human Rights and Fundamental Freedoms' (New York: United Nations, 2000).

4. Ignacio Martín-Baró, 'Reparations: Attention Must Be Paid: Healing the Body Politic in Latin America', *Commonweal* 117(6) (1990); Ignacio Martín-Baró, *Writings for a Liberation Psychology*, ed. by Adrianne Aron and Shawn Corne (Cambridge, MA: Harvard University Press, 1994); Paz Rojas Baeza, 'Mental Health Disturbances Caused by the Absence of Truth and Justice', Paper presented at the 6th International Conference for Health and Human Rights (Cavtat, Croatia, June 21–4, 2001); Nora Sveaass and Nils Johan Lavik, 'Psychological Aspects of Human Rights Violations: The Importance of Justice and Reconciliation', *Nordic Journal of International Law* 69 (1) (2000): 35–52.

5. Víctor Espinoza Cuevas, Maria Luisa Ortiz Rojas, and Paz Rojas Baeza provide an excellent comparative review of recommendations on reparations by truth commissions in Argentina, Chile, El Salvador, Guatemala and South Africa, in their study, *Comisiones de la Verdad, ¿Un Camino Incierto?* (Chile: Corporación de Promoción y Defensa de los Derechos del Pueblo, Asociación Para la Prevención de la Tortura, 2003), see especially 113–15. For more on the Chilean experience, see Elizabeth Lira Kornfeld, 'The Development of Treatment Approaches for Victims of Human Rights Violations in Chile', in *Beyond Trauma: Cultural and Societal Dynamics*, Rolf J. Kleber, Charles R. Figley, and Berthold P. R. Gersons, eds. (New York: Plenum Press, 1995), 115–31; and Lira's chapter in Part I of this volume.

6. See, for example, Cuevas et al., op. cit.; Trudy de Ridder, 'The Trauma of Testifying: Deponents' Difficult Healing Process', *Track Two* 6 (3/4) (1997), http://ccrweb.ccr.uct.ac.za/two/6_34/p30_deridder.html; accessed 8 October 2003; Cheryl de la Rey and Ingrid Owens, 'Perceptions of Psychosocial Healing and the Truth and Reconciliation Commission in South Africa', *Peace and Conflict: Journal of Peace Psychology* 4(3) (1998): 257–70.

7. Yael Danieli, ed., *International Handbook of Multigenerational Legacies of Trauma* (New York: Plenum, 1998); Sveaass and Lavik, op. cit.

8. David Becker, 'Dealing with the Consequences of Organized Violence', in *Berghof Handbook for Conflict Transformation*, Martina Fischer, Alex Austin, and Norbert Ropers, eds. (Berlin: Berghof Research Center for Constructive Conflict Management, 2003).

9. Sveaass and Lavik, op. cit. See also Paz Rojas Baeza, 'Ruptura Del Vínculo Humano: La Mirada Médica-Psiquiátrica De La Impunidad', in *Impunidad, Una Perspectiva Ética: Seis Estudios De Casos De América Latina*, Charles Harper, ed. (Geneva: World Council of Churches, 1996).

10. United Nations, *Impact of Armed Conflict on Children* (New York: UN, 1997).

11. International Rehabilitation Council for Torture Victims (IRCT), *Rehabilitation of Torture Victims—Global Directory of Centres and Programmes 2003–2004* (Copenhagen: IRCT, 2003).

12. American Psychiatric Association (APA), *Diagnostic and Statistical Manual of Mental Disorders*, 3rd edn. (Washington, DC: APA, 1980).

13. American Psychiatric Association, *Diagnostic and Statistical Manual of Mental Disorders*, 4th edn. (Washington, DC: APA, 2000), 169.

14. Vladan Starcevic and Slavoljub Durdic, 'Post-Traumatic Stress Disorder: Current Conceptualization: An Overview of Research and Treatment', *Psihijatrija Danas* 25(1/2) (1993).

15. Wilbur J. Scott, 'PTSD in DSM-III: A Case in the Politics of Diagnosis and Disease', *Social Problems* 37(3) (1990).

16. Patrick J. Bracken, Joan E. Giller, and Derek Summerfield, 'Psychological Responses to War and Atrocity: The Limitations of Current Concepts', *Social Science and Medicine* 40(8) (1995).

17. Ibid.; and Patrick Bracken, *Trauma: Culture, Meaning, and Philosophy* (Philadelphia, PA: Whurr Publishers, 2002).

18. Charles Figley, ed., *Trauma and Its Wake* (New York: Brunner/Mazel, 1985); Jonathan Shay, *Achilles in Vietnam: Combat Trauma and the Undoing of Character* (New York: Atheneum, 1994).

19. See, for example, Ronnie Janoff-Bulman, *Shattered Assumptions: Towards a New Psychology of Trauma* (New York: Free Press, 1992).

20. Ibid.

21. See, for example, Francine Shapiro, *Eye Movement Desensitization and Reprocessing: Basic Principles, Protocols, and Procedures* (New York: Guilford Press, 1995); Bessel A. van der Kolk, Jennifer A. Burbridge, and Joji Suzuki, eds., *The Psychobiology of Traumatic Memory. Clinical Implications of Neuroimaging Studies*, vol. 821, *Psychobiology of Posttraumatic Stress Disorder* (New York: New York Academy of Sciences, 1997).

22. See, for example, George S. Everly, Jr. and Jeffrey T. Mitchell, *A Primer on Critical Incident Stress Management (CISM)*, http://www.icisf.org/inew_era.htm; accessed July 5, 2004. For a critical review of this intervention strategy, see Beverley and Lenore Meldrum Raphael, 'Does Debriefing after Psychological Trauma Work? (Randomized Controlled Trials) (editorial)', *British Medical Journal* 310(6993) (1995).

23. Patrick J. Bracken, 'Hidden Agendas: Deconstructing Post-Traumatic Stress Disorder', in *Rethinking the Trauma of War*, Patrick J. Bracken and Celia Petty, eds. (London: Free Association Books, 1998).

24. Ibid.; and Becker, op. cit.

25. Raija-Leena Punamaki, 'Political Violence and Mental Health', *International Journal of Mental Health* 17(4) (1989).

26. Ibid., 4.

27. Ibid., 5.

28. Bracken et al., op. cit.

29. Bracken, 'Hidden Agendas: Deconstructing Post-Traumatic Stress Disorder', op. cit.

30. Arthur Kleinman, *Rethinking Psychiatry: From Cultural Category to Personal Experience* (New York: Free Press, 1988).

31. Bracken, *Trauma: Culture, Meaning, and Philosophy*, op. cit.

32. Veena Das, Arthur Klinman, Margaret lock, Mamphela Ramphele and Pamila Reynolds eds., *Remaking a World: Violence, Social Suffering, and Recovery* (Berkeley, CA: University of California Press, 2001).

33. Arthur Kleinman, *Writing at the Margin: Discourse between Anthropology and Medicine* (Berkeley, CA: University of California Press, 1995).

34. Anthony J. Marsella and Geoffrey M. White, eds., *Cultural Conceptions of Mental Health and Therapy* (Boston: Kluwer, 1982).

35. Janis Hunter Jenkins, 'The State Construction of Affect: Political Ethos and Mental Health among Salvadoran Refugees', *Culture, Medicine and Psychiatry* 15 (1991).

36. Maurice Eisenbruch, 'From Post-Traumatic Stress Disorder to Cultural Bereavement: Diagnosis of Southeast Asian Refugees', *Social Science and Medicine* 33(6) (1991). See also Maurice Eisenbruch, 'Cross-Cultural Aspects of Bereavement I: A Conceptual Framework for Comparative Analysis', *Culture, Medicine and Psychiatry* 8 (1984); Maurice Eisenbruch, 'Cross-Cultural Aspects of Bereavement II: Ethnic and Cultural Variations in the Development of Bereavement Practices', *Culture, Medicine and Psychiatry* 8 (1984).

37. Kleinman, *Writing at the Margin: Discourse between Anthropology and Medicine*, op. cit.

38. Allan Young, *The Harmony of Illusions: Inventing Post-Traumatic Stress Disorder* (Princeton, NJ: Princeton University Press, 1995), 5.

39. Ignacio Martín-Baró, 'War and Mental Health', in *Writings for a Liberation Psychology* (Cambridge, MA: Harvard University Press, 1994), 109–11.

40. Ibid.

41. Punamaki, op. cit.

42. Derek Summerfield, 'Addressing Human Response to War and Atrocity: Major Challenges in Research and Practices and the Limitations of Western Psychiatric Models', in Kleber, Figley, and Gersons, op. cit., 17–19.

43. Becker, op. cit., 4.

44. Ana Julia Cienfuegos and Christina Monelli, 'The Testimony of Political Repression as a Therapeutic Instrument', *American Journal of Orthopsychiatry* 53(1) (1983).

45. David Becker, Elizabeth Lira, Maria Isabel Castillo, Elena Gomez and Jauna Kovalskeys, 'Therapy with Victims of Political Repression in Chile: The Challenge of Social Reparation', *Journal of Social Issues* 46(3) (1990): 142.

46. Becker, op. cit., 8.

47. See Inger Agger and Soren Buus Jensen, *Trauma and Healing under State Terrorism* (London: Zed Books, 1996), for an evaluative study of the Chilean experience and a discussion of its implications beyond Chile.

48. Becker, op. cit.; Cienfuegos and Monelli, op. cit.

49. M. Brinton Lykes, 'Gender and Individualistic vs. Collectivist Bases for Notions About the Self', *Journal of Personality* 53(2) (1985).

50. Richard A. Shweder and Edmund B. Bourne, 'Does the Concept of the Person Vary Cross-Culturally?', in *Culture Theory: Essays on Mind, Self and Emotion*, Richard A. Shweder and Robert A. LeVine, eds. (Cambridge: Cambridge University Press, 1984), 158–99.

51. See, for example, M. Brinton Lykes and Dongxiao Qin, 'Individualism and Collectivism', in *Encyclopedia of Women and Gender*, Judith Worrell, ed. (New York: Academic Press, 2001), 625–31.

52. David M. Chavis and J. Robert Newbrough, 'The Meaning of "Community" in Community Psychology', *Journal of Community Psychology. Special Issue: Psychological Sense of Community: II. Research and Applications* 14(4) (1986).

53. Seymour B. Sarason, *The Psychological Sense of Community; Prospects for a Community Psychology* (San Francisco, CA: Jossey-Bass, 1974), 157.

54. Margarita Melville and M. Brinton Lykes, 'Guatemalan Indian Children and the Socio-cultural Effects of Government-Sponsored Terrorism', *Social Science and Medicine* 34(5) (1992).

55. M. Brinton Lykes, 'Meaning Making in a Context of Genocide and Silencing', in *Myths About the Powerless: Contesting Social Inequalities*, Ali Banuazizi, M. Brinton Lykes, Ramsay Liem and Micheal Morris, eds. (Philadelphia, PA: Temple University Press, 1996), 159–78. See also Commission for Historical Clarification [*Comisión para el Esclarecimiento Histórico*] (CEH), *Report of the CEH: Guatemala: Memory of Silence [Memoria del Silencio]*, vol. IV (Guatemala: CEH, 1999). Available at http://hrdata.aaas.org/ceh

56. Arthur Kleinman, Veena Das, and Margaret Lock, *Social Suffering* (Berkeley, CA: University of California Press, 1997); Veena Das, Arthur Kleinman, Manphela Ramphele and Pamela Reynolds, eds., *Violence and Subjectivity* (Berkeley, CA: University of California Press, 2000); Das et al., *Remaking a World: Violence, Social Suffering, and Recovery*, op. cit.

57. Hunter Jenkins, op. cit.

58. Becker, op. cit.

59. Africa News Service (ANS), 'Local Therapy to Heal the Trauma of War' (Johannesburg: ANS, October 7, 2002). See also Michael G. Wessells and Carlinda Monteiro, 'Healing the Wounds Following Protracted Conflict in Angola: A Community-based Approach to Assisting War-affected Children', in *Handbook of Culture, Therapy, and Healing*, Uwe P. Gielen, Jefferson M. Fish, and Juris G. Draguns, eds. (Mahwah, NJ: Lawrence Erlbaum, 2004), 597–641.

60. Ibid.; Michael G. Wessells and Carlinda Monteiro, 'Healing Wounds of War in Angola', in *Addressing Childhood Adversity*, David Donald, Andrew Dawes, and Johann Louw, eds. (Claremont, South Africa: David Philip, 2000), 176–201.

61. Teresa Durán Pérez, Roberta Bacic Herzfeld, and Pau Pérez Sales, *Memorias Recientes De Mi Pueblo, 1973–1990: Muerte Y Desaparición Forzada En La Araucanía: Una Aproximación Étnica* (Temuco, Chile: Centro de Estudios Sociocuturales, Universidad Católica de Temuco, 1997).

62. Gillian T. Eagle, 'Promoting Peace by Integrating Western and Indigenous Healing in Treating Trauma', *Peace and Conflict: Journal of Peace Psychology* 4(3) (1998).

63. Ibid., 273.

64. Noel Muchenga Chicuecue, 'Reconciliation: The Role of Truth Commissions and Alternative Ways of Healing', *Development in Practice* 7(4) (1997).

65. See Robert J. Lifton, *The Nazi Doctors: Medical Killing and the Psychology of Genocide* (New York: Basic Books, 1986); Danieli, op. cit.

66. Tamara Hareven, 'The Search for Generational Memory', in *Public History Readings*, Phyllis K. Leffler and Joseph Brent, eds. (Malabar, FL: Krieger, 1992), 207–83. See Ramsay Liem, 'History, Trauma, and Identity: The Legacy of the Korean War for Korean Americans', *Amerasia Journal* 29(3) (2003/4): 111–39, for a discussion of these ideas and another example.

67. Danieli, op. cit.; Dan Bar-On, 'Attempting to Overcome the Intergenerational Transmission of Trauma: Dialogue between Descendants of Victims and of Perpetrators', in *Minefields in their Hearts: The Mental Health of Children in War and Communal Violence*, Roberta J. Apfel and Bennett Simon, eds. (New Haven, CT: Yale University Press, 1996), 165–88; Dan Bar-On and Noga Gilad, 'To Rebuild Life: A Narrative Analysis of Three Generations of an Israeli Holocaust Survivor's Family', in *Exploring Identity and Gender: The Narrative Study of Lives*, vol. 2, Amia Lieblich and Ruthellen Josselson, eds. (Thousand Oaks, CA: Sage, 1994), 83–112.

68. Ibid.; see also Cienfuegos and Monelli, op. cit.

69. Ibid.

70. Carlos Martín Beristain, Darío Paez, and José Luis González, 'Rituals, Social Sharing, Silence, Emotions and Collective Memory Claims in the Case of the Guatemalan Genocide', *Psicothema* 12(suppl.) (2000).

71. Espinoza Cuevas et al., op. cit.

72. Mónica Muñoz and Mariana Perez, 'Reconstrucción De La Identidad De Los Desaparecidos. Archivo Biográfico Familiar De Abuelas De Plaza De Mayo' (Paper presented at the Segundas Jornadas Interdisciplinarias: Memoria, Historia e Identidad, Centro de Derechos Humanos 'Emilio Mignone' Universidad Nacional de Quilmas, Noviembre 2001), 2.

73. See Pumla Gobodo-Madikizela, *A Human Being Died That Night: A South African Woman Confronts the Legacy of Apartheid* (Boston: Houghton Mifflin, 2003) for a moving discussion of her therapeutic experience of accompanying Eugene de Kock, one of the commanding officers of state-sanctioned apartheid death squads, who is currently serving 212 years in jail for crimes against humanity, in his TRC testimony and beyond.

74. Women of PhotoVoice and M. Brinton Lykes, *Voces e imágenes: Mujeres Mayas Ixiles de Chajul/Voices and Images: Mayan Ixil Women of Chajul* (Guatemala: MagnaTerra, 2000).

75. See, for example, Martina Fischer, 'Recovering from Violent Conflict: Regeneration and (Re-) Integration as Elements of Peacebuilding', in Fischer, Austin and Ropers, op. cit., for a review of the literature and typology for humanitarian assistance and development work after violent conflict. This framework is important for those planning psychosocial reparations programs, as is argued by David Becker in another chapter, op. cit.

76. A review of the wide and growing literature about individual psychosocial workers, including long overdue attention to how caregivers 'care for themselves' and the potential of 'secondary trauma' for those who work over long periods of time in war-torn societies, is beyond the scope of this chapter.

77. Michael Wessells and Carlinda Monteiro, 'Psychosocial Intervention and Post-War Reconstruction in Angola: Interweaving Western and Traditional Approaches', in *Peace, Conflict, and Violence: Peace Psychology for the 21st Century*, Daniel J. Christie, Richard Wagner, and Deborah Du Nann Winter, eds. (Upper Saddle River, NJ: Prentice–Hall, 2000), 262–75.

78. Agneta M. Johannsen, 'Participatory Action-Research in Post-Conflict Situations: The Example of the War-Torn Societies Project', in Fischer et al., op.cit.

79. Women of PhotoVoice and Lykes, op. cit.

80. For details about the nearly 36-year civil war and genocide in Guatemala, see CEH, *Memory of Silence* op. cit., Conclusions and Recommendations.

81. Women of PhotoVoice and Lykes, op. cit.

82. Shari Eppel, 'Healing the Dead to Transform the Living: Exhumation and Reburial in Zimbabwe', Paper presented at Conference on Regional and Human Rights Contexts and DNA (University of California, Berkeley, April 26–7, 2001).

83. Ibid., 9.

84. Lawrence L. Langer, *Holocaust Testimonies: The Ruins of Memory* (New Haven, CT: Yale University Press, 1991).

85. See, for example, Espinoza Cuevas, op. cit.; Brandon E. Hamber, 'Does the Truth Heal? A Psychological Perspective on the Political Strategies for Dealing with the Legacy of Political Violence', in *Burying the Past: Making Peace and Doing Justice after Civil Conflict*, Nigel Biggar, ed. (Washington, DC: Georgetown University Press, 2001), 131–48; and Brandon E. Hamber, 'Healing', in *Reconciliation after Violent Conflict: A Handbook*, David Bloomheld, Jeresa Banes and Tue Huyse, eds. (Stockholm, Sweden: International Institute for Democracy and Electoral Assistance, 2003), 77–88.

86. Women of PhotoVoice and Lykes, op. cit.

87. Espinoza Cuevas et al., op. cit.

88. See, for example, ibid.; Trudy de Ridder, 'The Trauma of Testifying: Deponents' Difficult Healing Process', *Track Two* 6(3/4) (1997), http://ccrweb.ccr.uct.ac.za/two/6_34/p30_deridder.html; accessed October 8, 2003; Cheryl de la Rey and Ingrid Owens, 'Perceptions of Psychosocial Healing and the Truth and Reconciliation Commission in South Africa', *Peace and Conflict: Journal of Peace Psychology* 4(3) (1998): 257–70.

89. Rojas Baeza, 'Mental Health Disturbances', op. cit.; Sveaass and Lavik, op. cit.

CHAPTER 18

REPARATION OF SEXUAL VIOLENCE IN DEMOCRATIC TRANSITIONS: THE SEARCH FOR GENDER JUSTICE

COLLEEN DUGGAN AND ADILA ABUSHARAF

INTRODUCTION

Although notable advancements have been made in the articulation of an international legal framework responsive to the particular forms of violence that women suffer during periods of political turmoil and armed conflict, feminists continue to point out that during periods of political transition from previously abusive regimes to democracy, justice continues to fail the victims of gender-based violence. Indeed, a cursory glance at the literature on transitional justice reflects a striking absence of gender-differentiated analysis. The reasons for this failure, while frustrating, are not surprising: while policymakers are coming to understand that men and women experience political violence differently, the vast array of public policies being designed to redress the consequences of violence and facilitate democratic transition continue to be largely gender-blind. Such is the case of national reparations programs that have not yet specifically addressed the suffering of women and girls who have been victims of sexual violence.[1]

This chapter explores the challenge of repairing sexual violence perpetrated against women as one of the most egregious forms of gender-based violence, and the extent to which national reparations programs might provide short-term redress while contributing to the achievement of longer-term goals for gender justice.[2] While the authors recognize and are sensitive to the fact that both males and females are victims of sexual violence during times of political repression and social break-down, we have chosen to focus upon how this phenomenon impacts upon women[3] for several reasons. First, sexual violence has always affected women disproportionately, and in terms not just of frequency, but of effects; the socioeconomic impact of sexual violence upon female victims is part of a continuum of violence which is often so acute that it can undermine chances for recovery and for reintegration into the family, the community and the State. Second, at the local and national level, domestic laws for the criminal or civil prosecution and redress of sexual violence are often weak, discriminatory or nonexistent, which greatly reduces the possibilities of securing justice through the courts. This absence of judicial recourse is felt more keenly during moments of political transition when national justice systems are often so debilitated or compromised that they are ill-equipped to deal with the complexity of sexual violence which has often been widespread and systematic. Third, in many countries, the absence of effective domestic remedies for sexual violence in times of peace, during periods of political breakdown and in moments of democratic transition reinforces discriminatory public attitudes and gender in-equality. Finally, the gravity of sexual violence, whether perpetrated in the private or public domain, is at best weakly recognized and at worst blamed on the victim. As a result, survivors not only live with the severe physical or mental health conse-quences of the abuses suffered in the aftermath of political violence, but also fear ongoing nonconflict-related sexual violence, largely perpetrated with impunity.

Advancements in international law reflect the evolution of the treatment of sexual violence in international humanitarian and human rights law as well as international criminal law from a crime 'against family honor and rights' or as 'outrages against personal dignity' (Fourth Geneva Convention) to the recognition of rape and other forms of sexual violence as a crime against humanity (Statutes of the International Criminal Court, International Criminal Tribunal for the former Yugoslavia and International Criminal Tribunal for Rwanda).[4] Sexual violence is defined as '[a]ny violence, physical or psychological, carried out through sexual means or by targeting sexuality'.[5] For the purposes of this chapter, our discussion of sexual violence committed as part of a larger campaign of political violence is understood to include practices such as sexual slavery, forced pregnancy or abortion, and rape. In general terms, transitional governments design reparations programs that will deal with a wide range of human rights violations (e.g. torture and forced disappearance) committed by previous regimes. They often do this while concurrently addressing other social policy demands for economic and fiscal reform, poverty alleviation and citizen security.[6] It is therefore unimaginable and impractical to suggest that governments should design reparations for women victims of sexual violence alone. However, in light of the above observations, and as our analysis will make clear, sexual violence perpetrated by either State or non-State actors undermines not only the physical security of women—and therefore, their fundamental civil rights—but also violates a series of their substantive economic, social, and cultural human rights.[7] Hence, the authors consider that sexual violence perpetrated against women by both State and non-State actors should figure as a special category under State-sponsored programs for reparation in the aftermath of repressive political regimes or war.

The objective of this chapter, then, is to highlight the gendered impact of sexual violence so that victims, victim support groups, and policymakers will be better positioned to design and implement gender-sensitive reparation programs. Our discussion will be divided into three sections. Section 1 will outline key aspects for understanding the nature of sexual violence as part of a larger strategy of political violence and the rationale for ensuring that reparations programs specifically address the gendered harm caused to victims. Section 2 will focus upon some of the conceptual and normative barriers that affect the access that women victims have to reparations programs as well as those relating to the structure of the national regulatory framework within which reparations programs operate. The analysis offered in this section will be framed in terms of gender-discriminatory attitudes and structures—often referred to as 'bias' (defined as the leakage of patriarchal norms into purportedly impartial laws and social policy) and 'capture' (defined as the outright denial of rights and entitlements to women).[8] Bias and capture operate at the substantive, structural, and cultural levels and have a profound influence upon the environment in which reparations programs are carried out.[9] Section 3 will tease out some of the difficulties that bedevil the design and implementation of reparations programs. Reparations programs cannot be considered in a contextual vacuum but, rather, must be analyzed within a coherent framework for transitional justice. Such a framework can be said to generally include prosecutions, truth-telling processes, reparations and institutional reform policies as essential and complementary building blocks.[10] Our intent is to offer some guidance for current and future reparations programs, with a view to enhancing the role they should play as part of a transitional justice strategy and with a view to rebuilding the relationship between the State and female victims and these victims and their societies.[11]

1. SEXUAL VIOLENCE AS AN INDICATION OF GENDER BIAS AND THE RATIONALE FOR ITS REPARATION

Understanding the gendered impact of sexual violence is important: if we fail to grasp the complex web of motivations which underlie the commission of sexual crimes during periods of political violence, we cannot begin to design social policies which address the past, yet are forward-looking and preventive. A closer examination of how gender bias and capture undermine women's ability to access reparation indicates that the question of *how* to repair the harm done cannot be delinked from the question of *why* the harm was done and to *whom*.

Why Women Are Targeted for Sexual Violence

Many feminists correctly describe the logic of sexual violence during war or moments of civil upheaval as not a 'matter of chance'.[12] It is rather a question of power and control which is structured by male power-holders' traditional notions of their masculine privilege.[13] This 'entitlement approach' is often re-inforced by class and ethnic inequalities and entertained across military lines of command, either State or non-State.[14] For this reason, until recently, sexual violence perpetrated against women during moments of repression was largely seen as collateral damage or as a secondary effect of political authoritarianism and not as a human rights violation. Various forms of sexual violence, particularly rape, are now recognized as strategic weapons of political violence that serve both military and political ends. The pain and humiliation inflicted by the perpetrators dominates and degrades not only the individual victim, but also destroys cultural values and wider community relationships.[15] This linkage is particularly evident in the context of ethnic or identity-based conflicts such as those that have taken place in the former Yugoslavia and Rwanda; here, sexual violence was not 'exclusively an attack on the body—but an attack on the body-politic'—or against a social system.[16] As such, *realpolitik* apologies which stress the 'natural occurrence' of sexual violence including rape during moments of violent political repression or war mask the explicit targeting of women to intimidate, humiliate and even facilitate the elimination of specific political communities or certain ethnic groups.[17] Simply put, women become an indirect tool of political violence, a means to achieve a political end.

What Happens to Women Victims During Political Transition?

Research on violence against women has uncovered a most disturbing trend: while sexual violence is intensified during periods of political violence and social break-down, it continues unabated, most often in the home, during the aftermath.[18] According to UNIFEM's report on women, war and peace, women's suffering cannot be attributed solely to the conditions of political violence or regime change; it exists in their lives, even in times of peace.[19] Political violence tends to affect women disproportionately '*because* they are women, and often because they do not have the same rights, autonomy or social privileges that men do'.[20] Sexual violence reflects a deep-seated structural violence that, if not deterred, can persist during the transitional period and cut into women's socioeconomic role. Since violence has come to be understood as a legitimate means for waging and eventually ending conflict, men use violence against women in the aftermath of conflict in order to reestablish or retain control over family resources, and above all, over women's productive and reproductive rights.[21] At any rate, the reality is that women are often revictimized by returning husbands, sons, and uncles. These findings have been reflected in studies on domestic violence, which indicate an alarming increase in incidents of sexual violence in the home during moments of transition and reconstruction.[22]

Due to the absence of appropriate national legal measures that protect women's right to physical security, violence against women during periods of severe political breakdown continues unabated even after the turmoil is over. As mentioned earlier, if in some States national laws governing violent practices such as rape are insufficient even in relative peace, they will be even more incapable of addressing the complex aspects of the type of large-scale sexual violence that takes place during periods of political violence and transition. The weaknesses of national criminal laws in countries such as Rwanda and Sierra Leone have been well documented.[23] As will be discussed below, a large part of the problem hinges upon the fact that citizenship formation, even in countries undergoing democratic transition, is a highly gendered enterprise; that is, women are not treated as equal citizens. Their role is recognized in the confines of the private sphere (the family and the home, traditionally occupied by women) and they have no legal autonomy in the public sphere (public affairs and government, traditionally occupied by men). Gendered legislative and institutional frameworks create legal constructs that reinforce women's power-lessness and therefore need to be reformed. However, the transformation of norms and institutions can be a painfully long process. Reparations schemes— while not a panacea for reversing all forms of gender bias and capture—offer interesting possibilities to lay the social and political groundwork needed for this process to advance, and in the interim could offset some of the gendered harm caused by sexual violence.[24]

Long-Term Impact, Increased Socioeconomic Vulnerability

As a result of the latent gender bias that exists in many societies, men often have more opportunities to participate more widely in public life, have greater mobility and access to economic resources and education than women.[25] Ironically, for some women, peace does not necessarily mean an end to vulnerability. In the aftermath of political violence, women often find themselves faced with increasing responsibilities while living in extremely precarious conditions. The high mortality and/or disappearance rate of men during political conflict and the massive population displacements and migrations that often accompany such turmoil can have profound effects upon families. One of the most significant of these is the formation of female-headed households in which women suddenly find themselves responsible for senior family members, distant relatives, or numerous orphans. Research has proven that political violence shifts the economic burden of caring for and supporting the family further onto women and that their plight is exacerbated by a lack of financial resources and more people to feed.[26]

It has also been noted that in the aftermath of violence, women often lose what few material assets they have when widows return to villages to find that they have lost established property rights or that their land has been given by a local chief to a demobilized combatant.[27] In addition to general health and mental health problems, the precarious nature of women's living conditions, especially victims of sexual violence and those who are heads of family, can lead them into prostitution and other dangerous practices which put their health and lives at great risk.

The absence of men in transitional contexts gives rise to a particularly problematic situation: official statistics often count households that are headed *de jure* by women (widows or divorcees), ignoring those that are run *de facto* by women because their husbands have gone to fight, have been disappeared or have migrated.[28] This 'invisibility' is particularly problematic during transitional moments of regime change when new policies for rehabilitation and reconstruction are being defined. Outdated census information or new census information collected in a gender-blind fashion can serve to cut women out of important economic and social packages for development. For this reason, the collection of sex-disaggregated data is of particular importance for the design of reparations programs within which both men and women should be fairly represented.

The Other Side of the Equation: Increased Opportunities?

A number of feminist scholars also voice the opinion that while women's experiences have largely been documented and portrayed in terms of victimization, political violence itself and the transitional period can often open up 'intended or unintended spaces for empowering women, effecting structural social transform-ations and producing new social, economic and political realities that redefine gender and caste hierarchies'.[29] In most political conflicts, the traditional division between private and public space collapses. With the absence of men from trad-itional public spaces, women fill this vacuum and increasingly occupy a diversity of spaces and roles (from markets to government), often providing for the welfare and security of their families.[30] Consequently, periods of regime change and transition to democracy should offer historic opportunities for the redefinition of gender roles. And yet, the literature on postconflict and transitional societies indicates that often these opportunities are lost. At a time when women can move from being victims to being agents for positive social change, gender-discriminatory attitudes are often further entrenched when men return to their communities and their families, and traditional roles and duties are reestablished.

Discussion of a potential 'gender dividend' has been present in much of the literature dealing with gender mainstreaming into postconflict peace-building and reconstruction experiences.[31] Since much less has been said about how gender gains could be woven into transitional justice processes, this should perhaps give us pause to consider how reparations programs for victims of sexual violence might lay some of the groundwork required to transform authoritarian structures of governance into functional democratic institutions based upon principles of equity, equality, and nondiscrimination—for both men and women. For this reason, in our view, reparations programs as one facet of a transitional justice strategy should be based upon a nuanced understanding of the implications of gender bias and capture, and built on a solid foundation of gender justice.

2. Access to Reparation for Sexual Violence: Implications of Gender Bias and Capture

Women's Political Citizenship and Entitlements

Historically, citizenship formation in the liberal democratic sense has often resulted in the political exclusion of women in many countries. Feminists have also highlighted the general political exclusion of women by authoritarian regimes as part of their 'essentialist' approach in setting parameters for public/private space.[32] As a result, women are not treated as equal members of a 'political' community but rather as dependent family members, who should 'preserve' the values of this community. This is especially the case in ethnically based repressive regimes where women who belong to minority or marginalized groups are subjected to further discrimination.

The starting premise of van Boven and Bassiouni's principles on the right to reparation is that the State is responsible for ensuring that victims of gross human rights violations enjoy an individual right to reparation.[33] It follows that individuals are the holders of a series of personal entitlements and that one of the most important aims of reparations is to 'return (or in some cases, establish anew) the status of citizens to individuals'.[34] When viewed through a gendered lens, the idea of individualizing reparations as a means of granting political recognition to individuals as citizens, particularly in constitutional democracies, takes on multiple dimensions. The main problem facing women victims of sexual violence relates to the inadequacy (or absence) of legal mechanisms for the protection of their citizenship rights and the entitlements that go with them. This lacuna can in part be traced to the dominant role that patriarchy plays in defining and regulating social and power relations. During times of social breakdown the problem of protection of citizenship rights such as the right to physical security and the right to access justice is exacerbated by the absence of a system of accountability and impunity for those enjoying more social privileges, in this case male perpetrators of sexual violence.

Policymakers, when designing reparations programs, will need to pay particular attention to the socio-legal status of victims of sexual violence as it is these restrictive parameters which often throw up barriers to victims as they attempt to access justice in general, and reparations in particular. If one of the objectives of reparation is to restore civic trust—as de Greiff argues in this volume—transitional governments will also need to put the woman-citizen/State relationship on a more just and equitable footing. The following sections detail some of the principal obstacles pertaining to women's ability to exercise their right to reparation, including lack of legal autonomy, legal pluralism and cultural mores.

Legal Autonomy and Victims of Sexual Violence

Citizenship also consists of the legal processes by which subjects of a State are defined.[35] Citizenship constructs the subject of the law and also 'generates social processes by which subjects are made, invented and constructed'.[36] Much of the recent literature on citizenship reminds us that while in most countries of the world laws and constitutions are drafted in terms of an abstract, homogeneous citizen, citizenship is in fact a highly gendered enterprise,[37] both *de jure* and *de facto*. Emerging transitional societies such as the former Yugoslavia, Rwanda, Sierra

Leone, and Guatemala are characterized by myriad religious, linguistic, ethnic, and class differences. While competing identities and loyalties differ according to context, in many parts of the world there exists an unmistakable symbolic connection between the idea of woman and the idea of nation. This, in turn, has given rise to a system of beliefs rooted in ideals of 'authentic' national cultures, 'indigenous' religions and 'traditional' family norms.[38] The combination of these factors essentially influences social policies within which women's roles are largely confined within the private sphere of the family. As an outcome of these policies, the identity of women is subsumed in the family and women's role is far from being recognized as autonomous.

The complete absence of women's voice in the public domain acts as a distinct form of 'capture' of the right to reparation. This perception of women's role also often serves in justifying States' reluctance to issue legislation on gender-based violence or to modify existing national criminal laws to cope with everyday sexual violence, let alone with the level and intensity with which it occurs during moments of political upheaval. This reluctance is often born of an official perception of sexual violence against women as a stain upon the social fabric of the nation, rather than being interpreted as a violation of women's rights as individuals. Thus, official positions on sexual violence often function to close avenues for protection from sexual violence, including that resulting from political violence.

Reparation in the wide sense[39] is closely associated with construing and implementing reparations as a matter of individual legal rights.[40] The sort of individual recognition by the State—first of the harmful act and later of the individual herself—that a well-crafted reparations program manifests is an important facet of belonging to a political community.[41] However, feminist scholars are correct in insisting that the unequal treatment of women within nation-states must be addressed by strengthening the role of women as individual citizens within the larger collectivity, so the various transitional justice measures, including reparations, will need to take into account that in many contexts, in both law and practice, women's legal autonomy, and by extension the system of individual entitlements available to them, continue to face serious obstacles.

Similarly, there can be no doubt that in the aftermath of mass violence, the use of reparations to facilitate the construction of civic trust is a highly desirable goal.[42] The achievement of such a goal for both men and women will be a long-term process if we agree that western liberal understanding of citizenship is underpinned by a series of civic ideals that often conceal varying forms of substantive and structural gender bias and capture. In light of these concerns, it is essential that policymakers take steps to guard against gender-blind presumptions concerning citizenship and, by extension, women victims' ability to claim reparation. The exercise of this right risks being undermined by the social, cultural, and gender-based inequalities clearly manifested in the pluralistic legal systems which characterize many countries.

Legal Pluralism and the Right to Reparation: Which Law Trumps?

It has been pointed out that many women in parts of Africa, Asia and the Middle East live under more than one 'State'. Their daily behavior is regulated by more than one set of laws, and it is this reality which complicates our discussion of women's ability to access reparations in countries which, at least at the constitutional level, purport to be liberal democracies. Turshen reminds us that

> in Africa at least two legal regimes govern women's lives simultaneously: the statutory regime of the nation-state and the customary regime of their natal household or clan. When women marry into a society ruled by a different set of customary laws, they are subject to yet a third regime. Sometimes it is clear which law takes precedence, but that clarity might not be honored in practice or even in court, especially in the areas of personal law.[43]

It is the second and particularly the third regimes mentioned above, the customary and natal, that women have the most difficulty changing and which are most likely to affect the possibility of a survivor of sexual violence accessing reparations. In practice, customary law often takes precedence over national law when it comes to matters concerning how women might approach and make use of the formal mechanisms of justice. When coupled with other cultural specificities, it is not unusual for women to find themselves doubly penalized, losing both in customary law and in national law.[44]

   The coexistence of multiple statutory and customary legal regimes can severely curtail women's access to domestic remedies. To date, little (if any) research has been conducted on how legal pluralism operates as both a cultural and a structural bias that affects women's ability to exercise their right to reparation. What is clear, however, is that in many transitional societies, gender-biased social practices and the domestic legislation that governs women's socioeconomic and socio-legal entitlements are major stumbling blocks to accessing justice. This is obvious in cases where, for example, a wife must obtain her husband's consent to approach the legal system. A concrete example of this type of paternalistic approach is the strict interpretation of the principle of *Alwilaia* or 'guardianship', as applied in a number of Islamic communities. In such cases *Alwilaia* has been often interpreted to override the individual rights and choices of women and consequently the exercise and enjoyment of those rights. An

> *Alwali* can be the father, grandfather, husband, brother, or uncle with a mandate to exercise wide discretionary powers over the life of the women in their environment be they a daughter, granddaughter, wife, sister, or niece. The *Awali* exercises considerable influence over a woman's social and economic well-being, deciding whether or not she will be educated and whether she will be able to earn an independent living or will remain economically dependent on him. He can also decide whether to grant her protection in the family or to ostracize her from the family.[45]

This situation has become extreme in countries such as Somalia and Sudan where traditional leaders have introduced conservative interpretations of *Sharia* in local-level Islamic courts.[46] In contexts such as these, it is difficult to envision if and how a survivor of sexual violence might go about accessing a reparations program—indeed if she even has knowledge of such a program and of her claim to such measures vis-à-vis the State.

Social Attitudes and Cultural Mores: Taboos and Silence

Sexual violence—whether perpetrated in the private or public sphere—is a phenomenon not easily discussed by its victims. Indeed, it is the shroud of silence which envelopes sexual violence that has further complicated efforts to seek and provide appropriate remedies at both the national and international levels. Understanding why survivors of sexual violence often choose to 'leave the past in the past' is critical for the design of gender-sensitive measures for redress. Women who have survived sexual violence do not talk about it for a variety of reasons: some victims are afraid that they will never be able to marry, particularly in cultures where virginity is highly valued. Others fear that they will be shunned by their family, community or society as a whole, as has been reported by some survivors in Sierra Leone and Burundi.[47] Those who have been left behind and have been victimized, or have witnessed the victimization of others, sometimes fear reprisal from community members or former combatants who have been demobilized and have returned to communities once peace has been brokered.

In many contexts, women are viewed as pillars of their communities or vestibules and guardians of values of the linguistic, ethnic or cultural group to which they belong. Since the family and by extension the community are key actors in the political construction of the 'nation', women—and particularly their productive and reproductive capacity—are often viewed through a patriarchal lens as symbols and guarantors of nations and nationalist causes.[48] This delineation of 'woman' brings with it the imposition of specific forms of behavioral control and restricted understandings of women's value and virtues. Women's virtue is often tied to their sexuality. A number of respected feminist scholars have pointed out that many African and Asian societies distribute resources to women on the basis of women's purported virtue; 'virtuous women' are generally unmarried virgins, faithful wives and celibate widows. 'Non-virtuous women' are promiscuous women and women who have been raped.[49] In many societies, once lost, a woman's virtue can never be recovered. Sexual violence thus devastates women because it excludes them from both the private and the public life. Similarly, the loss of virtue besmirches not only the individual but also the honor of the men of her family and her clan or community. This places upon the victim of sexual violence an onerous responsibility to uphold the honor of the extended community and the nation.

The cultural stigma attached to rape and other acts of sexual torture have been well documented by national and international human rights organizations active in the majority of conflicts of the last decade, especially those in Africa, Asia, and the Balkans.[50] Feelings of guilt and overwhelming shame have been mentioned by survivors of sexual violence in high intensity wars such as those that took place in Bosnia Herzegovina and Kosovo and in low intensity conflicts such as those of Guatemala and Peru. The links between sexual violence and a perceived betrayal of the honor of husbands, fathers, or male family members is a common thread that runs through all of these situations in which the victims have admitted to contemplating or attempting suicide on more than one occasion. In societies such as Sudan, the relationship between honor and shame may have far-reaching social consequences for the eventual negotiation of reparations programs. Here it will be difficult to convince the government to acknowledge sexual violence since an admission of State responsibility will be tantamount to admitting to the dishonoring of an entire society.

While it is true that the social fabric of societies affected by mass violence is unmistakably altered in the transitional time, traditional views of women and the lower status they often occupy do not change as quickly.[51] Many of the mundane obstacles that feminize poverty can be exacerbated when victims of sexual violence find themselves ostracized from their family and/or community. In such circumstances women's access to productive activities (communal farms, local markets, etc.) can be denied. Acknowledgment of sexual violence can leave victims with limited social and economic options in the aftermath. For example, in Colombia, indigenous women of the Embera group have reported that women who have been raped by any one of that country's armed actors have been turned out of their community and been forced to live in the jungle.[52] The socioeconomic obstacles that constrain women's access to development resources and generally exacerbate women's economic vulnerability are equally applicable to the access that they might have to reparations programs. These include their inability to leave their children and/or place of employment, the limitations that family or social norms place upon travel to urban areas, lack of control over incoming resources, inability to open a bank account in the absence of legal standing or without endorsement by a male relative, etc.

Our discussion of how gender bias and capture influence women's ability to exercise their right to reparation suggests that State programs for reparation need to be contextually grounded and based upon a full understanding of how gender identities interact with race, class, age, religion, and other social divisions.[53] If one of the goals of a reparations program is to return or establish anew the status of citizens, then such programs will necessarily need to reexamine the terms of women's social and economic entitlements within society. This will necessarily require victim support groups and policymakers to consider the structural nature of violence against women and to ask themselves some difficult questions concerning women's legal status, social norms, and gender and power arrangements within their respective societies prior to determining who should have access to reparations programs and how these programs might be designed.

In the view of the authors, the particularities of sexual violence call for policymakers to adopt at least two fundamental complementary or supplementary goals.[54] These include first breaking the silence, by articulating processes of reparation that will contribute to the establishment of a societal conviction that victims of sexual violence must not be silenced and that accountability for these crimes must not be obscured.[55] Second, ensuring that measures for reparation take advantage of opportunities to redefine the social norms that have fostered sexual violence and underscore the importance of structural change, thus forging a critical link between the enforcement of the right to reparation and the elaboration of responsive public policies for prevention in the future.

3. Practical Dilemmas for Gendering the Design and Implementation of Reparations Programs

Acknowledging Sexual Violence in the Mandate and Jurisdiction of Reparations Programs

As mentioned earlier, advances in international law have ensured that sexual violence is now perceived not only as a gender-based crime but also as a crime against humanity. Widespread reports of sexual violence in the conflicts in the former Yugoslavia and Rwanda and subsequent efforts to prosecute perpetrators in international and national tribunals have been instrumental in putting sexual violence on the agenda of advocates of transitional justice. Practical experience demonstrates that the path to gender justice can be indirect and have many curves. For example, it was thanks to the efforts of the UN and human rights advocates that the truth commission (TRC) in Sierra Leone was established, mostly due to pressures to reverse the pardon of international crimes such as genocide underlying the Lomé Agreement. These efforts primarily relied upon the State's *erga omnes* obligation to investigate and prosecute crimes against humanity. This obligation provided an argument for victims' groups to lobby the transitional government to ensure that sexual violence appeared alongside other crimes against humanity in any future reparations program. Concretely, Sierra Leone's TRC has a mandate to 'create an impartial historical record of violations and abuses of human rights and international humanitarian law related to the armed conflict in Sierra Leone, from the beginning of the armed conflict in 1991 to the signing of the Lomé peace agreement; to address impunity; to respond to the needs of the victims; to promote healing and reconciliation; and to prevent a repetition of the violations and abuses suffered'.[56] However, it was only after national and international women's groups exerted significant pressure that the TRC was called upon to give special attention to the subject of sexual abuse and also to implement 'special procedures to address the needs of... those who have suffered sexual abuse'.[57] In this way, human rights activists and victim support groups have been able to use positive developments in the international arena to counteract incidents of substantive bias in the conceptualization of transitional justice processes at the national level.

This progression towards a more gender-sensitive approach to justice can be clearly tracked by comparing the processes of truth-telling and reparation in El Salvador (1993), Guatemala (1999), and Peru (2003). In the case of El Salvador, incidents of sexual violence were not mentioned as principal acts to be documented by the truth commission and do not figure significantly in that report.[58] Neither was reparation of sexual violence contemplated in any resulting program of reparation.[59] Guatemala's truth commission report dedicates significant space to reporting on incidents of sexual violence (particularly their impact upon victims and family members). However, this discussion is part of a larger analysis that focuses upon the impact of torture.[60] Reparation for sexual violence figures significantly in the State-proposed reparation program[61] (as yet underresourced and largely unimplemented). In Peru, documentation of incidents of sexual violence perpetrated against women were contemplated almost from the beginning. Although they are not specifically cited in the terms of reference of the Commission, they figure prominently in the report itself (some 120 pages are dedicated to documenting cases of sexual violence) and appear as a category in the proposed program for reparation.[62] This comparison suggests that reparations for sexual violence may be moving away from being an afterthought by policymakers, often tacked onto State programs in the wake of political pressure and lobbying especially from external groups, to becoming a more fundamental issue which appears more centrally on the agenda of transitional governments.

Another important issue relating to official acknowledgment of sexual violence relates to the decision of the government of Sierra Leone to postpone the work of the TRC allegedly out of fear that the issue would heighten tensions around elections. By recalling our discussion of Sudan (how recognition of structural violence could risk questioning the legitimacy of the State), it is essential to take into consideration the political climate in which reparations programs are to be launched. In order to minimize risks that sexual violence might fall off of the political agenda, it is critical that such abuses appear as part of an integral strategy for reparations. This is simply because a transitional government is not a single-minded actor with a unified set of interests. States are composed of different conflicting views and changing sets of social interests, and political leaders are embedded in local communities.[63]

The official reluctance to support public acknowledgment of sexual violence, a taboo subject in so many societies, might result in excluding a female victim from the very collective from which, as an individual, she draws her sense of identity and value. In light of these considerations, it is important at this point to recognize the urgent need to put in place adequate institutional policies for the immediate redress of sexual violence and strict measures to prevent its occurrence in the future, while being cognizant of the difficulties and dilemmas that victims may face in trading silence for recognition and material benefits.

Learning relevant lessons from previous experiences of reparation of sexual violence is also essential for longer-term goals of enhancing gender justice for female victims of sexual violence. For example, it has been noted that the Asian Women's Fund for Japanese financial compensation for the 'comfort women' was criticized for being 'a welfare-oriented system based on gender and development needs rather than an acceptance of responsibility and an obligation to provide reparation'.[64] In contrast, Chile's reparations for the victims of the Pinochet regime took the form of a continuing pension and it has been noted that this formula enabled the new government to address a number of longer-term needs including ongoing mental health care.[65] In the view of the authors, acknowledgment and apology in cases of sexual violence is of limited use if it ignores the structural dimension and is restricted to acknowledging the harmful act alone. Gendered violence is part of a socio-political economy based on the desire to control women's sexuality, especially their productive and reproductive capacity. Consequently, collective understanding of, and responsibility for, this type of violence as a socially constructed phenomenon is key to changing the status quo in many societies. The public debate which often accompanies the creation of reparations programs provides a historic opportunity not only to discuss why sexual violence figures so prominently as a tool for political repression but also to lay the groundwork for the social transformation of gender-discriminatory attitudes.

Legislative and Institutional Constraints: Sensitizing Information Collection and Verification of Facts

There also exists a series of legislative and institutional constraints that should be borne in mind by those interested in designing and implementing programs of reparation. One of the most glaring examples of gender bias operating upon State capacities to deliver justice for sexual violence can be found in the absence of strong national legislation that hands down stiff penalties for acts such as rape and the legal barriers embedded in time limits for bringing charges against perpetrators of sexual abuse (statutes of limitation). Such obstacles are insensitive to victims' need to overcome the traumatic experience of sexual violence.[66] Truth commissions and subsequent State-sponsored schemes for reparation could go a long way to re-dressing, in some way, women victims who have been disqualified from seeking justice through the courts for reasons of substantive bias or statutes of limitation.

It is also no secret that, throughout history, women have been underrepresented in judicial and administrative processes. Only one woman has served as a judge on the International Court of Justice since its establishment more than eighty years ago. Despite its fifty-five-year history, no woman participated in the International Law Commission until 2001, when two women were elected.[67] Underrepresentation of women in the legal profession, both nationally and internationally, sends a clear message that women's input is not recognized as important or valid. Hence, women often become intimidated, disillusioned, or distrustful of the justice system especially when their claims revolve around the remediation of sexual violence. Such attitudes are understandable. According to Ann Marie Goetz, acts of sexual violence carried out with impunity and without fear of persecution are a clear case of 'capture'.[68] For instance, incidents of rape in police custody are an example of the capture of state resources.[69] This is typically true in cases where sexual violence is carried out on a large scale by either State or non-State actors as part of a wider campaign of political violence. For example, the recently released Truth and Reconciliation Report in Peru (CVR) documents cases in which women who had been raped by leftist insurgents reported their experiences to the police, only to be raped by those same members of the State security force. Obviously, these crimes were never investigated despite the fact that, at the time, the Peruvian State would have had a clear political interest in prosecuting those acts committed by the insurgency. For this reason, it is not surprising that incidents of rape and other forms of sexual violence were consistently underreported during the years under study by the CVR.

At the practical level, this has very immediate and real consequences. The collection of testimonies and evidence, the building blocks of truth-telling and hence of access to reparations, is undermined. Fact-finding in the aftermath of mass violence is a traumatic experience and often doubly so for victims of sexual violence. Women victims in the context of the International Criminal Tribunal for Rwanda have reported being mocked and humiliated by officials.[70] Evidently, the presence of lawyers and other professionals trained in dealing with sexual trauma will be key to ensuring that victims' stories are told.

Similar problems can arise in the area of information collection for victim registration. Community spokespersons and representatives of victim support groups need to understand the significance of hearing first hand accounts—often in private—from women victims. While mechanisms for collective psycho-social recovery might suggest the creation of a nonthreatening and supportive atmosphere, this has not always been the case. In Guatemala, Mayan women victims often would not talk about what had happened to them in front of other female members of their community. The reasons behind this silence are complex and numerous. In some cases, victimizers had convinced victims that they were responsible for the death of a spouse or male family member. This sense of guilt left victims with the distinct impression that their own suffering was insignificant when compared with the death of a loved one.[71] Similarly, given the ethnic dimension of Guatemala's political violence and the breadth of provisions for indigenous rights included in the Guatemalan peace accords, some victims who had suffered at the hands of a Mayan community member felt that denouncing the perpetrator would be tantamount to betraying the larger political struggle of the Mayan people.

Yasmin Sooka of South Africa's Truth and Reconciliation Commission recognizes that the debate on reparation in that country, like the world debates, was not sensitive to gender differences. Specifically she notes that the TRC was weak in 'extracting the truth about women and giving them compensation'. She notes that although 55 percent of the statements made to the commission were delivered by women, invariably they talked about the experiences of their menfolk, their children, and their loved ones.[72] While the TRC did eventually open special hearings for women, evidence seems to suggest that many women did not look to the TRC as an appropriate mechanism for airing their personal violations.[73] At any rate, experiences in documenting the impact of political violence on women indicate that information collection needs to be understood as a contextually driven process. In some cases, the use of women interviewers might be sufficient. In other cases, particularly those in which victims are either too traumatized or hesitant to discuss their experiences, the use of third person narratives, story boards or other tools for the recuperation of historic memory might be more appropriate and yield better results.

Gendered Assets and Quantifying Harm

Reparative policies in the wake of massive human rights violations such as sexual violence should ideally be designed to provide full restitution to victims. Yet it has become increasingly obvious to legal experts, policymakers and victims that *restitutio in integrum* is often impossible in the aftermath of political violence.[74] This is especially the case for victims of sexual violence since the intangible assets that are often taken—purity, social standing—can never be returned. Some scholars maintain that monetary measures cannot remedy nonmonetary harms, like the loss of virginity. '[N]o market measures exist', writes Minow, 'for the value of living an ordinary life, without nightmares or survivor guilt.'[75] Putting a monetary value on tangible, not to mention intangible, assets is a complicated business. For example, in wars characterized by high levels of forced displacement, female victims suffer both moral and material damages. In such circumstances, as victims weigh up the costs of denouncing their suffering, they are forced to balance considerations of material loss (loss of property) and loss of gendered political assets (reputation).[76] In countries such as Colombia and Sudan, women have been compensated for neither and are thus forced into silence without necessarily having minimal guarantees of social and economic survival. This dilemma has become known as 'asset-stripping'.[77] In the most extreme circumstances of least-developed countries, a weak economy coupled with the social and communal fallout of sexual violence are so acute that they extinguish other traditional avenues of social and economic survival available to women victims.[78]

The above discussion begs the question whether individual compensation for sexual violence presents itself as the most appropriate form of redress.[79] Countries which have used individual payments as part of reparations have, as a general rule, some understanding of tort law. In such cases, the awarding of money for suffering is seen to represent something symbolic. However, as has been evident in cases where survivors have alleged that individual payments constitute 'blood money', female survivors of sexual violence might not necessarily view monetary damages through the same symbolic lens. Indeed, in some cultures, accepting money for sexual abuse might be extremely inappropriate and problematic.[80] Even if such payments are culturally appropriate, how should payments be calculated? It should be clear that if reparations benefits were calculated on the basis of lost income, in countries such as Peru, where a large percentage of the victims of sexual abuse were poor Quechua-speaking women engaged in informal economic activities particularly in rural areas, this approach would underserve the interests of women.[81]

Heavy payment burdens are a serious concern for transitional regimes that are often faced with the dilemma of simultaneously having to repair individual harm and harm to entire communities. In practice these two responsibilities often become superimposed and new governments must grapple with balancing their scarce resources to compensate individual victims and to rebuild a society victimized by poverty, unemployment and an appalling lack of basic social services such as health care and education. However, many victim support groups point out that in the aftermath of conflict or repressive regimes, States have the obligation to provide adequate policies for social and economic development in addition to reparations.

The cases of South Africa and Guatemala clearly highlight the obstacles that those countries are encountering in trying to distinguish between reparations for the individual and the collectivity while addressing wider social policy pressures for economic and fiscal reform, poverty alleviation, and citizen security. Ironically, while some scholars have argued that the collective approach to reparations adopted in Guatemala is more in keeping with the indigenous peoples' vision of justice, it is clear that Guatemala is still a long way from repairing violations perpetrated for reasons of racial and gender discrimination. The tensions between individual and collective measures are not likely to be easily dispelled in the near future. Compensation is in most cases likely to be grossly disproportionate to the damage caused, and, as alleged by some, to risk trivializing suffering.[82] Indeed, some scholars perceive the compensatory objective of compensation to be largely nominal or symbolic.[83] Symbolism, however, can be of practical importance to victims of sexual violence whose social and economic needs and gender-differentiated suffering have long been ignored or undermined by society in general.

Views on the need to limit or fix parameters for the scope of the sexual harm to be repaired should not discourage the adoption of reparations programs. While it is true that some harms are not easy to quantify, invoking intangibles should not become an excuse for avoiding any valuation.[84] 'Immeasurable' should not become 'forgettable'. Rather, such debates should be considered as demonstrative of the sort of public discussion that new democratic governments need to undertake if new values for promoting equity and equality—both essential components of gender justice—are to take root. Therefore, discussions on how to repair the proximate harm caused by sexual violence should, as part of the public discourse, redress historical injustices and challenge *status quo ante* perceptions that acts of sexual violence perpetrated during moments of political breakdown were somehow isolated incidents of 'out of control' State and non-State actors, completely unrelated to discriminatory structures and practices which not only leave women vulnerable to attack but perpetuate impunity and continued hardship during periods of democratic transition.

How Might the Reparation of Sexual Violence as a Special Category Be Financed?

As mentioned earlier, transitional governments often find themselves under pressure to prioritize spending on large national goals rather than financing reparation schemes.[85] A review of the experiences of Rwanda and Sierra Leone indicates that both countries have been faced with competing demands to finance mechanisms for retributive justice (tribunals) and mechanisms for reparative justice (national programs for reparations).[86] In both cases, the resources allocated for remedying gender crimes were meager. According to the governments in both countries, one of the reasons for under-funding can be traced to the serious economic problems inherited from the former regimes. This resulted in the diversion of resources from other national development priorities such as health and education reform.

However, at the end of the day, both governments have been influenced by victims, victim support groups and human rights advocates who are clamoring for justice and an accounting for past crimes, including sexual violence.

The experiences of both of these countries suggest that while aggregate benefits accruing from national development programs may be a government priority, they do not automatically offset individual costs. The immeasurable costs associated with the harm inflicted by sexual violence are both physical and psychological. As discussed above, the long-term costs of harm often severely curtail a victim's capacity for accessing opportunities for income generation and livelihood in the medium and long term. This is especially the case when victims have already experienced the loss of other material interests such as property and access to social services. A study on victims of sexual violence in Rwanda indicated that 66.7 percent of the women surveyed have AIDS.[87] Thirty-four percent of the households in Rwanda are headed by women who are caring for senior family members, distant relatives or orphaned children.[88] In situations where sexual violence has been massive and systematic, ignoring the social costs, intentionally or not, can result in under-financing of the greater goals of national economic development.

While it is beyond the scope of this paper to enter into a full discussion of the financing of reparations,[89] victims' groups and policymakers might find it useful to examine the growing body of country case studies on experiences in gender budgeting. The tools of gender-responsive budgeting are generally used by governments, intergovernmental organizations, public-interest groups and NGOs to 'analyze how governments raise and spend public money with the aim of mainstreaming gender equality in decision-making about public resource allocation; and gender equality in the distribution of the impact of government budgets, both in their benefits and in their burdens'.[90] Gender budget initiatives are diverse and may focus on national, regional or local budgets; activities may cover an entire State budget or selected areas (e.g. particular departments, new programs or specific revenue instruments).[91] All gender budget initiatives share a unifying objective:

to make more transparent the connections between two sets of knowledge ... hitherto kept separate: understanding about public money and public services, on the one hand; and awareness of the different and unequal life experiences of women and men, girls, and boys, on the other.[92]

While the vast majority of gender-budgeting experiences have taken place in countries in 'normal development circumstances' (i.e. countries that do not have a recent history of mass political violence or authoritarianism) there does exist an emerging set of case studies in countries undergoing processes of reconstruction and transition—these experiences offer not insignificant lessons for the design of policies for reconciliation, including reparations.[93] For example, the failure of certain transitional aid programs for women in Bosnia, Kosovo, and East Timor have been in part attributed to the absence of gender budget analysis. On the other hand, women in South Africa have reported some successes in integrating gender analysis into the work of different State departments involved in the process of reconciliation.[94]

Gender-budgeting tools offer advantages for reparation programs, in particular those programs that are designed to deliver long-term social services, such as trust funds for pension payments, scholarships for the children of victims of sexual violence and the provision of social security to victims. The tools could play an important role in assisting policymakers to 'see the big picture' from a gender perspective, as they go about the complex business of rebuilding democratic institutions, reactivating beleaguered economies and reconstituting the social fabric. They also allow policymakers to examine the level of socioeconomic impact that reparation might have on the lives of victims of sexual violence by comparing the advantages of direct financial payments to other reparation modes such as the provision of social services. Finally, gender-budgeting tools could also enable policymakers to track the transitional government expenditure priorities in order to ensure that victims will continue to receive reparation if it is paid out in installments.

4. REPARATION AND GENDER JUSTICE: LOOKING TO THE FUTURE

Upon reviewing the vast spectrum and diversity of experiences in reparations analyzed in this whole study, it is clear that divergent thinking is needed in addressing the parallel processes of democratic transition and the democratic representation of women's interests as part of transitional justice. While these two streams of thought do not always sit easily together, transitional governments would be well advised not only to include, but also to make good on promises for reparation of sexual violence, sooner rather than later.

We have endeavored to demonstrate that, in contrast to other types of harm, the gendered impacts of sexual violence often result in continued suffering for the victims even in the aftermath of mass violence. This suggests that reparations for victims will need to be understood as a long-term, multidimensional process. Accordingly, this chapter has touched upon some of the challenges and dilemmas that face victims, victim support groups and policymakers—all of whom are critical stakeholders involved in conceptualizing and implementing

State-sponsored initiatives for redressing sexual violence in the aftermath of political violence and during periods of transition.

Realization of the right to reparation will in many cases be tied to larger questions concerning women's access to social services and other entitlements. Gender equality in access to reparations during periods of democratic transition could therefore serve as an important stepping-stone for women. The right to monetary or nonmonetary reparation needs to be entrenched in both the legal framework and the economic institutions of the country in question, since these jointly influence the resources to which women have access, the activities they can undertake, and the ways in which they can participate in the political economy. Hence, the reparation of sexual violence should provide an opportunity to review the commitment to the citizens' rights of women. Equitable access to compensation is not only about giving cash or income-generation opportunities, it is also about empowering women to attain a basic quality of life, to be able to participate productively in society, and to have better opportunities to improve their lives and the lives of their children.

Evidently, it would be unrealistic to expect reparations programs alone to encompass the myriad of goals involved in the type of long-term processes required for building active citizenship, lasting democracy and sustainable human development. However, careful consideration by policymakers, victim support groups and donors of the role that gender relations within State and society might play in such programs would be an important first step in counteracting and dismantling the discriminatory structures that reflect the low status of women in many transitional societies.

NOTES

1. The Peruvian Truth and Reconciliation Commission, in its Final Report, made recommendations concerning reparations, and these include a variety of measures for the victims of rape. The Truth and Reconciliation Commission for Sierra Leone goes even farther. However, the recommendations have not been implemented yet in either country.
2. Gender justice is a broad concept that can be defined as 'the ending of, and if necessary the provision of redress for, inequalities between men and women that result in women's subordination to men'. Ann Marie Goetz, 'Conceptual Paper on Applied Research for Gender Justice' International Development Research Center (IDRC), Gender Unit Workshop on Gender Justice, Citizenship and Entitlement, November 13–14, 2003), 11. It also implies full citizenship for women. Maxine Moyneux, 'Gender Justice, Citizenship and Entitlement in Latin America, and the Caribbean' (IDRC, Gender Unit Workshop on Gender Justice, Citizenship and Entitlement, November 2003), 3.

3. While we recognize that sexual violence profoundly impacts both women *and* girls, this chapter will focus upon women, given that a discussion of girls' experiences as victims of political violence would involve reviewing a separate body of literature on children's experiences in war. This is considered to be beyond the scope of this chapter.

4. It should be noted that the most dramatic legal advancements in criminalizing sexual violence in war contexts emerged as a result of the conflicts of the former Yugoslavia during the 1990s. Due to considerations of scope and space we will not cover this ground, especially since it is known to most academics and practitioners in the area of human rights and international criminal justice.

5. Human Rights Watch, *We'll Kill You If You Cry: Sexual Violence in the Sierra Leone Conflict* (New York: Human Rights Watch, 2003), n. 1 citing definition from United Nations, *Contemporary Forms of Slavery: Systematic Rape, Sexual Slavery and Slavery-like Practices during Armed Conflict*, Final Report submitted by Gay J. McDougall, Special Rapporteur (New York: United Nations, 1998), E/CN.4/Sub.2/1998/13, 7–8.

6. See Segovia (Chapter 19, this volume) for an analysis of the demands and constraints faced by reparations programs and the consequences these have on their finances.

7. The detrimental impact of sexual violence is, then, certainly no less than that resulting from other human rights violations such as forced disappearance or arbitrary detention.

8. Goetz, op. cit., 26.

9. Goetz, op. cit., 26.

10. For an articulation of the variety of reasons that explain why it is important to establish relations between reparations programs and other transitional justice measures ('external coherence') see de Greiff, 'Justice and Reparations' (Chapter 12, this volume).

11. Admittedly, this will be a difficult task and much of our analysis will be prospective, as opposed to retrospective. A review of the countries in which reparations policies and programs have been implemented indicates that, until very recently, there is little evidence to suggest that transitional governments have understood the importance of, let alone included, reparations for women victims of sexual violence. It is this lacuna that has motivated the authors to draft the current chapter.

12. Scott Splittgerber, 'The Need For Greater Regional Protection for the Human Rights of Women: The Cases of Rape in Bosnia and Guatemala', *Wisconsin International Law Journal* 15(1) (1996): 185, 196.

13. Literature on the gendered nature of political violence in Rwanda, Guatemala, Peru and Sierra Leone during the 1980s and 1990s confirms the age-old tradition of viewing women as 'war booty'.

14. Christine Chinkin, 'Rape and Sexual Abuse of Women in International Law', *European Journal of International Law* 5 (3)(1994): 2. Available at: http://www.ejil.org/journal/vol5/No3/art2-02.html, accessed August 27, 2003.

15. Human Rights Watch, *We'll Kill You If You Cry*, 4.

16. Carolyn Nordstrom, 'What John Wayne Never Told Us', unpublished paper (1991), cited by Tina Sideris, 'Rape in War and Peace: Social Contexts, Gender Power, and Identity', in *The Aftermath: Women in Post-Conflict Transformation*, Sheila Meintjes, Anu Pillay and Meredith Turshen, eds. (London, New York: Zed Books, 2001), 142–57, 147.

17. Sideris, op. cit., 147.

18. Anu Pillay, 'Violence Against Women in the Aftermath', in Meintjes et al., op. cit., 35–44, 36–7; Richard Strickland and Nata Duvvury, 'Gender Equity and Peacebuilding.

From Rhetoric to Reality: Finding the Way' (International Center for Research on Women, Washington DC, 2003), 7.

19. Elisabeth Rehn and Ellen Johnson Sirleaf, *Report on Women, War and Peace* (New York: UNIFEM, 2002), 13.

20. Rehn and Sirleaf, op. cit, 13 (emphasis added).

21. Sheila Meintjes, Anu Pillay and Meredith Turshen, 'There is No Aftermath for Women', in Meintjes et al., op. cit, 3–17, 13.

22. See generally Caroline Moser and Cathy McIlwaine, 'Gender and Rebuilding Social Capital in the Context of Political Violence: A Case Study of Colombia and Guatemala'. Paper presented at Gender, Armed Conflict and Political Violence. Conference organized by the World Bank, Washington DC, June 10–11, 1999.

23. Human Rights Watch, *We'll Kill You If You Cry*, op. cit., 19–20; and Human Rights Watch Report on Rwanda cited at http://www.hrw.org/wr2k3/africa9.html; accessed January 9, 2004.

24. This is not to suggest that reparations programs can or should replace mechanisms for retributive justice such as tribunals; we believe that both types of mechanisms (the reparative and the retributive) have a role to play in ensuring justice for victims and to put an end to impunity. See Section III, subsection 'How Might the Reparation of Sexual Violence as a Special Category be Financed?' for a brief discussion of the tensions between these two sets of mechanisms.

25. Strickland and Duvvury, op. cit., 18.

26. Sunila Abeysekera, 'Maximizing the Achievement of Women's Human Rights in Conflict-Transformation: The Case of Sri Lanka', *Columbia Journal of Transnational Law* 41(5) (2003): 523, 531.

27. Codou Bop, 'Women in Conflicts, Their Gains and Losses', in Meintjes et al., *The Aftermath*, 19–33, 28.

28. Ibid., 27.

29. Machanda cited in Meintjes et al., 'There is No Aftermath', 7.

30. Strickland and Duvvury, op. cit., 7. citing: Bop, op. cit., Judy El Bushra, 'Transforming Conflict', in *States of Conflict: Gender Violence and Resistance* (London: Zed Books, 2000); Sheila Meintjes, 'war and Post-war shifts in Gender Relations', in Meintjes et al., *The Aftermath*.

31. The 2001 supplement to the OECD-DAC guidelines on conflict, peace and development reflects a more nuanced understanding of the gendered experience of war. See also the Genoa Agreement cited at http://www.mofa.go.jp/policy/economy/summit/2001/g8conclude2.html; accessed January 10, 2004.

32. See for example, Sondra Hale, 'Sudanese Women in National Service, Militias and the Home', in *Women and Globalization in the Arab Middle East: Gender, Economy, and Society*, Eleanor Abdella Doumato and Marsha Pripstein Posusney, eds. (Boulder, Colorado: Lynne Rienner Publishers, 2003), 25–43.

33. See 'Basic Principles and Guidelines on the Right to Reparation for Victims of Gross Violations of Human Rights and International Humanitarian Law', UN Doc. E/CN.4/1997/104, 16 January 1997.

34. de Greiff, op. cit.

35. Suad Joseph, *Gender and Citizenship in the Arab Region* (New York: United Nations Development Program, 2002), 2.

36. Ibid., 2.

37. Ibid., 2.

38. Ibid., 3.

39. See Brandon Hamber (Chapter 16, this volume).

40. Stef Vandeginste, 'Reparation', in *Reconciliation after Violent Conflict: A Handbook,* David Bloomfield, Teresa Barnes and Luc Huyse, eds. (Stockholm: International Institute for Democracy and Electoral Assistance, 2003), 145–61, 145.

41. See de Greiff, op. cit.

42. See de Greiff, op. cit.

43. Meredeth Turshen, 'Engendering Relations of State to Society in the Aftermath', in Meintjes et al., *The Aftermath,* 78–94, 78.

44. Atieno Mboya Samandari, *The Gender Impacts of the Coexistence of Statutory, Customary and Religious Laws and Institutions* (Washington, DC: World Bank, 2002), 8.

45. Salma Maoulidi, 'Alwilaia and Women's Status Issues for Tanzania' (Sahiba Sisters Foundation: Dar es Salaam, 2003), 2 (manuscript).

46. Rehn and Sirleaf, op. cit., 100.

47. See for example Human Rights Watch, *We'll Kill You If You Cry,* and Human Rights Watch on Burundi, *Everyday Victims: Civilians in the Burundian War,* cited at http://www.hrw.org/doc?t=africa&c=burund; accessed January 2, 2004.

48. Joseph, op. cit., 3.

49. Meintjes et al., 'There is No Aftermath', 11.

50. See, for example, the reports of Radhika Coomaraswamy, UN Special Rapporteur on Violence Against Women, Causes and Consequences; Human Rights Watch, 'Gender-based Violence Against Kosovar Albanian Women', http://www.hrw.org/reports/2000/fry/Kosovo03-02.htm; accessed August 22, 2003.

51. Meintjes et al. have noted that 'Whether men's fantasies or women's realities prevail depends on who controls the myths and the making of identities; the institutions that govern social and behavioural norms—the religious institutions, the schools, the different levels of state—do not change.' 'There is No Aftermath', 14.

52. Interview with Zoraida Castillo, Coordinator of the Human Rights Program of Project Counseling Services, Bogota, December 9, 2003.

53. Beth Woroniuk, *Women's Empowerment in the Context of Human Security: A Discussion Paper,* December 1999: 13.

54. For a full discussion of the legitimate goals that reparations programs can be expected to deliver, refer to de Greiff, op. cit.

55. This is a call for what de Greiff calls 'external coherence'.

56. Human Rights Watch, *We'll Kill You If You Cry,* 62.

57. Ibid.

58. United Nations Security Council, *From Madness to Hope: the 12-year war in El Salvador: Report of the Commission on the Truth for El Salvador,* S/25500 (1993).

59. The truth commission report suggested that the government should facilitate the creation of reparation measures, but these suggestions were never fully implemented.

60. Commission to Clarify Past Human Rights Violations and Acts of Violence that caused the Guatemala People to Suffer, *Guatemala: Memory of Silence,* United Nations, February 1999.

61. Instancia Multi Institucional por la Paz y la Concordancia. Programa Nacional de Resarcimiento. Guatemala, 2003 (authors' copy).

62. Truth and Reconciliation Commission of Peru (CVR), *Final Report,* http://www.cverdad.org.pe/ifinal/index.php. Peru's proposed Integral Program for Reparation suggests that sexual violence might have a good chance of staying on the political agenda.

63. Joseph, op. cit., 3.

64. Vandeginste, op. cit., 158.

65. See the paper by Elizabeth Lira (Chapter 2, this volume).

66. Goetz, op. cit., 27.

67. Rehn and Sirleaf, op. cit., 93.

68. Goetz, op. cit., 27.

69. Goetz, op. cit., 26.

70. Rehn and Sirleaf, op. cit., 97.

71. *Guatemala: Never Again* (Recovery of Historical Memory Project at the Human Rights Office (REMHI) of the Archdiocese of Guatemala, 1999).

72. Turshen, op. cit., 93. Antjie Krog provides a striking account of testimonies in the TRC: 'After the first five weeks of intensive hearings, six out of ten of the testimonies were made by women, but three quarters of the women's testimonies and 88 percent of the men's testimonies were about abuses to men. Twenty-five percent of the women's testimonies dealt with abuses to their sons, 11 percent to their spouses and 8 percent to their brothers. Only 4 percent of men spoke about their sons and none of them talked about their spouses or sisters.' (Cited in Woroniuk, op. cit., 7).

73. Tina Sideris, 'Problems of Identity, Solidarity and Reconciliation', in Meintjes et al., *The Aftermath*, 46–60, 57.

74. This is one of the motivating insights of this whole research project, and especially of de Greiff (Chapter 12, this volume).

75. Mariam J. Aukerman, 'Extraordinary Evil, Ordinary Crime: A Framework for Understanding Transitional Justice', *Harvard Human Rights Journal* 15 (2002): 39–97; 79, n. 236, citing Martha Minow, *Between Vengeance and Forgiveness: Facing History After Genocide and Mass Violence* (Boston, MA: Beacon Press, 1998).

76. Meintjes et al., 'There is No Aftermath', 12.

77. Bop, op. cit., 21.

78. For a more detailed discussion, see section 'How Might the Reparation of Sexual Violence as a Special Category Be Financed?'

79. Compensation is generally the payment of money as a recognition of the wrong done and to make good the losses suffered. A distinction can be made between nominal damages (a small amount of money symbolizing the vindication of rights), pecuniary damages (intended to represent the closest possible financial equivalent of the loss or harm suffered), moral damages (relating to immaterial harm, such as mental distress or harm to a person's reputation or dignity) and punitive damages (which are of a different nature, and intended rather to deter than to make up for the loss suffered). Vandeginste, op. cit., 145.

80. We are grateful to Brandon Hamber (Chapter 16, this volume) for bringing this observation to our attention.

81. Cases of rape reported indicate that 75 percent of the victims were Quechua-speaking women; 83 percent of these were of rural origin. CVR, op. cit., 276.

82. Aukerman, op. cit., 79, n. 237, citing Minow, op. cit.

83. See Brandon Hamber, op. cit., for a more detailed discussion of the symbolic role of reparations.

84. Michael Cernea, *The Economics of Involuntary Resettlement: Questions and Challenges* (Washington, DC: The World Bank, 1999), 5, 21.

85. Again, see Segovia (Chapter 19, this volume), and on El Salvador and Haiti (Chapter 4, this volume).

86. Human Rights Watch, *We'll Kill you If You Cry*, 5; Rehn and Sirleaf, op. cit., 93.

87. Bop, op. cit., 33.

88. Bop, op. cit., 27.

89. See the chapters on microfinance and reparations by Seibel (Chapter 20) and State financing of reparations by Segovia (Chapter 19) in this volume for more detailed discussion of these issues.

90. *Gender Budget Initiatives: Strategies, Concepts and Experiences* (UNIFEM, IDRC, 2002), 7.

91. Ibid., 7.

92. Ibid., 8.

93. See case studies on South Africa, the Andean region and Rwanda in *Gender Budget Initiatives* and Debbie Budlender and Guy Hewitt, *Engendering Budgets: A Parctitioner's Guide to Understanding* and *Implementing Gender Responsive Budgets* (London: Commonwealth Secretariat, 2003).

94. *Gender Budget Initiatives*, 130–1.

CHAPTER 19

FINANCING REPARATIONS PROGRAMS: REFLECTIONS FROM INTERNATIONAL EXPERIENCE

ALEXANDER SEGOVIA[1]

1. INTRODUCTION

One of the least studied aspects regarding programs of reparation both in theory and in practice is financing. This is odd if we take into account that mobilizing resources, domestic and foreign, is politically one of the most difficult tasks any society can undertake, and that the scarcity of public resources is a serious restriction which limits the options of transitional societies[2] for the advancement of political, social, and economic reforms required for the consolidation of democracy and social development.

One reason that explains this lack of interest in the study of financing programs of reparation—in addition to a traditional aversion to quantitative analysis by those involved in human rights—is the belief that governments have enough power and the political incentives to ensure the mobilization of domestic and foreign resources for financing reparations. This would explain in some measure why truth commissions tend to recommend tax increases, cuts in military spending, or a redistribution of public expenditure to finance their proposed programs of reparation without exploring the real possibilities these measures have of being implemented. In theory, it is assumed that with such recommendations the problems of financing are already solved, and hence there is no need for further elaboration on the subject. From this perspective, if the government does not comply with such recommendations, it would be due simply to a lack of 'political will' and therefore it should be prepared to pay the political consequences.

Nevertheless, the political and social reality of many transitional societies is much more complex. First, governments do not always have the political incentives—and hence the political will—to comply with the recommendations made by truth commissions, which means that they are willing neither to assign resources to finance reparations, nor to risk their political capital for seeking a mobilization of these resources. Second, even when it has the political incentives to follow these recommendations, the government is not the only actor (and sometimes not even the strongest one) intervening in the process of mobilizing public resources. Third, in transitional societies, governments have other economic and social priorities which could clash with reparations proposals due to limited public funds and to the considerable amount of resources these proposals require for their implementation, especially in places where human rights violations have been massive, as in Guatemala and Peru.

In addition to the complexities that transitional societies face, we must take into account those specific to reparation programs, which make their management a complicated and problematic subject as well. First, potential beneficiaries of reparations (the victims and their families) are not only viewed by some powerful élites with suspicion owing to their past political affiliations, but also looked upon with reluctance and little interest by political groups, since they frequently belong to traditionally marginalized groups of society, as is the case with peasants and indigenous peoples.

Second, reparations are not always a priority in the national and international agendas of transitional justice, since other subjects such as the establishment of a public truth and prosecutions receive more attention. As a result, political pressures directed toward reparations are usually weaker than those geared in favor of truth and justice.

Third, reparations are politically difficult issues to manage since they entail digging in the past, which goes against the tendency in the policy of most governments of *looking ahead into the future*. This is a vision that is reinforced by the fact that designing a policy of reparations involves making difficult decisions that could have political consequences most governments are not always willing to assume. This is the case with decisions regarding the types of crimes that merit reparations, the scope of beneficiaries to be included, and the number of reparation measures that will be part of the program.

In the fourth place, reparations are difficult to design and implement because in addition to requiring considerable amounts of public resources, they need the existence of qualified technical resources, public and private institutional resources, and reliable statistical data, all of which is not always available in transitional societies.

The previous analysis explains why the design and implementation of programs of reparation has had unsatisfactory results internationally, in addition to the enormous difficulties of financing them. This study centers on the subject of financing reparation programs and attempts to answer, even if only in part, the following questions: Which factors play a role in the process of mobilizing domestic and foreign resources to finance reparations? Is financing solely a technical-economic problem, or does it involve political, social and cultural factors? Why do governments prefer financing social programs instead of programs of reparation? How do the proposals made by truth commissions regarding financing affect the viability of programs of reparation? Which factors explain the efficacy of financing models of reparation programs?

In order to fulfill these aims, this study has been divided into three main sections. In the first, programs of reparation are analyzed from the perspective of political economy, which means that both economic and noneconomic factors that influence the mobilization of domestic and foreign resources by a transitional society are taken into consideration. The second section of this study focuses on international experiences in the area of financing programs of reparation, with the purpose of extracting some lessons from these experiences. Finally, in the third section, the main conclusions of this study are presented.

2. The Political Economy of Financing Programs of Reparation

Mobilizing Financial Resources in Transitional Societies

In any society, mobilizing the financial resources necessary for national development and the consolidation of democracy is a complex and difficult process, not only because of its political dimension (which involves negotiations between many actors and institutions on the mobilization and allocation of resources), but also because of the scarcity of public resources, which are always insufficient to satisfy the demands of a modern society, regardless of its degree of economic development.

In the case of transitional societies, such process is even more complex for a number of reasons.[3] First, the transition from authoritarian to democratic regimes and from war to peace is characterized by opening the areas of debate in the political arena, which in turn causes a considerable increase in social and economic demands by organized groups and those who have been traditionally marginalized.[4] In addition, political parties and/or coalitions in charge of the democratic transition have an interest in advancing their causes in the social agenda, strengthening democratic institutions, and generating conditions for governance. This increases the demand for public resources and, in turn, complicates fiscal management, since governments have to reconcile these demands with the aims of preserving (and sometimes instituting) macroeconomic stability, which is central for a strategy of economic growth. In societies that have suffered internal armed conflicts, demands for reconstruction place additional pressures on already scarce State resources.

In such circumstances, governments are forced to rationalize public spending and establish priorities in investment and expenditures, which do not necessarily coincide with those related to peace and the consolidation of democracy. This situation is further complicated by the existence of agreements with international financial institutions (IFIs),[5] since the latter are not always sensitive to the realities of each nation and have a tendency to subordinate social and political aims to financial stability. The case of El Salvador is paradigmatic in this respect. From 1992 to 1994, with support from IFIs, El Salvador implemented an economic reform that had financial and exchange-rate stability as one of its main goals. Such reform implemented a restrictive fiscal policy that ignored additional spending commitments derived from the Peace Agreements. The adjustment mechanism used for this was the reduction of public investment, especially in infrastructure and social programs related to peace and development.[6]

A similar situation has taken place in Guatemala in recent years. Governments have had to apply a policy of adjustment centered on the reduction of public investment, due to the fact that tax burden goals[7] contemplated in the Peace Agreements[8] have not been met, and that there has been a need for reaching social spending objectives. This has compromised the governments' capacity to comply with their commitments derived from the Peace Agreements, particularly those related to the creation and/or improvement of the economic and social infrastructure in rural areas of the country.[9] It has to be pointed out, however, that in the case of Guatemala, IFIs have displayed more sensitivity to the local situation than in El Salvador, and for this reason, they have implemented more adequate and flexible conditions in favor of the peace process. For example, the Stand-By Agreement signed by the Guatemalan government with the International Monetary

Fund (IMF) in 2002 established a 5 percent minimum for social spending, so that the policy of reduction of public spending, applied by the government to keep the fiscal deficit under control, would not compromise financing basic public spending related to peace (health, education, housing, national security, the judiciary and the Public Ministry [*Ministerio Público*]).[10]

Second, and with notable exceptions, the margin for definition and implementation of fiscal policy is generally narrow in transitional societies owing to, among other factors, the existence of groups with veto power (such as the corporate sector in Central America) and, consequently, the relative weakness of the State; the lack of consensus among political groups on the national agenda; and finally, the existence of a deeply-rooted social conflict typically linked to unequal distribution of wealth and income and extreme poverty. In such circumstances, the possibilities of applying fiscal measures directed towards increasing tax burdens in these countries are significantly reduced, even if they are necessary from an economic and social point of view.

This explains why there is a generalized tendency to postpone, sometimes indefinitely, such measures, either out of fear of unleashing a battle for the distribution of resources, which could lead to more social conflicts and violence, or because of strong opposition from influential financial sectors to tax increases that could affect their short-term interests. In the end, what prevails are fiscal adjustments which reduce spending or strictly control the growth-rate of State expenditures (generally social spending or public investment). As a consequence of this policy, the agenda for reform is seriously affected.[11]

Because of the above reasons, serious tensions emerge frequently in transitional societies between macroeconomic-management goals and those related to strengthening democracy and peace. As I have pointed out elsewhere,[12] the first of these tensions emerges in the fiscal area, where traditional financial restrictions of the State and the need to finance peace and political reforms clash strongly with the need to preserve macroeconomic stability. The level of tension will depend on the conditions which public finances are in at the start of the transition and the magnitude of additional financial demands to finance peace and democracy. The experience in Central America shows that political reform is usually subordinated to short-term goals for stability.

A variation of the previous tension occurs with programs of reparation when governments, faced with insufficient resources, have to choose between financing such programs or financing social programs. Unfortunately, international experience reveals that there is a tendency by political groups and governments to privilege the latter over the former. Such decisions are based on political considerations (social programs are easier to sell than reparations and they also serve as a political-electoral instrument for the governing party), as well as on the lack of knowledge about the nature of programs of reparation, which are often associated automatically with social programs, ignoring the substantial differences existing between the two.[13]

For these reasons, the cases of Guatemala and Peru show that in the face of strong financial restrictions, governments prefer to finance collective measures of reparation (which generally include social programs) rather than individual measures. Such preference, in addition to leading to strong political tensions, breaks down the internal integrity or coherence of programs of reparation.[14] The reason behind this conduct adopted by governments is simple: in general, collective reparations can be carried out in part by reformulating already existing social programs (which sometimes only entails a change in their name), while individual reparations require a large amount of additional resources, especially if human rights violations have been massive.

The Political Dimension of Programs of Reparation and the Political Nature of the Process of Public Financing

Programs of reparation are essentially political in nature even though their content may be charged with economic and social ingredients and their implementation may sometimes be motivated by judicial reasons. This is due to several factors. First, reparations have to deal with the abuse of power by the State and, consequently, with the political conduct adopted by the élites that control it. For this reason, the general aim of programs of reparation is political: recognition of the victims and acknowledgment of the abuses committed by authoritarian regimes and/or by the groups in conflict.[15]

Second, programs of reparation are part of a more general human rights agenda, which involves the defense of traditionally marginalized social groups and/or groups whose political conduct and actions are considered illegal or illegitimate by a segment of the population and by traditional political groups. Both circumstances place programs of reparation in the political arena related to the access and control of power.

From the point of view of public policies, the political nature of reparations makes governments approach them cautiously, since, on the one hand, they try to avoid damaging their relationship with *de facto* powers and factions within the State opposed to reparations, and on the other, they seek to appease the fears of the corporate sector and IFIs that reparation measures may cause fiscal deficits and increase inflationary pressures. For these reasons, governments limit the scope of programs of reparation, even if this means that recommendations made by truth commissions are not met.

Not only are the aims of programs of reparation political in nature, but their financing is also fundamentally a political process that requires considerable mobilization of public financial resources, achieved by either a reorientation of existing resources and/or obtaining additional resources. Since it is generally the case that available State resources are not sufficient to satisfy increasing social demands as well as to comply with the existing responsibilities and functions owed by the State, it necessarily has to allocate them according to priorities, which in general respond to political motivations coming as much from the government as from the political parties represented in Congress.

Indeed, political parties play a central role in the process of approving reforms of the national budget, and they do not always support programs of reparation owing to their ideological affiliations or to the fact that they themselves were linked to human rights violations in the past. Such is the case in El Salvador where the parliament was controlled by a right-wing coalition with close ties to the military during the entire transitional phase.[16] A similar situation exists in Peru nowadays, where the parties that formed the government during the period of internal conflict have an important presence in Congress.[17]

Political parties (including the party in power) generally act on behalf of partisan interests, and therefore, their stance is influenced by the different social groups that form civil society—including corporate groups and international cooperation organizations—that have the capacity to exercise pressure on them.

Programs of reparation, then, have to compete for scarce resources in a difficult and complex political arena, such as the process of budgetary allocation of resources, which typically includes two main phases. The first corresponds to the drafting of the public budget, which is generally the responsibility of the executive branch. Through a process of consultation and negotiation with the other State institutions (the legislature, the judiciary, the various ministries, regional and municipal governments, autonomous institutions, etc.), the executive defines budget priorities and the amounts for each program and institution. At the end of this process, the executive branch, through the Ministry of Finance, presents a draft bill of the budget to Congress for its approval.

Once the draft bill comes to Congress, the budget process enters a second phase, which is even more complicated than the first, especially when the ruling party does not have the majority in parliament: each political force represented in Congress would want to see its priorities and party interests reflected in the budget, and such priorities do not always coincide with those of the government and the party in power.

In the end, the budget approved reflects the balance of political forces within the society in transition, particularly among the branches of the State (executive, legislative, and judicial) and within each of them, as well as the balance between these branches and the different social pressure groups. For this reason, the priorities reflected in the budget do not always correspond to the needs of the victims of human rights violations. In this context, the financing of reparation programs confronts great difficulties, since not only must it compete with other priorities, but it also faces the veto power of some sectors opposed to establishing a public truth about the past and bringing those responsible to justice.

Owing to these factors, the process of financing reparations is strongly constrained by the possibility that political alliances might be generated with sufficient power to influence the budget. As it will be argued later, when political parties or coalitions that defend and promote reparations come to power in transitional societies, they do receive financial support at least in part, in spite of severe financial restrictions, since it is always possible to reallocate some of the scarcely available resources, or to define various strategies for the mobilization of domestic and foreign resources. By contrast, when parties or coalitions do not defend or promote reparations, they will run the risk of not having enough funding, regardless of the actual availability of financial resources.

The Economic-Financial Dimension of Programs of Reparation

The mobilization of resources necessary to finance programs of reparation is in the end the result of the balance of political forces; however, this does not mean that the lack of resources is not a real problem, which in many cases prevents these programs from being effectively implemented. As pointed out earlier, transitional societies are confronted with growing social demands that cannot be entirely satisfied, especially in cases of low development, insufficient tax burden, and where the existence of veto powers as well as deeply-rooted social conflicts do not allow the application of tax reforms that would increase fiscal revenues.

In the context of such restrictions, programs of reparation recommended by truth commissions—especially if these programs are far-reaching—face serious obstacles to their effective implementation because of a severe lack of fiscal resources and the slim political possibilities of mobilizing additional resources. In fact, in such cases, far-reaching programs of reparation give rise to fears— among political groups, the corporate sector, and the government—of undue pressures on public finances that in the long run may result in an unmanageable situation with exchange rates and in financial circles. As a result, such sectors are reluctant to finance programs of reparation and/or try to reduce their reach and scope, either by privileging the least expensive measures of the program (this is the case with interim reparations in South Africa), or by emphasizing collective reparation measures, which take as the starting point for their implementation already existing social programs (the cases of Guatemala and Peru).

Aside from political and ideological motivations underlying such proposals, the truth is that in transitional societies fiscal management is essential to institute and/or preserve macroeconomic stability, and therefore such a dimension has to be taken into account when designing programs of reparation. Specifically, it is important to design a financing strategy that takes into account the macroeconomic situation in general as well as the situation of public finances in particular. The different phases of the execution of the program should also be considered, with the purpose of spreading the need for resources over time and, hence, adjusting such needs in accordance with the short-term macroeconomic financial program.

Unfortunately, this exercise of adjusting the financial needs of reparation programs to macroeconomic restrictions is usually not performed, either by the truth commissions that propose reparations, or by government institutions in charge of their financial management.[18] As a result, financing programs of reparation is seen as something alien, and for this reason disturbing, to short-term financial planning.

Moreover, far-reaching programs of reparation confront additional obstacles to their implementation in countries with serious socioeconomic problems, such as generalized poverty. In such cases, scarce State resources are by no means sufficient to deal with social problems; thus, adequate financing of reparation programs seeking to benefit a large portion of the population and/or including several measures of reparation is even more problematic. In fact, in such circumstances, programs of reparation compete with other priorities in the budget, in particular with social programs, which enjoy higher levels of political support and which are generally better conceived technically, since they are usually elaborated by national and international agencies with ample experience in the formulation and evaluation of these projects. In this context, programs of reparation have a clear disadvantage not only because of the technical difficulties involved in their elaboration (due in part to the lack of experts in the field), but also because it is very difficult to prove their superiority (and relevance) in net additional benefits that their implementation would have for potential beneficiaries.

The previous considerations suggest the need to include realistic and concise financing proposals for programs of reparation in poor countries, as well as solid arguments for the positive effects that would be derived from their implementation, above all, in terms of strengthening democratic governance and of advancing the social, political, and economic inclusion of traditionally marginalized sectors of society.

Programs of Reparation and the Limits of Foreign Financing

There is broad consensus about the fact that the international community could and should contribute to financing programs of reparation, not only for humanitarian reasons and those of solidarity, but also because in some cases foreign actors supported the military regimes or participated directly in the internal conflicts of societies in transition.[19] For this reason, most truth commissions have in their recommendations called on the international community to help finance reparations. An extreme case is the recommendation made by the Truth Commission of El Salvador, conceiving the creation of a special fund to finance reparations, which should consist mainly of foreign resources (1 percent of international aid)[20] (see Section III).

Nevertheless, foreign contributions for financing reparations have been fairly modest,[21] and in most cases disappointing, and this has caused frustration in transitional societies. The obvious question that arises is the following: why does the international community resist contributing significantly to financing programs of reparation? There are at least two reasons that explain such behavior. The first is that foreign actors believe that financing programs of reparations is in itself an act of reparation, and as such, the responsibility for financing is mainly a duty of the State and the society in transition.[22] This is why foreign actors are only willing to contribute to financing reparations after the national government has shown a clear political commitment to the issue and has invested public funds for that purpose. The experience of El Salvador, Guatemala, and in some respects Malawi, confirms this position (see Section III).

The second reason has to do with the political nature of programs of reparation, which makes foreign actors extremely cautious over the issue for fear of entering into conflict with governments, especially those led by conservative sectors or with close ties to the military. From a different perspective, foreign governments who have supported repressive political regimes or financed internal conflicts in countries in transition are not always interested in contributing to building democracy and peace, including through policies of reparations.

The previous analysis suggests that it is not realistic to expect programs of reparation to be financed mainly with foreign resources. At best, these should be considered a complement to national resources, but never as substitutes. In addition, it issues a warning about the need to establish an open and constructive dialogue with the international community (including IFIs) regarding the form and concrete mechanisms in which international aid can cooperate with the financing and implementation of programs of reparation. In this sense, the financing proposal made by the Truth Commission of Peru is interesting, for it underlines the need for the proposed reparations program to be financed with a reparations fund provided mainly by the State through a special budgetary allocation. It also proposes the establishment of a round table of debate where the main domestic and external actors participate in order to design a realistic financial strategy compatible with macroeconomic goals.[23]

3. The Efficacy of Financing Models for Programs of Reparation: Some Lessons Learned from International Experience

The Main Financing Models

International experience related to financing programs of reparation indicates that there are two main models proposed by truth commissions. The first and the most frequently recommended consists in the creation of special funds financed by national and international resources. As can be seen in Table 19.1, the truth commissions of El Salvador, Guatemala, Haiti, Malawi, South Africa, and Peru recommended this plan. In addition to resources from the public budget, they recommend seeking alternative financing sources, such as the following: foreign resources stemming from international cooperation (donations and loans); the issuance of public bonds; the introduction of new taxes or the modification of existing rates; private resources (from individuals or corporations); and public funds obtained from special sources, such as the sale of State assets, the assets confiscated from corrupt officials, and exchanges of foreign debt for reparations. In some cases, there are recommendations to reallocate the military budget to reparations.

The second proposed model consists of direct financing of the reparations program by the State, using funds from the public budget. This is the case in Argentina, Brazil, and Chile, where resources were channeled through a special budgetary allocation, or through the budget of a specific ministry. The case of Argentina is a variation on this model: reparations have been financed by the State with the issuance of public bonds. In Guatemala, the Reparations Trust Fund was financed also in part with the issuance of bonds in dollars that were placed in the international markets, that is, through foreign debt.

A review of international experience reveals that the most effective model, in terms of financing programs of reparation in transitional societies, has been the second one,[24] that is, direct financing from the public budget. The cases of Argentina, Brazil, and Chile illustrate the point in question, since various reparation measures have been effectively applied and, even though their financing has been an important restriction (especially in Argentina), this has not been an insurmountable obstacle to the implementation of programs of reparation.[25]

By contrast, the financing model based on the creation of special funds, generally managed on an ad hoc basis, has been less effective in providing the financial

Table 19.1 Financial models for reparations (a selection of some countries)

Country	Tax burden (Tax income/ GNP)	Governments/ coalitions in favor of reparations	The reach of the program of reparations[a]	Proposed plan	Observations
Argentina	12.5 (1995–9)	Yes	Far-reaching	Direct financing with State funds	The National Commission on the Disappearance of Persons [*Comisión Nacional sobre Desaparicion de Personas* (CONADEP)] recommended that the reparation initiatives be financed by the State. In practice, the implemented reparations have been financed with bonds issued by the State.
Brazil	19.8 (1997)	Yes	Limited	Direct financing with State funds	The reparations have been financed with funds from the public budget through amendments made in Congress.
Chile	19.0 (1995–9)	Yes	Limited[b]	Direct financing with State funds	The Rettig Report establishes that it is the duty of the State to finance reparations, and for this reason, the Report makes an appeal to the Chilean State to increase its efforts in order to achieve this purpose. In practice, reparations have been financed mainly with public funds, although the international community has contributed by financing specific programs, such as the health program (PRAIS).

Table 19.1 (cont.)

Country	Tax burden (Tax income/ GNP)	Governments/ coalitions in favor of reparations	The reach of the program of reparations[a]	Proposed plan	Observations
El Salvador	11.1 (1995–9)	No	Far-reaching	Reparations Fund financed with 1% of international aid.	The fund was never created, since the international community claimed that reparations were the duty of the State, and the government argued an absence of public funds. The lack of support for reparations on the part of former guerrillas has also contributed to this breach of the recommendations.
Guatemala	8.1 (1995–9)	No	Far-reaching	Reparations Fund financed with the following sources: increases in tax burdens, as was contemplated in the Peace Agreements; redirecting public expenditures; cuts in military spending; and contributions made by the international community.	The very few reparation measures that have been implemented thus far have been financed by foreign donors and, to a lesser degree, by the government, which has repeatedly claimed a lack of resources for financing reparations. Nevertheless, after violent protests by former *patrulleros* (patrolmen) linked to the Guatemalan Republican Front [Frente Republicono Guatemalteco] (FRG) the government promised to pay each former *patrullero* (around 850,000 persons) the amount of 5,241.6 quetzales (around

					US$663). For this purpose, the government, with resources obtained through the sales of public bonds, created a trust of 75 million quetzales (around US$10 million) to finance compensations to these groups. At the end of 2003, the National Program of Reparation [*Programa National de Resarcimiento*] was approved, which, according to the law, will be financed with resources from the public budget for a period of ten years (300 million quetzales, or US$40 million per year).
Haiti	8.1 (2000)	No	Far-reaching	Reparations Fund financed with public, private, and foreign resources.	The National Commission for Truth and Justice recommended the creation of the Special Reparation Commission [*Commission Especial de Reparación*], which would manage a fund created with resources coming from the State; private national or international donors; and international assistance, in particular, from the United Nations Fund for Victims of Torture. In practice, however, neither the government nor the international community have given a substantial amount of resources to this fund.

Table 19.1 (cont.)

Country	Tax burden (Tax income/ GNP)	Governments/ coalitions in favor of reparations	The reach of the program of reparations[a]	Proposed plan	Observations
Malawi	17.3 (2000–1)	No	No data available	National Compensations Fund	The parliament has allocated resources for the National Compensations Fund. The tribunal has requested help from international donors, who, in turn, have refused to provide it since they believe this is a duty owed by the State.
Peru	11.9 (2002)	No	Far-reaching	Reparations Fund financed by the State and complemented with foreign funds. The proposal includes an appeal to the international community to support the program of reparation through new mechanisms such as the exchange of foreign debt for reparations.	As a response to the proposal by the Truth and Reconciliation Commission (CVR) to create the Comprehensive Program of Reparations [*Programa Integral de Reparaciones*], which would include individual and collective measures, as well as material and symbolic reparations, the government announced the implementation of the Peace and Development Plan [*Plan de paz of Desarrello*] in the areas most affected by violence. This plan consists mostly of social projects and plans for infrastructure.
South Africa	23.2 (2000–1)	No	Far-reaching	Reparations Fund financed with domestic (public and private) as	The government and the corporate sector have argued that the reparations proposed by the Truth Commission

well as	are not fiscally viable.
foreign	Furthermore, the gov-
resources. The	ernment discarded the
Truth and Rec-	adoption of the tax re-
onciliation	commendations. In the
Commission	end, the government
recommended	rejected all of the re-
a wealth tax, a	commendations by the
once-off levy	Truth Commission and
on corporate	decided to award a one-
and private in-	time payment of less
come; a dona-	than US$4,000 to each
tion by public	victim.
trade com-	
panies of 1% of	
their market	
capitalization;	
and a retro-	
spective sur-	
charge on	
corporate	
profits extend-	
ing back to a	
date to be	
suggested.	

[a] The reach refers to the amount and type of proposed measures, as well as the number of possible beneficiaries of the proposed reparation program. In other words, the term refers to the balance between the categories of complexity and completeness proposed by de Greiff.

[b] Recently, the Chilean program of reparations broadened its reach considerably with the inclusion as beneficiaries of victims of torture, who represent the largest group of victims of the political violence that took place in that country.

Source: From the author's own research based on studies included in this volume and information from the International Monetary Fund.

resources that enable the implementation of programs of reparation. The cases of El Salvador, Guatemala, Haiti, Malawi, and South Africa illustrate this. In all of these countries, it has not been possible to provide the fund with the necessary resources to finance the programs of reparation recommended by the truth commissions.

Two obvious questions arise from the previous analysis. If the financing model for programs of reparation based on direct contributions by the State through its public budget has been the most effective, why has it not been the most recommended in practice? And secondly, which factors explain the efficacy of different financing models for programs of reparation? Table 19.1 reveals some of the relationships that could be established in order to answer these questions.

Political Coalitions in the Government in Favor of Reparations and Degrees of Compliance for Programs of Reparation

According to the information contained in Table 19.2, there seems to be a direct relation between the degree of support for reparations from parties or coalitions in power and the degrees of compliance for such programs. For example, there is the case of Chile where financing reparations directly from the public budget has been done without any major obstacles, owing to the fact that the coalition of political parties that came to power after General Augusto Pinochet's dictatorship has supported reparations and has included them in its political agenda.[26] Such support has even strengthened, since over time the country has built a strong social and political coalition in favor of reparations, which has enabled the widening of the reach of its program.[27]

Something similar has taken place in Argentina, where democratic governments as well as most political sectors have supported the implementation of reparation measures by the State. Moreover, in recent decades an important social movement denouncing human rights violations has emerged in that country.[28] As a result,

Table 19.2 Chile: cost of the program of reparations (currency: pesos 2003)[a]

Reparations Pensions 1992–June 2003 (Law Num. 19.123)	86,238,49,633
Compensation Bonus 1992–2003 (Law Num. 19.123)	7,285,138,614
Education Benefits 1992–2003 (Law Num. 19.123)	12,205,837,923
Indemnification for Confiscated Property from Political Parties 2001–3 (Law Num. 19.568)	12,058,897
Program for Returning Exiles [*Programa Nacional del Retorno*] 1990–4 (Law Num. 18.994)	8,677,019,743
Legal Medical Services (Project for the Identification of Disappeared Detainees 2000–2)	1,109,987,815
Program for the Politically Dismissed [*Programa de Exonerados Politicos*] 1993–2003 (Laws Num. 19.234, Num. 19.582, and Num.19.881)	305,756,361,524
Program of Human Rights and Recognition for the Politically Dismissed [*Programa de Derechos Humanos y Reconociniento al Exonerado Politico*] 1997–2003	1,247,704,755
Program of Mental Health	No figures available
Total	422,532,258,904

[a] The average exchange rate in December 2003 was 602.9 pesos to US$1.

Source: Gobierno de Chile (2003), *Propuesta de Derechos Humanos del Gobierno.*

the program of reparations has been implemented in Argentina despite its economic problems and differences over the issue among some of the victims' organizations.[29] Finally, there is the case of Brazil, where the government and a large number of political groups have supported the policy of reparations, even though the number of victims is quite small.

By contrast, in societies where the government and/or political coalitions in power have not supported reparations, financing such programs has been extremely difficult. El Salvador, Guatemala, Haiti, Peru, and South Africa are examples of this.[30] In these countries, the lack of support from governments (and sometimes opposition) for programs of reparation has hindered their effective implementation. Another factor contributing to this is the weakness of social coalitions that support reparations in the face of government or *de facto* powers opposed to their implementation.[31] In fact, the absence of a strong social force with enough power to influence political decisions that could have electoral costs for governments has made it possible for the latter to avoid complying with their reparation commitments, for this subject is a source of constant friction with their allies, especially the military and conservative corporate sectors.

In the cases in which governments do not support or are opposed to reparations, the very few examples of successful financing of reparations have taken place precisely when specific social groups have achieved a high degree of organization and political influence, or have enough power of their own to generate social and political instability. The case of Guatemala illustrates this. As a result of the pressure exercised by paramilitary groups (former *patrulleros*),[32] and for electoral reasons, the government of the FRG created a trust aimed at compensating these former *patrulleros*, with resources obtained from the issuance of public bonds.[33] This commitment has been formally acknowledged by the new government that took office in January 2004; however, it has not been fulfilled owing to scarce public resources. This lack of compliance has generated a growing confrontation between paramilitary groups and the government.[34] El Salvador is another good example: wounded war veterans from the Army joined the former guerrilla movements to press the State to meet their demands, which have been finally met.[35]

The previous analysis suggests that there is a strong relationship between political forces in favor of reparations and the effective financing of such programs. In particular, there is a direct relation between the degree of support by the parties or coalitions in power and their level of compliance with programs of reparation. This means that the best way to insure financing is to design and implement a political strategy aimed at, on the one hand, making political groups aware of the importance of reparations, and on the other, building a social and political alliance in favor of such programs.

The Reach of Programs of Reparation, the Financial Capacity of the State, and the Chosen Financing Model

International experience demonstrates that there is a second relation in postconflict societies between the reach of reparation programs recommended by a truth commission, the financial capacity of the State, and the recommended financing model. As can be appreciated from Table 19.2, in each case where truth commissions recommended far-reaching programs of reparation and the governments were financially weak (low tax burdens),[36] the recommended financing model was the creation of reparation funds using both domestic and foreign resources. This was the case with El Salvador, Guatemala, Haiti, and Peru.

In each of these cases, truth commissions concluded that, given the country's situation and the reach of the recommended programs, it was not feasible to finance reparations with public funds exclusively, and for this reason, they suggested a model which in theory could mobilize greater amounts of resources: reparation funds using domestic and foreign resources. Indeed, some commissions, such as the ones in El Salvador and Haiti, even suggested that reparations be financed mainly with external resources, given the precarious situation of the country's finances and the prominent participation of foreign actors in their internal conflicts. Unfortunately, as stated before, in both cases the international community did not respond according to expectations. In other cases like Guatemala, it was recommended that reparations be financed through the implementation of far-reaching tax reforms. In this last case, the political weakness and lack of commitment of governments meant that these proposals could not be carried out.

By contrast, in the cases where the reach of reparation programs was limited, either because human rights violations did not achieve elevated proportions, as in Brazil, or because truth commissions excluded certain types of victims from the benefits of reparations (reducing in this way the scope of beneficiaries and, thereby, the costs of the program), as in Chile,[37] the recommended model was direct financing by the State. Given that the fiscal capacity of these states is high in comparison with other postconflict countries, and that coalitions in favor of reparations are strong, financing reparations has not represented a major problem.

The previous analysis indicates that the recommended financing model is related to the reach of the contemplated reparation program and to the assessment made by a truth commission of the fiscal situation of the government. In fact, there seems to be a widely shared perception that in fiscally weak countries, far-reaching reparation programs can only be financed with a model that contemplates the mobilization of domestic and foreign resources. International experience does not seem to confirm this perception, however, given the unpromising results with this type of model. Furthermore, there is the case of Argentina where in spite of the far-reaching nature of the reparations program and the low financial capacity of the government (12.5 percent tax burden), the truth commission recommended direct financing by the State. In our opinion, this is due to the strong commitment by Argentinean society to reparations, and especially to the political commitment of transitional governments to offer reparations to the victims of the military dictatorship and the strength of victims' organizations. In this way, they have overcome severe financial restrictions through the implementation of heterodox measures (payment of reparations with public bonds).[38]

The case of South Africa is an exception because although it presents a pattern of generalized human rights violations and the truth commission recommended a far-reaching program of reparations, the South African government has a financial capacity far superior to other postconflict societies (23.2 percent tax burden) and therefore, financing reparations directly by the State should not represent an insurmountable problem.[39] However, the truth commission in South Africa recommended the creation of a presidential fund to finance reparations, which had to be supported with domestic (public and private) as well as foreign resources. It appears that this recommendation has to do with the position taken by the government and some corporate sectors for whom a far-reaching program of reparations is not fiscally viable. This could also be related to the lack of political commitment by the South African government and the party in office (the African National Congress) to reparations.[40]

Degree of Development and the Economic and Political Viability of Programs of Reparation

The fourth relationship that can be established from international experience is the one between the degree of socioeconomic development in a country and the effective implementation of reparation programs. As can be seen in El Salvador, Guatemala, Haiti, and Peru, the possibilities of implementing far-reaching programs of reparation where there are serious problems of poverty, inequality, and exclusion are reduced substantially. One reason for this, of course, is that public resources are by no means sufficient to meet the almost unlimited socioeconomic needs of the majority of the population in these countries. In such circumstances, the possibilities of implementing far-reaching programs of reparation, which involve an additional mobilization of financial resources, are limited.

Nevertheless, the fact that countries with comparable degrees of development implement reparation programs of variable munificence[41] suggests that the relationship between economic development and reparations is more complex than it seems. Initially, it can be established that some minimum degree of economic development represents a threshold for implementing reparations, but that once that threshold is crossed, countries in similar economic situations may take quite different paths regarding the issue, because such choices are also related to the existing political balance in a transitional country.

In addition, the existence of deeply-rooted socioeconomic problems, especially generalized poverty, means that social programs of a broader scope have a higher priority among political groups and the government than reparation programs. The reason for this is quite simple: social programs have more social and political support than programs of reparation, and the latter also have the disadvantage of benefiting only one sector of the poor population with a political past that is generally questioned by conservative groups.

4. CONCLUSIONS

The arguments presented here allow us to derive some conclusions regarding financing programs of reparation, as well as the degrees of efficacy of the various financing models recommended by truth commissions. First, they suggest that the process of financing reparations is very complex and that it varies from country to country depending on the economic, social, and political conditions of each society in transition, and on the content and reach of the programs of reparation recommended by truth commissions. In this sense, there are no definitive recipes for financing that could be applied in every case, and for this reason, each experience has to be analyzed according to the specific aspects of each transitional society.

Second, this analysis demonstrates that apart from the proposed financing model, political factors, especially the degree of support for a policy of reparations from the parties or coalitions in power and the possibility of creating a balance of forces in favor of reparations, which could generate the necessary incentives to governments and political groups for advancing this cause, are crucial to the effective financing of programs of reparation. As international experience indicates, when there is a balance of political forces favorable to reparations, they are efficiently financed, even if partially and gradually. By contrast, when such a balance does not exist, governments will wield technical and economic arguments as an excuse to obstruct the provision of resources for reparations.

Given that the balance of political forces in favor of reparations depends directly on the possibility of creating a social and political coalition that defends them, the most certain way of ensuring the financing of programs of reparation is through the design and implementation of political strategies aimed at raising awareness among political groups on the importance of this issue, as well as building a broad coalition in favor of reparations. In such strategies, organizations for victims, human rights organizations, and truth commissions themselves play a central role.[42]

Third, international experience demonstrates that the proposals for financing reparations that are based on broad fiscal reforms, involving the introduction or increase of taxation and massive redistribution of existing resources (including military spending) face greater difficulties for their effective implementation, even more so in societies where the government is weak in relation to *de facto* powers, and where there are no strong domestic actors who support and promote reparations. This does not mean, of course, that truth commissions should not recommend these measures, especially the introduction of temporary taxes on the wealth and assets of privileged sectors of transitional societies, which often were the ones who supported or allowed the installation of repressive regimes. The reduction of military spending is another feature that could be recommended. What I am trying to emphasize is that such recommendations need to be technically and politically well founded and that they should be accompanied by clear strategies that would ensure their political viability.

Fourth, the analysis suggests that financing proposals based on the expectation of significant contributions from the international community is not realistic, for foreign actors believe that this is fundamentally a duty owed by the governments of transitional societies. Moreover, the political interest that some external actors display during postconflict periods is quite different from that which they had shown during such conflicts. To put it bluntly, many foreign governments are more willing to finance wars than to contribute to peace. In any case, governments and societies in transition should make every effort towards an involvement of the international community that complements national efforts to finance reparations. To this end, it is important to establish a frank and consistent dialogue with the international community in every phase of the process of elaboration and implementation of reparations. It is also important to find new mechanisms of cooperation that enable the community to finance reparations, at least in part. The exchange of debt for reparations, or help with confiscating and repatriating assets from corrupt and illicit activities, are some of the new mechanisms that truth commissions are recommending in order to achieve this aim.

Fifth, international experience indicates that far-reaching programs of reparation whose effective implementation requires a mobilization of considerable resources face serious political difficulties because of fears that they will produce undue pressures on public finances. In this sense, it is crucial that financing proposals for reparation programs be technically solid, which means that apart from performing a consistent and realistic cost analysis, they should establish plans for macroeconomic consistency so that the higher demand for public resources will be compatible with macroeconomic goals over time (fiscal deficit, inflation, etc.).

Also, each proposal included in the reparations program must be justified on its own, and should be defended in relation to other areas of policy making, in particular, in relation to social programs.

Sixth, the analysis suggests that even if there is no direct relationship between the degree of wealth in a given country and the effective implementation of programs of reparation, there seems to be a relationship between the reach of such programs, the magnitude of socioeconomic problems, and the degrees of compliance for reparation programs. In those countries where poverty is deep-rooted and generalized, and where inequality is high (El Salvador, Haiti, Guatemala, Peru, and South Africa), the possibilities of implementing far-reaching programs of reparation are considerably reduced, due to the severe budget restrictions these governments have to face and the narrow margin for mobilizing additional resources. In such circumstances, political groups and governments prefer to dedicate available public funds to finance social programs of a broader nature rather than financing programs of reparation, which benefit a social group with a political background considered questionable and even illegitimate.

Finally, this study clearly demonstrates that there is a serious lack of knowledge regarding the financing of reparation programs, and in general, regarding relations between economics and politics in transitional societies. In this sense, the findings of this research should be considered preliminary and the subject of further research.

(Translated from Spanish by Christian Gerzso)

NOTES

1. The author wishes to express his deepest gratitude to Pablo de Greiff, who with great patience made incisive comments on previous versions of this study, which helped improve considerably the quality of the present version. Of course, the content of this work is the exclusive responsibility of the author.
2. By *transitional societies* I mean those societies that after going through internal armed conflicts or a situation of political violence have instituted and/or restored democratic regimes. This is why Argentina, Brazil, Chile, El Salvador, Guatemala, Haiti, Peru, and South Africa are considered countries in transition in this study.
3. For a detailed analysis of the relationship between politics and economics in postconflict societies see Alexander Segovia (2002), *Las Relaciones entre Economia y Politica en Sociedades Post-belicas: Lecciones a Partir de la Experiencia Centroamericana*, www.pnud.org.co
4. After long periods of dictatorship or internal armed conflicts, transitional societies usually experience a reemergence of social movements, particularly workers' and peasants' unions as well as former combatants from both sides who, in addition to fighting for democratization, demand better labor and living conditions.

5. International Monetary Fund (IMF), the World Bank (WB), and the Inter-American Development Bank (IDB).

6. An analysis of fiscal management in the case of El Salvador can be found in Alexander Segovia, 'Domestic Resource Mobilization', in *Economic Policy for Building Peace. The Lessons of El Salvador*, James Boyce, ed. (London/Boulder, CO: Lynne Rienner, 1996).

7. Tax burden is defined as the relationship between tax income and the gross national product (GNP).

8. The Peace Agreements include the government's commitment for the year 2000 to increase the tax burden in relation to the GNP up to 50 percent more than what was registered in 1995 (about eight percent). This means that the tax-income goal is 12 percent.

9. See Manfredo Chocano, '*El Grado de Cumplimiento del Pacto Fiscal Tres Años Después de su Suscripción*', *Informe Preparado para la Comisión de Seguimiento del Pacto Fiscal* (Guatemala: Comisión de Seguimiento del Pacto Fiscal, July, 2003).

10. A detailed analysis of the role of the international community in the Guatemalan case can be found in Alexander Segovia, *El Rol de la Comunidad Internacional en el Proceso de Paz de Guatemala: Lecciones Aprendidas a partir del Tema Fiscal* (Informe de Consultoría PNUD-Guatemala, 2001).

11. It is well documented in Latin American economic literature that during the 1980s and 1990s, most fiscal adjustments focused on the reduction of public spending (including state investments), and not on the increase of taxation through far-reaching tax reforms.

12. Segovia, *Las Relaciones*, op. cit.

13. Some of these differences are the following: (*a*) the aim of social programs is to deal with general problems of a structural nature (e.g., poverty, inequality, exclusion), while the aim of programs of reparation is to compensate victims and their families for harms caused by political violence; (*b*) although reparation programs may include social components (e.g. infrastructure projects, housing, health, and education) they do not consider only these measures, but contemplate aspects directly related to the suffering and moral harm caused to the victims. This is why they include symbolic measures and mental health programs, among other types of measures.

14. For a definition of the concepts of internal and external integrity or coherence of programs of reparation see Pablo de Greiff, 'Introduction', in this volume.

15. As de Greiff has pointed out, in periods of transition, reparations seek to contribute (however modestly) to the reconstruction or construction of a new political community. Ibid.

16. The Nationalist Republican Alliance Party [Partido Alianza Republicana Nacionalista] (ARENA) and the Reconciliation Party [Partido de Conciliación] (PCN) have ties to the armed forces, who were responsible for most human rights violations during the period of conflict.

17. It is worth highlighting the case of the Aprista Party, the most important political force in the country, which during the 1980s was the party in power (during Alan Garcia's administration). This party, along with the Fujimoristas, was one of the main critics of the work carried out by the Truth and Reconciliation Commission.

18. On the one hand, most truth commissions are not concerned with technically grounding their recommendations for reparation programs. On the other, central banks and ministries of finance have a tendency to exclude reparation expenses from their

financial projections, unless they are certain that these expenses will have an appropriate source of funding.

19. Such is the case of the USA, which openly supported the military dictatorships in Central and South America, and was directly involved in the armed conflict in El Salvador.

20. See Segovia, *Las Relaciones*, op. cit.

21. The US Agency for International Development (USAID), for example, provided initial financial resources (US$600,000) for the Comprehensive Health Care Program [*Programa de Asistencia Integral en Salud*] (PRAIS) in Chile, and financed one of the three pilot programs for compensations that were implemented in some districts in Guatemala. Some European countries and Canada have also supported various compensation programs in Guatemala.

22. This is the same position as the one assumed by the international community regarding financing peace agreements in Central America. For an analysis of this situation see Segovia, 'Domestic Resource Moblization' and *El Rol de la Comunidad Internacional*, op. cit.

23. See Comisión de la Verdad y Reconciliación del Perú, *Informe Final*, vol. 9 (*Recomendaciones*) (Lima, 2003).

24. This statement does not take into account the cases of reparation funds financed by developed countries.

25. For an analysis of measures of reparation in Argentina, Brazil, and Chile see the case studies included in this volume.

26. In fact, reparations for victims were part of the political platform of the *Partidos de la Concertación*. See Elizabeth Lira (Chapter 2, this volume).

27. At the end of 2003, the Chilean government announced new measures of reparation, broadening the benefits of some already existing ones and introducing new reparations measures for cases of torture, which until that point had been excluded from the reparations program. See Gobierno de Chile, *Propuesta de Derechos Humanos del Gobierno* (2003).

28. As was the case in Chile, in Argentina victims of repression were, for the most part, educated members of the urban middle class, a sector that has great social and political influence throughout the country.

29. The issue of reparations created serious divisions within the *Madres de la Plaza de Mayo*, the main victims' organization in the country.

30. For the cases of El Salvador and Haiti, see Segovia (Chapter 4, this volume). For the case of Guatemala see International Center for Transitional Justice (ICTJ) and Asociación Pro Derechos Humanos (APRODEH), *Parámetros para el Diseño de un Programa de Reparaciones en el Perú* (New York/Lima: September, 2002). For the South African case see Colvin (Chapter 5, this volume).

31. In these countries, the weakness of political coalitions is directly related to the profile of victims of human rights violations: the overwhelming majority of them are members of the rural population, suffering from extreme poverty, and in the cases of Guatemala and Peru, part of the marginalized indigenous population. This type of victim is also characterized by low levels of social and political organization, and a virtual absence from urban centers, where the powers of the State reside.

32. These groups resorted to the use of force to put pressure on the government, including demonstrations and blocking roads. The most important actions were the violent

taking of the Peten Airport and building barricades on the main roads that communicate with the Peten region.

33. In order to justify this decision, the government argued that former *patrulleros* were also victims of the internal armed conflict (to the extent that they acted under duress) and for this reason deserved to be compensated. But in addition to this, the government also included among the beneficiaries of compensations, victims of abuse by the Army.

34. President Oscar Berger committed himself during his presidential campaign to complying with the commitments established with the FRG. It had been determined that the compensation to former *patrulleros* (each would receive a total amount of around US$663) would be carried out in three separate payments of US$221. However, up to this date, the government has not been able to fulfill this commitment owing to a lack of public resources, which in turn is a consequence of a low tax burden (the government needs around US$443 million to make the second payment to about 500,000 former *patrulleros*). As a result, former *patrulleros* have mobilized to close down roads and the main routes of access to the country.

35. See Segovia (Chapter 4, this volume).

36. A low tax burden means that the government only keeps a small portion of the wealth generated in a country during a year. This makes it difficult for such a government to meet the demands of society.

37. It is a well-known fact that the Rettig Report recommended reparations only for assassinations and the disappeared, excluding the tortured who represented the largest group of victims. Nevertheless, as has been mentioned before, at the end of 2003, the Chilean government announced the inclusion of the tortured as beneficiaries of reparations.

38. The *Bocon Proveedores* Series II bonds were issued in dollars and pesos on December 28, 1994, and the grace period ended in December 2000. It must be pointed out that owing to the financial crisis in 2002, Argentina declared a moratorium and stopped paying the public debt, which affected bonds destined to pay reparations. See María José Guembe (Chapter 1, this volume).

39. An evaluation of the costs of the reparations program in South Africa can be found in Colvin (Chapter 5, this volume).

40. Ibid.

41. For an analysis of munificence, in other words the magnitude of benefits of reparation programs, as well as other categories, see Pablo de Greiff, 'Reparations Efforts in International Perspective: What Compensation Contributes to the Achievement of Imperfect Justice', in *To Repair the Irreparable: Reparation and Reconstruction in South Africa*, Erik Doxtader and Charles Villa-Vicencio, eds. (Claremont, South Africa: David Philip Publishers, 2004).

42. An in-depth analysis of this point can be found in Segovia (Chapter 4, this volume).

CHAPTER 20

REPARATIONS AND MICROFINANCE SCHEMES

HANS DIETER SEIBEL
WITH ANDREA ARMSTRONG

1. INTRODUCTION: IN SEARCH OF SUSTAINABLE IMPACT OF REPARATION PAYMENTS

Once a transitional government has taken the difficult decision to issue reparations payments, or material compensation, to victims of human rights abuse, the question then becomes one of effectiveness. How should reparations payments be designed such that they best redress the claims of justice of victims and others, and ideally facilitate a qualitative improvement in the daily lives of victims? As articulated by Pablo de Greiff, although reparations programs cannot restore the *status quo ante* for victims, they can still have a political, social, medical, and economic impact on the lives of victims if, as the chapters in this volume suggest, they are rooted in a long-term vision for society as a whole.

In many countries, self-help groups and indigenous informal savings and credit associations are the only civil society institutions that survive the breakdown of society. They represent the social capital[1] for the reconstruction of local financial institutions and even of local social relationships. In short, they are a potential resource for societies transitioning to democracy and coming to terms with past histories of abuse. The challenge for many transitional societies becomes utilizing existing social resources to achieve broader political and economic goals through making institutional commitments to acknowledge the past and construct a positive future.

2. THE POTENTIAL CONTRIBUTIONS OF MICROFINANCE INSTITUTIONS

Designing reparations payments so that they contribute to such a vision and facilitate individual and societal investment in the future is an ambitious and in our opinion achievable goal if combined with a focus on microfinance institutions (MFIs). The development of informal institutional frameworks that facilitate cooperation and collaboration within communities provides a structure for individuals to discuss and debate their visions for the future. For example, after establishing a community banking institution, shareholders must choose among a variety of projects and enterprises, all of which have applied for a loan. Perhaps they decide to provide the first loan to a local farmer, increasing the food supply within the community. Perhaps the shareholders believe their most pressing need is education and provide the next loan to a trader specializing in school supplies and textbooks. Particularly in the beginning of the institution's life, with each loan decision, shareholders make important decisions regarding the future shape of their community.

Moreover, experience in many countries has shown that, without an appropriate institutional framework, the benefits of one-time payments tend to be short-lived and unsustainable. There are two prerequisites of sustainable impact, which are mutually reinforcing: sustainable income-generating activities (IGA) and sustainable local financial institutions for the financing of such activities and other needs. However, in postconflict and postauthoritarian societies, such institutions have been destroyed or disrupted.

In this study, the main focus is on the second prerequisite, that is, MFIs,[2] which in many countries have now evolved from unsustainable projects to sustainable organizations.[3] There appear to be real opportunities to enhance the lives of victims through linking reparations payments to the development of MFIs. MFIs are defined here as formal, semiformal, or informal institutions[4] providing financial services (microsavings, microcredit, microinsurance) of a scale significantly below those of commercial banks[5] and to customers normally considered unbankable. One simplistic analogy for MFIs is a communal savings account. To belong to this informal organization, an individual must contribute to the communal account, typically referred to as 'buying shares of the institution'. The contributors become owners of the institution and can participate in the management of the MFI. The MFI uses these contributions to fund small-scale loans to individual members, with varying rates of interest that increase the overall cash holdings in the MFI. As the resources of the MFI grow from interest payments and newly opened savings accounts, it is able to award a larger number of loans within the community, thereby supporting local entrepreneurship and development.[6]

By converting reparations payments into shares and beneficiaries into shareholders of MFIs, the former victims turn into owners of sustainable local institutions at the grass-roots level of an emerging civil society. Microfinance, as a system of self-reliant local financial institutions—fuelled by reparation payments in addition to other resources—can play a crucial role in sustainable economic and even political development.

Experience has shown that networks of such institutions can be successfully built within two to three years; sustainability in terms of self-management, self-financing and legal framework of the MFIs and their network may take another five years. In terms of sustainable impact, there is no alternative to institution-building.

MFIs could be instrumental in providing an institutional framework for sustainable impact on recipients of reparation payments in three ways:

1. by offering a secure place for the safe-keeping and accumulation of reparation payments and savings, thereby strengthening the self-financing capacity of the recipients of reparation payments and other depositors;
2. by offering credit for investments and working capital to small and microentrepreneurs and attracting external finance of increasing size;
3. by offering recipients of reparations the opportunity of building MFIs, thereby mobilizing the self-help capacity of the victims as shareholder-owners and users, particularly in situations where no functioning institutions exist.

The approach presented here applies to poor countries emerging from civil war, total crisis, or repressive regimes; and to situations where large numbers or clusters of people are eligible for reparations in the form of compensation. It is inspired by the concern for sustainable impact, in two respects: (*a*) Economically, reparation payments which are not invested profitably may be wasted and may deepen the existing sense of hopelessness. Investing them in MFIs creates a source of funding and initiates a process of sustainable growth from profits generated. (*b*) Politically, investing reparation payments in MFIs is a way of facilitating a common future. It creates a network of relationships based on positive and repeated interaction. It creates ownership and control of institutions; this is fundamental and far more important than ownership of things material. Local financial institutions owned and controlled by the community or community members, after being trained in bookkeeping and financial management, are among the basic building blocks of civil society. In this way, linking reparations programs to MFIs can contribute to goals of recognition, civic trust, and social solidarity.[7]

Their potential for growth, if maintained over long periods of time, is unlimited. Although MFIs are particularly well suited to some postconflict contexts, microfinance is not a poor solution for poor people in poor countries. In Germany, and similarly in other countries in the region, microfinance emerged from informal beginnings under conditions of extreme poverty but the resulting savings and cooperative banks now account for more than 50 percent of banking assets. This is the chance of reparation payments: to lay the foundation for the emergence of civil institutions which put large numbers of the poor in control of savings and credit as the fuel of growth and development.[8] The development of MFIs can serve two crucially important goals for societies in transition: (*a*) it can increase the sustained effectiveness of reparations payments themselves; and (*b*) through its facilitation of decentralized economic authority, it creates alternative nongovernmental sources of power and is a potential impediment to future abuses by the central government.[9]

3. The Potential Risks of a Microfinance Approach

The approach proposed here is novel. There is some experience with microfinance in postconflict situations, but none with the use of reparations in building MFIs as instruments in a political or economic transition. First, it must be acknowledged that linking reparations payments with MFIs creates risks for victims, many of whom suffer from poor physical and mental health as a result of their abuse. The basic premise of local MFIs is that the initial loan recipients will indeed repay the loan and accrued interest on schedule. Particularly in a transitional context, when remnants of the old regime may still rule and institutional reform has yet to be enacted, local entrepreneurs operate in an uncertain context that threatens their ability to repay the loans. The social ties that make loan recipients accountable not only to the MFI, but to the larger community, are still in flux as individuals reevaluate their relationship to their neighbors in light of the country's transition. Without an initially successful rate of repayment, the MFI will fail those who most need it to succeed.

Second, MFIs are owned and managed by the community of shareholders. It therefore requires some knowledge of accounting and banking procedures, which may not be present within small rural communities. So in addition to the issuance of reparations payments, the community will also require specialized training from either governmental or nongovernmental authorities. Particularly as the institution grows, in terms of both capital and new members, the risk of failure increases unless continuing training takes place.

Third, similar to other cash payments, reparations may reinforce existing gender inequalities within society. The existence of new sources of power and authority, whether institutions or cash, inevitably inspires new attempts to control or secure it for oneself. Historically, women have frequently borne the brunt of this trend, as patriarchal societies either exclude them from management of the MFI or seize control of the payments issued to women. Strategies that aimed to increase rural women's access to credit have sometimes led to their exploitation as sources of capital and credit rather than their empowerment.[10] In contrast, there are numerous other cases where microfinance has given women unprecedented control, as for example in India where, as of mid-2004, women constitute 90 percent of the membership in more than one million self-help groups linked to banks.[11]

As the challenges above illustrate, the failure of an MFI within a transitional justice context is not solely an economic event. Within the context of reparations payments, it has implications for the political project of building a new state and a common future. Just as the successful MFI can contribute to the key reparations goals of recognition, civic trust, and social solidarity, the failure of the MFI can contribute to ostracism, generalized distrust, and the single-minded pursuit of self-interest. So while the potential benefits of linking reparations programs with MFIs are great, so too are the risks.

Moreover, microfinance is no panacea; nor is there any single model that fits all cases. In each individual case, one has to study the local situation, examine the international experience, involve all stakeholders, and jointly arrive at an appropriate approach. While training, donor and stakeholder support, and a supportive transitional context can all reduce the risks inherent in this approach, they cannot eliminate them. But reparations programs that include a microfinance component can build on decades, if not centuries, of history[12] and lessons learned that illustrate how microfinance institutions can help to alleviate poverty, increase self-reliance, and improve people's quality of life.

4. THE MICROFINANCE REVOLUTION

During the last two or three decades, there have been fundamental changes in development finance, captured by such terms as financial deregulation, development bank reform and the so-called microfinance revolution. These changes have led to a *paradigm shift* from subsidized targeted credit to financial systems development and institution-building, opening up a world of new options for agencies providing reparation payments to victims of human rights abuses. In particular, consensus has developed around certain principles (*best practices*)[13] with a dual concern for institutional sustainability and outreach to the poor.

Inspired by the success of the Marshall Plan in reconstructing Europe and rehabilitating its institutions after World War II, *capital transfer* emerged as the principal strategy of growth and modernization during the 1950s and 1960s. This has shaped the economic environment of many developing countries until today, especially the poorest among them, by making governments policymakers, bankers, and investors. Yet, governments performed poorly in each of these tasks. Despite good intentions, government involvement in most countries resulted in totally inadequate financial infrastructures, the substitution of external debts for domestic resources, bank failures, and severe misallocation of scarce resources—all summed up in a single term: *financial repression*.[14] Vested interests and perverse incentives kept the repressive system alive, benefiting a select number of politicians, public servants, bank staff, and big borrowers.

Such policies also had political consequences of centralizing economic power in select hands and effectively undermining the emergence of alternative sources of power or authority. In many countries, financial repression was part and parcel of a larger political strategy, which relied on abusive tactics to maintain economic and political control.

Due to the dismal performance of development banks, many of the major donors, around 1980, pulled out their support, while governments found it increasingly difficult to provide budgets for loans that were not repaid. Many development banks collapsed or were technically bankrupt, which harmed the organizations and societies through which assistance had been channeled.

Instead, donor support, albeit on a reduced scale, shifted to nongovernmental organizations (NGOs), particularly credit NGOs. They were supported by international NGOs and eventually also by bilateral and multilateral donors. This shift was initially not accompanied by a new paradigm: donors supplied the funds for loans; credit NGOs were not authorized to encourage voluntary savings; interest rates were subsidized; repayment rates were low; viability was abysmally low and self-reliance nonexistent. The new concern with poverty alleviation seemed to justify the need for capital transfer and low interest rates. How could donors possibly expect the poor and the very poor to mobilize savings, build their own institutions, and invest their loans at profit rates that would enable them to pay market rates of interest and repay their loans on time?

Not surprisingly, many credit NGOs met with a fate similar to that of development banks, combining donor dependency with a lack of both sustainability and outreach. As in Ireland and Germany during the eighteenth and nineteenth centuries,[15] it took some trials and errors to realize that, given the right incentives and institutional framework, the poor do save; they are responsible investors; they do repay their loans; and they may even own their financial institutions. It was also found that in many countries, women figure prominently among the prudent borrower-investors.

In an increasing number of countries, including some transitioning from abusive regimes (e.g. the Balkans, Rwanda, Cambodia), there have been notable changes from the old world of directed credit to a new world of sustainable institutions. In this new world, governments make determined efforts to create a *conducive policy environment*, with

- new legal forms for local financial institutions,
- deregulated interest rates,
- prudential regulation and supervision of financial institutions, and
- a deregulation of foreign exchange and the trade regime.

Responding to the demands of their customers, institutions reform and provide a variety of savings and credit services with the potential for income-generating activities, which generate funds to issue loans and expand. A number of agricultural and rural banks, cooperatives and other rural and urban MFIs have learned *to manage their risks by:*

- diversifying their portfolio,
- analyzing the investment and repayment capacity of the entire household,
- providing a range of appropriate financial services,
- starting small and granting repeat loans of increasing size,
- providing incentives to both staff and borrowers to enforce timely repayment,
- changing from group to individual loans and offering opportunities for graduation to larger loans as need be, and
- expanding into remote areas through linkages with self-help groups.

The transition from the old to the new world of development finance, as described below, is a challenging framework to any institution and donor agency aiming at sustainable poverty alleviation and development.

The promise of this new world of finance, for transitioning and stable regimes alike, has only just started. In most countries, the situation is highly complex and frequently contradictory. For example, failing and prospering institutions may exist side by side; governments pass laws on market-driven institutions, yet continue subsidizing the interest rates of others; banks mobilize large amounts of

Table 20.1 From the old world of directed credit to the new world of financial systems development and institution-building: do's and don'ts

	Don't support: *The old world of directed credit*	Do support: *The new world of institution-building*
Policy environment	Financial repression	Prudential deregulation, development of financial systems
Legal framework	Lack of private MFIs	New legal forms for previously unregulated MFIs
Development approach	Supply-driven	Demand-driven
Institutional focus	Monopoly institutions	Various competing financial institutions
Clients perceived as	Beneficiaries	Customers
Selection of clients	Targeting by donors and governments	Self-selection
Incentives for bank staff and borrowers	Perverse: leading to fund misallocation	Efficient allocation of funds
Regulation and supervision (R&S)	Cooperatives, MFIs, development banks unsupervised; donors keep distressed institutions alive	Microfinance units in central banks; regulation of rural banks/MFIs; closing of distressed institutions
Agricultural finance	Lack of self-financing; restricted credit according to government directions	Self-financing from savings; external financing for profitable investments
Remote and marginal areas	Futile attempts of donors to drive ill-suited MFIs into remote areas	Self-managed savings-based self-help groups and cooperatives operating at low cost
Self-reliance	NGOs, agricultural development banks barred from deposit-taking; donor and government dependency	Self-financing through deposits and profits; institutional autonomy
Sustainability	Donors, governments fail to insist on performance standards and sustainability: lack of healthy banks	Increasing numbers of self-sustaining institutions of any type and ownership
Access to financial services	Very limited access to savings, credit, insurance	Spectacular increase in outreach to the poor; profitable if interest rates are free

excess liquidity,[16] yet the government borrows money from international donors and increases its external debts.

Under adverse conditions, as in transitional situations, governments and donors tend to ignore all lessons taught (and evidently not learned), reverting to the old world of development finance. Driven by pressures to show impact immediately, it is tempting for agencies administering reparations to pursue centralized, government- or donor-driven policies. Yet, *only the slow way of involving the victims of abuses as partners and owners in building sustainable institutions* will lead to sustainable program impact: on both the victims in their capacity as micro-entrepreneurs and on the institutions they create.

Box 20.1 Requirements of sustainable microfinance

Sustainable financial institutions mobilize their own resources, provide financial services according to demand, cover their costs from their operational income, have their loans repaid, make a profit, and finance their expansion from deposits and retained earnings. *Resource mobilization* comprises equity, savings deposits, retained earnings, and commercial borrowings, augmented by external resources such as soft loans and grants. Of these resources, three are fundamental to self-reliance and dynamic growth: savings deposits, retained earnings, and other equity. *Financial services* comprise credit for various purposes and savings deposit facilities; they may further include money transfer, check clearing, and insurance. Insurance may serve the triple function of borrower protection, loan protection and resource mobilization. *Sustainable institutions* need an appropriate legal status which authorizes them to carry out all these functions; and they need to be properly regulated and effectively supervised. *Financial systems development* comprises processes of establishing a conducive regulatory environment (including a legal framework, prudential norms and effective supervision), an adequate infrastructure of viable small and large financial institutions, adequate demand-oriented financial products and good operational practices.

Experience around the developing world shows that virtually any type of financial institution, including commercial banks, can fail in the face of bad policy and bad management. On the other hand, experience also shows that any type of financial institution, once reformed and well managed, can provide finance in a profitable and sustainable way for a wide variety of income-generating activities, emergencies and consumer purposes. Among the *flagships of rural and microfinance institutions* are:

- Agricultural development banks like BRI in Indonesia, BAAC in Thailand, BNDA in Mali, CNCA in Burkina Faso, BNA in Tunisia, BK in Iran;
- Specialized banks for the poor like Grameen Bank in Bangladesh;
- Rural and community banks in Nigeria, Ghana, Tanzania, the Philippines, Indonesia;
- Commercial mesobanks[17] like Centenary RDB in Uganda, CMF in Uganda, EBS in Kenya, Banco Caja Social in Colombia, Micro Enterprise Bank (MEB) in Bosnia;

- Member-owned financial cooperatives like SACCOs in Kenya and Tanzania, credit unions in Madagascar, People's Credit Funds in Vietnam, Small Farmers Cooperatives Ltd. in Nepal, savings and credit cooperatives in the Philippines;
- NGOs like CHF/JACP in Jordan, UMU in Uganda, EKI in Bosnia, ASA in Bangladesh;
- Credit-NGOs establishing banks like SEWA in India, ACLEDA Bank in Cambodia, CARD and others in the Philippines, Bina Swadaya and Purba Danarta in Indonesia, K-Rep in Kenya, BancoSol in Colombia, Compartamos in Mexico;
- Member-owned village funds like *sanadiq* (singular *sanduq*) in Syria, *caisses villageoises*/village banks in numerous countries;
- Member-owned self-help groups as autonomous financial intermediaries linked to banks in India, Indonesia, the Philippines, Nepal, Nigeria, Burkina Faso, Mali.

These institutions rely on four commercial principles for their success:[18]

- mobilizing financial resources locally;
- having their loans repaid;
- covering their costs; and
- financing the expansion of outreach from deposits and retained earnings.

5. DILEMMAS IN THE DESIGNING OF A REPARATIONS-MICROFINANCE FRAMEWORK

In recent years large numbers of developing and transitional countries have experienced situations of *crisis*, following political, economic or natural disasters, or *total crisis*, triggered by war or totalitarian oppression, in which the very structure of society has been put out of function. In a total crisis, the state virtually ceases to exist, national economies disintegrate, and social and political structures melt away. A significant number of people are exposed to a day-to-day struggle for survival, often separated from their homes and deprived of their usual sources of livelihood. In particular, total crisis means that national governmental and civil society organizations have been destroyed; the production and market distribution of goods and services has been disrupted; institutional capacity for policy decisions and planning at national level has been eliminated or curtailed; communities and informal or traditional institutions have been detached from the broader society and markets; household economies have reverted to subsistence and survival strategies; and large numbers of individuals have been physically and socially displaced and were subject to traumatizing experiences of violence. The problems are almost too numerous to name, and, combined, they create a context that threatens not only the viability of a reparations program, but also society's larger transition to a functioning, just, and peaceful state.

It is within this context that designers of reparations programs face intense and difficult decisions, such as whether to make microfinance institutions a mandatory aspect of the reparations programs and how victims and perpetrators should relate to one another within this process.

Governments face immense financial and political hurdles in designing reparations programs, which often leads to a governmental preference for collective reparations programs. Collective payments and programs allow them to spend less per individual, while still providing reparations to the majority of victims. Through collective programs, the government recognizes that pain and suffering occurred, although for victims, this falls short of recognizing their individual pain. The use of collective grants may also allow governments to label existing infrastructure and development funds as reparations funds, thereby enacting a reparations program with little additional expense. While this may occur because the transitional government is simply not committed to a reparations program, it is also an understandable attempt to stretch limited budgets and make each dollar count twice.

Governments also usually prefer to provide services in kind, rather than direct cash payments. As is common in many stable regimes, some proponents of in-kind services do not trust recipients to spend cash payments as intended, despite numerous studies that show cash payments to be more efficient economically and socially. Other proponents stress the state capacity-building aspects of in-kind services. Providing services such as health care can simultaneously create employment and strengthen the state system while caring for victims of the past regime. The issuance of direct cash payments, while perhaps providing an economic lift through consumer spending, does not have nearly the same state-strengthening effect as in-kind services. Through the provision of services, instead of cash, the government in effect invests in itself and builds its own capacity, while caring for the needs of victims.

Both of these preferences, for the collective and service or in-kind benefits, can lead to development policies that masquerade as reparations programs. Yet, as other chapters in this volume affirm, victims of human rights abuse have a right to reparations above and beyond their right as citizens to development initiatives.[19] Simply put, governments will significantly harm the political and social aims of reparations if they substitute the provision of clean water for reparations programs. Moreover, the reparations payments have a value above and beyond what they can materially purchase. In many societies, cash implies a tangible commitment to repair past wrongs—particularly when compared to lofty but unimplemented developmental goals and inspirational speeches. Hence, in a variety of ways, government preferences may conflict with preferences of victims and indeed, the original aims of the reparations program.[20]

Within this context, there are several scenarios for introducing microfinance institutions as part of a reparations program. States could issue collective grants to villages and subdistricts to be used as start-up capital for a local microfinance institution. All members of that particular community would become immediate shareholders and eligible for savings accounts and small-scale loans. Although no solution can be absolutely perfect, this option presents significant difficulties. First, it fails to distinguish between victims and those who did not suffer directly, or worse, those who aided or participated in the abuse. Therefore, this option may be more successful when abuses targeted particular areas or when victims are con-centrated in certain locations, such as townships or rural homelands. Second, because community members do not consciously choose to take part, this option can reduce the sense of local ownership and responsibility. The implications of this may vary from diminished perceptions of self-help to the failure of the MFI because members were not personally invested in the outcome.

In a second scenario, governments could issue smaller collective grants to villages or subdistricts as the start-up capital for local MFIs, but also individual cash payments, with which beneficiaries may choose whether to buy shares or open accounts in the newly created microfinance institution. Those who do not receive cash payments would have the option to buy shares as well, but no one would be required to participate. This option does recognize individual suffering, but also provides a neutral space where, finances permitting, other members of the com-munity may also participate. Low-level perpetrators would indeed be allowed to participate, but their cash contribution to an organization that at least initially would be owned by victims could contribute to restoring inequalities of power within the community. Particularly for victims that have suffered abuse which led to their subsequent ostracism, such as disfigurement, amputation, or rape, these types of institutions can promote social inclusion and participation by facilitating interpersonal contact.

Lastly, governments could issue individual grants with the advice that victims should use those funds to create a local MFI and buy shares. As in each of the scenarios, the government could provide training and assistance, directly or via NGOs, throughout the country to facilitate the creation of the MFIs. Of course, the difficulty here is that MFIs require a minimum number of members to be finan-cially viable, depending on the amount of the cash payment. If the majority of cash recipients choose not to participate, this denies others who may wish to buy shares the opportunity to do so. This option is also the least preferred by governments who hope to wring political, social, and economic results out of reparations programs.

6. MICROFINANCE STRATEGIES: DELIVERY MECHANISMS AND SUSTAINABILITY

Prerequisites of Sustainable Impact

In addition to delineating what kinds of benefits victims will receive, it is equally important to decide how those benefits will be delivered. The method of delivery, in this instance, of cash payments can impact the political goals of the reparations program through their economic impact on the lives of victims. As we have argued throughout this paper, having a sustainable economic impact increases the probability that the reparations program will meet its political aims.

For a sustainable impact, the following conditions have to be met:

- profitable investment of payments in income-generating activities;[21]
- access to deposit facilities for the safe-keeping and accumulation of savings (derived from reparation payments and profits) as a source of self-financing;
- access to credit (at commercial rates) as a source of external financing;
- the repayment of loans on time as a prerequisite for repeat loans of increasing size.

There appear to be four delivery vehicles for issuing reparations payments to victims: (1) Direct payment through specialized agencies; (2) Payment through commercial banks; (3) Payment through credit NGOs; or (4) Investment in local financial institutions (co-)owned by recipients of reparation payments. The likelihood of sustainable impact of reparations on the life and well-being of recipients depends on how payments are transacted, increasing from (1) to (4) on the scale above.

Direct payments through specialized agencies, channeling funds on a temporary basis, may have some positive impact in individual cases (likely to be reported as success stories), but are unlikely to substantially and durably benefit a larger number of recipients. Chances of sustainable impact may improve somewhat if payments are administered through commercial banks, which are usually among the first institutions re-established after a crisis. If the beneficiaries are required to open a bank account first and payment is made through this account, there is a modest chance that this might lead to a lasting bank relationship. In this case, some other agency would have to provide training and consultancy services to guide the beneficiaries in their banking relations as well as in their investments. However, exceptions notwithstanding,[22] few commercial banks have shown an inclination to deal with small customers; on the contrary, many erect formal and informal barriers to keep them away, for example, through sizeable minimum deposits and unfriendly treatment.

As the example above illustrates, economic sustainability is not the only factor in choosing a suitable delivery agent for issuing reparations payments. Disrespectful or denigrating treatment by the delivery agent will negatively affect the victim's overall perception of the reparations program.[23] In addition, the type of delivery agent chosen will impact how involved and empowered victims feel in the founding of their local MFI. For example, if recipients receive reparations payments along the same lines that they receive their social welfare assistance, then payments are more likely to be perceived as state charity instead of state obligation.

In most postcrisis situations, NGOs are the major agencies for providing financial services. They are capitalized by donor agencies, international NGOs, bilateral or multilateral agencies. They provide microcredit and rudimentary savings services, usually in the form of compulsory savings as part of the credit package. NGOs have a number of strengths, which are of particular importance in countries destroyed or distressed by crisis:

- they are easily and quickly established and do not require a complex legal framework;
- given their orientation to poor target groups, they are able to communicate with the poor and distressed;
- and they are flexible in providing a range of services, including, in addition to finance, microenterprise training and consultancy as well as education, health care, counseling and others directly related to demand and felt needs.

Yet, some of the strengths of the NGOs are also their weaknesses First, while NGOs are easily established in a legal void, they lack the legal status of a financial institution and tend to feel quite comfortable with donor support and the absence of regulation and supervision. Donor dependency and lack of self-reliance in terms of operational and loanable funds have two repercussions: lack of viability (with operational self-sufficiency rates frequently far below 100 percent); and lack of growth of outreach, which would require rapidly increasing internal resources derived from savings and retained earnings. In addition, without legal status and effective regulation and supervision, growth has invariably taken an inordinately long time and eventually hit a barrier which only well-managed and properly supervised financial institutions have overcome.

This first weakness of credit NGOs is surmountable, as evidenced by the transformation of credit NGOs to rural banks in Sierra Leone, the Philippines, and Uganda.[24] Issuing reparations payments through credit NGOs can lead to economically sustainable outcomes for a large number of recipients, if these NGOs plan for their eventual conversion into a formal institution.

The second weakness of NGOs—lack of local ownership and transparent governance—however, has yet to be successfully overcome. As a result, there is little orientation towards profit-making and growth and no accountability for losses. The problem of ownership for credit NGOs is also complicated by donor involvement. One solution would be cooperative ownership by the clients; this however has rarely been accepted by the board and management of NGOs. Converting credit NGOs into member-owned institutions may be a desirable option, but does not seem to meet with much sympathy among their donor-stakeholders.

So although credit NGOs can facilitate the issuance of reparations payments, they fail to achieve many of the political goals of reparations programs. The collaborative and interactive processes of institution-building and allocating loans are processes that belong to owners, not users. If stakeholders cannot meaningfully participate in the direction and purpose of their microfinance institution, then linking microfinance institutions with reparations programs is of little value politically.

7. INVESTING IN LOCAL FINANCIAL INSTITUTIONS: THE CONTRIBUTION OF REPARATION PAYMENTS TOWARDS SUSTAINABLE INSTITUTIONAL REHABILITATION AND CAPACITY-BUILDING

One of the biggest mistakes often made in a post-conflict environment is the focus on speed of loan disbursement. Getting money out the door quickly often entails a very limited institutional development focus, which is the core behind best practice microfinance principles. By not focusing on institution building, projects often pollute the environment for those who are attempting to abide by best practice microfinance.[25]

Types of Local Financial Institutions

A different approach, with ownership clearly established from the outset, would be to support locally owned financial institutions, (co-)owned by recipients of reparation payments. These are mostly small local institutions, which are flexible and adaptive. Because of their institutional size, their sole business is microfinance. They may be formal, semiformal or informal, or combine two levels, as in the case of a village bank with a surrounding network of informal savings and credit associations as retailers. They may have great evolutionary potential: from informal to semiformal, from semiformal to formal, and from unit banking to branching-out. There are three major types of locally owned institutions:

Member-owned institutions based on *social solidarity* are typically self-financed and self-managed. They can be formed by any type and number of people within or across neighboring communities, comprising microentrepreneurs, small farmers, women, and the poor. Membership is normally contingent upon an equity capital contribution but may also include other criteria (e.g. gender as in the case of a women's bank, occupation as in the case of a market or traders' bank) and is a prerequisite for access to the institution's services. In some cases such institutions are also open to nonmembers but on different terms. Member-owned institutions rely fully or largely on their own resources, i.e. on savings and equity including retained earnings. Equity contributions (*shares*) may be equal (as in formal cooperatives) or unequal (as in many indigenous savings and credit associations and in the financial services associations (FSAs) presented below); similarly, votes may be equal or tied to voting shares. Among the financially self-reliant institutions owned by their members are vast numbers of group-based informal financial institutions. Among them are the ubiquitous rotating and nonrotating savings and credit associations. Whether nonformal institutions can evolve into banks depends on the legal framework, which is of course subject to change.

Community-owned financial institutions may be people- or local government-based. They are *people-based* if the members of the community are either directly (through individual or household membership) or corporately owners of the institution. There must be a provision in the rules and regulations or bylaws that the community members or its recognized representatives have a say in the running of their affairs. This should also be reflected in the perceptions of the people, who should consider the institutions as *theirs*. In some developing countries community banks are *government-based*, be they government-owned or government-imposed and perceived as government institutions. In fact the dividing line between institutions owned by local government and those owned by the people of the community is not always sharply drawn and may be as much a legal as a social issue. A useful quantitative indicator may be the extent to which community banks depend on government resources versus savings and retained earnings as a source of funds.

Privately owned financial institutions are owned by one or several wealthier individuals. Examples are the rural banks in the Philippines and Indonesia. Sometimes they are owned by large numbers of not-so-wealthy individuals, with shares similar in size to those in cooperatives. The difference lies in governance: cooperatives are governed by the principle 'one person, one vote'; in privately owned institutions, registered perhaps as stock companies, voting power is by number of shares. Financial service associations in Benin, Guinea, and Uganda permit unlimited ownership of shares, but restrict the number of voting shares.

Strategies for Promoting Locally Owned Financial Institutions: Upgrading, Innovating, Linking[26]

Informal financial institutions (IFIs) of indigenous origin are widespread in many developing countries, particularly in Africa and Asia.[27] Organized self-help is part of the social capital of almost every ethnic group, comprising a range of institutions referred to by terms in the local language. In a stable environment, they typically mobilize their own resources, cover their costs, have their loans repaid, and finance their growth from their profits. They are generally renowned for the effectiveness of social control. There are two types: individual intermediaries, such as moneylenders and deposit collectors; and indigenous group-based intermediaries. The emphasis here is on the latter, i.e., self-help organizations owned and managed by groups of local people, poor and nonpoor.

When the state with its institutions collapses, institutions that are part of the traditional fabric usually remain. In fact, in the absence of other options, indigenous institutions may gain in outreach and vigor. For example, in many parts of Ethiopia, *edir*, the ubiquitous funeral society, has evolved during the crisis years into a village-based financial institution with a range of innovative financial services to its members. Some NGOs, like the Norwegian Redd Barna, have built on that basis.

In postconflict situations, informal finance as a *cooperative coping mechanism* has been found to develop much more quickly than semiformal or formal microfinance, to do so at low cost, and to be more appropriate in terms of products and services. With increasing stability in the postconflict environment, the following shifts have been observed: from loans in kind to loans in cash; from short-term to longer-term loans; from trust to trust-cum-collateral. Both consumption and production loans for low investments and quick returns are heavily in demand, in that order.[28]

Reparation payments may be used for groups of recipients, together with people who bring in resources of their own, first to establish such IFIs according to local traditions, and then to upgrade them. This may entail:

- enhancing management skills and operational practices;
- transforming rotating and nonrotating savings and credit associations, funeral societies and similar IFIs into permanent financial intermediaries;
- upgrading to semiformal financial institutions;
- mainstreaming and integrating into the formal financial sector.

Where informal financial institutions are lacking, new financial service associations (FSAs) can be established.[29] FSAs are built on the principles of indigenous nonrotating savings and credit associations: proximity, local financial intermediation, ownership and self-management by the poor, self-reliance, and sustainability. Thus, the FSA concept is a flexible model of microfinancial intermediation in rural areas, resting on member-owned financial structures that are initiated, owned, and operated by the villagers themselves. In the restrictive policy environments, many FSAs have preferred to remain informal rather than register as savings and credit cooperatives, which are regulated by the law. Operating outside any formal regulation and supervision certainly is a risk to their growth and long-term sustainability; but during the start-up phase, this would be an advantage in postconflict situations where a formal institutional framework has yet to evolve singular.[30]

Sanadiq (singular *sanduq*), a concept based on ancient Arab traditions, are member-owned local financial institutions in Syria, a command economy where all banks have been state-owned. With a mixture of member-equity and external equity contributions, the *sanadiq* have been shaped in their structure and functioning by the local people in Jabal al-Hoss through an intense participatory process and not by any authorities. Support has come from the Ministry of Agriculture and Agrarian Reform and UNDP. It is not rare that women—among them a mother of ten—are the better entrepreneurs, perhaps ushering in a small social revolution.[31]

Reparation payments can be instrumental in establishing *self-help groups as informal financial institutions* or in the upgrading of such groups to semiformal and perhaps formal levels. Yet, without integration into national financial markets and access to capital markets at a later stage, there are limits to their growth, which in turn imposes limits on the growth of the micro and small enterprises of the members of such institutions. Linkage banking, by contrast, has opened the way for virtually unlimited growth.

Linkage banking, or SHG banking, as a strategy for linking banks with informal financial intermediaries and self-help groups (SHGs), is a three-pronged approach:

- mobilizing local resources through member-owned local financial intermediaries and providing access to credit from commercial sources;
- integrating these SHGs/IFIs into national financial markets;
- enabling banks to reach out to smallholders and microentrepreneurs as a new market segment.

Linkage banking has widespread economic and political benefits for societies recovering from massive histories of abuse. It can reduce the transaction costs of lenders and borrowers and simultaneously of deposit-takers and depositors. NGOs and other nonfinancial organizations have contributed to social mobilization, training and consultancy services; some have also acted as financial intermediaries in the inception stage when banks lacked confidence in informal groups. SHGs also deposited substantial amounts of savings voluntarily in banks as reserves. In addition to direct effects on bank profits, SHG Banking has *indirect commercial effects* on banks in terms of improved overall vibrancy in banking activities. *Indirect benefits* at village level include the spreading of thrift and financial self-reliance and of a credit culture among villagers, microentrepreneurial experience, growth of assets and incomes, the spreading of financial management skills, and the decline of private moneylending. *Intangible social benefits* are reportedly many: self-confidence and empowerment of women in civic affairs and local politics, improved school enrolment and women's literacy, better family planning and health, improved sanitation, reduction of drinking and smoking among men, and a decline in adherence to local extremism.

8. CONCLUSION: NEW OPPORTUNITIES

Whether building on local custom or establishing new informal institutions, a growing body of evidence shows that MFIs are an important part of building sustainable economic futures. Designers of reparations programs can take advantage of these positive outcomes by linking the issuance of reparations payments to the establishment or development of microfinance institutions. Moreover, if successful, the development of MFIs will further the political aims of the overall reparations program and contribute to a qualitative improvement in the lives of victims.

The use of microfinance institutions also presents new opportunities to external donors to contribute to reparations programs.[32] As the case of El Salvador illustrates, external donors are extremely reluctant to fund reparations programs directly. In part, this stems from the conviction that the state should fund reparations itself, as a sign of good faith and apology. It also reflects more general donor imperatives to fund initiatives that will be popular at home, and ideally initiatives that can be captured in a photo prominently featuring the donor country's flag. However, external countries may be more willing to contribute funds to communal savings accounts and facilitate self-help programs.

The economic and political choices in designing sustainable reparations programs are complex, yet the potential contribution of sound and effective programs compels us to investigate new approaches. While the approach in this chapter has never been attempted, there are a variety of lessons to be learned from postconflict development, rural development programs, and the growing field of microfinance. The combination of these insights presents a unique challenge to designers of reparations programs to incorporate the economics of sustainability into political programs for social change.

Notes

1. Social capital is defined here as the shared normative system of a group or organization which shapes the capacity of people to work together and produce results according to the group's or organization's purpose. See Benjamín R. Quiñones and Hans D. Seibel, 'Social Capital in Microfinance Case Studies in the Philippines', *Policy Sciences* 33 (3/4) (2000): 421–33. Reprinted in *Social Capital as a Policy Resource*, John D. Montgomery and Alex Inkeles, eds. (Dordrechot: Kluwer, 2001), 195–207.

2. *Microfinance* was first introduced in 1990, referring to small-scale financial intermediation between savers and borrowers, moving away from a sole emphasis on credit. Meanwhile, the term has been used in many different ways. An MFI is thus not *a particular* type of institution, but *any* type of institution offering small-scale financial services to the poorer sections of society. Some now prefer the term *microbanking* to connote small-scale financial intermediation along commercial lines.

3. Margaret S. Robinson, *The Microfinance Revolution: Sustainable Finance for the Poor* (Washington DC: The World Bank, 2001); Hans D. Seibel, *Financial Systems Development and Microfinance* (Rossdorf: TZ-Verlag; Eschborn: GTZ, 1996); Hans D. Seibel, 'Rural Finance: Mainstreaming Informal Financial Institutions', *Journal of Development Entrepreneurship* 6(1) (2001): 83–95.

4. Formal financial institutions such as banks and finance companies fall under banking and corporate law and are supervised by the central bank or bank superintendency. Semiformal institutions, such as credit NGOs, and savings and credit cooperatives, are officially recognized, but not financially regulated and supervised. Informal institutions of traditional or recent origin, among them self-help groups, are not officially recognized, but may fall under customary law. Any such institution is referred to as a *financial intermediary* if it mobilizes deposits and transforms them into loans.

5. With regard to loan size, there is usually a wide gap between MFIs and commercial banks, the former most likely averaging in the hundreds and sometimes thousands of US dollars and the latter in the tens or hundreds of thousands of US dollars. Agricultural and other development banks frequently offer medium-or large-scale as well as micro-finance services. There is no way of generally defining microfinance in terms of size, as there is wide variation between countries.

6. The by-laws of a rotating savings and credit association (ROSCA) among the Mano in the hinterland of Liberia are an example of how one member-owned MFI operates: 'All members should agree upon one sum of money to be paid every Sunday. And one late to pay that Sunday five cents interest will be added to the sum he is supposed to pay. Members should always put in the income; No matter how hard money business might be; you will have to put in the income. The five officers should agree before the money should be loaned to someone. Any money missing from the bank the Treasurer is responsible to pay for what is missing. Time for the income: Every Sunday'. Hans D. Seibel and Andreas Massing, *Traditional Organizations and Economic Development: Studies of Indigenous Cooperatives in Liberia* (New York: Praeger, 1974), x.

7. See Pablo de Greiff, 'Justice and Reparations' (Chapter 12, this volume).

8. It should be noted that Seibel's personal experience in developing countries is limited to Africa, South and Southeast Asia, and the Middle East.

9. This aspect of government economic and political control is explored more fully in Section 4: 'The Microfinance Revolution'.

10. Anne Marie Goetz and Rina Sen Gupta, 'Who Takes the Credit? Gender, Power and Control Over Loan Use in Rural Credit Programs in Bangladesh', *World Development* 24(1) (1996): 45–63.

11. Hans D. Seibel and Shyam Khadka, 'SHG Banking: A Financial Technology for Very Poor Microentrepreneurs', *Savings and Development* 26(2) (2002): 132–50.

12. Hans D. Seibel, 'History Matters in Microfinance', *Journal of Small Enterprise Development* 14(2) (2003): 10–12.

13. The term *best practices* has been disseminated by the Consultation Group to Assist the Poorest (CGAP) and the World Bank. It refers to a set of principles and should not be understood as a model that can be blindly replicated around the world. This author considers the latter a real risk and prefers the term *good practices* or *sound practices*, indicating that institutional solutions, while adhering to fundamental principles of viability and sustainability, invariably need to be developed, or adapted, within given cultural, social, economic, and political conditions.

14. Ronald McKinnon, *Money and Capital in Economic Development* (Washingdon DC: Brookings Institute, 1973).

15. Dirk Steinwand, The *Alchemy of Microfinance* (Berlin: Verlag für Wissenschaft und Forschung, 2001); Seibel, 'History Matters', op. cit.

16. Since 1995, the Microbanking Division of Bank Rakyat Indonesia has been producing annually between US$1 billion and US$1.5 billion in excess deposits (over and above the amount lent).

17. Mesofinance is a new term suggested here to connote the next rung on the ladder of institutional size, referring to financial services beyond the scope of most MFIs but still far below that of commercial banks. One implication is that, given a general reluctance to take on joint liability beyond a certain magnitude of loans, mesofinance mostly refers to individual loans backed by collateral rather than peer guarantees. Collateral may be formal or nonformal, but is likely to be more formal if larger and longer-term loans are involved.

18. It should be noted that these principles are not new in rural and microfinance. In the absence of external support, they have always been fundamental to indigenous informal financial institutions around the world.

19. See de Greiff (Chapter 12) and Segovia (Chapter 4).

20. See Hamber (Chapter 16).

21. Payments may also be invested in housing, either as a source of rental income or, given the fungibility of money, freeing other income for profitable investments.

22. The Commercial Bank of Sierra Leone might turn out to be such an exception, as it is reportedly making preparations for a new window for small loans. American Refugee Committee (ARC), International Sierra Leone Program, *Finance Salone Business Plan 2002–2007* (Sierra Leone: American Refugee Committee, 2001), 2.

23. As seen in Ariel Colonomos' case study, this is a common criticism of German reparations post-World War II for 'harm to health'. Victims felt the examination procedures (required to qualify for reparations) and, in some instances, the subsequent care provided, were humiliating and demeaning.

24. From Sierra Leone to the Philippines to Uganda, a new generation of credit NGOs are transforming themselves into sustainable microfinance institutions. *Finance Salone* in Sierra Leone will remain under the international management of the American Refugee Committee initially, but the latter is already planning for *Finance Salone* to be 'spun off'

within three years and registered as a local microfinance institution, managed by national staff. With professional local staff and national outreach, *Finance Salone* will be operationally self-sufficient by 2007 and financially self-sufficient by 2009. The Center for Agriculture and Rural Development (CARD) in the Philippines has successfully transformed itself from a credit NGO to a sustainable rural bank using group-lending techniques pioneered by the Grameen Bank in Bangladesh. Similarly, among the credit NGOs in Uganda, there are some 40 or 50 large ones, which may now take advantage of the recently prepared microfinance law and convert into regulated deposit-taking institutions, or directly into a commercial bank, like Centenary RDB. Other examples of banks of NGO origin are BancoSol in Bolivia, Bank Purba Danarta and numerous other NGO banks in Indonesia. For more on these examples see CGAP, *Microfinance Policy Review Sierra Leone* (Washington DC: The World Bank, 2000), and ARC, op. cit., for Sierra Leone; Hans D. Seibel and Delores Torres, 'Are Grameen Replications Sustainable, and Do They Reach the Poor? The Case of CARD Rural Bank in the Philippines', *The Journal of Microfinance* 1(1) (1999): 117–30, for the Philippines; and Hans D. Seibel, 'Centenary Rural Development Bank, Uganda: A Flagship of Rural Bank Reform in Africa', *Small Enterprise Development* 14(3) (2003): 35–46, for Uganda.

25. CGAP, op. cit., 24.

26. Downgrading or downscaling commercial banks is a fourth microfinance development strategy. This is not discussed here, because it would be illusory to request co-ownership by local people. See Hans D. Seibel, 'Upgrading, Downgrading, Linking, Innovating: Microfinance Development Strategies—A Systems Perspective', *Economics and Sociology Occasional Paper No. 2371, Rural Finance Program* (Columbus, OH: Ohio State University, 1997).

27. The institution of rotating savings is ancient, dating back at least to the sixteenth century, when Yoruba slaves carried it to the Caribbean, as part of their institutional luggage—or social capital. Both the term *esusu* and the practice have persisted to this day, as *esu* in the Bahamas, *susu* in Tobago or *sou* in Trinidad. Among the Yoruba in Nigeria today, there is hardly a single adult who is not a member or one or even several *esusu*, numbering anything between two and several dozen of even hundreds of members. The institution exists all over West Africa as well as in many other parts of the world, where it is an integral part of the local microeconomy and referred to with its own vernacular term, e.g, *arisan* in Indonesia, *paluwagan* in the Philippines, *gameya* in Egypt, *ekub* in Ethiopia, and *cuchubal* in Guatemala. Substantial changes have occurred in recent decades. Although with no predetermined pattern, these changes have tended to be in the following directions: from labor, kind or premonetary currency, to cash; from nonfinancial to financial groups; from rotating to nonrotating patterns; from short-lived to permanent groups; from savings only to savings-driven credit. With the expansion of the money economy, they have multiplied, both in number and in diversity. See Seibel, 'Rural Finance', op. cit., 84–5.

28. Alison Williams, Uch Vantha, and Soeng Vouch Ngin, *Post Conflict Microfinance in Cambodia*, http://www.postconflictmicrofinance.org/; accessed 14 November 2005; Tamsin Wilson, 'Microfinance During and After Armed Conflict: Lessons from Angola, Cambodia, Mozambique and Rwanda', The Springfield Centre for Business Development, http://www.postconflictmicrofinance.org/; accessed 14 November 2005.

29. Promoted by the International Fund for Agricultural Development (IFAD), a UN agency.

30. Hans D. Seibel, *Les Associations de Services Financiers (ASF) du PAGER, Républic de Bénin: Institutions de micro finance autofinancées et autogenérées en milieu rural* (Rome: International Fund for Agricultural Development, 2003).

31. Omar Imady and Hans D. Seibel, *Sanduq: A Microfinance Innovation in Jabal Al-Hoss, Syria* (Amman, Jordan: Near East North Africa Regional Agricultural Credit Association, 2003). For further details and a pictorial view see http://www.undp-hoss.com

32. The financing of reparations programs is explored more fully by Segovia (Chapter 19, this volume).

PART III

PRIMARY DOCUMENTS AND LEGISLATION

ARGENTINA

NUNCA MÁS: THE REPORT OF THE ARGENTINE NATIONAL COMMISSION ON THE DISAPPEARED*

Part VI
Recommendations and Conclusions

Recommendations

The facts presented to this Commission in the depositions and testimonies speak for themselves. They lead us to recommend to the various State authorities certain measures which will help to ensure that this curtailment of human rights is never repeated in Argentina. The aim of these recommendations is also to press for a judicial investigation into the facts denounced to us. We therefore recommend:

(a) That the body which replaces this Commission speeds up the procedures involved in bringing before the courts the documents collected during our investigation.

(b) That the courts process with the utmost urgency the investigation and verification of the depositions received by this Commission.

* Source: *Nunca Más: The Report of the Argentine National Commission on the Disappeared* (New York: Farrar Straus Giroux, 1986), 446.

(c) That the appropriate laws be passed to provide the children and/or relatives of the disappeared with economic assistance, study grants, social security, and employment and, at the same time, to authorize measures considered necessary to alleviate the many and varied family and social problems caused by the disappearances.

(d) That laws be passed which:

1. Declare forced abduction a crime against humanity.
2. Support the recognition of and adhesion to national and international human rights organizations.
3. Make the teaching of the defence and diffusion of human rights obligatory in state educational establishments, whether they be civilian, military or police.
4. Strengthen and provide ample support for the measures which the courts need to investigate human rights violations.
5. Repeal any repressive legislation still in force.

LAW 23.466*
PENSIONS FOR RELATIVES OF DISAPPEARED PERSONS

Buenos Aires, October 30, 1986
Official Gazette, February 16, 1987
In force
Regulatory Decree
National Decree 1.228/87

The Senate and the Chamber of Deputies of the Argentine Nation, in solemn session of Congress, etc. pass into law:

Article 1. A tax-free pension is hereby awarded to those persons who make a showing of the following conditions from the moment this law is adopted: (a) Being under 21 years of age; (b) The forced disappearance of one or both parents having taken place before December 10, 1983, justified by complaint filed with a judicial authority with jurisdiction, the former National Commission on the Disappearance of Persons [Comisión Nacional sobre la Desaparición de Personas]

* Laws translated from Spanish by Christian Gerzso and revised by Charles Roberts.

(Decree-Law 158/83) or the Office of the Undersecretary for Human Rights of the Ministry of Interior [Subsecretaría de Derechos Humanos del Ministerio del Interior]. For the purposes of this law, a forced disappearance is understood as meaning when a person has been deprived of his or her personal liberty, followed by the victim's disappearance, or if the person has been detained in clandestine places of detention or deprived in any other way of the right to due process [*derecho de jurisdicción*].

Article 2. In addition, the following relatives of the disappeared person, in charge of the person at the moment of the disappearance or at the moment this law is adopted, shall be qualified to receive the benefits of this law: (a) The spouse or person living in consensual union for at least five (5) years immediately preceding the disappearance, concurrent with their minor children, if any; (b) The parents and/or siblings disabled for work who do not perform any remunerated activity or enjoy retirement benefits, a pension, or other tax-free benefit; (c) The minor siblings who are orphans without father or mother who normally lived with the disappeared person before the disappearance. Amended by: Law 23.690 Art. (O.G. 8/16/89). Clause (c) replaced.

Article 3. The total amount of the benefit established by the present law shall be equivalent to the minimum amount awarded by the pension system for ordinary retirement to workers in the employ of another. For the purposes of disability, the provisions of Law 18.037 (T.O. in 1976), as amended, shall apply. Amended by: Law 23.793 Art. 1 Replaced (O.G. 8/03/90). Statutory Reference: Law 18.037.

Article 4. All beneficiaries of this law may enjoy the coverage of the National Institute of Social Services for Retirees and Pensioners [Instituto Nacional de Servicios Sociales para Jubilados y Pensionados].

Article 5. The beneficiaries of this law may avail themselves of the benefits awarded by other provisions insofar as they are compatible with the present law.

Article 6. The benefits shall automatically expire when: (a) The beneficiary reaches 21 years of age, except for the spouse or person living in consensual union for at least five (5) years immediately preceding the disappearance, and in cases of disability; (b) If the persons mentioned in Article 1(b) of the present law appear alive, this situation must be made known within a period of 180 days. As amended by: Law 23.690 Art. (O.G. 8/16/89). Clause (a) replaced.

Article 7. The Ministry of Health and Social Action [Ministerio de Salud y Acción Social] shall be the institution with which applications for benefiting from this law must be filed.

Article 8. The present law shall enter into force the first day of the month following its publication and shall grant beneficiaries one year for filing the documentation required to benefit from it. Note. See: Law 23.552 Art. (O.G. 4/27/88). Extension of the period for filing documentation until 3/01/89.

Article 9. The expenditures required for complying with this law shall be charged to the special accounts with numbers 324, 325, and 326 of the current national budget, or 'General Revenues' until the specific budgetary allocation is created.

Article 10. The Executive Branch shall regulate the present law within sixty (60) days of its adoption.

Article 11. It shall be communicated to the Executive Branch.

Signers
Pugliese – Martínez – Bejar – Macris

NATIONAL DECREE 1.228/87
REGULATION OF LAW 23.466 ON PENSIONS FOR MINORS WHOSE PARENTS HAVE BEEN DISAPPEARED

Buenos Aires, July 30, 1987
Official Gazette, August 6, 1987
Law Regulated, Law 23.466

Having seen
Law 23.466 and
Considering

That according to Article 10 thereof the EXECUTIVE BRANCH must proceed to regulate it.

That the permanent legal service of the originating authority has intervened. That, in keeping with the authority granted by Article 86(2) of the National Constitution, that obligation is hereby complied with.

Article 1. Applications for benefits shall contain the following information:

(a)
   (i) First and last names of the applicant, address, civil status, nationality, date of birth, and age.
   (ii) Identification papers: D.N.I and/or C.I. numbers.

(iii) Mention of other benefits received or requested.

(iv) Specification of disabilities if any.

 (v) Relationship to the disappeared person.

(vi) Mention of the institution with which the complaint was filed and the date.

(vii) Date of the forced disappearance.

(b) For the specific case of minors and other situations in which this benefit is to be collected through a representative, the nature of this representation must be shown by clear and convincing evidence.

(c) The family relationships described in Law 23.466 shall be shown exclusively by the pertinent certificates or by judicial declaration.

(d) All the requirements established in this article should be filled out in the application form included as Annex 1 of this decree; it shall be filled out in triplicate, with one copy given to the interested party as a written acknowledgment at the moment of filing.

(e) The complaint mentioned in Article 1(b) of Law 23.466 should be shown with a certification issued by the authorities there mentioned, in which they shall corroborate the factual predicates required in the last paragraph of that article. If these facts cannot be shown from the complaint, they should be shown by the testimony of two or more persons. If that documentation cannot be provided by the applicant, the Secretariat of Human Development and Family shall collect it at its own initiative from the agencies mentioned.

(f) The testimony provided for in this regulation must comply with requirements established in Articles 426, 427, 440, 441, 499, and 472 of the federal Code of Civil and Commercial Procedure, and must be given in the manner provided for in Article 197(1) and (2), of said Code.

Statutory References: Law 17.454 Articles 426, 427, 440, 441, 449, 472, 197.

Article 2. (a) It is presumed that the spouse and minor children were under the charge of the disappeared person, unless there is evidence to the contrary. (b) A disability making it impossible to work, provided for in Article 2(b) of Law 23.466 must be total, and if partial, to such a degree so as to impede the performance of a remunerated activity; this must be shown by certification issued by a competent authority of the petitioner's place of residence. (c) The lack of enjoyment of retirement benefits, a pension, or other tax-free benefits must be shown by a sworn statement made by the petitioner. If it is verified that such a statement is false, the penalty shall be the loss of all benefits provided for by Law 23.466. (d) The requirement referring to living in consensual union must be proven by any clear and convincing evidence showing that the persons in question were living together at the same address.

Statutory Reference: Law 23.466 Article 2.

Article 3. The status of disabled shall be understood in the terms established by Law 22.431, which shall be shown by certification issued by the competent official authority. Statutory Reference: Law 22.431.

Article 4. Not regulated.

Article 5. Not regulated.

Article 6. In the circumstance described in Article 6(b) of Law 23.466, failure to file the complaint within One hundred and eighty (180) calendar days shall entail loss of the right to retain benefits received after that period. The implementing authority shall judicially seek the return of the benefits. Statutory Reference: Law 23.466.

Article 7. The authority in charge of implementing Law No. 23.466 shall be the Ministry of Health and Social Action, through the Secretariat of Human Development and Family. Agreements may be made with provincial governments, local governments, and human rights organizations, for them to receive applications in the interior. Abroad, applications shall be filed with the Consulates of the Republic. In the event that an application is denied, an appeal may be filed in keeping with the Law on Administrative Procedures, without prejudice to the pertinent judicial actions.

Article 8. If reasons of *force majeure* make it impossible to show some of the requirements of the application at the moment of filing, the status, place, and stage of the filing should be verified.

Article 9. The Secretariat of Human Development and Family shall enter into agreements with the Secretariat of Social Security of the Ministry of Labor and Social Security [Secretaría de Seguridad Social del Ministerio de Trabajo y Seguridad Social] for this agency to serve as paying agent.

Article 10. As a result of the provision of the previous article, the expense required for complying with this law shall be imputed to Purpose 7, Function 01, Jurisdiction 77, Program 010, Special Account 374, Administrative Service 352, Principal Line Item 3180, Partial 806. To this end, funds from games of chance shall be transferred to said Special Account, or, if these are lacking, funds from General Revenues.

Article 11. This decree shall be communicated, published, given to the National Bureau of the Official Registry [Dirección Nacional del Registro Oficial], and filed.

Signers
Alfonsín – Sourrouille – Brodersohn – Alderete

National Decree 70/91
Decree of Necessity and Urgency on Benefits for Detainees under the Control of the National Executive Branch during the State of Siege

Buenos Aires, January 10, 1991
Official Gazette, January 16, 1991

Having seen
and
Considering

That at the start of the previous administration a large number of persons who had been deprived of their liberty by order of the National Executive Branch brought claims for damages before the Federal Judiciary. In all cases, they were actions against the National State for its tort liability. That without prejudice to cases in which the Judicial Branch considered all factual requirements shown, and, accordingly, handed down a judgment favorable to the plaintiffs, it should be noted that there were also a number of actions in which the statute of limitations stood in the way of satisfying the claims. That in effect, in those cases, the judges ultimately verified the deprivations of liberty and determined that the conditions in which they took place were unlawful, yet also determined that the claims were filed after the time limit, in light of Article 4037 of the Civil Code, which establishes that the actions prescribe after two (2) years. That some of the claims invoked Article 3980 of the aforementioned Code in the knowledge that until the advent of democracy there were severe limitations to bringing any judicial action for reparations against the Argentine State. The Supreme Court of Justice of the Nation did not admit the lawsuits, pointing out—as it did in rulings 250:676, 251:270, 269:51, etc.—that the passage of time cannot be inoperative for the purposes of the legal protection of rights, without a specific law that so establishes. In this context, it established that the two-year statute of limitation provided for in Article 4237 of the Civil Code should be counted from the date on which the plaintiffs regained their freedom. That a small number of these plaintiffs filed their claims before the Inter-American Commission on Human Rights, pursuant to Article 44 of the American Convention on Human Rights, approved by Law 23.054, which entered into force for Argentina on September 5, 1984. That the Argentine Government expressed before this international forum that even if the legal provisions applicable to the cases brought there were to lead to the rejection of the petitioners' claims, by operation of the statute of limitations recognized in Article 46(1)(b) of the American Convention, the National Executive Branch had made the political decision to promote, once the legal remedies in the area of subjective rights were exhausted, the adoption of a special law providing for and giving satisfaction, based on considerations of equity, to those who could not receive a favorable judgment as a result of having claimed their rights too late. That the beneficiaries of this legal provision are all persons who were under the control of the National Executive Branch by executive order, before December 10, 1983, and who, having initiated a proceeding seeking compensation for damages for this reason before December 10, 1985, had not obtained satisfaction because of the application of the statute of limitations by a firm judgment. That, as can be noted, the scope of application of this decree includes every detainee under the control of the National Executive Branch until the reestablishment of the rule of law. It is also required that the judicial action have been initiated during the first two years of the previous constitutional administration, a period of time equal to that provided for by Article 4037 of the Civil Code, but tolling in a time when democratic institutions were fully in force. Obviously, the actions must have been declared as having prescribed by a firm judgment, for if this were not the case, the appeals could have been heard in court. That it is also provided that those who have a judicial case under way at the moment this decree enters into force and who comply with the other requirements may avail themselves of the benefits established in it. For this purpose, a choice is provided among various alternatives, from the abandonment of the action and the right to compensation, to the conclusion of the proceeding by a judgment that rejects the action on grounds of the statute of limitations, for which the requirements are spelled out. That the benefit anticipated is equivalent to one-thirtieth of the monthly remuneration assigned the highest category of the Roster of Civil Servants of the National Public Administration [Escalafón para el Personal Civil de la Administración Pública Nacional], approved by Decree 1,428 of February 22, 1973, or another decree replacing this one, for each day the measure lasted for each beneficiary. That those cases in which the victim died or suffered from grievous injuries be explicitly provided for, in the meaning of Article 91 of the Criminal Code, in the course of the measure addressed here. In both cases, the benefit will cover not only the time the measure lasted but also an increment by the sole fact of death or grievous injuries, which has been considered equitable in view of the particular circumstances of the cases in question. That receiving a benefit—which may also be requested by the successors of the deceased victims—entails waiving all rights to compensation for damages for deprivation of liberty, arrest, being placed under the control of the National Executive Branch, death or injuries, and shall be exclusive of any other benefit or compensation for the same reason. That it should be pointed out that the aim of this decree is not to fix levels of compensation, as this would entail subrogating judicial functions. The aim here is to provide an equitable solution to those situations in which the strict and objective application of legal norms leads to inequitable results. That in this context, the Government embraces the distinction drawn by the Inter-American Court of Human Rights in its judgments of July 21, 1989, setting compensation in the *Velázquez Rodríguez* and *Godínez Cruz* cases, nonetheless recalling that the facts that led to the deprivation of freedom here are not the same ones giving rise to these judgments. That the National Executive Branch promoted the adoption of a law that provides a solution to the situations being described in Message 1484 of August 3, 1990. That said bill is before the Honorable Congress of the Nation for its consideration. That the adjournment of this Body allows one to assume that it will not be possible for the bill to be taken up by both Houses before February 8, 1991, the date on which the Inter-American Commission on Human Rights has scheduled a hearing to reach a friendly settlement, prior to making its definitive pronouncement. That during the hearing held for the same purpose in May 1990, the National Executive Branch informed the Commission of its intent to support a law that would provide an equitable solution to the problems posed; this decision was set forth in Decree 798/90 and in the aforementioned Message 1484/90. That in response to that expression of the Argentine Government, the Commission postponed its decision; this situation requires that a solution to this matter be adopted urgently, since the Argentine Republic must honor its commitment adopted by subscribing to the American Convention on Human Rights, and contribute equitably to alleviating unjust suffering. That if this measure is not adopted, the country could be sanctioned internationally, with the serious consequences that this entails, which is why the state of necessity and urgency that authorizes the Executive Branch to issue provisions legislative in nature, when the necessity is present and the urgency so justifies, is totally shown here. That the exercise of legislative functions by the Executive Branch, when necessity is present and urgency justifies it, enjoys the support of the best constitutional doctrine. And so Joaquín V. González has stated in his *Manual de la Constitución Argentina* that 'the Executive Branch may, when issuing general regulations or resolutions, invade the legislative sphere, or in exceptional or urgent cases, deem it necessary to anticipate the adoption of a law'. (See also Bielsa Rafael-Derecho Administrativo, Vol. 1, p. 309.) Also, the case law of the Supreme Court of Justice of the Nation has favorably received this doctrine (rulings 11:405; 23:257).

Article 1. Those persons who, during the period in which the state of siege was in force, had been placed under the control of the National Executive Branch by an act emanating from it, may avail themselves of the benefits of this decree, provided that they meet the requirements set forth in the following articles.

Article 2. The persons mentioned in the previous article should meet the following requirements: (a) having been placed under the control of the National

Executive Branch before December 10, 1983; (b) having initiated a proceeding for compensation for damages before December 10, 1985; (c) that the action have been declared to have prescribed by a firm judgment.

Article 3. Those whose actions are under way at the moment this decree enters into force may avail themselves of its benefits, provided that they meet the requirements set forth in Articles 1 and 2(a) and (b), and the requirements set forth in the following article.

Article 4. The persons alluded to in the previous article may opt to: (a) Pursue the proceedings they have brought until obtaining a final judgment. If this judgment rejects the cause of action on grounds of the running of the statute of limitations, one may avail oneself of the benefits of this decree by filing the pertinent application with the Ministry of Interior; (b) Abandon the action and the right being claimed, so as to avail oneself of the benefits of this decree in the manner specified in the previous clause. This option may only be exercised when, in the proceeding, the litigation is at a standstill and an answer to the action has been filed, or when the time for doing so has been declared to have lapsed, by firm order. Under the assumptions of this clause, it shall also be shown that the action has not lapsed, and if the relevant motion is being processed, one must await the definitive ruling. If the action is abandoned and the right waived in the cases considered in this clause, court costs will be awarded in the order in which they were incurred. Before the action is considered abandoned and the right waived, the court shall hear from the opposing party, by order notice of which shall be made personally or by official document. Abandonment of the action and waiver of the right set forth in clause (b) should be done before one hundred and eighty (180) days have elapsed from the entry into force of this decree, and provided that on that occasion all requirements demanded here are met. After this period has expired, interested parties may only exercise the alternative provided for in clause (a) of this article.

Article 5. The application for benefits shall be filed with the Ministry of Interior, which shall expeditiously verify compliance with the formal requirements of the previous articles, and the time during which the measure mentioned in Article 2(a), lasted. A ruling that rejects the benefit in full or in part shall be appealable within ten (10) days after the National Court of Appeals for Federal Contentious-Administrative Matters of the Federal Capital [Cámara Nacional de Apelaciones en lo Contencioso Administrativo Federal de la Capital Federal] has been notified. The appeal shall be filed stating the grounds; the Ministry of Interior shall forward it to the Court of Appeals with its opinion within five (5) days. The Court of Appeals shall rule, without further proceedings, no later than twenty (20) days after receiving the pleadings.

Article 6. The benefit established by this decree shall be equal to one-thirtieth of the monthly remuneration assigned to the highest category of the Roster of Civil

Servants of the National Public Administration (approved by Decree 1,428 of February 22, 1973, or that which replaces it), for each day the measure mentioned in Article 2(a) lasted, for each beneficiary. To this end, monthly remuneration shall be considered as the totality of all the items that constitute the salary of those subject to contributions for retirement, excluding particular additional items (seniority, title, etc.), and corresponding to the month in which the benefit is awarded. In order to calculate the period alluded to in the previous paragraph, one shall take account of the act by the Executive Branch establishing this measure, or the actual arrest not determined by court order, in case it came first, and the act that definitively annulled it, be it particular or as a result of the end of the state of siege. House arrest or parole shall not be considered an end to this measure. If the persons in question died during the time the measure mentioned in Article 2(a) was in force, the benefit will be set as indicated above, fixed in the manner indicated above, calculating the period until the moment of death. Without prejudice to this, in these cases the benefit will be increased, due solely to the fact of death, by a sum equivalent to what is provided for by this law for five (5) years of the measure mentioned in Article 2(a). The benefit corresponding to the persons who in like circumstances suffered grievous injuries, according to the classification made in the Criminal Code, shall be increased, due solely to this fact, by an amount equivalent to the one provided in the previous paragraph, reduced by thirty percent (30%). Statutory Reference: National Decree 1,428/73.

Article 7. The rights granted by this decree may be exercised by the persons mentioned in Article 1, or if they have died, by their successors.

Article 8. The application provided for in Article 5 of this decree shall be filed, lest the right to file it lapses, within one hundred and eighty (180) days of its entry into force. In the conditions set out in Article 4, the application must be filed within sixty (60) days of the firm judgment rejecting the action on grounds of the running of the statute of limitations, or of the order considering the actions abandoned and the right waived, as the case may be.

Article 9. In all circumstances, the payment must be made within sixty (60) calendar days after the benefit has been granted. If after this period the payment has not been made, the beneficiary may demand it judicially, without need for prior judicial demand, process, or claim; to this end, the provisions that regulate the enforcement of judgments shall apply. The payment shall be considered to have been made and shall have full effect when the Ministry of Interior deposits it to the order of the Judge in the case. The Judge in the case shall be understood here as meaning the one before which the proceeding alluded to in Article 2(b) was held.

Article 10. If the benefit is not deposited within the period set in the previous article, the amount shall be updated from the day it was granted to the moment the deposit is made, taking account of changes in the consumer price index published by INDEC, plus annual interest of six percent (6%). For the purposes of calculating the amount, the index corresponding to the month prior to the granting of the benefit and the actual deposit will be taken into account.

Article 11. The payment of the benefit entails the waiver of every right to compensation for damages due to the deprivation of liberty, arrest, being placed under the control of the Executive Branch, death or injuries, and it shall exclude any other benefit or compensation for the same reason.

Article 12. The expenditures required to comply with this decree shall be charged to the general revenues.

Article 13. The Honorable Congress of the Nation shall be informed.

Article 14. This decree shall be reported, published, given to the National Bureau of the Official Registry, and filed.

Signers
Menem – Mera Figueroa – González

LAW 24.043
BENEFITS GRANTED TO PERSONS PLACED UNDER THE CONTROL OF THE NATIONAL EXECUTIVE BRANCH DURING THE STATE OF SIEGE

Buenos Aires, November 27, 1991
Official Gazette, January 2, 1992
In force
Regulatory Decree
National Decree 1,023/92

The Senate and the Chamber of Deputies of the Argentine Nation, in solemn Session of Congress etc. pass into law:

Article 1. Those persons who during the state of siege were placed under the control of the National Executive Branch by its decision, or who, being civilians, were detained pursuant to the orders of military tribunals, regardless of whether they have brought proceedings for damages, may avail themselves of the benefits of this law, so long as they have not received any compensation pursuant to a court judgment, pursuant to the acts provided for in the present law.

Article 2. In order to avail oneself of the benefits of this law, the persons mentioned in the previous article must meet at least one of the following requirements: (a) Having been placed under the control of the National Executive Branch before December 10, 1983. (b) Being civilians, having been deprived of liberty by acts of military tribunals, regardless of whether a guilty verdict was reached in the military jurisdiction.

Article 3. Applications for the benefit shall be filed with the Ministry of Interior, which shall expeditiously verify compliance with the formal requirements of the previous articles and the duration of the measure mentioned in Article 2(a) and (b). A ruling denying the benefit, in full or in part, may be appealed within ten (10) days of notice being given, before the National Court of Appeals for Federal Contentious-Administrative Matters of the Federal Capital. The appeal shall be filed stating the grounds for it, and the MINISTRY OF INTERIOR shall forward it to the Court of Appeals, with its opinion, within five (5) days. The Court of Appeals shall decide, without further proceedings, no later than twenty (20) days after receiving the pleadings.

Article 4. The benefit established by the present law shall be equal to one-thirtieth of the monthly remuneration assigned to the highest category of the Roster of Civil Servants of the National Public Administration (approved by Decree 1,428 of February 22, 1973, or that which replaces it), for each day the measure mentioned in Article 2(a) and (b) lasted, with respect to each beneficiary. For this purpose, the monthly remuneration shall be considered the totality of all the items that constitute the salary of the civil servant subject to contributions for retirement, excluding particular additional items (seniority, title, etc.), and corresponding to the month when the benefit is granted. In order to calculate the time period mentioned in the previous paragraph, one shall take into account the act by the Executive Branch decreeing the measure, or the actual arrest not ordered by a judicial authority with jurisdiction, and the act that definitively annulled the measure either in the particular circumstance or as a result of the end of the state of siege. House arrest or parole shall not be considered as ending the measure. If the persons in question died when subject to the measure mentioned in Article 2(a) and (b), the benefit shall be set as indicated above, and the period shall be calculated up until the moment of death. Without prejudice to this, the benefit shall be increased, due solely to the fact of death, by an amount equivalent to what is provided for by this law when the measure mentioned in Article 2(a) and (b) has been in effect for five (5) years. The benefit for those persons who under like circumstances suffered grievous injuries, according to the classification made by the Criminal Code, shall be increased, due solely to this fact, by an amount equivalent to the one provided for in the previous paragraph, but reduced by thirty percent (30%). Statutory Reference: National Decree 1,428/73.

Article 5. The rights granted by this law may be exercised by the persons mentioned in Article 1, or, in case of death, by their successors.

Article 6. The application provided for in Article 3 of this law shall be filed, lest it lapses, within one hundred and eighty (180) days of its entry into force. Note. See: Law 24.906 Art. (O.G. 12/19/97). Extends time limit.

Article 7. In all circumstances, the payment shall be made in six (6) installments, one every six (6) months, the first of these coming due sixty (60) calendar days after the moment the benefit is granted. In order to calculate the amount, the index corresponding to the month immediately preceding the one when the benefit is awarded and the month prior to the moment the payment is actually made shall be taken into account. If the term established for making the payment of each installment has lapsed without it being made, then the beneficiary may demand it judicially, without needing to file a demand for payment, further proceedings, or a previous claim; to this end the provisions regulating the enforcement of judgments shall apply. The amount of the compensation provided for in this law may be paid in keeping with the terms of Law 23.982. As amended by: National Decree 2,722/91 Art. (O.G. 1/02/92). Second sentence vetoed.

Article 8. The Ministry of Interior shall be the authority for carrying out the present law and it shall be in charge of making the payments of the benefits established by it, by making deposits in official banks in the jurisdiction of the beneficiary's domicile, to the order of the beneficiary.

Article 9. The payment of the benefit entails the waiver of any right to compensation for damages for deprivation of liberty, arrest, being placed under the control of the Executive Branch, death or injuries, and it shall exclude any other benefit or compensation for the same reason.

Article 10. The expenditures required to comply with this law shall be charged to 'General Revenues'.

Article 11. The adoption of this decree shall be communicated to the National Executive Branch.

Signers
Pierri – Menem – Pereyra Arandía de Pérez Pardo – Flombaum

Decree 205/97, Regulations of Law 24.043

[March 17, 1997]

Replacing Article 4 of the regulation of Law 24.043, approved by Decree 1,023/92, making the evidence required for receiving benefits more flexible.

The President of the Argentine Nation decrees:

Article 1. Article 4 of the regulation of Law 24.043, approved by Decree 1,023/92, shall be replaced by the following: in order to calculate the period subject to compensation in cases of actual arrest not ordered by a competent authority, the following types of evidence shall be accepted:

(a) Copy of the filing of the writ of habeas corpus or of the court's judgment on said writ.
(b) Reports or certifications issued by a competent authority. The Office of the Undersecretary for Human and Social Rights of the Ministry of Interior [Subsecretaría de Derechos Humanos y Sociales del Ministerio del Interior] shall issue the certifications of the facts alleged and that appear in the files of the National Commission on the Disappearance of Persons and in the Files of Complaints under its custody.
(c) Documents in judicial and administrative files.
(d) Documents at the Inter-American Commission on Human Rights of the Organization of American States and the Inter-American Court of Human Rights.

Documents in national and international human rights organizations, press articles, and consistent bibliographic material shall be evaluated together with the body of evidence produced.

When the identity of the beneficiary or the exact length of the detention he or she suffered cannot be confirmed beyond a doubt from the evidence produced, it may be shown by judicial declaration (judicial investigative hearing), which may be corroborated by the enforcing authority.

Grievous injuries shall be understood as those provided for at Article 91 of the Criminal Code. For the purposes of showing that such injuries occurred during the detention, at least one of the following types of evidence shall be required:

(a) Clinical records of the place of detention.
(b) Copy of the judicial judgment that considered the detentions shown.
(c) Medical or clinical records with the date corresponding to the period covered by the benefit, issued by an official health institution.

(d) If necessary, a medical consultation shall be ordered, for which purpose the Office of the Undersecretary for Human and Social Rights of the Ministry of Interior is authorized to enter into agreements with federal, provincial, or local hospitals.

In all cases, the documents should be submitted with certification by the issuing authority.

Article 2. The following shall be incorporated as Article 8 of the regulation of Law 24,043, approved by Decree No. 1,023/92: The Office of the Undersecretary for Human and Social Rights of the Ministry of Interior shall verify compliance with requirements established for granting benefits, and shall determine the period covered by compensation.

Article 3. This decree shall be communicated, published, given to the National Bureau of the Official Registry, and filed.

LAW 24.321
FORCED DISAPPEARANCE OF PERSONS

Declaration of absence. Judge with jurisdiction. Procedure. Time limits. Civil effects. Reappearance, alive, of the absent person. Provisions in relation to cases of absence with presumption of death.

Adopted: May 11, 1994.
Promulgated: June 8, 1994.

The Senate and the Chamber of Deputies of the Argentine Nation, in Solemn Session of Congress etc. pass into law:

Article 1. The absence by forced disappearance may be declared for every person who before December 10, 1983 disappeared against his or her will from his or her place of domicile or residence, without there being any news as to his or her whereabouts.

Article 2. For the purposes of this law, the forced disappearance of a person shall be understood as having occurred when someone has been deprived of his or her personal liberty, followed by the disappearance of the victim, or if he or she has been kept in clandestine places of detention or deprived, in any other manner, of the right to due process. A forced disappearance has to be shown by complaint filed with a judicial authority with jurisdiction, the former National Commission on the Disappearance of Persons (Decree 158/83), or the Office of the Undersecretary for Human and Social Rights of the Ministry of Interior or the former National Bureau for Human Rights [Dirección Nacional de Derechos Humanos].

Article 3. All those who have a legitimate interest subordinated to the absent person may petition for the declaration of absence due to forced disappearance. In the case of the spouse, ascendants, descendants, and relatives up to the fourth degree, such interest is presumed. The judicial proceeding, within the federal jurisdiction, shall be exempt from court fees.

Article 4. The judge of the civil court of the applicant's domicile, or otherwise of the place of residence of the disappeared person, shall have jurisdiction to hear the case. The proceeding, within the federal jurisdiction, shall be by summary procedure.

Article 5. Once the petition for a declaration of absence due to forced or involuntary disappearance has been received, the judge shall demand of the official agency to which the report of the disappearance was filed, or, if there is none, of the judge before whom the writ of habeas corpus was filed, information on the formal veracity of the act, and said judge shall order the publication of notice for three (3) consecutive days in a newspaper of the respective locality or in the Official Gazette, summonsing the disappeared person. In case of urgency, the judge may designate a provisional administrator or take the measures warranted by the circumstances. The publication in the Official Gazette shall be free of charge.

Article 6. After sixty (60) calendar days have elapsed after the last publication of the notices and after a hearing with the defense counsel for absent persons, who shall only verify compliance with the foregoing provisions, the absence due to forced disappearance shall be declared, setting as the presumptive date the one included in the original complaint before the competent official institution, or, as the case may be, the date of the last reliable news—if any—of the disappeared person.

Article 7. The civil effects of the declaration of absence due to forced disappearance shall be analogous to those prescribed by Law 14.394 for absence with presumption of death.

Article 8. In the event that the absent person reappears alive, he or she may claim the restitution of his or her property in the condition it was in, such property as was acquired from the value of that which is missing, the price owed for such property as was sold, and the proceeds not yet consumed. The reappearance shall not in itself void a new marriage or any other legal act that was entered into lawfully.

Article 9. The exercise of the rights granted by this law does not impede actions provided for by other legal provisions.

Article 10. Those cases that have already been declared as absence with presumption of death, in which the judgment has already been entered in the National Registry of Persons [Registro Nacional de las Personas], or is already firm and pending such entry, may be changed, upon petition by the party, to 'absence due to forced disappearance', by proving only the requirements established in Article 2 of this law before the same judge who declared the absence with presumption of death. After verifying the forced disappearance, the judge shall order, without further proceedings, the official letter modifying the judgment, declaring that the declaration of absence with presumption of death has been replaced by absence due to forced disappearance.

Article 11. The Executive Branch shall be informed.

Alberto R. Pierri–Eduardo Menem–Esther Pereyra Arandía de Pérez Pardo. Edgardo Piuzzi

Done at the Hall of Sessions of the Argentine Congress, in Buenos Aires, the Eleventh of MAY, nineteen hundred and ninety-four.

Decree 897/94 Buenos Aires, 6/08/94
Therefore:
This shall be considered as Law of the Nation 24.321, it shall be carried out, communicated, published, given to the National Bureau of the Official Registry [Dirección Nacional del Registro Oficial], and filed.
Menem. – Carlos F. Ruckauf

LAW 24.411
ABSENCE DUE TO FORCED DISAPPEARANCE

Buenos Aires, December 7, 1994
Official Gazette, January 3, 1995
In force
Regulatory Decree
National Decree 403/95

The Senate and the Chamber of Deputies of the Argentine Nation in Solemn Session of Congress, etc. pass into law:

Article 1. Those persons who at the time this law is promulgated are in a situation of forced disappearance shall have the right to receive, through their assignees [*causahabientes*], a special benefit equivalent to the monthly remuneration of civil servants at Level A of the roster of civil servants of the national public administration, approved by Decree 993/91, times the coefficient 100. For the purposes of this law, a forced disappearance is understood as having occurred when a person has been deprived of his or her personal liberty, followed by the disappearance of the victim, or if he or she was held in a clandestine place of detention, or deprived in any other way of the right to due process. Statutory Reference: National Decree 993/91.

Article 2. The assignees of every person who has died as a result of the actions of the armed forces, security forces, or any paramilitary group before 12/10/83, shall have the right to receive the same benefit as established in Article 1.

Article 2 bis. The compensation established by the present law is in the nature of property belonging to the disappeared or deceased person. In the event of disappearance and as long as it persists, the compensation shall be distributed in the same order of priority as established in Articles 3545ff. of the Civil Code, without detriment to the rights recognized by Article 4 of this law. As amended by: Law 24.823 Art. 1 Incorporated (O.G. 5/28/97).

Article 3. In order to show the aforementioned situations, and for the exclusive purposes of this law, one shall proceed as follows:

1. Under Article 1, the forced disappearance shall be proven by either of the following means: (a) The pertinent criminal complaint for unlawful deprivation of liberty, and by the ruling by the judge that *prima facie* the disappearance is due to that cause. In this respect, the judge should verify the formal veracity of the complaint and rule solely for the purpose of this law, and in very summary form; (b) Either by the complaint filed with the National Commission on the Disappearance of Persons, created by Decree 87/83, or with the Office of the Undersecretary for Human and Social Rights of the Ministry of Interior.
2. Under Article 2, by any of the means set forth in the previous clause, and by death, shown by the respective death certificate.

Article 4. The effects and benefits of this law shall also apply to consensual unions that lasted for at least two years before the disappearance or death, as the case may be, and when this is proved by clear and convincing evidence. It shall be presumed, unless there is evidence to the contrary, that consensual union existed when there are descendants recognized by the disappeared or deceased, or the filiation of the descendant has been judicially established. A person joined by consensual union shall benefit in the same proportion as a spouse. If there was concurrence of a spouse and one who has proven a consensual union lasting at least two years immediately preceding the disappearance or death, the amount corresponding to the spouse shall be distributed to both in equal amounts. As an exception to Title IV of Section Two, Book One of the Civil Code on Full Adoption, it is established that the children who as a result of the forced disappearance or death of one or both parents were given in full adoption shall have the right to receive the compensation established by the present law. As amended by: Law 24.823 Art. 2 (O.G. 5/28/97). Second paragraph incorporated. Law 24.823 Art. 3 (O.G. 5/28/97). Last paragraph incorporated.

Article 4 bis. The person whose absence due to forced disappearance has been judicially declared in the terms of Law 24.321 shall receive said pecuniary reparation through his or her assignees, who must show this relationship in court. The judge presiding over a matter of absence due to forced disappearance shall have jurisdiction to issue the declaration of assignees. Before the issuance of the declaration of assignees of the disappeared person, those claiming this right must come forward within thirty (30) days of the last publication. When this period has concluded, the judge, within thirty (30) days, shall declare who are his or her only assignees in a declaration with effects analogous to those of Article 700 of the federal Code of Civil and Commercial Procedure. Under penalty of annulment of the pertinent part, under no circumstance may the judge declare the death or set the presumed date of death. As amended by: Law 24.823 Art. 4 Incorporated (O.G. 5/28/97).

Article 4 ter. The payment of compensation to the heirs of the deceased or to the assignees of the disappeared person who have shown such status by judicial declaration, including the ruling on consensual unions, shall release the State of its liability under this law. Those who have received a pecuniary reparation legally shall be subrogated to the State if, afterwards, other assignees or heirs with the same or a better right apply for the same benefit. As amended by: Law 24.823 Art. 5 Incorporated (O.G. 5/28/97). Note. See: National Decree 479/97 Art. I (O.G. 5/28/97) Last paragraph vetoed when this article was incorporated.

Article 5. In case the persons mentioned in Article 1 appear alive, the judge with jurisdiction must be so informed, but there shall be no obligation to return the benefit if it has already been received.

Article 6. Applications for benefits shall be filed with the Ministry of Interior, which shall verify, in very summary form, compliance with the formal requirements for obtaining the benefit. In case of doubt about granting the compensation provided for by this law, one should adhere to whatever is more favorable to the beneficiary or his or her assignees or heirs, in keeping with the principle of good faith. A ruling that rejects the benefit, in full or in part, may be appealed within ten

(10) days of notification to the National Court of Appeals for Federal Contentious-Administrative Matters of the Federal Capital. The appeal shall be filed stating the grounds for it, and the Ministry of Interior shall forward it to the Court of Appeals with its opinion within five (5) days. The Court of Appeals shall decide without further proceedings no later than twenty (20) days after receiving the pleadings. As amended by: Law 24.823 Art. 6 (O.G. 5/28/97). Second paragraph incorporated.

Article 7. The application for the benefit shall be filed, lest the right lapse, within one hundred and eighty (180) days after the date on which this law enters into force. Note. See: Law 24.499 Art. (O.G. 7/03/95). It extends to five (5) years the time limit for filing the application for the benefit, to be counted from the expiration date established in this article.

Article 8. The Ministry of Interior shall be the authority for enforcing this law and shall be in charge of paying the benefit it establishes by making deposits in official banks within the jurisdiction that corresponds to the beneficiary's domicile; the payment shall be to the order of the beneficiary. The amount of the benefit provided by this law may be paid as per the terms of Law 23.982. After the established time limit for making payment of the benefit has lapsed without it being paid, the beneficiary or beneficiaries may demand it judicially without need to file a prior demand for payment, process, or claim; to this end, the provisions that regulate enforcement of judgments shall apply. Statutory Reference: Law 23.982.

Article 9. In those cases in which compensation for damages has been recognized by judicial resolution, or the benefit granted by Decree 70/91, Decree 1313/91, or for the grounds established in Article 4(4) of Law 24.043, and this benefit has been received, the beneficiaries may only receive the difference between the amount established by this law and the amounts actually collected under the other laws mentioned. If the amount received has been equal to or greater than what is provided for herein, they shall not be entitled to the new pecuniary reparation. As amended by: Law 24.823 Art. 7 Replaced (O.G. 5/28/97).

Article 9 bis. The following are derogated insofar as they may have been in force, and declared incurably null and void: the institutional act of the Military Junta of April 28, 1983, and the so-called Final Report on the fight against subversion, of the same date. All provisions contrary to Law 24.411 and the present law are hereby derogated. As amended by: Law 24.823 Art. 8 Incorporated (O.G. 5/28/97).

Article 10. All expenditures required for complying with the present law shall be charged to 'General Revenues'.

Article 10 bis. The compensation stipulated by this law shall be exempt from encumbrances, and the judicial or administrative procedures whose aim is to show the circumstances or relationship to the victim shall also be exempt from fees, in the federal jurisdiction. The publication of notices in the Official Gazette shall be free of charge. As amended by: Law 24.823 Art. 9 Incorporated (O.G. 5/28/97).

Article 10 ter. The Provinces are encouraged to adopt relevant laws to exempt from court and administrative fees the judicial and/or administrative proceedings and mandatory publications necessary for receiving the benefit. As amended by: Law 24.823 Art. 10 Incorporated (O.G. 5/28/97).

Article 11. This decree shall be communicated to the National Executive Branch.

Signers
Pierri – Menem – Pereyra Arandía de Pérez Pardo – Piuzzi

NATIONAL DECREE 403/95
DECREE REGULATING THE LAW ON ABSENCE
DUE TO FORCED DISAPPEARANCE

Buenos Aires, August 29, 1995
Official Gazette, September 4, 1995
Law Regulated: Law 24.411

Having seen:
Laws 24.411 and 24.499, and
Considering:

That the first law cited grants a benefit, through their assignees, to those persons who disappeared and also to those who have died as a result of the actions of the Armed Forces, Security Forces, or paramilitary groups. That it is necessary to establish clearly the procedural guidelines aimed at regulating its implementation and processing. That Law 24.499 extended for five (5) years the time limit of one hundred and eighty (180) days established in Article 7 of Law 24.411, for claiming the benefit granted by Law 24.411. That the present measure is issued using the authority granted by Article 99(2) of the National Constitution. Accordingly,

Article 1. The Regulations of Law 24.411, as amended by Law 24.499, which as Annex I is an integral part of the present decree, is hereby approved. Statutory References: Law 24.411, Law 24.499.

Article 2. This decree shall be communicated, published, given to the National Bureau of the Official Registry, and filed.

Signers
Menem – Bauza – Corach

Annex A: Annex I. Regulation of Law 24.411

Article 1. For the purposes of Article 1 of the law, a forced disappearance must have lasted until its entry into force. Therefore, the following are not considered to be in that situation: (a) those persons who have reappeared, alive; (b) those persons whose corpses have been identified; and (c) those persons whose death has been recorded in a death certificate.

Article 2. For the purposes of Article 2 of this law, a paramilitary group shall be understood to refer only those groups that participated in the fight against subversion without identifying their personnel by uniforms or credentials.

Article 3. In order to show the situations set forth in the law, one shall proceed as follows:

  I. The forced disappearance mentioned in Article 3(1)(b) shall be shown by one of the following means:
  I(a) By certified copy of the judicial order declaring the absence due to forced disappearance provided for by Law 24.321. If the absence with presumption of death has been declared judicially and it was caused by forced disappearance, the latter may be shown in the terms of Article 3 of Law 24.411 or Article 10 of Law 24.321.
  I(b) By a certificate issued by the Office of the Undersecretary for Human and Social Rights of the Ministry of Interior that shows that the complaint was filed in a timely manner before the former National Commission on the Disappearance of Persons (CONADEP) or the then Office of the Undersecretary for Human Rights (former Bureau for Human Rights [Dirección de Derechos Humanos]), currently the Office of the Undersecretary for Human and Social Rights of the Ministry of Interior. It should be stated in the document that the corresponding files have been compared and that it does not follow from that comparison that the person is in the conditions set out in Article 1(a), (b), and (c) of this regulation.
  I(c) If the forced disappearance cannot be proven by any of the means provided for in the law or this regulation, or by the certifications issued by the former National Commission on the Disappearance of Persons (CONADEP), a new file shall be opened. In that case, the Office of the Undersecretary for Human and Social Rights of the Ministry of Interior shall issue a 'certificate of report of forced disappearance' that will have

full effect for considering it shown in the following situations: (a) When the report of the disappearance can be shown by contemporaneous documentary evidence, such as requests to determine the whereabouts of the victim, filing a writ of habeas corpus, or certifications in the files or in other public or private agencies whose legal status is recognized nationally or internationally. (b) When the report is filed under the plaintiff's number in Annex I of the final report of the former National Commission on the Disappearance of Persons (CONADEP), published by Editorial Universitaria of Buenos Aires. (c) When none of the elements referred to in the previous subsections exists, the report can be shown by the types of evidence provided for by the federal Code of Civil and Commercial Procedure and the federal Code of Criminal Procedure. In these cases, documentary or testimonial evidence produced subsequent to the entry into force of the law may only be considered valid when it corroborates other evidence produced contemporaneous with the disappearance. The certificate may be requested by any person with a legitimate interest, which is presumed for direct relatives up to the fourth degree of consanguinity. When there is no such relationship, a legitimate interest must be proven. If more than one certificate of forced disappearance is required, the issuing agency must state in the successive certificates that it has already issued previous ones, and it will take note of who has requested them, setting forth their identity card.

II. Cases of death referred to in Article 3, clause 2 of this law shall be shown as follows:

II(a) By a judicial ruling or administrative records which show the participation in the act of personnel from the Armed Forces, the Security Forces, or paramilitary groups. It is presumed that the death occurred due to the actions of the Armed Forces, Security Forces, or paramilitary groups when: (a) The death occurred in places or establishments belonging to these groups. (b) These persons were reported as disappeared to the former National Commission on the Disappearance of Persons (CONADEP) and fall within the provisions of Article 1(b) or (c) of this regulation. (c) In all other cases, death caused by the actions of the Armed Forces, Security Forces, or paramilitary groups may be shown by the types of evidence provided for in the federal Code of Civil and Commercial Procedure and Code of Criminal Procedure. In these cases, the documentary or testimonial evidence produced after the entry into force of the law being regulated may only be considered valid when it corroborates other evidence produced at the time of the death. The aforementioned Office of the Undersecretary for Human and Social Rights of the Ministry of Interior shall be in charge of preparing the individual files of the deceased persons, which should include the necessary background information and evidence aimed at showing the factual requirements provided for by law. Requests for reports required by the enforcement authority to show the disappearance or death should be answered within twenty (20) working days. In cases in which there is sufficient proof that the death was caused by the Armed Forces, Security Forces, or any paramilitary group indicated by the law, the Ministry of Interior through its Office of the Undersecretary for Human and Social Rights shall issue an administrative act stating this and shall issue a certificate that should be attached to the pleadings filed pursuant to Law 24.411, which will authorize one to continue the procedure. Statutory References: Law 24.321 Art. 10.

Article 4. The consensual unions referred to in Article 4 of the law being regulated should be shown by a judicial investigative hearing, in which the procedure established in Article 322 of the federal Code of Civil and Commercial Procedure must be observed. Statutory Reference.: Code of Civil and Commercial Procedure Art. 322.

Article 5. If the persons mentioned in Article 1 reappear, any person may notify the judge with jurisdiction of this situation; such a person should, in the same act, make the report, state the basis for it, and offer the relevant evidence. Otherwise, it shall be rejected *in limine*.

Article 6. The application for the benefit shall be filed with the Office of the Undersecretary for Human and Social Rights of the Ministry of Interior by one who presumes to have a legitimate interest, or any of his or her assignees who would qualify as heirs in the terms of Articles 3545 to 3587 of the Civil Code and, as the case may be, by the person who complies with the provisions of Article 4 of this law. The status of beneficiary may be shown by testimony or certified copy of the declaration of heirs of the disappeared or deceased person, or—for the sole purpose of complying with this law—by a judicial investigative hearing, in which the procedure established in Article 322 of the federal Code of Civil and Commercial Procedure should be observed. The processing of the judicial investigative hearing referred to shall, if necessary, be in the presence of a government attorney (from the Ministerio Público) and with legal counsel free of charge from the official institutions authorized for that purpose. After petitioners have provided the required information, the Ministry of Interior shall decide whether it is proper to grant the benefit within three hundred and sixty (360) administrative working days. In those cases in which the action of filiation, aimed at establishing the true identity of a person presumably the child of a person who disappeared or who died in the circumstances referred to in Articles 1 or 2 of the law, is being processed, the presumed child may request the suspension of the processing until there is a firm judgment determining filiation. Before the benefit is granted, the Office of the

Undersecretary for Human and Social Rights of the Ministry of Interior should request the Argentine Federal Police to report whether it has any record of the disappeared person after the date of the reported disappearance; such a request should be answered within twenty (20) working days. Once the requirements referred to in this Article are shown, the Ministry of Interior, after a ruling by its Permanent Legal Service, shall issue the administrative act declaring whether it is proper to grant the benefit to those persons who have shown beneficiary status. Statutory References: Civil Code Articles 3545 to 3587, Code of Civil and Commercial Procedure Art. 322.

Article 7. Not regulated.

Article 8. The payment of the benefit shall be made in keeping with the terms of Law 23.982. Statutory Reference: Law 23.982.

Article 9. In a sworn statement, one should state that he or she has not received any compensation for damages stemming from the grounds that give rise to this benefit, and waive the filing of any judicial actions for the same reason. The present benefit shall be incompatible with any other benefit received or to be received in relation to persons deceased or found to be absent with presumption of death, provided for in Decree 70/91 and Law 24.043 and amending, complementary, and/or clarifying provisions. Statutory References: National Decree 70/91 Law 24.043.

Article 10. Not regulated.

Article 11. Not regulated.

LAW 24.823
FORCED DISAPPEARANCE OF PERSONS

Certain aspects of the compensation provided for by Law 24.411 are hereby regulated, establishing its nature, way in which it is received, and its beneficiaries.

Passed into law: May 7, 1997.
Partially Promulgated: May 23, 1997.
The Senate and the Chamber of Deputies of the Argentine Nation, in solemn session of Congress, etc. pass into law:

Article 1. The following is added as Article 2 bis of Law 24.411:

Article 2 bis: The compensation established by the present law is in the nature of property belonging to the disappeared or deceased person. In the event of disappearance and as long as it persists, the compensation shall be distributed in the same order of priority as established in Articles 3545ff. of the Civil Code, without detriment to the rights recognized by Article 4 of this law.

Article 2. The following is added as the second paragraph of Article 4 of Law 24.411:
Article 4:   It shall be presumed, unless there is evidence to the contrary, that consensual union existed when there are descendants recognized by the disappeared or deceased, or the filiation of the descendant has been judicially established. A person joined by consensual union shall benefit in the same proportion as a spouse. If there was concurrence of a spouse and one who has proven a consensual union lasting at least two years immediately preceding the disappearance or death, the amount corresponding to the spouse shall be distributed to both in equal amounts.

Article 3. The following is added as the last paragraph of Article 4 of Law 24.411:
Article 4:   As an exception to Title IV of Section Two, Book One of the Civil Code on Full Adoption, it is established that the children who as a result of the forced disappearance or death of one or both parents were given in full adoption shall have the right to receive the compensation established by the present law.

Article 4. The following is added as Article 4 bis of Law 24.411:
Article 4 bis: The person whose absence due to forced disappearance has been judicially declared in the terms of Law 24.321 shall receive said pecuniary reparation through his or her assignees, who must show this relationship in court. The judge presiding over a matter of absence due to forced disappearance shall have jurisdiction to issue the declaration of assignees. Before the issuance of the declaration of assignees of the disappeared person, those claiming this right must come forward within thirty (30) days of the last publication. When this period has concluded, the judge, within thirty (30) days, shall declare who are his or her only assignees in a declaration with effects analogous to those of Article 700 of the federal Code of Civil and Commercial Procedure. Under penalty of annulment of the pertinent part, under no circumstance may the judge declare the death or set the presumed date of death.

Article 5. The following is added as Article 4 ter of Law 24.411:
Article 4 ter: The payment of compensation to the heirs of the deceased or to the assignees of the disappeared person who have shown such status by judicial declaration, including the ruling on consensual unions, shall release the State of its liability under this law. Those who have received a pecuniary reparation legally shall be subrogated to the State if, afterwards, other assignees or heirs with the same

or a better right apply for the same benefit. (Paragraph vetoed by Art. 1 of Decree 479/97 O.G. 5/28/97.)

Article 6. The following is added as the second paragraph of Article 6 of Law 24.411:
Article 6: In case of doubt about granting the compensation provided for by this law, one should adhere to whatever is more favorable to the beneficiary or his or her assignees or heirs, in keeping with the principle of good faith.

Article 7. Article 9 of Law 24.411 is replaced by the following:

Article 9: In those cases in which compensation for damages has been recognized by judicial resolution, or the benefit granted by Decree 70/91, Decree 1313/91, or for the grounds established in Article 4(4) of Law 24.043, and this benefit has been received, the beneficiaries may only receive the difference between the amount established by this law and the amounts actually collected under the other laws mentioned. If the amount received has been equal to or greater than what is provided for herein, they shall not be entitled to the new pecuniary reparation.

Article 8. The following is added as Article 9 bis of Law 24.411:
Article 9 bis: The following are derogated insofar as they may have been in force, and declared incurably null and void: the institutional act of the Military Junta of April 28, 1983, and the so-called Final Report on the fight against subversion, of the same date. All provisions contrary to Law 24.411 and the present law are hereby derogated.

Article 9. The following is added as Article 10 bis of Law 24.411:
Article 10 bis: The compensation stipulated by this law shall be exempt from encumbrances, and the judicial or administrative procedures whose aim is to show the circumstances or relationship to the victim shall also be exempt from fees, in the federal jurisdiction. The publication of notices in the Official Gazette shall be free of charge.

Article 10. The following is added as Article 10 ter of Law 24.411:
Article 10 ter: The Provinces are encouraged to adopt relevant laws to exempt from court and administrative fees the judicial and/or administrative proceedings and mandatory publications necessary for receiving the benefit.

Article 11. The Executive Branch shall be informed.

Done in the Session Hall of the Argentine Congress, in Buenos Aires, the Seventh day of May, nineteen hundred and ninety-seven.

Registered under Number 24.823 Alberto R. Pierri–Carlos F. Ruckauf–Esther Pereyra Arandía de Pérez Pardo–Edgardo Piuzzi

Law 25.914
Human Rights

August 30, 2004

Benefits are hereby established for those persons who were born during the deprivation of liberty of their mothers, or who, being minors, were detained with their parents, provided that at least one of them was detained and/or disappeared for political reasons, whether under the control of the National Executive Branch and/or military tribunals. Particulars for victims of change of identity. Requirements that must be shown to avail oneself of the benefits of the law. Procedures for calculating compensation.

Passed into law Sanctioned 8/04/2004; promulgated 8/25/2004; published 8/30/2004

The Senate and Chamber of Deputies of the Argentine Nation, in solemn session of Congress etc. pass into law:

Article 1. Those persons who were born during the deprivation of liberty of their mother, or who, being minors, were detained under any circumstance in relation to either parent, provided that either of them was detained and/or disappeared for political reasons whether under the control of the National Executive Branch and/or military tribunals and/or military areas, independent of their judicial situation, may avail themselves of the benefits instituted in this law. Those persons who due to any of the circumstances established here were victims of change of identity will receive the reparation determined by this law. This benefit is incompatible with any other compensation received pursuant to a judicial judgment for the reasons set forth in the present law.

Article 2. In order to avail oneself of the benefits of this law, those persons mentioned in the previous article should make a showing before the authority entrusted with the enforcement of this law that he or she meets the following requirements:

(a) Those persons who were born during the detention and/or captivity of their mother will have to present their birth certificate, with a date prior to December 10, 1983, and show, by any type of evidence, that their mother was detained and/or disappeared for political reasons under the control of the National Executive Branch and/or military tribunals and/or military areas, independent of their judicial situation.

(b) For minors who were born outside prisons and/or captivity, they must show by any type of evidence that they stayed in these places and the conditions required by Article 1 of the present law for either of their parents.

(c) For those cases laid out in the second paragraph of Article 1, the judicial judgment rectifying their identity will have to be presented. Those who under this circumstance have been adopted fully and in good faith are exempt from presenting such a judgment, and must show the forced disappearance of their parents by any means.

Article 3. The application for the benefit shall be filed with the Ministry of Justice, Security, and Human Rights as the authority entrusted with the enforcement of the present law, and which shall in very summary form verify compliance with the requirements of the previous articles. In case of doubt about granting the benefit provided for by this law, one should adhere to what is most favorable for the victims or their assignees, in keeping with the principle of good faith. The ruling denying the benefit, in full or in part, shall be appealable within ten (10) days of notice, before the National Court of Appeals for Federal Contentious-Administrative Matters of the Federal Capital has been notified. The appeal shall be filed stating its grounds, before the Ministry of Justice, Security, and Human Rights, which will forward it to the Court of Appeals with its opinion on the case after five (5) days. The Court of Appeals shall decide, without need for further proceedings, within twenty (20) days of receiving the pleadings.

Article 4. The benefit established by this law shall consist of a one-time payment of a sum equivalent to twenty times the monthly remuneration of civil servants at Level A, Grade 8 of the National System of the Administrative Profession, Decree 993/91 T.O. 1995. Monthly remuneration is considered to be the entirety of the items that constitute the salary of civil servants subject to retirement contributions. When, under the circumstances and periods indicated in Articles 1 and 2, the beneficiary's identity was changed, he or she shall receive, in all, compensation equivalent to that fixed by Law 24.411, with its complementary and amending laws. If, by virtue of the circumstances established in Article 1, the beneficiary has suffered grievous or very grievous injuries, as per the classification of the Criminal Code, or has died, the benefit shall be increased by fifty percent (50%), seventy percent (70%), and one hundred percent (100%), respectively.

Article 5. The payment of the benefit entails the waiver of all rights to compensation for damages based on the grounds set forth by this law, and excludes any other benefit or compensation for the same reasons.

Article 6. The Ministry of Justice, Security, and Human Rights shall be in charge of paying the compensation established by the present law, making deposits in official banks within the jurisdiction that corresponds to the beneficiary's domicile.

Article 7. The compensation provided for by this law is exempt from encumbrances, and, as the case may be, the judicial or administrative procedures aimed at showing the circumstances or link, in the federal jurisdiction, shall be exempt from fees. The publication of notices in the Official Gazette of the Republic of Argentina shall be free of charge.

Article 8. The provinces are invited to adopt laws or issue the corresponding administrative acts so as to, as the case may be, exempt from payment of judicial and administrative fees those judicial and/or administrative procedures and mandatory publications necessary for receiving the benefit hereby established.

Article 9. The expenditures required for complying with the present law shall be charged to the budgetary allocations of the Ministry of Justice, Security, and Human Rights, to which end the Chief of the Cabinet of Ministers shall make the corresponding budgetary adjustments.

Article 10. This law shall be communicated to the Executive Branch.

Done in the Session Hall of the Argentine Congress, in Buenos Aires, the fourth day of August, two thousand and four.

Registered under Number 25.914

Eduardo O. Camaño – Daniel O. Scioli – Eduardo D. Rollano – Juan Estrada

Decree 1096/2004
of 8/25/2004; published 8/30/2004
Therefore:
Consider this as Law of the Nation 25.914, it shall be observed, communicated, published, given to the National Bureau of the Official Registry, and filed.

Kirchner – Alberto A. Fernández – Horacio D. Rosatti

CHILE

REPORT OF THE CHILEAN NATIONAL
COMMISSION ON TRUTH AND
RECONCILIATION*

Part IV
   Chapter 1
   Proposals for Reparation

A. INTRODUCTION

Previous chapters have enabled readers to come to an understanding of the truth about the grave human rights violations that have taken place and the injury borne by the victims' relatives. Following our mandate, we will present in this chapter the measures we regard as just for reparation and the restoration of the good name of the victims.

   Obviously, there can be no correlation between the pain, frustration, and hopes of the victims' families and the measures to be suggested here. The disappearance

* Source: *Report of the Chilean National Commission on Truth and Reconciliation* (Notre Dame, IN: University of Notre Dame Press, 1993), 837–51.

or death of a loved one is an irreparable loss. Nevertheless, moral and material reparation seem to be utterly essential to the transition toward a fuller democracy. Thus we understand reparation to mean a series of actions that express acknowledgment and acceptance of the responsibility that falls to the State due to the actions and situations presented in this report. The task of reparation requires conscious and deliberate action on the part of the State.

Furthermore, the whole of Chilean society must respond to the challenge of reparation. Such a process must move toward acknowledging the truth of what has happened, restoring the moral dignity of the victims, and achieving a better quality of life for those families most directly affected. Only in this fashion will we be able to develop a more just form of common life that will enable us to look with hope toward the future.

- Although the specific measures of reparation adopted must be designed to be effective, they will obviously be unable to accomplish anything by themselves. The great ideals—truth, justice, forgiveness, reconciliation—must come first.
- Measures of reparation must aim to bring society together and move toward creating conditions for true reconciliation; they should never cause division.
- Only within an atmosphere that encourages respect for human rights will reparation take on vital meaning and shed any accusatory trait that might reopen the wounds of the past. The reparation process means having the courage to face the truth and achieve justice: it requires the generosity to acknowledge one's faults and a forgiving spirit so that Chileans may draw together.

B. Recommendations for Restoring the Good Name of People and Making Symbolic Reparation

1. Publicly Repairing the Dignity of the Victims

For some people the very fact that this Commission was created by the president and exists may constitute an initial gesture of reparation. Out of our own experience we can attest that many of the victims' relatives who attended sessions throughout Chile saw it as such a gesture.

Moreover, there are already a number of spontaneous initiatives and gestures of reparation throughout the country. Each of them is valuable in itself for what it expresses. Such initiatives need not spring from a law. Indeed it would be beneficial if initiatives for reparation were to multiply throughout the country and in every segment of society. Our hope would be that the creativity of such gestures might add to the artistic and moral endowment of our nation. Thus some day we may have symbols of reparation that are national and others that are regional or local in nature.

However, it would seem that these things are not enough: the country needs to publicly restore the good name of those who perished and to keep alive the memory of what happened so that it may never happen again. Hence the State can take the lead in making gestures and creating symbols that can give a national impetus to the reparation process. Today more than ever our country needs gestures and symbols of reparation so as to cultivate new values that may draw us together and unveil to us common perspectives on democracy and development. If we know how to be attentive to details and observe the formalities, we will also know how to overcome the obstacles still dividing us.

It is to be hoped that as soon as it is prudently possible, the government will see fit to provide the means and resources necessary to set in motion cultural and symbolic projects aimed at reclaiming the memory of the victims both individually and collectively. Such projects would lay down new foundations for our common life and for a culture that may show more respect and care for human rights, and so provide us with the assurance that violations so threatening to life will never again be committed.

2. Some Suggestions for Restoring the Good Name of People and Making Symbolic Reparation

This Commission has decided to offer some criteria or suggestions to aid government officials in taking a position on the kind of gesture or creative expression that could best serve the proposed aims of restoring the good name of people and making reparation. We have received many interesting contributions and note that they have certain common features:

- People are looking for expressions of reparation that will be public and national in scope. At the same time there is a concern that regional and even local aspects be expressed forcefully and independently.
- People are aspiring to have each victim's good name and dignity restored: future generations should know and perpetuate their full name so that it may serve to teach and reaffirm the value of life.

- People are longing to see such expressions reflect a consensus and not be a sign of division exalting some and disparaging others. Such expressions could make a contribution to greater unity and social cohesion.
- People are especially aware of the role played by the mass media in symbolic acts of reparation in view of their impact in creating culture.

Simply by way of example we can report that we have received many suggestions for symbolic reparation. Most frequently they are along the lines of:

- setting up a commemorative monument that would list all the victims of human rights abuses from both sides;
- building a public park in memory of those who lost their lives, to serve as a place of commemoration and a lesson, as well as a place for recreation and for bolstering a life-affirming culture;
- giving the recently created 'National Human Rights Day' the importance it deserves so that each December 10 will be observed throughout the country with public observances and ceremonies in the schools and other gestures aimed at symbolic reparation;
- organizing campaigns, cultural celebrations, and the like, so that we may continue to move toward creating a climate of national reconciliation.

With regard to how to implement these and other possible proposals, this Commission can only urge government officials to invite the most representative social sectors to design projects that both have artistic value and are intended to help make social reparation. In particular, we would like to suggest that those who work in art and culture be invited to make their own specific contribution. Likewise family members could be consulted in the design phase of the project.

3. Solemnly Restoring the Good Name of the Victims

Before ending this section we would like to offer a suggestion we regard as extremely important. This Commission takes the liberty of suggesting that the State—whether represented by his excellency the president of the republic, or by the Congress, or by a law—solemnly and expressly restore the good name of the victims who were accused of crimes which were never proven and who were never given the opportunity or adequate means to defend themselves. It is our hope that such a gesture may initiate an era in our common life as a nation in which a reaffirmation of life may serve to guide us toward the future.

C. Legal and Administrative Recommendations

1. Unresolved Legal Issues

The Commission has found that the immediate family members of the victims of the most serious human rights violations are burdened by a whole series of legal and administrative problems. Some of these problems deserve particular attention. We are referring to those problems arising directly from the state of legal uncertainty of people who have disappeared after arrest, due to the lack of proof of what has happened to them.

In addition to the uncertainty and anguish of this situation, family members confront a long list of problems in connection with their civil status, inheritance, ownership of the disappeared person's property, school tuition for the children, wives' legal interest in marital property, and a host of situations that harm the family estate.

There have been two possible approaches to this problem, one provisional and the other more permanent. One is the judicial appointment of a legal caretaker for the missing person's property. The disadvantage of this approach is that it grants only provisional power to administer the victim's property. The other possibility is to ask that the person be declared to be presumed dead in accordance with Article 8 1ff. of the Civil Code. The problem with this approach has been that the family members have often preferred not to utilize this procedure because it seems to imply that they are somehow giving up their efforts to discover the truth or to find the person alive, or for some other reason. These reasons should be respected.

We think both of these approaches were designed in another context and for other purposes, and they are not adequate for resolving the present problem. Hence we would like to propose that consideration be given to a special procedure for declaring dead those persons in whose cases we arrived at the conviction that government agents were responsible for their arrest and disappearance.

2. Special Procedure for Declaring Persons Arrested and Disappeared to be Dead

Here we will merely state some criteria for the consideration of those persons authorized to enact laws.

(a) Criteria

We propose that a new criterion for declaring a person to be presumed dead be added to those which the law already stipulates. We are referring to those people who have undergone arrest and disappearance at the hands of government agents and are therefore victims of human rights violations and who are listed as such in this report. Since for lack of evidence, this Commission did not come to any conviction in some cases, we suggest that the possibility of applying this criterion to such cases be studied. It would have to be established before the relevant agency designated in the law and within the time limit set by the law that such persons were victims of human rights violations.

(b) Proof

We would recommend that the conviction of this Commission should constitute sufficient proof for such a court decision and be the only evidence required. In other words, the only proof needed would be that the person's name appear on the list of victims in this report; no other procedure would be required. Accordingly, we would like to propose that any other kind of evidence in this procedure, such as issuing a public summons for the missing person, be eliminated.

(c) Procedure

We believe that this procedure would have to be governed by the general rules of law. Those formulating the law should study changes to make it more accessible, simpler, and free of charge for persons requesting it. To that end we propose:

- that the petitioner be permitted to present the request for a declaration of presumed death to the judge with jurisdiction over the last domicile of the disappeared person or the judge with jurisdiction over the petitioner's domicile;
- that the presumed date of death be determined to be that of the last information indicating that the person was still alive (this would constitute a clear exception to normal procedure);
- that final possession of property be granted without passing through a prior provisional possession, in view of the circumstances peculiar to disappearance, which make it more likely that the disappeared person is indeed dead.

In view of the documentation the Commission has obtained, we would recommend that the lawmaking authority consider the possibility that this procedure and legal assistance be free of charge to petitioners.

It has been our intention to recommend a special procedure for clarifying the legal dimension of the problem. We hope that such a procedure might to some degree help alleviate the plight of the relatives of those persons who disappeared after arrest. We hope that measures such as these will enable those affected to have available a legal instrument adapted to the special requirements of such cases, and that the petitioners themselves will be able to use it when they so choose. The social, symbolic, and ethical dimensions of the problem of those persons whom government agents arrested and subjected to forced disappearance leads us to maintain profound respect for the different choices that their relatives may have made or be led to make in the future.

D. Recommendations in the Area of Social Welfare

1. Antecedents

The aim of our recommendations in the area of social welfare is to repair the moral and material harm that the immediate relatives of the victims have suffered. Their plans and hopes have been altered radically by the violations that this Commission has examined.

We believe that by its very nature the State is obligated to undertake measures which support the efforts the affected families have made to seek a better quality of life. Hence we now propose a series of social welfare measures specifically in the areas of social security, health care, education, and housing, as well as other needs and rights. All these areas have been affected and all need mending in order to restore our common life.

- The support provided should not only help people deal with particular problems concerning their welfare; it should also encourage the participation of the relatives themselves, since it is they who can best determine which of their needs are most urgent and how they may be satisfied.
- We would also suggest that the measures finally adopted aim at providing a quick and effective solution, since these problems have been mounting up over the years and they hinder efforts to reintegrate these families into Chilean society.
- Although there are social and economic as well as cultural differences between the victims' family members, we think it would be wise that there be a single set of welfare measures applicable to all so that the reparation made will be permanent rather than momentary. In other words, such measures should support a process in which their quality of life is enhanced. These welfare measures should take into account the irreparable loss of a family member as well as what many years of searching does to a family and its fortunes.

2. Recommendations in the Area of Pensions

A number of the statements we have received lead us to think that the right of the victims' relatives to social security should be reestablished. This is one of the tasks of reparation that the State should assume.

(a) Countless problems and the complexity of solutions

There are countless problems related to pensions, owing to the death, or arrest and disappearance of the victims of human rights violations. Solutions would be very complex, especially due to the changes in the social security system in recent years. The people who were killed or who disappeared after arrest may be regarded as the source of rights to an array of pension benefits that their relatives have never received or have collected only in part. Thus many are owed benefits as survivors (widows, or orphans), from life insurance, and so forth. Remedying this situation would require the removal of legal and administrative obstacles, such as extending the time limits for receiving benefits, certifying or presuming the death of the person who is the source of such a right, bringing the amounts of payments owed in line with increases in the cost of living, and retroactively paying the monthly allotments due.

(b) Proposal for a single reparation pension

In accordance with these antecedents and the interesting suggestions we have received, we think it possible to propose a single reparation pension for the immediate relatives of the victims. The only condition is that the name of the person who is the source of the right must appear on the list in this report. That is, the relatives of those who have disappeared after arrest need not go through the procedure of having the person declared to be presumed dead.

The reason for proposing a single reparation pension is that it would be difficult to resolve quickly and satisfactorily the pension problems we have noted by following the established procedures for providing survivors' pensions. In many of these cases the circumstances of the person's death are not established, and in others their situation vis-à-vis pensions is quite abnormal.

On the basis of our own judgment and many opinions we have received, we would like to recommend that special legislation be drawn up to create a single reparation pension. To that end we would like to present some ideas on the kinds of issues on which the lawmaker or lawmaking body will have to come to a decision.

- There is a convergence of opinion that the single pension should apply to all cases starting on a single date. That date should be at least twelve months prior to the day on which the law goes into effect, and the first payment should be accumulative. The victims' relatives would thus be able to receive a lump sum of money that could serve in part to cover the costs incurred thus far.

- In view of the documentation provided by specialized agencies and taking into account the needs of most of those affected, we suggest that the monthly sum given to each family be not lower than the average income of a family in Chile.
- There is good reason to propose that the people in whose name the single reparation is to be paid be those persons who suffered human rights violations in all the categories laid down in Chapter Three of this report and those who were killed as a result of political violence, as defined there. Their names are listed alphabetically in the final volume of this report [not translated into English].

We suggest that after this Commission is dissolved, those persons over whom it could not come to a conviction may be able to be defined as victims by an agency designated for that purpose, within a time frame to be established by the lawmaking body.

- Laws should be enacted to determine who the beneficiaries are to be, in what order of priority and in which proportion they are to share in any single pension like the one being proposed. We trust that the lawmaker will give due consideration to the most up-to-date standards for social security and will also take into account special cases that may present themselves.
- We would also like to pass on the suggestions that we have received that this pension be for life. We hope that the lawmaker will take this aspect into account and will also define to whom such lifelong benefits are to accrue.
- The observations we have received indicate that receiving a single reparation pension should be incompatible with any other pension arising from the same cause and provided by the existing social security systems in the country. However, should the beneficiaries have a right to more than one pension, they should be able to choose the one that is most advantageous to them.
- The Commission believes that it is the role of the lawmaker to define whether this pension is compatible with any other legal claim the relatives may make on the basis of the victims' death or disappearance after arrest.
- We believe that in view of the reason for the reparation it would be fitting that the pension be granted quickly, easily, and in a manner that makes it accessible to the victims' relatives; the time period for payment should be established by the lawmaker.
- The expenditures required by the single pension are to come from the general funds of the national budget, although the lawmaker may make it possible that funds be received from other sources, especially those donated or collected for that purpose.

3. Recommendations in the Area of Health Care

(a) Consequences from the standpoint of people's health

We have received significant and helpful opinions concerning health care. In general, they focus on the health of the family members of the victims and recommend that these people be provided special attention in view of the effects human rights violations have had on their health.

- Specialized agencies have declared that the victims and their relatives have particular problems in both physical and mental health. They add that these problems are different from the way illnesses affect that portion of the Chilean population that has been less exposed to such violations.
- The permanent stress to which these people have been subjected has made them more vulnerable. They manifest grave symptoms in the area of mental health. They have had traumatic experiences so intense and so strong that their psychic structure has not been able to process them. All their subsequent efforts at reorganizing their lives will be marked by the damage done unless they receive specialized help.
- In terms of bodily health, although the pathology is not notably different, these people have been observed to differ from others treated in hospitals in being more precocious and in their level of commitment. Many of these persons and families are from the popular sectors and have little money or have gradually become poorer from the time they were victims of human rights violations. In some instances serious nutritional problems have been observed. We are especially concerned for senior citizens and children. All indications are that they are going to be exposed to a biological, psychological, and social deterioration that must be treated directly.
- Such disruption of health is not limited to the immediate family circle of those who were killed or who disappeared after arrest, or the survivors of serious torture or acts of violence committed for political purposes. They also affect social relations, work situations, the neighborhood, and indeed the whole community. The health of individuals, families, and society has been harmed.
- Moreover, such harm is both manifest and still latent in the population. Specialists say it will be difficult to overcome such damage in the short term, since it may extend even to the third generation.

No matter how extensive it may be, the specialists who offered their opinions to this Commission believe that this problem is very serious from a qualitative standpoint and that it involves an extreme degree of trauma. The situation is complex because these illnesses have themselves become injustices, or may have taken the form of a mute or stigmatizing pain. Some people have experienced their health problems in the form of an obscure or confused punishment, or as a comforting explanation for why they are powerless to express their truth. Sometimes the passage of time has made certain illness chronic and renders a comprehensive solution difficult or impossible. In such cases regaining health is more complex since it also requires that the person revise what he or she expects to achieve in life.

(b) Need for specialized health care

These brief observations suggest the need for specialized health care for an unspecified number of families who have suffered very serious violations of their rights. The Commission believes that it is primarily the task of the state to respond to this situation. The Ministry of Health will be best able to develop a program or a number of programs aimed at the most directly affected population.

In accordance with our observations here and with suggestions we have received, we propose that the direct beneficiaries of such health programs be all those persons who have been subjected to extreme physical or mental trauma as the result of a grave violation of their human rights committed by government agents or by private citizens who used violence for obvious political reasons. We have in mind the immediate family members of all the persons listed in this report. We would also like to explicitly recommend that those persons who have been the victims of severe physical and mental torture also be included, along with those who have been seriously injured as a result of politically motivated terrorist actions committed by private citizens.

In the context of social reparation, we want to point to the need to serve the health needs of those persons who have been involved in practicing torture in detention sites and to those who have acknowledged their participation in actions whose grave results we have investigated, as well as to those who may require such care in the future for the same reasons. It would seem that both humanitarian and technical reasons converge to urge that this population be furnished with comprehensive health care. Starting with their recovery and physical and mental rehabilitation, such care should go on to encompass levels of prevention and positive action that may extend to broader sectors of society.

(c) Suggestions for organizing health activities

We have received numerous suggestions on how to organize health activities on behalf of this sector of the population that is most in need. We would like to single out some of the more interesting suggestions concerning the manner in which health care is provided:

- Such activities should incorporate the experience people had to undergo. Insofar as necessary, people should be allowed to express the personal and family experiences that have given rise to their need for treatment.
- The approach to each person seeking attention should be comprehensive (biological, psychological, and social). Hence it is desirable that the teams be interdisciplinary and be familiar with the various reasons leading them to seek care. Insofar as possible, they should be alert to the needs of the family as a whole, and kindness and understanding should be part of the treatment.

- Activities should be planned so as to involve not only persons affected by human rights violations but also groups of such people, when the representational character and experience of such groups make it appropriate.
- The projected time period for such health care activities should not be too short. However, such activities should ultimately be aimed at integrating those in most need into ordinary health programs.
- Necessary services should be provided with no regard for the ability to pay of those most directly affected by human rights violations.

(d) Responsibilities of the health care system

Beyond making some suggestions, it is not the role of this Commission to take a position on the most adequate ways to organize and carry out health activities. Health officials will have to devise a special program, and the funding and coordination will have to come from the Ministry of Health. Such a program should seek technical cooperation from nongovernmental health organizations, particularly those that have provided health care to this population and have accumulated valuable experience over all these years. It is suggested that the private health care sector be allowed access to these programs and their funding so as to allow the clientele a variety of alternatives from which to choose.

We think it will be the task of health care providers to determine the existing needs and resources. We are certain that carrying out programs of this nature will require substantial amounts of economic and human resources. The government will have to redouble its efforts to provide the funding and to attain the national coverage that the problem demands. We likewise assume that the contributions that the armed forces and police could make to the overall health care system should not be overlooked. Some of their beneficiaries or potential beneficiaries belong to the population affected by the kinds of problems considered here.

In the spirit of uniting the various segments of our nation, all institutions and care providers in the health care system should be concerned about satisfying the basic needs of such persons.

4. Recommendations in the Area of Education

(a) Need for a vast creative effort to devise ways to make reparation in the realm of education

At first glance it might seem that the educational problems of the immediate relatives of human rights victims have to do with younger children, but that is not the case. Most of the children are adolescents or even adults whose opportunities for attending school or the university can now hardly be recovered. The events that so radically altered people's future plans usually took place years ago. The situation of people who lost their opportunity to receive an education is of special concern to us.

The cases we have examined have shown us how the chances of entering and remaining in the various levels of the educational system were disrupted for children and adolescents who were not especially predisposed to take such a risk. Here again poverty and declining living conditions have aggravated the problem of education for many of these families. In addition such children and young people have had to bear with emotional upheaval and learning problems during their elementary and high school years.

As a result of all these factors combined it has not been easy for them to enter universities and institutes for advanced technical training. Our country needs the contribution of all its youth and particularly these young people who have been excluded from formal education by the facts and circumstances presented in the earlier chapters of this report. There is no need for a lengthy diagnosis. It is obvious that we need a vast creative and perhaps unprecedented effort in our country to find ways to make reparation in the realm of education before it is too late and the situation is irremediable. At the same time, the tasks of making reparation in the realm of education must be coordinated with the efforts to prevent human rights abuses and forge a culture respectful of human rights that we propose below.

(b) Measures to take as quickly as possible

In accordance with the nature of the problem and the opinions we have gathered on this issue, it would be desirable to implement measures on behalf of the children of persons whose names are listed in this report in any of its categories as soon as possible. Our recommendations in this regard are directed to the Ministry of Education so that it may study the possibility of devising a program of reparation. The starting point for the program should be a diagnosis of the problem and should involve the participation of those who have suffered, human rights organizations, professional associations, the National Teachers Association, and other relevant bodies.

Among the measures we regard as most interesting we suggest the following:

- A portion of scholarships for higher education should be reserved for the children of human rights victims who are ready for such studies.
- Study should be given to the possibility of canceling debts that the children, spouses, or other immediate relatives of such victims have incurred with the State or universities, provided the proper authority approves.
- Young people and adults who did not complete their studies and do not have a trade should be regarded as having a right to enroll in certain institutes and centers for technical training.

- Similar opportunities and incentives should be provided for surviving spouses or partners, or other immediate family members, should they request it.
- We urge that educational measures be organized in the framework of our recommendations for social reparation so that they may make it as easy as possible for people to acquire a profession or trade, complete their training, or retrain for that purpose. We also urge that the government assume the costs within certain limits and time frames, once the scope of the demand has been assessed. Finally we urge that the aim must always be to reincorporate the relatives of human rights victims into society and that the stigma and risks of isolation that might derive from granting special aid be avoided.

(c) Appreciation for the efforts of those teaching outside the government system

Finally, we have come to an appreciation of the various efforts made by nongovernmental agents to aid in the education of the victims' family members. We hope that their contribution will continue to complement the initiatives that the government may undertake in this area and that new study and training opportunities may open up for young people and even older adults who also need them.

5. Recommendations in the Area of Housing

(a) Different problems

Housing issues might seem minor when compared to the serious consequences already described. There is no point in debating the issue, however, since housing is a basic need, and the ability of those affected by human rights violations to satisfy that need has been seriously impaired. Insofar as possible, reparation for that impairment should be made in a social manner.

In many instances the events we have investigated have forced families to move to a different area, leaving their home and even losing it. In other instances, the family did not have a house of their own when these events occurred. Had they not taken place, however, it is quite possible that the now missing head of the house would have been able to obtain a house for his family as the fruit of his work.

This Commission has also learned of land and goods being confiscated, of houses damaged by violence, of debts owed for housing payments, of situations in which insurance policies that should have paid off the mortgage when the person was killed or disappeared did not do so, problems with deeds, and so forth.

(b) Special treatment

In view of these factors, we think it would be just for the government to offer special treatment for the housing problems of the relatives of victims of the most serious human rights violations whose names are listed in this report. In connection with the reparation that the State should make, we offer two suggestions by way of example:

- We urge the Ministry of Housing and Urban Planning to give priority to those immediate family members of the victims of human rights violations to participate in social programs, should they apply. The very fact that they can prove they are such family members should entitle them to participate. We have in mind people who have no house of their own, who want to apply for a subsidy, and who fulfill the other requirements. How they can do so is to be established by the proper authorities.
- We likewise urge the ministry to study the possibility of setting aside a certain number of places within special housing programs for the victims' immediate family members who desire to apply for them and who fulfill the other requisites.

As was the case in other areas, it would be interesting to encourage specialized nongovernmental agencies, building contractors, and professional associations to become involved and work together with those affected and their organizations to devise new and concrete solutions that may quickly remedy the housing needs of this portion of the population which is spread throughout the cities and rural areas of the whole country.

6. Further Recommendations in the Realm of Social Welfare

(a) Recommendations for canceling debts

In the general area of reparation, we suggest that study be given to the possibility of canceling some outstanding debts to the government owed by people who were killed or who disappeared after arrest and who are listed in this report. Such debts would include those related to social security, education, housing, taxes, or others that may still exist with government agencies because requirements were not met within pre-scribed time periods. The aim is to alleviate the burden that the families have had to bear. We are also assuming that the State has a responsibility in the area of reparation.

(b) Recommendations concerning obligatory military service

In view of the evidence the Commission has in hand, and following suggestions from eminent moral authorities, we suggest that within the climate of reparation needed if the various sectors of the nation are to come together, the competent authority should study the possibility of allowing the children of those who suffered the most serious human rights violations the option to accept or reject military service without suffering discrimination in other opportunities for study or employment. The only basis for making this recommendation is the understandable problem of sensitive feelings aroused by this matter. In no way are we motivated by any lack of esteem for military service, which deserves our wholehearted respect.

(c) Recommendations concerning most vulnerable groups

We could not end this chapter without noting a concern shared with other agencies with whom we consulted. That concern is the priority that should be given to serving the needs of certain groups in the population due to their vulnerability and what they represent to society. In this regard we single out older people who have been left alone as a result of the events we have been considering. The children who have also suffered from these events deserve a very special priority, as do a group of Mapuche families who have likewise been significantly affected. We would like to recommend that along with the efforts it organizes on behalf of these more vulnerable groups, the State take into account the experiences of reparation in this area already existing in our country and in other countries as well.

We believe that the obligation to make reparation to future generations falls on the whole society. However, it also benefits the whole society because insofar as we truly become concerned for these people, we are doing something to prevent such grave human rights violations from ever recurring in Chile.

E. THE MOST URGENT RECOMMENDATIONS

In concluding this chapter the Commission would like to note that the information it has gathered and a body of suggestions that it has received would seem to indicate that certain reparation measures deserve more urgent attention from government authorities. These measures have to do primarily with symbols, law and administration, and social welfare.

- There seems to be a need for a symbolic gesture that will meet the requirements outlined above for restoring the good name of the victims and so that Chile may never again endure the kinds of events we have had to bring to light.

- In the area of law and administration, a special procedure for declaring dead those persons who disappeared after arrest would help reestablish the necessary quality of life for their families.
- The social welfare of those families demands that lost or diminished pension rights be reestablished. The Single Reparation Pension would seem to be the most desirable means for doing so.

In pointing to the urgency of these three measures, it has not been our intention to simplify a situation that is inherently complex for the government. Our aim has been to convey the needs of those affected in order to set in motion the process of social reparation that his excellency, the president, announced when he created this Truth and Reconciliation Commission.

LAW 19.123*
ESTABLISHES THE NATIONAL CORPORATION FOR REPARATION AND RECONCILIATION AND GRANTS OTHER BENEFITS TO PERSONS AS INDICATED

Official Gazette No. 34,188, February 8, 1992
Last Amendment: Law 19.441
Date of last Amendment: 01/23/1996 Considering:
That the National Congress has approved the following Draft:

Title I
On the National Corporation for Reparation and Reconciliation Nature and Objectives

Article 1. The National Corporation for Reparation and Reconciliation, a decentralized, public service institution, under the supervision of the President of the Republic through the Ministry of Interior, is hereby established. Its domicile shall be in the city of Santiago.
Its purpose shall be to coordinate, carry out, and promote actions needed to comply with the recommendations contained in the Report of the National Truth and

* Translated from Spanish by Christian Gerzso and revised by Charles Roberts.

Reconciliation Commission, created by Supreme Decree 355 of April 25, 1990, and all other functions indicated in the present law.

Article 2.   In particular, the Corporation shall:

1. Promote reparations for the moral injury caused to the victims referred to in Article 18 and provide the social and legal assistance needed by their families so that they can access the benefits provided for in this law.
2. Promote and assist in the actions aimed at determining the whereabouts and circumstances surrounding the disappearance or death of the detained-dis-appeared persons and of those persons whose mortal remains have not been located, even though their death has been legally recognized. In pursuing this objective, the corporation should collect, analyze, and systematize all information useful for this purpose.
3. Serve as depository for the information collected by the National Truth and Reconciliation Commission and the National Corporation for Reparation and Reconciliation, and all information on cases and matters similar to those treated by it, that may be compiled in the future. It may also request, collect, and process existing information in the possession of public institutions, as well as request it from private institutions, in relation to human rights violations or political violence referred to in the Report of the National Truth and Reconciliation Commission.

Access to information must ensure its absolute confidentiality; however, the courts of justice may have access to such information in the proceedings brought before them.

4. Compile background information and perform the inquiries necessary to rule on the cases that were brought before the National Truth and Reconciliation Commission, in which it was not possible to reach a well-founded conclusion as to whether the person detrimentally impacted was a victim of human rights violations or political violence, or with respect to cases of the same nature that were not brought before the Commission in timely fashion, or, if they were, in which it did not reach a decision due to lack of sufficient information. In this regard, it shall proceed pursuant to the same rules established for said Commission in Supreme Decree 355, of the Ministry of Interior, of April 25, 1990, which established it.

The cases referred to in paragraph 3 above should be made known to the Corporation within ninety (90) days of the publication of its by-laws in the Official Gazette, and shall be resolved within one (1) year of said publication.* If the Corporation is able to reach a determination that a person is a victim, it shall

---

* Article 1 of Law 19.274, published in the Official Gazette of December 10, 1993.

immediately inform the relevant agencies of the State Administration so that they may grant beneficiaries the rights and benefits granted by this law.

5. Enter into agreements with nonprofit institutions or corporations so that they may provide the professional assistance needed to carry out the aims of the Corporation, including medical benefits.
6. Make proposals for consolidating a culture of respect for human rights in the country.

Article 3.   In order to attain its objectives, the Corporation may request the collaboration of different State agencies in those affairs under their jurisdiction and that are related to its functions.

Article 4.   Under no circumstance may the Corporation assume judicial functions properly vested in the Courts of Justice, or interfere in proceedings pending before them. Accordingly, it may not decide on the liability that, according to the law, may attach to individual persons.

If in the performance of its functions the Corporation learns of facts that appear to constitute the elements of a crime, it should, without any further processing, report them to the Courts of Justice.

Article 5.   The actions of the Corporation shall be carried out without publicity, and its counselors and officers shall be under an obligation not to disclose the information or documents they learn of in the performance of their functions.

Article 6.   It is hereby declared that locating the detained-disappeared persons, and locating the mortal remains of the persons executed and the circumstances surrounding their disappearances or deaths, constitute an inalienable right of the relatives of the victims and of Chilean society.

Section II
Organization of The Corporation

Article 7.   The management of the Corporation shall be entrusted to a Superior Council, which shall be structured as follows:

(a) One councilor who shall chair the Council, designated by the President of the Republic, and
(b) six councilors, designated by the President of the Republic, and ratified by the Senate.

The Councilors, with the exception of the Chairperson, shall receive an allowance that amounts to one-thirtieth part of the remuneration corresponding to a Minister of the Supreme Court, grade level II of the Scale of Remunerations established by Decree-Law 3,058 of 1979, for each session they attend.

The Councilors shall have the right to travel expense and per diem. The amount of the per diem shall be consistent with the per diem corresponding to the second category of the Judiciary.

The functions of the Chairperson of the Council and of the Councilors shall be compatible with any public function, except those established in the Constitution.

Even so, the incompatibility of remunerations shall apply to the Chairperson of the Council if he or she holds another job or public function, in which case he or she will have to choose between the remuneration assigned to him or her by this law and that of the other function or job.

Article 8.   The following are the functions of the Superior Council:

1. Undertaking the management of the Corporation and approving its plans and programs of action to carry out its mission.
2. Declaring the status of victim of human rights violations or political violence.
3. Making the proposals referred to in Article 2(6).
4. Ensuring that the agreements and instructions it adopts or imparts are carried out.
5. Issuing the by-laws of the Corporation, which should indicate, among other matters, the procedure to which applications for a hearing and decision of those cases and decisions referred to by Article 2(4) shall be submitted, the order of subrogation of the President among the members of the Council, that its decisions shall be adopted by the majority of its members, and that, in case of a tie, the Chairperson shall cast the tie-breaking vote.
6. Agreeing on those acts and contracts, which, according to the laws, require the granting of a special power.

Article 9.   The Chairperson of the Council shall:

1. Chair the sessions of the Council.
2. Represent the Corporation, judicially and extrajudicially.
3. Issue the resolutions needed to carry out the decisions and instructions of the Council.
4. Manage the Corporation, with the agreement of the Council.
5. Inform the President of the Republic of the work of the Corporation periodically.
6. Appoint the Executive Secretary and personnel, with the agreement of the Council.

Article 10.   The Corporation shall have an Executive Secretary, whose functions are as follows:

1. To execute the decisions of the Council and carry out the instructions of the Chairperson.

2. To serve as Secretary of the Council and Minister in Charge of Verification [Ministro de Fe]. The Executive Secretary shall have the right to speak in the sessions of the Council.

Section III
On Roster of Staff and Personnel

Article 11. The following roster of staff is established for the National Corporation for Reparation and Reconciliation:

Position	Grade Level	Number of Positions
Chairperson of the Council	1B	1
Executive Secretary	2nd	1
		2
Head of Department	4th	1
Head of Department	5th	1
		2
Professionals	5th	3
Professionals	6th	2
Professionals	7th	1
		6
Experts	10th	1
Administrative	13th	1
Administrative	17th	1
		3
Assistants	21st	2
Total Number of Positions		15

Article 12. The personnel of the Corporation shall be governed by the provisions of Law 834, Administrative Statute, and their remuneration shall be subject to the provisions of Decree-Law 49 of 1974, and its complementary legislation.

Article 13. The agencies and services of the State Administration may post staff members from their various offices, to be seconded to the National Corporation for Reparation and Reconciliation, without being subject to the limitation established in Article 70(1) of Law 8.834.

The grade-levels of the pay scales assigned to the employees, under contract or on grade-level-adjusted salary, of the Corporation, may not exceed the maximum for the personnel of the various staffing arrangements referred to in Article 5 of Law 18.834.

Section IV
On Assets and Financial Control

Article 14. The assets of the Corporation shall be constituted by all types of movables and real property it may acquire free of charge or by purchase, and in particular, by:

1. the contributions allocated to it annually by the Budget Law;
2. other contributions, national and international, and
3. the proceeds of such assets.

Donations to the Corporation shall not require the judicial approval procedure referred to in Article 1401 of the Civil Code, and shall be exempt from the tax on donations established by Law 16.271.

Article 15. The Corporation shall be subject to the financial control of the Office of the Comptroller General of the Republic [Contraloría General de la República] as regards the examination and evaluation of its accounts of revenues and expend-itures, and to control the legality of the acts in relation to its personnel and its regulatory framework.

Section V
On Extinction

Article 16. The National Corporation for Reparation and Reconciliation (Law 19.441 Art. 1) shall exist legally until December 31, 1996. After this period has elapsed, it shall extinguish by operation of law. Its assets shall be at the disposal of the National Treasury or one of its agencies, which shall be determined by a supreme decree issued by the Ministry of Interior.

However, if the aims of the Corporation are fulfilled before the period established in the previous clause, the President of the Republic, by decree signed by the Minister of Interior, shall be authorized to extinguish the Corporation with the anticipation he deems necessary.*

Title II
On the Pension for Reparation

Article 17. A monthly pension for reparation is hereby established for the relatives of the victims of human rights violations or political violence, who are named in the Second Volume of the Report of the National Truth and Reconciliation

* The amendment made to this article by Law 19.411, published in the Official Gazette of January 23, 1996, shall enter into force on January 1, 1996.

Commission and those who are recognized as such by the National Corporation for Reparation and Reconciliation, in keeping with the provisions of Articles 2(4) and 4(8).

Article 18. Those persons declared victims of human rights violations or political violence shall have the right to a pension for reparations, in keeping with the provisions of the previous article.

Article 19. The monthly pension established in Article 17 shall be for up to $140,000, plus the percentage equivalent to contributions for health care; it shall not be subject to any other contributions, and shall be adjusted in keeping with the provisions of Article 14 of Decree-Law 2,448 of 1979, or of the legal provisions replacing it. This pension may be waived.

Article 20. The beneficiaries of the pension established in Article 17 shall be the surviving spouse, the mother of the person with the right or the father in case of her absence, the mother of the victim's biological children or the father in case the mother was the person with the right, and his or her children under twenty-five (25) years of age, or disabled children of any age, be they legitimate, biological, adopted, or illegitimate in those cases provided for in Article 280(1), (2), and (3) of the Civil Code.

For the purposes of the present law, a disabled child shall be considered as one who has physical, intellectual, or psychological harm, or a considerable weakening of his or her physical or intellectual strength which, in a presumably permanent manner, causes a diminution of at least fifty percent (50%), in his or her ability to perform a normal job, mindful of his or her age, gender, and present strength, capacity, training, or education.

The declaration and review of the disablility * shall be done by the Commission of Preventive Medicine and Disabilities [Comisión de Medicina Preventiva e Invalidez] of the respective health service, in the manner determined by the Regulation.

Supervening disability shall entitle one to the pension, even if the right to it has ceased according to the provision of Article 22; in that case it shall be compatible with any other social security benefit established by law.

The pension shall be distributed among the aforementioned beneficiaries as follows:

(a) 40% for the surviving spouse;
(b) 30% for the mother of the person with the right, or the father in case of her absence;

---

* Supreme Decree 44 of the Office of the Undersecretary for Social Security, published in the Official Gazette of June 18, 1993, approved the Regulations for the Application of Article 20 of Law 19.123.

(c) 15% for the mother, or the father, as the case may be, of the victim's biological children; if more come forward, each shall receive the percentage indicated, even if with this one were to exceed the amount of the pension established in Article 19; and

(d) 15% for each one of the children of the person with the right under twenty-five (25) years of age, and disabled of any age.

In the event that more than one child comes forward, each and every one of them shall receive 15% of the pension, even if with this one were to exceed its amount established in Article 19.

If at the time of the call there is only one sole beneficiary, he or she shall have a total pension coming to $100,000, plus the contribution and readjustment established in Article 19.

If at the time of the call, there does not exist one or more of the beneficiaries as indicated in sections (a), (b), or (c) of this article, and more than one child comes forward, the amount that would have corresponded to the beneficiary lacking shall be earmarked, first, to satisfying, in whole or in part, the payments due to those children.

If, once this rule is applied, there is a residual amount, it shall preferentially be earmarked to satisfying, in whole or in part, the payments due to possible additional beneficiaries, of those indicated in section (c) of this article. If, even so, there is still a residual amount, it shall increase the benefit for all existing beneficiaries by an amount proportional to their rights, up to the total amount of the pension established in Article 19. The same increase shall operate if no children come forward.

If any of the beneficiaries should die or ceases to receive the benefit, in keeping with this law, or waives his or her right, the same increment shall apply, so that the pension is fully distributed, except when only one sole beneficiary remains, in which case the pension shall be reduced to $100,000, plus the contribution and adjustment established in Article 19 of this law.

Article 21. The benefit shall be paid at the moment the present law enters into force, and the beneficiaries shall be those persons who, existing at that time, had, as of the date of the death or disappearance of the person from whom the right arises, one of the family ties indicated in the preceding articles.

It shall be considered that the following had a family tie as of the date of the death or disappearance of the person from whom the right arises: posthumous legitimate children; biological children who obtained such recognition by a court judgment pursuant to Article 271(2), (3), (4), or (5) of the Civil Code; adopted children with respect to whom the registrations, subregistrations, and annotations established in

Article 7 of Law 7.613, Article 10 of Law 16.346, and Articles 12 and 34 of Law 18.703, were made after the date of death or disappearance of the person from whom the right arises, and the illegitimate children referred to in Article 20.

Article 22. The children shall receive the pension that corresponds to them, with the proper increments, until the last day of the year in which they turn twenty-five (25) years of age.

For all other beneficiaries, including disabled children, the pension shall be for life, with the proper increments.

The surviving spouse and the mother or father of the biological children of the person from whom the right arises, as the case may be, shall not lose this benefit due to marriage subsequent to the disappearance or death of the victim.

Regarding the beneficiaries of those who have been declared victims of human rights violations or political violence in the Report of the National Truth and Reconciliation Commission, the pension shall accrue as of July 1, 1991, provided that application for it is made within six (6) months of the entry into force of the present law; if the benefit is not claimed within this period, it shall accrue from the first day of the month following the one in which the right is exercised.

For the beneficiaries of those who have been declared victims of human rights violations or political violence by the National Corporation for Reparation and Reconciliation, the pension shall accrue from the date of the communication referred to in the last paragraph of Article 2(4), provided that they apply for it within six (6) months counted from that date.

Those who ask for it after this period shall begin to receive it, if there are already beneficiaries with a right to it, from the first day of the month following the one in which they file their applications.

Each time new beneficiaries appear and the right is awarded to them, the pension already determined must be recalculated. Such recalculation shall only be valid for the future, without prejudice to the provisions in clauses 4 and 5 of this article.

Article 23. Without prejudice to the provisions of Article 17, the families of the victims referred to in Article 18 shall be granted a lump sum compensatory allowance equivalent to twelve (12) months of pension, excluding the percentage equivalent to the contribution for health care, which will not be deemed income for any legal purpose.

This allowance shall not be subject to any contribution whatsoever, and shall be paid to the beneficiaries indicated in Article 20, in the proportions and with the proper increments indicated in that article.

This allowance shall be paid and its amount shall be determined definitively and irrevocably, payable to the beneficiaries who have filed the application provided for in clauses 4 and 5 of the previous article, within the time limits therein established; the right to this allowance shall extinguish for those beneficiaries who file after the time limits have expired.

Article 24. The pension for reparations shall be compatible with any other pension, of any kind, which is received or could correspond to the respective beneficiary.

In addition, the pension shall be compatible with any other social security benefit established by law.

Article 25. For all legal purposes, the Ministry of Interior shall grant, by petition of the interested parties or of the Instituto de Normalización Previsional, a certificate attesting that the National Truth and Reconciliation Commission, or the Corporation established in Title I of this law, has reached the conclusion that a given person has been the victim of a human rights violation or political violence.

Article 26. The monthly reparation pensions established in Articles 17 and 19 and the compensatory allowance of Article 23 shall be nonattachable.

Article 27. For the purposes of this law, the date of death or disappearance of the person from whom the right arises shall be that determined by the National Truth and Reconciliation Commission or that established by the National Corporation for Reparation and Reconciliation, if said Commission had not determined one.

Title III
On Medical Benefits

Article 28. The beneficiaries indicated in Title II, as well as the father and siblings of the person from whom the right arises in case they are not beneficiaries, are hereby granted the right to receive, free of charge, the medical benefits indicated in Articles 8 and 9 of Law 18.469, which in the modality of institutional care are provided in the establishments that are part of or attached to the National System of Health Services, created by Decree-Law 2,763 of 1979, and in the modality established by the Ministry of Health for specialized care.

The Ministry of Health or the corresponding Regional Ministerial Secretary of Health, by the sole merit of the documents that show the status of beneficiary, or of parent or sibling of the victim, shall order that a credential or special identification card be issued that will include the beneficiary's name, domicile, and national identity number. Said individual certificate shall be an essential requirement for the establishments that provide care that are part of or attached to the National System of Health Services at any level to provide medical assistance free of charge to the beneficiary.
The provisions of the foregoing clauses are without prejudice to the benefits arising from the contribution referred to in Article 19.

Title IV
On Educational Benefits

Article 29. The children of the persons from whom the right arises indicated in Article 18 of this law shall have the right to receive the educational benefits established in this title.

The age limit for claiming these benefits shall be thirty-five (35) years.

Article 30. The students of universities or professional institutes with fiscal contributions shall have the right to payment of their tuition fees and monthly stipend. The cost of this benefit shall be charged to the Scholarship and Development of Higher Education Fund of the Ministry of Education [Fondo de Becas y Desarrollo de Educación Superior del Ministerio de Educación]. The students at universities, professional institutes, and technical training centers without fiscal contributions and recognized by the Ministry of Education shall have the right to payment of tuition fees and the monthly stipend at each institution. The cost of this benefit shall be charged to the Scholarship Program of the President of the Republic, created by Supreme Decree 1,500, of the Ministry of Interior, of December 18, 1980.

Article 31. The students attending secondary school, as well as those indicated in both clauses of the previous article, shall have the right to receive a monthly subsidy that amounts to 1.24 monthly taxation units [unidades tributarias mensuales]. This subsidy shall be paid so long as the student shows his or her status as such, and shall accrue during the school year.

Title V
On Compliance with Compulsory Military Service

Article 32. The legitimate, biological, and adopted children of the persons referred to in Article 18 of the present law shall be in the category of available referred to in Article 30 of Decree-Law 2,306 of 1978, on Recruitment and Mobilization of the Armed Forces, when they so request directly or through the Corporation established in Title I of this law.

Title VI
On Financing

Article 33. The benefits established in Title II of the present law shall be administered by the Instituto de Normalización Previsional and shall be financed out of the resources provided for in item 15-08-01-24-30.002 Retirement, Pensions, and Pension Funds for Widows and Orphans of the budgetary allocation for the Ministry of Labor and Social Security of the Budget of the Nation for the current year.

Article 34. Without prejudice to what is indicated in the preceding article, the expenditure implied by this law in 1992 shall be financed from resources coming from item 50-01-03-25-33.104 of the Program of Complementary Operations of the Public Treasury. The President of the Republic, by supreme decree, issued through the Ministry of the Treasury, shall create the corresponding Chapter of revenues and expenditures of the budget of the National Corporation for Reparation and Reconciliation, with the pertinent budgetary allocations.

Transitory Article. Pending the time limits established in Article 22(4) and (5), and without waiting for their expiration, beneficiaries who show their right to the corresponding pension shall be paid provisionally, in keeping with the percentages established in letters in Article 20(5)(a), (b), (c), and (d).

In the same situation and manner, the compensatory allowance established in Article 23 shall be paid in an amount equivalent to twelve (12) months of the pension provisionally determined in keeping with the previous clause.

After the time limit has expired, these determined pensions and allowances shall be re-calculated retroactively.

And as I have seen fit to approve it and adopt it; therefore, it is promulgated and given effect as a Law of the Republic.

Santiago, January 31, 1992.

Patricio Aylwin Azócar, President of the Republic
Belisario Velasco Baraona, in lieu of Minister of Interior
Martín Manterola Urzúa, in lieu of Minister of Labor and Social Security
Jorge Rodríguez Grossi, in lieu of Minister of the Treasury
Enrique Correa Ríos, Minister Secretary General of Government

I hereby transcribe for your knowledge.
Sincerely Yours,

Gonzalo D. Manner Fanta,
In lieu of Undersecretary of Interior

BRAZIL

LAW 9,140 OF DECEMBER 4, 1995* RECOGNIZES AS DECEASED THOSE PERSONS WHO HAVE DISAPPEARED BECAUSE OF PARTICIPATION, OR ACCUSATION OF PARTICIPATION, IN POLITICAL ACTIVITIES IN THE PERIOD FROM SEPTEMBER 2, 1961 TO AUGUST 15, 1979, AND MAKES OTHER PROVISIONS

The President of the Republic

I hereby make known that the National Congress decrees and I sanction the following Law:

Article 1. The persons listed in Appendix I of this Law are recognized as deceased, for all legal purposes, for having participated, or having been accused of participation, in political activities in the period from September 2, 1961 to August 15,

* Translated from Portuguese by e-verba.

1979, and who, for this reason, were detained by government agents and subsequently disappeared without a trace.

Article 2. The application of the provisions of this Law and all of its effects will be guided by the principle of reconciliation and national pacification, expressed in Law 6.683 of August 28, 1979—the Amnesty Law.

Article 3. The spouse, male or female companion, descendant, ancestor, or relative to the fourth degree of the persons named on the list referred to in Article 1, who have proven this relationship, may petition the official of the civil registry of individuals of their domicile in order to obtain a death certificate; this petition must be presented with the original or a copy of the publication of this Law and its Appendices. In case of doubt, judicial justification shall be allowed.

Article 4. Given the political situation mentioned in Article 1, a Special Commission is hereby created with the following attributes:

I Proceed to the recognition of persons:

   (a) disappeared but not listed in Annex I of the present Law;
   (b) who, because of having participated or having been accused of participating in political activities during the period from September 2, 1961 until August 15, 1979 have died of nonnatural causes in police or similar premises.
II Take action to locate the bodies of persons who have disappeared if evidence exists as to where they may be deposited.
III Issue opinions on the petitions regarding compensation, which might be filed by the persons mentioned in Article 10 of this Law.

Article 5. The Special Commission shall be comprised of seven members, freely chosen and designated by the President of the Republic. The Commission will determine which of its members will preside over it and cast the deciding vote.

1. Of the seven members of the Commission, four shall be chosen:

   (a) from members of the Human Rights Commission of the House of Representatives [Câmara de Deputados];
   (b) from persons with family ties to the persons referred to on the list in Appendix 1;
   (c) from members of the Federal Public Prosecutor [Ministério Público Federal]; and
   (d) from members of the Armed Forces.

2. The Special Commission may receive assistance from federal public servants, designated by the President of the Republic, and may, moreover, request assistance from the Departments of Justice of the states, by means of an agreement with the (Federal) Ministry of Justice, if necessary.

Article 6. The Special Commission will function in conjunction with the Ministry of Justice, which will offer it the necessary support.

Article 7. To recognize persons who have disappeared and are not listed in Appendix 1 of this Law, petitions made by any of the persons mentioned in Article 3 shall be presented to the Special Commission within a period of one hundred and twenty (120) days, counting from the date that this Law is published, and shall be accompanied with the information and documents that verify the assertion. (1) An identical procedure shall be used in the cases based on Clause b of Paragraph I of Article 4. (2) The Special Commission's approval of the petitions for recognition of persons not mentioned in Appendix 1 of this Law shall accompany any petitions for a death certificate treated in Article 3 within a period of one hundred and twenty (120) days, counting from the notice of a favorable decision.

Article 8. If an express request is made by any of the persons mentioned in Article 3 during a period of one hundred and twenty (120) days counting from the founding of the Special Commission and the Commission concludes that sufficient evidence exists, the Commission may undertake measures to locate the remains of a disappeared person.

Article 9. For the purposes provided for in Articles 4 and 7, the Special Commission may request: (1) documents from any public agency; (2) the execution of expert investigations; (3) the collaboration of witnesses; (4) the intervention of the Ministry of Foreign Relations to obtain information from foreign governments and organizations.

Article 10. The compensation provided for in this Law is granted to the persons indicated below, in the following order: (1) to the spouse; (2) to the companion, defined by Law 8,971 of December 29, 1994; (3) to descendants; (4) to ancestors; (5) to relatives to the fourth degree removed. First, the petition for compensation may be submitted up to one hundred and twenty (120) days counting from the publication of this Law. In the case of recognition by the Special Commission, the period will be counted from the date of recognition. Second, if there is agreement among the persons indicated at the head of this Article, the indemnification may be petitioned for independently of the order provided herein. Third, after death is recognized, under the terms of Clause b of Paragraph I of Article 4, the persons mentioned at the head of this Article may, in the same order and conditions, petition the Special Commission for compensation.

Article 11. The compensation, intended as reparation, shall consist of the payment of a single amount equal to R$3,000.00 (three thousand réis) multiplied by the number of years corresponding to the life expectancy of the person who disappeared, taking into consideration the age at the time of disappearance and the criteria and amounts in the table found in Appendix II of this Law. First, in no case shall the amount of indemnification be less than R$100,000.00 (one hundred thousand réis). Second, the indemnification shall be granted by means of a decree issued by the President of the Republic, after the favorable report of the Special Commission created by this Law.

Article 12. If a disappeared person is found alive, or if existence of proof contrary to disappearance is presented, the respective acts resulting from the application of this Law shall be revoked, but regressive action for the reimbursement of any payment already made shall not be applied, except in the case of proven bad faith.

Article 13. Upon the conclusion of the judgment of the petitions, the Special Commission shall prepare a detailed report that shall be sent to the President of the Republic for publication, and the Commission shall terminate its activities. While its activities are underway, the Special Commission shall present evaluations on a quarterly basis.

Article 14. In compensatory judicial actions based on events resulting from the political situation mentioned in Article 1, appeals of unfavorable rulings shall be decided by the courts.

Article 15. The expenses resulting from the application of this Law shall be charged to the account of funds allocated in the Federal budget by the Budget Law.

Article 16. This Law will go into effect on the date of its publication.

Brasília, December 4, 1995; the 174th year of Independence and 107th year of the Republic.

Fernando Henrique Cardoso
Nelson A. Jobim

EL SALVADOR

FROM MADNESS TO HOPE: THE 12-YEAR WAR IN EL SALVADOR: REPORT OF THE COMMISSION ON THE TRUTH FOR EL SALVADOR*
[EXCERPTS]

Chapter V. Recommendations

[...]

Section IV. Steps Towards National Reconciliation

The Geneva Agreement of April 4, 1990, which provided the framework for the negotiations and thus for the peace agreements, defined as objectives of the process, in addition to guaranteeing unrestricted respect for human rights and promoting the democratization of the country, the restoration of peace, national reconciliation, and the reunification of Salvadorian society. These last two goals are complex and do not depend only on the cessation of hostilities but also on a process involving several stages that cannot be bypassed. We are again faced with inseparable goals. There will

* Source: UN Security Council, S/25500, 1993, Annex, *From Madness to Hope: the 12-year war in El Salvador: Report of the Commission on the Truth for El Salvador*, 184–7.

be no reunification of Salvadorian society without national reconciliation, and the latter will be impossible without the fraternal unity of the Salvadorian people.

The country must move on from a situation of confrontation to one of calm assimilation of all that has happened, in order to banish such occurrences from a future characterized by a new relationship of solidarity, coexistence, and tolerance. In order to achieve this, a process of collective reflection on the reality of the past few years is crucial, as is a universal determination to eradicate this experience forever.

One bitter but unavoidable step is to look at and acknowledge what happened and must never happen again. The Commission took on the difficult task of clarifying significant aspects of this reality, which it hopes it has fulfilled through this report. The truth is not enough, however, to achieve the goals of national reconciliation and the reunification of Salvadorian society. Pardon is essential: not a formal pardon which is limited to not imposing penalties, but one founded on a universal determination to rectify the mistakes of the past and on the certainty that this process will not be complete unless it emphasizes the future rather than a past, which, no matter how abhorrent the acts that occurred, cannot now be altered.

However, in order to achieve the goal of a pardon, we must pause and weigh certain consequences which can be inferred from knowledge of the truth about the serious acts described in this report. One such consequence, perhaps the most difficult to address in the country's current situation, is that of fulfilling the twofold requirements of justice: punishing the guilty and adequately compensating the victims and their families.

The Commission has already referred in its introduction to this chapter of the report to the insurmountable difficulties it has encountered in this regard. Such difficulties, which it is beyond its power to resolve directly, can be attributed to the glaring deficiencies of the judicial system.

In this connection, the Commission would simply add that, since it is not possible to guarantee a proper trial for all those responsible for the crimes described here, it is unfair to keep some of them in prison while others who planned the crimes or also took part in them remain at liberty. It is not within the Commission's power to address this situation, which can only be resolved through a pardon after justice has been served.

However, the Commission fervently hopes that knowledge of the truth, and the immediate implementation of the above recommendations, which can be inferred directly from the investigation, will be an adequate starting point for national reconciliation and for the desired reunification of Salvadorian society.

But justice does not stop at punishment; it also demands reparation. The victims and, in most cases, their families, are entitled to moral and material compensation. The Farabundo Marti National Liberation Front (FMLN) must provide such compensation where it is found to have been responsible, while this obligation devolves on the State in cases where the actions or omissions of the public authorities or their agencies were among the causes of the acts of violence described, or in cases where the persons responsible enjoyed impunity. However, since the country's financial constraints and national reconstruction needs cannot be ignored, complementary mechanisms along the lines recommended below should be envisaged.

A. Material compensation

   1. It is recommended that a special fund be established, as an autonomous body with the necessary legal and administrative powers, to award appropriate material compensation to the victims of violence in the shortest time possible. The fund should take into account the information on the victims reported to the Commission on the Truth contained in the annexes to this report.
   2. The fund should receive an appropriate contribution from the State but, in view of prevailing economic conditions, should receive a substantial contribution from the international community. Therefore, without prejudice to the obligations of the State and of FMLN, the Commission urgently appeals to the international community, especially the wealthier countries and those that showed most interest in the conflict and its settlement, to establish a fund for that purpose. It also suggests that the United Nations Secretariat promote and coordinate this initiative. It further recommends that not less than one percent (1%) of all international assistance that reaches El Salvador be set aside for this purpose.
   3. The fund could be managed by a board of directors consisting of three members: one appointed by the Government of El Salvador; a second appointed by the Secretary-General of the United Nations; and a third chosen by mutual agreement between the two appointed members.
   4. The fund must be free to establish its own rules of procedure and to act in accordance with the Commission's recommendations, Salvadorian law, international law, and general legal principles.

B. Moral compensation

The Commission recommends:

   1. The construction of a national monument in El Salvador bearing the names of all the victims of the conflict.
   2. Recognition of the good name of the victims and of the serious crimes of which they were victims.
   3. The institution of a national holiday in memory of the victims of the conflict and to serve as a symbol of national reconciliation.

C. Forum for Truth and Reconciliation

The Commission feels it would be useful if this report and its conclusions and recommendations and progress toward national reconciliation were analyzed not only by the Salvadorian people as a whole but also by a special forum comprising the most representative sectors of society which, in addition to the above-mentioned objectives, should strive to monitor strict compliance with the recommendations.

It is not for the Commission to indicate how such a forum should be established. However, a National Commission for the Consolidation of Peace (COPAZ) was established under the peace agreements as 'a mechanism for the monitoring of and the participation of civilian society in the process of change resulting from the negotiations'. It therefore seems appropriate that the task referred to by the Commission should be entrusted primarily to COPAZ. However, given the scope the [sic] importance of the subject matter dealt with in this report, the Commission would like to suggest to COPAZ that, to this end, it consider expanding its membership so that sectors of civilian society that are not directly represented in COPAZ can participate in this analysis.

Moreover, COPAZ is the body entrusted by the agreements with preparing preliminary legislative drafts related to the peace process. In this sphere, it has a crucial role to play in the implementation of the recommendations in the present report that call for legal reforms.

D. International follow-up

The Commission has carried out its mandate as part of an extraordinary process which is a milestone in the history of United Nations operations for the maintenance of international peace and security. The tragedy in El Salvador absorbed the attention of the international community. As a result, the current peace process continues to arouse expectations throughout the world. The United Nations is also responsible for verifying all the agreements, which includes ensuring that the recommendations of the Commission on the Truth, which the Parties undertook to carry out, are implemented.

The Commission requests the Independent Expert for El Salvador of the United Nations Commission on Human Rights, in the report he is to submit to the Commission on Human Rights pursuant to his mandate and to the extent allowed by that mandate, to make corresponding evaluation of the implementation of the recommendations of the Commission on the Truth.

HAITI

REPORT OF THE NATIONAL TRUTH AND JUSTICE COMMISSION CHAPTER VIII: RECOMMENDATIONS*

I.   Measures of Reparation

Special Commission for the Reparation of Damage to Victims of the de facto Regime

- Considering the State's obligation in international and domestic law to repair the damage to victims of human rights violations, to pursue those legally responsible and to prevent the repetition of such violations;
- Considering that this obligation is the sanction for failure by the State to meet its obligation to protect and to serve its citizens;
- Considering the Declaration of Basic Principles of Justice for Victims of Crime and Abuse of Power adopted by the United Nations General Assembly in its Resolution 40/34 of November 29, 1985;
- Considering that it is important for the collective memory of the Haitian people that those who have given their lives or suffered physical abuse for the survival of democracy not be forgotten symbolically, morally, or financially and that the State demonstrate its recognition and solidarity with these individuals at every level;

* Source: Report of the National Truth and Justice Commission, Embassy of the Republic of Haiti website: www.haiti.org/truth/chapit8.htm. Translated from French by e-verba.

The National Truth and Justice Commission recommends that a Special Commission be created to repair damage to victims of the de facto regime as a result of the *coup d'état* of September 29, 1991 in order to respond to the State's legal, moral, and financial obligations, set out above.

1. The Special Commission shall ensure the redress of damage suffered:
   (a) by victims identified by the National Truth and Justice Commission.
   (b) by other victims to be identified and selected according to the criteria proposed by the National Truth and Justice Commission, and who shall have presented themselves within six (6) months of the establishment of the Fund.
2. The Commission shall be temporary.
3. The Commission's resources shall come:

- from the State;
- from domestic or international private donors;
- from sympathetic countries or from the United Nations, mainly from the United Nations Voluntary Fund for Victims of Torture.

4. The Commission shall be managed by an administrative council that reflects the diversity of its members and which includes representatives of the victims.
5. The Commission shall minimally provide the victims with compensation as determined by a set scale. In addition, it shall offer other loans and services that take into account the legitimate needs of the victims.
6. The Commission shall operate regardless of whether the victims exercise their right to pursue judicial proceedings in order to obtain complete reparation.
7. The Commission shall eventually manage a system of legal aid for victims who do not have the financial means to pursue legal proceedings against the perpetrators of the violations suffered or to participate in such proceedings.
8. In addition to the victims identified by the National Truth and Justice Commission, the Commission will offer services to other victims who satisfy the following criteria:
   (a) suffered a serious human rights violation as defined by the National Truth and Justice Commission.
   (b) identified by the Commission within six (6) months of the establishment of said Commission.

The Commission recommends that in the case of minors under fifteen (15) years who have become orphans as a result of violations committed during the period concerned, the government take all necessary measures to ensure an appropriate education and a decent standard of living, as charges of the nation, so that their future not be biased by the execution or forced disappearance of their parents.

SOUTH AFRICA

PROMOTION OF NATIONAL UNITY AND RECONCILIATION ACT 34 OF 1995
[EXCERPTS]

(July 26, 1995)

It is hereby notified that the President has assented to the following Act, which is hereby published for general information.

Act

To provide for the investigation and the establishment of as complete a picture as possible of the nature, causes, and extent of gross violations of human rights committed during the period from March 1, 1960 to the cut-off date contemplated in the Constitution, within or outside the Republic, emanating from the conflicts of the past, and the fate or whereabouts of the victims of such violations; the granting of amnesty to persons who make full disclosure of all the relevant facts relating to acts associated with a political objective committed in the course of the conflicts of the past during the said period; affording victims an opportunity to relate the violations they suffered; the taking of measures aimed at the granting of reparation to, and the rehabilitation and the restoration of the human and civil dignity of, victims of violations of human rights; reporting to the Nation about such violations and victims; the making of recommendations aimed at the prevention of the commission of gross violations of human rights; and for the said purposes to provide for the establishment of a Truth and Reconciliation Commission, a Committee on Human Rights Violations, a Committee on Amnesty and a Committee on Reparation and Rehabilitation; and to confer certain powers on, assign certain functions to, and impose certain duties upon, that Commission and those Committees; and to provide for matters connected therewith.

Since the Constitution of the Republic of South Africa in 1993 (Act No. 200 of 1993) provides a historic bridge between the past of a deeply divided society characterized by strife, conflict, untold suffering, and injustice and a future founded on the recognition of human rights, democracy, and peaceful coexistence for all South Africans, irrespective of colour, race, class, belief, or sex;

And since it is deemed necessary to establish the truth in relation to past events as well as the motives for, and circumstances in which, gross violations of human fights [sic] have occurred, and to make the findings known in order to prevent a repetition of such acts in future;

And since the Constitution states that the pursuit of national unity, the well-being of all South African citizens and peace require reconciliation between the people of South Africa and the reconstruction of society;

And since the Constitution states that there is a need for understanding but not for vengeance, a need for reparation but not for retaliation, a need for ubuntu but not for victimization;

And since the Constitution states that in order to advance such reconciliation and reconstruction amnesty shall be granted in respect of acts, omissions, and offences associated with political objectives committed in the course of the conflicts of the past;

And since the Constitution provides that Parliament shall under the Constitution adopt a law that determines a firm cut-off date, which shall be a date after October 8, 1990, and before the cut-off date envisaged in the Constitution, and providing for the mechanisms, criteria, and procedures, including tribunals, if any, through which such amnesty shall be dealt with;

(English text signed by the President)
(Assented to July 19, 1995)

Be it therefore enacted by the Parliament of the Republic of South Africa, as follows.

CHAPTER 1

Interpretation and application

Definitions

1. (1) In this Act, unless the context otherwise indicates

[...]

(ix) 'gross violation of human rights' means the violation of human rights through

    (a) the killing, abduction, torture or severe ill-treatment of any person; or

    (b) any attempt, conspiracy, incitement, instigation, command or procurement to commit an act referred to in paragraph (a), which emanated from conflicts of the past and which was committed during the period 1 March 1960 to the cut-off date within or outside the Republic, and the commission of which was advised, planned, directed, commanded or ordered, by any person acting with a political motive;

[...]

(xiv) 'reparation' includes any form of compensation, ex gratia payment,

[...]

(xix) 'victims' includes

    (a) persons who, individually or together with one or more persons, suffered harm in the form of physical or mental injury, emotional suffering, pecuniary loss or a substantial impairment of human rights—

        (i) as a result of a gross violation of human rights; or

        (ii) as a result of an act associated with a political objective for which amnesty has been granted; and

    (b) persons who, individually or together with one or more persons, suffered harm in the form of physical or mental injury, emotional suffering, pecuniary loss or a substantial impairment of human rights, as a result of such person intervening to assist persons contemplated in paragraph (a) who were in distress or to prevent victimization of such persons; and

    (c) such relatives or dependants of victims as may be prescribed.

CHAPTER 2

Truth and Reconciliation Commission

Establishment and seat of Truth and Reconciliation Commission

2. (1) There is hereby established a juristic person to be known as the Truth and Reconciliation Commission.

(2) The seat of the Commission shall be determined by the President.

Objectives of Commission

3. (1) The objectives of the Commission shall be to promote national unity and reconciliation in a spirit of understanding which transcends the conflicts and divisions of the past by:

(a) establishing as complete a picture as possible of the causes, nature, and extent of the gross violations of human rights which were committed during the period from March 1, 1960 to the cut-off date, including the antecedents, circumstances, factors, and context of such violations, as well as the perspectives of the victims and the motives and perspectives of the persons responsible for the commission of the violations, by conducting investigations and holding hearings;

(b) facilitating the granting of amnesty to persons who make full disclosure of all the relevant facts relating to acts associated with a political objective and comply with the requirements of this Act;

(c) establishing and making known the fate or whereabouts of victims and by restoring the human and civil dignity of such victims by granting them an opportunity to relate their own accounts of the violations of which they are the victims, and by recommending reparation measures in respect of them;

(d) compiling a report providing as comprehensive an account as possible of the activities and findings of the Commission contemplated in paragraphs (a), (b), and (c), and which contains recommendations of measures to prevent the future violations of human rights.

(2) The provisions of subsection (1) shall not be interpreted as limiting the power of the Commission to investigate or make recommendations

concerning any matter with a view to promoting or achieving national unity and reconciliation within the context of this Act.

(3) In order to achieve the objectives of the Commission:

    (a) the Committee on Human Rights Violations, as contemplated in Chapter 3, shall deal, among other things, with matters pertaining to investigations of gross violations of human rights;

    (b) the Committee on Amnesty, as contemplated in Chapter 4, shall deal with matters relating to amnesty;

    (c) the Committee on Reparation and Rehabilitation, as contemplated in Chapter 5, shall deal with matters referred to it relating to reparations;

    (d) the investigating unit referred to in section 5(d) shall perform the investigations contemplated in section 28(4)(a); and

    (e) the subcommittees shall exercise, perform, and carry out the powers, functions, and duties conferred upon, assigned to, or imposed upon, them by the Commission.

Functions of Commission

4. The functions of the Commission shall be to achieve its objectives, and to that end the Commission shall:

    (a) facilitate, and where necessary initiate or coordinate, inquiries into

        (i) gross violations of human rights, including violations which were part of a systematic pattern of abuse;

        (ii) the nature, causes, and extent of gross violations of human rights, including the antecedents, circumstances, factors, context, motives, and perspectives which led to such violations;

        (iii) the identity of all persons, authorities, institutions, and organisations involved in such violations;

        (iv) the question whether such violations were the result of deliberate planning on the part of the State or a former state or any of their organs, or of any political organisation, liberation movement, or other group or individual; and

        (v) accountability, political or otherwise, for any such violation;

    (b) facilitate, and initiate or coordinate, the gathering of information and the receiving of evidence from any person, including persons claiming to be victims of such violations or the representatives of such victims, which establish the identity of victims of such violations, their fate or present whereabouts and the nature and extent of the harm suffered by such victims;

(c) facilitate and promote the granting of amnesty in respect of acts associated with political objectives, by receiving from persons desiring to make a full disclosure of all the relevant facts relating to such acts, applications for the granting of amnesty in respect of such acts, and transmitting such applications to the Committee on Amnesty for its decision, and by publishing decisions granting amnesty, in the Gazette;

(d) determine what articles have been destroyed by any person in order to conceal violations of human rights or acts associated with a political objective;

(e) prepare a comprehensive report which sets out its activities and findings, based on factual and objective information and evidence collected or received by it or placed at its disposal;

(f) make recommendations to the President with regard to

(i) the policy which should be followed or measures which should be taken with regard to the granting of reparation to victims or the taking of other measures aimed at rehabilitating and restoring the human and civil dignity of victims;

(ii) measures which should be taken to grant urgent interim reparation to victims;

(g) make recommendations to the Minister with regard to the development of a limited witness protection program for the purposes of this Act;

(h) make recommendations to the President with regard to the creation of institutions conducive to a stable and fair society and the institutional, administrative, and legislative measures which should be taken or introduced in order to prevent the commission of violations of human rights.

[...]

CHAPTER 5

Reparation and rehabilitation of victims

Committee on Reparation and Rehabilitation

23. There is hereby established a committee to be known as the Committee on Reparation and Rehabilitation, which shall in this chapter be referred to as the Committee.

Constitution of Committee

24. (1) The Committee shall consist of:
    (a) a Chairperson;
    (b) a Vice-Chairperson;
    (c) not more than five other members; and
    (d) in addition to the commissioners referred to in subsection (2), such other commissioners as may be appointed to the Committee by the Commission.
  (2) Commissioners designated by the Commission shall be the Chairperson and Vice-Chairperson of the Committee.
  (3) The Commission shall for the purpose of subsection (1)(c) appoint as members of the Committee fit and proper persons who are suitably qualified, South African citizens and broadly representative of the South African community.

Powers, duties, and functions of Committee

25. (1) In addition to the powers, duties, and functions in this Act and for the purpose of achieving the Commission's objectives referred to in section 3(1)(c) and (d):
    (a) the Committee shall
        (i) consider matters referred to it by (aa) the Commission in terms of section 5(e); (bb) the Committee on Human Rights Violations in terms of section 15(1); and (cc) the Committee on Amnesty in terms of section 22(1);
        (ii) gather the evidence referred to in section 4(b);
    (b) the Committee may
        (i) make recommendations which may include urgent interim measures as contemplated in section 4(f)(ii), as to appropriate measures of reparation to victims;
        (ii) make recommendations referred to in section 4(h);
        (iii) prepare and submit to the Commission interim reports in connection with its activities;
        (iv) may exercise the powers referred to in section 5(l) and (m) and Chapters 6 and 7.
  (2) The Committee shall submit to the Commission a final comprehensive report on its activities, findings, and recommendations.

Applications for reparation

26. (1) Any person who is of the opinion that he or she has suffered harm as a result of a gross violation of human rights may apply to the Committee for reparation in the prescribed form.

(2) (a) The Committee shall consider an application contemplated in subsection (1) and may exercise any of the powers conferred upon it by section 25.

(b) In any matter referred to the Committee, and in respect of which a finding as to whether an act, omission, or offence constitutes a gross violation of human rights is required, the Committee shall refer the matter to the Committee on Human Rights Violations to deal with the matter in terms of section 14.

(3) If upon consideration of any matter or application submitted to it under subsection (1) and any evidence received or obtained by it concerning such matter or application, the Committee is of the opinion that the applicant is a victim, it shall, having regard to criteria as prescribed, make recommendations as contemplated in section 25(1)(b)(i) in an endeavour to restore the human and civil dignity of such victim.

Parliament to consider recommendations with regard to reparation of victims

27. (1) The recommendations referred to in section 4(f)(i) shall be considered by the President with a view to making recommendations to Parliament and making regulations.

(2) The recommendations referred to in subsection (1) shall be considered by the joint committee and the decisions of the said joint committee shall, when approved by Parliament, be implemented by the President by making regulations.

(3) The regulations referred to in subsection (2):

(a) shall

(i) determine the basis and conditions upon which reparation shall be granted;

(ii) determine the authority responsible for the application of the regulations;

(b) may

(i) provide for the revision and, in appropriate cases, the discontinuance or reduction of any reparation;

        (ii) prohibit the cession, assignment, or attachment of any reparation in terms of the regulations, or the right to any such reparation;

       (iii) determine that any reparation received in terms of the regulations shall not form part of the estate of the recipient should such estate be sequestrated; and

      (iv) provide for any other matter which the President may deem fit to prescribe in order to ensure an efficient application of the regulations.

(4) The joint committee may also advise the President in respect of measures that should be taken to grant urgent interim reparation to victims.

President's Fund

42. (1) The President may, in such manner as he or she may deem fit, in consultation with the Minister and the Minister of Finance, establish a Fund into which shall be paid:

    (a) all money appropriated by Parliament for the purposes of the Fund; and

    (b) all money donated or contributed to the Fund or accruing to the Fund from any source.

(2) There shall be paid from the Fund all amounts payable to victims by way of reparation in terms of regulations made by the President.

(3) Any money of the Fund which is not required for immediate use may be invested with a financial institution approved by the Minister of Finance and may be withdrawn when required.

(4) Any unexpended balance of the money of the Fund at the end of a financial year, shall be carried forward as a credit to the Fund for the next financial year.

CONSTITUTIONAL COURT OF SOUTH AFRICA

Case CCT 17/96 [Excerpts]

The Azanian Peoples Organisation (AZAPO)—First Applicant

Nontsikelelo Margaret Biko—Second Applicant
Churchill Mhleli Mxenge—Third Applicant
Chris Ribeiro—Fourth Applicant

versus

The President of the Republic of South Africa—First Respondent
The Government of the Republic of South Africa—Second Respondent
The Minister of Justice—Third Respondent
The Minister of Safety and Security—Fourth Respondent
The Chairperson of the Truth and Reconciliation Commission—Fifth Respondent

Heard on: May 30, 1996
Decided on: July 25, 1996

Judgment
Mahomed D. P.:

[1] For decades South African history has been dominated by a deep conflict between a minority which reserved for itself all control over the political instruments of the state and a majority who sought to resist that domination. Fundamental human rights became a major casualty of this conflict as the resistance of those punished by their denial was met by laws designed to counter the effectiveness of such resistance. The conflict deepened with the increased sophistication of the economy, the rapid acceleration of knowledge and education and the ever increasing hostility of an international community steadily outraged by the inconsistency which had become manifest between its own articulated ideals after the Second World War and the official practices which had become institutionalised in South Africa through laws enacted to give them sanction and teeth by a Parliament elected only by a privileged minority. The result was a debilitating war of internal political dissension and confrontation, massive expressions of labour militancy, perennial student unrest, punishing international economic isolation, widespread dislocation in crucial areas of national endeavour, accelerated levels of armed conflict and a dangerous combination of anxiety, frustration and anger among expanding proportions of the populace. The legitimacy of law itself was deeply wounded as the country haemorrhaged dangerously in the face of this tragic conflict which had begun to traumatise the entire nation.

[2] During the eighties it became manifest to all that our country with all its natural wealth, physical beauty and human resources was on a disaster course unless that conflict was reversed. It was this realisation which mercifully rescued us in the early nineties as those who controlled the levers of state power began to negotiate a different future with those who had been imprisoned, silenced or driven into exile in consequence of their resistance to that control and its consequences. Those negotiations resulted in an interim Constitution committed to a transition towards

a more just, defensible and democratic political order based on the protection of fundamental human rights. It was wisely appreciated by those involved in the preceding negotiations that the task of building such a new democratic order was a very difficult task because of the previous history and the deep emotions and indefensible inequities it had generated; and that this could not be achieved without a firm and generous commitment to reconciliation and national unity. It was realised that much of the unjust consequences of the past could not ever be fully reversed. It might be necessary in crucial areas to close the book on that past.

[3] This fundamental philosophy is eloquently expressed in the epilogue to the Constitution which reads as follows:

'National Unity and Reconciliation

This Constitution provides a historic bridge between the past of a deeply divided society characterised by strife, conflict, untold suffering and injustice, and a future founded on the recognition of human rights, democracy and peaceful co-existence and development opportunities for all South Africans, irrespective of colour, race, class, belief or sex.

The pursuit of national unity, the well-being of all South African citizens and peace require reconciliation between the people of South Africa and the reconstruction of society.

The adoption of this Constitution lays the secure foundation for the people of South Africa to transcend the divisions and strife of the past, which generated gross violations of human rights, the transgression of humanitarian principles in violent conflicts and a legacy of hatred, fear, guilt and revenge.

These can now be addressed on the basis that there is a need for understanding but not for vengeance, a need for reparation but not for retaliation, a need for ubuntu but not for victimisation.

In order to advance such reconciliation and reconstruction, amnesty shall be granted in respect of acts, omissions and offences associated with political objectives and committed in the course of the conflicts of the past. To this end, Parliament under this Constitution shall adopt a law determining a firm cut-off date, which shall be a date after 8 October 1990 and before 6 December 1993, and providing for the mechanisms, criteria and procedures, including tribunals, if any, through which such amnesty shall be dealt with at any time after the law has been passed.

With this Constitution and these commitments we, the people of South Africa, open a new chapter in the history of our country.'

Pursuant to the provisions of the epilogue, Parliament enacted during 1995 what is colloquially referred to as the Truth and Reconciliation Act. Its proper name is the Promotion of National Unity and Reconciliation Act 34 of 1995 ('the Act').

[4] The Act establishes a Truth and Reconciliation Commission. The objectives of that Commission are set out in section 3. Its main objective is to 'promote national unity and reconciliation in a spirit of understanding which transcends the conflicts

and divisions of the past'. It is enjoined to pursue that objective by 'establishing as complete a picture as possible of the causes, nature and extent of the gross violations of human rights' committed during the period commencing 1 March 1960 to the 'cut-off date'. For this purpose the Commission is obliged to have regard to 'the perspectives of the victims and the motives and perspectives of the persons responsible for the commission of the violations'. It also is required to facilitate

the granting of amnesty to persons who make full disclosure of all the relevant facts relating to acts associated with a political objective...

The Commission is further entrusted with the duty to establish and to make known 'the fate or whereabouts of victims' and of 'restoring the human and civil dignity of such victims' by affording them an opportunity to relate their own accounts of the violations and by recommending 'reparation measures' in respect of such violations and finally to compile a comprehensive report in respect of its functions, including the recommendation of measures to prevent the violation of human rights.

[...]

[6] After making provision for certain ancillary matters, section 20(7) [of the Act] (the constitutionality of which is impugned in these proceedings) provides as follows:

'(7) (a) No person who has been granted amnesty in respect of an act, omission or offence shall be criminally or civilly liable in respect of such act, omission or offence and no body or organisation or the State shall be liable, and no person shall be vicariously liable, for any such act, omission or offence.

(b) Where amnesty is granted to any person in respect of any act, omission or offence, such amnesty shall have no influence upon the criminal liability of any other person contingent upon the liability of the first-mentioned person.

(c) No person, organisation or state shall be civilly or vicariously liable for an act, omission or offence committed between 1 March 1960 and the cut-off date by a person who is deceased, unless amnesty could not have been granted in terms of this Act in respect of such an act, omission or offence.'

[7] What is clear from section 20(7), read with sections 20(8), (9) and (10), is that once a person has been granted amnesty in respect of an act, omission or offence

(a) the offender can no longer be held 'criminally liable' for such offence and no prosecution in respect thereof can be maintained against him or her;

(b) such an offender can also no longer be held civilly liable personally for any damages sustained by the victim and no such civil proceedings can successfully be pursued against him or her;

(c) if the wrongdoer is an employee of the state, the state is equally discharged from any civil liability in respect of any act or omission of such an employee, even if the relevant act or omission was effected during the course and within the scope of his or her employment; and

(d) other bodies, organisations or persons are also exempt from any liability for any of the acts or omissions of a wrongdoer which would ordinarily have arisen in consequence of their vicarious liability for such acts or omissions.

[8] The applicants sought in this court to attack the constitutionality of section 20(7) on the grounds that its consequences are not authorised by the Constitution. They aver that various agents of the state, acting within the scope and in the course of their employment, have unlawfully murdered and maimed leading activists during the conflict against the racial policies of the previous administration and that the applicants have a clear right to insist that such wrongdoers should properly be prosecuted and punished, that they should be ordered by the ordinary courts of the land to pay adequate civil compensation to the victims or dependants of the victims and further to require the state to make good to such victims or dependants the serious losses which they have suffered in consequence of the criminal and delictual acts of the employees of the state. In support of that attack Mr Soggot SC, who appeared for the applicants together with Mr Khoza, contended that section 20(7) was inconsistent with section 22 of the Constitution which provides that

[e]very person shall have the right to have justiciable disputes settled by a court of law or, where appropriate, another independent or impartial forum.

He submitted that the Amnesty Committee was neither 'a court of law' nor an 'independent or impartial forum' and that in any event the Committee was not authorised to settle 'justiciable disputes'. All it was simply required to decide was whether amnesty should be granted in respect of a particular act, omission or offence.

[...]

[20] Is section 20(7), to the extent to which it immunizes wrongdoers from criminal prosecution, nevertheless objectionable on the grounds that amnesty might be provided in circumstances where the victims, or the dependants of the victims, have not had the compensatory benefit of discovering the truth at last or in circumstances where those whose [sic] misdeeds are so obscenely excessive as to justify punishment, even if they were perpetrated with a political objective during the course of conflict in the past? Some answers to such difficulties are provided in the sub-sections of section 20. The Amnesty Committee may grant amnesty in respect of the relevant offence only if the perpetrator of the misdeed makes a full disclosure of all relevant facts. If the offender does not, and in consequence thereof the victim or his or her family is not able to discover the truth, the application for amnesty will fail. Moreover, it will not suffice for the offender merely to say that his or her act was associated with a political objective. That issue must independently be determined by the Amnesty Committee pursuant to the criteria set out in section 20(3), including the relationship between the offence committed and the

political objective pursued and the directness and proximity of the relationship and the proportionality of the offence to the objective pursued.

[21] The result, at all levels, is a difficult, sensitive, perhaps even agonising, balancing act between the need for justice to victims of past abuse and the need for reconciliation and rapid transition to a new future; between encouragement to wrongdoers to help in the discovery of the truth and the need for reparations for the victims of that truth; between a correction in the old and the creation of the new. It is an exercise of immense difficulty interacting in a vast network of political, emotional, ethical and logistical considerations. It is an act calling for a judgment falling substantially within the domain of those entrusted with lawmaking in the era preceding and during the transition period. The results may well often be imperfect and the pursuit of the act might inherently support the message of Kant that 'out of the crooked timber of humanity no straight thing was ever made'. There can be legitimate debate about the methods and the mechanisms chosen by the lawmaker to give effect to the difficult duty entrusted upon it in terms of the epilogue. We are not concerned with that debate or the wisdom of its choice of mechanisms but only with its constitutionality. That, for us, is the only relevant standard. Applying that standard, I am not satisfied that in providing for amnesty for those guilty of serious offences associated with political objectives and in defining the mechanisms through which and the manner in which such amnesty may be secured by such offenders, the lawmaker, in section 20(7), has offended any of the express or implied limitations on its powers in terms of the Constitution.

[...]

Amnesty in respect of the civil liability of individual wrongdoers

[33] Mr Soggot submitted that chapter 3 of the Constitution, and more particularly section 22, conferred on every person the right to pursue, in the ordinary courts of the land or before independent tribunals, any claim which such person might have in civil law for the recovery of damages sustained by such a person in consequence of the unlawful delicts perpetrated by a wrongdoer. He contended that the Constitution did not authorise Parliament to make any law which would have the result of indemnifying (or otherwise rendering immune from liability) the perpetrator of any such delict against any claims made for damages suffered by the victim of such a delict. In support of that argument he suggested that the concept of 'amnesty', referred to in the epilogue to the Constitution, was, at worst for the applicants, inherently limited to immunity from criminal prosecutions. He contended that even if a wrongdoer who has received amnesty could plead such amnesty as a defence to a criminal prosecution, such amnesty could not be used as a shield to protect him or her from claims for delictual damages suffered by any person in consequence of the act or omission of the wrongdoer.

[...]

[36] What are the material circumstances of the present case? As I have previously said, what the epilogue to the Constitution seeks to achieve by providing for amnesty is the facilitation of 'reconciliation and reconstruction' by the creation of mechanisms and procedures which make it possible for the truth of our past to be uncovered. Central to the justification of amnesty in respect of the criminal prosecution for offences committed during the prescribed period with political objectives, is the appreciation that the truth will not effectively be revealed by the wrongdoers if they are to be prosecuted for such acts. That justification must necessarily and unavoidably apply to the need to indemnify such wrongdoers against civil claims for payment of damages. Without that incentive the wrongdoer cannot be encouraged to reveal the whole truth which might inherently be against his or her material or proprietary interests. There is nothing in the language of the epilogue which persuades me that what the makers of the Constitution intended to do was to encourage wrongdoers to reveal the truth by providing for amnesty against criminal prosecution in respect of their acts but simultaneously to discourage them from revealing that truth by keeping intact the threat that such revelations might be visited with what might in many cases be very substantial claims for civil damages. It appears to me to be more reasonable to infer that the legislation contemplated in the epilogue would, in the circumstances defined, be wide enough to allow for an amnesty which would protect a wrongdoer who told the truth, from both the criminal and the civil consequences of his or her admissions.

[37] This conclusion appears to be fortified by the fact that what the epilogue directs is that

amnesty shall be granted in respect of acts, omissions and offences.

If the purpose was simply to provide mechanisms in terms of which wrongdoers could be protected from criminal prosecution in respect of offences committed by them, why would there be any need to refer also to 'acts and omissions' in addition to offences? The word 'offences' would have covered both acts and omissions in any event.

[38] In the result I am satisfied that section 20(7) is not open to constitutional challenge on the ground that it invades the right of a victim or his or her dependant to recover damages from a wrongdoer for unlawful acts perpetrated during the conflicts of the past. If there is any such invasion it is authorised and contemplated by the relevant parts of the epilogue.

The effect of amnesty on any potential civil liability of the state

[39] Mr Soggot contended forcefully that whatever be the legitimate consequences of the kind of amnesty contemplated by the epilogue for the criminal and civil

lability [sic] of the wrongdoer, the Constitution could not justifiably authorise any law which has the effect of indemnifying the state itself against civil claims made by those wronged by criminal and delictual acts perpetrated by such wrongdoers in the course and within the scope of their employment as servants of the state. Section 20(7) of the Act, he argued, had indeed that effect and was therefore unconstitutional to that extent.

[40] This submission has one great force. It is this. If the wrongdoer in the employment of the state is not personally indemnified in the circumstances regulated by the Act, the truth might never unfold. It would remain shrouded in the impenetrable mysteries of the past, leaving the dependants of many victims with a grief unrelieved by any knowledge of the truth. But how, it was argued, would it deter such wrongdoers from revealing the truth if such a revelation held no criminal or civil consequences for them? How could such wrongdoers be discouraged from disclosing the truth if their own liberty and property was not to be threatened by such revelations, but the state itself nevertheless remained liable to compensate the families of victims for such wrongdoings perpetrated by the servants of the state?

[41] This is a serious objection which requires to be considered carefully. I think it must be conceded that in many cases, the wrongdoer would not be discouraged from revealing the whole truth merely because the consequences of such disclosure might be to saddle the state with a potential civil liability for damages arising from the delictual acts or omissions of a wrongdoer (although there may also be many cases in which such a wrongdoer, still in the service of the state, might in some degree be inhibited or even coerced from making disclosures implicating his or her superiors).

[42] The real answer, however, to the problems posed by the questions which I have identified, seems to lie in the more fundamental objectives of the transition sought to be attained by the Constitution and articulated in the epilogue itself. What the Constitution seeks to do is to facilitate the transition to a new democratic order, committed to 'reconciliation between the people of South Africa and the reconstruction of society'. The question is how this can be done effectively with the limitations of our resources and the legacy of the past.

[43] The families of those whose fundamental human rights were invaded by torture and abuse are not the only victims who have endured 'untold suffering and injustice' in consequence of the crass inhumanity of apartheid which so many have had to endure for so long. Generations of children born and yet to be born will suffer the consequences of poverty, of malnutrition, of homelessness, of illiteracy and disempowerment generated and sustained by the institutions of apartheid and its manifest effects on life and living for so many. The country has neither the resources nor the skills to reverse fully these massive wrongs. It will take

many years of strong commitment, sensitivity and labour to 'reconstruct our society' so as to fulfill the legitimate dreams of new generations exposed to real opportunities for advancement denied to preceding generations initially by the execution of apartheid itself and for a long time after its formal demise, by its relentless consequences. The resources of the state have to be deployed imaginatively, wisely, efficiently and equitably, to facilitate the reconstruction process in a manner which best brings relief and hope to the widest sections of the community, developing for the benefit of the entire nation the latent human potential and resources of every person who has directly or indirectly been burdened with the heritage of the shame and the pain of our racist past.

[44] Those negotiators of the Constitution and leaders of the nation who were required to address themselves to these agonising problems must have been compelled to make hard choices. They could have chosen to direct that the limited resources of the state be spent by giving preference to the formidable delictual claims of those who had suffered from acts of murder, torture or assault perpetrated by servants of the state, diverting to that extent, desperately needed funds in the crucial areas of education, housing and primary health care. They were entitled to permit a different choice to be made between competing demands inherent in the problem. They could have chosen to direct that the potential liability of the state be limited in respect of any civil claims by differentiating between those against whom prescription could have been pleaded as a defence and those whose claims were of such recent origin that a defence of prescription would have failed. They were entitled to reject such a choice on the grounds that it was irrational. They could have chosen to saddle the state with liability for claims made by insurance companies which had compensated institutions for delictual acts performed by the servants of the state and to that extent again divert funds otherwise desperately needed to provide food for the hungry, roofs for the homeless and blackboards and desks for those struggling to obtain admission to desperately overcrowded schools. They were entitled to permit the claims of such schoolchildren and the poor and the homeless to be preferred.

[45] The election made by the makers of the Constitution was to permit Parliament to favour 'the reconstruction of society' involving in the process a wider concept of 'reparation', which would allow the state to take into account the competing claims on its resources but, at the same time, to have regard to the 'untold suffering' of individuals and families whose fundamental human rights had been invaded during the conflict of the past. In some cases such a family may best be assisted by a reparation which allows the young in this family to maximise their potential through bursaries and scholarships; in other cases the most effective reparation might take the form of occupational training and rehabilitation; in still other cases complex surgical interventions and medical help may be facilitated; still others

might need subsidies to prevent eviction from homes they can no longer maintain and in suitable cases the deep grief of the traumatised may most effectively be assuaged by facilitating the erection of a tombstone on the grave of a departed one with a public acknowledgement of his or her valour and nobility. There might have to be differentiation between the form and quality of the reparations made to two persons who have suffered exactly the same damage in consequence of the same unlawful act but where one person now enjoys lucrative employment from the state and the other lives in penury.

[46] All these examples illustrate, in my view, that it is much too simplistic to say that the objectives of the Constitution could only properly be achieved by saddling the state with the formal liability to pay, in full, the provable delictual claims of those who have suffered patrimonial loss in consequence of the delicts perpetrated with political objectives by servants of the state during the conflicts of the past. There was a permissible alternative, perhaps even a more imaginative and more fundamental route to the 'reconstruction of society', which could legitimately have been followed. This is the route which appears to have been chosen by Parliament through the mechanism of amnesty and nuanced and individualised reparations in the Act. I am quite unpersuaded that this is not a route authorised by the epilogue to the Constitution.

[47] The epilogue required that a law be adopted by Parliament which would provide for 'amnesty' and it appreciated the 'need for reparation', but it left it to Parliament to decide upon the ambit of the amnesty, the permissible form and extent of such reparations and the procedures to be followed in the determination thereof, by taking into account all the relevant circumstances to which I have made reference. Parliament was therefore entitled to decide that, having regard to the resources of the state, proper reparations for those victimised by the unjust laws and practices of the past justified formulae which did not compel any irrational differentiation between the claims of those who were able to pursue enforceable delictual claims against the state and the claims of those who were not in that position but nevertheless deserved reparations.

[...]

Conclusion

[50] In the result, I am satisfied that the epilogue to the Constitution authorised and contemplated an 'amnesty' in its most comprehensive and generous meaning so as to enhance and optimise the prospects of facilitating the constitutional journey from the shame of the past to the promise of the future. Parliament was, therefore, entitled to enact the Act in the terms which it did. This involved more choices apart from the choices I have previously identified. They could have chosen

to insist that a comprehensive amnesty manifestly involved an inequality of sacrifice between the victims and the perpetrators of invasions into the fundamental rights of such victims and their families, and that, for this reason, the terms of the amnesty should leave intact the claims which some of these victims might have been able to pursue against those responsible for authorising, permitting or colluding in such acts, or they could have decided that this course would impede the pace, effectiveness and objectives of the transition with consequences substantially prejudicial for the people of a country facing, for the first time, the real prospect of enjoying, in the future, some of the human rights so unfairly denied to the generations which preceded them. They were entitled to choose the second course. They could conceivably have chosen to differentiate between the wrongful acts committed in defence of the old order and those committed in the resistance of it, or they could have chosen a comprehensive form of amnesty which did not make this distinction. Again they were entitled to make the latter choice. The choice of alternatives legitimately fell within the judgment of the lawmakers. The exercise of that choice does not, in my view, impact on its constitutionality. It follows from these reasons that section 20(7) of the Act is authorised by the Constitution itself and it is unnecessary to consider the relevance and effect of section 33(1) of the Constitution.

Order

[51] In the result, the attack on the constitutionality of section 20(7) of the Promotion of National Unity and Reconciliation Act 34 of 1995 must fail. That was the only attack which was pursued on behalf of the applicants in this Court. It accordingly follows that the application must be, and is, refused.

Chaskalson P., Ackermann, Kriegler, Langa, Madala, Mokgoro, O'Regan and Sachs J. J. concur in the judgment of Mahomed D. P.

DIDCOTT J.:

[52] I concur in the order that Mahomed D. P. proposes to make. I also agree in general with, and wish to add nothing to, the comprehensive and lucid reasons given by him for the conclusions to which he has come that the Promotion of National Unity and Reconciliation Act (34 of 1995) is not unconstitutional in absolving:

(a) all those to whom amnesties have been granted from personal liability, either criminal or civil, for their unlawful activities that are covered;

(b) everyone else and all bodies and organisations besides the state from civil liability, incurred vicariously or otherwise, for such activities on the part of persons who have obtained their own amnesties in respect of those.

After much hesitation, and without managing to shed altogether some doubts that linger in my mind even now, I feel persuaded on balance that the same must go for the civil liability of the state. Both my approach to that troublesome issue and the line I take in endeavouring to resolve it are narrower than, and, in their emphasis, different from, the ones preferred by Mahomed D. P. I shall therefore explain separately why, at the end of that particular journey, I nevertheless find myself arriving rather reluctantly at the same destination as his. The considerations which account largely for those qualms of mine will emerge too from the explanation.

[...]

[55] In investigating the tolerability of the denial I do not set the store that Mahomed D. P. does by the impossibility of compensating all the countless victims of apartheid in any adequate measure or form for the incalculable damage done to them during that era, and by the unavailability of legal redress to a large majority of the victims either because the harm suffered was not in the first place the type for which the law could offer some remedy or because, though it fell within that restricted field, their claims had lapsed with the passage of time. Such harm, the scale and horror of which Mahomed D. P. has described so vividly, is highly pertinent to the political and social policy animating the statute, indeed of crucial importance there. It has scant bearing that I can see, however, on the constitutional issue now under discussion, since the lack of a right by the many can scarcely provide a sound excuse for its denial to others, be they relatively but few, whose title to it is clear. Nor do I attach great weight to the cost that the state would inevitably incur in meeting not some obligations foisted freshly on it, but ones endured all along from which the legislature has now seen fit to release it. We have no means of assessing that cost, even approximately. But, unless perhaps its amount unbeknown to us is prohibitively high in relation to our national revenue and expenditure, it does not strike me as a strong reason for depriving the persons to whom the obligations are owed of their normal and legal due.

[...]

[62] The scales are tipped further that way [that is, 'in favour of amnesties embracing all bearers of liability, amnesties that consequently include the state among the beneficiaries'], in my final estimation, by an aspect of the matter which I

have not yet touched. It concerns the homage that the postscript pays to the 'need for reparation'. Reparations are usually payable by states, and there is no reason to doubt that the postscript envisages our own state shouldering the national responsibility for those. It therefore does not contemplate that the state will go Scot-free. On the contrary, I believe, an actual commitment on the point is implicit in its terms, a commitment in principle to the assumption by the state of the burden.

[63] What remains to be examined is the extent to which the statute gives effect to the acknowledgement of that responsibility. The question arises because it was said in argument to have done so insufficiently.

[64] The long title of the statute declares one of the objects which it promotes to be

the taking of measures aimed at the granting of reparation to, and the rehabilitation and the restoration of the human and civil dignity of, victims of violations of human rights.

Section 1 defines 'reparation' in terms that include

any form of compensation, ex gratia payment, restitution, rehabilitation or recognition.

The word 'victims' is said in the same section to cover

persons who . . . suffered harm in the form of physical or mental injury, emotional suffering, pecuniary loss or a substantial impairment of human rights . . . as a result of a gross violation of human rights or . . . as a result of an act associated with a political objective for which amnesty has been granted.

The section continues by adding to the 'victims' thus described a further class consisting of 'such relatives or dependants' of the ones already listed 'as may be prescribed' by regulation. Sections 26 and 27 provide for the process of awarding reparations. Everyone professing to be a 'victim' may apply for an award to the Committee on Reparation and Rehabilitation after the matter has been referred there. It must decide in the first place whether the applicant is truly a 'victim'. Its next task, having accepted him or her as one if it does so, is to consider the application and recommend to the President what should be done 'in an endeavour to restore the human and civil dignity of such victim'. The President is required in turn to submit to Parliament his own recommendations on the case and all others like it. A joint committee of both houses has to consider those. Its decision, should Parliament approve of that, must then be implemented by regulations emanating from the President that 'determine the basis and conditions upon which reparation shall be granted'. All reparations are payable ultimately, in terms of section 42, from a special fund stocked mainly with money allocated by Parliament to that purpose.

[65] The Statute does not, it is true, grant any legally enforceable rights in lieu of those lost by claimants whom the amnesties hit. It nevertheless offers some quid pro quo for the loss and establishes the machinery for determining such alternative redress. I cannot see what else it might have achieved immediately once, in the light of the

painful choices described by Mahomed D P* and in the exercise of the legislative judgment brought to bear on them, the basic decision had been taken to substitute the indeterminate prospect of reparations for the concrete reality of legal claims wherever those were enjoyed. For nothing more definite, detailed and efficacious could feasibly have been promised at that stage, and with no prior investigations, recommendations and decisions of the very sort for which provision is now made.

[66] Such are the reasons for my eventual agreement with the full range of the order dismissing the present application . . .

For the applicants: D. Soggot S. C. and M. Khoza instructed by C. O. Morolo and Partners

For the respondents: G. J. Marcus and D. G. Leibowitz instructed by the State Attorney

Amicus curiae: Centre for Applied Legal Studies, University of the Witwatersrand

Truth and Reconciliation Commission of South Africa Report[†]

Volume 5

Chapter 5

Reparation and Rehabilitation Policy

Introduction

1. During the period under review, the majority of South Africans were denied their fundamental rights, including the right to vote and the right to access to appropriate education, adequate housing, accessible health care and proper

---

* See para 50 of his judgment.
[†] Source: *Truth and Reconciliation Commission of South Africa Report*, Vol. 5 (Cape Town: Truth and Reconciliation Commission, 1998), 170–95.

sanitation. Those who opposed apartheid were subjected to various forms of repression. Many organisations and individuals in opposition to the former state were banned and banished, protest marches were dispersed, freedom of speech was curtailed, and thousands were detained and imprisoned. This gave rise to tremendous frustration and anger amongst the disenfranchised. Soon, each act of repression by the state gave rise to a reciprocal act of resistance. The South African conflict spiraled out of control, resulting in horrific acts of violence and human rights abuses on all sides of the conflict. No section of society escaped these acts and abuses.

WHY REPARATION?

2. Victims of human rights abuses have suffered a multiplicity of losses and therefore have the right to reparation. Without adequate reparation and rehabilitation measures, there can be no healing or reconciliation.

3. In addition, in the context of the South African Truth and Reconciliation Commission, reparation is essential to counterbalance amnesty. The granting of amnesty denies victims the right to institute civil claims against perpetrators. The government should thus accept responsibility for reparation.

The legal basis for reparation

4. The Promotion of National Unity and Reconciliation Act (the Act) mandates the Reparation and Rehabilitation Committee of the Commission to provide, amongst other things, measures to be taken in order to grant reparation to victims of gross human rights violations (see below).

5. The legal authority for reparation is further entrenched in domestic law by the judgment in the case of the *AZAPO and Others v. The President of the Republic of South Africa and Others* (1996(8) BCLR 1015 (CC), in which the applicants sought an order declaring section 20(7) of the Act unconstitutional. Section 20(7) states that a person who has been granted amnesty shall not be criminally or civilly liable in respect of that act. The court held that section 20(7) is not unconstitutional. In arriving at such decision Didcott J. held at paragraph 62:

Reparation is usually payable by states, and there is no reason to doubt that the postscript envisages our own state shouldering the national responsibility for those. It therefore does not contemplate that the state will go Scot-free. On the contrary, I believe an actual commitment on the point is implicit in its terms, a commitment in principle to the assumption by the state of the burden.

6. He stated further at paragraph 65:

The Statute does not, it is true, grant any legally enforceable rights in lieu of those lost by claimants whom the amnesties hit. It nevertheless offers some quid pro quo for the loss and establishes the machinery for determining such alternative redress. I cannot see what else it might have achieved immediately once, in the light of the painful choices described by Mohammed D P and in the exercise of the legislative judgment brought to bear on them, the basic decision had been taken to substitute the indeterminate prospect of reparations for the concrete reality of legal claims wherever those were enjoyed. For nothing more definite, detailed and efficacious could feasibly have been promised at that stage, and with no prior investigations, recommendations and decisions of the very sort for which provision is now made.

Review of the Act

7. The Preamble to the Act stipulates that one of the objectives of the Commission is to provide for:

the taking of measures aimed at the granting of reparation to, and the rehabilitation and the restoration of the human and civil dignity of, victims of violations of human rights.

8. Pursuant thereto, section 4(f) states that one of the functions of the Commission shall be to make recommendations to the President with regard to:

the policy which should be followed or measures which should be taken with regard to the granting of reparation to victims or the taking of other measures aimed at rehabilitating and restoring the human and civil dignity of victims; measures which should be taken to grant Urgent Interim Reparation to victims.

9. Furthermore, section 25(b)(i) stipulates that the Reparation and Rehabilitation Committee may

make recommendations which may include urgent interim measures as contemplated in section 4(f)(ii), as to appropriate measures of reparation to victims.

10. In terms of section 42, the State President, in consultation with the Ministers of Justice and Finance, will establish a President's Fund. All money payable to victims in terms of regulations promulgated by the President shall be disbursed from this fund.

International legal framework

11. The right of victims of human rights abuse to fair and adequate compensation is well established in international law. In the past three years, South Africa has signed a number of important international instruments, which place it under an

obligation[1] to provide victims of human rights abuse with fair and adequate compensation. The provisions of these instruments, together with the rulings of those bodies established to ensure compliance with them, indicate that it is not sufficient to award 'token' or nominal compensation to victims. The amount of reparation awarded must be sufficient to make a meaningful and substantial impact on their lives. In terms of United Nations Conventions, there is well-established right of victims of human rights abuse to compensation for their losses and suffering. It is important that the reparation policy adopted by the government, based on recommendations made by the Commission, is in accordance with South Africa's international obligations. The reparation awarded to victims must be significant.

12. What follows is a brief review of international law in this regard.

Universal Declaration of Human Rights[2]

13. Article 8 of the Universal Declaration of Human Rights stipulates that

Everyone has the right to an effective remedy by the competent national tribunals for acts violating the fundamental rights granted him by the constitution or by law.

14. The use of the words 'effective remedy' underscores the point that the reparation awarded must be meaningful and substantial.

The International Covenant on Civil and Political Rights[3]

15. Section 3(a) of the International Covenant on Civil and Political Rights reads:

Each State Party to the present Covenant undertakes:
  (a) To ensure that any person whose rights or freedoms as herein recognised are violated shall have an effective remedy, notwithstanding that the violation has been committed by persons acting in an official capacity.

16. The Human Rights Committee established under the Optional Protocol to the International Covenant on Civil and Political Rights to consider alleged breaches of the Covenant has considered a number of cases relating to the right to compensation arising from gross violations of human rights.[4] In all these cases, it has been held that, where the state or any of its agents is responsible for killings, torture, abductions or disappearances, it is under a legal obligation to pay compensation to the victims or their families. The fact that, in the majority of instances, the Committee has used the term 'compensation' implies that the award to victims should be substantial.

The Convention against Torture and Other Cruel, Inhuman or Degrading Treatment or Punishment⁵

17. The Committee against Torture, established to ensure compliance with the Convention against Torture and Other Cruel, Inhuman or Degrading Treatment or Punishment, has found that complaints relating to acts of torture which occurred before the Convention entered into force are inadmissible because the Convention cannot be applied retroactively. Consequently, the Committee declared inadmissible a series of complaints by Argentinean citizens who alleged that they had been tortured before the Convention had come into force. Despite this rather technical finding, the Committee stressed in its communication to the government of Argentina that it should, in order to comply with the spirit of the Convention against Torture, ensure that victims of torture receive 'adequate compensation'. This is another example of an international body requiring not just token but significant reparation to be made to victims of human rights abuse.

The Inter-American Convention on Human Rights

18. The Inter-American Convention on Human Rights contains provisions that grant victims of human rights abuse a right to compensation. In the famous *Velasquez Rodriguez* case,⁶ the Inter-American Court held that a state is under an obligation to 'provide compensation as warranted for damages resulting from the violations [of the rights recognised by the Convention]'. On numerous other occasions—most recently in 1992 with respect to the governments of Uruguay and Argentina—the Inter-American Court has reasserted its view that victims of human rights abuse are entitled to compensation.⁷

The moral argument

19. The South African conflict produced casualties. Many people were killed, tortured, abducted and subjected to various forms of severe ill treatment. This not only destroyed individual lives but also affected families, communities and the nation as a whole.⁸ As a result, the new South Africa has inherited thousands of people whose lives have been severely affected. If we are to transcend the past and build national unity and reconciliation, we must ensure that those whose rights have been violated are acknowledged through access to reparation and rehabilitation. While such measures can never bring back the dead, nor adequately compensate for pain and suffering, they can and must improve the quality of life of the victims of human rights violations and/or their dependants.

20. The present government has accepted that it is morally obliged to carry the debts of its predecessors and is thus equally responsible for reparation. Implementation of reparation will afford all South Africans an opportunity to contribute to healing and reconciliation.

21. Without adequate reparation and rehabilitation measures, there can be no healing and reconciliation, either at an individual or a community level. Comprehensive forms of reparation should also be implemented to restore the physical and mental well-being of victims.

22. The following policy proposals and recommendations in respect of both urgent interim reparation and reparation itself are, therefore, submitted to the State President for his consideration in terms of sections 27 and 40(1)(d) of the Act.

WHAT CONSTITUTES REPARATION AND REHABILITATION

23. Section 1(1)(xiv) of the Act defines reparation as including 'any form of compensation, ex gratia payment, restitution, rehabilitation or recognition'.

24. The proposed reparation and rehabilitation policy has five components:

Urgent interim reparation

25. Urgent interim reparation is assistance for people in urgent need, to provide them with access to appropriate services and facilities. It is recommended that limited financial resources be made available to facilitate this access.

Individual reparation grants

26. This is an individual financial grant scheme. It is recommended that each victim of a gross human rights violation receive a financial grant, according to various criteria, paid over a period of six years.

Symbolic reparation/legal and administrative measures

27. Symbolic reparation encompasses measures to facilitate the communal process of remembering and commemorating the pain and victories of the past.

28. Amongst other measures, symbolic reparation should entail identifying a national day of remembrance and reconciliation, erection of memorials and monuments, and the development of museums.

29. Legal and administrative measures will also be proposed to assist individuals to obtain death certificates, expedite outstanding legal matters and expunge criminal records.

Community rehabilitation programmes

30. The Commission consulted with relevant government ministries in preparing its proposals for the establishment of community-based services and activities, aimed at promoting the healing and recovery of individuals and communities that have been affected by human rights violations.

31. During the life of the Commission, a number of victims were referred to the relevant government departments for assistance. It is recommended that this process continue after the Commission closes.

Institutional reform

32. These proposals include legal, administrative and institutional measures designed to prevent the recurrence of human rights abuses.

Who Is Entitled to Reparation and Rehabilitation?

33. It is recommended that the recipients of urgent interim reparation and individual reparation grants should be victims as found by the Commission, as well as their relatives and dependants who are found to be in urgent need, after the

consideration of a completed prescribed application form, according to the proposed urgency criteria.

34. For the purposes of this policy, the Reparation and Rehabilitation Committee (Chapter 1 of the Act) defines relatives and dependants of a victim as:

(a) Parents (or those who acted/act in place of a parent);

(b) Spouse (according to customary, common, religious or indigenous law);

(c) Children (either in or out of wedlock or adopted);

(d) Someone the victim has/had a customary or legal duty to support.

35. It should be noted that, if the victim died as the result of the violation, the definition of relatives and dependants will apply to the situation at the time of the victim's death. If the victim is alive, the definition will apply to the situation as at December 14, 1997.

REPARATION AND REHABILITATION POLICY DEVELOPMENT

36. In formulating these policies and recommendations, the Reparation and Rehabilitation Committee collected information from a variety of sources. Specifically, the Committee collected information from victims and survivors, representatives of non-governmental organisations (NGOs) and community based organisations (CBOs), faith communities and academic institutions. Consultative workshops were held throughout the country. The information collected from deponents was processed and coded in the Commission database and assisted the Reparation and Rehabilitation Committee to:

(a) Establish harm suffered;

(b) Determine the needs and expectations of victims;

(c) Establish criteria to identify victims in urgent need;

(d) Develop proposals regarding long-term reparation and rehabilitation measures.

37. The Reparation and Rehabilitation Committee was also guided by internationally accepted approaches to reparation and rehabilitation:

(a) Redress: the right to fair and adequate compensation;

(b) Restitution: the right to the re-establishment, as far as possible, of the situation that existed prior to the violation;

(c) Rehabilitation: the right to the provision of medical and psychological care and fulfilment of significant personal and community needs;

(d) Restoration of dignity: the right of the individual/community to a sense of worth; and

(e) Reassurance of non-repetition: the strategies for the creation of legislative and administrative measures that contribute to the maintenance of a stable society and the prevention of the re-occurrence of human rights violations.

38. Policy development was also informed by the work and recommendations of other Truth Commissions, in particular the Chilean Commission, which awarded a 'pension' to the families of the dead and disappeared; by the decision of the United Nations to award financial compensation to the victims of the Iran–Iraq war; and, most pertinently, by the conclusions of the Skweyiya and Motsuenyane Commissions.

39. The Skweyiya Commission[9] recommended that victims of 'maltreatment during detention' should receive monetary compensation, appropriate medical and psychological assistance, assistance in completing interrupted education and compensation for property lost. The Motsuenyane Commission[10] also recommended compensation to those who suffered human rights violations and assistance with medical expenses.

40. In the process of developing policy, the Reparation and Rehabilitation Committee was faced with a number of decisions. Perhaps the most important of these was whether reparation should be financial and, if so, how much money should be given.

41. The alternative to a financial grant would be a 'service package'. Offering a service package has a number of pitfalls:

(a) The costs of administering the process might reduce the amount available to victims.

(b) Victims' needs change over time; thus, a service package tailored to meet present needs could well be inappropriate after a period.

(c) Dependants' needs (and status) also change over time.

(d) Giving preferential access to services to select individuals in a community could give rise to tensions.

(e) The way in which a distant implementing body chooses to service a need may not be the way the individual would have chosen himself or herself.

42. The Reparation and Rehabilitation Committee decided that a well-structured monetary grant would be preferable to a services package, providing it took two things into account:

(a) It should enable reasonable access to essential basic services.

(b) It should generate opportunities to achieve a dignified standard of living within the South African socio-economic context.

43. A monetary package also gives freedom of choice to the recipient. He or she can use the money in a way that is most appropriate to redress the injustice experienced. Because a monetary package provides government with a set of

predictable, limited expenses, it makes fiscal management more feasible. An appropriately organised package requires minimal bureaucratic oversight.

44. The final, and most important, factor in favour of an individual monetary grant was that analysis of a representative sample of statements revealed that most deponents requested reparation in the form of money or services that money can purchase (see Figure RR1). The highest expectation of the reparation process was for monetary assistance. Compensation, bursaries, shelter, medical care and tombstones occupied third to seventh places respectively in the most frequent requests (the second most commonly requested intervention was for investigation of the violation).

45. For all these reasons, it was decided to recommend the provision of urgent interim reparations and individual reparation grants in the form of money.

PRINCIPLES OF REPARATION AND REHABILITATION POLICY

Development-centred

46. This policy is development-centred. Central to the approach is a focus on resources, knowledge and choice. Development is not about provision of resources to passive individuals, but rather about actively empowering individuals and communities to take control of their own lives. In adherence to this principle, it is essential to provide individuals with sufficient knowledge and information about available resources and to help them utilise those resources to their maximum benefit.

47. Implementation must be a participatory process. This strengthens collective community development and local reconstruction and development initiatives.

Simplicity and efficacy

48. The policy should be simple, efficient and fair to ensure that the allocated resources are utilised to the maximum benefit of the recipients.

Cultural appropriateness

49. The services developed as a result of this policy should be responsive to the religious and cultural beliefs and practices of the community in which the services are provided.

Community-based

50. In consultation with appropriate ministries, community-based services and delivery should be strengthened and expanded to have a lasting and sustainable impact on communities.

Capacity development

51. Those community resources that are developed should focus not only on delivery of services but also on local capacity building, to ensure sustainability of programmes.

Promoting healing and reconciliation

52. The activities that emerge from this policy should aim to bring people together, to promote mutual understanding and reconciliation.

53. The Act provides for two stages in the process of Reparation and Rehabilitation, namely Urgent Interim Reparation and Final Reparation Measures.

URGENT INTERIM REPARATION

54. Urgent interim reparation is the delivery of reparative measures to victims who are in urgent need. During the life of the Commission, urgent interim reparation was granted to certain victims. It was further recommended that all applicants be considered for this grant while awaiting final reparation (see Table 1).

Benefits

55. It was recommended that beneficiaries be entitled to the following:

   (a) Information about and/or referral to appropriate services (government, non-government and/or private sector), depending on type of need.

   (b) Financial assistance in order to access and/or pay for services deemed necessary to meet specifically identified urgent needs. Payment will be based on a sliding scale according to number of dependants and need. Thus:

Intervention categories and eligibility criteria

56. Victims or their relatives and dependants who have urgent medical, emotional, educational, material and/or symbolic needs will be entitled to urgent interim reparations.

57. Urgency will be determined in each of the above categories using a detailed set of criteria available to the Committee and the proposed government implementing structure.

Implementation

58. The promulgation of government regulations on urgent interim reparation took longer than expected, which resulted in a delay in making this relief available. The time it would have taken for a multi-disciplinary implementing body (as originally envisaged) to be set up would, in turn, have meant further delay in delivering tangible reparation to victims.

Table 1. Number of people in need

One (i.e. applicant only)	R2,000
One plus one	R2,900
One plus two	R3,750
One plus three	R4,530
One plus four	R5,205
One plus five or more	R5,705

59. The Reparation and Rehabilitation Committee thus took responsibility for disseminating, receiving and assessing reparation application forms. Two committee members recommended a cash payment and made suggestions about appropriate services that the applicant could access. This information was forwarded to the President's Fund in Pretoria. The President's Fund made payment to the applicant, either via electronic bank transfer or a cheque posted by registered mail and, through a network of nodal points in provincial governments, informed applicants of available services.

60. While this system was being implemented (first payments were made in July 1998), ongoing discussion took place about the constitution of the implementing body that would eventually take over from the Reparation and Rehabilitation Committee. This matter had not been finalised at the time of reporting.

Implementation of urgent interim reparations before the date specified by the President in terms of section 43(1)

61. This section outlines the different ways in which urgent interim relief policy was implemented before the date specified by the President in terms of section 43(1).

62. Regional Human Rights Violations Committees made preliminary findings on victim statements gathered from their areas. Preliminary regional findings were considered by the national Human Rights Violations Committee and were either accepted or rejected. If the Human Rights Violations Committee found that a gross violation of human rights had occurred and was of the opinion that a person was a victim of such a violation, it referred the statement of the person concerned to the Reparation and Rehabilitation Committee. Moreover, if the Amnesty Committee granted amnesty in respect of any act and was of the opinion that a person was a victim of that act, it referred the identified individual to the Human Rights Violations Committee which, if it concurred, referred the matter to the Reparation and Rehabilitation Committee. In addition, if the Amnesty Committee did not grant amnesty for an act and was of the opinion that the act was a gross violation of human rights and that a person was a victim in the matter, it referred the matter to the Reparation and Rehabilitation Committee through the Human Rights Violations Committee.

63. Any person referred to the Reparation and Rehabilitation Committee, in terms of the steps outlined above, was entitled to apply for reparation on the prescribed form that was sent to them.

64. The Reparation and Rehabilitation Committee applied its mind to the information contained in the prescribed application form and other evidence or information of possible relevance in order to determine whether the applicant was a victim (i.e. whether he or she had suffered harm in terms of section 1(1)(xix) of

the Act), whether he she was in urgent need and to identify the nature of the urgency. The final decision was based on the information contained in the pre-scribed application form. If the applicant was found to be both a victim and in urgent need, the Reparation and Rehabilitation Committee conveyed this decision and all other relevant information regarding this application to the President's Fund.

65. Delivery of urgent interim reparation by the President's Fund involved the following steps:

   (a) receiving decisions from the Commission's Reparation and Rehabilitation Committee;
   (b) referring victims to appropriate service/s; and
   (c) making payment according to the approved sliding scale and/or type of need.

66. It is recommended that all those found to be victims will be eligible for final reparation, regardless of urgency of need.

INDIVIDUAL REPARATION GRANTS

67. In acknowledgement of victim's rights to reparation, it is recommended that final reparation involve an amount of money, called an individual reparation grant, to be made available to each victim (if he/she is alive) or equally divided amongst relatives and/or dependants who have applied for reparation (as defined above) if the victim is dead. The amount of the grant will be based on the formula outlined below. The formula is based on three components, namely an amount to acknowledge the suffering caused by the gross violation that took place, an amount to enable access to services and facilities and an amount to subsidise daily living costs, based on socio-economic circumstances.

Rationale

68. The individual reparation grant is an acknowledgement of a person's suffering due to his/her experience of a gross human rights violation. It is based on the fact that survivors of human rights violations have a right to reparation and rehabilitation. The individual reparation grant provides resources to victims in an effort to restore their dignity. It will be accompanied by information and advice in

order to allow the recipient to make the best possible use of these resources. Thirty-eight per cent of the Commission's deponents requested financial assistance to improve the quality of their lives. In addition, over 90 per cent of deponents asked for a range of services which can be purchased if money is made available—e.g. education, medical care, housing and so on.

Formula for calculating interim reparation grants[11]

69. The monetary package is based on a benchmark amount of R21,700, which was the median annual household income in South Africa in 1997. The Reparation and Rehabilitation Committee believes that this is an appropriate amount to achieve the aims of the individual reparation grant—that is, to enable access to services and to assist in establishing a dignified way of life. The poverty line of R15,600 per annum was rejected as a benchmark, as this would be condemning victims to a life of near poverty, rather than one of minimum dignity.

70. The actual amount that each victim receives will be based on an easily administered formula, which differentiates according to three criteria:

(a) An acknowledgement of the suffering caused by the violation (#1);

(b) An amount to facilitate access to services. Because services are less accessible in rural areas, those living in rural communities will receive a premium in this part of the grant. The difference is based on the assumption that accessing services in rural areas is 30 per cent more expensive than in urban areas (#2);[12]

(c) An amount to subsidise daily living costs. This will be differentiated according to numbers of dependants and/or relatives, which will be capped at nine. In addition, because the cost of living is higher in urban areas, people living in urban areas will be favoured in this portion of the grant. The difference is based on the assumption that the cost of living in urban areas is 15 per cent higher than in [rural] areas (#3).

71. Each portion of the formula is given a weighting or ranking as follows:

#1= 50%, #2 = 25%, #3=25% of total interim reparations grant.

72. The actual variation in amounts payable according to the formula and differentiation criteria is shown in Table 2.

73. Using the proposed projections, no individual will receive more than R23,023 per annum (the maximum individual reparation grant). This maximum amount would apply to an individual, living in a rural area, who has nine or more dependants.

Table 2. Reparation Payment Schedule (Per Annum Per Victim)

#1	#2	#3	
Acknowledgement of violation 50%	Access to services[13] 25%	Daily living costs[14] 25%	Total Annual Reparation
Rural			
0.5 × 21,700 = 10,850	0.25 × 24,630 = 6,157.5	Household size 0.25×	
		1 5,169	18,330
		2 8,396	19,107
		3 11,152	19,796
		4 13,640	20,418
		5 15,946	20,994
		6 18,117	21,537
		7 20,181	22,053
		8 22,158	22,547
		9+ 24,063	23,023
Urban			
0.5 × 21,700 = 10,850	0.25 × 18,771 = 4,693	Household size 0.25×	
		1 5,947	17,029
		2 9,660	17,958
		3 12,831	18,750
		4 15,693	19,466
		5 18,347	20,129
		6 20,844	20,754
		7 23,219	21,348
		8 25,494	21,916
		9+ 27,685	22,464

74. The annual individual reparation grant should be calculated for each beneficiary and paid as 50 per cent of the total every six months. The annual payments will continue for a period of six years.

Administration/President's Fund

75. The grant will be funded and administered by the President's Fund. The President's Fund will accrue resources through allocations from the national fiscus, international and local donations and earned interest on the funds. Based on the given policy and formula, and estimating 22,000 victims, the total cost of this policy will be R477,400,000 per annum or R2,864,400,000 over six years. The figure of 22,000 victims is based on the Commission's Human Rights Violations Statement as the only point of entry.

76. It is recommended that the President's Fund function on an interdepartmental or interdisciplinary basis as a dual structure with

(a) an administrative capacity to disburse the money which has been allocated;

(b) a multi-disciplinary Reparation Panel to assess application forms and to advise appropriately. While the Commission is still in existence, members of the Reparation and Rehabilitation Committee may sit on this panel.

Symbolic Reparation/Legal and Administrative Interventions

78. Symbolic reparation measures are aimed at restoring the dignity of victims and survivors of gross human rights violations. These include measures to facilitate the communal process of commemorating the pain and celebrating the victories of the past. Deponents to the Commission have indicated that these types of interventions are an important part of coming to terms with the past.

Individual interventions

79. The following services will be made available:

Issuing of death certificates

80. Many people making statements to the Commission highlighted the fact that they did not receive death certificates for deceased relatives. It is recommended that mechanisms to facilitate the issuing of death certificates be established by the appropriate ministry.[15]

Exhumations, reburials and ceremonies

81. In a number of cases, the need for exhumations and reburials became evident. It is recommended that mechanisms to expedite this process be established by the appropriate ministries. Alternative culture-specific ceremonies should similarly be facilitated. Costs associated with exhumations, reburials and alternative ceremonies will be met from the individual reparation grant.

Headstones and tombstones

82. In a number of cases, deponents asked for tombstones and headstones to be erected on the graves of the deceased. It is recommended that these will be paid for from the individual reparation grant.

Declarations of death

83. In many cases of disappearances reported to the Commission, people have not formally been declared dead. It is recommended that mechanisms to facilitate the declaration of deaths be established and implemented in those cases where the family requests an official declaration of death. This is an obligation of the Commission according to section (k) of the Act.

Expunging of criminal records

84. Many victims received criminal sentences for political activities. It is recommended that mechanisms to facilitate the expunging of these records be established by the appropriate ministry.

Expediting outstanding legal matters related to the violations

85. A careful analysis of statements indicates that there are still many outstanding legal matters that deponents would like to have resolved. Mechanisms to facilitate the resolution of outstanding legal matters which are directly related to reported violations should be established within the President's Fund.

Community interventions

86. It is recommended that the following measures be taken:

Renaming of streets and facilities

87. It is recommended that streets and community facilities be renamed to reflect, remember and honour individuals or events in particular communities. Local and provincial authorities should be informed about these requests.

Memorials/monuments

88. It is recommended that monuments and memorials be built to commemorate the conflicts and/or victories of the past. These monuments and memorials should be built in consultation with local government structures. Local and provincial authorities should establish the necessary mechanisms in this regard.

Culturally appropriate ceremonies

89. It is recommended that specific needs of communities regarding remembering and/or celebrating be honoured through culturally appropriate ceremonies. This, according to requests, could include cleansing ceremonies. Local and provincial authorities should establish the necessary mechanisms in this regard, in close cooperation with the appropriate faith communities and cultural and community organisations.

National interventions

90. The following measures need to be taken:

Renaming of public facilities

91. It is recommended that, after careful consideration and consultation, public facilities should be renamed in honour of individuals or past events. The necessary mechanisms should be put in place by the appropriate ministries.

Monuments and memorials

92. In response to the requests of many victims and the broader community, the erection of appropriate monuments/memorials should be considered. The appropriate ministries should put the necessary mechanisms in place to plan and implement this.

A day of remembrance

93. In response to the requests of many victims and the broader community, it is recommended that the government declare a National Day of Remembrance. The appropriate ministries should facilitate this, in close liaison with the different faith communities and cultural organisations in the country.

COMMUNITY REHABILITATION

94. Individuals eligible for individual reparation grants are members of communities that have been subjected to systemic abuse. Entire communities suffer the adverse effects of post-traumatic stress disorder, expressed by a wide range of deponents to the Commission. It is therefore recommended that rehabilitation programmes be established both at community and national levels.

95. Rehabilitation programmes should form part of a general initiative to transform the way in which services are provided in South Africa. Such programmes can also promote reconciliation within communities. The following possible rehabilitation programmes have been identified with reference to the needs expressed by deponents in their statements. For community rehabilitation programmes to have the desired positive effect and to be sustainable, relevant government ministries should facilitate their development, in consultation with other partners like representatives of organised businesses, victim support groups, NGOs, faith communities and so on.

Health and social services

National demilitarisation

96. Because of ongoing exposure to, and involvement in, political violence, young people have become socialised to accept violence as a way of resolving conflict. This issue needs to be addressed as a matter of urgency.

97. The demilitarisation programme should be systematic and assist in demilitarising youth, who have for decades been involved in violent activity to effect political change. Secondary and tertiary educational institutions and sporting bodies should be involved in the implementation of this programme. The programme should consist of a combination of social, therapeutic and political processes and interventions, appropriate to the area in which they are being implemented.

Dislocation and displacement

98. South Africa has thousands of 'internal' refugees, who have been driven from their homes by political conflict. Displacement can lead to psychological distress, unemployment and trauma.

99. It is recommended that a multi-disciplinary programme, involving all relevant ministries and departments (such as health, welfare and housing) be put

in place to resettle displaced persons and address the problems of displaced communities.

Appropriate local treatment centres

100. Victims and survivors of gross human rights violations have complex physical and emotional needs which can be most appropriately addressed by multi-disciplinary teams—taking cultural and personal preferences into account—at accessible local treatment centres. It is recommended that the Department of Health establish such centres.

Rehabilitation for perpetrators and their families

101. Perpetrators and their families need to be reintegrated into normal community life. This is essential to create a society in which human rights abuses will not recur. Individual and family rehabilitative systems need to be instituted to assist individuals and families in coming to terms with their violent past and learning constructive and peaceful ways of resolving conflict without resort to violence.

Mental health services

102. Prevailing negative perceptions of therapy and its practice prevent people from accessing mental health services. Individuals and communities should be educated about the link between mental health and conflicts of the past. Appropriate mental health initiatives should be linked with developmental projects, for example, the Reconstruction and Development Programme and Masakhane. Mental health cannot be seen in isolation from socio-economic development.

Community-based interventions

103. It is recommended that self-sustaining, community-based survivor support groups be established, staffed by trained facilitators from the community. This method of support and treatment is not a unique concept and enjoys success where facilitators focus on therapy. The support group method represents a cost-effective, accessible, non-threatening way in which people can access counselling.

Skills training

104. Community members should be trained in a variety of skills to enable them to assist victims of human rights abuses. These should include crisis management,

critical incident briefing, trauma awareness training, referral skills and knowledge of available resources.

Specialised trauma counselling services

105. Specialised emotional trauma counselling services should be established. A national strategy to train trauma counsellors should be developed.

Family-based therapy

106. The impact of gross human rights violations on the family is often underestimated. To address this issue, it is recommended that training programmes for health care workers, aimed at improving their skills in the family systems approach be instituted by the relevant ministries.

Education

107. The standard of black education was appalling and this aspect of the legacy of apartheid is likely to be with us for a long time to come. Education is ripe for reform and the possibilities for its transformation are exciting. However, one of the effects of the past is that it has resulted in a strong culture of often pointless conflict around education matters. The desire to learn in a disciplined environment no longer seems to prevail.

Assistance for continuation of studies

108. It is recommended that the establishment of community colleges and youth centres be prioritised, to facilitate the reintegration of affected youth into society.

109. Specific accelerated adult basic education and training (ABET) programmes should be established to meet the needs of youth and adults who are semi-literate and have lost educational opportunities due to human rights abuses.

Building and improvement of schools

110. Rebuilding of demolished schools, particularly in rural and disadvantaged areas, should be prioritised.

Special educational support services

111. Remedial and emotional support should be included in mainstream educational programmes.

112. Mainstream educational facilities should provide skills-based training courses in order to respond to the needs of mature students and to help them find employment.

Housing

Housing provision

113. It is recommended that specific attention be given to establishing housing projects in communities where gross violations of human rights led to mass destruction of property and/or displacement. The appropriate ministry should put the necessary mechanisms in place.

Institutional reform

114. One of the functions of the Commission is to make recommendations on institutional legislative and administrative measures designed to prevent the recurrence of human rights abuses in the future.[16]

115. The Reparation and Rehabilitation Committee recommends that the measures and programmes outlined in the chapter on Recommendations become part of the operational plans and ethos of a wide range of sectors in society including the judiciary, media, security forces, business, education and correctional services.

IMPLEMENTATION PROCESS AND RESPONSIBILITY

116. The nature and structure of the body which implements final reparation will need to be debated and will obviously depend on the decisions taken by

Parliament about the form that final reparation will take. Based on present policy proposals, the Reparation and Rehabilitation Committee believes that the following issues must be considered:

(a) Implementation must take place at national, provincial and local levels.

(b) The national implementing body should be located in the office of the State President or Deputy President. The body should not be allocated to one particular ministry, as its functions will require access to the resources, infrastructure and services of a number of ministries (such as housing, health, welfare and education).

(c) The national body should be headed by a National Director of Reparation and Rehabilitation, who will be advised by a panel or board of trustees, composed of appropriately qualified members from relevant ministries and human rights organisations.

117. The national body will have the following functions:

(a) Implementing and administering any financial reparation policy.

(b) Maintaining regular contact with relevant ministries, to ensure appropriate service provision.

(c) Establishing provincial reparation desks.

(d) Facilitating the formation of partnerships with NGOs, the private sector, faith communities and other appropriate groupings, in order to meet victims' needs.

(e) Promoting fund raising and communication strategies.

(f) Monitoring, evaluating and documenting the national implementation of reparation and rehabilitation.

(g) Reporting to the Inter-Ministerial Committee.

118. Provincial reparation desks should be established within existing provincial government structures.

119. Provincial reparation desks will have the following functions:

(a) Ensuring that reparation recipients are linked to appropriate service providers.

(b) Monitoring dispersal of financial reparation and providing suitable financial counselling to recipients.

(c) Taking particular responsibility for community reparation and symbolic reparation at a local level.

(d) Monitoring, evaluating and documenting implementation of reparation at a provincial level.

(e) Reporting to the National Director of Reparation and Rehabilitation.

NOTES

1. Once a treaty has been signed, a country is obliged, according to article 18 of the Vienna Convention on the Law of Treaties, to 'refrain from acts which would defeat the objects and purpose of such treaty'. South Africa is therefore bound by the provisions and jurisprudence of those treaties it has signed.
2. The Universal Declaration of Human Rights has been accepted as customary international law.
3. Signed by South Africa on October 3, 1994.
4. See *Bleier v. Uruguay* (Case No. 30/1978); *Camargo v. Columbia* (Case No. 45/1979); *Dermit v. Uruguay* (Case No. 84/1981); *Quinteros v. Uruguay* (Case No. 107/1981); *Baboerem v. Suriname* (Case Nos. 146/1983 & 148–54/1983); *Muiyo v. Zaire* (Case No. 194/1985). Scores more cases can be referred to. See generally T. van Boven, 'Study Concerning the Right to Restitution, Compensation and Rehabilitation for Victims of Gross Violations of Human Rights and Fundamental Freedoms' (Report submitted to the United Nations Commission on Human Rights, July 2, 1993).
5. Signed by South Africa on January 29, 1993.
6. Judgment, Inter-American Court of Human Rights, Series C. No. 4 (1988).
7. Inter-American Commission on Human Rights, Report No. 29/92 (October 2, 1992); Inter-American Commission on Human Rights, Report No. 28/92 (October 2, 1992).
8. See chapter on Consequences of Gross Human Rights Violations.
9. 'Report of the Skweyiya Commission of Enquiry into complaints by former African National Congress prisoners and detainees', August 1992.
10. 'Report of the Motsuenyane Commission of Enquiry into certain allegations of cruelty and human rights abuse against ANC prisoners and detainees by ANC members', August 1993.
11. The Commission acknowledges the assistance of the University of Cape Town Budget Project in this regard.
12. Rural versus urban to be determined by standard census delimitation.
13. The rural/urban difference for this category is based on the assumption that accessing rural health is 30 per cent more expensive in rural areas.
14. The rural/urban difference for this category is based on the assumption that the cost of living is 15 per cent lower in rural areas and the differences within rural and urban categories reflect differences in household size. Concerning household size, the calculations assume that a seven-person household will receive R21,700 on average. Households with less than seven members receive less than the anchor and larger households receive up to a maximum set by a nine-person household. It is also assumed that each additional household member costs the household slightly less than the preceding family member.
15. See chapter on Recommendations.
16. See chapter on Recommendations.

REGULATION 1660
PROMOTION OF NATIONAL UNITY AND RECONCILIATION ACT, 1995, ACT 34/95: REGULATIONS REGARDING REPARATION TO VICTIMS

Government Gazette
Republic of South Africa
Regulation Gazette No. 7821
Vol. 461, Pretoria, November 12, 2003, No. 25695
Department of Justice and Constitutional Development
No. R. 1660   November 12, 2003

The President has, under section 27(2) of the Promotion of National Unity and Reconciliation Act, 1995 (Act No. 34 of 1995), and after the procedures prescribed in sections 4(f)(i) and 27(1) and (2) of the said Act have been complied with, made the Regulations in the Schedule.

Schedule

Definitions

1. In these Regulations, any word or expression to which a meaning has been assigned in the Act shall bear the meaning so assigned and, unless the context otherwise indicates

   - 'accounting officer' means the officer appointed by the Minister under section 42(6) of the Act;
   - 'alive' means alive at the time of the request for payment in terms of regulation 4;
   - 'beneficiary' means a person contemplated in regulation 3;
   - 'completed request form' means a form contemplated in regulation 4(1) or(2), on which all the required information has been submitted;
   - 'child' means a child of an identified victim, irrespective of whether such child was born in or out of wedlock or was legally adopted;
   - 'Fund' means the Fund established under section 42(1) of the Act;
   - 'Fund administrator' means an officer designated by the Minister under section 42(5) of the Act;
   - 'identified victim' means a person who has been found by the Commission to be a victim of a gross violation of human rights;

- 'parent of a victim' means a parent of, or a person who exercises or has exercised parental responsibility over, an identified victim;
- 'reparation grant' means the reparation grant referred to in regulation 3(1);
- 'spouse' means the person married to an identified victim under any law, custom or belief; and
- 'the Act' means the Promotion of National Unity and Reconciliation Act, 1995 (Act No. 34 of 1995).

Authority responsible for application of regulations

2. The accounting officer is responsible for the application of these regulations.

Basis and conditions of individual reparation grant

3. (1) An identified victim is entitled to a one-off reparation grant in the amount of R30,000 as final reparation.
   (2) The reparation grant must be paid to an identified victim if he or she is alive.
   (3) If an identified victim is not alive, the reparation grant must, subject to the provisions of subregulation (7), be paid to the person to whom urgent interim reparation relating to that identified victim had been paid.
   (4) If both the identified victim and the person to whom urgent interim reparation relating to that identified victim had been paid are not alive, the reparation grant must
      (a) be paid to the spouse of the identified victim; or
      (b) in the case of the identified victim having more than one spouse, be divided equally among, and paid to, all the spouses of that victim.
   (5) If both the identified victim and the person to whom urgent interim reparation relating to an identified victim had been paid are not alive, and that victim is not survived by a spouse, the reparation grant is to be divided equally among and paid to the following persons in the following order of preference:
      (a) If the victim is survived by children, the reparation grant must be paid to those children;
      (b) if the victim is not survived by a child, the reparation grant must be paid to the parents of that victim;
      (c) if the victim is not survived by a parent, the reparation grant must be paid to other blood relations of that victim who are related to the victim nearest in degree; or

(d) if the victim is not survived by any person contemplated in this sub-regulation, the reparation grant must remain in the Fund.

(6) If an identified victim is not alive and no urgent interim reparation relating to that victim has been paid, the reparation grant must be paid to a person contemplated in subregulation (4) or (5) in the order of preference contemplated in the said subregulations.

(7) If an identified victim is not alive, the reparation grant may be paid to a person contemplated in subregulation (4) or (5) in the order of preference contemplated in the said subregulations, if such person, in the opinion of the Fund administrator, ranks higher than the recipient of the urgent interim reparation in terms of the order of preference referred to.

Request for payment

4. (1) A request by
   (a) an identified victim; or
   (b) a person to whom urgent interim reparation relating to that identi-fied victim had been paid, for payment of the reparation grant contemplated in regulation 3 must be made in the form of Request Form 1 contained in the Annexure.

   (2) A request by a beneficiary, excluding a person contemplated in subregula-tion (1), for payment of the reparation grant contemplated in regulation 3 must be made in the form of Request Form 2 contained in the Annexure.

   (3) A reparation grant must, subject to the provisions of regulation 5, be paid on receipt of a completed request form.

   (4) The completed request form must be submitted to the Fund administrator in one of the following ways:
   (a) By mail, in which case it must be addressed to the Fund Administrator of the President's Fund, Private Bag X81, Pretoria, 0001 ; or
   (b) by personal delivery to the Fund Administrator of the President's Fund, Presidia Building, comer of Paul Kruger and Pretorius Street, Room 245, Pretoria.

Processing of request

5. (1) On receipt of a completed request form the Fund administrator must
   (a) forthwith, for purposes of the speedy payment of the reparation grant, obtain any further information or documentation or clarify any uncertainties with regard to the information in that form;

(b) make arrangements with relevant persons or institutions to facilitate the payment of the reparation grant;

(c) satisfy himself or herself that the person requesting the payment is a beneficiary entitled to the reparation grant; and

(d) subject to the provisions of subregulation (2), make the payment in accordance with the manner specified by the beneficiary in the completed request form.

(2) The Fund Administrator must, before a reparation grant is paid to a person other than an identified victim, in a notice

(a) make known the particulars of the identified victim, the person to whom the reparation grant will be paid, the relation between the identified victim and the person and the amount to be paid; and

(b) invite the persons contemplated in regulation 3(4) and (5) to lodge, within 30 days after the date of the notice, an objection, if any, to the payment to be made.

(3) The notice contemplated in subregulation (2) must be displayed on the notice board at every magistrate's office or post office.

Payment of reparation grant

6. (1) The payment of the reparation grant is made from the Fund.

(2) The reparation grant may be paid

(a) by electronic bank transfer; or

(b) by cheque.

(3) The Fund administrator must

(a) inform the beneficiary when the payment of the reparation grant has been made; and

(b) retain proof of the payment.

Representations by aggrieved persons

7. (1) Any person who is aggrieved by a decision of the Fund administrator regarding the person to whom the reparation grant is to be, or was, paid may make representations to the accounting officer.

(2) The representations contemplated in subregulation (1)

(a) may be made at any time but not later than 30 calendar days after payment of the reparation grant to a beneficiary;

    (b) must be in writing;
    (c) must indicate the reasons why the person is aggrieved; and
    (d) must, where possible, be accompanied by documents as proof for the
        reasons why the person is aggrieved.
(3) The Fund administrator must, immediately upon notification by the
    accounting officer of representations received in terms of subregulation
    (1), submit to the accounting officer the documents in his or her posses-
    sion that relate to the matter, together with his or her reasons for the
    decision.
(4) The accounting officer may, in order to make a finding regarding the
    representations, make any enquiries that he or she deems fit.
(5) The accounting officer must make a finding in regard to the representa-
    tions and inform, in writing, the person who made the representations of
    his or her finding.

Cession, assignment or attachment of reparation

8. Despite any law to the contrary, no reparation grant shall
    (a) be capable of cession or assignment by the beneficiary to whom it has
        been awarded;
    (b) be capable of attachment under a judgment or execution of a judgment
        of a court of law; or
    (c) form part of the estate of the beneficiary, should such estate be seques-
        trated.

MALAWI

Constitution of the Republic of Malawi

Chapter 13

National Compensation Tribunal

The National Compensation Tribunal

137. There shall be a National Compensation Tribunal which shall entertain claims with respect to alleged criminal and civil liability of the Government of Malawi which was in power before the appointed day and which shall have such powers and functions as are conferred on it by this Constitution and an Act of Parliament.

Exclusive original jurisdiction

138. (1) No person shall institute proceedings against any Government in power after the commencement of this Constitution in respect of any alleged criminal or civil liability of the Government of Malawi in power before the commencement of this Constitution arising from abuse of power or office, save by application to the National Compensation Tribunal, which shall hear cases initiated by persons with sufficient interest.

(2) The National Compensation Tribunal shall have all powers of investigation necessary to establish the facts of any case before it.

(3) Notwithstanding subsection (1), the National Compensation Tribunal shall have the power to remit a case or a question of law for determination by the ordinary courts where the National Compensation Tribunal is satisfied that the Tribunal does not have jurisdiction, or where the Tribunal feels it is in the interest of justice so to do.

Composition

139. (1) There shall be a Chairman of the National Compensation Tribunal who shall be a judge and who shall
   (a) be appointed in that behalf by the Chief Justice on the nomination of the Judicial Service Commission; and
   (b) hold the office of Chairman of the National Compensation Tribunal for not more than three years or until such time as that person ceases to be a judge whichever is sooner.

(2) The Chairman of the National Compensation Tribunal shall be assisted by such additional members and by such assessors and other experts as may be appointed in accordance with the provisions of an Act of Parliament.

Procedure

140. (1) The rules of procedure of the National Compensation Tribunal and other matters of policy or principle concerning its powers and functions shall be prescribed by or under an Act of Parliament and shall be such as shall ensure expeditious disposal of cases, which may include an informal preliminary arbitration procedure.

(2) Notwithstanding subsection (1), the procedures of the National Compensation Tribunal shall
   (a) conform to the standards of proof required for a normal civil court unless the National Compensation Tribunal otherwise determines in the interest of justice in any particular case or class of cases; and
   (b) conform with the standards of justice set out in this Constitution and the principles of natural justice.

Protection of third party rights

141. Where a third party disputes a claim and has an interest in money or property that is the subject of a claim before the National Compensation Tribunal
   (a) that party shall be given adequate notification;
   (b) that party shall be entitled to legal representation; and
   (c) if the Chairman of the National Compensation Tribunal is satisfied that the person is of insufficient means to retain legal counsel, legal assistance shall be provided at the expense of the State.

Jurisdiction of ordinary courts

142. (1) The High Court shall not be excluded from hearing applications for judicial review of the decisions of the Tribunal nor shall a determination by the Tribunal be a bar to further criminal or civil proceedings in an appropriate court against a private person for the duration of the existence of the fund.

(2) A 'private person' for the purposes of this section means a person who was before the commencement of this Constitution a member of the Government or of an agent of the Government, who would, under the laws then in force, have been personally liable for an act that is the subject of the criminal or civil proceedings.

Power to waive statutory limitations

143. For the purposes of pursuing claims before the National Compensation Tribunal and criminal and civil proceedings against a private person within the meaning of subsection 142 (2), any statutory time limitation may be waived by the Tribunal or by a court if it seems to the Tribunal or the court equitable to do so.

National Compensation Fund

144. (1) There shall be a National Compensation Fund which shall be a trust vested in the Republic.

(2) The National Compensation Fund shall be used exclusively for the purposes assigned to it by this Constitution and shall

(a) be a trust, the purpose of which shall be for the exclusive benefit of those applicants to the National Compensation Tribunal who have been granted any award, gratuity, pension or other form of reparation according to the principles, procedures and rules of the National Compensation Tribunal;

(b) be held in a separate account within the Reserve Bank of Malawi; and

(c) have all of its reports, financial statements and information relating to its operation published and maintained for public scrutiny.

(3) Subject to this chapter, the only charges on, or disbursements to be made from, the National Compensation Fund shall be by

(a) the National Compensation Tribunal; or

(b) the trustees of the Fund in so far as such disbursements or charges are necessary and prudent for the efficient operation of the Fund in accordance with its purpose as declared in this subsection.

(4) There shall be not less than four trustees of the National Compensation Fund who shall be appointed from time to time by the Public Appointments Committee on the recommendation of the National Compensation Tribunal.

(5) A Trustee shall hold office for the duration of the Fund unless and only in such circumstances as that trustee is removed by the Public Appointments Committee on the grounds of
   (a) incompetence;
   (b) incapacity; or
   (c) being compromised in the exercise of his or her functions to the extent that his or her financial probity is in serious question.

(6) Trustees of the National Compensation Fund shall exercise their functions independent of any direction or interference by any body or authority, save as is provided by this section.

(7) The Auditor General shall make an annual report, to be laid before the National Assembly, on the conduct and status of the Fund which shall provide guidance to the National Assembly for voting an appropriation for the purposes of the National Compensation Fund.

(8) An appropriation for the purposes of the National Compensation Fund shall be laid before the National Assembly by the Minister responsible for Finance before the beginning, and with respect to, every financial year during the life of the Fund.

(9) With respect to any financial year, the Tribunal shall prescribe a period not being more than six months after the commencement of that financial year, after which the Tribunal shall not receive applications for compensation within that financial year from the National Compensation Fund.

Winding up of the National Compensation Fund

145. (1) The National Compensation Fund shall cease to be charged with new claims for compensation not later than ten years after the commencement of this Constitution at which time the National Compensation Tribunal shall dissolve.

   (2) If, with respect to any year within the period prescribed in subsection (1), and after the second year of it coming into existence, less than ten applications are made to the National Compensation Tribunal, then the Chairman of the Tribunal may direct the Minister responsible for Finance to lay before the National Assembly a Bill
      (a) to dissolve the National Compensation Tribunal; and
      (b) to confer on the High Court jurisdiction equivalent to that of the National Compensation Tribunal to determine claims against the Government within the meaning of this chapter.

(3) Where the National Compensation Tribunal has been dissolved, for the remaining duration of the period prescribed in subsection (1) the uncommitted residue of the Fund shall remain a separate fund within the accounts of the Consolidated Fund which shall be drawn upon by the Minister responsible for Finance in respect of awards made by the High Court in relation to claims that would otherwise have been determined by the National Compensation Tribunal.

(4) The National Compensation Fund shall continue until there is no longer a committed residue.

NATIONAL COMPENSATION TRIBUNAL (PROCEDURE) RULES, 1997

[The Malawi Gazette Supplement, October 17, 1997]

Rule   Arrangement of Rules

PART I PRELIMINARY

In exercise of the powers conferred by section 3 of the National Compensation Tribunal (Miscellaneous Provisions) Act, 1995, I, Richard Allen Banda, Chief Justice, make the following rules.

Part I: Preliminary

1. The Rules may be cited as the National Compensation Tribunal (Procedure) Rules, 1997.
2. In these rules, unless the context otherwise requires,

   - 'agent' means a person appointed by a claimant to act on behalf of the claimant;
   - 'claim' means an application by, or on behalf of, a claimant or joint claimants addressed to the Tribunal for an award in respect of a loss or injury;
   - 'claimant' means a person who suffered loss or injury or a person who has at law inherited an entitlement to claim in respect of a loss or injury, and includes a dependant of a claimant and a representative, but does not include an agent;
   - 'Fund' means the National Compensation Fund established under section 144 of the Constitution;
   - 'representative' means

     (a) a person through whom a claim is brought by a person beneficially entitled to claim but lacks legal capacity to act, or
     (b) a person who is authorized to act for another person, including a family unit;

   - 'Tribunal' means the National Compensation Tribunal established under Part XIII of the Constitution.

3. These Rules apply to all claims submitted before the Tribunal.

Part II: Notification and Registration of Claims

4. (1) Every person wishing to make a claim shall notify the Tribunal of his or her intention by submitting sufficient information to identify the claimant and the claim.
   (2) Where the Tribunal receives notification of a claim, it shall, unless it decides such step to be unnecessary, forward to the claimant such claim forms as will facilitate the efficient assessment of the claim.
   (3) Subject to subrule (4), every claimant shall append his or her signature or other identification mark to the notification and claim forms referred to in subrules (1) and (2), respectively.
   (4) The Tribunal may, in exceptional circumstances and under such conditions as the Tribunal may in the best interests of the claimant impose, accept the signature of an agent instead of the signature or other identification mark of the claimant.

5. (1) Subject to subtitle (3), the Tribunal shall upon receipt of a notification under rule 3 register the claim.

(2) Upon registration of a claim under subrule (1) the Tribunal shall within fourteen days send a written notice of the registration of the claim to the claimant.

(3) Subject to any deadlines that may be prescribed, from time to time, in respect of specific categories of claims, the Tribunal may register claims up to one year before the completion of the operations of the Tribunal.

PART III: FILING OF CLAIMS

6. Every person acting as a representative of the claimant shall produce evidence satisfactory to the Tribunal regarding his or her authority to so act.

7. (1) Every person acting as an agent of a claimant shall produce evidence satisfactory to the Tribunal regarding his or her authority to act as agent of the claimant for the purpose of making a claim, and such evidence shall include a letter of authority bearing the signature or other identification mark of the claimant authorizing the agent to act on behalf of the claimant.

(2) Where a claimant is represented by an agent,

(a) the claim shall continue in the name of the claimant who shall be entitled to receive a copy of all notices sent to the agent;

Provided that in the case of a claim by an unincorporated association the Tribunal may limit the number of persons entitled to receive copies of notices;

(b) the claimant shall have the right to terminate or limit the mandate of the agent at any time by written notice to the Tribunal;

(c) the Tribunal shall not entertain any claim in respect of fees or other expenses associated with the pursuit of a claim, either as an independent claim or as a charge against an award.

8. A claim by, or on behalf of, a minor may be made by his or her parent, guardian or person appointed by the court or by the Tribunal, and shall be styled 'X on behalf of Y, a minor'.

9. Where a claim arising from the same event or series of related events is bought by, or on behalf of, persons closely related, any person acting on behalf of the family shall be deemed to be an agent, unless the Tribunal determines otherwise, and payment may be made either to individual claimants or to the appropriate District Commissioner who shall pay the individual claimants.

10. Where a claim is made in respect of the loss of an unincorporated association, any two or more members of the association may represent the other members, if the Tribunal is satisfied that they are acting in the best interests

of, and with the approval of, the other members of the association, and the claim shall be styled, 'X, an unincorporated association'.

11. Where, in the opinion of the Tribunal, two or more claims may be conveniently assessed or determined at the same time, the Tribunal may order that the claims or parts of the claims be associated and where, in the opinion of the Tribunal, several claims may be conveniently treated as separate claims, it may likewise so order.

12. (1) Where a claimant seeks restitution of specific property the Tribunal shall within a reasonable time notify the current title holder of the property of the existence of the claim and of his and her rights, under these Rules.

(2) A third party who disputes a claim for restitution and who has a sufficient interest in the property which is the subject of a claim shall notify the Tribunal of his or her interest, and if the Tribunal finds the intervention or claim to be warranted, the Tribunal shall join that party to the proceedings.

(3) The title holder of any property notified under subrule (1) and any party joined to the proceedings under (2) shall, within the time set out in any notice by the Tribunal, provide such information concerning his or her acquisition of the property or interest, and any other relevant information that the Tribunal may request.

(4) A party joined to proceedings pursuant to subrules (1) and (2) shall be entitled to all notices of the proceedings and be given the same opportunity to be heard as claimant.

PART IV: SUBMISSION, PREPARATION, AND ASSESSMENT OF CLAIMS

13. (1) The claimant shall provide such evidence as may be required to establish the claim.

(2) Notwithstanding subrule (1), the Tribunal may consider or hear any other evidence or information that may otherwise be presented to it, and for this purpose the Tribunal shall

(a) have powers of the High Court in hearing evidence, summoning of witnesses and compelling the attendance of any person and production of documents;

(b) have power to obtain evidence abroad, and may give such directions for the taking of such evidence and for the manner thereof as may be deemed expedient.

14. The Tribunal may, in respect of any claim on category claims, appoint such experts or panels of experts as it considers necessary and for such period as it considers appropriate to establish facts and to make appropriate recommendations on matters of policy.

15. The Tribunal shall establish and publish assessment guidelines and tariffs for the expeditious processing of claims.

16. (1) The Tribunal shall review each claim and evidence in support of the claim, and may, by notice in writing addressed to the claimant, require the claimant to provide such further information or documents as in the opinion of the Tribunal may be necessary to facilitate the assessment of the claim.

    (2) A notice under subrule (1) may be supplemented by such additional requests and communications as the Tribunal may consider appropriate, and in each case the Tribunal shall specify the period within which the claimant shall respond.

PART V: DETERMINATION OF CLAIMS

17. (1) Subject to availability of funds for distribution and subrule (3), where the Tribunal considers that a claim is read for determination, or where no additional information or documents requested by notice to the claimant is supplied or expected, the Tribunal shall upon at least fourteen days written notice inform the claimant that the claim is ready for determination, and shall thereafter determine the claim.

    (2) The Tribunal shall within seven days of the date of an award notify the claimant of any particulars of the award.

    (3) Subject to rule 19 and subrule (1), the Tribunal shall determine claims in ascending order of size.

    (4) The Tribunal may make such interim awards from time to time as it may deem to be just in the circumstances, provided that such award does not exceed the anticipated total value of the claim.

18. (1) The Tribunal may of its own volition or upon the application of a claimant order an oral hearing of a claim, and where the Tribunal so orders, it shall notify the claimant in writing at least fourteen days before the date of the hearing.

    (2) Save as the Tribunal may otherwise order, an oral hearing shall be held in public at a place to be determined by the Tribunal.

19. Where a claimant:

    (a) has reached the age of sixty-five years or

    (b) produces a medical certificate, which, in the opinion of the Tribunal, provides strong evidence that, in light of the condition and prospects of the claimant, it would be inequitable not to expedite his or her claim, the Tribunal shall process the claim of the claimant on a priority basis.

    Provided that the Tribunal may order an independent examination of the claimant to establish the bona fides of any claimant seeking relief under this rule.

Part VI: Awards

20. (1) The Tribunal shall make payment of a monetary award to a successful claimant as expeditiously as possible in accordance with the following principles:

(a) Lump sum monetary awards not exceeding a prescribed payment threshold to be determined by the Tribunal from time to time shall be paid in full as soon as possible.

(b) Monetary awards exceeding or equal to a threshold determined by the Tribunal shall be paid up to the threshold amount, and any balance shall be discharged in a manner to be determined by the Tribunal having regard to amounts available for distribution in the Fund, and other available resources.

(c) All payments shall be made directly to the claimant or his or her legal representative, or a bank account or a building society account held in the name of the claimant.

(d) The Tribunal shall not entertain requests to make payments to third parties.

(2) Notwithstanding subrule (1), any monetary compensation payable to a minor shall be paid into court or to an appropriate District Commissioner, and shall be held in trust for the minor until such time as the minor reaches the age of majority.

(3) Where the Tribunal has made a monetary award in favor of an unincorporated association, the Tribunal may withhold payment until such time as the right of the representatives to receive funds has been established to the satisfaction of the Tribunal, and the Tribunal may for the purposes of making payment at any time appoint any other person in addition to, or in substitution for, any person previously accepted as representative.

21. (1) The Tribunal may, in respect of any claim, recommend a non-monetary award, including the restitution of property, and shall within seven days communicate its recommendation to the appropriate party.

(2) An order under this section shall have the same force and effect as an order of the High Court, and shall be enforced in the same manner.

22. Where it is in the interest of the parties and the Tribunal to do so, the Tribunal may negotiate the settlement of a claim or take part in any informal dispute resolution procedures, and any terms agreed as well as any recommendation arising from the procedures shall be subject to approval by the Tribunal.

Part VII: Review of Awards

23. (1) A claimant may, within twenty-one days of receipt of notification of an award, file with the Tribunal an objection to the amount or type of award.

    (2) An objection filed pursuant to subrule (1) shall state the reasons for the objection and may be supported by further information or documents made available by the claimant.

    (3) Where the Tribunal, after considering the reasons for the objection and any further information or documents made available by the claimant, is of the opinion that

       (a) there is sufficient grounds on which to renew an award, and

       (b) there is sufficient reason for the further information or documents not being available at an earlier date.

    It may, subject to rule 25, review the award and reverse its findings.

    (4) The Tribunal may, within seven days of a review of an award, notify the claimant of the amount and any particulars of the award as reviewed.

24. (1) The Tribunal may, subject to subrule (2), at any time before an award is paid out, of its own volition review an award.

    (2) In the case of a review other than to increase the amount of an award the Tribunal shall not proceed unless it has served twenty-one days' written notice on the claimant stating an intention to review the award and the reasons for the review, and the Tribunal shall accord the claimant sufficient opportunity to be heard prior to the review.

25. Except in cases of fraud, no review shall be made after the expiry of twenty-one days of the date of an award or where the amount of the award has been paid out to the claimant.

Part VIII: Amendment, Withdrawal and Abandonment of Claims

26. (1) A claimant may at any time before a claim is determined in accordance with rule 17 amend his or her claim.

    (2) Save as otherwise provided in subrule (1), a claimant shall not, without leave of the Tribunal, amend his or her claim.

27. (1) The Tribunal may, on application by a person with a sufficient interest in the claim, add to, or remove from, a claim any person or charge the particulars of any person to a claim:

    Provided that any person to be removed shall have the right to be heard in the same manner as a determination of a claim under rule 17.

(2) Every application under subrule (1) shall be in writing and shall state the reason for the removal or addition of a person to the claim, or the change of the particulars of that person, as the case may be.

28. (1) A claim may be withdrawn at any time:

Provided that where the claim was instituted or continued by an agent or representative, the claim shall not be withdrawn save with the written consent of the claimant signified in writing.

(2) A claim which has been withdrawn shall not be reinstituted without the leave of the Tribunal.

29. (1) Where a claim has been dormant for a period of two years from the date of the last unanswered communication from the Tribunal addressed to the claimant and reasonable efforts have been made to locate the claimant but no evidence of continued interest of the claimant has been received by the Tribunal, the claim shall be deemed to have been abandoned.

(2) Where a claim is deemed abandoned in accordance with subrule (1), the Tribunal shall send to claimant, at his last address, written notice of abandonment, and the notice shall be published in the Gazette and in at least two issues of any national newspaper in general circulation.

(3) An abandonment claim shall be deemed withdrawn ninety days after a notice of abandonment has been given to the claimant in accordance with subrule (2).

PART IX: MISCELLANEOUS

30. No claim shall be assigned and no form of reparation shall be awarded to the assignee of a claim.

31. In the event of the death of a claimant, an award shall be payable to the estate of the deceased unless the award is specified to the claimant such as medical care or job retraining.

32. Notwithstanding any other provision of these Rules, the Tribunal may, on application by the claimant, of its own volition, make any order or give any direction necessary to facilitate the fair and expeditious determination of a claim.

33. Notwithstanding any other provisions of these Rules, the Tribunal shall have the discretion to accept any communication in lieu of prescribed forms subject to such conditions as the Tribunal may in its discretion consider appropriate.

34. (1) The Tribunal shall maintain records of claims and the Fund in such a manner as to facilitate the periodic reporting of progress of the claims and to ensure transparency in the management of the Fund.

(2) The Tribunal shall publish in the Gazette beginning after the expiry of three months from the commencement of these Rules, a monthly progress report containing information covering:

(a) the total number of claims received;

(b) the number of claims in each category;

(c) the amounts awarded in each category;

(d) the total amount awarded;

(e) other forms of compensation awarded;

(f) the number of claims dismissed; and

(g) such other information as the Tribunal may consider appropriate.

35. Any notice or other document required or authorized to be served on any person for the purposes of these Rules may be sent by prepaid post to that person or a representative or both, as the case may be, at the last address notified to the Tribunal, and if so sent shall be deemed to have been duly served on the date of posting.

36. (1) All communications in respect of claims under these Rules may be in any of the principal languages of Malawi.

(2) All forms, instructions and communications issuing from the Tribunal shall be in English, with such supplementary translations in additional languages as may be required for the effective prosecution of claims.

37. Any clerical mistake or error in any determination, order or direction may at any time be corrected by the Tribunal of its own volition after giving notice to the claimant or at the request of the claimant.

Made this 25th day of September, 1997.

R. A. Banda
Chief Justice

USA

CIVIL LIBERTIES ACT OF 1988
[EXCERPTS]

PL 100–383 (HR 442) August 10, 1988

An Act to implement recommendations of the Commission on Wartime Relocation and Internment of Civilians.

Be it enacted by the Senate and House of Representatives of the United States of America in Congress assembled,

Section 1.   '50 USC app. 1989' Purposes
The purposes of this Act are to

(1) acknowledge the fundamental injustice of the evacuation, relocation, and internment of United States citizens and permanent resident aliens of Japanese ancestry during World War II;

(2) apologize on behalf of the people of the United States for the evacuation, relocation, and internment of such citizens and permanent resident aliens;

(3) provide for a public education fund to finance efforts to inform the public about the internment of such individuals so as to prevent the recurrence of any similar event;

(4) make restitution to those individuals of Japanese ancestry who were interned;

(5) make restitution to Aleut residents of the Pribilof Islands and the Aleutian Islands west of Unimak Island, in settlement of United States obligations in equity and at law, for

    (A) injustices suffered and unreasonable hardships endured while those Aleut residents were under United States control during World War II;

    (B) personal property taken or destroyed by United States forces during World War II;

    (C) community property, including community church property, taken or destroyed by United States forces during World War II; and

    (D) traditional village lands on Attu Island not rehabilitated after World War II for Aleut occupation or other productive use;

(6) discourage the occurrence of similar injustices and violations of civil liberties in the future; and

(7) make more credible and sincere any declaration of concern by the United States over violations of human rights committed by other nations.

Section 2. '50 USC app. 1989a' Statement of the Congress

(a) With regard to individuals of Japanese ancestry—The Congress recognizes that, as described by the Commission on Wartime Relocation and Internment of Civilians, a grave injustice was done to both citizens and permanent resident aliens of Japanese ancestry by the evacuation, relocation, and internment of civilians during World War II. As the Commission documents, these actions were carried out without adequate security reasons and without any acts of espionage or sabotage documented by the Commission, and were motivated largely by racial prejudice, wartime hysteria, and a failure of political leadership. The excluded individuals of Japanese ancestry suffered enormous damages, both material and intangible, and there were incalculable losses in education and job training, all of which resulted in significant human suffering for which appropriate compensation has not been made. For these fundamental violations of the basic civil liberties and constitutional rights of these individuals of Japanese ancestry, the Congress apologizes on behalf of the Nation.

(b) With respect to the Aleuts—The Congress recognizes that, as described by the Commission on Wartime Relocation and Internment of Civilians, the Aleut civilian residents of the Pribilof Islands and the Aleutian Islands west of Unimak Island were relocated during World War II to temporary camps in isolated regions of southeast Alaska where they remained, under United States control and in the care of the United States, until long after any potential danger to their home villages had passed. The United States failed to provide reasonable care for the Aleuts, and this resulted in widespread illness, disease, and death among the residents of the camps; and the United States further failed to protect Aleut personal and community property while such property was in its possession or under its control. The United States has not compensated the Aleuts adequately for the conversion or destruction of personal property, and the conversion or destruction of community property caused by the United States military occupation of Aleut villages during World War II. There is no remedy for injustices suffered by the Aleuts during World War II except an Act of Congress providing appropriate compensation for those losses which are attributable to the conduct of United States forces and other officials and employees of the United States.

Title I—United States Citizens of Japanese Ancestry and Resident Japanese Aliens

Section 101. '50 USC app. 1989b' Short Title

This title may be cited as the 'Civil Liberties Act of 1988'.

Section 102. '50 USC app. 1989b—1' Remedies with Respect to Criminal Convictions

(a) Review of Convictions—The Attorney General is requested to review any case in which an individual living on the date of the enactment of this Act was, while a United States citizen or permanent resident alien of Japanese ancestry, convicted of a violation of
  (1) Executive Order Numbered 9066, dated February 19, 1942;
  (2) the Act entitled 'An Act to provide a penalty for violation of restrictions or orders with respect to persons entering, remaining in, leaving, or committing any act in military areas or zones', approved March 21, 1942 (56 Stat. 173); or
  (3) any other Executive order, Presidential proclamation, law of the United States, directive of the Armed Forces of the United States, or other action taken by, or on behalf of, the United States or its agents, representatives, officers, or employees, respecting the evacuation, relocation, or internment of individuals solely on the basis of Japanese ancestry; on account of the refusal by such individual, during the evacuation, relocation, and internment period, to accept treatment which discriminated against the individual on the basis of the individual's Japanese ancestry.
(b) Recommendations for pardons—Based upon any review under subsection (a), the Attorney General is requested to recommend to the President for pardon consideration those convictions which the Attorney General considers appropriate.

(c) Action by the President—In consideration of the statement of the Congress set forth in section 2(a), the President is requested to offer pardons to any individuals recommended by the Attorney General under subsection (b).

Section 103.   '50 USC app. 1989b—2' Consideration of Commission Findings by Departments and Agencies

(a) Review of applications by eligible individuals—Each department and agency of the United States Government shall review with liberality, giving full consideration to the findings of the Commission and the statement of the Congress set forth in section 2(a), any application by an eligible individual for the restitution of any position, status, or entitlement lost in whole or in part because of any discriminatory act of the United States Government against such individual which was based upon the individual's Japanese ancestry and which occurred during the evacuation, relocation, and internment period.

(b) No new authority created—Subsection (a) does not create any authority to grant restitution described in that subsection, or establish any eligibility to apply for such restitution.

Section 104.   '50 USC app. 1989b—3' Trust Fund

(a) Establishment—There is established in the Treasury of the United States the Civil Liberties Public Education Fund, which shall be administered by the Secretary of the Treasury.

(b) Investment of amounts in the Fund—Amounts in the Fund shall be invested in accordance with section 9702 of title 31, United States Code.

(c) Uses of the Fund—Amounts in the Fund shall be available only for disbursement by the Attorney General under section 105 and by the Board under section 106.

(d) Termination—The Fund shall terminate not later than the earlier of the date on which an amount has been expended from the Fund which is equal to the amount authorized to be appropriated to the Fund by subsection (e), and any income earned on such amount, or ten years after the date of the enactment of this Act. If all of the amounts in the Fund have not been expended by the end of that ten-year period, investments of amounts in the Fund shall be liquidated and receipts thereof deposited in the Fund and all funds remaining in the Fund shall be deposited in the miscellaneous receipts account in the Treasury.

(e) Authorization of appropriations—There are authorized to be appropriated to the Fund $1,250,000,000, of which not more than $500,000,000 may be appropriated for any fiscal year. Any amounts appropriated pursuant to this section are authorized to remain available until expended.

Section 105.   '50 USC app. 1989b—4' Restitution

(a) Location and payment of eligible individuals:

    (1) In general—Subject to paragraph (6), the Attorney General shall, subject to the availability of funds appropriated to the Fund for such purpose, pay out of the Fund to each eligible individual the sum of $20,000, unless such individual refuses, in the manner described in paragraph (4), to accept the payment.

    (2) Location of eligible individuals—The Attorney General shall identify and locate, without requiring any application for payment and using records already in the possession of the United States Government, each eligible individual. The Attorney General should use funds and resources available to the Attorney General, including those described in subsection (c), to attempt to complete such identification and location within twelve months after the date of the enactment of this Act. Any eligible individual may notify the Attorney General that such individual is an eligible individual, and may provide documentation thereof. The Attorney General shall designate an officer or employee to whom such notification and documentation may be sent, shall maintain a list of all individuals who submit such notification and documentation, and shall, subject to the availability of funds appropriated for such purpose, encourage, through a public awareness campaign, each eligible individual to submit his or her current address to such officer or employee. To the extent that resources referred to in the second sentence of this paragraph are not sufficient to complete the identification and location of all eligible individuals, there are authorized to be appropriated such sums as may be necessary for such purpose. In any case, the identification and location of all eligible individuals shall be completed within twelve months after the appropriation of funds under the preceding sentence. Failure to be identified and located by the end of the twelve-month period specified in the preceding sentence shall not preclude an eligible individual from receiving payment under this section.

    (3) Notice from the Attorney General—The Attorney General shall, when funds are appropriated to the Fund for payments to an eligible individual under this section, notify that eligible individual in writing of his or her eligibility for payment under this section. Such notice shall inform the eligible individual that

        (A) acceptance of payment under this section shall be in full satisfaction of all claims against the United States arising out of acts described in section 108(2)(B); and

        (B) each eligible individual who does not refuse, in the manner described in paragraph (4), to accept payment under this section within eighteen months after receiving such written notice shall be deemed to have accepted payment for purposes of paragraph (5).

(4) Effect of refusal to accept payment—If an eligible individual refuses, in a written document filed with the Attorney General, to accept any payment under this section, the amount of such payment shall remain in the Fund and no payment may be made under this section to such individual at any time after such refusal.

(5) Payment in full settlement of claims against the United States—The acceptance of payment by an eligible individual under this section shall be in full satisfaction of all claims against the United States arising out of acts described in section 108(2)(B). This paragraph shall apply to any eligible individual who does not refuse, in the manner described in paragraph (4), to accept payment under this section within eighteen months after receiving the notification from the Attorney General referred to in paragraph (3).

(6) Exclusion of certain individuals—No payment may be made under this section to any individual who, after September 1, 1987, accepts payment pursuant to an award of a final judgment or a settlement on a claim against the United States for acts described in section 108(2)(B), or to any surviving spouse, child, or parent of such individual to whom paragraph (6) applies.

(7) Payments in the case of deceased persons:

(A) In the case of an eligible individual who is deceased at the time of payment under this section, such payment shall be made only as follows:

(i) If the eligible individual is survived by a spouse who is living at the time of payment, such payment shall be made to such surviving spouse.

(ii) If there is no surviving spouse described in clause (i), such payment shall be made in equal shares to all children of the eligible individual who are living at the time of payment.

(iii) If there is no surviving spouse described in clause (i) and if there are no children described in clause (ii), such payment shall be made in equal shares to the parents of the eligible individual who are living at the time of payment.

(iv) If there is no surviving spouse, children, or parents described in clauses (i), (ii), and (iii), the amount of such payment shall remain in the Fund, and may be used only for the purposes set forth in section 106(b).

(B) After the death of an eligible individual, this subsection and subsections (c) and (f) shall apply to the individual or individuals specified in subparagraph (A) to whom payment under this section will be made, to the same extent as such subsections apply to the eligible individual.

(C) For purposes of this paragraph

    (i) the 'spouse' of an eligible individual means a wife or husband of an eligible individual who was married to that eligible individual for at least one year immediately before the death of the eligible individual;

    (ii) a 'child' of an eligible individual includes a recognized natural child, a stepchild who lived with the eligible individual in a regular parent–child relationship, and an adopted child; and

    (iii) a 'parent' of an eligible individual includes fathers and mothers through adoption.

(b) Order of payments—The Attorney General shall endeavor to make payments under this section to eligible individuals in the order of date of birth (with the oldest individual on the date of the enactment of this Act (or, if applicable, that individual's survivors under paragraph (6)) receiving full payment first), until all eligible individuals have received payment in full.

(c) Resources for locating eligible individuals—In attempting to locate any eligible individual, the Attorney General may use any facility or resource of any public or nonprofit organization or any other record, document, or information that may be made available to the Attorney General.

(d) Administrative costs not paid from the Fund—No costs incurred by the Attorney General in carrying out this section shall be paid from the Fund or set off against, or otherwise deducted from, any payment under this section to any eligible individual.

(e) Termination of duties of Attorney General—The duties of the Attorney General under this section shall cease when the Fund terminates.

(f) Clarification of treatment of payments under other laws—Amounts paid to an eligible individual under this section

    (1) shall be treated for purposes of the internal revenue laws of the United States as damages for human suffering; and

    (2) shall not be included as income or resources for purposes of determining eligibility to receive benefits described in section 3803(c)(2)(C) of title 31, United States Code, or the amount of such benefits.

Section 106.   '50 USC app. 1989b—5' Board of Directors of the Fund

(a) Establishment—There is established the Civil Liberties Public Education Fund Board of Directors, which shall be responsible for making disbursements from the Fund in the manner provided in this section.

(b) Uses of Fund—The Board may make disbursements from the Fund only

    (1) to sponsor research and public educational activities, and to publish and distribute the hearings, findings, and recommendations of the Commission, so that the events surrounding the evacuation, relocation,

and internment of United States citizens and permanent resident aliens of Japanese ancestry will be remembered, and so that the causes and circumstances of this and similar events may be illuminated and understood; and

(2) for reasonable administrative expenses of the Board, including expenses incurred under subsections (c)(3), (d), and (e).

(c) Membership:

(1) Appointment—The Board shall be composed of nine members appointed by the President, by and with the advice and consent of the Senate, from individuals who are not officers or employees of the United States Government.

(2) Terms:

(A) Except as provided in subparagraphs (B) and (C), members shall be appointed for terms of three years.

(B) Of the members first appointed

(i) five shall be appointed for terms of three years, and

(ii) four shall be appointed for terms of two years, as designated by the President at the time of appointment.

(C) Any member appointed to fill a vacancy occurring before the expiration of the term for which such member's predecessor was appointed shall be appointed only for the remainder of such term. A member may serve after the expiration of such member's term until such member's successor has taken office. No individual may be appointed as a member for more than two consecutive terms.

(3) Compensation—Members of the Board shall serve without pay, except that members of the Board shall be entitled to reimbursement for travel, subsistence, and other necessary expenses incurred by them in carrying out the functions of the Board, in the same manner as persons employed intermittently in the United States Government are allowed expenses under section 5703 of title 5, United States Code.

(4) Quorum—Five members of the Board shall constitute a quorum but a lesser number may hold hearings.

(5) Chair—The Chair of the Board shall be elected by the members of the Board.

(d) Director and staff:

(1) Director—The Board shall have a Director who shall be appointed by the Board.

(2) Additional staff—The Board may appoint and fix the pay of such additional staff as it may require.

(3) Applicability of civil service laws—The Director and the additional staff of the Board may be appointed without regard to section 5311(b) of title 5, United States Code, and without regard to the provisions of such title governing appointments in the competitive service, and may be paid without regard to the provisions of chapter 51 and subchapter III of chapter 53 of such title relating to classification and General Schedule pay rates, except that the compensation of any employee of the Board may not exceed a rate equivalent to the minimum rate of basic pay payable for GS-18 of the General Schedule under section 5332(a) of such title.

(e) Administrative support services—The Administrator of General Services shall provide to the Board on a reimbursable basis such administrative support services as the Board may request.

(f) Gifts and donations—The Board may accept, use, and dispose of gifts or donations of services or property for purposes authorized under subsection (b).

(g) Annual reports—Not later than twelve months after the first meeting of the Board and every twelve months thereafter, the Board shall transmit to the President and to each House of the Congress a report describing the activities of the Board.

(h) Termination—Ninety days after the termination of the Fund, the Board shall terminate and all obligations of the Board under this section shall cease.

Section 107.   '50 USC app. 1989b—6' Documents Relating to the Internment

(a) Preservation of documents in National Archives—All documents, personal testimony, and other records created or received by the Commission during its inquiry shall be kept and maintained by the Archivist of the United States who shall preserve such documents, testimony, and records in the National Archives of the United States. The Archivist shall make such documents, testimony, and records available to the public for research purposes.

(b) Public availability of certain records of the house of Representatives:

(1) The Clerk of the House of Representatives is authorized to permit the Archivist of the United States to make available for use records of the House not classified for national security purposes, which have been in existence for not less than thirty years, relating to the evacuation, relocation, and internment of individuals during the evacuation, relocation, and internment period.

(2) This subsection is enacted as an exercise of the rulemaking power of the House of Representatives, but is applicable only with respect to the availability of records to which it applies, and supersedes other rules only to the extent that the time limitation established by this section

with respect to such records is specifically inconsistent with such rules, and is enacted with full recognition of the constitutional right of the House to change its rules at any time, in the same manner and to the same extent as in the case of any other rule of the House.

Section 108.   '50 USC app. 1989b—7' Definitions

For the purposes of this title:

(1) the term 'evacuation, relocation and internment period' means that period beginning on December 7, 1941 and ending on June 30, 1946;

(2) the term 'eligible individual' means any individual of Japanese ancestry who is living on the date of the enactment of this Act and who, during the evacuation, relocation, and internment period

(A) was a United States citizen or a permanent resident alien; and

(B)(i) was confined, held in custody, relocated, or otherwise deprived of liberty or property as a result of

(I) Executive Order Numbered 9066, dated February 19, 1942;

(II) the Act entitled 'An Act to provide a penalty for violation of restrictions or orders with respect to persons entering, remaining in, leaving, or committing any act in military areas or zones', approved March 21, 1942 (56 Stat.173); or

(III) any other Executive order, Presidential proclamation, law of the United States, directive of the Armed Forces of the United States, or other action taken by, or on behalf of, the United States or its agents, representatives, officers, or employees, respecting the evacuation, relocation, or internment of individuals solely on the basis of Japanese ancestry; or

(ii) was enrolled on the records of the United States Government during the period beginning on December 7, 1941 and ending on June 30, 1946 as being in a prohibited military zone; except that the term 'eligible individual' does not include any individual who, during the period beginning on December 7, 1941 and ending on September 2, 1945 relocated to a country while the United States was at war with that country;

(3) the term 'permanent resident alien' means an alien lawfully admitted into the United States for permanent residence;

(4) the term 'Fund' means the Civil Liberties Public Education Fund established in section 104;

(5) the term 'Board' means the Civil Liberties Public Education Fund Board of Directors established in section 106; and

(6) the term 'Commission' means the Commission on Wartime Relocation and Internment of Civilians, established by the Commission on Wartime Re-

location and Internment of Civilians Act (Public Law 96–317; 50 USC app. 1981 note).

Section 109.   '50 USC app. 1989b—8' Compliance with Budget Act

No authority under this title to enter into contracts or to make payments shall be effective in any fiscal year except to such extent and in such amounts as are provided in advance in appropriations Acts. In any fiscal year, total benefits conferred by this title shall be limited to an amount not in excess of the appropriations for such fiscal year. Any provision of this title which, directly or indirectly, authorizes the enactment of new budget authority shall be effective only for fiscal year 1989 and thereafter.

[...]

TITLE II—Aleutian and Pribilof Islands Restitution

Section 201. '50 USC app. 1989c' Short Title

This title may be cited as the 'Aleutian and Pribilof Islands Restitution Act'.

Section 202.   '50 USC app. 1989c—1' Definitions

As used in this title:

(1) the term 'Administrator' means the person appointed by the Secretary under section 204;
(2) the term 'affected Aleut villages' means the surviving Aleut villages of Akutan, Atka, Nikolski, Saint George, Saint Paul, and Unalaska, and the Aleut village of Attu, Alaska;
(3) the term 'Association' means the Aleutian/Pribilof Islands Association, Inc., a nonprofit regional corporation established for the benefit of the Aleut people and organized under the laws of the State of Alaska;
(4) the term 'Corporation' means the Aleut Corporation, a for-profit regional corporation for the Aleut region organized under the laws of the State of Alaska and established under section 7 of the Alaska Native Claims Settlement Act (Public Law 92–203; 43 USC 1606);
(5) the term 'eligible Aleut' means any Aleut living on the date of the enactment of this Act
    (A) who, as a civilian, was relocated by authority of the United States from his or her home village on the Pribilof Islands or the Aleutian Islands west of Unimak Island to an internment camp, or other temporary facility or location, during World War II; or
    (B) who was born while his or her natural mother was subject to such relocation;
(6) the term 'Secretary' means the Secretary of the Interior;

(7) the term 'Fund' means the Aleutian and Pribilof Islands Restitution Fund established in section 203; and

(8) the term 'World War II' means the period beginning on December 7, 1941 and ending on September 2, 1945.

Section 203. '50 USC app. 1989c—2' Aleutian and Pribilof Islands Restitution Fund

(a) Establishment—There is established in the Treasury of the United States the Aleutian and Pribilof Islands Restitution Fund, which shall be administered by the Secretary. The Fund shall consist of amounts appropriated to it pursuant to this title.

(b) Report—The Secretary shall report to the Congress, not later than sixty days after the end of each fiscal year, on the financial condition of the Fund, and the results of operations of the Fund, during the preceding fiscal year and on the expected financial condition and operations of the Fund during the current fiscal year.

(c) Investment—Amounts in the Fund shall be invested in accordance with section 9702 of title 31, United States Code.

(d) Termination—The Secretary shall terminate the Fund three years after the date of the enactment of this Act, or one year following disbursement of all payments from the Fund, as authorized by this title, whichever occurs later. On the date the Fund is terminated, all investments of amounts in the Fund shall be liquidated by the Secretary and receipts thereof deposited in the Fund and all funds remaining in the Fund shall be deposited in the miscellaneous receipts account in the Treasury.

Section 204. '50 USC app. 1989c—3' Appointment of Administrator

As soon as practicable after the date of the enactment of this Act, the Secretary shall offer to undertake negotiations with the Association, leading to the execution of an agreement with the Association to serve as Administrator under this title. The Secretary may appoint the Association as Administrator if such agreement is reached within ninety days after the date of the enactment of this title. If no such agreement is reached within such period, the Secretary shall appoint another person as Administrator under this title after consultation with leaders of affected Aleut villages and the Corporation.

Section 205.   '50 USC app. 1989c—4' Compensation for Community Losses

(a) In general—Subject to the availability of funds appropriated to the Fund, the Secretary shall make payments from the Fund, in accordance with this section, as restitution for certain Aleut losses sustained in World War II.

(b) TRUST:

(1) Establishment—The Secretary shall, subject to the availability of funds appropriated for this purpose, establish a trust for the purposes set forth in this section. Such trust shall be established pursuant to the laws of the State of Alaska, and shall be maintained and operated by not more than seven trustees, as designated by the Secretary. Each affected Aleut village may submit to the Administrator a list of three prospective trustees. The Secretary, after consultation with the Administrator, affected Aleut villages, and the Corporation, shall designate not more than seven trustees from such lists as submitted.

(2) Administration of Trust—The trust established under this subsection shall be administered in a manner that is consistent with the laws of the State of Alaska, and as prescribed by the Secretary, after consultation with representatives of eligible Aleuts, the residents of affected Aleut villages, and the Administrator.

(c) Accounts for the benefit of Aleuts:

(1) In general—The Secretary shall deposit in the trust such sums as may be appropriated for the purposes set forth in this subsection. The trustees shall maintain and operate eight independent and separate accounts in the trust for purposes of this subsection, as follows:

(A) One account for the independent benefit of the wartime Aleut residents of Attu and their descendants.

(B) Six accounts for the benefit of the six surviving affected Aleut villages, one each for the independent benefit of Akutan, Atka, Nikolski, Saint George, Saint Paul, and Unalaska, respectively.

(C) One account for the independent benefit of those Aleuts who, as determined by the Secretary, upon the advice of the trustees, are deserving but will not benefit directly from the accounts established under subparagraphs (A) and (B). The trustees shall credit to the account described in subparagraph (C) an amount equal to 5 percent of the principal amount deposited by the Secretary in the trust under this subsection. Of the remaining principal amount, an amount shall be credited to each account described in subparagraphs (A) and (B) which bears the same proportion to such remaining principal amount as the Aleut civilian population, as of June 1, 1942, of the village with respect to which such account is established bears to the total civilian Aleut population on such date of all affected Aleut villages.

(2) Uses of accounts—The trustees may use the principal, accrued interest, and other earnings of the accounts maintained under paragraph (1) for

(A) the benefit of elderly, disabled, or seriously ill persons on the basis of special need;

(B) the benefit of students in need of scholarship assistance;

(C) the preservation of Aleut cultural heritage and historical records;

(D) the improvement of community centers in affected Aleut villages; and

(E) other purposes to improve the condition of Aleut life, as determined by the trustees.

(3) Authorization of appropriations—There are authorized to be appropriated $5,000,000 to the Fund to carry out this subsection.

(d) Compensation for damaged or destroyed church property:

(1) Inventory and assessment of property—The Administrator shall make an inventory and assessment of real and personal church property of affected Aleut villages which was damaged or destroyed during World War II. In making such inventory and assessment, the Administrator shall consult with the trustees of the trust established under subsection (b), residents of affected Aleut villages, affected church members and leaders, and the clergy of the churches involved. Within one year after the date of the enactment of this Act, the Administrator shall submit such inventory and assessment, together with an estimate of the present replacement value of lost or destroyed furnishings and artifacts, to the Secretary.

(2) Review by the Secretary; deposit in the trust—The Secretary shall review the inventory and assessment provided under paragraph (1), and shall deposit in the trust established under subsection (b) an amount reasonably calculated by the Secretary to compensate affected Aleut villages for church property lost, damaged, or destroyed during World War II.

(3) Distribution of compensation—The trustees shall distribute the amount deposited in the trust under paragraph (2) for the benefit of the churches referred to in this subsection.

(4) Authorization of appropriations—There are authorized to be appropriated to the Fund $1,400,000 to carry out this subsection.

(e) Administrative and legal expenses:

(1) Reimbursement for expenses—The Secretary shall reimburse the Administrator, not less often than annually, for reasonable and necessary administrative and legal expenses in carrying out the Administrator's responsibilities under this title.

(2) Authorization of appropriations—There are authorized to be appropriated to the Fund such sums as are necessary to carry out this subsection.

Section 206. '50 USC app. 1989c—5' Individual Compensation of Eligible Aleuts

(a) Payments to eligible Aleuts—In addition to payments made under section 205, the Secretary shall, in accordance with this section, make per capita payments out of the Fund to eligible Aleuts. The Secretary shall pay, subject to the availability of funds appropriated to the Fund for such payments, to each eligible Aleut the sum of $12,000.

(b) Assistance of Attorney General—The Secretary may request the Attorney General to provide reasonable assistance in locating eligible Aleuts residing outside the affected Aleut villages, and upon such request, the Attorney General shall provide such assistance. In so doing, the Attorney General may use available facilities and resources of the International Committee of the Red Cross and other organizations.

(c) Assistance of Administrator—The Secretary may request the assistance of the Administrator in identifying and locating eligible Aleuts for purposes of this section.

(d) Clarification of treatment of payments under other laws—Amounts paid to an eligible Aleut under this section

   (1) shall be treated for purposes of the internal revenue laws of the United States as damages for human suffering; and

   (2) shall not be included as income or resources for purposes of determining eligibility to receive benefits described in section 3803(c)(2)(C) of title 31, United States Code, or the amount of such benefits.

(e) Payment in full settlement of claims against the United States—The payment to an eligible Aleut under this section shall be in full satisfaction of all claims against the United States arising out of the relocation described in section 202(5).

(f) Authorization of appropriations—There are authorized to be appropriated to the Fund such sums as are necessary to carry out this section.

Section 207.   '50 USC app. 1989c—6' Attu Island Restitution Program

(a) Purpose of section—In accordance with section (3)(c) of the Wilderness Act (78 Stat. 892; 16 USC 1132(c)), the public lands on Attu Island, Alaska, within the National Wildlife Refuge System have been designated as wilderness by section 702(1) of the Alaska National Interest Lands Conservation Act (94 Stat. 2417; 16 USC 1132 note). In order to make restitution for the loss of traditional Aleut lands and village properties on Attu Island, while preserving the present designation of Attu Island lands as part of the National Wilderness Preservation System, compensation to the Aleut people, in lieu of the conveyance of Attu Island, shall be provided in accordance with this section.

(b) Acreage determination—Not later than ninety days after the date of the enactment of this Act, the Secretary shall, in accordance with this subsection, determine the total acreage of land on Attu Island, Alaska, that, at the beginning of World War II, was subject to traditional use by the Aleut villagers of that island for subsistence and other purposes. In making such acreage determination, the Secretary shall establish a base acreage of not less than 35,000 acres within that part of eastern Attu Island traditionally used by the Aleut people, and shall, from the best available information, including information that may be submitted by representatives of the Aleut people, identify any such additional acreage on Attu Island that was subject to such use. The combination of such base acreage and such additional acreage shall constitute the acreage determination upon which payment to the Corporation under this section is based. The Secretary shall promptly notify the Corporation of the results of the acreage determination made under this subsection.

(c) Valuation:

(1) Determination of value—Not later than one hundred and twenty days after the date of the enactment of this Act, the Secretary shall determine the value of the Attu Island acreage determined under subsection (b), except that

(A) such acreage may not be valued at less than $350 per acre or more than $500 per acre; and

(B) the total valuation of all such acreage may not exceed $15,000,000.

(2) Factors in making determination—In determining the value of the acreage under paragraph (1), the Secretary shall take into consideration such factors as the Secretary considers appropriate, including

(A) fair market value;

(B) environmental and public interest value; and

(C) established precedents for valuation of comparable wilderness lands in the State of Alaska.

(3) Notification of determination; APPEAL—The Secretary shall promptly notify the Corporation of the determination of value made under this subsection and such determination shall constitute the final determination of value unless the Corporation, within thirty days after the determination is made, appeals the determination to the Secretary. If such appeal is made, the Secretary shall, within thirty days after the appeal is made, review the determination in light of the appeal, and issue a final determination of the value of that acreage determined to be subject to traditional use under subsection (b).

(d) In lieu compensation payment:

(1) Payment—The Secretary shall pay, subject to the availability of funds appropriated for such purpose, to the Corporation, as compensation for the Aleuts' loss of lands on Attu Island, the full amount of the value of the acreage determined under subsection (c), less the value

(as determined under subsection (c)) of any land conveyed under subsection (e).

(2) Payment in full settlement of claims against the United States—The
payment made under paragraph (1) shall be in full satisfaction of any
claim against the United States for the loss of traditional Aleut lands and
village properties on Attu Island.

(e) Village site conveyance—The Secretary may convey to the Corporation all
right, title, and interest of the United States to the surface estate of the
traditional Aleut village site on Attu Island, Alaska (consisting of approximately 10 acres) and to the surface estate of a parcel of land consisting of all
land outside such village that is within 660 feet of any point on the boundary
of such village. The conveyance may be made under the authority contained
in section 14(h)(l) of the Alaska Native Claims Settlement Act (Public Law
92–203; 43 USC 1613 (h)(1)), except that after the enactment of this Act, no
site on Attu Island, Alaska, other than such traditional Aleut village site and
such parcel of land, may be conveyed to the Corporation under such section
14(h)(l).

(f) Authorization of appropriations—There are authorized to be appropriated
$15,000,000 to the Secretary to carry out this section.

C Section 208. '50 USC app. 1989c—7' Compliance with Budget Act

No authority under this title to enter into contracts or to make payments shall be
effective in any fiscal year except to such extent and in such amounts as are
provided in advance in appropriations Acts. In any fiscal year, the Secretary, with
respect to

(1) the Fund established under section 203;
(2) the trust established under section 205(b); and
(3) the provisions of sections 206 and 207, shall limit the total benefits conferred
to an amount not in excess of the appropriations for such fiscal year. Any
provision of this title which, directly or indirectly, authorizes the enactment of
new budget authority shall be effective only for fiscal year 1989 and thereafter.

Section 209. '50 USC app. 1989c—8' Severability

If any provision of this title, or the application of such provision to any person or
circumstance, is held invalid, the remainder of this title and the application of such
provision to other persons not similarly situated or to other circumstances shall
not be affected by such invalidation.

[...]

Title III—Territory or Property Claims against the United States

Section 301. '50 USC app. 1989d' Exclusion of Claims

Notwithstanding any other provision of law or of this Act, nothing in this Act shall be construed as recognition of any claim of Mexico or any other country or any Indian tribe (except as expressly provided in this Act with respect to the Aleut tribe of Alaska) to any territory or other property of the United States, nor shall this Act be construed as providing any basis for compenstion in connection with any such claim.

Approved August 10, 1988.

Legislative History—HR 442:

House Reports: No. 100–278 (Comm. on the Judiciary) and No. 100–785 (Comm. of Conference)

Congressional Record: Vol. 133 (1987): Sept. 17, considered and passed House. Vol. 134 (1988): Apr. 20, considered and passed Senate, amended. July 27, Senate agreed to conference report. Aug. 4, House agreed to conference report.

Weekly Compilation of Presidential Documents, Vol. 24 (1988): Aug. 10, Presidential remarks. PL 100–383, 1988 HR 442

Amendment to the Civil Liberties Act of 1988 to Increase the Authorization for the Trust Fund under that Act [Excerpts]

102nd Congress; 2nd Session
In the House of Representatives as Enrolled

HR 4551
1992 HR 4551; 102 HR 4551

Synopsis: An Act to amend the Civil Liberties Act of 1988 to increase the authorization for the Trust Fund under that Act, and for other purposes.

Date of introduction: March 24, 1992

Date of version: October 28, 1992

Version: 5

Text: Be it enacted by the Senate and House of Representatives of the United States of America in Congress assembled,

Section 1.   Short Title.

This Act may be cited as the 'Civil Liberties Act Amendments of 1992'.

Section 2.   Authorization for Trust Fund.

Section 104(e) of the Civil Liberties Act of 1988 (50 USC app. 1989b—3(e)) is amended by striking '$1,250,000,000' and inserting '$1,650,000,000'.

Section 3.   Definitions.

Section 108(2) of the Civil Liberties Act of 1988 (50 USC app. 1989b—7(2)) is amended in the matter preceding subparagraph (A) by inserting ', or the spouse or a parent of an individual of Japanese ancestry,' after 'Japanese ancestry'.

Section 4.   Benefit of the Doubt; Judicial Review.

  (a) Benefit of the doubt—Section 105(a) of the Civil Liberties Act of 1988 (50 USC app. 1989b—4(a)) is amended:
    (1) by redesignating paragraphs (3) through (7) as paragraphs (4) through (8), respectively; and
    (2) by inserting after paragraph (2) the following:
    '(3) benefit of the doubt—when, after consideration of all evidence and relevant material for determining whether an individual is an eligible individual, there is an approximate balance of positive and negative evidence regarding the merits of an issue material to the determination of eligibility, the benefit of the doubt in resolving each such issue shall be given to such individual.'
  (B) Judicial review—Section 105 of such Act is amended by adding at the end the following:
  '(h) Judicial review—
    '(1) Review by the Claims Court—A claimant may seek judicial review of a denial of compensation under this section solely in the United States Claims Court, which shall review the denial upon the administrative record and shall hold unlawful and set aside the denial if it is found to be arbitrary, capricious, an abuse of discretion, or otherwise not in accordance with law.
    '(2) Applicability—This subsection shall apply only to any claim filed in court on or after the date of the enactment of this subsection.'
  (c) Conforming amendments—Section 105 of such Act is amended
    (1) in subsection (a):

(A) in paragraph (1) (i) by striking '(6)' and inserting '(7)'; and (ii) by
     striking '(4)' and inserting '(5)';
(B) in subparagraph (B) of paragraph (4) (as redesignated by subsec-
     tion (a)(1) of this section) (i) by striking '(4)' and inserting '(5)';
     and (ii) by striking '(5)' and inserting '(6)';
(C) in paragraph (6) (as redesignated by subsection (a)(1) of this
     section) (i) by striking '(4)' and inserting '(5)'; and (ii) by striking
     '(3)' and inserting '(4)'; and
(D) in paragraph (7) (as redesignated by subsection (a)(1) of this
     section) by striking '(6)' and inserting '(8)'; and (2) in subsection
     (b) by striking '(6)' and inserting '(8)'.

Section 5.   Termination of Duties of Attorney General

Section 105(e) of the Civil Liberties Act of 1988 (50 USC app. 1989b—4(e)) is
amended by striking 'when the Fund terminates.' and inserting 'one hundred and
eighty days after the Fund terminates.'

[...]

Section 7.   Compliance with Budget Act

Section 110 of the Civil Liberties Act of 1988 (50 App. 1989b—9) is amended

(1) by inserting '(a) In general' before 'Subject to';
(2) in subsection (a) (as so designated by paragraph (1))
    (A) in the first sentence, by inserting 'and except as provided in subsection
         (b)' after '105(g) of this title'; and
    (B) by striking the second sentence; and
(3) by adding at the end the following new subsections:
    '(b) Payments from discretionary appropriations:
        '(1) Payments—Any such payment made to an individual who is not
             of Japanese ancestry and who is an eligible individual on the basis
             of the amendment made by section 3 of the Civil Liberties Act
             Amendments of 1992 shall not be an entitlement and shall be made
             from discretionary appropriations.
        '(2) Authorization of appropriations—There are authorized to be
             appropriated for fiscal year 1993 and each subsequent fiscal year
             such sums as may be necessary for the payments from discretion-
             ary appropriations described in paragraph (1).
    '(c) Definitions—As used in this section:
        '(1) the term "discretionary appropriations" has the meaning
             given that term in section 250(c)(7) of the Balanced Budget and
             Emergency Deficit Control Act of 1985 (2 USC 900(c)(7)); and

      '(2) the term "entitlement" means "spending authority" as defined in section 401(c)(2)(C) of the Congressional Budget Act of 1974 (2 USC 651(c)(2)(C))..'.

Speaker of the House of Representatives

Vice President of the United States and President of the Senate

USA

AIR TRANSPORTATION SAFETY AND SYSTEM STABILIZATION ACT
[EXCERPTS]

Public Law 107–42, September 22, 2001 107th Congress

An Act to preserve the continued viability of the United States Air Transportation system.[1]

> Be it enacted by the Senate and House of Representatives of the United States of America in Congress assembled,[2]

Section 1. Short Title

This Act may be cited as the 'Air Transportation Safety and System Stabilization Act'.

Title I—Airline Stabilization

Section 101. Aviation Disaster Relief[3]

    a) In General—Notwithstanding any other provision of law, the President shall take the following actions to compensate air carriers for losses incurred by the air carriers as a result of the terrorist attacks on the United States that occurred on September 11, 2001:

1) Subject to such terms and conditions as the President deems necessary, issue Federal credit instruments to air carriers that do not, in the aggregate, exceed $10,000,000,000 and provide the subsidy amounts necessary for such instruments in accordance with the provisions of the Federal Credit Reform Act of 1990 (2 USC 661 et seq.).

2) Compensate air carriers in an aggregate amount equal to $5,000,000,000 for

    A. direct losses incurred beginning on September 11, 2001, by air carriers as a result of any Federal ground stop order issued by the Secretary of Transportation or any subsequent order which continues or renews such a stoppage; and

    B. the incremental losses incurred beginning September 11, 2001 and ending December 31, 2001, by air carriers as a direct result of such attacks.

b) Emergency Designation—Congress designates the amount of new budget authority and outlays in all fiscal years resulting from this title as an emergency requirement pursuant to section 252(e) of the Balanced Budget and Emergency Deficit Control Act of 1985 (2 USC 901(e)). Such amount shall be available only to the extent that a request, which includes designation of such amount as an emergency requirement as defined in such Act, is transmitted by the President to Congress.

Section 104. Limitation on Certain Employee Compensation.[4]

a) In General—The President may only issue a Federal credit instrument under section 101(a)(1) to an air carrier after the air carrier enters into a legally binding agreement with the President that, during the two-year period beginning September 11, 2001 and ending September 11, 2003, no officer or employee of the air carrier whose total compensation exceeded $300,000 in calendar year 2000 (other than an employee whose compensation is determined through an existing collective bargaining agreement entered into prior to September 11, 2001):

1) will receive from the air carrier total compensation which exceeds, during any twelve consecutive months of such two-year period, the total compensation received by the officer or employee from the air carrier in calendar year 2000; and

2) will receive from the air carrier severance pay or other benefits upon termination of employment with the air carrier which exceeds twice the maximum total compensation received by the officer or employee from the air carrier in calendar year 2000.

b) Total Compensation Defined—In this section, the term 'total compensation' includes salary, bonuses, awards of stock, and other financial benefits provided by an air carrier to an officer or employee of the air carrier.

Section 105. Continuation of Certain Air Service[5]

a) Action of Secretary—The Secretary of Transportation should take appropriate action to ensure that all communities that had scheduled air service before September 11, 2001 continue to receive adequate air transportation service and that essential air service to small communities continues without interruption.
b) Essential Air Service[6]—There is authorized to be appropriated to the Secretary to carry out the essential air service program under subchapter II of chapter 417 of title 49, United States Code, $120,000,000 for fiscal year 2002.
c) Secretarial Oversight:
   1) In general—Notwithstanding any other provision of law, the Secretary is authorized to require an air carrier receiving direct financial assistance under this Act to maintain scheduled air service to any point served by that carrier before September 11, 2001.
   2) Agreements—In applying paragraph (1), the Secretary may require air carriers receiving direct financial assistance under this Act to enter into agreements which will ensure, to the maximum extent practicable, that all communities that had scheduled air service before September 11, 2001, continue to receive adequate air transportation service.

Section 106. Reports[7]

a) Report—Not later than February 1, 2001, the President shall transmit to the Committee on Transportation and Infrastructure, the Committee on Appropriations, and the Committee on the Budget of the House of Representatives and the Committee on Commerce, Science, and Transportation, the Committee on Appropriations, and the Committee on the Budget of the Senate a report on the financial status of the air carrier industry and the amounts of assistance provided under this title to each air carrier.
b) Update—Not later than the last day of the seven-month period following the date of enactment of this Act, the President shall update and transmit the report to the Committees.

[...]

Title IV—Victim Compensation[8]

Section 401. Short Title[9]

This title may be cited as the 'September 11th Victim Compensation Fund of 2001'.

Section 402. Definitions[10]

In this title, the following definitions apply:

(1) Air carrier—The term 'air carrier' means a citizen of the United States undertaking by any means, directly or indirectly, to provide air transportation and includes employees and agents of such citizen.

(2) Air transportation—The term 'air transportation' means foreign air transportation, interstate air transportation, or the transportation of mail by aircraft.

(3) Claimant—The term 'claimant' means an individual filing a claim for compensation under section 405(a)(1).

(4) Collateral source—The term 'collateral source' means all collateral sources, including life insurance, pension funds, death benefit programs, and payments by Federal, State, or local governments related to the terrorist-related aircraft crashes of September 11, 2001.

(5) Economic loss—The term 'economic loss' means any pecuniary loss resulting from harm (including the loss of earnings or other benefits related to employment, medical expense loss, replacement services loss, loss due to death, burial costs, and loss of business or employment opportunities) to the extent recovery for such loss is allowed under applicable State law.

(6) Eligible individual—The term 'eligible individual' means an individual determined to be eligible for compensation under section 405(c).

(7) Noneconomic losses—The term 'noneconomic losses' means losses for physical and emotional pain, suffering, inconvenience, physical impairment, mental anguish, disfigurement, loss of enjoyment of life, loss of society and companionship, loss of consortium (other than loss of domestic service), hedonic damages, injury to reputation, and all other nonpecuniary losses of any kind or nature.

(8) Special master—The term 'Special Master' means the Special Master appointed under section 404(a).

Section 403. Purpose[11]

It is the purpose of this title to provide compensation to any individual (or relatives of a deceased individual) who was physically injured or killed as a result of the terrorist-related aircraft crashes of September 11, 2001.

Section 404. Administration[12]

a) In General—The Attorney General, acting through a Special Master appointed by the Attorney General, shall

1) administer the compensation program established under this title;
2) promulgate all procedural and substantive rules for the administration of this title; and
3) employ and supervise hearing officers and other administrative personnel to perform the duties of the Special Master under this title.

b) Authorization of Appropriations—There are authorized to be appropriated such sums as may be necessary to pay the administrative and support costs for the Special Master in carrying out this title.

Section 405. Determination of Eligibility for Compensation[13]

a) Filing of Claim:
1) In general—A claimant may file a claim for compensation under this title with the Special Master. The claim shall be on the form developed under paragraph (2) and shall state the factual basis for eligibility for compensation and the amount of compensation sought.
2) Claim form:
   A. In general—The Special Master shall develop a claim form that claimants shall use when submitting claims under paragraph (1).[14] The Special Master shall ensure that such form can be filed electronically, if determined to be practicable.
   B. Contents—The form developed under subparagraph (A) shall request
      I. information from the claimant concerning the physical harm that the claimant suffered, or in the case of a claim filed on behalf of a decedent information confirming the decedent's death, as a result of the terrorist-related aircraft crashes of September 11, 2001;
      II. information from the claimant concerning any possible economic and noneconomic losses that the claimant suffered as a result of such crashes; and
      III. information regarding collateral sources of compensation the claimant has received or is entitled to receive as a result of such crashes.
3) Limitation—No claim may be filed under paragraph (1) after the date that is two years after the date on which regulations are promulgated under section 407.

b) Review and Determination:
1) Review—The Special Master shall review a claim submitted under subsection (a) and determine
   A. whether the claimant is an eligible individual under subsection (c);
   B. with respect to a claimant determined to be an eligible individual
      I. the extent of the harm to the claimant, including any economic and noneconomic losses; and

II. the amount of compensation to which the claimant is entitled based on the harm to the claimant, the facts of the claim, and the individual circumstances of the claimant.

2) Negligence—With respect to a claimant, the Special Master shall not consider negligence or any other theory of liability.

3) Determination[15]—Not later than one hundred and twenty days after that date on which a claim is filed under subsection (a), the Special Master shall complete a review, make a determination, and provide written notice to the claimant, with respect to the matters that were the subject of the claim under review. Such a determination shall be final and not subject to judicial review.

4) Rights of claimant—A claimant in a review under paragraph (1) shall have
   A. the right to be represented by an attorney;
   B. the right to present evidence, including the presentation of witnesses and documents; and
   C. any other due process rights determined appropriate by the Special Master.

5) No punitive damages—The Special Master may not include amounts for punitive damages in any compensation paid under a claim under this title.

6) Collateral compensation—The Special Master shall reduce the amount of compensation determined under paragraph (1)(B)(ii) by the amount of the collateral source compensation the claimant has received or is entitled to receive as a result of the terrorist-related aircraft crashes of September 11, 2001.

c) Eligibility:
   1) In general—A claimant shall be determined to be an eligible individual for purposes of this subsection if the Special Master determines that such claimant
      A. is an individual described in paragraph (2); and
      B. meets the requirements of paragraph (3).
   2) Individuals—A claimant is an individual described in this paragraph if the claimant is:
      A. an individual who
         I. was present at the World Trade Center (New York, New York), the Pentagon (Arlington, Virginia), or the site of the aircraft crash at Shanksville, Pennsylvania, at the time, or in the immediate aftermath, of the terrorist-related aircraft crashes of September 11, 2001; and
         II. suffered physical harm or death as a result of such an air crash;
      B. an individual who was a member of the flight crew or a passenger on American Airlines flight 11 or 77 or United Airlines flight 93 or 175,

except that an individual identified by the Attorney General to have been a participant or conspirator in the terrorist-related aircraft crashes of September 11, 2001, or a representative of such individual shall not be eligible to receive compensation under this title; or

C. in the case of a decedent who is an individual described in subparagraph (A) or (B), the personal representative of the decedent who files a claim on behalf of the decedent.

3) Requirements:

A. Single claim—Not more than one claim may be submitted under this title by an individual or on behalf of a deceased individual.

B. Limitation on civil action:

I. In general—Upon the submission of a claim under this title, the claimant waives the right to file a civil action (or to be a party to an action) in any Federal or State court for damages sustained as a result of the terrorist-related aircraft crashes of September 11, 2001. The preceding sentence does not apply to a civil action to recover collateral source obligations.

II. Pending actions—In the case of an individual who is a party to a civil action described in clause (i), such individual may not submit a claim under this title unless such individual withdraws from such action by the date that is ninety days after the date on which regulations are promulgated under section 407.

Section 406. Payments to Eligible Individuals[16]

a) In General[17]—Not later than twenty days after the date on which a determination is made by the Special Master regarding the amount of compensation due a claimant under this title, the Special Master shall authorize payment to such claimant of the amount determined with respect to the claimant.

b) Payment Authority—This title constitutes budget authority in advance of appropriations Acts and represents the obligation of the Federal Government to provide for the payment of amounts for compensation under this title.

c) Additional Funding:

1) In general—The Attorney General is authorized to accept such amounts as may be contributed by individuals, business concerns, or other entities to carry out this title, under such terms and conditions as the Attorney General may impose.

2) Use of separate account—In making payments under this section, amounts contained in any account containing funds provided under paragraph (1) shall be used prior to using appropriated amounts.

Section 407. Regulations[18]

Not later than ninety days after the date of enactment of this Act,[19] the Attorney General, in consultation with the Special Master, shall promulgate regulations to carry out this title, including regulations with respect to:

(1) forms to be used in submitting claims under this title;
(2) the information to be included in such forms;
(3) procedures for hearing and the presentation of evidence;
(4) procedures to assist an individual in filing and pursuing claims under this title; and
(5) other matters determined appropriate by the Attorney General.

Section 408. Limitation on Air Carrier Liability[20]

a) In General—Notwithstanding any other provision of law, liability for all claims, whether for compensatory or punitive damages, arising from the terrorist-related aircraft crashes of September 11, 2001, against any air carrier shall not be in an amount greater than the limits of the liability coverage maintained by the air carrier.
b) Federal Cause of Action:
   1) Availability of action—There shall exist a Federal cause of action for damages arising out of the hijacking and subsequent crashes of American Airlines flights 11 and 77, and United Airlines flights 93 and 175, on September 11, 2001. Notwithstanding section 40120(c) of title 49, United States Code, this cause of action shall be the exclusive remedy for damages arising out of the hijacking and subsequent crashes of such flights.
   2) Substantive law—The substantive law for decision in any such suit shall be derived from the law, including choice of law principles, of the State in which the crash occurred unless such law is inconsistent with or pre-empted by Federal law.
   3) Jurisdiction—The United States District Court for the Southern District of New York shall have original and exclusive jurisdiction over all actions brought for any claim (including any claim for loss of property, personal injury, or death) resulting from or relating to the terrorist-related aircraft crashes of September 11, 2001.
c) Exclusion—Nothing in this section shall in any way limit any liability of any person who is a knowing participant in any conspiracy to hijack any aircraft or commit any terrorist act.

Section 409. Right of Subrogation[21]

The United States shall have the right of subrogation with respect to any claim paid by the United States under this title.

[...]

Title V—Air Transportation Safety

Section 501. Increased Air Transportation Safety[22]

Congress affirms the President's decision to spend $3,000,000,000 on airline safety and security in conjunction with this Act in order to restore public confidence in the airline industry.

Section 502. Congressional Commitment[23]

Congress is committed to act expeditiously, in consultation with the Secretary of Transportation, to strengthen airport security and take further measures to enhance the security of air travel.

[. . .]

Title VI—Separability

Section 601. Separability[24]

If any provision of this Act (including any amendment made by this Act) or the application thereof to any person or circumstance is held invalid, the remainder of this Act (including any amendment made by this Act) and the application thereof to other persons or circumstances shall not be affected thereby.

Approved September 22, 2001.

CODE OF FEDERAL REGULATIONS, TITLE 28, CHAPTER I, PART 104 SEPTEMBER 11TH VICTIM COMPENSATION FUND OF 2001

Subpart A—General; Eligibility

104.1   Purpose.

104.2   Eligibility definitions and requirements.

Subpart E—Payment of Claims

Subpart F—Limitations

Subpart G—Measures to Protect the Integrity of the Compensation Program

Authority: Title IV of Pub. L. 107–42, 115 Stat. 230, 49 USC 40101 note.

Subpart A—General; Eligibility

§104.1 Purpose.

This part implements the provisions of the September 11th Victim Compensation Fund of 2001, Title IV of Public Law 107–42, 115 Stat. 230 (Air Transportation Safety and System Stabilization Act) to provide compensation to eligible individuals who were physically injured as a result of the terrorist-related aircraft crashes of

September 11, 2001, and to the 'personal representatives' of those who were killed as a result of the crashes. All compensation provided through the Fund will be on account of personal physical injuries or death.

§104.2 Eligibility definitions and requirements.

(a) *Eligible claimants.* The term *eligible claimants* means:
    (1) Individuals present at the World Trade Center, Pentagon, or Shanksville, Pennsylvania, site at the time of, or in the immediate aftermath of, the crashes and who suffered physical harm, as defined herein, as a direct result of the terrorist-related aircraft crashes;
    (2) The Personal Representatives of deceased individuals aboard American Airlines flights 11 or 77 and United Airlines flights 93 or 175; and
    (3) The Personal Representatives of individuals who were present at the World Trade Center, Pentagon, or Shanksville, Pennsylvania, site at the time of, or in the immediate aftermath of, the crashes and who died as a direct result of the terrorist-related aircraft crash.
    (4) The term eligible claimants does not include any individual or representative of an individual who is identified to have been a participant or conspirator in the terrorist-related crashes of September 11.

(b) *Immediate aftermath.* The term *immediate aftermath* of the crashes shall mean, for purposes of all claimants other than rescue workers, the period of time from the crashes until 12 hours after the crashes. With respect to rescue workers who assisted in efforts to search for and recover victims, the immediate aftermath shall include the period from the crashes until 96 hours after the crashes.

(c) *Physical harm:*
    (1) The term *physical harm* shall mean a physical injury to the body that was treated by a medical professional within 24 hours of the injury having been sustained, or within 24 hours of rescue, or within 72 hours of injury or rescue for those victims who were unable to realize immediately the extent of their injuries or for whom treatment by a medical professional was not available on September 11, or within such time period as the Special Master may determine for rescue personnel who did not or could not obtain treatment by a medical professional within 72 hours; and
    (2) In every case not involving death, the physical injury must be verified by contemporaneous medical records created by or at the direction of the medical professional who provided the medical care.

(d) *Personal Representative.* The term *Personal Representative* shall mean the person determined to be the Personal Representative under Sec. 104.4 of this part.

(e) *Present at the site.* The term *present at the site* (i.e. the World Trade Center, Pentagon, or Shanksville, Pennsylvania, site) shall mean physically present at the time of the crashes or in the immediate aftermath:

    (1) In the buildings or portions of buildings that were destroyed as a result of the airplane crashes; or

    (2) In any area contiguous to the crash sites that the Special Master determines was sufficiently close to the site that there was a demonstrable risk of physical harm resulting from the impact of the aircraft or any subsequent fire, explosions, or building collapses (generally, the immediate area in which the impact occurred, fire occurred, portions of buildings fell, or debris fell upon and injured persons).

§104.3 Other definitions.

(a) *Beneficiary.* The term *beneficiary* shall mean a person to whom the Personal Representative shall distribute all or part of the award under Sec. 104.52 of this Part.

(b) *Dependents.* The Special Master shall identify as dependents those persons so identified by the victim on his or her federal tax return for the year 2000 (or those persons who legally could have been identified by the victim on his or her federal tax return for the year 2000) unless:

    (1) The claimant demonstrates that a minor child of the victim was born or adopted on or after January 1, 2001;

    (2) Another person became a dependent in accordance with then-applicable law on or after January 1, 2001; or

    (3) The victim was not required by law to file a federal income tax return for the year 2000.

(c) *Spouse.* The Special Master shall identify as the spouse of a victim the person reported as spouse on the victim's federal tax return for the year 2000 unless:

    (1) The victim was married or divorced in accordance with applicable state law on or after January 1, 2001; or

    (2) The victim was not required by law to file a federal income tax return for the year 2000.

(d) *The Act. The Act,* as used in this part, shall mean Public Law 107–42, 115 Stat. 230 ('Air Transportation Safety and System Stabilization Act'), 49 USC 40101 note.

(e) *Victim.* The term *victim* shall mean an eligible injured claimant or a decedent on whose behalf a claim is brought by an eligible Personal Representative.

§104.4 Personal Representative.

(a) *In general.* The Personal Representative shall be:
   (1) An individual appointed by a court of competent jurisdiction as the Personal Representative of the decedent or as the executor or administrator of the decedent's will or estate.
   (2) In the event that no Personal Representative or executor or administrator has been appointed by any court of competent jurisdiction, and such issue is not the subject of pending litigation or other dispute, the Special Master may, in his discretion, determine that the Personal Representative for purposes of compensation by the Fund is the person named by the decedent in the decedent's will as the executor or administrator of the decedent's estate. In the event no will exists, the Special Master may, in his discretion, determine that the Personal Representative for purposes of compensation by the Fund is the first person in the line of succession established by the laws of the decedent's domicile governing intestacy.
(b) *Notice to beneficiaries.* Any purported Personal Representative must, before filing an Eligibility Form, provide written notice of the claim (including a designated portion of the Eligibility Form) to the immediate family of the decedent (including, but not limited to, the decedent's spouse, former spouses, children, other dependents, and parents), to the executor, administrator, and beneficiaries of the decedent's will, and to any other persons who may reasonably be expected to assert an interest in an award or to have a cause of action to recover damages relating to the wrongful death of the decedent. Personal delivery or transmission by certified mail, return receipt requested, shall be deemed sufficient notice under this provision. The claim forms shall require that the purported Personal Representative certify that such notice (or other notice that the Special Master deems appropriate) has been given. In addition, as provided in Sec. 104.21(b)(5) of this part, the Special Master may publish a list of individuals who have filed Eligibility Forms and the names of the victims for whom compensation is sought, but shall not publish the content of any such form.
(c) *Objections to Personal Representatives.* Objections to the authority of an individual to file as the Personal Representative of a decedent may be filed

with the Special Master by parties who assert a financial interest in the award
up to thirty days following the filing by the Personal Representative. If timely
filed, such objections shall be treated as evidence of a 'dispute' pursuant to
paragraph (d) of this section.

(d) *Disputes as to identity.* The Special Master shall not be required to arbitrate,
litigate, or otherwise resolve any dispute as to the identity of the Personal
Representative. In the event of a dispute over the appropriate Personal
Representative, the Special Master may suspend adjudication of the claim
or, if sufficient information is provided, calculate the appropriate award and
authorize payment, but place in escrow any payment until the dispute is
resolved either by agreement of the disputing parties or by a court of
competent jurisdiction. Alternatively, the disputing parties may agree in
writing to the identity of a Personal Representative to act on their behalf,
who may seek and accept payment from the Fund while the disputing
parties work to settle their dispute.

§104.5 Foreign claims.

In the case of claims brought by, or on behalf of, foreign citizens, the Special Master
may alter the requirements for documentation set forth herein to the extent such
materials are unavailable to such foreign claimants.

§104.6 Amendments to this part.

Claimants are entitled to have their claims processed in accordance with the
provisions of this Part that were in effect at the time that their claims were
submitted under Sec. 104.21(d). All claims will be processed in accordance with
the current provisions of this Part, unless the claimant has notified the
Special Master that he or she has elected to have the claim resolved under
the regulations that were in effect at the time that the claim was submitted under
Sec. 104.21(d).

Subpart B—Filing for Compensation; Application for Advance Benefits

§104.21 Filing for compensation.

(a) *Compensation form; 'filing'.* Except for applications for Advance Benefits pursuant to Sec. 104.22, no claim may be considered until the claimant has submitted both an 'Eligibility Form' and either a 'Personal Injury Compensation Form' or a 'Death Compensation Form'. A claim shall be deemed 'filed' for purposes of section 405(b)(3) of the Act (providing that the Special Master shall issue a determination not later than one hundred and twenty days after the date on which a claim is filed), and for any time periods in this part, when a Claims Evaluator determines that both the Eligibility Form and either a Personal Injury Compensation Form or a Death Compensation Form are substantially complete. Provided, however, that if a claimant files an Eligibility Form requesting Advance Benefits pursuant to Sec. 104.22 of this part without filing either a 'Personal Injury Compensation Form' or a 'Death Compensation Form', the claim shall be deemed 'filed' when the Claims Evaluator determines that the Eligibility Form is substantially complete, but the time period for determination and any time periods in this part shall be stayed or tolled as described in Sec. 104.22(g) of this part.

(b) *Eligibility Form.* The Special Master shall develop an Eligibility Form that will require the claimant to provide information necessary for determining the claimant's eligibility to recover from the Fund.

   (1) The Eligibility Form may require that the claimant certify that he or she has dismissed any pending lawsuit seeking damages as a result of the terrorist-related airplane crashes of September 11, 2001 (except for actions seeking collateral source benefits) within ninety days of the effective date of this part pursuant to section 405(c)(3)(B)(ii) of the Act and that there is no pending lawsuit brought by a dependent, spouse, or beneficiary of the victim.

   (2) The Special Master may require as part of the notice requirement pursuant to Sec. 104.4(b) that the claimant provide copies of a designated portion of the Eligibility Form to the immediate family of the decedent (including, but not limited to, the spouse, former spouses, children, other dependents, and parents), to the executor, administrator, and beneficiaries of the decedent's will, and to any other persons who may reasonably be expected to assert an interest in an award or to have a cause of action to recover damages relating to the wrongful death of the decedent.

(3) The Eligibility Form may require claimants to provide the following proof:

    (i) Proof of death: Death certificate or similar official documentation;

    (ii) Proof of presence at site: Documentation sufficient to establish presence at one of the crash sites, which may include, without limitation, a death certificate, records of employment, contemporaneous medical records, contemporaneous records of federal, state, city or local government, an affidavit or declaration of the decedent's or injured claimant's employer, or other sworn statement (or unsworn statement complying with 28 USC 1746) regarding the presence of the victim;

    (iii) Proof of death on board aircraft: Death certificate or records of American or United Airlines or other sufficient official documentation;

    (iv) Proof of physical harm: Contemporaneous medical records of hospitals, clinics, physicians, licensed medical personnel, or registries maintained by federal, state, or local government, and records of all continuing medical treatment;

    (v) Personal Representative: Copies of relevant legal documentation, including court orders; letters testamentary or similar documentation; proof of the purported Personal Representative's relationship to the decedent; copies of wills, trusts, or other testamentary documents; and information regarding other possible beneficiaries as requested by the Eligibility Form;

    (vi) Any other information that the Special Master deems necessary to determine the claimant's eligibility.

(4) The Special Master may also require waivers, consents, or authorizations from claimants to obtain directly from third parties tax returns, medical information, employment information, or other information that the Special Master deems relevant in determining the claimant's eligibility or award, and may request an opportunity to review originals of documents submitted in connection with the Fund.

(5) Application for Advance Benefits: The Eligibility Form shall include a section allowing claimants to indicate that they wish to apply for Advance Benefits. Claimants who apply for such Advance Benefits must certify on that Form that they have not yet received $450,000 in collateral source compensation if they are bringing a claim on behalf of a deceased victim with a spouse or dependent, $250,000 in collateral source compensation if they are bringing a claim on behalf of a deceased victim who was single with no dependents, or an amount in excess of their lost wages plus out-of-pocket medical expenses if they are an injured claimant. All such claimants also must state on the Form facts

establishing financial hardship that would justify a determination that they are in need of Advance Benefits.

(6) The Special Master may publish a list of individuals who have filed Eligibility Forms and the names of the victims for whom compensation is sought, but shall not publish the content of any such form.

(c) *Personal Injury Compensation Form* and *Death Compensation Form.* The Special Master shall develop a Personal Injury Compensation Form that each injured claimant must submit. The Special Master shall also develop a Death Compensation Form that each Personal Representative must submit. These forms shall require the claimant to provide certain information that the Special Master deems necessary to determining the amount of any award, including information concerning income, collateral sources, benefits, and other financial information, and shall require the claimant to state the factual basis for the amount of compensation sought. It shall also allow the claimant to submit certain other information that may be relevant, but not necessary, to the determination of the amount of any award.

(1) Claimants shall, at a minimum, submit all tax returns that were filed for the years 1998, 1999, and 2000. The Special Master may, at his discretion, require that claimants submit copies of tax returns or other records for any other period of years he deems appropriate for determination of an award. The Special Master may also require waivers, consents, or authorizations from claimants to obtain directly from third parties medical information, employment information, or other information that the Special Master deems relevant to determining the amount of any award.

(2) Claimants may attach to the 'Personal Injury Compensation Form' or 'Death Compensation Form' any additional statements, documents, or analyses by physicians, experts, advisers, or any other person or entity that the claimant believes may be relevant to a determination of compensation.

(d) *Submission of a claim.* Section 405(c)(3)(B) of the Act provides that upon the submission of a claim under the Fund, the claimant waives the right to file a civil action (or to be a party to an action) in any Federal or State court for damages sustained as a result of the terrorist-related aircraft crashes of September 11, 2001, except for civil actions to recover collateral source obligations and civil actions against any person who is a knowing participant in any conspiracy to hijack any aircraft or commit any terrorist act. A claim shall be deemed submitted for purposes of section 405(c)(3)(B) of the Act when the claim is deemed filed pursuant to Sec. 104.21, regardless of whether any time limits are stayed or tolled.

(e) *Provisions of information by third parties.* Any third party having an interest in a claim brought by a Personal Representative may provide written statements or information regarding the Personal Representative's claim. The Claims Evaluator or the Special Master or his designee may, at his or her discretion, include the written statements or information as part of the claim.

§104.22 Advance Benefits.

(a) *Advance Benefits.* Eligible Claimants may apply for immediate 'Advance Benefits' in a fixed amount as follows:

   (1) $50,000 for Personal Representatives; and

   (2) $25,000 for injured claimants who meet the requirements of paragraph (d) of this section.

(b) *Credit against award.* The Advance Benefit shall be credited against any final compensation award so that the amount of the Advance Benefit is deducted from the final award under this program.

(c) *Application for Advance Benefits.* An otherwise eligible claimant may seek Advance Benefits to alleviate financial hardship faced by the claimant (or financial hardship faced by the beneficiaries of the decedent) by submitting an Eligibility Form described in Sec. 104.21(b) and indicating thereon that he or she is applying for Advance Benefits.

(d) *Eligibility for Advance Benefits.* In the case of a Personal Representative, the claimant may be deemed eligible for Advance Benefits if a Claims Evaluator or the Special Master or his designee determines that the claimant is eligible to recover under the Fund. In the case of an injured claimant, the claimant may be deemed eligible for Advance Benefits when the Special Master or his designee determines that the claimant is eligible to recover under the Fund and that the claimant's physical injury required hospitalization for one week or more.

(e) *Authorization of payments.*

   (1) Payment in the amount described in paragraph (a) of this section will be authorized immediately upon a determination that the claimant is eligible for Advance Benefits and the claimant is:

     (i) An injured claimant;

     (ii) A Personal Representative who was the spouse of the deceased victim on September 11, 2001; or

     (iii) A Personal Representative who has obtained the consent of the spouse of the deceased victim (or, if there is no surviving spouse, all of the dependents of the deceased victim) to file for Advance Benefits.

(2)(i) With respect to other Personal Representatives, payment will be authorized within fifteen days after the determination that the claimant is eligible for Advance Benefits, provided that no other individual has asserted a colorable conflicting claim as the Personal Representative with respect to the decedent and the Personal Representative identifies and has given notice to the beneficiaries to whom such Advance Benefits will be distributed.

(ii) In the event that a colorable conflicting claim has been asserted, no Advance Benefit will be paid until a final eligibility determination has been made.

(f) *Tolling of 120-day clock and other time periods.* A claimant filing an Eligibility Form requesting Advance Benefits before filing a Personal Injury Compensation Form or Death Compensation Form will be deemed to have waived his right to commencement of the one-hundred-and-twenty-day period in section 405(b)(3) of the Act (providing that the Special Master shall provide notice to the claimant of his determination within one-hundred-and-twenty days after the date on which a claim is filed). The one-hundred-and-twenty-day period and all other time limitations in this part, except those applicable to Advance Benefit payments, shall be stayed or tolled until such time that a Claims Evaluator determines that the claimant's Personal Injury Compensation Form or Death Compensation Form is substantially complete.

Subpart C—Claim Intake, Assistance, and Review Procedures

§104.31 Procedure for claims evaluation.

(a) *Initial review.* Claims Evaluators shall review the forms filed by the claimant and either deem the claim 'filed' (pursuant to 104.21(a)) or notify the claimant of any deficiency in the forms or any required documents.

(b) *Procedural tracks.* Each claim will be placed on a procedural track, described herein as 'Track A' and 'Track B', selected by the claimant on the Personal Injury Compensation Form or Death Compensation Form.

(1) Procedure for Track A. The Claims Evaluator shall determine eligibility and the claimant's presumed award pursuant to Sec. 104.43 to 104.46 of this part and, within forty-five days of the date the claim was deemed filed, notify the claimant in writing of the eligibility determination, the amount of the presumed award, and the right to request a hearing before the Special Master or his designee under Sec. 104.33 of this part. After an eligible claimant has been notified of the presumed award, the claimant

may either accept the presumed compensation determination as the final determination and request payment, or may instead request a review before the Special Master or his designee pursuant to Sec. 104.33. Claimants found to be ineligible may appeal pursuant to Sec. 104.32.

(2) Procedure for Track B. The Claims Evaluator shall determine eligibility within forty-five days of the date the claim was deemed filed, but shall not determine the claimant's presumed award; the Claims Evaluator shall notify the claimant in writing of the eligibility determination. Upon notification of eligibility, the claimant will proceed to a hearing pursuant to Sec. 104.33. At such hearing, the Special Master or his designee shall utilize the presumptive award methodology as set forth in Sec. 104.43 to 104.46 of this part, but may modify or vary the award if the claimant presents extraordinary circumstances not adequately addressed by the presumptive award methodology. There shall be no review or appeal from this determination.

(c) *Multiple claims from the same family.* The Special Master may treat claims brought by or on behalf of two or more members of the same immediate family as related or consolidated claims for purposes of determining the amount of any award.

§104.32 Eligibility review.

Any claimant deemed ineligible by the Claims Evaluator may appeal that decision to the Special Master or his designee by filing an eligibility appeal on forms created by the office of the Special Master.

§104.33 Hearing.

(a) *Supplemental submissions.* The claimant may prepare and file Supplemental Submissions within twenty-one calendar days from notification of either the presumed award (Track A) or eligibility (Track B). The Special Master shall develop forms appropriate for Supplemental Submissions.

(b) *Conduct of hearings.* Hearings shall be before the Special Master or his designee. The objective of hearings shall be to permit the claimant to present information or evidence that the claimant believes is necessary to a full understanding of the claim. The claimant may request that the Special

Master or his designee review any evidence relevant to the determination of the award, including without limitation: factors and variables used in calculating economic loss; the identity of the victim's spouse and dependents; the financial needs of the claimant; facts affecting noneconomic loss; and any factual or legal arguments that the claimant contends should affect the award. Claimants shall be entitled to submit any statements or reports in writing. The Special Master or his designee may require authentication of documents, including medical records and reports, and may request and consider information regarding the financial resources and expenses of the victim's family or other material that the Special Master or his designee deems relevant.

(c) *Location and duration of hearings.* The hearings shall, to the extent practicable, be scheduled at times and in locations convenient to the claimant or his or her representative. The hearings shall be limited in length to a time period determined by the Special Master or his designee.

(d) *Witnesses, counsel, and experts.* Claimants shall be permitted, but not required, to present witnesses, including expert witnesses. The Special Master or his designee shall be permitted to question witnesses and examine the credentials of experts. The claimant shall be entitled to be represented by an attorney in good standing, but it is not necessary that the claimant be represented by an attorney.

(e) *Waivers.* The Special Master shall have authority and discretion to require any waivers necessary to obtain more individualized information on specific claimants.

(f) *Track A review of presumed award.* For proceedings under Track A, the Special Master or his designee shall make a determination whether:

    (1) There was an error in determining the presumptive award, either because the claimant's individual criteria were misapplied or for another reason; or

    (2) The claimant presents extraordinary circumstances not adequately addressed by the presumptive award.

(g) *Determination.* The Special Master shall notify the claimant in writing of the final amount of the award, but need not create or provide any written record of the deliberations that resulted in that determination. There shall be no further review or appeal of the Special Master's determination. In notifying the claimant of the final amount of the award, the Special Master may designate the portions or percentages of the final award that are attributable to economic loss and noneconomic loss, respectively, and may provide such other information as appropriate to provide adequate guidance for a court of competent jurisdiction and a personal representative.

§104.34 Publication of awards.

In order to assist potential claimants in evaluating their options of either filing a claim with the Special Master or filing a lawsuit in tort, the Special Master reserves the right to publicize the amounts of some or all of the awards, but shall not publish the name of the claimants or victims that received each award. If published, these decisions would be intended by the Special Master as general guides for potential claimants and should not be viewed as precedent binding on the Special Master or his staff.

§104.35 Claims deemed abandoned by claimants.

The Special Master and his staff will endeavor to evaluate promptly any information submitted by claimants. Nonetheless, it is the responsibility of the claimant to keep the Special Master informed of his or her current address and to respond within the duration of this two-year program to requests for additional information. Claims outstanding at the end of this program because of a claimant's failure to complete his or her filings shall be deemed abandoned.

Subpart D—Amount of Compensation for Eligible Claimants.

§104.41 Amount of compensation.

As provided in section 405(b)(1)(B)(ii) of the Act, in determining the amount of compensation to which a claimant is entitled, the Special Master shall take into consideration the harm to the claimant, the facts of the claim, and the individual circumstances of the claimant. The individual circumstances of the claimant may include the financial needs or financial resources of the claimant or the victim's dependents and beneficiaries. As provided in section 405(b)(6) of the Act, the Special Master shall reduce the amount of compensation by the amount of collateral source compensation the claimant (or, in the case of a Personal Representative, the victim's beneficiaries) has received or is entitled to receive as a result of the terrorist-related aircraft crashes of September 11, 2001. In no event shall an award (before collateral source compensation has been deducted) be less than $500,000 in any case brought on behalf of a deceased victim with a spouse or dependent, or $300,000 in any case brought on behalf of a deceased victim who was single with no dependents.

§104.42 Applicable state law.

The phrase 'to the extent recovery for such loss is allowed under applicable state law', as used in the statute's definition of economic loss in section 402(5) of the Act, is interpreted to mean that the Special Master is not permitted to compensate claimants for those categories or types of economic losses that would not be compensable under the law of the state that would be applicable to any tort claims brought by, or on behalf of, the victim.

§104.43 Determination of presumed economic loss for decedents.

In reaching presumed determinations for economic loss for Personal Representatives bringing claims on behalf of decedents, the Special Master shall consider sums corresponding to the following:

(a) *Loss of earnings or other benefits related to employment.* The Special Master, as part of the process of reaching a 'determination' pursuant to section 405(b) of the Act, shall develop a methodology and publish schedules, tables, or charts that will permit prospective claimants to estimate determinations of loss of earnings or other benefits related to employment based upon individual circumstances of the deceased victim, including: the age of the decedent as of September 11, 2001; the number of dependents who survive the decedent; whether the decedent is survived by a spouse; and the amount and nature of the decedent's income for recent years. The decedent's salary/income in 1998–2000 (or for other years the Special Master deems relevant) shall be evaluated in a manner that the Special Master deems appropriate. The Special Master may, if he deems appropriate, take an average of income figures for 1998–2000, and may also consider income for other periods that he deems appropriate, including published pay scales for victims who were government or military employees. The Special Master's methodology and schedules, tables, or charts shall yield presumed determinations of loss of earnings or other benefits related to employment for annual incomes up to but not beyond the 98th percentile of individual income in the United States for the year 2000. In cases where the victim was a minor child, the Special Master may assume an average income for the child commensurate with the average income of all wage earners in the United States. For victims who were members of the armed services or government employees such as firefighters or police officers, the Special Master may consider all forms of compensation (or pay) to which the victim was entitled. For example, military service members' and uniformed service members' compensation includes all of the various components of compensation, including, but not limited to, basic pay (BPY), basic allowance for housing (BAH), basic allowance for subsistence (BAS), federal income tax advantage (TAD), overtime bonuses, differential pay, and longevity pay.

(b) *Medical expense loss.* This loss equals the out-of-pocket medical expenses that were incurred as a result of the physical harm suffered by the victim (i.e. those medical expenses that were not paid for or reimbursed through health insurance). This loss shall be calculated on a case-by-case basis, using documentation and other information submitted by the Personal Representative.

(c) *Replacement services loss.* For decedents who did not have any prior earned income, or who worked only part time outside the home, economic loss may be determined with reference to replacement services and similar measures.

(d) *Loss due to death/burial costs.* This loss shall be calculated on a case-by-case basis, using documentation and other information submitted by the personal representative and includes the out-of-pocket burial costs that were incurred.

(e) *Loss of business or employment opportunities.* Such losses shall be addressed through the procedure outlined above in paragraph (a) of this section.

§104.44 Determination of presumed noneconomic losses for decedents.

The presumed noneconomic losses for decedents shall be $250,000 plus an additional $100,000 for the spouse and each dependent of the deceased victim. Such presumed losses include a noneconomic component of replacement services loss.

§104.45 Determination of presumed economic loss for claimants who suffered physical harm.

In reaching presumed determinations for economic loss for claimants who suffered physical harm (but did not die), the Special Master shall consider sums corresponding to the following:

(a) *Loss of earnings or other benefits related to employment.* The Special Master may determine the loss of earnings or other benefits related to employment on a case-by-case basis, using documentation and other information submitted by the claimant, regarding the actual amount of work that the claimant has missed or will miss without compensation. Alternatively, the Special Master may determine the loss of earnings or other benefits related to employment by relying upon the methodology created pursuant to Sec. 104.43(a) and adjusting the loss based upon the extent of the victim's physical harm.

   (1) *Disability; in general.* In evaluating claims of disability, the Special Master will, in general, make a determination regarding whether the claimant is capable of performing his or her usual profession in light of the injuries.

   (2) *Total permanent disability.* With respect to claims of total permanent disability, the Special Master may accept a determination of disability made by the Social Security Administration as evidence of disability without any further medical evidence or review. The Special Master may also consider determinations of permanent total disability made by other governmental agencies or private insurers in evaluating the claim. The Special Master may require that the claimant submit an evaluation of the claimant's disability and ability to perform his or her occupation prepared by medical experts.

   (3) *Partial disability.* With respect to claims of partial disability, the Special Master may consider evidence of the effect of the partial disability on the claimant's ability to perform his or her usual occupation as well as the effect of the partial disability on the claimant's ability to participate in usual daily activities.

(b) *Medical expense loss.* This loss equals the out-of-pocket medical expenses that were incurred as a result of the physical harm suffered by the victim (i.e. those medical expenses that were not paid for or reimbursed through health insurance). In addition, this loss equals future out-of-pocket medical expenses that will be incurred as a result of the physical harm suffered by the victim (i.e. those medical expenses that will not be paid for or reimbursed through health insurance). These losses shall be calculated on a case-by-case basis, using documentation and other information submitted by the claimant.

(c) *Replacement services loss.* For injured claimants who did not have any prior earned income, or who worked only part-time outside the home, economic loss may be determined with reference to replacement services and similar measures.

(d) *Loss of business or employment opportunities.* Such losses shall be addressed through the procedure outlined above in paragraph (a) of this section.

§104.46 Determination of presumed noneconomic losses for claimants who suffered physical harm.

The Special Master may determine the presumed noneconomic losses for claimants who suffered physical harm (but did not die) by relying upon the noneconomic losses described in Sec. 104.44 and adjusting the losses based upon the extent of the victim's physical harm. Such presumed losses include any noneconomic component of replacement services loss.

104.47 Collateral sources.

(a) *Payments that constitute collateral source compensation.* The amount of compensation shall be reduced by all collateral source compensation, including life insurance, pension funds, death benefits programs, and payments by Federal, State, or local governments related to the terrorist-related aircraft crashes of September 11, 2001. In determining the appropriate collateral source offset for future benefit payments, the Special Master may employ an appropriate methodology for determining the present value of such future benefits. In determining the appropriate value of offsets for pension funds, life insurance and similar collateral sources, the Special Master may, as appropriate, reduce the amount of offsets to take account of self-contributions made or premiums paid by the victim during his or her lifetime. In determining the appropriate collateral source offset for future benefit payments that are contingent upon one or more future event(s), the Special Master may reduce such offsets to account for the possibility that the future contingencies may or may not occur. In cases where the recipients of collateral source compensation are not beneficiaries of the awards from the Fund, the Special Master shall have discretion to exclude such compensation from the collateral source offset where necessary to prevent beneficiaries from having their awards reduced by collateral source compensation that they will not receive.

(b) *Payments that do not constitute collateral source compensation.* The following payments received by claimants do not constitute collateral source compensation:

(1) The value of services or in-kind charitable gifts such as provision of emergency housing, food, or clothing; and

(2) Charitable donations distributed to the beneficiaries of the decedent, to the injured claimant, or to the beneficiaries of the injured claimant by privately funded charitable entities; provided however, that the Special

Master may determine that funds provided to victims or their families through a privately funded charitable entity constitute, in substance, a payment described in paragraph (a) of this section.

(3) Tax benefits received from the Federal government as a result of the enactment of the Victims of Terrorism Tax Relief Act.

Subpart E—Payment of Claims

§104.51 Payments to eligible individuals.

Not later than twenty days after the date on which a determination is made by the Special Master regarding the amount of compensation due a claimant under the Fund, the Special Master shall authorize payment to such claimant of the amount determined with respect to the claimant.

§104.52 Distribution of award to decedent's beneficiaries.

The Personal Representative shall distribute the award in a manner consistent with the law of the decedent's domicile or any applicable rulings made by a court of competent jurisdiction. The Personal Representative shall, before payment is authorized, provide to the Special Master a plan for distribution of any award received from the Fund. Notwithstanding any other provision of these regulations or any other provision of state law, in the event that the Special Master concludes that the Personal Representative's plan for distribution does not appropriately compensate the victim's spouse, children, or other relatives, the Special Master may direct the Personal Representative to distribute all or part of the award to such spouse, children, or other relatives.

Subpart F—Limitations

§104.61 Limitation on civil actions.

(a) *General.* Section 405(c)(3)(B) of the Act provides that upon the submission of a claim under the Fund, the claimant waives the right to file a civil action (or be a party to an action) in any Federal or State court for damages sustained as a result of the terrorist-related aircraft crashes of September 11, 2001, except that this limitation does not apply to recover collateral source obligations, or to a civil action against any person who is a knowing participant in any conspiracy to hijack any aircraft or commit any terrorist act. The Special Master shall take appropriate steps to inform potential claimants of section 405(c)(3)(B) of the Act.

(b) *Pending actions.* Claimants who have filed a civil action or who are a party to such an action as described in paragraph (a) of this section may not file a claim with the Special Master unless they withdraw from such action not later than March 21, 2002.

§104.62 Time limit on filing claims.

In accordance with the Act, no claim may be filed under this part after December 22, 2003.

§104.63 Subrogation.

Compensation under this Fund does not constitute the recovery of tort damages against a third party or the settlement of a third party action, and the United States shall be subrogated to all potential claims against third party tortfeasors of any victim receiving compensation from the Fund. For that reason, no person or entity having paid other benefits or compensation to, or on behalf of, a victim shall have any right of recovery, whether through subrogation or otherwise, against the compensation paid by the Fund.

Subpart G—Measures to Protect the Integrity of the Compensation Program

§104.71 Procedures to prevent and detect fraud.

(a) *Review of claims.* For the purpose of detecting and preventing the payment of fraudulent claims and for the purpose of assuring accurate and appropriate

payments to eligible claimants, the Special Master shall implement procedures to:

    (1) Verify, authenticate, and audit claims;

    (2) Analyze claim submissions to detect inconsistencies, irregularities, du-
plication, and multiple claimants; and

    (3) Ensure the quality control of claims review procedures.

(b) *Quality control.* The Special Master shall institute periodic quality control
audits designed to evaluate the accuracy of submissions and the accuracy of
payments, subject to the oversight of the Inspector General of the Department of Justice.

(c) *False or fraudulent claims.* The Special Master shall refer all evidence of false
or fraudulent claims to appropriate law enforcement authorities.

Notes

1. Sept. 22, 2001—[HR 2926].
2. Air Transportation Safety and System Stabilization Act. 49 USC 40101 note.
3. 49 USC 40101 President Terrorism.
4. 49 USC 40101.
5. 49 USC 40101.
6. Appropriation authorization.
7. Deadlines. President. 49 USC 40101.
8. September 11th Victim Compensation Fund of 2001. Terrorism.
9. 49 USC 40101 note.
10. 49 USC 40101.
11. 49 USC 40101.
12. 49 USC 40101.
13. 49 USC 40101.
14. Electronic document.
15. Deadline. Notification.
16. 49 USC 40101.
17. Deadline.
18. 49 USC 40101.
19. Deadline.
20. NOTE: 49 USC 40101.
21. 49 USC 40101.
22. 49 USC 40101.
23. 49 USC 40101.
24. 49 USC 40101.

GERMANY

JEWISH VICTIMS OF THE HOLOCAUST

LUXEMBOURG AGREEMENT
[EXCERPTS]

September 10, 1952

Agreement between the Federal Republic of Germany and the State of Israel

Whereas unspeakable criminal acts were perpetrated against the Jewish people during the National Socialist regime of terror and whereas by a declaration in the Bundestag on September 27, 1951, the Government of the Federal Republic of Germany made known their determination, within the limits of their capacity, to make good the material damage caused by these acts and whereas the State of Israel has assumed the heavy burden of resettling so great a number of uprooted and destitute Jewish refugees from Germany and from territories formerly under German rule and has on this basis advanced a claim against the Federal Republic of Germany for global recompense for the cost of the integration of these refugees now therefore the Federal Republic of Germany and the State of Israel have agreed as follows:

Article 1

(a) The Federal Republic of Germany shall, in view of the considerations hereinbefore recited, pay to the State of Israel the sum of DM3,000 million.

(b) In addition, the Federal Republic of Germany shall, in compliance with the obligation undertaken in Article 1 of Protocol No. 2 this day drawn up and signed between the Government of the Federal Republic of Germany and the Conference on Jewish Material Claims against Germany, pay to Israel for the benefit of the said Conference the sum of DM450 million; the said sum of DM450 million shall be used for the purposes set out in Article 2 of the said Protocol.

(c) The provisions hereinafter contained in the present Agreement shall apply to the total sum of DM3,450 million so arising, subject, however, to the provisions of Article 3, paragraph (c), and of Article 15.

Article 2

The Federal Republic of Germany will make available the amount referred to in Article 1, paragraph (c) of the present Agreement for the purchase, in pursuance of Articles 6, 7 and 8, of such commodities and services as shall serve the purpose of expanding opportunities for the settlement and rehabilitation of Jewish refugees in Israel. The Government of the Federal Republic of Germany shall, in order to facilitate the purchase of such commodities and the provision of such services, take the measures and accord the facilities as set out in Articles 5, 6 and 8.

Article 3

(a) The obligation undertaken in Article 1 of the present Agreement shall, without prejudice to the provisions of Article 4, be discharged by the payment of annual instalments, as follows:

(i) As from the coming into force of the present Agreement until March 31, 1954, an amount of DM200 million for each financial year. The first financial year shall be deemed to be the period commencing on the date of the coming into force of the present Agreement and ending on March 31, 1953; thereafter, each financial year shall be the period commencing on the first day of April of one year and ending on the thirty-first day of March of the following year;

(ii) As from April 1, 1954, nine annual instalments of DM310 million each and a tenth annual instalment of DM260 million, subject to the provisions of sub-paragraph (iii) hereof;

(iii) Should the Government of the Federal Republic of Germany be of opinion that they cannot comply with the terms of sub-paragraph (ii) hereof, they shall, three months before the beginning of the third financial year, give notice in writing to the Israel Mission referred to in Article 12, of a reduction of the annual instalments payable under sub-paragraph (ii) hereof, provided, however, that the said annual instalments shall in no circumstances be allowed to fall below the sum of DM250 million.

(b) The annual instalments hereinbefore referred to shall become due in equal amounts on the fifteenth day of April and on the fifteenth day of August of each year. The first annual instalment shall be paid as follows: DM60 million on the day of the coming into force of the present Agreement, and DM140 million three months thereafter, or on March 31, 1953, whichever date may be the earlier.

(c) Any annual instalments paid in pursuance of the provisions of this Article shall, when paid, diminish the obligation undertaken by the Federal Republic of Germany in Article 1, paragraph (b) in the proportion which that obligation bears to the total sum payable, and referred to in Article 1, paragraph (c). The Government of Israel shall, when such annual instalments have been received, pay to the Conference on Jewish Material Claims against Germany, or to its successor or successors, an amount in the proportion hereinbefore referred to, within one year from the receipt of such instalments.

[...]

Article 6

(a) The commodities and services to be purchased by the Israel Mission shall be comprised in Schedules.

(b) In laying down such Schedules account shall be taken especially of capital goods.

(c) Commodities delivered under the terms of the present Agreement may also be of non-German origin.

(d) The commodities and services included in the Schedule for the first two financial years shall be comprised in the following Groups:

Group I—Ferrous and non-ferrous metals;
Group II—Products of the steel-manufacturing industry;
Group III—Products of the chemical industry and of other industries;
Group IV—Agricultural products;
Group V—Services.

(e) The amounts by which the annual instalments under the present Agreement may increase shall be apportioned as follows among the Groups mentioned in paragraph (d) hereof:
13% of the increase to go to Group I;
30% of the increase to go to Group II;
45% of the increase to go to Groups III and IV;
12% of the increase to go to Group V.

[...]

Article 13

(a) The Contracting Parties shall set up a Mixed Commission composed of representatives of the Government of Germany and of the Government of Israel, respectively.

(b) The Mixed Commission shall meet at the request of the representatives of either Party.

(c) The Mixed Commission shall have the following functions:

   (i) To deal with all questions arising between the Contracting Parties out of, or in connection with, the implementation of the present Agreement, to review the progress of such implementation, to examine any difficulties that may arise, and to take decisions in order to resolve such difficulties;

   (ii) To lay down Schedules in accordance with the Provisions of Article 6.

[…]

In faith whereof the undersigned representatives duly authorized thereto have signed the present Agreement. Done at Luxembourg this tenth day of September, 1952, in two originals in the English language, one copy of which shall be furnished to each one of the Governments of the Contracting Parties.

For the Federal Republic of Germany
s/Adenauer
For the State of Israel
s/M. Sharett

Protocol No. 1

Drawn up by Representatives of the Government of the Federal Republic of Germany and of the Conference on Jewish Material Claims against Germany

Representatives of the Government of the Federal Republic of Germany and of the Conference on Jewish Material Claims against Germany have met in The Hague to discuss the extension of the legislation existing in the Federal Republic of Germany for the redress of National Socialist wrongs and have agreed on a number of principles for the improvement of the existing legislation as well as on other measures. The Government of the Federal Republic of Germany declare that they will take as soon as possible all steps within their constitutional competence to ensure the carrying out of the following programme:

I. Compensation

1. The Government of the Federal Republic of Germany is resolved to supplement and amend the existing compensation legislation by a Federal Supplementing and Coordinating Law [*Bundesergaenzungs- und -rahmengesetz*] so as to ensure that the legal position of the persecutees throughout the Federal territory be no less favourable than under the General Claims Law now in force in the US Zone. Insofar as legislation now in force in the *Laender* contains more favourable regulations these will be maintained. The provisions contained hereinafter shall apply throughout the whole territory of the Federal Republic.

2. Jurisdictional gaps resulting from the residence and date-line requirements of the compensation laws of the various *Laender* will be eliminated. A change of residence from one *Land* to another shall not deprive anyone of compensation.

3. Where residence and date-line requirements are applicable under compensation legislation, compensation payments for deprivation of liberty shall be granted to persons who emigrated before the date-line and had their last German domicile or residence within the Federal territory.

4. Persecutees who were subjected to compulsory labour and lived under conditions similar to incarceration shall be treated as if they had been deprived of liberty by reason of persecution.

5. A persecutee who, within the boundaries of The German Reich as of December 31, 1937, lived 'underground' under conditions similar to incarceration or unworthy of human beings shall be treated as if he had been deprived of liberty by reason of persecution, in the meaning of that term under compensation legislation.

6. Where a persecutee died after May 8, 1945, his near heirs (children, spouse or parents) shall be entitled to assert his claim for compensation for deprivation of liberty, if this appears equitable by reason of the connection between the persecutee's death and persecution or of the indigence of the claimant. This provision shall not apply if the deceased was at fault in failing to file his claim in time.

7. Where the computation of annuities payable to persecutees is or will be based on the amounts of pensions payable to comparable categories of officials all past and future changes in the pensions payable to comparable categories of officials will also be applied, as from the effective date of the future Federal Supplementing and Coordinating Law, to the annuities payable to persecutees. If at that time the persecutee has received no such annuities, such changes shall be effective as of April 1, 1952.

8. The future Federal Supplementing and Coordinating Law in supplementing the present legislation will grant to members of the free professions, including self-employed persons in trade and industry, agriculture, and forestry, the

choice between a capital payment and annuities as compensation for loss of opportunities to earn a livelihood [*Existenzschaeden*]. The capital payment shall be granted up to a ceiling of DM25,000 in each case as compensation for the damage suffered before the former vocation was fully resumed. Instead of the capital payment the persecutee may elect an appropriate annuity corresponding to his former living standards. The annuity shall, however, not exceed DM500 per month. The persecutee shall be entitled to such choice only if at the time the choice is made, he is unable to, or cannot be reasonably expected to, fully resume his former vocation. The choice shall be final. If the beneficiary elects annuities, payments will be computed as from the day one year prior to the date of election.

9. The Government of the Federal Republic of Germany will provide compensation to persons who suffered losses as officials or employees of Jewish communities or public institutions within the boundaries of the German Reich as of December 31, 1937. Insofar as these persons have a claim against public authorities for compensation under existing or future compensation legislation, they will receive temporary relief pending the beginning of these compensation payments. If the persons involved do not have such claims, their maintenance will be secured by monthly payments based on their former salaries.

10. The future Federal Supplementing and Coordinating Law shall, in providing compensation for damage to economic prospects, include in an appropriate manner provisions for compensation for damage to vocational and professional training.

11. Persecutees who have their domicile or permanent residence abroad shall be compensated for deprivation of benefits accruing to victims of the First World War if they were deprived of such benefits by the National Socialist regime of terror because of their political convictions, race, faith or ideology.

12. Persons who were persecuted because of their political convictions, race, faith or ideology and who settled in the Federal Republic or emigrated abroad from expulsion areas within the meaning of that term in the Equalization of Burdens Law shall receive compensation for deprivation of liberty and damage to health and limb in accordance with the [sic] up to a ceiling of RM150,000 in each case, and converted at the rate of DM6.5 for RM100.

If the claimant is aged or permanently incapable of earning a livelihood because of illness or physical disability and the compensation paid to him for personal damages and for special levies, together with his own property and his other income, is insufficient to provide for his livelihood he may elect, instead of a capital payment for damage to his economic prospects, a requisite annuity.

Compensation in accordance with Paragraph 1 shall also be paid to persecutees who emigrated abroad or settled in the Federal Republic during or after the time the general expulsions took place.

13. The residence and date-line requirements of the General Claims Law of the US Zone shall not be applied to persecutees who suffered damage under the National Socialist regime of terror and who, as political refugees from the Soviet Zone of occupation, moved into the Federal Republic and legally established their permanent residence there (so-called 'double persecutees').

14. Persons who were persecuted for their political convictions, race, faith or ideology during the National Socialist regime of terror and who are at present stateless or political provisions of the General Claims Law of the US Zone. This applies only if they settled in the Federal Republic or emigrated abroad before the general expulsions took place and if it may be assumed that the persecutee would have been subjected to the expulsion measures taken against German nationals and ethnic Germans in connection with the events of the Second World War. Survivors of such persecutees shall receive annuities if all other conditions prescribed in the General Claims Law of the US Zone for the grant of survivors' annuities are fulfilled.

Such persecutees shall receive compensation for special levies, including the Reich Flight Tax, which were imposed upon them as a result of acts of terror of the National Socialist regime, either by law or arbitrarily. Such special levies shall be taken into account up to a ceiling of RM150,000 in each individual case. The claim shall be converted at the rate of DM6.5 for RM100, in the same way as savings accounts of expellees from the East are being converted.

For damage to economic prospects compensation shall be paid insofar as such damage made it impossible for the persecutee to provide for old age maintenance, wholly or in part, out of his own resources. In such case the damage will be determined, taking into account also refugees, and those who were deprived of liberty by National Socialist terror acts shall receive appropriate compensation for deprivation of liberty and damage to health and limb in accordance with the basic principles of the General Claims Law of the US Zone and in line with [*in Anlehnung an*] the compensation payments established therein, i.e. as a rule, not less than 3/4 of those rates. This does not apply, however, if the persecutee's needs are or were provided for by a State or an international organization on a permanent basis or by way of a capital payment because of the damage suffered from persecution. Persecutees who acquired a new nationality after the end of persecution shall be assimilated to stateless persons and political refugees.

Survivors of such persecutees shall receive corresponding annuities if all other conditions established in the General Claims Law of the US Zone for the grant of survivors' annuities are fulfilled.

If the compensation granted to the claimant, together with his own property and other income, is insufficient to provide for his livelihood he shall, in recognition of the persecution, be granted a corresponding equalization payment out of the Hardship Fund referred to elsewhere which is to be established by the Government of the Federal Republic of Germany. The provisions contained herein shall not be applicable insofar as a persecutee is covered by the provisions of 12 above.

15. The Government of the Federal Republic of Germany will endeavour to carry out the whole compensation programme as soon as possible but not later than within ten years. They will see to it that the necessary funds shall be made available, as from the financial year 1953–54. The funds to be made available for any specific financial year shall be fixed in accordance with the Federal Republic's capacity to pay.

16. The Federal Supplementing and Coordinating Law shall in recognition of general social principles, provide that claims of persons entitled to compensation who are over sixty years of age, or who are needy, or whose earning ability has been considerably impaired because of illness or physical disability shall be accorded priority over all other claims, both in adjudication and payment. Full compensation for deprivation of liberty and for damage to life and limb shall in these cases be payable at once. Property damage and loss of opportunities to earn a livelihood insofar as they are compensated by capital payment shall be payable at once up to an amount of DM5,000 in each case. Insofar as payments are granted to such beneficiaries by way of annuities full payment shall begin at once.

17. The Government of the Federal Republic of Germany will see to it that, taking into account the principles contained in 15 above, funds shall be provided in such amounts, during the first financial years, that not only the claims referred to in 16 above can be satisfied but, in addition, claims of other beneficiaries can also be appropriately dealt with.

18. No distinction shall be made concerning the treatment of claimants living within and those living outside of the territory of the Federal Republic insofar as compensation is concerned.

19. Where evidence is required equitable consideration shall be given to the probative difficulties resulting from persecution. This shall apply particularly to the loss or destruction of files and documents and to the death or disappearance of witnesses. The compensation authorities shall ex officio make the investigations necessary to establish the relevant facts and seek appropriate evidence. The special conditions affecting the persecutees shall be taken into due consideration in interpreting the terms 'domicile' ['rechtmaessiger Wohnsitz'] or 'residence' ['gewoehnlicher Aufenthalt'].

20. A principle corresponding to the legal presumption of death contained in the restitution laws of the US and British Zones shall be inserted in the

Federal Supplementing and Coordinating Law. This presumption of death shall also be applied in the procedure before the Probate Courts dealing with the issuance of a certificate of inheritance [*Erbschein*], provided that the validity of the certificate of inheritance be restricted to the compensation procedure.

II. Restitution

1. The legislation now in force in the territory of the Federal Republic of Germany concerning restitution of identifiable property to victims of National Socialist persecution shall remain in force without any restrictions, unless otherwise provided in Chapter 3 of the 'Convention on the Settlement of Matters Arising out of the War and the Occupation'.

2. The Federal Government will see to it that the Federal Republic of Germany accepts liability also for the confiscation of household effects in transit [*Umzugsgut*] which were seized by the German Reich in European ports outside of the Federal Republic, insofar as the household effects belonged to persecutees who emigrated from the territory of the Federal Republic.

3. The Government of the Federal Republic of Germany will see to it that payments shall be ensured to restituees—private persons and successor organizations appointed pursuant to law—of all judgments or awards which have been or hereafter shall be given or made against the former German Reich under restitution legislation. The same shall apply to amicable settlements. Judgments or awards based on indebtedness in Reich Marks of the former Reich for a sum of money [*Geldsummenansprueche*] shall be converted into Deutsche Marks at the rate of RM10 for DM1. Judgments or awards for compensation for damage [*Schadenersatz*] shall be made in DM and assessed in accordance with the general principles of German Law applicable to the assessment of compensation for damage.

   In accordance with Article 4, paragraph 3 of Chapter 3 of the 'Convention on the Settlement of Matters Arising out of the War and the Occupation', the obligation of the Federal Republic of Germany shall be considered to have been satisfied when the judgments and awards shall have been paid or when the Federal Republic of Germany shall have paid a total of DM1,500 million. Payments on the basis of amicable settlements shall be included in this sum. The time and method of payment of such judgments and awards shall be determined in accordance with the Federal Republic's capacity to pay. The Government of the Federal Republic of Germany will, however, endeavour to complete these payments within a period of ten years. In settling the liabilities of the German Reich the claimants in the French Zone shall not be treated less favourably than those in other parts of the Federal territory.

4. Monetary restitution claims against the German Reich up to an amount of DM5,000 in each case, as well as claims of beneficiaries who are over sixty

years of age, or are needy or whose earning ability has been considerably impaired because of illness or physical disability shall be accorded priority over all other monetary restitution claims against the German Reich, both in adjudication and payment.

[...]

In witness whereof the Chancellor and Minister for Foreign Affairs of the Federal Republic of Germany, of the one part, and the representative of the Conference on Jewish Material Claims against Germany, duly authorized thereto, of the other part, have signed this Protocol. Done at Luxembourg this 10th day of September 1952, in the English and German languages, each in two copies, the texts in both languages being equally authentic.

For the Government of the Federal Republic of Germany
s/Adenauer

For the Conference on Jewish Material Claims against Germany
s/Goldmann

Protocol No. 2
Drawn up by Representatives of the Government of the Federal Republic of Germany and of the Conference on Jewish Material Claims against Germany

Consisting of the Following Organizations:

Agudath Israel World Organization
Alliance Israelite Universelle
American Jewish Committee
American Jewish Congress
American Jewish Joint Distribution Committee
American Zionist Council
Anglo-Jewish Association
B'Nai Brith
Board of Deputies of British Jews
British Section, World Jewish Congress
Canadian Jewish Congress
Central British Fund
Conseil Représentatif des Juifs de France
Council for the Protection of the Rights and Interests of Jews from Germany
Delegacion de Asociaciones Israelitas Argentinas (DAIA)

Executive Council of Australian Jewry
Jewish Agency for Palestine
Jewish Labor Committee
Jewish War Veterans of the USA
South African Jewish Board of Deputies
Synagogue Council of America
World Jewish Congress
Zentralrat der Juden in Deutschland

The Government of the Federal Republic of Germany, of the one part, and the Conference on Jewish Material Claims against Germany, of the other part,

Whereas
The National Socialist regime of terror confiscated vast amounts of property and other assets from Jews in Germany and in territories formerly under German rule;

and whereas
Part of the material losses suffered by the persecutees of National Socialism is being made good by means of internal German legislation in the fields of restitution and indemnification and whereas an extension of this internal German legislation, in particular in the field of indemnification, is intended;

and whereas
Considerable values, such as those spoliated in the occupied territories, cannot be returned, and that indemnification for many economic losses which have been suffered cannot be made because, as a result of the policy of extermination pursued by National Socialism, claimants are no longer in existence;

and whereas
A considerable number of Jewish persecutees of National Socialism are needy as a result of their persecution;

and having regard
To the statement made by the Federal Chancellor, Dr. Konrad Adenauer, in the Bundestag on September 27, 1951, and unanimously approved by that body;

and having regard
To the Agreement this day concluded between the State of Israel and the Federal Republic of Germany;

and having regard
To the fact that duly authorized representatives of the Government of the Federal Republic of Germany and of the Conference on Jewish Material Claims against Germany have met at The Hague.

Have therefore this day concluded the following Agreement:

Article 1

In view of the considerations hereinbefore recited the Government of the Federal Republic of Germany hereby undertakes the obligation towards the Conference on Jewish Material Claims against Germany to enter, in the Agreement with the State of Israel, into a contractual undertaking to pay the sum of DM450 million to the State of Israel for the benefit of the Conference on Jewish Material Claims against Germany.

Article 2

The Federal Republic of Germany will discharge their obligation undertaken for the benefit of the Conference on Jewish Material Claims against Germany, in the Agreement between the Federal Republic of Germany and the State of Israel, by payments made to the State of Israel in accordance with Article 3 paragraph (c) of the said Agreement. The amounts so paid and transmitted by the State of Israel to the Conference on Jewish Material Claims against Germany will be used for the relief, rehabilitation and resettlement of Jewish victims of National Socialist persecution, according to the urgency of their needs as determined by the Conference on Jewish Material Claims against Germany. Such amounts will, in principle, be used for the benefit of victims who at the time of the conclusion of the present Agreement were living outside of Israel.

Once a year the Conference on Jewish Material Claims against Germany will inform the Government of the Federal Republic of Germany of the amounts transmitted by Israel, of the amounts expended as well as of the manner in which such expenditure has been incurred. If, for any adequate reasons, the Conference on Jewish Material Claims against Germany has not spent the moneys it has received, it shall inform the Government of the Federal Republic of Germany of the said reason or reasons.

[...]

In witness thereof the Chancellor and Minister for Foreign Affairs of the Federal Republic of Germany, of the one part, and the representative of the Conference on Jewish Material Claims against Germany, duly authorized thereto, of the other part, have signed this Protocol.

Done at Luxembourg this tenth day of September, 1952, in the English and German languages, each in two copies, the text in both languages being equally authentic.

For the Government of the Federal Republic of Germany
s/Adenauer

For the Conference on Jewish Material Claims against Germany
s/Goldmann

FEDERAL LAW FOR THE COMPENSATION OF VICTIMS OF NATIONAL SOCIALIST PERSECUTION [BUNDESENTSCHAEDIGUNGSGESETZ – BEG] (FEDERAL COMPENSATION LAW) [EXCERPTS]*

FEDERAL COMPENSATION LAW THIRD LAW TO AMEND THE FEDERAL SUPPLEMENTARY LAW FOR THE COMPENSATION OF VICTIMS OF NATIONAL SOCIALIST PERSECUTION

Dated June 29, 1956

The Federal Diet by, and with the concurrence of, the Federal Council has enacted the following Law:

Article I

New Version of the Federal Supplementary Law for the Compensation of Victims of National Socialist Persecution

The Federal Supplementary Law for the Compensation of Victims of National Socialist Persecution (BEG) of September 18, 1953 (Federal Official Gazette, Part I, p. 1387), as amended by the Second Amending Law to the Federal Supplementary Law for the Compensation of Victims of National Socialist Persecution of August 10, 1955 (Federal Official Gazette, Part I, p. 506) will henceforth be titled 'Federal Law

---

* The ICTJ obtained a photocopy of the English translations of Germany's 1956 compensation law from the Conference on Jewish Material Claims against Germany, which stated that the translation was by the Institute of Jewish Affairs. The Institute of Jewish Affairs was a research agency of the World Jewish Congress, and as such collected legal and claimant materials on the indemnification policies around the world. The Institute also worked closely with the United Restitution Organization and the Claims Conference. The Institute of Jewish Affairs became the Institute for Jewish Policy Research based in London. The ICTJ received permission from the Institute for Jewish Policy Research to use its translation in this publication.

for the Compensation of Victims of National Socialist Persecution (Federal Compensation Law—BEG)' and will have the wording as contained in the Appendix hereto.

[...]

Article V

Effective Date

The Amending Law shall come into effect on April 1, 1956.

The Federal Government has granted to the foregoing Law its consent as required by Article 113 of the Basic Law.

The foregoing Law is hereby promulgated.

Bonn, June 29, 1956.

The Federal President	Theodor Heuss
The Federal Chancellor	Adenauer
The Federal Minister of Finance	Schaeffer
The Federal Minister of Justice	Neumayer

In Recognition of the Fact

that wrongs have been committed against persons who under the oppressive National Socialist regime, were persecuted because of their political opposition to National Socialism or because of their race, religion or ideology,

that the resistance to the oppressive National Socialist regime based on conviction, faith or conscience was a service to the welfare of the German people and state and,

that democratic, religious and economic organizations, too, have suffered damages by the oppressive National Socialist regime in contravention of the law,

the Bundestag with the consent of the Bundesrat has enacted the following Law:

Part One

General Provisions

First Chapter

Claim to Compensation

§1

(1) A victim of National Socialist persecution (persecutee) is a person who, because of political opposition to National Socialism, or because of race, religion or

ideology, was persecuted by National Socialist oppressive measures and, in consequence thereof, has suffered loss of life, damage to limb or health, liberty, property, possessions, or vocational or economic pursuits.

(2) Treated equally with persecutees within the meaning of sub-§ (1) are persons who were persecuted by National Socialist oppressive measures because,

1. at the dictates of their conscience, they had, at personal risk, actively opposed the disregard of human dignity or the destruction of human lives not morally justified even by the War;
2. they adhered to artistic or scientific creeds or tenets rejected by National Socialism;
3. they were closely connected with a persecutee.

(3) 'Persecutee' within the meaning of sub-§ (1) is also to embrace

1. the survivor of a persecutee who was deliberately killed or negligently killed, or was impelled to his death, or who died in consequence of damage to his limb or health;
2. a damagee who while committing an offense, in combating the National Socialist oppressive regime, or in warding off persecution, was able to conceal the motive for the offense;
3. a damagee affected by National Socialist oppressive measures because he was mistakenly regarded as belonging to a group of persons persecuted for the reasons specified in sub-§ (1) or (2).

§2

(1) National Socialist oppressive measures are measures directed against the persecutee for reasons of persecution specified in §1 by, at the behest of, or with the approval of, an agency or official of the Reich, a Land, or any other public law, body, institution or foundation, or the National Socialist German Workers Party (NSDAP), its divisions or affiliated associations.

(2) National Socialist oppressive measures are to be regarded as such even though they were based on provisions of law, or were directed against the persecutee by the misapplication of such provisions.

§3

The persecutee shall have a claim for compensation under this Law.

§4

(1) The right to claim compensation exists

1. if the persecutee
    a) had his domicile or the place of his permanent sojourn within the area of operation of this Law on December 31, 1952;
    b) died prior to December 31, 1952 and had his last domicile or permanent sojourn within the area of operation of this Law;

c) emigrated, was deported, or expelled prior to December 31, 1952, and had his last domicile or the place of his permanent sojourn in territories which, on December 31, 1937, belonged to the German Reich, unless at the time of the decision (in his case) his domicile or the place of his permanent sojourn is in countries with whose governments the Federal Republic of Germany does not maintain diplomatic relations;

d) as repatriate within the meaning of the Law of Assistance to Repatriates (Repatriates' Law), has taken or is taking up his domicile or the place of permanent sojourn within the area of operation of this Law;

e) is an expellee within the meaning of §1 of the Law governing the affairs of expellees and refugees (Federal Expellees' Law) and has taken or is taking up his domicile or place of permanent sojourn within the area of operation of this Law;

f) has been recognized as a refugee from the Soviet Zone within the meaning of §3 of the Federal Expellees' Law or considered as if he were a refugee from the Soviet Zone by the Decree of August 25, 1953, governing the refugee status of Germans forced out from the Saar Region (Federal Official Gazette I, p. 1074), and has taken or is taking up his domicile or place of permanent sojourn within the area of operation of this Law.

2. if the persecutee, on January 1, 1947, was in a Displaced Persons camp within the area of operation of this Law and either emigrated from the area of operation of this Law, or as a homeless alien became subject to the jurisdiction of the German authorities after December 31, 1946, or acquired German nationality.

(2) An expelled persecutee (sub-§ (1) Number 1(e)) shall have a claim to compensation even though his belonging to the German 'nation' is based on his having belonged to the German linguistic or cultural group; an explicit declaration of belonging to the German 'nation' shall not be deemed necessary for the claim to membership in a German linguistic or cultural group.

(3) The forced stay, due to deprivation of liberty, at a specific place and sojourn in a DP camp shall not be deemed to constitute a domicile or a permanent sojourn within the meaning of sub-§ (1).

(4) Where the Federal Republic of Germany does not maintain diplomatic relations with certain countries, the Federal Government may designate which of these countries shall be treated as if such diplomatic relations were being maintained.

(5) A claim for damages to real estate may be made regardless of the persecutee's domicile or permanent sojourn if the real estate is located within the area of operation of this Law.

§5

(1) A claim to compensation may be made to the extent that the claim for indemnification of damages, according to its legal nature, falls under special legislation for the indemnification of damages caused by National Socialist wrongs in force in the area of operation of this Law. Legislation within the meaning of this sentence includes in particular:

the legal provisions for the restitution of identifiable property and for the settlement of the restitutory monetary obligations of the German Reich or 'assimilated' legal entities,

the legal provisions for the assignment of the assets or organizations,

the legal provisions regulating the redress of National Socialist wrongs for public servants,

the legal provisions for the redress of National Socialist wrongs in the field of social insurance and the care of war victims.

(2) A claim to compensation may not be made if the claim for indemnification of the damages does not come under the special legislation within the meaning of sub-§ (1) solely because of the territorial limitations of its validity, or because the persecutee can no longer assert his claim under the special legislation within the meaning of sub-§ (1), owing to his failure to observe the time limits specified in such legislation.

(3) If an authority, or a court competent for the claims specified in sub-§ (1) has made a non-appellable determination that, in view of the legal nature of the claim, any special legislation referred to in sub-§ (1) is or is not applicable, the compensation agencies and the compensation courts shall be bound by such determination.

§6

(1) A person shall be disqualified from claiming compensation if
  1. he was a member of the NSDAP or of one of its divisions, or aided and abetted the National Socialist oppressive regime; nominal membership in the NSDAP or of one of its divisions does not serve as a disqualification for a claim to compensation, if the persecutee, at the risk of his liberty, life or limb, combatted National Socialism for reasons corresponding to the reasons of persecution specified in §1 of this Law and was persecuted in consequence thereof;
  2. after May 23, 1949, he fought against the free democratic basic order in the meaning of the Basic Law;
  3. after May 8, 1945, he has been deprived by non-appellable judgment of his civil rights;
  4. after May 8, 1945, he has been sentenced by a non-appellable judgment to penal servitude for a term exceeding three years.

(2) Sub-§ (1) numbers 3 and 4 shall not apply if the sentence was pronounced outside the area of operation of this Law, and if the action is not punishable within

this area, or the deprivation of civil rights or sentence to penal servitude for a term exceeding three years does not accord with the principles of states which are considered to be devoted to the Rule of Law.

(3) The claim to indemnification shall be forfeited if, after having been fixed or having been made on a non-appellable judicial decision, one of the grounds of disqualification specified in sub-§ (1) (2–4) should arise. The refund of any payments can be demanded if it is established that there is such a ground for forfeiture.

§7

(1) The claim to compensation may be denied, in full or in part, if in order to obtain compensation, the eligible person has used unfair means, or deliberately or through gross negligence made, caused, or permitted to be made wrong or misleading statements about the basis or the amount of the damage.

(2) The claim to compensation may be vitiated, in full or in part, if after it was fixed it is discovered that there is a ground for denying it pursuant to sub-§ (1) or that the decision was based on incorrect statements of the eligible person regarding the facts in case.

(3) The refund of payments already made may be demanded.

§8

(1) Without prejudice to the legislation referred to in §5 and to the provisions remaining effective pursuant to §228(2), claims against the German Reich, the Federal Republic of Germany and the German Laender may be asserted only in accordance with this Law if they are based on damages arising from measures deemed persecutory as specified in §1 or for the reason specified in §167(1).

(2) Claims against other bodies, institutions or foundations of public law or persons of private law shall not be affected by this Law. To the extent that compensation is paid under this Law, they shall devolve upon the Land which made the payments. The devolution cannot work to the disadvantage of the eligible persons.

§9

(1) The civil law rules governing the consideration of contributory guilt and the set-off of any benefits gained in connection with the damages shall apply *mutatis mutandis*.

(2) The persecutee's consent to the measure which had caused the damages given in connection with the persecution shall not vitiate the claim to compensation.

(3) If damages had arisen as a result of the persecutee's action or omission under pressure of the persecution, such action or omission shall not vitiate the claim to compensation.

(4) Payments which were or are being made by a third party to the persecutee in fulfilment of a legal or moral obligation of support shall not vitiate the claim to compensation even though the damages suffered have been compensated by such payments.

(5) No compensation shall be paid for damages which would have arisen even if no persecution had taken place.

§10

(1) Payments made out of German public funds in the process of compensating victims of National Socialist persecution shall be set off against the compensation under this Law. Payments which were or are being made with respect to a specific period or a specific category of damages shall be set off only against the compensation due for that period or for that category of damages. Public assistance grants are not to be set off.

[...]

(3) In the event an eligible person is entitled to several claims which are being satisfied at different times, no set-off shall be made of payments necessary to meet current living expenses or to build up an adequate subsistence basis to the extent that the set-off against later payments is safeguarded.

[...]

§12

No annuities shall be paid before November 1, 1953. They shall be paid monthly and at the beginning of the month.

Second Chapter

Succession to and Cession of the Claim to Compensation

§13

(1) The claim to compensation is inheritable.

(2) The claim lapses upon the death of the persecutee if the Treasury is the statutory heir. It shall likewise lapse if the persecutee had died before the claim was decided upon or a non-appellable court judgment in respect of the claim has been made and his estate devolves in its entirety to a person disqualified from compensation under §6 hereof. The claim shall not lapse insofar as the persecutee has willed it to a person who would not be disqualified from compensation. The bequest shall be invalid if the legatee would be a disqualified person.

(3) If the persecutee's estate devolves upon several heirs and only some of these heirs are disqualified, the remaining heirs shall be entitled to the claim to compensation as an 'advance'. The provisions governing bequests shall apply to such advances.

§14

The claim to indemnification may be ceded, pledged or attached. A cession, pledging or attachment of the claim shall be permitted only with the consent of the compensation agency.

Part Two

Categories of Damages

First Chapter

Loss of Life

§15

(1) A claim to compensation for loss of life exists if the persecutee has been deliberately or carelessly killed or driven to death. It suffices if the nexus between death and persecution is probable.

(2) If the persecutee died during deportation or during deprivation of liberty within the meaning of this Law or immediately thereafter, it shall be presumed that he was deliberately or carelessly killed or driven to death by National Socialist oppressive measures.

§16

Compensation is payable in the form of
1. an annuity,
2. a lump sum, in case of remarriage,
3. a capital indemnity.

§17

(1) The following survivors shall be entitled to an annuity:
1. the widow until remarriage or death;
2. the widower until remarriage or death provided the persecutee was maintaining him at the beginning of the persecution leading to her death or would maintain him if she were still alive;
3. the children for as long as children's allowances may be granted for them under civil service legislation; after completion of its sixteenth year even if the child should have a monthly income of its own as defined in the Federal Salaries Law exceeding DM75;
4. the fully orphaned grandchildren subject to the conditions set forth in number 3, provided the persecutee was maintaining them at the beginning of the persecution leading to his (or her) death or would maintain them if he (or she) were still alive;
5. the relatives in the ascending line for the period of indigence, provided the persecutee was maintaining them at the beginning of the persecution leading to his (or her) death or would maintain them if he (or she) were still alive;
6. the adoptive parents subject to the conditions set forth in number 5.

(2) Subject to the conditions set forth in sub-§ (1) numbers 1 and 2, the following shall be assimilated to the widow or widower:
1. the innocently divorced spouse;

2. the former spouse, assimilated to an innocently divorced spouse whose marriage has been annulled or declared void;

3. persons to whose relationship with the persecutee the Federal Law on the Recognition of Free Marriages of Racial or Political Persecutees or legislation of the Laender has accorded the legal effects of a lawful marriage;

4. the wife whose marriage to the persecutee has been subsequently solemnized by an order under the Federal Law on the Legal Effects of the Pronouncement of a Post-Dated Marriage.

(3) Sub-§ (2) numbers 1 and 2 shall not be applicable to a spouse who has turned away from the persecuted spouse for reasons corresponding to the reasons of persecution specified in §1.

§18

(1) The annuity is to be computed on the basis of the maintenance payments that would be granted to survivors of a federal civil servant who had died by an accident while on duty, and whose salary group with progressive salary increments, is comparable to the economic position of the persecutee, under the legislation covering accident maintenance of federal civil servants. The economic position shall be determined on the basis of the persecutee's average income during the last three years preceding his (or her) death; any reduction of the income as a result of preceding persecution shall be disregarded. In addition to the persecutee's economic position his social position shall be considered, only if such consideration would lead to the persecutee being classified as a member of a higher comparable civil servants' group.

(2) The annuity shall be computed at less than 100 per cent of the maintenance payments according to sub-§ (1) if the economic position of the survivor justifies such a reduction. In considering his or her economic position, account shall also be taken of amounts which the survivor could have been expected to earn but has not done so.

(3) The computation of the annuity shall be based on the amount of the maintenance payments of comparable civil servants' groups within the meaning of sub-§ (1), as fixed by law for the respective period.

§19

The monthly minimum amount of the annuity shall be for:

the widow	DM200
the widower	DM200
the orphan who has lost both parents	DM100
the first and second orphan who has lost one parent,	
if no annuity is paid to the widow or widower	DM75 each

if an annuity is paid to the widow or widower	DM55 each
the third and each further orphan who lost one parent	DM50 each
the grandchild who has lost both parents	DM100 each
the parents or adopting parents together	DM150 each
a surviving parent or adopting parent	DM100 each

§20

(1) The sum total of the annuities according to §18 must not exceed the accident pension payable to a comparable federal civil servant. Should the sum total of the annuities due to several survivors exceed such accident pension, the several annuities shall be reduced proportionately. §19 shall remain unaffected.

(2) If, on account of the provision of sub-§ (1), third sentence, the annuity of any survivor is not reduced, the annuity of another survivor may not be reduced by an amount larger than the one resulting from sub-§ (1), second sentence.

(3) Should any particular survivor qualify for several annuities under §17, then, if the annuities are equal, only one annuity shall be paid and, if they are of varying amounts it shall be the highest annuity.

§21

If the circumstances, which formed the basis for the computation of the annuity, should subsequently have changed to such extent that the annuity, newly computed on the basis of the changed circumstances, should differ by at least 10 per cent from the annuity previously fixed, the annuity shall be re-computed.

§22

The annuity shall remain in abeyance to the extent and as long as the survivor shall, because of the persecutee's death, derive from German public funds maintenance and allowances or other recurrent benefits of a monthly amount in excess of DM200. This provision shall not apply if the maintenance allowances or other recurrent benefits are due exclusively to the persecutee's own monetary contributions.

§23

On remarriage the widow or widower shall receive a lump sum payment amounting to twenty-four times the annuity paid for the last calendar month preceding the remarriage. Should the new marriage be dissolved or be declared void, the annuity shall revive and go into effect from the first day of the month following the month during which the marriage was dissolved or declared void, at the earliest, however, after the expiration of two years from the remarriage. Benefits to which the widow or widower shall be entitled by virtue of a new claim to maintenance or support acquired as a result of the marriage being dissolved or declared void, shall be set off against the annuity.

§24

The survivor (§17) is to receive a capital indemnity for the period between the persecutee's death and November 1, 1953.

§25

(1) The computation of the capital indemnity shall be based on the amount of the annuity computed in accordance with §§ 18 to 20, which is due for the month of November 1953. §22 shall apply *mutatis mutandis*.

(2) If no claim to an annuity existed as of November 1953, sub-§ (1) shall apply with the proviso that the computation of the capital indemnity shall be based on the amount due as of the last calendar month for which the prerequisites for the claim to an annuity existed.

(3) For the period prior to currency conversion the monthly amount on which the computation according to sub-§§ (1) and (2) is to be based shall equal two-tenths of the monthly amount calculated in Deutsche Mark.

§26

(1) The claim to the current annuity is neither cessable nor inheritable; this shall likewise apply to the claim of the widow or widower, on remarriage, to the lump sum payment.

(2) The claim to the annuity amounts in arrears and to the capital indemnity is inheritable before it was determined, or a non-appellable court judgment was reached, only if the survivor's heirs are his spouse, children, grandchildren or parents.

§27

(1) The Federal Government is authorized to issue regulations in implementation of §§ 15 to 26. In this connection it may, as a basis for the computation of the annuities and capital indemnities, draw up a salary table showing the average pensionable salaries (basic salary and housing allowance) of the federal civil servants in the lower, middle, higher and upper service grades. On the basis of that table the persecutee shall be classified as belonging to a comparable civil servants' group. Flat rates may be fixed for the determination of the percentage of the civil service pension payable as an annuity under the provisions of this Law.

(2) The Federal Government is further authorized to increase equitably, by regulation, the monthly minimum amounts of the annuities (§19), in the event salaries and allowances of the federal civil servants are increased by law.

Second Chapter

Damage to Limb or Health

§28

(1) A persecutee shall have a claim to compensation if he has suffered damage to limb or health that is more than insignificant. It shall suffice if there is a probable nexus between the damage to limb or to health and the persecution.

(2) §15(2) applies *mutatis mutandis.*

(3) The damage shall be deemed insignificant if it does not entail, nor will probably entail, a lasting impairment of the persecutee's mental or physical faculties.

§29

Compensation shall be furnished as:

1. medical treatment;
2. annuity;
3. capital indemnity;
4. out-of-hospital allowance;
5. retraining assistance;
6. maintenance of the survivors.

§30

(1) The extent and the implementation of the claim to medical treatment are governed by the rules covering the post-accident maintenance of federal civil servants.

(2) The claim shall not be barred because the medical treatment has taken place prior to the entry into force of this Law.

§31

(1) The persecutee shall be entitled to an annuity in the event that his earning capacity has been reduced by at least 25 per cent and the annuity shall continue for the duration of such impairment.

(2) The annuity shall be computed at a percentage of the service income (basic salary and housing allowance) of a federal civil servant in a salary group, with progressively rising pay, whose economic position is comparable to that of the persecutee. The economic position shall be established in accordance with the persecutee's average income during the three years preceding the start of the persecution directed against him; a reduction of his income during those years as a result of earlier persecution shall be disregarded. In addition to the persecutee's economic position his social position shall be considered, if such consideration could lead to the persecutee's classification in a higher comparable civil servants' group.

(3) In fixing the percentage appropriate consideration shall be paid to the current personal and economic position of the persecutee and, in particular, to his permanent income, inclusive of maintenance payments, benefits under the Law for the Maintenance of War Victims (Federal Maintenance Law), payments from the obligatory annuities insurance, and income which he could have been expected to earn but has not done so, as well as of the extent of the decrease of his earning capacity, and of the obligations imposed upon him by the care for members of his family entitled to support.

(4) The computation of the annuity shall be based on the amount of the salary of the comparable civil servants' groups within the meaning of sub-§ (2) for the respective period.

(5) The annuity shall amount, in the case of an impairment of the earning capacity of the salary which the persecutee would have been entitled to if he were classified as belonging to a comparable civil servants' group, according to his age on May 1, 1949.

By from	25 to 39 per cent	to at least	15	but not more than	40 per cent
"	40 to 49	"	20	"	45
"	50 to 59	"	25	"	50
"	60 to 69	"	30	"	55
"	70 to 79	"	35	"	60
by 80 and more per cent,		"	40	"	70

§32

(1) The monthly minimum amount of the annuities shall be in the case of a decrease of the persecutee's earning capacity

by	from	25	to	39	per cent	DM100
"	"	40	"	49	"	" 125
"	"	50	"	59	"	" 150
"	"	60	"	69	"	" 175
"	"	70	"	79	"	" 200
by 80 and more per cent						" 250

(2) The monthly minimum amount of the annuity shall be DM250 for any persecutee whose earning capacity has been decreased by at least 50 per cent and who, in the case of a male, is sixty-five years of age or older and in the case of a female, is sixty years of age or older. The first sentence of this sub-paragraph shall apply only to male persecutees born before January 1, 1900, and female persecutees born before January 1, 1905. The claim to the monthly minimum amount of DM250 shall not be dependent on the decrease of the earning capacity by 50 per cent being exclusively due to persecution.

§33

The extent of the decrease in, and the impairment of, the earning capacity shall be judged by the extent to which the persecutee is mentally and physically capable of satisfying the requirements of general economic life. Account shall be taken of the vocation which the persecutee followed before the start of the persecution or of the vocational training which he had already started, or to which he can prove to have aspired, prior to that date.

§34

If, in addition to the impairment by damage due to the persecution, the persecutee's earning capacity should have been decreased from other causes, only the impairment of the earning capacity resulting from the damage due to persecution shall constitute the basis for fixing the amount of the annuity. §33, second sentence, shall apply *mutatis mutandis.*

§35

If the circumstances which formed the basis for the computation of the annuity, should subsequently have changed to such extent that the annuity newly computed on the basis of the changed circumstances, should differ by at least 10 per cent from the annuity previously fixed, the annuity shall be recomputed. §32(2) shall remain unaffected.

§36

The persecutee shall be entitled to a capital indemnity for the period between the start of the impairment of his earning capacity of at least 23 per cent and November 1, 1953.

§37

(1) The computation of the capital indemnity shall be based on the amount of the annuity computed in accordance with §§ 31 to 34, which is due for the month of November 1953.

(2) If no claim to an annuity existed for the month of November 1953, sub-§ (1) shall apply with the proviso that the computation of the capital indemnity shall be based on the amount due as of the last calendar month for which the prerequisites for the claim to an annuity existed.

(3) For the period prior to currency conversion the monthly amount on which the computation according to sub-§§ (1) and (2) is to be based shall equal two-tenths of the monthly amount calculated in Deutsche Mark.

(4) §32(2) shall not apply.

§38

The persecutee shall be entitled to an out-of-hospital allowance if, as a result of medical treatment, he suffers a loss of earnings, and his remaining income amounts to less than the annuity which would be payable to him had his earning capacity been impaired by 80 or more per cent; the calculation for this purpose is to be based on 55 per cent of the service income to which the persecutee would be entitled if he were classified as belonging to a comparable civil servants' group according to his age on May 1, 1949 (§31(5)). The out-of-hospital allowance is based on the difference between the remaining income and the annuity derived in accordance with the first sentence of this paragraph, but shall not exceed the amount of the loss in earnings.

§39

(1) The claim to the recurrent annuity is neither cessable nor inheritable.

(2) The claim to the annuity amounts in arrears, to the capital indemnity, and to the out-of-hospital allowance, is inheritable before it was determined or a non-appellable court judgment was reached only if the persecutee's heirs are his spouse, children, grandchildren or parents.

§40

A persecutee who is prepared to train himself for another vocation may be granted allowances toward the costs to be incurred, provided that there is a reasonable probability that the retraining would restore or improve his capacities.

§41

If the persecutee died as a result of the damage to limb or to health, his survivors shall be paid compensation in accordance with §§ 15 to 26.

§42

(1) The Federal Government is authorized to issue regulations to implement §§ 28 to 41. In this connection, it may, as a basis for the computation of the annuities and capital indemnities, draw up a salary table showing the average salary (basic salary and housing allowance) of the federal civil servants in the lower, middle, higher and upper service grades sub-divided into age groups. On the basis of that table the persecutee shall be classified as belonging to a comparable civil servants' group.

(2) The Federal Government. is further authorized to increase equitably, by regulation, the monthly minimum amounts of the annuities (§32(1)), in the event that salaries and pension allowances of the federal civil servants are increased by law.

Third Chapter

Damage to Liberty

I. *Deprivation of Liberty*

§43

(1) A persecutee shall have a claim to compensation if, at any time between January 30, 1933 and May 8, 1945, he has been deprived of his liberty. This shall also apply if, in flagrant disregard of the principles of a state governed by the rule of law, he was deprived of his liberty by a foreign state and

1. the deprivation of liberty was made possible by the fact that the persecutee had lost the German nationality or the protection of the German Reich; or
2. the government of the foreign state was induced by the National Socialist German Government to effect the deprivation of liberty.

(2) Deprivation of liberty includes, in particular, police or military detention, arrest by the NSDAP, custodial and penal imprisonment, detention in a concentration camp and forced stay in a ghetto.

(3) A persecutee is also considered to have been deprived of liberty if he lived or did forced labor under conditions similar to those of detention, or did service in a penal or reform unit of the German Armed Forces.

§44

(1) If the deprivation of liberty has taken place in connection with a penal sentence, compensation may, in cases of doubt, be made conditional upon the conviction having been annulled or modified at a retrial on the basis of the rules governing the redress of National Socialist wrongs committed in the administration of criminal justice. For the purposes of this Law, a petition under such rules may be filed up to October 1, 1958.

(2) The annulment or modification of a penal sentence shall be proved by producing the decision of the court which has annulled or modified the sentence. In the case of a rescission or modification by virtue of statutory provisions, a certificate of the courts or authorities which are competent under the provisions of sub-§(1) shall be produced.

§45

The compensation under §43 shall be payable in the form of a capital indemnity. It shall be DM150 for each full month of the deprivation of liberty. It shall be computed on the basis of the whole calendar months during which the persecutee was deprived of his liberty, plus the sum of thirty days of the months during which he was intermittently deprived of his liberty. The several periods of deprivation of liberty shall be added together.

§46

(1) The claim to compensation for deprivation of liberty cannot be ceded before it was determined or a non-appellable court judgment was reached.

(2) The claim is inheritable before it was determined or a non-appellable court judgment was reached only if the persecutee's heirs are his spouse, children, grandchildren or parents.

(3) Compensation sums, in case of devolution by law of inheritance to the persecutee's spouse, children, grandchildren or parents shall be exempt from inheritance tax.

II.   Restrictions on Liberty

§47

The persecutee shall have a claim to compensation if, at any time between January 30, 1933 and May 8, 1945, he had worn the Star of David or had lived 'underground' under conditions unfit for a human being.

§48

The compensation under §47 shall be paid in the form of a capital indemnity. It shall be DM150 for every full month of the restriction on liberty. §45, third sentence, shall apply *mutatis mutandis*.

§49

If a persecutee has claim to compensation for deprivation of liberty under §43 with respect to any period in which he wore the Star of David or lived 'underground' under conditions unfit for a human being, he shall have no claim with respect to such period to compensation based on restrictions on liberty.

§50

The claim to compensation for restrictions on liberty is cessable and inheritable in accordance with §46. §46 sub-§ (3) shall apply *mutatis mutandis* to exemption from inheritance tax.

Fourth Chapter

Damage to Property

§51

(1) A persecutee shall have a claim to compensation for damage to property if any tangible object which belonged to him at the time of the damage was destroyed, defaced or left to be looted within the territory of the German Reich as of December 31, 1937.

(2) The phrase 'left to be looted' shall be applicable particularly if

1. tangible objects which belonged to the persecutee were appropriated by, or distributed among, a mob that had exercised or usurped powers of public authority;

2. the persecutee was deprived of his liberty in such circumstances that his tangible objects were left without supervision by anyone safeguarding his interests.

(3) The persecutee shall likewise have a claim to compensation if he had to abandon tangible objects belonging to him because he emigrated, fled or lived in illegality, to evade National Socialist oppressive acts, or because he was expelled or deported for reasons of persecution specified in §1.

(4) If the persecutee belonged to a group of persons whom the National Socialist German Government or the NSDAP intended to exclude in its entirety from the cultural or economic life of Germany, it shall be presumed that the damage to his property was caused by National Socialist oppressive measures.

§52

(1) The compensation under §51 shall be computed in Deutsche Mark.

(2) The amount of compensation for the objects destroyed or lost shall be computed at their replacement costs in the area where this heir operates. The determining factor shall be the replacement costs at the tide of decision with due regard to the value of the object at the time of the damage.

(3) Where compensation is due on the basis of defacement of an object, the amount of compensation shall be computed at the costs which, in the area of this Law's operation, would have to be incurred to restore it to its previous state at the time of decision. The same shall apply in cases of destruction of an object, if its restoration is possible.

§53

If a successor organization established under the restitution legislation has a claim to restitution, under the legislation relating to the restitution of identifiable property or to transfer on the basis of the rules governing the transfer of the assets of organizations, of a tangible object, such a successor organization shall, with respect to such objects, also have a claim to compensation in accordance with §51. Should the persecutee or his heirs file the same claim before the claim under §51 has been determined or a non-appellable court judgment has been reached with respect to this claim, the claim of the successor organization to compensation shall, at the time of its assertion, pass to the persecutee or his heirs.

§54

(1) If the persecutee had lost household goods through destruction, defacement, by leaving them to be looted, or because he had to abandon them, he may, before the claim under §51 was determined or a non-appellable court judgment with respect to such claim was reached, demand lump sum compensation in lieu of compensation under §51. Such lump sum payment shall amount, converted into Deutsche Mark at the ratio of 1:1, to one and a half times the persecutee's net income in 1932, but shall not exceed DM5,000.

(2) If a persecuted married couple has lost household goods, they shall be entitled to jointly claim the lump sum, regardless of which individual was the owner of the household goods. If one spouse has died, the surviving spouse shall be entitled to claim the lump sum payment. If, at the time of decision, husband and wife were living apart or were divorced, each of the spouses is entitled to half of the lump sum.

§55

(1) Compensation under §§ 51 through 54 shall not, for any single persecutee, exceed the amount of DM75,000. This rule shall also apply if the persecutee is entitled to compensation claims, partly on an individual basis or partly as a member of a group owning property, either in specific or undivided shares and which is neither an unincorporated association nor a company without legal personality under civil or commercial law.

(2) If claims to compensation are submitted by the successor organizations referred to in §53, the maximum amount specified in sub-§ (1) shall apply to the compensation to which such an organization is entitled instead of an individual persecutee.

Fifth Chapter

Damage to Possessions

§56

(1) A persecutee shall have a claim to compensation if he has suffered damage to his possessions which were located in the territory of the German Reich as of December 31, 1937. Impairment of the persecutee's use of his property or possessions shall also be deemed to be damage to possessions. A claim may also be asserted if the damages were caused by boycott. No compensation is payable for losses totaling less than RM500.

(2) If the persecutee in addition to suffering impairment of the use of his property or possessions also suffered damage to their substance, the impairment in the use shall be indemnified by adding 5 per cent thereof to the compensation payable for the damage to the substance of his property or possessions.

(3) The persecutee shall also have a claim to compensation if emigration or preparation thereto has led to a loss occasioned by transfer. This applies on condition that the persecutee was forced to emigrate for the persecutory reasons specified in §1 and that, for the amount transferred, he has received less than 80 per cent of the sum which he could have received had he been able to transfer free Reichsmark at the official rate of exchange valid at the time. The compensation shall be computed by converting the Reichsmark amount for which the persecutee has received no equivalent into Deutsche Mark at the ratio of 10:2. No compensation shall be paid for loss of income derived from the use of property.

(4) If the persecutee belongs to a group of persons whom the National Socialist German Government or the NSDAP intended to exclude in its entirety from the cultural or economic life of Germany, it shall be presumed that the damage to possession was caused by National Socialist oppressive measures.

§57

(1) A persecutee who, between January 30, 1933 and May 8, 1945, emigrated or was expelled from the territory of the German Reich as of December 31, 1937 for the persecutory reasons specified in §1 shall have a claim to a refund of the necessary expenditures entailed by the emigration or expulsion; the same shall apply to the necessary expenditures entailed by his return.

(2) If such expenditures were incurred in foreign currency, the compensation shall be computed on the basis of the rate of exchange of this currency at the time of decision.

(3) The compensation under sub-§§ (1) and (2) is not to exceed DM5,000 for any individual persecutee.

§58

The total indemnification under §§ 56 through 57 is not to exceed DM75,000 for any individual persecutee. §55 shall generally apply *mutatis mutandis*.

Sixth Chapter

Losses Incurred through Payment of Discriminatory Levies, Fines, Penalties and Costs

§59

(1) A persecutee shall have a claim to compensation if he paid discriminatory levies imposed upon him for the persecutory reasons specified in §1. No compensation shall be paid for losses of income derived from the use of property.

(2) The term 'discriminatory levies' shall include:
1. losses which the persecutee had suffered through a forced 'contract of admission to an old age home';
2. payments made to the German Golddiskontbank to obtain an export license;
3. payments of the Reich Flight Tax;
4. payment of surcharges for overdue payments, interest for default, bank charges and execution costs incurred in connection with the payment of discriminatory levies.

Payments to the German Golddiskontbank and of the Reich Flight Tax shall be regarded as discriminatory levies only if the persecutee was forced to emigrate for the persecutory reasons specified in §1.

§60

(1) The persecutee shall have a claim under §59 even if the discriminatory levy, in full or in part, was paid in property which as such is subject to restitution. Restitutory claims to which the persecutee is entitled shall, up to the amount of compensation payable under §59 in accordance with the value at which the respective alienated property was accepted, pass to the Land paying the compensation. The renunciation by the persecutee of the restitutory claim shall not affect the rights of the Land paying the compensation. If the persecutee had received any benefits by way of restitution, the value of these benefits shall be set off against the compensation. Advance payments and loans made or granted subject to their being set off against the future settlement of the restitutory monetary obligations of the German Reich and assimilated legal entities shall likewise be set off.

(2) If the persecutee had paid the discriminatory levy, in full or in part, with the proceeds of an item of property subject to restitution and, under the rules relating to the restitution of identifiable property, he is obliged to repay the purchase price or to cede the restitutory claim for the purchase price which he did not receive or of which he could not dispose freely, the claim under §59 shall to that extent be converted into Deutsche Mark at the ratio of 10:1. No claims under §59 exist, if the persecutee regained or regains the item of property subject to restitution, but neither repays the purchase price nor cedes the restitutory claim in respect of the purchase price not received or of which he could not dispose freely.

§61

(1) A persecutee shall have a claim to compensation for any fines and monetary penalties paid by him to the extent that they were imposed upon him for perse-cutory reasons specified in §1. The claim exists only if the fine or monetary penalty was paid or collected in the territory of the Reich as of December 31, 1937. If the persecutee is an expellee within the meaning of §1 of the Federal Expellee's Law, he shall have a claim also if the fine or monetary penalty was paid or collected in the expulsion area. §44 shall apply *mutatis mutandis*.

(2) §60 shall apply *mutatis mutandis*.

§62

Persecutees shall have a claim to compensation for court and necessary out-of-court costs if they derived from judicial or disciplinary criminal proceedings instituted against him for the persecutory reasons specified in §1. The claim exists only if the proceedings took place in the territory of the German Reich as of January 31, 1937. If the persecutee is an expellee within the meaning of §1 of the Federal Expellee's Law, he shall also have a claim if the proceedings took place in the expulsion area. §44 shall apply *mutatis mutandis*.

§63

If the persecutee belongs to a group of persons whom the National Socialist German Government or the NSDAP intended to exclude in its entirety from the cultural or economic life of Germany, it shall be presumed that the damages caused by the payment of discriminatory levies, fines, monetary penalties and costs were caused by National Socialist oppressive measures.

Seventh Chapter

Damage to Vocational and Economic Pursuits

I.   *Principle*

§64

(1) A persecutee shall have a claim to compensation for damage to his vocational and economic pursuits if, in the process of persecution begun in the territory of the German Reich as of December 31, 1937, he suffered damages to a more than insignificant extent in his vocational or economic pursuits. If the persecutee is an expellee within the meaning of §1 of the Federal Expellee's Law, he shall also have a claim if the persecution started in the expulsion area.

(2) If the persecutee belongs to a group of persons whom the National Socialist German Government or the NSDAP intended to exclude in its entirety from the cultural or economic life of Germany, it shall be presumed that the damage to the vocational and economic pursuits was caused by National Socialist oppressive measures.

II.   *Damage to Vocational Pursuits*

1.   *Definition*

§65

Damage to vocational pursuits exists if the persecutee suffered damage in his use of his working power.

2.   *Self-Employed Occupations*

§66

(1) A persecutee shall have a claim to compensation if he has been excluded from, or substantially restricted in, the exercise of an occupation on his own account (independent), including occupations in agriculture, forestry, or commercial and industrial activity.

(2) The conduct of business in a commercial law stock company by an active partner who owned 50 per cent or more of the capital of that company shall be deemed tantamount to an independent occupation.

(3) A restriction in an independent occupation shall, as a rule, be deemed to have been substantial if, throughout the whole period of the damage, the restriction has led to a reduction in earnings of over 25 per cent.

§67

(1) The persecutee shall have a claim to be assisted in resuming, through the issue of the requisite licenses, admissions and purchase permits, his former independent occupation, or to assume an independent occupation of equal standing. The question of public need may not be examined in this connection. If the issue of the licenses, admissions or purchase permits depends on special requirements, these prerequisites shall be regarded as fulfilled in the person of the persecutee if he does not satisfy them solely because National Socialist oppressive measures were directed against him.

(2) A persecutee who, prior to September 4, 1939, was, under German regulations, admitted but who has not yet been readmitted to health insurance practice as a physician or dentist shall henceforth be considered as admitted to such practice. A persecutee who was not admitted to health insurance practice, although he had fulfilled the personal and professional requirements, shall be admitted to such practice. The persecutee shall be considered as admitted or shall be admitted at the place where he applies for settlement; area of his activities selected by him shall be granted him regardless of the number of people already admitted in such area and without including him in the ratio.

(3) Sub-§§ (1) and (2) shall not affect the provisions regarding the personal and professional requirements on which the entry to certain vocations depends.

(4) The persecutee shall have a claim to being exempted from examinations or proofs of qualifications which were introduced in the meantime. The claim cannot be asserted if the examination or proof of qualification is required from all persons working in that particular vocation.

§68

(1) Without prejudice to the regulations concerning distressed areas, persecutees shall be preferentially considered in the placing of public orders. The same shall apply to enterprises in which persecutees hold a decisive participation.

(2) Financial subsidies by public authorities shall be granted on condition that the recipients of such subsidies undertake, when placing orders, to proceed in accordance with sub-§ (1).

§69

(1) A persecutee shall have a claim to interest-free loans or loans at a reduced rate of interest in the event he is unable to procure otherwise the funds which are needed for the resumption of his former independent occupation or to take up an independent occupation of equal standing.

(2) A persecutee shall have the claim pursuant to sub-§ (1) even though he has already taken up an independent occupation referred to in that sub-§, if the loan is required to render the basis of the occupation more secure. The same shall apply to a persecutee who was substantially restricted in the exercise of his independent occupation if he needs the loan to develop fully his former occupation.

(3) The maximum amount of the loan shall be DM30,000.

§70

(1) If the persecutee, at the start of the persecution, had followed several independent occupations, he shall have a claim to a loan for the resumption of any and all of the former occupations.

(2) The total amount of several loans may not exceed the maximum amount specified in §69(3).

§71

The loan agreement shall be made on the following conditions:

1. as a rule, the loan shall carry an interest of 3 per cent per annum;
2. after the lapse of the first two years during which no repayments shall be required, the loan shall be paid off at the latest in the course of another ten-year period;
3. the loan shall, as far as possible, be secured, primarily by the assignment of ownership on articles purchased with the loan monies;
4. the recipient of the loan must furnish information annually on the use of the loan; he shall, on demand, permit an examination of the conduct of his affairs and, in particular, an inspection of his business books; he shall report forthwith any deterioration in his professional and economic position which might endanger the repayment of the loan;
5. notice of cancellation of the loan agreement may be given at any time, for any important reason which arises about the personal qualifications or the position of the recipient of the loan.

§72

(1) If the persecutee has to take up his former occupation or some other occupation of equal standing under particularly trying conditions, and if, for that reason, his initial unreproductive expenses including reasonable costs of living cannot be adequately balanced by the loan, he shall have a claim to an additional loan, that repayment may be waived on proof of its being properly expended.

(2) Particularly trying conditions within the meaning of sub-§ (1) may be regarded as existing if the persecutee had to interrupt his occupation for more than five years; if he has had to resume it at another place; if he had lost his business substance and could not recover it adequately by way of restitution; if the persecution has substantially reduced the number of his business relationships, or if the

age which he has reached has made it unusually difficult for him to resume his occupation.

(3) The maximum amount of the additional loan shall be DM20,000.

(4) §71 shall apply *mutatis mutandis* except that the additional loan shall be granted without interest.

§73

(1) §§ 69(1) and (2), 70, 71, 72(1), (2) and (4) shall apply *mutatis mutandis* to the surviving spouse and the children of a deceased persecutee if they have resumed or intend to resume the former occupation of the persecutee.

(2) The total amount of several loans in case of the application of sub-§ (1) may not exceed the maximum amounts mentioned in §§ 69(3) and 72(3).

§74

The persecutee has a claim to compensation for the period of his exclusion from, or substantial restriction on, the exercise of his independent occupation. The compensation consists of a capital indemnity or a pension.

§75

(1) The capital indemnity shall not be paid for any time beyond the date on which the persecutee has taken up an occupation which provides him with an adequate subsistence basis. It shall be presumed that this was the case only on January 1, 1947, if, on that date, the persecutee had his domicile or permanent sojourn within the area of operation of this Law.

(2) A subsistence basis shall be deemed to be adequate if it provides the persecutee and the members of his family entitled to his support, on a permanent basis, with such a standard of living (including reasonable provision for his old age and for his survivor) as is generally enjoyed by persons with the same or a similar vocational training.

(3) If, either under the legislation referred to in §5 or under §56 hereof, the persecutee has already received indemnification for the loss of income due to the above exclusion or restriction, or a claim thereto has been granted to him by decision or a non-appellable court judgment or an amicable settlement, he shall have no claim to a capital indemnity to that extent.

§76

(1) If the persecutee was excluded from his occupation, the capital indemnity shall be computed on the basis of three quarters of the salary to which a comparable federal civil servant would have been entitled at the date of his discharge. In this connection, the age of the persecutee at the start of the damages shall replace the service age of the federal civil servant at the time of his discharge. Decisive for the classification of the persecutee into a comparable civil servants' group shall be his vocational training and his economic position prior to the start of the persecution. The economic position shall be established on the basis of the average

income of the persecutee during the three years preceding the start of the persecution. Reasonable consideration shall be given to the circumstance that the
persecutee would have advanced in his profession if such a persecutee was in an
early stage in the exercise of his vocation.

(2) If the persecutee was substantially restricted in the exercise of his occupation, sub-§(1) shall apply with the proviso that the capital indemnity shall be
computed on the basis of the proportion between the reduction in income caused
by the restriction and the attainable service income of a comparable civil servant.
'Attainable service income' is the emoluments which a comparable civil servant
would have received at the end of the compensation period. If the average income
of the persecutee during the three years preceding the start of the restriction were
higher than the attainable service income of a comparable federal civil servant, sub-
§ (1) shall apply with the proviso that the capital indemnity shall be computed on
the basis of the proportion between the reduction in income caused by the
restriction and such average income.

(3) For the benefit of the persecutee the lack of provision for his old age and his
survivors enjoyed by the comparable federal civil servant shall be compensated by
an addition of 20 per cent to the total of the emoluments computed in accordance
with sub-§ (1) or (2).

(4) The entire period during which the persecutee was excluded from his
occupation or substantially restricted in its exercise shall be treated as a single
period of claim. The same applies to separate periods during which the persecutee
was excluded from his occupation or substantially restricted in its exercise.

§77

The income derived by the persecutee during the entire compensation period from
the utilization of his working power shall be deducted from the amount computed in
accordance with §76(1), (3) and (4) to the extent that such income, together with the
amount computed in accordance with §76, shall exceed the attainable service income
of a comparable federal civil servant. §76(2) second sentence shall apply. However, no
account shall be taken of income earned prior to July 1, 1948.

§78

The capital indemnity is to be computed on the basis of whole months. It shall
be based on the whole calendar months during which the persecutee was excluded
from, or substantially restricted in, the exercise of his occupation, plus the aggregate of every thirty days of the period during which he was only temporarily
excluded or restricted.

§79

(1) The period for which capital indemnity is payable ends at the latest on the
day on which the persecutee is found incapable of further work. It is assumed that
this is the case when the persecutee has completed his seventieth year of age.

(2) Sub-§ (1) does not apply if his incapacity is, to at least 50 per cent, attributable to the persecution.

§80

If, after a decision or a non-appealable court judgment was obtained, the prerequisites for payment of a capital indemnity continue to exist, the annual amount, on which the computation of the capital indemnity pursuant to §76 has been based, shall continue to be paid by way of monthly installments, until such time as the maximum amount of the capital indemnity (§123) has been reached.

§81

The persecutee may elect an annuity instead of a capital indemnity. The annuity shall be paid for life, without regard to the amount of the capital indemnity.

§82

A prerequisite for the exercise of the right of election in accordance with §81 is that, at the time of the decision on the claim, the persecutee did not exercise an occupation that provided him with an adequate basis of subsistence and that he also could not have been expected to take up such an occupation. The persecutee especially cannot be expected to take up such an occupation if, at the time of the decision on the claim, he had completed his sixty-fifth year or, in the case of women, her sixtieth year of age. Recurrent payments accruing as a result of an occupation formerly followed shall be deemed equivalent to the exercise of an occupation affording to the persecutee an adequate basis of subsistence.

§83

(1) The annuity is to be computed on the basis of two thirds of the pension of a comparable federal civil servant. §76(1), second to fifth sentences, shall apply with the proviso that the age of the persecutee on the effective date of this Law shall be the basis of the computation.

(2) The maximum monthly amount of the annuity is DM600.

(3) If the persecutee has elected an annuity he shall receive for the period up to November 1, 1953 an indemnity in the amount of one year's annuity.

§84

The right of election under §81 must be exercised within a three-month period or, if the persecutee lives in a non-European foreign country, he must so elect within a six-month limit, by a declaration submitted to the competent compensation agency. The time limit begins on the day on which the decision of the compensation agency has become final or the court judgment non-appealable. The election is final.

§85

(1) If the persecutee has died after having exercised the right of election, the widow, until her remarriage, and the children, up to the age until which children's allowances may be granted for them under civil service regulations, are entitled to

an annuity. No claim may be asserted if the marriage was contracted after the effective date of this Law.

(2) The annuity of the widow shall amount to 60 per cent and that of each child to 30 per cent of the annuity to which the persecutee was entitled under §83. Other assistance payments from German public funds shall be set off against the annuity to the extent that they exceed the amount of DM150 per month.

(3) The total of all annuities pursuant to sub-§ (2) may not exceed the amount of the persecutee's annuity. If, upon adding the annuities, an amount higher than the persecutee's annuity is arrived at, the several annuities shall be proportionately reduced.

(4) Subject to the prerequisites of §17(1) No. 2, sub-§ (1) to (3) of this paragraph apply *mutatis mutandis* to the widower.

§86

(1) If the persecutee has died within the time limit specified in §84 without having exercised the right of election granted to him by §81, the widow may exercise this right. The time limit for the exercise of the right of election pursuant to §84 begins on the day on which the persecutee has died.

(2) If the persecutee has died after the effective date of this law but before the start of the time limit specified in §84 without having exercised the right of election, and if he possessed the prerequisites for the exercise of this right pursuant to §82 before his death, the widow may exercise the right of election if she herself is a persecutee or was affected by her husband's persecution. §84 applies *mutatis mutandis* to the exercise of the right of election by the widow.

(3) If the widow elects an annuity, §85(1) to (3) applies *mutatis mutandis*. For the period preceding the death of the persecutee, the widow and the children are to receive an amount equivalent to one year's annuity to which the persecutee would have been entitled under §83(3). That indemnity is divided between the widow and the children in accordance with §85(2), first sentence, and sub-§ (3).

(4) If any payments had already been made with respect to the persecutee's claim for damage to his vocational pursuits, such payments shall be fully set off against the amenity and the compensation for the period preceding the persecutee's death. This shall also apply if the payments were made to a third party.

(5) Subject to the prerequisites of §17(1), No. 2, sub-§ (1) to (4) of this paragraph apply *mutatis mutandis* to the widower.

3.   *Non-Self-Employed Occupations*

A.   *Private Employment*

§87

(1) A persecutee shall have a claim to compensation if he suffered damages by dismissal, (forced) premature retirement or transfer to an employment with substantially reduced pay.

(2) Transfer to an employment with substantially reduced pay shall, as a rule, be deemed to have taken place if the transfer led to a reduction in income of more than 25 per cent for the whole period of the impairment.

§88

§87 shall apply *mutatis mutandis* if,

1. the persecutee was given notice of dismissal by his employer in compliance with the then legal employment contract or agreed upon employment requirements, but if none of the reasons of persecution specified in §1 had existed, the employment would have been continued either on the basis of usage or by taking into account the circumstances of the individual case;
2. an employment limited in time was not renewed, but if none of the reasons of persecution specified in §1 had existed, a renewal could have been expected on the basis of usage or by taking into account the circumstances of the individual case;
3. the persecutee lost his employment because he was deprived of liberty, was prohibited from pursuing his vocation, has emigrated, fled or lived illegally in order to escape National Socialist oppressive measures, or was expelled or deported for the reasons of persecution specified in §1;
4. the unemployed persecutee did not find employment for the reasons referred to in number 3 or, for the reasons of persecution specified in §1, was excluded from assistance by labor exchanges;
5. the employee lost his employment because his employer discontinued his activities because of persecution and the employee subsequently could not find equivalent employment because he had worked for that employer;
6. the tasks of the employee's organization were, in the process of the National Socialist reorganization measures, transferred to another organization, and the employee, for the reasons of persecution specified in §1, was excluded from the general transfer of the staff to the latter organization.

§89

(1) The persecutee shall have a claim to be restored to his former or an equivalent employment unless he has become in the interim sixty-five years old or is incapable of working. Such incapacity shall be measured by the persecutee's mental and physical abilities as are generally required in economic life.

(2) The obligation of restoring the persecutee to his former employment or giving him an equivalent position devolves upon every employer from whose service the persecutee was dismissed or has prematurely retired or upon such employer's successor in right.

(3) The employer or his successor in right, required to comply with this obligation, may refuse to satisfy the claim to the former or an equivalent position only if,

1. he is unable to satisfy the claim for compelling economic or business reasons;
2. in the case where several persons are under such an obligation, another employer, with due regard to all relevant circumstances, should on balance be considered under the greatest obligation to satisfy the claim.

(4) If the obligation to restore the persecutee to his former or an equivalent position has been established by an uncontestable decision or a non-appellable court judgment, the employment relationship shall be deemed to have been restored.

§90

If the persecutee has taken up self-employed occupation, or he has proved that he possesses the qualifications necessary to succeed in such an occupation, he may be granted a loan as provided for in §§ 69 and 71. §72 shall apply *mutatis mutandis.*

§91

The persecutee has a claim to compensation for the losses incurred by his dismissal, (forced) premature retirement or transfer to an employment with substantially reduced pay. The compensation consists in either a capital indemnity or an annuity.

§92

(1) §§ 75, 76(1), (2) and (4), 78, 79 and 80 apply *mutatis mutandis* to the capital indemnity.

(2) If the persecutee has neither a claim to an annuity from the annuities insurance based on law, because he has completed his sixty-fifth year of age, nor a claim to compensation under §§ 134 to 137 below, the total of the compensation computed in accordance with sub-§ (1) above shall be increased by 20 per cent.

(3) §77 applies with the proviso that, in addition to the income derived by the persecutee from his work, all compensations, grants, contributions toward maintenance or similar payments which the persecutees received from a former employer or his successor in right shall be taken into account.

§93

The persecutee may elect an annuity instead of the capital indemnity. In computing the annuity the persecutee's age and the capital indemnity due to him under §92 shall be adequately taken into account.

§94

It shall be a prerequisite to the exercise of the right of election pursuant §93 that, at the time of the decision of the claim, the persecutee has completed his sixty-fifth year or, in the case of women, her sixtieth year of age, or that his working capacity, in his particular vocation, has been reduced by more than half.

§95

(1) The maximum monthly amount of the annuity is DM600.

(2) The minimum monthly amount of the annuity is DM100.

(3) The minimum monthly amount of the annuity shall be reduced to the extent that such minimum amount together with maintenance allowances or recurrent benefits from German public funds exceeds the amount of DM300 per month. The amount of DM300 shall in the case of married persecutees be increased by DM60 per month, and for every child for which children's allowances may be granted under civil service regulations by DM20 per month. The persecutee shall, however, receive minimally the amount of the annuity computed in accordance with §93.

§96

The right of election under §93 shall be exercised before the expiration of a three-month period or, if the persecutee lives in a non-European foreign country, within a six-month limit, by a declaration submitted to the competent compensation agency. The time limit begins on the day on which the decision of the compensation agency has become final or the court judgment non-appellable. The election is final.

§97

(1) If the persecutee has died after having exercised the right of election, §85 shall apply *mutatis mutandis*. The computation of the annuity shall be based on the annuity to which the persecutee was entitled under §§ 93 and 95.

(2) The monthly minimum amount of the annuity for the widow or widower shall be DM60, for each child DM30; §95(3) applies *mutatis mutandis*. If, upon adding the minimum amounts of the annuities pursuant to the first sentence of this sub-section, an amount higher than the minimum amount of the persecutee's annuity is arrived at, the several minimum amounts of the annuities shall be reduced in proportion to their respective amounts.

§98

If the persecutee has died before exercising the right of election, §86 applies *mutatis mutandis*. The annuity shall be computed in accordance with §97.

B. *Public Service*

(a) *Common Provisions*

§99

(1) A persecuted member of the public service (§§ 1, 2, 2a of the Law regulating the Redress of National Socialist Wrongs Committed Against Members of the Public Service) has a claim to compensation for the period prior to April 1,1950 if he had lost emoluments as a result of the execution of one of the following measures:

    1. in the case of civil servants and professional soldiers:

        (a) termination of the service on the strength of a criminal sentence;

    (b) dismissal from service;

    (c) discharge without, or with, a reduced pension;

    (d) premature placing on the retired list;

    (e) placing on the waiting list;

    (f) transfer to an office or to a service post with a lower final basic salary;

2. in the case of pensioners:

    (a) non-payment of pensions;

    (b) reduction in the pensions;

3. in the case of employees and workmen:

    (a) discharge;

    (b) premature termination of the employment;

    (c) employment in a position with a lower remuneration or wage;

4. in the case of non-officials, extraordinary professors and extramural lecturers, at the scientific colleges:

    (a) revocation of the authorization to lecture (*venia legendi*).

It shall be presumed that the service or employment would have continued beyond May 8, 1945, if, without the persecution, it would have existed on that date.

(2) Equivalent to discharge, premature placing on the retired list, nonpayment of pensions or revocation of the *venia legendi* within the meaning of sub-§ (1) are measures which, as a result of the wording of the law, had the same consequences. In the case of persecuted members of the public service in the territories mentioned in §1(2) of the Law regulating the Redress of National Socialist Wrongs Committed against Members of the Public Service, the refusal to continue their employment and, in the case of persecutees whose services were terminated after they had passed the final examination of the preparatory service, their non-appointment to a post of an extraregular civil servant shall likewise be deemed to constitute a discharge.

(3) §§ 1 to 14, 64, shall apply.

§100

A claim to compensation cannot be asserted if, according to present legal concepts, the same measure would have been justified on grounds of civil service regulations or contractual employment rules, unconnected with National Socialist oppressive measures. The marriage of a persecuted member of the public services of the female sex shall not constitute a 'ground of civil service regulations or contractual employment rules' in the sense of the preceding sentence.

§101

If one of the measures referred to in §99(1), No. 1 and 2 has been pronounced by, or has been the consequence of, a criminal sentence or a disciplinary sentence, § 44 shall apply *mutatis mutandis*. The annulment, as an act of clemency, of the consequences of the sentence with regard to the civil service or pensions shall be considered equivalent to the voiding of the sentence.

(b) *Civil Servants*

§102

(1) A civil servant who was deprived of service pay as a result of any of the measures referred to in §99(1) is entitled to the following capital compensation:

1. if he has not received any pension, to compensation amounting to three quarters of the service pay last paid him;

2. if he has received a pension or the emoluments of a civil servant on the waiting list or had a lower service pay, to compensation equalling the amount by which these payments fell short of three quarters of the service income received up to the time when the said measures were taken.

(2) Reductions in salaries under the Decree of the Reichspresident to Safeguard the Economy and Finances of December 1, 1930 (Reich Official Gazette I, p. 517, 522), the Second Decree of the Reichspresident to Safeguard the Economy and Finances of June 5, 1931 (Reich Official Gazette I, n. 279/282) and the Fourth Decree of the Reichspresident to Safeguard the Economy and Finances for the Protection of the Internal Peace of December 8, 1931 (Reich Official Gazette I, p. 699/738) shall be considered only with respect to the period in which they were applicable to the Reich and federal civil servants.

(3) If at the time when the damage was caused the civil servant was on the waiting list (temporary retirement) sub-§§ (1) and (2) apply with the proviso that instead of the capital indemnity in the amount of three quarters of the last service pay, a capital indemnity amounting to three quarters of the pay of a civil servant on the waiting list shall be paid.

(4) If at the time when the damage was caused the civil servant had passed an examination prescribed or customary for a certain position but had not yet been appointed to permanent position, sub-§§ (1) and (2) apply with the proviso that instead of the capital indemnity in the amount of three quarters of the last service pay a capital indemnity amounting to three quarters of the service pay of the initial grade of his particular service career shall be paid. The same applies in case of his non-acceptance as a non-permanent civil servant (§99(2), second sentence).

(5) §§ 75(1) and (2) apply *mutatis mutandis.*

§103

Civil servants in retirement, widows and orphans who were deprived of pensions either in full or in part (§99(1) No. 2) have a claim to a capital indemnity in the amount of the pensions lost.

§104

(1) A survivor of a persecuted civil servant or pensioner entitled to maintenance payments who did not receive any, or received only reduced maintenance payments as a result of a measure directed against the persecutee (§99(1), No. 1 and 2), has a claim to a capital indemnity in the amount of the survivors' emoluments com-

puted in accordance with the general civil service regulations, based on the capital indemnity which the persecutee would have been entitled to pursuant to §§ 102 and 103.

(2) It suffices if the survivor entitled to maintenance payments satisfies the requirements of §4. In all other respects §§ 5 to 14 apply *mutatis mutandis.*

§105

In the case of a civil servant or pensioner who suffered losses as a result of a series of measures (§99(1), No. 1 and 2) the capital indemnity shall be computed on the basis of the legal situation which existed at the time of the initial damage. If the civil servant was, at the time of a later measure, employed in accordance with his previous legal position, the capital indemnity for the later period is to be computed on the basis of the last service relationship.

§106

The pay and pension regulations for federal civil servants effective as of April 1, 1951 shall apply to the computation of the indemnity under §§ 102 to 105. In this connection only that part of the service income shall be considered by which the pension is determined.

§107

(1) Against the capital indemnity payable pursuant to §§ 102 to 106 are to be set off in full all maintenance payments, lump sum payments, contributions toward maintenance, grants and similar payments out of German public funds made for the same period, with the exception of benefits from unemployment insurance or unemployment assistance funds. Payments already taken into account in the computation of the capital indemnity (§§ 102(1) No. 2, 103, 104) shall not be set off.

(2) Beneficiaries who have derived income through the use of their working power shall receive the capital indemnity only to the extent that the indemnity together with such income and the payments referred to in sub-§ (1) shall not exceed

1. in the case of a civil servant dismissed, or placed prematurely on the retirement or the waiting list, the service pay which the civil servant would have attained, if he had been retained in the service, in the course of his regular service career;
2. in the case of a civil servant on the retirement or waiting list, the pensionable service pay on which the retirement pension or waiting status pay is based;
3. in the case of a widow, 75 per cent of the service income pursuant to number 2;
4. in the case of an orphan, 40 per cent of the service income pursuant to number 2.

In this connection no account shall be taken of income earned prior to May 1, 1948.

(c) *Professional Soldiers*

§108

(1) §§ 102 to 107 shall apply *mutatis mutandis* to professional soldiers of former German Defense Forces as well as their surviving dependents.

(2) The computation of the pensionable service pay according to Salary Schedules A and B shall be based on the table annexed to §20(1) No. 2 of the Law regulating the Redress of National Socialist Wrongs Committed against Members of the Public Services, the pay for seniority status in the groups of Salary Schedule A shall, in particular with respect to the determination of what pay shall be considered pensionable service pay, be established on the basis of the provisions of the Salaries Law that are applicable to civil servants in accordance with the Ordinance for the Implementation of §20 of the Law regulating the Redress of National Socialist Wrongs Committed against Members of the Public Service.

(3) The term 'former German Defense Forces' shall include the Defense Force within the meaning of the National Defense Law of May 21, 1935 (Reich Official Gazette I, p. 609), the Reich Defense and the old Defense Forces (Army, Navy, Protective Force).

(d) *Employees and Workmen*

§109

§§ 102 to 107 apply *mutatis mutandis* to employees and workmen (§99(1) No. 3) who have a contractual claim to maintenance payment in accord with the rules governing the civil service, or to retirement benefits, as well as to their survivors.

§110

(1) §§ 87, 88, 90 to 98 apply *mutatis mutandis* to employees and workmen (§99(1) No. 3) who do not possess a contractual claim to maintenance pay in accordance with the rules governing the civil service, or to retirement benefits, as well as to their survivors.

(2) As an exception to the provisions of §99(1), employees and workmen referred to in sub-§ (1), as well as their survivors, have a claim to compensation for the period following April 1, 1950, but not beyond the date from which they received recurrent payments under §21a of the Law regulating the Redress of National Socialist Wrongs Committed against Members of the Public Services.

(e) *Extraordinary Professors and Lecturers, Non-Officials*
at Universities and Colleges

§111

(1) Extraordinary professors and extramural lecturers at scientific colleges (§99(1) No. 4), who were not members of the civil service, have a claim to capital indemnity amounting to three quarters of the service pay to which they would have

been entitled if, at the time when the damaging measures were applied against them, they had been given a lectureship with fees, provided that, at that time, the Colleges Scientific Personnel Pay Law of February 17, 1939 (Reich Official Gazette I, p. 252) had already been in force.

(2) §§ 104 to 107 apply *mutatis mutandis.*

C. *Service with Religious Associations*

§112

§§ 109, 110, 88 apply *mutatis mutandis* to persecutees who were employed and suffered damage in the services of religious bodies, as well as to their survivors. The claim to compensation can also be made for the period after April 1, 1950, but not beyond the date from which they received recurrent payments under the Law regulating the Redress of National Socialist Wrongs Committed against Members of the Public Services.

4. *Losses Suffered in Self- and Non-Self-Employed Occupations*

§113

(1) If a persecutee was engaged both in a self-employed and non-self-employed occupation but has been damaged in only one of these activities, only the provisions relating to that damage shall apply.

(2) If a persecutee was damaged both in his self-employed and non-self-employed occupation, his claim to a capital indemnity or an annuity shall be based on the activity from which he derived the higher income, if it was not a temporary activity.

(3) If the persecutee's income from his self-employed and non-self-employed occupation was approximately the same, he shall be treated, with regard to his claim to a capital indemnity or annuity, as a self-employed person.

5. *Non-Assumption of an Occupation Despite Accumulated Vocational Training*

§114

(1) A persecutee who, although he had completed a vocational training, was unable for the reasons of persecution specified in §1, to assume an occupation corresponding to that training has a claim to compensation pursuant to §§ 66 to 86. His survivors possess, as well, the claim.

(2) If, after examination of the specific circumstances of the case, it can be inferred that the persecutee had no intention of assuming a self-employed occupation, both the persecutee and his survivors shall have a claim to compensation pursuant to §§ 87 and 90 to 98.

(3) The classification of the persecutee in a comparable civil servants group shall be determined by his vocational training and what his income would have probably been.

(4) Sub-§§ (1) to (3) do not apply, if the persecutee or his survivors receive an indemnity under §102(4), second sentence, or §§ 104 to 107.

6. *Damage to Training*

§115

(1) Damage to vocational pursuits in the meaning of §65 is also deemed to be damage which a persecutee has suffered in his vocational or his prevocational training by having been excluded from the training to which he had aspired or by having been compelled to interrupt such training.

(2) §67 applies *mutatis mutandis* with the proviso that the claim under §67(2), second and third sentences, exists as from the date on which, but for the exclusion from the training to which he had aspired or the interruption of such training, the persecutee would have been admitted to practice in social insurance institutions against sickness.

§116

(1) The persecutee shall be entitled to a grant to enable him to defray the expenses which he will incur or has incurred in the resumption of his training. The grant shall amount to DM5,000. When his costs of training shall be proven to exceed that figure he shall be refunded the additional expenses up to an amount of DM5,000.

(2) Any payments from German public funds which the persecutee has received under other laws to further his training shall be set off against the grant. §10 remains unaffected.

§117

(1) Upon successful completion of his training the persecutee shall have a claim to a loan. §69(1) and (2) apply *mutatis mutandis*.

(2) The maximum amount of the loan shall be DM10,000. §71 applies *mutatis mutandis*.

§118

(1) If the persecutee does not desire to resume his training, he shall be entitled to an indemnity in the amount of DM5,000 as compensation for the training which he has not received.

(2) If the persecutee has entered on the resumption of his training, but does not desire to complete it, the grant and other payments which the persecutee received from German public funds under other laws toward the resumption of his training shall be set off against the indemnity pursuant to sub-§ (1).

§119

(1) Children who, as a result of the persecution of their parents, were unable to commence or to complete vocational or prevocational training to which they had aspired shall be entitled to a grant toward the necessary expenditures arising from the resumption of their training for as long a period as children's allowances may

be granted for them under civil service regulations. Such claims exist only to the extent that the parents, because of persecution, are unable to defray themselves the costs of the training.

(2) It suffices with regard to these claims that the children satisfy the require-ments of §4. In all other respects §§ 5 to 14 apply *mutatis mutandis.*

(3) The grant shall be paid in installments corresponding to the costs rising in the training. For each child the total amount of the grant shall not exceed DM5,000. §116(2) applies *mutatis mutandis.*

7. Concurrence of Claims for Compensation for Damage to Vocational Pursuits and of Claims for Compensation for Loss of Life, or Damage to Limb or Health

§120

If a survivor of a persecutee has a claim to an annuity for damage to vocational pursuits under paragraphs 85 and 86 or paragraphs 97 and 98 as well as a claim to an annuity for loss of life, he shall receive the full amount of the higher annuity plus 25 per cent of the lower annuity.

§121

(1) If a persecutee has a claim to a capital indemnity or to an annuity or damage to vocational pursuits as well as a claim to an annuity and capital indemnity for damage to limb or health in the same compensation period, he shall receive the full amount of compensation for the damage on which the higher claim is based and 25 per cent of the compensation for the damage on which the lower claim is based.

(2) In computing the amount of the claim for damage to vocational pursuits account shall be taken of the fact that, because of the damage to limb or health, the persecutee was, or is, not fully capable or working.

(3) Sub-paragraphs (1) and (2) shall not apply in the cases covered by para-graphs 115 to 119.

§122

(1) If the compensation for the damage on which the lower claim is based has already been determined by a final decision or by a non-appellable court judgment, 75 per cent of that compensation shall be set off against the compensation or the damage on which the higher claim is based.

(2) Sub-paragraph (1) shall also apply if the compensation for the damage on which the lower claim is based has been established in some other manner, in particular, through amicable settlement or by a lump sum payment.

8. Maximum Amount of Capital Compensation

§123

(1) The capital indemnity for damage to vocational pursuits shall, for the benefit of any one particular persecutee, not exceed the amount of DM40,000.

(2) Grants and compensation for damage to training as well as compensation under paragraph 19 of the Law regulating the Redress of National Socialist Wrongs Committed against Members of the Public Services shall be included in the maximum amount.

§124

If a survivor entitled to maintenance pay has a claim to compensation under paragraphs 99 to 109 or 111, the maximum amount specified in paragraph 123 shall be reduced in the proportion existing under maintenance pay regulations between survivor's emoluments and the retirement salary or retirement pay of the deceased public servant.

§125

The maximum amount specified in paragraph 123 also applies if capital indemnities under paragraphs 99 to 109 or 111 are payable to several eligible persons because of a service relationship.

[...]

III. *Damage to Economic Pursuits*

1. *Damage to Insurance Other than Social Insurance*

§127

(1) A persecutee is entitled to claim compensation if, as an insured party or as a beneficiary, he has lost, in full or in part, the protection of a life insurance (capital or annuity insurance) entered into with an insurance institution under private or public law, other than social insurance, because his right to insurance benefits or his right under the assumption of a risk, which existed under the statutes or under the terms of the policy, was impaired.

(2) A beneficiary who is not a persecutee shall have a claim to compensation if the insured was a persecutee and the beneficiary is either the spouse of the persecutee or, in case of intestate succession, would be an heir of the first or second degree. It suffices if the beneficiary satisfies the requirements of paragraph 4. In all other respects paragraphs 5 to 14 apply *mutatis mutandis.*

[...]

§133

(1) The compensation under §§ 127 to 130 may, with respect to any particular insured person or to all the beneficiaries combined, not exceed a total of DM25,000. This likewise applies if an injured person or a beneficiary suffered damage with respect to several insurance policies.

(2) The capital value of the annuity is to be computed by application, *mutatis mutandis*, of the assessment law.

2. *Damage to Maintenance*

§134

(1) A persecutee has a claim to compensation if, as an employee in private employment, or as the survivor of such an employee, he was entitled to, or could reasonably expect, maintenance benefits for old age or disability, and if he suffered damage in such maintenance.

(2) A survivor of a persecutee also has a claim to compensation if, as a result of National Socialist oppressive measures directed against the latter, he did not or does not receive any, or only reduced, maintenance benefits. It suffices if the survivor satisfies the requirements of §4. In all other respects §§ 5 to 14 apply *mutatis mutandis.*

[...]

§137

(1) The compensation under §§ 134 to 136 may not exceed for any one persecutee and his survivors a total of DM25,000.

(2) The capital value of the annuity is to be computed by application, *mutatis mutandis*, of the Assessment Law.

3. *Damage to Social Insurance*

§138

The redress of losses which a persecutee or his survivors suffered in social insurance is governed by the special legislation applicable thereto and, in particular, the Law Concerning the Treatment of Persecutees of National Socialism in Social Insurance; applications under that legislation may be filed until the expiration of the time limit for applications specified in §189(1).

4. *Damage to War Victims' Benefits*

§139

The redress of losses which a persecutee or his survivors suffered with respect to war victims' benefits is governed by the Law Concerning the Treatment of Persecutees of National Socialism in Social Insurance and the Law for the Redress of National Socialist Wrongs with Respect to War Victims' Benefits for Claimants Living Abroad; applications under this legislation may be filed until the expiration of the time limit for applications specified in §189(1).

[...]

Eighth Chapter

Immediate Aid to Repatriates

§141

(1) A persecutee of German citizenship or the German 'nation' who, for reasons of persecution specified in §1 had emigrated, been deported or expelled during the

period from January 30, 1933 to May 8, 1945 and who has had the place of his last domicile or permanent sojourn in territories which, on December 31, 1937, formed part of the German Reich, has a claim to an immediate aid payment in the amount of DM6,000 if, after May 8, 1945, he has taken up or is taking up his domicile or permanent sojourn within the area of operation of this Law.

(2) Half the immediate aid payment is to be set off against compensation payable for damage to property or possessions.

(3) The claim to immediate aid is, before it was determined or a non-appellable court judgment was reached, neither cessible nor inheritable.

Part Three

Special Provisions for Legal Persons, Institutions or Associations

§142

(1) A legal person, institution or association (unincorporated society, association under civil or commercial law not endowed with legal personality) shall have a claim to compensation if they have suffered damage by National Socialist oppressive measures.

(2) If a legal person, institution or association referred to in sub-§ (1) has ceased to exist and there is also no successor in right, the claim to compensation may be asserted by that legal person, institution or association which, according to its statutes, objectives, composition or organizational status and according to its actual activities shall be deemed to be a successor in objective. The term 'successor in right' includes, for the purposes of the preceding sentence, with respect to claims under §51, successor organizations established under restitution legislation.

§143

(1) The claim to compensation exists only if the legal person, institution or association

1. on December 31, 1952, had its seat or its administrative center within the area of operation of this Law;

2. prior to December 31, 1952, for reasons of persecution specified in §1, transferred its seat or administrative center abroad from territories which, on December 31, 1937, formed part of the German Reich, except if its seat or administrative center is, at the time of the determination of the claim, located in areas with whose governments the Federal Republic of Germany does not maintain any diplomatic relations; §4(4) applies *mutatis mutandis.*

(2) If a legal person, institution or association has ceased to exist, a claim to compensation exists only if either entity had its seat or administrative center in territories which, on December 31, 1937, formed part of the German Reich and if, on December 31, 1952, the seat or administrative center of a successor in right or objective was within the area of validity of this law.

§144

A claim to compensation may not be asserted if it is probable that, on the basis of its present statutes, objectives, composition, organizational status or actual activities, the legal person, institution or association or its successor in right or objective would not have been persecuted.

§145

(1) A legal person, institution or association is disqualified from receiving compensation if, on the basis of their statutes, objectives, composition, organizational status or actual activities they

1. aided and abetted the National Socialist oppressive regime;
2. after May 23, 1949 fought against the free democratic basic order as defined in the Basic Law.

(2) The claim to compensation is forfeit if, after it was determined or an appellable court judgment was reached, the ground for disqualification specified in sub-§ (1), No. 2 arises. A refund of any benefits paid after the ground for forfeiture has arisen may be demanded.

(3) Sub-§§ (1) and (2) also apply to the successor in right or objective to a legal person, institution or association.

§146

(1) A claim to compensation exists only with respect to damage to property and possessions and only insofar as the damage occurred within the area of validity of this Law.

(2) Associations which were established or recognized by religious bodies and whose members have undertaken certain work solely in behalf of the association, may claim as damage to possessions also the loss, which the association sustained as a result of the loss of the work of its members.

(3) No compensation is payable for loss of contributions, donations and similar revenues.

§147

If a legal person, institution or association or their successor in right or objective have obtained benefits under the legislation relating to the transfer of the assets of organizations, a claim to compensation under this Law exists only to the extent to which the damage has not been made good by such benefits.

§148

(1) The maximum amount specified in §§ 55(1) and 58 also apply to the claims of a legal person, institution or association or their successor in right or objective.

(2) The maximum amounts specified in §§ 55(1) and 58 apply in favor of persecuted religious bodies and their institutions or their successors in right or objective with respect to each item of property for which a claim to compensation

for or damage to property or possessions may be asserted. In cases covered by §146(2) the maximum amount specified in §58 applies to the total loss the individual legal body has sustained.

(3) The maximum account may be exceeded insofar as this is necessary to fulfill the functions of the religious bodies or their institutions or their successors in right or objective within the area of validity of this Law. The religious bodies or their institutions or their successors in right or objective have to claim that the prerequisites for exceeding the maximum amount exist; the amount in excess of the maximum amount shall be paid to the religious bodies or their institutions or their successors in right or objective. §142(2) second sentence is not applicable.

(4) §55(2) applies *mutatis mutandis*.

Part Four

Special Groups of Persecutees

First Chapter

General Rules

§149

If persecutees from expulsion areas as well as persecuted stateless persons and refugees within the meaning of the Geneva Convention, and the survivors of such persecutees, do not satisfy the requirements of §4, they shall have a claim to compensation limited in kind and scope.

Second Chapter

Persecutees From the Expulsion Areas

§150

(1) A persecutee from expulsion areas who is an expellee as defined in §1 of the Federal Expellees Law has a claim to compensation for damage to limb and health, for damage to liberty, for losses through payment of discriminatory levies, and for damage to vocational pursuits. §4(2) shall apply.

(2) A survivor of a persecutee who belongs to the group of persons described in sub-§ (1) above has a claim to compensation for loss of life. The claim to compensation may also be asserted if the survivor belongs to the group of persons described in sub-§ (1).

§151

Compensation for damage to limb and health is to be paid in accordance with §§ 28 to 40.

§152

Compensation for damage to liberty is to be paid in accordance with §§ 43 to 50.

§153

(1) Compensation for losses through payment of discriminatory levies is to be paid in accordance with §§ 59 and 60. A prerequisite for such compensation is that the persecutee emigrated abroad before the general expulsion.

(2) The amounts paid as discriminatory levies shall be considered up to a maximum amount of RM150,000. The Reichsmark amount thus ascertained is to be converted into Deutsche Mark at the ratio of 100:6.5.

(3) The claim is inheritable before a decision has been made or a non-appellable court judgment reached only if the heir is the spouse of the persecutee or, in the event of intestate succession, would be an heir of the first or second degree.

§154

(1) Compensation for damage to vocational pursuits is payable in accordance with §§ 64 to 66, 87, 88, 112 and 114. A prerequisite to such compensation is that the persecutee emigrated abroad before the general expulsion.

(2) The compensation consists of a capital indemnity or an annuity.

§155

The capital indemnity amounts to DM10,000.

§156

(1) The persecutee may elect an annuity instead of the capital indemnity. A prerequisite to the exercise of right of election is that, at the time of the decision, the persecutee shall have completed his sixty-fifth year, or, in the case of women, her sixtieth year, or that his capacity to work, in his particular vocation, has been reduced by over half.

(2) §84 shall apply.

(3) The monthly amount of the annuity shall be DM200.

§157

(1) If the persecutee died after exercising the right of election the widow shall be entitled to an annuity. In the event of the remarriage or death of the widow, the claim to an annuity shall devolve upon the children for as long a period as children's allowances may be granted for them under civil service regulations.

(2) The monthly amount of the annuity for the widow, or, in the cases provided for in sub-§ (1), second sentence, for all the children together shall be DM150. if [sic] there is only one child, the monthly amount of the annuity shall be DM75.

(3) The claim according to sub-§§ (1) and (2) does not exist if the marriage has been contracted after the effective date of this Law.

(4) Subject to the prerequisites of §17(1) No. 2, sub-§§ (1) to (3) above apply *mutatis mutandis* to the widower.

§158

§140(1) to (3) apply *mutatis mutandis* to the inheritability and cessibility of the claim to compensation under §§ 154 to 157.

§159

Compensation for loss of life is payable in accordance with §§ 15 to 26 and 41. The claim to the capital indemnity exists only for the period beginning with January 1, 1949.

Third Chapter

Stateless Persons: Refugees within the Meaning of the Geneva Convention

§160

(1) A persecutee who, on the effective date of this Law, is a stateless person or a refugee within the meaning of the Geneva Convention of July 28, 1951, and has not been cared for with recurrent payments with respect to the damage suffered, by grants from any state or intergovernmental organization or has not been so cared for by a lump sum instead of recurrent payments shall have a claim to compensation for damage to limb and health and for damage to liberty.

(2) The right to the claim in accordance with sub-§ (1) also exists for a persecutee who, as a stateless person, or a refugee within the meaning of the Geneva Convention, acquired another nationality after the end of the persecution. This shall not apply if the persecutee was an Austrian who had acquired German nationality through the unification of Austria with the German Reich and had become stateless by the loss of such nationality.

(3) The survivor of a persecutee who belonged to the group of persons described in sub-§§ (1) and (2) has a claim to compensation for loss of life. The claim also exists if the survivor belongs to the group of persons described in sub-§§ (1) and (2) above.

(4) This provision shall not vitiate the rights which may be asserted under §§ 150 to 159.

§161

Compensation for damages to limb or health shall be paid in accordance with §§ 28, 29 No. 1 to No. 3, §§ 30 to 37 and 39. The claim to the capital indemnity exists only for the period beginning with January 1, 1949.

§162

Compensation for damage to liberty shall be paid in accordance with §§ 43 to 50.

§163

(1) Compensation for loss of life is payable in accordance with §§ 15, 16 No. 1 and No. 3, §§ 17 to 22, 24 and 25. The claim to the capital indemnity exists only for the period beginning with January 1, 1949.

(2) The claim to the current annuity is neither cessable nor inheritable. The claim to the annuity amounts in arrears and to the capital indemnity is neither cessible nor inheritable before it has been determined or a non-appellable court judgment rendered.

§164

(1) A persecutee who belongs to a group of persons described in §160(1) and (2) and who, on the effective date of this Law, is a national of a state being repaid by the Federal Republic of Germany for the costs of integration, shall have a claim only to compensation for damage to liberty.

(2) The survivor who belongs to the group of persons described in §160 (3) and who, on the effective date of this Law, is a national of a state being repaid by the Federal Republic of Germany for the costs of integration shall have a claim to an annuity for loss of life.

§165

If due consideration of the persecutee's possessions and other income having been given, the compensation according to §§ 161 to 164 does not suffice to cover his subsistence costs, he shall be granted adequate hardship-mitigation payments. This shall also apply if the persecutee belongs to a group of persons for whom funds or special purposes are otherwise provided for.

§166

§§ 160 to 165 do not apply to stateless persons who, under Article 1 F of the Geneva Convention, would be disqualified from recognition as refugees.

Part Five

Persons Damaged Because of Their Nationality

§167

(1) Persons who, in violation of human rights, were damaged, under the National Socialist oppressive regime on the basis of their nationality, and who, on the effective date of this Law, were refugees within the meaning of the Geneva Convention of July 28, 1951, shall have a claim to compensation for permanent damage to limb or health.

(2) Any person shall be disqualified from compensation under sub-§ (1) who
1. has committed a crime against peace, a war crime or a crime against humanity as defined in international agreements;
2. has committed a grave non-political crime outside the receiving country before he was granted refuge in that country;
3. has been guilty of acts contrary to the aims and principles of the United Nations.

(3) §§ 6 to 10 and 12 apply *mutatis mutandis.*

§168

(1) It shall be deemed to be a permanent damage to limb or health in the meaning of §167 if, at the time of the decision on the claim, the damagee's earning capacity has still been reduced by at least 25 per cent and there is no prospect of a substantial improvement therein.

(2) The compensation consists in an annuity. That annuity amounts monthly in the case of an impairment of the earning capacity

By from 25 to 49 per cent	to DM100
By from 50 to 59	to DM120
By from 60 to 69	to DM140
By from 70 to 79	to DM160
By from 80 and more per cent	to DM200

(3) §§ 28 and 33 to 35 apply *mutatis mutandis.*

(4) The claim to the current annuity and to the annuity amounts in arrear is neither cessible nor inheritable.

Part Six

Payment of the Compensation Claims

§169

(1) The claims to be satisfied by payments in money, insofar as they do not involve recurrent payments for future periods, shall be satisfied at the latest by end of the fiscal year 1962.

(2) The payments are due at once. This shall not apply to claims for damage to property and possessions, or to claims for the payment of a capital indemnity for damage to vocational and economic pursuits to the extent that these claims exceed an amount of DM10,000 in each case and as long as the claimant has not completed his sixtieth year of age. The payment for their claims shall become due on April 1, 1957.

(3) If the claimant has died and the claim is inheritable, the age requirement of sub-§ (2) must be satisfied by the heir. In the event there are several heirs it shall suffice if one of them satisfies the requirement as to age. If the heir has been ceded, pledged or attached, the age of the original claimant shall continue to govern the maturity.

§170

(1) Advances may be granted if a claim with respect to any particular damage has been substantiated by prima facie evidence and if the grant of an advance is necessary to alleviate existing distress. Advances may also be granted for other substantial reasons which make an advance appear a reasonable necessity. The advance may be paid at one time or in installments limited in time.

(2) The advance is to be set off against the claim for which it has been given. If this is not possible, it may either be set off against other claims or its refund may be demanded.

Part Seven

Mitigation of Hardship

§171

(1) In order to mitigate hardships, persons whose damages are due to the reasons of persecution specified in §1 and for, whom funds for special purposes are not otherwise provided for, may be granted hardship-mitigation payments. The payments may take the form of grants for sustaining the costs of subsistence, for carrying on a medical treatment, for purchasing household goods, for building up a basis of self-sustenance and for vocational training. To enable persons to build up a basis of self-sustenance loans may also be extended to them. The grants shall, as a rule, not exceed the maximum amounts provided for in this Law.

(2) Mitigation of hardship under sub-§ (1) may also be granted to persons who have suffered damage through the dissolution, by National Socialist oppressive measures, of the institution which provided their maintenance if, because of such damage, they are in financial distress. The Federal Government is authorized to determine by regulation which of those institutions are regarded as having been dissolved by National Socialist oppressive measures.

(3) Sums for hardship-mitigation may further be granted to

1. damagees who have been sterilized, without previous proceedings, under the Law for the Prevention of the Procreation of Progeny Afflicted with Hereditary Diseases, dated July 14, 1933 (Reich Official Gazette I, p. 529);
2. survivors of persons who under the National Socialist oppressive regime were victims of euthanasia, if it may be assumed that had such persons not been killed their survivors would now be supported by them.

(4) In certain instances payments may also be made to recognized charity organizations or to a Jewish dispensing charity, if such grants appear necessary for the establishment or maintenance of charity institutions for the benefit of persecutees. This does not apply to organizations or agencies dispensing charity for which funds for special purposes are otherwise provided for.

[...]

Part Nine

Compensation Authorities and Procedure

[...]

§189

(1) Compensation shall be granted only upon application. The applications shall be filed with the competent compensation agency before October 1, 1957.

(2) The cut-off time for applications shall be deemed to have been observed, if the application was filed in time with an authority not competent for the claim under this Law or if the claim was asserted by action in a court.

(3) If the claimant was prevented from observing the time limit for reasons beyond his control, he shall, on application, be granted reinstatement to a position entitling him to file a claim.

§190

The application should contain:
1. data concerning the person and the claimant's economic position;
2. a statement of the facts on which the claim is based;
3. listing all available evidence;
4. data concerning the kind and amount of the claim;
5. a statement as to whether and, if so, where the applicant has already made an application or filed a claim;
6. a statement concerning payments which, in the process of compensation to victims of National Socialist persecution, have been made from German public funds or by a party liable in damages under civil law;
7. a statement as to whether restitution proceedings have been instituted with regard to items of property which, prior to the alienation, belonged to the claimant or his predecessor in right, and the disposition of such proceedings.

§191

(1) Except as otherwise provided by this Law or *Land* law referred to in §184(1), §§ 355 ff. of the Code of Civil Procedure shall apply *mutatis mutandis* to the taking of evidence by the compensation agencies. The compensation agencies shall not administer oaths.

(2) The compensation agencies are authorized, by corresponding application of §287 of the Code of Civil Procedure, to estimate the amount of damage.

(3) Legal and official assistance is to be given to the compensation agencies. No fees or costs shall be reimbursed for such assistance if they are rendered in Germany.

(4) The compensation agency may request in particular:
1. the public prosecutor's offices or the police authorities directly to investigate the facts of a persecution case;
2. the *Amtsgericht* in whose district the applicant, a witness or an expert is staying, to take the testimony of the applicant, witness or expert, advising that court of the facts and occurrences in respect to which the testimony is required;
3. a representative of the Federal Republic in foreign countries to take testimony of the applicant, witness or expert residing in the area in which the representative exercises his function. The compensation agency shall supply the

representative with all the facts of, and events with regard to, the testimony which is required;

4. the Penal Registration Authorities for unrestricted information, including information on convictions eliminated from the penal register.

(5) The provisions of the Code of Civil Procedure concerning the taking evidence by interrogation of the parties, evidence by witnesses, evidence by experts, and the procedure for the administration of oaths shall apply *mutatis mutandis* in the cases referred to in sub-§ 4 No. 2.

§192

(1) With the assent of the applicant the compensation agency may obtain for inspection records of illnesses, notes, histories of sicknesses, post-mortem findings and examination of results as well as x-rays from public, free caritative [charitable]and private hospitals, as well as hospitals of corporations under public law and social insurance institutions. The compensation agency shall safeguard the applicant from having medical information disclosed.

(2) Subject to the conditions of sub-§ (1), the compensation agency may obtain information and examination records for inspection from private physicians who have treated or are treating the persecutee.

§193

(1) The applicant and his representative may inspect the records of the compensation agency. They may make extracts and copies from such records or obtain them by payment of the expenses involved.

(2) The applicant may, for special reasons, be denied the right to inspect a whole or part of the records and to obtain extracts and copies thereof.

(3) Only attorneys at law admitted to practice at a court in the area of generation of this law are entitled to inspect the records and have them handed over to them.

§194

The compensation agency shall serve a certified copy of the application upon an employer against whom a claim is being filed in accordance with §89 and, before rendering a decision, hear such employer on the claim, the claimant's statements, and the results of the investigations.

§195

(1) The determination of the compensation agency shall be made by decision. Partial decisions are permissible.

(2) The decision must contain:

1. the designation of the compensation agency;
2. the formula of the decision including any reservations as to payment and the date on which the compensation becomes due in the event the amount of the claim is not due forthwith;

3. a reference to the fact that a court claim may be instituted to the extent that the claim has been denied; information as to the form in which, the time limit within which, and the designation of the court where, such action may be taken.

(3) The decision should contain:

1. the personal data about the applicant;

2. a statement on the facts of the case;

3. the reasons for the decision.

§196

(1) The decision shall be served upon the applicant. If a representative has been appointed, the decision is to be served upon the latter.

(2) In the cases referred to in §§ 86(2) and 98 the decision shall be served upon the widow or the widower even if they are not heirs.

§197

(1) Service shall be made in accordance with the provisions of the Administrative Service Law.

(2) If the person on whom service is to be made resides outside the area of operation of this Law, §§ 174 and 175 of the Code of Civil Procedure shall apply *mutatis mutandis*. Service may also be made by mail with postal receipt.

§198

(1) A separate decision shall be rendered regarding the employer's obligation to place the persecutee in his former or an equivalent position.

(2) The decision shall be also served on the employer. §197(1) shall apply.

§199

If the right of election is provided for claims for damage to vocational pursuits, the compensation agency shall, in its decision, also state the amount of the claim with respect to which the election may be exercised. It need not do so if the right of election has been exercised prior to the decision on the claim.

[...]

§207

(1) No fees and disbursements are to be charged in proceedings before the compensation agencies. Costs may, however, be charged to the applicant in the case of obviously unfounded applications. The award as to costs shall be made simultaneously with the decision on the merits of the claim.

(2) Fees and disbursements shall not be refunded.

(3) Certificates of vital statistics required for production to the compensation agencies shall be issued free of charge.

[...]

Second Law to Amend the Federal Compensation Law [Bundesentschaedigungsgesetz – BEG] [Excerpts]*

Dated September 14, 1965

Collection of the Federal Law (Bundesrecht), Federal Law Gazette (Bundesgesetzblatt) III 251–4[1]

The Federal Diet by and with the concurrence of the Federal Council has enacted the following Law:

Article I

Amendment to the Federal Compensation Law[2]

[...]

1. §1, sub-§ (3) is changed as follows:
   a) In number 1 the words 'deliberately or negligently' are deleted.
   b) The following number 4 will be added:
   '4. The damagee, who as a close relative of the persecutee was affected by National Socialist oppressive measures; "close relative" includes the spouse of the persecutee and the children for as long as children's allowances may be granted to them under civil service legislation.'

2. §4 is changed as follows:

'§4

(1) The right to claim compensation exists
1. if the persecutee

[...]

   (e) is an expellee within the meaning of §1 of the Law governing the affairs of expellees and refugees (Federal Expellees' Law) and has taken or is taking up his domicile or place of permanent residence within the area of operation of this Law before April 30, 1965 or after this date takes it within six months of leaving the territory of the country from which he is expelled or resettled;

[...]

   (g) has moved or moves his domicile or place of permanent residence through family reunification from the area of the Soviet-occupied Zone

* Translated from German by Karin Beck Gallagher.

of Germany or from the Soviet-occupied Sector of Berlin into the area of operation of this Law, because he is in constant need of nursing and care due to physical or mental frailty, or because he is at least sixty-five years old; §3 sub-§ (2) of the Federal Expellees' Law shall apply *mutatis mutandis*.

2. if the persecutee, on January 1, 1947, was in a Displaced Persons camp within the area of operation of this Law and either died in the Displaced Persons camp or emigrated from the area of operation of this Law, or as a homeless alien became subject to the jurisdiction of the German authorities after December 31, 1946 or acquired German citizenship.

[. . .]

(3) The claim to compensation does not cease to apply if the deported persecutee (sub-§ (1), No. (1)c was forcefully returned to the territory of the German Reich as of December 31, 1937 or to the Free City of Danzig.

[. . .]

(5) Family reunification means reuniting with a spouse, a first-degree relative or collateral relatives to the second degree or step- and foster children, adopted children or children-in-law. Reuniting with step- or foster children or adopted children is only possible, if they lived with the moving person in one household before their 18th birthday or for at least three years.'

[. . .]

3. The following new §4a is added:

'§4a

(1) If the persecutee died before December 31, 1952 and if he had his last domicile or place of permanent residence outside of the area of operation of this Law but within the territory of the German Reich as of December 31, 1937 or the Free City of Danzig, his not-remarried widow who was affected by the persecution has a right to claim compensation, as long as she fulfils the conditions of §4. This shall not apply, if the persecutee only established his domicile or place of permanent residence after the end of the despotic National Socialist regime in the area defined in sentence 1.'

[. . .]

7. §10 is in the following new version:

'§10

[. . .]

(5) persecutees are not required to reimburse costs of Social Welfare Assistance according to §92, sub-§ (3) of the Federal Social Welfare Assistance Law. Insofar as the persecutee received unemployment benefits before November 1, 1953 the claim of compensation cannot be transferred to the Federal Government.'

[. . .]

11. §15 is in the following new version:

'§15

(1) A claim to compensation for loss of life exists if the persecutee has been killed or driven to death and his death occurred during the persecution or within eight months after the end of the persecution that caused his death. It suffices if the nexus between death and persecution is probable.

(2) If the persecutee died during deportation or during deprivation of liberty according to this Law or within eight months after the end of the deportation or deprivation of liberty, it shall be presumed that the conditions defined in sub-§ (1), sentence 1 are fulfilled.'

[. . .]

13. §19 is in the following new version:

'§19

The monthly minimum amount of the annuity shall be for:

	Through March 31, 1957 (DM)	From April 1, 1957 through May 31, 1960 (DM)	From June 1, 1960 through December 31, 1960 (DM)	From January 1, 1961 through June 30, 1962 (DM)	From July 1, 1962 through September 30, 1964 (DM)	From October 1, 1964 (DM)
the widow	200	220	236	255	270	292
the widower	200	220	236	255	270	292
the orphan who has lost both parents	100	110	118	128	136	147
the first and second orphan who has lost one parent						
if no annuity is paid to the widow or widower	75	83	89	97	103	111
if an annuity is paid to the widow or widower	55	61	66	72	76	82
the third and each further orphan who lost one parent	50	55	59	64	68	73
the grandchild who has lost both parents	100	110	118	128	136	147

the parents or adopting parents together	150	165	177	192	204	220
a surviving parent or adopting parent	100	110	118	128	136	147

[...]

21. §31 is changed as follows:

a) A new sub-§ (2) is added:

'(2) If the persecutee was detained in a concentration camp for at least one year and his earning capacity has been reduced by at least 25 per cent, it is favor presumed in his favour that his reduction in earning capacity due to persecution is 25 per cent for his claim to an annuity.'

[...]

22. §32 is changed as follows:

[...]

'(1) The monthly minimum amount of the annuities accounting for curtailing of the persecutee's earning capacity

		%	%	Through March 31, 1957 (DM)	From April 1, 1957 through May 31, 1960 (DM)	From June 1, 1960 through December 31, 1960 (DM)	From January 1, 1961 through June 30, 1962 (DM)	From July 1, 1962 through September 30, 1964 (DM)	From October 1, 1964 (DM)
by	from	25 to	39	100	110	118	128	136	147
"		40 to	49	125	138	148	160	170	184
"		50 to	59	150	165	177	193	204	220
"		60 to	69	175	192	207	224	237	256
"		70 to	79	200	220	236	255	270	292
		80 and more		250	275	295	319	338	365

[...]

32. In §43(1), sentence 2 Number 2, the period is replaced by a semicolon and the following sub-clause is added:

'April 6, 1941 is considered the starting date for the beginning of German responsibility for the deprivation of liberty due to race that occurred under the governments of the states of Bulgaria, Rumania, and Hungary.'

[...]

35. In §47 the following sub-§ (2) will be added:

'(2) If the persecutee lived under a false name it is assumed that during his clandestine life he lived under conditions incompatible with human dignity.'

36. §51 (1) through (3) is in the following new version:

'(1) The persecutee is entitled to claim compensation for damage to property if an object which belonged to him at the time the damage occurred was destroyed, disfigured, or exposed to plunder within territory of the German Reich as of December 31, 1937 or the Free City of Danzig.
(2) Exposure to plunder shall be deemed to have occurred especially if objects belonging to the persecutee were embezzled or distributed to a mob by persons exercising or usurping powers of public authority.
(3) The persecutee is also entitled to claim compensation as well if he had to leave objects behind in the territory of the German Reich as of December 31, 1937 or the Free City of Danzig without supervision to safeguard his interests, because
    1. he had been deprived of his freedom or lived clandestinely;
    2. he emigrated or fled to escape National Socialist despotic measures;
    3. he was expelled or deported by reasons of persecution as defined in §1.
[...]

38. §57 is changed as follows:

[...]

b) The following sub-§ (2) will be added:
'(2) Sub-§ (1) shall apply *mutatis mutandis*, if the persecutee after completed emigration continued to emigrate due to impending National Socialist despotic measures.'

[...]

44. §75 will be changed as follows:

[...]

c) The following new sub-§ (3) will be added:
'(3) If the persecutee does not have the claim to or the expectancy of lifelong support according to the civil service rules or principles or of retirement annuity or survivor's annuity, 20 per cent shall be added to the average income according to sub-§ (2). Upon attaining the age of sixty-five, this sum shall be raised to 30 per cent; for women the age of sixty replaces the age of sixty-five.'

[...]

48. §83 is changed as follows:

[…]

   b) sub-§ (2) is in the following new version:

'(2) The maximum monthly amount of the annuity is

through March 31, 1957	DM600
from April 1, 1957 through May 31, 1960	DM630
from June 1, 1960 through December 31, 1960	DM660
from January 1, 1961 through June 30, 1962	DM700
from July 1, 1962 through September 30, 1964	DM735
from October 1, 1964 through December 31, 1965	DM785
from January 1, 1966	DM1,000'

[…]

53. The following new §89a is added:

'§89a

Persecutees, who without fault have not yet started a constant regular occupation in their former or aspired profession, shall be given preference in the referral to a vacant position by the public employment agency.'

[…]

57. §95 is changed as follows:

   a) Sub-§ (1) is in the following new version:

'(1) The maximum monthly amount of the annuity is

through March 31, 1957	DM600
from April 1, 1957 through May 31, 1960	DM630
from June 1, 1960 through December 31, 1960	DM660
from January 1, 1961 through June 30, 1962	DM700
from July 1, 1962 through September 30, 1964	DM735
from October 1, 1964 through December 31, 1965	DM785
from January 1, 1966	DM1,000'

[…]

65. In §112 sentence 1 the words 'or Jewish public institutions' will be added after 'religious bodies'.

[…]

69. §116 will be in the following version:

'§116

The persecutee has a claim to a capital indemnity in the amount of DM10,000.'

[...]

80. §141 will be in the following version:

'§141

(1) ... The following sentence will be added: §4(3) shall apply *mutatis mutandis*. The spouse and the descendants of the persecutee have a claim to an emergency aid payment under the conditions of sentence 1 even if they were not persecuted themselves but were affected by the persecution.

(2) For persecutees, who have had the place of their last domicile or permanent residence in the territory of the German Reich as of December 31, 1937, a transfer into a concentration camp outside of this territory is considered a deportation. For deportees, who have had the place of their last domicile or permanent residence in the Free City of Danzig, the transfer into a concentration camp outside of the territory of the German Reich as of December 31, 1937 and outside of the Free City of Danzig is considered a deportation.

(3) A persecutee of German origin also has a claim according to sub-§ (1), if between September 30, 1938 and May 8, 1945 he emigrated or was expelled due to persecution reasons defined in §1 and if he has had his last domicile or permanent residence in a territory that was annexed to the German Reich after September 30, 1938, including the Protectorate of Bohemia and Moravia, if he, after the end of the National Socialist despotic regime moved or moves his domicile or permanent residence into the area of operation of this Law. The right to claim only exists if the persecutee is a German citizen at the time of the decision. Sub-§ (1), sentence 2 shall apply *mutatis mutandis*.

[...]

(6) Persecutees, who were deprived of their liberty for at least three years and who were German citizens at the time of incarceration have a claim to an emergency aid payment of DM3,000. Sub-§ (4) shall apply *mutatis mutandis*. The right to claim does not exist, if the persecutee has a claim to an emergency aid payment according to sub-§ (1) or (3).'

[...]

81. After §141 the following new Ninth Chapter 'Health Care' will be added:

'§141a

(1) A persecutee, whose claim to annuity payments due to damage to life or damage to limb and health or to an emergency aid payment has been established through ruling, settlement or non-appealable judicial decision, has a claim to health care for ailments not due to persecution. The claim exists only as long as the persecutee has his domicile or permanent residence in the area of operation of this Law.

(2) The persecutee (sub-§ (1)) has a claim to health care for spouse and children for as long as children's allowances may be granted to them under civil service

legislation, as long as they live in a common household or are mainly supported by him. Sub-§ (1), sentence 2 shall apply *mutatis mutandis.*

(3) The claim according to sub-§ (1) and (2) is barred

1. insofar as an equivalent claim exists toward a social insurance institution or the agency for aid to tuberculosis patients,

2. insofar as an equivalent claim exists due to a contract (with the exclusion of private health or accident insurance),

3. if the income of the persecutee exceeds the limit of annual earnings for the compulsory health insurance; in case of sub-§ (2) the claim is also excluded if the income of the spouse or the children exceeds this limit.

(4) The claim according to sub-§ (1) and (2) is neither transferable nor inheritable.

§141b

(1) Health care will only be provided in case of an illness according to the rules of the compulsory health insurance.

(2) Within the framework of health care the persecutee only has a claim to services that are suitable and sufficient for curing or relief of suffering according to medical science. The persecutee cannot claim services that are not necessary or uneconomical for a cure.

§141c

(1) The health care includes

1. outpatient medical and dental treatment;

2. drugs and dressing material as well as small remedies.

(2) Instead of outpatient medical or dental care, stationary treatment in a hospital (hospital care) can be provided.

(3) Otherwise the rules of the compulsory health insurance apply.

(4) If the persecutee receives health care, according to this Law, he is exempt from payment for the gazette of ordinances and the fee for the health insurance certificate (§§ 182a and 187b RVO).

(5) If the persecutee incurred costs for health care according to sub-§§ (1) and (2) prior to his claim for annuity payments due to damage to life or damage to limb or health or for an emergency aid payment, then the costs for these necessary treatments shall be adequately refunded. The same applies, if a persecutee, who has a claim according to §29(1), had expenses for health care and it turns out later that the health care was not necessary for the ailment due to persecution. §141a/(4) shall apply *mutatis mutandis.*'

82. After §141c the following new Tenth Chapter 'Concurrence of Claims for Damage to Life, Damage to Limb or Health and Damage to Professional Advancement' will be added:

'1. Concurrence of two claims

[...]

§141e

(1) If the persecutee has for the same compensation period a claim for annuity payments and capital indemnity for damage to limb or health and a claim to capital indemnity or pension for damage to professional advancement, he receives the full compensation for the damage related to the higher claim and 25 per cent of the compensation for the damage related to the lower claim. Therefore §31(3), (4) and §95(3) shall not be applicable.

(2) For the assessment of the claim for damage to professional advancement it remains out of consideration that the persecutee was or is not at his full achievement potential due to damage to limb or health.

(3) If the persecutee has a claim to compensation for the time before November 1, 1953 according to §83(3), then this claim is to be offset only with capital payments for claim for damage to limb or health for the period from November 1, 1952 through October 31, 1953.'

[...]

86. The following new §148a is added:

'§148a

(1) If a juridical body, institution or association or its legal successor that was damaged due to National Socialist despotic measures is considered as working for the benefit of the public according to the Ordinance regulating tax advantages for promotion of public benefits, then it can be granted a hardship allowance on application for mitigation of a hardship due to §§ 142–148, insofar as this is necessary for the fulfillment of its duties.

(2) Applications for mitigation of hardship according to sub-§ (1) are due by December 31, 1965.

(3) For the granting of hardship allowances a special fund of DM10 million will be established. It will be administered by the Land of Baden-Wuerttemberg.'

[...]

99. After §166 the following new Fourth Chapter 'Common Rules' is added:

[...]

'§166c

The rules of §§ 149–166 shall not apply to persecutees that were or are citizens of a state to whose financial expenses for the victims of National Socialist persecution the Federal Republic of Germany contributes according to a special contract in the form of an explicit contribution, unless the persecutee only acquired this citizenship after the end of the persecution.'

100. The former Part Five 'Persecutees on Grounds of Nationality' including §§ 167 and 168 are removed.

[...]

103. §171 is changed as follows:

[...]

b) In sub-§ (1) the following new sentence 5 is added:

'The maximum rate for a housing credit is DM5,000.
c) (2) A hardship mitigation may also be granted
    a) if the probability of the nexus between a damage to limb or health and the persecution cannot be proved only because the cause of the ailment is not known to medical science.'

[...]

112. The following new §189 is added:

'§189a
(1) If an application for a claim to compensation according to §189 was legally submitted, then claims that were not registered with this submission can still be registered until December 31, 1965.

(2) After January 1, 1966 a further claim can only be registered insofar as the claim is based on events that only occurred after December 31, 1964. In this case the claim has to be registered within one year after the occurrence of the fact. §189 sub-§ (3) shall apply *mutatis mutandis*.'

[...]

128. After §227 the following Fifth Chapter 'Rules of Procedure for the Claim to Health Care' is added:

'§227a
(1) The local branch of the National Health Insurance of the district, where the persecutee resides or, if such a branch does not exist, the Land Health Insurance, manages the health care.

[...]

§227b
(1) The expenses of the Compulsory Health Insurance that occur due to §§ 141a through c, plus 8 per cent administrative expenses will be refunded by the Land that is responsible according to §185.

(2) Claims to refund according to sub-§ (2) prescribe after two years. The period of limitation starts with the end of the year in which the expenses for the health insurance occurred.

(3) Sub-§ (2) shall apply *mutatis mutandis* for claims for recovery by the land for wrongfully provided refunds. The period of limitation starts with the end of the year in which the refund had been provided to the health insurance.'

[...]

130. The following new §238 a is added:

'§238a

(1) A claim to compensation according to this Law only exists if the claimant has his domicile or permanent residence at the time of the decision in a country, with which the Federal Republic of Germany maintains diplomatic relations at the time of operation of this Law or on January 1, 1963. For juridical bodies, agencies or associations and their legal successors the domicile is replaced by the place of business and the permanent residence is replaced by the place of administration.'

[...]

Article V

Special Regulations for Supra-Regional Groups of Persecutees

1. (1) A persecutee, who had been deprived of his liberty for at least six months (§43 BEG) or who can prove a lasting reduction in earning capacity of at least 80 per cent at the time of the decision, receives an assistance grant from a special to-be-established fund according to the requirements of this fund. The same shall apply to the widow of a persecutee, who suffered damage to life (§15 BEG), as well as for the widower of a persecutee under the conditions of §§ 15, 17 sub-§ (1), No. 2 BEG; in these cases the grant is only provided, if the widow or widower did not remarry.

   (2) The persecutee, who had been wearing the Star of David or who lived clandestinely under conditions incompatible with human dignity (§47 BEG) receives an assistance grant from the fund to be established. A claim to this grant does not exist if the persecutee receives a grant according to sub-§ (1).

   (3) The Special Fund will be endowed with DM1.2 million.

   (4) The applicant is only entitled to the assistance grant if he
      a) does not fulfill the conditions of §4 BEG or the general conditions of §§ 150 or 160 BEG
      and
      b) has his domicile or place of permanent residence on December 31, 1965 outside of the territories named in §1, sub-§ (2), No. 3 of the Law on Expelled Persons (Bundesvertriebenengesetz) and the Soviet-occupied Zone or the Soviet-occupied Sector of Berlin.

   (5) the assistance will not be granted, if the applicant
      a) does not have a claim to compensation according to §160 BEG because of the care through another country or an international organization
      or
      b) belongs to a group of people whose benefit contracts or accords for global reparation of the Federal Republic of Germany have been concluded,
      or

c) is on December 31, 1965 a citizen of a state that is mentioned in §1 sub-§
(2) No. 3 of the Expelled Persons Law, unless he was before this time a
refugee according to the Geneva Convention of July 28, 1951.

(6) The basic amount of the assistance grant according to sub-§ (1) sentence 1
is DM2,000. The basic amount is raised to DM2,500, if the persecutee has
reached the age of sixty-five at the time of proclamation of this Law.

(7) The basic amount of the assistance grant according to sub-§ (1) sentence 2
is DM3,000. It is raised to DM5,000 if the widow or widower was deprived of
their liberty for at least one year.

(8) The assistance grant according to sub-§ (2) is DM1,000.

(9) The assistance grant according to sub-§ (2) and the basic grant according
to sub-§§ (6) and (7) are due immediately after determination.

(10) The following rates of increment shall be paid in addition to the basic
amounts of sub-§§ (6) and (7):

    a) simple rate of increment
       in case of deprivation of liberty for one to two years or
       in case of a lasting reduction in earning capacity at the time of decision
       of at least 80 per cent;

    b) double rate of increment
       in case of deprivation of liberty for more than two and up to three
       years;

    c) triple rate of increment
       in case of deprivation of liberty for more than three and up to four
       years;

    d) quadruple rate of increment
       in case of deprivation of liberty for more than four years;

    e) quintuple rate of increment
       in case of damage to life under the conditions of sub-§ (1) sentence 2.

(11) In cases of sub-§ (10) only one of the five rates of increment can be asserted.

(12) The amount of the rate of increment according to sub-§ (10) is determined according to the proportion of the remaining amount in the fund after
payment of the basic assistance grants according to sub-§§ (6) and (7) and the
assistance grants according to sub-§ (8) to the total number of the determined
rates of increment. Amounts that are contestable through reference to the
compensation courts have to be taken into account.

[...]

Article VI

Special Regulations for Persons Damaged because of their Nationality

1. (1) Persons who were damaged under the National Socialist despotic regime
    by reason of their nationality in disregard of human rights and who on

October 1, 1953 were refugees according to the Geneva Convention of July 28, 1951, are entitled to claim compensation for lasting damage to limb or health. It is considered damage by reason of nationality if the damaging measure was fully or partly due to the person's citizenship of a foreign country or to a non-German people. If no other reasons for the damaging measure in disregard of human rights are apparent, it is assumed for the persons as defined in sentences 1 and 2 that the damage happened due to reasons of nationality.

[...]

2. Any person shall be disqualified from compensation who
   1. has committed a crime against peace, a war crime or a crime against humanity as defined in international agreements;
   2. has committed a grave non-political crime outside the receiving country before he was granted refuge in that country;
   3. has been guilty of acts contrary to the aims and principles of the United Nations.

[...]

4. (1) Persons, who were damaged according to the requirements of No. 1, can be granted a one time grant up to DM6,000, if the compensation according to No. 1 is excluded because the damagee
   a) turned refugee according to the Geneva Convention of July 28, 1951 only after October 1, 1953 or
   b) after the end of the damage and before October 1, 1953 as a refugee within the meaning of the Geneva Convention of July 28, 1951 acquired a new citizenship.

[...]

Article VIII

Cessation of Compensation

(1) Claims to compensation according to the BEG and to this Law can no longer be registered after December 31, 1969. This does not apply to the claim to compensation for the costs of treatment to damage to limb or health that has been approved as due to persecution according to §29, No. 1 BEG and article VI, No. 1, sub-§ (3), No. 1 of this Law, if the treatment was provided only after December 31, 1968 as well as for the claim to support of survivors according to §29 No. 6 BEG. §206 BEG is not affected.

[...]

Article IX

Rehabilitation in Criminal Justice

(1) The regulations for rehabilitation of National Socialist wrongs in the criminal justice system that set a time limit for registration of the claim for nullification are repealed.

(2) If neither the land regulations nor the Amendment Law Regulating Sphere of Jurisdiction of August 7, 1952 can determine jurisdiction within the area of operation of this Law, then the court of competent jurisdiction is the criminal division of the district court or the jury court of the district where the convicted person has his domicile at the time of proclamation of this Law or where he moves first after its proclamation. In the case that the convicted has his domicile outside of the area of operation of this Law, the Federal High Court [Bundesgerichtshof] determines the court of competent jurisdiction.

(3) In the case that an application for nullification of a criminal justice decision according to the regulations described in sub-§ (1) was denied merely due to the expiry of a time limit, then the validity of this decision does not contradict the permissibility of a new application. The same applies, if in the cases regulated in sub-§ (2) an application was denied due to lack of competent jurisdiction.

[…]

The Federal Government has given the present Law the approval necessary under Article 113 of the Constitution.

The present Law is hereby promulgated. Bonn. September 14, 1965.

For the Federal President the President of the Bundesrat, Zinn
Federal Chancellor, Ludwig Erhard
Federal Minister of Finance, Dr. Dahlgruen

NOTES

1   Changes Federal Law Gazette III 251–1 and 251–1/1.
2   Federal Law Gazette III 251–1.

GERMANY

FORCED AND SLAVE LABOR

FEDERAL LAW ON THE CREATION OF A FOUNDATION, 'REMEMBRANCE, RESPONSIBILITY AND FUTURE'

of August 2, 2000, which entered into force on August 12, 2000

(Federal Law Gazette I 1263) amended by the Law of August 4, 2001, which entered into force on August 11, 2001 (Federal Law Gazette I 2036) as well as by the Law of August 21, 2002, which entered into force on August 28, 2002 (Federal Law Gazette I 3347) as well as by the Law of August 19, 2004, which entered into force on August 25, 2004 (Federal Law Gazette I 2166)

Preamble

Recognizing

that the National Socialist State inflicted severe injustice on slave laborers and forced laborers, through deportation, internment, exploitation which in some cases extended to destruction through labor, and through a large number of other human rights violations,

that German enterprises which participated in the National Socialist injustice bear a historic responsibility and must accept it,

that the enterprises which have come together in the Foundation Initiative of German Industry have acknowledged this responsibility, that the injustice committed and the human suffering it caused cannot be truly compensated by financial payments,

that the Law comes too late for those who lost their lives as victims of the National Socialist regime or have died in the meantime,

the German Bundestag acknowledges political and moral responsibility for the victims of National Socialism. The Bundestag intends to keep alive the memory of injustice inflicted on victims for coming generations as well.

The German Bundestag presumes that this Law, the German–US intergovernmental agreement, the accompanying statements of the US Government as well as the Joint Declaration by all parties to the negotiations provide adequate legal security for German enterprises and the Federal Republic of Germany, especially in the United States of America.

With the concurrence of the Bundesrat, the Bundestag has passed the following Law:

Section 1: Establishment and Headquarters

(1) A legally recognized foundation with the name 'Remembrance, Responsibility and Future' shall be established under public law. The Foundation comes into being as of the entry into force of this legislation.
(2) The headquarters of the Foundation shall be in Berlin.

Section 2: Purpose of the Foundation

(1) The purpose of the Foundation is to make financial compensation available through partner organizations to former forced laborers and to those affected by other injustices from the National Socialist period.
(2) A 'Remembrance and Future' fund will be established within the Foundation. Its continuing task is to use the income primarily produced by the

means allocated to it from Foundation monies to foster projects that serve the purposes of better understanding among peoples, the interests of survivors of the National Socialist regime, youth exchange, social justice, remembrance of the threat posed by totalitarian systems and despotism, and international cooperation in humanitarian endeavors. In commemoration and respect of those victims of National Socialist injustice who did not survive, it is also intended to further projects in the interest of their heirs.

Section 3: Donors and the Foundation's Capital Assets

(1) Contributors to the Foundation's capital fund shall be the companies joined together in the Foundation Initiative of German Industry, and the Federal Government.

(2) The Foundation shall be endowed with a capital fund consisting of the following:

1. Five billion deutsche marks that the companies joined together in the Foundation Initiative of German Industry have agreed to make available, including the payments that German insurance companies have provided to the International Commission on Holocaust Era Insurance Claims or will provide in the future.

2. Five billion deutsche marks that the German Federal Government is making available in the year 2000. The contribution of the Federal Government includes the contributions of enterprises of which the Federal Government is sole owner or in which it has a majority interest.

(3) There is no obligation for the donors to make supplementary payments.

(4) The Foundation is authorized to accept contributions from third parties. It shall endeavor to obtain additional contributions. The contributions are exempt from inheritance tax and gift tax.

(5) Income from the Foundation's capital fund and other income is to be used only for the purposes of the Foundation.

Section 4: The Bodies of the Foundation

The bodies of the Foundation are:

1. the Board of Trustees; and
2. the Board of Directors.

Section 5: The Board of Trustees

(1) The Board of Trustees is made up of 27 members, namely:
1. the chairman, to be named by the German Chancellor;
2. four members to be named by the companies joined together in the Foundation Initiative of German Industry;
3. five members to be named by the German Bundestag and two by the Bundesrat;
4. one representative of the Federal Ministry of Finance;
5. one representative of the Federal Ministry for Foreign Affairs;
6. one member to be named by the Conference on Jewish Material Claims against Germany;
7. one member to be named by the Central Council of German Sinti and Roma, the Alliance of German Sinti, and the International Romani Union;
8. one member to be named by the Government of the State of Israel;
9. one member to be named by the Government of the United States of America;
10. one member to be named by the Government of the Republic of Poland;
11. one member to be named by the Government of the Russian Federation;
12. one member to be named by the Government of Ukraine;
13. one member to be named by the Government of the Republic of Belarus;
14. one member to be named by the Government of the Czech Republic;
15. one lawyer to be named by the Government of the United States of America;
16. one member to be named by the United Nations High Commissioner for Refugees;
17. one member to be named by the International Organization for Migration in accordance with Section 9, Paragraph 2, Number 6; and
18. one member to be named by the Federal Information and Counseling Association for Victims of National Socialism e.V. [Registered Association].

The sending body may designate a substitute for each member of the Board.

A different composition of the Board of Trustees may be decided by a unanimous decision of the Board of Trustees.

(2) The term of office for members of the Board of Trustees shall be four years. If a member should resign before the end of his term, a successor may be appointed for the remainder of the term. The members of the Board of Trustees can be recalled by the sending body at any time.
(3) The Board of Trustees shall establish its own rules of procedure.

(4) The presence of half the membership of the Board of Trustees plus one shall constitute a quorum. The board shall make decisions on the basis of a simple majority. In case of a tie, the vote of the chairman shall determine the outcome.

(5) The Board of Trustees has the right to decide on all fundamental matters that have to do with the tasks of the Foundation, specifically with regard to budgetary plans, the annual report, and the existence of the specific characteristics referred to in Section 12, Paragraph 1. It monitors the performance of the Board of Directors.

(6) The Board of Trustees makes decisions regarding the projects of the 'Remembrance and Future' Fund based on proposals by the Board of Directors.

(7) The Board of Trustees establishes guidelines for the use of resources insofar as their use is not already specified in this Law. In this connection, it shall particularly endeavor to see to it that the partner organizations are able to draw in fair shares upon the eligibilities for payment referred to in Section 11, Paragraph 1, Sentence 1, Numbers 1 and 2.

(8) Members of the Board of Trustees serve in a 'pro bono' capacity; necessary expenses will be reimbursed.

Section 6: The Board of Directors of the Foundation

(1) The Board of Directors shall consist of the chairman and two additional members. Members of the Board of Trustees may not at the same time belong to the Board of Directors.

(2) The members of the Board of Directors will be named by the Board of Trustees.

(3) The Board of Directors shall direct the day-to-day business of the Foundation and shall implement the decisions of the Board of Trustees. It is responsible for distributing the resources of the Foundation to the partner organizations and for the management of the 'Remembrance and Future' fund. It oversees the purposeful and prudent expenditure of the Foundation's funds, in particular adherence by the partner organizations to the provisions of this Law and the guidelines established by the Board of Trustees for the use of its funds. The Board of Directors shall represent the Foundation, both in judicial and extrajudicial matters.

(4) The details shall be determined by the by-laws.

Section 7: The By-Laws

The Board of Trustees shall adopt a set of by-laws by a two-thirds majority vote. If a set of by-laws has still not been adopted within three months of the initial meeting of the Board of Trustees, the chairman shall propose a set of by-laws that will be passed by a simple majority. The Board of Trustees may amend the by-laws on the basis of a two-thirds majority.

Section 8: Oversight, Budget, Auditing

(1) The Foundation is subject to legal oversight by the Federal Ministry of Finance; starting with the second period in office of the Board of Trustees, it shall be subject to legal oversight by the Federal Ministry for Foreign Affairs.

(2) The Foundation shall prepare a budget in timely fashion before the start of each fiscal year. The budget shall require the approval of the Federal Ministry of Finance.

(3) The Foundation shall be subject to being audited by the Federal Court of Audit. Without prejudice hereto, the Foundation's accounts and the management of its budget and finances are to be audited by the Federal Office for the Settlement of Open Property Matters.

Section 9: Use of Foundation Resources

(1) Resources of the Foundation that serve the purpose of the Foundation, referred to in Section 2, Paragraph 1, will be allocated to partner organizations. They are to be used for one-time payments to persons eligible pursuant to Section 11, as well as for covering the personnel and non-personnel expenses of the partner organizations. Persons eligible under Section 11, Paragraph 1, Sentence 1, Number 1, or Sentence 5 can receive up to DM15,000, and persons eligible under Section 11, Paragraph 1, Sentence 1, Number 2, or Sentence 2 can receive up to DM5,000. Receiving a payment under Section 11, Paragraph 1, Sentence 1, Number 1 or 2 does not preclude receiving a payment under Section 11, Paragraph 1, Sentence 1, Number 3, or Sentence 4 or 5.

(2) The partner organizations shall have available DM8.1 billion including DM50 million in accrued interest for payments to persons who suffered

personal damage as referred to in Section 11, Paragraph 1, Sentence 1, Numbers 1 and 2, and Section 11, Paragraph 1, Sentence 2, insofar as [the payments are] intended for compensation for forced labor. The total amounts shall be divided into the following maximum amounts:

1. for the partner organization responsible for the Republic of Poland, DM1,812 million;
2. for the partner organization responsible for Ukraine and the Republic of Moldova, DM1,724 million;
3. for the partner organization responsible for the Russian Federation and the Republic of Latvia and the Republic of Lithuania, DM835 million;
4. for the partner organization responsible for the Republic of Belarus and the Republic of Estonia, DM694 million;
5. for the partner organization responsible for the Czech Republic, DM423 million;
6. for the partner organization responsible for the non-Jewish claimants outside the states referred to in Numbers 1 through 5 (the International Organization for Migration), DM800 million; the partner organization must pay over up to DM260 million of this amount to the Conference on Jewish Material Claims against Germany;
7. for the partner organization responsible for the Jewish claimants outside the states referred to in Numbers 1 through 5 (the Conference on Jewish Material Claims against Germany), DM1,812 million.

The partner organizations must use these monies to make the stipulated payments for all persons who on February 16, 1999 had their principal domicile in their [the organizations'] individual regional areas of responsibility and on that date belonged to their material sphere of responsibility. The partner organizations referred to in Numbers 2, 3, and 4 are also responsible for those persons who on February 16, 1999 had their principal domicile in other states, which were republics of the former USSR; in each case that partner organization is responsible from whose area the claimant was deported.

(3) DM50 million are intended for compensation of other personal injuries in connection with National Socialist injustice. Claims are to be addressed to the partner organizations referred to in Paragraph 2. These organizations shall determine the merits and amount of the damage claimed. The amount of the compensation payments shall be determined by the Commission referred to in Paragraph 6, Sentence 2, in accordance with the ratio between the totality of the damages recognized by the partner organizations and the total amount of the monies referred to in Sentence 1, with due consideration given to Section 11, Paragraph 1, Sentence 5. The partner organizations may request the Commission referred to in Sentence 4 to assign the determinations referred to in Sentence 3 to an independent

arbitrator. A partner organization that prefers not to make the determinations referred to in Sentence 3 itself must bear the costs of the arbitrator.

(4) The sum of DM1 billion of the Foundation's monies is intended for payments to persons who suffered property loss. This amount is divided into the following maximum amounts:

1. DM150 million for property losses resulting from persecution within the meaning of Section 11, Paragraph 1, Sentence 1, Number 3;

2. DM50 million for other property losses within the meaning of Section 11, Paragraph 1, Sentence 4;

3. DM150 million for the International Commission on Holocaust Era Insurance Claims to compensate unpaid or revoked and not otherwise compensated insurance policies of German insurance enterprises, including the costs incurred in this connection;

4. DM300 million for social purposes to the benefit of Holocaust survivors through the Conference on Jewish Material Claims against Germany; DM24 million of this shall be paid over to the partner organization referred to in Paragraph 2, Number 6, which shall use it for social purposes vis-à-vis the similarly persecuted Sinti and Roma;

5. DM350 million for the humanitarian fund of the International Commission on Holocaust Era Insurance Claims.

(5) If additional interest is earned from the monies made available to the Foundation except for the monies intended for the Future Fund, up to DM50 million of this shall be made available to the International Commission on Holocaust Era Insurance Claims to compensate insurance losses within the meaning of Paragraph 4, Sentence 2, Number 3, for foreign subsidiaries of German insurance enterprises and for costs incurred in this connection, as soon as the monies are available. Monies referred to in Sentence 1, and Paragraph 4, Sentence 2, Number 3, may also be used for the other purpose in each case.

(6) Claims for payments from the monies envisaged in Paragraph 4, Sentence 2 Numbers 1 and 2, are to be addressed to the partner organization referred to in Paragraph 2, Number 6, regardless of the claimant's residence. Determinations concerning these payments shall be made by a commission to be formed under this partner organization. The commission shall consist of one member each to be named by the Federal Ministry of Finance and the Department of State of the United States of America and a chairperson to be chosen by those two members. The commission shall establish supplemental principles concerning the content and procedure of its determinations, insofar as these are not already established under this Law or the by-laws. The commission shall rule on the submitted applications within a year after expiration of the application deadline. The Property Claims Commission shall rule on appeals against its initial determination subsequent to renewed

consultation as the appeals organ within the meaning of Section 19. The costs of the commission, the appeals organ, and the partner organization are to be covered pro rata from the total amount referred to in Paragraph 4, Sentence 2, Numbers 1 and 2. If the amount of damages recognized by the commission exceeds the monies available under Paragraph 4, Sentence 2, Number 1 or 2, the payments to be made are to be reduced in proportion to the available monies.

(7) DM700 million including the interest accruing thereto are to be used for projects of the 'Remembrance and Future' Fund. Of this amount, DM100 million may be made available for other than its intended purpose, if well-founded requests are filed based on insurance claims that could not be met under Paragraph 4, Sentence 2, Number 3, and Paragraph 5.

(8) In concert with the Board of Trustees, the partner organizations may subdivide the category of forced laborers, within its quota, in accordance with Section 11, Paragraph 1, Sentence 1, Number 1, insofar as this involves persons interned in other places of confinement, as well as affected persons within the meaning of Section 11, Paragraph 1, Sentence 1, Number 2, into subcategories depending on the severity of their fate and may set correspondingly gradated maximum amounts. This shall also apply to the eligibility of legal successors.

(9) The maximum amounts under Paragraph 1 may only be paid out for the time being in the amount of 50 percent for claimants under Section 11, Paragraph 1, Sentence 1, Number 1, and 35 percent for claimants under Section 11, Paragraph 1, Sentence 1, Number 2, or Sentence 2. Another payment of up to 50 percent of the amounts mentioned in Paragraph 1 for claimants under Section 11, Paragraph 1, Sentence 1, Number 1 and up to 65 percent of the amounts mentioned in Paragraph 1 for claimants under Section 11, Paragraph 1, Sentence 1, Number 2, or Sentence 2 shall be paid out after conclusion of the processing of all applications pending before the respective partner organization, to the extent possible within the framework of the available means. The partner organizations may set up a financial reserve for appeals under Section 19, in the amount of up to 5 percent of the monies allocated. To the extent the reserve has been set up, payment of the second installment under Sentence 2 may be made before the conclusion of the appeal proceedings. The Board of Trustees has the right, at the request of individual partner organizations, to allow an increase in the installment payments laid down under Sentence 1, insofar as it is assured that the monies allocated in Paragraph 2 are not exceeded.

(10) Payments under Section 11, Paragraph 1, Sentence 1, Number 3, with the exception of the payments of the International Commission on Holocaust Era Insurance Claims and payments under Section 11, Paragraph 1, Sentence

4 or 5, can take place only after all applications pending before the competent commission have been processed.

(11) Monies allocated under Paragraph 2 but not completely depleted are to be used for persons entitled to payments under Section 11, Paragraph 1, Sentence 1, Numbers 1 and 2. Should the funds provided under Paragraphs 2 and 3 not be completely depleted in spite of payment of the maximum amounts under Paragraph 1, Sentence 3, the Board of Trustees shall decide how they shall be used. Just as in the case of the use of additional monies, the Board must compensate, in particular, any shortage incurred by individual partner organizations in making payments under Section 11, Paragraph 1, Sentence 1, Numbers 1 and 2. Monies referred to in Paragraph 4, Sentence 2, Numbers 1 and 2, which are not drawn down despite full compensation of damages shall go to the Conference on Jewish Material Claims against Germany; those referred to in Paragraph 4, Sentence 2, Number 3, to the International Commission on Holocaust Era Insurance Claims. The Board of Trustees may allow the maximum amounts under Paragraph 1, Sentence 3 to be exceeded if all partner organizations have been able to make payments in the amounts of these maximum amounts.

(12) Personnel and non-personnel costs shall be paid from the Foundation's funds, insofar as they are not to be assumed by the partner organizations in accordance with Paragraph 1, Sentence 2. The costs to be borne by the Foundation also include outlays for attorneys and counsel whose activity on behalf of persons entitled to payments under Section 11 contributed to the establishment of the Foundation or otherwise were favorable to its creation, particularly by taking part in the multilateral negotiations that preceded the establishment of the Foundation or by filing suits on behalf of claimants under Section 11 between November 14, 1990 and December 17, 1999. There is no legal claim to payments pursuant to Sentence 2. An arbitrator named by the Foundation will determine the allocation of an amount set by the Board of Trustees, based on guidelines that shall be determined and published by the Board of Trustees. Requests for the payments stipulated in Sentence 2 are to be submitted to the Foundation by the attorneys and counsel themselves and on their own behalf within eight months after publication of the guidelines. They must be accompanied by documentation of the outlays claimed. Every attorney and counsel shall make a declaration in the request proceedings to the effect that he waives any claims against his clients upon receipt of a payment under Sentence 2. He is under obligation to advise his clients that he has waived any claims.

(13) For pending litigation concerning matters covered in this Law, court costs shall not be levied.

Section 10: Distribution of Resources through Partner Organizations

(1) The approval and disbursal of one-time payments to those persons eligible under Section 11 will be carried out through partner organizations. The Foundation is neither authorized nor obligated in this regard. The Board of Trustees may decide for another mode of payment. The partner organizations shall cooperate with appropriate associations of persecutees and local organizations.

(2) Within two months after entry into force of the Law, the Foundation and its partner organizations are to publicize the possibility of compensation under this Law in an appropriate manner to all groups of eligible people in their respective countries of residency. These publications shall specifically include information about the Foundation and its partner organizations, the conditions on which compensation can be awarded, and application deadlines.

Section 11: Eligible Persons

(1) Eligible under this Law are:

1. persons who were detained in a concentration camp as defined in Section 42, Paragraph 2 of the German Indemnification Act or in another place of confinement outside the territory of what is now the Republic of Austria or a ghetto under comparable conditions and were subjected to forced labor;

2. persons who were deported from their homelands into the territory of the German Reich within the borders of 1937 or to a German-occupied area, subjected to forced labor in a commercial enterprise or for public authorities there, and detained under conditions other than those mentioned in Number 1, or were subjected to conditions resembling detention or similar extremely harsh living conditions; this rule does not apply to persons who because their forced labor was performed primarily in the territory of what is now the Republic of Austria can receive payments from the Austrian Reconciliation Foundation;

3. persons who suffered property loss as a consequence of racial persecution with essential, direct, and harm-causing collaboration of German businesses as defined by the laws on indemnification and who could not receive any payment or could not file their claims for restitution or compensation by the deadline because they either did not meet the

residency requirements of the Federal Indemnification Act or had their domicile or permanent residence in an area with whose government the Federal Republic of Germany did not maintain diplomatic relations, or because they could not prove that an asset that had been expropriated due to persecution outside the territory of the German Reich in its 1937 borders, and could no longer be located there, had been removed to the Federal Republic of Germany, or the proofs of the validity of their claims under the Federal Restitution Act [*Bundesrückerstattungsgesetz*] and the Federal Indemnification Act [*Bundesentschädigungsgesetz*] became known and available only due to German reunification, and the filing of the claims under the Law on the Settlement of Open Property Matters or the Law on Indemnification of Victims of Nazism was not allowed, or to the extent that restitution payments for monetary claims expropriated outside Reich territory were denied for lack of the possibility of assessing them, and no payments could be claimed either under the Currency Conversion Act, the Federal Indemnification Act, the Equalization of Burdens Act, or the Reparation Losses Act; that also applies to other persecutees within the meaning of the Federal Indemnification Act; special arrangements within the framework of the International Commission on Holocaust Era Insurance Claims shall remain unaffected.

The partner organizations may also award compensation from the funds provided to them pursuant to Section 9, Paragraph 2 to those victims of National Socialist crimes who are not members of one of the groups mentioned in Sentence 1, Numbers 1 and 2, particularly forced laborers in agriculture. These awards, with reservation as to Section 9, Paragraph 8, must not result in any reduction in the payments to persons eligible under Paragraph 1, Sentence 1, Number 1. The funds provided for in Section 9, Paragraph 4, Sentence 2, Number 2 are intended to compensate property damage inflicted during the National Socialist regime with the essential, direct, and harm-causing participation of German enterprises, but not inflicted for reasons of National Socialist persecution. The funds referred to in Section 9, Paragraph 3 shall be awarded in cases of medical experiments or in the event of the death of, or severe damage to the health of, a child lodged in a home for children of forced laborers; in cases of other personal injuries they may be awarded.

(2) Eligibility shall be demonstrated by the applicant by submission of documentation. The partner organization shall bring in relevant evidence. If no relevant evidence is available, the claimant's eligibility can be made credible in some other way.

(3) Eligibility cannot be based on prisoner-of-war status.

(4) Payments from the Foundation are exempt from inheritance tax and gift tax.

Section 12: Definitions

(1) Specific characteristics of other places of confinement referred to in Section 11, Paragraph 1, Number 1 are inhumane conditions of detention, insufficient nutrition, and lack of medical care.

(2) German enterprises referred to in Sections 11 and 16 are those that had their headquarters within the 1937 borders of the German Reich or have their headquarters in the Federal Republic of Germany, as well as their parent companies, even when the latter had or have their headquarters abroad. Enterprises situated outside the 1937 borders of the German Reich in which, during the period between January 30, 1933 and the entry into force of this Law, German enterprises as described in Sentence 1 had a direct or indirect financial participation of at least 25 percent are also considered German enterprises.

Section 13: Application Eligibility

(1) Awards under Section 11, Paragraph 1, Sentence 1, Numbers 1 or 2, or Sentence 2 or Sentence 5 are strictly personal and individual and must be applied for in one's own name. In a case where the eligible person has died after February 15, 1999, or where an award under Section 11, Paragraph 1, Number 3 or Sentence 4 is being applied for, the surviving spouse and children shall be entitled to equal shares of the award. If the eligible person left neither a spouse nor children, awards may be applied for in equal shares by the grandchildren, or if there are no grandchildren living, by the siblings. If no application is filed by these persons, the heirs named in a will are entitled to apply. Special arrangements within the framework of the International Commission on Holocaust Era Insurance Claims shall remain unaffected. The claim to payment cannot be ceded or attached.

(2) Juridical persons shall not be eligible. They can file applications as representatives of their shareholders eligible under this Law if specifically authorized by these shareholders. If a religious community or organization suffered property losses with the essential, direct, and harm-causing participation of German enterprises, Sentence 1 does not apply to them or their legal successors.

Section 14: Cut-off Dates

(1) Eligibility pursuant to Section 11 can no longer be determined if an application has not been received by a partner organization by the end of December 31, 2001. This shall also apply if upon conclusion of processing by the respective partner organization within the meaning of Section 9, Paragraph 9, Sentence 2 the application forms, documentation and evidence required to take a decision on the application have not been received.

(2) Applications that are received directly by the Foundation or by an inappropriate partner organization shall be forwarded to the appropriate partner organization. Special arrangements within the framework of the International Commission on Holocaust Era Insurance Claims shall remain unaffected.

(3) If an application has been filed within the application period specified in Paragraph 1 and if within six months after the death of the eligible person none of the persons eligible as legal successors pursuant to Section 13, Paragraph 1, Sentences 2 through 4 have notified the partner organization of their legal succession, the eligibility for an award shall expire. Paragraph 2 shall apply to the notification of legal succession *mutatis mutandis.*

Section 15: Treatment of Other Payments

(1) Payments for injustices suffered under National Socialism are supposed to benefit the persons eligible and not lead to a reduction of income received from the social security or health care system.

(2) Payments made earlier by enterprises in compensation for forced labor and other National Socialist injustices, even if made through third parties, shall be counted against payments under Section 9, Paragraph 1. Special arrangements within the framework of the International Commission on Holocaust Era Insurance Claims shall remain unaffected.

Section 16: Exclusions from Claims

(1) Payments from public funds, including social security, and from German business enterprises for injustice suffered under National Socialism as defined in Section 11 may be claimed only under the terms of this Law. Any further claims in connection with National Socialist injustices are excluded.

This applies also to cases in which claims have been transferred to third persons by operation of law, transition, or a legal transaction.

(2) Each claimant shall provide a statement within the framework of the application procedure irrevocably renouncing, without prejudice to Sentences 3 through 5, after receipt of a payment under this Law any further claim against the authorities for forced labor and property damage, all claims against German enterprises in connection with National Socialist injustice, and forced labor claims against the Republic of Austria or Austrian enterprises. The renunciation becomes effective upon receipt of a payment under this Law. Accepting payments for personal damage under Section 11, Paragraph 1, Sentence 1, Number 1 or 2, or Sentence 2 or 5 shall not mean the renunciation of payments for insurance or other property damage in accordance with Section 11, Paragraph 1, Sentence 1, Number 3, or Sentence 4, and vice versa. Sentence 1 does not apply to claims arising from National Socialist injustice committed by foreign parent companies with headquarters outside the 1937 borders of the German Reich without having any connections with their German subsidiaries and the latter's involvement in National Socialist injustice. Sentence 1 also does not apply to any claims to restitution of artworks, insofar as the applicant undertakes to pursue this claim in Germany or the country from which the artwork was taken. The renunciation also pertains to compensation of legal costs for the prosecution of the claim, insofar as Section 9, Paragraph 12 does not provide otherwise. The details of the procedure shall be determined by the by-laws.

(3) More extensive compensation arrangements and settlements of the consequences of war at the public expense shall not be prejudiced by the above.

Section 17: Transfer of Funds

(1) The Foundation is to make funds available quarterly to the partner organizations according to their documented need as outlined in Section 9, Paragraphs 2 and 3. The utilization of funds will be appropriately monitored by the Foundation.

(2) The first allocation of funds to the Foundation requires as a precondition the entry into force of the German–US Intergovernmental Agreement Concerning the Foundation 'Remembrance, Responsibility and Future', and the establishment of adequate legal security for German enterprises. The German Bundestag shall determine whether these preconditions exist.

Section 18: Requests for Information

(1) The Foundation and its partner organizations are authorized to receive information from agencies and other public bodies that is necessary for the fulfillment of their responsibilities. Information will not be provided if this would be contrary to specific official regulations on the use of the information, or when justifiable protection of the interests of the party concerned outweighs the general interest favoring disclosure.

(2) The information received may be used only for the purpose of carrying out the goals of the Foundation, and an applicant's personal data may be used only for the grant procedure under Section 11. The use of these data for other purposes is admissible only with the express consent of the applicant.

(3) Applicants under this Law may request information from enterprises in Germany for which or for whose legal predecessors they performed forced labor, insofar as this is requisite for determining their eligibility for awards.

Section 19: Appeals Process

The partner organizations are to create appeals organs that are independent and subject to no outside instruction. The appeals process itself is to be free of charge. However, costs incurred by the applicant are not to be reimbursed.

Section 20: Entry into Force

This Law enters into force on the date after its promulgation. Section 14 in the version of the Law of August 4, 2001 shall enter into force at the latest as of August 11, 2001.

Property Claims Commission Supplemental Principles and Rules of Procedure
[Excerpts]

The Property Claims Commission,

Pursuant to section 9, paragraph 6 of the Law on the Creation of the Foundation 'Remembrance, Responsibility and Future' of August 2, 2000, entered into force on August 12, 2000 (the 'German Foundation Act' and the 'German Foundation', respectively);

Recalling that under section 9, paragraph 6 of the German Foundation Act, the Commission is responsible for making determinations on property claims within the meaning of section 11, paragraph 1, sentence 1, number 3 and section 11, paragraph 1, sentence 4 of the German Foundation Act;

Noting that under section 9, paragraph 6 of the German Foundation Act, claims for property losses are to be addressed to the International Organization for Migration ('IOM'), regardless of the claimant's residence;

Recalling that under section 9, paragraph 3 of the German Foundation Act, the Commission is also responsible for the pro rata determination of the amount of compensation payments for personal injury claims within the meaning of section 11, paragraph 1, sentence 5 of the German Foundation Act;

Noting that under section 9, paragraph 3 of the German Foundation Act, partner organizations of the German Foundation may request the Commission to assign the determination of the merits and quantum of personal injury claims to an independent arbitrator;

For the purpose of establishing supplemental principles concerning the substance and procedure of its determinations;

Hereby adopts the following:

Section 1
Definitions

For the purposes of the present Supplemental Principles and Rules of Procedure:

'Commission' means the Property Claims Commission established to determine property claims pursuant to section 9, paragraph 6 of the German Foundation Act.

'Foundation's By-Laws' means the document ('Statutes') adopted by the Board of Trustees of the German Foundation on August 31, 2000 pursuant to section 7 of the German Foundation Act.

'German enterprises' means enterprises referred to in section 12, paragraph 2 of the German Foundation Act.

'German Foundation Act' means the Law on the Creation of a Foundation 'Remembrance, Responsibility and Future' of August 2, 2000, entered into force on August 12, 2000.

'IOM' means the International Organization for Migration.

'National Socialist era' means the period from January 30, 1933 through May 9, 1945.

'Other property loss' means a property loss suffered in connection with National Socialist wrongs but not because of National Socialist persecution, within the meaning of section 11, paragraph 1, sentence 4 of the German Foundation Act.

'Partner organizations' means organizations, including IOM, participating in making financial compensation available, pursuant to the terms of the German Foundation Act, to former slave and forced laborers and other victims of National Socialist injustice.

'Persecution' means persecution as defined in the German Federal Indemnification Act [*Bundesentschädigungsgesetz*, or 'BEG'].

'Persecution-related property loss' means a property loss suffered as a result of National Socialist persecution, within the meaning of section 11, paragraph 1, number 3 of the German Foundation Act.

'Personal injury claims' means claims referred to in section 11, paragraph 1, sentence 5 of the German Foundation Act.

'Property' means any and all immoveable, moveable, tangible and intangible assets.

'Rules' means these Supplemental Principles and Rules of Procedure.

General Principles

Section 2
Scope and Effect

These Supplemental Principles and Rules of Procedure (the 'Rules') contain supplemental principles concerning the substance and procedure of the determinations of the Commission insofar as such principles and procedures are not already established under the German Foundation Act and the By-Laws of the German Foundation.

Section 3
Eligibility to File a Claim

3.1 A claim may be made by the individual who suffered the property loss. If the individual who suffered the property loss is no longer alive, the surviving spouse and children shall all be entitled to equal shares of the award. If neither a spouse nor children survive, the grandchildren, or in the absence of grandchildren, the siblings, are eligible. If none of the above files a claim, then a claim may be filed by the beneficiaries named in the will of the individual who suffered the property loss.

3.2 Religious communities and religious organizations that suffered a loss of or damage to their property during the National Socialist era as a result of essential, direct, and harm-causing participation of German enterprises are eligible to file a claim for compensation. If the religious community or religious organization has ceased to exist, the legal successor of such a community or organization is eligible.

Section 4
Representation

4.1 Individual claimants may be represented by a lawyer or another representative of their choice. Representatives shall submit a written authorization from the claimant stating that the claimant is aware that the procedure before IOM and the Commission is free of charge, that neither IOM nor the Commission will reimburse lawyers' or any other fees, and that payment will not be made to the representative but only to the person entitled to payment.

4.2 Legal entities are entitled to make claims on behalf of individual shareholders or other owners who suffered a property loss as specified in sections 18 and 19 below, if specifically authorized by such shareholders or other owners.

Section 5
Cost of Claims Processing

5.1 The processing of claims shall be free of charge.

5.2 Expenses incurred by claimants, including expenses for representation, shall not be reimbursed.

Section 6
Waiver

6.1 Prior to their receipt of compensation payments, Claimants shall have signed a waiver waiving any and all National Socialist era claims against German enterprises and the German Government, and all forced labor claims against Austrian enterprises or the Austrian Government. The waiver shall be deemed to take effect with respect to a claimant on the date on which such claimant receives a compensation payment.

6.2 The waiver shall not preclude claimants from being eligible to receive payments under the German Foundation Act for slave or forced labor or personal injury.

6.3 The waiver shall not preclude the claimant from bringing an action against a specific German entity for the return of a specifically identified piece of art if the action is filed in the Federal Republic of Germany or in the country in which the art was taken.

6.4 The waiver shall not preclude insurance claims brought in the framework of the International Commission on Holocaust Era Insurance Claims (ICHEIC).

Section 7

(Deleted)

Chapter II
Submission of Claims

Section 8

Claim Form

8.1 Claims shall be submitted on the official IOM claim form for property losses. The claim form shall be made available in the following languages: Czech, English, German, Hebrew, Hungarian, Polish, and Russian.

8.2 A claim form from an individual claimant shall be accepted in Czech, English, German, Hebrew, Hungarian, Polish, and Russian. A claim form from a religious community or religious organization, or an individual claimant who is represented by a lawyer is expected to be submitted in English or German.

8.3 All claimants, whether represented or not, must sign the claim form before a notary public or other official authorized to attest to the authenticity of signatures. If the claimant is homebound, the claimant may sign the claim form before an attending physician.

8.4 Claim forms shall be available free of charge.

Section 9

Submission of Claim

9.1 The duly completed IOM claim form must be submitted in one original and one copy. All accompanying documents must be submitted in two copies.

9.2 If a claim is submitted in a formless manner, IOM shall set the claimant a deadline to submit a duly completed IOM claim form for property loss and to remedy any other formal deficiencies as defined in section 15.1 below.

9.3 Only one claim shall be filed by persons other than the person who suffered a property loss. Should more than one claim be filed, IOM may consolidate them or set the plural claimants a 90-day deadline to submit a common claim.

9.4 Individuals representing a religious community or religious organization must submit documentation demonstrating their authority.

9.5 Other legal entities submitting a claim on behalf of shareholders or other owners shall attach documentation demonstrating that eligible shareholders or other owners have authorized the entity to submit the claim as their representative. Documentary evidence shall be attached showing that the shareholders or other owners are themselves eligible for compensation under the German Foundation Act.

Section 10
Statement of Claim

10.1 Claims shall be accompanied by a Statement of Claim that explains for each item lost:

   a. the circumstances of the loss;
   b. who caused the loss and the reasons as to why the loss should be considered to have resulted from National Socialist persecution or in connection with National Socialist wrongs, as the case may be, with the essential, direct, and harm-causing participation of German enterprises;
   c. in case the claim is for a persecution-related property loss, the reasons why no claim could be made under previous German restitution or indemnification laws;
   d. the location of the property at the time of loss;
   e. the value of the property at the time of loss; and
   f. the method used to calculate the value of the property.

10.2 The Statement of Claim shall be in English or German. A Statement of Claim from an individual claimant shall also be accepted in Czech, Hebrew, Hungarian, Polish, and Russian. A Statement of Claim from a religious community or religious organization, or an individual claimant who is represented by a lawyer, is expected to be submitted in English or German.

Section 11
Evidence

11.1 Claims should be supported by written evidence. If a claimant is unable to provide written evidence in support of the claim, the claimant must explain why written evidence cannot be submitted.

11.2 If the evidence submitted by the claimant in support of the claim is not in English or German, it shall be translated into one of these languages. Evidence submitted by an individual claimant shall also be accepted in Czech, Hebrew, Hungarian, Polish, and Russian. Evidence submitted by a religious community or religious organization or an individual claimant who is represented by a lawyer is expected to be translated into English or German, if it is not in one of these two languages.

11.3 Claimants other than the person who suffered a property loss shall provide proof of their relationship with that person by submitting a copy of a marriage certificate, birth certificate, family registration booklet, will, or other relevant document.

Section 12
Claimant Assistance

12.1 IOM shall provide information to claimants on the eligibility criteria specified in section 3 and sections 17–19 and on the formal filing requirements specified in section 15.1 below.

12.2 IOM shall provide assistance to claimants in filling in the claim form by establishing helpline operations in countries where claimants are likely to reside.

Section 13
Filing of Claims

13.1 Claims shall be submitted to IOM Geneva at an address specified in the information materials prepared by IOM.

13.2 Claims shall be submitted in an envelope that is post-marked no later than August 11, 2001, subject to any extension of the filing deadline by the German Foundation.[1]

13.3 The submission of a formless claim is sufficient for the claimant to comply with the filing deadline, if the claimant submits the completed IOM claim form within the deadline established pursuant to section 9.2 above.

Chapter III
Registration, Initial Review and Translation of Claims

Section 14
Registration

IOM shall register all claims as they are received and issue a receipt to the claimant confirming that the claim has been received.

Section 15
Initial Review

15.1 IOM shall perform an initial review of the claims prior to their submission to the Commission. The initial review will consist of checking whether

    a. the claim form is duly completed;
    b. the claim form, including the waiver clause, is duly signed;
    c. the claim is accompanied by a Statement of Claim; and
    d. documentary and other evidence is submitted with the claim.

15.2 If the claim does not meet the formal requirements set out in paragraph 1 above, IOM will provide the claimant with an opportunity to remedy the identified deficiencies within a deadline set by IOM. After the expiration of the deadline, IOM will submit the claim to the Commission, whether or not all the deficiencies have been remedied.

15.3 IOM shall carry out inquiries itself to ascertain the information required to verify a claim and include any such additional information in the submission of the claims to the Commission.

15.4. IOM shall submit claims arising from the same original property loss in the same file.

Section 16
Translation of Claim Files

To the extent that the claim files are not in English or German, IOM will arrange for the translation of the files into one of these two languages prior to their submission to the Commission, unless otherwise determined by the Commission.

Chapter IV
Substantive Criteria and Causation

Section 17
Causation

17.1 Compensation shall only be paid for losses that were caused by the essential, direct, and harm-causing participation of German enterprises during the National Socialist era.

17.2 The Commission shall make its determinations regarding causation pursuant to the terms of the German Foundation Act, these Rules, and on the basis of respect for established principles of international law and practice regarding causation and directness of loss. In applying these principles, the Commission shall take into account the evidentiary standard set out in section 22 below.

Section 18
Persecution-Related Property Losses

18.1 Persons who, during the National Socialist era, suffered a property loss within the meaning of the German Federal Indemnification Act (BEG), as a result of persecution for their race or other grounds of persecution, with the essential, direct, and harm-causing participation of German enterprises, are eligible for compensation.

18.2 Compensation for persecution-related property losses is available to these persons only if they were unable to make timely applications and who could not receive payment under previous German restitution or indemnification laws for any of the following reasons:

  a. because they did not meet the residency requirements of the German Federal Indemnification Act (BEG); or
  b. because they could not file their claims for restitution or indemnification by the deadline because they had their domicile or permanent residence in an area with whose government the Federal Republic of Germany did not have diplomatic relations; or
  c. because proof of the validity of their claims under the German Federal Indemnification Act (BEG) or the German Federal Restitution Act [*Bundes-rückerstattungsgesetz*, or 'BRückG'] became available only after the reunification of the Federal Republic of Germany, provided the claims were not covered by post-reunification restitution or compensation legislation, i.e. the Law on the Settlement of Open Property Matters [*Gesetz zur Regelung offener Vermögensfragen*] or the Law on Indemnification of Victims of Nazism [*NS-Verfolgtenentschädigungsgesetz*]; or
  d. because their claims concerning moveable property were denied or would have been denied under the German Federal Indemnification Act (BEG) or the German Federal Restitution Act (BRückG) because the claimant, while able to prove that a German company was responsible for seizing or confiscating property, was not able to prove (as required by law) that the property was transferred into then West Germany or, in the case of bank accounts, that compensation was or would have been denied under the Currency Conversion Act [*Gesetz zur Neuordnung des Geldwesens*], the German Federal Indemnification Act (BEG), the Equalization of Burdens Act [*Lastenausgleichsgesetz*], or the Reparation Losses Act [*Reparationsschädengesetz*] because the sum was no longer identifiable, where either (a) the claimant can now prove the property was transferred into then West Germany or (b) the location of the property is unknown.

Section 19
Other Property Losses

Persons who suffered a property loss in connection with Nazi wrongs with the essential, direct, and harm-causing participation of German enterprises, but not because of National Socialist persecution, are eligible for compensation under the provisions of the German Foundation Act.

Chapter V
Substantive Determinations and Evidentiary Standard

Section 20
Submission of Claims and Support

20.1 IOM shall submit the claims received by IOM to the Commission in installments. To the extent possible, claims raising similar factual and legal issues shall be processed together.

20.2 IOM shall provide administrative, legal, and technical support to the Commission during and outside its sessions.

Section 21
Review Period

The Commission will endeavor to complete its review of, and make its determinations on, the compensability of the claims within a year after the expiration of the deadline for filing of claims as set out in section 13.2 above, subject to any extension of the filing deadline by the German Foundation.

Section 22
Evidentiary Standard

22.1 The Commission's decisions on compensability shall be based on relaxed standards of proof taking into account the lapse of time between the date the loss occurred and the date the claim was made; the circumstances in which the specific loss or types of losses occurred; the information available from other cases; and the background information available to the Commission regarding the circumstances prevailing during the National Socialist era and World War II and the participation of German enterprises in the commitment of National Socialist wrongs.

22.2 A fact shall be considered established if it has been credibly demonstrated. A claim cannot be rejected on the sole ground that it is not supported by official documentary evidence.

Section 23
Decision-Making; Form of Decisions

23.1 A decision shall be made by a majority of the Commissioners. Should a Commissioner be unable to attend a meeting of the Commission, decisions shall be taken provisionally by the remaining Commissioners with the Chairman having the casting vote. On individual cases, no decisions may be taken by the remaining Commissioners. Any provisional decision shall be resubmitted to the Commission at the next meeting at which the full Commission is present.

23.2 The Commission's decisions on compensability shall be made in writing and in a form to be determined by the Commission. The Commission shall provide reasons for the decisions and shall include a statement informing the claimant of a right to request reconsideration of the decision in respect of the grounds of the decision or the compensable amount.

23.3 A decision shall be communicated to the Claimant in an English original. In case the individual Claimant has submitted the claim in Czech, German, Hebrew, Hungarian, Polish, or Russian, a translation of the decision into the language of his claim shall be provided upon request.

Chapter VI
Notification of Decisions, Appeals, Pro Rata Allocation and Payment

Section 24
Notification of Decisions

24.1 IOM shall communicate the Commission's decisions to the claimants.

24.2 A claimant shall be notified of the decision on compensability as soon as the Commission has made it.

24.3 Any written communication from IOM to a claimant who has filed a claim on behalf of one or more other persons shall be sent by IOM to all such co-claimants.

Section 25
Request for Reconsideration

25.1 Claimants shall have a right to file a Request for Reconsideration of the decision of the Commission taken pursuant to section 23 above with respect to the claim.

25.2 The only grounds for reconsideration are (i) manifest error or (ii) new evidence previously unavailable to the Claimant. Only new evidence that the

Claimant shows was unavailable to the Claimant at the time of submission of the Claim or its supplements will be considered.

25.3 The Claimant must submit a detailed, written statement requesting reconsideration of the Decision. The statement must contain the following:

a. the Claim Number;
b. the names and addresses of all Co-Claimants, if any;
c. the grounds and reasons for supporting the Request for Reconsideration, and in particular the part of the Decision to which the Request for Reconsideration relates;
d. if the basis for the Request for Reconsideration is new evidence (not manifest error), then the Request for Reconsideration must include the new evidence, and the Claimant's statement must specify how the new evidence submitted with the statement is relevant, why the new evidence was unavailable to the Claimant at the time of submission of the Claim or its supplements, and the date on which the new evidence became available to the Claimant; and
e. the signature of the person requesting the Request for Reconsideration.

A Request for Reconsideration (and the accompanying evidence) (i) may be filed in English, German, Czech, Hebrew, Hungarian, Polish, or Russian, if the person filing the request is an individual without representation, and (ii) shall only be filed in English or German, if the person filing the request is either an individual with representation or a religious community or religious organization.

25.4 A Request for Reconsideration may be filed by the Claimant or by any Co-Claimant. A Claimant may file a Request for Reconsideration on behalf of all of the Co-Claimants.

25.5 A Request for Reconsideration must be received by IOM within three (3) months of the date of the decision of the Commission.

25.6 The Claimant must file the Request for Reconsideration at the following address:

International Organization for Migration
German Forced Labor Compensation Program
IOM Appeals Body (PROP)
17 route des Morillons, P.O. Box 174
CH-1211 Geneva 19
Switzerland

25.7 The other Rules contained herein shall apply, as appropriate, to the Request for Reconsideration and the decision thereon, including the provisions of Section 23 regarding the Form of Decision (except Section 23.2, second sentence, final clause) and Section 24 regarding Notification of Decisions.

Section 26
Pro Rata Allocation

26.1 Once the Commission has determined all claims filed with IOM and no requests for reconsideration are still pending or possible, it shall determine whether the total amounts available for the compensation of property losses are sufficient to satisfy the compensable amounts in full, as specified in paragraphs 2 and 3 below.

26.2 Persecution-related property losses are compensated in full if the total amount available for the compensation of these losses under section 9, paragraph 4, Number 1 of the German Foundation Act is sufficient to satisfy all awards made by the Commission in compensation for persecution-related property losses. If the total amount available for such property losses is not sufficient to satisfy the compensable amounts, the Commission will allocate the funds on a pro rata basis according to the ratio between the compensable amounts and the total amount available for compensation.

26.3 Other property losses are compensated in full if the total amount available for the compensation of these losses under section 9, paragraph 4, Number 2 of the German Foundation Act is sufficient to satisfy all awards made by the Commission in compensation of other property losses. If the total amount available for the compensation of such property losses is not sufficient to satisfy the compensable amounts, the Commission will allocate the funds on a pro rata basis according to the ratio between the compensable amounts and the total amount available for compensation.

26.4 There shall be no request for reconsideration of the pro rata allocation of compensation amounts made by the Commission.

Section 27
Payment

Payments may be made only as permitted by the German Foundation Act.

Chapter VII
Assignment of Personal Injury Claims to Arbitration

Section 28
Request for Assignment

28.1 At the request of a partner organization of the German Foundation, including IOM, the Commission shall appoint an independent arbitrator to determine personal injury claims within the meaning of section 11, paragraph 1, sentence 5 of the German Foundation Act, filed with such partner organization.

28.2 The request shall be in English and addressed to the Chairman of the Commission in writing.

Section 29

Decision

29.1 The Commission shall assign the determination of personal injury claims to an independent arbitrator who is knowledgeable and experienced in making such determinations and is fluent in the language or languages in which the claims are made.

29.2 The Commission's decision under paragraph 1 above is final and not subject to appeal.

Chapter VIII
Decisions on Compensation Payments for Personal Injury Claims

Section 30

Jurisdiction

30.1 The Commission shall determine the pro rata amounts for claimants whose claims have been found to be compensable by partner organizations based on the total amount available for the compensation of personal injury claims under section 9, paragraph 3 of the German Foundation Act.

30.2 When making the pro rata allocation referred to in paragraph 1 above, the Commission may not review the merits of the claims or the amounts found to be compensable by the partner organizations.

Section 31

Procedure

31.1 The partner organizations, including IOM, and the sole arbitrator(s), as the case may be, shall forward to the Commission a list of all personal injury claims found to be compensable by each such partner organization or sole arbitrator as soon as they have completed the review of all personal injury claims falling under their respective jurisdiction.

31.2 The list shall be in English or German and shall identify each individual whose claim has been found to be compensable and the compensable amount.

31.3 If a partner organization has not received any personal injury claims it shall inform the Commission accordingly.

Section 32

Decision

32.1 Having received the lists of compensable claims from all partner organizations pursuant to section 31.1–2 above, or a notification that no personal injury claims have been received by a particular partner organization, the Commission shall determine whether the total amount available for compensation of personal injury claims under section 9, paragraph 3 of the German Foundation Act is sufficient to satisfy in full all the claims found to be compensable by the partner organizations.

32.2 If the funds are sufficient to satisfy all the compensable claims in full, the Commission shall make no reductions from the compensable amounts.

32.3 If the funds are not sufficient to satisfy all the compensable claims in full, the Commission shall determine the pro rata amounts for all compensable claims based on the total amount available for the compensation of personal injury claims under section 9, paragraph 3 of the German Foundation Act, taking into account the German Foundation's decision with respect to the priority of the payments for the various types of claims for persons injured pursuant to section 11.1(5) of the German Foundation Act.

Section 33

Notification of Decisions

IOM shall communicate the Commission's decision taken pursuant to section 32 above to the other partner organizations. If the Commission's decision affects the amounts awarded by the partner organizations, the partner organizations are responsible for notifying their claimants of the Commission's decision in accordance with their ordinary procedures.

Section 34

Appeals

34.1 Claimants whose claim is affected by a decision taken by the Commission pursuant to section 32 above shall have a right to appeal.

34.2 The Commission's determinations on compensation payments for personal injury claims are subject to appeal only in respect of quantum.

Chapter IX
Final Provisions

Section 35
Amendments to the Rules

These Rules may be amended or supplemented by the Commission as appropriate.

Section 36
Language

The English text of these Rules shall govern, regardless of the existence of any translations of these Rules into other languages.

Section 37
Conflict

37.1. These Rules shall be interpreted, where necessary, in order to avoid the existence of a conflict between these Rules and the German Foundation Act.

37.2 In the event of a conflict between these Rules and the German Foundation Act, the provisions of the latter shall prevail.

Geneva, June 5, 2001, as amended on September 17, 2001, December 3, 2001, January 29, 2002, and August 28, 2002.

Pierre A. Karrer
Chairman

Eberhard Hubrich
Commissioner

Richard M. Buxbaum
Commissioner

NOTE

1 This deadline was extended by the German Foundation to December 31, 2001.

INDEX

Entries appearing as boxes, notes or tables are indexed in bold e.g. 646n

Brazil (*cont.*)
    victims 108, 115, 116–117, 119, 123, 124–125, 125t,
        139, 145t, 146t, 147t, 148t
        exclusions after 1979 138; families of 113,
            118, 129, 131, 140; fatal 102–152; in
            custody 119, 123; in hiding 105, 106;
            information on 117, 119; of police
            violence 107; of political violence 114,
            137; restrictions in types of 141; use of
            false names for burial 107
Brecher, Michael 414n
Brownlie, Ian 535n
Brunkhorst, Hauke 477n
budgets 656
    public 660
Burbridge, Jennifer A. 618n
burden of proof 540, 550
    Brazil 115–116, 118, 137, 138, 141
    Chile 540, 550
    forced labor 434
    United Nations Compensation
        Commission 346, 359, 365, 373
Burundi 633
Busch, Almirante Jorge Martínez 95n
Bush, George W. (President, USA, 2000 to
    present) 269, 288, 291, 294, 307, 309
Business Trust (South Africa) 574

Cambodia 597, 682
Cammack, Diana 247n
Caracazo Case, El (Venezuela) 513, 516, 517, 521, 522
Carron, David B. 352, 385n, 388n
Castillo, M. I. 583
Castro, Mercedes 101n
Catholic Church:
    Brazil 103, 104, 105
    Chile 55–56, 83–84, 90
causality 604
Cavallo, Ascanio 99n
Cédras, Raoul (President, Haiti, 1991–1994) 166
censorship:
    Brazil 103, 104
Central America 597, 654
Central Europe 431, 435
Centre for the Study of Violence and
    Reconciliation (South Africa) (CSVR) 200
Cernea, Michael 648n
Chanika, Emmie 255n
Chapman, Audrey R. 172n, 175n
Chaskalson, M. 210n, 212n, 213n
Chavis, David M. 620n
Chen, David 319n, 320n
Chicuecue, Noel Muchenga 604, 620n
children;

see also orphans
Angola 603
Argentina 48n, 51n, 54n
    disappearances of 23; disappearances of
        parents 7–8, 42; of detainees 34, 42
    benefits 26
    Chile 61, 67
    development 570
    Japanese-American Internment 273
Chile 3–4, 5, 9–10, 11–12, 18n, 42, 293, 294, 577;
    beneficiaries 59, 61, 62–63, 67, 69, 70–71, 74,
        76, 77, 81, 82–83, 84, 85, 92, 93
    benefits 4, 59, 61, 67, 79, 83, 85, 87
    compensation claims 55–56, 60, 66, 77–78,
        82–84, 87–89, 90, 506
        rejection of 544–546, 550
    crimes 9, 86
    deaths 57–59, 66, 93
    detainees 62, 63 , 69, 75, 92
        deaths 56; disappearances 65, 66, 82, 86–87,
            90, 93
    disappearances 56, 57–67, 80, 83
        final whereabouts 64; forced 66; of family
            members 87
    executions 56, 82, 83
        of family members 87; political 57–67, 69,
            90, 93
    exiles 55, 69, 71–74, 80, 81, 82, 87, 88
    harms 77, 87, 90, 93
        recognition for 62
    Human Rights Program 65, 66
    human rights violations 757
    indemnification 86, 87, 89, 90, 93, 94
    justice 56, 58, 62, 66–67, 92, 93, 94
    legislation 15, 55–101
    Military Justice Code 75
    payments 13, 56, 61, 67, 82, 88–90
        non-monetary forms of 63; one-off 76
    peasants:
        expelled from land 56, 69, 83–86;
            reparations funding 84, 84t, 85
    pensions 4, 61, 62–63, 66, 81–82, 84, 84–86,
        90, 93
        contributions 80–81; expenditure 60t;
            for peasants 87; for unfair
            dismissals 78;
        grace 85–86; life 85, 93; monetary 79;
            monthly 59–60, 67, 84, 86;
    people confined to a region 69
    reconciliation 58
        national 79; political 62, 87, 92
    reparations 453, 528, 637
        education 743–745; financing 660, 666;
            health care 754;

Milton Keynes UK
Ingram Content Group UK Ltd.
UKHW022116230624
444583UK00007B/63